1986

Psychology

Its Study and Uses

Psychology

Its Study and Uses

Louis H. Janda
Old Dominion University

Karin E. Klenke-Hamel
Old Dominion University

St. Martin's Press
NEW YORK

Library of Congress Catalog Card Number: 81–51857

Manufactured in the United States of America.
65432
fedcba
For information, write St. Martin's Press, Inc.,
175 Fifth Avenue, New York, N.Y. 10010

cover design: Tom McKeveny

typography: Murray Fleminger Associates

picture editor: Inge King

ISBN: 0–312–65241–0

CHAPTER OPENER PICTURE CREDITS

1. © Joel Gordon
2. © Rota/American Museum of Natural History
3. © Ken Karp Photography
4. © Marilyn Schwartz/Photo Researchers, Inc.
5. © Frank Siteman MCMLXXX/Taurus Photos
6. © M. E. Warren/Photo Researchers, Inc.
7. © David Powers/Stock, Boston, Inc.
8. © Hella Hamid/Photo Researchers, Inc.
9. © Dennis Stock/Magnum Photos
10. © Magnum Photos
11. © Suzanne Szasz
12. © Collection Guttmann-Maclay
13. © Paul Fusco/Magnum Photos
14. © Dennis Brack/Black Star
15. © Susan Lapides/Design Conceptions
16. © Marjorie Pickens
17. © Steve Hansen/Stock, Boston, Inc.
18. © Burt Glinn/Magnum Photos
19. © Stock, Boston, Inc.
20. © Photo Researchers, Inc.

To our children
Christopher and Michael
Katja and Max

Contents

4 Sensation and Perception 81

5 Principles of Learning 111

8 Life-Span Development 203

9 Gender Identity and Sex Roles 239

10 Theories of Personality 267

12 Abnormal Behavior 327

13 Treatment of Abnormal Behavior 365

15 Social Perception, Social Attraction, and Love 419

16 Groups 441

Special Features: Applications and Critical Issues

Preface

In a number of ways, the introductory course in psychology offers a greater challenge than any other to both instructors and textbook writers. It is here that the students are both largest in numbers and most diverse in their backgrounds, abilities, interests, and expectations. Since a majority of these students will not be psychology majors, and for many the course will be the only formal exposure to the field that they will ever have, it is inevitable that their lifelong view of psychology will be strongly influenced by their introductory textbook and classroom lectures. The impact on declared and potential psychology majors is equally important, for it will have a decided effect both on their individual careers and on the future of the discipline. The ranks of psychologists are filled with people who as undergraduates had an awakening interest in psychology fostered by an exciting introductory course. We hope this book will help instructors perform the same task for a new generation.

Psychology: Its Study and Uses covers all of the basic areas of psychological investigation: physiological, experimental, developmental, clinical, and social. We discuss the theoretical aspects, the major research findings, and, where possible, the controversies and the social and ethical implications that are related to these various areas. Further, as our subtitle is meant to suggest, this text gives more attention than most to the applications of psychology—the ways in which psychological concepts and findings are put to work in a great variety of everyday situations. A distinctive feature of the book is the inclusion of three chapters that use insights and techniques from all the basic areas of the field to explore particular topics: human sexual behavior, violence and aggression, and applications of psychology in environmental, industrial, community, and educational contexts. Each chapter in the book was written to provide a thorough introduction to the subject under consideration and to suggest the limits of our present knowledge concerning it.

We planned *Psychology: Its Study and Uses* to be substantial enough for a two-semester course and flexible enough for a single semester. Although we carefully selected the sequence of chapters, it need not be adhered to strictly. For example, some instructors may wish to emphasize the scientific aspects of psychology, while others may prefer to stress the applications of psychology. Both will be able to assign chapters that fulfill their objectives. Here is one possible organization of chapters for each of these two emphases, and other sequences are also feasible:

Science of Psychology

1. The Nature of Psychology
20. Statistics and Research Methods
2. The Physiological Basis of Behavior
3. States of Consciousness
4. Sensation and Perception

Applications of Psychology

1. The Nature of Psychology
3. States of Consciousness
5. Principles of Learning
6. Motivation and Emotion
8. Life-Span Development

5. Principles of Learning
6. Motivation and Emotion
7. Language, Thinking, and Memory
8. Life-Span Development
10. Theories of Personality
11. Psychological Assessment
12. Abnormal Behavior
13. Treatment of Abnormal Behavior
16. Groups
17. Human Sexual Behavior
18. Violence and Aggression

9. Gender Identity and Sex Roles
10. Theories of Personality
11. Psychological Assessment
12. Abnormal Behavior
13. Treatment of Abnormal Behavior
14. Attitudes and Attitude Change
15. Social Perception, Social Attraction, and Love
16. Groups
17. Human Sexual Behavior
18. Violence and Aggression
19. Applications of Psychology

Chapters 17 and 18, "Human Sexual Behavior" and "Violence and Aggression," were included for two reasons. First, the topics are of great interest to students. Second, the chapters illustrate that a variety of approaches and methods is necessary to make a topic fully understandable. By its very nature as a survey, the introductory psychology course tends to make the discipline appear far more fragmented than it is. Students study learning one week, sensation the next, development the following week, and so on, without ever having the opportunity to cover a particular aspect of human behavior in depth. These two chapters afford that opportunity, each demonstrating how the interests of all the basic areas within the discipline can be brought to bear on a single subject.

Our experience indicates that when most beginning students think of careers in psychology they have visions of therapists and clients. They are surprised to discover that psychologists work in business, industry, and government as environmental planners, as personnel directors, or as researchers in a host of specialties; that others are employed in community mental health programs as administrators, consultants, or social workers; that still others are in education as counselors or as teachers of handicapped children. Chapter 19, "Applications of Psychology," and the "Training and Employment" section of Chapter 1, "The Nature of Psychology," inform students about some of the employment options available to them should they choose to continue their study in the discipline.

Perhaps we should say a word about our boxed discussions—some entitled "Critical Issues," some entitled "Applications"—which appear throughout the book. We have chosen the topics for these, first of all, to help sustain the student's interest. For example, one box describes recent and exciting research suggesting that tears may be the body's way of ridding itself of stress-related biochemicals; another discusses Ralph Nader's controversial criticism of the Educational Testing Service; a third examines an amusing study testing the hypothesis in the title of the song "Don't the Girls Get Prettier at Closing Time." Some of the boxes explore theoretical or empirical issues—for instance, "Sex Differences in the Brain." Others suggest practical uses of research findings—for example, "Breaking the Smoking Habit." A good many consider social or ethical implications—for instance, "Tests as an Invasion of Privacy" or "Confidentiality between Therapist and Client." A complete list of the boxes appears at the end of the table of contents.

We recognize that if our goal of conveying the nature of psychology in an exciting fashion is to be met, the text must be accessible to students. We open each chapter with a short anecdote or case history that gets the student thinking early about the questions addressed later in the chapter. From the outset of our work on the book, we have been conscious of the crucial importance of readability. We were especially gratified by the comments of our manuscript reviewers that our text was unusually easy to read, and certainly we have worked hard to make it even more so. Part of the task of any introductory text is to teach the basic vocabulary of the discipline, but technical jargon can be bewildering to the beginning student, and we have avoided it whenever possible. To aid students in mastering the language of psychology, we have printed important terms in boldface type, defined them as early as possible in each chapter, listed them in the "Key Terms for Review" at the end of each chapter, and defined them again in the "Glossary" at the end of the book. We believe that graphic materials—tables, figures, and photographs—are immensely helpful to students in understanding the text, and we have provided them in abundance.

In any task as large as preparing an introductory psychology text, many people play an indispensable role. First, we are grateful to the reviewers who offered their time and expertise to help us provide an accurate and representative account of the various areas of psychology. Their names are listed here:

Nancy S. Breland, Trenton State College
Elliot E. Entin, Brandeis University
Halford Fairchild, University of California—Los Angeles
Joshua Gerow, Indiana University—Purdue University at Fort Wayne
Mark G. McGee, University of Colorado Medical Center
Gerald Mikosz, Moraine Valley Community College
Dan Motet, Seattle Pacific University
Samuel H. Osipow, The Ohio State University
Robert A. Osterhouse, Prince George's Community College
Janat Parker, Florida International University
Bobby J. Poe, Belleville Area College
Francis Terrell, North Texas State College
Sol Schwartz, Kean College of New Jersey

Of course, any errors of fact or interpretation remain our responsibility.

Several people at St. Martin's Press made essential contributions. Tom Broadbent was always willing to contribute his support and resources when they were needed. Helen Greer and Jinny Joyner helped to turn our drafts into polished prose. Inge King did an excellent job in obtaining the photographs. Ron Aldridge made the process of transforming typewritten copy into printed pages as painless as possible. Special thanks go to Walter Kossmann, our editor and friend. He guided the process of producing this book from its inception to bound copies. Not only is he a first-rate editor, but he also manages to remain cheerful and encouraging throughout the difficult times.

In addition, several people at Old Dominion University merit our gratitude and appreciation. Our colleagues in the Psychology Department were always willing to help when we asked. Perry Duncan and Steve Klein deserve special mention for offering their comments on first drafts of the physiological chapters. Margueritte Lucas gracefully performed the tedious chore of turning our handwritten pages into typed copy. Finally, we wish to thank our chairman Ray Kirby, our students, and our families, who offered their support and encouragement and tolerated our preoccupation with the manuscript over the past three years.

Louis H. Janda
Karin E. Klenke-Hamel

Psychology

Its Study and Uses

1

The Nature of Psychology

Tom decided that he was going to major in psychology when he began college in the fall. He was not sure what psychologists did exactly, but he had always been interested in why people behave the way they do and what might be done for those whose behavior got them into difficulties. He did know, from hearing Dr. Robinson speak at his high school's career day, that these were the kinds of things that some psychologists studied. Dr. Robinson was a clinical psychologist who specialized in treating people with marital and family problems. Tom talked with her after her lecture, and she told him that anyone who wanted to devote a career to helping others was to be commended.

Tom's parents also approved of his decision. His mother mentioned that her college roommate, Emily Hopkins, was now a professor of psychology at the state university and was very happy with her work. In fact, Tom's mother thought her old roommate would be willing to meet with Tom and answer any questions he might have. Tom's father offered to introduce him to some of the psychologists at his company, a research and development firm. Tom was enthusiastic about both ideas.

Driving back from the visit with his mother's friend, Tom felt somewhat bewildered and a little depressed. If Professor Hopkins's work was representative of how psychologists spent their time, he wanted no part of it. He had expected to see a throng of students outside her office waiting for the advice that would turn their lives around. Instead, he found her in a laboratory, where she and her students were surrounded by cages and cages of rats! They all spoke enthusiastically about their research on rats, but Tom was too taken aback to understand much of it. His only comfort was that tomorrow he would visit his father's company and meet the psychologists who worked there. At least they worked with people!

Tom's introduction to psychology's role in research and development left him feeling even more unsure of his choice of a major. Dr. Heath, an engineering psychologist, spent more than an hour showing Tom the project he was conducting. It seems that Dr. Heath asked people to stay awake for 24 hours and then had them push knobs and turn dials on a control panel that did not control anything at all. When Dr. Heath commented that he was sure Tom could see the importance of the work, Tom nodded politely, but he could not begin to fathom its importance.

That night, out of a sense of desperation, Tom called his older brother Bob, a college sophomore. Bob listened to Tom's story and, after making a few sympathetic comments, suggested that Tom talk to his roommate, who was already majoring in psychology. Bob's roommate had taken introductory psychology and was currently taking psychological statistics. That did it for Tom. Psychological statistics! He thought psychology was about people, not numbers.

Lying in bed that night, Tom reflected on his experiences of the past few days. While Dr. Robinson's lecture provided a ray of hope, he did not know what to think about Professor Hopkins and Dr. Heath. Although they all called themselves psychologists, their jobs seemed to have little in common. What could psychology possibly be about?

Many introductory psychology students experience Tom's confusion about the nature of psychology. Tom is unusual only in that his confusion began before he enrolled in the college-level introductory course. The impression of psychology that most people have is based on what they see on television and in the movies and what they read in newspapers and magazines. These sources imply that most psychologists spend their time providing services for people who have problems. Psychologists are shown administering psychological tests, conducting psychotherapy, or working in programs for drug addicts and juvenile delinquents. Occasionally the public may be made aware of the research role of psychologists. But the research they are likely to hear about tends to be sensational and unrepresentative of real psychological research.

So what *is* psychology all about? The definition of psychology that is usually offered in introductory texts does not answer the question completely. Psychology is generally defined there as the *scientific study of the behavior of organisms.* We shall examine the elements of this definition later in the chapter, but already you can probably think of several things psychologists do that the definition does not seem to cover.

For instance, some psychologists conduct encounter groups. Do encounter groups involve the scientific study of behavior? The answer could be yes, but more often it would have to be no. As we shall see in Chapter 13, many scientific studies have been made of the effects that encounter groups have on participants. But more often psychologists who conduct encounter groups are utilizing the art of psychology. This means that, although they may base their encounter-group techniques on psychological theory, much of what they do involves their intuition of what might work. In other words, what they are doing has not been scientifically demonstrated to be effective. Much of the applied work that psychologists do falls under the heading of "art" rather than "science." However, applied work is often the outcome of scientific findings and may in turn generate scientific research in a particular area. Both art and science have a role in psychology.

"Behavior" is a key word in our definition of psychology. But many areas of research bear at most an indirect relation to behavior. As you will see in Chapter 4, many psychologists have conducted extensive research to learn about the operation of our sensory mechanisms. For instance, they are interested in how the physical energy of light or sound is converted into information that we can understand. In fact, physiologists could do the same research just as well and never concern themselves with the relation between sensory reception and behavior.

At this point you may be wondering, Can psychology be defined? The answer is no if you insist on a strict definition. Psychology encompasses a diverse group of activities. The activities and interests of psychologists may overlap, but they may also bear little relation to one another. After all, it is difficult to imagine what the encounter-group leader and the researcher studying sensory mechanisms have in common other than the title of psychologist. Any definition that attempts to bridge the gap between the two is bound to be somewhat artificial.

To understand how this diversity came about, let us briefly review the historical highlights of psychology. We shall then take a look at the major areas of interest in psychology and examine the scientific method and the art of psychology.

Wilhelm Wundt (1832–1920) set up the first experimental laboratory in psychology. (© *The Bettmann Archive, Inc.*)

HISTORICAL DEVELOPMENTS

The development of psychological thought can be traced back to the ancient Greek philosophers Socrates, Plato, and Aristotle. They and numerous others debated various conceptualizations of the human mind and behavior in the fifth century B.C. It was not until the late 1800s, however, that psychology gained recognition as a formal and independent discipline. Two milestones that are recognized as marking the birth of psychology were the publication of Gustav Fechner's *Elements of Psychophysics* in 1860 and the founding of the first psychological laboratory in Leipzig, Germany, in 1879 by Wilhelm Wundt.

The early psychologists disagreed on the content and methods of their discipline. This disagreement led to the formation of schools or "isms" in psychology. The members of each school naturally believed that their definition of the content of psychology and their methods of studying it were the only appropriate ones. Let us examine the major schools in psychology: structuralism, functionalism, behaviorism, Gestalt psychology, psychoanalysis, the study of individual differences, and humanism.

Structuralism

Wundt and one of his students, Edward Bradfort Titchener, believed that the task of psychology was to analyze the elements of consciousness. They believed that our complex conscious experiences could be broken down into fundamental components in much the same way that chemists have broken down physical substances into 105 or so basic elements. They intended to discover the *structure* of the mind and founded the school called **structuralism.**

William James (1842–1910) taught philosophy and psychology at Harvard University and expanded the domain of psychology with his concept of functionalism. (© *Culver Pictures, Inc.*)

Their method of accomplishing this task was to place subjects in standardized laboratory settings. There the subjects would report their conscious experiences in great detail and broken down into basic components. Instead of saying, "I see a picture of a tree," for example, they would report their sensations of the various colors and degrees of brightness they associated with trees. On the basis of his experiments, Wundt concluded that the mind is made up of three basic elements: sensations, the reactions generated by external stimuli; images, the reactions produced by the mind itself; and feelings, the emotions associated with various experiences.

Working alone, Titchener took these ideas a step further. Using the methods outlined in Fechner's 1860 book, he attempted to quantify the sensations of the "generalized human mind." He concluded that we can discriminate about 35,000 colors, 600 to 700 degrees of brightness, 11,000 auditory tones, and 4 taste, skin, and internal organ sensations. He believed there were a total of 46,708 basic sensations! Like Wundt, Titchener believed that all conscious experience was a result of blending these sensations with images and feelings. Notice that the structuralists had no interest in behavior as we generally think of it. They defined psychology as the study of the mind.

Functionalism

The name most closely associated with **functionalism** is that of William James, the first prominent native-born American psychologist. James was a physiology professor at Harvard in the 1870s. He also had a strong interest in philosophy, and before long he began to see connections between the two disciplines. In 1875 he initiated a course in psychology and began to conduct psychological experiments. His work resulted in the publication of *The Principles of Psychology* in 1890.

James disagreed with the structuralists on a number of points. Perhaps his most important contribution was the idea that the workings of the mind are functional—they allow us to survive and to adapt to everyday occurrences. This idea provided a link between consciousness and behavior. While Titchener believed that psychology should focus only on the mind, James argued that the relation between the mind and behavior was of crucial importance.

Behaviorism

Shortly after the turn of the century, John B. Watson received his doctorate in psychology from the University of Chicago. His dissertation was concerned with learning in rats. In accord with the emphasis placed on consciousness at that time, one of Watson's assigned tasks was to speculate about the impact of the rats' consciousness on their behavior. Watson thought this requirement was absurd, but he complied in order to receive his degree. Ten years later, however, he published a monograph, "Psychology as the Behaviorist Views It" (1913), in which he made known his feelings about consciousness.

Watson's thesis was that consciousness could not be defined, measured, or located. In short, there is no evidence that it exists. Watson wrote that the belief in consciousness, or the mind, was a superstition left over from the Middle Ages. Psychology could never aspire to be a science if it was to be based on something so vague. It should concern itself only with observable and measurable behavior.

Watson's ideas presented a severe challenge to both the structuralists and the functionalists. Perhaps because Wundt's type of experiments had lost their novelty, Watson's **behaviorism** was enthusiastically received.

Gestalt Psychology

About the same time that behaviorism was gaining acceptance in the United States, a group of German psychologists mounted an attack against

John B. Watson (1878–1958) founded behaviorism, which aims to make psychology more scientifically rigorous by concentrating on measurable behavior. (© *Culver Pictures, Inc.*)

structuralism from another direction. These theorists agreed with Watson that it was absurd to try to identify the elements of consciousness, but for a different reason. They argued that we do not see a combination of 10,000 colors and 700 degrees of brightness when we look at a tree—we see a tree. In other words, we see a whole structure (*Gestalten* in German).

To illustrate this point, Max Wertheimer, the founder of **Gestalt psychology,** discussed the phenomenon of apparent movement. We see this when a series of individual neon lights is turned on and off in such a way that we perceive a single moving light. Wertheimer and the other Gestaltists believed that it was useless to try to reduce such a perception to elementary sensations. Our

The work of Max Wertheimer (1880–1943) contributed to the founding of Gestalt psychology. (© *The Bettmann Archive, Inc.*)

conscious experience of the world is more than just the sum of the individual elements. One blinking light plus one blinking light do not necessarily add up to two blinking lights; they may add up to apparent movement.

Psychoanalysis

Sigmund Freud was not involved in the early struggle to define the content and methods of psychology, but his work resulted in yet another school, **psychoanalysis.** As a Viennese physician, Freud became interested in patients who had physical symptoms that did not appear to have any organic basis. He came to believe that these symptoms were based on childhood experiences that were repressed, or driven out of conscious awareness, because the memories of such experiences were extremely frightening or threatening. Although these memories were unconscious, Freud believed that they served as a basis for motives, desires, and fantasies that continued to exert an influence on overt behavior throughout adulthood (see Chapter 10). On the basis of his observations, Freud developed a method of psychological treatment and a comprehensive theory of personality, both of which have come to be known as psychoanalysis.

Freud's theory was totally incompatible with Watson's behaviorism, which reached its peak of popularity in the 1920s. Watson believed that behavioral scientists should ignore mental events, whereas Freud argued that these events were the primary determinants of behavior. Freud's ideas began to attract interest, however, and during the 1930s and 1940s psychoanalysis flourished in the United States.

During the 1960s and 1970s, psychoanalysis began to slip in prestige in academic circles, but it has continued to exert a powerful influence in clinical settings. Many psychotherapists use methods based on Freud's ideas. The public, although probably unaware of it, is influenced strongly by psychoanalytic thought. Take the lovelorn columns, such as the one by Ann Landers. When readers ask about the "strange uncle" in their family or their compulsive overeating, Landers often suggests that such problems result from deep personality problems and urges the reader to seek psychotherapy. In contrast, a behaviorist would suggest that the causes of the problem were probably to be found in the person's environment.

The Study of Individual Differences

Sir Francis Galton is an important historical figure in psychology, even though he did not establish a school. During psychology's early years, theorists were interested in discovering laws of behavior that could be applied to everyone. There was little, if any, interest in the differences among individuals. When **individual differences** did show up in experiments, they were thought to reflect the need to develop more precise laws of behavior. Galton helped to make the study of individual differences respectable through his study of intelligence.

Galton, a half-cousin to Charles Darwin, was an English biologist who had diverse interests. His interest in human intelligence prompted him to devise methods for measuring it. He believed that a person's sensory acuity provided an index of intellectual level. In pursuit of this idea, Galton gave visitors at a World's Fair in 1884 a variety of tests measuring their visual acuity, muscular strength, and reaction time. He borrowed ideas from mathematicians to summarize and analyze the data he collected.

Although Galton's attempt to measure intelligence through physical characteristics proved to be a failure, he laid the groundwork for mental, or psychological, tests, and his work served as a model for future psychologists who wished to quantify their observations. Most important, Galton's work served as a stimulus for researchers to explore differences among people.

Humanistic Psychology

Many schools of psychology were developed largely in protest to existing theories of human behavior. **Humanistic psychology** is one example. During the middle of this century, psychoanalysis and behaviorism were the dominant schools of thought. But a growing number of psychologists were dissatisfied with both. They objected to behaviorism as too mechanistic and to psychoanalysis as too strongly oriented toward the pathological. Humanistic psychologists, such as Abraham Maslow and Carl Rogers, emphasized the unique qualities of human beings. In contrast to behaviorists, humanistic psychologists believe that goals, values, thoughts, and aspirations play an important role in influencing human behavior. Unlike psychoanalysts, they believe that people can transcend unfavorable environments and adverse childhood experiences. They can strive to fulfill themselves and to find peace and happiness.

In recent years, the debate between humanists and behavior-oriented psychologists has been heated. The former argue that a science of behavior will be deficient unless it studies the unique qualities of human beings, such as values and aspirations. The behavior-oriented psychologists argue that any approach that attempts to discover how to live wisely and well is philosophy and not science (Hebb, 1973). The debate is likely to continue for some time.

The above represent only the major "isms" of psychology. Other schools of thought have had an impact on the study of human behavior. One of these is cognitive psychology. Unlike the behaviorists, cognitive psychologists believe that we think about our environment and process information. We do not simply learn stimulus-re-

Sigmund Freud's (1856–1939) school of psychoanalysis searches for the key to many psychological problems in repressed memories of childhood experiences. (© *The Bettmann Archive, Inc.*)

sponse associations. Like the behaviorists, cognitive psychologists believe that our thoughts, as well as our behavior, are influenced by learning experiences and biological predispositions. Another current "ism," existential psychology, has had an impact on psychotherapy. An outgrowth of humanistic psychology, it holds that we should look to the writings of Heidegger and Kierkegaard, which stress human freedom and personal responsibility, to find out how to deal with alienation and a depersonalized world. Throughout the text we shall discuss these schools where relevant.

Current Status of Schools of Psychology

Over the past 30 to 40 years, the struggle to define the content and methods of psychology has largely faded away. Few psychologists today believe that psychology should focus on a narrow aspect of the human experience. Most recognize that a variety of topics can be made understandable by psychological investigation. They also recognize that in order to understand a particular phenomenon in psychology fully, a variety of methods must be employed.

In addition, psychologists are less likely to confine themselves to one school than they were 50 years ago. They may still think of themselves as principally behaviorists, psychoanalysts, or Gestaltists, but they are more open to ideas from other schools. In fact, a majority of psychologists today would probably identify themselves as **eclectics.** Rather than identify with any particular school, they select worthwhile principles and findings from a variety of schools in developing their own theoretical approach.

The diversity that existed in psychology around the turn of the century continues today, however, making it as hard as ever to define the term. The difference is that today psychologists tend to align themselves with certain interest areas rather than with schools of thought.

Francis Galton (1822–1911) explored differences between human beings in his psychological experiments. He is also known for his work in eugenics, meteorology, and fingerprint classification. (© *The Bettmann Archive, Inc.*)

MAJOR INTEREST AREAS OF PSYCHOLOGY

One often hears descriptive words applied to the title psychologist—clinical psychologist, school psychologist, experimental psychologist, consumer psychologist, industrial psychologist. The list is seemingly endless. It reveals the many areas of specialization that are available to the aspiring psychologist.

Attempts to categorize interest areas in psychology are somewhat arbitrary. This text describes five major interest areas—physiological, experimental, developmental, clinical, and social psychology. These categories are by no means mutually exclusive. In fact, it is nearly as difficult to define these interest areas as it is to define psychology as a whole. With this caution in mind, let us examine some of the features of these major areas.

Physiological Psychology

Physiological psychologists are generally interested in the biological basis of behavior. For example, they might investigate the relation between activity in certain areas of the brain and behavior or emotion. The role of hormones in influencing aggressive or sexual behavior would interest them. Or they might attempt to understand how our sense organs convert physical energy into meaningful experiences. The overlap between **physiological psychology** and other areas can be seen readily in research investigating biological factors associated with psychological disorders, such as schizophrenia or depression. The diversity of topics associated with physiological psychology will be explored in Chapters 2, 3, and 4.

For a more detailed example of the types of problems investigated by physiological psychologists, consider the following experiment conducted by Ronald Johnson (1979) at the University of Hawaii. He had men and women, who ranged in age from 44 to 79, wear earphones that transmitted a different series of numbers to each ear at the same time. The results indicated that people could generally recall more digits heard in the right ear than in the left ear. This is not surprising since the left side of the brain is largely responsible for processing verbal information. Information from the right side of the body is generally received by the left side of the brain and vice versa, so the right ear had an advantage (see Chapter 2).

What was surprising was that there were sharp differences between the age groups. While the number of correctly identified digits heard by the right ear remained relatively constant, the number heard by the left ear and the right side of the brain dropped from 63 correct out of 90 for the youngest group to 34 out of 90 for the oldest group. This suggests that the functions associated with the right hemisphere of the brain may deteriorate with age more rapidly than left-hemisphere brain functions. This finding may provide an important clue for researchers interested in the relation between aging and various abilities. Thus this basic research conducted by physiological psychologists also has implications for developmental psychologists.

Carl Rogers (1902–) espoused humanistic psychology, which looks at the effect of values and attitudes on human behavior. (© *Nozizwe S.*)

Experimental Psychology

Experimental psychology is generally associated with basic research into determinants of behavior. Some experimental psychologists perform theoretical research into basic psychological processes, such as learning, perception, memory, and comparisons of the behavior of different animal species (see Chapters 5 and 6). Others investigate practical concerns, such as alcoholism, anxiety, and maternal deprivation. All experimental psychologists adopt the experimental method, which allows them to identify cause-and-effect relationships (see Chapter 20 for a discussion of the various research methods).

Experimental psychology overlaps with several other interest areas. For example, experimental and developmental psychologists work together to

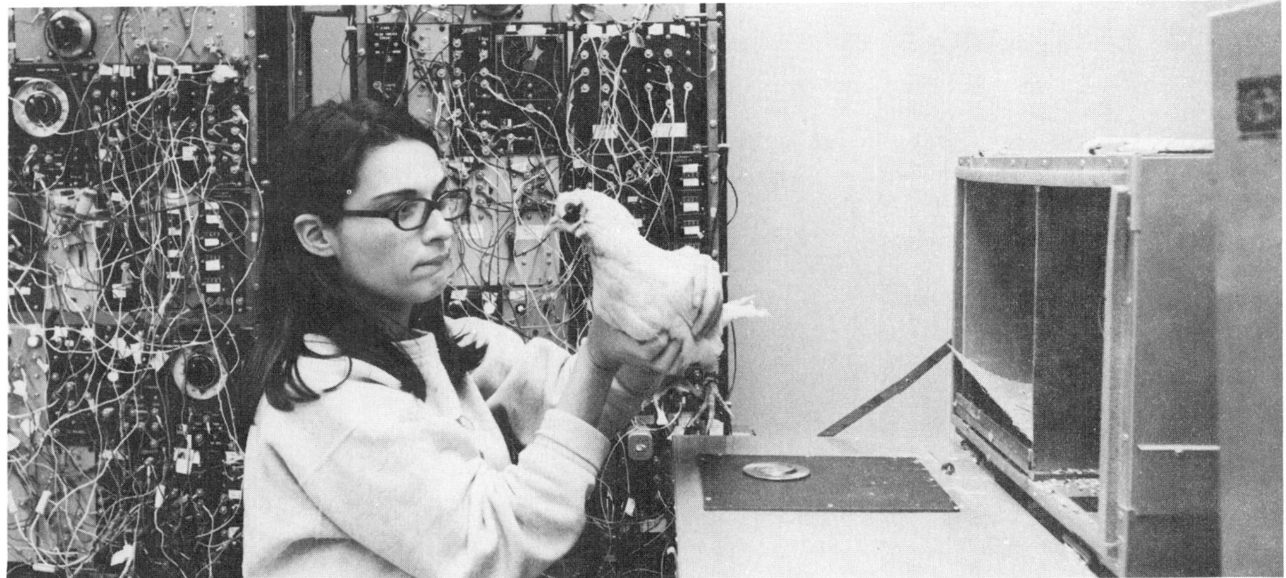

By studying the behavior of a chicken, this experimental psychologist can make inferences about human behavior. (© *Van Bucher/Photo Researchers, Inc.*)

study learning processes in children. As you will see in Chapter 4, both experimental and physiological psychologists are interested in sensation and perception. Experimental psychologists like Martin Seligman conduct research with animals that has implications for clinical psychologists.

Seligman's work provides one example of theoretical research that quickly generated practical applications. Some 15 years ago, he and his colleagues were conducting laboratory research on dogs to learn more about the relation between two basic learning processes (Overmier & Seligman, 1967; Seligman & Maier, 1967). Their procedure involved immobilizing the dogs in a harness and then administering brief and painful, but not permanently harmful, electric shocks. The dogs were then moved to a shuttlebox, which is a large box with a shoulder-high barrier dividing it in half. One half of the box contains an electric grid on the floor. Usually dogs placed in the electrified half learn very quickly to jump over the barrier to the safe half. If a tone precedes the onset of the shock by a few seconds, most dogs will learn to avoid the shock entirely. This phenomenon, discussed in Chapter 5, is called avoidance learning. Seligman's dogs, however, behaved in a surprising way. Instead of learning to avoid the shock in the shuttlebox, they lay down on the floor and accepted it with only a few whines in protest.

Puzzled by the dogs' unusual behavior, Seligman conducted several additional experiments before he felt confident of the explanation (cf. Seligman, 1975). He concluded that the dogs, having been exposed in the first part of the experiment to painful stimulation they could do nothing about, apparently believed there was nothing they could do about the shocks they received in the second part of the experiment. They had learned to be helpless.

This phenomenon of **learned helplessness,** as Seligman has called it, has been offered as one possible cause of depression in humans, a subject that will be discussed more fully in Chapter 12. Seligman has suggested that the depression suffered by many young adults may have resulted from their growing up in affluent families. Because as children they were given things they wanted without working for them, they failed to learn that their own efforts can make a difference in what they can have. Thus, like Seligman's dogs, these individuals learned to be helpless, and became easily depressed.

Such an explanation for the apparent increase in depression that has occurred in the past few years is, of course, highly speculative and has received criticism. But it is of interest that Seligman began by conducting pure experimental research with animals and within a few years was suggesting hypotheses that had broad and practical implications.

Developmental Psychology

Developmental psychologists are interested in the relationship between age and behavior. This interest can include a variety of topics. Some psychologists may focus on the acquisition of language skills in very young children. Others may be interested in the development of moral reasoning in children and adolescents. In recent years, the development of gender identity and the acquisition of sex roles have been popular topics of investigation. The goal of these specialists is to understand complex types of behavior by studying their origins.

For many years, the terms "developmental psychologist" and "child psychologist" were virtually synonymous. The focus of **developmental psychology** was on children, because physical and mental changes occur most rapidly during childhood. Over the past decade, however, developmental psychologists have become increasingly aware that these changes do not end at age 16, 18, 21, or any other arbitrarily chosen age. These psychologists have begun to explore life-span development. That is, they investigate critical developmental periods right through adulthood up to, and including, the process of dying. These topics are discussed in Chapters 8 and 9.

One example of research in this area is a study of intellectually gifted children begun by Lewis Terman of Stanford University in 1921. Terman, who is best known for developing the Stanford-Binet test of intelligence, was interested in learning whether stereotypes applied to exceptionally intelligent children were accurate. To this end he selected 1,000 children with IQs of 135 or above. This score placed them in the top 1 percent of the population. Terman compared these gifted children with their more average peers in a variety of intellectual, physical, and social characteristics.

The project did not end there, however. Terman was interested in how these children would fare as adults, so he conducted several follow-up studies. After Terman's death, the project was taken over by the husband-and-wife team of developmental psychologists, Pauline and Robert Sears. The most recent follow-up study, the seventh, was conducted in 1977, after a majority of the subjects had retired (Goleman, 1980).

The early studies tested the belief that intellectually gifted children were likely to be inferior in other ways. At the time, the stereotype of the frail, sickly, socially inept egghead was common. Terman's results showed the stereotype to be false. Not only were the gifted children superior in their academic achievement, but their teachers also rated them as above average in will power, self-confidence, sense of humor, leadership, truthfulness, health, and physical energy.

The more recent surveys have examined differences between the gifted children who achieved high levels of success as adults and those whose vocational success was average. The researchers became aware early in the study that there was wide variability in achievement in their sample of subjects. To understand the source of this variability, they compared 100 of the most successful, called group A, with 100 of the least successful, called group B. In 1959 the median income for the A's was about $24,000 and for the B's slightly more than $7,000. At that time the national median was about $5,000.

A number of differences were found between the two groups, but an important variable appeared to be the desire to succeed. The A's differed from the B's for this variable as children in the original study, and the difference was maintained throughout the years. In surveys made in

1940 and 1950, parents and spouses of the subjects rated them on a number of characteristics, and only three differences were found. Compared to the B's, the A's were more goal oriented, had greater perseverance, and had more self-confidence. The more recent surveys found that the A's derived more satisfaction from their vocations, their marriages, and their lives in general than did the B's.

This study, perhaps the most ambitious developmental study ever conducted, has yielded many important findings. It demonstrated that intelligence measured in childhood is related to success in later life. By comparing the A's and the B's, the research also showed that intelligence alone does not guarantee outstanding success. Having goals and the energy and persistence to accomplish them also contributes a great deal.

This clinical psychologist is counseling a client. (© *Erika Stone*)

Clinical Psychology

Clinical psychology involves assessing and treating psychological disorders. It is the largest interest area, consisting of about one-third of all psychologists. It tends to be more application oriented than research oriented. While many **clinical psychologists** teach and conduct research at colleges and universities, a majority of them are employed at psychiatric hospitals and outpatient clinics or are engaged in private practice.

Many people are confused about the distinction between **psychiatrists** and clinical psychologists. The activities of the two are similar, centering around the diagnosis and treatment of psychological disorders. An important difference between the two professions lies in their academic training. A psychiatrist is an M.D. who after medical school completes psychiatric residency of three to four years. A residency can be thought of as on-the-job training. While working at a psychiatric facility the resident attends seminars and conferences and is closely supervised. Like other M.D.'s, psychiatrists can prescribe medicine for their patients.

The clinical psychologist receives training in four to five years of graduate work in psychology. This study includes all of the basic areas of psychology and specialized work in clinical methods of assessment and treatment. Clinical psychologists must complete a one-year internship that is similar to the psychiatric residency before they can receive their Ph.D. (Doctor of Philosophy) degree. During the past decade several universities have introduced the Psy.D. (**Doctor of Psychology**) degree for clinical psychologists. Work for this degree is similar to that done for the Ph.D., but training in clinical skills is emphasized while training in research skills is deemphasized. A clinical psychologist is not a physician and cannot prescribe medicine.

Because clinical psychologists are trained to be scientists, research is often an important part of their activities. Their research can be application oriented, such as testing the effectiveness of a method of treatment in a psychiatric setting, or it can be highly theoretical, such as using rats to test hypotheses regarding psychological disorders.

Anthony Graziano and Kevin Mooney (1980) conducted an experiment that provides a good example of research in clinical psychology. They developed and evaluated a treatment program for children who had intense nighttime fears. By placing a notice in the local newspaper, they were able to recruit 30 children between the ages of 6 and 13 for their project. The parents of the children reported that the problem was indeed serious. Bedtime had become a highly emotional and disruptive event. Crying and severe panic were frequent and often lasted past midnight. Many of the children insisted on sleeping with the lights and the radio or television on in their rooms. Parents and children both were eager to receive help and were involved in treatment. At an initial meeting, the children were told:

> All of you have told us you are afraid of the dark or being alone. As you know, some kids are afraid in the dark and others are not. The main difference between you and those other kids who are not afraid is that those other kids know how to *make* themselves not be afraid. In this class, we are going to teach you how to make yourselves less afraid. We are going to teach you how to relax, think pleasant thoughts, and say special words, all of which will help you become braver (p. 209).

The special words were phrases such as "I am brave" and "I can take care of myself when I am in the dark." The parents were encouraged to help their child practice the exercises and were instructed in the awarding of "bravery tokens." The tokens were to be given out for practicing bravery exercises and for being brave at bedtime and throughout the night. Once the child had 10 consecutive fearless nights, he or she could exchange the bravery tokens for a McDonald's hamburger party.

The experiment was a success. Two months after treatment began, 24 of the 30 children had had 10 consecutive fearless nights. Parents were encouraged to continue with the treatment procedures, and by the end of one year only two children had failed to meet the criterion. Almost without exception, the parents reported that the treatment had resulted in improvements in family tranquility. Bedtime panic and the resulting tension was virtually eliminated.

Social Psychology

Social psychologists are interested in the effects of groups on an individual's behavior. We all recognize that our behavior is influenced by norms established by others. We want to dress, act, and *be* like the particular group with which we identify. Topics that interest social psychologists include conformity, prejudice, attitude formation, and leadership. **Social psychology** differs from sociology in that the latter is more interested in the behavior of groups, while the former focuses on the behavior of the individual within a group.

Social psychologists Judith Rodin and Ellen Langer conducted an experiment that illustrates the type of work done in this area and its relevance to important social problems (Rodin & Langer, 1977). They were concerned with the decline in alertness, health, and activity that often occurs in elderly people once they are admitted to nursing homes. On the basis of Rodin and Langer's theoretical laboratory research, they suspected that these declines might be caused by a perceived loss of control over one's life.

As a test of the hypothesis, one group of nursing-home residents heard a talk by the administrator stressing their responsibility for themselves. To bolster this theme, the residents were *offered* plants and were told that it was their responsibility to care for them. A comparison group heard a talk emphasizing the staff's responsibilities for caring for the patients. At the end of the talk, these patients were *given* plants and were told that the staff would care for them.

The responsibility-induced group showed increases in alertness, happiness, and activity in relation to the comparison group. The former group attended more movies, socialized more with friends, and participated more actively in a variety of activities. Most important, within 18 months after the experiment, 15 percent of the responsibility-induced group had died and 30 percent of the comparison group had died. This difference appeared to be a result of the experimental manipulation, since there were no differences in initial health ratings made by physicians and nurses between the two groups. Obviously, such research has implications for policies of nursing homes.

Other Interest Areas

The five areas discussed above, while comprising the major areas of psychology, are not exhaustive. For example, industrial, personnel, and organizational psychologists may work in business settings. They may help companies with the hiring and training of employees, or in finding ways to increase productivity and raise employee morale. The purpose of the tests conducted by the engineering psychologist Tom talked to was to learn how fatigue affects job performance.

Counseling psychology, still another interest area, is similar to clinical psychology. Counseling psychologists tend to deal with everyday problems and may work with students in schools and colleges or employees in large companies. Some school or educational psychologists attempt to identify children who require special attention and develop special programs for exceptional children. They also design new teaching methods and develop standardized tests of achievement. These interest areas will be discussed further in Chapter 19.

The range of activities open to the psychologist is extremely broad. This breadth accounts for much of psychology's appeal as a profession. Table 1-1 lists the divisions in the American Psychological Association and provides an index of the interest range of psychologists.

It is important to remember that the problems psychologists study do not fall into neat categories. Aggression and violence, for example, cannot be categorized as an appropriate topic of study only for social psychology or only for physiologi-

Table 1–1. Divisions in the American Psychological Association

1. General Psychology	22. Rehabilitation Psychology
2. Teaching of Psychology	23. Consumer Psychology
3. Experimental Psychology	24. Philosophical and Theoretical Psychology
5. Evaluation and Measurement	25. Experimental Analysis of Behavior
6. Physiological and Comparative Psychology	26. History of Psychology
7. Developmental Psychology	27. Community Psychology
8. Personality and Social Psychology	28. Psychopharmocology
9. Society for the Psychological Study of Social Issues	29. Psychotherapy
10. Psychology and the Arts	30. Psychological Hypnosis
12. Clinical Psychology	31. State Psychological Association Affairs
13. Consulting Psychology	32. Humanistic Psychology
14. Industrial and Organizational Psychology	33. Mental Retardation
15. Educational Psychology	34. Population and Environmental Psychology
16. School Psychology	35. Psychology of Women
17. Counseling Psychology	36. Psychologists Interested in Religious Issues
18. Psychologists in Public Service	37. Child and Youth Services
19. Military Psychology	38. Health Psychology
20. Adult Development and Aging	39. Psychoanalysis
21. Society of Engineering Psychologists	40. Clinical Neuropsychology
	41. Psychology and Law

cal psychology. Each interest area has contributions to make. So while psychologists tend to specialize, their training must be broad enough to ensure that they can understand what other interest areas have to say about a topic. To do otherwise would be analogous to the proverbial group of blind men who tried to describe an elephant after each one felt a different part of its body.

PSYCHOLOGY: A SCIENCE AND AN ART

Let us return for a moment to the usual definition of psychology—the scientific study of the behavior of organisms. This definition implies that psychology is a science. As we have seen, many psychologists are involved primarily in applying psychology to practical problems and never conduct scientific research, but every psychologist does receive training in scientific methods. Even those who do not conduct research themselves must be able to evaluate research findings in order to apply them in their professional activities. On the other hand, psychologists involved with practical problems quickly learn that the science of psychology does not provide them with all the answers they need. They are forced to rely on the art of psychology. Let us explore the dimensions of psychology as a science and as an art.

The Science of Psychology

When we use the term "science," we are actually speaking of certain methods of collecting information and arriving at conclusions. Psychologists who identify with "psychology as a science" use these scientific methods to conduct research in order to increase their understanding of human behavior. These methods, which will be discussed in Chapter 20, allow researchers to collect information in such a way that they can be confident of their results. It is a process of formulating hypotheses about behavior and then conducting experiments to test those hypotheses. The science of psychology is built upon the findings from such research and the methods used to generate new empirical findings.

As an example, suppose Mr. Jones, a kindergarten teacher, believed that preschool children who receive training in gymnastics adjust to school better than children who do not receive such training. He believed that mastering these exercises gives children more self-confidence, which in turn helps them cope with the separation from home and the new situation of school. To test his hypothesis, Mr. Jones placed a notice in the local newspaper, and 20 parents enrolled their children in his gymnastics class. Six months later, after the school year was half over, he compared the children who had received the special training with those who had not and found that the former had fewer discipline problems, were more cooperative, and performed better on assigned tasks. Mr. Jones concluded that gymnastic training did increase self-confidence and hence improved adjustment to school.

Are Mr. Jones's conclusions justified? While he did use elements of the scientific method, other aspects of his approach were too flawed to warrant his conclusions. He formulated a hypothesis and conducted an experiment to test his hypothesis. His experiment, however, was not designed in a way that could provide support for his ideas.

There were at least three major problems with his experiment. First, he used as subjects only children whose parents volunteered for a special program, and he compared them to children of parents who showed no such interest. It is likely that parents who show an interest in such special programs are particularly concerned with their children's adjustment to school. Thus the parents who volunteered may have spent more time preparing their children for school, and their children would have done better even without the gymnastics class. Second, Mr. Jones should have compared the children who received gymnastic training with children who received some other form of special training that was not believed to help prepare children for school. As the experiment was conducted, it is impossible to know whether it was the gymnastic training that produced the results or simply the children's getting to know the teacher. Third, although Mr. Jones believed that the gymnastic training was effective because it increased self-confidence, he never actually measured the self-confidence of the children. Perhaps the gymnastic training was beneficial because it taught the children how and why to follow directions.

The importance of the science of psychology is evident in this example. If Mr. Jones were able to convince his school principal that the experiment was meaningful, the school might require all children to complete a gymnastics class before entering kindergarten—even though it was of no value. Similar decisions have to be made about a number of important social issues, such as the effectiveness of Head Start programs, violence in the media, legislation directed at discrimination, and sex education in the schools. By using the science of psychology, researchers can provide public officials with information to help them make sound decisions such as these.

The Art of Psychology

Psychologists perform many tasks for which the science of psychology provides little guidance. In these situations psychologists must rely on their skill, experience, and subjective or intuitive feelings. When they do this, they are practicing the art of psychology.

Suppose Dr. Smith, a personnel psychologist for a large company, has been asked to recommend one of two candidates for the position of sales manager. Both are men who have worked for the company for several years as sales representatives. For the past five years, Dr. Smith has used the science of psychology to identify valid predictors of success for executive positions. But the two candidates, Mr. Harris and Mr. Davis, are similar on all these predictors—aptitude test scores, past sales records, and supervisors' ratings. In other words, the science of psychology will not help Dr. Smith with her decision.

Dr. Smith decides to interview the two men with the hope of finding some information that will help her. Mr. Harris turns out to be a pleasant and outgoing man. He is enthusiastic about his possible promotion and has many ideas about how to increase sales. But Dr. Smith is troubled by Mr. Harris's response to the question about how to deal with sales representatives who fail to meet their quota. Although she cannot put her finger on what bothers her, she feels that Mr. Harris would have difficulty in confronting subordinates who are not performing as they should. In the interview with Mr. Davis, she does not get the same feeling. Although Mr. Davis is not as outgoing as Mr. Harris, he communicates a sense of self-assurance that would enable him to deal with unpleasant situations effectively. Dr. Smith recommends that Mr. Davis receive the promotion.

Dr. Smith practiced the art of psychology in this instance because she had no concrete evidence to go on in making her decision. She had to rely on her knowledge of and experience with people and how they functioned in various capacities. When people are interviewed for a promotion, they try to present themselves in the most favorable light. Mr. Harris and Mr. Davis were no exceptions, so Dr. Smith had to rely on her subjective reactions to the way in which the two men presented themselves.

Some psychologists argue that there are many situations in which the science of psychology will never be able to replace the art of psychology. Just as you cannot train someone to be a Picasso or a Beethoven, neither can you train someone to be perceptive and sensitive to the nuances of human behavior. Artistic, musical, and psychological abilities may be enhanced by training, but individuals have to have the basic skills and qualities to begin with to be successful at the art.

The difference between psychology as a science and psychology as an art is largely a difference in approach. The scientific approach tries to identify principles of behavior that can be applied to people in general. It tends to minimize individual differences. The artistic approach focuses on the individual. It emphasizes the uniqueness of individuals and attempts to understand the causes of individual differences.

To illustrate, suppose a researcher discovers that a particular type of psychotherapy results in a reduction in the average level of anxiety for 10 subjects. Psychologists sympathetic to the scientific approach would be pleased with such findings. They would suggest the general principle that this form of therapy is effective in treating anxiety.

Psychologists sympathetic to the artistic approach would point out any variability among the ten subjects. Perhaps seven showed some improvement, two showed no change, and one was more anxious at the end of therapy than at the beginning. The "artist" would argue that we cannot rely on the general principle that brand-X therapy is effective in treating anxiety. Instead we would have to take individual differences into account and use expertise and intuition to decide which individuals will respond favorably to this form of therapy.

The controversy between the artists and the scientists goes on. It is our belief that both approaches are necessary. For example, one would not want to recommend that all preschool children take gymnastics without scientific evidence that such a program would make a difference. To do otherwise would be a waste of resources. On the other hand, one would not hire Mr. Harris over Mr. Davis simply because he scored two points higher on an aptitude test, no matter how valid the test may be. The personnel psychologist would need to consider other characteristics that cannot be measured scientifically. The skillful psychologist is one who knows how to integrate the science and the art of psychology.

TRAINING AND EMPLOYMENT IN PSYCHOLOGY

A few years ago, a student who asked a psychology professor what one should do with a major in psychology could expect to be told to go to graduate school. Unfortunately, the days of steadily expanding college enrollments are over. Similarly, good jobs are getting harder to obtain. More than ever before, students are concerned with acquiring marketable skills. They are passing over psychology in favor of majors in fields such as business and engineering. Psychology professors can no longer ignore the question of career prospects for their increasingly precious majors.

During the past decade, the American Psychological Association has recognized the problem of what students can expect to do with a major in psychology. Their interest has resulted in the publication of two books, *Career Opportunities for Psychologists* (Woods, 1976) and *The Psychology Major* (Woods, 1979). These references provide encouragement that there are indeed many things one can do with training in psychology, with graduate school being just one of the opportunities.

Psychologist Paul Woods, who edited the two books for the American Psychological Association, reported that he first became concerned about the prospects for psychology students in the early 1970s. As a result of his work on the two volumes, he is now enthusiastic about the future of psychology. He believes that in any service-oriented occupation, a person trained in the methods and content of psychology can make an important contribution. He feels that the future will find psychologists employed in vocations that do not even exist now. Psychologists will continue to discover new ways in which their talents will prove useful.

In *The Psychology Major,* Woods included several surveys conducted by departments of psychology to discover what students were actually doing with an undergraduate degree in psychology. The diversity of postgraduate experiences was surprising. Nearly half of the students went on to obtain a graduate degree—although a majority of these degrees were in fields other than psychology, such as education, business, law, and medicine. About 75 percent reported that they would select psychology as a major again if they had a second chance. There was no relation between whether students would major in psychology again and the type of graduate training they received. This suggests that a major in psychology is perceived as good preparation for advanced study in a variety of fields.

The surveys also indicated that the prospects for students who wished to begin their careers immediately after college were relatively good. Unlike accounting and engineering majors, psychology majors are not wooed by corporate representatives on college campuses. But it does appear that about two-thirds of psychology majors are able to obtain a position related to their career choices within six months of graduation. Many of these positions, such as probation counselor, social worker, counselor for learning-disabled children, and mental-health worker, are in fields directly related to psychology. Others are not related to psychology. These include positions in fields ranging from business to acting.

Woods maintained that students who planned ahead were more successful in obtaining satisfying positions than those who waited until late in their senior year to ask themselves what they would do upon graduation. Let us review some of the things students can do to facilitate finding a job or gaining admittance to a graduate program. We shall also discuss what psychology has to offer to the nonpsychology major.

Strategies for Career Preparation

Perhaps, as Woods suggested, the most important thing a student can do to prepare for a career is to plan ahead. This means that as early as possible students should begin to think about what types of careers are appealing and then to learn as much

Many psychology majors pursue careers in social work. This social worker is counseling a pregnant woman. (© *Erika Stone*)

as they can about those careers. Then courses and extracurricular activities can be selected accordingly.

Suppose Tom, whose initiation to psychology was described at the beginning of this chapter, decided that he wanted to work with disturbed adolescents after he graduated. The first things he would want to know are what agencies employ people with a background in this area and what specific positions are available. The place to begin might be his adviser at the university. Many psychology professors engage in professional activities in their communities and are knowledgeable about such opportunities. They would be able to provide Tom with the information he wants or to refer him to someone who can.

Next, Tom would want to talk with people who are currently working in agencies that he is interested in. They might be able to give him valuable advice concerning the courses he should take. And Tom would have a useful contact when it came time to look for a job.

Developing contacts is extremely important because they can serve as a source of recommendations as well as a pipeline to jobs. Students are often reluctant to approach professionals in their communities for fear they will be rebuffed. Of course this may happen, but many professionals are flattered to be able to serve as a mentor to an interested and motivated student.

A third important strategy is to acquire skills through course work. While this may appear obvious, too many students select courses on the basis of scheduling convenience or the reputation of the instructor. Because of Tom's interests, he should take as many clinical courses as possible. He might also take courses in education, since adolescents are likely to have school-related problems. Business courses might be valuable, since even psychologists have to be concerned with matters such as budgets, income, and expenses. A sequence of accounting courses could mean the difference between advancement and stagnation within a particular organization.

Tom should select these courses with an eye to developing specific areas of competence. For instance, a student interested in a research career might take three or four advanced courses in statistics, rather than a greater number of lower-level statistics courses. A student interested in a business career might take a series of advanced courses in accounting or business management rather than a variety of survey courses in business. It is helpful to be able to offer a prospective employer more than a well-rounded background.

The fourth important recommendation is to acquire relevant experiences during the college years. This can be done through volunteer activities or part-time employment. Many social-service agencies are happy to have psychology majors serve as volunteers for a few hours a week. Activities may range from working as an aide in a psychiatric hospital to tutoring a child who comes from a disadvantaged background. Such volunteer activities often develop into paid positions as students gain more experience.

Part-time jobs, even if they are not directly related to career goals, can often provide invaluable experience. A part-time job as a bank teller can pave the way to a management position for a student interested in personnel work. Volunteer work for a charity can lead to a paid position in the organization upon graduation. And part-time jobs also serve the important function of increasing one's contacts.

As Woods suggests, an undergraduate degree in psychology will not qualify one to be a psychologist, but a number of career opportunities are available to the psychology major. It requires advance planning and extra effort, but the student interested in a career related to psychology should not be dissuaded by the notion that the only thing he or she can do with a degree in psychology is to go to graduate school. It simply is not true!

Strategies for Graduate Training Preparation

The strategies for being admitted to graduate school are similar to strategies for career preparation. Planning ahead is crucial. Every spring psychology professors are approached by seniors who say they have decided to go to graduate school and ask for advice. By then, of course, it is too late. The professor can only suggest that they plan for the following year.

During the first two years of college, students should start to consider what type of graduate training they are interested in. Again, the best way to do this is to make contacts and ask questions. Psychology professors are the best place to start. They can provide information about the various areas of specialization and the schools that offer such training. Psychologists who work in the community are usually pleased to spend time with students. Tom learned about two areas of specialization that he was not interested in by talking with psychologists working in those areas. By continuing to make contacts, he could find areas that did appeal to him. College catalogues, which can be found in almost every college library, provide information about different programs and the types of courses required. It is important to gather this objective information because it is easy to develop an inaccurate idea of what various kinds of psychologists do. Television, movies, and newspaper accounts may create an image of clinical or experimental psychologists that bears little relation to reality.

Planning ahead includes selecting courses that will satisfy the requirements of the graduate programs to which the student intends to apply. This information can be obtained from college catalogues. Course requirements will rarely be a problem for psychology majors who apply to psychology programs. But for students who intend to receive graduate training in fields such as education or business management, course selection should be carefully considered.

The most important thing students can do to increase their chances of getting into graduate school is to get to know their professors. Every college professor has had the experience of hearing a student's voice for the first time when he or she asks for a letter of recommendation. These students may have done very well in their courses, but they never participated in class or stopped by the professor's office to chat about a course. The professor can say little about such students in letters of recommendation beyond describing their grades. Such letters do not impress graduate admissions committees.

Getting to know professors not only provides a basis for receiving helpful letters of recommendation, but it also can help the student grow professionally. It may be possible to assist in research the professor is conducting. Or the student may do volunteer work at an agency with which the professor is associated. And just by having informal discussions with professors, the student's grasp of and appreciation for the discipline of psychology is likely to increase.

Many students may not qualify for the graduate program at the top of their list. Admissions to well-known graduate programs are highly competitive. Given sufficient interest, motivation, and planning, however, the majority of students will be able to find placement in a program that will enhance their chances of reaching their career goals.

What Psychology Has to Offer the Nonmajor

Because psychology is concerned with human behavior, and because virtually everyone must interact with other people in their vocations and avocations, a series of courses in psychology can be valuable for almost anyone. Students majoring in fields that require extensive contact with others, such as education or business management, can enhance their skills with courses in psychology. Courses such as those that cover exceptional children, theories of motivation, and psychological testing can complement majors in several other fields. They can provide knowledge and skills that will make one more employable.

Several of the surveys discussed by Woods (1979) reported results that have important implications for course selection. These surveys found that many respondents, regardless of their occupations, believed that courses in behavioral methodologies were most valuable to them. These are courses such as psychological statistics and experimental methods in psychology. Unfortunately, these courses tend to be difficult and hence are avoided by many nonmajors. But they do provide skills that can be useful in a variety of occupational settings.

Psychology courses can also make a valuable contribution at a personal level. Most people must deal with stressful situations, rear children, form friendships, be members of a group, and go through transitional periods. Psychology courses can help make these roles and relationships more understandable and perhaps help individuals make more effective choices in dealing with them.

Summary

Psychology is typically defined as the scientific study of the behavior of organisms. While adequate at a general level, this definition fails to do justice to the diversity of interests and activities of psychologists.

Defining psychology has been a problem from the beginning of its history. Wilhelm Wundt and his student, Edward Titchener, believed that psychology was the study of the mind. Their approach, called structuralism, attempted to identify the elements of consciousness. William James, the first native-born American psychologist of renown, helped to establish functionalism. He argued that the workings of the mind are functional in that they help us survive. He believed psychology should focus on the relation between the mind and behavior. A group of German psychologists also attacked structuralism. Their approach, called Gestalt psychology, suggested that our conscious experience was more than just the sum of individual elements. John B. Watson, the father of behaviorism, argued that the mind, or consciousness, was a myth. He believed that psychologists should focus only on observable behavior. Sigmund Freud was not concerned with defining psychology, but his work resulted in a school of thought called psychoanalysis. His theory suggested that behavior is influenced by unconscious memories, motives, and fantasies. Francis Galton did not initiate a school of psychology, but his work on heredity and intelligence provided the basis for the psychological assessment and study of individual differences.

While schools of psychology continue to exist, psychologists today are more likely to identify with a particular interest area of psychology. Physiological psychology is concerned with the biological basis of behavior. Experimental psychologists study basic foundations of behavior such as learning and memory, but the experimental method is applicable also to the study of any number of practical problems. The relation between behavior and age is the domain of the developmental psychologist. Diagnosis and treatment of psychological disorders are the primary interests of clinical psychologists. Social psychology focuses on the influence of groups on the behavior of individuals.

Psychology is both a science and an art. It is a science because it utilizes the scientific method to acquire knowledge about behavior. It is an art because psychologists work in many settings where they must make decisions without having a scientific basis for doing so. They must rely on their knowledge, experience, sensitivity, and insight to make the correct decisions.

Students who major in psychology need to plan ahead for either a career or graduate training. Despite popular stereotypes, individuals with an undergraduate degree can find jobs that are relevant to their career goals. While well-known graduate schools are extremely competitive, most students can obtain graduate training that will enhance their qualifications. Students will improve their chances of finding a job or being admitted to a graduate school if they plan ahead, build a network of contacts, and gain relevant experience through part-time jobs or volunteer activities. Psychology courses can also provide nonmajors with knowledge and skills that they will find valuable in a variety of careers and in their personal lives.

Key Terms For Review

behaviorism
clinical psychologist
clinical psychology
developmental psychology
Doctor of Psychology
eclectic
experimental psychology
functionalism
Gestalt psychology
humanistic psychology
individual differences
learned helplessness
physiological psychology
psychiatrist
psychoanalysis
social psychology
structuralism

Suggested Readings

American Psychological Association. *Graduate study in psychology.* Washington, D.C.: Author, 1977.

This is an invaluable resource book for anyone contemplating graduate training in psychology. It provides general pointers regarding the process of planning for graduate work and applying to graduate schools, and it provides descriptions of all graduate training programs in psychology. Details such as requirements for admission, expenses, and names and addresses are given.

Evan, R. I. *The making of psychology.* New York: Knopf, 1976.

Twenty-eight of the most important figures in modern psychology discuss their contributions to the field. This book provides an overview of the different interest areas that concern psychologists.

Watson, R. I. *The great psychologists* (3rd ed.). Philadelphia: J. B. Lippincott, 1971.

This book offers an enjoyable method of learning about the history and major theories of psychology by presenting them through the stories of the people who contributed to psychology's development.

Woods, P. J. (Ed.). *Career opportunities for psychologists: Expanding and emerging areas.* Washington, D.C.: American Psychological Association, 1976.
This book discusses positions open to psychologists, educational and job requirements, and potential salaries. It also speculates about roles psychologists may fulfill in the future. It is an important resource for any student contemplating a career in psychology.

Woods, P. J. (Ed.). *The psychology major: Training and employment strategies.* Washington, D.C.: American Psychological Association, 1979.
This text offers practical advice to students who plan to begin their careers immediately after college and discusses the types of jobs available to them.

2

The Physiological Basis of Behavior

In 1966 a 25-year-old student of architectural engineering climbed to the top of the tower on the campus of the University of Texas in Austin and methodically began shooting everyone in sight. He killed 13 people and wounded 31 before he was shot dead by the police. Later it was discovered that the sniper had also slain his wife and mother before his shooting spree.

*Like many mass murderers, Charles Whitman was described by his acquaintances as an exemplary boy, the kind that neighborhood mothers hold up as a model to their own youngsters (*Time*, 1966). His upbringing could not have been more typically middle class—he was an altar boy in his church, delivered newspapers in his neighborhood, became an Eagle Scout, and managed the football team of his parochial school. The only atypical aspect of this middle-class background was that Charles's father was a gun fanatic who trained his son to use a gun as soon as he could hold it.*

During the spring preceding the mass murder, Charles complained to the University of Texas staff psychiatrist about the intense anger he felt toward his father, whom he held responsible for his parents' divorce. He told the psychiatrist that he was "thinking about going up on the tower with a deer rifle and . . . shooting people."

The evening before the shooting, Whitman wrote a note that began: "I've been having fears and violent impulses. I've had some tremendous headaches. I am prepared to die. After my death, I wish an autopsy on me to be performed to see if there's any mental disorder." He also stated in his note: "I intend to kill my wife after I pick her up from work. I don't want her to have to face the embarrassment that my actions will surely cause her." Whitman's autopsy uncovered that he had a malignant tumor in an area of the brain known as the amygdala. Did the tumor cause Whitman's violent behavior? Would earlier detection and removal of the cancerous tissue have prevented the tragedy?

The intention of this chapter is to relate behavior to its biological foundations. Psychologists are interested in the role played by genes and by the brain in influencing human behavior. Although most research in behavioral genetics and physiological psychology uses animals as experimental subjects, we shall present human data wherever possible. Such human data are readily available, for example, in cases of genetic disorders or brain abnormalities and injuries.

HEREDITY AND BEHAVIOR

Human beings have always been interested in their origins. The young child will inevitably ask, "Where did I come from?" Adults have long been engaged in tracing their ancestry and making up family trees. It has been suggested that people had an intuitive feel for heredity and its effects long before the science of genetics was born.

The study of heredity, or **genetics,** is concerned with the transmission of physical and psychological traits from parents to offspring and with the relationship between inherited characteristics and environment. Genetics helps explain why human beings are alike as a species, yet different as individuals. The color of your hair and eyes and the shape of your nose are characteristics that you inherited from one or more ancestors, and so are aspects of your personality.

Genetics is a relatively young science. Its foundations were laid by an Austrian monk, Gregor Mendel (1822–1884), at about the same time that Charles Darwin published his book *Origin of Species* (1859). Over the past 80 years, the science of genetics has been moving forward at an astonishing rate. We have come to see that surprisingly simple rules underlie the bewildering complexities of inheritance. (Dobzhansky, 1964).

Genes and Chromosomes

The basic unit of inheritance is genes, which are found in the nucleus of all living cells. Genes are composed of DNA, or **deoxyribonucleic acid.** DNA has become the symbol of life, because encoded in its chemical script are the instructions that direct our development from a single-cell organism to a complex adult.

The DNA is divided into segments, each of which consists of a series of proteins called amino acids. Each of the DNA segments is built up from four chemical subunits that combine and repeat themselves in various ways to write the messages of heredity in our genes. The four chemicals, which are themselves composed of proteins, are the same in people, animals, and plants, but they differ in the order in which they are strung together. Every human being is thought to be the product of literally billions of DNA subunits, arranged in different ways in different individuals (except in the case of identical twins). Figures 2–1 and 2–2 illustrate the structure and replication of DNA.

One of the most important characteristics of DNA is its ability to reproduce itself in cell division. During the self-copying process, each DNA segment in a gene forms a replica of itself, so that every newly produced gene is composed of one old strand and one new strand of DNA.

Genes are located, by the hundreds and perhaps thousands, in every **chromosome.** Chromosomes are microscopic particles that occur in pairs in the nucleus of every human cell. Each cell typically contains 46 chromosomes, or 23 pairs. Twenty-two pairs of chromosomes carry the genes for general body characteristics and functions, but the 23rd pair are the so-called sex chromosomes.

Every human life begins with a single cell weighing about one twenty-millionth of an ounce.

Figure 2–1. The structure and replication of DNA. The ribbons in the shape of a double helix represent the backbones of the DNA strands. They are made up of alternating sugar and phosphate groups (not shown). The strands are kept together by weak hydrogen bonds (· · ·) between nucleic acid bases: adenine (A) pairs with thymine (T), and guanine (G) pairs with cytosine (C). The lower part of the diagram shows what happens when the DNA double helix is replicated. Note that each of the resulting double helices contains one old strand and one newly made one. (Adapted from James D. Watson, *Molecular Biology of the Gene*).

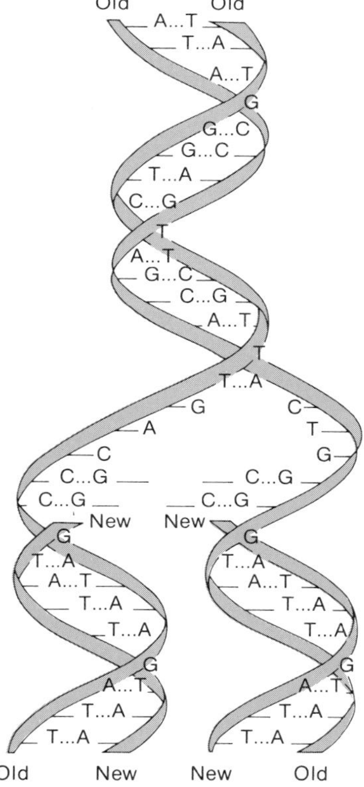

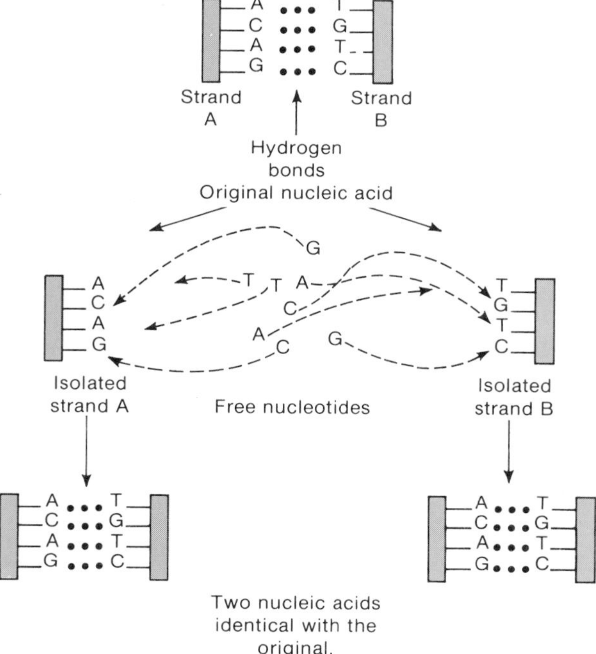

Figure 2–2. Detail of replication.

This tiny bit of matter was created by the union of an egg cell from the mother and a sperm cell from the father, a process known as fertilization. Both egg and sperm contribute a genetic message encoded in DNA. The combined message in the new cell carries the entire genetic blueprint of the person. The new cell divides into two, four, eight, and ultimately billions of cells and grows into an embryo, a fetus, an infant, and an adult.

The sex of the new organism is determined by the type of sex chromosomes transmitted during fertilization. The typical process is as follows. The mother's egg transmits an X chromosome. Half of the father's sperms have an X chromosome, and half have a Y chromosome. When a sperm with an X chromosome fertilizes the egg, the offspring is female (XX). When a Y-chromosome sperm fertilizes the egg, the offspring is male (XY). Virtually all people have either XX or XY chromosomes, but, as we shall see later, there are exceptions.

It should be noted that sexual reproduction does not equal genetic replication, since your children will be only half you and your grandchildren only a quarter you. That is, parents and their children share 50 percent of a common gene pool, whereas grandparents have only 25 percent of genes in common with their grandchildren. In a few generations the most you can hope for is a large number of descendants, each of whom bears only a tiny portion of you in the form of a few genes.

It used to be fashionable to debate how much of our characteristics are due to heredity, or genes, and how much to the environment in which we grow up. This debate is known as the nature-nurture controversy. Today, however, extreme positions in this controversy are outmoded. Advances in genetics have reduced the argument of heredity (nature) versus environment (nurture) to futility, because any trait or characteristic is both genetic and environmental. Without genes there can be no organism, and without a supportive environment an organism cannot survive and therefore will be unable to display behavioral characteristics. It is reasonable, then, to assume that behavior is a function of an interaction between genes and the quality of the environment to which the person is exposed. Take the case of someone who has excellent bodily coordination. If that person is not given the opportunity to use and develop that coordination, it will not show up as a trait. But if a coach or a parent spots the potential of the child in, say, tennis and provides a way to develop it, he or she may turn into a Bjorn Borg or Chris Evert. Thus we may say that genes determine a range of potential for a given trait, and environment shapes the person's actual behavior within that range.

Down's syndrome, the most prevalent chromosomal aberration, is also the most common cause of mental retardation. With IQs below 70, Down's children develop basic language skills around the age of five. *(© Rick Winsor/Woodfin Camp & Associates)*

Effects of Genes on Behavior

The influence of genes on behavior manifests itself in a number of ways. For example, we know that certain psychological disorders, such as schizophrenia (see Chapter 12), tend to run in families. Data from family studies indicate that the closer the blood kinship and the more similar the genetic background, the greater the possibility of schizophrenia. Schizophrenia is found more frequently in first-order relatives, such as siblings, children, and parents of schizophrenic patients, than in second-order relatives, such as aunts, uncles, nieces, and nephews. The greatest degree of similarity for schizophrenia is found among identical twins, who are genetic carbon copies of each other.

Research also suggests that personality traits may be transmitted genetically. For example, a study of identical twins and fraternal twins (who do not share the same genes) found strong evidence that there is an inherited component to anxiety reactions (Slater & Shields, 1969). Similarities between parents and children have been reported for many traits, including intelligence, aggression, and level of activity.

Table 2–1. Incidence of Human Chromosome Aberrations

Clinical Syndrome	*Chromosome Number*	*Estimated Incidence*	*Calculated Number in U.S.*
Down's syndrome	47	1 in 600	288,571
Klinefelter's syndrome	47	1 in 400 males	252,500
Turner's syndrome	45	1 in 5,000 females	20,500
Double Y syndrome	47	1 in 250 males	404,000

Source: Adapted from Mertens, 1975

Chromosome Aberrations and Behavior

Much of what we know about the effects of specific genes has been obtained from the study of genetic defects, abnormalities in either the structure or the number of chromosomes. The most common of these conditions is **Down's syndrome,** also known as mongolism because of the almond-shaped, slanted eyes that give the person a somewhat oriental appearance. About 1 in every 600 babies born in the United States is diagnosed as having Down's syndrome, a condition that occurs more often in children born to older mothers (age 35 and older).

Individuals with Down's syndrome have 47 rather than the usual 46 chromosomes in their cells, since they carry chromosome 21 in triplicate. The condition may also be caused by breaks or translocations of genetic material in chromosome 21. **Translocations** involve the attachment of a whole chromosome or a fragment to another chromosome.

The most important behavioral characteristic in Down's syndrome is mental retardation. Intelligence quotients range from 20 to 70, compared with the normal range of 85 to 115. Down's syndrome is the single most common cause of mental retardation and accounts for 10 percent of the population in institutions for the mentally retarded.

In physical appearance individuals with Down's syndrome are usually very short. They have flattened faces and a thick, fissured tongue. Development in Down's children is slow, but it does occur. Most of them can walk by the third and fourth year, and nearly all have simple language skills by the age of five. Most Down's children are very affectionate and respond to affection from others.

Aberrations of the sex chromosome are also common but much rarer than Down's syndrome, as can be seen from Table 2–1. The most important ones are Klinefelter's syndrome in males and Turner's syndrome in females. Men with **Klinefelter's syndrome** carry an additional X sex chromosome (XXY), making 47 chromosomes in all. According to Hamerton and his co-workers (Hamerton, Canning, Ray, & Smith, 1975), Klinefelter's syndrome is caused by a fault in the genetic control of cell division in the mother's ovum. Most often this condition occurs in children of mothers age 35 or older.

Men with Klinefelter's syndrome have underdeveloped male sex characteristics, such as small testes or lack of facial and body hair. Frequently they show breast enlargement and a widening of the pelvic area. Some degree of mental retardation is present in most affected men. Various forms of psychopathology are more common among Klinefelter's men than among men in the general population (Nyhan, 1971). Unconventional sexual identities, such as transvestism, transsexualism, homosexuality, and bisexuality, are particularly common (Money & Ehrhardt, 1972). Some of the men with this condition appear normal physically and mentally. Nonetheless, all Klinefelter's men are sterile.

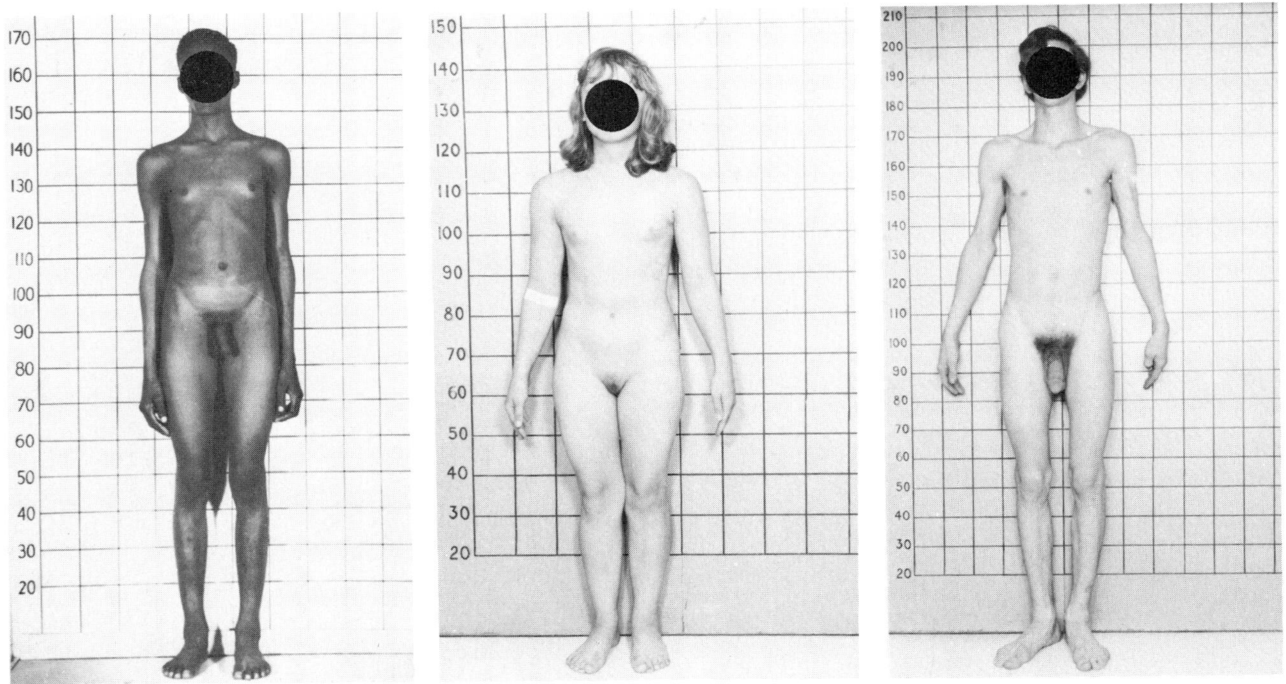

Physical abnormalities can result from one missing or extra chromosome. Left: Klinefelter's syndrome triggers underdeveloped sex characteristics and sterility. Center: Turner's syndrome in women causes shortness, sterility, and rudimentary reproductive organs. Right: The only known physical trait of the double Y syndrome is extraordinary height.

Whereas Klinefelter's syndrome in men is characterized by the presence of an additional X chromosome, **Turner's syndrome** in women is caused by the absence of one X sex chromosome (XO), making a total of 45 chromosomes. Physical abnormalities in Turner's women include shortness in stature (they rarely reach more than 4½ feet as adults), a short, webbed neck, and underdeveloped breasts with widely spaced nipples. The internal reproductive organs are rudimentary, and ovaries are replaced by narrow streaks of nonfunctional tissues. Because ovaries are missing, the hormones necessary for the initiation and regulation of the menstrual cycle cannot be secreted. If the condition is recognized early enough, hormone-replacement therapy can bring about a normal menstrual cycle. Like the Klinefelter's males, Turner's women are sterile, though they may have a normal uterus and menstruation can be induced. Some, but not all, are mentally retarded.

Psychologically, girls with Turner's syndrome are unequivocally feminine in their gender identity. They experience the same romantic fantasies of courtship and marriage that normal girls do. Those who marry and adopt children display strong maternal interests and behavior.

Another chromosomal abnormality, an extra Y sex chromosome in men (XYY, 47 chromosomes), has caused considerable public controversy. Its only apparent physical manifestation is unusual height, but the condition has also been associated with criminality. Early surveys of prisons, mental institutions, and detention homes revealed a disproportionately large percentage of XYY men present (Jacobs, Brenton, Melville, Brittain, & McClermont, 1965). But many of these early surveys were biased, because these XYY males may represent the more severe cases of the condition rather than the entire group. Many XYY men show up on basketball teams rather than in criminal institutions. Although violent murders have been committed by XYY men, it is not yet justified to label the XYY condition a "criminal syndrome." Owen (1972) concluded that XYY men in nonprison populations do not seem more aggressive than normal men but that the XYY pattern carries a greater risk of mental retardation.

Genetic Engineering

Imagine programming an astronaut to be born without legs to be better able to endure prolonged confinement in a space capsule. Or imagine creating groups of soldiers or scientists who are genetic xerox copies of a famous military leader or eminent scientist. Although fiction today, these events may become reality through genetic engineering, or the technological use of genetic knowledge. Genetic engineering is an adventurous and morally complex science that can involve manipulating genetic material to alter human characteristics.

Amniocentesis. One genetic-engineering technique in use today is **amniocentesis,** a procedure to detect genetic disorders before birth (see Figure 2–3). In this procedure a needle is inserted through the abdomen of a pregnant woman into the amniotic cavity of the uterus and a small amount of amniotic fluid is removed. Since the amniotic fluid contains fetal cells, probably sloughed off from the skin, urinary tract, or respiratory system, it can be examined for genetic disorders. If chromosomal abnormalities are found, the mother has the choice of continuing the pregnancy or requesting a therapeutic abortion. The artificial interruption of any pregnancy, however, creates many moral, legal, and medical problems. At the present time, amniocentesis must be performed in the first 20 weeks of pregnancy and is mainly used to diagnose gross chromosomal abnormalities, such as Down's syndrome. Amniocentesis is generally justified in the cases of women of advanced maternal age, particularly those over 35, and of women who have already had a child with a chromosomal abnormality.

Ectogenesis. **Ectogenesis** uses genetic-engineering techniques to allow the fertilized or nonfertilized ovum to complete some or all of its prenatal development outside the female reproductive tract (Marx, 1973). This procedure is applicable to couples who are infertile because blockages in the woman's fallopian tubes impede conception. Prior to ovulation, the ovum is withdrawn and placed in a fertilization medium. The sperm provided by the husband by masturbation is also placed in a culture. When the egg is placed into the sperm suspension, sperm penetration usually occurs within three or four hours. Fertilization takes place "in vitro" (literally, in the glass). After the fertilized egg has been allowed to develop for a few days, it can be implanted in the mother's uterus for a normal pregnancy. The first successful birth of an in-vitro fertilized baby occurred in 1978 (see page 34).

While in-vitro fertilization is a boon to couples who have been unhappy in infertile marriages, the procedure does raise some important ethical issues. Proponents of the procedure argue that parents who are willing to go to such lengths to have a baby will probably go out of their way to provide an optimal environment for the child. Others question whether we are justified in de-

Figure 2–3. Amniocentesis.

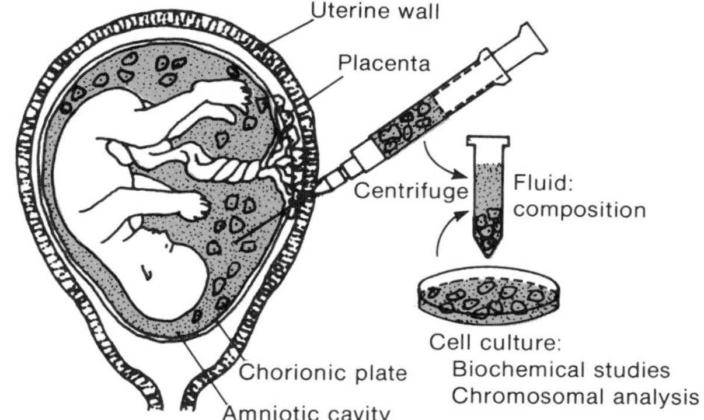

APPLICATION

Louise Brown: The World's First Test-Tube Baby

The first test-tube baby was safely delivered by Caesarean section on July 25, 1978, to John and Lesley Brown at Oldham Hospital in Oldham, England. After nine years of infertility due to blocked fallopian tubes, Lesley Brown was referred to gynecologist Patrick Steptoe, a pioneer in in-vitro fertilization. Steptoe worked in collaboration with Robert Edwards, a physiologist who had perfected a means of fertilizing human eggs and improved chemical solutions necessary to keep them alive outside the body.

Louise Brown was conceived in November 1977 after Steptoe had extracted an egg from one of Lesley's ovaries and placed it in a laboratory dish where it was fertilized with John Brown's sperm. After two and a half days, during which the fertilized egg underwent three cell divisions and reached the eight-cell stage, it was reimplanted into Lesley's uterus, where it developed into a normal embryo. Amniocentesis at 16 weeks revealed no abnormalities in the fetus's 46 chromosomes (Steptoe & Edwards, 1978).

When Lesley developed mildly high blood pressure, threatening complications in the delivery, Steptoe decided on the Caesarean section. The delivery itself was uneventful. Louise, blue-eyed and just under six pounds, was described by her father as "beautiful, with marvelous complexion and not red and wrinkly at all." Edwards added, "The last time I saw the baby, it was just eight cells in the test tube. It was beautiful then and it's beautiful now." Three days after birth, Louise had gained two ounces and was being breastfed.

Reactions to the news of the first test-tube baby came from many quarters. Some hailed it as a medical miracle, some as an ethical mistake or the beginning of a new age of genetic manipulation. Naturally the event has given hope to other childless couples who would like to see the procedure applied to their own cases.

veloping new ways of producing babies, thereby playing a superhuman kind of role.

In addition, lawyers are envisioning the possibility of malpractice suits by in-vitro fertilized children, either against their parents or against the physician who created them, if they are born with mental or physical abnormalities. The potential legal complications that may arise from this kind of fertilization were illustrated in the case of couple in New York who sued a gynecologist, a hospital, and Columbia University for 1.5 million dollars in emotional and physical damages. A fertilized egg ready for implantation into the wife had to be destroyed after the physician inadvertently disturbed the egg by opening the jar containing it.

Ethical questions also arise concerning how to deal with extrauterine fertilizations that use a foster mother in cases where the genetic mother is unable to bear the child. Whose child would it be—the genetic mother's or the foster mother's?

Artificial Insemination. Another genetic-engineering technique that has been put into practice is artificial insemination, using either the husband's sperm obtained by masturbation or sperm from a donor. The actual insemination procedure is quite simple. At the estimated time of ovulation, a small volume of semen is introduced into the cervix. When fresh semen is used, approximately 35 percent of women conceive during the first attempt and 75 percent by the fourth attempt. When frozen semen is used, an eventual 50-percent rate of success is usual (Karp, 1977).

Like in-vitro fertilization, artificial insemination presents many moral and ethical problems. Several religions, including orthodox Judaism and Roman Catholicism, hold that artificial insemination with sperm other than that of the woman's husband is immoral and indefensible because the procedure involves both masturbation and adultery. The adultery issue is particularly interesting because most people, including some courts of law, believe that the sexual act is at the core of adultery.

The issue of semen donors also raises ethical issues. Most such donors are paid for their services. As in the case of paid blood donors, this procedure runs the risk that prospective donors will falsify their genetic or medical history to avoid being rejected.

A Look at the Future. Scientists today are fascinated by the prospects for genetic engineering. New techniques and advanced technology are rapidly unraveling the secrets of DNA combinations. One study estimates that the deciphering of genetic messages is increasing at the rate of 15 percent a month (Schmeck, 1981). In time we shall have all the genetic information needed to create a complete human being. We shall be able to make genes to order.

One technique of genetic manipulation that looms not far in the future is **cloning,** a process that produces genetic carbon copies of a person. Scientists have produced clones in the laboratory by taking an unfertilized egg cell from a frog and destroying its nucleus by radiation. The nucleus was then replaced with the nucleus of a cell from the intestines of a tadpole. The egg began to divide as if it had been normally fertilized. The result: a twin of the donor tadpole (Mertens, 1975, p. 10).

Cloning offers the possibility of endlessly reproducing individuals who are valued by society and of creating large numbers of people to predetermined specifications. Someone with superior intellectual ability, such as an Einstein, or athletic talent, such as a tall basketball player, can be cloned.

Cloning has been found in nature. Amoebas, for instance, reproduce asexually by transferring the nucleus to the interior of a different type of cell (Briggs & King, 1952). Cloning of humans is more problematic because it does not duplicate the effects that environment has on a person's psychological makeup (Thomas, 1972). Even though members of a common clone would be genetically identical, it seems virtually impossible to create identical environments for them to grow up in.

If clonal reproduction of humans were ever practiced widely, human evolution would certainly take an entirely different course. For one thing, sexuality would begin to lose its connection with reproduction. The family as we know it would no longer exist, and the idea of parenthood would change completely.

A number of other genetic-engineering techniques have been investigated for several years. Gene therapy, the introduction of foreign DNA into patients with genetic disorders, has been attempted. In the view of many geneticists, gene therapy may provide a cure for some human genetic diseases. Recently a group of scientists at Harvard University reported they had identified for the first time a single gene among the millions in a human cell (Gwynne, et al, 1978). Their finding promises the possibility of detecting genetic diseases in embryos and fetuses as well as altering genetic material. For example, if scientists can

Genetic counseling is increasingly recommended for pregnant women over the age of 35. *(© Catherine Ursillo/Photo Researchers, Inc.)*

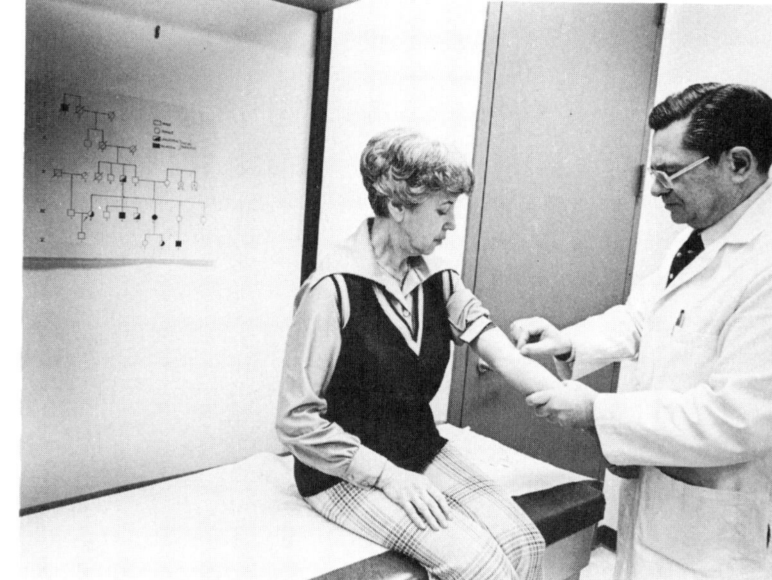

identify the gene involved in the transmission of diabetes or sickle cell anemia, they may be able to correct the defect before the condition develops in a person.

Advancing knowledge in genetics will soon force us to make decisions on issues never faced before. Dr. James Watson (1971), the co-discoverer of DNA, believes that the legal and ethical problems involved in genetic manipulation should not be left to scientists or politicians but should be examined by society as a whole. He recommends decision making through public discussion, much as that which took place during nuclear testing. However, the crucial and controversial issue remains: How should public policy decisions be made on potentially dangerous new technologies? The main challenge for the decades to come may well be to assure that people control science and that scientific advances do not gain control over us.

THE ENDOCRINE GLANDS AND THEIR FUNCTIONS

Human life is highly dependent on the adequate functioning of two important communication systems—the nervous system and the endocrine system. The nervous system, which we will examine later in the chapter, provides a very rapid communication service, not unlike that of a telephone system of a large city. The endocrine system of glands provides a rather slow form of communication. The messages of these glands are carried through the bloodstream by highly specialized substances known as **hormones,** which regulate physiological processes such as how we grow and mature and how we respond to danger.

The **endocrine glands** are located in separate areas of the body, but collectively they make up an interlocking system in which each gland depends on the others (see Figure 2–4). Balance among these glands is necessary for a mentally and physically healthy individual. The major endocrine glands are the **pituitary,** the **thyroid,** the **adrenals,** and the **gonads.**

The Pituitary Gland

Because the pituitary controls the functions of most of the other glands, it is often referred to as the master gland. Located at the base of the brain, to which it is attached by a thin stalk, the pituitary consists of two regions, or lobes—anterior and posterior. The anterior lobe secretes a variety of hormones that primarily govern normal growth and metabolism. This lobe is also involved in sexual maturation, since it controls the release of hormones that regulate the activities of the ovaries and testes. The posterior lobe produces two important hormones that raise the blood pressure, enhance the retention of body water, promote contractions of the uterus at the onset of labor in pregnancy, and initiate the emission of milk from the glandular tissue of the breasts when the mother is nursing a child.

If either lobe of the pituitary does not function properly, a number of pathological conditions may result. For instance, a child deficient in anterior pituitary hormones may fail to grow properly and become a dwarf. Excessive functioning of the anterior pituitary, on the other hand, may lead to overgrowth. People with this condition have been found to reach a height of eight feet.

The Thyroid Gland

The thyroid gland, located in the middle of the neck, secretes the hormone thyroxin, which is intimately involved in the control of normal growth and the development of the body. Too little thyroxin secretion, or **hypothyroidism,** results in a condition known as cretinism. Usually the symptoms make their appearance around the age of six months, when parents notice that the physical and mental development of the child is obviously retarded. As the child grows older, he or she fails to pass important developmental milestones, such as learning to walk and talk at the usual age. Most cretins are dwarfs and have severely impaired mental abilities. If the condition is promptly diagnosed, treatment through injections of extra thyroxin can restore the deficiency and renew the process of normal growth (Levinthal, 1979).

The Adrenal Glands

The two adrenal glands are found in the mid-region of the body above the kidneys. Each gland has two portions—an outer section called the adrenal cortex and an inner section called the adrenal medulla. The adrenal medulla secretes two hormones. The first is **epinephrine** (adrenaline), which is produced primarily during times of stress or emotional crisis. Release of epinephrine causes the heart to beat faster, raises the blood pressure, and elevates the blood-sugar level, thereby providing extra fuel for the brain in emergency situations. The second hormone of the adrenal medulla is **norepinephrine,** which acts upon the pituitary to stimulate the adrenal cortex, which in turn secretes hormones called **steroids.** Steroids are also released under stress and enable the body to be more responsive. The adrenal hormones, then, help determine the behavior of humans as well as that of many animals in situations of danger. By a complicated mechanism, the adrenal glands produce most fear responses.

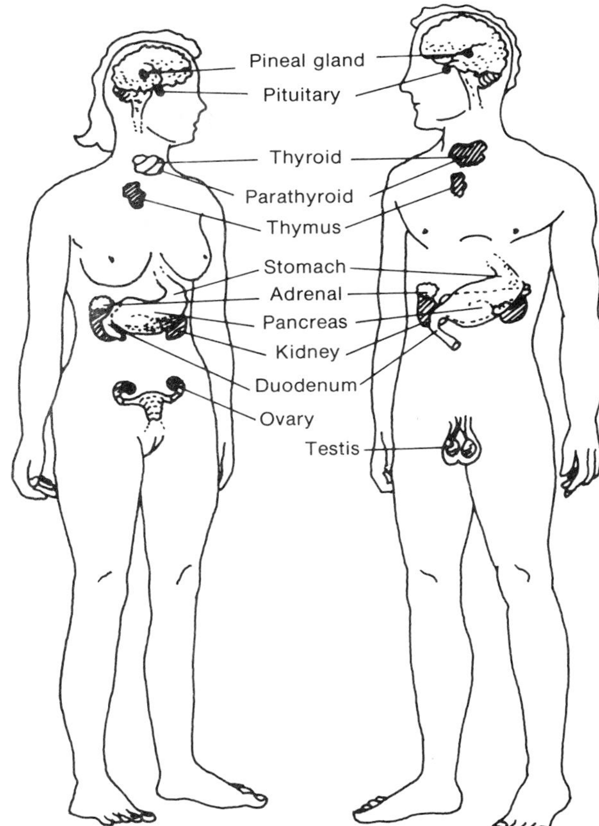

Figure 2–4. Major glands of the body.

The Gonads

The glands that produce sex hormones are the ovaries in females and the testes in males, together called the gonads. The major male sex hormones are **androgen** and **testosterone,** which are responsible for the maturation of male sex organs and the development of secondary sex characteristics, such as the growth of facial hair and change of voice at puberty. More specifically, androgen is a steroid hormone that produces masculine sex characteristics and has an influence on body and bone growth and on the sex drive. Testosterone induces and maintains male secondary sex characteristics.

An excess or deficit of male sex hormones is associated with a number of behavioral phenomena. For example, Rose, Holiday, and Bernstein (1971) reported that aggressive male monkeys tend to have higher levels of testosterone than their more placid cagemates, suggesting that hormone levels affect behavior (see Chapter 18). At the same time, there are cases of individuals who are chromosomally normal males (XY) but who appear to be totally unresponsive to testosterone, while estrogen, the female sex hormone, in their bodies produces breast development and feminine contours (Unger, 1979). Such a person combines the male internal reproductive apparatus with the external sex organs of a normal female and is usually classified as female at birth.

Estrogen is the major female sex hormone. (Males also produce small amounts of estrogen and women small amounts of androgen.) Estrogen accounts for the maturation of female internal reproductive structures and the emergence of secondary sex characteristics, such as breasts and pubic hair. It also plays an important role in the regulation of the menstrual cycle, not only physiologically but also behaviorally. It has been suggested, for instance, that women feel depressed, tense, and irritable just before the onset of their menstrual period, when estrogen levels are low (Bardwick, 1973). Conversely, women report feelings of physical and emotional well-being around the middle of the cycle, just around ovulation, when estrogen levels peak.

The relationship between changes in hormone levels and changes in mood is more complex, however. For example, women who use contraceptive pills, which maintain female sex hormones at a constant level until just before menstruation, do not show the mood changes associated with the menstrual cycle (Paige, 1971; Marinari, Lesher, & Doyle, 1976). And not all women experience high or low moods as a function of changing hormone levels. The effect of hormone levels on mood depends on the individual's physiology, her attitude toward menstruation, and a host of other factors.

Another hormone secreted by the ovaries, called **progesterone,** prepares the uterus for implantation of the fertilized egg and for the nourishment of the embryo during the early stages of prenatal development (see Chapter 8).

THE NERVOUS SYSTEM

Much of our behavior and many of our sensations and skills are governed by the nervous system: rolling our eyes or swinging a tennis racket, the pleasure we experience during orgasm or the pain during hunger, our ability to read language or understand numerical symbols. Damage to certain areas of the nervous system produces physical or behavioral impairments, such as partial blindness, paralysis, or inappropriate behavior. Charles Whitman's abnormal aggressiveness, described at the beginning of this chapter, was probably caused by a disorder in his nervous system.

Divisions of the Nervous System

The nervous system is organized into two major divisions—the **central nervous system,** consisting of the **brain** and the **spinal cord,** and the **peripheral nervous system,** consisting of the autonomic and somatic divisions. The autonomic nervous system has two additional branches, the sympathetic and parasympathetic. The basic building block of the nervous system is the neuron, or nerve cell, which sends messages through the various parts of the nervous system.

The Neuron

The individual nerve cell, or **neuron** (see Figure 2–5), is specialized to receive and transmit information in electrochemical form. The cell body of the neuron performs all the chemical transformations necessary to keep the nerve cell functioning. Each neuron has a fiber called an **axon** that transmits information to other neurons as well as to the muscles or glands. Each axon ends in an enlarged branch known as an **axon terminal.** Axons vary considerably in length. The axons of the spinal motor neurons that send impulses to the muscles of the foot can be several meters long, while axons in the brain can be less than a millimeter long (Ganong, 1975). Some axons are covered by a fatty substance, the **myelin sheath.** The presence of myelin and the diameter of the axon help determine the speed with which nerve impulses travel along the axon. Impulses travel along thick myelinated axons at about 300 feet per second and along thin, unmyelinated ones at about 3 feet per second (Grossman, 1973).

Protruding from the cell body are a number of irregular branching fibers known as **dendrites** (from the Greek *dendron,* "tree"). Like axons, the

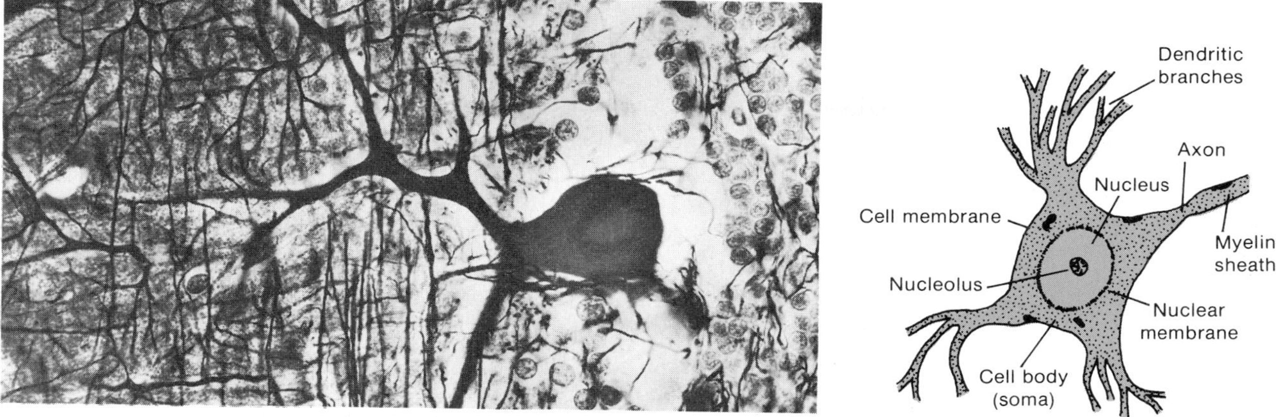

Figure 2–5. Photograph and cross section of a single neuron in the brain. *(© Manfred Kage/Peter Arnold, Inc.)*

dendrites vary in length from as short as one millimeter to as long as one meter. They act as receivers of information from adjacent cells.

Much of the neuron's activity depends on the difference between the chemicals inside and outside the nerve cell. The neuron functions like a slightly porous bag full of fluid. Certain electrically charged chemical particles known as ions pass through the cell membrane. Small ions, such as potassium, can pass through, while larger ones, such as sodium, cannot. In a typical neuron that is at rest, the concentration of sodium (Na^+) is much higher on the outside of the cell, while the concentration of potassium (K^+) is much higher inside the cell. This creates a difference in electric charge when the cell is not firing an impulse. Thus the resting state of the cell is said to be in the polarized condition. When the cell changes from a resting to an excited stage, the electrically charged particles flow across the membrane, which becomes depolarized. This is how a nerve impulse is freed.

Transmission of Nerve Impulses

As long as the cell membrane remains undisturbed, the electrical charge remains the same. However, if a point along the membrane is sufficiently stimulated, sodium can rush into the cell, thereby causing a shift in voltage. This change in electric potential, called **action potential,** sets up a disturbance that spreads like a lighted fuse along the length of the axon. Actually all this consists of is a sequence of rapid changes from resting to excited state back to resting state all down the axon. Even while the sodium ions are rushing in at each point on the axon, potassium ions are being replaced, bringing about the resting state again. Note that nothing physically moves down the axon: all movement is of particles going into and out of sequential points.

The neuron is said to fire in an all-or-nothing fashion, somewhat like a gun. Until a large enough stimulus is reached, the "trigger" will not function. Stimuli that exceed the action potential, no matter how strong, produce a "shot" of the same intensity. The intensity of a stimulus affects the rate of firing, not the size of the nerve impulse. A bright light, for example, will stimulate a neuron carrying visual information from the eye to fire rapidly; a dim light will stimulate the same neuron to fire more slowly. Immediately after an impulse has passed along the axon, there is a **refractory period.** During this period the cell cannot transmit another impulse unless a much stronger stimulus can evoke a second action potential (see Figure 2–6).

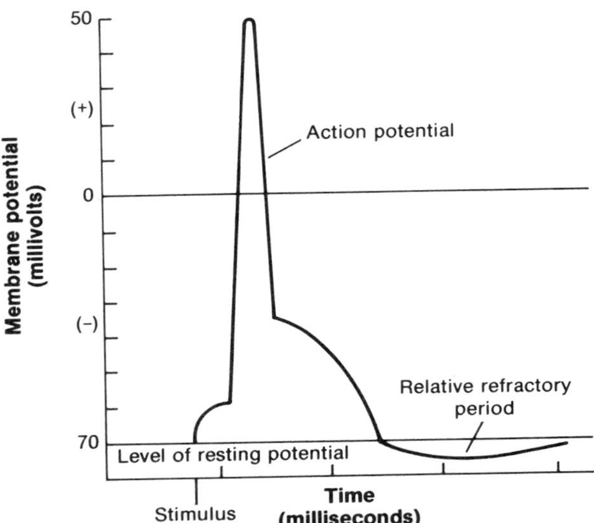

Figure 2–6. This graph illustrates how action potential might appear on an oscilloscope screen.

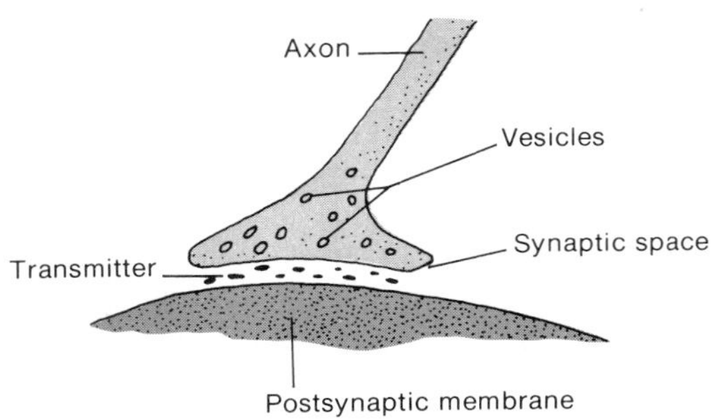

Figure 2–7. Neural structures involved in the transmission of signals.

While nerve impulses are transmitted electrically from one end of the neuron to the other, they are transported *chemically* from one neuron to the next. When the nerve impulse arrives at the axon terminal, it has to cross a gap to get to the next neuron. This gap is called the **synapse,** a minute, fluid-filled junction through which neurons communicate chemically. The neural impulse causes the end of the axon to release a chemical substance. This transmitter chemical interacts with a chemical in the receiving cell, which sets up an electrical charge that may or may not be sufficient to fire an impulse in that cell (see Figures 2–7 and 2–8).

Currently we know only a small number of transmitter substances responsible for synaptic communication. Snyder's recent work at Johns Hopkins University suggests that there may be as many as 200 different transmitter substances in the brain that may influence our behavior in ways now completely unknown (Snyder, 1980). We do know, however, that each neurotransmitter is associated with specific behavior functions and psychological states. For example, supplying the brain with the transmitter substance **serotonin** relieves the symptoms of depression (see Chapter 12). Reducing the activity of the transmitter dopamine with drugs called phenothiazines helps in treating schizophrenia. A recently discovered transmitter called **enkephalin** has been found to mimic the effects of opiates and seems to inhibit pain.

Figure 2–8. Electrochemical events at a synapse. A nerve impulse (action potential) travels along an axon until it reaches the presynaptic membrane, where the transmitter is released. The transmitter crosses the synapse and alters the permeability of the postsynaptic membrane, producing a flow of ions in the dendrite of the adjoining neuron.

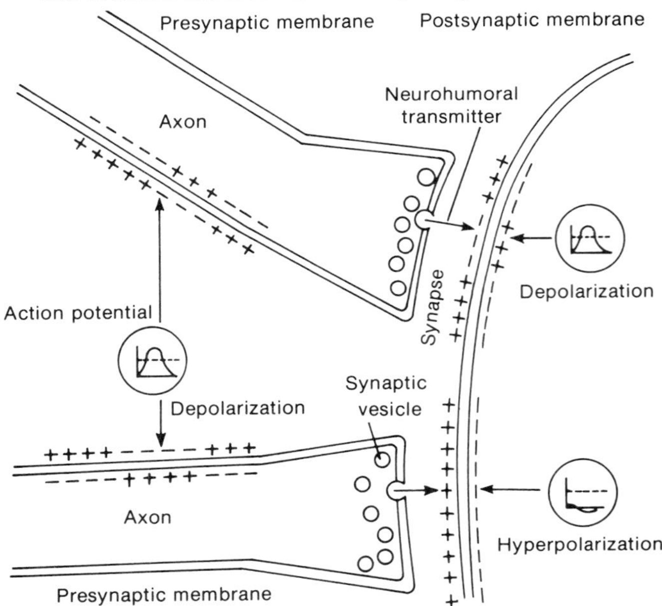

THE CENTRAL NERVOUS SYSTEM

The central nervous system is composed of the nerves in the spinal cord and the brain. Since the anatomy of the central nervous system, especially of the brain, is extraordinarily complex, we shall limit our discussion to the major structures. Before doing so, let us briefly review some of the techniques physiologists use to study the central nervous system.

Studying the Brain

One technique for studying brain-behavior relationships is the **lesion,** a procedure that damages neural tissue and is used only with laboratory animals. Lesion studies have generated a great deal of knowledge about the functions of specific parts of the brain. The most widely used apparatus for producing lesions is the **stereotaxic instrument** (see Figure 2–9). This instrument consists of a metal frame that holds the animal's head in position. With the help of brain atlases, the physiologist locates the specific structure to be destroyed. The lesion is made by implanting **electrodes** and passing a direct current through the area. After the animal has recovered from the surgery, the effects of the lesion on behavior can be evaluated.

A second technique of investigating the functioning of the brain is **electrical stimulation.** Electrodes are implanted in much the same way as for a lesion. Passing small amounts of electrical current through intact brain tissue allows the researcher to measure the animal's behavior as a function of electrical changes in the brain. The electrical stimulation of the brain can excite or inhibit behavior. For example, by stimulating certain areas of the brain, the neurophysiologist can make an animal become obese, put it to sleep, or awaken it.

Still another way of studying the brain is to record the bursts of electrical activity rippling through the brain. This technique is known as electroencephalography. An **electroencephalogram (EEG)** monitors the collective activity of the

Figure 2–9. Rat held in a stereotaxic instrument for implantation of electrodes.

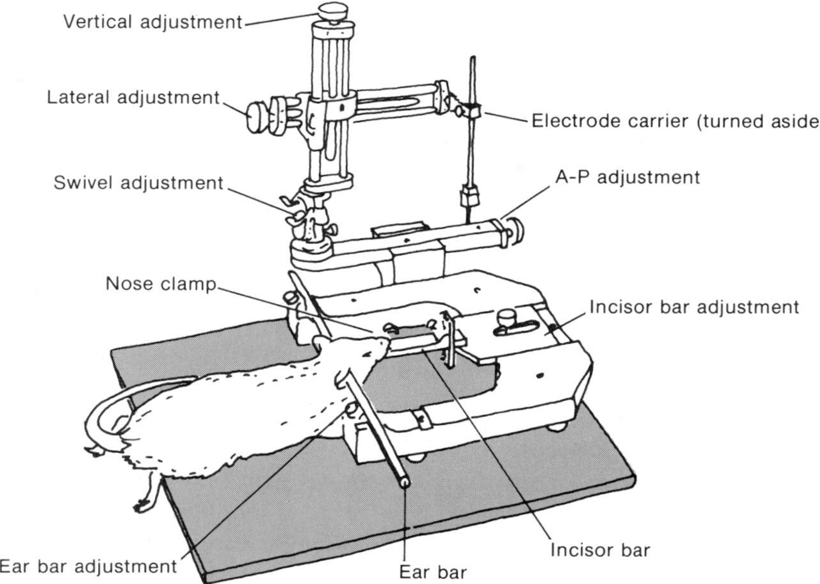

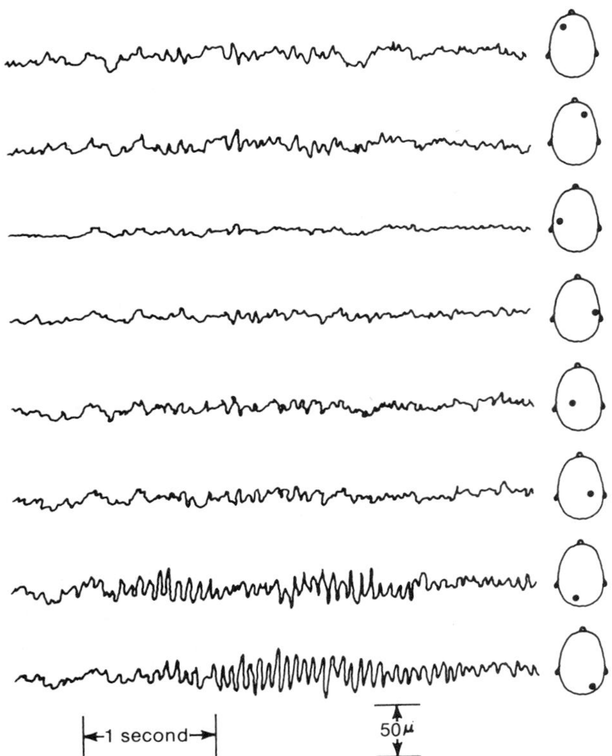

Figure 2–10. A typical EEG. (From VanderArk, G. D., & Kempe, L. G. *A primer of electroencephalography* [2nd Ed.]. Nutley, New Jersey: Hoffman La Roche Inc., 1970, p. 7.)

neurons immediately surrounding the electrode and provides an index of overall brain activity. Neurologists routinely use EEG's to check for malfunctions of the central nervous system. EEG's of several brain areas are shown in Figure 2–10.

The Spinal Cord

The spinal cord receives messages from various parts of the body and conducts them to the brain. It also carries messages from the various centers of the brain to all parts of the body. The major functions of the spinal cord include the maintenance of posture, the initiation and integration of motor sequences, the protection of the organism from injury, and the withdrawal of limbs from noxious stimulation, such as pain or heat.

The spinal cord contains circuits capable of generating relatively stereotyped responses. Consider sitting with your knees crossed loosely; the muscle that extends the knee joint is relaxed. Within the joint there are nerves whose axons run to the spinal cord. When the knee is tapped with a hammer, the muscles attached to the tendon are stimulated to contract, which results in a swift jerk of the knee.

The Brain

The brain is a sophisticated machine for communicating, for receiving and storing information and for issuing instructions concerning all our bodily functions and mental activities. In this section we shall tour the brain and describe what it looks like to the naked eye and under the microscope. Figures 2–11, 2–12, 2–13, and 2–14 show the main structures and functions of the brain.

The human brain, which tops the scale at some 1,500 grams, is heavier than most organs of the body (Rose, 1973). The brain is not a solid mass of cells; instead it consists of a system of interconnected spaces, or **ventricles,** filled with **cerebrospinal fluid,** which plays a part in the nutrition of the brain and the spinal column (Schwartz, 1978). If excessive cerebrospinal fluid accumulates in an infant's brain, a condition called **hydrocephalus** (literally, "water on the brain") develops. The excess fluid forces the skull bones of the infant apart, greatly increasing the size of the head. Hydrocephalus can be corrected by implanting a pressure-sensitive valve that drains excess cerebrospinal fluid into the bladder.

Anatomists divide the brain into three regions: the hindbrain, the midbrain, and the forebrain.

The Hindbrain. The hindbrain is the oldest and most primitive part in terms of evolutionary history. It contains three separate structures—the medulla, the pons, and the cerebellum—each of which can be easily identified by the naked eye if the brain is exposed for surgery. The **medulla** is the continuation of the spinal cord. Its primary function is the coordination of vital bodily processes, such as breathing, heart rate, and gastrointestinal functions. The next higher structure of the hindbrain is the pons. The **pons** serves as a relay station for the auditory system and contains nuclei influencing respiration, movement, and facial expressions. The pons forms a bridge to the **cerebellum,** a highly convoluted, fist-sized structure. The cerebellum appears to monitor all fine muscular movements, from playing the violin to tying shoes. In addition, the cerebellum is directly concerned with sense of balance, posture, and muscle tone, and perhaps with overall motor coordination. If the cerebellum is removed, or if the nerve tracts connecting it with the rest of the brain are damaged, then one loses control of fine motor movement. This kind of impairment is often seen in the shaking and hand tremors of elderly people.

The size and the development of the cerebellum vary in different species. In general, the cerebellum tends to be large and well-developed in organisms capable of precise, graceful movements. The well-developed cerebellum in a bird's brain, for instance, may be related to the need for coordination and control of balance in flight. Most animals and people become clumsy and uncoordinated after the removal of the cerebellum.

The Midbrain. A major portion of the midbrain is taken up by a dense network of neurons that are part of the **reticular activating system (RAS),** which originates in the hindbrain and extends into the hypothalamus and thalamus. Under the microscope this system appears as a criss-crossed, or reticulated, set of fibers running up and down through a large portion of the brain. The ascending RAS plays a decisive role in regulating our state of alertness. Electrical stimulation of the RAS of anesthetized or sleeping animals induces quick arousal. If that part of the brain is damaged, the animal becomes apathetic and drowsy, sleeps much of the time, and may even lapse into coma. The descending fibers of the RAS are part of a large system that mediates movement.

The midbrain also governs reflex movements of the head and neck that are triggered by sensory stimuli. For example, if you are sitting in a movie theater and a bright light from the projector appears, you will contract the pupils of your eyes and turn your head to the source of the light. This chain of motor responses is coordinated by centers in the midbrain.

The Forebrain. When most people think of the brain, they have the forebrain in mind. As the highest portion of the central nervous system, the forebrain is enormously complicated and its potential is staggering. It is not only involved in many kinds of emotions and motivations (see Chapter 6), but it also governs our higher mental processes of problem solving, language, thinking, and memory. Among the many centers and tracts found in the forebrain, four structures are of particular importance. They are the thalamus, the hypothalamus, the limbic system, and the cerebral hemispheres.

The **thalamus,** a large mass of gray matter divided into a number of nuclear groups, is the major relay station for almost all sensory messages. Pathways from all senses except touch connect to the thalamus.

Figure 2–11. Structures of the brain important to physiological psychology.

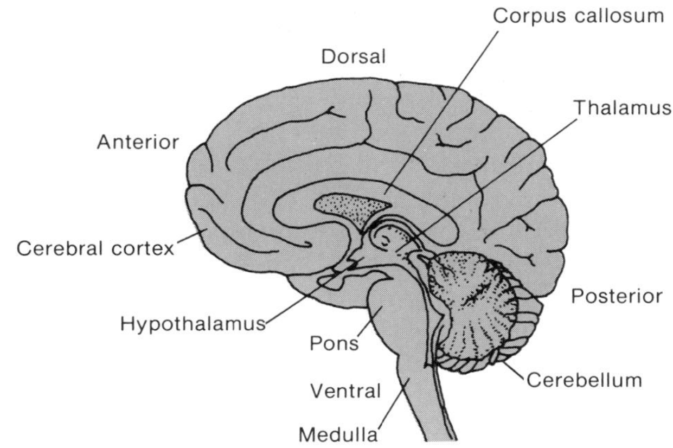

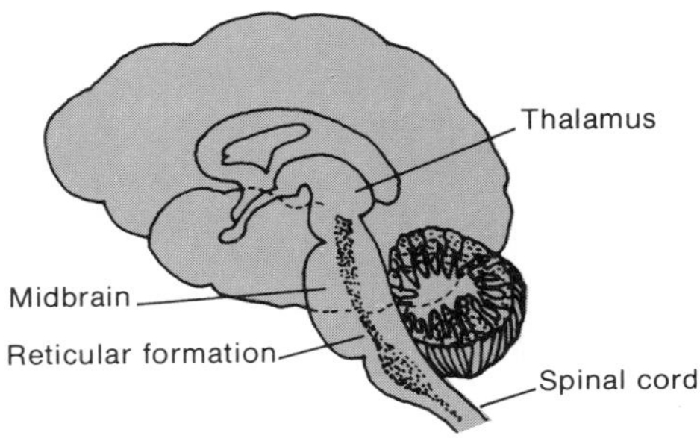

Figure 2–12. Location of the reticular formation in the human nervous system.

The thalamus is particularly important in lower organisms, such as the frog, which has highly developed senses of sight and hearing. In this species the thalamus is the principal coordinator of sensory information, but in mammals and humans the cerebral hemispheres have taken over some of the thalamic functions. Various regions of the thalamus then became staging posts or relay stations to the cortex.

The **hypothalamus** forms a junction between the midbrain and the thalamus. It consists of several nerve-cell nuclei with functions vital to the survival of the individual and the species. For example, the hypothalamus contains the cells that govern the regulation of eating, drinking, and sexual behavior (see Chapter 6), as well as emotional reactions such as fear. Hypothalamic cells form centers that excite and inhibit behavior. If an inhibitory center is damaged, the organism will find itself unable to stop eating and will become obese. However, if the injury occurs in the excitatory center, the animal will not eat at all and may starve to death in the presence of plenty of food. In addition to regulating vital functions, the hypothalamus is also instrumental in the control of the internal environment of the body, including heart rate, blood pressure, and temperature.

Suspended from the hypothalamus is the pituitary gland, which, as we have seen, secretes many hormones affecting behavior and controls the hormonal activities of other endocrine glands. The secretions of the pituitary are controlled by hypothalamic cells. Thus the hypothalamus is the brain's most important link with the endocrine system, demonstrating the complex interaction between hormonal and nervous systems. Finally, the hypothalamus is also that part of the brain that controls an important division of the nervous system, the autonomic nervous system.

The **limbic system** consists of a group of interconnected structures primarily concerned with emotions. Damage to this system causes intense emotional reactions turning highly excitable animals, such as lions or monkeys, into docile pets, or tame laboratory animals into ferocious creatures. One of the major structures of the limbic system is the **amygdala,** which appears to be particularly important in aggression. As you may recall from our chapter opening, a tumor near the amygdala may have played a role in Charles Whitman's violent behavior.

The cerebral hemispheres, or **cerebrum,** constitute a very large and important part of the forebrain. If you look at the top of an exposed brain, you will see that the cerebrum is separated into two halves, somewhat like a giant walnut. It consists of the cerebral cortex, or **neocortex** (gray matter), and the **corpus callosum** (white matter), a fiber tract connecting the two hemispheres. Since the neocortex was the last region of the brain to evolve, it is greatly enlarged in humans and other primates. The cortex has many indentations (fissures) and ridges (convolutions), which make up the surface of the cerebral hemispheres.

The cerebral hemispheres are commonly divided into four lobes, according to the physical and mental activities they control. The **frontal lobe,** located in the front of the head behind the forehead, is involved in learning, memory, and reasoning. People with frontal-lobe injuries may display subtle personality changes. Often they are described as unable to plan ahead, unreliable, rude, and impulsive. Despite the fact that they score normally on most standardized intelligence tests, they are often unable to hold a job for a long time. During the first part of this century, it was popular to perform lobotomies on certain mental patients, since the operation seemed to alleviate the symptoms of a number of disorders characterized by anxiety, fear, and excessive emotional activity (see Chapter 13 for a detailed discussion of frontal lobotomies).

The **temporal lobes** are located above the ears and contain the major auditory reception areas. Damage to the temporal lobes has been associated with epilepsy in many cases. In a series of dramatic studies, Dr. Wilder Penfield (1975), a Canadian neurophysiologist, showed that the surgical removal of a small part of the temporal lobes reduced the frequency of seizures in epileptic patients. However, this treatment was used only in intractable cases where the seizures threatened to incapacitate the person. More recently, new drugs have reduced the need for surgery in epileptic cases.

The **parietal lobe** occupies the region at the top of the head. In general, it contains those areas responsible for the coordination and control of sensory input and motor output. The parietal lobe also contains two speech areas, and it receives information about bodily position. Electrical stimulation of the parietal lobe produces peculiar sensations, such as tingling or itching. Destruction of the lobe dulls all skin sensations. In extreme cases parietal-lobe damage may lead to unusual difficulties with spatial organization and distorted perceptions of one's body image.

Finally, at the rear of each hemisphere we find the **occipital lobes,** which receive and analyze visual information (see Chapter 4). Information detected by the eye is projected onto a region in both occipital lobes. Damage to these areas in humans can lead to total or partial blindness, even though the eyes may be in perfect anatomical order.

Cerebral Dominance. The brain is uniquely organized so that each of the two hemispheres deals with the opposite side of the body. Damage to the right side of the cortex, for instance, results in blindness in the left eye; similarly, stimulation of the left motor cortex produces movement of the right side of the body.

For some functions, however, only one hemisphere is in control. This is particularly true for speech. In most people, for example, the left hemisphere is the dominant hemisphere for language functioning.

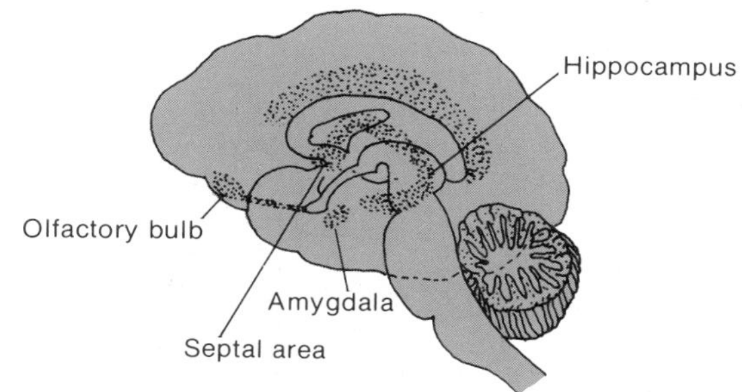

Figure 2–13. Location of the principle structures that constitute the limbic system.

Hemispheric dominance is roughly correlated with handedness. In more than 90 percent of right-handed men and women, speech is controlled by the left hemisphere of the brain. Speech is controlled by the right hemisphere in about two-thirds of left-handed individuals (Milner, 1974). In a few individuals, neither hemisphere seems to be dominant for language.

Early brain damage in the left hemisphere leads to compensatory lateralization of language functions in the right hemisphere. That is, although speech or another function is localized in one hemisphere, the other hemisphere can take over that function early in life because the brain is then a highly plastic organ.

The study of brain-damaged patients has provided some interesting clues about the organization of language functions and language-related functions in the brain. Some stroke victims who have lost the ability to read are still able to write, suggesting that activities such as reading and writing are in some way separate in the brain.

Many of our nonverbal skills, such as spatial organization and the processing of perceptual information, are handled more efficiently by the hemisphere not dominant for speech. Many people can rightly think of their left brain talking, rationalizing, reasoning its way through life, while their right half rides silently along, absorbed in its own mental work, contemplating life in its own nonverbal way (Sage, 1976). Integration of the two

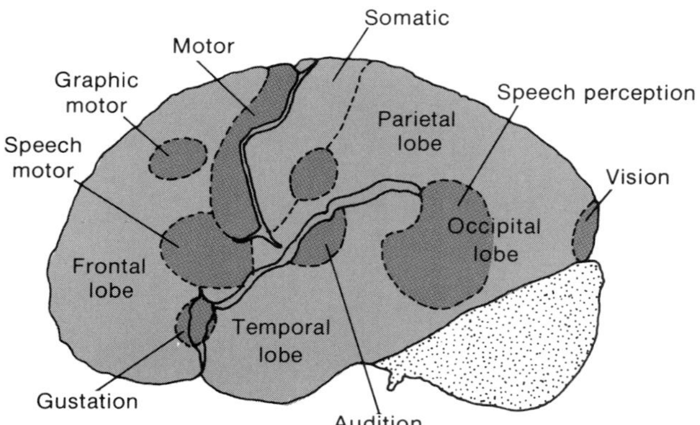

Figure 2–14. Major areas of the brain.

hemispheres, which is accomplished through the corpus callosum, is crucial for certain experiences. The left hemisphere, for instance, can produce speech, and the right hemisphere can visualize a rainbow, yet they must work together to describe that rainbow (Schwartz, 1978). In general, it appears that the dominant hemisphere, whichever it is, represents the analytical, linguistic side of the brain, whereas the nondominant hemisphere controls artistic and intuitive activities.

Some activities, however, contradict both the straightforward duality of the brain and its localization of functions. One example is singing. Singing uses four elements simultaneously: pitch, rhythm, intonation, and lyrics. Of the four, lyrics seems to fit most easily into the hemispheric model of the brain; that is, we would expect lyrics to originate in the verbal hemisphere. So it may seem surprising that people with severe damage to this hemisphere are able to sing familiar tunes. Buck reported such a case. A 46-year-old man's speech was limited to a few automatic words and short phrases after the removal of the left hemisphere because of a recurrent tumor. Although the man could learn single words, he could not put them together in any kind of structure. Yet his singing of some songs remained unimpaired; he retained not only the skills involved in melody, rhythm, and intonation but also in lyrics (Buck, 1976, p. 29).

Effects of the Split Brain. The cerebral hemispheres are mirror images of each other, completely symmetrical in structure. The corpus callosum acts as a transmission cable between them and helps to synchronize their activities. If the brain is split down the middle by severing the corpus callosum, a split brain is produced. A split-brain operation is sometimes performed with epileptic patients whose seizures are so severe that they cannot be controlled by medication. The study of such patients has revealed some interesting effects.

In a famous series of studies, Sperry and Gazzaniga (1967) devised a number of tests to investigate the way the two independent hemispheres function. For example, they flashed words or pictures on either the right or left side of a screen in front of which a patient with a split brain was sitting. When the picture appeared on the right side of the screen, the patient could immediately name it, since the information was going to the left hemisphere. However, the same person could not say anything about a picture flashed on the left side of the screen, only notice that there was a flash. The right hemisphere apparently "knows" that it has seen something but cannot verbalize it. This was demonstrated by flashing an emotionally arousing picture—say, that of a nude woman—in the left field of a split-brain man. The instant such a picture appeared, the subject blushed, but when asked to explain what caused the reaction, he was unable to do so.

A more conclusive demonstration is to ask the split-brain person to select an object similar to one that has been flashed into his or her left field from an array of objects placed behind a screen. The person is able to do so, but only with his or her left hand. If forced to use the right hand, the person performs at a chance level. After locating the object, the individual is still not able to tell what it is unless he or she is allowed to feel the object with the right hand (Milner, 1970). The reason is that only information from the right half of the body reaches the left hemisphere, which verbalizes the information and enables the person to name the object.

THE PERIPHERAL NERVOUS SYSTEM

The second major division of the nervous system is the peripheral system. Peripheral nerves connect the central nervous system with the rest of the body and serve both sensory and motor functions. Most of the neurons that make up the peripheral nervous system lie outside the brain and the spinal cord.

The Autonomic Nervous System

The peripheral nervous system consists of two branches, **the autonomic nervous system** and the **somatic nervous system.** The autonomic nervous system (ANS), illustrated in Figure 2–15, controls virtually all the internal functions of the body—breathing, blood circulation, stomach contractions, salivation—as well as many of our emotional reactions. The autonomic nervous system is also referred to as the involuntary nervous system because it is primarily concerned with reflex control of the internal organs.

The autonomic nervous system has two subdivisions, whose activities are opposite to each other. The sympathetic system mobilizes and organizes the body for emergency reactions, whereas the parasympathetic system runs the body under normal conditions and is most active when a person is in a resting state.

The Sympathetic Nervous System. The **sympathetic nervous system** consists of a group of nerve centers located near the spinal cord. From these

CRITICAL ISSUE

Sex Differences in the Brain

There is increasing evidence from research in biochemistry and neuropsychology that the brains of men and women differ. Although scientists have not been able to pinpoint all the physiological differences between male and female brains, they think that the development of the brain parallels that of the genitals (Weintraub, 1981). It has been suggested, for example, that if the fetus is a boy, secretions of testosterone not only stimulate the development of the male sex organs but also masculinize the tissue in the hypothalamus and other structures in the brain. Similarly, if the fetus is a girl, the estrogen secreted by the ovaries feminizes brain tissue in the cerebral cortex.

Other researchers (e.g., Timiras, 1971) have suggested that hormones can permanently affect the physical structure of the brain, thereby producing permanent sex differences. Both estrogen and testosterone, for instance, increase the branching of hypothalamic cells in animals (Toran-Allerand, 1976). By giving female rats testosterone shortly after birth, scientists have created large clusters of cells in the hypothalamus of female animals that resembled that of males.

Anatomical differences in male and female brains do not stop at the hypothalamus. Nash (1970) claimed that the gray commissure is more often absent from male than from female brains. In addition, he stated that the female brain has simpler and more regular convolutions. Other anatomical differences have also been discovered in the thinking part of the brain, the cerebral cortex. The right hemisphere of the cortex in male rats, for instance, has been found to be thicker than the left, while in female rats the left hemisphere is thicker than the right. Administering female hormones to males and male hormones to females can affect the width of the cortex.

These findings suggest that the cortex in men and women may also be different, largely because of hormones that early in life alter the organization of the two hemispheres (Weintraub, 1981). However, since scientists cannot dissect the living human brain, future evidence regarding the existence of physical differences between male and female brains must come from animal research. Generalizing about the human brain from such research remains speculative and inconclusive.

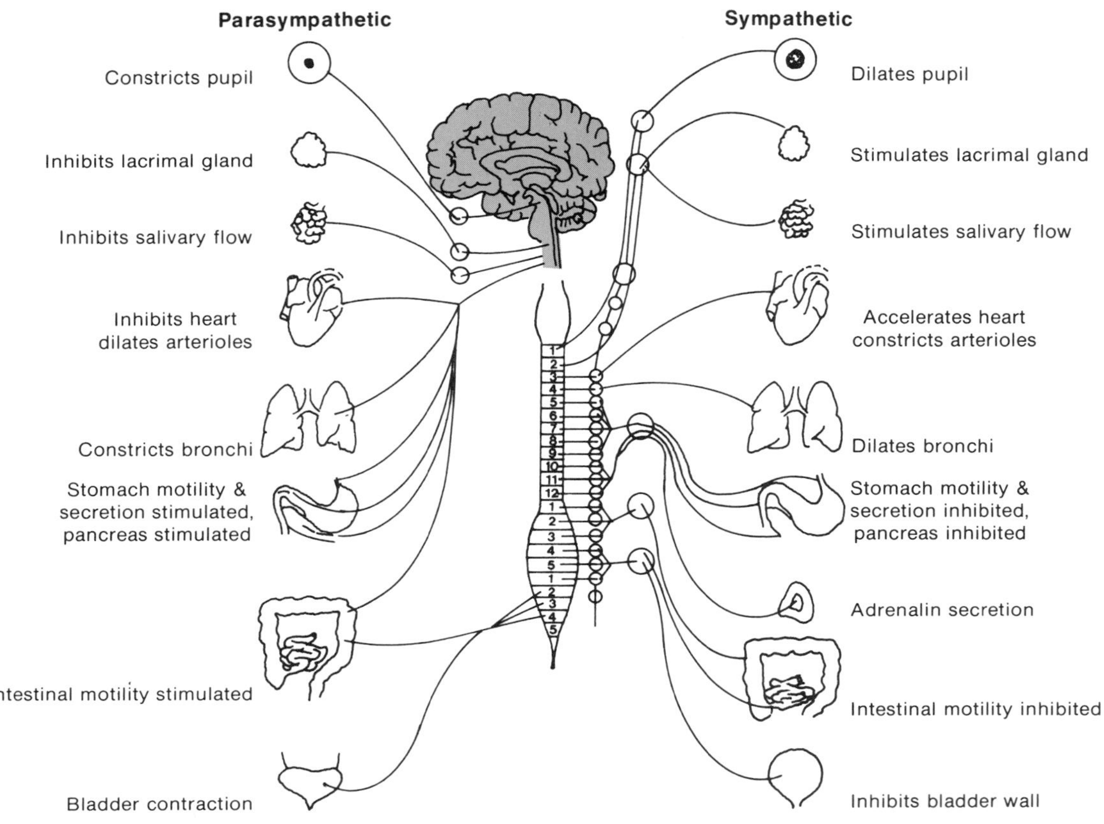

Figure 2–15. The anatomy and functions of the sympathetic and parasympathetic nervous systems. (From Bruce, R. L. *Fundamentals of physiological psychology.* New York: Holt, Rinehart & Winston, 1977, p. 77.)

centers fibers branch out to the major organs of the body, such as the heart, lungs, stomach, and liver.

When your sympathetic system is activated, your body enters a state of arousal and alertness. Your heart beats faster, you breathe more deeply, and your liver secretes extra sugar into the blood for additional energy. All these automatic physiological reactions take place when you are afraid, startled, moved by a strong desire, or sexually aroused. The sympathetic division also governs orgasm and ejaculation during sexual stimulation.

The Parasympathetic Nervous System. Instead of expending energy, the **parasympathetic system** conserves it. For example, stimulating the sympathetic nerve that travels to the heart will speed up the heart rate, while stimulating the parasympathetic nerve will slow it down. The parasympathetic system is by and large concerned with building up bodily resources. It slows the heart rate and breathing, stops the flow of sugar into the blood, and enhances digestive activity. Whenever your body quiets down and you feel calm and relaxed, your parasympathetic system is responsible. Taken together, the two divisions of the autonomic nervous system control many of your bodily functions in a coordinated fashion. Various functions of the respective nervous systems are represented in Figure 2–15.

THE SOMATIC NERVOUS SYSTEM

Whereas the autonomic division controls the body's internal environment, the somatic division of the peripheral nervous system is generally concerned with the regulation of the external environment. Its specific functions include the control of skeletal muscles, such as those used in raising your arms or wiggling your toes. In general, we can say that the somatic nervous system is primarily in charge of voluntary activities, while the autonomic nervous system principally controls involuntary functions, such as the constriction of blood vessels or the regulation of the respiratory system.

We have seen in this chapter that human behavior is controlled partially by biological and physiological conditions. But this does not mean that biological drives or innate instincts control human behavior to the same extent that they control animal behavior. Much of our behavior is also governed by psychological, social, and cultural factors. We shall examine these factors throughout the rest of this book.

Summary

Every human life begins as a single-cell organism that contains the entire program for future development embodied in the substance of the genes. Genes, composed of DNA, not only include the blueprint for later behavior but also play a primary role in the transmission of the physical and behavioral characteristics that we inherit from our parents.

In spite of the crucial role of heredity, a person's development, once genetically programmed, can be modified by external influences. For many years psychologists have argued over the relative contributions of genetic (nature) versus environmental (nurture) factors to behavior. Although the nature-nurture controversy continues, many psychologists now assume that behavior results from a complex interaction of both genetic and environmental forces.

Much of our knowledge of genetic mechanisms is derived from the study of genetic abnormalities. The most common one is Down's syndrome; three others are Klinefelter's syndrome in males, Turner's syndrome in females, and the XYY syndrome in males. The effects of these conditions range from mental retardation to sterility.

Although the science of genetics is barely a hundred years old, the last few decades have seen a number of exciting advances, particularly in genetic engineering. Scientists are developing techniques that may one day allow us to manipulate genes to gain control over reproduction and the quality of life. Currently both in-vitro fertilization and artificial insemination are successfully practiced. In the near future, geneticists hope to make significant advances in gene surgery and gene therapy, and perhaps some day they will be able to produce clones of highly valued individuals.

Behavior is also influenced physiologically by the hormonal secretions from the endocrine glands. The most important hormonal center in the human body is the pituitary, or master gland, which governs the activities of many of the other glands, such as the adrenals or gonads.

The nervous system controls our behavior in many important ways. It is organized into two major divisions: the central nervous system and the peripheral nervous system. In both divisions the neuron is the basic building block. Anatomically, the neuron consists of three parts: the cell body, the dendrites, and the axon. The axon plays a central role in transmitting nerve impulses electrochemically from one nerve cell to the next.

The central nervous system is composed of the spinal cord and the brain. The spinal cord controls a number of automatic responses, among them the knee-jerk reflex and erection during sexual excitement. The brain consists of three subdivisions: the hindbrain, the midbrain, which includes the reticular activating system, and the forebrain. Many sensory, motor, and motivational functions are controlled by the various structures located in the hindbrain and the midbrain. For human behavior the forebrain is of vital importance because its structures are concerned with our faculties of speech, thought, and consciousness. The highest center of the brain, the cerebral hemispheres, is commonly divided into four lobes that govern learning and memory (frontal lobe), auditory reception (temporal lobe), bodily position (parietal lobe), and vision (occipital lobe). The left hemisphere controls the right side of the body and vice versa. Observations of split-brain patients, whose hemispheres had to be surgically disconnected, have revealed some interesting behavioral deficits related to speech functions. The study of split-brain patients shows clearly that each hemisphere is responsible for certain functions. In most people, for instance, the left hemisphere is dominant for speech.

The second major division of the nervous system, the peripheral nervous system, consists of nerve centers located outside the spinal cord and the brain. One part of the peripheral nervous system is the autonomic nervous system with its two subdivisions, the sympathetic and the parasympathetic. These divisions operate in opposition to each other. The sympathetic system is responsible for activating bodily resources in preparation for emergency situations. The parasympathetic system, in contrast, works to maintain and restore the body to a state of relaxation and repose. The other part of the peripheral system is the somatic division, which governs the regulation of the external environment.

Key Terms For Review

action potential
adrenal glands
amniocentesis
amygdala
androgen
autonomic nervous system
axon
axon terminal
brain
central nervous system
cerebellum
cerebrospinal fluid
cerebrum
chromosome
cloning
corpus callosum
dendrite
deoxyribonucleic acid (DNA)
Down's syndrome
ectogenesis
electrical stimulation
electrode
electroencephalogram (EEG)
endocrine glands
enkephalin
epinephrine
estrogen
frontal lobe
genetics
gonad glands
hormones
hydrocephalus
hypothalamus
hypothyroidism
Klinefelter's syndrome
lesion
limbic system
medulla
myelin sheath
neocortex
neuron
norepinephrine

occipital lobe
parasympathetic nervous system
parietal lobe
peripheral nervous system
pituitary gland
pons
progesterone
refractory period
reticular activating system (RAS)
serotonin
somatic nervous system
spinal cord
stereotaxic instrument
steroids
sympathetic nervous system
synapse
temporal lobe
testosterone
thalamus
thyroid gland
translocation
Turner's syndrome
ventricles

Suggested Readings

Gazzaniga, M. *The bisected brain.* New York: Appleton-Century-Crofts, 1970.
A fascinating report of split-brain behavior reported by one of the original researchers.

Jensen, D. *The human nervous system.* New York: Appleton-Century-Crofts, 1980.
This book provides a detailed introduction to the structure and functioning of the nervous system, including both the peripheral and the central nervous system. Special topics such as the cerebral blood flow, higher cortical functions, and the senses of vision, audition, gustation, and olfaction are discussed.

Valenstein, E. *Brain control: A critical examination of brain stimulation and psychosurgery.* New York: Wiley, 1973.
An excellent account of the history of psychosurgery, beginning with the review of animal experiments that eventually led to attempts to treat mental disorders by brain surgery. The book includes a discussion of the recent controversy over psychosurgery and criticism of brain surgery.

Watson, J. *The double helix.* New York: Atheneum, 1968.
The now classical history of the discovery of DNA, the heredity molecule.

Windle, W. *The spinal cord and its reaction to traumatic injury.* New York: Marcel Dekker, 1980.
The purpose of this book is to summarize current knowledge about the spinal cord. It begins with a description of the anatomy and physiology of the spinal cord and explores the changes brought about by various types of trauma. The newest therapeutic procedures for dealing with spinal-cord injuries are also discussed.

3

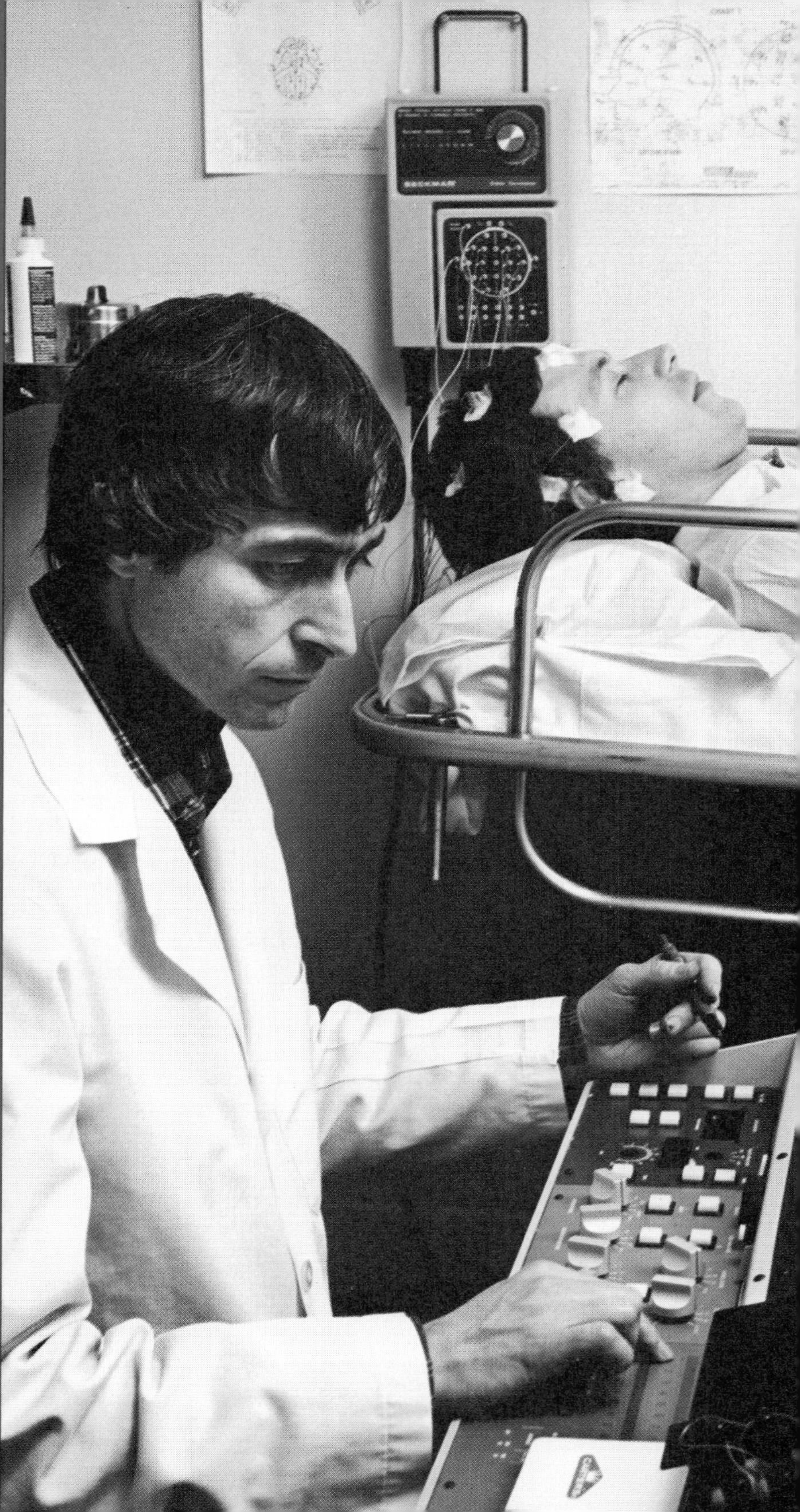

States of Consciousness

Jim is a chronic alcoholic. He goes off on a bender about once a month, leaving his law practice and disappearing for several days to a week. In the past ten years, he has been briefly hospitalized more than 20 times for alcohol-related difficulties.

In a recent episode, Jim's girlfriend called the emergency ward at the local hospital because he was jabbing himself with a fork "to get those miserable gnats out of my body." He was screaming and delirious upon admission to the hospital, terrified not only by the hallucinated gnats, but by "crazy shapes" and "smelly queeries" that were coming after him. Nothing could be done to comfort Jim for several hours. He continued to have tremors, cowered in a corner, drew his blanket over his head, twisted and turned anxiously, and kept screaming about hallucinated images that "attacked" him and "ate up" his skin (Millon & Millon, 1974, p. 398).

Liz once took LSD. She now realizes the dangers she risked by doing so. She makes this report about her experience:

> *Everything perceived—colors, textures, lines—attained beauty and richness never seen before. Perception seemed to be so incisive that the pores in my skin almost stood out and clamored for recognition. I felt that my visual powers penetrated other people to plumb their secret lives. For example, if I looked at my hand and focused upon the thumb, my thumb proceeded to swell and undulate and began moving toward me. . . . My sense of time changed dramatically . . . the very sense of future lost all meaning. . . . My perceptions and feelings were so heightened that they intensively recorded every instant. . . . Closing my eyes produced remarkable visions filled with vivid and persistent imagery (adapted from Snyder, 1974, pp. 42–43).*

Two entirely different states of consciousness are reflected in the above examples. And both are considerably altered from what is thought of as the normal state of consciousness. People of all cultures and all ages, from the Egyptian priests to the Australian bushmen, from the ancient Chinese to contemporary American Indians, have sought to expand or alter their consciousness in some way. Many Eastern civilizations have developed elaborate techniques, such as those of yoga and Zen Buddhism, to induce altered states of consciousness. People in Western countries used adaptations of Eastern techniques, such as transcendental meditation, as well as marijuana, LSD, and other mind-altering drugs to serve the same purpose. In this chapter we are concerned with all of these states of consciousness. Before discussing the various ways that can be used to change our normal, waking consciousness, let us see what psychologists mean by consciousness.

THE NATURE OF CONSCIOUSNESS

Consciousness is a complex concept that entails many, often unresolved philosophical and physiological implications regarding our fundamental human nature. The study of consciousness was introduced into psychology by the philosopher William James, who described consciousness as a continuously changing stream. There have been two philosophical approaches to consciousness—dualistic and monistic. Dualistic doctrines emphasize that mental and physical states are totally distinct from each other. Monistic approaches contend that mental and physical states constitute different aspects or hierarchical levels of a single, unified reality.

Some psychologists define consciousness in terms of its physiological aspects. Robert Ornstein (1973), for example, based his view of consciousness on the physiological evidence that the two halves of the brain differ in structure (see Chapter 2). According to Ornstein, two major modes of consciousness exist, the intellectual and the intuitive.

Since the science of consciousness is still in the embryonic stage, we have to accept the fact that the phenomena it purports to study are often ill-defined and not fully agreed upon (Davidson & Davidson, 1980). Those most commonly agreed upon include: (1) ordinary perceptual awareness; (2) self-consciousness; (3) dreams; (4) hypnogogic states; (5) socially induced trances or trance-like states; (6) drug-induced states; (7) meditative states; and (8) dissociative states as experienced under the influence of alcohol or in cases of multiple personality (see Chapter 10).

As you might expect, a single definition of consciousness that encompasses all of its diverse aspects is not easy to come up with. Singer proposed the following definition:

> Human consciousness, the subtle interplay of fleeting images, perceptions of the immediate environment, memories of long-gone events, and daydreams of future or impossible prospects, all carried along the stream of thought, represent a true miracle of our experience of being (1974, p. 1).

Some of the best-known descriptions of the stream of consciousness are found in the writings of Virginia Woolf and James Joyce. The following passage, taken from Joyce's *Ulysses*, reflects the stream of consciousness as defined by Singer—thoughts, speculations, plans, and memories:

> Better not stick here all night like a limpet. This weather makes you dull. Must be getting on for nine by the light. Go home. Too late for *Leah, Lily of Kilarney*. No. Might be still up. Call to the hospital to see. Hope she's over. Long day I've had. Martha, the bath, funeral, house of keys, museum with those goddesses, Daedalus' song. Then that bawler in Barney Kiernan's. Got my own back there. Drunken ranters (1961, p. 380).

Ordinary Consciousness

In our description of consciousness, we have referred to two major states: ordinary and altered. We use the terms ordinary, or normal, consciousness to refer to our waking state; although some researchers include dreaming and dreamless sleep as ordinary states of consciousness (e.g., Campbell, 1974).

Ordinary consciousness is something with which everyone is familiar, but few people study it in detail. Consider your own consciousness at this moment. Look around you. What do you see? What do you hear? Focus on the various parts of your body. What are your hands doing? What are the muscles of your leg doing? Try to take all this in and whatever else goes on in the back of your mind. You discover a mixture of sensations, perceptions, feelings, fantasies, and ideas. These constitute your ordinary consciousness at this particular moment.

Obviously attention, or our ability to select what sort of information enters the stream of consciousness, determines our state of awareness to some extent. The selective attention that is part of our ordinary consciousness is easily illustrated by everyday examples. When was the last time you found yourself having an exciting conversation and crossed the street oblivious to the traffic? When you are hungry, you may fantasize about your favorite foods—something you would not do when satiated. By the same token, you may be unaware of the signals from your stomach at lunchtime because you are daydreaming about an attractive person you met in one of your classes. Examples such as these show that we attend to some aspects of the environment while discarding others.

Altered States of Consciousness

Altered states of consciousness are those that differ significantly from our normal state of awareness. Since the term "altered" implies that these states are a deviation from the way consciousness should be, some writers (e.g., Zinberg, 1977) prefer to call them alternate or expanded states of consciousness. Ludwig (1969) defined such states as follows:

> Any mental state(s) induced by various physiological, psychological, or pharmacological maneuvers or agents which can be recognized subjectively by the individual himself (or by an objective observer of the individual) as representing a sufficient deviation in subjective experience or psychological functioning from certain general norms for that individual during alert, waking consciousness. This sufficient deviation may be represented by a greater preoccupation than usual with internal sensations or mental processes, changes in formal characteristics of thought, and impairment of reality testing to various degrees (p. 225).

The experiences of Jim and Liz described at the beginning of this chapter would qualify as altered states of consciousness. Probably the most familiar alternate state is daydreaming, followed by sleep. Other states most of us have experienced come from the changes produced by the consumption of alcohol or other consciousness-changing chemicals. Some altered states are so marked and so easily observable that they are readily accepted as such. Sleep and dream states or intense intoxication are clear-cut cases. In cases such as meditative states, the boundaries between altered and ordinary states become more tentative. It is difficult to determine exactly where deep contemplation in a state of ordinary consciousness changes into a meditative state of altered consciousness. Ludwig (1969) in his list of altered states also mentions specific alterations of consciousness, such as the ecstatic trance experienced by the "whirling dervishes" during their religious dance and the changes in consciousness that may occur following bilateral cataract operations.

According to Tart (1969), an altered state of consciousness is one in which a person clearly feels a *qualitative* shift in his or her pattern of mental functioning rather than just a *quantitative* shift (more or less alert, more or less visual imagery, sharper or duller). That is, the individual feels that some quality or qualities of his or her mental processes are different. Mental functions operate that ordinarily do not operate at all, and perceptual qualities appear that have no normal counterpart. There are many borderline cases in which the affected persons cannot clearly distinguish just how their state of consciousness is dif-

"Whirling dervishes" attain a heightened state of consciousness in their ritualistic dances. (© *Ira Friedlander/Woodfin Camp & Associates*)

ferent from normal and where quantitative changes in mental functioning are marked. Such borderline states and difficult-to-describe effects, however, do not negate the existence of feelings of clear, qualitative changes in mental functions that are the criterion of altered states of consciousness.

Again, as we saw in Ludwig's definition, the above description of altered states of consciousness encompasses a broad range of phenomena. It also implies that every person, whether he or she retains the awareness of them, spends some time in states other than the normal waking state. Some psychologists (e.g., Weil, 1977) even suggest that we are born with a drive to experience modes of awareness other than the normal waking one and that altered states of consciousness allow us to tap our full human potential.

MIND-ALTERING DRUGS

Psychoactive drugs represent one way of changing our state of consciousness. A **psychoactive drug** is a substance that, when taken into the body, changes a person's characteristic mode of functioning or thinking or both. Psychoactive drugs can be classified according to their chemical structure, their legality or illegality, and their potential hazard to health and public safety. The classification that best serves our purpose groups psychoactive drugs according to their most salient behavioral effects. Such a classification scheme is presented in Table 3–1, which lists the three major classes of psychoactive drugs: the stimulants, the depressants, and the psychedelic drugs, or hallucinogens.

The Stimulants

Amphetamines, cocaine, caffeine, and nicotine are classified as behavioral stimulants. They elevate the mood, increase alertness, produce an exaggerated sense of well-being or euphoria, and generally activate and speed up the central nervous system. They also produce feelings of increased physical and mental power. In high doses these stimulants are capable of producing anxiety, irritability, and patterns of psychotic behavior.

The **amphetamines** are a group of drugs that have been used as stimulants for a number of years. Amphetamines are potent stimulants in the central nervous system, producing signs of increased excitement both in behavior and in the electrical activity of the brain.

Usually amphetamines are taken orally. Some users prefer to inject the drug because the injection provides a sudden "rush," described as being extremely pleasurable and similar to an intense orgasm. High-dose injections may induce behavior resembling schizophrenia.

Amphetamines are often taken as a means of weight control, since they strongly depress appetite. Although amphetamines can aid in weight reduction, hunger is suppressed only while the drug is taken. Many authorities (e.g., Ray, 1978) believe that the euphoric effect of amphetamines is the real basis for their continued use in weight control. Some students use amphetamines when studying long hours for exams, and some truck drivers take them to stay awake.

One controversial use of amphetamines involves athletes. Studies in the late 1950s of the effects of amphetamines on the performance of swimmers (e.g., Smith & Beecher, 1959) showed that highly trained athletes could improve their performance by taking amphetamines. Amphetamines became especially popular among basketball players who needed extra motivation and energy in all-important tournament games.

Today amphetamine use by sports figures is widely disapproved of. In the 1976 Olympic games, the Sport Medicine Committee ordered urine samples from each of the top four finishers in each competition as well as from a random group of participants. In the 1980 games, all competing finalists had to undergo a urinalysis.

Long-term use of amphetamines can cause physical damage from appetite loss and the overstimulation of bodily functions and can lead to addiction or psychological dependence. Psychological dependence means that the drug plays a prominent role in the individual's repertoire of coping mechanisms (Ray, 1978). Overdoses can also produce severe mental illness known as **amphetamine psychosis.**

Cocaine, or "coke," is a stimulant derived from the leaves of the coca plant, which grows exclusively on the eastern slopes of the Andes in South America. Cocaine can be ingested by sniffing and swallowing and rarely by injecting. It is a powerful drug that produces short-term mind-altering effects and, like the amphetamines, psychological dependence (Fischman, Schuster, & Resnekov, 1976). The drug produces extreme euphoria, increases energy levels, and induces sleeplessness. Cocaine users may ascend to heights of mood elevation and elation to the point of experiencing feelings of grandiosity. Whereas the high produced by amphetamines may last for several hours, the effects of cocaine last only a few minutes because the drug is rapidly metabolized by the liver.

Cocaine is often called the "darling of the drug culture." The powerful and initially pleasant effect

Table 3–1. Classification of Psychoactive Drugs (brand names shown in parentheses)

1. Stimulants (uppers)
   - Amphetamines (Benzedrine, Dexedrine)
   - Cocaine
   - Caffeine
   - Nicotine
2. Depressants (downers)
   - Barbiturates (Nembutal, Seconal)
3. Hallucinogens
   - LSD
   - Marijuana

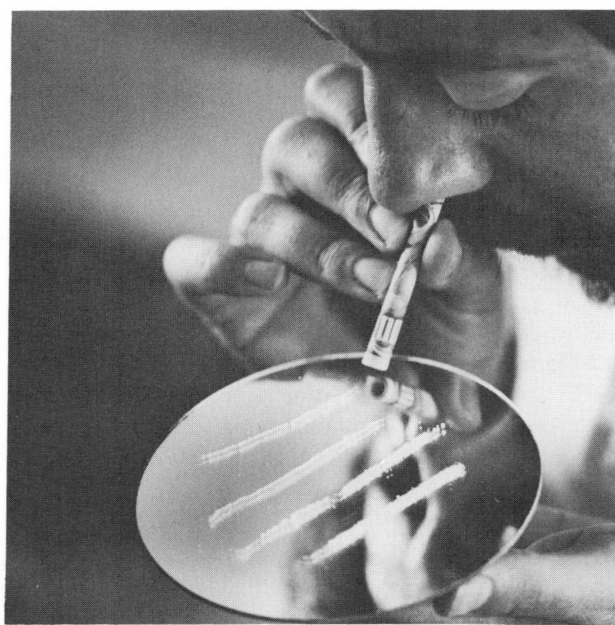

One common method of ingesting cocaine is to spread it in lines on a clean surface and sniff it through rolled-up paper. (© *Joel Gordon*)

allows the user to shift rapidly from one state of consciousness into another. Recently its popularity has grown among adolescents as well as among middle- and upper-class adults. Confiscation of cocaine by the United States Department of Justice doubled from 1969 to 1971 and increased sevenfold from 1969 to 1974 (Ray, 1978).

Continued use of cocaine leads to loss of appetite and weight, insomnia, and hallucinations, especially tactile hallucinations known as "cocaine bugs." This common effect refers to the feeling of bugs crawling under the user's skin. The sensation may become so intense that the person is tempted to take a knife to cut them out. Even without taking such an extreme measure, the heavy cocaine user may produce open sores from scratching and picking at the "bugs." Ellinwood (1969) suggested that the basis for this experience is a drug-induced stimulation of nerve endings in the skin.

Caffeine is one of the most widely used stimulants in the world. It is found in significant concentration in coffee, tea, and cola drinks. Compared with the amphetamines and cocaine, caffeine is a relatively mild stimulant. In normal doses, it promotes wakefulness and improved psychomotor performance. Like amphetamines, but to a much smaller degree, caffeine prolongs the amount of time a person can engage in physically exhausting work. The behavioral effects of moderate amounts of caffeine appear to be largely related to its stimulating properties, which cause an increased alertness and "brighter spirits" (Select Committee Report to the FDA, 1977, p. 21). In most adults, these effects are not associated with altered states of consciousness.

However, large doses (about 500 mg: a 5 oz. cup of brewed coffee contains between 80 and 150 mg of caffeine) can promote alterations in consciousness. Many persons believe with Goodman and Gilman (1975) that caffeine produces "a more rapid and clearer flow of thought . . . a greater sustained effort and a more perfect association of ideas" (p. 368).

Nicotine is a widely used psychoactive agent, most commonly found in tobacco. Nicotine affects the central nervous system by acting at the level of the cortex and produces electrical arousal patterns in the brain. It also affects areas outside the central nervous system, causing the release of adrenalin from the adrenal glands.

The ingestion of nicotine through smoking creates physiological dangers. Chronic smoking has been proven to be a major contributor to a variety of health problems. For instance, a correlation has been established between cigarette smoking and lung cancer. Nicotine also has a toxic effect on the cardiovascular system. Statistics indicate that smokers have a higher mortality rate from coronary disease than nonsmokers. Since nicotine increases both heart rate and blood pressure, smokers typically respond with sustained increases in blood pressure, which in turn increase the workload of the heart. Prolonged use of nicotine produces physiological addiction and psychological dependence.

The hold that nicotine can have on a person was dramatically demonstrated by Sigmund Freud, whose habit of consuming 20 cigars a day was ruining his health. When his doctor ordered him to stop smoking, he did so for a time and described his suffering during abstinence as follows:

> Soon after giving up smoking, there were tolerable days. . . .Then there came suddenly a severe affection of the heart, worse than I ever had when I was smoking . . . and with it an oppression of mood in which images of dying and farewell scenes replaced the more usual fantasies. . . . [Although] the organic disturbances have lessened in the last few days, the hypomanic mood continues (Jones, 1953, p. 179).

Soon after he wrote this, Freud was smoking as heavily as ever.

The Depressants

The depressants produce states of awareness exactly opposite to those produced by stimulants. Instead of exciting and speeding up our system, downers produce a relaxed, sleep-like state of consciousness. Moreover, these drugs are capable of inducing various degrees of behavioral depression ranging from mild sedation through anesthesia to coma and death. The two major depressants are barbiturates and alcohol.

Barbiturates are often prescribed to induce sleep, to sedate a person, or to treat epileptic seizures. Many people use barbiturates to reduce tension, anxiety, and nervousness.

Barbiturates are powerful and highly addictive drugs. Habitual users may require such great dosages to go to sleep and stay asleep that they have a barbiturate hangover in the morning because the sedative effects continue after the user awakens. Overdoses, accidental or intentional, may end in coma or death. Such problems can occur with insomniacs, who need to take increasing doses of sleeping pills to put them to sleep. Death may also occur if a person takes barbiturates after drinking a large amount of alcohol.

Alcohol is a drug that, contrary to popular belief, depresses many of the activities of the brain. In small quantities alcohol appears to be a stimulant because it produces a sense of expansiveness and well-being and reduces inhibitions and social constraints. After a few drinks, unpleasant realities seem to be less disturbing and our self-esteem rises. Changes in behavior result from a depression of the inhibitory centers of the brain and from socially learned expectations about what it feels like to be high.

Alcohol produces a continuum of states of consciousness ranging from ordinary states of awareness to total blackouts. Below a certain concentration of alcohol in the blood, no mood changes result (see Table 3–2). When the alcohol content of the bloodstream reaches 0.1 percent, the person is considered to be intoxicated. Further alcohol consumption leads to clouding of memory, dissociative states, and total lapses of memory.

About 90 percent of habitual drinkers may experience a clouding of memory called the alcoholic haze, which does not seem to result from irreversible changes in the brain (Loftus, 1980). These memory problems usually disappear if the person stops drinking. The dissociative state is best illustrated by a concept known as **state-dependent learning** (Overton, 1972). If you try to learn something while you are drunk and hope to remember that material when sober, you cannot expect to do well. This concept suggests that something learned in state A can be forgotten in state B and be recalled again in state A. Alcohol-induced blackouts are total lapses of memory. Many years ago, Crothers (1884) described this state as an "alcoholic trance":

> This trance state is a common condition of inebriety, where . . . a profound suspension of memory and consciousness and liberal paralysis of certain brain functions follow. This trance state may last from a few moments to several days during which the person may appear [rational] and act rationally and yet be actually a mere automaton without consciousness or memory of his actual condition (p. 189).

Thus an intoxicated person may engage in relatively complex activities such as driving a car (long after it is safe for the person to drive) and have absolutely no trace of recall the next day. Blackouts are not necessarily determined by the amount of alcohol consumed, for heavy drinkers may experience them after relatively moderate drinking. However, drinking large amounts of distilled liquor rapidly, drinking on an empty stomach, or drinking after having taken tranquilizers increase the chances of blacking out.

Two other states associated with alcohol intoxication deserve mention. In **delirium tremens (DTs),** the state that Jim, the chronic alcoholic described at the beginning of the chapter, experienced, the person is disoriented and has vivid visual hallucinations, particularly of small, fast-moving animals like rats and roaches. The person may react to these hallucinated animals with terror, trying desperately to fight them off. Individuals with DTs tremble furiously and perspire profusely. DTs usually begin after a period of nondrinking and are preceded by restlessness and insomnia; they can last from three to six days and are generally followed by deep sleep. In **alcoholic hallucinosis** the main symptoms are auditory hallucinations such as hearing the clanking of chains, the sharpening of knives, or the firing of pistols.

The Hallucinogens

The two major psychedelic drugs are LSD and marijuana, both of which enlarge the realm of consciousness. Liz, the college student we met earlier in this chapter, described an LSD experience that took her to new heights of consciousness.

APPLICATION

Breaking the Smoking Habit: A Behavioral Approach

Virtually everybody—smokers, ex-smokers, and nonsmokers alike—agrees that smoking is not a good thing (Hunt & Matarazzo, 1973). The growing evidence, documented in the Surgeon General's report (U.S. Public Health Service, 1964), indicates that cigarette smoking is causally linked to a number of serious physical disorders. The growing concern over nicotine-related health problems has given impetus to an increasingly large number of behavior-modification programs for smokers. The American Psychiatric Association in its official classification system of mental disorders has even created a separate subcategory entitled "tobacco use disorders" under the general category of "substance use disorders."

The person for whom the termination of smoking involves nothing more than the decision to quit, and a supportive environment in which to make this decision, is not the problem. Therapists are concerned with the many people for whom smoking is an addiction—those who experience the negative effects, declare their intention of quitting, and try unsuccessfully to eliminate smoking from their behavior repertoire. For these people the commitment to smoking may be viewed as analogous but not identical to the drug addict's commitment to drugs (Sarbin & Nucci, 1973).

A variety of treatment programs have been developed, ranging from hypnosis to traditional psychotherapy. Many of them report the same results that Freud repeatedly showed with his cigar habit: kicking the habit temporarily and then relapsing. One study that examined several techniques indicated that the percentage of people who had stopped smoking completely at the conclusion of a stop-smoking program ranged from 7 to 40 percent, with an average abstinence rate of 26 percent. Six months later, an average of 13 percent were not smoking (McFall & Hammen, 1971). Long-term abstinence rates (a year or more after termination of therapy) are generally less than 15 percent with most of these techniques (Pomerlau & Pomerlau, 1977).

Behavior-therapy programs, some of which have included aversive-conditioning procedures, offer more promising results. In a program of aversive conditioning, the chronic smoker may volunteer for sessions in which rapid smoking is followed by electric shock to link the smoking to unpleasant consequences. These sessions would continue until the smoker indicated no further desire for cigarettes. Lichtenstein and Penner (1977) reported a success rate of 34 percent when they interviewed partici-

The **hallucinogens** have a profound effect on all our senses but particularly on vision. Colors seem dazzlingly bright and intense, contours are sharpened, and ordinary objects take on new significance. Depth perception (see Chapter 4) is heightened, and objects change their size and shape. Walls and floors undulate as if breathing, and spatial perception is distorted into exaggerated depth or flatness (Grinspoon & Bakalar, 1979). The senses of hearing, touch, and smell are similarly enhanced. Feelings toward other people become much more intense.

Striking effects also occur in the perception of time. In states of normal consciousness time unfolds in a linear and regular sequence. Time passes in recognizable units—seconds, hours, days, and weeks—in a strict pattern of past, present, and future. Psychedelic drugs distort this linear movement. Time may pass more slowly, or run backwards. Past, present, and future may seem to converge and happen all at once. The whole idea of temporal succession may become meaningless.

Psychedelic drugs, in addition to greatly enlarging our conscious realm, also diminish our capacity to think rationally and behave adaptively.

Lysergic acid diethylamide (LSD) is a hallucinogen developed in 1938 by Dr. Albert Hoffman, a Swiss scientist. He discovered its ability to cause visions and hallucinations when he swallowed

pants two to six years after the program ended. However, rapid-smoking procedures may be dangerous, particularly for smokers with cardiovascular or pulmonary problems. Good results were also obtained when shock was self-administered in response to the thoughts that trigger smoking (Berecz, 1976).

Some of the most successful behavioral techniques are those using self-control techniques in which the therapist teaches the person how to control his or her own behavior by manipulating environmental conditions. Self-control procedures involve three basic steps (Kanfer, 1970): (1) Clients must learn to monitor their own behavior to become more aware of the response to be changed; (2) They need to evaluate the response in relationship to some personal goal; and (3) They must apply their own reward or punishment. In the case of a person who is trying to quit smoking, he or she may set a limit to how many cigarettes are to be allotted each day and specify a reward (e.g., going to a movie) for staying within the limit. Whenever the person exceeds the limit, something enjoyable must be given up. According to the U.S. Department of Health, Education, and Welfare (1979), 95 percent of smokers who quit do so on their own, probably using self-control techniques. The majority of successful stop-smoking programs administered by professionals, including the withdrawal clinics sponsored by the American Cancer Society and the American Lung Association, combine a variety of techniques. Bernstein and McAlister (1976), for instance, described a successful therapy program that involved the identification of situations that precipitate smoking, group contacts and support, and extensive follow-up.

Group therapy has been effective in helping people break the smoking habit. (© *American Cancer Society*)

Table 3–2. Alcohol levels in the blood after drinks taken on an empty stomach by a 150-pound male drinking for one hour*

Effects	*Time for all alcohol to leave the body—Hours*	*Alcohol concentration in blood—Percent*	*Amount of beverage*
Gross intoxication	10	0.15	5 highballs (1½ oz. whiskey each) *or* 5 cocktails (1½ oz. whiskey ea.) *or* 27½ oz. ordinary wine *or* ½ pint whiskey
Clumsiness-unsteadiness in standing or walking	8	0.12	4 highballs *or* 4 cocktails *or* 22 oz. ordinary wine *or* 6 bottles beer (12 oz. ea.)
Exaggerated emotion and behavior—talkative, noisy, or morose	6	0.09	3 highballs *or* 3 cocktails *or* 16½ oz. ordinary wine *or* 4 bottles beer
Feeling of warmth, mental relaxation	4	0.06	2 highballs *or* 2 cocktails *or* 11 oz. ordinary wine *or* 2 bottles beer
Slight changes in feeling	2	0.03	1 highball *or* 1 cocktail *or* 5½ oz. ordinary wine *or* 1 bottle beer

*Blood alcohol level following given intake differs according to the person's weight, the length of the drinking time, and the sex of the drinker (*Time*, 1974).

some by accident. Until the 1950s, however, LSD was little more than a laboratory curiosity. Since then, it has been widely publicized and both praised and condemned. When Dr. Timothy Leary, a Harvard professor, told people to "tune in, turn on, and drop out" with LSD in the 1960s, he made thousands of people aware of the "mind drug." For some, LSD became the center of a new pseudoreligion.

LSD stimulates pupil size, pulse rate, brain-wave activity, environmental inputs, and judgmental errors. Most LSD users, like Liz, report unique sensory experiences, intense emotions, and a profundity of thought not encountered in ordinary states of consciousness. For artists such distortions are particularly fascinating.

As LSD begins to affect the nervous system, other changes occur. Sensitivity to color and form increases. Colors grow richer and deeper. Visions of multicolor geometric patterns occur. These abstract patterns are generally three-dimensional and constantly change in a steady rhythmic flow, resembling a view through a kaleidoscope (Tart, 1972).

These perceptual changes represent only a very shallow level of heightened consciousness. Beyond the colors and patterns, a person may experience more profound imagery and vision. At this deeper, more mystical level, a person may envision himself or herself walking through a magic garden, ancient cities, or futuristic communities. Such an altered state of awareness is illustrated by the following account:

> I lay on my stomach and closed my eyes and brilliantly colored patterns of fantastic beauty collided, exploded, raced by. Other things, too . . . teeth, pearls, and precious stones, and lips, and eyes. Outside of the window, the branches of the trees were gigantic arms with transparent muscles, now threatening, now embracing. Glasses started rolling on the table, the bookcase was full of swimming books, the door bulged like a balloon, the carpet in the other room was full of thousands of little green snakes. The dial on the telephone was a huge pearl-studded wheel. The shapes and colors of objects got more and more intense, the outlines etched with luminous clarity and depth. Anything with a polished metal surface turned into gleaming silver and gold. The faces of other people became clear and beautiful and open. At one point all the faces were colored green. (Pahnke & Richards, 1972, p. 419–420).

Good trips, or psychedelic experiences with pleasant imagery, a variety of interesting bodily sensations, sexual pleasure, and aesthetic experiences encourage the continued use of hallucinogens. However, not all LSD experiences lead to heightened or inspiring states of consciousness. The drug can also produce bad trips, in which the user responds to the changed perceptions with terror, acute panic, disorganization, and confusion. Thought disturbances and loss of contact with reality may be experienced, resulting in psychotic-like states. Although the chaotic states of consciousness are more likely to be experienced by individuals who have a history of emotional instability, such is not always the case. In most cases the person using LSD to expand his or her awareness cannot be sure whether the trip will be good or bad. Going into the LSD experience with the expectation of reaching a heightened state of consciousness is often unrealistic and may be the cause of a bad trip. Even if exciting and spectacular events occur during a psychedelic experience, most of them are too unintelligible to be coordinated into daily life (Girando & Girando, 1973).

Psychedelic drugs are rarely dangerous physically. The only problem that has aroused serious concern is the possibility of chromosome breakage after LSD. This problem was first reported in 1967 (Cohen & Marmillo), when researchers found a higher proportion of chromosome breaks in paranoid schizophrenics who had been treated with LSD. They also found that LSD caused chromosome breaks in white blood cells artificially cultured in the lab. The publication of these findings became the basis for a rather sensational propaganda campaign featuring pictures of deformed children born to LSD users—children with club feet, protruding abdomens, and vertebral abnormalities. However, many studies find no evidence for a relationship between parental use of LSD and major congenital defects in children.

Conclusions about the relationship between birth defects in children and maternal use of LSD

Delirium tremens produces feelings of disorientation and hallucinations that often include small animals. (© *Culver Pictures, Inc.*)

are difficult to draw because this type of research is confounded by a number of other factors. Erickson, Catz, & Yaffee (1973) concluded that it is almost impossible to isolate the specific effects of the drug. Reports of chromosome damage frequently come from studies in which the pregnant women ingested impure LSD. Moreover, these prospective mothers were often multiple-drug users, were malnourished, or had poor prenatal care. Any of these other factors could have contributed to the observed abnormalities in the children.

After examining nearly 100 studies, Dishotsky, Loughman, Mogar, and Lipscomb (1971) concluded that only very high dosages of LSD cause chromosome damage in humans. There was no evidence of a high rate of birth defects in children of LSD users. Later studies and experiments on rats and other animals confirmed this conclusion

The flowers and leaves of the Indian hemp plant are used to make marijuana. (© *United Press International Photo*)

(Dorrance, Janiger, & Teplitz, 1975; Amarose, Schuster, & Muller, 1973).

Current data indicate that the risk of genetic damage from LSD is small, but the possibility has not been excluded. Rice (1972), considering the inconclusiveness of the current data, still warns pregnant women away from LSD. According to him it requires a bizarre form of courage to take LSD trips for which one's children may pay with deformed bodies and ineffective minds, even if the probability of such an outcome is slim.

Marijuana is classified as a hallucinogen, but it is often treated separately from LSD because its effects are considerably milder. Marijuana is sometimes referred to as a minor hallucinogen, compared with the major hallucinogen LSD. Although LSD is widely used, the use of marijuana is far more common.

Marijuana is derived from the flowers and top leaves of the Indian hemp plant known by the generic name *cannabis*. Cannabis is usually inhaled as a smoke since it is not soluble in water and therefore not suitable for injection. Inhalation of the smoke produces an almost immediate effect.

The effects of marijuana on consciousness vary considerably from person to person depending on the dose, the quality of the drug, and the setting in which marijuana is taken. The setting in this context refers to the expectancies, attitudes, and motivations that the person brings to the drug experience as well as the physical and social environment in which it occurs. The powerful effects of setting on smoking marijuana were illustrated in a study in which experimental subjects who expected to become high were given a very small dose of the drug; they were then exposed to other people who were acting as if high (Carlin, Bakker, Malpern, & Post, 1972). The experimental subjects behaved in ways typical of people who have been given a much larger dose of marijuana. To a great extent people learn the subjective or psychological effects of marijuana from being told about the drug, from reading about it, and most often from watching and being taught by others who have experienced its effects (Becker, 1953).

Marijuana enhances sensory experiences in

both intensity and quality. Sounds become much more distinct. One person observed, "I can hear more subtle changes in sounds, e.g., the notes of music are purer, more distinct, the rhythm stands out" (Tart, 1971, p. 72). Marijuana also distorts time. Events seem to last longer; one side of a record may seem to play for hours. The feeling that a certain event has happened before is a common experience. Under marijuana a person seems to have more time, and much more of his or her awareness is filled with perceiving objects, not through one but through many senses. Thus the color, shape, and aroma of a flower are experienced simultaneously and with a heightened sense of awareness.

Marijuana use has also been linked with a heightened sense of sexuality, although the effects are not altogether clear. For practically all experienced users, marijuana greatly intensifies the sensations experienced in sexual intercourse. Sex is generally desired more, and feelings of greater responsiveness, sharing, and generosity are often experienced (Tart, 1971). Some of Tart's subjects made comments such as "When making love, I feel in much closer contact with my partner" or "Sexual orgasm has new qualities when I'm stoned."

As in the case of LSD, the marijuana user can become overwhelmed by intense negative emotions. Users term such an event "freaking out."

One particular type of marijuana user, the "pot-head," is a dropout from society who centers his or her life on marijuana. Smith (1968) proposed that the proportion of such people in the total population of marijuana users parallels that of alcoholics in the total population of alcohol users. Thus not all marijuana smokers become dependent upon it, just as not all alcohol users become alcoholics.

The Behavioral Effects of Mind-Altering Drugs

In addition to their ability to induce altered states of consciousness, psychoactive drugs have a number of other behavioral effects, including physiological dependence, psychological dependence, and various side effects.

Physiological Dependence. A person who habitually uses some drugs develops a **tolerance** for them and must constantly increase the dosage in order to produce any effect. This is the result of the condition of physiological dependence, which may be defined as a state of progressively decreased responsiveness to a drug. Some alcoholics, for example, can drink a quart of whiskey a day without seeming intoxicated. Both physiological dependence and tolerance are commonly recognized as factors necessary for true addiction. The following description of addiction was offered by the World Health Organization:

> Drug addiction is a state of periodic or chronic intoxication detrimental to the individual and to society, produced by repeated consumption of a drug (natural or synthetic). Its characteristics include: (1) an overpowering desire or need to continue taking the drug and to obtain it by any means, (2) a tendency to increase the dosage, and (3) a psychic [psychological] and sometimes physical dependence on the effects of the drug (1965, p. 722).

A person who is physically dependent on drugs suffers **withdrawal symptoms** when deprived of them. Withdrawal symptoms take the form of perspiration, tremors or convulsive seizures, loss of appetite, vomiting, and diarrhea and they may end in coma or death.

Psychological Dependence. When a person discovers that he or she derives pleasure, a greater sense of well-being, or a new state of awareness from a drug, the desire to continue taking it develops. This desire, which may range from a mild need to an uncontrollable craving, is a sign of **psychological dependence.** The individual may become increasingly preoccupied with obtaining drugs, often discarding values concerning family, job, studies, or personal appearance. In the most serious cases, the addict may resort to criminal behavior to procure drugs. A user can become psychologically dependent on a drug that is not physiologically addictive.

Side Effects. Physical reactions that a drug user is not interested in obtaining are known as side effects. For example, LSD is taken to expand consciousness, not to experience a temporary psychotic state, which sometimes happens. A person who takes barbiturates for pain relief is not interested initially in the mild euphoria induced by this drug. However, that person may begin to take barbiturates primarily to obtain a high. In that case, a side effect has turned into a main effect.

By far the most common side effect is the **flashback,** or spontaneous recurrence of emotions and perceptions originally experienced under the influence of a psychedelic drug. Although flashbacks are briefer and less florid than the original experience, they may cause a person considerable anxiety about his or her sanity. Flashbacks may produce feelings of paranoia and estrangement along with distorted visual perceptions and prickly or tingling sensations.

Flashbacks have been known to last from a few minutes to several hours, to occur once a month or several times a day, up to 18 months after drug use. According to Shick and Smith (1970), there are three kinds of flashbacks: perceptual, somatic, and emotional. The first two usually elicit reactions of panic, fear, and hysteria, but the third type may be the most dangerous because the persistent feelings of fear, remorse, or loneliness may lead to suicide.

Societal Implications

Mind-altering drugs can produce extremely pleasant or heightened states of awareness, but they are subject to abuse. Some of the psychoactive agents are so powerful that their use needs to be supervised. This is particularly important in the case of drugs that may produce psychotic reactions, such as the amphetamines or hallucinogens.

Ray (1978) summarized the societal implications of psychoactive drugs:

1. Psychoactive drugs per se are not good or bad. Only the use to which they are put should be judged.

2. Psychoactive drugs have multiple effects. Altering consciousness or affecting mood are but two of them. Although most drug users seek only these effects, they cannot avoid side effects as well.

3. The effects of a mind-altering drug depend on the dose the individual has taken.

4. The effects of psychoactive drugs depend on the person's mental state and expectations. The more stable and psychologically adjusted the person, the less likelihood there is of a bad trip (p. 11).

From this it follows that maladjusted, irresponsible individuals who experiment with psychoactive agents may create problems for themselves and place a burden on community resources. After a bad trip, a drug user may need medical help in an emergency room or psychological assistance in a crisis-intervention center (see Chapter 19).

Addiction to drugs is damaging to society. To solve the problem of addiction-related crimes, it has been suggested that drugs be legalized and dispensed at a minimal cost to addicts, who are under medical supervision. Such a system has been implemented in Great Britain. The growing black market that controls the distribution of psychoactive drugs generates another set of social problems. Tracking down street dealers as well as those on a higher level requires the involvement of law-enforcement officers.

NON-DRUG TECHNIQUES OF CONSCIOUSNESS ALTERATION

In addition to mind-altering drugs, a number of nondrug techniques produce altered states of awareness.

Meditation

Meditation is one of the classical ways of reaching altered states of consciousness without drugs. It involves a deliberate attempt to separate oneself for a short period from the flow of daily life and "turn off" the active mode of normal consciousness in order to enter the complementary mode of darkness and receptivity (Ornstein, 1973). Meditation requires a passive, receptive attitude.

Those who meditate assume a comfortable position that can be maintained for about 15 minutes. The body should be in such a position that no physical strains are created and only minimal attention need be given to the physical self.

Meditation embraces a diverse group of mental and physical practices. It may involve focusing on a mentally generated sound, or mantra, or contemplating an external object (Goleman, 1977). Some meditation exercises concentrate directly on the content of consciousness. For example, Chandhuri (1965), drawing on yoga practices, writes:

> The radical approach begins with the resolve to do nothing, to make no effort of one's own, to relax completely and to let go one's mind and body . . . stepping out of the stream of ever-changing ideas and feelings that your mind is. Watch the onrush of the stream. Refuse to be submerged in the current. Changing the metaphor, it may be said, watch your ideas, feelings, and wishes fly across the mental firmament like a flock of birds. Let them fly freely. Just keep a watch. Don't allow the birds to carry you off into the clouds (p. 13).

Some people like to meditate in front of a specific object, such as a vase. But the object used is not the chief concern; it is the concentration on it for a certain period of time that counts. Let us look at a meditation exercise taken from yoga:

> The point of primary importance is that one should create a meditation image to accompany him continuously; only as a secondary consideration does it matter what this particular image is. Instead of contemplating a disc of earth, for example, one can meditate on an evenly ploughed field seen from a distance. In the Water Kasina the yogi concentrates either on the circular surface of the water in a jar, or on a lake seen from a mountain. So, too, the fire on the hearth, the flame of a candle, the wind that sways the crests of the tree may also be used as Kasina. The exercise of Color Kasina makes use of round, colored discs, and even of bright-colored flags and flowers. In Space Kasina, one meditates on a circular window opening, the attention in this case being directed primarily to the dimensional proportions of the opening (Spiegelberg, 1962, p. 46).

Meditation involves concentrating on one object or sound and eliminating all other stimuli from consciousness. (© *Watriss-Baldwin/Woodfin Camp & Associates*)

There are many different practitioners of meditation—Zen Buddhists, followers of yoga, the Sufis. One form of meditation that has become fairly popular in Western cultures is transcendental meditation (TM). Transcendental meditation is a form of yoga in which the person is given a specific mantra (significant word) and repeats it over and over for about one-half hour at least twice a day. As soon as the meditator realizes that his or her attention is no longer focused on the mantra, a deliberate effort is made to return to it. The thoughts that arise during meditation are considered to be of no importance.

All forms of meditation are means of expanding and developing our sense of awareness. Common to all meditation practices is the goal of passive awareness—a state in which the mind becomes still and consciousness transcends thought (Schuman, 1980).

It has been shown that meditation produces changes in the electrical activity of the brain. In meditating monks, for instance, alpha waves, ordinarily present when a person is thoroughly relaxed, increased in amplitude and regularity (Wallace & Benson, 1972).

Hypnosis

An important state of consciousness that can be studied in the laboratory is **hypnosis.** Although defining a hypnotic trance is difficult, we do know that hypnosis focuses consciousness very intensely.

Hypnosis is a trancelike state characterized by extreme suggestibility in the subject. (© *Mimi Forsyth /Monkmeyer Press Photo Service*)

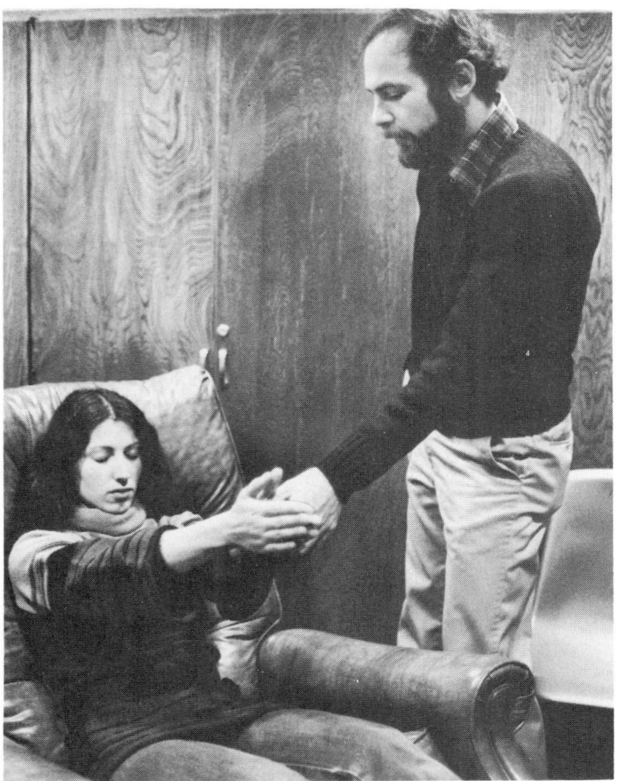

The hypnotist induces a hypnotic trance by focusing the person's attention wholly on him or her. First, the person is asked to relax. The hypnotist describes the phenomenon, assures the subject of the safety of the procedure, and then hypnotizes the person by rhythmic and soothing verbalizations, somewhat as follows:

> I want you to pay close attention to what I say. Now close your eyes and listen carefully; that's fine, just relax your mind and shut out everything except what I say. Think of nothing else. Now your eyes are shut and you are relaxed and feeling drowsy. You can hear only my voice. Now you are breathing regularly and deeper. You can only hear my voice. Your sleep is getting deeper and deeper. When I count from one to ten, your sleep will get even deeper; one, deeper, deeper; two, still deeper; three, you can hear only my voice as your sleep becomes deeper . . .

As the hypnotist induces the trance, his or her voice becomes increasingly softer, slower, and more monotonous. Hypnosis is generally easy to produce unless the subject resists. A person who does not wish to be hypnotized cannot be put into a hypnotic trance. Many of us experience mildly hypnotic experiences in everyday life. It has been suggested, for instance, that the TV commercial is the commonest light-trance induction technique in our culture (Muses & Young, 1974). We allow ourselves to be hypnotized by the commercial and then follow its suggestion.

The trance is terminated at a prearranged signal given by the hypnotist. Sometimes a posthypnotic suggestion is given so that the subject performs a particular act or thinks certain thoughts upon awakening. Hilgard (1970) cited the example of a young subject who was told that she would awaken from hypnosis to find that she had no hands but that this discovery would not bother her. When her "absent" hands were given a rather strong electric shock, the subject reported that she felt nothing, although there had been no specific analgesic suggestions.

Some researchers (e.g., Barber, 1976) doubt that there is a unique state of consciousness involved in hypnosis. Others (e.g., Ornstein, 1972) consider the extreme suggestibility of the hypnotized person to be the only justification for calling hypnosis a state of consciousness. The hypnotic state is usually described as a state of enhanced suggestibility and heightened physiological responsiveness (Wolberg, 1972). Hypnotic suggestions can have specific uses, such as helping a person relax or remember early childhood experiences or reducing pain (Hilgard, 1969). Whether hypnosis really produces a state in which a person attains a more vivid imagination is not clear.

Sensory Deprivation

Still another technique for inducing altered states of consciousness is **sensory deprivation.** This is a state of perceptual isolation in which the person does not receive enough information from the senses to maintain a normal balance. Typically people who are systematically deprived of sensory cues from the environment are likely to exhibit various degrees of disturbance.

One of the first systematic studies of sensory deprivation was carried out by Heron (1957) at McGill University. Male college students were paid $20 a day to participate in a study that required each one to lie on a bed in a lighted cubicle for 24 hours a day. The subjects were encouraged to participate as long as they wanted to but were assured that they could withdraw at any time. Time out was given only for meals, which were consumed sitting at the edge of the bed, and for going to the toilet. The students wore translucent plastic visors that transmitted light but prevented patterned vision. Cotton gloves and cardboard cuffs prevented any tactile sensations. Auditory perception was restricted by a foam-rubber pillow on which the subject's head rested and by the drone of the air-conditioning equipment.

The results of this experiment indicated that sensory deprivation can have severe effects on personality. The thinking of the experimental subjects was impaired, their emotional responses became childish, their perceptions were disturbed, and they had visual hallucinations. One student repeatedly saw visions of a rock shaded by a tree; another saw pictures of babies that he could not erase from his mind. Other sensations reported were tactile experiences, such as being hit on the arm with pellets, electric shock, and a sense of movement while motionless. Brain-wave patterns also indicated changes from the normal state of consciousness.

Some of the phenomena experienced in sensory deprivation are similar to those reported by individuals who practice meditation: feelings of estrangement, increased brightness of color, movement of stationary objects, and hallucinations. In comparison to the usual experiences in sensory deprivation, however, the meditation experience is more rewarding and pleasurable. Most people find the absence of physical and social stimulation stressful and extremely unpleasant.

Biofeedback

An altered state of consciousness can be brought about by machines using a technique known as **biofeedback.** Biofeedback instruments monitor physiological activities such as heart rate, temperature, and brain waves, and feed back biological information through lights or tones (Brown, 1974). The primary purpose in biofeedback training is to help the person become aware of his or her physiological functioning and modify it as warranted.

In this chapter we are mainly concerned with biofeedback training that focuses on the electrical signals emitted from the brain. Researchers who studied the brain-wave patterns of Zen monks, yogis, and other practitioners of meditation discovered that they produce brain-wave states different from those of the average person. While most people in the waking state exhibit irregular brain rhythms of varying frequency, meditators produce even brain waves, called alpha waves, of one predominant frequency (8–12 cycles per second).

Dr. Joe Kamiya of the Langley Porter Neuropsychiatric Institute in San Francisco discovered in 1952 that normal people can be trained to pro-

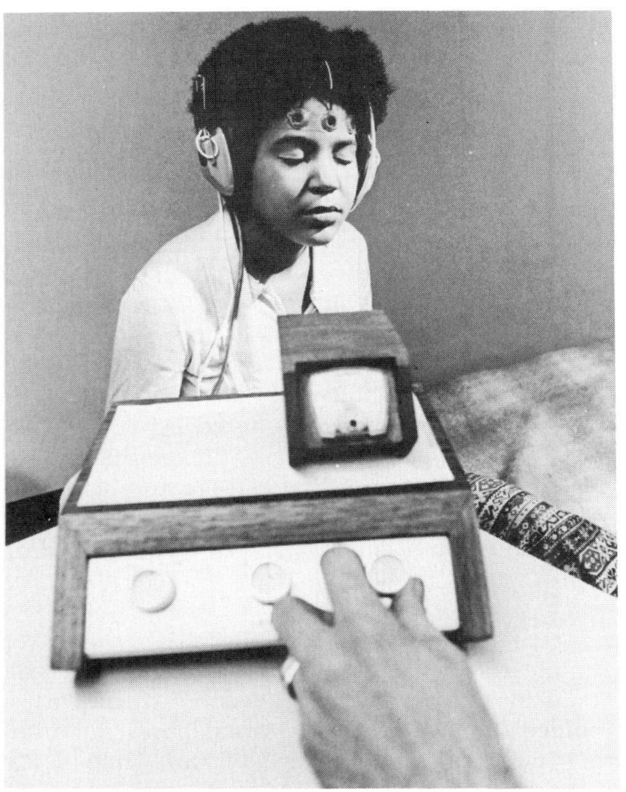

By recording various mental functions electronically and showing the readings to the subject, biofeedback enables him or her to control certain elements of consciousness. (© *Monkmeyer Press Photo Service*)

duce more alpha waves if they are given immediate feedback of their brain-wave pattern. The alpha state is frequently described as follows:

> an increase in smooth, flowing energy, a release of tension and a spreading of attentional focus. . . . Alpha has generally been associated with relaxed wakefulness. Subjects report that while producing alpha, they attend more effortlessly to either internal or external stimuli. While producing alpha, their perceptions are inclined toward larger gestalts; they appear more expansive and more accepting of the objects of their attention. . . . A frequent observation by subjects, after some hours devoted exclusively to alpha training, is that they get along with people better than before training (Payne, 1973, pp. 70–71).

Most people who learn to increase their alpha waves report feeling relaxed and peaceful. Like those who practice meditation, they may experience a feeling of depersonalization, a loss of individual identity, and an awareness of a unifying thread of life. In fact, meditation and alpha biofeedback appear to produce states of concsiousness that are quite similar.

Biofeedback has generated a lot of excitement in the scientific as well as in the lay community. It has been used as a therapeutic technique for a variety of psychosomatic disorders, such as headaches, insomnia, asthma, and high blood pressure. Although scientists urge us to be skeptical about some of the "miracle cures" brought about by biofeedback, there seem to be grounds for optimism. In the future, biofeedback research may help clarify to what extent the ability to control our autonomic processes, such as blood flow, may be related to the capacity to change our state of consciousness (Miller, 1973).

SLEEP AND DREAMING

Sleeping and dreaming are the most common of the altered forms of consciousness. They have been fascinating subjects throughout history. Although our knowledge of sleep and dreams is far from complete, the research of the last twenty years has produced some unexpected findings that have helped to unravel the mysteries of sleeping and dreaming.

Sleep, as a state of consciousness, differs from the waking state in two important aspects: there is (1) less responsiveness to the external world and (2) a change in bodily functions and central-nervous-system activity. When we go to sleep, our physical activity decreases sharply. Our eyes are closed, and our brain, although still receiving incoming information from our senses, no longer processes this information. During sleep, heart and respiration rates decrease, and our level of arousal is lowest. Yet although sleep appears to be a quiet, detached state of consciousness, a lot of exciting things happen.

Patterns of Sleep

Sleep is usually operationally defined with respect to EEG recordings characteristic of its rhythmic patterns (Williams, Karacan, & Hursch, 1974). In general, lower-voltage, faster-frequency EEGs indicate arousal, and higher-voltage, slower-frequency EEGs indicate lessened arousal, sleep, or similar states.

Two Types of Sleep. Take the opportunity to observe someone sleeping—a person, a cat, or a dog—and you will notice two discernible types of sleep that alternate rhythmically. One type is characterized by **rapid eye movements (REM)** and the other by the absence of these movements (non-REM, or NREM). NREM sleep is very quiet, characterized by regular eye movements and little body movement. The organism is motionless, and contact with the environment is entirely lost. Brain waves are slow and regular. Dement (1974) noted, however, that at least in one respect the term "quiet sleep" is a misnomer because it is during this period that snoring occurs.

REM sleep was discovered almost accidentally. In 1952, Dr. Nathaniel Kleitman, a pioneer in sleep research, studied the slow, rolling eye movements that typically accompany the onset of sleep. He was interested in finding out whether these movements continued throughout the night. Kleitman assigned the task of watching the sleeping subjects to one of his graduate students, Eugene Aserinsky, who made a discovery that was a breakthrough in sleep research. Aserinsky noticed that at certain times during the night very rapid eye movements occurred that were entirely different from the slow movements he was told to observe. When Aserinsky woke the subjects from sleep stages that were characterized by rapid eye movements, they reported dreams more frequently than if he awakened them from NREM stages. In addition, dreams reported from the REM period tended to be emotional and organized into recognizable events, while NREM dreams tended to be vague and fragmentary. The onset of REM sleep is clearly observable. The sleeper's face twitches, breathing becomes irregular, and any snoring ceases. In infant and adult males, penile erections may occur. Brain waves go into bursts of activity. Many sleep researchers have compared the REM period to electric seizures. As we noted earlier, the most exciting aspect of REM sleep is its relation to dreaming. During the REM stage a person may be literally watching his or her dream. (Webb, 1975).

Stages of Sleep. Suppose that you have just climbed into bed and are ready for sleep. You are now in the state of relaxed wakefulness (see Figure 3–1), which is characterized by alpha waves. If

Sleep laboratories are enabling psychologists to understand the mysteries of sleep. (© *News and Publications Service, Stanford University*)

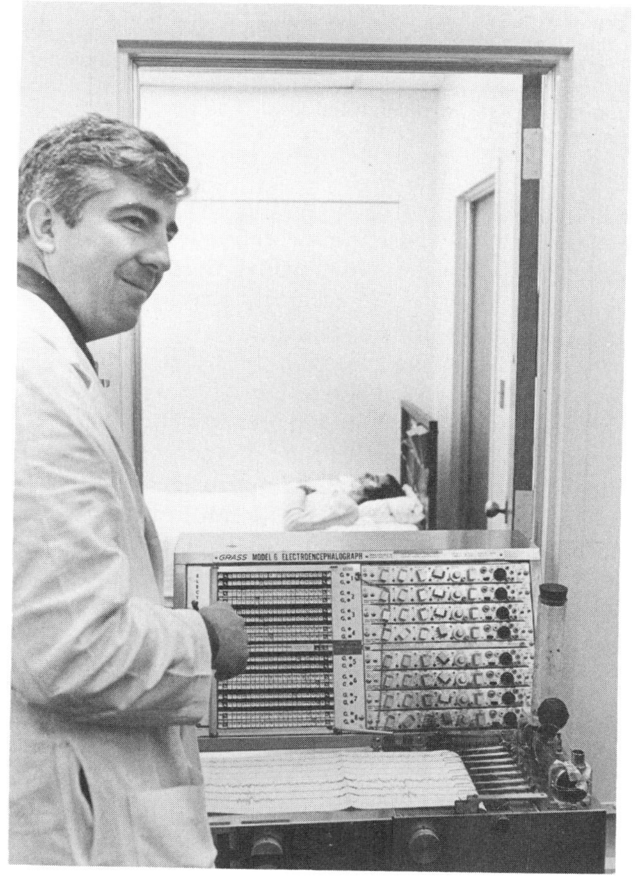

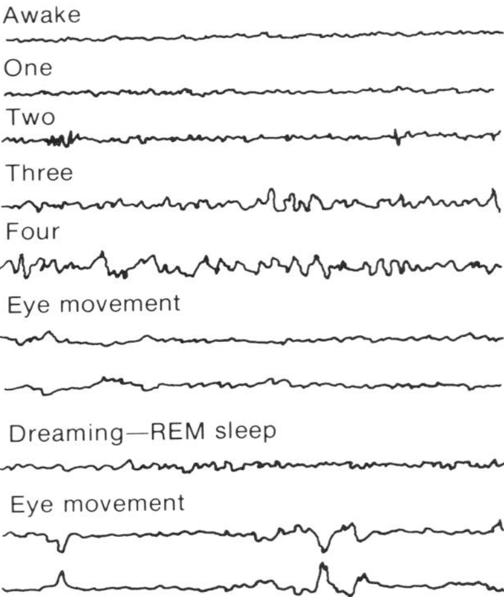

Figure 3–1. Human EEG illustrating Dement-Kleitman classification of EEG stages of sleep and eye movements. The eye movements at the bottom of the figure are the rapid eye movements characteristic of REM sleep. (From Johnson, L. C., Sleep and sleep loss: Their effects on performance. *Research Reviews*, 1967.)

you allow yourself to drift into sleep, the alpha waves gradually disappear. Many sleep researchers (e.g., Hartman, 1967) define the actual onset of sleep as the time when alpha activity occurs in less than one-half of each minute.

Upon the onset of sleep, a person goes through four NREM stages of sleep. During *Stage 1*, some examples of waking behavior, such as body movements or eye blinks, are no longer observable. Brain waves have a low amplitude and a frequency in the 2–7 cycles-per-second range, just a bit slower than in the waking state (Bennett, 1977). While in this stage you can be relatively easily awakened. During *Stage 2*, brief bursts of electrical activity called **sleep spindles** appear. These are short, fast waves (14–16 cycles per second), which resemble the way a thread is wrapped around an old-fashioned sewing spindle. As *Stage 3* approaches, the characteristic **delta waves**—high-amplitude, slow waves of 1–2 cycles per second—begin to be interspersed with the spindles. Stage 3 is defined by an EEG record in which more than 20 percent but less than 50 percent of the record consists of delta waves. In the course of a night's sleep approximately 5 percent of sleep is spent in Stage 3. *Stage 4* is often referred to as deep sleep, defined by an EEG record consisting of more than 50 percent delta waves. We normally spend about 15 percent of the night's sleep in Stage 4. If we are prevented, by some annoyance or tension, from getting our 15 percent quota, we will make up for it by spending more than 15 percent of subsequent nights in Stage 4 (Bennett, 1977).

About 30 to 40 minutes after the onset of sleep, the first REM period begins. For the rest of the night, REM periods will recur about every 80 to 90 minutes and comprise 20 to 25 percent of the total sleeping time. As sleep becomes deeper, REM periods become progressively longer. The first REM period is the shortest, lasting 5 to 10 minutes. Later REM periods may last 50 to 60 minutes. About 80 percent of the time, subjects awakened during such periods report that they had been dreaming (Schwartz, 1978). As William Dement remarked: "After offering us several short episodes early in the night, the brain may produce an hour-long feature film."

The World of Dreams

All human beings have dreams. Dreams have been described as a series of thoughts or images and feelings passing through the mind in sleep. They constitute a kind of awareness that is different from ordinary consciousness and sleeping.

As we have seen, the dream state is associated with REM sleep. Dement and Kleitman (1957) found that dream recall was obtained on 80 percent of REM period awakenings but only on 7 percent of NREM awakenings. In addition to the differences in recall frequencies, there are important qualitative differences between REM and NREM dreams. Compare the following two dreams reported by a student:

> *Dream 1:* He is in a sleep laboratory, filling out a paper-and-pencil form. Someone passes by, commenting that the task is a stupid one (NREM).

> *Dream 2:* In the first scene, he is standing on a street corner, holding his bicycle and talking to someone about a girl who wanted to be a striptease dancer. In the second scene, he is a doctor with two women. They are discussing two books. The heroine in the first book was a striptease dancer but now is a nurse. The women are discussing how much hardship the nurse has (REM) (Foulkes, 1974, p. 301).

Generally NREM recall is more like thinking, less visual, more concrete, and more concerned with actual events or people than is REM recall. REM dreams correspond more closely to vivid, hallucinatory experiences that we associate with altered states of consciousness.

Dream Recall

Dream recall is a skill that improves with practice. If you want to recall a dream, you need to plan to remember it. Before you fall asleep, you might use autosuggestion, telling yourself several times, "I am going to wake up after a dream."

The best time for dream recall is in the morning. When you wake up spontaneously (not by the alarm clock or the phone ringing), you are awakening from a REM period. As we have seen, the morning dream is the longest, sometimes lasting half an hour to an hour.

Dream research has clearly established that dream recall is richest and most detailed *immediately* after a REM period ends. Sleepers who were awakened five minutes after REM sleep stopped could only remember vague snatches of the dream. Dreamers who were awakened ten minutes after the REM period stopped had no dream recall or only a blurry impression that they had had a dream (Garfield, 1974).

After you wake up, it is important to stay relaxed with your eyes closed. Lie still and let the dream images flow through your mind. When the images are fixed in your mind, sit up gently, switch on the light, and write down the dream or tape-record it in as much detail as possible. Date your dreams and keep them together with your interpretations in a notebook. Dream sequences give insight into a person's own personality as well as into his or her relationships with others. As Carl Jung wrote over 40 years ago, "The dream is the small hidden door in the deepest and most intimate sanctum of the soul."

Dream Interpretation

The nature of dreams and their meanings are a puzzle, delight, and source of fear for many people. Interest in dreams was stirred by Sigmund Freud in his book *The Interpretation of Dreams* (1953), originally published in 1900. According to Freud, dreams represent the fulfillment or attempted fulfillment of *unconscious* wishes.

The wish-fulfilling component of dreams can be seen in a dream of a young woman who was undergoing therapy with Freud. She dreamed that she was having her menstrual period. Freud's interpretation of the dream was that in real life she had missed her period. She *wished* she had had it because she was not sure whether she wanted to be pregnant.

Freud believed that the two principal wishes or impulses gratified in dreams are those of sex and aggression. Freud referred to the dream's facade, or mask, consisting of all those recalled sights, images, sounds, and smells that compose the story of the dream. Behind that facade lie the unacceptable impulses that are far commoner in mental life than straightforward, undisguised urges (Freud, 1925, p. 132). Freud distinguished between the *manifest* and *latent* content in the dream. The *manifest* content corresponds to the mask in the part of the dream that is easily recalled by the dreamer. The *latent* content refers to the impulses that are disguised, like "masked criminals," and can only be revealed through careful interpretation.

Let us look at two examples of dreams with sexual and aggressive imagery. Here is the dream of a young man:

> I was at an amusement park with several male friends. The booths were attended by gorgeous-looking girls and we divided into separate groups to see what we could do for ourselves. I went up to one of these beautiful girls and asked her where she

> lived, walked away, then returned and asked her if I could take her home that night. She said I could and just after that I remembered going on the merry-go-round. When the park closed, I called for her. We got into a car and drove to her apartment. She asked me in and told me to wait until she changed into something more comfortable (Hall, 1966, pp. 49–50).

Obviously the dreamer was hesitant about making advances to a girl. Nevertheless, the amusement park created a setting of fun and excitement that was conducive to a sexual encounter. Note that the dream ended before the sexual relationship was consummated.

Here is an example of a dream with strong aggressive undertones: a young woman dreamed that her whole family, save herself, was swept to death by a tidal wave. By such a ruse she got rid of her family, which she hated, and then pitied herself because she was all alone in the world. The aggressive, destructive symbolism of this dream is obvious.

Peter Tripp suffered a bout of depression after staying awake for more than eight days. (© *Wide World Photos*)

Freud stressed the idea of symbolism in dreams as a means of reaching into different realms of consciousness. A symbol, according to Freud's definition, is a mental representation of a particular concept. For example, riding a horse, ploughing a field, climbing stairs, or shooting a gun symbolize sexual intercourse. Freud believed that sharp, elongated objects are symbolic representations of the penis. By the same token, cups, boxes, houses, and other containers symbolize the vaginal opening. Much of dream symbolism is based on the notion that dreams go by opposites. To dream of being in a crowd, for instance, means being alone; to dream of being clothed means being naked.

Of course, not everyone accepts the Freudian interpretation of dreams. Some sleep researchers argue that before the discovery of REM sleep as an indicator of dreaming, scientific research on dreams was impossible. It was, as van de Castle (1971) put it, "like trying to lasso a cloud on a windy day while perched in wet sneakers on a mountaintop." Reviewing Freudian dream theory in the light of recent physiological evidence, Webb (1975) concluded that it is unlikely that unconscious wishes seek satisfaction regularly during REM periods, as Freud contended. Although wish-fulfillment may be one of the functions of dreams, it is unlikely that it figures in all dreams.

Effects of Sleep Loss

Research has shown that lack of sleep affects personality. After 40 hours without sleep, irritability, tension, lack of perseverance, and distortions in perception occur. After 100 sleepless hours, psychotic symptoms in thinking, mood, and motor activity occur. Hallucinatory episodes make the sleep-deprived person unable to distinguish between real and imagined events. Occasionally a sensation of a band extending around the head,

CRITICAL ISSUE

Sleep Learning

Although our level of arousal is lowest when we are asleep, many people believe that we are able to learn while asleep. In fact, a small industry has grown up, promising to make useful the time we "waste" sleeping by providing us with pillow speakers, tape recorders, and foreign-language tapes to promote learning during sleep (Hintzman, 1978).

The concept of sleep learning is based on audiovisual learning that occurs during reduced conscious awareness (Rubin, 1971). Soviet scientists who initiated research on sleep-assisted instruction called it hypnopaedia (*hypno* meaning sleep; *paedia* meaning education). In sleep-assisted instruction, the training material is introduced during the waking state just before sleep and is subsequently repeated during states of drowsiness and light sleep. Most sleep-learning lessons last from 6 to 10 minutes and are repeated several times during a 40-to-50-minute sleep-learning session.

The learning material presented in the Soviet studies ranged from nonsense syllables to readings in a foreign language. In a typical study, 120 Hungarian words were paired with their Russian translation and presented over a five-night training period. After the subjects had become accustomed to the laboratory setting, they were instructed to spend their time in the lounge and then go to bed at 10:50 P.M. The "conditioning tape" started to play at 10:55 P.M. and made certain suggestions:

> You know that your ability to memorize while you are asleep depends entirely on your willingness to cooperate, because if you don't want to learn while you are asleep we won't be able to make you do it. But if you pay close attention to what I say and then follow what I tell you to do, it will be very easy for you to learn while you sleep and you will learn. We are confident of your ability to learn while you are asleep. But you must relax and now go to sleep. Pay careful attention to what I will say and you will go to sleep very soon; you will fall asleep and retain the Hungarian (Rubin, 1971, p. 53).

Each afternoon following instruction the subjects were given a multiple-choice test using one training word and four control words. The subjects recognized about 40 percent of the material that had been presented during sleep.

Soviet investigators (e.g., Maksimov, 1968) reached the following conclusions regarding sleep learning:

1. The most suitable stage for sleep learning is the light-sleep stage, in which alpha waves are easily provoked by the learning procedure.
2. The repetitive presentation of the learning material is a prerequisite of the learning effect.
3. The possibility of sleep learning depends primarily on EEG changes from the sleep pattern to mixed-activity wave patterns.

Many of the experiments conducted in the Soviet Union and Eastern Europe have not been rigorously designed; very few, for instance, reported control groups.

Evidence collected in the United States provides little basis for optimism (Aarons, 1976). In a review of Soviet and Western research on sleep-assisted instruction, it was found that Soviet studies are largely positive, while Western studies found little or no learning during sleep. Although there may be some learning of material presented during sleep, most learning takes place during intervals of waking.

known as the "hat illusion," is reported. This sensation may be accompanied by subjective feelings of depersonalization, that is, thinking that one is not oneself.

The experience of a New York disc jockey named Peter Tripp highlights the major effects of sleep deprivation (Dement, 1974). Tripp stayed awake for 200 consecutive hours to raise money for the March of Dimes. He conducted his waking marathon in a glass booth on Times Square, making a daily broadcast to the crowd below. Through most of the sleepless period, he was witty and talkative. However, toward the end of the marathon dramatic changes occurred. His speech began to slur. One night he went into an acute paranoid stage during which he experienced auditory hallucinations and believed that his enemies were trying to slip sedatives into his food and drink. After the marathon was over, Tripp suffered a three-month depression.

Sleep Disturbances

Most of us take sleep for granted; it is as natural and necessary as breathing. However, on occasion most of us have been plagued by a sleep problem of one sort or another. The most common one is probably insomnia, but sleepwalking, night terrors, and a sleep disorder called narcolepsy are also fairly prevalent.

Insomnia. This common sleep disturbance affects about 20 million Americans. Although most of us have experienced periods when we found it difficult to fall or remain asleep, for the insomniac this is a chronic problem.

Much of **insomnia** is due to poor sleep habits. Some people have a tendency to vary when and where they sleep. One night they go to bed at 4 A.M.; the next night they retire at 9 P.M. to catch up on sleep lost the previous night. Or, if they travel a great deal, they sleep in different places night after night. Such irregularities prevent sleep from developing a systematic pattern. A regular bedtime in the same sleep environment is often necessary to guarantee an even sleep rhythm. Many insomniacs compound the problem with worry.

Sleepwalking. Contrary to what cartoons show, sleepwalkers do not walk with arms outstretched and eyes closed. In sleepwalking, or **somnambulism,** a person gets out of bed spontaneously and walks about rigidly with eyes open. Often sleepwalkers act as if searching for something specific. If you live with a somnambulist, it is wise to lock the doors and remove dangerous objects. The sleepwalker's recovery of consciousness is usually sudden and spontaneous. On command from an authoritative voice the sleepwalker may stop what he or she is doing or may return to bed voluntarily.

Until quite recently sleepwalking episodes were thought to be an acting out of a dream or a symptom of personality disturbance. Now sleepwalking is established as an NREM disturbance. According to psychoanalytic theory, somnambulism indicates the flight into a different state of awareness, a form of personality dissociation in which the person acts out deep-seated psychological problems during the sleepwalking episode. Today somnambulism is looked on as a developmental rather than a personality disturbance. Sleepwalking is common among children, but most of them outgrow it by adolescence.

Night Terrors. A night terror refers to a sudden awakening from sleep in a state of extreme panic. Most night terrors are experienced by children. Typically the child screams and groans and may appear to be fighting or running away from some terrifying situation or person. Even when awakened, the child may continue to scream and remain disoriented and confused for a while.

Like sleepwalking, night terrors have been erroneously linked with dreams. Night terrors are not considered dreams since they occur during NREM rather than REM cycles (Fisher, Kahn, Edwards, & Davis, 1973).

Narcolepsy. **Narcolepsy** is a sleep disorder in which the individual periodically suffers from a sudden and overpowering desire to sleep. These sudden sleeping attacks, which usually last from a few minutes to a half hour, often come at inappropriate times. Dement (1974) cites one case of a fireman who had an attack while climbing a ladder on a burning building and another case in which a woman fell asleep while scuba diving 20 feet under water. Many times these sleep attacks are triggered by monotonous activities. Listening to a dull lecture, eating a big meal, or lying down in the sun are examples of activities that bring on sleep attacks in narcoleptics. It has also been suggested that many automobile accidents are caused by sleep attacks, though not all of these attacks are narcoleptic.

Although the exact cause of narcolepsy is not known, it appears to be associated with an abnormality of the REM-stage sleep process. Dement (1974) discovered that in a narcoleptic attack the person does not begin sleep in the conventional NREM manner but goes immediately from wakefulness into a REM sleep. As we have seen, the REM stage does not normally appear until some 30–40 minutes after sleep onset.

Narcoleptics sometimes experience a forewarning. The sleep attack may be signaled by an **aura,** or a period of unusual feelings or perceptions, before the person lapses into an overwhelming sleep. The aura may be followed by hallucinations and vivid dreams. Presently there is no cure for narcolepsy. Treatment usually involves the administration of antidepressants (Wyatt, Fram, Buchbinder, & Snyder, 1971).

Summary

Our awareness is an ever-changing phenomenon. Many different states of consciousness exist, and most of us function at different levels of awareness. Definitions of consciousness usually include references to mental images, memories, perceptions of the immediate environment, daydreams, and fantasies. Psychologists distinguish between two major states of consciousness: ordinary, or waking, consciousness and altered states of awareness.

Alterations of consciousness can be produced by a variety of means. Psychoactive drugs, particularly the hallucinogens LSD and marijuana, provide many people with the opportunity to expand their consciousness and explore dimensions of awareness not available to them in the normal waking state. Stimulants produce states of consciousness characterized by excitation and euphoria, while depressants produce a calmer mood. Although these drugs have the power to shift a person into a different realm of consciousness, they may also have harmful side effects.

Changes of consciousness can also be brought about without drugs through the techniques of meditation, hypnosis, sensory deprivation, and biofeedback. People who utilize these techniques to alter their levels of awareness typically believe that higher states of consciousness can guide them through the maze of daily living by providing a source of inspiration and creativity.

Sleep is a unique and familiar state of consciousness in which most people spend about one-third of their lives. Although the essential facts about sleep have been available since the 1930s, the discovery of REM sleep did not occur until the 1950s. NREM sleep has been divided into four stages based on the predominant EEG characteristics that correlate with the depth of sleep. REM sleep is associated with mixed-frequency EEGs. One of the most dramatic discoveries in sleep research has been the association of REM sleep and dreams. The nature of our dreams and their interpretation has always fascinated people. Freud proposed that dreams represent the fulfillment of unconscious wishes, most of which are sexual or aggressive. Psychologists also study and develop strategies for treating several common problems that are associated with sleep, including insomnia, sleepwalking, night terrors, and narcolepsy.

Key Terms For Review

alcohol
alcoholic hallucinosis
amphetamines
amphetamine psychosis
aura
barbiturates
biofeedback
caffeine
cocaine
delerium tremens (DTs)
delta waves
flashback
hallucinogens
hypnosis
insomnia
lysergic acid diethylamide (LSD)
marijuana
meditation
narcolepsy
nicotine
psychoactive drug
psychological dependence
rapid eye movements (REM)
sensory deprivation
sleep spindles
somnambulism
state-dependent learning
tolerance
withdrawal symptoms

Suggested Readings

Dement, C. *Some must watch while some must sleep.* San Francisco: W. H. Freeman, 1974.
A brief and informal account of the major findings from 20 years of sleep research, written for a general audience.

Josephson, B., & Ramachandran, V. *Consciousness and the physical world.* New York: Pergamon Press, 1980.
This book, based on an interdisciplinary symposium, presents various topics related to consciousness in a scientific form. Among the topics are altered states of consciousness and personal identity, split-brain patients, and social aspects of consciousness.

McKean, M. *The stop smoking book.* San Luis Obispo, Cal.: Impact Publishers, 1976.
This book is written from a highly personal point of view and offers behavior-change techniques, including checklists, journal entries, and other helpful ways to break the smoking habit.

Ornstein, R. *The psychology of consciousness* (2nd ed.). New York: Harcourt Brace Jovanovich, 1977.

A survey of topics related to consciousness ranging from physiological studies of hemispheric functions and behavioral analyses of time perception to Eastern philosophy and meditation.

Teyler, T. *Altered states of consciousness: Readings from Scientific American.* San Francisco: W. H. Freeman, 1972.

A collection of articles providing the student with insight into several states of consciousness, including those produced by meditation, drugs, sensory deprivation, dreams, and dreamless sleep.

4

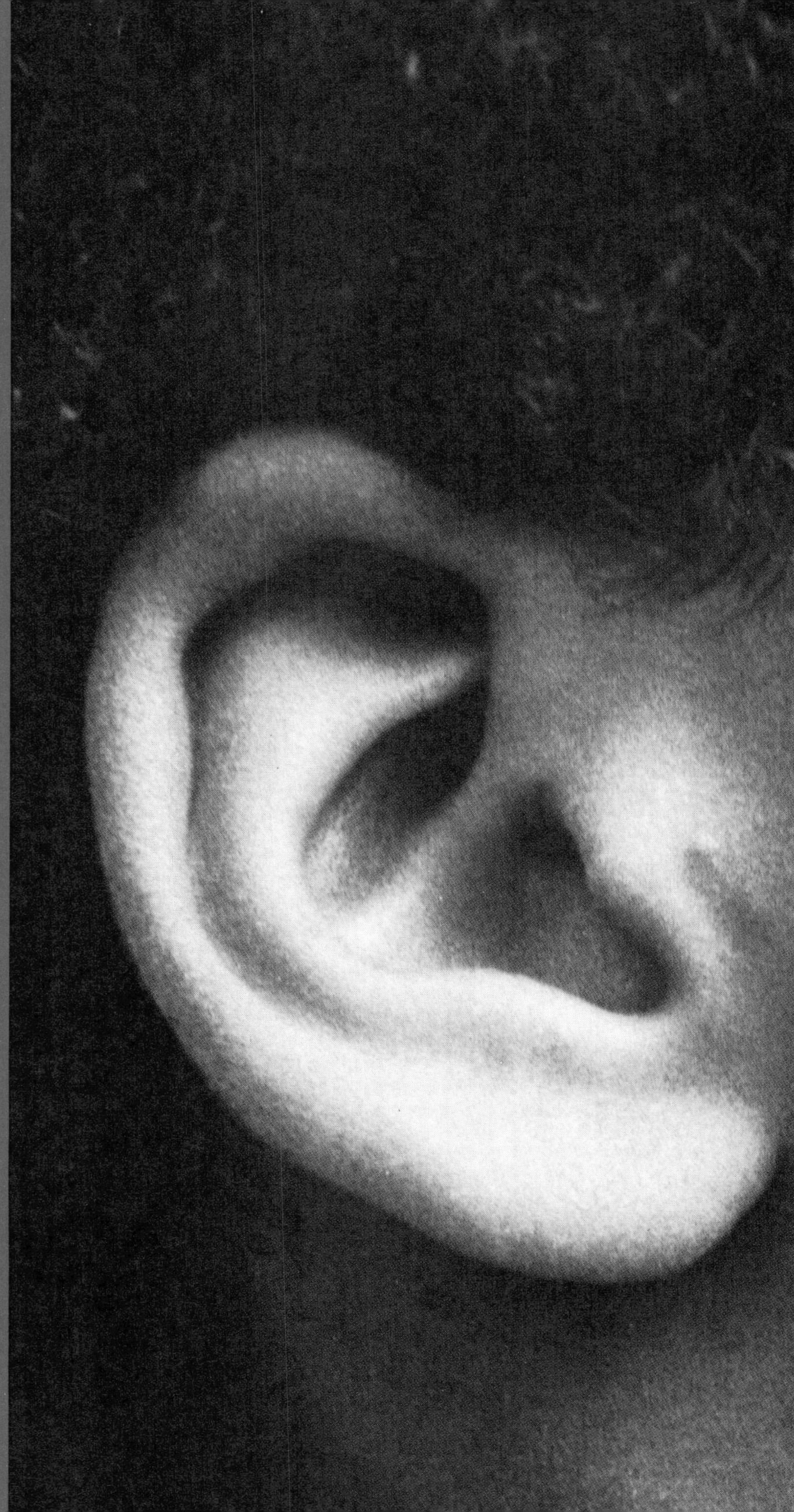

Sensation and Perception

Kenge looked over the plains and down to where a herd of about a hundred buffalo were grazing some miles away. He asked me what kind of insects they were, and I told him they were buffalo, twice as big as the forest buffalo known to him. He laughed loudly and told me not to tell such stupid stories. . . . We got into the car and drove down to where the animals were grazing. He watched them getting larger and larger, and though he was as courageous as any Pigmy, he moved over and sat close to me and muttered that it was witchcraft. . . . Finally, when he realized that they were real buffalo he was no longer afraid, but what puzzled him still was why they had been so small, and whether they really had been small and suddenly grown larger, or whether it had been some kind of trickery.

(TURNBULL, *1961)*

The above quotation was provided by an anthropologist who studied the behavior of the Bambuti Pygmies, who live in the Ituri Forest in the Congo. It illustrates how we tend to take for granted our sensations and perceptions. If we look out a window and see a parked car across the street and another one a block away, we see them as being the same size. Kenge would have seen the car that was a block away as being much smaller but as close to him as the car across the street. A knowledge of the processes of sensation and perception can make differences such as this understandable—as we shall see shortly.

The importance of our senses was recognized as early as 450 B.C., when the Greek philosopher Protagoras stated that "man is nothing but a bundle of sensations." Perception, as illustrated with the example of Kenge, has taken on equal importance. You may recall from Chapter 1 that the German physicists and physicians who founded psychology considered sensation and perception to be basic issues. In fact, the first English textbook on psychology, written by Alexander Bain in 1855, was titled *The Senses and the Intellect*. Our senses make it possible to experience the world: without them there would be no conscious existence—at least none as we know it.

This chapter will provide an overview of the complexities of our sensory world and the ways that we perceive it. First, however, we should note where sensation ends and perception begins.

Suppose you visit an art museum and become interested in its collection of impressionistic paintings. As you look at a particular painting, electromagnetic energy (i.e., light) strikes your eyes. You see a picture of a man seated in a room. How does this happen? How does physical energy become translated into a meaningful and coherent conscious experience?

The distinction between sensation and perception refers to different aspects of this question. Psychologists who are interested primarily in sensation might investigate the way in which the eye converts electromagnetic energy into neural activity. They would be interested in how the neural activity moves from the eye through the visual pathways to the visual centers in the brain. And they would ask how the activity in the brain is transformed into conscious experience of color, shape, and brightness.

Psychologists who are interested primarily in perception would want to know how colors, shapes, and brightness are organized into a coherent experience. For instance, an impressionistic painting of a man may not resemble any man we have ever seen before, yet we recognize instantly that it is a man. Very slight differences in color or brightness may mean the difference between perceiving the painting as reflecting happiness or sadness. The shape of a door in the painting may be a parallelogram, but we perceive it to be rectangular. These phenomena are included under the heading of perception.

Obviously the topics of sensation and perception are closely related, and the dividing point between them is somewhat arbitrary. But we shall make use of the distinction noted here. In the first half of the chapter we shall examine the workings of the senses, and in the second half we shall explore the factors that influence perception.

SENSATION

Each one of our senses may be thought of as a channel that, when stimulated, will lead a person to a certain type of experience. What is experienced is activity in the nervous system rather than the external world per se. That is, we do not experience the external world directly. We experience it through the processes of **sensation** and **perception.** In response to the philosophical question, "If a tree falls in the forest and no one is near, is there any sound?," the psychologist would argue that there is sound but no hearing. The falling tree would generate sound waves, but this physical energy would not be transformed into neural activity since no one was around. Our sensory receptors and central nervous system receive, process, and analyze physical energy in a way that enables us to have a meaningful and coherent experience of the world around us.

Most people believe they have five senses, but the actual number is close to twice that. Along with vision, hearing, smell, taste, and the skin senses are kinesthesis (movement) and the vestibular sense (equilibrium). In addition, the skin senses consist of four types of distinct sensory experiences: pain, touch, cold, and warmth. And taste consists of four sensations: sweet, sour, bitter, and salty. Because vision is such an important sense, it will be explored in detail. The other senses will be discussed more briefly.

Vision

Most of us believe that vision is our most important sense. Consider the weight an eyewitness in court carries, or the expression "I saw it with my own eyes." There is also experimental evidence that our perception of the world is strongly influenced by what we see. Two psychologists asked subjects to view a number of objects, such as blocks of various shapes, and simultaneously to feel them with their hands. Their view, however, was distorted by a series of mirrors. The experiment showed that vision, in relation to touch, is so powerful that the experience of touch underwent a change. The subjects believed the objects "felt" the way they appeared visually (Rock & Victor, 1964).

The eye responds to electromagnetic energy. This form of energy has wave-like properties and can be described in terms of the distance between the peaks of successive waves. At one end of the electromagnetic spectrum are gamma rays, which have very short wavelengths (measured in trillionths of an inch). The longer wavelengths consist of radio and television waves and may measure many miles. The human eye is sensitive to a very narrow range of electromagnetic energy, measuring from about 380 to 780 nanometers (billionths of a meter). Within this visible spectrum, as it is called, various wavelengths are associated with different colors (see color insert).

A working knowledge of how our sense of vision functions is important to psychologists because many practical problems revolve around our ability to see. Children with learning disabilities may have subtle visual disturbances. Industrial psychologists who are called upon to help design complex instruments for occupations such as pilot or air traffic controller must know about the capabilities and limitations of our visual system. And psychologists are interested in studying the visual system simply to increase their knowledge of the human organism. Let us examine how this electromagnetic energy is translated into visual experiences.

Structure of the Visual System. The human eye is an extremely complex organ. Figure 4–1 illustrates the important structures of the eye. The outer covering, called the **sclera,** is a strong elastic membrane that serves to protect the eye. In the front of the eye, the sclera bulges forward to form the **cornea.** The function of the cornea is to gather and concentrate light.

The colored membrane, ranging in color from blue through black, is called the **iris;** to some extent, it controls the amount of light entering the eye. The **pupil** is the dark circle in the center of the eye that admits light. Its size is controlled by a light reflex. In dim light it may dilate to more than 8 mm, while in bright light it may constrict to as little as 2 mm. Pupil size is also influenced by emotional and motivational factors. When we are interested in something we see, our pupils will dilate. This fact was discovered by American psychology only in the 1960s (Hess, 1965), but other cultures may have been using this piece of knowledge in their interpersonal relations for centuries. Anthropologist Edward T. Hall (1979) believes the Arabs have known about the pupil response for hundreds, if not thousands, of years. He further believes that this explains why they maintain a conversational distance of about two feet compared with the five feet used by Americans. It may also explain why many Arabs, such as PLO leader Yasir Arafat, wear dark glasses even indoors. At two feet one can see another's pupils dilate or constrict, and the dark glasses prevent another person from learning about one's mood or interest.

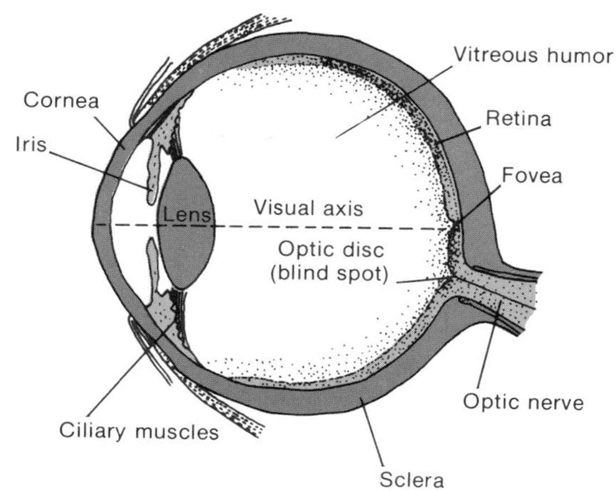

Figure 4–1. The anatomy of the eye.

The **lens,** located directly behind the pupil, controls the degree to which light entering the eye is bent. The shape of the lens changes in order to bring near and far objects into focus in the rear of the eye. This process, called **accommodation,** involves the lens becoming more spherical when one is viewing close objects. When more distant objects are viewed, the lens will flatten. This process is illustrated in Figure 4–2.

In many individuals, the focusing ability is less than perfect, and artificial lenses (glasses) must be used to help the human lens focus the light rays on the back of the eye. Figure 4–3 illus-

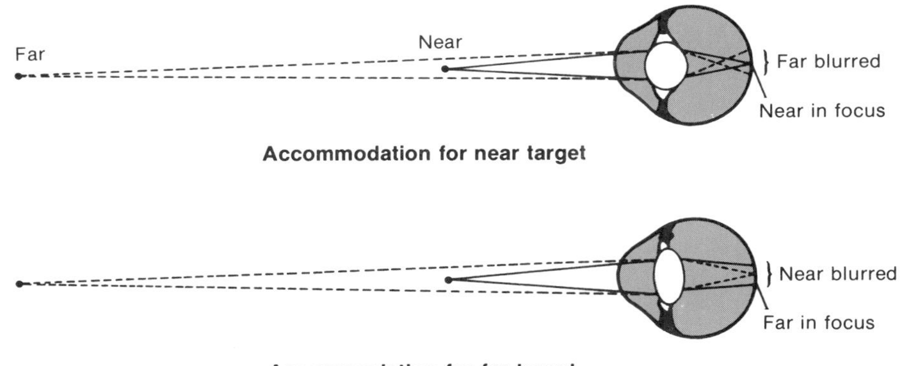

Figure 4–2. Accommodation. Changing the shape of the lens allows the eye to focus on either far or near objects.

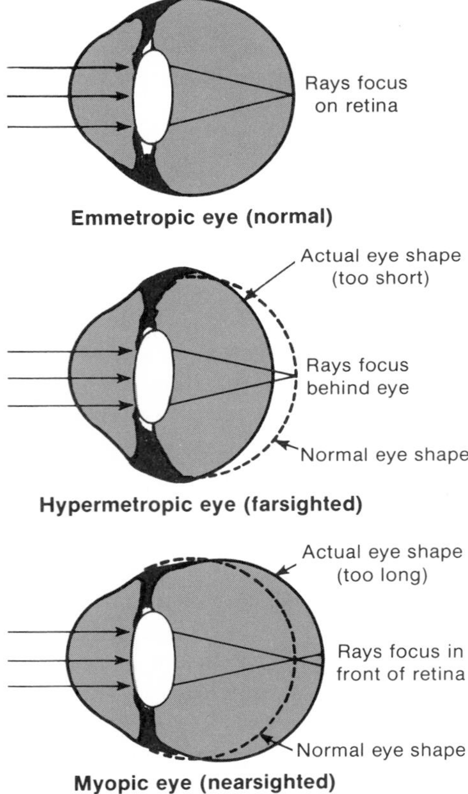

Figure 4–3. Normal and abnormal refraction.

trates three common conditions. The top drawing represents normal vision, in which the lens is able to focus light on the back of the eye. The middle figure represents a case of **hypermetropia**, or farsightedness. In this condition the lens cannot accommodate adequately, or the shape of the eye is too short so that close objects cannot be brought into focus. In the bottom figure, the shape of the eye is too long so that distant objects cannot be focused. This condition is referred to as **myopia**, or nearsightedness.

The back of the eye is covered with a thin layer of tissue called the **retina.** The retina consists of three major layers of cells. The first layer consists of two types of photoreceptive cells called **rods** and **cones.** These cells convert light into neural activity, which is then transmitted to the second major layer, the bipolar cells. From the bipolar cells, the information is transmitted to the ganglion cells, the third layer, which are the nuclei of the cells forming the optic nerve. The schematic representation of the retina presented in Figure 4–4 illustrates that the photoreceptors do not have separate pathways to the higher visual centers. There are some 126 million photoreceptors in the human eye and only about 1 million optic nerves. So, several photoreceptors will stimulate each bipolar cell, and several bipolar cells will stimulate each ganglion cell. This process of convergence provides the first step in the analysis of visual information. It is at this point that the transformation of physical energy into perceptual experience begins.

In the mid-1800s it was discovered that nocturnal animals, such as owls, have retinas that contain only rods. The retinas of animals active during the day consist of cones only, while animals that are active during the twilight have both rods and cones. This observation led to the **duplicity theory** of vision, recognizing two visual systems. Over the past century much evidence has accumulated that there are indeed two systems. The first is for vision in dim light and is dependent primarily on the rods, and the second is for vision in bright light, and is dependent primarily on the cones. Individuals who are born without rods have normal vision during daylight, but at twilight they become functionally blind. Those who are born without cones find daylight to be extremely painful and are unable to discriminate among colors. Under dim light, however, their eyesight appears to be normal.

In the normal human eye there are approximately 120 million rods and 6 million cones. The rods and cones are not distributed evenly on the retina. Cones are concentrated at a depressed spot at the back of the eye called the **fovea.** Rods have their greatest concentration about 20 degrees either side of the fovea (see Figure 4–5). Along with being responsible for day vision, cones are responsible for color vision and fine visual acuity, or sharpness of vision. When one wishes to view an object clearly, it will be focused on the fovea where the concentration of cones is greatest. Rods do not allow for fine visual discrimination, nor do they respond to differences in color.

Color Vision. Our ability to distinguish nearly 200 different colors not only adds an aesthetic quality to our lives, but it can help us in making important discriminations. Imagine trying to distinguish between ripe and nearly ripe tomatoes without color vision. In earlier times, when survival depended upon hunting, color vision made it possible to pick out animals in a forest, a jungle, or on the plains. Many animals depend on their ability to discriminate among colors. Bees might find it nearly impossible to find nectar-bearing flowers hidden in shrubs or leaves without their color vision. Color vision helps us to adapt to our world.

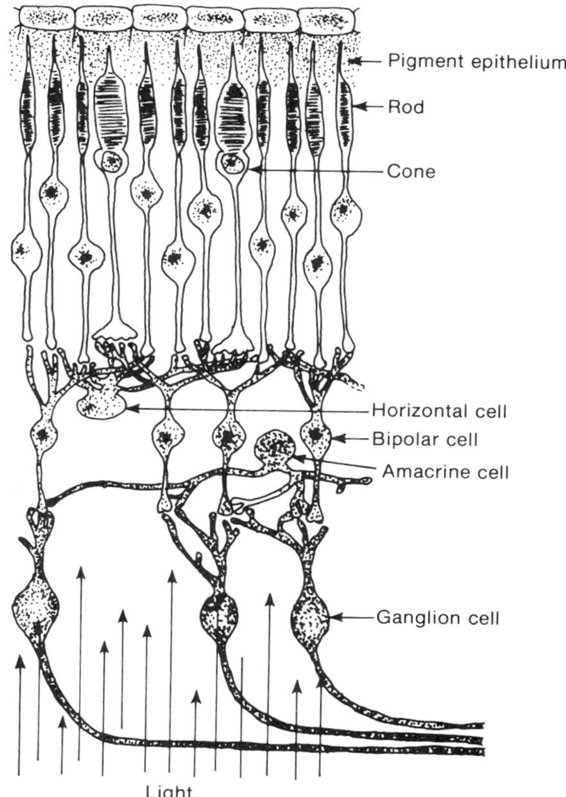

Figure 4–4. Schematic diagram of the human retina.

Two major theories of color vision have been proposed. The Young-Helmholz theory, or **trichromatic theory,** suggests that all colors can be made by mixing the three basic colors of red, green, and blue. As mentioned earlier, the cones are responsible for color vision. According to the trichromatic theory, there are three types of cones, with each being particularly sensitive to one of the basic colors. Seeing the color purple, for ex-

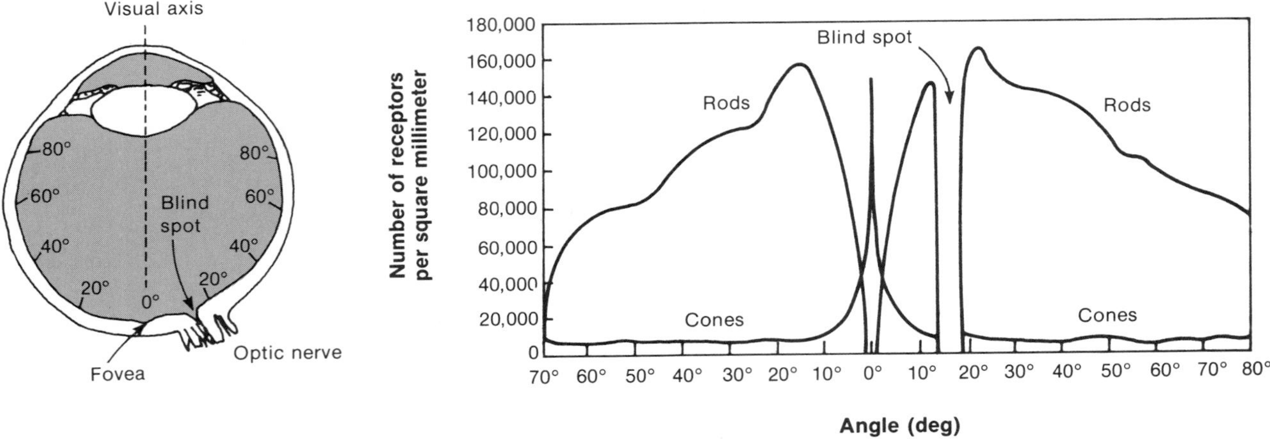

Figure 4–5. The distribution of rods and cones in the human retina. The graph gives the concentrations on the retina based on the angle of refraction shown in the diagram of the eye (from Lindsay & Norman, 1977).

ample, would result from strong responses of the red-sensitive and blue-sensitive cones and a weak response of the green-sensitive cones.

In the late nineteenth century the German physiologist Ewald Hering (1878) made several observations that created doubts about the trichromatic theory of Young and Helmholz. He noticed that when people were asked to identify pure colors, they typically selected red, green, blue, and yellow. This suggested to Hering that there might be four primary colors rather than three. He also noticed that certain color combinations were never reported by people. For instance, everyone can recognize yellowish-green, but we do not see yellowish-blue or greenish-red. This led Hering to suggest that the four primary colors were arranged in opposing pairs. He suggested that there are three types of receptor cells: red-green, yellow-blue, and black-white. The first two types of cells would be associated with our perception of colors, while black-white receptor cells would account for brightness perception.

This theory, called **opponent-process theory,** suggests that activity in a cell is either increased or decreased depending on the wavelength of light that strikes it. For instance, if we were exposed to light waves associated with the color blue, activity would increase in the yellow-blue receptor cells. Light waves associated with yellow would inhibit activity in these same cells. In other words, processes associated with yellow would oppose or cancel the processes associated with blue. This theory would account for why we cannot see combinations of yellow and blue or of red and green.

Both the trichromatic theory and the opponent-process theory have been supported by empirical evidence. It now appears that both theories are correct but that they apply to different stages of processing information regarding color. Evidence supports the notion that there are three kinds of cones, which is consistent with the trichromatic theory. So, this theory explains the first stage of perceiving color when light waves strike the retina. After the cones convert the physical energy into neural energy and these impulses leave the eye through the optic nerve, the opponent-process theory fits best with empirical observations. So, the opponent-process theory describes how information regarding color is coded in the higher visual pathways, which we will discuss next. It is worth noting that color-television cameras use a very similar system to convert physical energy into electrical energy (Coren, Porac,

& Ward, 1979). The camera first analyzes color in the original scene into its red, green, and blue components. It then transforms the color into two opponent-process signals plus an intensity signal. The television set reconverts these signals into the red, green, and blue signals. This technique was selected by engineers because it could provide good fidelity with economy. Perhaps these same considerations of fidelity with economy underlie the development of our visual system.

Higher Visual Pathways. The visual pathways begin a short distance away from the fovea, where the ganglion cells gather together to form the optic nerve (see Figure 4–1). Because there are no photoreceptor cells at this area, it is called the blind spot.

The optic nerve transports impulses from the retina to certain visual areas in the brain. The two most important areas are the lateral geniculate body and the visual cortex. These tissues are responsible for processing and analyzing the visual impulses that result in our perceptions.

As can be seen from Figure 4–6, some portion of the optic nerves from the right and left eye cross before they reach the brain. The crossover spot, called the **optic chiasma,** allows certain stimuli received by the left eye to reach the right side of the brain and certain stimuli from the right eye to reach the left side of the brain. In lower animals, all nerves cross over; that is, all stimuli received by the left eye proceed to the right half of the brain and vice versa. But in mammalian species, including humans, some of the fibers do not cross over. This may facilitate depth perception for those animals whose survival is dependent on it. As we shall see later in the chapter, each eye has a slightly different view of the world. The partial crossover of optic fibers may enable us to integrate these two views more effectively.

Within the visual cortex, there is a fairly direct point-for-point mapping of the external visual world. That is, each point in the environment corresponds to electrical activity at a specific point in the visual cortex. The point-for-point representation is not exact, however. If you look at a tree, there will not be a pattern of electrical activity in the visual cortex in the shape of a tree. Much of this information was obtained by studying war casualties who had wounds that destroyed a specific part of the cortex. These patients were blind in a part of their visual field. It is interesting to note that if the damage is small, and not too close to the region of the cortex that corresponds to the fovea, the patient may not be aware of the blindness prior to testing.

Certain cells in the brain appear to be especially sensitive to specific forms of visual stimulation (Hubel, 1963; Hubel & Wiesel, 1962). For instance, some cells are activated when the indi-

Figure 4–6. The optic chiasma.

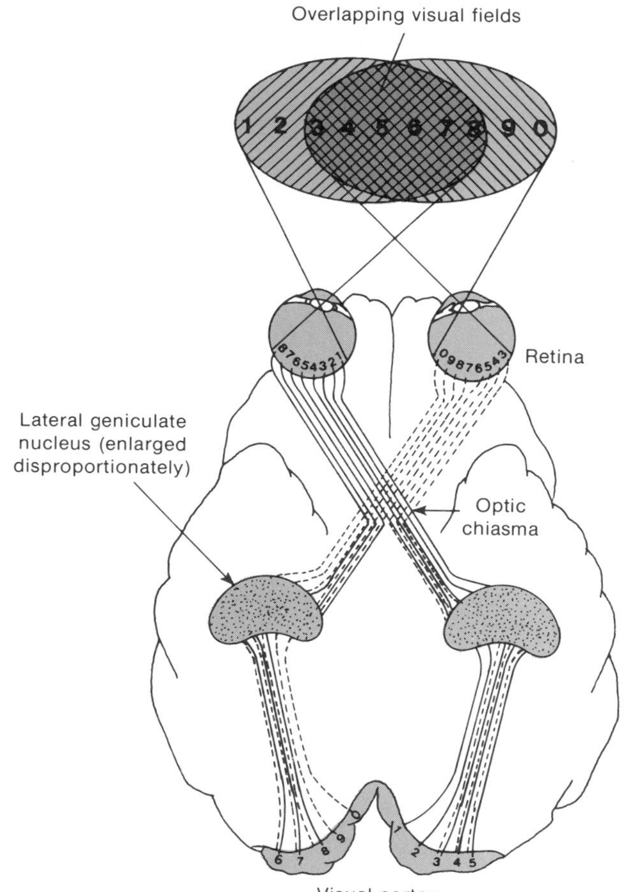

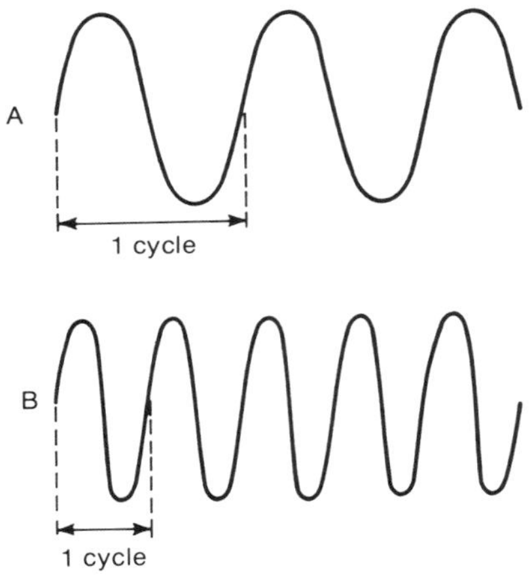

Figure 4–7a. The frequency (measured in Hertz, or cycles per second) of sound wave B is twice that of sound wave A. Wave B has a pitch one octave above that of wave A. The amplitudes, or wave heights, of A and B are equal.

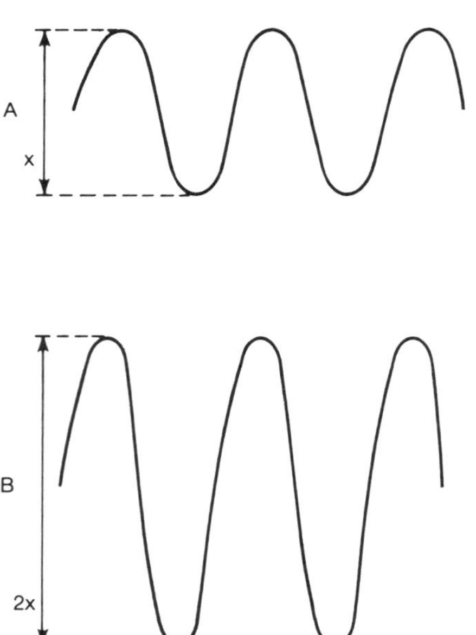

Figure 4–7b. The amplitude of sound wave B is twice that of sound wave A. Wave B is twice as loud as wave A. The frequency, and thus the pitch, of A and B is the same.

vidual views a horizontal line, while other cells are activated when he or she views a vertical line. Even more complex cells exist that are activated by more complex forms and a specific direction of movement of visual stimuli.

The existence of these orientation-specific or feature-specific cells, as they are called, suggests that our visual experiences are broken down into specific components and then resynthesized at some later point. At this time it is not known how this process operates. The process does appear similar, however, to machines that read numbers on checks or price codes on grocery-store items. It is readily apparent from this brief overview that the processing and analysis of visual stimuli are extremely complex.

Hearing

Along with vision, hearing provides a crucial vehicle for interacting with other people and the world. Our sense of hearing helps us form close relationships, acquire information, and enjoy our environment. Even minor impairments in hearing can lead to significant problems. For example, it has been found that for elementary-school children living in apartment buildings in Manhattan, reading scores on standardized tests are related to the floor on which they live; the higher the floor the higher the reading score (Glass, Cohen, & Singer, 1973). Street noises produce a higher noise level on the lower floors, which apparently interferes with the children's ability to discriminate between similar sounds, such as "cope" and "coke." This impairment was thought to be responsible for their difficulties in learning to read.

The physical stimulus for hearing is sound. Sound essentially consists of changes in the air pressure that surrounds us. The vibration of air molecules by a sounding object produces waves of compression and expansion. As in the case of light waves, the frequency of sound waves, or the distance from one peak to the next, is an important characteristic. Frequency is related to our perception of pitch (see Figure 4–7a). Although it is not a one-to-one relationship, in general the greater the frequency of sound waves, the higher we perceive the pitch to be. The human ear is capable of detecting sounds that range from about 20 Hz (Hertz, cycles per second) to about 20,000 Hz. Certain animals, such as bats and dogs, can detect sounds at much higher frequencies. Whistles are now manufactured that dogs can hear but humans cannot.

A second important characteristic of sound waves is their amplitude, or the height of the wave from crest to dip (see Figure 4–7b). The amplitude of sound waves plays a major role in our perceptions of loudness. The loudness of a sound is measured in units called decibels. The human ear is responsive to a tremendous range of decibels. The loudest sound we can listen to without discomfort has an amplitude of about 1 million times that of the weakest sound we can perceive. Table 4–1 provides a gauge of a variety of sounds. Prolonged exposure to sounds around 100 decibels can lead to hearing impairment.

Table 4–1. Representative sounds and their decibel level

Decibels	*Sound*
150	Jet airplane
130	Pain threshold
125	Loud music
120	Loud thunder
100	Subway train
70	Automobile
60	Ordinary conversation
40	Business office
25	Whisper
0	Threshold of hearing

Source: Adapted from Kagan and Havemann

Structure of the Ear. The human ear can be divided into three parts—the outer, middle, and inner ear. The outer ear, the fleshy part that we typically call the ear, consists of the pinna, the auditory canal, and the eardrum (see Figure 4–8). The function of the **pinna** is to collect and channel the sound waves into the auditory canal. The **auditory canal** is shaped so as to concentrate the sound waves and increase their force against the **eardrum.**

The middle ear consists of the three small bones called the **malleus** (hammer), **incus** (anvil), and **stapes** (stirrup). The sound waves cause the eardrum to vibrate, which in turn produces vibrations in the three small bones. The shape and relative sizes of the parts of the middle ear produce further amplification of the sound waves. Up to this point, the processing of sound waves is entirely mechanical.

The primary structure in the inner ear is a snail-shaped tube called the **cochlea,** which is filled with fluid. Within the cochlea is the basilar membrane, which contains millions of tiny hair cells. The vibrations from the bones of the middle ear set the fluid in the cochlea in motion, which, in turn, pushes and pulls the hair cells. The stimulation of these hair cells is believed to be the mechanism by which mechanical energy is transformed into neural activity. The neural activity is then sent to the brain through the auditory nerve.

Auditory Pathways. The auditory pathways are somewhat more complex and indirect than the visual pathways, but there are many similarities. For instance, it has been found that certain cells in the auditory system are maximally sensitive to certain frequencies of sound. Other cells are particularly sensitive to sounds of certain intensities. That is, just as there are cells in the visual cortex that are particularly responsive to, say, vertical lines, there are cells in the auditory cortex that are especially sensitive to certain sound characteristics. As you might expect, the process by which sound waves are coded into neural messages is incredibly complex. But it is this process that allows us to recognize an almost infinite variation in pitch and loudness of sounds.

The auditory pathways are also similar to the visual in that each ear sends information to both halves of the brain. Thus damage to one half of the brain through a stroke or injury will not pro-

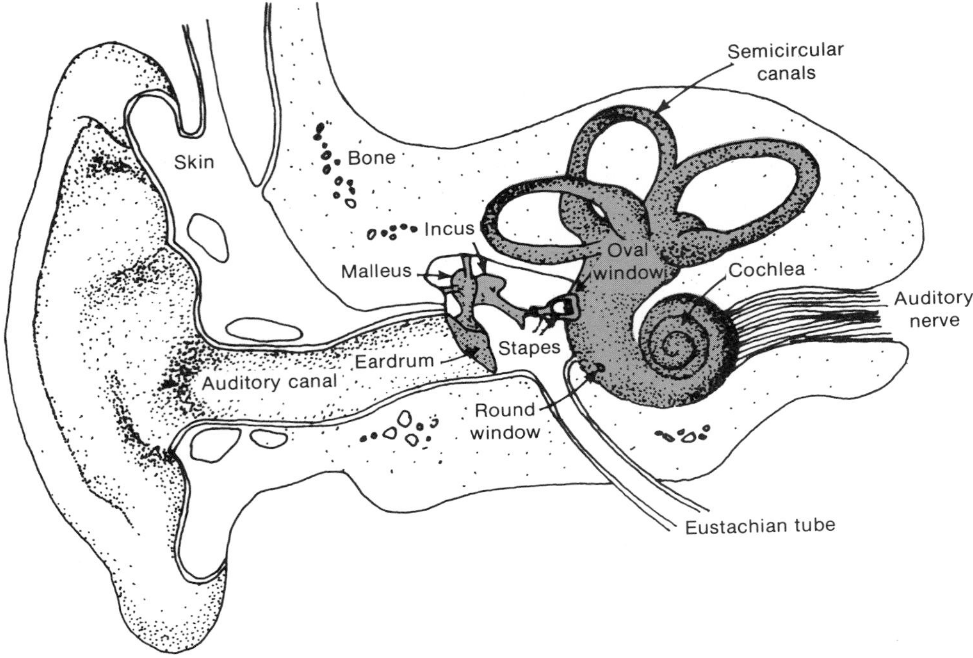

Figure 4–8. The human ear.

duce deafness in either ear. The primary destination of sound messages is the auditory areas of the cerebral cortex, but messages are also sent to brain centers that coordinate movements of the eyes, head, and ears.

There are two basic ways in which one's hearing can be impaired. In the first, called **conduction deafness,** sound waves are unable to activate the mechanism of the inner ear. Causes can include a buildup of wax in the auditory canal, a loss of flexibility of the eardrum, and diseases that affect the middle ear. Some forms of hearing impairment caused by conduction problems may be overcome by the use of a hearing aid. **Nerve deafness,** the second basic type of impairment, involves damage to the cochlea mechanism or to the auditory nerve. The most common cause of this type of impairment is prolonged exposure to loud noises. For several years rock musicians such as Alice Cooper have been aware of the risks to their hearing that their profession entails.

Taste

Taste is considered to be a chemical sense. This is because the receptors, or **taste buds,** are stimulated by chemicals in the food we eat. The taste buds are primarily located in the crevices between the small bumps on the tongue (see Figure 4–9). Each taste bud consists of a number of hair cells that are sensitive to chemical substances that can be dissolved in the saliva. The nerves that carry information about taste to the brain also transmit information about textures and temperatures that the tongue can feel.

The average adult has about 10,000 taste buds. These taste buds are continually being replaced, since their life span is only a few days. As we get older, the total number of taste buds decreases, so children have even more taste buds than adults. Since children seem to be especially sensitive to taste, they generally prefer bland foods. And since elderly people become more and more insensitive

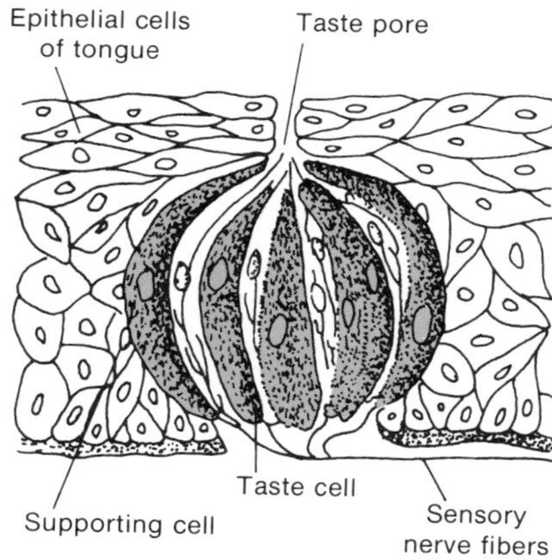

Figure 4–9. Taste buds are located on the top and sides of the tongue, at the back of the mouth and the insides of the cheeks, and in the throat. They are especially dense on the bumps, or papillae, of the tongue. Material enters taste pores and activates nerve fibers in the taste cells.

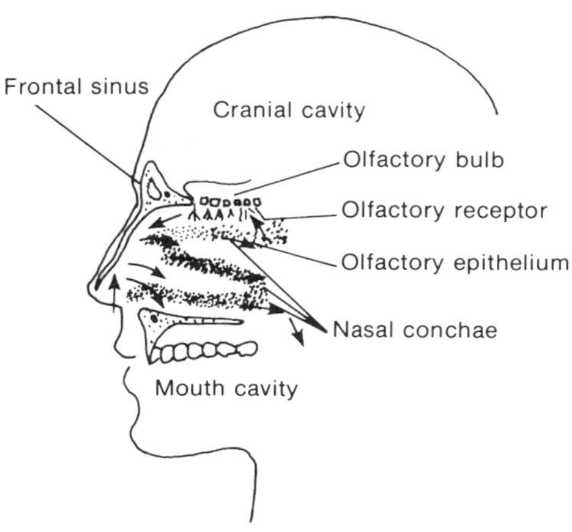

Figure 4–10. A cross section of the nose. Air currents inhaled through the nostrils are carried to the upper part of the nasal cavity, where they stimulate the olfactory, or smell, receptors.

to taste, they tend to lose interest in food altogether.

It has been accepted for some time that there are four basic taste sensations—sweet, sour, salty, and bitter. All tastes essentially possess these qualities alone or in combination. It has also been established that different areas of the tongue are especially sensitive to specific tastes. The tip of the tongue is especially sensitive to sweetness. There are a few taste receptors located in other areas of the mouth, but these seem to play a minor role in the sensations of taste.

One interesting finding has been that the various taste qualities interact or blend with one another in different ways (Bekesy, 1964). For instance, two different taste sensations applied to different sides of the tongue may combine to produce a taste sensation in the middle of the tongue. Sweet substances generally interact or blend with bitter substances, as do salty and sour sensations. Neither bitterness nor sweetness, however, interacts with saltiness or sourness. The proficient chef is undoubtedly aware of these qualities.

Much about our sense of taste remains a mystery. At one time it was thought that four types of taste receptors corresponded to the four taste sensations. It now appears that every receptor cell responds to the four basic taste stimuli with varying patterns of neural activity (Kimura & Beidler, 1961). The precise mechanism by which taste stimuli activate the taste receptors, however, remains unclear.

Smell

While the sense of smell is extremely important to many animals, for humans it is almost a bonus. Smell enhances the taste of food, and it helps us in detecting whether certain foods are spoiled, but we do not rely on it, as do animals, to find food, detect enemies, or to determine which females are sexually receptive. Smell does enrich our sensual experiences. The fragrance of a flower, perfume, or a gourmet meal are certainly pleasant sensations.

Like the sense of taste, smell is a chemical sense. A membrane, called the **olfactory epithelium,** contains the receptor cells for our sense of smell (see Figure 4–10). The receptor cells are stimulated directly by the molecules that make up the odorous substance, although how this is done is unclear. One theory is that there are seven basic classes of odorous molecules, which vary in size, shape, and electrical charge. These seven odors are etherlike, camphorlike, musky, flowery, minty, pungent, and putrid. According to this theory, each type of molecule fits a particular receptor in the olfactory epithelium in much the same way a key fits into a lock (Amoore, Johnson, & Rubin, 1964). Other researchers have argued that other characteristics of the molecules, such as vibration frequency, are the crucial characteristics (Wright & Burgess, 1975).

The Skin Senses

The skin senses, also known as the **cutaneous senses,** are made up of four basic sensations; pressure, warmth, cold, and pain. All our tactile sensations result from these elements or combinations of them. Some areas of the human body are more sensitive to these sensations than others. For example, the hands, feet, and face are much more sensitive than the back and the upper arms.

The skin senses fooled researchers for many years. Since there are four basic sensations and a variety of sensory receptors in the skin, it was assumed that each type of receptor was associated with one of the skin sensations. Evidence for specific types of receptors, however, could not be discovered. Currently researchers suspect that some types of receptors are more sensitive to certain forms of stimulation than others. For instance, the nerve-end structures that end directly at the epidermis (the outer layer of the skin) are especially sensitive to pain, but they are also responsive to warmth and cold. Similarly, the nerve endings that end at the base of hair follicles are associated with the sensation of pressure, but some of our most sensitive areas of the body—such as the lips—have no such nerve endings. It appears, therefore, that the total pattern of activity in the receptors carries information to the brain about the nature of the stimulus.

Researchers who mapped the skin for receptors made an interesting discovery (Zotterman, 1959). When the skin is touched by a small rod heated to about 110° Fahrenheit (45°C) or more, the subject will report it as feeling cold. Temperatures between about 80° and 110°F (25° and 45°C) are perceived as being warm. This phenomenon is referred to as **paradoxical cold** and may explain how we can distinguish between objects that are hot and those that are merely warm. When one set of temperature receptors sends messages to the brain, they are perceived as cold. When the other set of receptors is activated, the brain registers "warm." When both sets of receptors are activated, however, the stimulus is perceived as being hot.

Pain is a sense that we often would be happy to do without, but it serves the very important function of warning us of danger to our body. Congenital analgesics, persons who are born without a sense of pain, are known to receive severe burns and other injuries because their bodies cannot warn them.

Pain is different from the other senses in that receptors exist not just in the skin but throughout our muscles and internal organs. A bad case of gas in the alimentary canal can cause extremely painful distention of the intestines. Yet the intestines, for example, do not respond to pain in the same way that the skin does. Intestines can be burned or cut without any resulting pain. Because so many people suffer from chronic pain, researchers are expending much effort to arrive at an understanding of this sensation.

The Body Senses: Kinesthesis and Equilibrium

Up to this point all the senses we have discussed have been responsible for gathering and processing information about the outside world. Two important senses, kinesthesis and the sense of equilibrium, provide us information about our body. Without them it would be extremely difficult even to walk down a flight of stairs or scratch our back.

Kinesthesis is the sensory system that informs us about the position and movement of our body parts. It allows us, for example, to describe accurately the position of our legs, toes, and arms

CRITICAL ISSUE:

Extrasensory Perception

It has only been in the past decade or so that extrasensory perception, or ESP, has achieved any degree of scientific respectability. While most scientists remain highly skeptical, there are many scientists conducting research in an attempt to prove the existence of ESP, and articles dealing with the topic have appeared in prestigious journals such as the British scientific journal *Nature.*

Four basic types of ESP have been examined:

1. *Mental telepathy,* also known as mind reading, is the ability of one person to transmit messages to a second person without use of the usual sensory channels.
2. *Clairvoyance* is the ability to see things hidden from sight, such as a message in a sealed envelope.
3. *Precognition* is the ability to foresee events.
4. *Psychokinesis* is the ability to control objects without touching, such as controlling the outcome of a throw of dice.

Scientists who take ESP seriously believe that these powers may result from the use of undiscovered forms of energy and sensory receptors. For example, mental telepathy may involve the transmission of brain waves from one person to another. While this may be possible, no one has been able to demonstrate that brain waves pass through space, nor has anyone discovered potential receptors for such forms of energy. For other forms of ESP, such as clairvoyance, it is difficult to imagine what forms of energy could possibly be involved.

Despite these conceptual limitations, thousands of studies have been conducted, and a sizable number purportedly demonstrate the reality of ESP. Unfortunately for those who want to believe in ESP, most of these experiments cannot be replicated. In fact, many of the successful experiments involve subjects and experimenters who are committed to the notion of ESP. When more skeptical experimenters conduct this type of research, the results are generally unfavorable.

Another problem is that many supposed demonstrations of ESP have been exposed as outright trickery. Many well-known psychics are accomplished magicians. While their performances may impress scientists, they are often transparent to other magicians. Because of this it has been suggested that research teams investigating ESP should be comprised of both magicians and scientists.

So can we say that ESP does not exist? The answer is no. The scientific evidence is certainly not sufficient to convince skeptics that it does exist, but neither does it rule out the possibility that it does. Perhaps our trying to understand ESP within the context of our current science and technology is analagous to the medieval sorcerers trying to understand atomic power. After all, as recently as 1940 many reputable scientists believed that the idea of an atomic bomb was pure science fiction.

without looking at them. The kinesthetic receptors are located in the muscles, tendons, and joints. Without the information they provide, the simplest movements such as walking, would be difficult, and more complex movements, such as dribbling a basketball, would be next to impossible.

The **sense of equilibrium** also known as the vestibular sense helps us to maintain our balance and gives us information about our head position. It is this sense that tells us whether we are going up or down in an elevator when we have no visual cues to rely on. It is also the sense that causes us to feel dizzy if we spin around rapidly.

The receptors for this sense are located in the inner ear. Two different structures, the semicircular canals and the vestibular sacs, contain a fluid that shifts with movements of the head. The fluid stimulates receptors that send information about the position of the head with respect to gravity. Because gravity is important to the vestibular sense, there was concern about the potential effects of weightlessness on astronauts. It seems that the human body can adapt to such conditions, but many astronauts reported that it was more difficult to adapt to earth's gravity once they returned home than to adapt to the weightlessness of space (Kopaner, 1972).

Sensory Mechanisms

We have seen the variety of receptor cells, but these cells have several characteristics in common. All of them are stimulated by some form of external or internal energy (e.g., light waves, sound waves, movement of fluid in the inner ear). All receptor cells are able to change the energy they receive into electrochemical neural impulses. This process is known as **transduction.** The neural impulse is then coded and sent along sensory pathways to the brain. Along its way to the brain the neural impulse may be coded further so the brain receives a partially analyzed message. The final analysis of the neural energy occurs in the brain and provides the basis of our perceptions.

Another characteristic that our senses have in common is that of adaptation. The senses are particularly sensitive to changes in stimulation, but once they are exposed to a constant level of stimulation, they get used to it and become less sensitive to it. In other words, they adapt. For example, if you walked into a chemical plant, you might be repelled by the strong odors that the workers are unaware of. If you were to get a job in an office where several typewriters were clacking, you may feel that you will never be able to concentrate. After a few hours you probably will not even hear the background noise.

PSYCHOPHYSICS

At this point you might be wondering if this chapter has not been mistakenly taken from a textbook in physiology. It may be hard to see what connection this material has with human behavior. As you will recall from Chapter 1, however, the scientists who were responsible for establishing psychology as a scientific discipline were very interested in the problem of sensation. At that time they questioned whether it was possible to relate the physical energy that generated sensations to the subjective experience of sensations in a meaningful and consistent way. The work done by these early researchers provided one of the first bridges between events in the external world and processes within the human psyche.

The study of the relationship between physical stimuli and subjective experience is called **psychophysics.** This field of research is concerned with questions in three general areas: stimulus detection, stimulus discrimination, and stimulus scaling. Let us briefly review some of the work in these three areas.

Detection of Stimuli

How much of a physical stimulus is necessary before an individual can detect the presence of that stimulus? This minimum level is referred to as the **absolute threshold.** To illustrate, suppose you were to find the absolute threshold of a tone of a particular frequency. What you might do is ask subjects to wear earphones through which the tone can be presented and which blocks out background noises. Then you would present the tones at various intensities and ask the subjects to indicate whether or not the tone was present. If you were to plot the data, you would obtain a graph that looked something like Figure 4–11. At extremely low levels of volume, the subjects would almost always report that no sound was present. At higher levels of volume, they would almost always hear a sound. The point at which subjects hear a sound 50 percent of the time would be the absolute threshold for that stimulus.

The S-shaped curve shown in Figure 4–11 is typical of results obtained in experiments in absolute thresholds of all sensory systems. Detecting the presence of a stimulus increases gradually as the intensity increases.

The human sensory systems are remarkably sensitive. For instance, on a clear, dark night an adult with normal vision can detect a candle flame nearly 30 miles away. The ticking of a wristwatch can be heard from 20 feet in a quiet room. And a drop of perfume diffused throughout an average three-room apartment can be detected (Galanter, 1962).

Experiments in finding the absolute threshold have several drawbacks. Suppose a subject who was asked to detect a tone wanted to show the experimenter that he or she had particularly acute hearing. Or suppose a second subject was very concerned about making the mistake of saying the tone was present when, in fact, it was not. As you might guess, the curves describing these two subjects' auditory thresholds would be considerably different. In other words, subjects use a variety of decision-making strategies in deciding whether or

APPLICATION:

Messages that Manipulate

Psychologists have known for a number of years that people can detect stimuli of which they are not consciously aware. For example, if an experimenter flashes a very faint photograph on a screen, subjects can guess what was shown, even though they insist that they did not see anything. These stimuli, which are strong enough to excite sensory receptors but not strong enough to be perceived, are referred to as subliminal, since they are below the threshold of conscious awareness.

In the mid-1950s James Vicary, a public-relations executive, claimed to have discovered a new advertising technique: subliminal advertising. Vicary claimed that he had used a special projector to flash very faint and very rapid messages to buy popcorn and soft drinks at a movie theater. Although the viewers were unaware of the messages, popcorn sales were said to have increased by 50 percent. Advertising executives were very excited about the possibilities of the technique, but it soon fell out of favor. Studies showed that it was not very effective after all, and many people were frightened and indignant about the possibility of having their behavior controlled without their awareness.

Subliminal messages may be making a comeback, however. Recently *Time* magazine (1979) reported that an inventor named Hal C. Becker devised a black box that blends subliminal messages with background music. One East Coast chain of department stores claims to have reduced shoplifting by 37 percent by repeating the message "I am honest. I will not steal" 9,000 times an hour at a very low volume. Other applications are said to include real-estate offices that motivate their sales agents with the message "I love real estate. I will prospect for new listings for clients each and every day," and professional sports teams that want to increase the motivation of their players. Becker's ideas for other potential applications approach the grandiose. For example, he believes that by placing subliminal messages on television about the hazards of overeating, the problem of obesity could be eliminated in one generation.

Becker's claims are bound to rekindle the controversy surrounding subliminal advertising. Psychologists may conduct a new series of studies, politicians and advertisers may attempt to use the technique once again, and Vance Packard may publish a revised edition of *The Hidden Persuaders,* which exposed subliminal advertising the first time around. But if the results of research conducted in the 1950s are to be trusted, which showed that such methods are not effective, the controversy will fade rather quickly. In 1959, when psychologist Israel Goldiamond was asked to comment on the potential of subliminal advertising, he replied:

> Rather than protesting against the alleged invasion of privacy of our homes by the subliminal advertisers, those of us who are concerned with obnoxious advertising on TV might welcome this occurrence. It would be welcome because it can render obnoxious advertising *less* effective. If the advertiser wishes to reduce the force of his message and to reduce its effectiveness, I can think of few better ways for him to do so than by blanket use of this procedure (Goldiamond, 1966, p. 277).

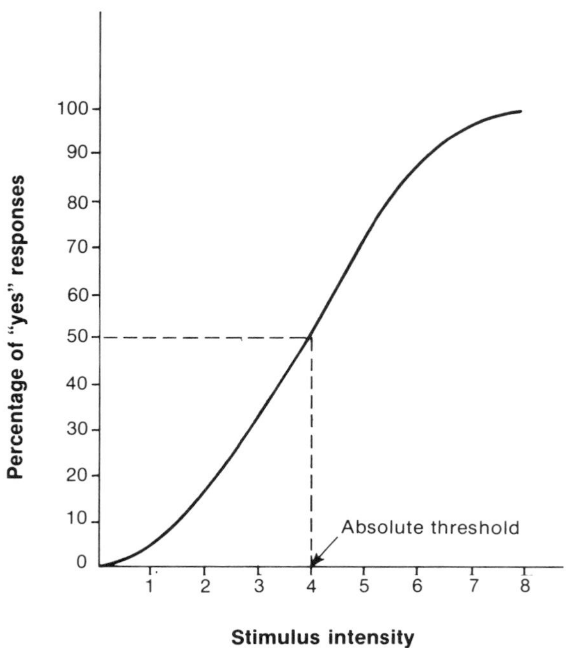

Figure 4–11.

not to indicate that they heard the tone. The study of the factors that influence an individual's decision-making strategy is known as **signal-detection theory.** Signal-detection theory recognizes that factors other than the presence or absence of a stimulus will influence an individual's response. Motivation and the consequences of making an incorrect response are also important factors.

The importance of signal-detection theory can be illustrated with the following examples. Imagine a radiologist examining a set of X-rays for a spot that might indicate cancer. If he or she decides that signs of cancer exist, when in fact they do not, the costs are not that great. It will only require that the patient take some additional tests. If, however, the radiologist fails to detect an existing spot that signals the presence of cancer, the costs could be enormous. It might mean the death of the patient. On the other hand, an observer looking at a radar screen for enemy missiles may have quite a different decision-making rationale. Reporting a blip indicating an enemy missile when it does not exist could lead to a war, whereas not detecting a blip that does exist might mean only the loss of a few seconds until the signal becomes stronger. Because important decisions involving the detection of sensory stimuli have to be made every day, researchers are attempting to learn everything they can about signal-detection theory.

Discrimination of Stimuli

Psychophysicists are also interested in the smallest difference in similar stimuli that can be detected. For example, how much lower does tone A have to be, compared with tone B, before they are perceived as being different? Or suppose you are in a darkened room lighted by a single candle. The addition of a second candle would be easily noticeable. The room would appear to be considerably lighter. If the same room, however, were lighted by 1,000 candles, the lighting of one additional candle would be imperceptible. Although the amount of physical energy added is the same in both cases, the difference can be discriminated in the first case but not in the second case.

The smallest difference that can be discriminated between two stimuli is referred to as the **just noticeable difference (JND).** In research attempting to establish JNDs for various stimuli, it was found that the ratio of the amount of energy added to the amount of energy already present in order to result in a JND was a constant. For example, if you were to hear a 50-decibel sound, it would require 5 more decibels before you noticed a difference in loudness. But if you were to hear a 100-decibel noise, it would require 10 decibels more to notice a difference. The ratio in both cases is constant: 1/10 ($\frac{5}{50} = \frac{10}{100} = 1/10$). This has come to be known as **Weber's Law** and can be summarized in the following formula:

$$\text{K (constant)} = \frac{\text{I (energy added)}}{\text{I (energy present)}}$$

Except for extreme stimulus intensities, Weber's Law describes the research data surprisingly well.

Stimulus Scaling

The third general issue psychophysicists are interested in is whether sensory experiences can be measured and plotted as a mathematical function of levels of physical energy. The nineteenth-century researchers quickly found that this was indeed possible, but for a number of years there was some controversy about the best method for scaling stimuli.

The method that is most widely accepted today is called **magnitude estimation.** To illustrate its use, imagine you are participating in an experiment in which the task is to judge the loudness, or intensity, of tones. The experimenter would present you with a standard tone and assign it an arbitrary numerical value—say, 20. Then, you would be presented with test tones and asked to assign numerical values to them based on their relation to the standard. If you perceived the test tone to be half as loud as the standard, you would assign it the number 10. If it were three times as loud as the standard, you would assign it the number 60, and so on.

The psychologist who popularized this technique, S. S. Stevens (1956), found that the perceived intensity of a particular stimulus is a function of the physical intensity of the stimulus raised to some power or exponent. The formula for the relationship, called **Stevens's Power Law,** is:

$$S = aI^n$$

where S is the perceived stimulus intensity and I is the physical intensity of the stimulus. The a is a constant and n is the exponent. Both of these must be determined for each particular stimulus. Because the power exponents for some stimuli are less than one and for others they are greater than one, the relation between stimulus intensity and perceived stimulus intensity can vary considerably. In Figure 4–12, this relation is illustrated for electric shock, apparent length of lines, and loudness of a noise. As you can see for electric shock, with an exponent of 3.5, at the higher intensity levels it takes only a very slight increase in the physical intensity of shock for subjects to perceive a very large change. At the higher intensity for loudness, with an exponent of 0.6, a very large increase in the physical stimulus will be perceived as only a small change. Because apparent length has an exponent of 1, there is a close correspondence between the physical stimulus (the length of a line) and the sensory experience (the perceived length of the line).

One interesting sidelight to Stevens's Power Law is that it can be used to describe social judgments. For example, seriousness of theft has an exponent of 0.2. This means that a thief must steal about $160 before the crime is considered to be twice as serious as the theft of $5 (Stevens, 1972). It is surprising to note that the methods of psychophysics may extend from the study of sensory experience to sociology.

PERCEPTION

The processes through which we organize and interpret information received by our senses are involved in perception. For most of us the study of

Figure 4–12.

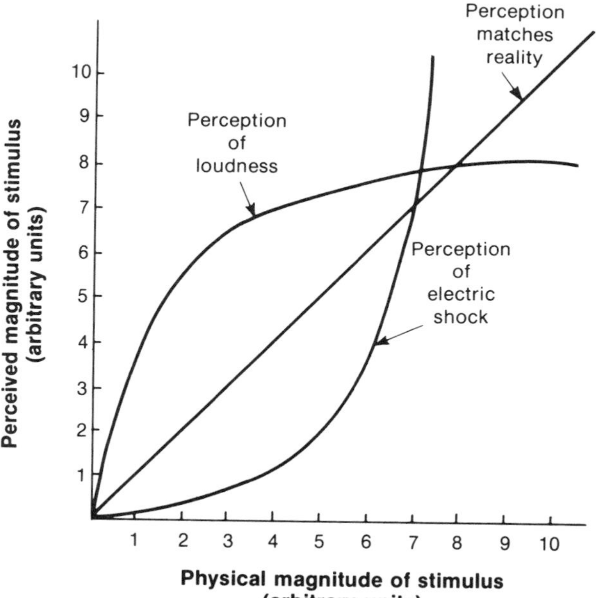

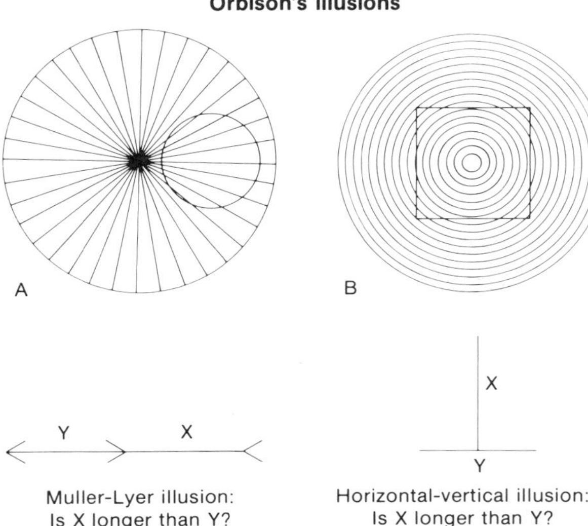

X
Y X
Y

Muller-Lyer illusion:
Is X longer than Y?

Horizontal-vertical illusion:
Is X longer than Y?

Figure 4–13. Top, the enclosed circle in A and the enclosed square in B seem to be distorted. But if you check your perceptions with a compass and a ruler you will find that the measurements (also perceptions) disagree with your first perceptions. Illusions are examples of perceptual organization at work: they are not tricks (After Orbison, 1939). Bottom, X appears larger than Y, but measurement will show that they are equal.

perception involves the study of phenomena that we take for granted. For instance, if you look out your window you might see a bush a few feet away and a tree farther down the street. You know immediately that the bush is closer to you than the tree, and you know that the tree is larger than the bush. The "obvious" perceptions do not correspond to the sensory evidence. Because the bush is closer to you, it projects a larger image on your retina than does the tree, yet it is *perceived* as smaller. Also, the retina is capable of processing visual stimuli in only two dimensions—up and down, and left and right. But as you look out the window you *perceive* the third dimension of depth, which lets you know that the tree is farther away from you than the bush. So our ability to "know" the world depends on our perceptions.

Illusions are a common method of illustrating that there is not necessarily a direct correspondence between sensory evidence and perception. Figure 4–13 illustrates some examples for which our perceptions are not consistent with the information received by our senses. This inconsistency is fortunate. As we saw with the example of the tree and bush, if there were a direct relationship between our sensory experience and our perceptions, our world would be a very confusing place. Let us examine some of the factors that influence our perceptions—attention, organization into forms, perceptual constancies, perception of depth, and our experiences.

Attention

Think about the last time you went to a restaurant. As you were seated, you were probably aware of a variety of sensations: how the chair felt, the aroma of food, the conversation of the people in the restaurant, and so on. If you were fortunate enough to have an engrossing dinner companion, your awareness of these stimuli probably diminished rather quickly. You probably had little difficulty in listening to and understanding your companion. In fact, you probably could not recall anything of the conversation of the people next to you even if they were talking in loud voices. Your focus on your dinner companion illustrates the process of attention.

Because we are constantly being bombarded with sensory stimuli, the ability to "tune out" some stimuli while attending to others is crucial. The process by which we do this has undergone considerable research. In a well-known set of experiments, psychologist Colin Cherry (1953) asked subjects to wear earphones that were capable of sending different messages to the two ears. The subjects were asked to repeat aloud, or "shadow," one of the messages. This forced the subjects to pay attention to the shadowed message and allowed the experimenter to discover later how much information had been processed from the competing, or nonshadowed, message.

The results of experiments such as this have found that very little information from the nonshadowed message is processed if the two messages are similar—for example, if they are both prose. It is somewhat easier to detect information in the nonshadowed message if it differs from the message being attended to. For example, subjects are relatively successful at perceiving the sound of a bell or their own name in the nonshadowed message (Treisman, 1969). Attending to two different messages is considerably easier if they involve different sense organs. For instance, it is not difficult to listen to someone on the telephone and read a note at the same time. It is, however, almost impossible to listen to someone on the telephone and listen to someone in the same room simultaneously.

The mechanism that limits our ability to attend to numerous stimuli is not fully understood. One hypothesis has suggested that a filtering process occurs immediately after sensory registration at the receptors. Stimuli that are not being attended to do not even reach the higher cortical levels for processing. This hypothesis, however, is not consistent with our everyday experiences. If it were correct, it would be impossible for us to hear our name being called while engrossed in conversation with someone else.

A more reasonable hypothesis suggests that a filtering process occurs at the level of memory. The sensory stimuli are sent to the higher levels for processing, but they are not necessarily stored in our memory. This view has received support in shadowing experiments. If subjects are interrupted in the middle of a task, they can repeat more information from the nonshadowed message than they can if the experimenter waits several seconds after the messages have been completed. Regardless of the mechanism involved, our ability to filter out some stimuli while attending to others is a crucial part of perception.

Form Perception

Once again, look out your window. You undoubtedly see a variety of forms, such as trees, grass, and cars. The sensory input we receive is not perceived as patches of color, a series of lines, or a variety of unintelligible noises. Sensory input is *organized* into meaningful forms. Let's see how this is done.

Figure and Ground. Perhaps the most basic process in form perception is that of seeing a figure on a ground. As you read this page, you do not see a jumble of black and white but rather black figures *on* a white background. The background appears to be formless and appears to continue behind the figures.

Figure 4–14 illustrates a reversible figure-ground relation. When you first look at it, you probably perceive the darkened area to be the background and, hence, see a vase. If you try to see the white as background, you will see two profiles. Notice that it is very difficult to see the vase and the profiles simultaneously.

Some Principles of Organization. As we saw in Chapter 1, in the early 1900s a group of German psychologists were interested in how people organized their perceptions so as to perceive forms. Their work resulted in what is known as the Gestalt school of psychology. There is no English word equivalent to the word *Gestalt* but roughly it means "whole form."

The Gestaltists believed that several principles describe the way we organize elements within a pattern so that we perceive meaningful figures. In Figure 4–15a the Law of Proximity leads us to perceive the dots as comprising two figures rather than as 14 individual dots. The Law of Similarity

Figure 4–14. Sometimes a figure can become a ground and vice versa. This reversible figure-ground may be perceived as either a vase or two profiles.

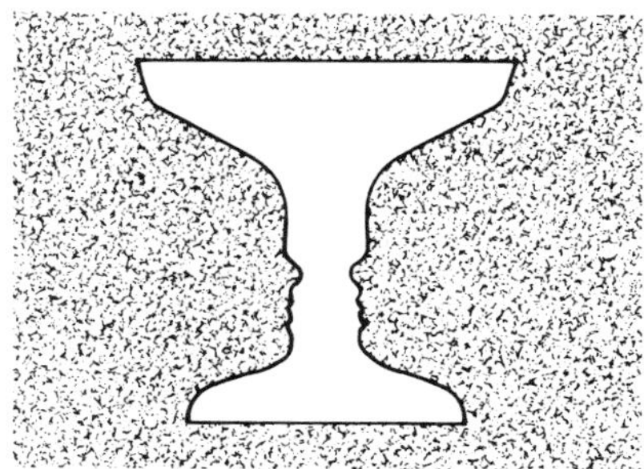

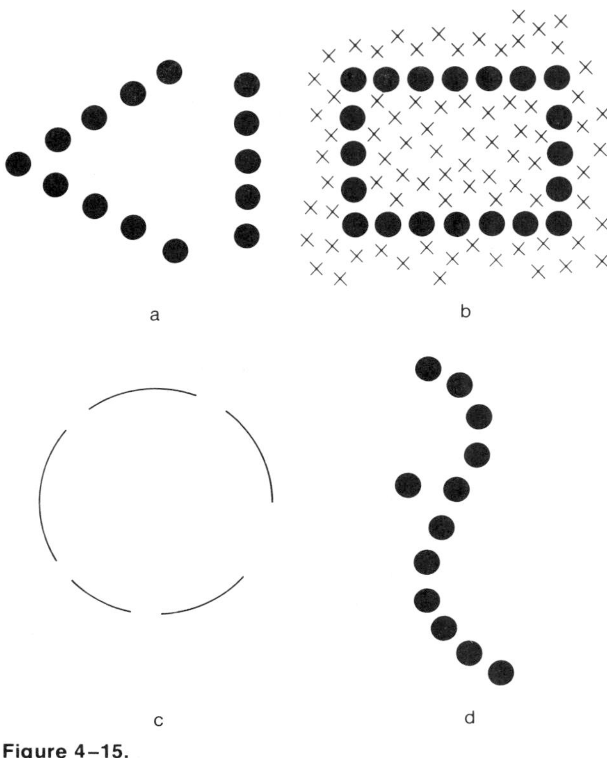

Figure 4–15.

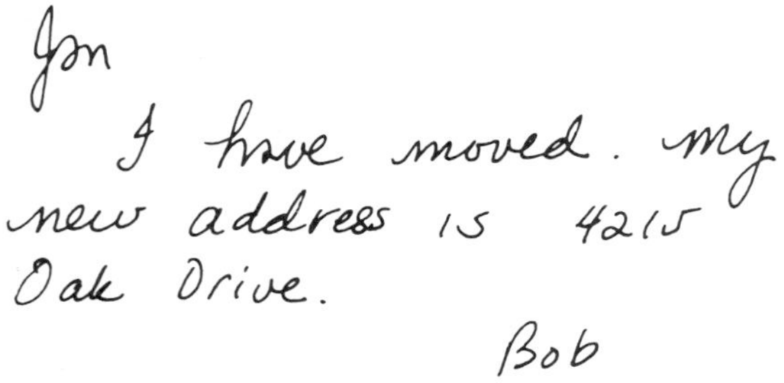

Jim
I have moved. My
new address is 4215
Oak Drive.
Bob

Figure 4–16.

leads us to see Figure 4–15b as a square made up of black dots against a background of Xs because we tend to group similar objects together. In Figure 4–15c the Law of Closure is illustrated; it causes us to see the figure as a circle rather than as a number of curved lines. Figure 4–15d illustrates the Law of Continuity. We tend to see the dots as forming a curved line with one extra dot along the side. These examples illustrate our tendency to perceive order rather than a series of unrelated dots and lines.

The Role of Context. Before reading any further, look at the message in Figure 4–16. You probably had no difficulty in reading it, but if you look closer you will notice the word "is" is nearly identical to the 15 in the address. Yet you probably saw the figures as being letters in the first instance and as being numbers in the second instance without giving it a thought. The context in which we view an object will influence our perception of it.

The influence of context can be seen in many types of everyday behavior. If one of two people who do not like each other makes a sarcastic remark, it will probably be perceived as hostile. The same remark occurring between two people who are good friends may be perceived as affectionate. The importance of context can be observed readily by those who do not want their actions or remarks to be taken out of it. For example, in the last Presidential campaign, President Reagan was accused of opposing Medicare because he wanted a piece of Medicare legislation voted down. Reagan claimed he was quoted out of context and that he actually favored a more generous bill.

Perceptual Constancies

We perceive the world to be consistent and stable even though the stimuli that reach our sense receptors are varied and inconsistent. As an illustration, look out your window again and hold a pencil about 18 inches in front of your eyes. If you line up your pencil with a tree in the distance so that the bottom of the pencil and the bottom of the tree are even, the top of the pencil will extend beyond the top of the tree. And yet you perceive the tree to be considerably larger than the pencil. The factors that describe this type of perceptual organization are called the **perceptual constancies.**

Size Constancy. The example of the tree and the pencil illustrates the constancy of size. The information received by our sense receptors is not consistent with our perceptions since the image of the pencil on our retina is larger than that of the tree. As another example, imagine yourself walking toward your car, which is a block away. As you approach it, the image of the car on your retina is growing larger, yet you perceive that the car remains the same size. Figure 4-17 shows other examples of our perception of size.

Various factors influence the constancy of size. First, we make assumptions based on our experiences. Because we know something about the relative sizes of pencils and trees, it would be virtually impossible for us to perceive a pencil as being larger than a tree regardless of the evidence provided by our senses. Second, there is a relationship between assumed size and assumed distance. Because we perceive the tree as being some distance away, we know that it must be relatively large. Third, the background information available helps our perception of relative sizes. We see the tree against a background of houses, cars, streets, and other objects with which we are familiar. Our knowledge of the characteristics of the background provides us with cues about the size of the tree.

Brightness and Color Constancy. A snow-covered field would be perceived to be the same under moonlight as it would on a bright, sunny day; the snow would seem white both times. Yet the amount of light reflected by the snow under the two conditions would be considerably different. If you hold a colored piece of paper under a fluorescent light and then under an ordinary light bulb, it will seem to be the same color on both occasions, even though the light waves reflected by the paper will be slightly different. These experiences reflect our perceptual constancies for brightness and color.

Shape Constancy. As a final example of perceptual constancies, look at a dinner plate while standing several feet away from a table. Then look at it from directly above. You undoubtedly perceived the plate as being round in both cases, even though from several feet away the image on your retina was oval-shaped. Our experience with and knowledge of objects help us to perceive their shape as unchanging, even though the evidence reaching our receptors would suggest otherwise.

The Perception of Depth

Artists as well as psychologists are interested in depth perception. The basic question that both ask is how can a three-dimensional world be translated onto a two-dimensional surface? The surface of interest to the artist is the canvas, while the psychologist is interested in the retina. The techniques mastered by artists to convey depth, however, have provided many clues to the psychologist.

Figure 4–17. (A) Although to our sense perceptors the two logs appear to be different sizes, background information contributes to our perception of size constancy. (B) Our knowledge of the relationship between assumed size and assumed distance contradicts our sense perception that the logs are the same size. (C) The Ponzo illusion. In the absence of any context for distance or depth, the perception is similar to that in (B).

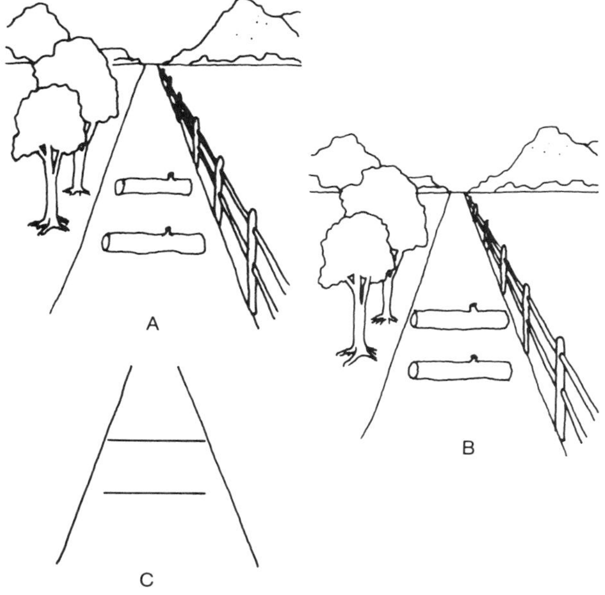

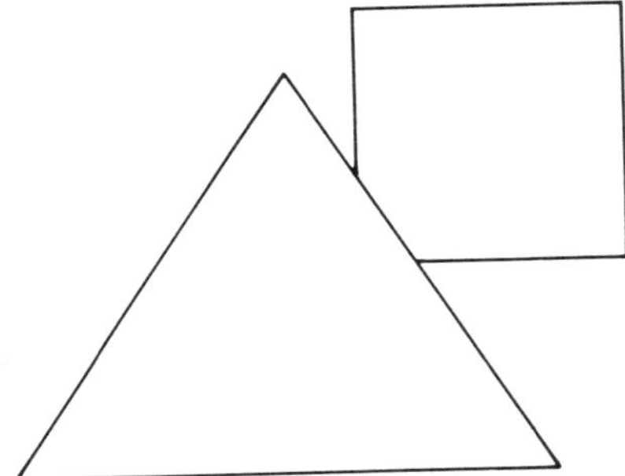

Figure 4–18.

Monocular Cues. This term refers to cues provided about depth that we can obtain when using only one eye. One of the most powerful of these cues is called **interposition,** which is illustrated in Figure 4–18. The triangle appears to be closer because it seems to be partially blocking our view of the square.

Linear perspective refers to the phenomenon that parallel lines seem to be converging as they recede into the distance. This can be seen in the skylines of buildings on either side of an avenue. Differences in perceived texture of the buildings also add to the perception of depth: coarser texture is associated with closeness and finer texture is associated with distance. Clearness also contributes to the perception of depth. If you live close to hills or mountains, you have undoubtedly noticed that they seem closer on a clear day than on a hazy day.

Two additional monocular cues are relative size and shadows. Figure 4–19 illustrates how perceived distance or depth can vary with perceived size. Once we know something about the size of an object, then the smaller its image on our retina, the farther away we will perceive it to be. The addition of shadows in Figure 4–20 can transform a two-dimensional circle into a three-dimensional sphere.

A monocular cue not available to the artist involves movement. If you move your head from left to right, you may notice that objects nearer you appear to be moving from right to left, while more distant objects appear to move in the same direction as your head. Furthermore, as you may have noticed when driving along a highway, objects close to us appear to be passing by much more rapidly than distant objects. These movement cues provide important information about the relative distance of objects.

Retinal Disparity. Because our two eyes are separated by a nose and some 65 mm, each eye receives a somewhat different view of the world. These two views are integrated in the brain to produce a single image. This process adds greatly to our perception of depth. This binocular cue, as it is called, is illustrated in Figure 4–21. The principle is used in children's stereoscopic viewers, which allow each eye to see a slightly different view of the same scene in order to give the illusion of depth.

Experience and Perception

In the early stages of research into problems of sensation and perception, scientific views often fell into one of two schools of thought. The first school, known as the nativists, believed that perceptual abilities are mostly innate. The second school of thought, the empiricists, believed that learning and experience play important roles in shaping one's perceptual experiences. Both sides conducted experiments to support their point of

Figure 4–19. The lamppost and block of wood at the far right look much bigger than the lamppost at the far left and the block of wood in the foreground. We perceive them as larger because we perceive them as farther away. Actually the two lampposts and blocks of wood are exactly the same size.

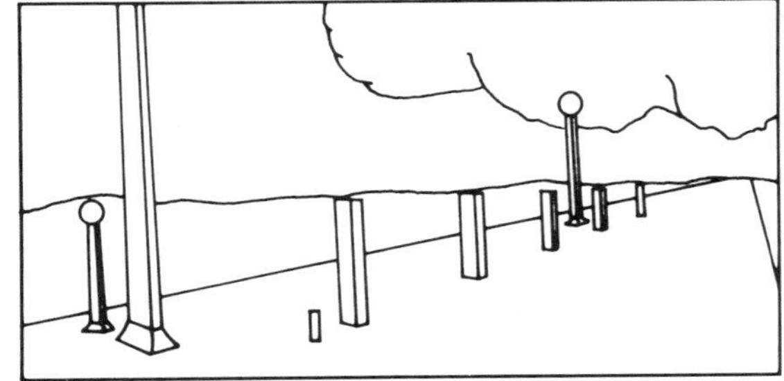

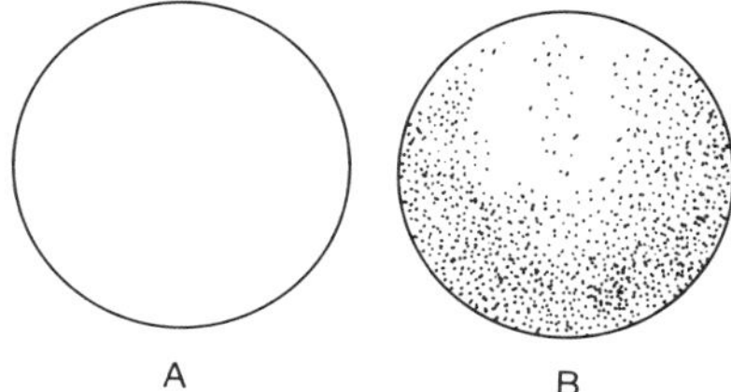

Figure 4–20.

view, and both sides were often successful in doing so.

This controversy, although quite heated at one time, has passed by the wayside. Most psychologists today recognize that both groups of factors are necessary for sensory and perceptual experiences. Without the sensory and perceptual mechanisms innate in the physiology of most people, there would be no sensation or perception. And without relevant experience and learning, perceptual mechanisms would not develop. Let us review a few examples that illustrate the interaction between the innate mechanisms and relevant experiences.

One dramatic example of the importance of experience in the development of perception concerns people born with cataracts. Cataracts, disorders of the lens of the eye, prevent patterned vision, although some diffuse light can reach the eyes. When these individuals have their cataracts removed, their eyes are normal (Von Senden, 1932, 1960). Many patients have difficulty recognizing familiar objects, but they can readily identify them if they are allowed to touch them. Most patients have extreme difficulty in recognizing faces—even those of close friends and relatives. One particularly bright patient could recognize only four or five faces two years after his surgery.

Some patients were overwhelmed by their new visual experiences. One man, who had his cataracts removed at the age of 52, became terrified of traffic. Prior to his operation he had no qualms about crossing even the busiest of streets with his cane in hand. Most patients showed considerable improvement after months and years of visual experiences, but it is questionable whether their visual perception would ever be normal. Their reactions to having their sight restored clearly illustrates the importance of learning and experience in visual perception.

Recall Kenge, the Pygmy whose reaction to a distant herd of buffalo opened this chapter. His reaction illustrates the importance of experience in developing size constancy in perception. Because he lived in dense forests, where his vision was limited to distances of about 30 yards, he did not have the opportunity to learn the maintenance of size constancy at greater distances.

A series of experiments to test the roles of heredity and experience have used the **visual cliff** (Walk, 1962, 1964; Walk & Gibson, 1961). This apparatus, illustrated in Figure 4–22, consists of two sections divided by a platform. On one side of the platform, called the shallow side, a piece of glass is placed directly on a patterned surface. On the other side, the deep side, the patterned surface is some distance below the glass. It is assumed that

Figure 4–21. You can see the difference between the views of your eyes by holding a pencil up near your nose. The tip of the pencil should be toward you and pointed slightly downward. Now close one eye and then the other. The pencil seems to swing back and forth. With your right eye open, it seems angled toward the left, while with the left eye open, it seems angled toward the right. With both eyes open, the combined view is of a pencil straight ahead of your nose.

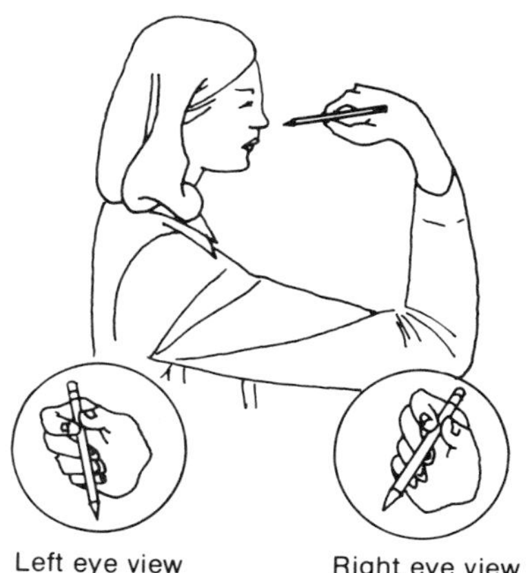

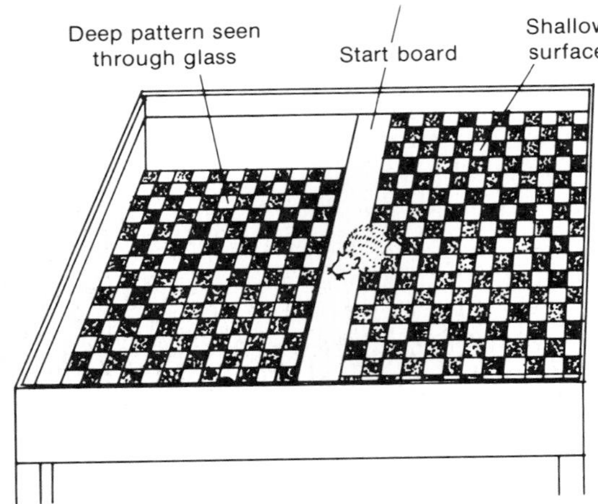

Figure 4–22. The visual cliff.

the deep side appears dangerous to subjects since it simulates a cliff-like dropoff.

Animal studies clearly indicate that both innate mechanisms and visual experiences are important to depth perception (Tees, 1974). Rats who were reared under normal conditions were compared with rats who were reared in the dark. It was found that both groups of rats avoided the deep side when the dropoff was 20 to 25 cm. When the dropoff was 15 cm or less, however, only the normally reared rats avoided the deep side. This suggests that the mechanism for depth perception is innate, but experiences with relevant cues in the environment are necessary for it to be fully developed. Adult animals invariably prefer the shallow side. Interestingly, this only holds for landbound animals. Aquatic animals, such as ducks and turtles, do not show a strong preference for one side over the other. Perhaps the survival value of depth perception is not so pronounced with these animals since lakes and ponds contain few cliffs that need to be avoided.

Human infants who are able to crawl show a clear preference for the shallow side (Campos, Langer, & Krowitz, 1970). But since they have had about six months' worth of visual experiences, this does not necessarily indicate that depth perception is innate. When infants as young as two months of age are placed on the deep side of the apparatus, their physiological reaction (deceleration of heartrate) indicates that while they can perceive the difference between the deep and shallow sides, they are not sensitive to the dangers of the dropoff. So once again, relevant experiences appear to be necessary for innate mechanisms to develop fully.

A dramatic experiment conducted by two British physiologists, Colin Blakemore and Grahame Cooper (1970), demonstrated that experience can modify physiological responses in the brain. As you recall, earlier in the chapter we mentioned that certain cells in the visual cortex respond most strongly to vertical lines, while other cells respond most strongly to horizontal lines. In this experiment, one group of kittens' visual experiences were limited to an environment with vertical lines, while a second group was exposed to horizontal lines only. At five months of age, both groups of kittens showed evidence of perceptual difficulties related to the type of environment in which they were reared. But even more striking was the finding that cats reared with vertical lines did not have cells in the visual brain that usually become excited when the subjects are viewing horizontal lines. Conversely, cats reared in the environment with horizontal lines showed no relevant visual brain activity when viewing vertical lines. Additional research demonstrated that there is a critical period, extending from birth to about four months of age in the kittens, for this effect to occur. After this critical period, restriction of visual stimulation will have little effect. It is noteworthy, however, that for a certain period of time some types of experiences can actually modify the functioning of the brain.

Perception and the Perceiver

Although many of the early researchers were interested in discovering general principles of sensation and perception that were applicable to everyone, it has been recognized for some time that one individual's motives, emotions, interests, and personality will influence his or her percep-

Above: When visible light passes through a prism, refraction causes it to be separated into colors. The shorter the wavelength of each color the greater it is bent. **Below:** Visible light is a type of electromagnetic radiation having a wavelength between 400 and 700 nanometers (billionths of a meter). Other types of radiation and their wavelengths are shown.

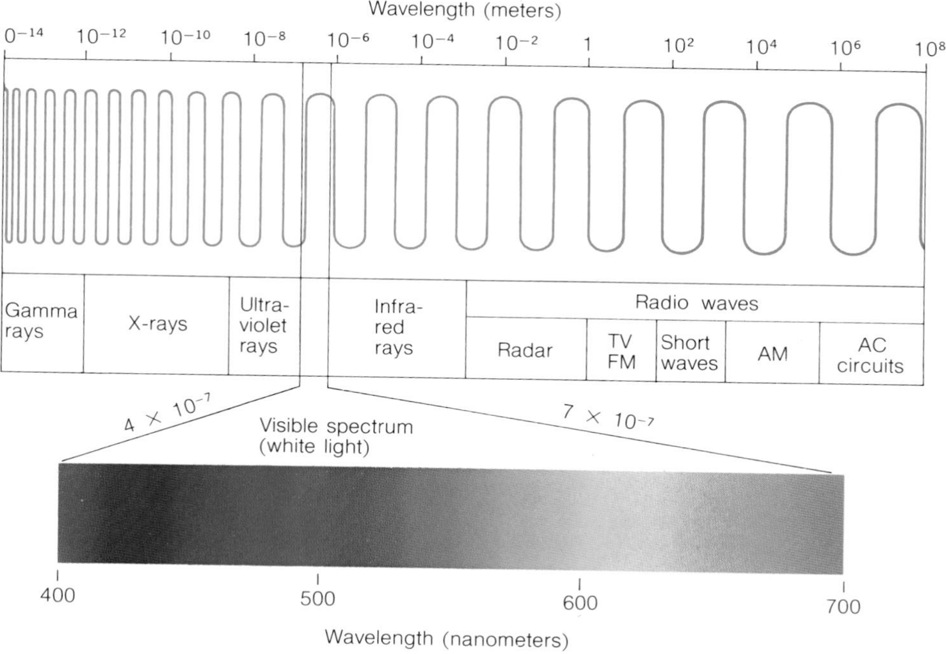

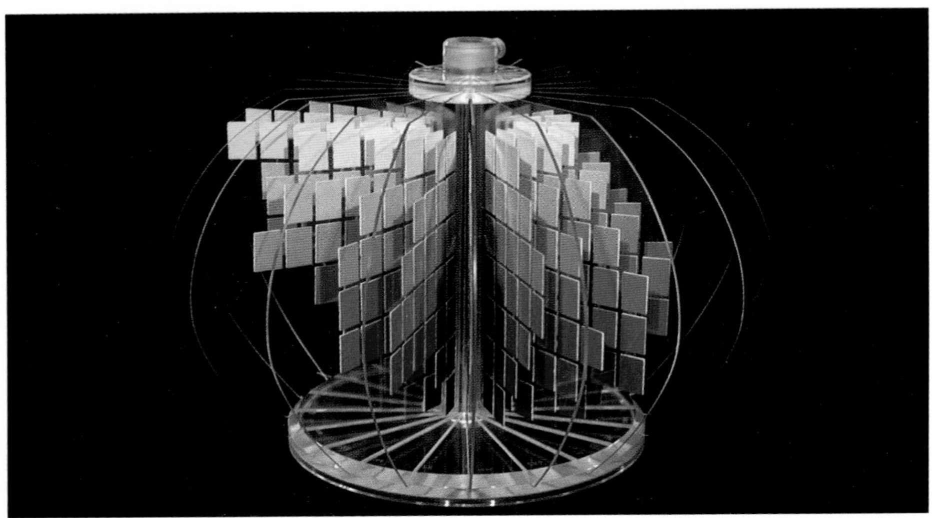

Above: A color solid conveys three aspects of color change in three dimensions. Tints and hues are illustrated vertically, with each square whiter than the one below it. Intensity is represented horizontally, with each square more concentrated in pure color than the one inside it. Hue is shown circularly, covering the entire spectrum. **Below:** Television sets use a system of additive color mixture similar to this one. Blue, red, and green are basic colors. The three colors that result from equal mixtures of two basic colors are shown. Other colors (not shown) can be produced from different ratios of the basic colors. Equal mixtures of all three basic colors produce white.

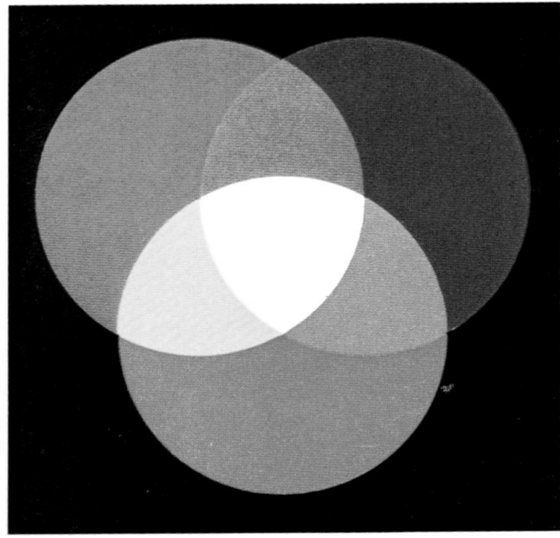

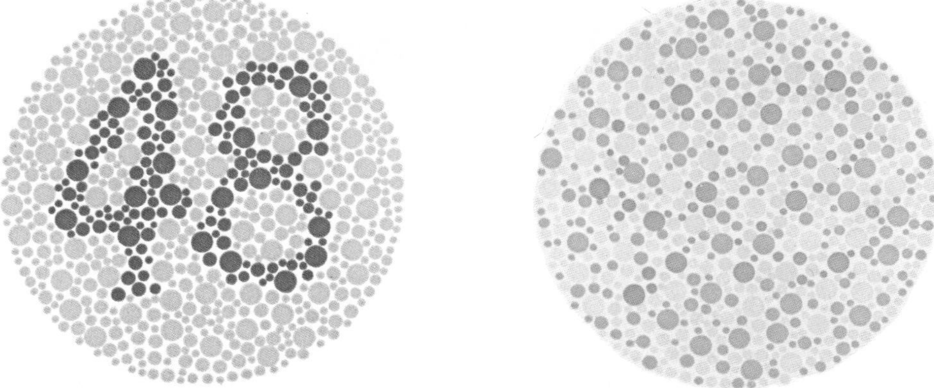

Above: People with normal color vision see the numbers 48 and 92. Those with red-green impairment cannot detect either number. **Below:** These four pictures show the impression of a bowl of fruit and flowers as seen by people with normal color vision (upper left), monochromatic vision (upper right), red-green impairment (lower left), and blue-yellow impairment (lower right).

Above: You will see the after image of this flag by staring at it for 15 seconds and then looking at a white background. **Below:** This painting by Alfred Sisley illustrates two visual principles. Through *perspective* Sisley helps the viewer's eyes to interpret the smaller trees in the middle of the painting as farther away and about the same size as those on the left. Impressionist painters like Sisley experimented with *color mixture*. They were interested in capturing the transient effects of light on a subject. One method they used was to place blotches of pure color side by side on the canvas rather than mixing colors on the palette. This enabled the viewer's eyes to do the mixing.

CRITICAL ISSUE:

Dreams of the Blind

I'm flying in a little silver-colored spaceship with a few other people (whose identities I don't now recall). We are approaching a tiny planet which is composed solely of ice, a planet even smaller than the moon. Its orbit is extremely irregular, almost chaotic, as it bounces and wobbles along in an aimless fashion; or perhaps it is completely out of orbit and simply wandering through space; but the sun or some other star to which it may belong is dimly visible in the distance. Then we land but decide not to get out of the ship because outside it is very cold and dark—we've come down on a vast, desolate glacial plain, surely an environment hostile to life. There is nothing living in sight, only ice—plains, mountains, hills, and valleys of it. The sun is so far away that its light is reduced to a slight phosphorescent glow along the horizon (Kirtley, 1975, pp. 254–255).

Does this dream sound unusual? It is, but not because it's about silver spaceships and alien planets. It is unusual because it was reported by a man, aged 31, who had been blind for nearly 20 years. Yet it sounds like a dream anyone could have.

Although dreams of the blind are not a widely researched topic, there are several dozen studies, dating back to the mid-1800s, which provide us with some understanding of the issue. One finding, as suggested by the above example, is that blind people do have visual imagery in their dreams, especially if they had their sight up to the ages of four to seven. For those who became blind before this critical period, dreams primarily involve the senses of hearing and touch. One man, for example, reported hearing entire lectures in his dreams. Dreams involving smell and taste are reported less frequently among these persons.

The intensity of the visual images in blind people's dreams varies widely. Although the vividness of the imagery tends to fade with time, some people continue to have extremely vivid dreams years after becoming blind. Others report that they can perceive only degrees of lightness and darkness. Some individuals who lose their sight little by little, report that the visual imagery in their dreams is never more vivid than what they can see while awake (Kirtley, 1975).

Dreams of the deaf and blind seem similarly varied. Consider the following dream reported by Helen Keller, who became deaf and blind at the age of 19 months:

> Once in a dream I held in my hand a pearl. . . . It was a smooth, exquisitely molded crystal. As I gazed into its shimmering deeps, my soul was flooded with an ecstasy of tenderness, and I was filled with wonder, as one who should for the first time look into the cool, sweet heart of a rose.

In contrast, a woman who became blind and deaf at the age of two reported that she had frequent dreams but that she could not recall them. She described a typical dream simply as "hard, heavy, thick." This same woman was observed using the touch language to form a few letters or words with her fingers while sleeping. Apparently, this was her way of talking in her sleep.

These reports illustrate that the loss of a sensory capacity can affect us 24 hours a day—while we are awake *and* asleep.

tions. Perhaps the effects of these kinds of variables can be seen most clearly in social perceptions. Take the case of a husband and wife who attend a party and spend much of the evening with another couple. While driving home they may exchange impressions of the couple they met. The husband may be surprised to learn that his wife did not like the other woman. He was impressed by her warm smile and sparkling eyes, while his wife perceived her makeup and dress to be gaudy and ostentatious. The husband may remark that the other man seemed shallow and ill-informed on current issues, while his wife was struck by his compassion and understanding. Obviously, the motives and interests of the husband and wife influenced their perceptions of the second couple.

Laboratory research has confirmed the importance of such variables. Using a tachistoscope, a device that can flash images on a screen for very brief periods of time, researchers have found that interests and motives are related to the ability to perceive words. Individuals who have a strong desire to achieve are more likely to perceive words such as "strive" and "perfect" than are subjects with low levels of achievement motive (McClelland & Liberman, 1949). Likewise, individuals with a strong interest in religion are more likely than others to perceive words such as "sacred," while those interested in economics are particularly quick to recognize words such as "income" (Postman, Bruner, & McGinnies, 1948).

Perhaps the most intriguing and comprehensive theory relating differences in perception to personality variables is that proposed by the British psychologist Hans Eysenck (1967). He suggested that the personality dimension of extraversion-introversion is based on physiological differences and might hold implications for individual differences in sensation and perception. According to this theory, extraverts, who tend to be outgoing and sociable, have a low level of physiological arousal, which causes them to be relatively insensitive to external stimulation. Introverts, who tend to be more withdrawn and introspective, are thought to have high levels of physiological arousal, which makes them especially sensitive to external stimuli. Studies have shown that there do appear to be differences between the two groups in sensory thresholds. Introverts have lower thresholds for vision (Siddle, Morish, White, & Mangen, 1969), hearing (Stelmack, Achorn, & Michand, 1977), touch (Coles, Gale, & Kline, 1971), pain (Halsam, 1967), and taste (Eysenck, 1973). Eysenck's theory, and the supporting research, raises the interesting possibility that one's sensations and perceptions may influence personality development. At the very least it suggests that sensation and perception should not be viewed as isolated aspects of human functioning.

Summary

Sensation and perception are the processes by which we know the world. The senses consist of vision, hearing, taste, smell, the skin senses, kinesthesis, and equilibrium. Perception involves the processes by which information from these senses is transformed into meaningful experiences.

The eye is our most complex and probably our most important sense receptor. The lens of the eye focuses light onto the retina, which contains a variety of photoreceptive cells. Two important types of cells are rods and cones. Rods are responsible for vision in dim light, and cones are responsible for vision in bright light, discrimination of colors, and acuity of vision. These photoreceptive cells transform the light waves into neural activity, which is carried by the optic nerve to the visual areas of the brain for processing.

The ear can be divided into the outer, middle, and inner ear. The outer ear amplifies and channels sound waves so that they cause vibrations in the eardrum. The eardrum sets three tiny bones in the middle ear into motion. The vibrations from these bones set fluid in the inner ear into motion, which in turn stimulates tiny hair cells. These hair cells convert mechanical activity into neural activity, which is transmitted along the auditory nerve to the brain.

Taste and smell are known as the chemical senses because molecules of the food and odoriforous substances stimulate their receptor cells directly. The four basic taste sensations are bitter, sweet, sour, and salty. It has been suggested, but not confirmed, that there are seven basic odors. Contrary to what was once believed, there are not separate receptor cells for each taste sensation. The mechanism by which odors are discriminated is not known.

The skin senses consist of four basic sensory experiences: warmth, cold, pressure, and pain. There are several types of receptors, but they are not associated with a specific sensation. Although some types of receptors respond most strongly to a particular type of stimulation, it is the overall pattern of activity in the receptors that produces our sensory experiences.

Kinesthesis and the sense of equilibrium provide us with information about the orientation of our body. Kinesthesis tells us about the position and movement of our body parts. The sense of equilibrium allows us to know the position of our head in respect to gravity and hence is responsible for our sense of balance.

Psychophysics is the study of the relation between physical energy (such as light and sound waves) and sensory experience. It is concerned with three general issues: the minimum amount of energy that can be detected, the difference in levels of energy that can be detected, and the scaling of physical energy as it relates to sensory experience. The smallest amount of energy that can be detected on 50 percent of all trials is the absolute threshold. Signal-detection theory examines the decision-making process of individuals who are involved in this task. The smallest difference between two levels of energy that can be discriminated is called the just noticeable difference (JND). Weber's Law describes the amount of energy that must be added before a difference can be detected. The relation between physical energy and sensory experience can best be described by Stevens's Power Law. It states that sensory experience is a function of the intensity of the physical stimulus raised to some exponent. The exponent's value must be determined for each stimulus.

Perception involves the process by which the information received by our senses is translated into meaningful experiences. Illusions illustrate that there is not necessarily a direct relation between sensation and perception.

The attention we pay to a stimulus plays a large role in our perception of it. The perception of form is one of the most important of the perceptual experiences. Our tendency to view objects as figures against a ground is basic to form perception. The early Gestalt psychologists identified several principles that contribute to our perception of form. These include the principles of proximity, similarity, closure, and continuity. Context also influences perception of the form of figures.

The perceptual constancies allow us to view the world as stable, even though the evidence received by our senses is not. The size constancy causes us to perceive an object as being the same size as we move toward it or away from it. We view an object as having the same brightness and color under a variety of lighting conditions because of brightness and color constancy. And shape constancy allows us to perceive objects as retaining their shape while we view them from different angles.

The perception of depth is of interest because our sensory evidence utilizes only two dimensions. The monocular cues that contribute to depth perception are interposition, linear perspective, texture, clearness, relative size, shadows, and movement. Because our eyes are about 65 mm apart, each eye receives a slightly different view when we focus on an object. This retinal disparity contributes to our perception of depth.

An early controversy in psychology concerned whether perceptual processes were largely inborn or acquired on the basis of experience. Currently, most psychologists recognize that both factors play a crucial role. While many basic perceptual processes are innate, the organism must have relevant learning experiences for them to be fully developed. Psychologists have known for some time that our perceptions are also influenced by our motives, interests, and personality.

Key Terms For Review

absolute threshold
accommodation
auditory canal
cochlea
conduction deafness
cones
cornea
cutaneous senses
duplicity theory
eardrum
fovea
hypermetropia
incus
interposition
iris
just noticeable difference (JND)
kinesthesis
lens
linear perspective
magnitude estimation
malleus
myopia
nerve deafness
olfactory epithelium
opponent-process theory
optic chiasma
paradoxical cold
perception
perceptual constancies
pinna
psychophysics
pupil
retina
rods
sclera
sensation
sense of equilibrium
signal-detection theory
stapes
Stevens's Power Law
taste buds
transduction
trichromatic theory
visual cliff
Weber's Law

Suggested Readings

Bartoshuk, L. Separate worlds of taste. *Psychology Today*, September 1980, pp. 48 ff.
This article discusses the influence of heredity on the way that we taste. It explores the sources of individual differences in taste for a variety of foods.

Coren, S., Porac, C., & Ward, L. M. *Sensation and perception.* New York: Academic Press, 1979.
A well-written and comprehensive text for the student who is interested in learning about the topic in detail.

Fisher, J. *Body magic.* New York: Stein & Day, 1980.
Fisher explains how magicians and psychics utilize knowledge of perception to fool us.

Fisher, S. Experiencing your body: You are what you feel. *Saturday Review*, July 8, 1972.
An interesting article that discusses the difficulties many people have in maintaining an accurate body image.

Gibson, E. J. The development of perception as an adaptive process. In I. L. Janis (Ed.), *Current trends in psychology*, Los Altos, Calif.: William Kaufman, 1977.
This article discusses various perceptual processes in animals and humans. It discusses the role of experience in developing these processes and their evolutionary significance.

Hall, E. T. *The silent language.* New York: Fawcett, 1959.
This paperback is a classic exploration of cultural differences. It provides numerous fascinating examples of how people from different cultures perceive phenomena such as time and interpersonal distances in quite different ways.

Kirtley, D. D. *The psychology of blindness.* Chicago: Nelson-Hall, 1975.
Kirtley, who is blind, discusses the effects of losing one's sight. The book includes information on attitudes toward the blind, adjustment in the blind, and dreaming in the blind.

5

Principles of Learning

Linda is a 23-year-old teacher. She works with children who are several years behind academically because they lack motivation, study skills, and home support. Most of them are considered to have behavior problems. As part of her classroom management Linda uses the following procedure for one and a half hours each day: She tapes spiral notebooks to each seat and writes these words on the blackboard: in seat, face front, raise hand, working, paying attention, desk clear. *The children are told that they can earn from 1 to 10 points each 15 minutes for following the rules or showing improvement. The points can be exchanged for prizes worth up to 99¢, which are grouped in boxes labeled 10, 25, and 50 points. Linda arranges the instructional units so she can stop each 15 minutes, take 2 minutes to write the points earned on the notebooks, and tell the children what they have done to earn them. While she is handing out points, the class can earn a group point toward a Friday popsicle party for good behavior.*

After a few days, Linda changes the time period from 15 to 30 minutes. Then, progressively over several weeks, the children are required to save points for two days, three days, and four days. The number of points required for various prizes increases. The children have to work harder and longer for a smaller reward. Over a period of a month, the number of incidents of inappropriate behavior decreases and the children begin to succeed in learning and to take pride in being productive (Walker & Buckley, 1974).

Learning is a central process in our life. All of us learn something new every day, and this learning produces changes in our behavior. Having read the first chapters in this book, you can now use words or terms you did not know before. After taking diving lessons, you can expect to dive better than before those lessons. A child who touches a hot pan will not repeat that behavior. Learning, then, refers to relatively permanent changes in behavior as a result of training or experience.

Learning is one of the key phenomena in psychology. It applies to a great many kinds of behavior, ranging from flipping a light switch to mastering a foreign language or matrix algebra. Most higher organisms continually demonstrate the ability to learn complex tasks. For human beings, these tasks include playing a musical instrument, memorizing a mathematical formula or classroom lecture, or driving a car. By learning we gain mastery over our environment. In fact, there are few abilities as basic to the survival of most organisms as learning.

Most psychologists use the term "learning" more broadly than lay people use it. What is learned need not be "correct," that is, we can learn poor habits along with good ones. Moreover, learning can be subtle, involving attitudes and emotions as well as knowledge or skills. Many aspects of our social life, such as language, religious beliefs, and prejudices regarding race, sex, and social class, are learned and relearned through experience.

Animal trainers often use learning theory. This trainer rewards a dog with attention and petting after it has learned to shake hands. *(© H. Armstrong Roberts)*

Learning principles and problems are of central interest to all psychologists, regardless of their area of specialization. For example, many clinical psychologists assume that psychological and behavioral problems such as social anxiety or irrational fears can result in part from adverse learning experiences. Consequently, these clinical psychologists use learning principles to help their clients unlearn types of maladaptive behavior. Industrial psychologists use learning principles to improve the skills and motivation of employees. Developmental psychologists consider the basic laws of learning to be crucial determinants in child development. Physiological psychologists who wish to learn more about the biological basis of behavior also closely follow the developments in the area of learning.

People from all walks of life have shown interest in the practical ramifications of studies in learning. Professional animal trainers use learning principles to teach their animals tricks. Pet owners teach their animals to learn good habits and eliminate bad ones. Parents wanting their children to learn appropriate behaviors and correction officers interested in rehabilitating their prisoners make use of learning principles.

At one time or another, most of us have been interested in how we can direct and facilitate the learning process. Consider adults in such roles as parents, teachers, supervisors, business executives, military officers, ministers, or politicians. Men and women in these capacities have considerable influence and control not only over what their protégés learn but also over the conditions under which learning occurs. Educators, for instance, study educational environments. They ask questions such as: How can instructions be given more effectively? Can forgetting be slowed or even prevented? What kinds of students derive maximal benefits from which teaching methods?

In our society, which places a high premium on formal education and in which training of some sort has become a lifelong activity for many people, it is particularly important that we understand basic learning processes. In this chapter, then, we shall examine the key concepts and principles of learning and illustrate them in a variety of applications.

THE NATURE OF LEARNING

As noted earlier, we shall define learning as follows: a relatively permanent change in behavior as the result of training and experience. Let us examine some of the properties of this definition more closely.

Our definition implies that certain conditions in the environment produce fundamental changes in behavior that persist over time. But not all changes in behavior can be related to learning through training and experience. Some behavioral changes are a function of biological development or maturation (see Chapter 8). The young child learns to stand upright as a result of biological maturation. An old person's strength of grip may weaken as a result of aging. These changes do not depend on the person's experience and are excluded from our definition of learning. Other changes are due to transient motivational, emotional, or physiological states. For example, a person who is intoxicated may exhibit marked changes in behavior. Normally such changes are short-lived and do not fit into our definition of learning.

A second important aspect is that the learning process is not directly observable but must be inferred from performance. The distinction between learning or acquiring knowledge (a capability) and performance (exhibiting this capability in some form of action) is an important one. When an organism has learned something, the effects of this learning, although not immediately observable, can still change later behavior.

Most of our knowledge of learning processes and principles comes from laboratory research. Much of what we have to say in this chapter is based on information collected from experiments on rats, dogs, pigeons, or monkeys. Why has most research in learning involved animals rather than people? First, lower animals breed rapidly, are genetically pure, and can be maintained in the laboratory under controlled conditions (Hulse, Egeth, & Deese, 1980). Second, the scientifically controlled environment of the laboratory makes it possible to carry out hazardous experiments not suitable for human subjects. However, laboratory animal research is limited in scope. Typically laboratory investigations single out phenomena and study them out of their usual context; they often fail to explain how these phenomena work in the real world. What laboratory research does do, however, is help psychologists discover general principles of the learning process. These principles can then be applied to more complex forms of behavior and to all species capable of learning.

LEARNING THROUGH CONDITIONING

Conditioning has to do with two kinds of behavior: respondent and operant. **Respondent behavior** is a reflex evoked by a stimulus. For example, if a bright light shines into your eye, your pupil will automatically constrict. In this case a stimulus (the bright light) evoked, or *elicited,* the response (pupil constriction). All organisms are provided by nature with **reflexes.** These reflexes are innate, spontaneous responses to certain environmental events. Though innate, reflexes are subject to modification, typically through classical-conditioning procedures.

Not all behavior is evoked by stimuli, however. Waving your hand in class to attract the attention of your professor, for instance, is not elicited by an inborn need for attention. Instead, it occurs because it is an effective way of attracting attention. The class of responses not elicited by specific stimuli is called **operant behavior.** Operant responses are said to be *emitted* by the organism, because there is no easily identifiable stimulus provoking the behavior. Operant behavior is voluntary; it "operates" on the environment to produce consequences for the organism. As we shall see, operant responses can be conditioned by manipulating the consequences of the responses. Examples of operant responses are rats pressing levers to get food or children searching for candy.

PRINCIPLES OF CLASSICAL CONDITIONING

Classical conditioning refers to the model of learning developed by the Russian physiologist Ivan Pavlov. The term is used interchangeably with respondent, or Pavlovian, conditioning.

Pavlov, after obtaining his medical degree, was appointed professor at the St. Petersburg Medical Academy, where he conducted a monumental series of studies on the physiology of digestion that eventually won him the Nobel Prize. Pavlov was interested in the digestive reflexes that occur in response to clear-cut, measurable stimuli such as food. One such reflex is salivation in response to food placed in the mouth. To study salivary secretions Pavlov had dogs brought into a soundproof room and strapped into a harness that secured their necks and legs, thereby making gross body movements impossible. Usually the duct of the dog's salivary gland was moved to the outside of the cheek by minor surgery and connected to a recording instrument that measured the exact amount of salivation in drops. He then placed meat powder in the dog's mouth and recorded his results.

Pavlov noticed that if the same dog was used repeatedly, salivation soon began to occur even before the food was placed in the dog's mouth. Not just the sight of food, but even the sight of the experimenter or his footsteps were often enough to produce salivation. Pavlov viewed this response as a learned reflex that was produced by the pairing of a neutral stimulus with food in the dog's mouth. Initially Pavlov labeled this phenomenon "psychic secretions" and recognized them as a simple form of learning. At the time, the learning process was a complete mystery to science. In 1902 Pavlov decided to turn all his efforts to the investigation of learning, a decision that was to make him as famous in psychology as he was in physiology.

Pavlov ran a large and efficient laboratory that would be the envy of any experimenter. Thousands of experiments were performed systematically, many of them variations of the same basic scheme. Inside the laboratory Pavlov was justly respected for his astuteness and even feared by his associates. In private life, by contrast, he was absent-minded, impractical, and often sentimental. It was not unusual for him to forget to pick up his salary or lend it to an unscrupulous acquaintance who would never return the money. After a number of disastrous financial affairs, Pavlov's wife took over the management of the family finances, and he was seldom allowed to carry more than loose change (Fancher, 1979).

Pavlov insisted to the end of his life that he was a physiologist whose work was of no interest to psychologists. Psychologists, he believed, were scientists who exclusively studied subjective states of consciousness. Little did he imagine that psychologists would use objective techniques and that his study of the reflexive salivary response in dogs would have a lasting influence on learning theory.

The Classical-Conditioning Model

Pavlov referred to the meat powder in his experiment as the **unconditioned stimulus (US)** and the dog's salivation as the **unconditioned response (UR).** Such stimuli and responses are called unconditioned because they occur without prior training. The unconditioned response is both predictable and measurable. Other examples of unconditioned stimuli are a puff of air to the eye, electric shock to the sole of the foot, or the stroking of an infant's palm. The corresponding unconditioned responses are blinking of the eye, leg flexion, and grasping.

First Pavlov established the relationship between the unconditioned stimulus and the unconditioned response. Then he started the conditioning procedure by pairing a **neutral stimulus**—one

Pavlov and his laboratory assistants developed the principles of classical conditioning through meticulous experimentation. *(© Culver Pictures, Inc.)*

that will not produce the unconditioned response when presented alone initially—with the unconditioned stimulus, food. The neutral stimulus he used was an auditory tone, which naturally by itself did not cause the dog to salivate. When paired with an unconditioned stimulus, a neutral stimulus becomes a **conditioned stimulus (CS).** One of the crucial characteristics of the CS is that it must act upon the senses of the organism, i.e., it must be hearable, tastable, touchable.

In a typical CS-US pairing, the CS (tone) was presented first for about five seconds. Then the US (a piece of food) was placed in a tray in front of the dog. The dog picked up the food and salivated. Each CS-US pairing constituted a trial. For the first few trials, there was no noticeable response during the presentation of the CS (tone), whereas there was much salivation during the presentation of the US (food). After about a dozen trials, the dog began to salivate reliably at the sound of the tone in anticipation of food. This anticipatory salivation is the **conditioned response (CR),** which is a reflex reaction given in response to the conditioned stimulus alone. Although the CR may be similar to the UR, it is never exactly the same (Lovell, 1980). **Classical conditioning,** then, is a procedure in which a conditioned stimulus (CS, tone)—through repeated pairings with an unconditioned stimulus (US, food)—comes to elicit the conditioned response (CR). Classical conditioning requires that the neutral and unconditioned stimuli be paired relatively closely in time. This closeness in time, referred to as **temporal contiguity,** is the single most important factor in classical conditioning.

Since Pavlov's original investigations, thousands of experiments have been done using the classical-conditioning model with a variety of conditioned stimuli and many variations of the basic procedure. Evidence of classical conditioning has been found in organisms as simple as flatworms and as complex as humans. Many reflexes other than the salivary response have been studied, including the kneejerk, the eyeblink, vomiting, changes in respiration, heartbeat, and the constriction of blood vessels.

Most of us do not realize how familiar we are with the results of classical conditioning in our own experience. Feeling uncomfortable at the sound of the dentist's drill, feeling your heart skipping a beat when the telephone rings, or feeling upset when passing a place where a terrible car accident had once been witnessed are examples familiar to most of us. Classical conditioning is involved in the development of many involuntary emotional responses. For instance, a young child who on his way to school every day must pass a fierce dog tied up in someone's yard may be fearful of going to school because he associates it with the barking, growling dog.

Becoming anxious at the sound of a dentist's drill is an example of classical conditioning. *(© Rick Winsor/Woodfin Camp & Associates)*

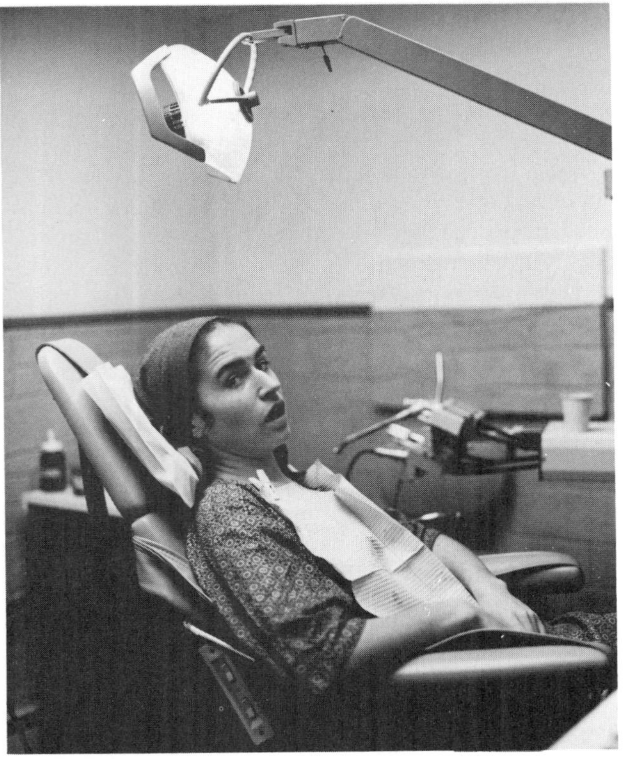

Extinction and Spontaneous Recovery

Pavlov varied his experiments to find out how strong the conditioned response was. He found that if the conditioned stimulus is presented several times without the unconditioned stimulus, the conditioned response, no matter how well established, becomes progressively weaker. If this procedure is continued until the CS no longer elicits a response, **extinction** is said to have occurred (see Figure 5–1). But extinction should not be equated with the loss of the conditioned response. This can be easily demonstrated by a phenomenon known as **spontaneous recovery.** If the animal is returned to the experimental environment an hour or two after extinction first occurred and is then presented with the conditioned stimulus, the conditioned response will reappear spontaneously Although the magnitude of the response does not return to the level reached before extinction, the existence of any recovery indicates that the conditioned reflex was not lost during extinction. As Pavlov put it, there must still remain in the nervous system some "trace" or memory of the association even after the disappearance of the response.

Pavlov (1927) thought that the operation of the nervous system was based on two opposing tendencies—excitation and inhibition. He assumed that the conditioned reflex was based on excitation of the CS-CR pathway in the brain. In other words, if the previously neutral CS is paired with a US, the CS acquires excitatory properties since it produces the CR. Extinction was thought to be due to the temporary blocking of the CS-CR pathway by inhibitory processes opposed to the reflex.

Generalization and Discrimination

In another series of experiments Pavlov investigated the effects of a stimulus somewhat different from the original conditioning stimulus. Suppose a dog has been conditioned to salivate to a 500-Hz tone. Pavlov discovered that if the dog was tested with tones of somewhat higher or lower frequen-

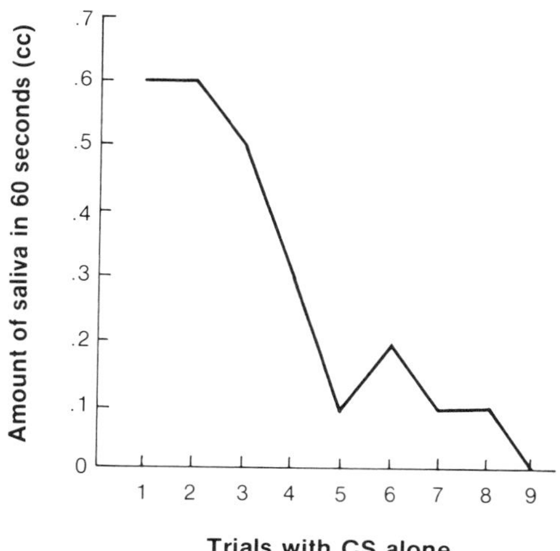

Figure 5–1. The graph shows the extinction of a conditioned salivary reflex. CS presentations occurred 16 minutes apart. (Data from *Pavlov, 1927.*)

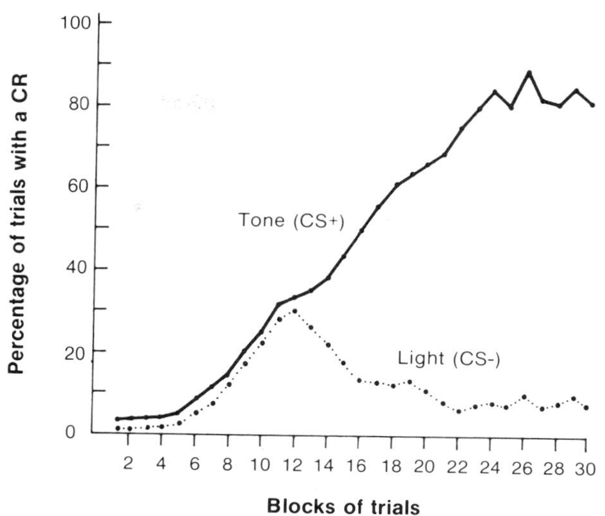

Figure 5–2. Stimulus Discrimination.

cies (300, 400, 600, 700), these new conditioned stimuli also elicited the conditioned response. When an organism that has been conditioned to respond to one stimulus responds to similar stimuli that have not been paired with the original US, we encounter a phenomenon known as **stimulus generalization.** The greater the similarity between the original CS and other stimuli, the more likely we are to respond to those stimuli in place of the original stimulus. The gradual drop in response strength associated with the decreasing similarity to the original conditioned stimulus is referred to as the **generalization gradient.** Stimulus generalization may be viewed as a very primitive form of categorization, or the treatment of similar events as identical or nearly identical because of shared properties.

Classical conditioning can also teach subjects to discriminate between stimuli. When an organism responds differentially to previous generalized stimuli, we say that the organism has learned a **stimulus discrimination.** In a typical Pavlovian discrimination experiment, a dog generalizes two conditioned stimuli, such as a tone and a light, each paired with food (US). After a period, food is withheld for one stimulus, light. The dog learns not to salivate for the withheld stimulus (see Figure 5–2). Experiments involving discrimination of more similar conditioned stimuli, such as two types of sounds, have also been successful.

At this point you may wonder how the simple association of two stimuli relates to many of the complex types of behavior that we learn in everyday life. After all, our daily experiences are not always characterized by CS-US pairings. However, another classical-conditioning principle seems to be more relevant to everyday experiences. It is called **higher-order conditioning.** Pavlov (1927) demonstrated higher-order conditioning in the following way. First a dog was trained to salivate to the sound of a metronome by pairing the sound with food. When the sound controlled salivation, a new stimulus—sight of a black square—was paired with the sound of the metronome, but food was no longer presented. The critical question now was: Would the new stimulus also come to elicit salivation? After ten pairings of the black square and the sound of the metronome, salivation occurred on presentation of the black square alone. This is an example of second-order conditioning, which is schematized in Figure 5–3. In principle, higher-order conditioning

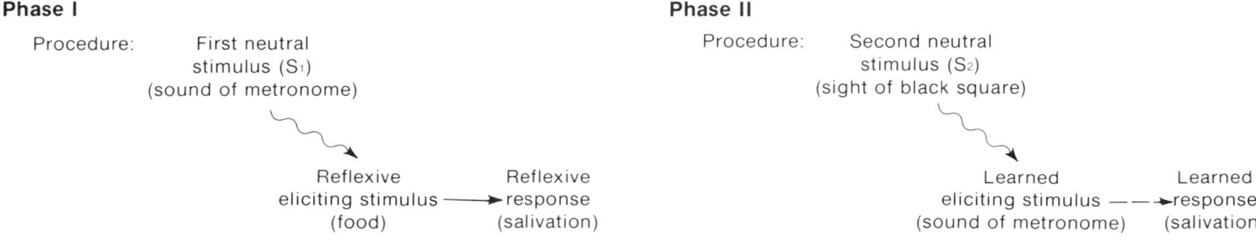

Figure 5–3. The procedure for producing higher-order conditioning. In Phase 1, a reflexive elicitation process depends on a neutral stimulus (S_1). As a result, S_1 comes to control a response similar to the reflexive response. In Phase II, a learned elicitation process depends on a second neutral stimulus (S_2). As a result, S_2—which has never been paired with the reflexive elicitation process—acquires control over a response similar to the learned response from Phase I. The wavy lines indicate the contingencies that the experimenter imposes. The dashed lines indicate the new, learned functional relationships between the environment and behavior.

APPLICATION

Uses of Classical Conditioning to Modify Human Behavior

From the beginning of Pavlov's research, American psychologists have been interested in how classical-conditioning principles can be applied to the problems of ordinary life.

In one of the earliest applications of Pavlovian principles to human behavior, Watson and Rayner (1920) extended classical-conditioning procedures to the learning and extinction of a commonly experienced emotional reaction, fear. They chose for their experimental subject an 11-month-old infant named Albert. The goal of the study was to determine whether Albert would learn to show fear to a neutral stimulus (CS) when it was paired with another stimulus (US) that already produced the fear reaction (UR). For their neutral stimulus Watson and Rayner chose a white rat, an animal of which Albert showed no fear. The unconditioned stimulus was a loud noise, which Albert spontaneously responded to with fear. Watson and Rayner's laboratory notes (1920, pp. 4–5) described Albert's classically conditioned fear of the white rat as follows:

Age 11 months 3 days

1. White rat suddenly taken from the basket and presented to Albert. He began to reach for rat with left hand. Just as his hand touched the animal, the bar was struck immediately behind his head. The infant jumped violently and fell forward, burying his face in the mattress. He did not cry, however.
2. Just as the right hand touched the rat, the bar was again struck. Again the infant jumped violently, fell forward, and began to whimper.

In order not to disturb the child too seriously no further tests were given for one week.

Age 11 months 10 days

1. Rat presented suddenly without sound. There was steady fixation but no tendency at first to reach for it. The rat was then placed nearer, whereupon the infant began tentative reaching movements with the right hand. When the rat nosed the infant's left hand, the hand was immediately withdrawn. He started to reach for the head of the animal with the forefinger of the left hand, but withdrew it suddenly before contact. It is thus seen that the two joint stimulations given the previous week were not without effect. He was tested with his blocks immediately afterwards to see if they shared in the process of conditioning. He began immediately to pick them up, dropping them, pounding them, etc. In

can be extended to third- and fourth-order conditioning. Much of the recent evidence for higher-order conditioning comes from the work of Rescorla (1977, 1978, 1979).

Higher-order conditioning is common in the real world. Suppose you are afraid of thunder. The sound of thunder is the unconditioned stimulus for the fear response. A variety of stimuli frequently precede a thunderstorm, such as a drop in temperature, an increase in wind, or the darkening of the sky (all of these are CS_2). Any of these stimuli can function as second-order conditioning stimuli, so that the dark sky, for instance, would come to elicit the fear response. Higher-order conditioning results in the acquisition of many phobias or prejudices. Unlike stimulus generalization, higher-order conditioning involves an association with new stimuli that need not bear any physical similarity to the original CS (Wingfield, 1979). Once the CS-CR relationship has been established, new associations can be conditioned using the CS itself as reinforcement.

To sum up, classical conditioning is a model of learning that consists of the association of two classes of stimuli: the unconditioned stimulus, which elicits a spontaneous, reflexive response whenever presented, and the neutral stimulus, which initially fails to produce the response. Through repeated pairings with the unconditioned stimulus, the neutral stimulus becomes a conditioned stimulus and acquires the power to elicit the conditioned response. In classical con-

the remainder of the tests the blocks were given frequently to quiet him and to test his general emotional state. They were always removed from sight when the process of conditioning was under way.

2. Joint stimulation with rat and sound. Started to touch rat, then fell over immediately to right side. No crying.
3. Joint stimulation. Fell to right side and rested upon hands, with head turned away from rat. No crying.
4. Joint stimulation. Same reaction.
5. Rat suddenly presented alone. Puckered face, whimpered, and withdrew body sharply to the left.
6. Joint stimulation. Fell over immediately to right side and began to whimper.
7. Joint stimulation. Started violently and cried, but did not fall over.
8. Rat alone. The instant the rat was shown, the baby began to cry. Almost instantly he turned sharply to the left, fell over on left side, raised himself on all fours and began to crawl away so rapidly that he was caught with difficulty before reaching the edge of the table.

When Watson and Rayner tested for generalization, they found that the conditioned fear response had transferred to other furry objects such as a rabbit, cotton, a fur coat, a dog, and even a mask of Santa Claus. Prior to the conditioning Albert was not afraid of any of these. On the basis of this experiment classical conditioning has been used as a model to explain the acquisition of certain phobias that are maladaptive, irrational fears.

Classical-conditioning procedures have also been applied to the treatment of certain behavioral problems. In one typical treatment program (Foreyt & Kennedy, 1971), classical aversive conditioning was used to help overweight women achieve an initial weight loss and then maintain that loss over an extended period of time. The US, consisting of the women's favorite high-caloric foods, such as doughnuts, pie, and french fries, was heated in front of the women, who were asked to smell the food and think about putting it into their mouth. Immediately afterwards they were asked to place a mask over their face, and a noxious odor was blown through the mask. The US (favorite food)-CS (noxious odor) pairings were repeated 15 times during each session. The women exposed to this conditioning procedure lost on the average approximately 13 pounds, whereas women who were not exposed to this treatment lost an average of only 1 pound. Forty-six weeks after completion of the treatment program, five of the six women still showed some weight loss but not as much as after conditioning. Thus the use of noxious smells when paired with the favorite foods eventually made these foods less desirable.

ditioning the emphasis is placed on the association between the CS and US, that is, on the temporal arrangements between the two stimuli. Although this learning model appears to be relatively simple, it would be erroneous to dismiss classical conditioning as unimportant to learning in higher organisms, because it is the mechanism through which many of our responses of fear, anxiety, or pleasure are acquired.

PRINCIPLES OF OPERANT CONDITIONING

Only a small part of an organism's behavior consists of involuntary responses elicited by particular stimuli. Much of the behavior of animals as well as humans is voluntary. At the beginning of this chapter, we made the distinction between respondent and operant behavior. As you recall, we stated that operant behavior produces consequences for the organism. To explain the complex interplay of voluntary responses and their consequences that characterize our natural environment, we need to introduce the second major model of learning known as **operant,** or **instrumental, conditioning.**

B. F. Skinner used pigeons as experimental subjects in his investigations of operant conditioning. (© *Ken Heyman*)

The discovery of operant conditioning is often attributed to Thorndike (1898), who attempted to investigate how specific responses become linked with specific stimuli. After conducting numerous experiments with animals, Thorndike concluded that the development of connections between stimulus and response resulted from a process of trial and error. Thorndike's most significant contribution to learning was his formulation of the **law of effect,** which states that the future frequency of a response is related to its past consequences. In other words, the law of effect stresses the learner's efforts being followed by success. Thorndike's trial-and-error learning was a form of operant conditioning, and many of Thorndike's ideas have been carried much further in the work of B. F. Skinner, who is credited with the development of the fundamental principles of operant conditioning.

B. F. Skinner, one of the most prominent contemporary psychologists, originally wanted to become a writer. After graduation from high school, he built himself a study in the attic of his parents' home and tried to write. The experience was a total disaster and was later referred to by Skinner as his "dark year." Looking for alternative ways of studying human behavior, Skinner took up formal study of psychology.

In the laboratory Skinner used the law of effect to develop operant-conditioning procedures. Taking a radical position, Skinner believed that theoretical abstractions are unnecessary in explaining behavior (Skinner, 1972). He relied entirely upon accurate descriptions of behavior and of the relations between behavior and measurable variables. His prime concern was first to predict behavior accurately and then to modify it.

Skinner's early success was due in part to the development of an ingeniously simple piece of laboratory apparatus, the Skinner box. It consists of a soundproof chamber, with a lever mounted on one wall near a food tray. The lever is connected to the food storage, and the laboratory animal has to learn to manipulate it. By pressing the lever, the animal activates a mechanism that dispenses food pellets into the tray. The floor of the apparatus may be electrified to study the effects of electric shock. This highly automated device avoids laboratory drudgery since it requires little or no active participation by the experimenter once the animal is placed inside the box. Skinner also used a similar apparatus designed for pigeons. Instead of the lever it has a key that can change colors. Both devices restrict the experimental animal to a relatively small amount of space.

Behavior in the Skinner box is recorded by a cumulative recorder outside the box. The **cumulative record** is made with a pen that leaves a continuous line on a roll of paper moving at a constant speed. Each time the animal presses the lever or pecks the color key, the pen records the response. If the animal responds quickly, the resulting curve is steep. If responding is slow, the slope of the curve is more gradual.

In *The Shaping of a Behaviorist* Skinner (1979) described the upbringing of his daughter Deborah, who was raised in a scientific environment modeled after the Skinner box. The "baby tender," as it is called, is a crib-sized box with sound-absorbing walls and a large picture window. A thermostat keeps the temperature constant, and moist air is piped through the floor.

Although Skinner admitted that the baby tender would have been an ideal apparatus for experimentation, he actually conducted few experiments with his daughter. He did, however, record some of Deborah's early motor activities inside the tender.

Since Skinner was convinced that the baby tender was the ideal environment for infants, he embarked on an ambitious campaign to market it commercially under the label "heir conditioner." In 1945 he received some publicity when the *Ladies' Home Journal* published his article under the unfortunate title "Baby in a Box." Inevitably criticism arose. Many people compared the baby tender with the Skinner box for pigeons and rats, assuming that the infant was just another experimental subject like a laboratory animal. Others accused Skinner of misusing an innocent child in the name of science. Although we cannot assess the effects of being raised in a highly controlled early environment such as the baby tender, we do know that this experience did not have the harmful effects many people had feared. Today Deborah is an accomplished artist who lives in London with her husband.

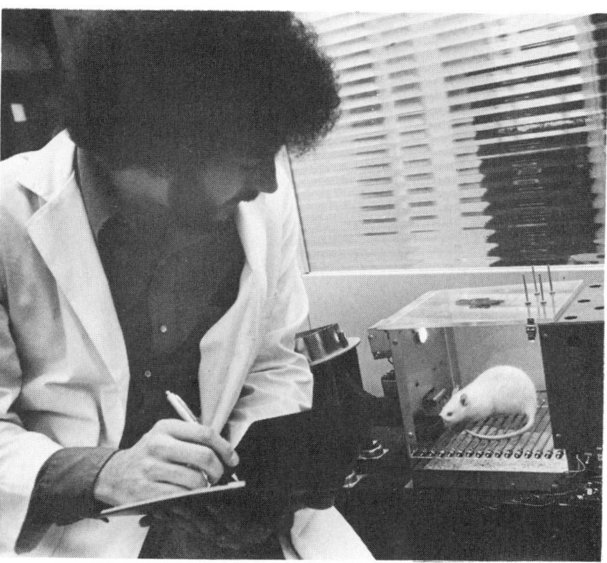

An experimental psychologist studies the behavior of a mouse in a Skinner box. *(© Sybil Shelton/Monkmeyer Press Photo Service)*

The Operant-Conditioning Model

The basic procedure in operant conditioning is very simple. When the laboratory animal is placed in the Skinner box, it will engage in exploratory behavior and in doing so accidentally depress the lever. The depression of the bar activates the food-dispensing mechanism that delivers food pellets.

In this experiment food serves as a reward, or **reinforcement,** for the operant response.

Behavior is said to be operant when it can be modified by its consequences. The response is termed operant because it "operates" on the environment to produce the reinforcing event. As mentioned earlier, operant behavior is said to be emitted rather than elicited. For learning to take place in operant conditioning, a response must be emitted and then followed by a reinforcer.

Looking back at Linda's case, the teacher whose procedures were described at the opening of this chapter, let us identify the basic components of operant conditioning. Linda was concerned with establishing appropriate classroom behavior; she wanted her pupils to stay in their seats, face her, and pay attention to her or work on their assignments. Any of these types of behavior constitutes a response that has to be emitted in order to earn one of the prizes. The prizes represent the reinforcing stimuli, which will be delivered only if students respond appropriately.

The fundamental principle in operant conditioning, then, is the notion that behavior is governed by its consequences. We do not behave in a random fashion but to bring about certain desired objectives.

Reinforcement

The key concept in operant conditioning is reinforcement. Whereas classical conditioning is concerned with the association between two stimuli, operant conditioning deals with the association between a response and its consequences, i.e., reinforcement. Learning theorists distinguish between two types of reinforcement: primary and secondary. A **primary reinforcer** is usually a stimulus that a deprived organism will approach, such as food for a hungry animal or water for a thirsty one. Primary reinforcers typically interact directly with the physiological state of the organism.

A **secondary reinforcer** is a stimulus that reinforces because it was initially associated with a primary reinforcer. Secondary reinforcers do not have intrinsic reinforcing properties; their reinforcing values are learned through experience. Money is a good example of a secondary reinforcer. Of no intrinsic value itself, money gains reinforcing properties because it allows us to take care of basic necessities of life, such as shelter and food. Similarly, stock-market quotations are a list of dull numbers for some people, but these numbers can be extremely reinforcing for the skilled investor.

Our daily lives are filled with examples of secondary reinforcement. We work for money to meet our basic needs or for the pleasure derived from doing a job well; we write or paint because creating something new is a rewarding experience; we maintain physical fitness and a good appearance because these things bring us social approval. Praise, warmth, smiles, attention, money, and free time are reinforcing for most people, children as well as adults. The concept of secondary reinforcement, then, allows for a wide range of learning experiences to occur.

As we have seen, responses that are closely followed in time by reinforcing consequences are likely to recur. This reinforcement is as important for the maintenance as for the learning of behavior. Initially Linda reinforced her deserving pupils every 15 minutes. Then the interval between reinforcers became progressively longer, from 30 minutes to several days. Skinner would say that these pupils were on a **schedule of reinforcement.**

Schedules of reinforcement allow the experimenter to control the rate of responding. In all schedules of reinforcement, of course, reinforcement is not delivered until the desired response occurs. Rewarding an organism for every desired response is known as **continuous reinforcement.** Under continuous reinforcement an organism acquires a new response very rapidly. In most real-life situations, however, we do not receive reinforcement every time we make an appropriate response. Reinforcement on some occasions and not on others is an **intermittent schedule of reinforcement.** Under this schedule the rate of acquisition of a new response is much slower than under a continuous schedule.

A simple type of intermittent schedule is a **fixed-ratio schedule.** In this schedule the experimenter determines a fixed number of responses that must occur before reinforcement is delivered. For example, if a fixed ratio of 5:1 is chosen for a Skinner-box experiment, the animal has to depress the lever five times for every reward. In a **variable-ratio schedule,** the ratio of responses to rewards can be determined in the long run through averaging but is unpredictable in the short run. The rat in the Skinner box might average one reward for each five responses, but these rewards could come in any pattern, not simply one for each group of five responses. Examples of variable-ratio schedules are found in gambling or other games of chance. Since variable-ratio schedules are only predictable in the long run, they are likely to result in high rates of responding to maximize the certainty of reinforcement.

Ratio schedules provide reinforcement after a certain number of responses occur. In interval schedules the delivery of reinforcement is defined in terms of time instead of the number of responses. On a **fixed-interval schedule,** reinforcement depends on the passage of a set period of time. An example in the everyday world is the wage earner who receives reinforcement—wages—for work performed at the end of every week. Similarly, students receive feedback and reinforcement from their teachers when the weekly assignment is handed back marked. Since reinforcement is defined in terms of time, it makes no difference on interval schedules how rapidly the response occurs. For that reason, interval schedules generally produce slower rates of responding than ratio schedules. Usually the rate of responding is very slow immediately after reinforcement and then gradually increases as the time for the next rein-

Gambling produces unpredictable short-term results characteristic of a variable-ratio schedule of reinforcement. *(© Dan Brinzac/Peter Arnold, Inc.)*

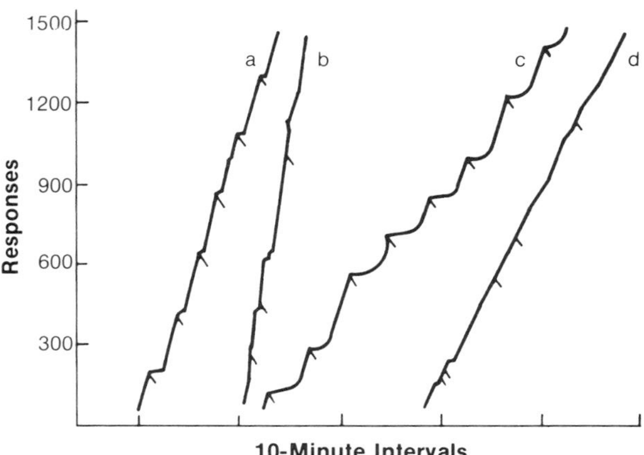

Figure 5–4. Cumulative records produced by four schedules of reinforcement: (a) fixed ratio, 200 responses per reinforcement; (b) variable ratio, 100 responses per reinforcement; (c) fixed interval, 4 minutes; (d) variable interval, 3 minutes. (Adapted from *Ferster and Skinner, 1957.*)

forcement approaches. As a result, the cumulative record of a fixed-interval schedule shows the characteristic scalloped pattern depicted in curve c in Figure 5–4. You may find that you follow this pattern if you examine your study habits. Immediately after a test, especially if you earned a good grade, you do little studying, but the rate increases as the next test date approaches and probably reaches a peak immediately before the next examination.

Another schedule of reinforcement that depends on the passage of time is the **variable-interval schedule.** Under this schedule the time between reinforcements varies. Since the time interval between reinforcements is unpredictable, it is not easy to learn the nature of this relationship. As a result, responding occurs at a much steadier rate than under a fixed-interval schedule, although there is some tendency to respond more slowly immediately after reinforcement. As an example of a variable-interval schedule in the real world, consider the behavior of many parents in response to the cries of young children. These parents may attend to the child immediately or let the child fuss for a while before giving it attention. On different occasions variable time intervals pass before the child can command the attention of the parent.

In Figure 5–4 typical cumulative records of the four schedules of reinforcement that we discussed are shown. As can be seen, ratio schedules generally produce faster rates of responding than interval schedules.

Superstitious Behavior

Skinner (1948) trained food-deprived pigeons to eat grain from a feeder that dispensed it at regular intervals irrespective of what the pigeons were doing. At the time the grain was delivered, the bird was typically making some random response, such as pecking at the floor, turning around in the cage, or tossing its head about. As the result of the first accidental reinforcement of the pigeon's idiosyncratic response, it was likely to be doing that same activity again at the time of the next food delivery. Eventually learning became the result of a vicious cycle—the more reinforcement the random, stereotyped response received, the greater the likelihood of its recurrence. All experimental animals developed some stereotyped pattern of behavior, although the particular activity varied from pigeon to pigeon.

Skinner labeled this phenomenon **superstitious behavior** because some response totally irrelevant to the reinforcing event is strengthened by being accidentally paired with the reinforcement. Superstitious behavior is not restricted to laboratory animals. Athletes often have stereotyped ways of performing. A basketball player, for instance, may bounce the ball five times before taking a free throw. Or a baseball pitcher may rub the ball before winding up for a pitch. You can probably identify some of your own superstitious behavior. In most cases, the more often a successful performance reinforces the stereotyped response, the more strongly the person attributes his or her success to it, even though it did not contribute at all.

Latent Learning

One of the most important theoretical issues in operant conditioning involves the question of reinforcement as a necessary condition for learning. Learning that takes place in the absence of reinforcement is called **latent learning.** The now classic experiment in latent learning was conducted by Tolman and Honzik (1930), who ran three groups of rats in a complex maze illustrated at the left in Figure 5–5. One group was trained over a two-week period with food always found at the correct goal arm of the maze. The graph in Figure 5–5 shows the expected gradual reduction of errors as this group learned the most efficient route to the goal. The second group was allowed to run freely through the maze, but without any reinforcement. As expected, the animals in this group showed no preference for the unreinforced goal arm. To see whether reinforcement was actually necessary for learning, the experimenters took a third group of rats and let them run through the maze for the first 10 days without reinforcement. As can be seen from Figure 5–5, up to that point their performance matched that of the second group, showing no apparent learning. On the eleventh day, however, the correct arm of the maze was reinforced with food. The results were dramatic: by the next training session, the performance of the third group matched and even slightly surpassed the performance of group one, which had been reinforced from the very beginning. Clearly, the third group must have learned something about the maze during the first 10 days without reinforcement. In Tolman's terms, the rats learned a cognitive map of the maze, an integrated representation including not only the chain of events that leads from the start to the goal box but also the chain that leads into various blind alleys and thus to no food.

For Tolman and others this experiment implied that learning can take place in the absence of re-

Figure 5–5. Latent Learning. Tolman and Honzik sent three groups of rats through a maze similar to the one below, containing both curtains and one-way doors. One group never received food at the goal box, and one group always did. The group of principal interest was not reinforced until the eleventh day, after which it was continually reinforced until the end of the experiment. (Source: E. C. Tolman and C. H. Honzik, Introduction and removal of reward and maze performance in rats. *University of California Publications in Psychology*, vol. 4, fig. 4, 267. Published in 1930 by the Regents of the University of California.)

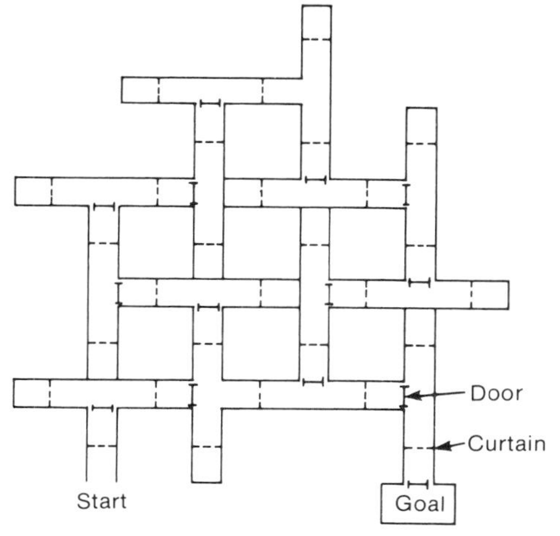

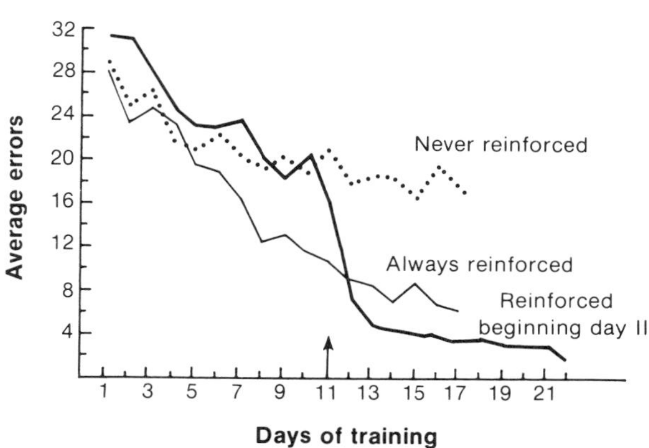

inforcement. This learning does not manifest itself in performance; it is only when reinforcement is introduced that we are able to see what has been learned. Latent learning was a controversial issue at first because it implied that we need to make a distinction between learning and performance. Gradually, however, latent learning faded as a critical experimental issue.

Extinction and Spontaneous Recovery

Extinction in operant conditioning simply involves nonreinforcement of a previously reinforced response. Withholding reinforcement sooner or later leads to a reduction in the frequency of responding until the subject completely ceases to respond. Other things being equal, the past history of reinforcement determines how rapidly the behavior is extinguished. Behavior reinforced on a continuous schedule extinguishes most rapidly. If you are accustomed to your radio's playing every time you turn it on, you will soon put it aside if nothing happens when you try to play it. Responses reinforced on intermittent schedules extinguish more slowly. Fishermen, for instance, may cast for hours even though no fish bites. Since most learned behavior in our environment is maintained by intermittent reinforcement, it often takes consistent nonreinforcement to eliminate them from our behavior.

Tennis lessons involve the shaping of behavior. *(© Ken Karp Photography)*

As in the case of classical conditioning, if the operant-conditioning subject is returned to the test chamber, the experimental response may reappear, producing the familiar phenomenon of spontaneous recovery. Psychiatric patients, for instance, who had their maladaptive behavior extinguished and replaced with more socially acceptable forms, still revert occasionally to their inappropriate behavior.

Shaping

Skinner (1953) stated that operant conditioning shapes behavior as a sculptor shapes a lump of clay. By using the method of **successive approximations** it is possible to train an animal to come closer and closer to the desired response. Suppose our food-deprived pigeon is back in the experimental chamber, where it tends to explore the environment. Typically the pigeon will pick at various objects, and sooner or later it discovers the food tray. Since the key the bird is to peck is located above the food tray, the bird is rewarded at first for remaining close to the food tray and approaching the key. On successive trials reinforcement is delivered only when the pigeon brings its beak close to the key. During further trials reinforcement becomes dependent on touching the key. By rewarding successive approximations to the desired response, the experimenter is able to shape it, even though the operant level of that response was initially low.

Shaping is a step-by-step process in which better and better approximations are required if reinforcement is to occur. Thus the reinforcement contingency is shifted closer and closer to the desired response. Suppose your tennis coach wants to improve your backhand stroke. At first the coach may positively reinforce you by expressing his or her approval for a clumsy version of the desired stroke. After several attempts the coach becomes more demanding and does not praise you unless you have improved the quality of your stroke a bit. This process of differential reinforcement, praising you when you come a little closer to the correct stroke and withholding approval if your stroke does not improve, is continued until the correct response is established or shaped.

Generalization and Discrimination

Suppose a pigeon has learned to peck the key in the Skinner box in the presence of a 500-Hz tone. If the experimenter varies the intensity of the tone over a range of values, say from 200 Hz to 700 Hz, the pigeon continues to peck the key. This phenomenon, as we have seen, is stimulus generalization, the process by which an organism responds to stimuli similar to the original stimulus but not specifically paired with reinforcement. Generalization in operant conditioning, as in classical conditioning, is facilitated by the degree of similarity between the original test stimulus and the subsequent stimuli. Our trained pigeon will respond to tones of varying degrees of intensity, but it is unlikely that the bird will generalize the response to a series of lights.

In operant conditioning our ability to respond to a range of similar stimuli serves many adaptive purposes. This is readily apparent when children respond to a teacher's affection like they would to that of a parent. An example of stimulus generalization in a psychiatric hospital was reported by Bennett and Maley (1973), who reinforced psychiatric patients for conversing with one another in daily 30-minute sessions. The amount of talking among the patients not only increased markedly during the experimental sessions but also generalized to the ward. Stimulus generalization is important because although training may take place in a restricted setting (institution, special classroom, hospital, day-care center, home), it is desirable that the types of behavior developed in these settings generalize or transfer to other settings (Kazdin & Bootzin, 1972).

Complete generalization, however, is not always adaptive; it can prevent us from learning new responses. Overgeneralization may be illustrated by the following letter, which appeared in the advice column of a local newspaper.

> Dear Abby:
>
> When my girlfriend fixed me up with a blind date, I should have known that he could not be trusted the minute he walked into my apartment in his bow tie. Nevertheless I fell head over heels in love with him. We started dating but he lied to me and cheated on me like all men who wear bow ties. This has happened to me every time I got involved with a man wearing bow ties. To help other girls not to fall into the same trap, please print a letter warning them about men who wear bow ties.
>
> Against Bow Ties
>
> Dear Against:
>
> It has been my experience that many men in bow ties are perfectly trustworthy individuals. Because of your experience with them you should not condemn all men wearing bow ties.

Many of our cultural stereotypes, such as that the English are reserved and proper, the French are good lovers, or the Italians are unpredictable in temperament, are based on overgeneralizations that have little basis in reality.

Like stimulus generalization, stimulus discrimination also occurs in both classical and operant conditioning. Let us look at a laboratory example of stimulus discrimination in operant conditioning. Suppose a pigeon is placed in a Skinner apparatus in which the key can be made two different colors. Initially the pigeon will peck both colors indiscriminately. To train for discrim-

APPLICATION

Uses of Operant Conditioning to Modify Human Behavior

Operant-conditioning principles have been applied in a variety of complex, practical situations. Academic skills have been acquired through operant conditioning, and disruptive classroom behavior has been reduced by using negative reinforcement. Skinner (1970) described a utopian community, Walden Two, that operates on the principle of positive reinforcement.

One of the most effective applications of operant principles has been the use of the **token economy.** A token is an object that can be exchanged for items or activities of value. Token economies are based on contingent reinforcement, that is, tokens are rewarded when the behavior is satisfactory and withheld when it is unsatisfactory.

One of the earliest token programs involved psychiatric patients (Ayllon & Azrin, 1965). Patients on the ward could earn tokens for various activities, such as making their beds, cleaning dishes or the floor, grooming other patients, or participating in housekeeping or secretarial duties. They could also earn tokens for self-care. The tokens could be exchanged for a large number of back-up reinforcers. A back-up reinforcer might be actual goods, such as food or cigarettes, or it might be a privilege, such as watching television or visiting a friend. The dramatic effect of tokens in this early token economy is illustrated in Figure 5–6. When the tokens were eliminated, job performance dropped drastically, indicating that the presentation and withholding of token reinforcement controlled patient performance.

After the work of Ayllon and Azrin, token economies were implemented not only in psychiatric wards but also in classrooms, prisons, homes, and organizations. Token programs have been employed successfully with students at all levels, juvenile delinquents, adult offenders, drug addicts, and problem drinkers. They are effective in modifying a wide range of behavior, including social withdrawal, aggression, self-help, study, academic achievement, and disruption of classrooms. Sachs (1975) employed social and token reinforcement for diverse types of behavior with residents of a nursing home. Other investigators (Libb & Clements, 1969) used token reinforcement to develop exercise in geriatric patients with chronic brain disorders.

With the exception of psychoactive drugs (see Chapter 3), no other innovation has so dramatically affected the policies and organization of our institutions (Kazdin, 1977a). Token economies are set up so that recipients can spend tokens any way they

ination, reinforcement is delivered only for pecking when the key is green, but not when it is red. A stimulus whose presence is associated with reinforcement is referred to as an S^D; in our case, it is the green key. A stimulus whose presence is associated with nonreinforcement is referred to as an S^Δ (S delta). After a number of nonreinforced responses following the presentation of the red key, the pigeon quickly learns to peck only the green key. At this point, we say the pigeon has learned a discrimination.

There are many examples of discriminative control of behavior in everyday life. Crossing an intersection when the light is green but not red, eating differently at home than in an expensive restaurant, or behaving one way with one's coworkers and another with the boss are instances that readily demonstrate the value of discriminations.

Complex Behavior Sequences: Chaining

Thus far we have discussed relatively simple, single operant responses. But the operant-learning model applies to more complicated forms of behavior as well. The process of linking entire series of operant responses is known as **chaining.** Let us look at examples of this procedure both in the laboratory and in everyday life.

wish. Thus the back-up reinforcers allow for personal preferences.

Despite their successes, token economies have been criticized on several grounds. First, in many institutional settings the behavior learned is relevant only to the particular institution rather than to life in general. In many applications, token economies are implemented in facilities that may contribute to the problems the programs are designed to ameliorate (Kazdin, 1977b). Experience with released patients who had been in a token economy program suggests that behavioral improvement continues only while the environment supports it. In a comprehensive review of token-economy programs, Kazdin and Bootzin (1972) offer the pessimistic conclusion that although token economies have been dramatically effective within the psychiatric hospital, there is little evidence that improvement is maintained outside the institution.

Token economies, like many other behavior-modification techniques, raise important ethical questions. Token economies are a form of behavioral control that potentially jeopardizes the freedom of the participant. Being able to control a person's behavior implies the possibility of manipulating the person. One way of protecting people against coercive behavioral control and manipulation is by making them aware of the factors that control their behavior and the principles upon which such control is based.

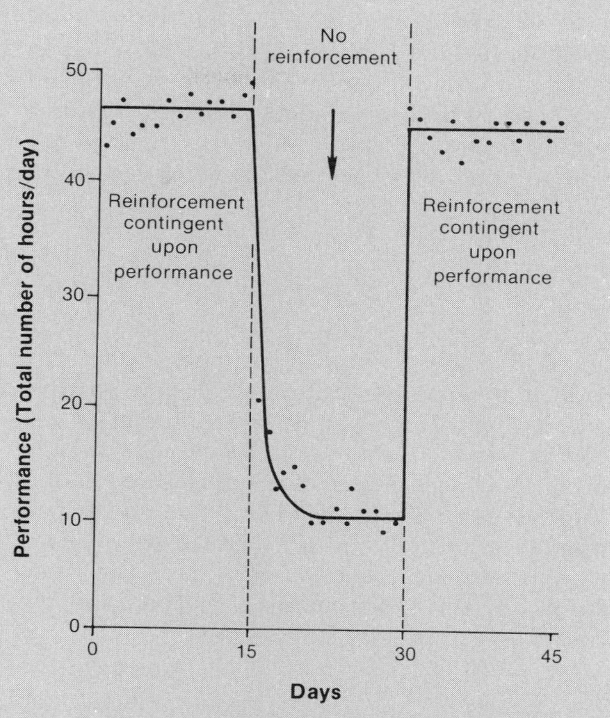

Figure 5–6. Token Economy. Giving or withholding token reinforcement greatly affected behavior. (From Ayllon & Azrin, 1965; Society for the Experimental Analysis of Behavior).

In a typical laboratory experiment, a rat is trained to press the lever when a light is on. When this response is established, a cord is suspended from the ceiling of the Skinner box. To obtain the reinforcement, the animal has to pull the cord, which will turn on the light; in the presence of the light the rat depresses the bar, and this response is followed by reinforcement. If we were to add another link to the chain, we might introduce a small tunnel into the box. The rat would be required to perform the following series of responses: crawl through the tunnel, then pull the chain, then press the bar while the light is on to obtain the food. The last stimulus in the chain is usually a primary reinforcer, while the other stimuli serve as secondary reinforcers for the responses preceding them. Professional animal trainers who teach a bear to dance or a dog to walk on a tightrope use the principle of chaining to establish complex responses.

In humans, chaining accounts for many of the complex types of behavior that we engage in daily. Consider the chain of responses involved in going out to dinner (Reynolds, 1968). The decision to eat out may be initiated by a dinner invitation, a phone call, hunger, or some other event. After the decision has been made, several types of behavior occur in a sequence, including dressing to go out, leaving the house, driving the car, entering the restaurant, ordering the meal, and eating. Note that this chain of responses is relatively fixed in the sense that earlier behavior must precede later behavior. The last response in the chain is ordering the meal, which is reinforced with food. Building response chains requires working backward from the last response in the sequence that precedes reinforcement (Kazdin, 1975).

AVERSIVE CONTROL OF BEHAVIOR

Thus far we have focused our attention primarily on operant responses acquired through positive reinforcement, such as rewards, success, and items of value. In this section we shall examine the consequences of aversive, unpleasant stimuli, or negative reinforcement. These stimuli play an important role in learning, since we are exposed to unpleasant experiences every day. The three approaches to aversive control of behavior involve avoidance, escape, and punishment.

Avoidance

Avoidance conditioning involves the presentation of an aversive event, which is signaled by a discriminative stimulus. The subject has the opportunity to avoid or prevent the recurrence of the event by responding to the discriminative stimulus.

Many laboratory experiments of avoidance conditioning use a shuttle box as the basic experimental apparatus and electric shock as the aversive stimulus. The shuttle box consists of a chamber with two compartments, the floor of which has an electrified grid. The animal, usually a rat, is placed in one compartment with the door between the two compartments closed. Then a tone or light (the discriminative stimulus) comes on, and the door between the two compartments opens. Shortly thereafter, the electric shock is delivered through the grid floor. During the first trials the subject attempts to escape the shock by running into the opposite compartment, where there is no shock. Sooner or later, however, the animal learns to avoid the shock altogether by crossing over to the safe compartment while the light or tone is on.

Mowrer (1947) proposed one of the first and most popular theories of avoidance, suggesting that both classical and operant conditioning (hence called the **two-factor theory**) are involved in avoidance learning. During the early learning trials, before the subject learns to make the avoidance response of crossing into the safe compartment, classical conditioning occurs. The aversive stimulus (shock) serves as the unconditioned stimulus that elicits the unconditioned fear response. The conditioned stimulus (tone or light), through repeated pairing with the aversive event, develops the capacity to elicit the conditioned fear response. This is a clear example of classical conditioning.

The next step, according to Mowrer, is the acquisition of the avoidance response, which is learned through operant conditioning. The avoidance response reduces fear and is therefore reinforced by this fear reduction. The classically conditioned fear state and the operantly conditioned avoidance response combined are thus responsible for avoidance behavior. Put another way, Mowrer's theory suggests that the avoidance response is acquired through the reduction of conditioned fear.

Although the two-factor theory seems to provide a plausible explanation for avoidance learning, the theory has come under heavy attack. Several empirical investigations (e.g., Bolles, 1970, 1978) found conflicting results regarding the relationship between the classically conditioned fear response and the operantly conditioned avoidance response. For example, Bolles argued that neither escape nor the termination of the light or tone (the conditioned stimulus as stated above) are necessary for the establishment of avoidance behavior. According to Bolles, if a particular avoidance response is to be acquired, it must be a species-specific defense reaction, such as fleeing, freezing, and fighting. For example, a gazelle does not flee from a lion because it fears the lion's bite: it does so because running away from any approaching large object is one of its species-specific defense reactions. Thus Bolles's interpretation of avoidance learning rests on the importance of the avoidance response: in order for an avoidance response to be rapidly learned in a given situation, it must be an effective species-specific defense reaction in that situation.

Avoidance responses are very resistant to extinction. Solomon and his co-workers (Solomon, Kamin, & Wynne, 1953; Solomon & Wynne, 1954) reported that once an animal made a single successful response, it would persist for hundreds of trials, even in the absence of the aversive stimuli. That is, the response was essentially nonextinguishable unless special procedures were used. One procedure, called flooding, introduced a glass barrier at the hurdle dogs had to jump to get from one compartment into the other (Baum, 1971). At first, the dogs crashed into the glass barrier, but eventually they were forced into learning that the discriminative stimulus was no longer followed by shock in the "dangerous" compartment.

All of us are familiar with many common varieties of avoidance behavior: the child who stays away from hot stoves to avoid getting burned, the driver who obeys traffic signals to avoid automobile accidents, the beach lover who uses tanning lotion to avoid sunburns, the student who studies hard to avoid failure. Each day we all expend considerable effort to avoid painful or unpleasant experiences.

As in the laboratory, avoidance responses in real life are not extinguished easily, and often counseling or psychotherapy is necessary to extinguish them. Patterson (1965) reported the case of a seven-year-old boy named Karl who would not stay in school (avoidance response). During therapy a doll-play situation was used in which the male doll "enacted" situations that were problematic for Karl, such as going to school. Karl was asked questions about the doll such as "Is he afraid to leave his mother?" The child was rewarded with praise and candy whenever he indicated that the doll had little difficulty going places. After ten sessions a similar procedure was repeated at the school. Within a few weeks Karl was in school full time, attending with no apparent fear.

Escape

In **escape conditioning** the subject cannot avoid the noxious stimulus but can terminate it by making the appropriate response. A rat in the shuttle box will actively seek to escape the shock during the first trials by random movements such as running or leaping. Accidentally it will hit the bar, and this response is reinforced by the termination of the shock. Once the animal learns the relationship between pressing the bar and its consequences, the escape response tends to occur much sooner on subsequent trials.

Familiar examples in everyday life are leaving the house to escape from an argument with your spouse or roommate, closing the window to escape from the street noise, or taking medication to escape pain.

Figure 5–7. Using the shuttle box for escape conditioning.

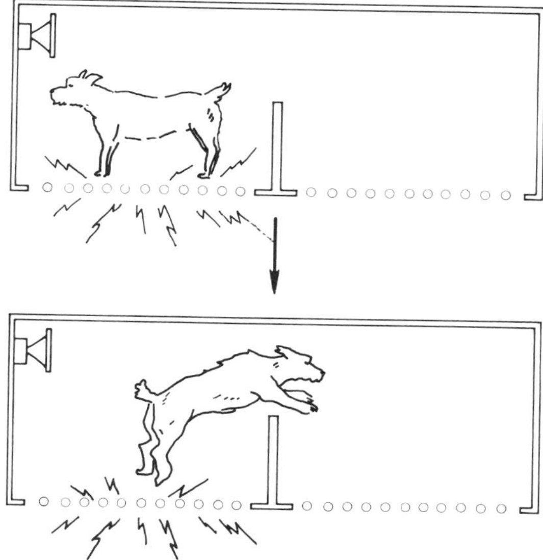

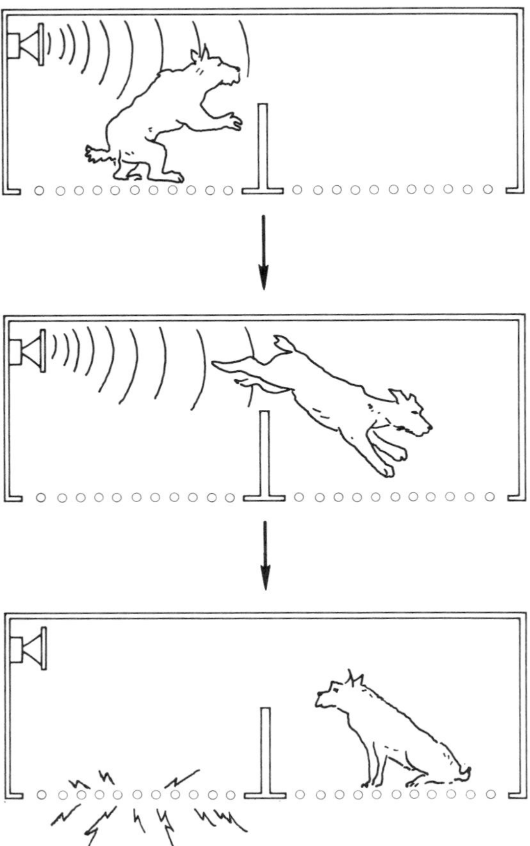

Figure 5–8. Using the shuttle box for avoidance conditioning.

Avoidance conditioning and escape conditioning are easily confused. The major difference between the two is that in escape conditioning the subject makes a response that terminates a noxious stimulus *after* it has been experienced (see Figure 5–7). In avoidance conditioning the subject makes a response that terminates a potential stimulus *before* it has been experienced. The subject learns to avoid the aversive event altogether (see Figure 5–8). If you are caught in the rain (aversive event), you can escape it by running under some shelter. You can avoid getting caught in the rain in the first place by seeking shelter when dark clouds signal the coming rain.

Punishment

Punishment is a learning procedure in which responses are followed by aversive events in an attempt to decrease their frequency. The most characteristic feature of punishment is to reduce, at least temporarily, the strength of the response that is being punished.

Both punishment and negative reinforcement are aversive events. Negative reinforcement refers to the removal of a noxious stimulus, which has the effect of *increasing* the probability of a response being performed. In escape conditioning, the shock can be called the negative reinforcer. When the lever is pressed, the shock is turned off, and this increases the likelihood of the animal's pressing the lever on later occasions. In contrast, punishment refers to the presentation of a noxious stimulus that *decreases* the probability of the occurrence of the response. For example, if our laboratory animal received a shock when it pressed the lever, this would be called punishment since it would reduce the likelihood of the animal's pressing the lever on subsequent occasions.

A variety of punishments can be used to decrease undesirable behavior. Spanking, reprimands, threats, or humiliation are relatively common means of suppressing behavior. Punishment can also take the form of removing a positive event after an inappropriate response has been made. Time-out and cost-contingency are two punishment techniques involving the withdrawal of reinforcers.

Time-out refers to a temporary withdrawal of all positive reinforcers. In many applied settings time-out is physically accomplished by isolating the person in a special room that is devoid of all objects or situations, including social contacts with peers. Younger children may be requested to go to the time-out room for three to five minutes; for older children and adults, the time is longer. Time-out has been effective in decelerating or eliminating various types of undesirable behavior, including hitting and temper tantrums.

Cost contingencies, or fines, refer to the withdrawal of reinforcers that have already been earned. In a cost-contingency program with psychotic patients, for instance, fines were levied whenever the patients violated a rule of the ward (Upper, 1973). Transgressions of patients included getting up late in the morning, undressing or exposing oneself, shouting, sleeping in unauthorized areas, and neglecting personal hygiene. Whenever one of these rules was broken, the patients received a ticket indicating that a predetermined amount was subtracted from their earnings. As a result of this cost-contingency program, violations of the ward rules dropped very rapidly.

All of us are familiar with everyday applications of cost contingencies: parents withhold privileges such as watching television to alter disruptive behavior of their children in the home; taxpayers are charged late fees for filing their income tax after the due date; or pupils have to give up minutes from recess for inappropriate classroom behavior (Kazdin, 1972).

In contrast to time-out, there is no fixed time during which positive reinforcers are not available in cost contingencies. The interval between the occurrence of the undesirable behavior and the payment of the fine should be relatively short; otherwise the procedure may be rendered ineffective. Also, feedback procedures should be set up so that the person knows exactly which type of inappropriate behavior resulted in the fine. More serious transgressions should be subject to heavier fines than milder transgressions.

An important factor in punishment is the intensity and duration of the aversive event. Generally the more intensive the punishment and the longer its duration, the greater will be the suppression of the response. Behavior that is pun-

Cost contingencies effectively alter behavior by taking away previously earned reinforcers, such as money. *(© Paul S. Conklin/Monkmeyer Press Photo Service)*

ished on every occurrence is most reliably reduced. Very intensive punishment can completely eliminate a type of behavior, while weak punishment may have little or no effect. As most of us know, mild forms of punishment are often not very effective and even some of the more severe forms of punishment such as incarceration for an adult do not always produce the desired results.

Punishment is most effective when it is delivered immediately after the occurrence of the undesirable behavior. A mother's threat, "Just wait until your father gets home tonight and he will give you a good spanking," does little to suppress the target response in the child. The longer the delay between the undesirable response and the punishment, the less likely the person will be to associate the two events with one another.

When punishment is necessary, it should be used with care. For parents who rely heavily on punishment to discipline their children, learning theorists call attention to the possible side effects of punishment. Punishment may arouse anger in the child and can promote a counterattack. Punishment can also teach the child to avoid or escape from the punisher, thereby lessening the influence the adult has over the youngster.

When using punishment with children it is also important to specify the rules before the undesirable behavior occurs. Parents are also cautioned not merely to threaten the child but to carry through with the consequence the first time, and every time, the deviant behavior occurs to assure its eventual suppression. And finally it is important for the punisher to make sure that the consequence is unpleasant enough for the child to stop the inappropriate behavior rather than risk the consequences. For example, a child may behave so aggressively in school that he or she is sent home. In this case the aversive event, being sent home, will do little to suppress the child's fighting in school. Punishment is probably most effective when it is coupled with positive reinforcement for alternate responses (Azrin & Holz, 1966). For example, in teaching language to retarded children, instructors have used mild shock for incorrect responses combined with token reinforcement for correct responses (Kirchner, Pear, & Martin, 1971). Many experiments involving punishment include reinforcement of appropriate behavior to maximize behavior change.

To evaluate the effectiveness of punishment, we need to know about the person's previous history of reinforcement, the kinds of behavior he or she has typically been punished for, and what punishments have been used. Unless we can specify these conditions, it is difficult to predict the effects of punishment with any degree of accuracy.

CLASSICAL AND OPERANT CONDITIONING COMPARED

We now need to ask whether classical and operant conditioning produce entirely different or similar types of learning. As we have seen, the procedures involved are rather different. In classical conditioning a conditioned stimulus is presented in contiguity with an unconditioned stimulus, which elicits a reflexive unconditioned response prior to any learning. In operant conditioning reinforcement is presented following the performance of some response. If learning is to take place in operant situations, a response must first be emitted and then followed by a reinforcer. In classical conditioning, by contrast, a stimulus-response connection must exist, and responses are said to be elicited. Classical conditioning involves reflexes and the autonomic nervous system, while operant conditioning usually involves voluntary responses and the somatic nervous system.

It has often been claimed that operant conditioning depends solely on reinforcement, whereas classical conditioning does not. This is a misleading statement. As early as 1937 Skinner noted that in both conditioning procedures reinforcement is utilized but administered in a different sequence. In classical conditioning the unconditioned stimulus (food) serves the function of the reinforcer, and it *precedes* the conditioned response. In operant conditioning reinforcement *follows* the response since the reward is contingent on the oc-

CRITICAL ISSUE

Limitations of the Laws of Learning: Preparedness

Since the discovery of classical- and operant-conditioning principles, psychologists have hoped to discover general laws of learning in the simple, controlled world of levers and mechanical feeders, of metronomes and salivation (Seligman, 1970). Seligman, however, suggests that biological constraints may limit the acquisition of certain responses in certain organisms. He argues that preparedness may be one of these constraints, i.e., some responses are innately better prepared to be modified than others. The notion of preparedness implies that every organism is programmed by the evolution of its species to associate a given response with a certain outcome. In other words, certain responses are learned very easily, whereas others are almost impossible to condition. Laboratory rats, for instance, require a considerable amount of training to learn to depress a lever to avoid electric shock. The animal's instinctual response in this situation is to flee or fight, a response called a species-specific defense reaction (Bolles, 1970). In a biological sense, pigeons are prepared to learn pecking or pigs to learn rooting. As humans, we are probably prepared to learn language (Chomsky, 1972; see Chapter 7).

At one end of the preparedness continuum, then, we have behavior for which the organism is innately prepared. At the other end are responses for which the organism is, in Seligman's terminology, contraprepared—that is, the organism's biology or sensory apparatus is such that these behaviors are extremely difficult if not impossible to learn. Seligman suggests that most behavior falls around the middle of the continuum, meaning that the organism is essentially unprepared but can learn the responses with moderate difficulty. In the prepared category biological aspects facilitate learning, whereas in the contraprepared category biology places constraints on learning. In a sense, then, the preparedness continuum is an ease-of-learning dimension. A contingency that is very easy to learn for one organism (a pigeon pecking a key for food) may be impossible to learn for another organism (a cat).

The concept of preparedness presents a challenge for learning theorists who believe in general laws of learning because it implies that the laws of learning, whether classical or operant, may vary with the preparedness of the organism. Seligman suggests that before learning theorists can formulate general laws of learning, they must first investigate the extent to which organisms are prepared or contraprepared to learn certain classes of responses.

currence of the response. Another way of looking at the differences in the manipulation of reinforcement is to note that in classical conditioning reinforcement is independent of the subject's response (since the unconditioned and the conditioned responses are always paired), whereas in operant conditioning the subject must make the response first in order to obtain the reinforcement.

Another difference between the two procedures is that in classical conditioning the relationship between the conditioned and the unconditioned stimulus produces the conditioned response. In operant conditioning the important relationship is between the response and its consequences, that is, the reinforcing event that follows the response.

Classical conditioning is a more passive form of learning in the sense that the unconditioned stimulus occurs independent of the behavior of the organism and it elicits the response. In operant conditioning the organism is active and has to initiate a response because reinforcement is contingent upon the occurrence of the response.

Finally, if we look at the types of behavior people learn through the two models of learning, we note that many of our emotional responses, such

Table 5–1. Model of Conditioning

	Classical Conditioning	*Operant Conditioning*
1. Assumption	A stimulus must precede a response; if there is no stimulus, there will be no response; stimuli elicit responses.	The emphasis is on responses that operate on the environment to produce consequences; responses are emitted.
2. Type of response	Involuntary reflexes.	Voluntary behavior.
3. Reinforcement	Reinforcement precedes the response because it is temporally associated with a stimulus.	Reinforcement follows the response because it is contingent upon the occurrence of the response.
4. Subject-environment relationship	Importance of what the environment does *for* the subject.	Importance of what the subject does *to* the environment.
5. Basis of learning	Conditioned stimulus-unconditioned stimulus pairings; contiguity of stimuli.	Response-reinforcing stimulus pairings; consequences of responding.

as feelings, attitudes, and fears, are acquired through classical conditioning, whereas operant conditioning is involved in most of our goal-seeking behavior where we operate actively on our environment. The major differences between classical and operant conditioning are summarized in Table 5–1 and Figure 5–9.

Although classical and operant conditioning employ dissimilar procedures, they share a number of learning processes, such as extinction, spontaneous recovery, generalization, and discrimination, which tend to produce similar effects attained by different procedures. In order to determine adequately whether the same or different types of learning underlie classical and operant conditioning, more research is needed. Presently many learning theorists and researchers assume that similar learning processes take place in both types of conditioning.

The distinction between classical and operant conditioning has been blurred by a series of experiments conducted by the physiological psychologist Neal Miller and his co-workers (Miller, 1969; DiCara, 1970). Traditionally it had been assumed that involuntary responses, such as heart rate and blood pressure, which are controlled by the autonomic nervous system, can only be modified by classical conditioning. This view assumed that involuntary responses cannot be brought under the control of reinforcing stimuli. In fact, this argument was used to support the notion that classical and operant conditioning represent two different models of learning rather than reflect different manifestations of the same model with different conditions.

Neal Miller, however, argued that there is only one kind of learning and challenged the view that operant learning of visceral responses was impossible. In a remarkable series of experiments, he was able to show that presumably involuntary responses, such as salivation, heart-rate changes, and the rate of urine formation, can be controlled by reward contingencies. Rats were trained, for instance, to increase or decrease their heart rate, to dilate or constrict their blood vessels of the tail, or to dilate the blood vessels in one ear while constricting those of the other ear—all for the reinforcing stimulus of electrical stimulation of the brain.

Recent studies conducted at the Harvard Medical School indicated that human subjects can be trained through feedback and reinforcement to modify their blood pressure. In one experiment male volunteers were conditioned to increase or decrease their blood pressure. Each successful trial was signaled by a flashing light and followed by the reward, a glimpse of a nude pin-up picture.

If visceral responses can be modified by operant-learning techniques, it may be possible to train people with certain psychosomatic disorders to overcome their symptoms. Disorders of heartbeat rhythm have been treated successfully through such training (DiCara, 1970).

SOCIAL LEARNING

The range of social settings in which we have to learn to interact with others is extremely diverse, ranging from the close circle of the family to the many formal and informal groups that are part of our social environment (see Chapter 16).

Figure 5–9. Summary of two types of learning—classical conditioning and operant conditioning. Classical conditioning (top) begins with an unconditioned stimulus. The conditioned stimulus that is paired with it is substituted for it in producing the unconditioned response. In operant conditioning (*bottom*) a conditioned stimulus is presented along with an opportunity to respond in various ways. The correct response is reinforced, or rewarded, several times until the stimulus serves as a signal to perform the learned response.

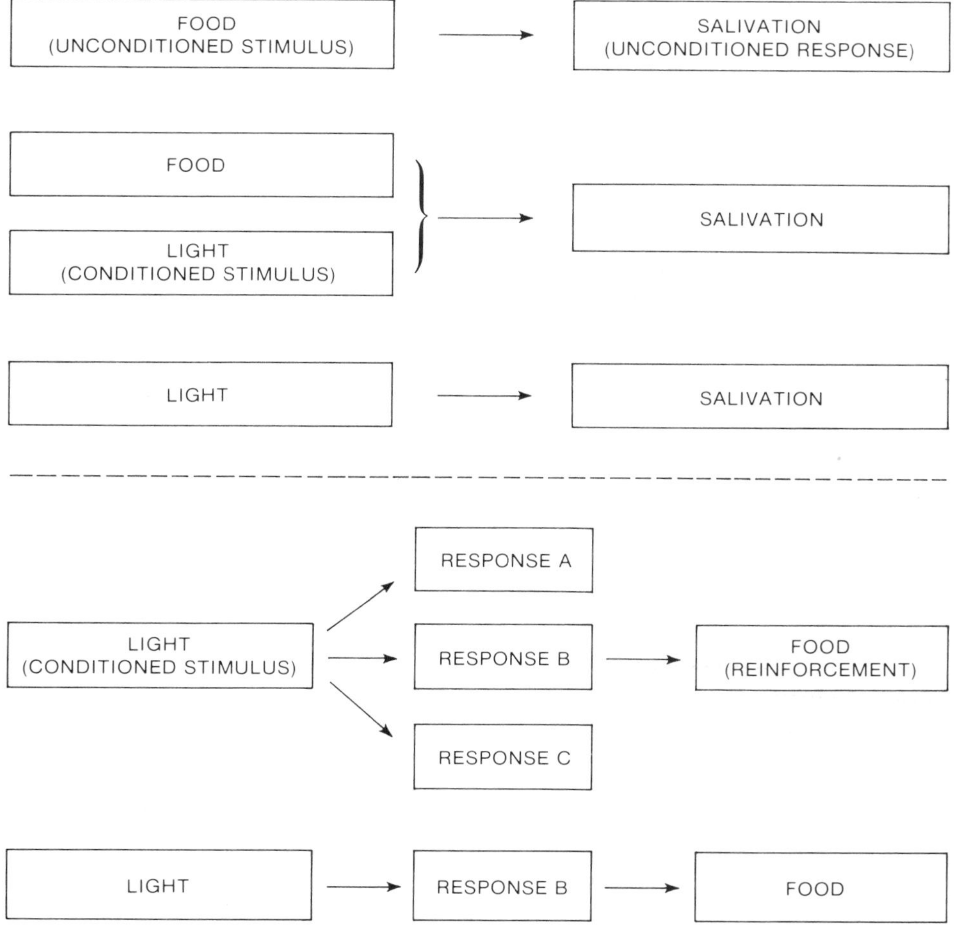

In the sections on operant and classical conditioning we analyzed learning in terms of the reinforcement conditions that increase, decrease, or shape behavior. Some learning theorists argue that reinforcement contingencies are not sufficient to explain adequately how we acquire most of our social behavior. Social-learning theorists contend that much of social learning occurs as the result of casual or directed observation or is mediated through cognitive processes, such as internal dialogues, attributions, or self-appraisals.

Observational Learning

Social-learning theorist Albert Bandura (1977) suggested that most of our social behavior is picked up from **observational learning** through **modeling.** Bandura argued that because we can learn how to behave from the example of a person we observe, we can be spared needless errors.

Albert Bandura's theory of observational learning attributes some learning to the mimicking of live models. *(© Beryl Goldberg)*

Our social behavior can be learned not only through observation of a live model, but also by exposure to symbolic models. Symbolic models may be presented in oral or written matter, in pictures, or in a combination of verbal and pictorial materials. Today television and movies are highly influential sources of symbolic modeling, especially in view of the amount of time young people spend before the television set. It has been repeatedly shown that both children and adults acquire attitudes, emotional responses, and new ways of behaving through models on film and television.

Bandura points out that three processes—attentional, retentional, and motor-reproduction—are crucial if learning through modeling is to take place. **Attentional processes** are based on the notion that people cannot learn much by observation unless they attend to and perceive accurately the significant features of the behavior to be modeled. Models, live as well as symbolic, differ in the degree to which they can hold the attention of people. Models with competent qualities are more likely to be imitated than models who lack such characteristics. Similarly, attention to models is facilitated by interpersonal attraction. Some models are so intrinsically attractive or compelling that they hold the attention of people of all ages for extended periods. This is nowhere better illustrated than in certain television personalities who serve as models (Bandura, 1977).

Attending to a model's behavior, however, is not sufficient for learning. There must also be **retentional processes** at work. That is, we must remember the behavior observed, since models will not always be present to provide guidance. To retain the activities of the model, we must hold them in memory in some symbolic form, either through verbal coding or imagery. Many times we retain a clear mental image of what we have seen; at other times we supply verbal descriptions instead. For example, the route of a model seen on television may be converted into verbal codes of right and left turns. Observers who code a model's activities into concise labels or vivid imagery learn better than those who simply watch a model or are mentally preoccupied with other matters while watching (Bandura & Jeffery, 1973).

The third process in observational learning concerns the conversion of symbolic representations into appropriate actions. Bandura thought that **motor-reproduction processes** serve this purpose. After observing a professional play golf, you retain a mental image of his or her activities and try to imitate them when you get on the golf course yourself. In observational learning, then, a person moves from focusing attention on a model to remembering the person's activities through verbal or visual codes and then translating these symbolic representations into motor actions. For example, the child who observes an aggressive act on television (attentional process) may retain a mental image of the situation (retention processes). As a result, the child may hit another child (motor process) who is trying to take away his or her toy.

According to social-learning theorists, reinforcement serves a facilitative rather than a necessary function. This is not to say that mere exposure to a model is, in itself, sufficient to produce observational learning. Reinforcement does play a role, but as an antecedent rather than a consequent influence (Bandura, 1977). For example, knowing that a model's behavior is effective in producing a conditioning, a great deal of learning takes place through direct contact with the environment. In addition, learning through observation illustrates that learning can occur vicariously as well. Children and adults can expand their range of behavior merely by observing the behavior of others.

Summary

Two basic models of learning are classical and operant conditioning. In classical conditioning two stimuli, such as a noise and food, are paired until both the noise and the food elicit a reaction (salivation) that was previously linked only with the food. Classical conditioning applies primarily to involuntary, reflexive behavior. Operant conditioning, unlike classical conditioning, requires that the organism first make a response in order to experience some consequences. Conditioning occurs when a response is consistently followed by a reinforcing event.

Reinforcement can be administered according to a number of basic schedules. Continuous schedules produce a rapid rate of response. Of the intermittent schedules, those based on fixed or variable ratios tend to produce faster rates of responding than those based on fixed or variable intervals. In addition to being reinforced positively, operant behavior can be brought under the control of aversive stimuli, or negative reinforcement. This allows for the conditioning of avoidance and escape and the suppression of behavior through the use of punishment.

Both classical and operant conditioning share a number of phenomena such as extinction, spontaneous recovery, stimulus generalization, and discrimination. To learn effectively, an organism must learn to notice similarities as well as distinctive features of the environment. The processes occurring in both classical and operant learning are similar, despite considerable procedural differences.

Learning by observation is an effective way to

learn social behavior. We can acquire new responses or modify existing behavior as a result of exposure to competent models. A common way of learning by observation, for children in particular, is observation of symbolic models on television.

Taken together, the three models of learning presented in this chapter—classical, operant, and observational—account for the acquisition of a good part of involuntary, voluntary, and social behavior.

Key Terms For Review

attentional processes
avoidance conditioning
chaining
classical conditioning
conditioned response (CR)
conditioned stimulus (CS)
conditioning
continuous reinforcement
cost contingencies
cumulative record
escape conditioning
extinction
fixed-interval schedule
fixed-ratio schedule
generalization gradient
higher-order conditioning
intermittent schedule
latent learning
law of effect
learning
modeling
motor-reproduction processes
neutral stimulus (NS)
observational learning
operant behavior
operant conditioning
primary reinforcer
punishment
reflex
reinforcement
respondent behavior
retentional processes
schedule of reinforcement
secondary reinforcer
shaping
spontaneous recovery
stimulus discrimination
stimulus generalization
successive approximations
superstitious behavior
temporal contiguity
time-out
token economy
two-factor theory of avoidance
unconditioned response (UR)
unconditioned stimulus (US)
variable-interval schedule
variable-ratio schedule

Suggested Readings

Carpenter, F. *The Skinner primer.* New York: The Free Press, 1974.
A paperback describing Skinner's basic ideas, methods, and procedures.

Kazdin, A. *Behavior modification in applied settings.* Homewood, Ill.: Dorsey Press, 1977b.
This book presents a good introduction to behavior-modification techniques employed in applied settings. It focuses on the application of the various operant principles in schools, psychiatric hospitals, day-care centers, and outpatient settings, as well as private homes.

Nye, R. *What is B. F. Skinner really saying?* Englewood Cliffs, N.J.: Prentice-Hall, 1979.

This book aims to inform the reader about B. F. Skinner in a relatively quick and easy way. The author discusses the basic principles of Skinnerian psychology and some common misunderstandings about Skinner. It also compares Skinner's ideas with other major schools of psychology, such as humanism and psychoanalysis.

Reynolds, G. *A primer of operant conditioning.* Glenview, Ill.: Scott, Foresman, 1975.

This primer presents a detailed account of the theory and principles of operant conditioning derived from the work of B. F. Skinner and his followers. Separate chapters discuss conditioned reinforcers, schedules of reinforcement, aversive control, and a comparison between operant and classical conditioning.

Skinner, B. F. *The shaping of a behaviorist.* (Vols. 1, 2). New York: Knopf, 1979.

These two volumes of a projected four-volume life history cover Skinner's most significant achievements from his entry to graduate study to his return to Harvard in 1948 as a full professor in psychology. Personal and familial events alternate with professional advancements in a detailed account.

Swenson, L. *Theories of learning: Traditional perspectives/contemporary developments.* Belmont, Cal.: Wadsworth, 1980.

This book is an excellent scholarly combination of a historical perspective on the development of major learning theories, an exposure to major principles of learning, and information about how learning principles and theories are applied in the real world.

6

Some Definitions

Biological Drives
Hunger
The Problem of Obesity
Thirst
Other Biological Drives
Environmental Cues and Biological Drives

Psychological Motives
Need for Achievement
Anxiety
Hierarchy of Motives
Unconscious Motivation
Intrinsic versus Extrinsic Motivation

Conflict of Motives
Approach-Approach Conflict
Avoidance-Avoidance Conflict
Approach-Avoidance Conflict
Double Approach-Avoidance Conflict

Emotion
The James-Lange Theory
The Cannon-Bard Theory
A Two-Component Theory of Emotion
Differential-Emotion Theory
The Role of Emotions

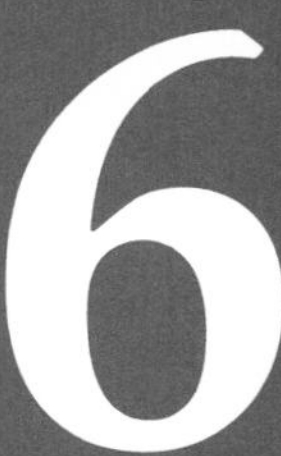

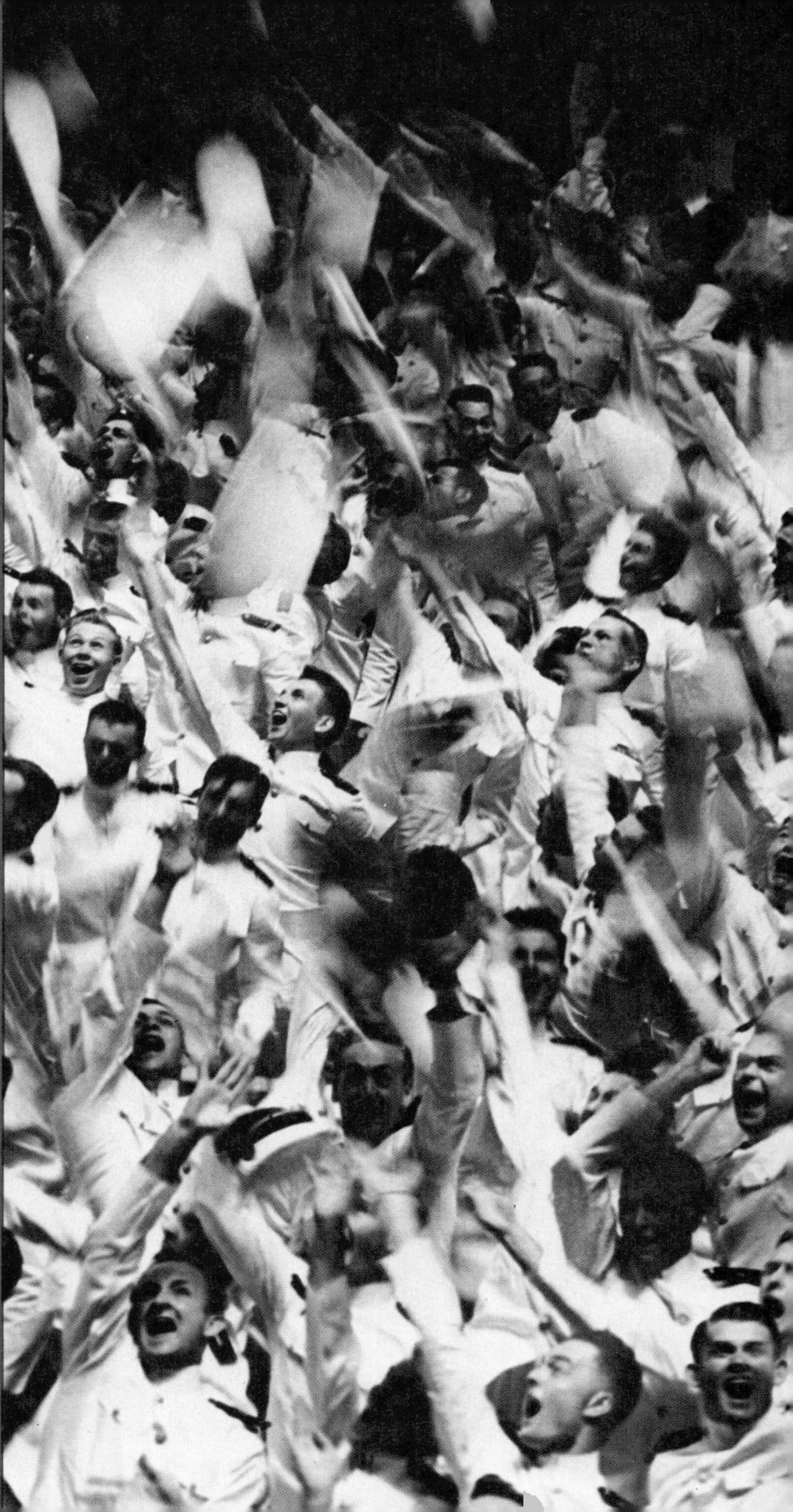

Motivation and Emotion

Mr. and Mrs. Scott were concerned about their six-year-old son, Michael. He spent most of his time at home alone in his room and appeared to be a very unhappy child. He seemed to have no interest in playing with other boys and girls his own age. Most of the neighborhood children had learned that it was little use to ask if Michael would come out to play, but now and then a child, desperate for a playmate, would ask for him. On these rare occasions Michael's parents would virtually push him out the door and encourage him to have fun with his friend.

Mr. and Mrs. Scott's worries were compounded when Michael's first-grade teacher asked them to have a conference with her. Miss Bradley told them that she too was worried about Michael. He preferred to sit alone in the corner and showed little interest in what was going on in class. The teacher believed that Michael had a problem with motivation—in fact, he did not appear to have any at all. He was not motivated academically or socially, and he seemed to be devoid of any curiosity. Confident of her assessment of Michael's problem, Miss Bradley recommended that Mr. and Mrs. Scott consult with the school psychologist to learn what could be done to increase Michael's level of motivation.

The school psychologist, Dr. Engle, spent several hours with Michael and several more hours interviewing his parents. Her assessment of Michael's case was considerably different from Miss Bradley's. Dr. Engle believed that Michael's problem was emotional. She said that Michael was severely depressed, withdrawn, and fearful of other people. If Michael's emotional state could be changed, Dr. Engle was confident that his problems at home and at school could be dealt with easily.

Puzzled by these divergent views of Michael's problem, Mr. and Mrs. Scott took him to a private clinic. They were seen by Dr. Lloyd, a clinical psychologist. After a careful assessment of the case, Dr. Lloyd told Mr.

and Mrs. Scott that Michael's problems did not involve either motives or emotions. He explained that when a young child is having problems, the best approach is to see how the child's environment can be changed. Changing the environment would be likely to produce changes in the child's personality and behavior. Dr. Lloyd pointed out that Michael was an exceptionally bright child; by providing him with a more challenging environment, his parents could probably make him happier.

Mr. and Mrs. Scott were now thoroughly confused. Was Michael's problem motivational or emotional? Or was the problem in Michael's environment? They did not know where to turn.

Motivation and emotion are of particular interest because they deal with the "why" of behavior. Questions such as Why does he work 18 hours a day? or Why does she spend so much time alone? are often answered in terms of motives or emotions. The psychologist, however, must be extremely careful to ensure that such questions and answers do not become circular. For instance, if you said that the rat ran directly to the food because it was hungry and that you knew that the rat was hungry because it ran directly to the food, you would be adding nothing to our knowledge of animal behavior. But if you could specify the physiological and environmental conditions that are associated with hunger and if you could use the construct of hunger to make predictions about the rat's behavior, you would be making an important contribution. In this way concepts such as motivation and emotion can be an invaluable tool in the study of animal and human behavior.

Although Michael's case is fictional, the scenario is plausible. Most psychologists believe that motives and emotions are important concepts that help us understand behavior. They may, however, disagree about the relation between the two concepts or the relative importance of each or whether a particular concept is a motive or an emotion. Some psychologists, like Dr. Lloyd, may argue that both motivation and emotion are irrelevant. Behaviorists such as B. F. Skinner and John Watson would argue that because motives and emotions cannot be directly observed, they have no place in a science of behavior. This is an extreme view, of course, and a majority of psychologists do find them to be useful concepts. This chapter will explore the nature of motivation and emotion and how they can help us to understand human behavior.

SOME DEFINITIONS

Several terms are used by psychologists when discussing motivation and emotion. A **motive** can be defined as a condition that causes an individual to engage in goal-directed behavior. Some theorists prefer to reserve the term "motive" for social or psychological conditions, such as the motive to achieve or the motive to affiliate with other people. They generally use the term **drive** to refer to motivational states that have a physiological basis, such as hunger or thirst. **Emotion** is the word used by psychologists to describe our feelings, such as happiness, anger, sadness, and surprise. **Affect** is used to describe the observable component of an emotion. Thus a psychologist who observed a person giggling at a funeral would describe the emotional response as an inappropriate affect. The distinctions presented here are not rigidly adhered to by all psychologists, and we have presented them only to help students become familiar with the jargon used by psychologists.

Suppose you were observing a friend's psychology experiment. A rat placed in a simple maze runs to the end where there is a box of food pellets. A second rat placed in the maze seems to have no interest in the food. It scampers back and forth, sniffing at the edges of the runway. How would you explain the differences in the rats' behavior? The simplest explanation might be that the first rat was motivated to seek the food and the second rat was not.

Regardless of whether your explanation is correct, what you have done is made an inference. You decided that the first rat was hungry because it ran directly toward the food. You could not observe the rat's hunger; you could only make an inference of hunger based upon your observation of the rat's behavior. Other observations may increase your confidence in your inference. The rat's blood-sugar level, stomach contents, and brain activity may all point to the drive of hunger. The important point to remember is that at no time did you observe hunger directly. You inferred that the rat was hungry because of its behavior and physiological condition.

The same would be true if you were to make statements about emotions. You may infer that your roommate is sad because he or she is crying and refusing to talk to anyone, but you cannot see sadness—you can only see signs that may cause you to infer sadness. Thus both motives and emotions are concepts that can only be inferred. Psychologists and lay people use them to help understand behavior. Let us take a look now at some common drives and motives.

BIOLOGICAL DRIVES

Biological drives are those that arise from states of physiological deprivation or imbalance. They include hunger, thirst, sex, temperature regulation, and the need for sleep. These drives generally result in a particular pattern of brain activity and are accompanied by certain sensations. For example, when we are deprived of food for five or six hours, certain messages are being processed by our brain, and we experience relevant sensations—namely, hunger pains. The same phenomena would occur if our bodies were in a state of imbalance, such as being too hot or too cold. These drives impel us to action—to eat something, or to cool off or to warm up. When we perform these actions our brain processes messages that tell us our biological drives have been satisfied.

Even though such drives have a strong physiological basis, they can still be affected by learning or psychological factors. For instance, we may all have a biological drive to eat, but some people eat to the point of obesity while others diet to the point of starvation. Thirst is a biological drive, but psychological factors may dictate that we satisfy this drive by drinking water, beer, soda, or any number of beverages. As always, the psychologist studying biological drives will be interested in examining the interaction between biological and psychological factors.

Hunger

Most people tend to believe that stomach contractions are responsible for the sensation of hunger and the drive to eat. This view was shared by psychologists during the first three decades of this century. In a classic experiment physiologist Walter Cannon (1929) had one of his students swallow a rubber hose with a balloon attached to its end. (Reportedly, with practice this can be done with little discomfort.) Cannon's results showed that there was a very close correspondence between his subject's stomach contractions and subjective feelings of hunger. Thus hunger seemed to be a relatively straightforward matter. It was caused by contractions of the stomach.

This conclusion, which was widely accepted at the time, has been discredited by more recent research. For example, it has been found that individuals who have their stomachs removed for medical reasons still experience hunger sensations. Both stomach contractions and sensations of hunger can be eliminated by injecting a sugar solution directly into the blood stream.

Currently it is believed that two small areas of the brain, located in the hypothalamus, regulate eating behavior. The first of these, called the lateral hypothalamus, is referred to as the "start eating" center. When this center is stimulated electrically in a laboratory animal, the animal will begin to eat even if it has just finished eating to satiation. The "stop eating" center is known formally as the ventromedial nucleus. When stimulated electrically it will cause laboratory animals to discontinue eating, even if they have been food-deprived (Anand & Brobeck, 1951). If the stop-eating center is destroyed, the animal will eat constantly and become grossly obese (Teitelbaum, 1967).

The mechanism by which the start-eating and stop-eating centers are activated appears to be changes in blood chemistry. The important factors are levels of fatty compounds and blood sugar. If a person goes without eating for a period of time, there is a substantial drop in the level of these substances. The body will then begin to draw upon reserves stored in the tissue. This process will continue until the person eats again to provide a new source of energy.

The importance of blood chemistry has been vividly demonstrated in an experiment involving two dogs (Tschukitscheff, 1930). One dog was permitted to eat until it no longer was interested in food. The second dog was deprived of food for some time. The experimenter gave a blood transfusion taken from the hungry dog to the sated dog. Although it had just finished eating its fill, this dog immediately began to search for more food.

Very minor changes in food intake or in exercise can have a significant effect on a person's weight over a period of a year. For instance, a secretary who shifts from a manual to an electric typewriter will gain five pounds in a year if all other factors are held constant. One extra apple per day will lead to a weight gain of about nine pounds over the course of a year. In view of this, the mechanisms that control our eating have to be remarkably sensitive to keep our weight constant. Nonetheless, a significant number of people in our society have problems of weight regulation. One condition, called anorexia nervosa, involves an inability to maintain normal body weight and may even result in death. A more common problem is that of obesity.

The Problem of Obesity

Psychological factors play an important role in eating. Almost everyone has had the experience of suddenly feeling hungry after smelling a favorite food cooking or of losing a strong appetite after smelling one's least favorite food. The role that psychological factors play in hunger for obese people has received much attention in recent years.

Social psychologist Stanley Schachter has conducted several studies that have compared the eating behavior of obese and normal people. In one experiment both normal and obese individuals were invited to taste-test two different kinds of ice cream. They were both expensive brands of French vanilla, but one brand had a bitter substance added to it. Schachter found that the obese subjects ate much more of the untainted ice cream and less of the bitter-tasting ice cream than did the normal subjects. He concluded that obese individuals depend more on taste cues than do individuals of normal weight. In other experiments Schachter has found that obese people will eat more if the clock tells them it is time to eat and will eat less if they must work for their food. Also, obese subjects will eat just as much food after recently completing a meal as they would if it had been several hours since they had eaten. Under these conditions, normal individuals will eat considerably less than obese individuals (Schachter & Rodin, 1974). Schachter's conclusion is that, contrary to the popular view, obese people are not driven to overeating by irresistible cravings and desires. Rather than listening to their bodies, they are oversensitive to external cues related to food and eating. Schachter's theory alone cannot account for all cases of obesity, but insensitivity to internal cues does appear to play a role.

Not all researchers agree that obesity is a psychological matter. Psychologist Richard Nisbett (1972) has suggested that obese people are genetically programmed to be fat. He cites evidence that overweight people have up to three times as many fat cells—the special cells that store fatty compounds—as do people of average weight. If these obese people diet, there will be a reduction in the size of the fat cells but no reduction in their number. An obese person who has dieted successfully and reduced the size of the fat cells may actually be in a state of food deprivation. Consistent with this idea are the reports by dieting obese people of being constantly hungry. Nisbett argues that one's normal weight is determined by his or her number of fat cells. Thus it is possible that for two people of the same weight and height, one may be overweight and the other underweight.

There is some disagreement as to what factors are responsible for determining the number of fat cells an individual possesses. Some researchers have shown that it may be a matter of heredity (Schemmel, Michelsen, & Gill, 1970). Others suggest that overeating in the first few months of life may be the responsible factor. Many parents are convinced that fat babies are healthy babies. Pediatricians who are concerned that an infant's weight might correspond to weight later in life find it difficult to persuade these parents to keep their infant's weight at an average level.

The research of Schachter and Nisbett suggests that there may be different kinds of obesity. Some overweight individuals may have extreme difficulty in maintaining an average weight because of their genetic makeup or their early eating experiences. The weight problems of others may have resulted from faulty learning; they may have learned to eat in response to situational cues rather than in response to their own internal signals. And, of course, many cases of obesity probably result from a combination of biological and psychological factors.

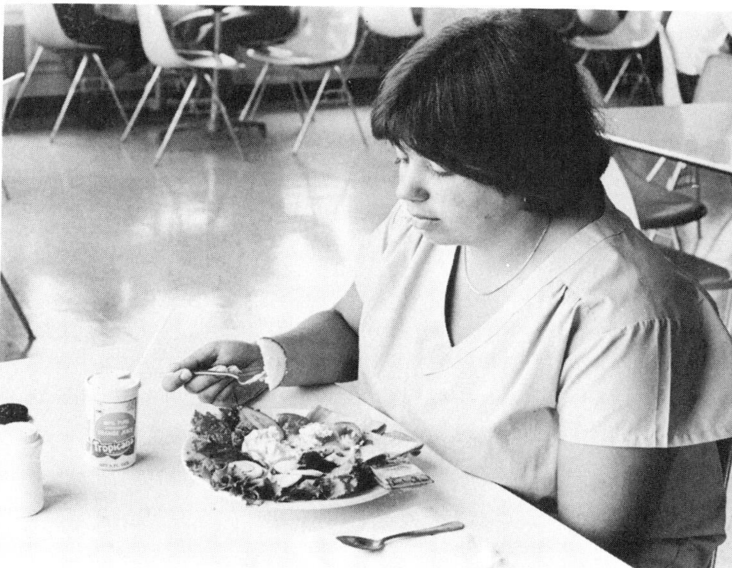

Many recent studies concern the pyschological factors involved in obesity. *(© Teri Leigh Stratford/Monkmeyer Press Photo Service)*

Thirst

One mechanism believed to be important in controlling the level of fluids in our body is located in the hypothalamus. Certain cells in that area are especially sensitive to fluid dehydration. Another mechanism for regulating fluid intake is located in the kidneys. When dehydration reduces the volume of blood flowing through the body, the kidneys produce a chemical that activates the thirst center in the hypothalamus.

As is the case with hunger, an imbalance in the body triggers the thirst drive. The bodily sensations that accompany thirst—dryness in the mouth and throat—play only a secondary role. We drink to satisfy the imbalance of fluid in our body, not to reduce the sensations of thirst. This has been demonstrated with laboratory animals. They can learn very rapidly to regulate their fluid intake by pressing a bar that injects water directly into their stomachs. Thus they never drink to satisfy their thirst; they merely press a lever (Solarz, 1958).

Other Biological Drives

Several other drives must be satisfied to ensure survival. The sleep drive was discussed in Chapter 3. If it is not satisfied, the organism will die of exhaustion. We humans also have a drive to maintain our bodies at a temperature of 98.6 degrees Fahrenheit. This drive is controlled by cells in a lower part of the brain. Breathing is taken for granted, but anyone who has held his or her breath for a minute or so is aware of the strength of the breathing drive. Our drive to avoid tissue damage will cause us to pull our hand away from a hot stove.

Two additional drives that are believed to have a biological basis are the sex drive and the drive to have sensory stimulation. As you will see in Chapter 17, there is a strong biological basis for sexual behavior in lower animals. For humans, biology serves as an impetus to engage in sex, but the manner in which this drive is satisfied is dependent on matters of experience. Some people have little difficulty in abstaining from sexual activity for their entire lives, while others appear driven to have numerous and diverse sexual experiences.

Environmental Cues and Biological Drives

The biological drives depend primarily on brain activity in response to certain physiological conditions. There is, however, an important interaction between physiological events and environmental cues. As we saw in Schachter's research, some people may eat in response to cues in their environment. In fact, probably everyone is susceptible in some degree to environmental cues that are relevant to a person's physiological needs. Who has not suddenly become hungry when walking by a restaurant and smelling pizza in the oven?

These environmental cues, called **incentives,** influence animal behavior as well. For instance, male rats will copulate more often if they are presented with a different female after each act than if left with just one partner (Beach & Ransom, 1967). Also, animals (and many people) who have eaten their fill will begin to eat again if presented with a preferred kind of food. Many a dessert has been consumed on a "full" stomach.

PSYCHOLOGICAL MOTIVES

Psychological motives are those needs that are acquired primarily on the basis of learning or experience. Our needs to affiliate with others, to achieve success, to be competent, to be liked and respected, as well as the less desirable motives such as anxiety, fear, and avoidance of success, are thought to be acquired. This is not to say that biological factors are totally unimportant. For instance, the need to affiliate probably has survival overtones and may be a product of the evolutionary process. Nevertheless, the strength of these acquired needs can vary considerably from person to person depending on the individuals' experiences. The division of motives into the biological and the psychological, or acquired, reflects the *relative* importance of each set of factors and not an all-or-none phenomenon.

Psychologists have hypothesized dozens of different psychological motives, several of which are identified in Table 6–1. Two of the most researched motives are the need for achievement and anxiety.

Need for Achievement

Psychologist David McClelland of Harvard University is largely responsible for the interest shown in the **need for achievement** (McClelland, 1961; McClelland, Atkinson, Clark, & Lowell, 1953), which can be defined as a motive to strive for success. He measured the need for achievement with the Thematic Apperception Test (TAT; see Chapter 11). The TAT is a series of pictures about which people are asked to tell a story. One of the cards used was a picture of an adolescent boy apparently looking off into space, with an operating room in the background. One person might tell a story in which the boy is dreaming about the day he will become a great surgeon. He will study hard to complete medical school, develop new surgical techniques, save many lives, and become world renowned for his dedication and skill. A story told by another person might center on the man on the operating table. He may be the boy's father, who was in an automobile accident. The boy is hoping his father will be all right and is promising to be a good son if his father's life is spared. These two types of stories are thought to reflect different needs or motives. The first reflects a strong need for achievement. The second may reflect needs for love and dependency.

After McClelland and his colleagues devised their method of measuring need for achievement, they attempted to find out how those who were low and those who were high in this motive differed. Numerous studies have found a variety of important differences between these two types of individuals. For example, when the two types of people are given a word-scrambled task in which they must rearrange the letters to spell a word, those with a high need for achievement improve with practice. Subjects with a low need show little, if any, improvement over numerous trials (Lowell, 1952). Supposedly, people with a high need strive to find new and better ways of performing the task.

A second difference concerns the risks the two types are willing to take. One experiment required subjects to participate in a ring-toss game (Atkinson & Litwin, 1960). They were instructed to see how well they could do and were allowed to stand anywhere from 1 to 15 feet away from the peg. Individuals with a low need for achievement were just as likely to stand 1 foot away as 15 feet away. Those with a high need, however, were most likely to stand about 9 to 10 feet away. This experiment, taken together with other research (Atkinson & Feather, 1966), suggests that those high in need for achievement prefer tasks of intermediate difficulty. They are not interested in tasks that are so simple that success is virtually assured, nor are they interested in tasks for which the probability of success is extremely small.

The need to affiliate begins in early childhood. *(© Nancy Hays/Monkmeyer Press Photo Service)*

The need for achievement appears to have a significant effect upon one's life. Compared with those who have low levels of this motive, individuals with high levels are likely to do better in college, are more apt to be business people than professionals, and are more likely to become entrepreneurs. Boys high in the need for achievement are likely to surpass their fathers in occupational status, while those low in need for achievement are likely to have the same or lower occupational status as their fathers (Crockett, 1962). Interestingly, McClelland has argued that the economic productivity of a nation as a whole is related to the emphasis it places on need for achievement.

Table 6–1. Examples of Acquired Motives

Motive	*Definition*
Abasement	To accept blame, criticism, or punishment.
Affiliation	To be around others and win their love and affection.
Aggression	To cause harm to others.
Autonomy	To act in accord with one's own feelings; to be independent.
Certainty	To be able to predict one's future.
Dependence	To view others as strong and capable so they may care for and protect one.
Dominance	To control others or one's environment.
Exhibition	To be seen and heard; to be noticed.
Mastery	To be in control of one's environment; to be competent.
Nurturance	To care for and satisfy the needs of those that appear helpless.
Sentience	To seek and enjoy sensual impressions.
Succorance	To be cared for and loved.

The need for achievement appears to have its origins early in life. An important factor seems to be independence training on the part of the parents. Parents who demand that their children do things on their own at an early age, and do them well, are likely to instill the need for achievement (McClelland, et al., 1953; Winterbottom, 1958). For example, mothers of eight-year-old boys who had high levels of this motive expected their sons to earn their own spending money, to know their way around the neighborhood, and to participate in the parent's conversations and interests.

A second factor concerns the use of rewards and punishments by parents. It has been found that mothers who reward their sons for satisfactory behavior while ignoring unsatisfactory behavior are more likely to induce the need for achievement than mothers who ignore their sons' satisfactory behavior while punishing their unsatisfactory behavior (Teevan & McGhee, 1972). It appears that independence training combined with rewards and affection for behaving independently are responsible for instilling the need for achievement in young boys.

Most of the research on the need for achievement has been conducted with men. McClelland et al. (1953) reported that women did not respond to conditions designed to elicit this need the same way that men did, so they concentrated their efforts on males. Several explanations have been offered for this sex difference. One possibility is that need for achievement in women is related to different situations (such as social skills) than for men (Stein & Bailey, 1973). Another possibility is that women fear success and strive to avoid it (Horner, 1972). Achievement motivation in women will be considered in more detail in Chapter 9.

While many people in our society value achievement motivation, the drive to be successful is not without liabilities. It may mean long hours at work that take away time from family and friends. It may also mean the possibility of developing a stress-related medical disease. More than one person has reached the pinnacle of success only to find the achievement somewhat hollow.

Anxiety

Although many motives can be classified as positive because they propel us to seek desirable goals, motives can be negative or disruptive as well. Perhaps the most important of these is **anxiety,** or irrational fear. Anxiety can influence behavior in a variety of ways. People with high levels of this motive may avoid high places, public-speaking opportunities, social situations, dentists, sexual relationships—the list could go on and on. These effects of anxiety make it of particular interest to clinical psychologists. Many psychotherapy techniques are intended to reduce anxiety levels so that people can take part in activities they are fearful of.

Although some theorists believe that anxiety or the potential to develop anxiety is innate, most psychologists agree that learning plays a major role in its development. People may learn to be anxious about certain situations by association with pain. For example, if a child is bitten by a dog, he or she may come to feel anxious around all dogs. Just observing and learning from others can generate anxieties. Many people with a fear of snakes, for instance, have acquired it by observing that reaction in movies and television shows, or seeing their parents exhibit a fear of snakes. Developmental psychologists have found that certain types of parental behavior, such as expressing negative evaluations of their children's behavior and accomplishments, are likely to instill anxiety in the children (Mussen, Conger, & Kagan, 1974). These are but a few examples of the ways in which anxiety can be learned or acquired.

Although most people tend to think of anxiety as something they would be happy to do without, it can have beneficial effects. For instance, we seek and even enjoy feelings of apprehension and tension when we go to horror movies or sporting events. Many performers try to "psych themselves up" before they appear in public. Several years ago Johnny Carson had a cardiologist as a guest, and Carson wore a telemetric device to record his pulse rate during the monologue. When the cardiologist appeared, he reported that Carson's pulse rate was 150 per minute when Carson first appeared on stage. (A normal adult pulse rate is 70 to 90 beats per minute.) Carson responded that he had to be "up" if he was going to perform well.

Anxiety can also serve to increase our desire to complete certain tasks. For instance, anxiety in students about the possibility of receiving bad grades may motivate them to study for an upcoming exam. But this beneficial effect seems to work only for moderate intensities of anxiety. Students with no anxiety whatsoever may not be able to resist the temptation to put off their studying until it is too late. And students with extremely high levels of anxiety may have their performance impaired. They may be so anxious about the possibility of doing poorly on the exam that they are unable to concentrate on studying. Research has confirmed that students with moderate levels of anxiety tend to receive better grades in college than students who have low anxiety levels (Sarason, 1957; Suinn, 1965).

This type of relationship between motivation level and performance has been observed in many situations and was first described over 70 years ago by R. M. Yerkes and J. D. Dodson. This relation is now referred to as the Yerkes-Dodson Law. When motivation level is at moderate intensities, performance will be relatively good. When motivation is either very low or very high, performance will suffer. Up to now, the Yerkes-Dodson Law has been demonstrated primarily

Wilma Rudolph won three gold medals in the 1960 Olympics, although pneumonia and scarlet fever prevented her from walking until age nine. Her success can be attributed to a need for achievement. *(© Associated Press / Wide World Photos)*

The best tests produce moderate anxiety—enough to stimulate maximum effort but not more than can be coped with. *(© Hugh Rogers/Monkmeyer Press Photo Service)*

with regard to negative motives, such as fear and anxiety. It is conceivable, however, that it holds for other drives and motives as well. Perhaps a person suffering from extreme hunger would be unable to seek food as effectively as someone with only moderate hunger.

Hierarchy of Motives

Early in his career humanistic psychologist Abraham Maslow was puzzled by his observation that people exhibit such a variety of motives. Some people seem to be concerned primarily with winning the approval of others, while other individuals care most about doing a good job regardless of what people think. Some people appear to have strong social needs; their primary interest is to have lots of friends. Others seem to care little about companionship and spend much of their time alone. To understand these differences, Maslow developed a hierarchical theory of motivation. Certain lower-level, basic needs must be satisfied before the individual can be motivated by higher needs. Maslow suggested that the level of a person's motivations or needs depends on the circumstances of his or her life.

At the bottom of the hierarchy are the **physiological needs.** These include hunger, thirst, sex, and the need for warmth. If these needs are satisfied, the person will move to the next level, **safety needs,** which involve avoiding both physical and psychological abuse. It is likely that many people who live in politically unstable countries, such as those in the Middle East or Southeast Asia, are concerned primarily with the motive to avoid injury or death from terrorists or enemy armies. Similarly, people who cannot tolerate even a hint of criticism may have strong psychological safety needs.

The third level is the **need for acceptance.** People who are operating at this level desire to be liked and loved and to belong. Professors who are so concerned that their students like them that they cannot bring themselves to give a poor grade have strong acceptance needs. The professor who is more concerned that students learn the course material than with being liked is operating at the next level of **esteem needs.** These people are concerned with their evaluations of themselves. They care about other people, but they want to see themselves as adequate, competent, and useful.

Maslow (1972) called the highest level of motivation **self-actualization.** This level is reached by relatively few people. Self-actualized individuals derive satisfaction from personal growth and development. Because they are relatively free from fears, anxieties, and defenses, they are able to have unusually accurate perceptions of other people or situations. They tend to have a fresh appreciation of life. They have what Maslow called **peak experiences,** feelings of awe and pleasure that may be elicited by such ordinary events as a sunset, the touch of a child, or a piece of music. Maslow pointed out that self-actualized individuals are by no means perfect—they can be boring, irritating, stubborn, and vain—but they are extraordinarily strong, competent, and independent. Perhaps six-year-old Michael's lack of interest in others resulted from his need to be alone to pursue his self-development.

A crucial concept in Maslow's theory is that an individual's needs must be met at one level before he or she can progress to a higher level. For instance, an adult who was reared by parents who never demonstrated their love may go through life trying to win the love and approval of others. Such an individual's acceptance needs may never be satisfied, regardless of how many people profess love for them. This theory may explain the suicides of some movie stars who felt lonely and unloved despite their millions of adoring fans.

Maslow's theory is difficult to prove, but its intuitive appeal has made it very popular. It seems to fit in with many everyday observations, and it may explain individual variability in motivations.

Unconscious Motivation

Most of us have known someone who seemed to behave continually in ways that were self-destructive. Take the alcoholic who continues to drink, even though he or she knows the drinking may result in the loss of family or job or both. Or take the person who is chronically hostile or aggressive, even though it is apparent that such behavior is alienating friends and business associates. How can such self-defeating behavior be explained?

Sigmund Freud asked himself the same question, and his answer resulted in the concept of **unconscious motivation.** Freud believed that many people have motives that are so frightening to them that the motives are repressed into the unconscious (see Chapter 10). Even so, these motives continue to exert an influence on behavior. Thus the alcoholic or the hostile person may be behaving to satisfy needs that he or she is totally unaware of.

One of the basic motives, according to psychoanalytic theory, is to protect one's self from threatening situations. That is, we may have an unconscious need to reduce or eliminate anxiety. This need can result in the formation of **defense mechanisms,** which are processes that our unconscious uses to ward off anxiety. Once again this is a concept with intuitive appeal for many psychologists but difficult to prove with research.

Social-learning theorist Brenden Maher (1966) has offered another explanation of this kind of self-defeating behavior—the concept of **learning without awareness.** Consider a preschool boy who tends to be aggressive and forceful with other children. He *learns* that by being aggressive he can obtain toys from the other children and get to the head of the line to use the playground equipment. At the same time he is learning these things, his preschool teacher and parents are instructing him in the virtues of sharing, getting along, and nonviolence. So the boy learns that if he talks as if he believes in sharing and getting along with the other children, he will win the approval of his teacher and parents. In other words, the boy has learned one kind of behavior on a verbal level, but quite another one on a nonverbal level. It is likely that as he grows up he will believe in the virtues of sharing and respecting the rights of others, but in competitive situations he may nevertheless behave in an overaggressive fashion. Some theorists would attribute his behavior to unconscious motivation. Freudians might argue that he has unconscious hostility or an unconscious need to dominate others. But Maher and other social-learning theorists would point to his case as an example of learning without awareness. For them, the concept of motivation would not even arise.

Intrinsic versus Extrinsic Motivation

Are people motivated by extrinsic rewards, such as money, a plush office, or, in the case of children, a cookie or an extra late bedtime? Or are they motivated by intrinsic rewards, such as the satisfaction of completing a task successfully or of satisfying their curiosity? Is one type of motivation to be preferred over the other? These are questions that psychologists, parents, and school administrators grapple with continually. For example, should children be given an allowance for making their bed and carrying out the trash, or should they learn to do these things for the satisfaction of knowing that they are contributing to the family?

The case of Michael, which opened this chapter, may reflect this distinction. Michael's teacher suggested that Michael's problems centered on a deficit of intrinsic motivation. She recommended that Michael receive counseling to increase his intrinsic motivation. The psychologist who saw Michael recommended that his environment be changed. For example, he could be offered rewards for completing his schoolwork or presented with challenges that would be more appropriate for his ability. Which is the best way to proceed?

The answer seems to be that it depends on the situation. People do have intrinsic motivation to perform some tasks, and in these cases the offer of extrinsic rewards may actually reduce interest. In one experiment it was found that college students who were paid to work interesting puzzles spent less time with the puzzles during a free-choice period than did a group of students who were not paid initially (Deci, 1972). The extrinsic reward appeared to have reduced the intrinsic motivation of the subjects. Thus a parent may not want to offer a child money if the child seems to enjoy helping with the household tasks. To do so may cause a shift in motives. The child will subsequently help with the housework for the money rather than for the intrinsic satisfaction.

On the other hand, it is unrealistic to expect people to perform many tasks for intrinsic rewards only. How many people working at unskilled jobs would be satisfied with knowing they are making a contribution to society? And how many children do their schoolwork because they want to learn? The teacher or parent who refuses to employ external rewards (such as grades) to motivate children has only punishment to rely on. In Michael's case it is obvious that intrinsic rewards are not working. It would seem reasonable to introduce external rewards to promote behavioral changes.

Often some combination of intrinsic and extrinsic motives works best. For instance, as authors of this book we would like to believe that the intrinsic satisfaction of communicating knowledge about our profession motivated us to write it. However, if our publisher had announced that our royalties would be given away, our typewriters would soon have gathered dust. Many companies attempt to improve employee morale by promoting both intrinsic and extrinsic rewards.

CONFLICT OF MOTIVES

Everyone is motivated by a variety of drives and needs. In a given situation, one specific drive or need may be dominant, and the behavior of the individual will be relatively straightforward. There are many occasions, however, when two drives or needs are elicited that place the individual in a state of conflict. The conflict can range from the mild (a dieter choosing between pie or no dessert after dinner) to the severe (a destitute person choosing between going hungry and stealing). Social psychologist Kurt Lewin (1935/1972) has described four basic types of conflict.

Approach-Approach Conflict

An **approach-approach conflict** occurs when we are motivated to seek two equally desirable but mutually exclusive goals. To illustrate, consider a person who has strong needs for achievement in her career as well as strong motives to start and raise a family. Such a conflict might be severe. Most cases of approach-approach conflict, however, are not serious and are usually resolved without much difficulty. In fact, many people relish the situation in which they have to choose between equally desirable alternatives.

Avoidance-Avoidance Conflict

A situation in which a person must choose between two equally undesirable goals or needs is known as an **avoidance-avoidance conflict.** For instance, college students may have to choose between studying for a boring course or failing the final exam. Michael, the child described at the opening of the chapter, may have had to choose between doing schoolwork that was boring to him or being disapproved of by his teacher. Avoidance-avoidance conflicts can result in serious psychological disorders. Psychiatrist Gregory Bateson (Bateson, Jackson, Haley, & Weakland, 1956) has suggested that this conflict may contribute to some cases of schizophrenia—a type of psychosis (see Chapter 12). He described the case of a girl whose mother would badger her for details of her personal life. When the girl finally told her mother these details, the mother would promptly tell the father, who would then punish his daughter severely. Thus the girl was placed in a no-win situation. She could withhold information and incur her mother's wrath or give it and incur that of her father.

One way in which people often try to deal with this conflict is to avoid the situation altogether—either physically or psychologically. Students may try to find a way to withdraw from a course at the last moment, or a person in a position like that of the schizophrenic girl may retreat into an internal world and simply cease responding. And Michael's withdrawn behavior may have been his way of avoiding the two unpleasant alternatives.

Approach-Avoidance Conflict

A single goal that has both desirable and undesirable qualities produces an **approach-avoidance conflict.** For example, a person may want to be a performer but may fear getting up in front of a crowd. Such anxiety or fear is generally involved in approach-avoidance conflicts.

Neal Miller (1959) has developed the concept of goal gradients to describe this form of conflict. A gradient can be defined as the strength of the motive to either approach or avoid a particular goal in relation to the distance from the goal. As a person approaches the goal the strength of the avoidance gradient increases more rapidly than the approach gradient. When the person is some distance from the goal, the approach gradient will be stronger than the avoidance gradient, inducing the person to move closer to the goal. As he or she gets close to the goal, the strength of the avoidance gradient becomes stronger, so the person will then retreat. When the person reaches the point where the gradients cross, he or she is likely to be uncertain as to which course of action should be taken because the two gradients are of equal strength. The point of crossing is called the vacillation point.

As an example, suppose you want to ask your boss for a raise. You feel that you deserve it and you certainly could use the extra money. Your boss, however, is an intimidating figure, and you are anxious about approaching her. Sunday night your approach gradient will be quite high, and you will be determined to speak to your boss first thing in the morning. When you wake up on Monday, your approach gradient is still going strong, but now your avoidance gradient is showing some strength. You begin to worry about your boss's reaction, and when you reach the office your approach gradient is only slightly higher than your avoidance gradient. You are still determined to ask for the raise, but you are feeling very nervous. You are near the vacillation point. As you walk toward your boss's door, your avoidance gradient suddenly becomes stronger than your approach gradient. You now believe your boss will be angry with you for asking, and you humbly walk back to your desk. That night, when you are removed from the goal once again, you berate yourself for being so timid, and you resolve to ask for the raise the very next day.

This type of conflict is a component of many minor psychological disorders. People have needs or goals that they cannot achieve because of their fearfulness—or, in Miller's terms, their avoidance gradients.

Double Approach-Avoidance Conflict

Double approach-avoidance conflicts present themselves to us every day. They involve situa-

APPLICATION

Cigarette Smoking: A Destructive Motive

People are subject to a variety of negative motives. Among them are the so-called addictions—to alcohol, heroin, and barbiturates, to name just a few. One addiction that is particularly perplexing is to cigarettes. Evidence has been accumulating over the past 30 years that smoking contributes to potentially fatal diseases such as cancer, heart disease, and emphysema. Yet millions of people continue to smoke, and cigarettes are sold side by side with candy and soft drinks. One branch of the federal government warns us that cigarette smoking is hazardous to our health and spends millions of dollars in antismoking campaigns, while another branch spends millions to subsidize farmers who grow tobacco.

The general public and the government are not the only ones who are confused about cigarette smoking. Psychologists have conducted numerous studies that have produced contradictory results. One unresolved issue concerns what it is that causes people to smoke cigarettes. If smokers are asked why they smoke, the most common answer is that it is relaxing. Physiological indices of relaxation, such as heart rate and blood pressure, however, increase rather than decrease as a result of smoking.

People are also said to smoke because they are addicted to nicotine. Social psychologist Stanley Schachter (1977) has reported data to support this notion. Heavy smokers smoked more when they were given low-nicotine cigarettes than when they were given high-nicotine cigarettes. They appeared to be regulating their nicotine intake. There are, however, at least ten studies that have failed to find any evidence supporting the idea of nicotine regulation. It would seem that both psychological and physiological factors are involved in cigarette smoking. The degree to which the various factors are important probably varies from individual to individual.

Psychologists have developed treatment techniques to help people stop smoking. Many of these techniques involve aversion therapy. By administering an electric shock or blowing stale smoke at people while they smoke, therapists hope to create an aversion to smoking cigarettes. Most of these treatments have been spectacularly unsuccessful.

Perhaps one reason they have failed is that people do not take cigarette smoking as seriously as other addictions. People who are addicted to alcohol or drugs are willing to be admitted to hospitals for a month or so for treatment. And insurance companies are willing to pay for such treatment. Cigarette smokers, however, are expected to quit on their own or with the assistance of a few hours of therapy. If we were willing to recognize cigarette smoking as the health problem and life-threatening habit it is, we might find that more intensive treatment methods would be effective.

tions in which we must select one of two alternatives, each of which has positive and negative elements. To illustrate, imagine that when you graduate you are one of the fortunate few who are offered two jobs. One is with a large company that offers security and a good starting salary. Opportunities for advancement, however, are severely limited. The second job is with a small company that offers you the opportunity to grow with it. If the company is successful, you will be in the top levels of management within a few years. You are concerned, however, about the modest starting salary and by the knowledge that if the company is a failure you could be out of a job within a few years. In short, there are both desirable and undesirable elements to consider in pursuing either position.

People react to this type of conflict similarly to the way they react to the other forms. They are likely to vacillate between the two goals without being able to make up their mind. Some individuals may become emotional and have feelings of anxiety or distress. When people finally do make up their mind, they may accentuate the desirable aspects of the goal they select and the negative aspects of the goal they reject.

EMOTION

Most people would agree that emotions are necessary to add richness and meaning to human existence. What would life be like if we could not experience the pride of accomplishment, the contentment of a good friendship, or the joy of being in love? Along with making life meaningful, our emotions can cause us great pain. The emptiness of feeling totally alone, the sorrow of losing a loved one, or the despair of a failure can cause us temporarily to lose our will to go on. These positive and negative emotions often seem interrelated. Philosophers, poets, and psychologists have all wondered if the joy of being in love would be so intense if it were not for the pain of unrequited love. Or would the feeling of accomplishment we have after a victory be the same if it were not for the agony of defeat?

Since emotions are such an important aspect of life, one might expect that psychologists would have devoted substantial time and energy to studying them. Such has not been the case. Although the early psychologists, such as Wundt and James, did write about emotion, and research about emotions has continued since that time, the study of emotions has not received the attention it seems to deserve. Currently, psychologists disagree about a number of issues related to emotions and even whether emotions deserve to be studied at all! Some theorists have argued that emotions are unnecessary concepts for the science of behavior (Duffy, 1962; Lindsley, 1957). Others believe that emotions are the primary motivational system of human beings and hence an indispensable concept (Arnold, 1960; Izard, 1977). Some psychologists believe that emotions are, for the most part, a source of problems in that they disrupt and disorganize behavior (Lazarus, 1968; Young, 1961). Other researchers argue that although emotions can be disruptive, they can also serve to organize, motivate, and sustain desirable behavior (Tomkins, 1962, 1963; Izard, 1972, 1977). And as we shall see in the sections that follow, there is very little agreement about the process of creating emotions.

The James-Lange Theory

Shortly before the turn of the century, William James (1884) offered the first formal theory of emotion. Although it contradicted ideas about emotion prevalent at the time, it gained popularity rapidly and continues to be influential. James argued that we do not cry because we are sad or run away because we are afraid; rather, we are sad *because* we cry and afraid *because* we run away. According to James, emotions are based on physiological reactions. We are exposed to some stimulus, experience physiological changes, and then experience emotions.

As an example, suppose you were walking down the street, when you suddenly saw a large vicious-looking dog approaching you. First you would experience physiological changes: "knots" in your stomach, trembling, increased heart rate, rubbery knees, and changes in your facial expression. The physiological changes would probably include your turning in the other direction and moving very rapidly. These changes, taken together, would serve as the basis for your experience of the emotion of fear. The changes occur before the emotion is experienced.

About the same time that James developed his theory, the Danish psychologist Karl Lange (1885/1922) offered a similar theory. Together, their theories have come to be known as the **James-Lange theory,** although there are important distinctions between the two approaches. Lange believed that the physiological changes that led to the experience of emotion were limited to changes in the visceral and glandular organs—sensations such as butterflies in the stomach and a pounding heart. James included voluntary muscle changes, arguing that changes in facial expressions and the act of running, as well as sensations in the stomach, could elicit the experience of emotion.

The Cannon-Bard Theory

Some 40 years after the formulation of the James-Lange theory, physiologist Walter Cannon (1927) presented evidence that seemed to disprove it. Supported by the work of L. L. Bard on brain functioning, the **Cannon-Bard theory** suggested that the viscera (internal organs of the body) cannot be a cause of emotional experiences. In a series of experiments in which the nerves of the visceral organs of animals were severed, Cannon found that the animals continued to exhibit emotional responses. Furthermore, the same visceral changes occurred in a variety of emotional states. If changes in the viscera caused emotions, we should expect to find many distinct changes, each of which would correspond to one of the various emotions. Finally, not all visceral changes lead to emotional experience. If you exercise vigorously, your heart pounds but you do not experience fear.

The Cannon-Bard theory suggests that there are specific brain centers, in the thalamic and hypothalamic regions, that are involved in the experience of emotion. According to this theory, once a person is exposed to a stimulus (the vicious-looking dog), nerve impulses pass through the thalamus. From there, some impulses are sent to the cortex, where the stimulus is perceived and emotion is experienced, while other impulses travel to the muscles and viscera, where the physiological changes occur. So Cannon and Bard would argue that when you see a vicious-looking dog, you run *and* you are afraid. Both the experience of emotion and the physiological changes occur as a result of nervous activity in the thalamus and hypothalamus. This theory has received support from a variety of experiments that have shown that electrical stimulation of these areas of the brain does result in emotional experiences (Hess & Akert, 1955; Olds, 1973).

A Two-Component Theory of Emotion

While few psychologists would deny the importance of brain activity in the experience of emotion, many believe that the Cannon-Bard theory fails to explain many phenomena. Suppose you are awakened in the middle of the night by the telephone. Your first reaction may be fear of bad news, but you may experience relief as soon as you discover that it is a wrong number. What accounts for your change in emotional reactions?

Many theorists would argue that how you appraise an external stimulus (a ringing telephone) is a key element in the emotion you experience. A leading proponent of this view is social psychologist Stanley Schachter. He argues that emotions are caused by two components: (1) a physiological arousal, which alone tends to be vague and diffuse, and (2) a cognitive process by which individuals label their physiological arousal by looking toward their environment for cues.

Schachter conducted an experiment that he believed offered support for this two-component theory of emotion (Schachter & Singer, 1962). He gave three groups of subjects an injection of epinephrine, a drug that produces physiological arousal, and a control group an injection of a saline solution. One-third of the subjects in the three experimental groups were given accurate information about the effects of the drug (e.g., increased heart rate). One-third were misinformed about the effects of the drug (e.g., light-headedness), and the remaining subjects were given no information about what they could expect. Each subject was then asked to have a seat in a waiting room with another "subject"—actually a confederate of the experimenter. The subjects were told that the confederate had received the same injection a few minutes earlier. For half of the subjects, the confederate began to act giddy after a few minutes. He folded a questionnaire into an airplane and sailed it across the room. Later, he would crumple it into a ball and use the wastebasket as his target. In general, he acted as if he were having a good time and were in high spirits.

The other half of the subjects were exposed to a confederate who behaved aggressively and hostilely. Schachter was interested in learning under what conditions the subjects' behavior and emotional reactions would be influenced by the behavior of the confederate.

Consistent with his theory, Schachter found that subjects who were given the injection of epinephrine and either not informed or misinformed about its effects were influenced by the confederates' actions and behaved like them. Subjects who were accurately informed about the effects of the drug and subjects who were given only an injection of saline solution were not as likely to be influenced by the confederate in either case.

The explanation for the results was that subjects who were not informed or were misinformed about the effects of the drug relied on their environment (that is, the confederate's behavior) to label their own physiological arousal. The failure of the subjects who received the saline injections to mimic the behavior of the confederate illustrates that both physiological arousal and cognitive appraisal of the environment are necessary to produce emotion.

As additional support for a **two-component theory,** Schachter (1970) argued that people learn which emotions they can expect to experience when they smoke marijuana. If first-time smokers are around other smokers who act giddy and happy, they are likely to label their physiological arousal, which tends to be diffuse and vague, in similar ways. Conversely, novice smokers who are around smokers who are withdrawn and intro-

CRITICAL ISSUE

Tears: Do They Play a Role in Emotion?

For years many scientists have accepted Charles Darwin's assertion, made in the late 1800s, that while the act of weeping can serve to reduce suffering, tears themselves are a purposeless by-product. Recently a biochemist and professor of psychiatry, William Frey (1980), has reported data suggesting that tears do have a function—it may be that we are literally crying our grief out of our bodies when we shed tears.

Frey found that tears shed in response to emotion differ chemically from tears shed in response to eye irritation. Emotional tears contain greater concentrations of protein and the catecholamines epinephrine and norepinephrine than do irritant-induced tears. Our bodies produce these and certain other biochemicals during periods of stress, and these chemicals can, in turn, affect the way we feel. Frey believes that shedding tears may be a way of relieving stress. He points out that men who are taught that it is unmasculine to cry have a higher incidence of stress-related disorders—such as high blood pressure and ulcers.

This type of research is very difficult to do. The technology for measuring the biochemical make-up of very small quantities of tears is just being developed. And the practical problem of getting research participants to catch their tears in test tubes while weeping is no small matter. Frey found that many people could not cry with an experimenter present. He was finally able to collect emotional tears from 100 volunteers by showing them sad movies.

Frey recognizes that this hypothesis is speculative. The research is in the preliminary stages, and it may be some time before we know to what degree the failure to cry is associated with stress-related disorders.

Tears shed in sorrow differ chemically from those shed to cleanse the eyes. The former contain substances that the body creates during times of stress. (© Ken Karp)

Izard concluded that cultures interpret facial features differently. What emotions do you ascribe to the people pictured here? *(left to right: © Frank Siteman/Stock, Boston, Inc.; © Marjorie Pickens; © Ken Heyman; © Rick Smolan/Stock, Boston, Inc.; © Marjorie Pickens; © Suzanne Szasz)*

spective are likely to report those emotional reactions.

Schachter's theory and research have been very influential. The conceptualization of emotion as a two-component process has been used to explain phenomena as diverse as fear and romantic love. The debate about the nature of emotions, however, is far from resolved. Attempts to replicate Schachter's experiment described above have not been successful (Marshall & Zimbardo, 1979; Maslach, 1979). And other experiments have shown that some of Schachter's assumptions were incorrect (Valins, 1966). For instance, subjects who are aroused but have no explanation for their reaction report that the experience is unpleasant—not neutral, as Schachter assumed.

Differential-Emotion Theory

One controversy concerning emotions is whether they are innate or learned. Perhaps the most prevalent position among psychologists is that the capacity to have emotional reactions is innate, but learning plays an important role in influencing what emotions will be experienced and how they will be expressed. Once again, an either-or position seems to be oversimplistic. An interaction between innate biological factors and learned environmental factors is responsible for determining one's emotional experiences.

Certain theorists have been particularly interested in the innate-acquired controversy. Their theories suggest that certain basic emotions are indeed innate. These basic emotions each have their own specific neurological pattern. That is, if there are ten fundamental emotions, then there are ten different patterns of neurological activity in the brain that correspond to these emotions. This theory is known as **differential-emotion theory.** Differential-emotion theorists hypothesize that each fundamental emotion has evolutionary significance and that learning factors will influence the way these emotions are expressed and experienced. For instance, Japanese and Americans learn to express anger in different ways.

These theorists suggest that the fundamental emotions can be blended to produce the wide variety of emotions we experience (see Table 6–2).

One of the most prominent of the differential-emotion theorists is Carroll Izard (1977). His theory grew out of the work of Charles Darwin and William James and emphasizes the role of facial expressions in the emotional process. As Darwin hypothesized some 100 years ago, Izard believes that facial expressions provide feedback to the brain that can intensify, inhibit, or modify the experience of an emotion. Each fundamental emotion is associated with a specific facial expression. Note that Izard's theory is consistent with James's version of the James-Lange theory. James believed that voluntary muscle activity, such as facial expressions, can influence the experience of emotions. You might try to frown in an exaggerated way for a minute or two. Many people are surprised to discover that when they do this they begin to feel sad.

Feedback from facial expression is but one component in this theory. Two other components of emotions are (1) neural activity of the brain and somatic nervous system and (2) subjective experience. Since no single component alone can determine emotional experience, it is possible to experience emotion without accompanying facial expressions or to have a particular facial expression without the relevant emotional experience. For instance, everyone has had the experience of trying to maintain a blank expression while fighting the urge to laugh. Also, when a photographer asks you to smile, you do not necessarily feel happy when you comply. The importance of facial expression, however, can be seen in research that has found that an emotional experience may be accompanied by a change in facial expression that is so rapid it is not usually perceived by an observer (Haggard & Isaacs, 1966). So when you suppress laughter, your facial expression probably does change, but so rapidly and subtly that an observer could not detect it. Even when facial expression does not change discernibly, facial-muscle tension may change (Schwartz, Fair, Greenberg, Freedman, & Kleiman, 1974).

Table 6–2. Differential Emotions

Emotion	*Description*
Interest	To be engaged, fascinated, anxious; to want to investigate or become involved.
Joy	To feel confident, significant, content; to feel loved or lovable.
Surprise	To be amazed or astonished; a fleeting emotion in which the mind seems to go blank.
Distress	To be sad, discouraged, miserable; to feel out of touch with people, especially those who care for one.
Anger	To feel powerful and want to strike out.
Disgust	To feel sick to one's stomach and want to get away from a repellent object.
Contempt	To feel superior and somewhat hostile.
Fear	To be apprehensive, uncertain, insecure; to feel threatened physically or psychologically.
Shame/Shyness	To be aware of one's incompetence, inadequacy, or transgressions.
Guilt	To be preoccupied with perceived wrongdoing and want to set things right again.

One line of evidence that Izard presents to support his hypothesis that the ten fundamental emotions listed in Table 6–2 are innate comes from cross-cultural research. He and his colleagues have presented photographs of different facial expressions to people from a variety of cultures and asked them to identify the emotion being experienced. The cultures studied ranged from Western European countries to isolated preliterate cultures in New Guinea and Borneo. The percentage of agreement is remarkably high, averaging around 80 percent. But the importance of learning can be seen in the cultural differences. For example, the French are much better at identifying anger-rage (91.5 percent agreement) than are the Japanese (56.8 percent agreement). These differences are likely to have resulted from their different cultural values with regard to anger.

Differential-emotion theory is appealing because it, more so than other theories, takes the complexity of emotional experience into account. Izard's hypothesis regarding the role of facial expressions is particularly provocative and interesting. While the empirical support for this theory is impressive, it is by no means conclusive. For instance, while research has shown that electrical stimulation of certain areas of the brain can produce emotional reactions (Delgado, 1971), no one has been able to identify ten different patterns of neurological activity or ten specific areas of the brain that correspond to ten emotions.

The Role of Emotions

What role do emotions play in determining human behavior? The answer depends on whom you ask. As mentioned earlier, Izard believes that emotions are the primary motivational system for human beings. He suggests that emotions influence not only behavior, but one's perceptions, memory, thinking, imagination, and personality development as well. As just one example, the person who is usually joyful will tend to view the world through "rose-colored glasses," while the depressed or sad individual will tend to have a more pessimistic outlook. In contrast, theorists such as O. H. Mower (1961) believe that thoughts and attitudes are most important. His view suggests that emotions are an effect and not a cause.

The debate about the role of emotions has more than theoretical significance. A clinical psychologist's view of the role of emotions will influence the type of therapy he or she practices. As will be seen in Chapter 13, some psychotherapists, such as Albert Ellis, believe that a person's beliefs, thoughts, and attitudes are the source of psychological problems. Ellis attempts to modify his clients' thoughts in the belief that these changes will produce changes in emotional reactions. In contrast, much of the personal-growth movement is either implicitly or explicitly based on the notion that emotions are the primary causal factor in psychological disorders. Therapists who take this approach use techniques to help people remove emotional blocks and to get in touch with their feelings. Thus the way in which one views the role of emotions has practical implications; the controversy is not merely an esoteric debate among scientists.

Summary

Motivation and emotion are concepts that psychologists use to make behavior more understandable. Because motives and emotions must be inferred and cannot be directly observed, some psychologists believe they do not have a place in a science of behavior. Most feel, however, that as long as motives and emotions can be tied in to specific physiological and environmental conditions to predict behavior, they are useful concepts.

The term "drive" is generally used for motives that have a strong physiological basis. These include hunger, thirst, sex, temperature regulation, sleep, and breathing. Hunger, perhaps the most researched of these drives, is believed to be controlled by the activity of nerves in a "start eating" center and a "stop eating" center in the hypothalamus. These areas are sensitive to changes in blood chemistry. Other cells in the hypothalamus are sensitive to dehydration and arouse thirst.

Learning factors can shape the manner in which drives are expressed. Research has shown that obese people tend to eat in response to external cues, such as the taste of food or the time of day, while people of average weight seem to eat in response to internal cues. Obese people may also have a large number of fat cells, either through heredity or early nutritional experience.

Psychological motives are acquired primarily through learning. Two of the most researched psychological motives are the need for achievement and anxiety. The need for achievement is thought to be instilled by parents who encourage their children to be independent and reward them for being so. Individuals with high needs for achievement tend to prefer tasks of intermediate difficulty; they generally receive higher grades in college and are more likely to go into business or to become entrepreneurs than those with low motivation.

Anxiety is generally regarded as a negative drive because it often prevents people from engaging in rewarding activities. It can, however, have positive effects as well. It can facilitate performance and motivate individuals to work toward desirable goals. Research has shown that there is a complex relation between level of anxiety and performance. Moderate levels of anxiety tend to be associated with high levels of performance, while both low and high levels are associated with poorer performance. This relationship is called the Yerkes-Dodson Law.

Maslow proposed a hierarchy of motives to explain why people's motives differ. In ascending order, his hierarchy comprises physiological, safety, acceptance, esteem, and self-actualization needs. Once lower-level needs are satisfied, one can progress to the higher levels.

Psychoanalysis suggests that people can have unconscious motives, which influence our behavior without our awareness. This concept, although widely used by psychotherapists, has received little empirical support.

The issue of intrinsic versus extrinsic motivation concerns whether we behave in certain ways to satisfy internal needs or to obtain external rewards. Both intrinsic and extrinsic motivation are useful concepts, and researchers are concerned with how they interact with various situations. Probably both types of motivation play a role in most situations.

When two or more motives are active at the same time, conflict can result. In approach-approach conflicts, a person is motivated to approach two equally desirable but mutually exclusive goals. In avoidance-avoidance conflicts, a person must choose between two equally undesirable goals. Approach-avoidance conflicts are those in which a person is motivated both to approach and to avoid the same goal. Double approach-avoidance conflicts involve two goals, both of which have desirable and undesirable aspects. These types of conflict have been used to conceptualize various psychological disorders.

Four theories of emotion are the James-Lange theory, the Cannon-Bard theory, the two-component theory of emotion, and differential-emotion theory. The James-Lange theory suggests that the experience of emotion is produced by physiological changes. That is, we are afraid *because* we are running away. The Cannon-Bard theory suggests that specific brain centers are associated with emotion. Physiological changes in the viscera and the experience of emotion are produced by activation of these brain centers. According to this theory, we run *and* we are afraid. The two-component theory emphasizes cognition as well as physiological changes. It hypothesizes that we experience emotion by looking to the environment to provide labels for our physiological arousal. Differential-emotion theory suggests there are three components to emotions: activity of the brain and somatic nervous system, subjective experience, and feedback from movements in the voluntary muscles. The most important muscles, according to one version of this theory, are those involved in facial expressions. It further suggests that certain fundamental emotions are innate, having characteristic neural patterns in the brain.

Psychologists disagree about the role of emotions in influencing behavior. Some theorists believe that emotions are the primary motivational system of human beings. Others believe that emotions are an effect of cognition and behavior and have no causal role of their own. These theoretical differences have important implications for the practice of psychotherapy.

Key Terms For Review

affect
anxiety
approach-approach conflict
approach-avoidance conflict
avoidance-avoidance conflict
Cannon-Bard theory
defense mechanisms
differential-emotion theory
double approach-avoidance conflict
drive
emotion
esteem needs
incentive
James-Lange theory
learning without awareness
motive
need for acceptance
need for achievement
peak experience
physiological needs
psychological motives
safety needs
self-actualization
two-component theory of emotion
unconscious motivation

Suggested Readings

Beck, R. C. *Motivation: Theories and principles.* Englewood Cliffs, N. J.: Prentice-Hall, 1978.

A comprehensive text covering the theories and issues in motivation, for the student who wants to learn about the topic in detail.

Douglas, M. Accounting for taste. *Psychology Today,* July 1979, pp. 44 ff.

An interesting article that suggests that feelings of hunger and satiation are influenced by cultural patterns of preparing and serving food.

Fisher, S., & Fisher, R. L. Schlemiel children. *Psychology Today,* September 1980.

The authors describe the behavior and background of children who can be described as the class clown. It is suggested that such children develop this pattern to deal with conflict in the home.

Izard, C. E. *Human emotions.* New York: Plenum, 1977.

This text provides a review of the various theories of emotion and presents differential-emotion theory in detail.

Schachter, S. Some extraordinary facts about obese humans and rats. *American Psychologist,* 1971, *26,* 129–144.

Schachter reviews several of his studies that show the importance of external factors in the eating habits of the obese. He also discusses parallel findings in experiments with rats.

Suedfeld, P. The benefits of boredom: Sensory deprivation reconsidered. In I. L. Janis (Ed.), *Current Trends in Psychology,* Los Altos, Calif.: William Kaufmann, 1977.

Suedfeld reviews the research dealing with the effects of sensory deprivation. Rather than inducing pathology, the boredom associated with sensory deprivation may have useful therapeutic effects.

7

Language, Thinking, and Memory

After H. M. had an operation, his progress was followed for a considerable length of time. He showed no decrement in intelligence. In fact, his measured intelligence quotient actually increased by 13 IQ points to 117. This increase was attributed to the cessation of fits. The outstanding change was in his memory. Immediately following the operation there was marked retrograde and anterograde amnesia. The **retrograde amnesia** *(loss of memory for events preceding the operation) was quite severe but gradually shrank with time. Twelve years after the operation H. M. sometimes mixed up the temporal order of events before the operation.*

The severe **anterograde amnesia** *(failure to remember events occurring after the operation) persisted for at least 14 years with little, if any, improvement. H. M. was unsure of his new address six years after the family had moved. He was unable to learn where constantly used objects, such as the lawnmower, were kept. H. M. would amuse himself by reading the same magazines and solving the same jigsaw puzzles over and over again without giving any evidence of having seen them before. This lack of ability to register information was almost total and led to a lack of appreciation of the passage of time. When asked his age, H. M. would appreciably underestimate it in his answer (Miller, 1972, pp. 48–49).*

Memory, one of the higher mental functions, is responsible for our feelings of identity and continuity. These feelings give us the sense of being a person with a past, a present, and a future. Two other important mental functions are language and thinking. In this chapter we shall examine how these processes develop and what role they play in our daily interactions.

LANGUAGE

The use of language is one of the most important aspects of human behavior. Language permits us to express our innermost feelings and thoughts, exchange information, and transmit our knowledge, wisdom, and beliefs from generation to generation. Thus our culture firmly rests on the use of language, and language depends on specialized processes in the brain.

Language involves the use of arbitrary sounds that have accepted referents and that can be arranged in different ways to have different meanings (Lefrancois, 1980). This definition includes the three characteristics of language described by Brown (1973): displacement, meaning, and productiveness. Language involves displacement in both time and space because it permits reference to things and events that are removed from the language user. Language must also be organized semantically, since the communication of meaning is one of the primary functions of language. The third characteristic of language, productiveness, implies that given a set of speech sounds and a system of rules necessary for pairing sounds with meaning, we can generate an infinite number of combinations.

The Functions of Language

Language serves a vast variety of purposes. Halliday (1975) isolated the following basic functions:

1. *The instrumental function.* Language permits us to satisfy our needs and to express our desires.
2. *The regulatory function.* This function allows us to control the behavior of others by issuing demands and requests; it may be described as the "do that" function.
3. *The interpersonal function.* Language facilitates our encounters with others in social situations. Through language we identify our "me and you" interactions.
4. *The personal function.* Our personal identity, our expressions of unique views, feelings, and attitudes, is established in part by the way we express ourselves.
5. *The heuristic function.* We use language to understand and explore our environment. Halliday refers to this questioning process as the "tell me why" function of language.
6. *The imaginative function.* Through language we can escape from reality into a universe of our own making. The "let's pretend" or poetic function of language takes us into the world of fantasy.
7. *The informative function.* Finally, language allows us to communicate new information. Consider the importance of language when you feel like saying: "I've got something to tell you."

The Elements of Language

The study of language is usually divided into three areas: phonology, syntax, and semantics. **Phonology** describes the system of sound for a language. The elementary sounds of language are **phonemes,** which, for the most part, roughly correspond to the vowels and consonants of the letters of the alphabet. There are 45 phonemes in the English language, including vowel sounds like *e,* as in *he,* consonant sounds like *m* as in *mother,* and combination consonants like *th* as in *the.* Phonemes combine into larger units called **morphemes,** which are the smallest meaningful units of language. A morpheme may be a word (*pig*), or it may be part of a word, such as a prefix or suffix (*sub, ing,* etc.).

The second element of language is **syntax,** or grammar, which describes the structure of language and the ways words are put together to form sentences. Each language has its own set of rules for creating sentences from words and for expressing grammatical relations among words.

The third central aspect of language is **semantics,** which refers to the study of the meaning of words and sentences. Experience with words and an understanding of how words represent external objects and events are the raw materials for the acquisition of language.

The Development of Language

The study of language development is both dramatic and exciting. There are striking similarities among children from all cultures, most of whom normally acquire their native language reasonably well by the time they are age four or five. This is an impressive achievement considering the complexity of the process of language acquisition. In spite of the similarities in language acquisition among cultures, individual children vary considerably. Some children are completely verbal by the time they are 18 months old; others may be two and a half before they speak their first word. In this section we shall trace the development of language from the first vocal sound to the mastery of complete sentences. As we shall see, language acquisition entails the unfolding of an orderly sequence of events.

Early Vocalizations. The first vocal response is the birth cry. Although crying is a relatively simple response, it serves an important communicative function. The infant's cry initiates contact with the outside world, conveying basic physiological needs, such as being hungry, thirsty, or otherwise discontented. Crying sounds are characteristically made during periods of distress.

After the third month, crying usually decreases and noncrying sounds increase. The nondistress vocal productions of the infant in the second to sixth month are referred to as **cooing.** Most cooing sounds consist of long vowels like *umm* or gurgling sounds. They convey the kind of contentment associated with smiles and chuckles.

Sometime around the sixth month the child's vocalization changes, both qualitatively and quantitatively. The infant is now ready to enter the babbling period. **Babbling** includes a wider variety of sounds than cooing and is rich in both consonants and vowels. The early consonants include *p*, *m*, and *b*, which are sounds produced with the tongue in front of the mouth. Adults who are struggling to learn the gutteral sounds of the German language are surprised to hear infants spontaneously babble these sounds. Much of the infant's babbling, which is still meaningless speech, seems to serve no particular communicative function, but it is a necessary step in language development. Babbling helps to strengthen the muscles used in speech and provides a means for controlling and coordinating the sounds. Listening to an infant babbling, one gets the impression that the child finds the sound of his or her voice reinforcing. Babbling allows the child to vary sounds purposely in order to hear their consequences.

Is there any relationship between babbling and later language? There are a number of reasons for believing that babbling is not strictly necessary for later speech. It has been observed, for instance, that deaf children babble, although they make little progress toward adult speech. In addition, some theorists have held that the sounds of babbling are not the same as sounds used during the early word phase (Jakobson, 1968). This seems to indicate that the babbling child is not practicing sounds that will be used in later speech.

Recently, however, some researchers have challenged the assumption that there is no continuity between the child's babbling and later speech. Oller and Warren (1976), for example, studied the early babbling of infants and found that babbled syllables did indeed resemble the child's first meaningful words. According to these authors, babbling utterances are not random vocalizations but rather systematic expressions manifesting many of the same phonetic preferences that are found in later childhood pronunciations of adult words.

In any case, the infant's early speech productions indicate that the child is remarkably well prepared to learn to talk. Even before their first words children produce sounds in an orderly sequence, which was summarized as follows by Kaplan and Kaplan (1971):

1. Crying, which begins at birth.
2. Other (nondistress) vocalizations and cooing.
3. Babbling, which begins around the middle of the first year.
4. Finally, patterned speech toward the end of the first year.

This orderly sequence of sound production has been found to be universal.

The Holophrastic Stage. Somewhere around the age of ten months to a year, the child says the first meaningful word. For the next few months the child's speech consists of one-word utterances. When a single word stands for a phrase or sentence, it is referred to as a holophrase. In **holophrastic speech,** then, the child utilizes single-word utterances to express complex intentions or ideas. Generally, holophrases are labels for persons, objects, or acts. For example, the word "cookie" may mean "I would like a cookie," "I dropped my cookie and cannot reach it," "Give me another cookie," and so on. To extract the appropriate meaning from holophrastic speech, it is necessary to know what the child is doing or what situation the child is in.

Patricia Greenfield and her colleagues (Greenfield & Smith, 1976) suggested that children's single words progress in stages during the early part of the second year. Initially single words represent a combination of language and action. For example, the child may say "hi" or "bye-bye" when coming or going. During the next stage the child begins to use words that can be specifically attached to a person or object. Thus the child may say "ball" in the presence of that toy or "daddy" in the presence of the father. During the third stage holophrases represent requests and demands. The word "milk" indicates that the child wants something to drink.

These two-year-old children are learning to construct their first sentences. (© *Ed Lettau/Photo Researchers, Inc.*)

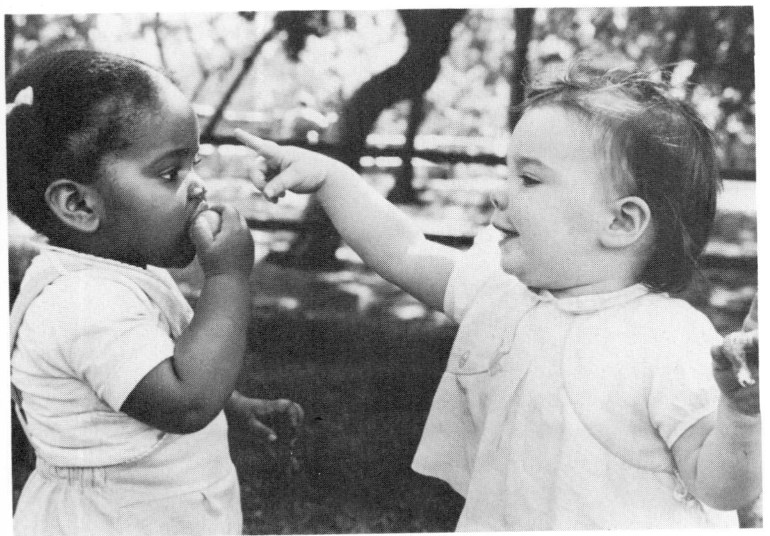

During the latter part of the holophrastic stage children use single-word utterances to express more complex relationships, such as an entire situation. For instance, the child may say "on" when the air conditioning is on.

While Greenfield and her co-workers attribute considerable meaning to the single words of children, other developmental psychologists are more conservative, assuming that single-word utterances are simply labels for familiar objects. Most interpretations of holophrastic speech, however, assume that the single-word utterance expresses more than just a label for an object.

The First Sentences. The next important step in language development occurs somewhere between 18 and 24 months, when the child begins to put two words together. These are generally simple contractions such as "where daddy" or "allgone milk." The two-word utterances express many relationships that were only implied in the child's holophrastic speech. Although the child's first sentences are quite simple, they are novel and creative and not merely a copy of the speech the child hears. Roger Brown (1973), a prominent psycholinguist, found that children express at least seven forms of knowledge in their two-word sentences (see Table 7–1).

As in holophrastic speech, two-word utterances cannot be understood by an examination of the syntax and grammatical relations alone. A knowledge of the context in which the sentence occurs is critical for capturing the meaning of the child's sentence.

Until the age of two, a child's language consists primarily of a mixture of single words and two-word sentences. Later, three- and four-word sentences appear, until the child's speech gradually takes on adult-like qualities.

Later Language Development. Usually around three years of age, rudimentary forms of more grammatical complexity begin to appear. Children begin, for instance, to join related ideas with con-

Table 7–1. A Child's First Sentences

Type of knowledge	Understanding implied by two-word sentences	Example
Naming	There exists a world of objects, whose members bear names.	It ball. There doggie.
Recurrence	A substance or activity can be prolonged, made to reappear, added to, or otherwise enriched or lengthened.	More ball.
Nonexistence	An object can disappear from a situation.	Allgone ball. No doggie.
Agent-action	People do things.	Johnny fall.
Action-object	Objects are acted upon.	Put truck. Change diaper.
Agent-object	A person can perform actions on an object.	Johnny stone. Me milk.
Action-location	An action can occur in a specific place.	Sit chair. Fall floor.
Object-location	An object occupies a specific place.	Book table.
Possessor and possession	People possess objects.	My ball. Adam ball.
Attribution	Objects have characteristics.	Big ball. Little story.
Demonstrative entity	One of a set of objects can be specified.	That ball.

Source: Adapted from Brown, *A First Language: The Early Stages* (Cambridge, Mass.: Harvard University Press, 1973).

junctions such as "and" and "but." By the time children have reached the age of four to five years, most of them have acquired the basic syntax of their language.

One striking characteristic of early syntactic development is that children omit words, such as "of," "or," and "the," that carry little meaning to them. The child's version of the sentence "I showed you the book" may be "I show book." Speech that consists largely of meaningful or content words has been called **telegraphic speech.** Telegraphic sentences are abbreviations of adult speech that sound like telegrams.

Between ages three and six, overgeneralizations and underextensions are common errors. In **overgeneralization** the child uses a word in a much broader sense than adults. For example, a two-year-old may say "dog" when referring not only to dogs but to all four-legged animals. In **underextension** the child fails to include objects in a particular category because they are unfamiliar or atypical. Children, for instance, may not include "worms" in the animal category because "animal" means four-leggedness and animation.

Although the basic language structure is acquired during the first three to five years, both semantic and syntactic development continue for many years. Comprehension of passive forms such as "the cart is pulled by the horse" develop relatively late. Large increases in grammatical constructions are made between kindergarten and first grade and between the fifth and seventh grades. Children make the greatest semantic gains during the school years.

With the acquisition of language the child attains a level of sophistication unknown heretofore. Once armed with the symbol system of language, the child's interactions with people and the environment begin to assume a new importance. Table 7–2 and Figure 7–1 summarize the development of language during the first six years.

It appears that in order to learn a language a child must be able to interact with people in that language. Of all the adults whose speech the child is exposed to, the mother or primary caretaker has the greatest influence on the child's language development. The speech of the caretaker is distinctively different from that of others. Typically, mothers use a simplified vocabulary, higher pitch, and exaggerated intonation when talking to their young children. In addition to short simple sentences, a high proportion of questions among mothers and imperatives among fathers was reported by Moskowitz (1978). Curiously, as the child begins to utter meaningful words, adults invariably speak to the child in very simple sentences; during the babbling stage, many parents address the baby in long, complex sentences.

Table 7–2. Overview of Language Development

Age	Description	Example
First year: babbling	Babbling sounds appear around six months. They include a variety of sounds, both consonants and vowels, many of which are duplications of monosyllables.	"baba" "mama"
Second year: holophrases	This stage is characterized by single-word utterances, which are used to express more complex meanings. Most holophrases are labels for persons, objects, or actions.	"cookie"
Second year: two-word sentences	Toward the end of the second year the child begins to speak in two-word sentences. Language at this stage is novel and creative.	"Adam hit." "My ball." "Allgone milk."
Third year: complex constructions	Grammar is fairly well developed, although not always correct. Around age three the child learns the use of auxiliaries and can change word order to produce grammatically correct negatives.	"I no want apple." "It broke." "I am playing." "Don't go away."
Fourth year: correct, concrete, simple language	Use of correct but relatively simple language. No use of passive forms or conditional sentences. Future tense and adult question forms are developing.	"Will Adam go?" "Why is he singing?"
Fifth year: approximation of adult speech	Two or more ideas are expressed in one sentence.	"I see what I made."

One familiar type of caretaker speech is known as baby talk. Most baby talk consists of simplified vocabulary items for food, animals, body functions, and toys. Some words are simply duplications of syllables, such as "wa-wa" for water or "choo-choo" for train.

Psychologists are not sure of the exact functions of the modifications in the caretaker's speech. It has been suggested that the purpose of baby talk is to make the speech more affectionate. Exaggerated intonations may alert the child to the spoken language. In many instances it seems that by modifying their speech caretakers try to simplify the child's task of analyzing the language it hears.

Many studies have shown that vocabulary grows faster in children who are spoken to a great deal. In addition, Katherine Nelson's (1973) extensive study of vocabulary growth in one- and two-year-old children found that those who had more experiences outside the home (outings, visits, field trips) and contacts with different adults developed their vocabulary more rapidly than children who spent most of their time at home with their mothers. It seems safe to say, then, that the child's language is affected by the quality and quantity of the language of the caretaker.

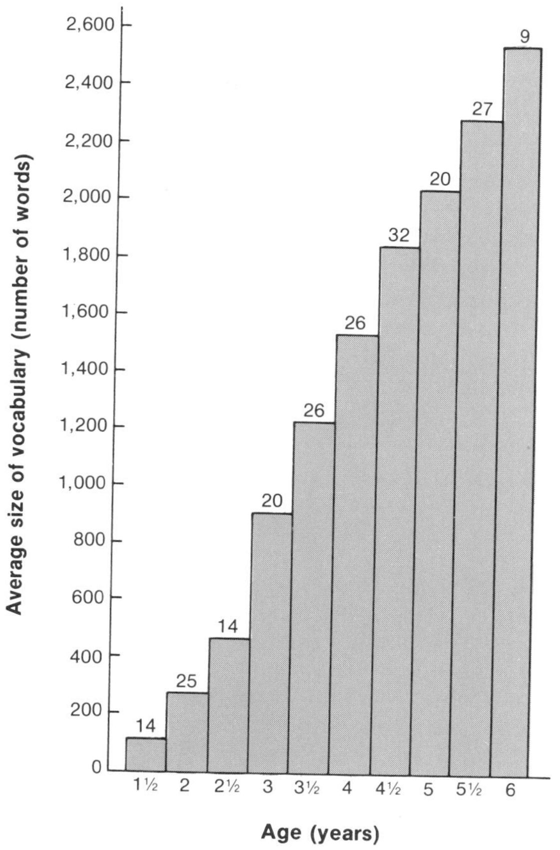

Figure 7–1. The average size of children's vocabulary grows enormously between the ages of one and a half and six. The number of children tested for each age group is shown above each bar. Data are based on work done by Madorah E. Smith of the University of Hawaii.

Theories of Language Development

The field of language development has been influenced heavily by theoretical views. One view holds that language ability is innate; another argues that language is learned by imitating others. A third view recognizes the importance of both biological, or innate, determinants and environmental influences. We shall briefly examine each of these views next.

The Nativist Perspective. According to this view, language acquisition is an innate ability. Historically, our understanding of the biological basis of language has been rooted in the study of language disorders resulting from brain damage (Geschwind, 1972). For example, a person with **expressive aphasia** has difficulty expressing thoughts in speech or writing. Someone with **receptive aphasia** has trouble understanding written or spoken communications.

We have selected Chomsky's (1968) work to illustrate the **nativist perspective,** and we shall also consider Lenneberg's contribution. Noam Chomsky proposed that the human nervous system is equipped with what he called the **language-acquisition device,** a neurological system prewired in such a way that the person is able to process and receive language. This language-acquisition device is, of course, not actually a structure in the brain but the innate capacity to learn grammar. Slobin (1972) noted grammatical errors such as "goed," "sayed," or "runned" that are common among young children. According to Slobin, such errors seem to support the existence of a language-acquisition device because they result from irregularities in the language rather than from the misapplication of rules.

The most thorough and precise case for biological determinants of language was presented by Lenneberg (1967), who considers language acquisition to be a function of biological maturation. Lenneberg argued that the ability to generate and understand language is uniquely human and inherited as a species-specific characteristic. The inherited biological determinants include, among other things, the structure of the articulatory apparatus, including the mouth and larynx; specific brain centers that process language; and a specialized auditory system.

APPLICATION

Nonverbal Communications

During the past decade increasing attention has been paid to nonverbal aspects of human communication. The popularizers of the body-language concept have pointed out that we often communicate far more with our body—through gestures, postures, facial expressions, and body motion—than with the words we speak. In fact, a number of researchers contend that we not only reveal our thoughts, intentions, and personality through nonverbal communications, but that the nonverbal aspects of our interactions are more important than the verbal messages in determining social meaning (Mehrabian, 1972).

Obviously there are different types of nonverbal behavior just as there are different types of verbal behavior. Moreover, nonverbal communications vary not only from culture to culture, but also with a person's age, sex, and social status. It has been found, for instance, that women smile and laugh more and pay more visual attention to their partners than men do (Frances, 1979). Similarly, men have been reported to make significantly more postural shifts, such as shifting seat or leg positions, than women do. According to Henley and Freeman (1975), the differences in nonverbal communications between men and women are related to the status differences between the sexes.

Let us look more closely at two examples of nonverbal communications that all of us use daily and the types of meanings that psychologists extract from such communications.

Most of us would agree that the human face is rich in communicative potential. It is the primary site of communication of emotional states; it reflects interpersonal attitudes; and some say its power to communicate is second only to human speech (Knapp, 1972). Consequently most of us pay a great deal of attention to the messages we receive from the faces of others.

Much of the research examining facial expressions is concerned with the question of how accurately we can interpret facial expressions as mirrors of emotions. Friedman and his co-workers (Friedman, DiMatteo, & Mertz, 1980) recently studied the facial expressions of broadcasters during coverage of the 1976 presidential election campaign. They prepared brief videotape segments of the facial expressions of five anchorpersons (Brinkley, Chancellor, Cronkite, Reasoner, and Walters) while saying "Gerald Ford" (or "Mr. President" or "President Ford") or "Jimmy Carter" (or "Governor Carter" or "the Democratic presidential nominee").

The judges, a group of untrained college students who had volunteered to participate in this study, were asked to assess the facial expressions of each broadcaster, rating them from extremely positive to extremely negative. They found that four of the anchorpersons showed reliable differences in facial expressions while saying the candidates' names. Cronkite, Brinkley, and Reasoner were judged as having a more positive facial expression when saying Carter than when saying Ford. Chancellor's expression was more positive when saying Ford. For Barbara Walters the difference was not significant.

Lenneberg pointed out that children around the world acquire language in a strikingly similar order, despite vast cultural variations. As we have seen, children everywhere begin to babble when six months old, say their first word near the end of the first year, use two-word combinations near the end of the second year, and master basic syntax about age four or five. The similarities in language learning for different children and different languages are so great that it is tempting to assume that the human brain is preprogrammed for language acquisition.

The notion of language as an innate ability is also supported by the fact that people learn language far more quickly and easily during a certain period of biological maturation, from infancy to puberty. Before adolescence a child can achieve the fluency of a native speaker in any language without much training. Later, learning is more difficult and usually requires study. When a fam-

One possible explanation for the differences in facial expressions is that they reflected differences in the broadcasters' attitudes toward the two candidates. If this conclusion is accurate, nonverbal communications may transmit important attitudinal and emotional information to TV viewers that an objective press would work to eliminate.

Our second example of nonverbal communications, tactile communications, is probably the most basic form of communication. Our skin is equipped with thousands of tactile receptors (see Chapter 4) specialized to receive nonverbal messages from pressure, temperature, texture, and pain. The newborn child uses tactile explorations to gain knowledge about the environment; for the adolescent tactile experiences with members of the same and then of the opposite sex become increasingly important; and throughout adulthood touching plays a crucial part in human relationships. As in the case of facial expressions, the amount and kind of tactile contact varies with age, sex, and the relationship of the partners. Men, for instance, have been found to touch women more than the reverse. Psychologist Nancy Henley (1975), after recording many instances of touching in places such as a shopping center, a bank, and a college campus, suggested that touch is a means by which men express dominance over women.

Perhaps the most dramatic testimony of the communicative potential of touch comes from the blind. Here is how Helen Keller described her dog: "He was rolling on the grass . . . his fat body revolved, stiffened and solidified into an upright position and his tongue gave my hand a lick. . . . If he could speak, I believe he could say with me that paradise is attained by touch" (Knapp, 1972, p. 112).

Willis and Hamm (1980) recently reported that touch is important in securing compliance, especially if a request is difficult. In a series of experiments, the researchers asked university students to sign a petition for a popular cause (easy request) and shoppers to take a few minutes of their time to make several ratings of photographs (difficult request). In both situations half of the participants were slightly touched by the experimenter on the upper arm prior to the request, while the other half were not touched. In both experiments compliance was more likely for subjects who had been touched. It was suggested that touch may increase compliance by increasing attention and involvement.

Although the communication systems of the body may not operate exactly like a linguistic system, these examples indicate that nonverbal communications by themselves or in combination with words produce important shades of meaning.

A politician knows that touching someone can influence his or her behavior. *(© Vicki Lawrence/Stock, Boston, Inc.)*

ily moves to a foreign country, children pick up the language much more quickly than their parents, who often must depend on them as translators. In cases of speech disruption caused by brain damage, young children often recover their language capacity, whereas older persons who suffer brain damage have a poor prognosis for the recovery of language.

Although we are probably biologically prepared for language, it is unlikely that biological principles alone account for all aspects of language development.

The Learning-Theory Perspective. Ask most people how children learn to speak, and they will probably say the child learns by imitation. This position is maintained by many learning theorists who emphasize reinforcement principles (Skinner, 1957) or the role of imitation (Bijou, 1976). Skinner, for instance, maintained that language is learned through operant conditioning. According to this view, parents selectively reinforce those parts of the child's speech that approximate adult language. Generally, the child is rewarded for closer and closer approximations of adult speech. The fundamental notion in Skinner's theory of language acquisition is that the child learns language because he or she is shaped into it. For example, sounds like "kuh" may be reinforced with a cookie, "wa" with a drink, or "da" with a smile from daddy. As the child's language repertoire grows, reinforcement is withheld unless the boy or girl says something closer to the adult version of the word.

The **learning-theory perspective** of language development assumes that children learn to imitate the speech responses of their parents through reinforcement. However, acquiring speech responses is not sufficient to be verbally effective. The child must also learn to use language in its appropriate context. In Skinner's terminology this means that speech must come under stimulus control. For example, the child just having learned the word "daddy" is initially likely to say "daddy" in the presence of many different men. A child of one of the authors, whose father wears a beard, ran toward a bearded sailor on a beach shouting "Daddy, daddy" while his father was out of town. Children soon learn that they are only reinforced for the use of words in their appropriate context. At that point we can say that speech has come under stimulus control.

Learning-theory accounts of language development have been criticized because they emphasize the role of imitation without taking into consideration the unique contribution of the child to language acquisition. We do know, for instance, that children extract simple rules (such as making a noun plural by adding *s*) from the speech they hear and use them in their own language. Gradually these rules help them approximate the speech of adults, to whom the child listens more and more. We also know that most children practice their language and try out new grammatical forms when no one is around. According to learning theory, however, the child is a hollow organism who responds only to external stimulation, that is, reinforcement.

Learning theory assumes that children learn what to say and when to say it because they are rewarded for speaking correctly and not rewarded for violating the rules of speech. But observational studies made of parents and children together find that parents are just as likely to reward their children for incorrect statements as they are to reinforce them for correct ones. Roger Brown and Camille Hanlon (1970) examined whether parents approved or disapproved their children's syntactic errors in verb forms ("swammed"), plurals ("foots"), and subject-verb agreement ("they smiles"). Their findings revealed that the parents responded to the child's meaning of the sentence and not to the grammar. The parents corrected the child's factual inaccuracies and insults but paid little attention to grammatical mistakes. This study, along with others (e.g., Brown, 1973), makes it difficult to see how adult reinforcement alone can explain the child's learning of correct grammar. Instead, it appears that children pass at their own rate through the principal stages of syntactic and semantic development, regardless of the pattern of reinforcement.

In contrast to the learning perspective, in which the child is essentially viewed as a passive observer, many current theorists emphasize the active role that the child plays in the process of language acquisition. Tagatz (1976) summarized this viewpoint as follows:

> Children compile specific information from what they hear and formulate hypotheses concerning the nature of this language. Children are instrumental in the language development process. . . . Not only do they formulate, test, and evaluate hypotheses concerning the rules of their language, but they also actively compile linguistic information to use in the formulation of hypotheses (p. 90).

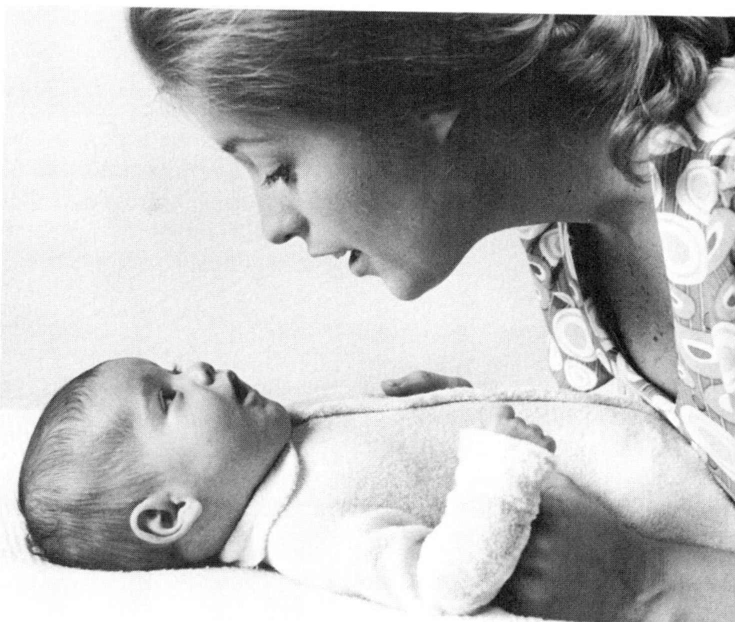

The interactionist perspective emphasizes the role of the environment—here, the way a mother talks to her child—in language development. *(© Suzanne Szasz)*

The Interactionist Perspective. Most psychologists today accept the notion that language is learned in the context of spoken language as well as the idea that there is some kind of innate biological preparation for learning to speak. However, there is considerable disagreement over the extent to which the child has to be directly taught to speak. Clearly certain biological factors predispose us to acquire language. At the same time, our environment contributes to how, and how well, this innate potential is realized. Part of the child's early linguistic environment, for instance, receives important contributions from the speech of parents and other adults.

The basic assumption of the **interactionist perspective** is that although we may know that basic language abilities are governed by biology, environmental factors are also important in language acquisition. In other words, while the pattern of language development may reflect certain ways in which the information is processed by the brain, the speed with which children pass through the stages of language development may be more susceptible to the effects of family and environment (Bloom, Rocissano, & Hood, 1976). In addition, the interactionist stresses the importance of the role of the child in language mastery.

Adequate explanations of language acquisition today seem to depend on a closer linkage between language and thinking (see Brown, 1973; Bruner, 1975). The simplistic notions of a biological or learning-theory perspective have come under considerable attack. The interactionist theory represents an attempt to combine biological heritage with a number of different environmental determinants. It currently offers the most encompassing theory of language acquisition.

Sex and Social-Class Differences in Language Development. It used to be widely believed that girls acquire language more rapidly than boys. In fact, our sex-role stereotypes assume that women are much more verbal than men. Presumably the earlier verbal fluency of females begins during infancy. Moss (1967), for instance, found that by the age of three months baby girls babble and vocalize more than boys.

After reexamining the available evidence, Maccoby and Jacklin (1974) concluded that sex differences in language acquisition have been greatly exaggerated. In spite of some small advantages for girls in the early years of life, from age three onward there appears to be no overall superiority among girls in sentence length, vocabulary size, and linguistic complexity.

We find similar results about differences in linguistic abilities among people from different social classes. It has long been asserted that upper- and middle-class children are verbally superior to lower-class children. Lower-class children have smaller vocabularies and are likely to complete language mastery later than upper- and middle-class children.

The differences are usually explained in terms of the different types of language training children receive. Middle-class mothers verbally interact more frequently with their children than do lower-class mothers. Similarly, middle-class parents tend to ask more questions of their children and elaborate on their statements, thereby helping the child to express connections between abstract ideas. In lower-class families, language tends to be more concrete and is often restricted to verbal communication in connection with discipline. In contrast to middle-class mothers, lower-class mothers often do not encourage their children to develop formal, conceptually ordered speech.

Black English is an expressive, sophisticated idiom and not the inferior dialect it is sometimes thought to be. (© *Ken Heyman)*

Some of the most interesting studies of social-class differences compared black ghetto children and white middle-class children (see Dale, 1972; Labov, 1970). Black children often use two modes of communication, one in school and another at home and among friends. The language the child speaks in school is characterized by nonfluency, simplified syntax, and lack of expressiveness. However, the language the child speaks at home is rich and fluent. Labov found that the black adolescent gang members he studied displayed a highly sophisticated verbal system and placed high value on verbal skills. The gangs often had a "verbal leader" who would direct the group in gang-oriented epic poems, which frequently had high literary value. The boys would partly recite epic poems from classical literature and supplement the original with gang-relevant activities.

In a sense, then, black children have to be bilingual—speaking one language (standard English) in the school and another (black English) in the home and neighborhood. Contrary to popular belief, black English is not a collection of random mistakes but a distinct, complex dialect that is governed by rules and capable of carrying shades of meaning, as is standard English (Dillard, 1972).

The incorrect notion that black English is inferior puts many black children in a perplexing situation. Often they are scolded by teachers for violating language rules that they may not have acquired. At the same time, they are expected to learn rules that are incorrect from their perspective. The language discrepancies between standard and black English contribute to the problems black children experience in school.

Language in Apes

Our discussion of language development would be incomplete without mentioning the research conducted on language learning in apes.

David Premack (1971) at the University of California at Santa Barbara trained a chimpanzee named Sarah to use plastic symbols in a manner suggestive of language. Taking advantage of chimpanzees' ability to discriminate shapes, he taught Sarah to use various visual forms to represent "words" (see Figure 7–2). Employing principles of operant conditioning, Premack reinforced her with an apple whenever she placed the correct plastic "word" on a metal slate. The if-then concept illustrated in Figure 7–2 was taught using sentences such as the following:

Sarah take apple
if-then
Mary give chocolate Sarah
Sarah take banana
if-then
Mary no give chocolate Sarah

Sarah demonstrated her understanding by taking the apple in the first case and not taking the banana in the second case (Premack & Premack, 1972). The Premacks successfully showed that chimps can be trained to use language concepts creatively and "say" things they did not learn during training.

Another well-known subject of language-learning experiments was the chimpanzee Lana (Rumbaugh, Gill, von Glasersfeld, Warner, & Pisani, 1975). Lana's language training utilized a special computer keyboard, from which she would make requests such as the following:

Please machine give coffee
Please Tim tickle Lana

(Lana was particularly fond of coffee and liked being tickled.)

As part of her language training Lana would monitor her sentences on a computer display and erase those with grammatical mistakes. One time when Lana was in the middle of constructing an elaborate sentence, her trainer Tim deliberately interspersed a word from his separate computer console that made nonsense of Lana's sentence. She gazed at her own computer display and responded with the sentence, "Please, Tim, leave room."

Lana had acquired the correct use of the concept "name-of" in response to the question "What name-of this?" She had not, however, been taught

Lana's ability to communicate with plastic symbols shows that some animals can learn primitive forms of language. (© *Yerkes Regional Primate Research Center, Emory University*)

to ask for the name of an object. One day Tim was sitting in front of Lana's cage holding three objects. Lana knew the names of two of them (a can and a bowl, both empty), while the third object (a box filled with M&Ms) was unfamiliar to her. The following dialogue between Lana and Tim was recorded by the computer:

Lana: Tim give Lana this can. (11:36 a.m.)
Tim: Yes. (And Tim gave her the empty can, though apparently she wanted the box with the M&Ms.)
Lana: ? Tim give Lana this can. (11:42 a.m.)
Tim. No can. (Which meant that Tim did not have the can to give her as it had just been given to her.)
Lana: ? Tim give Lana this bowl. (11:43 a.m.)
Tim: Yes. (And Tim gave the empty bowl to her.)
Lana: ? Shelley (sentence unfinished) (11:43 a.m.)
Tim: No Shelley. (Shelley, the technician, was not present.)
Lana: ? Tim give Lana this bowl. (Before Tim could answer, she continued . . .) (11:44 a.m.)
Lana: ? Tim give Lana name-of this. (11:45 a.m.)
Tim: Box name-of this. (Thereby giving her the name of the vessel which she apparently wanted.)
Lana: Yes. (11:46 a.m.)

Lana: ? Tim give Lana this box. (11:47 a.m.)
Tim: Yes. (Whereupon Tim gave it to her, and she immediately ripped it open and extracted the M&M candies.) (Rumbaugh et al., 1975, p. 368.)

Still other chimps, like Washoe, acquired an impressive repertoire of signs in American Sign Language that could be used in meaningful communication (Gardner & Gardner, 1969, 1974).

Although there is little doubt that apes have the ability to communicate through means suggestive of language, the question remains whether they have the capacity for language. Hewes (1977) concluded that on the basis of the evidence available now, we may say that chimps have a rudimentary capacity for language, but it remains to be seen whether that capacity is rooted in psychological processes that are fundamentally similar to those involved in the linguistic performance of humans (p. 356). Wilson (1972) concluded that the language difference between humans and primates may be quantitative rather than qualitative, but at the very least our own species must still be ranked as unique in its capacity to transform a large vocabulary into sentences that touch on virtually every experience and thought (p. 60).

Figure 7–2. Sarah's language board.

THE CONCEPT OF THINKING

In contrast to language, cognitive processes are private events, since we cannot see what somebody else is thinking. Thinking, thinking of, thinking up, thinking about are some of our most important mental activities. The question of central concern in this section is: What is thinking and how do we acquire this important mental capacity?

The Nature of Thinking

Say you walk down the street and notice a brand new Porsche. The idea occurs to you, "It would be nice to own that car." The common-sense term for this kind of mental process is thinking. In everyday usage thinking refers to reasoning, reflection, judgment, or more generally to the fact that "something is going on in the mind."

More formally defined, however, thinking involves the organization and reorganization of past learning in present situations. Thinking is closely linked to other mental activities, especially perception and memory; psychologists usually refer to these interrelated processes as cognition. **Cognition** is concerned with how we gather knowledge about the world around us and how we store, retrieve, and use that knowledge.

Thinking is a complex, multifaceted human phenomenon. Consider the many uses of the word "think."

1. Can you think of (remember) the name of the street she lives on?

CRITICAL ISSUE

Language and Thought

The relation between language and thought has puzzled psychologists for many years. There are two major views regarding this relationship.

One view assumes that language determines thought. It claims that our world view and nonverbal behavior are affected by the language we speak. The chief adherent of this perspective is Benjamin Lee Whorf (1956). As a linguist, Whorf was interested in the vocabulary and sentence structure of people from different cultures. He thought that differences in language—92 words for snow in one, words for only three colors in another, or no separate words for wide and fat in still another language—must influence the ways members of different cultures think. Since most of the world's languages differ markedly from one another, Whorf assumed that children in sophisticated cultures must think differently from those in remote and linguistically distant cultures. Although the **Whorf hypothesis** is interesting and attractive, there is little experimental evidence supporting it. Nevertheless, the idea that language influences thought is consistent with daily observations. Describe a young lady as a "free spirit" or "tramp" to a friend and you find radically different trains of thought.

The second viewpoint suggests that language and thought are interrelated. Vygotsky (1962) suggested that there is a mutual interdependence between language and thought, that is, language determines thought and thought determines language. He contends that thought and speech are initially separate streams that develop parallel for a time. Near the age of two, however, the two independent streams merge—thought becomes verbal and speech becomes rational. According to Vygotsky, language and thought serve each other.

The interdependence of language and thought is supported by many experiments (e.g., Bruner & Kenney, 1966). Bruner points to the errors that children under seven or eight years typically make on problems of conservation, hypothesizing that these errors may be due partly to the child's underdeveloped system of verbalization. To support the relationship between language and thought, Bruner cites a study of transposition. The experimental apparatus consisted of a tray of nine glasses of three different heights and three different widths, arranged in three rows of equal heights and three columns of equal diameters (see Figure 7–3). Children ages five to seven were asked to perform one of three tasks related to the matrix of glasses: copy the original matrix when all the glasses had been removed, properly replace missing glasses in the otherwise unchanged matrix, or rebuild the matrix with one of the corner elements transposed to the diagonal corner. Throughout the experiment the children were encouraged to verbalize their attempts. The experimenters noted three classes of verbal descriptions. The first class, observed among the youngest subjects, was labeled **global descriptions,** which included terms such as "smaller," "littler," "gianter." Older children used **dimensional descriptions,** words that were related to one of the specific dimensions of the glasses. A third type of description was called a **confounded description,** since it included both dimensional and global terms.

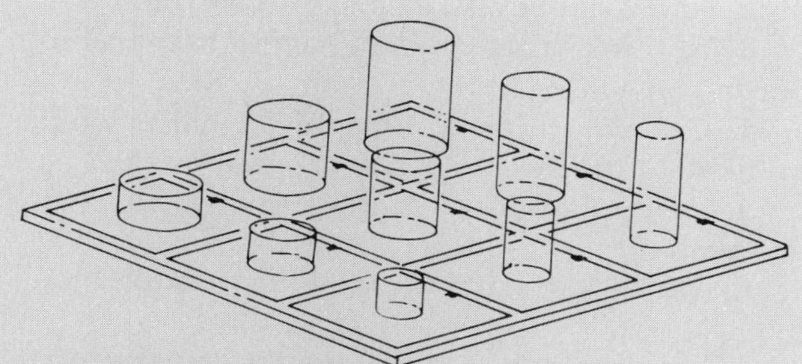

Figure 7–3. Matrix of glasses employed in the Bruner and Kenney experiment. (From J. S. Bruner, Rose R. Oliver, and Patricia M. Greenfield, *Studies in Cognitive Growth*. Copyright © 1966 by John Wiley & Sons, Inc.)

The results of this experiment indicated that children who employed dimensional descriptions to describe the matrix were more likely to succeed in transposing the matrix correctly than children who used either global or confounded descriptions. The authors concluded that language is closely related to the level of thinking.

2. I think (believe) I will skip class tomorrow.
3. To think of (anticipate) having to cancel the party is upsetting.
4. Can you think of (imagine) what it would be like not having to go to work every day!
5. Dropping out of school is unthinkable (unacceptable).
6. He did it without thinking (unintentionally).
7. I am thinking of taking (tentatively planning to take) a trip.
8. I think highly of my friend (judge her approvingly).

This list of meanings of the word "think" captures some of the different cognitive functions that underlie our thought processes.

Cognitive Development

According to most theories of cognitive development, thinking depends on how a person perceives his or her environment and in what ways he or she can act upon this internal representation. The most important contribution in the area of cognitive development was made by the Swiss zoologist Jean Piaget, who formulated a detailed and provocative theory of intellectual development.

Piaget (1960) viewed cognitive growth as a progressive change in mental functioning. Although cognitive growth varies from person to person, Piaget assumed that it follows a fixed sequence. Children may not go through the various stages of cognitive development at the same age, but they do pass through the stages in the same order. Piaget was convinced that the intellectual attainments in earlier stages were prerequisites for progress in the later stages.

Piaget's theory recognizes four main periods of cognitive growth: the sensory-motor stage, the preoperational stage, the stage of concrete operations, and the stage of formal operations. Let us examine the progression toward cognitive maturity during each of these periods.

The Sensory-Motor Stage. For approximately the first two years of life children progress through a number of different substages or circular reactions making up the **sensory-motor stage.** The child makes a dramatic transition from a reflexive organism to one possessing rudimentary symbolic thought. During this early stage of cognitive development the child represents the world in terms of actions—sucking, looking, grasping, and holding.

Several interesting accomplishments are achieved during the sensory-motor stage. The child becomes aware of spatial relationships through motor activity, such as reaching and grasping. And the infant develops a concept of the passing of time.

Another important discovery during the sensory-motor stage involves the development of **object permanence.** Object permanence refers to the child's knowledge that objects continue to exist even though they are no longer in sight. At birth the infant has no conception of object permanence. When objects are out of the visual field, they no longer exist. As the concept of object permanence develops, the baby will actively search for a vanished object. For example, if you move a ball behind a screen on the left side of the infant's vision, the baby will move his or her head or eyes to look for the reappearance of the ball on the right side.

During the sensory-motor stage the infant also shows a growing ability to solve simple problems. The child now uses an already known response to a specific end. Thus the child may knock down a pillow or push your hand away to obtain a toy hidden behind it. According to Piaget, this is a clear intention on the child's part to solve a problem by inventing a strategy that will work.

Finally, toward the second half of the second year we come to the beginning of what we normally call thought. The child now has the ability to invent new means through mental combinations rather than through overt explorations or manipulations. An observation Piaget made of his own son Laurent may illustrate the rudimentary ability to think through a problem and find a so-

APPLICATION

Cognitive Growth: From Reflexes to Thought

Some of the changes that take place in the sensory-motor stage of cognitive development can be seen in the diary Piaget (1954) kept for his three children—Laurent, Lucienne, and Jacqueline:

> *0 months, 20 days.* (Adaptation of reflexes.) He bites the breast which is given him, 5 cm from the nipple. For a moment he sucks the skin when he lets go in order to move his mouth about 2 cm. As soon as he begins sucking again he stops. . . . When his search subsequently leads him accidentally to touch the nipple with the mucosa of the upper lip (his mouth being wide open), he at once adjusts his lips and begins to suck.
>
> *1 month, 1 day.* (Primary circular reactions.) . . . His right hand may be seen approaching his mouth. . . . But as only the index finger was grasped, the hand fell out again. Shortly afterward it returned. This time the thumb was in the mouth. . . . I then remove the hand and place it near his waist. . . . After a few minutes the lips move and the hand approaches them again. This time there is a series of setbacks . . . [but finally] the hand enters the mouth. . . . I again remove the hand. Again lip movements cease, new attempts ensue, success results for the ninth and tenth time, after which the experiment is interrupted.
>
> *3 months, 5 days.* (Secondary circular reactions.) Lucienne shakes her bassinet by moving her legs violently (bending and unbending them, etc.), which makes the cloth dolls swing from the hood. Lucienne looks at them, smiling, and recommences at once. . . . Lucienne, at 4 months, 27 days, is lying in her bassinet. I hang a doll [from the hood] over her feet which immediately sets in motion the schema of shaking. But her feet reach the doll right away and give it a violent motion, which Lucienne surveys with delight. Afterward she looks at her motionless foot for a second, then recommences.
>
> *10 months, 11 days.* (Tertiary circular reactions.) Laurent is lying on his back. . . . He grasps in succession a celluloid swan, a box, etc., stretches out his arm and lets them fall. He distinctly varies the positions of the fall. Sometimes he stretches out his arm vertically, sometimes he holds it obliquely, in front or behind. . . . When the object falls in a new position (for example, on his pillow), he lets it fall two or three times more in the same place . . . then he modifies the situation.
>
> *1 year, 4 months, 0 days.* (Beginning of thought.) I put [a] chain into a box and reduce the opening to 3 mm. It is understood that Lucienne is not aware of the functioning of the opening and closing of the matchbox. . . . She only possesses the two preceding schemata: turning the box over . . . and sliding her fingers into the slit to make the chain come out. It is, of course, this last procedure that she tries first: she puts her finger inside and gropes to reach the chain, but fails completely. A pause follows during which Lucienne manifests a very curious reaction. . . . She looks at the slit with great attention; then, several times in succession, she opens and shuts her mouth, at first slightly, then wider and wider! . . . [Then] Lucienne unhesitatingly puts her finger in the slit and, instead of trying as before to reach the chain, she pulls so as to enlarge the opening. She succeeds and grasps the chain.

lution with little or no overt trial-and-error behavior. During his first year Laurent had often played with sticks but never used them as a means of reaching for objects. Even at 14 months he would hold the stick in one hand while stretching out the other hand for some distant object. One day, when Laurent was over 16 months, he held the stick in the middle trying to pull a cookie toward him. He soon switched his hand to the end of the stick and successfully got hold of the

Realizing that the toy continues to exist while out of sight, this child has mastered the concept of object permanence. *(© George Zimbel/Monkmeyer Press Photo Service)*

cookie. From that time on, Laurent would use the stick whenever he wanted a distant object.

The Preoperational Stage. The **preoperational stage,** ages two to six, is characterized by the development of language. During this period the child develops the ability to treat objects as symbolic of things other than themselves. The three-year-old may treat a stick as if it were a candle and blow it out, or a block as if it were a car and push it across the floor. With the use of language symbols the child's problem-solving abilities become much more diversified.

One outstanding characteristic of the child's thought during this time is what Piaget called **egocentricity.** The preoperational child is unable to see the world from anyone else's point of view and believes that everything centers on her or him. What the child is experiencing is what everyone else is experiencing. Consider Piaget's dialogue with a preoperational girl (Piaget, 1960):

Piaget: Does the sun move?
Child: Yes, when I walk, it follows. When I turn around, it turns around, too. Doesn't it ever follow you?
Piaget: Why does it move?
Child: Because when I walk, it walks.
Piaget: Why does it move?
Child: To hear what we say.
Piaget: Is it alive?
Child: Yes, of course; otherwise it would not follow us, it wouldn't shine (p. 215).

The Stage of Concrete Operations. Around the age of seven, as the child enters the period of **concrete operations,** several complex mental activities are gradually acquired. Let us take a look at these new operations.

The concrete operation of **conservation** demonstrates the child's understanding of the fact that solids and liquids can be transformed in shape without changing their mass or volume. In the classic experiment liquid is poured from a short, fat glass into a tall, thin glass (see Figure 7–4). A preoperational child who is asked about the amount of liquid in the two glasses will insist that there is more liquid in the tall, thin glass. The child who has acquired the concrete operation of conservation will say that the amount of liquid is the same in both containers. This child recognizes that height and width compensate for each other.

Figure 7–4 gives some additional examples of simple tests for conservation. The child who grasps this principle will know that the number of pennies in a row does not change when spread out, nor does the amount of plasticene in a ball change when made into a different shape.

Another concrete operation that the child in this stage can perform is **serial ordering,** that is, arranging objects according to some quantified dimension such as weight or size. Typically, a four-year-old child cannot arrange eight sticks of different lengths from the shortest to the longest whereas the eight-year-old can.

According to Piaget the preoperational child cannot reason simultaneously about part of the whole and the whole. If you show a five-year-old eight yellow M&Ms and four brown ones and ask,

"Are there more yellow M&Ms or more M&Ms?" the child is likely to say, "More yellow M&Ms." The child in the stage of concrete operations would answer correctly. This child knows that some classes can be included in others, that a cat is both a cat and an animal and that there are more animals than cats.

A final important concept of this stage is **reversibility,** or the ability to reverse mental actions. Irreversibility of thought in the preoperational child is demonstrated by a four-year-old boy who recognizes that he has a brother but fails to see that his brother has a brother—himself (Philips, 1969, p. 61). The child in the stage of concrete operations would not make this mistake. He or she can mentally reverse actions, such as going back to the beginning of a chain of reasoning. The ability to undo an action conceptually is important in the development of reasoning.

The Stage of Formal Operations. By early adolescence, around age 11, the period of **formal operations** begins. The child is more sophisticated and is able to think about problems that are not based in reality. During this period the child develops the ability to generate hypotheses, to think abstractly in terms of probabilities and possibilities rather than concretely in terms of here and now.

The adolescent in the formal-operations period also systematically searches for an answer to a problem and explores all possible alternatives. Scientific reasoning begins to emerge during this stage. For the first time the adolescent is able to use deductive logic, going from the general to the specific rather than vice versa. Piaget believed that the preoccupation with thought is the principal characteristic of the stage of formal operations.

Piaget's theory of cognitive development is a comprehensive attempt to describe and explain the unfolding of rational thought processes. This development begins with the newborn, whose repertoire consists of reflexes and basic perceptual skills. In the relatively short period of time from birth to age 11, cognitive growth progresses dramatically. By adolescence children are able to perform complex logical operations, break out of the confines of concrete experience, imagine things they have never seen, and think about thinking. Table 7–3 highlights the major developmental milestones of this remarkable process.

By observing the same amount of fluid in containers of different shapes, this boy comes to understand the concept of conservation. *(© George Roos/Peter Arnold, Inc.)*

As the new mental operations, or processes, emerge and become functional, learning becomes more economical and effective. Long after physical maturation has ceased, the cognitive structure continues to develop as an adult continues to learn. As more individual meanings are learned, they are organized into increasingly comprehensive conceptual cores (Klausmeier, 1979) throughout adult development.

Creativity

One particular aspect of our thought processes involves creative thinking. Creativity refers to our ability to see things in a new, unusual light. It is the antithesis of routine, stereotyped patterns of thinking. Most definitions of creativity include novelty, spontaneity, and the production of rare or unusual ideas or objects (see Figures 7–5 and 7–6).

Creative thinking appears marvelous and mysterious. Who can explain the creative powers of a Leonardo da Vinci, a Marie Curie, or a Thomas Edison? Who can explain the mental processes involved in a new discovery, invention, theory, solution to a problem, or aesthetic vision?

Recently much attention has been devoted to the personality characteristics of creative individuals. Several salient themes have emerged from that research. Creative people are curious and enjoy thinking; they like to manipulate ideas; and

Figure 7–4.

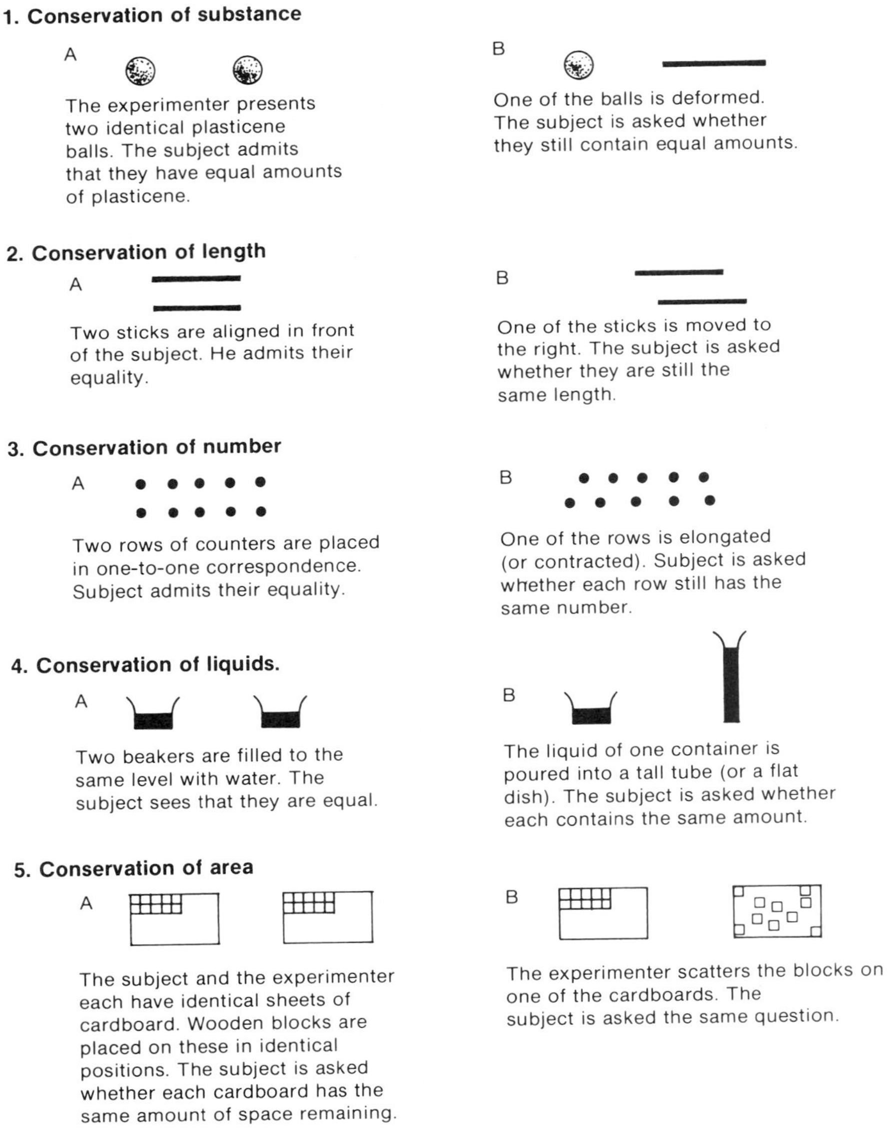

1. Conservation of substance

A

The experimenter presents two identical plasticene balls. The subject admits that they have equal amounts of plasticene.

B

One of the balls is deformed. The subject is asked whether they still contain equal amounts.

2. Conservation of length

A

Two sticks are aligned in front of the subject. He admits their equality.

B

One of the sticks is moved to the right. The subject is asked whether they are still the same length.

3. Conservation of number

A

Two rows of counters are placed in one-to-one correspondence. Subject admits their equality.

B

One of the rows is elongated (or contracted). Subject is asked whether each row still has the same number.

4. Conservation of liquids.

A

Two beakers are filled to the same level with water. The subject sees that they are equal.

B

The liquid of one container is poured into a tall tube (or a flat dish). The subject is asked whether each contains the same amount.

5. Conservation of area

A

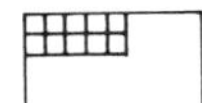

The subject and the experimenter each have identical sheets of cardboard. Wooden blocks are placed on these in identical positions. The subject is asked whether each cardboard has the same amount of space remaining.

B

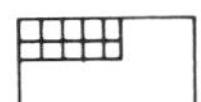

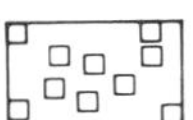

The experimenter scatters the blocks on one of the cardboards. The subject is asked the same question.

they crave variety. Parnes and Harding (1962) found that the creative person can tolerate ambiguity and apparent disorder. Creative people often spend a great deal of time turning problems over in their mind. They are able to let a problem "simmer" in their heads while turning attention to other activities. High energy levels and vast work output are usually associated with creativity.

Although many great discoveries follow periods of intensive work, the new idea or solution to the problem seems to spring full-blown from an observation of the moment. For example, when Marie Curie realized that the radioactivity she was studying could not be accounted for by a description of the known elements, the daring thought that she might have discovered a new element

Table 7–3. Piaget's Stages of Cognitive Growth

Stage	*Age Range*	*Major Developments*
Sensory-Motor Period	Birth to 2	Development of object permanence; rudimentary understanding of time and space; means-end manipulations and explorations.
Preoperational Period	2 to 6	Development of language; use of symbols; rudimentary problem-solving abilities; egocentricity of thought.
Period of Concrete Operations	6 or 7 to 11 or 12	Conservation of mass; serial ordering; class inclusion; logical thinking through concrete operations.
Period of Formal Operations	11 or 12 on	Abstraction; generation of hypotheses; deductive logic; consideration of possible alternatives in complex problems.

Figure 7–5.

	Common answer	**Creative answer**
How many things could these drawings be?		
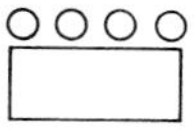	Table with things on top	Foot and toes
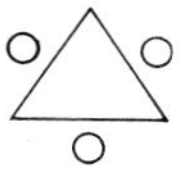	Three people sitting around a table	Three mice eating a piece of cheese
	Flower	Lollipop bursting into pieces
	Two igloos	Two haystacks on a flying carpet
What do these things have in common?		
Milk and meat	Both come from animals.	Both are government-inspected.
How many ways could you use these objects?		
Newspaper	Make paper hats	Rip it up if angry.

Figure 7–6. Drawing-Completion Test, devised by Kate Franck. Subjects were asked to elaborate on the simple figures at top left. A typical response of a subject chosen at random is shown in the second set of boxes. The responses of creative individuals are shown in the third and fourth sets of boxes.

popped into her head. Similarly, after trying for years to fit together the anthropological puzzle of culturally determined sex roles, Margaret Mead suddenly hit upon the notion of inborn temperamental types. But neither of these discoveries would have come about if their creators had not prepared themselves by years of arduous work.

The Relationship between Creativity and Intelligence. Are creative people more intelligent than noncreative people? The bulk of evidence indicates that creativity is independent of intelligence, as measured by standard tests (Dellas & Gaier, 1970). Although little or no creativity is found at relatively low levels of intelligence, a high level of intelligence does not necessarily mean one is creative. You probably know bright people who do well in school or on the job but exhibit little evidence of creativity. You probably also know people who muddle their way through college but constantly come up with original ideas. Although highly creative people are often highly intelligent, the reverse does not necessarily hold true (Torrance, 1964).

Creativity is not the mysterious prerogative of a special group of gifted people. Creative situations are common to everyone, from the experienced artist to the college student taking an introductory psychology course. When a problem arises for which there is no predetermined correct answer, we combine imagination and realistic thinking in a creative endeavor to arrive at the solution.

Problem Solving

We have examined only a few research samples in the area of cognition. Since many of the issues in cognition are closely related to problem solving, let us briefly turn to an analysis of this process.

A typical problem studied by cognitive psychologists is that of the hobbits and orcs (Thomas, 1974; Greeno, 1974). Three hobbits and three orcs are traveling together. The orcs will not leave the hobbits behind, but they will overpower them if ever any hobbits are outnumbered by orcs. As the group reaches a river that must be crossed, it finds a boat that can only hold one or two creatures at a time. How do the hobbits organize the crossing to assure that no hobbits are ever outnumbered by orcs?

Figure 7–7 presents the most efficient solution to this problem. It is based on larger units consisting of sequences of moves that lead to some intermediate arrangements of hobbits and orcs on the two sides of the river. It is interesting to note that except for an alternative first move not shown and the two cases of branching moves at the beginning and end of the sequence, the only allowable alternatives to correct moves are moving backward through the sequence. Errors were more likely at some points of the sequence (states 321 and 110) than at others.

Problems tend to focus on the solution because a person's objective in problem solving is to arrive at the correct outcome, which is usually specified in advance. The problem is solved when the solution is produced.

Stages of Problem Solving. Research on problem solving (Greeno, 1973; Jackson, 1975) suggests that we pass through four different phases when we attempt to solve a problem. The first phase is a *period of preparation.* Before beginning to do anything about looking for a solution, we have to detect and define the problem. If we start to work on a problem without being absolutely clear what it is, we are bound to waste time and effort. The preparatory period is concerned with the inspection of the problem and the collection of information. It is often a period of intensive work, concentration, and study, characterized by trial and error.

The period of preparation is followed by a phase in which there seems to be little progress in the direction of a solution. This stage is the *period of incubation.* It is a time when the solution germinates or ripens. During this time we systematically "search in the back of our minds" for the solution. We call on past experience, manipulate materials, and examine our personal resources. Often this is a period of frustration characterized by restlessness.

Eventually the incubation stage is followed by *the period of insight.* As a result of the reorganization of the available material and resources during the incubation period, insight finally comes. Many times insight comes in a flash. The problem solver suddenly has a hunch and sees the answer. Such moments are extremely rewarding, marked by feelings of success and accomplishment. The

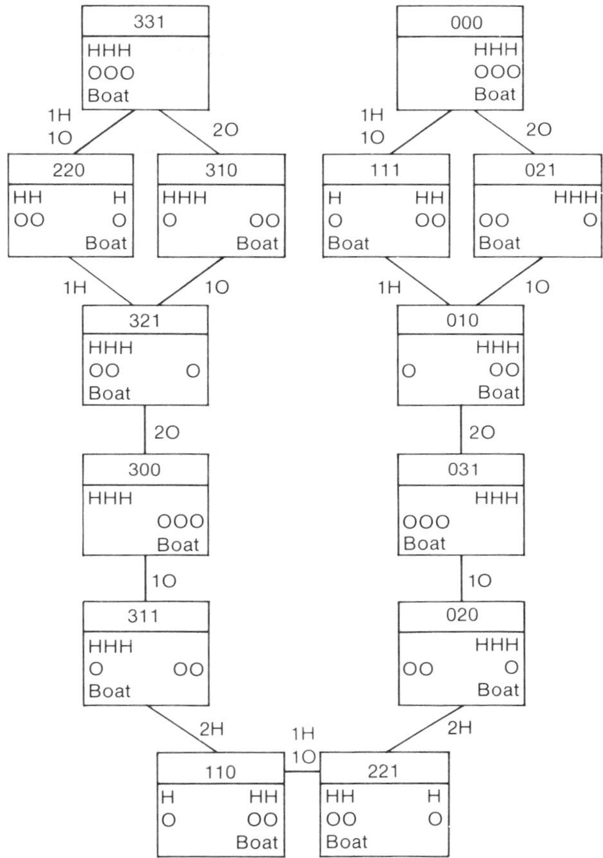

Figure 7–7. Successive stages in the solution of the hobbits-and-orcs problem. Three hobbits and three orcs must cross a river. They have one boat that can hold only one or two creatures, and hobbits may never be outnumbered by orcs. Each stage is represented by three digits: the number of hobbits on the starting side, the number of orcs on the starting side, and the boat on the starting side. In each stage, the positions of the hobbits (H), the orcs (O), and the boat are shown below the digit code, and the hobbits and orcs transported by the boat are shown in the transitions between stages. Except for a transition to stage 320 from the first state (crossing of one orc and the boat, not shown), no other moves in which hobbits are not outnumbered by orcs are possible. (Adapted from Thomas, 1974, Figure 1.)

insight period is the most dramatic stage of problem solving.

The process of problem solving terminates with the *period of verification.* During this stage the problem solver painstakingly evaluates, criticizes, tests, and polishes the solution until satisfied. A problem is solved when a person successfully undertakes some purposeful action.

In our everyday life we usually turn first to our repertoire of strategies for problem solving that have been successful in the past. Gagné (1977) stated that the strategies we adopt to solve problems depend on the rules we have available. According to Gagné, the problem-solving process involves discovering how a combination of previously learned rules can be applied in order to achieve a solution to a novel situation. This new solution will then be retained and is available the next time a similar problem is encountered.

Not all problem-solving efforts result in successful solutions. If the problem has not been fully grasped and no clue has been found to eliminate the various alternatives, the solution attempt is chaotic. A satisfactory solution is one in which the problem solver successfully combines experience and imagination to come up with a workable idea. From our assessment of the situation we begin to form a number of hypotheses about the possible cause of the problem and then attempt to evaluate the evidence that supports or contradicts these hypotheses.

Obstacles to Problem Solving. Many times we encounter obstacles that stand in the way of solving a problem. Sometimes we have emotional reactions that hinder the solution of a problem. If you are very upset, for instance, you may not be able to think clearly at all. Pressure to solve a problem may cause us to flit from one potential solution to another, anxiously trying to come up with an answer.

Another impairment in our ability to solve problems is termed **functional fixation** (Scheerer, 1963), a concept explored by early Gestalt psychologists who tried to explain why people gain or fail to gain insight into problems. They found that insight is often delayed or thwarted by fixation on an inappropriate solution. In functional fixation we take a habitual approach to problem solving and overlook the creative solution. As a result of education and experience we develop inhibitions that tend to make our thinking rigid and that militate against an imaginative approach toward problem solving. For example, functional fixation makes the discovery of out-of-the-ordinary functions of a common idea or object unlikely. If we are familiar with the use of an electric drill, it might not occur to us to employ it for cleaning the boiler, although all that is needed is replacing the bit with one containing an abrasive disc.

A related tendency that militates against successful problem solution is conformity. The fear of looking foolish by taking risks usually goes with not wanting to be different. Many people hold back an inventive idea because they are afraid that others may consider it outlandish or inappropriate.

Other factors that may prevent successful problem solving are the complexity of the outcome, the degree to which the solution is conceptualized, and the kind of resources that are available (Vinacke, 1974). Such conditions impose definite limitations, determining what is possible or necessary for a person to solve the problem.

One way of overcoming blocks to problem solving is by **brainstorming.** Brainstorming is a concentrated assault on the barriers of routine and stereotypic thought habits. Most brainstorming takes place in groups where each participant can voice opinions, offer suggestions, and thrash out ideas. The unrestrained atmosphere encourages the people in the group to be creative and come up with new ideas.

Successful problem solution calls for us to keep going. We often give up too easily and too early. If we would keep our imagination to the grindstone a little bit longer, we might spark more and better ideas.

MEMORY

Both language and cognitive integration require memory. A person with a deficient memory becomes lost in his or her environment or, like the man H. M., described at the beginning of this chapter, lives with a shattered mind (Gardner, 1975).

People can learn a remarkable number of things. We can learn languages and mathematical equations. We can learn to repair cars and stereo equipment. We can learn to play the piano and to ski. We can learn to balance our checkbook and prepare our income-tax return. All this learning would, of course, be useless if we could not remember it. In this section we shall examine the processes and structures that account for remembering and forgetting. Let us begin with a look at how psychologists measure memory.

How Can We Study Memory?

There are three principal ways to measure memory. We can ask a person whether he or she remembers something, we can ask the person to select previously learned items from a larger group of items, or we can measure how fast the person learns material a second time. These approaches are referred to as recall, recognition, and relearning, respectively.

The ability to remember your date of birth or experiences from early childhood is an example of **recall.** In college, recall is the task you are given in an essay exam. Recall may be tested in two ways. In free recall the person is asked to reproduce the material from memory without any cues. In cued recall the person is presented with a special cue such as the first letter of the word to be recalled.

The second procedure for studying memory is **recognition.** In recognition we perceive that something is familiar, that we have encountered it before. In a recognition test the person is required to identify items previously learned or experienced. Multiple-choice exams illustrate the recognition task. Recognition is usually easier than recall since we do not have to search our minds for the information. The principle that recognition is easier than recall is not only reflected in the comment "I'll know it when I see it" but also explains the apparent preference of some students for multiple-choice tests over essay examinations.

If we cannot recall or recognize the material, we may still show evidence of remembering through **relearning.** If we learn material faster the second time than the first time, we show that we have some memory of the material. Relearning is a common experience among adults who learned a foreign language in childhood. They may not be able to recall any of the language or even recognize many of the words. However, as they begin to study the language again, they find that vocabulary and grammar come back to them rather easily. Information that is not available for recall may nevertheless be accessible by recognition or relearning.

The Structure of Memory

For convenience, the human memory system can be divided into three different components: **sensory memory, short-term memory (STM),** and **long-term memory (LTM).** As we shall see, in addition to these three different memory stores there are several control processes for transforming the material from one store to another.

The Sensory-Information Store (SIS). The first component in our memory system is a short-term **sensory-information store** that receives information from our various sense receptors. It has been observed in the visual, tactile, and auditory modalities. Sensory memory refers to the brief retention of raw, unprocessed information.

The Short-Term Memory Store. The next memory store is a short-term information store with limited storage capacity. Remembering a telephone number for at least as long as we need to dial it illustrates the operation of short-term memory.

Perhaps the most important characteristic of STM is its limited storage capacity. Miller (1956), in a now classic paper entitled "The Magic Number Seven Plus or Minus Two," suggested that this capacity is about seven items for most people. To increase the limited capacity of STM, we can employ a process that Miller called **chunking.** Chunking consists of grouping separate bits of information. For example, the number 4671363 is more easily retained if it is chunked as 467, 13, 63. Without skills in chunking we could not recall strings of more than seven digits or, for that matter, sentences of more than seven words.

To illustrate the principle of chunking, Miller compared the short-term memory to a purse that can hold seven coins. If the coins are pennies, then the capacity of the purse is only seven cents. But if the coins are dimes, the capacity is increased to 70 cents. Although STM may only be able to hold about seven items, we can increase the amount of information in these items by chunking. People who have a good short-term memory have typically increased this facility.

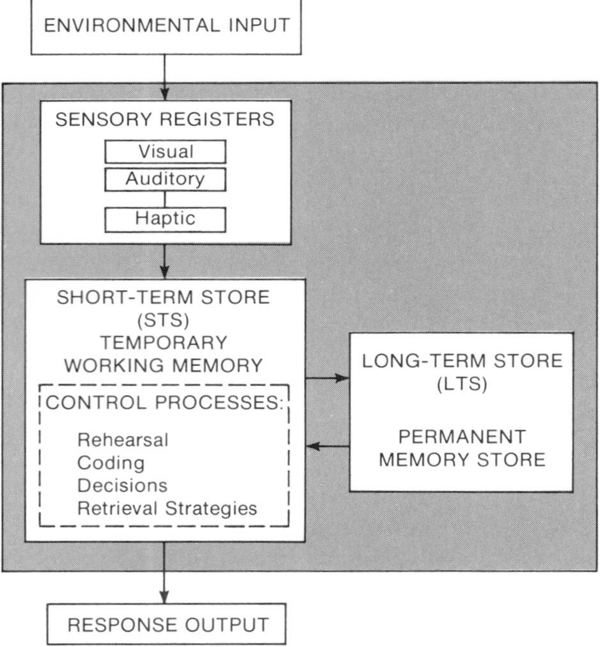

Figure 7–8. The interaction of the three components of human memory. (Adapted from Richard C. Atkinson and Richard M. Shiffrin, "The Control of Short-Term Memory."

Information stored in STM decays very quickly, usually in less than 30 seconds unless we rehearse the material. **Rehearsal** consists of repeating the information over and over. To understand the effectiveness of rehearsal, try the following exercise. Ask a friend to write down five phone numbers with which you are unfamiliar. Then have your friend read the numbers to you, one at a time, with a three-second pause in between. During the pause try to remember each number by rehearsing it. After the three seconds are up, write down the numbers. Repeat the process until you have recalled all five phone numbers. Then write down five new numbers and test your friend's memory. However, this time ask your friend to recite the alphabet backwards during the three-second interval. You will probably find that you were able to recall all of the numbers, while your friend was able to remember only portions of each. By being prevented from rehearsing the numbers, your friend was unable to retain them in STM. Items in STM must be periodically rehearsed or they will fade away. Our short-term memory is a working memory where information is being held temporarily while it is being rehearsed, recoded, and related to past knowledge.

The Long-Term Memory Store. Long-term memory is what most people mean when they talk about memory. It is relatively permanent, and its storage capacity is virtually infinite. Some of the most convincing evidence for the immense capacity of the LTM store comes from demonstrations of hypnosis and from electrical stimulation of the brain. Under both conditions people have recalled early childhood experiences or reported reliving previous events with all the sensations experienced at the earlier time.

The characteristics of LTM are quite different from SIS or STM. LTM can survive many assaults on the activity of the brain, such as electric shock, epileptic seizures, or long periods of coma. The fact that memory remains intact for many years without apparent rehearsal of information suggests a structural change of some permanence in the brain (Beatty, 1975).

The long-term memory store has been compared to a filing cabinet, whereas the STM store is like an in-basket on an office desk. The in-basket has limited storage capacity. When the basket is filled it has to be emptied out to make room for more. Some of the material will be thrown out; other material will be filed in the large cabinet. Nothing can be put into the large file cabinet without first going through the in-basket. In the same way, information received by the STM is continually being processed into the more permanent LTM store. This transformation process, which is not under voluntary control, is called **consolidation.**

The concept of two distinctive memory systems linked by a consolidation process came originally from observations of amnesic patients. Typically patients with amnesia have marked deficits in LTM, but the characteristics of STM are quite normal. For example, amnesic patients do not differ significantly from normal individuals in the number of items they can hold temporarily in memory (Shallice & Warrington, 1970). The disease processes in amnesia appear to interfere only with long-term information processing.

The relationships between the three components of the human memory system are diagrammed in Figure 7–8.

Memory Processes

There are three basic control processes in our memory system: encoding, storage, and retrieval. These processes can be thought of as the "three Rs" of remembering: recording (encoding), retaining (storage), and retrieving.

Encoding refers to the formation of a memory trace. Anatomical theorists generally contend that memory traces are physically represented in the brain by reverberatory circuits that encompass the neurons involved in processing the information. Encoding, then, is the process by which information in the form of physical energy from the environment is translated into some more suitable state for memory storage. For example, as you listen to a lecture, you do not remember every word but encode the essential features of the material. Underlining key concepts in an assigned chapter is another example of encoding. By encoding we convert information into a form that is meaningful and easily retained. We easily encode most everyday events into our memory. However, the effectiveness of encoding depends on the type of material we are trying to retain. Some information is encoded much better than other material. Historical dates and chemical formulas, for instance, are notoriously difficult to remember, while poems and pictures are considered easier to remember.

The second memory process, **storage,** refers to the holding or retention of encoded information while it is not being used. Thus storage involves the maintenance of information over time.

Finally, **retrieval** refers to the active search for stored information. Given that a certain memory has survived the passage of time and is available in storage, we need to gain access to it in order to retrieve it. Memory can be retrieved from either STM or LTM. Getting information out of STM is not difficult, but searching for and locating specific information in LTM is sometimes a problem because the information is not always stored in an orderly way. Occasionally retrieval, like encoding, is automatic and effortless, especially if the material has been well learned.

Think of LTM as a giant library in which ideas are stored and referenced on the main floor on shelves surrounded by similar ideas. Ideas may be unavailable for retrieval because the catalog cards are misplaced or because ideas on the same shelf get mixed up.

Although we talk about memory stores as if they occupy specific areas in the brain, we need to remind ourselves that memory refers to a set of attributes and activities rather than to a particular area of the brain. There are many things we do not know about human memory—is it chemical or electrical, highly structured or random? A great deal of research is devoted to the study of memory. As a result of this research some very useful hypotheses about remembering and forgetting have emerged.

Remembering and Forgetting

Forgetting is a familiar plight for most of us. We search our mind for a fact that we know should be there, only to find a jumble of more or less related ideas and soon a total blank. There is hardly a student who has not experienced sudden panic in an exam because he or she could not remember a fact that had seemed solidly entrenched in the mind the night before. Most of us often find ourselves groping in vain for a name or the ending of a joke. We lose, on the average, more than 80 percent of all the information we receive through our senses during a lifetime because we cannot locate it in LTM.

Over the past years psychologists have devoted considerable efforts to the study of forgetting in an attempt to explain some of the factors responsible for remembering and forgetting. Most definitions of forgetting define our memory lapses as the inability to recall learned material after a certain period of time, but this does not necessarily mean that the loss is permanent.

The rates of forgetting are different for STM and LTM. Information in STM is much more rapidly forgotten than information in LTM. Research on memory also indicates that we do not forget at a constant rate. Instead, most forgetting occurs shortly after we have learned something.

Theories on Why We Forget

The question of why we forget is central to memory. Several explanations have been offered for why we forget. Let us briefly consider four of the classical interpretations.

Decay Theory. Perhaps one of the oldest explanations for forgetting is that memories decay over time. **Decay theory** suggests that memories leave some physical trace in the brain that gradually fades away and eventually is permanently lost. Unfortunately, decay theory cannot explain why we are occasionally able to remember things we have previously been unable to recall. Also, studies of older people have shown that some memories are reasonably permanent and show little decay over time. Often an older person accurately remembers events that occurred much earlier in life, while forgetting many of the more recent experiences. Although the idea that memories fade spontaneously with time may seem reasonable, it is surprisingly difficult to prove.

The Junk-Box Theory. The **junk-box theory** suggests that all forgetting is caused by retrieval failure. Our memory is compared to a disorganized junk box. We find things in the box that have been placed there recently and are typically found on top. However, when it comes to finding objects placed in the box some time ago, we must search longer. Often we give up our search for the item because we conclude it is no longer in the box. According to the junk-box theory, true forgetting does not occur; memory lapses are simply a matter of our inability to retrieve items.

The Switchboard Theory. Many scientists today subscribe to one form or another of the so-called **switchboard theory** of forgetting. They believe that the 10 billion neurons that compose our brain arrange themselves into interconnected electrochemical circuits called **engrams.** According to this view, the engram is the pathway of memory. Like the light bulbs that flash on and off to spell out words in advertising signs in front of buildings, each neuron may be turning off and on an infinite number of engrams. Switching engrams off accounts for forgetting. The problem with this theory is that physiologists have not been able to trace the engram in the brain. Karl Lashley (1950), a prominent physiologist, spent over 30 years in the search for engrams but was never able to locate them.

The Interference Theory. Perhaps the most powerful explanation of forgetting is **interference theory.** According to this theory, we forget because other similar material that we have learned interferes with the recall of the material we want to remember.

There are two main sources of interference: information learned before and information learned after the material to be remembered. Information you have learned in the past may interfere with your memory for something you have learned recently. Psychologists refer to this type of interference as **proactive.** Suppose you are studying for an exam in English composition first and then for a test in American literature. When you try to remember the highlights of the assigned literature chapters, you may find that material from English composition keeps popping into your head. This material has thus become proactive and interferes with the recall of the material you studied more recently.

In a typical proactive interference experiment, experimental subjects are required to learn a list of words (List A), a second list of words (List B), and then are tested for recall of List B. A control group is required only to learn List B and be tested. The experimental model looks as follows:

Table 7–4. The Proactive Interference Model

	Experimental Treatment		
Group	*Phase 1*	*Phase 2*	*Phase 3*
Experimental	Learn A	Learn B	Recall B
Control	Rest	Learn B	Recall B

Studies of this type have shown that the experimental subjects have greater difficulties in recall than the control subjects. In this case the material learned in List A interferes with the recall of List B.

Interference can also be produced by material that you learned *after* the acquisition of the target information. Suppose you met a number of people at a football game last week, then met some more people at a party last night. If you try to recall the names of the people at the football game, you may find that the names of the party guests get in the way. Psychologists refer to this type of interference as **retroactive** and test for it with the following model:

Table 7–5. The Retroactive Interference Model

	Experimental Treatment		
Group	*Phase 1*	*Phase 2*	*Phase 3*
Experimental	Learn A	Learn B	Recall A
Control	Learn A	Rest	Recall A

Here, too, the recall of experimental subjects is typically poorer than that of control subjects. Retroactive interference, produced in Phase 2, has a detrimental effect on the recall of material learned in Phase 1. Thus forgetting is caused by information learned after the test material.

Improving Your Memory

Psychological research has focused on a number of basic principles that help memory: meaningfulness, organization, association, and visualization. Many students are aware of some of these principles when memorizing; they try various techniques to recode the material, reorganize it, give it meaning, or in some way make sense of it (Montague, 1972). It is useful to know how these principles work.

Meaningfulness affects memory at all levels. Information that does not make any sense to you is difficult to remember. There are several ways in which we can make material more meaningful. Many people, for instance, learn a rhyme to help them remember. Do you know the rhyme "Thirty days hath September, April, June, and November . . ."? It helps many people remember which months of the year have 30 days. Making up acronyms by taking the first letters of the items to be remembered may also increase their meaningfulness. An acronym most schoolchildren learn is HOMES, composed of the first letters of each of the five Great Lakes: Huron, Ontario, Michigan, Erie, and Superior.

Organization also makes a difference in our ability to remember. How useful would a library be if the books were shelved in random order?

Several mnemonic devices can help people remember useful information, such as telephone numbers. *(© Joel Gordon)*

Material that is organized is better remembered than jumbled information. One example of organization already described is chunking. Categorizing, grouping by first letters, and sequencing are other means of organization. Suppose you are asked to remember the following list of words: man, rose, dog, pansy, woman, horse, child, cat, carnation. Many people will group the words into similar categories and remember them during the recall test as follows: man, woman, child; cat, dog, horse; rose, pansy, carnation. Or compare the following two shopping lists: List One—milk, chicken, beans, cheese, corn, pork, hamburger meat, butter; List Two—dairy: milk, butter, cheese; meat: chicken, pork, hamburger meat; vegetables: beans, corn. Needless to say, the second list can be remembered more easily than the first one.

Association refers to taking the material we want to remember and relating it to something we remember accurately. In memorizing an unfamiliar number, you might try to associate it with familiar numbers or events. For example, the height of Mount Fuji in Japan—12,389 feet—might be remembered using the following associations: 12 is the number of months in the year, and 389 is the number of days in a year (365) added to the annual number of months twice (24). Or we can remember that stalagmites come from the ground and stalactites hang from the ceiling by associating the *g* in stalagmites with ground and the *c* in stalactites with ceiling. Associations can occur in the form of analogies, metaphors, comparisons, or contrasts, all of which can aid us in remembering.

The last principle is visualization. Research has revealed striking improvements in many types of memory tasks when people are asked to visualize the items to be remembered. In one study, subjects in one group were asked to learn some words using imagery, while the second group used repetition to learn the words (Groninger, 1974). Those using imagery recalled an average of 80 to 90 percent of the words, compared with 30 to 40 percent of the words for those who memorized by rote. Thus forming an integrated image with all the information placed in a single mental picture can help us to preserve a memory.

Another memory-improvement method relevant to studying is the **chain technique.** Chains are constructed by selecting cue words under the following rules: (1) the cue word must be one that will allow you to recall the sentence or paragraph from which it is chosen; and (2) all the cue words must be easily linked together to form a chain. The chain method emphasizes continuity of cue words and links them together in such a way that each cue word gives you a recall cue for the next cue word in the chain.

Suppose you are trying to memorize the Declaration of Independence. Using the chain method you might set up a list of the following cue words for the preface (Fuerst, 1972, pp. 94–95).

When in the course of human events . . .
one people to dissolve the political bands . . .
declare the causes: all men are created equal . . .
unalienable rights . . .
life, liberty, and the pursuit of happiness . . .
absolute despotism . . .
it is the right of the people to alter or to abolish it . . .
governments long established should not be changed for light and transient causes . . .
a long train of abuses . . .
it is their right, their duty, to throw off such government . . .
the history of the present king of Great Britain is a history of injuries and usurpations.

The number of cue words you use to build your chain depends on both familiarity with the material and the length of the material to be remembered. However, a 20-page article does not necessarily require 10 times as many cue words as a two-page article. As you gain experience with the chain method, you will become more proficient and will need fewer cue words.

Memory Tricks

Some people are capable of performing remarkable memory feats. Napoleon, for instance, reputedly knew the name of every officer in his army. General George Marshall was able to quote from memory almost every event in World War II. For the countless people who cannot remember the name of someone they met a few days ago or cannot speak at a meeting without notes, who forget where they left their keys last night or cannot retain the content of a book they have read only recently, such memory feats are overwhelming.

Faced with the task of having to memorize detailed, unfamiliar information, students seem to have only two alternatives: either learn it by rote until the material becomes familiar enough by sheer repetition or transfer it into a different memory code that is easier to work with.

The art of applying memory devices is called **mnemonics.** Mnemonic techniques are simple mental tricks, such as rhymes or visual images, that help us to improve our memory, mainly our long-term retention. Probably the oldest mnemonic trick, known as the **method of loci,** is credited to the Greek poet Simonides, who lived about the year 3000 B.C. According to the story, Simonides had been reciting a poem at a banquet when he was abruptly called away. While he was outside the banquet hall, the roof caved in, crushing all the guests to death. Because the disaster had mutilated the bodies beyond recognition, the relatives desperately needed a way of identifying their loved ones. Simonides was able to walk through the rubble and identify the bodies because he knew the exact place where each person had been sitting. How did Simonides remember this? As a reciter of long poems, Simonides needed some device to keep him from forgetting his lines. He had come to rely on a method whereby he thought beforehand of the place where he would be reciting and assigned each part of his recitation to a spot in the room. By looking from spot to spot, he could remember the complete poem. In doing so, at actual events, he associated the people he saw with the spots they occupied—and so Simonides was able to remember where everyone at the banquet had been sitting.

The trick of Simonides can be used in practical tasks, such as remembering a grocery list or important dates for a history exam. For example, a student might imagine a systematic walk from one distinctive campus landmark to another: from the gymnasium to the dormitories to the classroom; then to the library, the computer center, and the student center. To learn a series of ordered historical dates, the student imagines a date at each successive location. To recall the series of dates, the student would take an imaginary walk across campus, remembering each date in its appropriate place (Christen & Bjork, 1976).

Another popular mnemonic device that includes visual imagery, rhyme, and meaningful transformations is the "one-is-a-bun" mnemonic, otherwise known as the **pegword system.** Miller, Galenter, and Pribram (1960) suggested the following standard rhyming pegword list:

One is a bun.	Six is sticks.
Two is a shoe.	Seven is heaven.
Three is a tree.	Eight is a gate.
Four is a door.	Nine is wine.
Five is a hive.	Ten is a hen.

Suppose you are trying to learn the following list of words: (1) ashtray; (2) firewood; (3) picture; (4) cigarette; (5) table; (6) matchbook; (7) glass; (8) lamp; (9) shoe; (10) phonograph. You can do so simply by pegging each word to the rhyme. The idea is first to learn the pegwords and then to imagine a picture combining each numbered item with a pegword. For example, think of a bun (the first pegword) sitting on an ashtray (the first word to be learned). Move on to the next pegword, and "hang" the next item of the list on it. Apparently pegwords help us by providing a sort of internal imagery comparable to the method of loci, which focuses on external imagery. The pegword system has the advantage that the learner can recall any item without necessarily starting from the beginning of the list (e.g., to recall the third item, the learner has only to remember what was imagined with tree).

Various schemes have also been developed to help us memorize digit sequences. After all, we live in an age of numbers: highway numbers, social security numbers, license numbers, zip-code numbers, charge-account numbers, telephone numbers. How can we remember all these numbers, especially since numbers have no meaning in themselves?

Here is one system, known as the **digit-letter system.** Its aim is to break up numbers—dates, telephone numbers, statistics—and convert them into words. A code that is commonly used adopts the following series of letter-number correspondences:

0 = Z or S	5 = L
1 = T or D	6 = J, CH, or SH
2 = N	7 = K or C
3 = M	8 = F or V
4 = R	9 = P or B

"Thus 32, a friend's apartment, becomes MN," writes Bower (1970), "and can be sounded out as MAN or MOON, so that I remember my friend lives on the moon; a colleague's extension number, 8741, translates as VCRD and can become VICE RAID." It takes practice, Bower notes, but the time spent in learning the code can repay the student who needs to remember many numbers.

Mnemonic devices have their limitations. They are of little use in helping you to integrate knowledge from diverse sources and make critical judgments. Alan Baddely, a British psychologist, noted that mnemonic systems are not particularly helpful in remembering the sort of information we acquire in daily life. "They are, of course, excellent for learning strings of unrelated words which are so close to the hearts of many experimental psychologists, but I must confess that if I need to remember a shopping list, I do not imagine strings of sausages festooned from my chandeliers and bunches of bananas sprouting from my wardrobe. I simply write it down" (1978, p. 34).

Although education systems tend to emphasize learning through understanding rather than memorization, it is unlikely that the learner will be disadvantaged by learning in more than one way. Mnemonic techniques can supplement other methods of study effectively (Higbee, 1977).

Summary

Language, thinking, and memory are our most important higher mental processes. Language serves a variety of functions, not only in interpersonal communication but also in thinking and learning. The three major elements of language are phonology, syntax, and semantics. Phonology describes the sound system for a language. Syntax describes the grammatical structure of a language. Semantics studies the relation between words and meaning.

In the first two years of life language develops from the birth cry through cooing, babbling, one-word (holophrase) utterances, and two-word sentences. While children usually acquire the basic vocabulary and syntax by the time they are four or five years old, important language development takes place during the school years.

Various theoretical positions have provided us with explanations for the acquisition of language. The nativist perspective holds that important aspects of language development are innate and biologically based. Learning theory stresses the role of parental reinforcement and limitation on the part of the child. It is questionable whether either innate abilities or learning processes alone can explain language development. A third perspective, the interactionist view, combines the nativist and learning views. Interactionists assume that although language abilities are governed by biology, environmental factors also make important contributions to language development.

Girls' superiority over boys in language development has probably been exaggerated. Social class can be influential in the early years due to differences in language training in middle- and upper-class homes and in lower-class homes. Primates have been taught to communicate using symbols, such as shapes, but humans are still unique in the sophistication of their use of language.

Language is intimately linked with thinking. Like language development, cognitive development proceeds in an orderly sequence. The most comprehensive account of cognitive growth was suggested by Piaget, who proposed that cognitive development goes through a fixed sequence of stages: the sensory-motor stage, the preoperational stage, the stage of concrete operations, and the stage of formal operations.

Creative thinking and problem solving are two particular thought processes. Creative thought is novel and spontaneous and leads to unusual outcomes. Creative individuals do not necessarily have above-average intelligence, but they share a number of personality traits, including curiosity, liking to think, and tolerance for ambiguity. Problem solving, which we are faced with daily, is an act of creative thinking. Research suggests that we go through a series of stages—preparation, incubation, insight, and verification—when we try to solve a problem. Psychologists have identified several generalized obstacles to successful problem solving. These include functional fixation, or focusing on ineffective approaches, and conformity, or the unwillingness to take risks because of the fear of others' opinions. Both obstacles can be overcome by brainstorming.

To learn to speak or think requires memory. The principal ways of testing for memory are through recall, recognition, and relearning. We have three kinds of memory stores: sensory, short-term, and long-term. Most of the available evidence supports the notion that our memory is organized, rather than being simply a dumping ground of randomly arranged facts and ideas. We constantly encode, store, and retrieve memories, thereby reorganizing our memory representations. Of particular importance for the study of memory is forgetting. Several explanations for forgetting have been advanced. One suggests that the strength of the memory trace decays over time. The junk-box theory holds that memories are never lost but that sometimes we fail to retrieve them. A third idea is that electrochemical circuits form memory pathways in the brain; however, these pathways, or engrams, have never been traced. Perhaps the most powerful explanation is that forgetting results from interference of learned material that is similar to what we are trying to remember; this interference can be proactive or retroactive.

Certain basic principles can help us remember: meaningfulness, organization, association, and visualization. In addition, a number of memory tricks have been recommended to help us combat forgetting. These mnemonic devices imply that we do not actually remember; instead, we remember how to remember.

Key Terms For Review

anterograde amnesia
babbling
brainstorming
chain technique
chunking
cognition
concrete operations
confounded description
conservation
consolidation
cooing
decay theory
digit-letter system
dimensional description
egocentricity
encoding
engram
expressive aphasia
formal operations
functional fixation
global description
holophrastic speech
interactionist perspective
interference theory
junk-box theory
language-acquisition device
learning-theory perspective
long-term memory (LTM)
method of loci
mnemonics
morpheme
nativist perspective
object permanence
overgeneralization
pegword system
phoneme
phonology
preoperational stage
proactive interference
recall
receptive aphasia
recognition
rehearsal
relearning
retrieval
retroactive interference
retrograde amnesia
reversibility
semantics
sensory-information store (SIS)
sensory memory
sensory-motor stage
serial ordering
short-term memory (STM)
storage
switchboard theory
syntax
telegraphic speech
underextension
Whorf hypothesis

Suggested Readings

Brown, R. *A first language: The early stages.* Cambridge, Mass.: Harvard University Press, 1973.
A detailed description of the early development of language in infants.

Fuerst, B. *Stop forgetting.* New York: Doubleday, 1972.
Dr. Fuerst provides the reader with scientific and educational guidelines for memory training. The emphasis is on teaching students the rules and principles through which they can improve their memory and concentration. The author also applies the various memory techniques to specific occupations and professions.

Pribram, K. *Languages of the brain.* Englewood Cliffs, N.J.: Prentice-Hall, 1971.
A challenging and provocative treatise of a wide range of language-related physiological topics, including an extended description of Pribram's optical-hologram model of memory.

Puff, R. *Memory organization and structure.* New York: Academic Press, 1979.
This book is a scholarly portrayal of our present understanding of the ways in

which the human memory is organized and the role organization plays in memory.

Rotman, B. *Jean Piaget: Psychologist of the real.* Ithaca, N.Y.: Cornell University Press, 1977.
The author traces the development of Piaget's theory of cognition and his philosophy of the mind.

Wilson, E. Animal communication. *Scientific American*, 1972, *227*, (3), 52–60.
The author discusses animal communications using chemicals, movements, and sounds. Included are the waggle dance of the honeybee, the courtship rituals of the penguins, the call of the indigo bunting, and the communication codes of mammals.

8

Theories of Human Development
- Biological Theory
- Psychoanalytic Theory
- Erikson's Eight Stages of Psychosocial Development
  - *1. Infancy: Trust versus Mistrust*
  - *2. Early Childhood: Autonomy versus Shame*
  - *3. Preschool Age: Initiative versus Guilt*
  - *4. School Age: Industry versus Inferiority*
  - *5. Puberty and Adolescence: Identity versus Role Confusion*
  - *6. Early Adulthood: Intimacy versus Isolation*
  - *7. Middle Adulthood: Generativity versus Stagnation*
  - *8. Old Age: Integrity Versus Despair*
- Learning Theory
- Cognitive-Developmental Theory

Childhood Development
- Prenatal Development
- Infancy
  - *Motor Development*
  - *Perceptual Development*
  - *Emotional and Social Development*
- Early Childhood
  - *Motor Development*
  - *Emotional and Social Development*
- Late Childhood
  - *Motor Development*
  - *Social Development*
  - *Moral Development*

Adolescence
- Physical Development
- Emotional Changes
- Psychosocial Development

Early Adulthood
- Marriage
- Parenthood
- Career Choice

Middle Adulthood

Late Adulthood

Death and the Life Cycle

Life-Span Development

"I am considering leaving the firm. I've been there four years now. I'm getting good feedback, but I have no clients of my own. I feel weak. If I wait much longer, it will be too late, too close to that fateful time of decision on whether or not to become a partner. I'm success-oriented. But the idea of being 35 years old and stuck in a monotonous job drives me wild. It drives me crazy now, just a little bit. I'd say that 85 percent of the time I thoroughly enjoy my work. But when I get a screwball case, I come away from court saying, 'What am I doing here?' It's a visceral reaction that I'm wasting my time. I'm trying to find some way to make a social contribution or fill a slot in city government. I keep saying, 'There's something more.' "

"The concept of a home has become meaningful to me, a place to get away from troubles and relax. I love my son in a way I could not have anticipated. I never could live alone."

The man making the comments in the first paragraph wants to broaden himself professionally. At the same time he wants to expand his personal life and have two or three more children. Consumed with the task of making critical decisions about the direction his life will take, he demonstrates the essential shift at this age: an absolute requirement to be more self-centered. The self has a new value now that his competency has been proved.

His wife is struggling with her own priorities. She is 30 and wants to go to law school, but he wants more children. If she is going to stay home, she wants him to make more time for the family instead of taking on more professional commitments. His view of what he would most like from his wife is this: "I'd like not to be bothered. It sounds cruel, but I'd like not to have to worry about what she's going to do next week. Which is why I have told her several times that I think she should do something. Go back to school and get a degree in social work or geography or whatever. Hopefully that would fulfill her, and then I wouldn't have to worry about her line of problems. I want her to be decisive about herself."

The trouble with his advice to his wife is that it comes out of concern with his convenience rather than with her development. She quickly picks up on his lack of goodwill. He wants to be rid of her problems. At the same time, he refuses her the latitude that he has to be "selfish" in making an independent decision to broaden her horizons. Both perceive a lack of mutuality. And this is what "Catch-30" is all about for the couple (Sheehy, 1976, p. 29).

Writer Gail Sheehy describes the life cycle as a series of predictable crises. She thinks of these events not as catastrophes but as turning points. In accordance with this conceptualization of the life cycle, this chapter will provide a broad overview of the major periods of the life span: infancy, childhood, adolescence, adulthood, and middle and old age.

Psychologists believe that children acquire certain abilities, such as walking, at critical periods of development. (© *Suzanne Szasz)*

The study of life-span development is the province of developmental psychologists, who are concerned with the ways people change over the life cycle, beginning at birth and ending at death. Life-span development is a story of continuous change. The change may be progressive or regressive, rapid or almost static. Generally the rate of change is more rapid during the earlier than the later years of life. The growth, maturation, and learning of a child are readily apparent. Once a person has reached maturity, however, changes over time are more subtle and gradual. Through adulthood and old age the developmental processes may not be readily measured in terms of quantitative changes.

Developmental psychologists are interested in studying common and characteristic age changes. Although most individuals follow a similar pattern of development, changes do not take place at precisely the same time. Both children and adults vary in the ages at which they attain certain levels of maturity. For example, not all 1-year-olds can walk and not all 65-year-olds are ready to retire.

Perhaps one of the most basic and yet complex problems in understanding the developing organism is the influence of genetic and environmental factors. This issue, as we saw in Chapter 2, is known as the nature versus nurture controversy. It was once the source of many heated debates among psychologists. At one extreme were those who believed that our genes are the chief determinants of the developmental process. At the other extreme were those who argued that the infant is born as a *tabula rasa,* or blank tablet, upon which environmental forces impress their marks. Few psychologists today fall into either camp. Instead it is recognized that both heredity and environment contribute to development. In order to become a ballet dancer, for instance, our bone structure and muscles must be ready, but we also need some exposure to the world of dance and music. Similarly, before we can adopt a sex-role identity we must be physically differentiated. The critical question, then, is how these two forces interact with each other to affect the course of development.

The interaction of genetic and cultural influences is particularly important during certain periods of development when the organism is maximally sensitive to external influences. During these periods the individual is physiologically ready to take on new developmental tasks and requires the opportunity to acquire and practice new skills. For example, a critical period for social development is the first months of infancy, when the child forms an attachment, or bond, with the mother or primary caretaker. Similarly, abilities such as walking, talking, or abstract thinking depend on physiological readiness and practice time. If an individual experiences unfavorable conditions during critical periods, such as the absence of a mother or lack of intellectual stimulation, his or her adjustment in later life may be adversely affected. An extreme case is the "closet" child who grows up under conditions of total sensory and emotional deprivation.

THEORIES OF HUMAN DEVELOPMENT

Many attempts have been made to conceptualize and explain the progressive series of changes that occur over the life cycle from conception to death. Notable among these are biological theory, psychoanalytic theory, Erikson's theory of psychosocial development, learning theory, and cognitive-developmental theory. As yet, no theorist has managed to come up with a unified and comprehensive theory to explain completely the phenomena of growth and change.

Biological Theory

One approach to human development may be labeled biological theory. Theorists in this category argue that foremost attention must be given to our genetic makeup and the process of maturation because these biological factors determine the evolution of the person. As we have suggested, however, while most people are willing to recognize that biological forces have an important influence on human development, few would agree that the vast changes we see over a person's lifetime can be explained solely in biological terms.

Psychoanalytic Theory

A second major theoretical perspective is provided by psychoanalytic theory. According to Freud, whose theory is more fully explained in Chapter 10, human development is a series of successive stages. Each stage is defined in terms of attributes and types of behavior characteristic of a dominant way of functioning. Most early psychoanalytic theorists assume that development essentially ceases at the end of childhood and that progression from stage to stage is inevitable, except under highly unusual circumstances.

Erikson's Eight Stages of Psychosocial Development

In contrast to Freud, Erik Erikson (1963) believes that development continues throughout the life span. Erikson also shifted the emphasis from biological determinants such as physical maturation to social demands as major influential factors. Erikson described eight stages of psychosocial development (see Table 8–1), each of which represents a critical period during which development may take place successfully or unsuccessfully. Successful mastery of the developmental tasks of each stage will add strength to an individual's personality, whereas failure results in various maladaptive behavior patterns. In accordance with Erikson's theory, which is summarized below, the remainder of this chapter will focus on the developmental successes and failures of each period of the life span.

1. Infancy: Trust versus Mistrust. The major developmental task during infancy is the establishment of a loving, reliable relationship between the child and the mother or primary caretaker.

Table 8–1. Erikson's Eight Stages of Psychosocial Development

Stage (ages are approximate)	*Psychosocial Crisis*	*Significant Relations*
1. Birth through first year	Trust vs. mistrust	Maternal person
2. Second year	Autonomy vs. shame	Parental persons
3. Third year through fifth year	Initiative vs. guilt	Basic family
4. Sixth year to onset of puberty	Industry vs. inferiority	Neighborhood, school
5. Adolescence	Identity vs. role confusion	Peer groups
6. Early adulthood	Intimacy vs. isolation	Partners in friendships and sexual relationships
7. Middle adulthood	Generativity vs. stagnation	Divided labor and shared household
8. Old age	Integrity vs. despair	Humankind

Gratification of the infant's physical needs and parental affection establish basic trust. Infants who are not given continuity of care or who are neglected develop an overwhelming sense of mistrust during this stage.

2. Early Childhood: Autonomy versus Shame. Between the ages of two and three, children develop some degree of independence and a sense of control over bodily functions. Autonomy allows children to view themselves as persons in their own right. Unsuccessful resolution of this developmental task leads to feelings of inadequacy and self-doubt. A child who is constantly browbeaten by a parent will grow up feeling ashamed and doubtful and lack the spirit necessary for healthy autonomy (Turner & Helms, 1979).

3. Preschool Age: Initiative versus Guilt. When children reach the age of four, new skills must be developed. The newly acquired skill of language enables them to initiate a variety of activities. On the one hand, they are experiencing themselves as more powerful than ever before; on the other hand, they are beginning to realize that they must control their behavior and that failure to do so leads to feelings of guilt. "The child indulges in fantasies of being a giant and a tiger, but in his dreams he runs in terror for dear life" (Erikson, 1963).

4. School Age: Industry versus Inferiority. During middle childhood the central scheme is to develop scholastic and social competency. It is a period of sexual latency, a lull before the storm of puberty, during which children acquire a sense of duty and accomplishment and set out to win recognition. A sense of inferiority may develop if they do not receive recognition for their accomplishments.

5. Puberty and Adolescence: Identity versus Role Confusion. The developmental task of the fifth stage is to integrate childhood identifications with biological drives and social roles. Bodily and social identifications must merge to bridge the division between childhood and adulthood. The healthy adolescent will emerge from this stage with a firm sense of identity. Role confusion may manifest itself in juvenile delinquency, truancy, or in the inability to decide which adult role is to serve as a model.

6. Early Adulthood: Intimacy versus Isolation. After young adults have begun to feel secure in their identity, they are expected to make an intimate commitment to another individual as well as to a meaningful line of work. Freud termed the central task of this stage "to love and to work." Failure to do so may lead to promiscuity and isolation.

7. Middle Adulthood: Generativity versus Stagnation. During this period, the developmental task is to abandon self-related interests in favor of the younger generation. Generativity may be expressed not only by parents but also by adults without children who in some way guide younger people. The danger of this stage lies in a middle-aged person's inability to find value in aiding the next generation. As a result, the person experiences a pervasive sense of stagnation, boredom, and personal impoverishment.

8. Old Age: Integrity versus Despair. Integrity is the culmination of successful growth. It implies the acceptance of the life a person has lived without regrets for what might have been. It also implies an acceptance of death; the individual sees old age as a link between past heritage and future generations. Despair, on the other hand, is the protest of the person who is not satisfied with his or her life. Despair indicates an unwillingness to end a life that failed to bring personal fulfillment.

Although several investigators (e.g., Neugarten, 1977) have been unable to demonstrate that people actually pass through the stages delineated by Erikson, the theory has generally been well received, particularly because it includes a description of growth and change in the latter part of the life span.

Learning Theory

For learning theorists the key to psychological development is found in environmental influences. According to these theorists, much of human development throughout the life cycle can be accounted for by the basic learning principles, such as reinforcement, modeling, and observational learning (Chapter 5). Social-learning theory, for instance, notes that infants are born with certain physiological needs, such as hunger and thirst. Usually an adult, typically the mother, satisfies these needs. As we saw in Chapter 5, food and liquid are considered primary reinforcers, whereas the mother who is associated with the primary reinforcers serves as a secondary reinforcer. So far as other humans resemble the mother, they will elicit similar positive reactions by the process of stimulus generalization. Social-learning theory in particular emphasizes the acquisition of socially acceptable behavior as the foundation of human development, a process that is best explained in terms of the reinforcement that society provides for acceptable behavior. Thus through learning principles the behavior of the developing child will be shaped so as to be socially acceptable.

Cognitive-Developmental Theory

A final approach to life-span development is provided by cognitive-developmental theorists. Whereas psychoanalysis-oriented theorists are primarily concerned with personality development, and whereas learning theorists emphasize the acquisition of socially acceptable behavior, cognitive theorists focus on intellectual development. The chief representative of this approach is

A loving relationship between mother and child normally begins during infancy. *(© Jean-Claude Lejeune/Stock, Boston)*

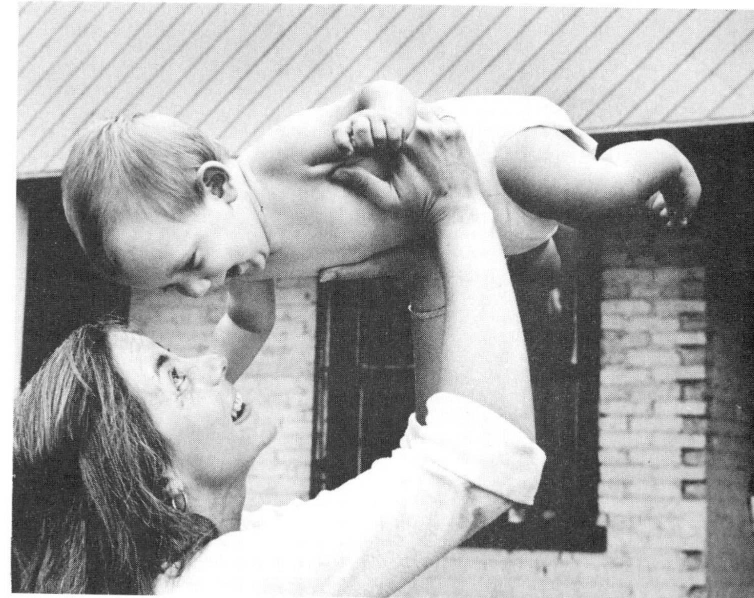

During middle childhood children begin to strive for scholastic excellence. *(© Stan Goldblatt/Photo Researchers, Inc.)*

Establishing intimacy with another person is an important challenge of early adulthood. *(© Susan Lapides/Design Conceptions)*

Jean Piaget, whose theory we introduced in the last chapter. For Piaget, the story of development is a story of adaptation (Piaget, 1926). The mechanisms of adaptation, according to Piaget, take place through the interplay of two related processes, assimilation and accommodation. **Assimilation** refers to the use of aspects of the environment for activities that are already in the child's repertoire (Lefrancois, 1980). For example, when infants suck a nipple, they can be said to be assimilating properties of the nipple to the activity of sucking. In other words, assimilation involves exercising previously learned behavior. **Accommodation** refers to modifications in existing behavior to meet environmental demands. Based on the interaction between assimilation and accommodation, the child (and adult) adapts to a progressively more complex environment.

In addition to specifying the mechanisms of adaptation, Piaget has also outlined a series of stages that characterize the intellectual development of the child (see Chapter 7). Piaget, like most cognitive theorists, concentrated largely on changes in higher mental processes, such as language and thought. Social, emotional, and personality development are areas that still need to be investigated in more detail from the cognitive-developmental perspective.

Regardless of which theory of development one adopts, the actual sequence of developmental events unfolds in an orderly fashion. In other words, we move from childhood through adolescence and adulthood to old age. Let us now turn to the major developmental tasks that characterize each phase of the life cycle. These tasks are outlined in Table 8–2.

CHILDHOOD DEVELOPMENT

Development during childhood is characterized by rapid changes in all areas of human growth. It covers the time span from conception to the beginning of puberty, during which we develop from a single-cell organism to a highly complex person. For convenience we may divide childhood into the following stages: prenatal, development, infancy, early childhood, and late childhood.

Prenatal Development

Prenatal development begins at the moment of conception, when two cells, the sperm from the father and the egg (ovum) from the mother, unite. Fertilization of the ovum usually takes place in the middle section of the fallopian tube. The fertilized egg, called the **zygote,** then travels from the fallopian tube to the uterus. On its way to the uterus the zygote undergoes a series of cell divisions. At the end of the germinal period the zygote buries itself in the lining of the uterus, which has been prepared by maternal hormones to provide nourishment for the developing organism. This anchoring process, referred to as **implantation,** marks the end of the **period of the ovum.** Figure 8–1 illustrates the events of the first ten days of the zygote.

During the **period of the embryo,** which covers the following six weeks of prenatal development, the various organ systems begin to develop. A rudimentary heart, brain, kidneys, liver, and digestive tract are formed. At the beginning of this period the human embryo looks very much like that of other animals. Toward the end of the period, however, it has a definite human appearance. The ears, nose, lips, tongue, and even buds of teeth are discernible. The brain sends out impulses that coordinate the functions of the organ systems. At the end of the embryonic period at eight weeks (see Figure 8–2) the embryo measures approxi-

Table 8–2. Examples of Developmental Tasks for Each Period of the Life Span

Period	*Tasks*
Infancy (0–2)	Forming an emotional attachment to caretaker; learning to walk; learning to take solid food; learning to control bladder and bowel movement.
Childhood (2–12)	Learning to talk; learning to get along with age mates; learning an appropriate sex role; developing academic skills; developing a conscience and a scale of values; achieving independence in self-help area; becoming a member of a social group.
Adolescence (12–20)	Accepting a masculine or feminine role; developing new relations with age mates of both sexes; developing emotional independence of parents; selecting and preparing for an occupation; developing intellectual skills and social competence; integrating physical changes into a sense of self.
Early Adulthood (20–45)	Selecting a mate; learning to live with a marriage partner; starting a family; rearing children; managing a home; finding a congenial social group.
Middle Adulthood (45–65)	Establishing and maintaining an economic standard of living; accepting and adjusting to the physiological changes of middle age; assisting adolescents to become responsible adults; adjusting to aging parents.
Old Age (65–death)	Adjusting to decreasing physical strength; adjusting to retirement and reduced income; establishing satisfactory physical living arrangements; overcoming the death of a life-time partner; accepting one's own death.

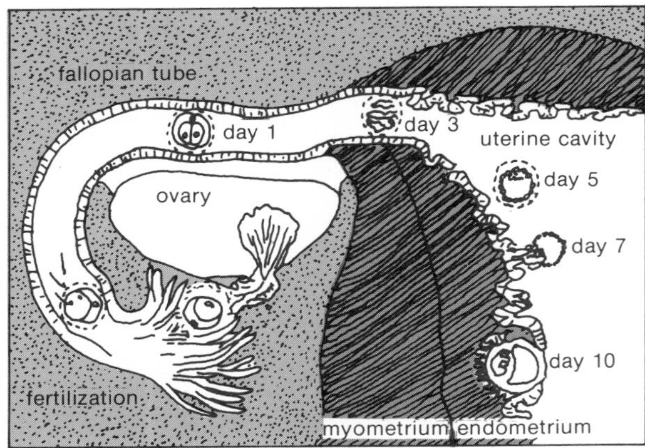

Figure 8–1. The first ten days of the embryo. (Adapted from Smith, D. W. and Bierman, E. L., Eds.; *The Biologic Ages of Man*. Philadelphia, W. B. Saunders Company, 1973.)

mately one inch in length and weighs one thirteenth of an ounce.

The **period of the fetus** begins about two months after conception and extends to birth. During this phase most of the organ systems that had existed in rudimentary form during the embryonic stage become functional. Body proportions of the fetus change due to accelerated growth of the lower part of the body during the fourth month. As a result, the head, which had been disproportionately large because of the sudden growth during the embryonic period, begins to blend in with the rest of the body.

During the remainder of the prenatal period the fetus continues to increase in weight and length. Reflexes become brisker and fetal movements can be perceived by the mother. The seventh month of prenatal development is a landmark because at that time the fetus is capable of independent life. At birth, a full-term infant weighs about 7 pounds, although the weight may vary from 5 to 12 pounds. The average length of the baby is about 20 inches. (Figure 8–2 and Table 8–3 summarize the major events in the development of a zygote into a newborn child.)

Normal prenatal development depends on good maternal health. It is particularly important for the mother to maintain an adequate and balanced diet. A proper environment is also necessary for healthy physical and psychological development. For example, drugs, radiation, or infectious diseases may interfere with the development of vital organ systems, particularly the brain.

Our growing knowledge of the importance of early influences on later development has made many parents more aware of their role during the prenatal period. For example, we know that an expectant mother's emotional state can bring about changes in her body chemistry. Emotions such as anger or anxiety may release into the bloodstream certain hormones that can be irritating to the fetus (Janda & Klenke-Hamel, 1980). As a result of this increased awareness, more and more couples are demanding excellent prenatal care. Many are also choosing to have their children by natural childbirth, without drugs, since it has been found that infants are more responsive when the mother did not receive medication during delivery. In most natural-childbirth methods both parents share the prenatal experience by developing a thorough understanding of the physiological and psychological processes involved in giving birth, and ideally the father is willing to participate in the birth experience.

One popular natural-childbirth method that requires the presence of the father during labor and delivery is the Leboyer approach (Leboyer, 1975). Leboyer proposed that standard hospital delivery procedures assault the infant's sensibilities. To reduce the birth trauma, auditory and visual stimulation are reduced during delivery; for example, overhead lights are dimmed. After birth the father places his child in a warm-water bath for approximately five minutes. Leboyer's technique provides both parents and infants with psychological experiences that are likely to have positive effects (Blum, 1980). Some researchers (e.g., Klaus & Kennell, 1976) believe that the hour immediately after delivery is critical for successful later development in the child. During this hour the process of parent-child attachment, referred to as **bonding,** can be either significantly enhanced or disrupted.

Infancy

Infancy is the developmental period that covers the first two years of a child's life. It is a time of remarkable motor, perceptual, and emotional development.

Motor Development. At birth the infant is primarily a motor creature who confronts the world with a number of reflex responses. Even though the responses of the newborn appear to be relatively simple compared with later development, newborns have many more competencies than scientists originally granted them. For example, newborn infants show discriminative responses to tones in the range of the female voice (Hutt, 1973; Kearsley, 1973). Similarly, as early as nine

Table 8–3. Prenatal Development

Trimester	*Major Characteristic*
First: 0–3 months	Beginning development of all internal organs, appendages, sense organs.
Second: 4–6 months	Continuation of development of organs plus growth from 3 inches to 1 foot in length and 1 ounce to 1½ pounds in weight.
Third: 7–9 months	Additional growth of about 8 inches in length and about 6 pounds in weight.

Source: Turner & Helms (1979).

Figure 8–2. The development of the zygote, embryo, and fetus. Teratogens are substances that produce abnormalities.

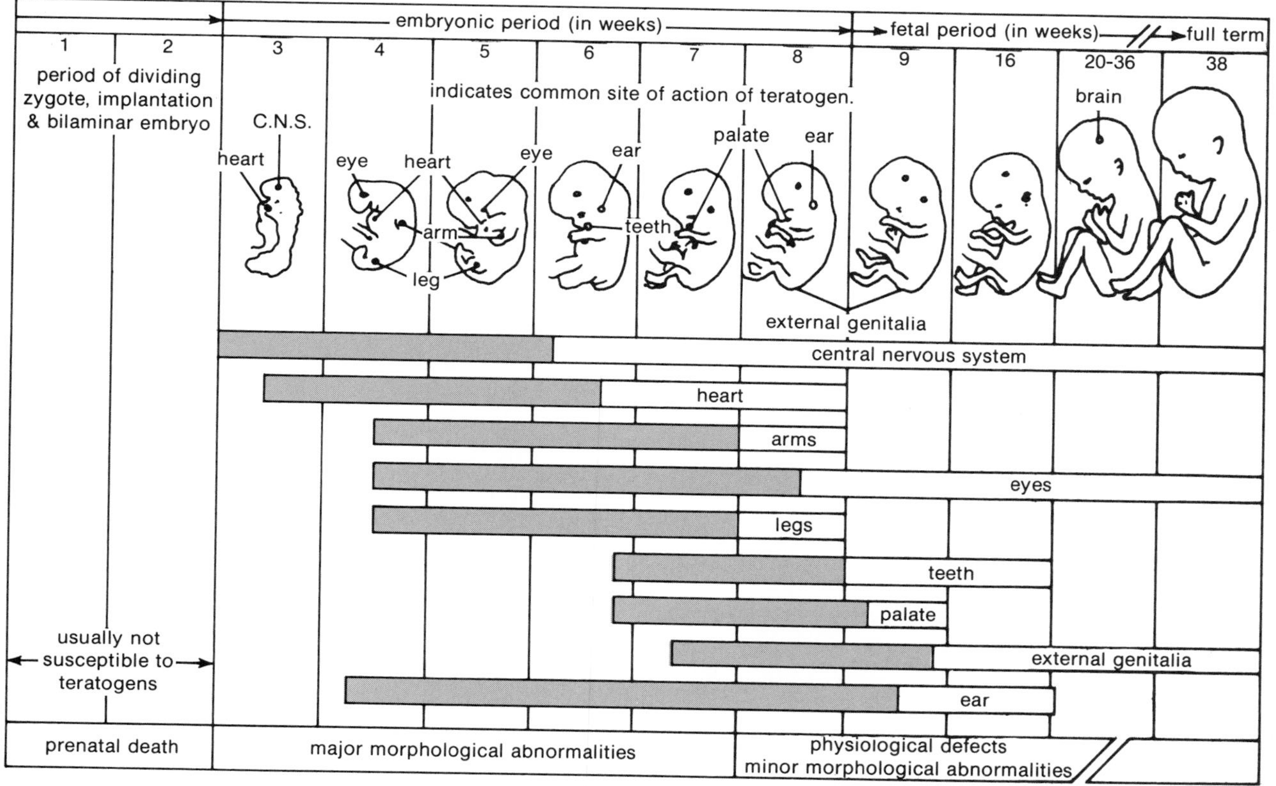

minutes after birth, infants will track a moving two-dimensional representation of a face by moving their heads and eyes (Goren, Sarty, & Wu, 1975). Thus only to the casual eye does the infant do little except eat, sleep, and excrete.

All the reflexes of the newborn are automatic responses that facilitate adaptation to the external world (see Table 8–4). The **Moro reflex** is the newborn's startle response. Making a sudden noise by slamming the door will cause the infant to fling its arms out and then bring them together as the hands open and then clench. If this reflex is weak or absent, it is a sign that the central nervous system is severely disturbed (Ambron & Brodzinski, 1979). The **grasping reflex** applies to the infant's toes as well as fingers. The baby will close its fingers firmly over any object placed on the palms. A finger placed under the infant's toe will produce a curling of the toes over the finger. If you tickle the sole of the foot, the big toe will lift up while the others fan out. This is the **Babinski reflex.**

Good prenatal care includes the expectant mother's maintaining a balanced diet. *(© Erika Stone)*

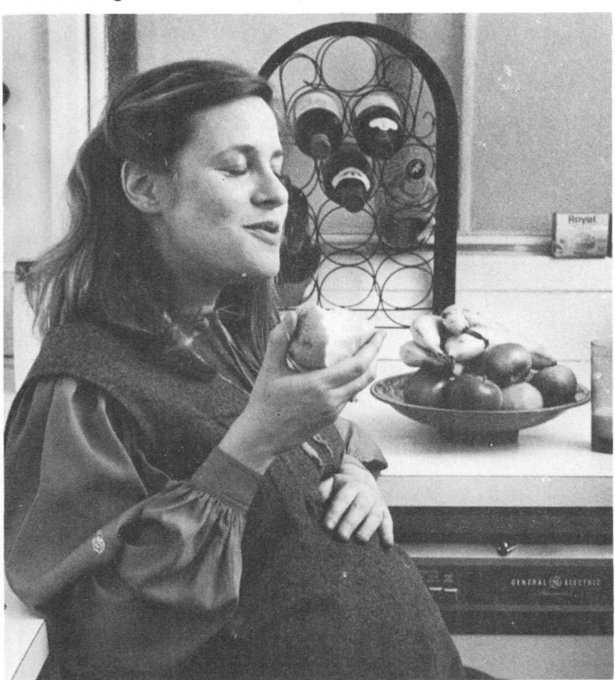

A necessary reflex of the mouth is the **rooting reflex.** When the baby's cheek is touched, its head will turn toward the finger and the mouth will make sucking movements. The **sucking reflex,** like the rooting reflex, is clearly necessary for survival. The **swimming reflex** allows infants to survive for a short time under water. They keep their heads down and exhale slowly through the mouth until there is no more air in their lungs.

In addition to the major reflexes, a baby is born with a number of other reflexes. They include coughing, sneezing, and several reflexes of the eye and serve various protective functions.

Normal physical development in infancy follows an orderly course. During the first year infants usually double their height and triple their weight. Dramatic changes in motor ability accompany physical growth. Over a two-year period the infant's motor skills develop in a sequence that progresses from sitting with support, to sitting alone, to crawling, creeping, standing, and finally taking the first step alone (see Figure 8–3).

Perceptual Development. People used to think that the sensory world of infants was a confusion of sounds, lights, touches, and odors. Experiments investigating the perceptual competence of infants have shown that this is not the case. Even very young infants are perceptually quite selective. Studies using sounds, for instance, revealed that infants can distinguish between pitches and have distinct preferences among them. Even the newborn pays more attention to higher-pitched female voices than to lower-pitched, male ones.

Research on visual perception has also produced some interesting discoveries. Fantz (1961) presented infants with three ovals shaped like human heads (see Figure 8–4). One of these shapes looked like a stylized human face, another showed the same facial features but scrambled them, and a third was a plain black and white oval. Infants showed a clear preference for the stylized human face and paid least attention to the black and white oval.

By the time infants are about two months old, they develop a preference for three-dimensional

Table 8–4. Major Reflexes Present at Birth

Reflex	*Stimulus*	*Response*	*Meaning*	*Other Comments*
Moro or startle	Sudden movement or loud noise, such as bumping of crib, slamming of door.	Legs draw up, back arches, arms are brought forward in hugging or embracing motion.	Absence indicates immaturity, or edema of brain or brain damage. Presence indicates awareness of equilibrium.	Basic reflex is lost 3 to 6 months after birth. Can appear in modified form even in adult.
Grasp or Palmar	Any object placed on palms or soles.	Hands grasp object with firm grip, then let go; toes curl downward.	Absence indicates neural depression.	No thumb is involved. Reflex is lost by 12 months. Infant can sustain own weight when lifted.
Sucking (accompanies swallow reflex)	Touch on lips.	Mouth makes sucking movements.	Absence indicates immaturity, narcosis, brain injury, or retardation.	Reflex is lost if not stimulated (Gesell) and Ilg, 1937), generalized at first but with time becomes more efficient.
Rooting	Touch on cheek.	Head turns toward touch.	Prepares infant for sucking.	Inexperienced mothers will touch cheek to push it toward nipple, and infant will root (i.e., turn the other way).
Babinski	Any stimulation of soles.	Toes fan out (spread).	Persistence indicates lack of myelination or other malfunction.	Reflex is lost at 4 to 6 months; convenient for noting cerebration progress.
Swimming	Placement in water.	Head goes down, breath is exhaled slowly through mouth.		Reflex is present at 6 to 12 months; infant probably can make smooth transition to voluntary swimming.

Source: Helms and Turner (1976).

forms. A commonly used apparatus testing the infant's depth perception is the visual cliff. Gibson and Walk (1960) created this special box to simulate depth. On one side a heavy piece of glass covered a solid surface. On the other side the heavy glass was two to three feet above the floor, simulating the cliff effect. Infants of six months or older refused to crawl across the surface that ap-

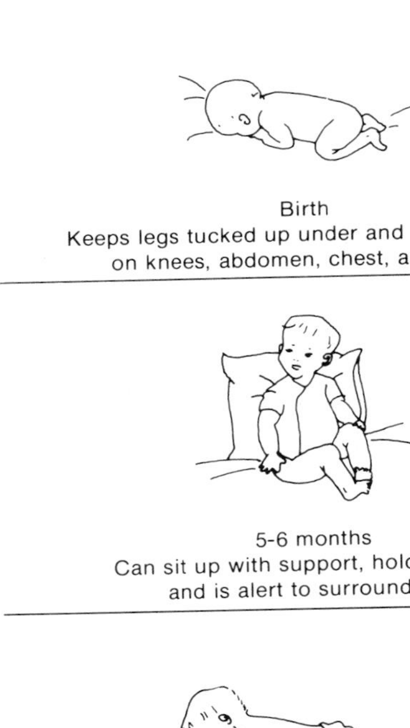

Birth
Keeps legs tucked up under and bears weight on knees, abdomen, chest, and head.

2-3 months
Extends legs and lifts chest and head to look around.

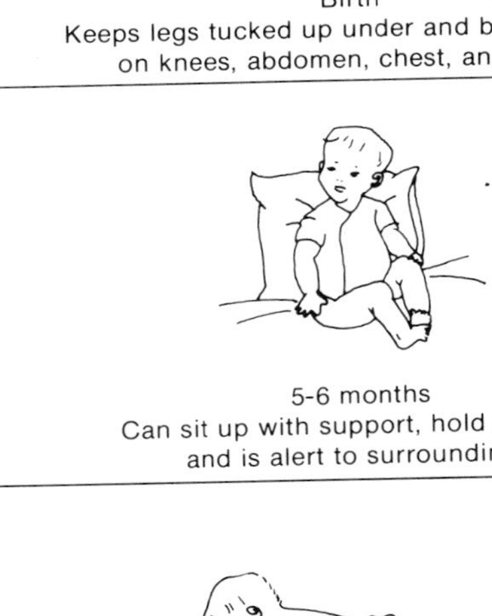

5-6 months
Can sit up with support, hold head up, and is alert to surroundings.

6½-7½ months
Sits up alone and steadily without support. Legs are bowed to help balance.

8-9 months
Creeping; the trunk is carried free from floor. With practice, rhythm appears and only one limb moves at a time.

9-11 months
Pulls self up and stands holding onto furniture. Feet far apart, head and upper trunk carried forward.

11-12 months
Stands alone, can walk with help.

12-14 months
Walks alone on wide base with legs far apart.

Figure 8–3. Development of posture and locomotion in infants. (From Ingalls, A. J., and Salerno, M. C.: Maternal and child health nursing, ed. 2, St. Louis, 1971, The C. V. Mosby Co.)

peared to be the cliff. Younger infants who were not able to crawl yet showed distress when looking over the cliff (see Chapter 4).

Emotional and Social Development. As we have seen, according to Erikson, basic trust or mistrust develops during infancy as the result of the baby's first interaction with the environment. Many developmental psychologists (e.g., Kagan, Kearsley, & Zelazo, 1978) agree that infancy and early childhood are developmental periods during which the child acquires a basic sense of emotional security. Psychologists have applied the term "attachment" to the creation of the first emotional bond between the infant and its caretaker. Attachment is seen in various types of behavior, including crying, smiling, approaching, or clinging, all of which promote contact or proximity with a specific person to whom the infant is attached (Craig, 1976). For a long time it was believed that the infant becomes attached to the caretaker because that person fulfills the baby's primary needs. But research with animals as diverse as goslings and rhesus monkeys have shown that this is only part of the picture.

The Austrian zoologist Konrad Lorenz (1952) described a process known as **imprinting** by which newborn animals form a relatively permanent bond with the parent during a critical period in the young animal's life. Dr. Lorenz observed that goslings would follow their mothers almost immediately after hatching. But if the natural sequence was altered, some bizarre forms of attachment would occur. For example, if Dr. Lorenz nurtured motherless goslings during the first 24 hours after they hatched, they would follow him rather than another goose. In fact, by waddling, honking, and flapping his arms he would get the new goslings to treat him like a mother.

Studies of imprinting, which occurs during a critical period varying from species to species, are important because they provide an explanation for early social attachment in animals and human infants. They imply that the presence of a stimulus, usually the mother, during this early period facilitates emotional attachment to the caretaker and later types of social behavior.

A second important series of experiments was conducted by the Harlows (1962) at the Primate Laboratory at the University of Wisconsin. In one of the experiments infant monkeys were placed in individual cages, each of which contained two surrogate mothers. One of the mothers consisted of a bare cylindrical wire frame topped with a wooden head. The other surrogate mother was essentially identical in form, except that she was covered with terry cloth. In each cage one of the surrogate mothers held a bottle of milk; half of the

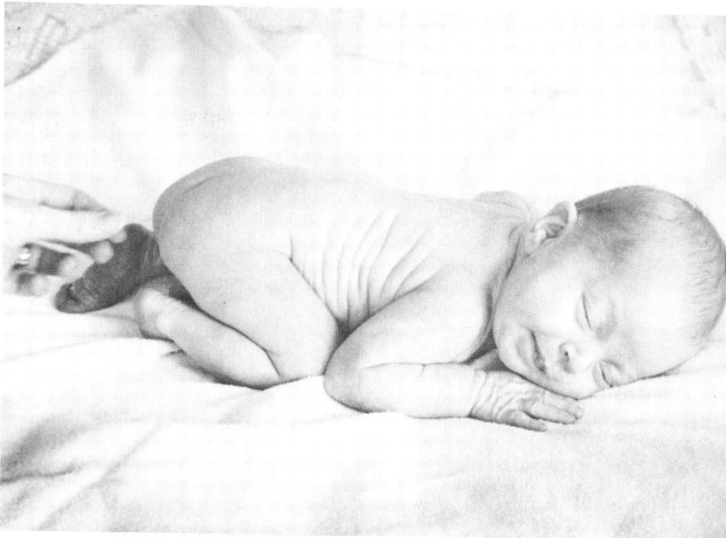

The Babinski reflex causes a baby to spread out its toes when the bottom of its foot is tickled. *(© Suzanne Szasz)*

Figure 8–4. Fantz's experiment on pattern perception. Infants, ranging in age from 4 days to 6 months, spent the most time looking a human face (above) and the least time looking at a bicolored oval (below). (*Adapted from* Fantz, R. L. *The origin of form perception.* Scientific American, May 1961, pp. 66–72.)

A baby's depth perception is confirmed when it does not crawl across the visual cliff. *(© William Vandivert)*

baby monkeys were fed on the bare-wire mother, the other half on the terry-cloth mother. The results showed that regardless of which surrogate mother supplied the food, the monkeys would spend most of their time clinging to the cloth mother, who was the object to which the attachment had developed (Figure 8–8). The Harlows concluded that the essential feature of the mother-infant relationship was not the provision of food but close physical contact. Since contact with the terry-cloth mother was so much more comfortable, the baby monkeys preferred to spend the time with her.

If we generalize the Harlow findings to human infants, we can assume that the formation of an attachment relationship is an essential part of normal development in infancy. We can further assume that severe emotional or social deprivation may result in long-term emotional disturbances. This conclusion is supported by observations of infants brought up in orphanages and institutions (Bowlby, 1960; Dennis, 1973). Even among infants brought up in homes, disruption of the early bonding between the infant and its caretaker may lead to disturbances in mother-infant interactions (Stern & Wasserman, 1979).

Most of the psychological literature concerning emotional development in infancy has focused on the bonds between babies and their mothers. The father has been a rather shadowy figure in the background. In recent years, however, the father-infant bond has received more attention. Greenberg and Morris (1974) interviewed a group of new fathers and found that almost all of them had formed a close attachment with their babies by the third day after birth. The authors labeled the father's attachment to his child **engrossment,** a term that refers not only to the father's involvement with the child but also to the father's sense of self-esteem that grows from this bond.

If attachment is the first emotional landmark in infancy, the second one is **stranger anxiety.** The presence of strangers causes infants to cry, cling, or hang on to their mother. Because the phenomenon occurs almost universally around the age of 28 weeks, some psychologists refer to it as the seventh-month anxiety. No traumatic event is necessary; no experience of a sudden or harsh separation needs to take place. The appearance of a familiar baby sitter, for example, is sufficient to produce a strong negative reaction in the baby.

Many psychologists see stranger anxiety as characteristic of infant development. As the infant's cognitive abilities mature, the child develops images of the familiar and notices discrepancies. When the child detects discrepancies from the known or expected, he or she experiences anxiety.

At the end of infancy the child has acquired the ability to move around and begins to join vocabulary items into two-word phrases (see Chapter 7). Development has proceeded from a primarily reflexive infant to a child who shows rudimentary foresight. According to Erikson's theory, the healthy child is now ready to assert his or her independence.

Early Childhood

During the preschool years between the ages of two and six the child experiences much that is new, exciting, and rewarding. There are changes in motor, emotional, and social development.

Motor Development. Increased mobility allows children to participate in many activities that will test and train their abilities. Running, jumping, throwing a ball, and playing competitive games with peers are some of the new challenges. During the preschool years children expend energy and develop initiative in many kinds of physical activities.

Emotional and Social Development. The preschooler must learn to handle a variety of feelings. Language acquisition alone makes the child much more responsive to the environment. As the child's awareness of the environment increases, so does the capacity for emotional response. Many positive emotions, such as joy and the pleasure of discovery, that children experience during this period are only possible because of their greater mastery over the environment.

Some emotions are likely to create conflict. For example, preschoolers often fluctuate between dependence and independence and must learn to find their own solutions to such conflicting feelings. Fears, anxieties, and socially disapproved emotions such as anger and aggression must also be dealt with. At the preschool level fears and anxieties are common among children of both sexes. Although some children are likely to have frightening experiences, such as getting lost or being bitten, many of the fears that preschoolers harbor have little basis in reality. Fears of supernatural dangers, for instance, are common at this age. Learning to manage these emotions is an important part of a child's growth.

Strong aggressive feelings must also be handled. Aggression may be expressed verbally or by shouting, crying, pulling, stamping feet, or biting. Observations of nursery-school children show that as children progress through the early years their behavior involves less physical and more verbal aggression.

Intellectually the child is now in the stage of preoperational thought. One important characteristic of preoperational thought is the child's egocentric style of thinking. Piaget (1926) stated that children below the age of seven do not communicate at all. According to Piaget, the typical form of egocentric speech is a kind of collective monologue where two or more children talk to themselves but take turns doing so as if engaged in a dialogue (Bower, 1979).

Cognitive growth is also reflected in the preschooler's social development. The child's interactions with family and peers change dramatically after infancy. Preschoolers greatly expand their

Through imprinting, Konrad Lorenz taught goslings to respond to him as if he were their mother. (*© Thomas McAvon/Life Picture Service*)

For monkeys the essential feature of the mother-infant relationship is physical contact, not food. *(© Primate Laboratory, University of Wisconsin)*

The bond between father and child was a long-neglected subject in developmental psychology. *(© Erika Stone)*

social environment, especially by means of their peers, who become a major source of reinforcement for many activities.

The young child who does not have real playmates will often create imaginary ones. Donna, for example, has five imaginary husbands (she is four years old). They ride the school bus with her every day and often throw salt at cars, just for fun (Pines, 1978). Jeff's friend is Tony, a mouse. Tony hides under the table and eats the food when nobody is looking. Parents often have to go along with invisible playmates, even to the extent of setting an extra plate at the table "for my friend Julie."

Interest in imaginary playmates begins at age 2½ and reaches a peak around 3½ or 4. Children discover imaginary playmates in books or simply invent them. Imaginary friends are typically loyal, reliable, and always available. They talk a lot and listen even more, thereby filling up the empty space in children's lives when they are without any real playmates. Although imaginary playmates can serve a variety of purposes, in most children they fulfill some inner need for companionship, giving the child someone to look up to or to boss.

Late Childhood

Erikson's fourth stage, industry versus inferiority, is the period of late childhood, which covers the years from 6 to 12. The development of academic and intellectual skills is a major task, and productivity in school as at play becomes important for the child's sense of self-esteem. Most children in this age group enter school, if they have not been enrolled in preschool programs. As we saw in Chapter 7, the child develops complex classification skills during this period and learns more realistic ways to categorize the environment. One of the most important milestones of the school years is the emergence of a sense of right and wrong. In a way, late childhood may be seen as a time of apprenticeship that prepares the child for the challenges of adulthood.

Motor Development. Physical development is on a kind of plateau. Although the child continues to grow, the rate of growth is considerably slower than it was earlier or will be later. Because of the steady, gradual progress in physical and motor growth, the school years are one of the most comfortable periods of physical adjustment for many children and one of their healthiest times.

Social Development. The school is a major socializing agent for the child. The world of the child begins to center on school. For more than a decade school and its activities serve as a training ground for children to develop what Erikson called a sense of industry. The concepts, symbols, and logic learned in school provide a major thrust for intellectual growth.

For many children, going to school is a rewarding and challenging experience. Some children, however, develop **school phobia,** an unrealistic fear of going to school. School phobias most commonly occur among children in kindergarten to fourth grade. Many times school phobias have little to do with anything that happens at school. Instead, it is the separation from the parent that makes the child anxious. Most children have outgrown school phobias by the time they are ten years old.

During the school years children form many ties with people outside the home. The peer group and its culture play an increasingly important role in molding children's attitudes and behavior. In a very real sense, the child lives in two worlds—that of parents and other adults and that of the peer group. Both boys and girls initially form informal groups, which become more highly structured as the child gets older. However, the social structure of boys' and girls' groups is usually different.

Boys at this age are interested in developing and asserting their masculinity. They tend to be involved in gangs and action-oriented activities, such as sports teams or Boy Scouts. The qualities that boys most admire are competence in group games, fearlessness, toughness, and the willingness to take risks. Girls, in contrast, tend to stay

Young children often find companionship in imaginary playmates. *(© Suzanne Szasz)*

The formation of peer groups in middle childhood allows children to develop social skills. *(© Ken Heyman)*

Table 8–5. Age Profiles for Late Childhood

Age	Outstanding Characteristics	Self-Concept	Social and Family Relationships	Work Habits
6	Very active physically; self-centered.	Begins differentiation of self.	Has difficulty relating to parents and siblings; forms erratic friendships.	Works and plans in spurts. Does not know when to stop; tires easily.
7	More active mentally; almost brooding as compared with a 6-year-old.	Less self-centered; more concerned with others' reactions to self.	More polite, likes to help at home. Has close peer friendships.	Persistent and careful with work. Better perspective of how much can be done.
8	Newly outgoing; curious; not as comfortable with the world as when younger.	Critical and self-evaluative; demanding and critical of others, too. Likes to compare self with others.	Highly critical of parents; has poor relationships with siblings. Peer friendships with same sex very important.	Social interests may interfere with schoolwork. Self-criticism may discourage work ("I can't spell").
9	Outgoing; curious; involved in personal interests; self-confident.	Still self-evaluating but more at ease with self. Can admit mistakes without feeling threatened.	Better relationships at home because less critical. Very close peer friendships.	Very persistent, self-absorbed. Academic achievement very important.
10	Stable; at ease with the world. Sex differences emerging.	Less self-evaluative; more self-satisfied.	Likes almost everyone in family. Closer peer friendships, with sex differentiation (boys in larger groups; girls in small groups). Likes organized clubs.	Likes school, has responsible work habits.
11	Very active physically; very curious; no longer quite at ease with self and others.	Newly doubtful and tense as adolescence approaches; moody, sensitive.	Challenges parents and all adults; has conflicts with siblings. Peer friendships very important.	Personal and social interests overwhelming; often has difficulty sustaining interest in schoolwork.
12	Outgoing; open; beginning to see self as no longer a child.	Less self-centered; capable of some self-criticism. Shows a need to define self.	Participates less in family activities; considers friends more important.	Difficult in school. More interested in expressing self than in working with others.

Source: Adapted from Elkind (1971, pp. 64–89, 129–131).

somewhat more closely tied to their parents. Girls form groups as a way to develop interpersonal relationships. Qualities such as being friendly, attractive, and "more grown up" are more important than excellence in competition.

Peer groups in middle childhood, then, are not just a gathering of children. Group members share many values and are expected to conform to the norms of the group, which govern the interactions of its members. Boys and girls travel different social routes, but both sexes are expected to conform to the standards of parents and other authority figures as well as to the demands of the peer group.

As a result of these complex social interactions the child's budding self-concept undergoes a number of critical changes. Typically children reach middle childhood with a self-concept that is likely to be incomplete or even distorted since it is derived through parents and family. Exposure to peer-group influence and greater freedom from parental supervision encourage the child to make some value judgments and decisions on his or her own. With this increase in freedom a more realistic self-concept develops. Table 8–5 presents an age profile of social development during middle childhood.

Moral Development. Although the development of a sense of right and wrong is a lifelong process, the school years represent the critical period during which conscience develops. This is when children develop their basic philosophical orientation to life.

The development of conscience is closely related to cognitive growth. As the thinking processes of children mature, their standards of right and wrong become less confined to specific types of behavior and less determined by external rewards.

Piaget believed that from the ages of 5 to 12 a child's concept of morality passes from a rigid notion of right and wrong learned from the parents to internalized standards. Piaget studied the ways children think about rules, the motivation behind actions, lying, cheating, and punishment to investigate changes in children's moral thinking. Here is a typical moral dilemma that Piaget would present to children:

> Once upon a time there were two boys, Augustus and Julian. Augustus noticed one day that his father's ink pot was empty and he decided to help his father by filling it. But opening the bottle, he spilled the ink and made a large stain on the table cloth. Julian played with his father's ink pot and made a small stain on the table cloth (Piaget, 1932, p. 64).

Piaget then would ask: "Which boy is naughtier?"

Most adults and older children would consider Julian guiltier, since the small stain he made was caused by doing something he was not supposed to be doing. Augustus's larger stain, on the other hand, was an accidental by-product of a considerate intention. But children under seven usually think Augustus to be the greater offender since he made the larger stain. Young children tend to make immature moral judgments because they are concerned with the magnitude of an offense rather than with the intention behind the act.

On the basis of children's responses to such stories, Piaget suggested that moral development proceeds in two stages. The earlier stage (seven- to eight-year-olds) is known as **morality of constraint,** or heteronomous morality, which is based on the belief that an act is bad because it will result in punishment. It is a stage when the child's moral judgments are subject to external control. Morality at this level is absolute because underlying intentions are not considered. Piaget believed that the cognitive limitations of the child during this stage lead him or her to confuse moral rules with physical laws.

Among 8- to 11-year-old children **morality of cooperation,** or autonomous morality, replaces the more immature morality of constraint. Whereas the younger child's moral judgments are built on punishment, the older child believes that an act is bad because it violates a rule or does harm to others. The older child no longer makes absolute judgments but sees a situation from more than one perspective, realizing that there are exceptions and that under certain circumstances transgressions may be justifiable. Morality of cooperation is a more relative moral system in which intentions are important. Reciprocity of behavior, such as that embodied in the golden rule is the most desirable manifestation of morality of cooperation. The two types of morality as distinguished by Piaget are outlined in Table 8–6.

Inspired by the work of Piaget, Lawrence Kohlberg's research (1964, 1968) essentially confirmed Piaget's findings that the level of a child's moral reasoning depends on the age and cognitive

Table 8–6. Piaget's Stages of Moral Development

	Stage I (ages 7–8)	*Stage II (ages 8–11)*
Moral Concepts	Morality of constraint (heteronomous morality) built on punishment	Morality of cooperation (autonomous morality) built on cooperation
Point of View	Child views an act as either totally right or totally wrong, and thinks everyone sees it the same way. Cannot put self in place of others.	Child can put self in place of others. Not absolutistic in judgments; sees possibility of more than one point of view.
Intentionality	Child tends to judge an act in terms of actual physical consequences, not the motivation behind it.	Child judges acts by intentions, not consequences.
Rules	Child obeys rules because they are sacred and unalterable.	Child recognizes that rules were made by people and can be changed by people. Considers self just as capable of changing rules as anyone else.
Respect for Authority	Unilateral respect leads to feeling of obligation to conform to adult standards and obey adult rules.	Respect for both authority and peers allows child to value own opinion and ability more highly and to judge other people realistically.
Punishment	Child favors severe, vengeful punishment. Feels that punishment itself defines the wrongness of an act; an act is bad if it will elicit punishment.	Child favors milder punishment that entails making restitution to the victim and helping the culprit understand why an act was wrong, thus leading to reform.
"Immanent Justice"	Child confuses moral law with physical law and believes that any physical accident or misfortune that occurs after a misdeed is a punishment willed by God or some other supernatural force.	Child does not confuse natural misfortune with punishment.

Source: Adapted partly from Kohlberg (1964); Hoffman (1970).

maturity of the child. Like Piaget, Kohlberg used stories to test the levels of children's moral maturity on basic moral concepts such as the value of human life. Here is an example:

> Heinz, whose wife was dying from a special kind of cancer, learned that there was one drug that might save her life. It was a kind of radium for which the druggist charged $2,000 for a small dose, although he paid only $200 for it. The husband went to all his friends and relatives asking for money. He was able to borrow $1,000, which he took to the druggist, pleading with him to sell the radium cheaper or to let him pay the rest later. After the druggist refused, the husband was desperate and broke into the drugstore to steal the drug for his dying wife. Should the husband have done what he did?

Kohlberg distinguished among three levels of moral development corresponding to six stages (see Table 8–7). Level I, or **preconventional morality,** emphasizes external control. At this level, the child makes moral judgments solely on the basis of anticipated punishment and reward. Stage-1 morality at this level is called punishment-and-obedience orientation, i.e., children obey the rules of others to avoid punishment. Stage 2 is characterized by a naive hedonism of the type

Table 8–7. Kohlberg's Three Levels of Moral Development

Levels	*Stages*	*Illustrative responses to story of Heinz stealing the drug*
Level I: Preconventional level (early middle childhood)	Stage 1: Obedience and punishment orientation.	It isn't really bad to take it—he did ask to pay for it first. He wouldn't do any other damage or take anything else and the drug he'd take is only worth $200, not $2,000.
	Stage 2: Naively egoistic orientation	Heinz isn't really doing any harm to the druggist, and he can always pay him back. He should take the drug because it's the only thing that will work.
Level II: Conventional (late middle childhood)	Stage 3: "Good-boy orientation."	Stealing is bad, but this is a bad situation. Heinz isn't doing wrong in trying to save his wife, he has no choice but to take the drug. He is only doing something that is natural for a good husband to do. You can't blame him for doing something out of love. You'd blame him if he didn't love his wife enough to save her.
	Stage 4: Respect for authority and social order. Orientation to "doing duty" and to showing respect for authority.	The druggist is leading a wrong kind of life if he just lets somebody die like that, so it's Heinz's duty to save her. But Heinz can't just go around breaking laws and let it go at that—he must pay the druggist back and he must take his punishment for stealing.
Level III: Postconventional moral principles (adolescence)	Stage 5: Contractual legalistic orientation.	Before you say stealing is wrong, you've got to really think about this whole situation. Of course, the laws are quite clear about breaking into a store. And, even worse, Heinz would know there were no legal grounds for his actions. Yet, I can see why it would be reasonable for anybody in this situation to steal the drug.
	Stage 6: Conscience or principled orientation.	Where the choice must be made between disobeying a law and saving a human life, the higher principle of preserving life makes it morally right—not just understandable—to steal the drug.

Source: Rest (1974, pp. 92–93).

"You scratch my back, I'll scratch yours." According to Kohlberg, children conform to rules out of self-interest and consideration of what others can do for them in return.

At Level-II morality, or the **conventional morality,** children are able to understand the roles of authority figures well enough to decide whether some action is good by their standards. At Stage 3, the "good boy, good girl" orientation, children want to please and help others and can judge the intentions of others. Stage 4 has been called "law and order" morality because the focus is on obeying the rules for their own sake. Children and adults at this stage are concerned with doing their duty, showing respect for higher authority, and maintaining societal order.

Figure 8–5. The peak in the bar labeled "height spurt" represents the age at which the spurt is greatest. The bars represent the average beginning and ending of the events of puberty. (Adapted from Tanner, I. M. *Growing up*. Scientific American, September 1973, p. 40.)

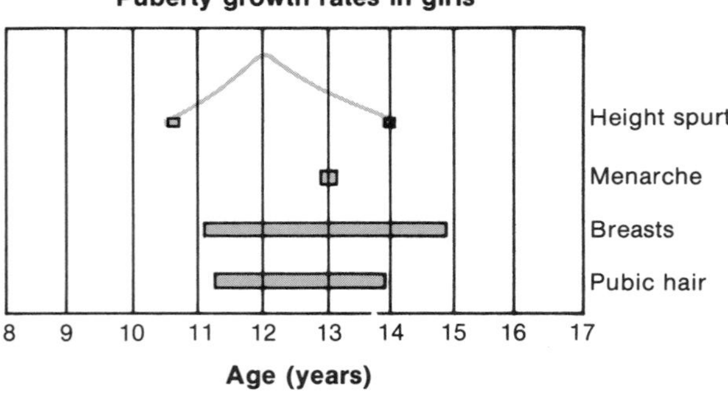

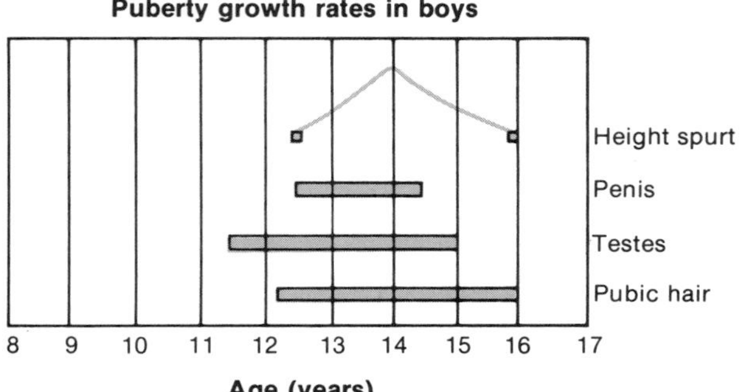

Finally, at Level III, the **postconventional level,** morality is based on self-accepted principles. For the first time, the individual recognizes the possibility of conflict between two socially acceptable standards and tries to decide between them. Stage 5 deals with the morality of contract, of individual rights, and of democratically accepted law. People at Stage 6, the morality of individual principles of conscience, essentially do what they as individuals think right regardless of legal sanctions or the opinion of others. On the basis of his studies, Kohlberg concluded that children arrive at their own moral judgments in a surprisingly independent fashion rather than merely absorbing the standards of their parents, teachers, or peers (Kohlberg, 1968).

ADOLESCENCE

Puberty, the period that signifies sexual maturity, marks the transition from childhood to adolescence. It is a time of rapid biological changes and emotional turmoil marked by a spurt in physical growth, changes in body proportions, and the development of secondary sex characteristics in boys and girls. It is generally accepted that the average age for sexual maturity is 12 for girls and 14 for boys (Lefrancois, 1980). The physical changes of puberty are often upsetting to a young person. It is a period of whispered conversations about sexual matters: "Have you had your period yet?" "How did you feel?" "Weren't you scared to tell your mother?" There are furtive looks at nudie magazines and exchanges of sexual jokes, often poorly understood.

Physical Development

The biological hallmark of puberty is sexual maturation in boys and girls. The two sexes develop at different rates, with girls rather uniformly experiencing extensive bodily changes two years before boys (Tanner, 1973). The growth spurt reaches a peak at 12 years for girls and 14 years for boys, as can be seen from Figure 8–5.

For a girl, breast buds and the first menstruation, or **menarche,** represent the most significant events of puberty. The normal age range for the first menstrual period is from 10 to 17 years. It is experienced by American girls when they are around 12½ years old. Evidence from many parts of the world indicates that the average age of menarche has dropped at least two and perhaps as many as five years in the last 100 years. Better nutrition and better living conditions are the reasons for the younger age of first menstruation. Menarche should not be equated with sexual maturity. The first menstrual periods tend to be irregular, and relatively few girls are able to reproduce immediately after their first menstrual periods.

In boys, one of the first indications of puberty is an accelerated growth of the testes, usually followed by that of the penis. **Nocturnal emissions,** or the ejaculation of semen while asleep (also known as "wet dreams"), signal the beginning of reproductive capacity. Often, but not always, such emissions occur in connection with erotic dreams. Additional physical changes in boys include the deepening of the voice and the appearance of facial hair.

Transition into adolescence for boys and girls depends on whether the teenager physically matures early or late. Generally it has been found that early-maturing boys have fewer adjustment problems than late-maturing boys. In one detailed longitudinal study (Jones, 1957, 1965), it was reported that early-maturing boys were more popular, appeared to be more self-confident and more independent and adept in interpersonal relationships, and were more successful in heterosexual relationships. Late-maturing boys tended to be more restless and more attention-seeking and had less positive self-concepts.

Whereas the findings regarding early- and late-maturing boys are generally consistent, the effects of early versus late maturation on girls are more ambiguous. Some studies report that early-maturing girls are at an advantage (e.g., Douglas & Ross, 1964), while others find just the opposite. Because girls mature two years earlier than boys on the average, the early-maturing girl may be three or four years ahead of like-aged boys, a fact that may complicate her social life (Faust, 1960). Although recent comparative studies of early and late adolescent girls are missing, some researchers speculate that being an early maturer may be more of an advantage for a girl in 1980 than it was for a girl before 1960.

Emotional Changes

Psychological reactions to the physical changes of puberty range from elation to shock. Discrepancies between a teenager's body and male or female ideals can be source of anxiety. In boys this anxiety typically focuses on the size of their penis, while girls are concerned with the size and shape of their breasts.

The emotions of teenagers tend to vacillate. One moment they are up in a cloud and the next moment down in the pits. Effective strategies for coping with frustrations and conflicts during childhood are suddenly undermined or no longer appropriate. During the adolescent years the physically mature boy or girl needs to bridge the gap between childhood and adulthood.

Psychosocial Development

Adolescence is the span of the life cycle bounded by the beginning of puberty on one side and the attainment of full adult status on the other. In Western societies it begins at the age of 12 or 13 and ends either in the late teens or early twenties. There is no exact criterion for the end of adolescence in our society.

In less complex cultures a young person has little or no difficulty in knowing when he or she passes from childhood to adulthood. In many of these societies puberty rites, or "rites of passage," celebrate and signal the attainment of adult status. This makes the transition from childhood to adulthood relatively smooth and problem-free.

In the mainstream of our society we do not have symbolic events or customs by which a young person knows that he or she has entered adulthood. Although ceremonies such as confirmation, first communion, and bar mitzvah may give an adolescent a sense of identity with an adult group, they are not a confirmation of adult status or an acceptance of the young person into the social world of adults. Instead we use a variety of criteria, such as economic independence, reaching the age of majority, or marriage. Prolonged higher education is steadily extending adolescence. This means that large numbers of young people become biologically and psychologically adult before society considers them adults.

Psychologically the most important developmental task of adolescence is the search for identity. For some young people this means conflict, unrest, and turmoil, turning adolescence into a period of "storm and stress." If we look at the number of choices and life decisions the adolescent must make concerning career planning, role choices, personal values, sexual identity, and willingness to conform to society's standards or peer-group pressures, adolescence seems to be a chaotic period.

An important stage in the transition from childhood to adulthood is the increased sexual awareness of adolescence. *(© Stephen Shames/Woodfin Camp & Associates)*

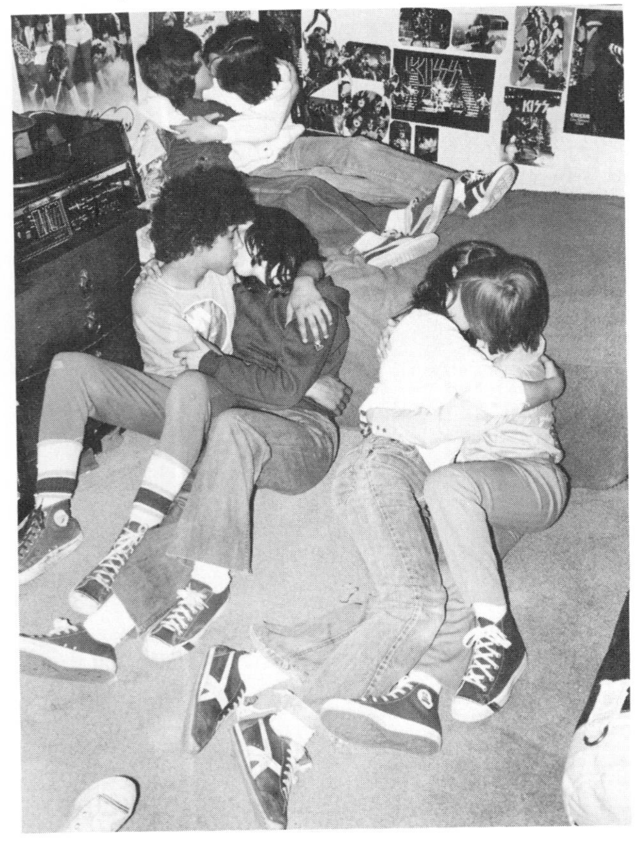

In the struggle for identity adolescents must liberate themselves from parental dependence and dominance without quite knowing which direction to take. Many concerns of adolescents center on the question "Who am I?" To find the answer, adolescents explore a variety of opportunities without making a commitment. In the process they oscillate between child and adult. Parents are frequently exasperated, antagonized, and frightened. As one father said about his adolescent daughter:

> I never know what to expect from her. One minute she is crazy. Her room looks like a pigpen, with cookie crumbs all over the floor. If I ask her to clean up she sulks and closes the door on me. The next minute she is sweet and lady-like. Her room is immaculate and she reminds me a little of my wife coming down the stairs all dressed up for a big date. What really bothers me are all the different ways she acts.

During later adolescence dating takes on a more serious pattern than it had during puberty, and questions over sexuality are of major concern. Competition for dates and the desire to be popular can put considerable strain on adolescents of both sexes.

Dates give adolescents a chance for sexual experimentation. Theoretically there are strict mores and built-in safety catches dictating just how far an adolescent boy or girl can go "without going too far." Nevertheless, many youths feel pressured by their peers into intimate relationships. This brings the adolescent face to face with his or her sexuality often before knowing how to deal with it.

The increase in adolescent sexual activities is seen in the decline of virginity among teenage girls and the increase in teenage pregnancies. Although teenage virgins are not extinct, they are

CRITICAL ISSUE

Teenage Pregnancy

With the apparent trend toward earlier sexual activity among adolescents, it is not surprising that teenage pregnancy in the United States is on the rise. About one out of ten teenage girls in the general population, four out of ten black girls, and three out of ten non-virgins have been pregnant (Sorenson, 1973; Shah, Zelnik, & Kanter, 1975). In 1976, 600,000 adolescent pregnancies resulted in live births, a rate surpassed by few Western industrialized nations (Monthly Vital Statistics Report, 1978). The number of births to adolescents might be even higher were it not for the liberalization of abortion laws and the increased availability of contraceptives. It has been estimated that approximately 300,000 teenagers obtain abortions annually, a figure that represents about one-third of the total number of abortions performed (Center for Disease Control, 1977).

Although the majority of teenage mothers (about 94 percent) keep their babies, they face a number of adverse consequences. Babies born to teenage mothers are much more likely to be premature and low in birth weight than infants born to mothers in their twenties. The teenage mother herself is more likely to suffer from complications. In addition to health hazards to mother and child, teenage mothers also face a bleak educational future and a stunted career. There is a good chance they will live in poverty (more than 15 percent of teenage mothers under 17 are dependent on welfare). And if they are married, there is a good chance their marriage will not last. (One half to two thirds of teenage marriages end in divorce).

Teenage mothers are also likely to undergo an altered relationship with their parents, particularly their mothers. Ninety percent of teenage mothers who keep their infants care for them in their parents' home. Roles may become blurred as the grandmother acts as primary caretaker for the infant, sharply diminishing the teenager's self-esteem and ability to develop a mothering relationship with her child (Marks, 1980).

One of the major factors in teenage pregnancy is the lack of or ineffective use of contraceptives. In the study by Shah and his co-workers (1975) it was found that seven out of ten girls were ignorant about birth-control methods. Some girls said they did not use contraceptives because they thought they were too young to get pregnant. Other reasons for not using contraception were because they had intercourse infrequently or because it was the "safe" time of the month. Even those girls who used contraception relied on the least effective methods.

While the news is full of stories about teenage mothers, little has been said about the impact of early fatherhood on teenage boys. We are almost led to believe that the experience leaves them untouched. Many of the teenage fathers, however, are willing to face their feelings and responsibilities and receive counseling. But the father is often forbidden to see his girlfriend after her parents discover her pregnancy because they believe it is the boy's fault.

---

becoming less common than they once were. In 1953, when Kinsey reported on the sex life of women, only 3 percent had parted with their virginity by age 15. A generation later, Zelnik and Kanter (1972) found that 11 percent of white females at 15 were no longer virgins. When the figures included 15-year-old black girls, who tend to be sexually more active, the nonvirgin rate went up to 14 percent. Late adolescent girls who worry about their normality if they are still virgins may engage in intercourse before they are ready for it.

Erikson viewed the period of adolescence as a "psychological moratorium." According to Erikson, "The adolescent mind is essentially a mind of the moratorium, a psychosocial stage between childhood and adulthood, and between the morality learned by the child, and the ethics to be developed by the adults" (Erikson, 1963, pp. 262–263). Others consider adolescence an uncharted stage of life that has been interposed between the attainment of physiological maturity and entry into the adult world. Ideally adolescents

For many young adults the establishment of an intimate relationship culminates in marriage. *(© Suzanne Szasz)*

emerge from this period with a true commitment to themselves. Commitment to self refers to an understanding of one's basic worth, a conviction that "I am a worthy being." This commitment underlies all other commitments adolescents make; it represents the successful resolution of the identity crisis that allows the adolescent to state, "This is me!" Since role choice is very much a process of self-definition, adolescence may be viewed as a time of self-discovery.

EARLY ADULTHOOD

No sharp line marks the moment when adolescence ends and the adult years begin. The 20-year span from the end of adolescence at about 20 to mid-life at about 40 is a busy time for most young adults. It is the time when most men and women get married, establish a home, and have children. It is a time when they get settled in an occupation and career and invest considerable amounts of energy in their work. During early adulthood people also widen their circle of friends, extend their social contacts, join organized social groups, and become involved in civic and community affairs.

After the rapid growth during adolescence, adult changes are more subtle, extending over long years. Adult development is so gradual that some people believe that adulthood is a static state of existence that lasts until old age sets in.

The completion of the major developmental tasks in early adulthood varies widely from person to person. Marriage may take place during adolescence, early adulthood, old age, or not at all. Similarly the choice of an occupation or the birth of the first child may occur at age 20 or 40. Because of the great variation in the timing of the main events, it is difficult, if not impossible, to pinpoint stages of adult development on the basis of age. Instead, in most Western societies a person is considered an adult if he or she has achieved one or more of the following: marriage, parenthood, or commitment to an occupation. For example, a youth who has a wife and a family is considered a man, whereas a single male of the same age may be regarded as a boy.

Again, the central tasks of young adulthood may be viewed from Erikson's perspective. Young adults must learn to relate unselfishly on a deeply intimate level, as required in a wholesome heterosexual relationship, and they must achieve generativity by becoming creative or parental (Rogers, 1979). The young lawyer we encountered at the beginning of the chapter was very much preoccupied with the major developmental tasks of early adulthood. Let us review each of these tasks in turn.

Marriage

In our society marriage is the most popular life style; some 95 to 98 percent of men and women marry. Most people marry for the first time during their young adult years. Although a vast amount of literature deals with marriage, particularly problems and failure in marriage, little is known about the specific contributions that marriage makes to adult development.

The idea that people marry only for love is a myth, although some couples do. According to Clayton (1975), motives that influence a couple to marry may be divided into "push" and "pull" factors. In the "push" category we find motives such as conformity to social expectations, legitimization of sex and children, and tax breaks. Among the "pull" factors are interpersonal attraction (see Chapter 15), similar value systems and goals, and, of course, love.

Marriage partners are typically of the same race, social class, religion, and educational background. Shared value systems and love are probably the basis for most successful marriages in our country.

As a developmental process marriage evolves into a relatively stable pattern of intimacy. In the course of this evolution the conditions of marriage are continually modified as husband and wife adjust to life's changing circumstances. A successful marriage requires both partners to make frequent adjustments. Adjustment, among other things, means the acceptance of the fact that marriage is not always a 50-50 affair. Instead, it is a relationship in which one partner may give more in certain situations than the other.

Not everyone wants to get married, however. People today feel less pressure to get married and are freer to remain single for a longer period of time. Many young adults choose to live together without being married. Each of these life styles—marriage, living together, and the single life—has its own cultural demands, social roles, and stresses.

Parenthood

Parenthood in early adulthood requires new roles and responsibilities on the part of the mother and father, which many couples are unprepared to fulfill. Motivations for becoming a parent are often difficult to determine. Some couples have ideal reasons, such as extending oneself beyond the present generation, whereas others are motivated by more subtle social pressures and policies. Childlessness, for example, has traditionally been associated with "irresponsibility, unnaturalness, immaturity, emotional instability, marital unhappiness, divorce, psychological maladjustment, and generally unsatisfactory mental health" (Veevers, 1974, p. 398). Parenthood is also encouraged in our society by preferential tax treatment.

The initial adjustment to parenthood is likely to be both exciting and frustrating. Once the child is born, family life revolves around it for some time. During this time parents have to adjust to the new demands placed on them. Child-care tasks are time consuming. The mother is likely to be tired, and the father may resent having to share her attention with the baby.

Most new parents also find their personal freedom curtailed. The spontaneous dinner at a new restaurant or the romantic candlelight evening at home often have to be sacrificed to satisfy the baby's needs. Disruption of sleep and sexual patterns, additional routines, and new financial responsibilities call for added sacrifices on the part of the parents.

Career Choice

A person's ability to become involved in meaningful work requires a series of commitments to some vocation or career. Some researchers (e.g., Shertzer & Stone, 1976) have found that the process of choosing an occupation is often a matter of rejecting alternatives. Most people are settled into a final occupation by the time they are 30 years old. Among the middle-aged persons that were questioned by Flaste (1976), the average age at which they chose their present occupation was 28.

The attitudes of men and women toward work vary considerably according to social class and sex. For lower- and middle-class people, for instance, work is often an economic necessity, something that must be done to survive. On the other hand, upper-class people are more likely to

CRITICAL ISSUE

The Midlife Crisis

Although for many people middle adulthood appears to be a prime time marked by good health, stable relationships, and a peaking career, it still has its crises. Many men and women find this period of life painful because they become aware of an aging body and the limitations of personal and professional potential. Somewhere in their forties, they realize that their lives are half over and they begin evaluating what they have done and whether they have achieved their goals. As a result, people at middle age often redefine their identity.

Midlife crisis is a relatively new concept. Writers have given this period of the life span a number of different names to call attention to some of the problems that may occur. These names include "mid-career crisis" (Rogers, 1973), "deadline decade" (Sheehy, 1976), and middle-age slump.

Middle-aged people in careers begin to face the prospects of retirement. As they evaluate their earlier expectations, they must come to terms with their ultimate career potential and the fact that they will never be the president of a company or earn a million dollars. For some people middle age brings the painful realization that they have lagged behind the goals set in early adulthood.

Some women who have devoted themselves to raising a family go through a crisis when children leave home to go to college or to get married. The empty-nest syndrome, as psychologists refer to it, may leave the middle-aged women feeling empty and depressed. The loss of physical attractiveness and reproductive ability may be other sources of depression. Sheehy (1976) pointed out that women approach the midlife crisis earlier than men, often by the age of 35.

Yet there is also conflicting evidence. The departure of children can lead to improved life satisfaction during middle age (Neugarten, 1970). Menopause for many women is less stressful than commonly assumed, and some women even view it as a positive event (Chiriboga & Thurnher, 1975).

view their work as an opportunity to be productive or creative or as a means of achieving personal fulfillment.

The sex of a person often determines his or her eventual career more than interests and abilities. Many occupations have disproportionate distributions of one sex or the other. For example, 97 percent of registered nurses but only 5 percent of attorneys are women. However, in some professions that were traditionally male-dominated the figures have changed considerably. Psychologists are a good example; today about 20 percent of the members of the American Psychological Association are women.

At the threshold of age 40, most men and women recognize that their time is limited. They begin to wonder what the future holds for them and question whether they have taken the right course in their life. Early adulthood as a developmental period is preceded by the stormy years of adolescence and is followed by the troublesome middle age.

MIDDLE ADULTHOOD

For most people middle age means "the other side of 40." Chronologically middle adulthood covers the years from 40 to 60, but it may be shorter or longer. In this time of life, as in most previous periods, there are wide differences among people. While one 40-year-old person may fit the stereotype of the settled and mature citizen, another may undergo a second identity crisis, striving frantically to carve out a new life. A successful 48-year-old physician, for instance, decided one day to leave his practice, family, and community to try out a new life style as a painter in a commune. Middle age is a period of being in between, a time when a man or woman is no longer a young adult but not yet an old person.

According to Erikson, the major task in middle adulthood is the development of generativity, which, as we have seen, refers to a concern for the younger generation. Parents can express generativity most obviously, yet all men and women can

Neugarten noted that when role changes of middle-aged women are predictable and occur "on schedule," they can be anticipated and worked through without disrupting her sense of self.

As couples, middle-aged men and women have to cope with still other stressful events. It is a time when their parents are likely to die. If their parents are still alive, they may be disabled enough to need their middle-aged children to take care of them. At the same time the children of middle-aged parents may be passing through their adolescent crises and testing new life styles that are unacceptable to the parents.

Many writers stress that the midlife crisis is not surprising. A person has to give up accustomed behavior patterns that are no longer viable and must search for new ways. In addition, people experience a series of losses: loss of hopes and ambitions, loss of the capacity to procreate, loss of parents and friends, loss of activities they formerly enjoyed. Like adolescence, middle age may be a time of profound change (Schreiber, 1977). At best, it allows the individual after a turbulent period to emerge with a kind of wisdom, maturity, and insight that are beyond the grasp of youthful capacity (Rosenberg & Farrell, 1976). Since research on the midlife crisis is a fairly recent phenomenon, there are few guidelines for successfully passing through this developmental crisis.

For many people middle age represents both the time of deepest satisfaction and that of a midlife crisis. *(© Maureen Fennelli/Photo Researchers, Inc.)*

display generativity by sharing their experience with the young and by teaching and guiding them.

Most men and women in middle age are in good health. Nevertheless, gradual physical changes occur. Although the aging process begins in the early twenties, most people pay little attention to it until they reach their forties. Then the muscles begin to lose their flexible tone, wrinkles crease the once-smooth skin, and visual acuity begins to decline. For women **menopause,** the cessation of menstruation, which marks the end of their reproductive ability, is often the sign that youth is over.

Many people believe that intellectual functions decline during the later part of adulthood. Recent studies reveal contradictory findings about intelligence in middle age. Some elements of intelligence, such as verbal understanding or reasoning ability, remain stable or broaden over the adult years, while others, such as motor speed or memory, show an apparent decline.

For many middle-aged couples the middle years bring increased marital satisfaction. Married people over 40 usually have found the person they want to stay married to. Most of them have done their duty by their children and now have time for each other. Some couples experience this time as a "second honeymoon," enjoying privacy they have not had for years, freedom to be spontaneous, and a new opportunity to get to know each other. Other couples are faced with the task of finding each other again as individuals after having been parents for more than a decade.

LATE ADULTHOOD

For the first time in our history we have a society with a mass population of elderly people. Since 1960 the elderly population has increased by 35.3 percent, compared with an overall population growth of 19 percent. In 1975 people between the ages of 65 and 74 made up 61.9 percent of the elderly population, those between the ages of 75 and 84 years 29.7 percent, and those 85 and over, 8.4 percent. Butler (1975) views the "elderly population explosion" as follows:

> Every day 1,000 people reach 65; each year 365,000. More than 70 percent of the 65-and-over age group in 1970 entered that category after 1959. With new medical discoveries, an improved health-care delivery system and the presently declining birth rate, it is possible that the elderly will make up one quarter of the total population by the year 2000. Major medical advances in the control of cancer or heart and vascular diseases could increase the average life expectancy by 10 or even 15 years. Discovery of deterrents to the basic causes of aging would cause even more profound repercussions. The presence of so many elderly, and the potential of so many more, has been a puzzlement to gerontologists, public-health experts and demographers, who don't know whether to regard it as "the aging problem" or a human triumph over disease. What is clear is that it will result in enormous changes in every part of our society. (pp. 16–17).

This rise in the population of the elderly has led to a new discipline called gerontology, or the study of aging.

There is more to aging than just getting old. Aging involves at least three kinds of changes: biological, psychological, and social. Most of the effects of **biological aging** are readily apparent and fairly predictable. Most older people develop sensory dysfunctions and are more susceptible to illnesses. The body of the older person shrinks in size and has a reduced ability to recover from stress. Most elderly people have to accept a decline in their energy level.

Individual differences in physical changes are probably greater in old age than at any other time. Certainly not all old people are senile or infirm. Many factors, including the kind of life the individual has led, nutrition, illness, and activity, affect the chances of having a long life.

One of the many stereotypes of old age is the senile old woman who cannot remember how to complete the sentence she has just started. Yet most of the research regarding intellectual functioning in old age indicates that the presumed intellectual decline in old age is mostly a myth. Many functions of intelligence do not decline at all in old age. One key function, short-term memory, does degenerate, and it is the decline of this function that has led people to believe that all mental processes slow down in the elderly. In fact, old people are able to learn new skills and information, although they need more time for learning than a younger person does.

The **psychological aging** and developmental tasks that face the elderly person were first brought to our attention by Erik Erikson. Peck (1968) expanded Erikson's eighth stage of development (integrity versus despair) to include three major crises that the aged must resolve. The first involves coming to terms with retirement. The second task is accepting and adjusting to a debilitating body. Peck suggested that it is important for the old person to turn away from preoccupation with physical discomforts and focus instead on satisfying relationships with other people. Finally, the old person needs to find ways to contribute to the happiness and well-being of others, as he or she had done earlier in life.

Psychological aging is measured by the capacity of the older person to adapt to the demands of the environment and of other people. Many people experience the last stage of life positively and make a variety of healthy adjustments as they grow old. Two theories have been proposed to explain successful aging: activity theory and disengagement theory.

Activity theory is based on the assumption that successful aging is related to the degree of activity an older person maintains. According to this theory, the more active old people remain, the more successfully they will age. Ideally, the old person remains as active as he or she was in middle age. For many old people this means finding substitutes for lost activities resulting from retirement or death of a spouse or friends.

The second theory, **disengagement theory,** proposed by Cumming and Henry (1961), characterizes aging by a mutual withdrawal of the old person, who decreases his or her activities and commitments, and of society, which forces retirement and encourages segregation by age. Disen-

CRITICAL ISSUE

Ageism

Ageism is a new word in our vocabulary that refers to discrimination against the old. Old people are often treated as children or as though they are no longer people. Like sexism and racism, ageism is based on many negative stereotypes. Old people are considered cranky and self-pitying (Butler, 1975), boring, senile, less intelligent than when they were younger, sickly, ugly, socially and sexually finished, and burdensome parasites living off welfare or their children. Yet there are millions of productive, vigorous, cheerful old people whose lives belie these stereotypes.

Ageism has become a social problem similar to sexism and racism. Old people are discriminated against in many ways. They are not hired for new jobs, and they are phased out of the ones they have. After a lifetime of hard work, many become poor for the first time. Old people are also discriminated against sexually because people assume that old age and sexual relationships are incompatible. Our humor about the sexual lives of old people implies wickedness in old men (old goat, dirty old man) and ugliness in women (hag, biddy) (Anderson, 1978).

Socially many old people are frequently shunned. For women social status drops rapidly when they "lose their looks," and the same happens for men when they retire. Intellectually old people also face a wall of discrimination because they are thought incapable of learning new things, rigid and inflexible in their thinking, and passé in their morality.

As Rogers (1979) pointed out, the effects of ageism are often subtle but always damaging. Like all prejudices, it affects older persons' views of themselves. The elderly not only tend to adopt the stereotypes but by doing so tend to perpetuate them.

The stereotype of the entire elderly population as infirm and senile is increasingly being broken down. *(© Peter Menzel/Stock, Boston)*

A number of reasons have been suggested to explain ageism in our society. Among them are our nation's youth cult, the limited contact younger people have with the elderly, the relatively few elderly men and women portrayed by the media, and a general ignorance about the aging process and old age (McKenzie, 1980). As the population of the elderly continues to grow, old persons will become more visible socially, economically, and politically. Also, our growing knowledge in the field of gerontology may contribute to the reduction of ageism.

gagement is a normal process because old people become more preoccupied with themselves and have decreased emotional ties with others. Since the withdrawal of the old person is usually voluntary, morale is generally high.

Social aging is gauged by the social roles and habits maintained by the older person (Smith, 1973). For example, forced retirement at 65 redefines the retiree's social role. Although retirement from work is only one facet of aging, it is clear-cut and easy to recognize. And it is another crisis of life. The old person must accept the fact of retirement. Old people, especially men, approach retirement from work reluctantly. For some it marks the step from a productive lifelong employment to what seems an unproductive old age.

Retirement can bring both stress and satisfaction. It may be stressful for a number of reasons: the loss of the dominant role, that of worker (Darnley, 1975), and the end of the work career. Retirement usually adds to financial worries since the retired person frequently must live on Social Security or a small pension. Retirement also brings feelings of emptiness because of reduced social contacts. Learning how to occupy leisure time so that life is meaningful is not an easy task.

Retirement can also put a strain on the marriage of an elderly couple. After a lifetime of individual schedules, the husband and wife find themselves together 24 hours a day. Many old people try to overcome the problem by finding part-time employment, devoting their energies to volunteer work, or starting projects they have put off.

Women are generally less affected by retirement than men because most of the women in our present elderly population have worked at home or have fluctuated between working at home and in the marketplace. The majority of older women today have had the opportunity to adjust to a less structured life at home. However, this will change in the next generation since more women are working outside the home. In 10 to 15 years psychologists will undoubtedly study the effects of retirement on women and compare their adjustment to that of men.

Retirement can, and often does, bring a variety of satisfactions, such as freedom from routine and time to pursue special interests. Successful adjustment to retirement depends on many factors, including economic security, life satisfaction, health, and the need for activity and a sense of fulfillment. Old people who have been active all their lives and have enjoyed their work are likely to remain busy after retirement.

The death of a spouse is an integral part of old age that affects women in particular. While most elderly men are married, nearly two-thirds of elderly women are widowed. This disproportionate ratio of widows to widowers is due to the longer life expectancy of women. In our society women tend to outlive men by seven or eight years. Moreover, widowers have twice as much chance of remarrying as widows because there are fewer possible mates for elderly women to choose from.

Being a widow or widower means changing one's social life. The surviving spouse inevitably experiences feelings of isolation and loneliness. Men try to fill the void by remarrying, while women seek the companionship of other widows.

In general, then, the needs of older people are not much different from those of younger people. Older men and women do best when they enjoy friendships and social contacts, keep busy with work, hobbies, or leisure activities, and maintain reasonable health.

DEATH AND THE LIFE CYCLE

The final developmental task of life is dying. Like old age, dying may be viewed from biological and psychosocial perspectives. **Biological death** is defined medically by a number of possible criteria: when the heart stops beating, when breathing stops, or when the electrical activity of the brain ceases. By nature's rules, death is an organic falling apart. According to one theory of dying, except in cases of fatal accidents or genetic disorders, we are biologically programmed to die because a clock of aging lies in each of our cells, where DNA molecules carry a gene or genes for our physical destruction. Another biological theory proposes that death is controlled by the endocrine system through some as yet undefined death hormones.

The psychological reality of death has only been studied recently. **Psychosocial death** refers to the ways we feel about our own impending death and about the death of those close to us. Elizabeth Kübler-Ross (1969) described five stages in the process of adjusting to death. The first stage involves **denial and isolation.** The person who learns about his or her impending death simply refuses to believe it. Terminally ill patients during this stage have a tendency to isolate themselves from objective information such as X-rays or lab reports. During the second phase **anger** is the pre-

CRITICAL ISSUE

Life after Death

Glimpses from the beds of the dying, from near-fatal accidents, and from individuals who claim to have come back from the brink of death reflect the intense curiosity and apprehension people have always had about the experience of dying. The promise of life after death is central to many religions and is an important part of the personal philosophy of many people (Siegel, 1981).

There is a growing body of popular and scientific books on life after death (Bayless, 1976; Fiore & Landsberg, 1979; Meek, 1980). According to physician Raymond Moody (1975, 1977), the prototypical experience of dying may include the following elements: being unable to describe the experience in words; hearing doctors and relatives pronouncing one dead; feeling a sense of peace and quiet; hearing a loud ringing or buzzing noise; feeling oneself moving through a dark tunnel having out-of-the-body experiences; meeting others, including guides, spirits, relatives, and friends; seeing a glowing light with a human shape; seeing a panoramic view of one's life; having visions of great knowledge; and seeing cities of light. Here are two testimonies of individuals who have stood at the threshold of death:

> There were colors—bright colors—not like here on earth, but just undescribable. I could see a city. There were buildings, separate buildings . . . a city of light (Moody, 1977, p. 17).

> I floated down to a grassy field which had horses, cows, lions, and all kinds of wild and tame animals. It was a painting at first, then it became real. I was in that field looking at all those great things when you [indicating doctors] pulled me back (Wheeler, 1976, p. 88).

Persons who have journeyed to the threshold of death generally say that there is much less terror and discomfort than they had expected, and some of them even report happiness and ecstacy. One individual's experience unfolded as follows:

> Her last violent reaction was fighting against the sense of dying, even though she was no longer afraid. She then gave in, knowing that she wanted it, death. Next she witnessed in rapid succession a great many scenes from her life. They began around the age of five and were marked by vivid impressions of colors. She had the sense of a beloved doll and was impressed with how bright the glass eyes were. She also had a picture of herself on a red bicycle on an equally bright green lawn. Other scenes followed, not from her whole life, but of her early childhood and she emphasized that the death scenes all made her ecstatically happy (Holcomb, 1975, p. 256).

While such accounts may offer some assurance for people who associate death with the fear of the unknown, other reports are highly speculative. Keleman (1975), for instance, believed that humans have a natural genetic programming for dying, which is an essential part of life's total developmental plan. According to Keleman, at impending death excitement can build up to a point of something resembling orgasm. He suggested that the "orgasm of dying" is similar to the excitement of other life experiences when we meet the unknown.

Psychologist Ronald Siegel (1980, 1981) noted a striking similarity between the descriptions given by dying persons and those reported by persons experiencing drug-induced hallucinations (see Chapter 3). Siegel speculated that both experiences result from activating stored images in the brain.

The belief in life after death is more a question of personal faith than scientific proof. If there is an afterlife, its proof will probably have to await changes in scientific and psychological thinking, not to mention future technology that may be necessary for its demonstration (Siegel, 1980, p. 927).

dominant reaction. The dying person asks, "Why me?" and bitterly envies those who live longer. Doctors become terrible people, and healthy friends are enemies.

During the **bargaining** stage the person says in one way or another, "Maybe death can be postponed; maybe I can ask God for an extension." In this stage some people make secret pacts with

God, promising that they will dedicate their lives to Him if He grants them more time. After bargaining comes **depression.** The dying person still asks "Why me?" but this time with a sense of sadness knowing that life will be over and that no one can stop the process.

In the final stage **acceptance** emerges. The person is neither angry nor depressed. Often there is an absence of feelings and conversation. The dying person may wish for the silent companionship of other people, such as family, friends, doctors, or nurses.

According to Butler (1975), the process of life review is the most important part of the person's adjustment to death. Both old and young people who know they will die soon look back on their lives, reevaluating and reliving old conflicts, pleasures, and pains. In the process they review the meaning of their existence. The life review can be one more step in the process of dynamic growth. In the course of this review the dying person must adjust the perception of life as it was lived to the way he or she would have liked to live it.

The final task the dying person faces is to adapt to a transition to an unknown state. Most religious teachings promise either restoration or another life after death. In this afterlife some people believe that recollections of the previous life are retained, while others believe in metamorphosis, where one is reborn after death without consciousness of a previous existence. Even though religious teachings may influence a person's reaction to the thought of impending death, the transition itself remains a mystery.

Summary

Life-span development can be approached from a number of theoretical perspectives, including biological, psychoanalytic, learning, and cognitive-developmental theories. This chapter used Erikson's eight stages as a basis for examining the developmental tasks of the life cycle.

Unique as each person's life is, development consists of the same stages that are encountered at about the same age and resolved in the same manner. Developmental stages are growth processes that all humans share.

Infancy and childhood are periods of rapid growth in all areas of development. In the course of the first two years a normal infant learns to walk and to talk, expands his or her emotional repertoire, and develops many different social skills. At the same time, the infant's perceptual and intellectual growth becomes more and more complex.

From age 6 to 12 a child's development is influenced by the school and the peer culture. Academic success and popularity have a profound effect on the child's growing self-concept. After the turmoil of puberty, adolescence is the developmental period that bridges the gap between childhood and adulthood, dependence and independence. It is a time of uncertainty, trials, and experimentation with new roles.

Young adulthood is a period of serious and presumably permanent commitments: commitment to a marriage partner, to a career or occupational choice, and to parenthood. Successful passage through middle age requires a series of adjustments to changes in life style. Toward the end of this stage women experience the cessation of reproductive function and men face retirement. Finally, during old age men and women must come to terms with the decisions and choices they made during their earlier years. Retirement, one of the major crises of old age, may mean a variety of restrictions during the last years of life. Personal preparation for death is difficult and complex. Acceptance of our mortality is the quintessential adjustment for many philosophical and religious doctrines.

Key Terms For Review

acceptance
accommodation
activity theory
ageism
anger
assimilation
Babinski reflex
bargaining
biological aging
biological death
bonding
conventional morality
denial and isolation
depression
disengagement theory
engrossment
grasping reflex
implantation
imprinting
menarche
menopause
morality of constraint
morality of cooperation
Moro reflex
nocturnal emission
period of the embryo
period of the fetus
period of the ovum
postconventional morality
preconventional morality
psychological aging
psychosocial death
rooting reflex
school phobia
social aging
stranger anxiety
sucking reflex
swimming reflex
zygote

Suggested Readings

Bloom, M. *Life span development.* New York: Macmillan, 1980.
This book provides a broad range of readings about various stages of growth and development in the young, the middle-aged, and the old; in men and women; and in blacks and whites.

Feifel, H. *New meanings of death.* New York: McGraw-Hill, 1977.
This book presents clinical and empirical findings in the areas of dying, death, and bereavement. The meaning of death for specific populations, such as children and college students, as well as responses to death and its impact on survivors are discussed.

Lefrancois, G. *Of children: An introduction to child development.* Belmont, Calif.: Wadsworth, 1980.
This book covers the periods of development from the prenatal period to adolescence and discusses topics such as sex roles, sex differences, social-emotional development, language development, and exceptional children.

McKenzie, S. *Aging and old age.* Glenview, Ill.: Scott, Foresman, 1980.
An introductory gerontology text, this book provides students with a basic understanding of the last stage of the human life span. It discusses the myths of growing old and presents an overview of the aging process. Other topics include the impact of stress on old people, psychological disorders of old age, sexual behavior, and social relationships of the elderly.

Nilsson, L. *A child is born.* New York: Delacorte, 1977.
A Scandinavian photographer captures the mystery of birth. The book contains excellent photographs of human reproduction from conception to birth.

9

Gender Identity and Sex Roles

"He is playing masculine. She is playing feminine.

"He is playing masculine because *she is playing feminine. She is playing feminine* because *he is playing masculine.*

"He is playing the kind of man that she thinks the kind of woman she is playing ought to admire. She is playing the kind of woman that he thinks the kind of man he is playing ought to desire.

"If he were not playing masculine, he might well be more feminine than she is—except when she is playing very feminine. If she were not playing feminine, she might well be more masculine than he is—except when he is playing very masculine.

"So he plays harder. And she plays . . . softer. He wants to make sure that she could never be more masculine than he. She wants to make sure that he could never be more feminine than she. He therefore seeks to destroy the femininity in himself. She therefore seeks to destroy the masculinity in herself.

"She is supposed to admire him for the masculinity in him that she fears in herself. He is supposed to desire her for the femininity in her that he despises in himself.

"He desires her for her femininity which is his *femininity, but which he can never claim. She admires him for his masculinity which is* her *masculinity, but which she can never lay claim to. Since he may only love his own femininity in her, he envies her her femininity. Since she may only love her own masculinity in him, she envies him his masculinity.*

"The envy poisons their love" (Roszak & Roszak, 1969, p. 1).

The differences between men and women, both behavioral and psychological, have puzzled laymen and social scientists for many years. Social scientists study sex differences because they assume that they can more effectively understand or predict behavior if they know the sex of a person. The opening quotation illustrates how much of our behavior depends on our perceptions of what is masculine and what is feminine.

But who are the sexes? In the minds of most people the separation between the two sexes is made on the basis of certain reproductive capacities such as the production of sperm in men or the maturation of fertile eggs in women. However, defining male and female on the basis of their reproductive functions alone does not tell us much about the behavior of men and women.

In this chapter you will learn about the processes that influence sex-related behavior. We shall explore how most of us develop sex-typed behavior through the process of sex-role socialization and where we find sources of sex-role information in our environment. As you will see, people acquire through interactions with others the personality characteristics and behavior that they and others perceive to be appropriate to members of the sex to which they belong.

WHAT IS GENDER IDENTITY?

Gender identity is the life style we project to society as a man or woman. This is not the same as sexual identity, which refers to our biological sex. Thus the term "gender" is used to designate the psychological, social, and cultural aspects of femaleness and maleness as manifested in our behavior. Sex-appropriate behavior that is most often displayed by women is considered feminine, and that which is most often displayed by men is considered masculine. Money and Ehrhardt (1972) explained gender identity as "all those things that a person says or does to disclose himself or herself as having the status of a boy or girl, man or woman."

From the moment a child is born and labeled a girl or boy, people have certain expectations that are different for male and for female children. For example, immediately after birth both the infant and the nursery are usually given the blue or pink treatment. One researcher who was interested in studying sex differences in infancy asked the mothers who had volunteered to participate in the study to dress their infants in overalls so that the observers would not know whether they were watching a baby boy or girl. Nevertheless, the girls were brought to the lab in pink overalls and the boys in blue ones.

Very early in life children observe that each parent has a distinct behavioral pattern that is in accordance with culturally prescribed stereotypes for males and females. Thus women tend to kiss, fondle, dress the child, and prepare the child's meal, while men tend to do the roughhousing and play outdoor sports with the child.

Leafing through any popular magazine will give you a quick idea of the types of behavior that our culture ascribes to men and women. The male is typically portrayed as a strong, active, courageous, competitive, adventurous person who assumes leadership and is rational and unemotional. Men are believed to be good at math and science and relatively unconcerned with their physical appearance. Moreover, according to psychoanalytic theory, men have a stronger superego (see Chapter 10). Thus men are ideally suited to take care of women, who lack all these characteristics.

The corresponding image of women is altogether different. In a *Playboy* article (Gunther, 1972) a woman described herself as follows: "I am a woman, scared, a pussycat, a lover, a crazy something, a child, a body, lots of tingles, eyes reaching out, afraid of anger, a caring person who needs attention, who loves the sun, who loves to dance, who loves quiet times, who loves to be touched, who wants to feel wanted, who wants to share" (p. 139).

These portrayals of men and women are called stereotypes. A **stereotype** is a set of beliefs about the characteristics of a person in a certain role, such as man or woman. According to Wrightsman (1977), a stereotype is a "relatively rigid, oversimplified conception of a group of people in which all individuals in the group are labeled with the so-called group characteristics" (p. 672). In other words, stereotypes are strongly held generalizations made about people in some designated social category. Such beliefs tend to be universally shared within a given society and are learned as part of the process of growing up in that society. Stereotypes are not necessarily based on the real characteristics of a person. If you were to accept what Hollywood or the mass media have to say about men and women, you would believe that the male is constantly demonstrating his virility, while the female is generally willing to submit to it.

In addition to ascribing certain characteristics to men and women, most stereotypes have an evaluative component. Certain behavior that is expected of women and men is evaluated as desirable or undesirable, good or bad. For example, psychologist Inge Broverman and her co-workers (Broverman, Broverman, Clarkson, Rosenkrantz, & Vogel, 1972) clearly demonstrated that in our culture the stereotyped female role consists of traits with low social value, such as passivity, helplessness, irrationality, and dependency. In contrast, male traits, such as competence, assertiveness, rationality, self-confidence, and ease at decision making, are highly valued because they are considered essential for personal, interpersonal, and professional success.

In the Broverman study a sex-role questionnaire (see Table 9–1) was given to a group of psychologists, psychiatrists, and social workers, who were asked to identify the characteristics of a normal, psychologically healthy adult of unspecified sex, of a normal man, and of a normal woman. In their responses they checked the same traits when describing a healthy adult for a healthy male, but the mature healthy woman was assigned traits that the same group of mental-health professionals rated as less healthy traits. In other words, the attributes of men became the standard against which women were judged and deemed inferior.

The manner in which parents interact with children can reflect different sex-role expectations. (*© Ken Karp*)

Thus the study revealed a double standard of mental health for men and women.

Many social scientists are seriously questioning the concepts of masculinity and femininity as mutually exclusive (e.g., Bem, 1974). But the majority of people still treat masculine and feminine characteristics as dichotomous. Many people do not recognize that masculine and feminine traits can coexist in a person. Let us examine how we develop our gender identity as men and women and how we come to learn and accept certain sex roles and kinds of stereotyped behavior, much of which is in accordance with sex-appropriate behavior prescribed by our culture.

DETERMINANTS OF GENDER IDENTITY

The development of gender identity is a complex process in which biological, psychological, and social forces interact. Since we attribute masculin-

Table 9–1.

Competency Cluster: Masculine Pole Is More Desirable	
Feminine	**Masculine**
Not at all aggressive	Very aggressive
Not at all independent	Very independent
Very emotional	Not at all emotional
Does not hide emotions at all	Almost always hides emotions
Very subjective	Very objective
Very easily influenced	Not at all easily influenced
Very submissive	Very dominant
Dislikes math and science very much	Likes math and science very much
Very excitable in a minor crisis	Not at all excitable in a minor crisis
Very passive	Very active
Not at all competitive	Very competitive
Very illogical	Very logical
Very home oriented	Very worldly
Not at all skilled in business	Very skilled in business
Very sneaky	Very direct
Does not know the way of the world	Knows the way of the world
Feelings easily hurt	Feelings not easily hurt
Not at all adventurous	Very adventurous
Has difficulty making decisions	Can make decisions easily
Cries very easily	Never cries
Almost never acts as a leader	Almost always acts as a leader
Not at all self-confident	Very self-confident
Very uncomfortable about being aggressive	Not at all uncomfortable about being aggressive
Not at all ambitious	Very ambitious
Unable to separate feelings from ideas	Easily able to separate feelings from ideas
Very dependent	Not at all dependent
Very conceited about appearance	Never conceited about appearance
Thinks women are always superior to men	Thinks men are always superior to women
Does not talk freely about sex with men	Talks freely about sex with men
Warmth-Expressiveness Cluster: Feminine Pole Is More Desirable	
Feminine	**Masculine**
Doesn't use harsh language at all	Uses very harsh language
Very talkative	Not at all talkative
Very tactful	Very blunt
Very gentle	Very rough
Very aware of feelings of others	Not at all aware of feelings of others
Very religious	Not at all religious
Very interested in own appearance	Not at all interested in own appearance
Very neat in habits	Very sloppy in habits
Very quiet	Very loud
Very strong need for security	Very little need for security
Enjoys art and literature	Does not enjoy art and literature at all
Easily expresses tender feelings	Does not express tender feelings at all easily

Source: Broverman et al. (1972)

ity or femininity to every person we see, we know that gender pervades our daily interactions with people.

Biological Determinants

How and to what extent is gender identity of men and women influenced by chromosomal, hormonal, or other biological factors? Many investigators have attempted to determine this. Researchers who accept a biological interpretation of the behavioral differences observed in men and women would assume, for example, that innate biological factors make women naturally poor at being engineers and men naturally poor at being nurses. Gender identity is seen as an expression of an unchangeable biological foundation.

From the biological perspective, a person's sex is basically determined by sex chromosomes. As we saw in Chapter 2, normal men and women have 23 pairs of chromosomes. The last pair consists of two sex chromosomes, designed as XX in women and XY in men. It is the X or Y chromosome transmitted by the father that determines a child's sex.

The second important factor in male and female sex differentiation is the presence of sex hormones, estrogen in women and androgen in men. In men androgen is responsible for the development of the male sex organs and secondary male sex characteristics, such as facial hair or the deepening of the voice. In women estrogen is necessary for the development of the female reproductive system and secondary sex characteristics, such as breasts. Contrary to popular belief, androgen and estrogen in differing quantities are found in both sexes.

The biological determinants of sex-specific behavior have been investigated in several ways. The two major approaches are animal studies and observations of men and women with chromosomal or hormonal abnormalities (see Chapter 2).

The most common procedure in animal research is to inject young animals with sex-related hormones and to observe their behavior in adulthood. Evidence from this type of research suggests that sex hormones act on the brain during critical periods of development. For example, female animals that were given androgen before birth did not display behavior typical of their sex as young females. Instead, they engaged in play behavior typically associated with the males of the species. Female monkeys, for instance, liked rough-and-tumble play and were aggressive with their playmates. This behavior was absent or much less noticeable in female monkeys of the same age who did not receive the androgen treatment.

Generalizing the findings—and we need to keep in mind the problems that arise when we use animal studies to make conclusions about human behavior—Diamond (1978) stated:

> Primarily owing to prenatal genetic and hormonal influences, human beings are definitely predisposed at birth to a male or female gender orientation. Sexual behavior of a person and thus gender role are not neutral or without initial direction at birth. . . . We are dealing with an interaction of genetics and experience; the relative contribution of each, however, may vary with the particular individual concerned. . . . It is the genetic heritage of an individual which predisposes him or her to react in a particular manner so that the learning of a gender role can occur.

Even if some of the sex-associated behavior was found to be universal among all nonhuman primates or indeed among all mammalian species, generalizations to human behavior and social relationships would have to ignore the five million years of evolutionary development of the human brain that resulted in the development of the cortex (Hubbard & Love, 1979). It is the cortex that provides for symbolization, verbal communication, and association of experiences and ideas that permit humans plasticity of behavior.

The biological interpretation of gender identity, however, does not deny the effects of learning or experience; it does suggest that the interaction of genetic and experiential forces is organized primarily at a biological level. In short, men and women differ at birth, and sex differences in adults merely reflect biologically determined capacities. After all, men and women have different sex chromosomes, differing quantities of sex-related hormones, and different reproductive systems. From a biological point of view, chromosomal and hormonal differences cause, directly or indirectly, the differences in the behavior of men and women.

The second approach to learning about the effect of biology on gender identity involves the study of human chromosomal and hormonal abnormalities. The findings of many of these studies suggest that socialization plays a stronger role than biological factors. In a relatively rare condition known as **hermaphroditism,** male infants are born with the normal male sex chromosomes (XY) but with external sex organs that look more like those of a female. If the condition is not recognized, the biologically incorrect sex (i.e., female) may be assigned to these infants at birth. A number of cases have been reported of parents who raised the child as a girl and did not learn about the biological error until puberty, when female secondary sex characteristics failed to develop. In most of these cases the children's gender identity was in accordance with the sex assigned to them and the way they were socialized, even though it was not their biological sex. Money (1977) concluded that socialization plays such an important (if not the only) role in gender identity that no attempt should be made to change that identity after 18 months of age lest severe psychological traumatization of the child result.

Another source of sexual ambiguity is found in the case of females exposed to an excess of androgen. Ehrhardt and Money (1967) studied ten girls whose mothers had been given **progestin** during pregnancy, a medication that relieves some of the discomforts of pregnancy and contains some of the chemical properties of androgen. These girls were born with external sex organs that were masculine in appearance (an enlarged clitoris resembling an underdeveloped penis). In childhood, the girls enjoyed vigorous outdoor sports, competed with boys, and considered themselves tomboys. In adolescence and adulthood many expressed interest in traditionally masculine professions and careers. Nevertheless, they expected to live normal female lives; they planned to get married, but in conjunction with having a professional career and few children. Thus in spite of their female chromosomal makeup, these girls showed interests and engaged in activities more frequently associated with men than with women.

There are disorders in women who are born with less than the normal two X chromosomes, men born with two or more Y chromosomes, and various other rare conditions. In all these cases the evidence overwhelmingly illustrates that human beings assume the mannerisms, habits, interests, and fantasies typical of the sex they were brought up to be, even if this was not their biological sex.

Most of the scientific evidence we have today indicates that even major biological determinants of sexual identity have little or no direct influence on whether a person *feels* male or female. That chromosomes, hormones, and internal reproductive organs are unimportant in the development of gender identity is illustrated by the gender attributions that children make long before they learn even the simplest biological criteria for being a girl or boy (Kessler & McKenna, 1978).

Psychological Determinants

The development of gender identity has been explained from a number of psychological perspectives. The three major interpretations come from psychoanalytic, social-learning, and cognitive-developmental theory.

Psychoanalytic Theory. Although we have ample evidence today that gender-characteristic patterns of behavior seem closely tied to the socialization process, early psychologists proposed that biology is responsible for gender development. Freud's theory of gender development is largely a biologically based interpretation. He viewed the sequence of development as innate proceeding from an awareness of the anatomical sex difference to identification with the same-sexed parent and eventually to adoption of sex-typed behavior.

According to Freudian theory of personality (see Chapter 10), each person, male or female, passes through a series of stages: oral, anal, phallic, latent, and genital. Freud considered the third, or phallic, stage (ages 3 to 5) to be the crucial one for gender identity.

Freud (1965/1933) believed that the mother is the first love object for boys and girls. Between the ages of 3 and 5 the boy's love for his mother unconsciously turns into sexual desires (Oedipal complex). The boy comes to view his father as the main rival in this incestuous mother-son relationship. Consequently he develops intense fears that his father will punish him by cutting off his penis (castration anxiety). This fear of mutilation causes the boy to repress his sexual desires for his mother and to identify with his father. According to Freud, the boy's degree of masculinity as an adult is determined by successful identification with the father. Successful resolution of the Oedipal complex during the phallic stage leads to the development of the superego, or conscience.

For the girl the Oedipal complex (also referred to as the Electra complex) begins with the discovery that she does not have a penis. She is "mortified by the comparison with the boy's far superior equipment." As a result the girl develops "penis envy." According to Freud (1965/1933),

> She [wishes] for a long time to get something like it and believes in the possibility for an extraordinary number of years; even at a time when her knowledge of reality has long led her to abandon the fulfillment of this desire as being quite unattainable (p. 160).

The girl's desire for a penis is translated into a wish for a baby from the father: "the feminine situation is only established, if the wish for a penis is replaced by one for a baby" (Freud, 1965/1933, p. 128). The previously active little girl now becomes passive and receptive and identifies with the mother.

In the normal course of development, then, children come to know what genitals they have

A child's sexual self-categorization is one stage in lifelong gender identity. *(© Peter Arnold, Inc.)*

and through identification with the same-sexed parent develop the behavior and values appropriate to their sex.

Freud's theory has been severely criticized for its equation of genital awareness with gender identity. It has also come under attack because it maintains that gender identity is completed in childhood, overlooking all that is learned about masculine and feminine behavior during preadolescence and adolescence (Maccoby & Jacklin, 1974).

Psychoanalyst Erik Erikson (1964) agrees with Freud that the biological framework is very influential in explaining sex differences; but his emphasis is different. Erikson argues that the shape of the male and female sex organs is translated into a profound difference in the sense of space in men and women.

According to Erikson, female gender identity is not so much the result of penis envy as it is of a constructive, creative, vital sense of **inner space.**

This sense of inner space reflects a woman's biological role in reproduction and accounts for her psychological and ethical commitment to raise children.

Erikson arrived at his theory of the phenomenon of inner space by observing play constructions of children. Boys and girls between 11 and 13 were asked to pretend that they were movie directors and to construct an exciting scene out of a selection of toys. Erikson noted that girls produced interior scenes, while boys constructed exterior scenes. The girls' constructions showed the people inside in static, peaceful positions. The boys' configurations, on the other hand, depicted people outside in exciting actions, such as falling from a height or meeting with an accident. In short, boys built towers (external spaces) and girls built enclosures (inner spaces). Erikson concluded that the spatial constructions of male and female children closely parallel the morphology of male and female sex organs: the external, erectible, and intrusive penis versus the internal, receptive vagina. Therefore, behavioral differences between men and women must be due to inherent biological differences.

Erikson's conclusions have been criticized because the boys and girls used in the study were old enough to be affected by cultural stereotypes. Thus socialization cannot be ruled out as a cause of the observed sex differences. Later attempts to replicate the study with two-to-four-year-old children failed to show sex differences in spatial constructions.

Social-Learning Theory. Instead of viewing gender identity as an innate, biologically determined development, social-learning theory sees it as a product of various forms of learning (see Chapter 5). According to social-learning theorists, parents serve as primary models for the development of gender identity during the early years of life (Mischel, 1970). In addition, parents reinforce male and female children differentially for sex-typed behavior. For example, by watching the mother put on makeup and dress to go out and by hearing the father compliment her on how nice she looks, both sons and daughters learn to "dress up." However, when the daughter imitates this particular behavior, she may be praised for "looking cute," while the son who does so may be reprimanded or called a "sissy" because "boys don't wear dresses." Eventually, the child learns his or her role directly through differential reinforcement and punishment and indirectly through observational learning and modeling.

Cognitive-Developmental Theory. In contrast to both Freudian and social-learning theory, which assign a relatively passive role to children, cognitive-developmental theorists (e.g., Kohlberg, 1966, Kohlberg and Ullian 1974) argue that children actively structure their gender-role concepts in accordance with how mature their thinking and reasoning are. According to Kohlberg, gender identity starts with the child's self-categorization as a "boy" or "girl." This self-categorization is rooted in the child's concepts of physical characteristics of maleness and femaleness, such as differences in physique, clothing, and hair style.

When a child first conceives of himself as a boy, he begins to reason: "I am a boy; therefore I want to do things that boys do." Moreover, he comes to understand that he is similar not only to other boys but also to men, one of which is his father. Consequently he wants to be like his father (identification). Similarly, a girl may say to herself: "I am a girl since I am more like my mother and other girls; therefore I want to dress like a girl."

Kohlberg asserts that gender-identity development "starts directly with neither biology nor culture, but with cognition and with the child's cognitive organization of his or her social world along sex-role dimensions." Once children have acquired their gender label, they come to value behavior and attitudes consistent with that label.

Kohlberg's theory is essentially cognitive because it suggests that children learn their sex role as a function of their level of understanding of the world. As we saw in Chapter 7, before the age of five children do not understand the idea of physical constancy (conservation). They do not under-

Table 9–2. Theoretical Models of Gender-Identity Development: Sequence of Events

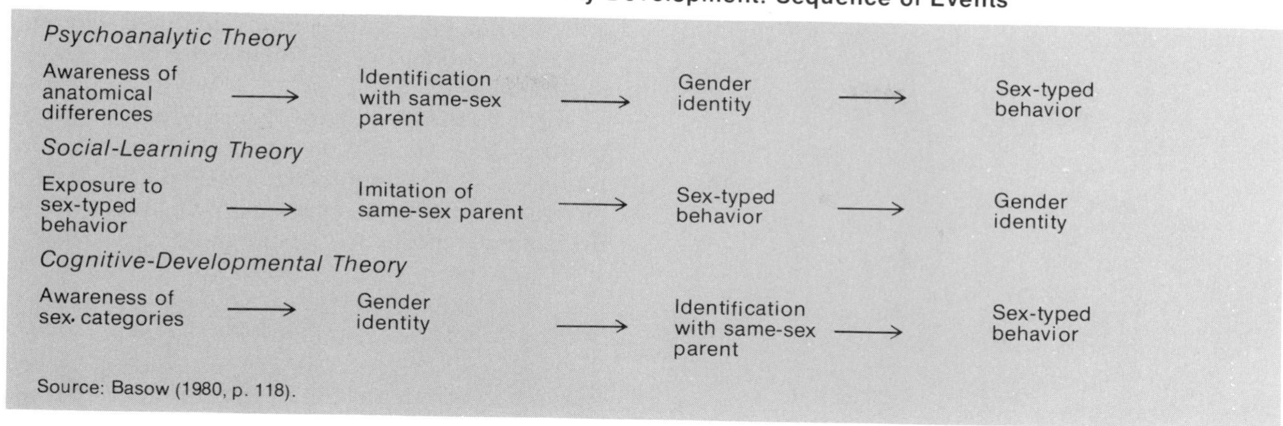

Psychoanalytic Theory						
Awareness of anatomical differences	→	Identification with same-sex parent	→	Gender identity	→	Sex-typed behavior
Social-Learning Theory						
Exposure to sex-typed behavior	→	Imitation of same-sex parent	→	Sex-typed behavior	→	Gender identity
Cognitive-Developmental Theory						
Awareness of sex categories	→	Gender identity	→	Identification with same-sex parent	→	Sex-typed behavior

Source: Basow (1980, p. 118).

stand, for instance, that water poured from a narrow glass into a wide glass is still the same amount of water. Therefore, before the age of five or so, they cannot have a firm gender identity.

While their cognitive development is still tied to concrete operations, children around the ages of six or seven have simplistic and exaggerated pictures of male and female roles and have sharp sex-role stereotypes. It is only with further cognitive development that these stereotyped conceptions can become modified to incorporate exceptions and personal preferences (Basow, 1980). Cognitive-developmental theory, then, although not ruling out learning principles, subordinates them to the cognitive processes occurring in the child's mind.

Comparing the three psychological theories of gender-identity development (see Table 9–2), you will notice that they all insist on the development of unique "masculine" and "feminine" behavior. There is no clear evidence, however, that people exhibit only these sex-exclusive patterns. In addition, none of these theories takes cross-cultural variations into consideration. Anthropological research has shown that culture strongly influences gender identity. The definition of masculinity-femininity varies in Arabia and Scandinavia, in India and Russia, just as it varies within our own culture among socioeconomic classes and different ethnic groups.

Sociocultural Determinants

According to Gagnon and Simon (1973), society prescribes "sexual scripts" for each gender. The script tells us what is and what is not socially appropriate behavior for our sex. In our society the male role is much more clearly defined than the female role since we have traditionally been a male-oriented culture. Consequently there is greater social pressure for boys to conform to sex-role stereotypes. For example, tomboyish girls are tolerated, but boys who are "sissies" are rejected or ridiculed. Similarly, girls may dress in jeans but boys can't wear skirts. As a result, boys often develop sex-appropriate behavior earlier and more consistently than girls do.

The development of gender identity and sex-typed behavior also appears to be a function of social class. Lower-class boys and girls are more rigid in their sex-role perceptions and develop sex-typed behavior earlier than do children from the middle or upper class (Weitzman, 1979). Lower-class parents seem to demand greater conformity to sex-role standards and present more conventional masculine and feminine models. Middle-class fathers, for example, are likely to share household chores, whereas lower-class fathers consider them a "feminine" responsibility (Block, 1978). Similarly, middle-class mothers are less likely than lower-class mothers to make

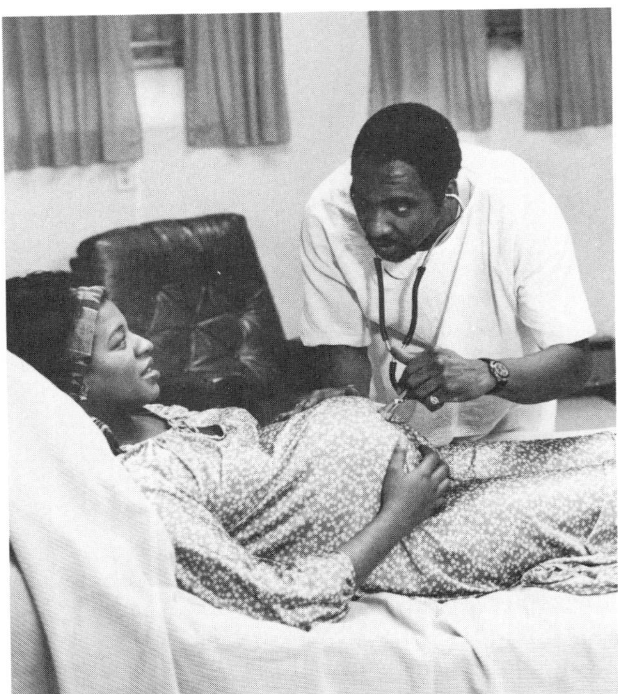

Parents' sex-role expectations can begin even before birth. *(© Mariette Pathy Allen/Peter Arnold, Inc.)*

homemaking a full-time occupation. Today many middle-class women have careers outside the home, providing their children with a different female role model from that found in the lower classes. Lower-class women, if they are employed outside the home, usually occupy service positions, such as housekeeper or cook.

Although roles related to gender (wife, mother, widow; husband, father, widower) change considerably over the life cycle, most people are fairly consistent over time in their gender identity. However, the two sexes perceive gender-related roles differently. Familial roles seem to be more salient for women, while work roles stand out for men. Stasz Stroll (1974), for instance, reported that only 19 percent of the fathers in her sample described themselves as fathers, while 54 percent of the mothers identified themselves as mothers. Similarly, only 29 percent of the husbands called themselves husbands, while 41 percent of the wives called themselves wives. Thus being a wife and mother was more significant for a woman's self-concept than being a husband and father was for a man's.

Such findings suggest that the acceptance of traditional sex roles runs deep. The importance of biological determinants notwithstanding, it is to environmental influences that we must look to understand conformity to sex-role expectations.

THE DEVELOPMENT OF SEX ROLES

There are three main forces that influence people to behave according to culturally prescribed sex roles. They are family, peers, and the media.

Family Influences

Parents start to treat their infants in accordance with the baby's sex at birth. Rubin and his colleagues (Rubin, Provenzano, & Luria, 1974) asked 30 pairs of parents of one-day-old infants to describe them as they would to a close relative or friend. Half of the infants were boys and half were girls. The fathers had never had physical contact with their babies; they had only viewed them through the glass window of the nursery. The mothers had held their babies before they were asked to describe them. The results of this study are impressive in view of the fact that the male and female babies did not differ in average length, weight, or Apgar scores (see Chapter 8). Both mothers and fathers described their daughters more often as little, beautiful, cute, weaker, and as resembling their mothers. Boys were described more often as firmer, larger featured, better coordinated, more adult, and hardier. The fathers made more extreme and stereotyped judgments of their newborns than the mothers did. The differences the parents perceived in the children seemed to be a pure case of parental labeling. Rubin et al. concluded that "sex typing and sex role socialization appear to have already begun their course at the time of the infant's birth when information about the label is minimal and these labels may well affect subsequent expectations about the manner in which their infant ought to behave as well as parental behavior itself" (p. 517).

In fact, sex-role stereotyping actually begins before birth, when parents make predictions about the sex of their unborn babies based on stereotypical notions of masculine and feminine characteristics. If the fetus is active, moving and kicking a great deal, the mother is likely to interpret this behavior as evidence of a male child.

Research on differential treatment of boys and girls is still in its infancy, but a number of conclusions can be drawn. Overall, boys are handled somewhat more roughly than girls. Fathers are more likely to be boisterous or to use such terms as "Hello Tiger" or "Come here, Ding-Bat" with their sons than with their daughters (Parke & Sawin, 1977). They are also more likely to gently cuddle their daughters than their sons. Mothers are more likely to look at and talk to their daughters than their sons. After the age of six months girls are more encouraged than boys to touch and to remain near their mothers.

From infancy on, children are given sex-specific toys, although most parents would deny any intention to distinguish between their sons and daughters when they are selecting toys. Usually boys have more toys of more different types than girls. By the age of two, boys are provided with objects such as cars and animals that encourage activities directed away from home, while girls are given objects like baby dolls that encourage activities toward the home (Rheingold & Cook, 1975).

The available research suggests that fathers may be more important in sex-role socialization than mothers. Fagot (1974), for instance, found that fathers rate more types of behavior as sex-appropriate than mothers do. Fathers, but not mothers, seem to discourage aggression more in their daughters than in their sons. Fathers, more than mothers, also reinforce feminine activities in their daughters. Femininity in daughters has been found greatest when fathers are nurturant and participate actively in child rearing (Biller, 1978). Boys with strongly masculine traits generally have fathers who play an active role in disciplining their sons.

A number of parental characteristics interact with the development of sex-typed behavior in boys and girls. Nurturance and warmth in the same-sex parent, for instance, have been found to facilitate the development of sex-appropriate roles in boys and girls (Mussen & Distler, 1960; Lefrancois, 1980). In addition, dominant mothers and ineffective passive fathers have a destructive influence on the sex-role perceptions of boys but rarely interfere with the development of sex-typed behavior in girls. The relationship between parental characteristics and the development of sex roles in children is by no means simple or direct, however. Studies of preschool children, for instance, do not report significant relationships between personality traits of children and those of either parent, even though the children are strongly sex-typed at that age (Maccoby & Jacklin, 1974).

Sex-appropriate behavior is fostered by nurturance by the same-sex parent. (© *Erika Stone*)

CRITICAL ISSUE

Effects of Father Absence on Sex-Role Socialization

Since the father plays such a critical role in sex typing, we might expect children who grow up in homes without a father to show disruptions in sex-role socialization. Father absence has been associated with disruptions in the way girls relate to males (Hetherington, 1972). But the form of these disruptions was different for daughters of widows and daughters of divorcées. Daughters of divorcées were sexually more promiscuous and more eager to leave home than daughters of widows. Whereas the daughters of divorcées harbored critical or hostile attitudes toward the divorced father, daughters of widows often retained an aggrandized image of their father and felt that few males could compare favorably with him.

The following are two representative descriptions of daughters in father-absent families. The first one comes from a divorced mother, the second from a widow.

"That kid is going to drive me over the hill. I'm at my wits' end. She was so good until the last few years, then Pow! When she was only twelve I came home from a movie and found her in bed with a young hood and she has been bouncing from bed to bed ever since. She doesn't seem to care who it is, she can't keep her hands off men. It isn't just boys of her own age; when I have men friends here she kisses them when they come in the door and sits on their knees all in a very playful fashion but it happens to all of them. Her uncle is a 60-year old priest and she even made a pass at him. It almost scared him to death. I sometimes get so frantic I think I should turn her in to the cops but I remember what a good kid she used to be and I do love her. We still have a good time together when we're alone and I am not nagging her about being a tramp. She's smart and good-looking—she should know that she doesn't have to act like that.

———is almost too good. She has lots of girlfriends but doesn't date much. When she is with girls, she's gay and bouncy—quite a clown—but she clams up when a man comes in. Even around my brother she doesn't say much. When

Regardless of whether parents are conventional or liberal with regard to sex roles, they are likely to provide many cues that children pick up. Even parents who think of themselves as nontraditional with respect to sex roles can inadvertently communicate sex-typed principles to their children (Fagot, 1974). A working mother, for instance, may ask her daughter rather than her son to help with kitchen chores.

Sex-role development is also influenced by the ordinal position of the child and the sex of siblings. First-born children receive more attention than those born later; first-born sons are touched more by their fathers than later-born boys (Parke, 1976). Apparently the first-born child and the only child are subjected to more intense sex differentiation than are later-born children. Children who grow up with siblings of the same sex acquire sex-appropriate roles earlier than children who grow up among both brothers and sisters. For example, a girl with an older sister acquires sex-typed behavior faster than a girl with an older brother.

Extrafamilial Influences: Teachers and Peers

Although parents are very influential in shaping their children's sex-role behavior, once school begins, other people share the responsibility for sex-role socialization. From the time the child starts school, which for some children may be as early as three years old, teachers provide additional messages regarding sex-role behavior. In most cases, these messages reinforce those received at home, strengthening sex typing.

boys do phone she often puts them off even though she has nothing else to do. She says she has lots of time for that later, but she's sixteen now and very pretty, and all her friends have boyfriends (Hetherington, 1972, p. 322).

This study and others indicate that girls need to interact with a warm, effective father who rewards and enjoys their femininity. Through this interaction girls learn to feel competent in their sex role and to value and acquire the social skills necessary for later heterosexual partnerships. The effects of father absence on daughters can, however, be moderated by maternal behavior. Mothers who have positive attitudes toward their ex-husbands and who present them in a positive manner lessen the deleterious effects of father absence.

Effects of father absence on boys are apparent at all ages. Disruptions in sex-role socialization in boys are most severe if the separation has occurred before the age of five. Preschool boys have been found to be less aggressive and more dependent if they were separated from their fathers early in life. They also displayed more feminine behavior patterns in play and social interactions. In other words, these boys exhibited behavior more characteristic of girls than of boys.

The impact of father absence on older boys seems to be less consistent. Some studies found no differences between adolescent boys whose fathers were absent and those whose fathers were present. Others reported that older boys from father-absent homes engaged in a pattern labeled "compensatory masculinity," which refers to the exhibition of inconsistent patterns of both masculine and feminine behavior. In older boys the presence of other models, such as peers, male relatives, surrogate fathers, and male figures presented by the media, may partially moderate the effects of father absence on sex-role learning.

Hartley (1959) has suggested that boys growing up in father-absent families have the additional problem shared by all boys of more rigid sex-role definitions; demands that boys conform to social notions of what is manly come much earlier and are enforced with much more vigor than similar attitudes with respect to girls. These demands are frequently enforced harshly, impressing the small boy with the danger of deviating from them, although he does not quite understand what they are (p. 461). The boy growing up without a male model is likely to be exposed to a constricted range of behavior, which makes deviations from stereotypical sex roles difficult.

At school most children develop clear perceptions of sex-typed activities. For example, science and math are labeled "boyish," while reading and artistic endeavors are considered "girlish." Reviewing the types of games schoolchildren play, Sutton-Smith and Sovasta (1972) found that boys between the ages of 8 and 12 preferred games involving strength, body contact, and a clear outcome of winning and losing. In contrast, girls of the same ages preferred games that could be characterized by taking turns, choral activities, and verbalism.

Because boys and girls have been reinforced for different types of behavior, school affects them differently. In many ways our nursery and elementary schools foster feminine qualities, such as being quiet, obedient, and passive. It is therefore not surprising that boys have more difficulties than girls adjusting to school and create more problems for their teachers. Teachers report boys much more frequently than girls for offenses such as playing truant, stealing property, bullying others, or being rude. In addition, many boys view school as a sex-inappropriate institution because they are usually exposed to female teachers who emphasize feminine activities. Hetherington and Parke (1979) suggested that it may be the feminine environment of the early school years that accounts for the lower academic achievement of boys during these years.

Like parents, teachers treat their female and male pupils differently. Serbin and O'Leary (1975) described a situation in which the teacher was demonstrating to preschoolers how the same quantity of water can be poured to fill different containers of varying heights (the conservation

CRITICAL ISSUE

Anatomy Is Not Destiny

If there is an example that dramatically illustrates the importance of nonbiological factors in the development of gender identity, it is a case of male identical twins, whose prenatal development was normal (Money & Ehrhardt, 1972). In infancy, however, one twin's penis was accidentally destroyed during circumcision. After much agonizing the parents agreed with the physicians to reclassify the child as female, which was formally done at the age of 17 months. This reassignment was based on the belief that gender identity is basically a learned, social phenomenon and that a child without a penis would be able to function more adequately as a female than as a male. Reclassifying the child meant surgical and hormonal treatment.

Because of the unique situation—a pair of identical twins of two sexes—the children were studied extensively throughout childhood. It was interesting to observe how the parents began to treat the reassigned child and her previously identical brother. The mother reported:

> I started dressing "her" not in dresses but, you know, in little pink slacks and frilly blouses . . . and letting her hair grow. . . . I even made all her nightwear into granny gowns. (Money & Ehrhardt, 1972, p. 119).

By age 4 the mother reported that the female twin preferred dresses over slacks, wore bracelets and rings, and was much cleaner and neater than her brother. Nevertheless, the feminized twin had many tomboyish traits. The parents encouraged the girl to be less rough than her brother and to be quieter and "more ladylike." The male twin was reported to be physically protective of his sister.

If the female twin continues to maintain a strong feminine identity, she provides evidence that biological components of gender identity are far less, if at all, important compared with social conditioning.

---

principle). Three children, Michael, Patty, and Daniel, sat nearby, obviously fascinated by the demonstration. The teacher let Michael pour the water himself, explaining how the water can change shape without changing volume. Patty asked if she could try and was told to wait. The teacher gave Daniel a chance to pour the water and then put the materials away. Despite another request, Patty never got her turn.

Teachers have been found to reinforce conformity to the traditional female role rather than present exciting new role models. This tendency may be one reason why girls are more likely to exhibit learned helplessness in school than boys (see Chapter 12). Learned helplessness exists when children reduce their efforts because they assume that failure is inevitable. Girls are likely to blame a poor performance on their own lack of ability, while boys are likely to say that they did not try hard enough (Dweck & Reppuci, 1972). Even when girls are proficient at a task, they are more likely to assume that a failure reflects lack of ability and subsequently do less well at the task.

Several studies have reported that teachers respond more to boys than girls who are involved in task-oriented activities (e.g., Fagot, 1977), provide more individual instruction for boys, and criticize them more. In many ways, then, the same types of stereotypic behavior, such as dependency in girls and acting out in boys, that are reinforced by the parents are also encouraged in the classroom.

As we saw in Chapter 8, as the child approaches school age and widens his or her social circle beyond the immediate family, peers become more and more influential. Peer popularity appears to be related to how closely one's sex-typed behavior matches the stereotype. For boys dominance and aggression are criteria for peer status. For girls peer status is determined by conformity to the requirements of the group and social acceptance by peers (Hartup, 1970). It has often been observed that few leaders of groups of children are female. Thus children's differential criteria for peer status seem to be consistent with the sex stereotypes of society as a whole.

Peer pressures lead to a number of additional sex differences. For example, boys compete more but share significantly less than girls. For girls competition may simply seem less relevant; nothing they can do will change their relative position among their peers since boys are perceived as dominant and leaders. Also, girls tend to imitate one another more readily than boys. Imitation is particularly likely to occur in situations in which little information concerning appropriate or expected behavior is provided (Geshuri, 1975).

Teachers and peers, like parents, perceive boys and girls differentially. They encourage dependency in girls and power and competence in boys. Moreover, most schools have tracking systems in which girls are channeled into "feminine" subjects (English and social studies or typing and bookkeeping).

Sex Roles and the Media

As everyone knows, the media are filled with stereotypes of men and women. Pingree and her colleagues (Pingree, Hawkins, Butler, & Paisley, 1976) developed a consciousness scale for media sexism that classified the portrayal of women and men on five different levels.

At Level I a woman is presented as the dumb blonde, the sex object, and the whimpering victim. Correspondingly, the male is used to decorate advertisements for products that require the presence of a handsome, physically fit, sexy, and well-groomed man. At Level II we find women depicted in terms of traditionally accepted feminine qualities and "womanly" roles: wives, mothers, secretaries, clerks, teachers, and nurses. In other words, the message here is that a woman's place is in the home or in some feminine occupation, the only places where she is considered competent. Men at Level II occupy the world of work and the traditional "manly" activities.

As we move up the scale of consciousness, women's opportunities increase. At Level III a woman can be a lawyer or an architect, providing, however, that she has dinner ready at six. Housework and mothering come first, and a career is viewed as something extra. One example of a woman at this level is a "housewife" with an advanced degree in biochemistry who discusses the benefits of a certain breakfast food. The male at this level may be willing to help out at home, but his primary interests and loyalties are vested in his occupation or profession. Although Level III allows men and women to transcend rigid stereotypes, traditional activities remain primary for both sexes.

At Level IV, which is infrequently represented in the media, men and women are equal. Women are portrayed as professionals; they hardly mention their private lives, their favorite recipes, or their cleaning products. They do not remind you that housework or mothering are inevitable components of womenhood. Men at Level IV are essentially identical in commitment and attitudes to Level IV women.

The greater freedom in dress that society allows girls serves to slow down their development of sex-appropriate behavior. *(© Joel Gordon)*

Level V is almost never presented by the media. To use a term discussed later in this chapter, men and women at this level are androgynous people, that is, they are free of sex-role stereotyping and exhibit masculine and feminine behavior in accordance with the demands of the situation.

Pingree and her co-workers applied their consciousness scale to advertisements portraying women in four major national magazines: *Ms.*, *Time*, *Newsweek*, and *Playboy*. *Playboy* had significantly more Level 1 ads than any of the other magazines. There women were portrayed as perfect sex partners, sex goddesses, models, and beauty queens whose sexuality was exploited to sell merchandise. *Ms.* had more Level IV and a few Level V ads. *Time* and *Newsweek* each took the middle road. Both magazines contained more Level II ads than *Playboy*.

A number of different analyses of the content of women's magazine fiction have been made. Franzwa (1975) found that women's magazine stories from 1940 through 1970 stressed the following themes: marriage is inevitable for every normal female; to catch a man women must be less competent than men; married women do not work; being a housewife-mother is the best of all careers; the childless woman has wasted her life. The widow-divorcée is portrayed as being hopelessly incompetent without a man; spinsters are useless creatures, even if they hold high-status jobs.

Even though soap operas have introduced such controversial subjects as extramarital affairs and abortion, their characters still respond in stereotyped ways. Women appear more often in home settings and men in work situations (Finz & Waters, 1976). Conversations between men and women are likely to take place in the home. Even in series that use hospitals as the major setting and doctors and nurses as the leading characters, roles are allocated in a stereotypic way.

A much-discussed source of sex-role socialization for young children is television. It has been estimated that children spend one-third of their lives at home and sleeping, one-third at school, and one-third in front of a TV set. The average child watches between three and four hours a day (Nielsen, 1978). Gardner's (1970) study of the program "Sesame Street," a supposedly educational and innovative show for young children, suggests that even educational TV contributes to sex-role stereotypes. On one program, Big Bird (having said that he would like to be a member of a family and having been told that Gordon and Susan would be his family) is told that he will have to help with the work. Since he is a boy bird, he will have to do men's work—the heavy work, the "important" work. He is also told that he should get a girl bird to help Susan with *her* work of arranging flowers and the like. There was more, and virtually all of it emphasized that men's work is outside and women's work inside the home.

Dominick and Rauch (1972) observed that women are overrepresented in female cosmetics and household-product advertising categories, whereas men are most often found in commercials or ads for home appliances and cars. In other words, the media are suggesting that women are mostly concerned with decisions relating to the home and personal appearance, while men make decisions dealing with more costly and complex purchases. Moreover, the media give the impression that there are certain business and social activities that are still inappropriate for women to perform. The media today fail to acknowledge the fact that over 50 percent of all women over age 16 are in the labor market (U.S. Department of Labor, 1977).

MALE AND FEMALE DIFFERENCES

Although it is a fact that women excel in some tasks and men in others and that certain personality traits are skewed in the direction of one sex or the other, there are many more similarities than differences between men and women. Yet people continue to hold strong beliefs about sex differences, even when their beliefs fail to find any empirical support. Let us see what research tells us about male-female differences in three major areas: personality, achievement, and intelligence.

Sex Differences in Personality

Are there personality traits that you consider characteristic of most men and others characteristic of most women? As mentioned earlier, many people believe that certain personality traits apply to one sex only. For example, women are typically thought of as the talkative sex and men the more active sex. However, several studies have shown that men do at least as much, if not more, talking and gossiping (e.g., Kramer, 1974). In one society studied by anthropologist Margaret Mead, men were the idle gossipers in the village while the women worked (Mead, 1961).

Maccoby and Jacklin (1974) have dispelled many of the myths about male-female personality differences. For example, they provided ample evidence that girls are no more social or suggestible than boys. They also refuted the notion that women have a lower sense of self-esteem than men.

Of all the personality dimensions Maccoby and Jacklin studied, only one yielded significant differences between the sexes. In almost all cultures males are more aggressive than females. This difference in aggression manifests itself as soon as social play begins, around age two to two and one-half. As we have seen, there is some evidence that male-female differences in aggression have a biological basis, or more specifically a hormonal basis. As in so many cases, however, biological factors seem to interact with learning factors in the ways men and women express their aggressive feelings. For example, men are more likely to learn to express anger directly, either physically or verbally, while women often prefer more subtle strategies, such as pouting or ignoring the person who made them angry.

Sex Differences in Achievement

A great deal of research in the last two decades has focused on achievement motivation. This is not surprising since our society rates success very highly. Advertisements in magazines and on TV stress the importance of personal advancement and accomplishments. Novels, movies, and plays all trade in on the same theme of success.

Achievement motivation is defined as our desire to accomplish something of value or importance through effort and to meet standards of excellence in what we do (McClelland, et al., 1963) (see Chapter 6). There are a number of ways to measure this psychological construct. The most commonly used technique is to ask people to tell a short story about a somewhat ambiguous picture. The story is then scored according to specified criteria that reflect the strength of the subject's motive to achieve.

Research on achievement motivation originally focused primarily on males and male achievement behavior (Alper, 1974) since social prestige was traditionally awarded to men on the basis of their

In most cultures boys are more aggressive than girls. (© *Erika Stone)*

success in their work or other areas such as sports or politics. Women, on the other hand, have not been encouraged to succeed in those areas traditionally defined as male. Consequently it was assumed that females have lower levels of achievement motivation than males. The early data also suggested that successful women were not so much motivated by the need to achieve as by social concerns or by the need for affiliation. In other words, a desire for social approval rather than an internalized standard for excellence was thought to motivate women. According to this view, the differences in achievement behavior in men and women reflected two different needs, the need for achievement in men and the need for affiliation in women.

Psychologist Matina Horner (1972) first postulated the **motive to avoid success** in women as a stable personality disposition that is acquired early in life in conjunction with sex-role standards and that acts as an inhibiting factor in women's achievement motivation. This "fear of success" in girls and women presumably resulted from their being afraid of social rejection and loss of their femininity if they were to become successful. Horner's research suggested that fear of success is aroused in women especially in competitive situations with men.

The motive to avoid success has generated an enormous quantity of research, and many of Horner's original conceptions of fear of success have not been supported by empirical data. In fact, fear of success is not only experienced by women but appears to have become more and more common in men (Tresemer, 1974). Thus even if the motive to avoid success is valid, it does not appear to be experienced only by women and therefore cannot be used as an explanation for differential achievements in men and women.

Another interpretation of the sex differences in achievement suggests that men and women are both motivated by the needs for success but have different goals or areas of achievement in mind. Women are said to be concerned with success in the social or interpersonal realm, while men are concerned with success in academic or intellectual performance. Women's achievement in the social realm is an end in itself rather than a means of satisfying the need for affiliation. According to this position, "the hostess with the mostest" displays the same kind of achievement orientation as the upwardly mobile executive—only the area in which excellence is sought is different.

Differences in achievement motivation have also been attributed to differences in attribution processes. Typically four kinds of causes of success have been studied: ability, effort, luck, and task ease. Suppose a college woman gets an A on a physics exam. She might believe that she received the A because she was good in physics (ability), because she studied hard (effort), because she was lucky, or because the exam was easy. There seem to be important gender differences in attributions: males tend to attribute their success more to ability, and females tend to attribute both their successes and failures more to luck (Deaux, 1976). The implication is that, at least within traditionally male areas, women take less responsibility for and feel less pride in their successes and feel less shame about their failures (Hartnett, Boden, & Fuller, 1979).

Sex Differences in Intelligence

Stereotyped notions of different intellectual abilities in men and women have little basis in reality. One myth is that boys are more analytic than girls. However, Maccoby and Jacklin (1974) found that men and women generally do not differ on tests that measure analyzing or problem-solving abilities.

Boys do excel in spatial ability, an important intellectual function measured by many intelligence tests (see Chapter 11). **Spatial ability** refers to the visual perception of figures or objects in space and how they are related to each other. Male-female differences in spatial ability have not been observed in childhood but appear fairly consistently in late childhood and adolescence. There is some evidence that spatial ability is genetically determined. Stafford (1972), for instance, has suggested that one of the genes responsible for good mathematical ability and one of the genes coding for good space-form ability are both X-linked and recessive. A trait coded by an X-linked recessive gene will always be expressed in the male who inherits an X chromosome with that gene, because he has only the one X.

Other sex differences in intellectual performance seem to be largely a function of socialization. For example, children of all ages tend to stereotype math and science as masculine (Dwyer, 1973). Presumably they are responding to the fact that relatively few problems in grade-school math and science textbooks mention girls or relate to female interests. Even when problems mention both sexes, they often include such comments as "Susan could not figure out how to . . ." or "Jim showed her how . . ." (Federbush, 1974).

There is also evidence that differential practice with mathematics accounts for some of the sex differences in this subject. Boys are supposed to be good at math because many adult male-dominated occupations deal with figures and budgets. Consequently boys take more math courses than girls. In high school girls choose fewer advanced math and science courses since they have been socialized to believe that such careers are not appropriate to females.

According to Keniston and Keniston (1964), high school girls believe they must hide their intelligence if they are to be popular with boys. Girls soon learn that "popularity"—that peculiar American ecstacy from which all other good things flow—accrues to her who suppresses any mental powers she may have, flatters the often precarious maleness of adolescent boys, and devotes herself to activities that can in no way challenge their sex. The popular girls in high school are seldom the brilliant ones, or if they are, it is only because they are also smart enough to hide their intellectual gifts from less brilliant boys. Some American public and private schools make a girl with a passionate intellectual interest feel a strong sense of her own inadequacy as a woman, feel guilty about these "masculine" outlooks, and perhaps even wonder about her normality (p. 363).

If boys are superior to girls in mathematics and science, the demands of society rather than innate abilities account for this superiority. *(© Jean-Claude Lejeune/Stock, Boston, Inc.)*

Overall, we can conclude that men and women are equal in general intelligence but differ in some specialized abilities. A national assessment of educational progress (Sauls & Larson, 1975), which involved almost one million students throughout the United States, found that male and female performances were equal in science, mathematics, and social studies up to the age of 9. By the age of 13, however, girls began to fall behind in these subjects. Girls, on the other hand, were ahead in reading ability and literary knowledge.

In view of the similarities (see Table 9–3), you may wonder why so much attention is given to male-female differences in intelligence. Superiorities of each sex are slight, representing perhaps only a few IQ points. Again, the answer may be found in social factors. Small and seemingly unimportant differences may lead to more important ones if they are reinforced by the person's own behavior or by that of others. Liking words a bit more than numerals may induce a girl to do better homework in English during her grammar school years, to take history rather than physics as an elective in high school, to take a nonscience major in college, and to become an English teacher

Table 9–3. Sex Differences and Similarities

Abilities	
General intelligence	No difference on most tests.
Verbal ability	Females excel after age 10 or 11.
Quantitative ability	Males excel from the start of adolescence.
Creativity	Females excel on verbal creativity tests; otherwise, no difference.
Cognitive style	No general difference.
Visual-spatial ability	Males excel from adolescence on.
Physical abilities	Males more muscular; males more vulnerable to illness, disease; females excel on manual-dexterity tests when speed important, but findings ambiguous.
Personality Characteristics	
Sociability and love	No overall difference; at some ages, boys play in larger groups; some evidence that young men fall in love more easily, out of love with more difficulty.
Empathy	Conflicting evidence.
Emotionality	Self-reports and observations conflict.
Dependence	Conflicting findings; dependence probably not a unitary concept.
Nurturance	Little evidence available on adult-male reactions to infants; issue of maternal vs. paternal behavior remains open; no overall difference in altruism.
Aggressiveness	Males more aggressive from preschool age on.

rather than a dentist. Thus a small initial preference becomes more and more binding as the child grows into an adult (Wesley & Wesley, 1977).

IMPLICATIONS OF SEX-ROLE STEREOTYPING

As we have seen, sex typing begins at birth. The stereotypes can be seen in child-rearing practices, in the school system, in children's books, in textbooks, in magazines, and in television programs and commercials. Men and women who deviate from the stereotyped image are usually less liked; that is, both the masculine, competent woman and the feminine, expressive man are not as popular as the feminine woman or the masculine man. In addition, the stereotype of men is more favorable than the stereotype of women.

A strongly sex-typed man or woman is at a disadvantage since sex roles inhibit the expression of nonstereotyped behavior. Strongly sex-typed behavior may be especially troublesome for women because our society values the female role less than the male role. The most traditionally feminine women experience the most psychological difficulties. Heilburn (1968) found that women who combine desirable traits from masculine and feminine roles manage best in college.

Although sex typing decreases with education, cultural stereotypes prevail in all segments of our society. Sometimes these stereotypes may create sex differences where none exist; at other times sex typing exaggerates differences that may have an innate basis. Many men and women evaluate themselves and others according to the prevailing stereotypes, often with unfortunate consequences for their own self-image or mental health. Since in most instances sex differences are rarely viewed as mere differences, they also imply value judgments that influence social and educational policies. They are often used to justify the differential treatment of the sexes in many educational, occupational, and mental-health settings. Although individual potential is a far better predictor of behavior than membership in any particular group—racial, ethnic, or sexual—a lot of effort has been spent separating men and women along traditional cultural stereotypes.

Unfortunately an examination of the research on sex differences obscures the examination of sex similarities. The fact that men and women are similar in far more ways than they are different is not considered startling news among psychologists. Yet reports of sex differences are more likely to be published than reports of sex similarities.

ANDROGYNY

In recent years social scientists have noted a lessening of sex-typed expectations among parents concerning the interests, abilities, and personality characteristics of their sons and daughters. As we have seen, these trends are stronger in some sections of our society than in others: they are more characteristic of the middle than the lower class and more prevalent among the well-educated segment of the population.

The move away from rigid sex typing reflects the idea that our traditional concepts of masculinity and femininity may be inappropriate to the kind of world we live in today. Psychologists use the concept of **androgyny** to indicate that the whole repertoire of characteristics and behavior of human beings may be available to members of either sex. An androgynous conception of sex roles views each sex as free to cultivate some of the characteristics traditionally associated with the opposite sex. Thus tenderness and expressiveness should be cultivated in boys and socially approved in men. At the same time women should be encouraged to fulfill their need for achievement, and constructive aggression in women should be socially condoned. (Rossi, 1964).

In a way androgyny would appear as the best of two worlds since it allows men and women to be aggressive and submissive, daring and cautious, independent and dependent. An androgynous person is one who has both masculine and feminine characteristics and displays both depending on the situational appropriateness of these types of behavior (Bem, 1975). Androgyny as described by Bem and refined by Kaplan (1979), then, refers to the flexibility of the sex role, the integration of strong masculine and feminine traits in unique ways, influenced by individual differences across situations. Individuals who alternate between masculine and feminine behavior in inflexible ways are not androgynous according to this definition (Basow, 1980).

The concept of androgyny is not a new one in psychology. Carl Jung (1953, 1971), the founder of analytical psychology (see Chapter 10), introduced the concepts of **anima** (female aspects in males) and **animus** (male aspects in females) in the belief that a well-integrated person must possess both male and female characteristics. More recently psychologist Sandra Bem (1974, 1975) developed a personality test, the Bem Sex Role Inventory (BSRI), to identify androgynous individuals (see Table 9–4). This scale consists of a list of traits, such as independence, forcefulness, compassion, and affection. Based on the responses of college students, these traits were divided into equal numbers of masculine traits, feminine traits, and socially desirable traits that belong to no particular sex role. This inventory defined androgyny as the possession of a balance between the characteristics culturally defined as masculine or feminine. Truly androgynous persons have a large measure of the characteristics of both sexes, which makes them more flexible in their sex-role behavior. Each can then develop his or her potential to the fullest, without the restrictions imposed by fidelity to stereotypes.

Using the BSRI, Bem found androgynous people were less conforming. For example, the androgynous male, in contrast to a masculine male, expressed a wide range of behavior, includ-

Table 9–4. Measurement of Psychological Androgyny

1. self-reliant	31. makes decisions easily
2. yielding	32. compassionate
3. helpful	33. sincere
4. defends own beliefs	34. self-sufficient
5. cheerful	35. eager to soothe hurt feelings
6. moody	36. conceited
7. independent	37. dominant
8. shy	38. soft-spoken
9. conscientious	39. likable
10. athletic	40. masculine
11. affectionate	41. warm
12. theatrical	42. solemn
13. assertive	43. willing to take a stand
14. flatterable	44. tender
15. happy	45. friendly
16. strong personality	46. aggressive
17. loyal	47. gullible
18. unpredictable	48. inefficient
19. forceful	49. acts as a leader
20. feminine	50. childlike
21. reliable	51. adaptable
22. analytical	52. individualistic
23. sympathetic	53. does not use harsh language
24. jealous	54. unsystematic
25. has leadership abilities	55. competitive
26. sensitive to the needs of others	56. loves children
27. truthful	57. tactful
28. willing to take risks	58. ambitious
29. understanding	59. gentle
30. secretive	60. conventional

The listing above is the Bem Sex Role Inventory. To find out whether you score as androgynous, first rate yourself on each item, on a scale from 1 (never or almost never true) to 7 (always or almost always true). First add up your ratings for items 1, 4, 7, 10, 13, 16, 19, 22, 25, 28, 31, 34, 37, 40, 43, 46, 49, 52, 55, and 58. Divide the total by 20. That is your masculinity score. Then add up your ratings for items 2, 5, 8, 11, 14, 17, 20, 23, 26, 29, 32, 35, 38, 41, 44, 47, 50, 53, 56, and 59. Divide the total by 20. That is your femininity score. If your masculinity score is above 4.9 (the approximate median for the masculinity scale) and your femininity score is above 4.9 (the approximate femininity median), then you would be classified as androgynous on Bem's scale.
Source: Bem (1977); Hyde and Rosenberg (1980).

ing nurturance. The androgynous female had higher self-esteem, received more honors in school, and dated more than other females. Heilbrun (1976) found that androgynous people are more consistent in saying what their behavior would be in various situations, showing that they were more independent of the situation.

From this research, it seems as though the androgynous person is physically and psychologically healthier than the more sex-typed person. Androgynous women are more interested in education and achievement, more likely to make sexual relationships a dual concern, and less interested in having large families. Androgynous men are more expressive and nurturant than masculine males. For both sexes androgyny is associated with personal satisfaction and a more spontaneous expression of basic human feelings and values. For example, in a survey conducted by *Redbook* magazine (Levin & Levin, 1975) it was found that initiation of sexual intercourse and methods of sexual satisfaction are becoming a dual concern of men and women rather than a strictly male responsibility. Although many people continue to adhere to the traditional assumptions of sex-typed behavior, there are some indications that perhaps the androgynous person will come to represent a more human standard of psychological health.

New Directions for Women

Androgynous women are primarily concerned with transcending the stereotyped boundaries of the traditional feminine role. They aspire to educational and occupational levels that are similar to men's. Between 1965 and 1976 the number of female college graduates almost doubled. However, although one half of all Bachelor's and Master's degrees are earned by women, the number of female Ph.D.'s is still disproportionately small.

In the occupational sphere, women are becoming more interested in traditionally masculine activities, such as medicine and architecture. A steadily increasing number are employed outside the home, thereby altering the dynamics of family relationships. Still, there are often only token changes in the traditionally male professions. The number of women firefighters, police officers, or school principals is still minimal. An important goal for women in the future is to reduce the inequity that currently exists in the professional status (and hence power) of men and women.

Women are becoming interested in traditionally masculine professions. *(© Ken Karp, Ira Berger)*

New Directions for Men

Just as the concept of androgyny calls for women to develop and express masculine traits, men are encouraged to display feminine characteristics, such as intimacy, emotionality, and dependency. Jack Nickols (1975), in his book *Men's Liberation*, argues that traditional macho values have outlived their usefulness and are obsolete today. Nickols envisions men as surrendering dominance, aggression, and violence and becoming more sharing, gentle, and caring.

As a result of the changes women have been making, men, too, have changed their thinking. They have begun to realize the oppressiveness of the male role:

> Placing women in heaven (Mary) or hell (Eve) became a convenient way of removing her from earth where she would compete with men for a just share of material and human resources. . . . I labelled this well-entrenched masculine mentality a psychic celibacy. Although distinct from physical celibacy as practiced by Catholicism, psychic celibacy is a more pervasive and imposing phenomenon. It consists in keeping women mentally and emotionally at arm's length. It is in fact the core dogma of our patriarchal era. Women can be exalted as wife, virgin, mother or depreciated (and enjoyed) as temptress, playmate or whore. In whatever way this male projection works, woman is object, nonequal, manipulated, distanced. . . . Such a world is profoundly celibate (Bianchi & Reuther, 1976, p. 61).

Men apparently have not embraced the concept of androgyny as eagerly as women have. A survey at an Ivy League college by Mirra Komarovsky (1973), for instance, showed that only seven percent of the males of the androgynous type would be willing to modify their career if it would conflict with the career of their wife. Infant care and household work are still not very popular with the majority of men. Moreover, the number of males who have made inroads into traditionally female occupations, such as nursing or elementary-school teaching, is much smaller than the number of women who have entered traditionally male occupations.

Greater flexibility of male sex roles resulted from the dramatic change of women's definitions of themselves and of their place in society (Pleck, 1976). Men who are confronted with accepting women as peers in work settings or men who recognize female careers and power sharing in marital or other heterosexual relationships are most likely to feel the impact of the changing ideas concerning sex roles.

Sex-Role Transcendence

Men and women appear to be different in performance but not in potential. Society enforces different behavior patterns on men and women, resulting in the stereotypes of the masculine male and the feminine female. Recent research suggests that both stereotypes, the macho male and the inept female, may be on their way out. Because of the dissatisfaction with the masculine-feminine stereotypes, there is a need for a wider range of acceptable behavior for men and women. In an extensive survey, Tavris and Offir (1977) found that fewer women are now looking for strong, masculine men. Instead most women are seeking sensitivity and responsiveness in men to whom they wish to relate.

In view of the harm that adherence to masculine and feminine stereotypes may do, the current theme of **sex-role transcendence** (Rebecca, Hefner, & Oleshansky, 1976) seems to be particularly timely. According to this model, there are three stages in sex-role development. During Stage I (infancy) the child is unaware of culturally imposed restrictions of sex-typed behavior. This stage lasts through early childhood, until children begin to become aware of society's sex-role expectations.

The second stage begins during childhood and for many people continues through life. Stage II involves active acceptance of the stereotyped role and sex-typed behavior. Masculinity and femininity are dichotomies in this stage. Stage III is reached when we are no longer bound by rigid sex-role conformity and feel free to express ourselves without regard to sex roles. Men and women achieve sex-role transcendence, which implies that men and women no longer fear violating the stereotyped norms and actively pursue an androgynous identity. Rebecca and her colleagues suggested that Stage III is a dynamic process that involves an unending process of conflict and conflict resolution.

Summary

The development of gender identity and sex-typed behavior and values is influenced by a complex network of biological, psychological, and cultural factors. Since none of these factors alone offers a satisfactory explanation of the development of sex-role stereotyping, gender identity has become an interdisciplinary study.

Hormonal studies of animals and observations of people with chromosomal or hormonal abnormalities attempt to account for the differences between the sexes from a biological perspective. Even if biologically based sex differences in behavior do occur, most evidence suggests that socialization exerts a stronger influence than biological factors.

Several psychological theories have been proposed to explain the development of gender identity. According to Freudian theory, the child incorporates the qualities of the same-sex parent through the process of identification with that parent during the phallic stage of psychosexual development. In social-learning theory, modeling and differential reinforcement lead to gender identity. In the cognitive-developmental model, gender identity precedes identification with the parent and does not result from it, as Freud believed. According to Kohlberg, identity comes first based on cognitive maturity and makes the performance of sex-typed activities differentially reinforcing. A person's gender identity is also influenced by a number of cultural variables such as social class.

Sex-role training begins at the moment of birth, when boys and girls are exposed to different sex-role standards and treatment. Fathers seem more concerned than mothers about sex-appropriate behavior in their children and play a more important role in sex typing of boys and girls. Schools and the media reinforce the sex-role training that children receive at home. In later childhood and adolescence the peer group assigns status based on one's adherence to masculine and feminine norms. Conformity to stereotyped role expectations is part of being popular for children and adolescents.

Data relevant to behavioral differences between men and women focus on three major areas: personality, achievement, and intelligence. Contrary to popular belief, men and women share most personality traits. The only significant exception is aggression; in most cultures males are more aggressive than females. Some evidence supports the idea that a chromosomal difference affects sex differences in aggression. Sex differences in achievement motivation have been interpreted as a function of socialization; that is, men and women in our society have been socialized either to differentially value achievement itself or to differentially value various kinds of achievements.

No sex differences in general intelligence have been found between men and women. However, some sex differences are commonly found in certain intellectual skills. Women tend to score higher on verbal tasks, while men score higher on spatial and mathematical tasks. There is evidence of a biological influence on sex differences in spatial ability. Other cases of intellectual differences are probably accounted for by systematic differences in role assignment and socialization.

In recent years increasing emphasis has been placed on androgyny as a desirable model of mental health for both men and women. The androgynous person is someone free of the constraints of stereotyped sex-role standards. Androgyny and sex-role transcendence are concepts that permit men and women to exercise greater flexibility in developing their gender identity, since a person of either gender may incorporate the best aspects of the other gender.

Key Terms For Review

achievement motivation
androgyny
anima
animus
gender identity
hermaphroditism
inner space
motive to avoid success
progestin
sex-role transcendence
spatial ability
stereotype

Suggested Readings

Basow, S. *Sex-role stereotypes: Traditions and alternatives.* Monterey, Calif.: Brooks/Cole, 1981.

This book explores the origins and effects of sex-role stereotyping and discusses current findings in the area of sex differences and similarities. Consequences of sex-role stereotyping are presented in terms of individual, interpersonal, and societal consequences.

Bear, S., Berger, M., & Wright, L. Even cowboys sing the blues: Difficulties experienced by men trying to adopt nontraditional sex roles and how clinicians can be helpful to them. *Sex Roles,* 1979, 5 (2), 191–198.

This article discusses the impact of changing sex roles of women on men. The research indicates that men who are violating stereotypic sex-role expectations by becoming more active in fathering and household activities are exposed to pressures to conform to traditional sex roles by employers and organizations.

Forisha, B. *Sex roles and personal awareness.* Glenview, Ill.: Scott, Foresman, 1978.

The author examines the impact that sex roles have on our lives and explores alternative patterns of development. Numerous exercises and case histories highlight the various topics presented.

Maccoby, E., & Jacklin, C. *The psychology of sex differences.* Palo Alto, Calif.: Stanford University Press, 1974.

Presently the most comprehensive and scholarly review of male and female differences in personality, intelligence, achievement, and socialization.

Schaffer, K. *Sex roles and human behavior.* Cambridge, Mass.: Winthrop, 1981.

The book covers a variety of topics related to sex roles, including current and historical perspectives, sex-role socialization; career behavior; racial, social-class, and cross-cultural perspectives of sex roles; and sex roles and psychotherapy.

10

Theories of Personality

Jay, a thirty-year-old single physician, is described by friends and relatives as being highly motivated, intelligent, creative, attractive, and charming. "If they only knew," thinks Jay frequently. Unknown to others Jay feels insecure and anxious. According to her own description, Jay is introverted, shy, overweight, dull, unhappy, and inadequate.

Jay was the first-born in a family of two boys and one girl. Jay's father, a successful medical researcher, had especially high aspirations for his oldest child. Her mother, busy with a full-time career and housekeeping, often communicated her frustrations over her several roles to Jay, especially when Jay was young. Throughout elementary and high school, Jay was popular and did well academically. Before she was ten years old, Jay was determined to go into medicine, a goal that was strongly encouraged by her father. Yet despite Jay's popularity and ambitions, she felt lonely, depressed, and insecure throughout her childhood and adolescence.

The college years seemed a period of both personal growth and pain for Jay. Although successful academically, Jay had difficulties establishing a stable relationship with men. After several unsuccessful romantic involvements she became worried about her inability to maintain a relationship for any length of time. In medical school severe pressures and a heavy workload forced Jay to ignore potential romantic involvement. Although Jay tried not to dwell on her personal feelings, thoughts such as "I don't deserve to be a doctor," "I won't pass my exams," or "Why can't I meet that special person?" often went through her mind.

At the medical-school graduation ceremonies Dr. and Mrs. Smith were proud to congratulate their daughter, now officially Dr. Jaylene Smith, who graduated at the top of her class (Lazarus & Monat, 1979).

Now that you have learned something about Jay, what can you say about her personality? Are ambition and achievement orientation her major characteristics? What are the reasons for her repeated difficulties in heterosexual relationships? Could her position in the family, being first-born and female with two brothers, have had an influence on her personality development? These are the kinds of questions personality theorists ask.

There are many different approaches to personality. Some theorists, like Sheldon, focus on biological aspects, while others, like Adler, prefer a social perspective. In this chapter we shall examine the study of personality from a number of perspectives by surveying the definitions and dimensions of personality, by reviewing the major theories, and by sampling personality research.

WHAT IS PERSONALITY?

The term "personality" has many definitions, both popular and formal. Everyday definitions often equate personality with social skills or with a person's dominant characteristic. For example, we may describe a person as aggressive, truthful, or anxious, thereby selecting a particular quality that forms the basis of our overall impression.

Formal definitions proposed by theorists of personality show the same variety. Gordon Allport (1937) collected no fewer than 50 definitions, which he grouped into five categories. One is the **omnibus definition,** which includes everything about an individual. Another type is the **arrangement definition,** which puts personality traits into some kind of order to arrive at a total description of the person. The **adjustment definition** of personality views the individual as struggling to find his or her identity and to adjust to the environment. This type of definition tries to ascertain the person's degree of adjustment, ranging from mental health to personality disintegration. A fourth type, the **hierarchical definition,** interprets personality traits as stages of development that appear in a fixed order. Finally, Allport listed the **distinctiveness definition,** which equates personality with unique and individual aspects of behavior.

Clearly no single definition of personality can be applied with any generality. Moreover, these varied types of definitions are not necessarily mutually exclusive. The point is that there are many ways to define personality, and each one provides valid information about the underlying conceptualization of personality.

Dimensions of Personality

Personality has at least four dimensions: traits, character, motivation, and temperament. **Traits** are stable and distinctive characteristics that cause a person to act in some consistent way. Trait theorists observe and measure these enduring behavioral tendencies in order to compare variations in individuals' traits. We often use the trait approach to describe people. We may say, for example, that Bob is uninhibited or Janet is aggressive, thereby categorizing the person according to a distinguishing quality.

According to trait theorists, traits are presumably "carried around" by the person from situation to situation as relatively enduring psychological characteristics. However, many investigators have failed to find the trait consistency that the concept implies (Monte, 1977), leading some contemporary personality theorists (e.g., Mischel, 1968) to question the utility of the trait concept.

Character, according to dictionary definitions, refers to moral excellence. If we say that a person has good character, we are making a value judgment about his or her moral habits. When we say that someone has a character defect, we mean that the person in question tends to act unethically in certain circumstances. In personality theory the term character is used to mean "personality evaluated." Thus character refers to a dimension of personality that is evaluated by others as either ethical and moral or the reverse. In the past the study of character focused on negative qualities, such as high levels of anxiety or aggression. Recently, instead of studying criminals, delinquents, and psychopaths, theorists have begun to investigate positive aspects of character, such as sympathy, responsibility, integrity, and helping behavior.

A third dimension of personality is **motivation** (see Chapter 6). Some personality theorists make use of complicated motivational principles such as instincts, drives, needs, or other internal states. All of them agree, however, that motivation needs to be present if certain types of behavior are to be maintained. Some of the motivations that have been of interest to personality theorists are the needs for achievement, power, understanding, and independence.

Temperament is a fourth personality dimension. Terms used to describe an individual's temperament include irritable, nervous, or sensitive. Or we may speak of an even-tempered person. Most personality theorists assume that temperament is biologically based, a characteristic that we are born with.

While there are many other dimensions of personality, these four examples illustrate the complexity of the subject. The dimension of temperament raises the question of whether there is a biological basis for personality; the dimension of character emphasizes society's evaluation of personality; and the dimension of motivation implies internal psychological processes.

Contemporary Issues

Personality theorists are currently disputing a number of issues that are either controversial or difficult to settle. One such issue deals with semantics. A major problem in personality theory is the lack of clarity in the language used to express theoretical concepts. Many critics have accused personality theorists of creating a "semantic morass" by packaging their theories in ambiguous, misleading, ill-defined terms. Concepts such as Freud's "death instinct," or "thanatos," or Jung's "shadow" may be vivid and picturesque but fail to communicate the essence of the concept. In part, the semantic problem has arisen because many important theories have been translated from foreign languages. In some cases there simply was no translation for certain concepts, while in others certain terms were inaccurately translated. Many theorists have been highly creative in inventing an intuitively appealing terminology. However, most of these terms remain semantic curiosities that cannot be empirically tested (Schultz, 1981).

Several additional issues are open to debate (Corsini, 1977). One is the way in which personality theorists evaluate time. Some, such as Freud, stress the importance of the past, whereas others, such as Jung and Adler, propose that our future goals and aspirations determine our behavior. And still others, such as the learning theorists and existentialists, suggest that the present is most important.

Philosophically a theorist can take either the inductive or deductive approach. Deductive reasoning involves starting with a law or other generalization and applying it to particular cases. Inductive thinking starts with particular cases in the attempt to form a law or other generalization. In the following section you will meet representatives of both approaches.

Finally, there is the question of how much personality theories reflect the sociocultural climate of the time when they were formulated. For example, to what degree is Freudian theory a product of the declining Victorian era? How different would psychoanalytic theory be if it were written during the 1980s? The prevailing social, philosophical, and political climate at any given time is known as ***Zeitgeist;*** most personality theorists are influenced by it, and this influence is reflected in their theories.

WHAT IS A THEORY?

Just as all of us know what personality is, we are also familiar with the concept "theory." Yet when asked to define what a theory is, many people are at a loss. Generally theories are tools used by scientists to organize knowledge in such a way that it helps us understand the phenomena under investigation. Technically a theory is defined as an unsubstantiated hypothesis that needs to be confirmed or refuted by empirical data. Once a theory has been confirmed it becomes a fact.

Ideally a theory consists of two components: a set of assumptions that the investigator makes about the concept, idea, or subject he or she wishes to study and a set of empirical definitions. The **assumptions** must reflect the behavior, dimensions, or events with which the theory is concerned as well as the types of behavior that the theorist attempts to predict. Freudian theory, for example, assumes that behavior is biologically determined and that women are inferior. A theory that fails to make adequate statements about its underlying assumptions has little use since it cannot be tested.

The second component, **empirical definitions,** specifies the operations by means of which the theory can be tested. By means of these definitions the theory comes into contact with reality or observational data (Hall & Lindzey, 1978). A theory with well-defined assumptions and empirical definitions helps us to expand our knowledge systematically and is useful in predicting behavior in different situations.

The major theories of personality can be grouped according to common themes into three main categories: psychoanalytic theories (Freud, ego psychology, Jung, Adler); learning theories (Skinner, Bandura, Rotter); and humanistic-existential theories (Rogers, Maslow, existentialists). Each of these approaches represents a different although sometimes overlapping view of human behavior. Some of the theorists in these three main groups attempt to explain the same phenomena differently, while others explore entirely different events.

THE PSYCHOANALYTIC THEORY OF FREUD

Classical psychoanalysis, formulated by Sigmund Freud (1961, 1969), is not only one of the most comprehensive approaches to personality but has also become one of the major intellectual traditions of our century. Sometimes psychoanalysis is referred to as psychodynamic theory because it focuses on "inner dynamics" or "psychic processes" such as drives and instincts (Mischel, 1968, 1973). This label emphasizes an important principle of Freud's theory (and that of some of his followers), namely, that behavior is always the symbolic equivalent of psychic processes that lie below the surface of observable events. In making inferences about the nature of internal states, Freud relied heavily on two concepts: instincts and the unconscious.

Instincts

Basic to Freud's theoretical position as well as to the rationale of his work as a therapist is the concept of instincts. Freud believed that all human beings are born with a number of instinctual drives. He divided instincts into two categories: **eros,** or life instincts, and **thanatos,** or death or destructive instincts. The life instincts serve the purpose of individual survival and propagation of the species. Although Freud never specified the number of life instincts, he paid greatest attention to sexual energy, which he called **libido.** Freud insisted that most of our overt actions are motivated by sexual drives.

The second group of instincts, the death instincts, involve the wish to die. As Freud stated it, "the goal of life is death." Death instincts cannot be observed in their pure form. Instead, their existence is inferred from the tendency to behave aggressively and destructively. Aggression, according to Freud, is self-destruction turned outward; we act aggressively against another person because our death instincts have been blocked.

The Unconscious

Freud argued that we are strangers to ourselves, unaware or unconscious of the motives for our actions, and he presupposed three levels of con-

Table 10–1. Freud's Psychosexual Stages and Consequences for Later Development

Psychosexual Stage	*Erogenous Zone*	*Major Consequence for Personality*
Oral (birth to age 2)	Mouth	Ability to form interpersonal attachments
Anal (age 2 to 3)	Anus	Ability to work and feel competent
Phallic (age 3 to 5)	Genitalia	Development of conscience and guilt
Latent (age 6 to puberty)	None	Ability to be with others without sexual or aggressive feelings
Genital (puberty and on)	Genitalia	Ability to sustain a loving heterosexual relationship

sciousness: the unconscious, the preconscious, and the conscious. He also believed that a large portion of the unconscious cannot be penetrated because "in the depths of the unconscious are hurtful memories, forbidden desires, and other experiences that have been repressed, that is, pushed out of the conscious" (Freud, 1969, p. 38). To illustrate the distribution of consciousness and unconsciousness Freud used the analogy of an iceberg: only about 10 percent of its total mass is above the water. Similarly, we are conscious only of a small fraction of our mental life. Consciousness and unconsciousness are separated from each other by the **preconscious,** which contains repressed thoughts and feelings that are more easily accessible.

Freud quoted many kinds of evidence that reflect the working of the unconscious: jokes, slips of the tongue, dreams, neurotic symptoms, and even works of art. He also developed two specific techniques to retrieve unconscious thoughts and feelings in his patients: free association and dream analysis. **Free association** is the classic psychoanalytic technique that encourages a person to say whatever comes to mind without being on guard or fearing censorship. For Freud dreams were the "royal road to the unconscious"; **dream analysis** was seen as a means of putting a person in touch with threatening impulses or thoughts that were believed to produce psychological defenses such as repression. One of the major goals of psychoanalysis is to bring repressed thoughts and feelings to the surface.

The concept of the dynamic unconscious is a cornerstone of psychoanalytic theory. Although some of Freud's followers have placed more emphasis on conscious control, most have not entirely negated or surrendered the concept of the unconscious.

Psychosexual Development

According to Freud, each person goes through a series of psychosexual stages, the outcome of each having major consequences for personality (see Table 10–1). In the course of this development the child derives pleasure from the body's **erogenous zones,** which are highly sensitive openings such as the mouth or genitals. At specific psychosexual stages, different erogenous zones become the source of erotic pleasure. Based on the shift of erogenous zones, Freud outlined five stages of psychosexual development.

Oral Stage. During the oral stage (birth to age two) the mouth is the principal erogenous zone. Oral activities such as nursing from the mother's breast or the nipple of a bottle, sucking the thumb, or biting objects that can be placed in the infant's mouth provide maximal pleasure and gratification of libidinal drives. At this stage of

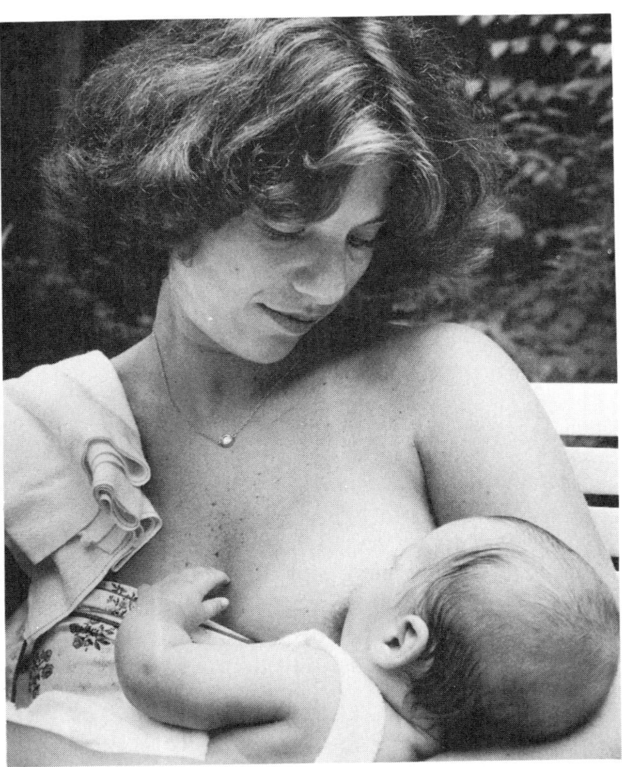

Freud's theory of psychosexual development contends that a baby derives pleasure principally through its mouth up to the age of two. (© *Erika Stone)*

development the infant is basically controlled by biological impulses and completely dependent upon others for basic physiological needs. According to Freud, if these drives are not sufficiently satisfied in infancy, certain oral traits such as overeating, excessive smoking or talking, or "having a biting tongue" can probably be observed in the adult. Such a person is an "oral character type." For Freud the person is an example of arrested development, or **fixation,** in the oral stage. Some research supports the hypothesis of oral personality types (Fisher & Greenberg, 1977).

Anal Stage. During the anal stage of psychosexual development (age two to three) pleasurable sensations focus on the anal region. Elimination of feces removes discomfort and tension and produces feelings of relief and pleasure. For the child this stage represents the first decisive experience with external control (parental prescriptions regarding appropriate toilet behavior) of an innate need (elimination). In a way, the anal stage may be viewed as a power struggle between the child and the parent in the conscious control over bladder and bowel. Conflicts that arise over the regulation of bladder and bowel movements may lead to fixations in the anal stage and the formation of an "anal-retentive character type." Children who resist parental efforts at toilet training by deliberately retaining their feces and refusing to move their bowels grow up to be stingy, obstinate, orderly adults. Like the oral character type, the anal type is supported by some research findings (Kline, 1972).

Phallic Stage. As psychosexual development continues, the erogenous zone shifts from the anal region to the sexual organs (age three to five). This is the time when many young children discover the pleasures of masturbation. The most important event in this period is the emergence and resolution of the **Oedipal complex.** Oedipus, according to Greek mythology, unknowingly killed his father and married his mother. Each little boy, Freud thought, symbolically relives the Oedipal drama at some time. The boy's desires for and sexual attraction to his mother bring him into conflict with his father, whom he views as his rival for his mother's love. He also, however, fears the wrath of his father, fantasizing that his father will punish him for his "incestuous" desires by removing his penis. This **castration anxiety** forces the boy to repress his desires for his mother and his hostility toward his father. If all goes well, the boy resolves the Oedipal conflict by identifying with the father and converting his dangerous erotic feelings for his mother into harmless affection for her. Resolution of the Oedipal complex results in the emergence of the superego, which Freud called the "heir of the Oedipal complex."

Although a corresponding conflict, the **Electra complex,** occurs in girls, the sequence of events and the resolution of the conflict are different. For the little girl, the discovery that she is lacking a penis is at the source of the conflict. As a result of her discovery she develops not only **penis envy** but also holds her mother responsible for her "castrated" condition. Thus penis envy is the female equivalent of castration anxiety; however, the underlying dynamics are different. The girl imagines that she has lost something valuable, that is, the penis, whereas the boy fears that he will lose it. To compensate for her "deficiency" the little girl turns to her father, who has the prized organ. The father becomes the desired love object replacing the mother, whom the girl begins to devalue. Although the process by which the Electra complex is resolved is not clear, Freud argued that girls eventually identify with their mothers as a means of vicariously obtaining the desired love object, i.e., the father (Freud, 1969, pp. 44–51). In Freud's opinion women tend to search for a penis substitute in adulthood by wishing for a male child. Thus for the girl the Oedipal complex persists in modified form and is never completely resolved. As a result her moral development is less adequate.

The major problem with the Electra complex is that its key concept, penis envy, cannot be evaluated scientifically. Although case histories are available to document the existence of penis envy among women in therapy (see Application, page

APPLICATION

A Case History Illustrating Penis Envy

Jane is a 20-year-old woman who sought therapy because she felt very depressed and anxious. As long as she could remember, she had resented being female. She described her marital relationship as tense and competitive, particularly since her husband had recently become highly successful, whereas she considered herself an unsuccessful artist. Since she could not compete with her husband professionally, she decided that the best way to compete was to do the one thing he could not do—bear a child.

Her childhood history revealed that Jane despised her mother, whom she described as dependent, ineffective, and prone to periodic depression, and adored her father, an unsuccessful artist. In fact, she spent almost 10 years of her childhood trying to be her father's son. Her fantasy of being like a boy was brutally crushed when she was preparing for a bar mitzvah. She thought she would be allowed to have one "as good as a boy's" but was sent home from the synagogue because it was decided that she was now a woman and could no longer compete with the boys.

When Jane started menstruating, her resentment of female functions and the female role increased. She compensated, however, with fantasies of having a son. After a brief stay in Europe, during which Jane felt she had attained self-sufficiency and no longer needed her father, she returned home to her ill father. He lived long enough to see her first one-person art show, but he teased her by saying, "Why not give it up, go home, and make babies."

After her father's death Jane became more and more depressed, thinking of herself as a failure. After four years of marriage, during which she had an irrational fear about pregnancy, she decided to get pregnant. Now she was overwhelmed by feelings of being trapped; having a baby would prevent her from trying to be like a man.

Psychoanalysis-oriented therapists would find plenty of evidence for penis envy in Jane's case. As a child she tried to compete with boys; as a woman, she envied and was attracted to powerful and achievement-oriented men. At the same time she was jealous of them because they were free to pursue their goals. For Jane, power, achievement, and success were symbolized by the penis; to have one would save her from being like her mother. According to Freudian theory, she wanted a baby as a substitute for not having a penis. Similarly, her reluctance to have one stemmed from her fear of relinquishing her fantasy penis. (Moulton, 1970).

273), it remains to be demonstrated that penis envy is common among women or that it has a profound influence on the development of personality in women. Freud, however, believed that many of the most important forces in human behavior are unconscious and thus cannot be studied by any of the usual scientific methods.

Latency Stage. During this stage (age six to the beginning of puberty) sexual drives are relatively quiet since they have come under the censorship of the conscience. Sexual instincts are now sublimated or channeled into socially acceptable activities such as learning and play.

Genital Stage. After puberty, with the maturation of the reproductive organs in both sexes, the person enters into the stage of mature heterosexuality, providing that no traumatic experiences occurred earlier. Sexual drives are awakened again, but now the person is able to invest his or her sexual interests in a loving relationship with a

Table 10–2. Traits of Psychosexual Stages of Development

	Abnormal	*Normal*	*Abnormal zero (absence of trait)*	*Normal*	*Abnormal*
Oral Traits	optimism	(←		→)	pessimism
	gullibility	(		)	suspiciousness
	manipulativeness	(		)	passivity
	admiration	(		)	envy
	cockiness	(		)	self-belittlement
Anal Traits	stinginess	(		)	overgenerosity
	constrictedness	(		)	expansiveness
	stubbornness	(		)	acquiescence
	orderliness	(		)	messiness
	rigid punctuality	(		)	tardiness
	meticulousness	(		)	dirtiness
	precision	(		)	vagueness
Phallic Traits	vanity	(		)	self-hate
	pride	(		)	humility
	blind courage	(		)	timidity
	brashness	(		)	bashfulness
	gregariousness	(		)	isolationism
	stylishness	(		)	plainness
	flirtatiousness	(		)	avoidance of heterosexuality
	chastity	(		)	promiscuity
	gaiety	(		)	sadness
Genital Traits	sentimental love	(		)	indiscriminate hate
	compulsive work	(		)	inability to work

The ideal personality should possess each of the above pairs of traits to a moderate degree. There must be a proper balance between opposing traits. Lack of balance among the traits constitutes a less than ideal personality. Abnormality in a personality may be determined in three ways: (1) possession of a trait to an extreme degree, (2) lack of the trait altogether, (3) imbalance between pairs of traits.
Source: From Di Caprio (1974, p. 52).

member of the opposite sex. During the genital stage successful personal growth means a shift from narcissistic, self-centered love to altruistic love in which a concern for the other person overrides selfish interests. Table 10–2 summarizes the character traits associated with each psychosexual stage.

Personality Structure

Freud's concept of personality assumed the existence of three constructs—the id, the ego, and the superego—which continually interact with each other in a mutual exchange of energy. The **id** is the source of all biological drives, the "reservoir of all psychic energy" containing all the primitive, untamed urges and desires. The id operates on the **pleasure principle,** striving for the immediate gratification of primitive drives and operating on the assumption that whatever satisfies an impulse is good and whatever blocks or frustrates such satisfaction is bad. Freud said that "the id, of course, knows no judgments of value: no good and evil, no morality" (Freud, 1933, p. 74). Although the id can generate mental images and wish-fulfillment fantasies, it cannot undertake the realistic actions needed to meet its demands.

The **ego** is the mediating force that balances the demands of the id and the external realities. Since the ego develops out of the id, the energy for ego functions must come from the id. In contrast to the pleasure principle of the id, the ego is governed by the **reality principle.** Characterized by realistic thinking or problem solving, the ego can postpone immediate gratification until an appropriate object or situation has been discovered in the real world. Whereas the id knows only subjective reality (e.g., an image of food), the ego distinguishes between subjective and objective reality and creates strategies for actually obtaining the desired satisfaction (e.g., getting food from the refrigerator).

The third construct, the **superego,** emerges after the Oedipal complex has been resolved. It is a moral or ethical agency that serves as the internal representative of parental and societal values; it is the voice of conscience, caution, and inhibition. As children grow up, various socializing agents, such as parents, schools, and churches, indoctrinate them into standards of right and wrong, good and bad, which they internalize. Transgressions of these internalized ethical and moral values result in feelings of guilt.

These three aspects of personality merely represent different psychological processes that obey different principles. It would be misleading to think of them as separate, independent subsystems. As Freud stated:

> In thinking of this division of personality into an ego, a superego, and an id, you will not, of course, have pictured sharp frontiers like the artificial ones drawn in political geography. We cannot do justice to the characteristics of the mind by linear outlines like those in a drawing or a primitive painting but rather by areas of color melting into one another as they are presented by modern artists. After making the separation we must allow what we have separated to merge once more (Freud, 1933, p. 79).

To draw an analogy, we may say that the id represents the motor of a car, the ego the driver who controls the power system (presumably with libido as gasoline), and the superego the police. Put another way, the id may be thought of as the product of evolution or the biological component of personality, the ego as the province of higher mental processes, and the superego as the product of socialization and the vehicle of cultural tradition.

Anxiety and Ego Defenses

The concept of anxiety, or psychic pain, is a central construct in psychoanalytic theory. Freud recognized three types of anxiety: (1) **reality anxiety,** or fear of real dangers in the external world; (2) **neurotic anxiety,** or the fear that threatening impulses will break down ego controls; and (3) **moral anxiety,** or fear of one's conscience.

The function of anxiety is to warn the ego to prevent the occurrence of inappropriate or traumatic experiences. In reality anxiety the danger is external, and the ego can deal with the threat by taking realistic steps to remove the danger. Neurotic and moral anxiety, however, cannot be handled realistically and rationally since they result not from real danger but from intrapsychic dangers. To cope with these internal threats the ego has to resort to unrealistic measures. These are the **defense mechanisms** of the ego, which are unconscious processes that keep disturbing and unacceptable impulses from being expressed directly (see Table 10–3).

All defense mechanisms deny, falsify, or distort reality to protect the ego from overwhelming anxiety. **Repression** is an attempt by the ego to prevent painful and dangerous thoughts and impulses from entering consciousness. **Projection** is an ego defense that externalizes the threatening feelings by attributing them to someone else. For example, a girl who hates her mother may unconsciously convince herself that it is her mother who hates her. **Reaction formation** involves the conversion of an undesirable impulse into its opposite. Thus the husband who hates his wife may shower her with kindness and gifts. In **rationalization** a person attempts to justify his or her behavior through the use of plausible but inaccurate excuses. Most rationalizations take the "sour grapes" form; for example, a student who has flunked out of college may argue that practical, real-life education is superior to any college degree. In **denial** the person simply refuses to acknowledge the existence of disturbing impulses. In **regression** the person retreats to an earlier period when life was less taxing and more pleasant. Adults, for instance, at times display childish behavior. **Sublimation** refers to the symbolic expression of a forbidden act by using acceptable and even admirable behavior. Freud proposed that many socially valued activities are sublimations of dangerous or unacceptable id impulses. A surgeon or a basketball player, for instance, may have found an acceptable outlet for aggressive drives. Of all ego defenses, sublimation has the most positive effects because it permanently channels forbidden impulses into acceptable activities. Finally, **compensation,** which substitutes a strength for a weakness, can be a healthy defense also. A boy, for instance, who is too frail to succeed in football may handle his feelings by excelling in scholastic endeavors.

Fear of external danger, or reality anxiety, is one of the three types of anxiety identified by Freud. (© *Joel Gordon*)

Can Freudian concepts help us understand the personality of Jay, the doctor described at the beginning of this chapter? Given Jay's difficulty with heterosexual relationships, Freud would suggest that she did not resolve the Oedipal complex successfully. She also had a much closer relationship with her father than with her mother when she was young. Jay probably kept her incestuous feelings toward her father and her hostile emotions toward her mother under control by defense mechanisms, probably repression. Some of her behavior at medical school, which requires a con-

Table 10–3. Defense Mechanisms

Mechanism	Description
Repression	Thoughts, feelings, or desires are barred from consciousness and deposited in the unconscious.
Identification	A person takes on mannerisms or behavior of another person viewed as powerful to deal with feelings of inferiority.
Projection	An undesirable impulse or behavior is attributed to others in the effort to deny its existence in one's self.
Displacement	A person expresses feelings toward another person to whom they do not apply because to express them toward the appropriate person is too frightening.
Denial	The person pretends an undesirable feeling or event does not exist.
Reaction formation	Threatening feelings are repressed and an opposite feeling is expressed; e.g., a person who is threatened by feelings of sexual attraction may express feelings of dislike or hatred.
Isolation	Feelings that accompany a painful memory are excluded from consciousness.
Sublimation	Unacceptable impulses are expressed in a socially desirable manner; e.g., an artist may express sexual impulses in sculpture or painting.
Regression	A person returns to an earlier level of psychological functioning under times of stress; e.g., an adult may have temper tantrums when frustrated.
Rationalization	After an unpleasant occurrence, a person provides rational and logical reasons; e.g., a person whose application is rejected by medical school explains that he or she did not want to work that hard anyway.

siderable degree of persistence, orderliness, and concern for detail, may also have been vestiges from the oral or anal stage.

Freud deserves credit for having developed a very comprehensive description of personality. Still, many valid criticisms have been made over the years. Since the theory is essentially presented in metaphors and other nonscientific terms, it does not lend itself to empirical testing and verification. Many critics have argued that Freudian theory also lacks cultural universality, that is, Freud's propositions may have explained behavior in late Victorian society but do not explain behavior in other cultures at other times. Another criticism often raised is that Freud derived his ideas almost exclusively from work with patients who were in therapy with him. Consequently his theory may describe not so much human behavior in general as disturbed behavior.

At the present time it is unrealistic to hope for any real confirmation or refutation of Freudian theory. Many psychologists (e.g., Marx & Hillix, 1979) are willing to argue that it is time to throw aside tradition and stop giving attention to psychoanalytic theory, even if there is nothing to replace it. In spite of its limitations, the theorizing

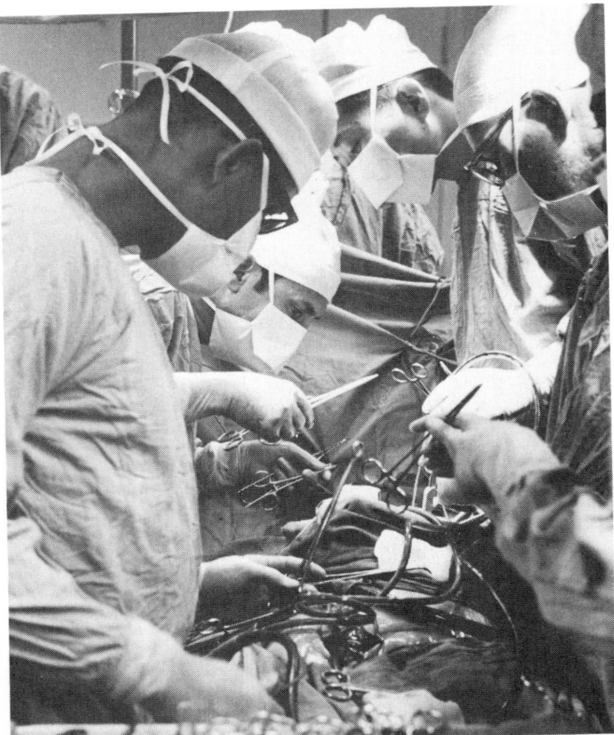

Surgeons may find an outlet for aggressive drives in their work. *(© Ken Heyman)*

of Freud has had a fundamental impact on our concept of human nature and behavior. Presently, however, psychoanalytic theory no longer directs psychological research on personality.

EGO PSYCHOLOGY

As psychoanalysis continued to develop, it became clear that Freud's view of the conflict-ridden, id-dominated personality was limited. Anna Freud (1936), his daughter, suggested that psychoanalysis could profit from more direct investigation of the conscious ego. A new branch of psychoanalysis called **ego psychology** arose.

A number of theorists have contributed to the development of ego psychology, among them Anna Freud and Heinz Hartman. Hartman (1964), for example, characterizes such functions as language, memory, and thinking as a "conflict-free ego sphere." Anna Freud is widely regarded as a prominent ego psychologist. Ego psychology deemphasizes the role of the id, postulating that ego functions are unrelated to the satisfaction of id impulses. In addition, ego psychologists recognize that personality development continues throughout the whole life cycle from infancy to old age. In general, ego psychology presents us with a much more optimistic view of human nature than does orthodox psychoanalysis because greater strength is attributed to the rational and adaptive ego (Ewen, 1980). Table 10–4 summarizes the major differences between Freudian theory and ego psychology.

JUNG'S ANALYTIC THEORY

Carl Jung was an early associate of Freud, but he was also the first psychoanalytic theorist to break away from Freud. He did so because he considered Freud's emphasis on the sexual nature of the life instincts too narrow. Jung constructed a theory of personality that is a unique blend of psychology, philosophy, anthropology, ancient myths, modern beliefs, religions of Eastern and Western civilizations, and themes of the occult. Perhaps because he drew his ideas from so many diverse sources, Jung's theory is in many ways more complex than that of any other theorist.

Personality Structure

Jung's theory of personality has three structural components: the ego, the personal unconscious, and the collective unconscious. The ego, or conscious mind, is made up of conscious perceptions, memories, feelings, and thoughts. Through the ego each person knows himself or herself. Eventually the ego gives way to the self, which inherits the role of the ego at a midpoint between consciousness and unconsciousness. The self does not emerge until middle age, which Jung considered a crucial transition period.

Of all the psychoanalytic theorists Jung placed the most emphasis on the unconscious. He distinguished between two types of unconscious: the personal unconscious and the collective unconscious. The **personal unconscious** begins at birth and consists of personal experiences, memories, and thoughts that have been removed from consciousness but still exist in a forgotten state. As was the case with Freud's preconscious, there is a great deal of interaction between the ego and the personal unconscious. Memories stored in the personal unconscious can be easily recalled to con-

Table 10–4. Ego Psychology Compared with Freudian Theory

	Freudian (id) Theory	*Ego Psychology*
The Id	The sole component of personality present at birth; entirely unconscious, amoral.	Similar, but less powerful.
The Ego	*Origin:* Begins to develop out of the id at age 6–8 months. *Characteristics:* A weak "rider" struggling desperately to control its instinctually energized "horse." Concerned solely with satisfying id impulses in a way that will also please its other two masters, the superego and external world. *Defense Mechanisms:* Used solely to ward off intrapsychic or external threats, primarily illicit id impulses and anxiety.	*Origin:* Begins to develop independently of the id very soon after birth. *Characteristics:* A relatively powerful and autonomous entity that encompasses important capacities of its own, which are directed toward such constructive goals as mastery of and adaptation to the environment. These ego functions are unrelated to the satisfaction of id impulses, yet are pleasurable in their own right. *Defense Mechanisms:* Are adaptive as well as defensive, as when fantasy anticipates a way of solving one's problems and becomes the basis for forming realistic goals.
The Superego	Includes introjected ideals and restrictions; may be overly harsh and oppressive.	Essentially similar.
Personality Development	Virtually complete by about age 5 years.	Continues throughout the whole life cycle from infancy to old age.
Society	An inevitable source of frustration and conflict, since illicit and irrational id impulses must be sublimated. An external burden imposed on the ego.	Not necessarily a source of frustration and conflict, since the ego functions are constructive and can therefore be expressed directly. An essential support (as well as sometime impediment) that provides the ego with fortifying social roles and identities.
Libido	The psychic energy that fuels all mental activity.	Essentially similar; but accorded considerably less emphasis, so that greater attention can be devoted to ego and societal forces.
View of Human Nature	Pessimistic, because of the emphasis on powerful illicit id impulses.	More optimistic, because greater strength is attributed to the rational and adaptive ego.

Source: Ewen (1980).

sciousness. Associated with the personal unconscious are **complexes,** which Jung defined as groups of feelings, thoughts, or memories centering on a dominant theme. A strong complex may dominate the rest of the personality. For example, if we say that a person has a power complex, we mean that power is the organizing principle that determines his or her behavior.

At a much deeper, mostly inaccessible level of personality is the **collective unconscious.** This is the most influential system in the personality. It is also Jung's unique and most controversial contribution to personality theory. The collective unconscious is the storehouse of universal evolutionary experiences that are transmitted from generation to generation by means of heredity. Jung believed, however, that it is not the memories themselves that are inherited, but the potential for having the same experiences as earlier generations. In other words, Jung proposed that we are predisposed to think and feel about certain universal experiences in the same way as our ancestors did. One example of such an inherited potential is the perception of mother as warm, nurturant, and protective since, supposedly, all infants throughout history perceived their mother in this way. Similarly, according to Jung, we are predisposed to fear darkness and worship the sun, because darkness and the sun generated reactions of fear and worship over many generations.

In contrast to the personal unconscious, the collective unconscious is said to be independent of personal experiences. Jung postulated that, just as a person accumulates and files all of his or her past experiences (the personal unconscious), so does humankind collectively do so as a species. Thus a child whose mother is cold and punitive nevertheless retains the universally transmitted memory trace of mother as warm and cherishing. Although the collective unconscious is the same in all people, this does not imply that all of us behave identically. The collective unconscious, then, contains the entire catalog of experiences that characterize human evolution, which is repeated in the brain of every man and woman in every generation.

The collective unconscious contains **archetypes,** or universal thought patterns and visions, which can appear in various symbolic forms. Archetypes serve as models for our actions and reactions; they are "inherited modes of psychic functioning which can be found in myths and dreams in every time and every place" (Kopp, 1977, p. 186). Among these universal experiences that are found repeatedly in the lives of people generation after generation are: the hero, the child, God, magic, power, and the wise old man.

Although Jung believed that archetypes are innumerable, he singled out the persona, the shadow, the anima, the animus, and the self as particularly well-developed archetypes. The **persona,** also known as the archetype of adaptation, refers to the mask we wear in response to the demands of social convention. It is our public personality, the facade we present when playing our various roles. Jung believed that the persona is necessary because we must function in a variety of roles, such as student, spouse, and parent, and interact with a diversity of people from co-workers to professors. The **shadow,** on the other hand, is the dark side of our nature, the evil Mr. Hyde underlying the impeccable Dr. Jekyll. The shadow archetype consists of all the animal instincts that, Jung suggested, we have inherited in the process of evolution from lower forms of life. Thus the shadow represents the evil, inferior, and primitive side of our nature.

According to Jung, no man is entirely masculine and no woman is entirely feminine. Instead each sex exhibits some of the characteristics typically associated with the opposite sex. Jung accounted for this complement of masculine and feminine characteristics with two archetypes known as the anima and the animus (see Chapter 9). The anima is the feminine archetype in men that is responsible for emotions and the ability to relate to and understand women. The animus is the masculine side in women's personality, which manifests itself in traits such as discipline, aggressiveness, and rational judgment.

Finally, the most important archetype is the self. It represents our constant striving for unity, harmony, and stability. The archetype of the self is best symbolized by the mandala, the magic circle of Eastern civilizations.

Attitudes and Functions

Jung distinguished between two fundamental attitudes or orientations of personality: **introversion** and **extraversion.** The introvert lives within himself or herself and enjoys a quiet, subjective world of solitude. In contrast the extravert is most interested in the external world and is oriented toward action and people. In the healthy individual both attitudes are balanced.

Jung also postulated four fundamental functions that he saw as techniques for orienting ourselves in life. Thinking is the rational function by which we try to comprehend our experiences in a logical fashion. Feeling is a subjective, evaluating function; we use it to reflect how certain experiences make us feel. Sensing is a perceptual function; it allows us to take in the external world much like a camera taking a picture. Intuiting, or perceiving through the unconscious, helps us to gain a glimpse of what lies behind our overt experiences and gives us an insight into the subliminal content of our existence.

To understand what Jung means, let us take the example of four people sitting on a rock overlooking the Grand Canyon. The thinking type follows the contours of the rocks and valleys, perhaps studying and comparing different stone formations or other geophysical elements. The feeling type is carried away by the sight below, experiencing joy, perhaps, or sadness. The sensing type listens to the sounds and enjoys the various colors. The intuiting type's mind may wander away from the sight of the canyon into higher realms of consciousness.

Although everyone possesses all four capacities, usually one or two functions serve as a basis for organizing one's personality. In introverts, the reflexive functions of sensing and intuiting tend to predominate. The rational functions of thinking and feeling are more prevalent in extraverts.

An introvert prefers to cultivate an inner life of quiet rather than participate actively in the external world. *(© Peter Menzel/Stock, Boston, Inc.)*

Personality Development

Jung did not delineate specific stages of development but described the process of psychological maturation as an arc ascending to a peak around middle age. Sometime in the late thirties or early forties a person must make the transition from youthful, self-directed interests and extraversion to more outer-directed and spiritual concerns. Instead of fulfilling primarily personal goals that have their roots in biological needs, the person turns his or her attention to social, civic, religious, or philosophical matters. For Jung this transition in the middle years is the most critical period in a person's life. His conceptualization of the midlife transition period, sometimes called the midlife crisis (see Chapter 8), is consistent with recent research (e.g., Levinson, 1978), which indicates that the middle years can be unsettling.

Jung's theory of personality is more esoteric and spiritual than other personality theories and also more difficult to grasp. One of the major problems is that of reading and understanding Jungian concepts. Jung's works are filled with apparent inconsistencies, contradictions, and a lack of logical order (Hogan, 1976). Although some of Jung's concepts, particularly the two attitudes (extraversion and introversion), have been widely accepted, the bulk of his theory has not been well received. Like psychoanalysis, his theory is criticized for lacking scientific methodology and empirical data.

A child's sense of weakness and desire for strength is summarized in Adler's inferiority-superiority concept. *(© Joel Gordon)*

ADLER'S INDIVIDUAL PSYCHOLOGY

For Alfred Adler (1964) the fundamental human motive is the striving for superiority as a compensation for feelings of inferiority. In fact, it was this principle that caused Adler to break away from Freud and the psychoanalytic movement. Adler was the first psychoanalytic theorist who recognized the fundamentally social nature of personality.

In contrast to Freud and Jung, Adler did not invent an elaborate terminology but presented his concepts in everyday language. One of the strong points of Adler's theory is its simplicity. In his view, all the important issues in the psychic life of the individual can be explained by a few concepts. First among these principles is the **inferiority-superiority concept.** Adler proposed that the determining movement in life is from "feeling minus to feeling plus." The child, born small, helpless, weak, and inferior, develops the need to become strong and powerful. In children as well as in adults, perceived feelings of inferiority, whether from biological, psychological, or social weakness, produce the need to become superior, to gain a sense of competence and fulfillment. This need was well illustrated in the case of Jay. Adler believed that the need to overcome inferiority and the desire to become superior are the basic motivating forces that account for individual growth and social improvement. Personality development for Adler, then, simply means overcoming minus estimates of ourselves and arriving at plus estimates.

A second important concept in Adler's theory is **social interest.** Adler proposed that we must develop social interests, or the desire to aid others, rather than pursue selfish interests. As Adler stated it; "Social interests mean a striving for a form of community which must be thought of as everlasting, as it could be thought of if mankind reached the goal of perfection" (Adler, 1973, pp. 34–35). Adler devoted considerable attention in his later works (1964, 1973) to the ways in which social interests contribute to adjustment, believ-

CRITICAL ISSUE

Birth-Order Effects on Personality

According to Adler, the child's first socialization experiences within the family are the most important ones. These experiences, in turn, are strongly influenced by the child's birth-order position. In other words, according to Adler, your place in the family largely determines how you cope with people and the world. Take a moment and consider your position in the family. Your life was probably affected by being a first- or last-born, or perhaps by being an only child. For example, did you have to prove yourself to a powerful older brother or mothering sister?

Adler recognized five basic birth-order positions. The first-born child is in a fortunate position since he or she receives all the love and attention of the parents, as well as their standards, values, and attitudes. On the other hand, most first-borns are not spared the traumatic experience of being "dethroned" when the second child is born. As adults, first-born children tend to strive for dominant positions among their peers. They tend to be more conscientious and achieve at higher levels scholastically. They are more apt to become scientists or eminent in their chosen career than later-born children. However, the experience of having lost the favorite place in the family also leaves scars. More so than later-born children, first-borns are prone to anxiety and jealousy.

The second child is characterized by a desire "to get ahead" or "to catch up." Second-born children tend to be very ambitious, constantly trying to surpass the older sibling. Having to work their way around an older, stronger sibling tends to make second-borns diplomatic and good at negotiating. They also profit from the opportunity to observe the successes and failures of the older child.

The middle-born child, that is, the one with both older and younger siblings, has neither the advantages of the oldest nor those of the youngest. Middle children learn early in childhood to adjust to both adults and children. Unless middle children make a firm place for themselves, they sometimes get lost in the shuffle.

The youngest child is in a special position since there is always someone to take care of him or her. Many youngest children are charming, playful, and lighthearted. Typically the youngest child either becomes the most successful member of the family or remains in the dependent position of the baby.

The final birth-order position is that of the only child, who never has to struggle or compete with other siblings for a place of importance in the family. According to Forer (1977), the world is his or her oyster, and there is no competition that cannot be met satisfactorily. Thus only children are likely to be dominating and perfectionistic; however, they are not usually jealous since their position in the family has never been threatened. Since only children sometimes do not have opportunities to share with others, they may develop a peculiarly dependent relationship to the parents or may be relatively insensitive to the needs of others.

Adler's observations of birth-order effects have been amply supported, but interpretations of birth-order positions have changed. Schachter (1959), for instance, also found that first-borns are more anxious than later-borns. However, Schachter contended that first-borns are more anxious not because they were dethroned by younger siblings but because they were handled by inexperienced parents. According to this interpretation, parents tend to be uncertain and worry about the proper ways of treating their first child. Their fears make them overattentive and create anxiety in the child.

ing that life's major problems all require social interest and cooperation for their solution. Social interest leads to willingness to cooperate with others and facilitates productive conflict resolution. For Adler lack of social interest is a major contributing factor in many forms of abnormal behavior.

Finally, a well-balanced person requires a master plan, or **style of life,** that directs the way goals will be pursued and individual inferiorities overcome. The style of life, a guiding ideal as well as an organizing principle, encompasses all drives, impulses, traits, and desires. Each individual has a unique style of life. A child who is neglected may choose a style of life characterized by feelings of revenge and hostility, whereas a child who is pampered may choose one characterized by an excessive need for attention. Adler believed that the style of life, and therefore the personality, is well developed by the age of four or five (agreeing with Freud on this issue and disagreeing with Jung). It represents both the child's life goals and the methods contemplated to achieve them and is strongly influenced by the child's birth order in the family (see Critical Issue, page 283).

Adler's theory has been criticized for being oversimplified and for overemphasizing the role of the conscious ego. According to Freud, the ego (in Adler's theory) plays the ludicrous part of a circus clown who by his gestures tries to convince the audience that every change in the circus is being carried out under his orders. But only the youngest spectators are deceived by him (Freud, 1914/1967, p. 53). Adler has also been criticized for his excessive optimism, which sharply contrasts with Freud's pessimism, and for his lack of quantitative analyses. Adler's conclusions, like Freud's, are drawn from his own subjective observations.

We have traced the psychoanalytic movement from its original conception to contemporary ego psychology, noting differences and similarities among the various theorists. Adler was the first psychodynamic theorist to attend to social determinants of personality, an important factor not addressed by Freud and Jung. Ego psychology recognizes the importance of individual and social factors interacting while at the same time recognizing that biological factors are operating but in no way determine an individual's personality.

LEARNING THEORIES

Learning theories are based on principles of learning developed in the experimental laboratories of Pavlov and Skinner (see Chapter 5). In contrast to Freud, who saw humans as being pushed from within by uncontrollable instincts, learning theorists assume that our personality is malleable and shaped by external forces (Skinner, 1953, 1974). They avoid any inferences to internal, hypothetical states, such as the ego or the collective unconscious. Instead they confine their analyses to observable responses. Skinner (1953) stated:

> The practice of looking inside the organism [as demonstrated by Freud] for an explanation of behavior has tended to obscure the variables which are immediately available for scientific analysis. These variables lie outside the organism, in its immediate environment and its environmental history (p. 31).

Skinner's Reinforcement Theory

B. F. Skinner, a fervent opponent of traditional constructs such as personality, traits, motives, drives, and other "explanatory fictions," argued that the most understandable and important causes of change in behavior come from outside the organism. For Skinner, complex behavior is shaped by reinforcement strategies (discussed in Chapter 5). Reinforcement is seen as a process that will increase the future probability of behavior. Applying the same principles and schedules of reinforcement used with laboratory animals to human beings, Skinner assumed that a person's behavior is determined by his or her past history of reinforcement and presently prevailing reinforcement conditions.

As we saw in Chapter 5, reinforcers can be divided into two classes, primary and secondary, or unlearned and learned. Learned reinforcers such as money and medals maintain various types of behavior. Learned reinforcers such as affection, approval, and attention, which Skinner called **generalized and conditioned reinforcers,** are rewarding for many different types of behavior. Some people, for example, will do almost anything for attention, approval, or affection. Skinner assumes that each of us has "reinforcing power," and consequently we are able to shape the behavior of others. We can reinforce them with smiles or attention for behavior we like, and we can withhold such reinforcement for behavior we do not like. Skinner advised against the use of punishment as a means of control because of its negative side effects (see Chapter 5).

Skinner examined personality through a functional analysis of behavior, that is, an analysis of cause-and-effect relationships. The causes are prior events composed of observable stimuli, and the effects are the consequences of these events. This approach allows the theorist to control, manipulate, and explain behavior without having to perform a "psychological autopsy" or infer any internal states. For Skinner, behavior (and consequently personality) is orderly and lawful, and our primary purpose is to understand and exercise control over it. Skinner is interested only in modifiable aspects of personality; consequently he deemphasizes aspects of personality such as temperament, which may be innate and hence unalterable.

Skinner's influence on contemporary psychology has been tremendous. Operant-conditioning principles have been successfully employed in the treatment of personality disturbances such as alcoholism and overeating, in the management of classrooms and mental hospitals (see the description of token economies in Chapter 5), and in the development of experimental communes. Skinner discussed not only methods of controlling the behavior of others but also means of self-control in which the individual is both the controller and the controlled. He makes that distinction to demonstrate that personal management of behavior like overeating or smoking can be corrected by removing oneself from food or tobacco, thereby increasing control over one's behavior. According to the behaviorist perspective as represented by Skinner, we could explain Jay's behavior if we had full knowledge of her history of reinforcement. Later reinforcements would be cues to earlier reinforcements. For example, her meticulous study habits in medical school were probably reinforced when she was young, particularly by her father and teachers. Her poor heterosexual relationships may have been shaped by a combination of rewards (warm relationship with father) and punishment (aversive experiences with men of her age).

Smiling is an important reinforcer for desired behavior. *(© Maureen Fennelli/Photo Researchers, Inc.)*

Skinner's approach to personality sharply contrasts with the psychoanalytic perspective not only in subject matter but also in methodology. Skinner proposed that all behavior is determined by prior conditioning, usually operant. We engage in the behavior we do because we have previously been reinforced for it. Skinner, whose approach follows the behaviorist tradition originated by Watson (see Chapter 1), does not study people, but rats and pigeons. This comes as a surprise to many people interested in personality. A strong advocate of applying scientific techniques to the study of human behavior, Skinner is well aware of the implications of his approach:

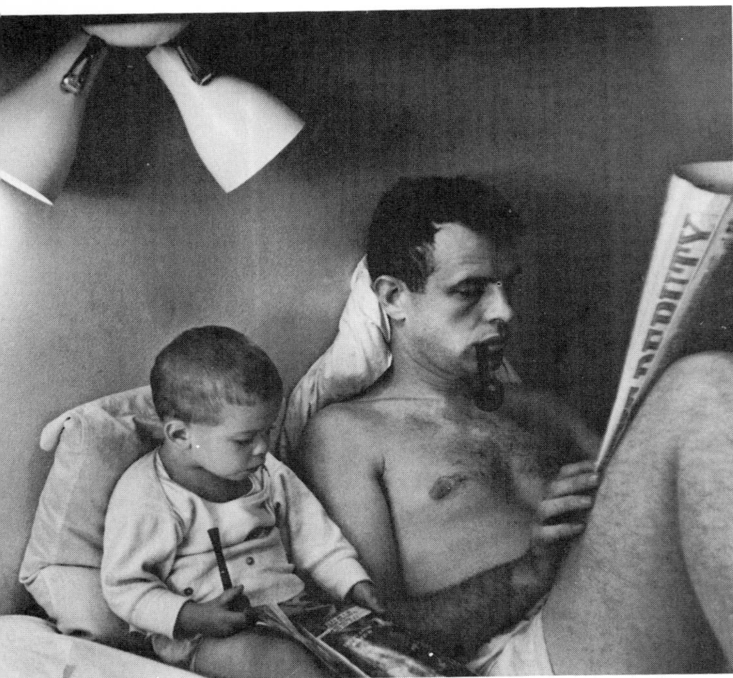

Much of our behavior derives from observational learning. (© Erika Stone)

> The possibility is offensive to many people. It is opposed to a tradition of long standing which regards man as a free agent whose behavior is the product, not of specifiable antecedent conditions, but of spontaneous inner changes. . . . To suggest that we abandon this view is to threaten many cherished beliefs—to undermine what appears to be a stimulating and productive conception of human nature. The alternative point of view insists upon recognizing coercive forces in human conduct which we may prefer to disregard. . . . Regardless of how much we stand to gain from supposing that human behavior is the proper subject matter of a science, no one who is a product of Western civilization can do so without struggle. We simply do not want such a science (1953, p. 7).

Critics have accused Skinner of developing an oversimplistic, mechanistic view of human nature that makes a person a pawn of environmental forces and fails to account for the complexity of human behavior. In addition, Skinner's view of personality was derived from experimentation with relatively simple organisms observed under relatively simple conditions. Nevertheless Skinner's approach is well respected because of the amount of carefully conducted research, the breadth of application of his principles, and the number of followers who, stimulated by Skinner's work, have continued and expanded operant theory.

Social-Learning Theories

Social-learning theorists share Skinner's assumption that most of our behavior is learned. However, they contend that social interactions are important agents of reinforcement and that learning theorists should not restrict their attention to the effects of reinforcement on voluntary responses like those investigated in Skinner's laboratory. Social-learning theorists see a need to discuss internal states in order to explain complex learning (Bandura, 1974).

According to Albert Bandura, a person's behavior can be shaped not only by appropriate schedules of reinforcement but also by the person's acting as his or her own reinforcing agent. As Bandura stated, "The development of self-reactive functions gives humans a capacity for self-direction . . . and self-worth and they refrain from behaving in ways that evoke self-punishment" (Bandura, 1974, p. 86). Social-learning theories thus broaden the Skinnerian perspective by including internal factors such as cognition, needs, and traits as legitimate topics in personality.

Bandura's Observational-Learning Theory. Bandura (Bandura and Walters, 1963; Bandura, 1965) introduced the idea that we may acquire responses in the absence of direct reinforcement through **observational learning.** As defined in Chapter 5, observational learning is learning new ways of behaving simply by observing others. This has also been called modeling or imitation. Our behavior is therefore not only controlled by immediate external reinforcement but is also affected by cognitive factors such as anticipated out-

APPLICATION

Studies in Locus of Control

Rotter's integration of personal and situational factors led him to develop a personality construct known as internal-external locus of control of reinforcement (I-E). According to Rotter (1966), people acquire the expectancy of perceiving reinforcing events either as dependent upon their own behavior or as beyond their control. Internally oriented people believe rewards occur as a result of their own skills and are consequently under their control. Externally oriented people see little or no connection between their behavior and reinforcement. For example, students who fail an examination will blame themselves if they are internally oriented, but will blame external reasons or bad luck if they are externally oriented.

To measure the internal-external personality dimension, Rotter constructed the I-E scale, which consists of 29 paired items. Here are some sample items of the I-E scale (adapted from Rotter, 1966, p. 11):

> I have often found that what is going to happen will happen (E).
> Trusting to fate has never turned out as well for me as making a decision to take a definite course of action (I).
>
> Getting a good job depends mainly on being in the right place at the right time (E).
> Becoming a success is a matter of hard work; luck has little or nothing to do with it (I).
>
> Unfortunately, an individual's worth often passes unrecognized no matter how hard he tries (E).
> In the long run people get the respect they deserve in this world (I).

A person's score on this scale is simply the number of times he or she responds in the external direction. High scores reflect an expectancy of reinforcement by luck, fate, or other factors beyond a person's control. Research with the I-E scale has shown that belief in internal control is learned in families in which parents are warm, supportive, and nonauthoritarian. The acquisition of internal control also seems to be a developmental process, that is, it tends to increase with age. Externally oriented individuals have been found to be subject to anxiety and depression (Naditch, Gargon, & Michael, 1975), while those who are internally oriented are more likely to use denial (Phares, 1976).

Internal-external locus of control as a personality style has been widely used to predict a broad array of behavior, from the use of birth-control techniques (MacDonald, 1970) to political activism (Gore & Rotter, 1963). Prociuk and Lussier (1975) reported that this personality dimension has generated more research (277 studies in the 1973–1974 period alone) than any other contemporary concept.

---

comes. Most of us, for instance, do not wait until we have a car accident to buy insurance.

Observational learning accounts for the acquisition not only of new types of behavior but also of maladaptive responses. As you will see in Chapter 18, children have been found to acquire aggressive behavior through modeling the behavior seen on TV shows.

According to Bandura, the behavior of our young physician, Jay, would be a function of the models she has been exposed to and the reinforcements she received. Bandura believed that modeling develops over time as a function of age and of the level of cognitive maturity. As Jay's cognitive abilities matured, she was more and more capable of self-control and became independent of external reinforcement.

Rotter's Expectancy Model. Julian Rotter (1966, 1970) constructed a theory of personality based on four major concepts: behavior potential, expectancy, reinforcement value, and the psychological situation. **Behavior potential** refers to the probability of a person's response when certain environmental conditions are present. Behavior potential is used by psychologists to predict the likelihood that a subject will exhibit a particular type of behavior.

Behavior potential is determined in part by **expectancy** which is "the probability held by the individual that a particular reinforcement will occur as a function of a specific situation or situations" (Rotter, 1954, p. 107). Rotter emphasized the role of cognitive and subjective probabilities held by the person regarding behavioral outcomes, but he also recognized that expectancies are substantially influenced by a person's reinforcement history. Suppose you are with a group of people who are discussing a subject you know very well. Although you are eager to participate in the discussion, you are afraid of being ignored. The reason you have this expectancy is that you have been ignored in similar situations in the past. For example, a man who has been unsuccessful in his request for dates may develop an expectancy of being rejected and hesitate to approach women in the future.

Behavior potential is also determined by the **reinforcement value** we attach to different types of rewards. For example, a child may be offered either a quarter or a candy for cleaning his or her room; the child will select the reinforcer he or she values most. Like expectancies, the values we associate with different reinforcers are in part determined by our past experiences. If the reinforcement value of a given type of behavior is high, such as gaining wealth or status, a person may give up everything to achieve that goal. Some people, for example, are tied so closely to their professions that they neglect health and family. People differ in terms of what they find reinforcing. Some find disco dancing reinforcing, while others prefer to listen to a symphony; some people select tennis and others, football.

Rotter's fourth major concept is the **psychological situation,** which refers to both internal and external environments. With this concept Rotter acknowledges the fact that behavior does not take place independent of a context but is influenced by specific situations. Take the example of the little boy who enjoys being held and kissed by his mother at bedtime but violently objects to such signs of affection in the presence of his friends. The physical stimulus (holding and hugging) is the same in both cases, yet the psychological situation (or the perception of the stimulus) differs. Consequently the little boy will behave differently in the two situations.

Rotter recognized the importance of both personal and situational influences on personality, a viewpoint that places him midway between theorists like Freud who stress internal motives, such as instincts, and those like Skinner who emphasize environmental determinants. Rotter's theory implies that we pay attention to our past experiences as well as to situational cues.

HUMANISTIC-EXISTENTIAL THEORIES

Humanistic psychology emerged as the third force in psychology (after psychoanalysis and behaviorism) in the 1950s and 1960s. Existential theories, most of which were a reaction against the dehumanizing tendencies of industrialized mass societies, had been developed earlier by European writers such as Kierkegaard and Nietzsche but came into popularity when a "new" psychology emerged in which the proper object of study was human existence itself, in all its complexity and confusion.

In contrast to the negative and pessimistic picture of human nature portrayed by Freudian theory, humanistic-existential theorists stress our positive nature. They focus on the importance of inner experience and our potential for self-direction. The theorists in this group are concerned with the individual's need to find meaning in existence, attain fulfillment, and decide what is right and good and act accordingly. In essence humanistic-existential theorists argue that modern psychology has failed to address itself to crucial problems in our daily life.

The humanistic perspective in personality is also referred to as the phenomenological approach because of each of us exists at the center of our own private, everchanging world of inner experience, the **phenomenal field** (Rogers, 1959).

Phenomenology (from the Greek root meaning "to appear" or "to show") emphasizes immediate sensory experiences and how we interpret them. Shlien (1963) describes the concerns of phenomenology well:

> If the mind could not think silently, if there were outwardly audible and visible signs directly indicating specific mental abilities, we would all be ranked behaviorists, and the history of psychology, to say the least, would have hinged on a very different set of data. But this is not the case. As things stand, we have both internal and external events experienced by the total organism, experienced, recorded, at some level of awareness, and in some cases given meaning. The phenomenologist is convinced that much goes on inside (pp. 291–292).

The theorists represented in this section of the chapter are concerned with the self as a unifying theme of personality. In both the humanistic and the existential framework the self is used as the basic principle to account for subjective experiences as well as a person's sense of identity and tendencies toward self-evaluation and self-fulfillment.

Rogers's Self Theory

From his pioneering research into the nature of the psychotherapeutic process, Carl Rogers developed a theory of personality, personality change, and psychotherapy (see Chapter 13). Theory and therapy are so closely interwoven in Rogers's system that it is almost impossible to separate them. It is equally as difficult to separate the man Rogers from his work. Because of his compassion and empathy for others, Rogers has not only been extremely successful in therapy but also has become internationally known and popular in the world of psychology.

Personality Structure. Rogers's theory of personality, like the theories of Freud and Jung, grew out of his experiences with his clients. Rogers insists that a theory of personality has to emerge from therapeutic relationships and is strongly opposed to any theory building that precedes therapy. Rogers's theory was originally presented in a book entitled *Client-Centered Therapy* (1951) and later more formally described in *On Becoming a Person* (1961). Although Rogers does not emphasize structural components of personality as Freud and Jung did, there are at least three fundamental constructs upon which the structure of personality rests: the organism, the phenomenal field, and the self.

The **organism** refers to the totality of all experiences. Based on his own experiences, Rogers explains that trusting one's organism makes a person open to all experiences. The opposite of trusting one's organism is to behave with too many constraints, which takes spontaneity and freshness out of our behavior. The phenomenal field refers to the individual's frame of reference based on his or her actual experience. The **self** is the major structure in Rogers's theory. Although the concept of the self is somewhat akin to the psychoanalytic ego, Rogers extended the self to include a person's self-concept and sense of identity. In contrast to Freud's concept of ego, this self is entirely conscious and consciously attempts to realize its full potential.

Rogers proposed two basic kinds of relationships between the self and the organism. If a person's self-concept is in line with his or her actual experiences, a state of congruence exists. Congruence means that the self-concept is a mirror reflection of what the person experiences in reality. Congruence also implies that the individual is open to new experiences. Incongruence, on the other hand, means disharmony between a person's behavior and his or her perception of it. Rogers argued that distorted perceptions are the source of many psychological disturbances. When the self clashes with the actual experience of the person (such as when a person has a positive sense of self but is not accepted by significant others), incongruence occurs and the person experiences anxiety and confusion.

Personality Development. Rogers does not provide a timetable of significant stages through which the individual must pass in traveling from infancy to maturity. In discussing personality development, Rogers focused on the way we are evaluated by people important to us, such as parents, spouses, or co-workers. If the evaluations are and always have been entirely positive—what Rogers calls **unconditional positive regard**—a perfect state of harmony or congruence exists between the organism and the self. However, since most of us are exposed to negative as well as positive evaluations, we learn to differentiate between those of our actions and feelings that are worthy (approved) and those that are unworthy (disapproved). Unworthy experiences gradually tend to be excluded from our self-concept. This exclusion, says Rogers, causes us to create a self-concept that is out of line with our actual experience.

Table 10–5. Traits of the Fully Functioning and Incongruent Selves

The Fully Functioning Self	*The Incongruent Self*
Self-aware	Out of touch with the self
Creative	Lacks firm sense of identity
Spontaneous	Introjects
Open to experience	Frustrated impulses
Self-accepting	Negative emotions
Self-determining	Distorted self-structure
Free from constraints	Antisocial behavior
Lives in his or her "now"	Puts forth masks
Allows full outlet of potentials	Unrealistic appraisal of potentials
Trusts his or her organism	
Possesses firm sense of identity	
Avoids facades	
Has sense of free choice	
Moves from introjection	
Moves toward self-direction	
Willing to be process	
Lives existentially	

Note: Represented here are the *extremes* of a continuum on the potentials of self, as considered by Rogers.
Source: DiCaprio (1974).

How can the breach between the self and the organism be healed? Rogers proposed client-centered therapy, a form of psychotherapy that emphasizes the client's individuality (see Chapter 13) and provides a warm, accepting, nonjudgmental relationship between the therapist and the client. In this way the client can explore threatening experiences and feelings, learn to assimilate them into his or her self-concept, and become more understanding and accepting of others.

Personality development culminates in the emergence of the **fully functioning self**, an individual who is open to experiences, is free of defenses, and has unconditional positive regard for self and others. Such a person also has a self-concept that is congruent with his or her actual experiences and lives wholly and freely in each moment (Rogers, 1961). The characteristics of the fully functioning self and the incongruent self are presented in Figure 10–1 and Table 10–5.

Recently Rogers suggested that a new, more fully human person has begun to emerge in our society. This "homo novus" has a distaste for phoniness, a relative unconcern with material possessions, a desire for intimacy and closeness with others, and a healthily critical attitude toward science and technology. This is a person who is aware that he or she is continually changing (Evans, 1975).

Overall there has been no change in Rogers's position since he first presented his theory. His implicit faith in the goodness of each person and his emphasis on growth rather than disease were readily accepted by professionals as well as the lay population as a welcome change from the pessimistic view of psychoanalysis. Rogers's theory is reflected not only in his client-centered therapy and his recent work with encounter and sensitivity groups but has also been applied to diverse areas such as education, family life, and leadership. With respect to education, for example, Rogers points out how a person-centered teacher, like a client-centered therapist, can create a psychological climate in the classroom that facilitates learning. Such a teacher shows unconditional positive regard and empathy for students, encouraging them to express their interests freely.

Rogers's major contribution is seen in the client-centered psychotherapy he developed. His theory has been criticized by some for failing to state the dimension of personality precisely. Other critics have argued that a theory like Rogers's, which grew out of subjective experiences of his clients, is inherently unsound because clients have a tendency to distort their recollections and feelings.

Maslow's Self-Actualization Theory

Abraham Maslow, like Rogers, stresses the importance of values and fulfillment in personality, not only for the sake of the individual but also for the sake of society. Maslow (1969) argued that it is essential to develop a "good society" because the actualization of human potential is possible only under favorable social conditions. Actualization refers to our tendency to enhance our experiences through personal growth; it is a tendency that both Rogers and Maslow considered a fundamental need of all human beings.

Maslow believed that we must study the best, healthiest, and most mature examples of the human species to understand the full range of human potential. Maslow himself was privileged to meet with two individuals who he believed qualified for this description: one of the founders of Gestalt psychology, Max Wertheimer, and the anthropologist Ruth Benedict. Spurred by these encounters, Maslow began to examine prominent personalities, both living and dead, to find those who might be called models of psychological health. From the case studies of these individuals, based on the interviews and biographical and autobiographical material, Maslow formulated his theory of personality. In addition, Maslow studied some 3,000 college students and found that only a small percentage of them met his criteria for self-actualization. Like Jung, Maslow believed that we do not attain full personality maturity until middle age.

A person-centered teacher fosters learning by offering attention and empathy to the student. *(© Ken Heyman)*

Hierarchy of Needs. Maslow proposed that our needs can be arranged in a hierarchy of potency or importance. Basic needs such as hunger, security, and self-esteem need to be fulfilled first before we can concern ourselves with justice, order, or beauty. Maslow labeled the basic needs deficiency needs and the higher needs **metaneeds,** or growth needs.

At the bottom of the hierarchy are the most urgent physiological needs, including hunger, thirst, and sex. Unless these biological needs are satisfied we are unlikely to worry about higher level needs such as safety, belongingness, self-esteem, or self-actualization. In addition to the basic needs Maslow postulated a number of metaneeds, among them truth, justice, order, meaningfulness, beauty, and unity. In contrast with the basic needs, metaneeds coexist rather than being arranged hierarchically. Maslow's metaneeds are

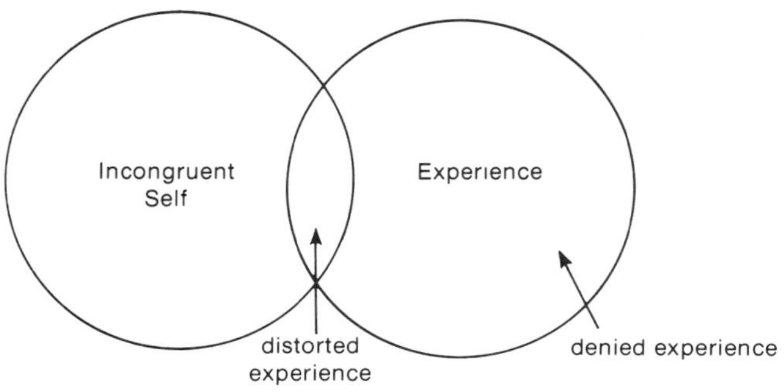

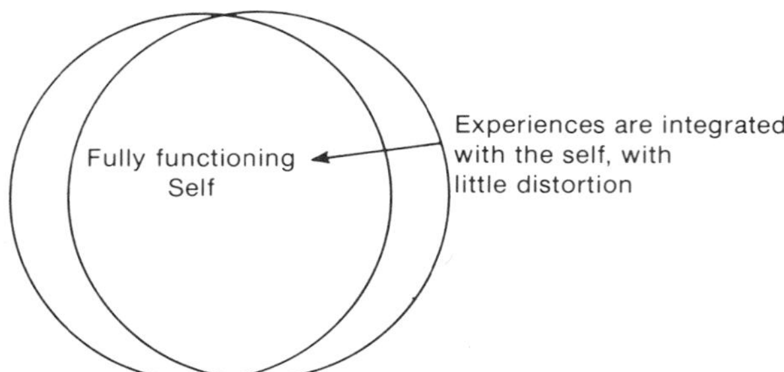

Figure 10–1. An important aim of client-centered therapy is to eliminate distortion and denial by helping the individual to bring "into one consistent and integrated system all his sensory and visceral experiences" (Rogers, 1951, p. 520). (Adapted from *Client-Centered Therapy*, Houghton Mifflin, 1951, p. 527.)

listed in Table 10–6 along with the psychological consequences that arise from the frustration of metaneeds. Maslow called these conditions **metapathologies.** Metapathologies prevent us from expressing, utilizing, and fulfilling our potential.

The Self-Actualizing Person. Just as Rogers tried to describe the fully functioning self, Maslow attempted to describe the **self-actualizing person.** To begin with, self-actualizers are people who have satisfied their need for food, shelter, and intimacy. They are reality oriented, accepting themselves and others for what they are. They are spontaneous and enjoy solitude. They are also independent and truly democratic in the sense of being free of prejudice. Self-actualizers are creative and nonconformist and have a sense of humor about themselves and life in general. Although the self-actualizing person possesses some of the finest human qualities, he or she is not perfect. Self-actualizers can be boring, stubborn, irritating, prone to temper outbursts, and capable of extraordinary and unexpected ruthlessness (Maslow, 1963, p. 550).

Maslow fully recognized that few people in our society—probably less than one percent—achieve self-actualization. Although he insisted that all of us have the potential for reaching this ideal state, he offered several possible explanations to account for the fact that so few people attain it. One is that self-actualization involves more persistence, courage, hard work, and willingness to transcend conventional standards than most people have at their command. Some critics have pointed out that self-actualization is reserved for a relatively small group—those with above-average intelligence, education, and incomes. Men and women with little education, who find themselves locked in dead-end, low paying jobs, are simply not in a position to admire the majestic quality of a sunset or the intricate beauty of a poem. As long as people are concerned with the satisfaction of physiological and safety needs, self-actualization needs cannot be attended to.

Maslow offered a very optimistic view of personality, emphasizing that all of us are capable of reaching our full potential. The theory has been particularly well received by the business community, which uses the concept of self-actualization to improve the productivity and morale of employees.

Existential Theories

The existential view of personality is based on the philosophies of Kierkegaard (1818–1855), Nietzsche (1844–1900), and Heidegger (1889–1976). In many ways the existential movement may be seen as a reaction to the conditions surrounding World War II. Prominent in the development of existential thought in the United States has been psychologist Rollo May, who started publishing during the 1950s. Contributions to the existential approach have come from philosophers, psychologists, artists, writers, and intellectuals. Like the humanistic psychologists, existential theorists emphasize our uniqueness as individuals, our quest for values and meaning, and our capacity for self-direction and self-fulfillment. Existential theorists, however, stress the difficulties that lie in our path.

Personality Structure. Like humanistic psychologists, existentialists show little concern for structural components of personality, such as Freud's id, ego, and superego. The concepts of existence, meaning, and freedom of choice are the key ideas in existential thought.

Table 10–6. Maslow's Need Hierarchy and Levels of Personality Functioning

Need Hierarchy	*Condition of Deficiency*	*Fulfillment*	*Illustration*
Physiological	Hunger, thirst Sexual frustration Tension Fatigue Illness Lack of proper shelter	Relaxation Release from tension Experiences of pleasure from senses Physical well-being Comfort	Feeling satisfied after a good meal
Safety	Insecurity Yearning Sense of loss Fear Obsession Compulsion	Security Comfort Balance Poise Calm Tranquility	Being secure in a full-time job
Love	Self-consciousness Feeling of being unwanted Feeling of worthlessness Emptiness Loneliness Isolation Incompleteness	Free expression of emotions Sense of wholeness Sense of warmth Renewed sense of life and strength Sense of growing together	Experiencing total acceptance in a love relationship
Esteem	Feeling of incompetence Negativism Feeling of inferiority	Confidence Sense of mastery Positive self-regard Self-respect Self-extension	Receiving an award for an outstanding performance on some project
Self-Actualization	Alienation Metapathologies Absense of meaning in life Boredom Routine living Limited activities	Healthy curiosity Peak experiences B-values Realization of potentials Work that is pleasurable and embodies values Creative living	Experiencing a profound insight

Source: DiCaprio (1974).

Existence. Existence, or being, is the basic theme in existential theory. Although existence is given to us, we have the responsibility of shaping our existence and thereby the kind of person we want to become. There are three worlds in which we exist: the inner experiential world, the physical world around us, and the social world in which we interact (Binswanger, 1963). Our existence is fluid, perpetually in search of meaning. With existence comes the struggle to overcome physical shortcomings, intellectual deficiences, hunger, poverty, and personal inadequacies. Rollo May (quoted in Maddi, 1976, p. 127) described the dilemma of existence as follows:

> Being [existence] in the human sense is not given once and for all. It does not unfold automatically as the oak tree does from the acorn. For an intrinsic and inseparable element in human being is self consciousness. Man is the particular being who has to be aware of himself, be responsible for himself, if he is to become himself. He also is that particular being who knows that at some future moment he will not be; he is the being who is always in dialectical relation with nonbeing, death. And he not only knows he will sometime not be, but he can, in his own choices, slough off and forfeit his being.

Existential theorists see two solutions to the problems of existence. We can either give up the quest for satisfaction by blindly conforming, or we can strive for deeper insight. Only the second choice brings fulfillment and meaning and leads to an authentic life, which is characterized by the recognition that the individual is not all-powerful.

Meaning. One of our most fundamental motivations, according to existential theory, is the need to find meaning in our lives (Frankl, 1963; 1969); we strive for goals that supply that meaning and accept the challenge of finding new purposes. Abandoning the search for meaning leaves us bored and apathetic; psychiatrist Victor Frankl noted that if we have no reason to continue living, life becomes empty and meaningless. After an intensely degrading personal experience in the grim world of the German concentration camps, Frankl still believed that there is meaning in every situation and that we are free to find it and are responsible for doing so. He was also convinced that conditions in modern society have caused many of us to lose the "why" to live, which makes it more difficult to cope with the "how."

Freedom of Choice. According to the French writer and philosopher Jean-Paul Sartre, freedom of choice is a fundamental aspect of our existence (Sartre, 1956). As Sartre stated, "I am my choices." While Freudian theory proposed that we have little choice, and behaviorists argue that we are shaped by environmental forces, existentialists place all responsibility on the person. According to these theorists, we have real choices, even in the face of death. Joseph Steiner (1967), in his account of the German death camp Treblinka, described one such choice—the choice by a camp inmate whether to be killed or to kill himself. After one person hanged himself, other choices appeared: attempting to break out, to confront death as a meaningful choice, or to give meaning to one's existence with a sense of future and transcendence. As Frankl said, "To live is to suffer; to survive is to find meaning in the suffering" (1963, p. 6). For many people the idea that what we make of our life is our own choice is frightening or unacceptable. Moreover, having choices does not guarantee that we make the right ones.

Personality Development. Personality development in existential theory is best understood as a series of confrontations between psychological, social, and biological needs and the environment that frustrates these needs (Maddi, 1970). Like Rogers and Maslow, existential theorists offer no theory of how the personality develops; all they say is that healthy maturation leads to authenticity. The authentic individual takes risks beyond his or her typical life style and accepts the responsibility for what happens. The search for authenticity in modern society is reflected in part by the growing number of people who find themselves dissatisfied with their lives and seek psychotherapy to help find meaning and direction.

Since finding meaning in our existence is a major human motivation, inability to do so creates feelings of nothingness. For existential theorists nothingness is a psychological state characterized by feeling empty and unreceptive. The ultimate form of nothingness is death, the inescapable fate of all of us. The vision of nothingness creates existential anxiety and guilt when the person finds himself or herself aimlessly searching for goals.

If we were to apply humanistic-existential theory to Jay's behavior, we would focus on her need for unconditional positive regard, her attempts to become a fully functioning person, and her search for the meaning of her life.

For a comparison of the major personality theories, see Table 10–7.

Feelings of boredom and emptiness characterize existential crisis. *(© Joel Gordon)*

OTHER CONTEMPORARY APPROACHES TO PERSONALITY

In contrast to the global theories presented thus far, the theories in this section may be described as limited-domain theories. They are typically more experimental and less clinical.

Reality Theory

Reality theory (Glasser, 1965) represents a relatively simple conceptualization of personality that shows little concern with an individual's past. A practical theory, it focuses on the present and is designed to help a person achieve precisely formulated goals. Although exploring a person's past may help explain how the individual came to be what he or she is now, this knowledge does not necessarily explain present behavior. Glasser argues that present behavior can be explained from a "here and now perspective" (Glasser, 1975).

Involvement. Glasser proposed that basic to all of us is the need for involvement. We must become involved with ourselves as well as with those such as friends, relatives, or therapists who are trying to help. In reality therapy the ability of the therapist to get involved with the client forms the basis of the therapeutic relationship. Reality theory focuses on current behavior, which is examined matter-of-factly. One way we avoid facing our present actions is by shifting our attention from what we are doing to how we are feeling. According to reality theory, the logical progression is not "When I feel better, I do better" but rather "When I do better, I feel better." Reality therapists do not deny the importance of emotions but are convinced that by concentrating on behavior they can best help their clients.

Evaluating Behavior. Once our attention is called to our present behavior, we must evaluate it critically. If we evaluate our behavior as incompetent or if we are hurting ourselves and others, we have established reasons for change. We must then take charge of our life and accept the responsibility to plan responsible behavior. Glasser believed that one of the major shortcomings in the lives of so many of us is our inability to come up

Table 10–7. Comparison of the Major Personality Theories

Emphasis	Freud	Jung	Adler	Rogers	Existentialists	Skinner
Purpose	H	H	H	H	H	L
Unconscious determinants	H	H	M	L	L	L
Reward	H	M	L	L	L	H
Learning process	M	L	L	L	L	H
Personality structure	H	H	M	L	L	L
Early developmental experience	H	M	H	L	L	M
Uniqueness	M	M	H	M	H	L
Psychological environment	H	H	M	H	H	L
Self-concept	H	H	H	H	M	L
Biology	H	H	M	L	M	L
Ideal personality	H	H	H	H	H	L

Key: H-high (emphasized); M-moderate; L-low (deemphasized).
Source: Adapted from Hall and Lindzey (1978).

with realistic plans for responsible, competent behavior.

Once we have decided on a realistic and responsible path of action, we need a total **commitment,** a single-minded determination to carry out the plan. This means following it through step by step and disallowing any excuses that would justify any deviations from the plan.

Glasser reasoned that by examining the past, we tend to emphasize our past failures, thereby developing a self-concept that he called a failure identity. In reality theory, psychological health is attained when we change our self-concept from a failure to a success orientation.

Gestalt Theory

Gestalt theory was founded by Frederick (Fritz) Perls (1969), whose provocative and inspiring personality attracted many people. A Gestalt is an organized pattern or structure that exists in its totality. Somewhat akin to existential theory, Gestalt theory emphasizes awareness and the need to change.

According to Kempler (1973), whose account we shall follow, Gestalt theory suggests that the evolving personality passes through a social, a psychophysical, and a spiritual stage. All three phases exist as potentials from birth on and are conceived as sequential stages of development. The **social phase** begins shortly after birth and is characterized by an awareness of others, mainly the parents. The second stage, the **psychophysical phase,** is the one in which most people spend their lives. In this phase a person has dimensions of awareness: an awareness of the self and an awareness of the social environment.

In the final stage, the **spiritual phase,** which encompasses both the social and the psychophysical phase, awareness goes beyond physical and material awareness of the self and others. Although most people never reach the third stage, they are intuitively aware of it. Devotion to religious beliefs or use of the mind-altering powers of drugs can establish a sense of continuity between the self and the universe at large. While Gestalt theory does not explain how we move from stage to stage, it assumes that we have the potential for reaching increasingly higher levels of personality integration.

Like many other theories, Gestalt theory has been mainly utilized in psychotherapy. Overall, the goal of Gestalt therapy is to create experiences for the client that increase the range of awareness and thereby facilitate progression through the phases. The therapist may, for example, help the client to enact different roles or parts of himself or herself. Thus, when there is conflict between the "top dog" (the superego) and the underdog (the depreciated self), the client has to act out each portion in turn, presenting the top dog's and then the underdog's viewpoint.

Transactional Analysis

Transactional analysis (TA) was introduced by Eric Berne (1963, 1964) and popularized by Thomas Harris (1969). TA became popular rapidly for a variety of reasons. The vocabulary is clear and precise, free of the ambiguous terms so often found in personality theories. The conceptualization of human relationships is also straightforward, stressing basic human needs directly related to types of everyday observable behaviors.

As described by TA theory the personality has three primary components; the Parent, Child, and Adult (P-A-C). This partition of the self is similar to Freud's scheme in that Parent = superego, Child = id, and Adult = ego. According to Berne, at any given time each person operates in one ego state, which he defined as a coherent system of feelings with its related set of behavior patterns (1963, p. 241). **Structural analysis** is the process of identifying and clarifying the ego state involved in a given situation.

The Parent is the "taught" concept of personality containing the values, attitudes, and behavior incorporated from external sources, primarily parents and authority figures (James & Jongeward, 1973). The Child is the "felt" concept, which recapitulates the feelings and attitudes experienced up to age 6. The Adult is the "thought" concept, which deals with facts and is devoid of feelings. The Adult acts in much the same way as a computer, gathering information, storing it in memory banks, and arriving at decisions and evaluations. In a healthy personality the P-A-C components are well developed and balanced, and the person is able to operate in the Child, Adult, or Parent state appropriate to the situation.

Scripts in TA language represent our fundamental attitudes toward ourself and others and reflect our individual way of operating. According to Harris (1969), there are four scripts representing four existential positions.

I'm OK, You're OK is the position of psychological health that makes the person outgoing and friendly. I'm OK, You're Not OK is the script of the person who feels everyone else is inferior and looks for things to criticize and make fun of. I'm Not OK, You're OK is the position of the person who tends to be self-depreciating and finds it difficult to accept compliments. Finally, I'm Not OK, You're Not OK is the script of hopelessness and futility.

TA is an appealing approach to personality because it provides us with a clear-cut picture of where we stand in relation to our attitudes toward ourselves and others. The goal of personality development is to turn each of us into an OK person who deals with situations at the appropriate level. For example, a man's Adult may be contaminated by the Child, resulting in self-indulgent behavior that the man engaged in as a boy. Through TA the man would learn to suppress the Child in his behavior when Adult-Adult transactions are required.

Direct-Decision Theory

Harold Greenwald's direct-decision theory (1975) assumes that our behavior is determined by the anticipated payoffs of our actions. However, we are likely to operate according to a well-established modus operandi that is not always appropriate. Moreover, many of us have a narrow vision and see only a few of the many possibilities for action. According to Greenwald, most of us are simply afraid to try something new.

Greenwald views our daily life as a process of constant decision making. Some of the decisions are trivial: when to get up, what to wear, what to eat; others are more crucial: whom to marry or what position to accept. Since our judgment is imperfect, we are prone to make poor decisions even under the best circumstances. We may say the wrong thing at the wrong time or select the wrong mate and thus become one of life's losers.

Greenwald believes that people become losers because they make a basic mistake at a turning point in their life, "going off the track" by finding an inferior solution. This crucial error predisposes them to repeat the same mistake; having gone in the wrong direction, they keep going that way. As a result, they move farther and farther away from their goals.

Making poor decisions, telling lies, or avoiding problems "work" in the sense that we do not have to face a painful confrontation or feel overwhelmed. Such circumventions exact a high price, however; we learn a useless strategy that we are likely to fall back on in similar situations. Thus we get enmeshed in our mistakes and life becomes increasingly twisted. The only way out is to discover our original mistake and try to rectify it.

To become winners, we must constantly weigh the advantages and disadvantages of each decision we make. This implies that we must operate from a cognitive rather than an emotional framework. Since we often think incorrectly, we also often act incorrectly and consequently feel bad. In direct-decision therapy the therapist helps the client to see his or her generalized errors and find new solutions to the problem.

Direct-decision theory represents an attempt to bring together elements from various contemporary theories. It is similar to reality theory and TA in that it is oriented toward the present and emphasizes cognitive processes and problem solving. It is also a school of psychotherapy.

FUTURE TRENDS IN THE STUDY OF PERSONALITY

Research in personality is plagued by many problems: problems of semantics, inadequate methodologies, opaqueness of concepts. Carlson (1971) noted:

> We cannot study the organization of personality because we know at most only one or two facts. We cannot study the stability of personality nor its development over epochs of life because we see our subjects for an hour. We cannot study the problems or capacities of the mature individual because we study late adolescents [i.e., college students] (p. 207).

In spite of these limitations, explorations in the field of personality continue to flourish, and psychologists have begun to conduct longitudinal studies on various aspects of personality.

What can we infer from the theories of personality discussed in this chapter? One implication is obvious: none of the theories are identical, yet all make similar assertions about the nature of personality. Comparing the various perspectives, we find that there are more agreements than disagreements. For example, most of them assume that learning processes influence personality and that personality is modifiable.

Looking forward we notice that computer simulations are looming large in the study of personality. The application of computer technology to human behavior opens a new range of possibilities. For example, the computer is a useful device for testing theories of personality. Some theorists (e.g., Simon, 1969) see computer programs and simulation of human behavior as the theoretical path of the future.

Psychobiological and biochemical advances also offer new ways of studying personality. The extensive investigations of genetic and hormonal determinants of personality over the past decades have broadened our understanding of how biological factors influence, and are influenced by, behavior. Freud's biological determinism is in dire need of updating. In the future we can expect that biology will make different contributions to personality than in the past.

Changes in our social structure and values are also likely to be integrated in future personality theories. Changing sex roles of women, for instance, have led to the development of a new personality type, the androgynous individual. Similarly, Carl Rogers's homo novus may reflect goals and strivings of men and women specific to our era.

And finally, there are theorists who wish to see a synthesis of existing personality theories into a global theory that is truly comprehensive and acceptable. At this time, however, it is debatable whether such a general theory would serve a meaningful purpose. Many theories, as we have seen, are characterized by imprecise concepts. There are also a considerable number of points where theories are in flat disagreement. As Hall and Lindzey (1978) asked, "When so little is known with certainty why place all of the future's hopes in one theoretical basket?" (p. 704). Instead of developing more new mini-theories or concentrating on the synthesis of a single global theory, personality theorists would profit more from a refinement of their methodologies and a broadening of their empirical findings.

Summary

The study of personality encompasses many dimensions, including traits, character, motivation, attitudes, and cognitive styles. Freud's psychoanalytic model, including his theorizing about instincts, psychosexual development, and the structure of the mind, is one of the intellectual landmarks of our century. Freud's ideas regarding the unconscious and psychic determinism have changed not only how professionals deal with their clients but also how all of us have come to understand human behavior. Jung enlarged the Freudian framework by reading deeper into the mind and stressing the importance of spiritual-religious experiences. Jung's account of personality draws from many different disciplines to arrive at a highly complex picture of the individual. Adler, although in an entirely different manner, also enlarged orthodox psychoanalysis. He believed that social interest and striving for perfection are innate tendencies, as innate as Freud's id impulses and Jung's archetypes. In contrast to the pessimism of Freud, Adler takes the optimistic view that people are able to produce a healthy society. Contemporary variations of psychoanalytic theory, known collectively as ego psychology, have deemphasized unconscious and sexual determinants of behavior and concentrate on the adaptive responses of the rational, conscious ego.

Learning theorists take the stand that most human behavior is shaped by external forces. Greatly expanding early behavioral principles, Skinner built a theory of personality based on operant conditioning. Although Skinner's theory is a product of laboratory experimentation, it has been widely applied to people of all ages in many diverse settings. Social-learning theory combines operant and classical conditioning with internal states such as cognition that mediate the overt behavior of the individual. One of the most powerful concepts in social-learning theory, observational learning, incorporates personal, situational, and cognitive factors.

The humanistic-existential theorists share a concern with individual expressions of growth potential, self-direction, self-fulfillment, and a meaningful existence. Both Rogers and Maslow recognize the self-actualizing tendency as a fundamental need in all people. In contrast to humanistic psychology, existential theories are less optimistic.

Over the last two decades a number of minitheories have been proposed. Some of them are concerned only with a particular domain of behavior, such as interpersonal interactions or decision making (direct-decision theory). Others, such as reality theory or transactional analysis, represent an approach that is direct, pragmatic, clad in everyday language, and consequently popular with professional and laypeople alike. Students often ask, "But which one of all these theories is the best?" The best answer probably is, "The one (or the combination) that applies and appeals to you most, or the one that works for you."

Key Terms For Review

adjustment definition
archetypes
arrangement definition
assumptions
behavioral potential
castration anxiety
character
collective unconscious
commitment
compensation
complex
defense mechanism
denial
distinctiveness definition
dream analysis
ego
ego psychology
Electra complex
empirical definition
erogenous zones
eros
expectancy
extraversion
fixation
free association
fully functioning self
generalized and conditioned reinforcers
hierarchical definition
id
inferiority-superiority concept
introversion
libido
metaneeds
metapathology
moral anxiety
motivation
neurotic anxiety
observational learning
Oedipal complex
omnibus definition
organism
penis envy
persona
personal unconscious
phenomenal field
pleasure principle
preconscious
projection
psychological situation
psychophysical phase
rationalization
reaction formation
reality anxiety
reality principle
reality theory
regression
reinforcement value
repression
self
self-actualizing person
shadow
social interest
social phase
spiritual phase
structural analysis
style of life
sublimation
superego
temperament
thanatos
trait
transactional analysis (TA)
unconditional positive regard
Zeitgeist

Suggested Readings

Chiang, H., & Maslow, A. *The healthy personality.* New York: D. van Nostrand, 1977.

A collection of articles from humanistic psychology that focus on the concept of psychological health.

Eysenck, H., & Wilson, G. *Know your own personality.* New York: Penguin, 1978.

This book was written to help readers see themselves as others see them. The authors present scales measuring various aspects of personality, including extroversion-introversion, emotional instability-adjustment, sense of humor, and social attitudes, and suggest interpretations for the profiles derived from the scales.

Frankl, V. *Man's search for meaning.* New York: Pocket Books, 1963.

Victor Frankl's personal account of his three years in Nazi concentration camps, which ultimately resulted in Dr. Frankl's own version of existential analysis.

Freud, S. *The complete psychological works of Sigmund Freud: Standard Edition.* London: Hogarth Press, 1952–1974.

This comprehensive collection of all Freud's psychological papers, lectures, books, and monographs delineates the development of Freud's ideas and concepts leading to the construction of psychoanalysis as a system of psychotherapy.

Pervin, L. *Current controversies: Issues in personality.* New York: Wiley, 1978.

This book looks at a number of current issues in personality research, including internal and external determinants of aggression, altruism and prosocial behavior, self-concept and ethics of personality research, from a variety of theoretical positions. The author demonstrates how such issues become controversial when seen in a broader social context.

11

Psychological Assessment

Kevin was a junior in college and he felt rather lost. He believed it was important to finish college and get his degree, but he was not very interested in his course work and had difficulty forcing himself to study. His ambivalence was reflected by his changing his major several times, from chemistry to engineering to accounting and back to chemistry. He also felt somewhat lonely and isolated. Although he lived in the college dorm, he had few acquaintances and no close friends. He could count on one hand the number of dates he had had since beginning college.

The past semester he had taken introductory psychology. The chapter in his textbook covering abnormal psychology depressed him. After reading it he was convinced he had several different psychological disorders. The chapter on psychological assessment, however, gave him hope. It made him believe that it would be possible to find out precisely what his problem was. Resolved to take a battery of intellectual, aptitude, and personality tests, Kevin made an appointment at the college counseling center.

He was somewhat disappointed after his first interview. His counselor was unwilling to give him any tests that day but wanted to talk with Kevin about his situation. At the end of the interview, the counselor told Kevin that an intelligence test and a vocational aptitude test might indeed be helpful. She believed, however, that she had learned enough about Kevin to make personality testing unnecessary.

After Kevin took the tests, he met with his counselor to talk over the results. She told him that he was in the superior range of intelligence and that he had the ability to get mostly A's and B's in his course work. The results of the vocational aptitude test surprised Kevin. They indicated that his interests were in the liberal arts rather than in the sciences. In discussing this contradiction between his interests and his variety of majors with his counselor, Kevin came to realize that he was majoring in the sciences to please his father. Kevin's father had impressed on him the importance of acquiring practical and marketable skills in college, and Kevin had attempted to do this even though the courses held little interest for him.

The counselor also discussed with Kevin her assessment of his interpersonal difficulties, namely his feelings of isolation and loneliness. She recommended that they meet occasionally for a few months to work on developing his social skills. Kevin agreed, and after a few sessions he found himself interacting with others more and feeling better about himself. He also changed his major to English and became more involved with his courses than he had been previously. By the end of the semester Kevin still had a few problems to work on, but he felt more optimistic about the future than he had in some time.

Psychological assessment was one of psychology's first contributions to human welfare. Historians disagree as to the origins of this specialty, but one account credits an astronomer with making the observations that provided the groundwork for psychological testing (Boring, 1950). In the late 1700s the German astronomer Maskelyne was timing stellar transits with a technique known as the eye-ear method. To do this, a star would be observed through a telescope with parallel cross-wires, and the time it took the star to cross the wires was measured to the nearest one-tenth of a second. Maskelyne had an assistant named Kinnebrook, whose observations consistently lagged about one-half second behind his. Maskelyne attributed this to laziness or sloppiness and consequently fired his assistant. Some 25 years later, another astronomer named Bessel reviewed this incident and concluded that it reflected a stable individual difference in perception and reaction time. Bessel developed a formula that allowed all astronomers to check their transit-tracking lag times against a standard and then subtract out any individual error.

This incident was important because the early psychologists were primarily interested in developing general principles of behavior that would be applicable to everyone. They tended to view individual differences as a source of error and paid little attention to them. Bessel's formula was evidence that stable individual differences did exist and that it was possible to measure them. Late in the 1800s several psychologists became interested in measuring individual differences in intelligence. By World War I these efforts were becoming increasingly sophisticated, and the practice of psychological assessment became firmly established. As we shall see in this chapter, assessment has become one of the most potentially helpful as well as one of the most controversial applications of psychology.

THE NATURE OF PSYCHOLOGICAL TESTS

The basic purpose of psychological tests is to measure differences between individuals or between types of behavior of the same individual on separate occasions. To do this effectively, a psychological test must have certain characteristics. Articles in popular magazines or newspapers that contain questions to measure one's ability as a lover, spouse, or parent are ordinarily not tests at all because they usually do not meet the necessary technical standards. A test that has been carefully developed, however, can be useful in a variety of situations.

The Uses of Psychological Tests

Psychological tests can be useful any time decisions have to be made about people. In the case history that opened this chapter, both Kevin and his counselor probably had several decisions to weigh. Should Kevin continue with college? If so, should he change his major? Because of his own concerns, might counseling be called for? In Kevin's case, the assessment procedure, including both the formal psychological testing and the less structured evaluations made by the counselor, provided useful information to help them make these decisions.

You can probably think of dozens of additional examples of when a test would be helpful in making a decision. Should company X hire Mr. Smith or Mr. Jones? Should an employee be transferred to the production or the sales department? Should student X be admitted to college? What grade should student Y receive in her English class? Should Mrs. Smith have psychotherapy? What type of therapy would be best for her? The list could go on indefinitely.

A related use of psychological tests is to evaluate programs. For example, schools routinely administer achievement tests to students. One reason for doing so is to obtain some idea about the effectiveness of the schools' programs. If students in a particular school receive scores that are considerably below the average for similar schools, then the school program is probably not as effective as it might be. Similarly, a mental-health clinic may evaluate its programs by testing clients and making relevant comparisons. Even when the goal of testing is the evaluation of school programs, the tests are still measuring differences between individuals.

One other important example of the use of tests concerns research. Psychologists interested in a variety of topics use psychological tests to provide objective information about human behavior. The study of personality, human development, cross-cultural differences, biological bases of behavior, and even topics as esoteric as the effects of lighting on work performance are all made possible by the use of well-constructed psychological tests. Psychological tests are not only a product of psychological knowledge but also a vehicle for acquiring new knowledge.

Characteristics of Psychological Tests

A widely accepted definition of a psychological test is provided by Anastasi (1976): "A psychological test is essentially an objective and standardized measure of a sample of behavior (p. 23)." There are several key terms in this definition.

The first important term is **sample.** Every time a person takes a test, the psychologist is collecting a sample of his or her behavior in much the same way that a physician takes a sample of a patient's blood. The psychologist is not interested in the specific sample of behavior elicited by the test but in how well the sample corresponds to some other real-life behavior. For example, on an IQ test the psychologist is not concerned with whether the examinee can define specific words or arrange blocks in a particular design. These types of behavior are only of interest insofar as they relate to other types of behavior, such as success in school.

The sample of behavior measured by the test may vary in terms of its similarity to the real-life behavior of interest. An aptitude test used to select workers for an assembly line in an electronics plant may contain tasks that are virtually identical to the tasks required on the job. By contrast, a person who is being considered for psychotherapy may be asked to say what he or she sees in a series of inkblots. There is, of course, no obvious similarity between seeing various objects in an

All psychological tests should be administered in standardized settings to avoid introducing unwanted variables. (© *Cary Wolinsky/Stock, Boston, Inc.*)

inkblot and responding well to psychotherapy. But in both cases, the psychologist is interested in the tested sample of behavior because it has been found to correspond to other important types of behavior. For example, some psychologists believe that people who see mostly animal figures in an inkblot test have difficulties in their interpersonal relations.

Because tests are generally used to compare individuals, they must be **standardized.** One aspect of standardization requires that all persons who take the test should do it under as nearly identical conditions as possible. Numerous studies have found that relatively subtle differences in test administration can affect test scores, so the psychologist will take care that such differences are kept to a minimum. Identical testing materials will be used for all examinees. Each person will have a comfortable chair in reasonably comfortable surroundings. The directions will always be followed precisely for everyone taking the test. The psychologist will attempt to develop a uniform way of interacting with those taking the test, and he or she will attempt to respond to questions about the testing procedures in a uniform manner. In other words, an individual's test score should not be dependent on the conditions under which the test was taken.

A second aspect of standardization is the development of test norms. **Norms** are scores that are based on the performance of a standardized group of people, and they give raw test scores meaning. For instance, if we are told that an individual answered 65 items on an intelligence test correctly, we really have not learned anything about that person. If we are told that this individual received an IQ score of 110—one type of normative score—we immediately know that the individual is of slightly above-average intelligence. Norms allows us to make interpretations about the relative performance of individuals who take a given test.

Two additional characteristics that all psychological tests must have are **reliability** and **validity.** The reliability of a test refers to its consistency of scores when an individual is retested with the identical test or an equivalent form of the test. If a person received a Scholastic Aptitude Test (SAT) score of 400 and a week later, upon retaking the test, received a score of 600, one would have little confidence in either score. But if the same individual received SAT scores of 590 and 600, this would be evidence that the test was highly reliable. When psychologists establish the reliability of a test, they must ensure that the interval between the two testings is not so long that actual changes in the examinee could occur. For instance, if a student received an SAT score of 500 and a year later received a score of 600, it may mean that he or she studied hard and learned a lot rather than that the test is unreliable. The time interval usually ranges from one to four weeks when establishing reliability.

Validity of a test refers to how well it measures what it is supposed to be measuring. The validity of a test can be established in several ways. One is to measure the degree of association between a set of test scores and a set of criterion scores. To illustrate, suppose a psychologist were interested in the validity of a new aptitude test in terms of predicting success in college. To validate the test, the psychologist might administer it to a group of high school seniors. After these students had completed their first year of college, the degree of association between their college grade-point average, which would be the criterion scores, and their test scores would be computed. If there was a high degree of association, the test would have validity. The test could then be used to predict the college performance of graduating high school students.

Standardization, reliability, and validity are three characteristics that all useful tests must possess. But not every test that meets these three criteria will be useful in every situation. The psychologist must evaluate each situation carefully and select the test that is most appropriate. To use psychological tests effectively, the psychologist must possess considerable knowledge and expertise.

INTELLIGENCE TESTS

For many people, the term "psychological test" means an intelligence test. This is not surprising, since tests of intelligence are among the most widely used psychological tests. Rare indeed is the individual who has not taken such a test at some point in life. Until a few years ago, schoolchildren across the country were routinely given intelligence tests.

Intelligence is a hypothetical construct, and not all psychologists are in agreement about its nature. Intelligence tests typically sample a variety of cognitive abilities, such as verbal reasoning and arithmetic skills, and there is some controversy about what these abilities reflect. Because many intelligence tests have been validated by demonstrating the ability of those who do well on them to succeed in school, some theorists have argued that intelligence tests measure nothing more than the ability to profit from formal education. Others point to cases in which individuals who receive high scores on intelligence tests do poorly in school, arguing that these tests are measuring something more. Regardless of what it is that intelligence tests are sampling, they are useful in a variety of situations. Let us examine two widely used tests of intelligence.

Stanford-Binet Intelligence Scale

The first test of intelligence with any degree of validity was developed by the French psychologist Alfred Binet in 1905. He developed a scale containing 30 problems that would identify mentally retarded children. Binet's problems emphasized judgment, comprehension, and reasoning. This was an important development, because for the previous two decades psychologists trying to construct such tests believed that intelligence should be measured by physical characteristics such as reaction time and perceptual acuity. These attempts did not meet with success, while Binet's scale was effective.

An American psychologist, Lewis Terman, was impressed with Binet's work. Using Binet's test as a framework, he conducted extensive revisions that resulted in virtually a new test. This test, published in 1916, was called the Stanford-Binet, reflecting the fact that Terman did his work at Stanford University. It was subsequently revised in 1937 and 1960 and restandardized in 1972. The test can be used with children between the ages of 2 and 18, although its validity for children beyond the age of 13 becomes questionable since it was developed primarily for younger children (Kennedy et al., 1960).

The test contains a large number of items that are grouped into age levels according to the average performance of the corresponding group of children. Thus a good item for 6-year-olds is one that 50 percent of all 6-year-olds can answer correctly; a good item for 8-year-olds is one that 50 percent of all 8-year-olds can answer correctly; and so on.

When administering the test, the psychologist must first find the child's **mental age.** This is done by first finding the highest age group of items of which the child can answer all of the items cor-

Table 11–1. Classifications of Intelligence-Test Scores

IQ	*Classification*	*Percent Included—Theoretical Normal Curve*	*Percent Included—Actual Sample*[a]
130+	Very Superior	2.2	2.6
120–129	Superior	6.7	6.9
110–119	High Average[b]	16.1	16.6
90–109	Average	50.0	49.1
80–89	Low Average[b]	16.1	16.1
70–79	Borderline	6.7	6.4
69–	Mentally Retarded[b]	2.2	2.3

[a] The percents shown are for Full Scale IQ, and are based on the total standardization sample (N = 1,880). The percents obtained for Verbal IQ and Performance IQ are essentially the same.
[b] The terms *High Average, Low Average,* and *Mentally Retarded* correspond to the terms *Bright Normal, Dull Normal,* and *Mental Defective*, respectively, used in the 1955 *WAIS Manual.*
Source: Wechsler (1981).

rectly. This level is referred to as the child's **basal age.** The psychologist then proceeds to administer groups of items until the child answers all the items within a particular group incorrectly. This is the child's **ceiling age.** By adding together all the correct responses, the mental age can be calculated. For example, if a 7-year-old child can answer all the items for 6-year-olds (the basal age), half of those for 7- and 8-year-olds, and none of those for 9-year-olds (the ceiling age), the mental age would be 7 ($6 + \frac{1}{2} + \frac{1}{2}$).

In the first two editions of the Stanford-Binet, the total test score was obtained by dividing the mental age (MA) by the chronological age (CA) and multiplying by 100. The resulting formula, $\frac{MA}{CA} \times 100$, resulted in an intelligence quotient, or IQ. More recent editions use norms by comparing an individual's mental age and chronological age with the large representative sample of children who initially took the test. So modern intelligence test scores are not really quotients, but through common usage the term "IQ" has been retained. Table 11–1 classifies IQ scores.

The content of the Stanford-Binet varies as one moves from the items intended for younger children to those intended for older children. Children two and three years of age are given tasks that emphasize eye-hand coordination, perceptual discrimination, the ability to follow directions, and the recognition of common objects. For older children the tasks emphasize verbal content, such as vocabulary, analogies, and the interpretation of proverbs. This difference in test content has been offered as one possible explanation for why a child's IQ score at age two has only a moderate relation to his or her IQ at age eight or nine (Anastasi, 1976). Examples of test items are shown in Table 11–2.

Wechsler Adult Intelligence Scale

In response to the need for an individual test of intelligence for adults, Dr. David Wechsler of Bellevue Psychiatric Hospital published the Wechsler Adult Intelligence Scale (WAIS) in 1955. It has become the most widely used intelligence test for individuals aged 16 and older. There is also a Wechsler test for children that is very similar in format, called the Wechsler Intelligence Scale for Children (WISC). The most recent version of this test was published in 1974 (WISC-R).

Table 11–2. Representative Test Items on the Stanford-Binet

Age Level	*Description of Item*
2	Building a tower four blocks high.
3	Identifying pictures of ten common objects (e.g., hat, ball).
5	Defining simple words (e.g., hat, stove).
7	Describing similarities between two objects (e.g., wood and coal).
10	Repeating a sequence of six digits.
14	Describing similarities between two concepts (e.g., winter and summer).

Unlike the single IQ score provided by the Stanford-Binet, the WAIS can provide scores for 11 different intellectual abilities. These separate subtest scores, which fall under two general categories called verbal intelligence and performance intelligence, may be useful in identifying an individual's particular strengths and weaknesses. hence the WAIS may be used to diagnose abilities as well as to provide an overall IQ score. The 11 subtests are given in Table 11–3.

Because intellectual development begins to level off during adolescence, the concept of mental age is inapplicable to adults. An individual's mental capacity does not change between the ages of 20 and 25 the same way that it did between the ages of 5 and 10. Because of this relative stability in adults, the use of the formula $\frac{\text{MA}}{\text{CA}} \times 100$ would suggest that people are deteriorating intellectually as they grow older. Because of this problem with the concept of mental age, Wechsler devised the "deviation IQ," a type of norm based on the mean and standard deviation (see Chapter 20) of the standardization group. The standard deviation of IQ scores on the WAIS is 15 and the mean is 100. So a person who obtains an IQ of 115 is one standard deviation above average. This score would be higher than about 84 percent of all those taking the test.

Table 11–3. Subtests on Wechsler Adult Intelligence Scale

Verbal	*Performance*
Information	Digit symbol
Comprehension	Picture completion
Arithmetic	Block design
Similarities	Picture arrangement
Digit span	Object assembly
Vocabulary	

The Nature of Intelligence

Recall the opening anecdote about Kevin. He was given an intelligence test—the WAIS, say—and was told that his score indicated that he was in the superior range of intelligence. What does this mean to Kevin? Does it mean he will be adept at learning anything he tries—such as chemistry, English, or even playing the piano? Or does his overall score reflect an average of his abilities on the various subtests on the WAIS? In other words, perhaps he did especially well on subtests such as vocabulary and not so well on items measuring mathematical ability. If this is the case, perhaps the single IQ score is an average that blurs one's strengths and weaknesses and hence is of limited value. In short, what is the nature of intelligence?

Psychologists do not completely agree on what intelligence is or how it should be defined. Is intelligence a single, general type of ability? Or is it a collection of relatively distinct abilities? Considerable research has been devoted to answering such questions, but the use of different research methods and statistical techniques has produced results that are often inconsistent.

One theory, developed by the British psychologist Charles Spearman (1927), suggests that a single factor, known as a general or "g" factor, is related to all intellectual abilities. Spearman argues that intelligence is a single or unitary characteristic. Other theorists, such as the American psychologist L. L. Thurstone (1938), have proposed that intelligence is comprised of about a dozen distinct or primary abilities. This view suggests that it is misleading to speak of a single intelligence; there are in fact several different types of intelligence.

It must be remembered that terms such as intelligence, verbal ability, and mathematical aptitude are descriptive terms. They are used by psychologists as labels to summarize their observations of people and may say nothing about the true underlying nature of intelligence. Thus the way in which intelligence is conceptualized may very well depend on the kinds of people that have been observed. To illustrate, consider two individuals with disparate interests. Suppose John is very interested in engineering and devoted his educational years to this subject. He is likely to have highly developed skills in math and spatial

CRITICAL ISSUE

Intelligence and the Nature-Nurture Controversy

One of the most controversial issues regarding the nature of intelligence is the extent to which its development is influenced by hereditary and environmental factors. Before World War II the prevailing view was that intelligence was largely determined by genetic factors; in fact at that time most definitions of intelligence referred to it as an "inherited capacity." Since then many researchers have attempted to establish the relative contributions of genetics and environment to intellectual development. This can be done in many ways, but one common method is to compare the similarity of IQ's of identical twins with that of fraternal twins. Because identical twins are genetically identical, these comparisons can be used to estimate the relative contributions of genetics and the environment. These studies found that identical twins are more likely to have similar IQs. The studies generally report that genetics is responsible for 70 to 80 percent of the variability associated with IQ scores in twins, while the environment accounts for 20 to 30 percent of the variability in scores. These figures reflect the heritability of intelligence.

This controversy acquired a new urgency in 1969 when educational psychologist Arthur Jensen published an article entitled "How Much Can We Boost IQ and Scholastic Achievement?" Although it was not the major thesis of his article, Jensen did argue that at least part of the black-white difference in IQs that has been found in numerous studies is caused by genetics. Jensen's arguments rested on the assertion that the heritability of intelligence is approximately .80—which means that genetic factors are about four times as important as environmental factors in determining intelligence. His article touched off a flurry of rebuttals and research that attempted to show that the difference in IQ between blacks and whites is caused not by genetics but by the impoverished conditions under which many blacks in the United States have lived for several generations.

There are two problems with estimates of the relative contributions of nature and nurture. First, they apply only to the sample from which they were derived. Thus while it may be accurate to say that heredity accounts for 70 to 80 percent of the variability in IQ scores for a sample of white, middle-class people, we still know nothing about groups that have had different kinds of experiences. Unfortunately for science (but fortunately for potential human subjects) it is not possible to conduct the type of research that would be needed to provide conclusive answers (see Chapter 20). The available research does suggest, however, that groups from lower socioeconomic backgrounds do have lower heritability of intelligence than middle-class individuals (Scarr-Salapatek, 1971).

Second, heritability of intelligence says nothing about modifiability. To use an absurd example, suppose a man and a woman with IQs of 150 have a child. We know from past research that this child, reared under normal conditions, can be expected to have a very high IQ as well. But suppose this child was given absolutely no stimulation during the first five years of life. The child was never spoken to, allowed to hear noises, or allowed to see and manipulate objects. At the time of the fifth birthday, this child would probably attain a score of near zero on an intelligence test. Even if the heritability of intelligence is high, it is quite possible that environmental factors can have a major impact on test scores.

The issue of nature-nurture and ethnic-group differences in intelligence is far from resolved. Shortly after the turn of the century, Jews who were immigrating to the United States were thought to be intellectually inferior. During processing at Ellis Island, immigrants were given intelligence tests, and the pattern of deficits exhibited by Jews was remarkably similar to the pattern of deficits exhibited by blacks today. No one today, of course, would argue that Jews are intellectually inferior. It is equally plausible that in the future, after blacks and whites have lived under similar conditions and had equal opportunities for several generations, the difference in their IQs will disappear. Perhaps then Jensen's controversial article will be of historical interest only.

relations, but he may have a limited vocabulary and little patience for anything the least bit abstract. Susan, in contrast, values a well-rounded education and took a variety of college courses. If these two individuals were administered the WAIS, it would be reasonable to predict that Susan would do equally well on all the subtests, while John would have an uneven performance. He might have exceptionally high scores on the arithmetic and block-design subtests but do poorly on the vocabulary, information, and comprehension subtests. If John's and Susan's types of intelligence were analyzed, Susan's intelligence might be described best by a "g" factor, and John's by several primary and distinct abilities. Thus the nature of intelligence seems to depend on the nature of one's experiences (Anastasi, 1976), and the search for the true nature of intelligence may be futile (see Chapter 7 for more information about intelligence).

This woman is being given a WAIS test. (© *Van Bucher / Photo Researchers, Inc.*)

PERSONALITY TESTS

Personality tests are intended to measure nonintellectual human characteristics, such as emotional adjustment, attitudes, motivations, and interpersonal relations. Kevin's counselor could have used personality tests to understand his loneliness and ambivalence toward college. While intelligence tests attempt to find out how well people are capable of performing in certain situations, personality tests are intended to discover how people typically behave in a given context.

Personality testing is of perhaps most importance to clinical psychologists, but research psychologists, educational psychologists, and industrial psychologists may all make use of these tests on occasion. In research settings, tests of personality are useful in helping psychologists to understand human behavior. In applied settings, these tests may be used as an aid to making decisions about people. Selecting clients for psychotherapy, teachers for positions working with exceptional children, or business executives for management positions may be facilitated by the careful use of personality tests.

Minnesota Multiphasic Personality Inventory

One of the most carefully constructed and well researched tests of personality is the Minnesota Multiphasic Personality Inventory (MMPI). There are well over 3,500 scientific articles in the literature concerning its use and effectiveness. Needless to say, with such a vast amount of available information, the effective use of the MMPI requires a great deal of expertise.

The MMPI was constructed in the late 1930s and early 1940s to serve as an aid in making psychiatric diagnoses (Hathaway & McKinley, 1967). It consists of 550 true-false items that can be scored for ten clinical and three validity scales. The clinical scales are described in Table 11–4.

When the MMPI was first developed, the emphasis was on interpretation of individual scales.

Current usage, however, emphasized interpretation of the profile. The profile is simply the line drawn to connect the scores on the individual scales. The peaks and slopes of the profile can be important diagnostic cues. For example, the first three scales, Hs, D, and Hy, are referred to as the **neurotic triad.** Elevated scores on all three of these scales may be more meaningful than an elevated score on any one particular scale. Various code books are available to aid in interpreting profiles (e.g., Marks, Seeman, & Haller, 1974).

The three validity scales, labeled the Lie (L), Validity (F), and Correction (K) scales, provide a means for monitoring carelessness, misunderstanding, and dishonesty in the examinee. Elevated scores on these scales may invalidate the clinical profile.

The MMPI is probably the best example of what is known as the empirical approach to test construction. In the development of the test, specific criterion groups were identified on the basis of extensive psychiatric evaluation. These consisted of groups of people who were selected because they possessed a certain characteristic, such as depression or schizophrenia. Their responses to the true-false items were then compared to those of a normative group—a group of people with no known psychological disorder. If there was a substantial difference between the criterion group and the normative group in the way they answered a particular item, then that item would be included on the relevant scale. For example, if 70 percent of a group of hypochondriacs said true to the item "I often feel dizzy," while only 30 percent of the normative group said true to the item, that item would be included on the hypochondriasis scale.

This approach to test construction may result in the inclusion of items that appear to bear little relation to the characteristic being measured. For example, one item on the hysteria scale asks if the examinee enjoys reading newspaper articles about crime. There is no apparent or theoretical reason why hysterics should answer this item differently from normal people, but nonetheless it does discriminate between the two groups. Items such as this illustrate the importance of collecting data to ensure the validity of a test. Simply because an item, or test, appears to bear a relation to the characteristic being measured is no assurance that it does.

A significant development in the past decade is the use of computers with the MMPI. A clinician can send an MMPI to one of several companies that will score and interpret the results. Interpretations vary from highly detailed ones, which

Table 11–4. MMPI Clinical Scales

1. Hypochondriasis (Hs). Extreme and persistent concerns about one's bodily health.
2. Depression (D). Poor morale, pessimism, feelings of hopelessness and sorrow.
3. Hysteria (Hy). Physical ailments that have no organic basis and feelings of sadness and lack of satisfaction.
4. Psychopathic deviation (Pd). Difficulty in forming satisfactory personal relationships and inability to anticipate consequences of one's behavior.
5. Masculinity-feminity (Mf). Traditional masculine and feminine interest patterns.
6. Paranoia (Pa). Feelings of sensitivity, suspiciousness, persecution, and grandiosity.
7. Psychasthenia (Pt). Vague anxieties, insecurity, self-doubt, phobias, and obsessive-compulsive reactions.
8. Schizophrenia (Sc). Emotional isolation and poor reality contact, sometimes accompanied by hallucinations.
9. Hypomania (Ma). Hyperactivity, restlessness, distractibility, and unrealistic optimism.
10. Social introversion (Si). Shyness and feelings of uneasiness in, and/or withdrawal from, social situations.

might be used by a therapist who plans intensive therapy with a client, to more general descriptive summaries that are useful as a screening device. There are dangers, however, in such impersonal approaches to personality description, and they can be misused. Because of the sophisticated technology associated with computerized interpretations, there can be a tendency to place more weight on the test results than is justified. The sophisticated clinical psychologist would view computerized test interpretations as just one source of data about the client that would have to be integrated with other types of data—such as that obtained in interviews.

The TAT involves creating stories based on carefully chosen pictures. (© *Sybil Shelton/Peter Arnold, Inc.*)

Projective Tests

In contrast to the MMPI, which is often referred to as a paper-and-pencil personality test, projective tests present the examinee with ambiguous stimuli. It is hypothesized that individuals will "project" their own needs, fantasies, and defenses onto the test materials. The two most widely used projective techniques are the Thematic Apperception Test (TAT) and the Rorschach Inkblot Technique.

Projective tests are most often used in clinical situations, and the client is administered the test individually. Projective tests are thought to provide a more global approach to personality. While structured personality tests such as the MMPI are used to measure specific traits, projective tests are believed to provide a picture of the entire personality. They are thought to measure unconscious fears and fantasies, defense mechanisms, and coping strategies. Anastasi (1976) has commented that a discrepancy exists between research and practice regarding projective tests. While the research data suggest that projective tests have serious deficiencies in their technical qualities, they continue to be widely used.

The TAT was developed by psychologists Henry Murray and Christina Morgan of the Harvard Psychological Clinic in the 1930s. It consists of four overlapping sets of 20 pictures that can be used with men, women, boys, and girls. The person taking the test is asked to make up a story about each picture. Each story is supposed to include a description of the events that led up to the scene pictured and how the situation was resolved.

Most clinical psychologists do not use a formal scoring system when evaluating the results of the TAT, but look for recurrent themes in the stories. For example, does the hero of the stories express any consistent needs, fears, or defenses? Does the hero have noteworthy problems in interacting with members of the opposite sex or persons of authority? If similar themes can be found in several of the stories, the clinician will suspect that the examinee has these as personal concerns. Consider the following story told in response to a card depicting a woman holding a man's arm as he is turning away:

> I think this is a couple that has been married for several years. They've been fighting and the husband said he's leaving and the wife is begging him to stay. [What have they been fighting about?] The wife accused him of not loving her. She thinks he

may be seeing other women. [How does the story end?] Well, . . . he tells her that he does love her, but she still feels insecure. . . . A few months later he does leave her for someone else.

This response was made by a 34-year-old woman who sought therapy to overcome her feelings of insecurity and inferiority. These feelings are clearly reflected in her story. The therapist also has learned something about how she deals with these feelings. Her story suggests that she may demand reassurance and declarations of love from those close to her.

The Rorschach Inkblot Technique was developed by the Swiss psychiatrist Hermann Rorschach in the 1920s. Drops of ink are placed on a piece of paper, which is then folded in half. The ink is spread out, creating a design that is bilaterally symmetrical. Rorschach experimented with a variety of designs before settling on the ten blots that make up the test. Figure 11–1 is similar to the blots used in the test. These stimuli are more ambiguous than the TAT cards and are generally believed to tap deeper levels of personality. While the TAT is believed to tap ego functions, such as conflicts and defenses, the Rorschach is thought, by some theorists, to detect unconscious motives and fantasies. Not all psychologists subscribe to this distinction between the two tests since there is little, if any, empirical evidence supporting it.

Figure 11–1. A Rorschach-type inkblot.

Examinees are asked to tell the psychologist what they see in the inkblots. They are free to turn the card sideways or upside down and are encouraged to give more than one response to each card. After this part of the test has been completed, examinees are asked to go through the cards again and explain their earlier responses in detail.

There are several scoring systems available for the Rorschach, but virtually all of them emphasize the categories of location, determinants, and content. **Location** refers to the portion of the blot that the examinee responded to. The **determinants** are those characteristics of the blot, such as color, shape, and shading, that led the examinee to make a particular response. **Content** refers to what was actually seen—animals, humans, landscape scenes, internal organs. Interpretations made from the Rorschach tend to be made in accord with psychoanalytic theory. Psychologists who use the test believe it can not only provide an index of the general level of psychological functioning, but also detect such variables as psychosexual development and unconscious motives.

Problems with Personality Tests

Personality tests pose special problems for psychologists who want evidence that the tests they use are reliable and valid. The ways that psychologists use these tests make it extremely difficult, if not impossible, to collect such information. If one wants to establish the validity of a test of intellectual aptitude, it is relatively simple. As we mentioned earlier, one could administer the SAT to a group of high-school students and use performance in college as the criterion. If there is a significant association between the test scores and the criterion scores, the test is valid. But what criterion does the psychologist use to discover if the MMPI, TAT, or Rorschach provide insights about clients that facilitate the process of psychotherapy? Or, how can we prove that the Rorschach can yield valid statements about unconscious motives? The use of personality tests tends to fall into "the art of psychology" category that we discussed in Chapter 1. Many psychologists believe that the research evidence does not justify their continued use. Many others point to the difficulties in conducting meaningful research on these issues and believe that by using such tests they can be of greater service to their clients.

The answers to those questions have not been resolved. There is considerable evidence that personality tests are of questionable usefulness in predicting specific criteria. The primary justification for their use is that they may provide information that can aid therapists in helping their clients. As we shall see later in the chapter, a growing number of psychologists believe that there are more effective ways of collecting such information.

TESTS OF INTERESTS, ATTITUDES, AND VALUES

Kevin, whose case opened this chapter, obviously had ambivalent feelings about his major in college. His counselor administered an interest inventory to him to help him clarify his goals. It enabled him to decide to change his major from the physical sciences to the liberal arts.

There are many situations in which psychologists find it useful to administer tests of interests, attitudes, or values. As in Kevin's case, students may be given an interest inventory to help them clarify their educational and career goals. Couples in marital counseling might be given a test measuring values to help them pinpoint their areas of conflict. And people in consciousness-raising groups dealing with sexism or racial prejudice may be given an attitude survey to help them become aware of how their views coincide or contrast with the views of others.

Tests of interests, attitudes, and values rarely provide clients with information about themselves that they were previously completely unaware of. For instance, Kevin probably already knew that he liked English better than chemistry. And if his counselor had decided to adopt a different strategy, she could probably have helped Kevin solve his academic problems without giving him the test. But the test may have expedited the process since it provided Kevin with objective evidence regarding his interests. Tests can also make the counseling process more efficient. The high-school vocational counselor who must see several hundred students every year can accomplish much more if each student first takes a vocational interest test.

There are dozens of available tests to measure interests, attitudes, and values. In practice the distinctions between these terms can sometimes blur. These tests generally measure the individual's educational and vocational goals, interpersonal relationships, leisure activities, and many other aspects of everyday life. To illustrate these types of tests we shall focus on one of the most thoroughly developed and validated—the Strong-Campbell Interest Inventory (SCII).

The Strong-Campbell Interest Inventory (SCII) (Campbell, 1977) was one of the most thoroughly developed and validated test of interests, attitudes, and values. It was developed to help determine an individual's interests in different types of work. We might wonder why the psychologist does not simply ask people what kinds of vocations they would like to pursue, but it has been found that the answers to such direct questions tend to be superficial and unrealistic. Many people form stereotypes about certain vocations on the basis of novels, television shows, movies, or hearsay. A television show about a physician may depict the profession as being full of excitement and challenge but say nothing about the years of training, the tedium of paperwork, or the emotional strain of making decisions about other people's lives. Most people are not able to evaluate their aptitude and liking for a vocation until they are in it, and then it may be too late to change. Hence the indirect method of assessing vocational interests provided by the SCII is often of value.

The test consists of 325 items of three different types. The first type requires the examinees to indicate whether they like, dislike, or are indifferent to certain activities (e.g., making a speech, raising money for charity). The second type requires the examinee to select a preference between paired statements (e.g., reading a book versus watching TV). The third category is a list of personal characteristics, and the examinees are asked to indicate whether the statements describe them (e.g., win friends easily, have patience when teaching others).

The SCII results in three sets of scores. The first group consists of six general occupational themes: realistic, investigative, artistic, social, enterprising, and conventional. These themes, referred to as general "vocational personalities," provide an overview of one's vocational orientation and cut across a variety of specific occupations. The second category of scores consists of 23 Basic Interest Scales. These scales, such as mechanical and artistic, measure the strength of specific interest areas. The final category of scores are the 124 Occupational Scales. These scales reflect similarities between the examinee's interests and those of people employed in those occupations.

The construction of the SCII proceeded along lines very similar to the construction of the MMPI. The responses of men and women who had been employed in a given occupation for at least three years, were satisfied with their occupation, and had achieved certain minimum standards of success were compared to a reference, or normative, group. Items that were able to differentiate between the people in the various occupations and the reference group were included on the scale. So, an examinee who receives a high score on the engineer scale, for example, has interests, attitudes, and values that are similar to those of employed engineers who are successful and who obtain satisfaction from their work.

The SCII has undergone continual revision since it was first introduced in 1927, and extensive research has demonstrated its usefulness. Studies have followed the careers of individuals for up to 30 and 40 years and have found a good correspondence between test profiles and occupational choices (Campbell, 1971; Vinitsky, 1973). Individuals who are uncertain about career choices may indeed profit from taking this test as part of vocational counseling to clarify their goals.

BEHAVIORAL ASSESSMENT

Up to this point the psychological assessments we have discussed have consisted exclusively of the administration of formal tests. Although formal tests are an important part of the assessment procedure as conducted by many psychologists, virtually all psychologists collect data about clients in another way—by observing their behavior. Kevin's counselor, as you will recall, did not feel that personality testing was required in his case. She was able to obtain the information she felt she needed by observing his behavior in the initial interview. Perhaps she noticed that he had difficulty in making eye contact with her and that he talked in a meek, submissive manner. These behavioral observations may have provided her with important clues as to why Kevin had so few social contacts.

Also, as you will recall from the preceding chapter, many theorists view personality traits as fixed characteristics that are related to various types of behavior in consistent ways. Thus a person who possesses the trait of honesty might be expected to behave in an honest fashion in a variety of situations. Many personality tests, particularly those used in clinical situations, are intended to measure these underlying and fixed traits. The increasing influence of the social-learning-theory approach to personality, however, has led to doubts about the utility of measuring such traits. Social-learning theorists have suggested that behavior itself should be assessed rather than underlying hypothetical constructs.

With the growth of behavior-modification programs—therapy procedures that attempt to change the client's behavior directly using principles of learning (see Chapter 13)—a variety of behavioral assessment methods have been developed. While they are generally quite different in format from more traditional psychological tests, they should still meet the necessary characteristics of psychological tests—that is, they should be standardized, reliable, and valid. Because most methods of behavioral assessment are of recent origin, sufficient data regarding these qualities remain to be collected. However, behavioral assessment methods are proving to be quite useful in behavior-therapy programs, and there is reason to believe such data will be forthcoming. Two examples of behavioral assessment are direct observation and role-playing techniques.

Direct Observation

The most straightforward method of assessing behavior is to have a trained observer simply record his or her observations. Thus a psychologist may observe the frequency of certain types of social behavior in hospitalized psychiatric patients, or the number of times overly aggressive children hit others on a playground. These direct observations can be performed in a number of ways.

To illustrate one approach, suppose an elementary-school teacher requested help from the school psychologist to control a class of unruly children. The psychologist's first step would be to make preliminary observations to arrive at a concise definition of the types of problem or target behavior. Terms such as "unruly," "overly aggressive," and "discipline problem" are too vague for behavioral psychologists. So, after observing the teacher's class for a period of time, the psychologist may decide to focus on three problems: inappropriate talking, inappropriate out-of-seat behavior, and throwing spitballs.

The next step would be to conduct a period of baseline assessment. This is a period of assessment that gives the psychologist an accurate picture of the extent of the problem. Some teachers may overestimate the extent of the problem because the discipline problems are so disagreeable to them. Other teachers may underestimate problems because they have a higher tolerance for such behavior. A second reason for collecting baseline data is that it provides a gauge against which improvement can be evaluated once the behavior-modification program is begun.

Table 11–5. Time-Sampling Chart

Johnny	S O T —	S O T —	S O T —	S O T —	S O T —	S O T —	S O T —	S O T —
Susan	S O T —	S O T —	S O T —	S O T —	S O T —	S O T —	S O T —	S O T —
Michael	S O T —	S O T —	S O T —	S O T —	S O T —	S O T —	S O T —	S O T —
Beth	S O T —	S O T —	S O T —	S O T —	S O T —	S O T —	S O T —	S O T —

One way of conducting a baseline assessment is to do time sampling. For the sake of efficiency, the psychologist may decide to observe the class one hour each morning and afternoon over a one-week period. During each hour he or she may observe each child for a 30-second interval to see if one of the three types of problem behavior occurs. Thus for a class of 20 children, each child would be observed six times each hour.

The observations might be recorded on a chart similar to that presented in Table 11–5. If Johnny threw a spitball during the 30-second interval when he was being observed, the S would be circled. If he did not engage in any inappropriate behavior, the — would be circled. At the end of the hour, the observations can be converted to a percentage by dividing the number of observation periods into the number of intervals in which a particular type of problem behavior occurred and multiplying by 100. In this example, suppose there were 25 spitballs thrown, 40 cases of inappropriate talking, and 15 cases of out-of-seat behavior. The percentages based on 120 30-second intervals would be:

$$\frac{25}{120} \times 100 = 20.8\% \text{ for spitballs}$$

$$\frac{40}{120} \times 100 = 33.3\% \text{ for talking}$$

$$\frac{15}{120} \times 100 = 12.5\% \text{ for out-of-seat}$$

One-way mirrors allow behavior to be observed that might ordinarily be suppressed in the presence of a psychologist. (© *Cary Wolinsky/Stock, Boston, Inc.*)

These data collected over a week's time would constitute the baseline assessment.

Psychologists who use this method must be sensitive to several issues. First, it is best to collect the data without the children's knowledge because the presence of an outside observer is likely to have an effect on their behavior. A one-way mirror is ideal for this purpose. Second, it is desirable to have two observers collect data on some occasions so that the accuracy or reliability of the primary observer's assessment can be evaluated. These and other techniques are employed to insure that the behavioral sample (recall our definition of a psychological test) provides a meaningful index of the situation under consideration.

Role-Playing Techniques

When behavior therapists see clients on an individual basis, it becomes impractical to make direct observations. As a substitute many therapists may ask their clients to simulate their problem behavior in the consulting room. Not all problems that clients bring to their therapists can be role-played (e.g., sexual problems), but for many problems, such as phobias and deficits in assertiveness, **role-playing** is an effective strategy for assessment of problems.

For example, psychologists Craig Twentyman and Richard McFall (1975) conducted an experiment to improve the dating skills of shy college men. Their assessment strategy consisted of several components. Along with asking the men for their own evaluations of their shyness, observers rated their social skills while the men role-played with an attractive woman. The men were asked to imagine that they were seated next to a woman in class whom they wanted to get to know. The man and woman then engaged in conversation for several minutes while the observations were being made. The shy men were rated as being lower in social skills than a control group of confident men. After treatment to enhance these skills, the shy men were rated as being much more confident and skillful in the role-playing task than they had been previously.

Behavioral methods of assessment also include paper-and-pencil tests that, on the surface, are very similar to many traditional psychological tests. One of these, called the Fear Survey Schedule, consists of some 50 common fears or phobias. The examinee is asked to indicate, on a seven-point scale, to what degree he or she experiences each fear. Even with these paper-and-pencil tests the distinction between behavioral and traditional assessment is apparent. The behavioral assessments are more direct than traditional assessments and focus on specific acts or types of behavior of the individual.

We have described only a very small sample of the various psychological tests available to the psychologist. The specific tests used will depend on the psychologist's job and theoretical orientation. For instance, psychologists employed by school systems to evaluate children are likely to use intelligence tests frequently. Those who offer vocational guidance are likely to rely on tests of interests. Psychologists who subscribe to psychoanalytic theory are most likely to use the projective tests. Behavior therapists will, of course, use behavioral assessment methods. Whichever method of assessment is used, all psychologists have the responsibility to use tests in a professional and ethical manner. Ethical questions are particularly problematical.

ETHICAL CONSIDERATIONS

The use of psychological tests began shortly after the turn of the century and grew rapidly for some 50 years. Psychological testing reached its zenith around the late 1950s and early 1960s (Maloney & Ward, 1976). During this period psychologists and the public alike had confidence in tests, and millions of people were tested each year. Unfortunately, the use of tests often outstripped their technical capabilities, and an era of discontent began to set in. Several popular books critical of tests were best-sellers in the 1960s. Courts of law

CRITICAL ISSUE

Tests As an Invasion of Privacy

It is virtually impossible to live in our society and not be required to take a psychological test on occasion. One concern that many people have when they take such tests is that some of the questions may constitute an invasion of privacy. And because the purpose and technique of some tests, such as the TAT and Rorschach, are disguised, many people are concerned that they may be revealing information about their motives, emotions, or attitudes of which they themselves are unaware. This possibility is actually relatively remote, but the concerns that many people have are very real and must be faced by psychologists.

This issue reached a peak in the 1960s when congressional leaders accused psychologists of wholesale violations of human dignity. Their attacks focused on the MMPI, which was being used by several governmental agencies as a screening instrument. The MMPI contains several items about religious beliefs and sexual practices, and many people objected to having to answer these questions as a condition of employment. They felt particularly strongly about items dealing with religion, since the Constitution prohibits discrimination on the basis of religious beliefs.

Psychologists were able to defend the MMPI with some success since interpretations do not depend on the content of specific items. Items are scored on the basis of the relative frequencies of endorsement of an item by various criterion groups. But the issue remains and is still being debated.

In fact, the issue has been broadened to include all types of tests. In the late 1970s the governor of New York signed a law that requires users of tests to allow all examinees to have complete access to test results. This means that anyone taking aptitude tests for college or graduate school can demand to see the test after it has been scored to determine which items were answered correctly and which were answered incorrectly. Tests such as the SAT can only be used once. New items now have to be developed for each group of people being tested since it is impossible to protect the confidentiality of the test materials. Rather than incur the costs of constructing new tests, the educational testing companies have reduced the number of times these tests are administered in the State of New York.

Needless to say, some compromise needs to be reached. Tests can be and have been abused. But to make it impossible for tests to be used would do little to promote human dignity. By following the guidelines for ethical practice, psychologists can use tests to promote the welfare of the people they serve.

banned the use of certain types of tests for job selection. School boards prohibited the use of intelligence tests. By the 1970s it was possible to receive a Ph.D. in clinical psychology without even taking a course in psychological testing. The specific reasons for this growing distrust of tests are numerous, but essentially people were beginning to wonder if tests were not hurting them more than they were helping them. Two issues related to this concern are the tendency of tests to categorize people and bias in tests.

Classification versus Diagnosis

World War I provided a tremendous impetus for psychological tests. Large numbers of men had to be classified in an efficient manner, and psychologists demonstrated that their tests were capable of accomplishing the task. They were able to classify men into those fit for military service and those who were not, and this was considered to be a valuable contribution to the war effort.

The World War I experience, however, may have started an unfortunate tradition—namely, using tests as a vehicle to place people in categories rather than to diagnose problems that might be resolved by treatment. Not only was the military classifying men as to their fitness to serve, but schools began to classify children, clinical psychologists began to classify clients, and employers began to classify potential employees. Under these conditions, it is not surprising that many people began to approach psychological tests with suspicion and fear. The results of a psychological test could mean the difference between approval and rejection.

There are occasions, of course, when the needs of an organization, such as the military in time of war, must take precedence over the needs of the individual. But in the history of psychological testing, there are far too many occasions when the needs of the individual have been neglected for no good reason. For instance, how does an intelligence test help children who are classified as intellectually deficient and placed in groups of slow learners for the rest of their school years? It probably doesn't help at all.

As we stated at the beginning of the chapter, psychological tests should be used to help people. To say that a child is doing poorly in school because that child is of low intelligence tells us nothing of any value. On the other hand, if tests can identify a specific weakness, so that remedial programs can be instituted to help the child catch up with school work, then tests can be truly helpful. In other words, if tests are used to diagnose difficulties with an eye to remedying those difficulties, they can be helpful to the individual.

Perhaps psychology's greatest failure of responsibility lies in not promoting the proper use of tests. In the first half of the twentieth century psychologists were primarily interested in developing valid and useful tests. They may have neglected to point forcefully enough to the limitations of their tests and to insure that they were being used in the proper context. They were often too successful in promoting their tests. In addition, tests were frequently used by people who did not have sufficient background and training. For example, school personnel routinely administered intelligence tests, even though they may not have had formal training in their use. Many children from ethnic minority groups have been classified as mentally retarded on the basis of taking an intelligence test that was constructed for white middle-class children.

At their best, psychological tests are tools to be used by a professional psychologist. Tests provide only one source of information about an individual, and test results must be interpreted in light of the total context. In the hands of a competent psychologist, test results, taken together with interview data, social history, and other pertinent sources of information, can indeed be helpful to individuals.

Test Bias

Tests may also hurt people when they are unfair to some segment of the population. The charge of

APPLICATION

Ralph Nader and Educational Testing Service

Reflecting the general public's growing suspicion of psychological tests, Ralph Nader, the prominent consumer advocate, has recently focused his efforts on Educational Testing Service (*APA Monitor,* 1980). Educational Testing Service, commonly called ETS, publishes and administers several tests used by colleges and professional schools to aid in the selection of students. These include the Scholastic Aptitude Test (SAT), the Graduate Record Examination (GRE), and the exams used by law schools, medical schools, and business schools.

The following statement was made by Nader:

> ETS is the largest standardized testing corporation in America and one of the most powerful—though little known—corporations in the world. They have assumed a rare kind of corporate power, the power to change the way people think about their own potential, and through the passive acceptance of their test scores by admissions officers, to decide who will be granted and who will be denied access to education and career opportunities. . . . ETS's claims to success are false and unsubstantiated, and can be described as a specialized kind of fraud (*APA Monitor,* 1980, p. 1).

These harsh words are based on Nader's interpretation of the research that has been conducted to establish the validity of these tests. Nader asserts that this research shows that "90 percent of the time, the tests predict first-year grades no better than a random-selection process." He further asserts that while the tests do not provide an accurate indication of an individual's chances of success, they do correlate with family income level. Nader concludes, therefore, that the tests are biased—they rank people by social class, not by merit.

Needless to say, ETS and psychologists who are actively involved with psychological testing have not accepted Nader's report uncritically. William Turnbull, president of ETS, claims that Nader's conclusions are based on the use of statistical methods designed to support his position (*APA Monitor,* 1980). Turnbull also states that current criticisms of tests are based on several misconceptions. As one example, he cites the belief that a difference in average scores between groups on a test automatically means that the test is biased (Turnbull, 1980). It may be the case that the group receiving the higher test scores will also perform better on the criterion. Or, the psychologist using the test may develop separate norms for each group so that the test can be used fairly for both groups.

We, the authors, take the view that Nader does make some valid points, even though his conclusions may be questionable. Nader and the public certainly have the right to demand evidence that the tests used by colleges and professional schools be as valid as technically possible. They also have the right to express the desire to do away with tests completely regardless of their validity.

Psychologists do not have the responsibility to decide whether tests should or should not be used by schools, but they do have the responsibility to evaluate their efforts critically so that the tests can be improved. If Nader's attack on standardized tests spurs psychologists on in this effort, then he has provided an invaluable service.

---

test bias is most closely associated with intelligence tests, but of more practical concern is bias in tests used for selection of employees. In the past, tests have been used as a means of discriminating against minority groups. Some employers required job applicants to take tests that had no relation to the job requirements. Because minority-group members often did poorly on such tests, they were effectively barred from employment. Court cases have prohibited the use of tests that are unrelated to job performance. As a result, psychologists now must demonstrate the validity and fairness of all tests that are used in employee selection.

The issue of what constitutes a fair test is complex, and there are several technical ways in which it can be defined. One definition states that a fair test will select applicants from various ethnic groups in the same proportions as they would succeed, if given a chance, on the job (Cole, 1972). For example, if we know that one half of all members of a particular minority group will succeed on a particular job if given a chance, but the selection test predicts that only one fourth of them will succeed, the test is biased.

To illustrate this point further, consider the two diagrams in Figure 11–2. These represent the relationship between test scores (on the X axis) and job performance (on the Y axis). As can be seen from the dark lines, called regression lines, the higher an individual's test score, the better we expect him or her to perform on the job. Suppose a company were using this test to select employees and set the cutoff score (the dotted line) at point X. Everyone with a score higher than this point would be hired. In Case 1, the test would be fair. The average Group A applicant would be hired, while the average Group B applicant would not, but a corresponding difference in job performance can be expected.*

Case 2 provides an example of test bias. In this situation the average Group A member would be hired, and the average Group B member would be rejected once again. But because the relationship between test scores and job performance differs for the two groups, we can see from the figure that the average job performance for the two groups is the same. So even though Group B members can be expected to perform as well on the job as Group A members, their test scores are lower, and hence they are less likely to be hired. In such a case it would be necessary to set different cutoff scores for the two groups.

The situation represented by Case 2 has been found to occur when predicting college grades (Temp, 1971) and law-school grades (Linn, 1975)

* The guidelines of the Equal Employment Opportunity Commission state that when fair tests result in disproportionate rejection rates for minorities, steps such as on-the-job training programs must be initiated to reduce the discrepancy as much as possible. This requirement is an attempt to compensate for past social inequities.

Figure 11–2. Examples of fair and unfair tests.

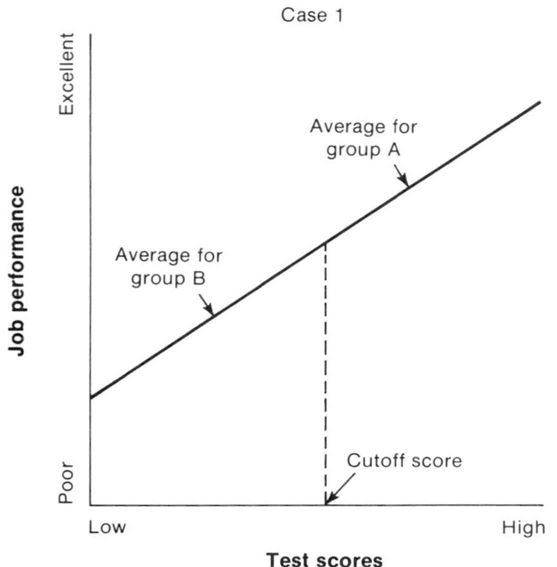

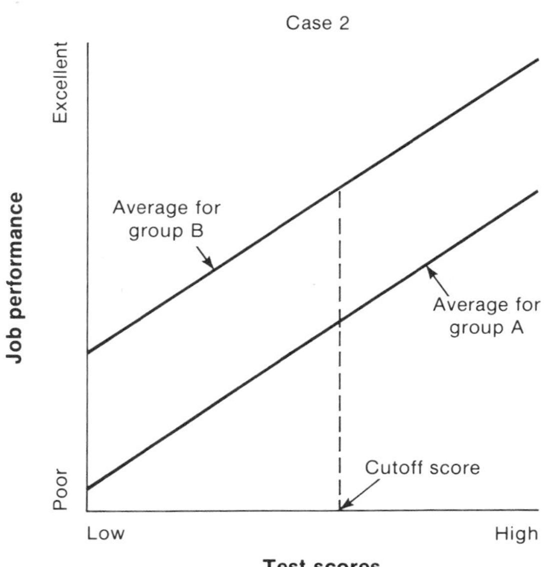

and in a variety of industrial settings (Campbell, Crooks, Mahoney, & Rock, 1973). This problem exists with regard to types of group differences other than ethnic-group differences. As just one example, aptitude tests used by the army are likely to discriminate against high-school dropouts. Test results for college graduates, on the other hand, lead to unrealistically high predictions of their job performance.

Once again it is important to keep in mind that the appropriate focus of the test-bias controversy should be on how tests are used. There is no justification for eliminating tests, as some have advocated, simply because they have been misused in the past. Psychological tests, when used properly, can actually provide a safeguard against favoritism and prejudice. One psychologist, commenting on the use of tests in schools, wrote, "The tests couldn't see whether the youngster was in rags or in tweeds, and they couldn't hear the accents of the slum. The tests revealed intellectual gifts at every level of the population" (Gardner, 1961, pp. 48–49). Assessment is a crucial part of the psychologist's role, and tests, when used properly, can serve as an invaluable aid in promoting human dignity and welfare.

Summary

Psychological tests are used to make comparisons between individuals or between different occasions for a single individual. Tests can be useful whenever decisions about people have to be made, such as in selecting employees, choosing a form of therapy for a client, or admitting students into graduate programs. Psychological tests are only one source of assessment data. When evaluating individuals, psychologists interpret test scores in light of other pertinent sources of information, such as interview data and social history.

Psychological tests are more than mere compilations of questions and answers. A definition of a psychological test is that it is an objective and standardized measure of a sample of behavior. Psychologists are interested in performance on specific test items insofar as they are associated with other types of real-life behavior. To be standardized, test scores must not be dependent on the conditions under which the test was taken, and scores must be interpreted in reference to the performance of a normative group. Reliability and validity of a test are essential to insure its objectivity.

Two major tests of intelligence are the Stanford-Binet Intelligence Scale for children and the Wechsler Adult Intelligence Scale for adults. The latter provides scores on 11 subtests as well as a global IQ score. Two controversial issues regarding intelligence concern its nature and the extent to which genetics and the environment contribute to its development. There are no conclusive answers for either issue. The answers probably depend on the specific individual being studied. Experiential factors may shape both the nature of intelligence and the degree to which environment influences its development.

Major tests of personality include the Minnesota Multiphasic Personality Inventory (MMPI), the Thematic Apperception Test (TAT), and the Rorschach Inkblot Technique. The MMPI is a paper-and-pencil test that consists of 550 true-false items. The TAT consists of a series of pictures about which examinees are asked to tell a story. For the Rorschach, examinees are asked what they see in ten inkblots. The TAT and the Rorschach are called projective tests because examinees are thought to project their own feelings, motives, and conflicts onto the unstructured stimuli.

The Strong-Campbell Interest Inventory (SCII) is an example of tests that measure interests, attitudes, and values. It is used to measure vocational interests and has proven to be quite valuable in helping people to make career decisions.

Behavioral methods of assessment are becoming increasingly popular with the advent of behavior-modification programs. Two such methods are direct observation, in which the psychologist makes systematic observations of real-life behavior, and role-playing, in which clients are asked to simulate types of problem behavior in the consulting room. Behavioral assessment differs from traditional tests in that it is more direct and less concerned with underlying personality traits.

Psychological testing enjoyed much popularity during the first half of this century, but by the 1960s an antitesting sentiment had begun to develop. Two factors that contributed to this feeling were the tendency to use tests to place people into categories rather than help them identify and resolve problems, and the discovery that some tests were biased against minority groups. These problems arise not because psychological tests are flawed but because they are misused. Psychological tests, when used properly by trained psychologists, can be an invaluable aid in promoting human dignity and welfare.

Key Terms For Review

basal age
ceiling age
content
determinants
location
mental age
neurotic triad
norms
reliability
role-playing techniques
sample
standardized tests
test bias
validity

Suggested Readings

Dobzhansky, T. Race, intelligence and genetics: Differences are not deficits. *Psychology Today*, December 1973, pp. 97 ff.

The author, a geneticist, discusses some of the difficulties of research in this area and suggests why it is impossible to draw any firm conclusions.

Dunnette, M. An evaluation of test critics and their assumptions. In D. A. Payne & R. F. McMorris (Eds.), *Educational and psychological measurement*. Morristown, N.J.: General Learning Press, 1975.

In this article Dunnette summarizes the points made in a best-selling book critical of psychological testing and suggests why the criticisms are not valid.

Jensen, A. Race, intelligence and genetics: The differences are real. *Psychology Today*, December 1973, pp. 81 ff.

Jensen summarizes the evidence that he believes supports the notion that part of the black-white difference in IQ is caused by genetic factors.

Kamin, L. J. The politics of IQ. In P. L. Houts (Ed.), *The myth of measurability*.

Kamin, a distinguished psychologist, traces the history of IQ testing and argues that it has always been used as an instrument of oppression against the poor.

Rice, B. Brave new world of intelligence testing. *Psychology Today*, September 1979, pp. 26 ff.

Rice describes several current lines of research that may result in radically different tests of intelligence. For example, intelligence tests of the future may measure brain activity in response to certain stimuli.

Rice, B. Race, intelligence and genetics: The high cost of thinking and the unthinkable. *Psychology Today*, December 1973, pp. 89–93.

This article describes some of the behind-the-scenes and often unprofessional behavior of scientists with regard to the IQ controversy.

12

Abnormal Behavior

George, age 32, had worked for the last seven years as an accountant for the same firm. He seemed content with his life, which centered on his family and a few hobbies. One day he left his wife and children, took up the guitar, and started singing in bars to make a meager living. Within a week he was arrested on a street corner for carrying a small quantity of marijuana.

Jane is a high-school teacher in her early fifties. She has never been married and has practically no social contacts. Although known as a good teacher, she is disliked by students because she is strict and demanding. Late or sloppy papers infuriate her, and she is likely to punish students whose work does not meet her standards. Jane collects dolls as a hobby and often talks about her new acquisitions in class. Students both fear and ridicule her.

Dave, age 22, liked to say, "Sleeping is a bad habit; Thomas Edison never slept more than 45 minutes a night." Although Dave could never reduce his sleep to an hour or less, he often worked through the night without tiring, and a catnap was all he needed to be revitalized completely. Most people admired Dave because he was always involved in several projects, working at all of them energetically and enthusiastically. Few knew that Dave seldom finished what he began because carrying out an idea bored him. Nor were many of his friends aware of his restlessness, which drove him crazy when he found himself between projects.

Hilda is a 71-year-old woman who cares for an older sister she cannot get along with. She tends to dwell on the prominence of her family, the luxuries of her early life, and her popularity during her younger years. She constantly apologizes for her appearance, emphasizing how beautiful she was when she was younger. Few men, she claims, could resist her. One day, during an argument with her sister, who complained about her bragging, Hilda broke down and was admitted to a mental hospital.

Jim and Judy have an open marriage. Both agree that marriage partners need variety and novelty in their sexual relationships. Each has intimate friends of the same and the opposite sex. They sometimes meet with other couples who also practice open marriage, and they swap spouses on occasion.

Consider these brief sketches for a moment and ask yourself which of these individuals you would consider abnormal and for what reasons. Think about whether your attitude would change if any of these persons were a friend or relative.

DEFINING ABNORMAL BEHAVIOR

Many psychologists (e.g., Poland, 1974) assert that our mental balance rests on sometimes fragile connections among the biological, psychological, and social factors of our existence. Most of us shift from one place to another along a continuum that ranges from normal to abnormal depending on life stresses and the resources available to us for coping with these stresses. In extreme cases of abnormal behavior a person may be severely handicapped and suffer subjective distress and may even evoke fear and revulsion from others. Milder forms of psychological disturbance are experienced by the majority of us, who fall around the middle of the hypothetical continuum between perfect mental health and abnormality (see Figure 12–1). Who among us does not have an occasional reaction that impairs our productivity or work efficiency, disrupts our interpersonal relationships, or otherwise hampers our ability to cope with the daily demands of life?

Abnormality has been defined in many different ways. For the lay person, an individual whose behavior is strange or unusual is abnormal. There is little doubt, though, that most of our evaluations of normality and abnormality depend on the social context. For example, a person who shakes a head or fist at a football game probably goes unnoticed, whereas the person who engages in the same behavior in a church or library is likely to be reprimanded or punished. Defining abnormality is a difficult task, since each definition has its strengths and its limitations. The four major definitions examined here are: statistical, subjective-distress, sociocultural, and legal.

The Statistical Definition

One common definition approaches normality and abnormality from a statistical perspective. Statistically, normality is what is usual or average, and abnormality is what is unusual or exceptional. To establish whether a certain characteristic or type of behavior is normal or abnormal, we simply count the number of people displaying it. If the majority of people exhibit it, we label it normal. For example, if statistics were to tell us that most people have dental cavities, we would be abnormal if we did not have them.

The only assumption of this definition of abnormality is that the types of behavior in question distribute themselves along the continuum of the normal or bell-shaped curve (see Chapter 20). Most biological and psychological traits, such as height, weight, intelligence, and anxiety, are normally distributed in the general population. The number of people who deviate from the average becomes increasingly smaller as we move to the right or left of the middle of the continuum on which the trait is plotted. For example, the majority of people have intelligence quotients falling between 85 and 115, the middle range of the distribution. Statistically, a similar distribution applies to normal and abnormal types of behavior. The major problem with the statistical definition is that normality cannot always be equated with the type of behavior displayed by the majority of the people. For example, many people would consider the Germans who became blind followers of Hitler during the Third Reich abnormal. Another problem with this definition is that people who occupy the tail areas of the normal curve are equally abnormal. According to this definition the genius at the high end of the IQ continuum would be no more normal than the mentally defective person who scores at the low end. Statistically speaking, George, Jane, Dave, Hilda, Jim, and Judy from our opening sketches would be labeled abnormal.

The Subjective-Distress Definition

A second definition of abnormality focuses on the personal discomfort or subjective pain experienced by the abnormal person. Subjective distress may manifest itself in physical symptoms, such as insomnia or loss of appetite, or in psychological problems, such as the inability to get along with others or the fear of failure.

Figure 12–1.

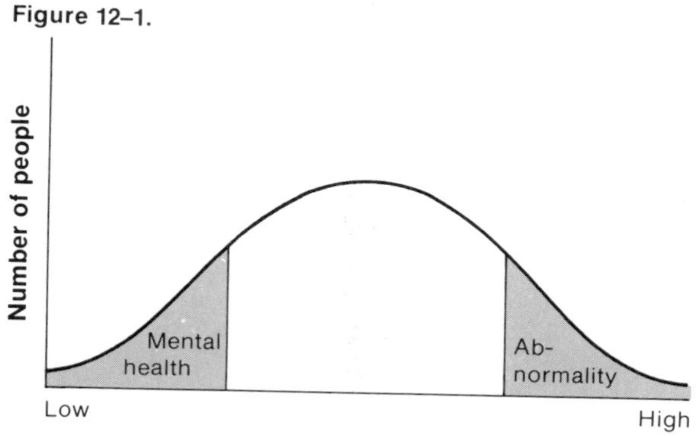

Shaking one's fist at traffic is often considered normal behavior, but shaking one's fist in a church might be thought abnormal. (© *Charles Gatewood*)

Unfortunately the most severely disturbed people are least likely to be able to describe or complain about subjective pains. For example, the severely retarded person or the schizophrenic patient in the advanced stage of disorder seldom provides meaningful descriptions of his or her inner experiences. Consequently we know very little about the subjective pain and inner turmoil that these individuals go through.

The Sociocultural Definition

The sociocultural definition of abnormality is based on the premise that abnormality cannot be judged outside the societal context. All societies provide their members with rules that govern social norms of appropriate and inappropriate types of behavior and with punishments for violations of the norms (see Figure 12–2). Normal behavior, then, is behavior that adheres to the norms, while abnormal behavior is behavior that deviates from them. Homosexuality is a good illustration of the

One means of defining abnormality is in terms of subjective pain. (© *Bob Henrioues/Magnum Photos, Inc.*)

dependency of normal and abnormal behavior on social standards. In ancient Greece homosexuality not only was accepted as a legitimate, normal life style but also supposedly served important pedagogic functions, since the mature man in these relationships was to pass on his knowledge of the virtuous life to the younger one. In our own culture, homosexuality was labeled a mental disorder until just recently.

The Legal Definition

Our fourth definition of abnormality comes from the legal profession. Legally a person is judged insane if it can be demonstrated in a court of law that the individual did not know what he or she was doing or could not judge between right and wrong at the time of the offense. This decision, known as the **McNaughten rule,** was announced in the aftermath of a murder trial in England. The judges at the time ruled that "to establish a defense of insanity, it must be clearly proved that, at the time of the committing of the act, the party accused was laboring under such a defect of reason, from disease of the mind, as not to know the nature and quality of the act he was doing; or if he did know it, that he did not know he was doing what was wrong." This "right-wrong" concept has been applied in the United States for many years and still is the sole test in some states (Davison & Neale, 1978, p. 569). Another court ruling, known as the **Durham decision** (*Durham* v. *United States*, 1954), specifies that an accused is not criminally responsible if his or her unlawful act was the product of a mental disease or mental defect. Although legal definitions vary considerably from state to state, a person must at least meet the following conditions to be labeled abnormal (Schwitzgebel & Schwitzgebel, 1980):

1. The person must be dangerous to himself, herself, or others if allowed to remain at liberty.
2. The person must be gravely disabled so as to be unable to provide for his or her basic physical needs.

Figure 12–2. Sample scale of inappropriate behavior and punishment. (Haas, 1975)

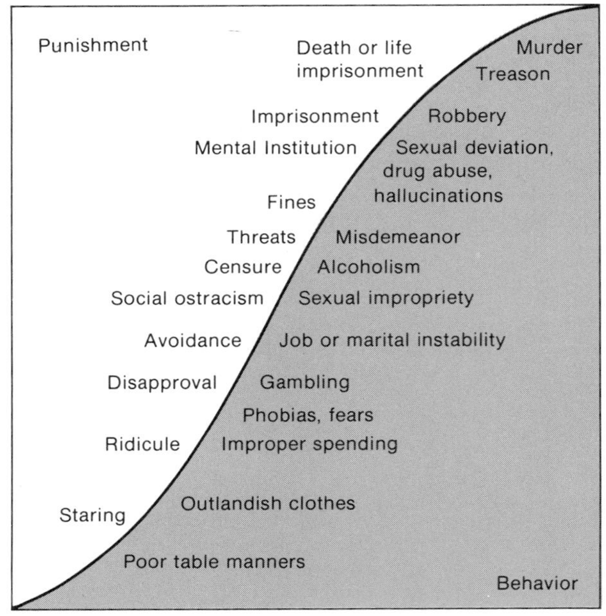

3. The person must be lacking sufficient insight or capacity to make responsible decisions concerning hospitalization.
4. The person must be in need of care and treatment in a hospital.

Legal definitions of normality and abnormality are confusing and inconsistent. For example, sexual acts that are considered misdemeanors in one state may lead to a prison sentence in another. Similarly, sexual practices considered normal under some circumstances may be unlawful under others. Having sexual intercourse with one's spouse, for instance, is not illegal, but having sex with one's mate while others are looking on is a legal offense.

No totally satisfactory definition of abnormal behavior exists. Each definition focuses on certain aspects of abnormal behavior, such as infrequency or lack of social appropriateness, but none captures all the factors involved in abnormal behavior.

MODELS OF ABNORMAL BEHAVIOR

To gain a better understanding of abnormal behavior, behavioral scientists have developed a number of models, each of which presents a different perspective (Price, 1978). Whenever we are confronted with a set of events that we do not understand well, or for which only limited data are available, we look to more familiar events for an explanation. For example, scientists have approached the study of the brain as if it were a computer, and they have compared the heart to a pump. Models help us to select certain events or characteristics for investigation and to organize them. In addition, scientific models help us to make future predictions about behavior based on data collected in accordance with the assumptions of the model.

In this section we present the three major models of abnormal behavior, each with its own assumptions, definitions, and language. Although each one exists in several variations, our interest here is primarily in the features shared by the medical, psychoanalytic, and learning models.

The Medical Model

The medical model, also referred to as the illness or disease model, borrows its definitions and terms from medicine and applies them to behavior disorders. As Brendan Maher (1966) pointed out:

> Society currently uses the model of physical illness as the basis for the terms and concepts to be applied to deviant behavior. Such behavior is termed *pathological* and is classified or diagnosed on the basis of *symptoms*. If the deviant behavior ceases, the *patient* is described as *cured*.

The terminology of the medical model is presented in Table 12–1.

The illness perspective has a long history. One of the first to view mental disorders as a product of illness was the Greek physician Hippocrates (460–377 B.C.). More than two thousand years later, in 1825, the discovery of a disorder known as **general paresis** greatly stimulated the development of biological theories of abnormal behavior. General paresis, a mysterious disorder characterized by progressive paralysis and mental deterioration, was inevitably fatal. In 1905 the specific infectious agent for syphilis, a spirochete called ***Trepomena pallidum,*** was discovered in the brain tissue of patients with general paresis. After this discovery numerous other biological factors, such as chemical imbalances in the central nervous system, structural damage to the brain, genetic defects, and virus infections, were examined as possible sources of behavior disorders.

At the turn of the last century the German psychiatrist Emil Kraeplin noted that there is a tendency in mental disorders for a certain set of symptoms to appear together so that they clearly define a specific disorder. This cluster of symptoms is known as a **syndrome.** Kraeplin developed a comprehensive description of psychiatric disorders, each of which was presented with its characteristic symptoms, believed to have a specific

Table 12–1. Language and Concepts of the Medical Model

Symptom A physical or behavioral manifestation of illness.

Syndrome Patterns or constellations of symptoms that are typical of a disorder.

Disorder One or more syndromes with common etiological factors.

Acute disorder Disorder with a sudden onset and of short duration. Acute disorders are usually considered reversible.

Chronic disorder Disorder that is longlasting and tends to be irreversible.

Disease Disorder characterized by symptoms, either mental or bodily, that indicate mental or physical dysfunction.

Nosology The classification of diseases.

Diagnosis The determination of the nature of a disease or abnormality based on symptoms displayed.

Etiology Causation; the systematic study of the causes of disorders.

Precipitating cause A cause of psychological disorder that serves as a "trigger" for the disorder. A precipitating life event could be a sudden loss of a loved one, a disaster, a major failure in one's life, or a sudden physiological change.

Predisposing cause An event or condition that occurs long before any abnormal behavior is observed, yet may predispose a person to later difficulties.

Specific etiology A causal condition that is necessary but not sufficient for an illness to occur; it does not by itself produce the illness.

Therapy The application of various treatment techniques either to affect symptoms or to affect etiological factors.

Prognosis Statement concerning the likely course and outcome of a disorder.

Source: Price (1978).

organic cause somewhere in the body. Kraeplin's work remains one of the most elaborate interpretations of the disease model.

A look at depression will help us gain a better understanding of the disease model. This type of disorder consists of a group of symptoms characterized by feelings of inadequacy, decreased activity levels, loss of energy, and loss of sleep, appetite, and sexual interest. Prognosis varies considerably from good to poor depending on the severity of the depression. The etiology, or causes, of depression are unknown, but some forms seem to involve biochemical abnormalities of the central nervous system. Treatment frequently involves various drugs or the use of electric convulsive shock. Mental-health professionals who follow the medical model see as their major task the identification of the symptoms and the attachment of the appropriate diagnostic label.

Like all models of abnormal behavior, the medical model has its advantages and disadvantages. Labeling a mental disorder an illness relieves the affected person from his or her responsibility for the condition. Under the medical model much of the disgrace associated with being abnormal was reduced. As a result, beginning in the eighteenth century, patients in mental hospitals received more humane treatment and were considered less of a threat to society.

Nevertheless, there have been numerous criticisms of the medical model. Psychiatrist Theodore Sarbin (1969), for instance, argued that psychopathology is not a medical issue like heart disease or cancer. He viewed the psychiatric syndromes as "social roles" that are forced upon a person by commitment to a hospital. Being hospitalized provides the person with a "sick role" that he or she is expected to fill.

Others (e.g., Davison & Neale, 1978; Goldstein, Baker, & Jamison, 1980) call our attention to the circular effect inherent in the disease model. These psychologists point out that certain types of behavior or symptoms are characterized as mental illness and given a name but then the name of the illness is often cited as an explanation for the cause of the symptoms. For example, a person who withdraws from all social contact and hears voices threatening to poison him or her is diagnosed as a schizophrenic. When we ask why the person is withdrawn, however, we are told it is because he or she is schizophrenic. Thus the label "schizophrenia" is used for both the symptoms and the cause of the symptoms, making an independent assessment of symptoms and causes impossible.

Finally, the medical model assumes that hospitals and mental-health clinics are the only appropriate environments for mental disorders to be treated. Although the treatment of the mentally ill has been the prerogative of the medical profession for centuries, we know today that numerous forms of mental disorder, such as the anxiety disorders, alcoholism, or antisocial behavior, do not require medical treatment and are much more amenable to other forms of therapy (see Chapter 13).

The Psychoanalytic Model

The psychoanalytic model of abnormal behavior was derived from Freud's theory of personality, discussed in Chapter 10. The language and concepts of this model are given in Table 12–2.

Freud believed that the root of all psychopathology could be found in the frustration of basic biological instincts. Instead of looking for organic disease as the cause of mental disorders, Freud emphasized the importance of psychic factors: unconscious motives, ego defenses, and the importance of early childhood experiences in adult personality functioning. Our discussion in Chapter 10 of the Freudian structure of personality, the stages of psychosexual development, and the protective mechanisms of the ego gave an idea of how normal personality development can be affected.

Freud was primarily interested in the anxiety disorders, or neuroses. He believed that neurotic symptoms are manifestations of traumatic childhood experiences or compensations for needs not met during childhood.

Although Freud's theory of psychopathology deals primarily with the origins of neurotic disorders, Freud also attempted to explain psychotic behavior, which he attributed to a poorly developed superego. For Freud, abnormal behavior, regardless of how bizarre or unmanageable, differed only quantitatively from normal behavior; thus the distinction between normality and abnormality was a matter of degree rather than kind.

Table 12–2. Language and Concepts of the Psychoanalytic Model

Unconscious The portion of the psychological structure of the individual where repressed or forgotten memories or desires reside. These memories or desires are not directly available to consciousness but can be made available through psychoanalysis or hypnosis.

Id The reservoir of instinctual drives in the psychological structure of the individual. It is the most primitive and most inaccessible structure of the personality.

Ego That part of the psychological structure which is usually described as the "self." It is the aspect of the personality that mediates between the needs of the id and reality.

Superego That structure of the personality which is concerned with ethical and moral feelings and attitudes. The superego is usually identified with the "conscience."

Pleasure principle In Freudian theory, the demand that an instinctual need be gratified at once. The principle that guides the id.

Reality principle Means by which ego balances the person's pursuit of gratification with the demands of external reality.

Neurotic anxiety Reaction when the ego is aroused by its perception of the possibility of being overwhelmed by the instincts of the id. Free-floating anxiety, phobia, and panic reactions are all forms of neurotic anxiety.

Defense mechanism A reaction designed to maintain the individual's feelings of adequacy and to reduce anxiety. Defense mechanisms operate at an unconscious level and tend to distort reality. Examples are denial, projection, reaction formation, regression, and repression.

Repression One of the fundamental defense mechanisms. Repression removes psychologically painful ideas from the individual's awareness. Dangerous desires or intolerable memories are kept out of consciousness by this mechanism as well.

Regression Retreat to an earlier stage of development in behavior to allow the id impulses expression at a level not possible at higher levels of development.

Source: Price (1978).

The psychoanalytic model undoubtedly enlarged our thinking about abnormal behavior and represents an influential model in the study of abnormal behavior. It was the first systematic attempt to show how psychological processes may result in mental disorders. As such, Freud's model of abnormal behavior was instrumental in developing an alternative to the medical model. Although psychoanalysis may be on the decline, as Szasz has been quoted as saying (Leó, 1968), there are few mental-health professionals who have not come into contact with the psychoanalytic model.

Many of the attacks directed at psychoanalysis as a theory of personality (see Chapter 10) also apply to psychoanalysis as a model of abnormal behavior. Since all the concepts used in the psychoanalytic perspective were derived from uncontrolled clinical observations and subjective reports and cannot be quantified, the prediction of future behavior, one of the primary functions of a model, becomes impossible. In addition, because of the lack of scientific evidence, the psychoanalytic model has been criticized for overemphasizing the importance of sexual motivation in abnormal behavior. And finally, by focusing on a relatively small number of cases in a highly culture-bound society (the declining Victorian era in Vienna), Freud neglected to examine the effects of cultural differences in shaping abnormal behavior.

The Learning Model

The concepts of this model come from experimental learning research, presented in Chapter 5. The learning perspective applies basic learning principles, such as classical and operant conditioning, modeling, extinction, and generalization, to abnormal behavior. For the learning theorist abnormal behavior is not a symptom of some underlying disease (as in the medical model) or unconscious conflict (as in the psychoanalytic model) but results from faulty learning. Consequently it can be "unlearned." The maladaptive behavior is itself the disorder. As Eysenck and Rachman (1965) explicitly put it:

> The point, however, on which the theory here advocated breaks decisively with psychoanalytic thought of any description is this: Freudian theory regards neurotic symptoms as adaptive mechanisms which are evidence of repression—they are the visible upshot of unconscious causes. Learning theory regards neurotic symptoms as simply learned habits; there is no neurosis underlying the symptom itself. Get rid of the symptom and you have eliminated the neurosis (p. 10).

Learning theorists argue that maladaptive behavior is acquired in the same way as is normal behavior. That is, maladaptive behavior is learned as a result of a person's past history of reinforcement and can be unlearned if reinforcement contingencies are changed. The learning model minimizes the importance of biological factors and subjective processes.

In the terminology of the learning model, which is presented in Table 12–3, abnormal behavior can be conditioned in many different ways: fear and anxiety can develop through classical conditioning, aggression can be shaped through modeling, and social approval (secondary reinforcement) of the peer group can maintain delinquent behavior of adolescents. Similarly, aversive conditioning, such as giving alcoholics a substance that makes them very ill, or extinction may be employed to eliminate maladaptive behavior.

One of the greatest strengths of the learning model is the precision with which the observations are made. Learning theorists concentrate on observable behavior rather than internal processes and avoid unverifiable explanations. The learning perspective provides many therapeutic applications of learning principles, which are designed to identify both the maladaptive behavior and the environmental conditions that sustain them. Thus the learning model offers not only a conceptualization of abnormal behavior but also a well-defined program of therapy.

The learning model, despite its preciseness and objectivity, has not been spared criticism. Opponents have argued that this model is too mechanistic and focuses on specific behavior rather than the total person. Learning theorists have been faulted for failing to consider subjective experiences, such as self-awareness, personal values, and the search for meaning. The latter criticism has become less valid in recent years since, as we saw in Chapter 10, many learning theorists are now including internal processes as mediating agents. Bandura (1974), for instance, emphasizes our capacity for self-determination and views the recognition of this capacity "as a substantial departure from exclusive reliance upon environmental control" (p. 863).

Implications of Models

Adopting a model helps us select certain events that are relevant to our study of abnormal behavior. Models allow us to make decisions about the kind of data that will be collected and how they will be interpreted. All models therefore affect both diagnosis and treatment. The psychiatrist who defines abnormal behavior on the basis of physical symptoms, for instance, will make a diagnosis after a careful physical examination and is likely to prescribe medical treatment, such as drug therapy, electric shock, or surgery. The psychoanalyst, who follows Freudian theory, will analyze childhood experiences before assigning the person to a particular psychiatric category. For the psychoanalyst, possible treatments include Freudian analysis (see Chapter 13) and free association. Finally, psychologists endorsing the learning model will make their diagnosis on the basis of observable behavior and may advocate one of the many behavioral techniques for treatment.

Adopting a single model necessarily results in decisions that may exclude alternative explanations for the disorder observed. This means that we may ignore possibilities or overlook other data. Of the models described, none in itself can completely explain or accommodate the complex and diverse nature of abnormal behavior. However, each does help us to understand certain aspects of it. Table 12–4 sums up the characteristics of the three models of abnormal behavior.

Table 12–3. Language and Concepts of the Learning Model

Stimulus Any objectively defined situation or event that is the occasion for an organism's response.

Response Any behavioral event whose strength can be manipulated by changing antecedent stimuli or consequent events.

Reinforcer Any event following a response that changes the strength of that response.

Reinforcement The process by which response strength (i.e., the probability of a response) is changed as a result of either classical conditioning or operant conditioning.

Classical conditioning The process whereby an originally neutral conditioned stimulus, through continuous pairing with an unconditioned stimulus, acquires the ability to elicit a response originally given to the unconditioned stimulus.

Instrumental conditioning Process of development of behavior in which the organism must emit the response before reinforcement can occur. Therefore, the response is instrumental in receiving reinforcement.

Modeling A learning mechanism involving the observation and imitation of others. Advocates of the learning perspective believe it is one mechanism by which abnormal behavior develops.

Discrimination The reinforcement of a response in the presence of a particular stimulus but not in the presence of other stimuli. The outcome of this procedure is that the response will occur in the presence of the stimulus associated with reinforcement and not in other situations.

Generalization A failure of discrimination. A response reinforced in the presence of a particular stimulus may also occur to stimuli that are similar to the original stimulus, even though the response was never reinforced in their presence.

Extinction The removal of the reinforcer used in conditioning a response; the resulting decline in response strength.

Maladaptive behavior Behavior that (1) is inappropriate in the eyes of those who control the reinforcements for the person, and (2) leads to a decrease in the amount of positive reinforcement given the person behaving abnormally.

Source: Price (1978).

Table 12–4. Major Models of Abnormal Behavior

	Medical Model	*Psychoanalytic Model*	*Learning Model*
Basic assumption (i.e., how abnormal behavior is conceptualized)	Disease based on organic, genetic, or biochemical factors	Intrapsychic conflict resulting from id, ego, and superego demands or early childhood trauma	Maladaptive behavior caused by faulty learning
Major concepts	Symptom, syndrome, etiology, prognosis	Id, ego, superego, anxiety, defense mechanisms	Reinforcement, classical and operant conditioning, observational learning, mediating cognitive events
Major proponents	Kraeplin	Freud	Skinner, Bandura
Implications for therapy	Medical treatment, including shock and surgery	Psychoanalysis	Behavior therapy

CLASSIFICATION OF ABNORMAL BEHAVIOR

Psychological disorders are classified according to a scheme developed by the American Psychiatric Association (APA) and known as the Diagnostic and Statistical Manual of Mental Disorders (DSM). In 1952 the APA adopted the first classification scheme, which has since undergone two revisions: DSM II was published in 1968 and DSM III in 1980. All three systems are based on the medical model, because historically the treatment of mental disorders fell into the realm of medicine (see Chapter 1 for the distinction between psychiatrist and clinical psychologist). This classification serves as a basis for the collection of statistics on the diagnostic characteristics of patients admitted to U.S. mental hospitals (DSM II, 1968).

For each DSM category, such as mental retardation or anxiety disorders, a description and a diagnostic label are given. This allows mental-health professionals throughout the world to compare the various types of mental disorders.

The Traditional Classification System

All sciences need to set up categories in which the subjects under study (people, animals, plants, or objects) can be grouped according to certain dimensions. Classification systems of abnormal behavior contain descriptive categories for identifying crucial similarities in symptoms, causes, and treatment choices of various pathological behavior patterns. The underlying assumption of such classification is that by grouping types of problem behavior into categories, psychologists can tell more about the nature of a given disorder. Ideally, the label for each category should provide accurate information about the characteristics of a person within that category. Moreover, we can expect that members within a category resemble one another with respect to the common dimensions, such as response to treatment, defining the category. Classification systems, then, are designed to provide a description of the problem behavior and to allow predictions of its future course as well as recommendations for treatment.

The present classification system, DSM III, differs from its predecessors in significant ways. Most important, there has been a considerable increase in the number of diagnostic categories, from 60 in DSM I to 145 in DSM II to 230 in DSM III. In the course of the revisions some diagnostic labels have been changed, some new ones added, and some subdivided in new ways to produce a classification system that reflects our current state of knowledge.

The second significant change involves the multidimensional, or multiaxial, approach to diagnosis. Multiaxial diagnosis leans on five dimensions, or axes, which provide information about the following areas:

Axis I: formal psychiatric syndrome: description of abnormal behavior patterns in terms of clear-cut symptoms.

Axis II: personality disorders: recurrent patterns of adult disturbances or specific developmental disorders in childhood or adolescence.

Axis III: physical disorders: nonmental medical disorders associated with psychological disturbances.

Axis IV: severity of psychosocial stress one year prior to the onset of the disorder.

Axis V: highest level of adaptive behavior one year prior to the onset of the disorder.

Axes IV and V (see Tables 12–5 and 12–6) are important additions that are included to predict the course of the disorder. In contrast to DSM II, which basically yielded a simple diagnostic label, DSM III requires much more information about a person in order to make a diagnosis.

Let us see what kind of information seeking the classification suggests about a depressed woman whom we shall call Liz.

Axis I requires the naming of the psychiatric condition, such as depression, which is Liz's psychiatric label. Axis II (which describes types of problem behavior of lasting durations in adults or transient developmental difficulties in children) alerts the diagnostician to look for chronic feelings of inadequacy, loneliness, and guilt, which are characteristic of depressed people. Axis III calls attention to specific medical problems that may be associated with psychological disturbances. In the case of Liz, it turns out that she complains about a variety of physical symptoms, including lack of appetite, insomnia, and irregular menstrual periods. Axes IV and V, the new additions to DSM III, are designed to assess the degree of life stress and the degree of coping ability one year prior to the onset of the disorder. On Axis IV stress can range from minimal (such as taking out a bank loan) to extreme (death of a family member). In Liz's case, the major stress factor was having to

Table 12–5. Axis IV Scale for Rating Severity of Psychosocial Stressors

Code	Term	Adult examples	Child or adolescent examples
1	None	No apparent psychosocial stressor	No apparent psychosocial stressor
2	Minimal	Minor violation of the law, small bank loan	Vacation with family
3	Mild	Argument with neighbor, change in work hours	Change in school teacher, new school year
4	Moderate	New job, death of a close friend, pregnancy	Parental fighting, change to new school, illness of close relative, birth of sibling
5	Severe	Major illness in self or family, bankruptcy, marital separation, birth of child	Death of peer, divorce of parents, arrest
6	Extreme	Death of close relative, divorce, jail term	Death of parent or sibling
7	Catastrophic	Concentration camp experience, devastating natural disaster	Multiple family deaths

Source: From DSM-III (APA, 1980).

Table 12–6. Axis V Scale for Rating Level of Functioning

Levels	*Adult examples*	*Child or adolescent examples*
1 *SUPERIOR* Unusually effective functioning in social relations, occupational functioning, and use of leisure time.	Housewife takes excellent care of children and home, has warm relations with family and many close friends, and is effectively involved in several community activities.	12-year-old girl is getting superior grades in school, is extremely popular among her peers, and excels in many sports.
2 *VERY GOOD* Better than average functioning in social relations, occupational functioning, and use of leisure time.	A 65-year-old retired widower does some volunteer work, often sees old friends, and pursues many life-long hobbies.	An adolescent boy is getting average grades, works part-time, has several close friends, and plays banjo in jazz band.
3 *GOOD* No more than slight impairment in either social or occupational functioning.	A man functions extremely well at a difficult job, but has only one or two good friends.	An 8-year-old boy is doing well in school and has several friends but bullies younger children.
4 *FAIR* Moderate impairment in either social relations or occupational functioning OR some impairment in both.	A female lawyer has trouble carrying through assignments and has several acquaintances but hardly any close friends.	A 10-year-old girl is doing poorly in school but has adequate peer and family relations.
5 *POOR* Marked impairment in either social relations or occupational functioning OR moderate impairment in both.	A man with one or two friends has trouble keeping a job for more than a few weeks.	A 14-year-old boy is almost failing in school and has trouble getting along with his peers.
6 *GROSSLY IMPAIRED* Marked impairment in both social relations and occupational functioning.	A woman is unable to do any of her housework and has violent outbursts towards family and neighbors.	A 6-year-old girl needs special help in all subjects and has virtually no peer relationships.

Source: From the DSM-III (APA, 1980).

move from a town where she had lived for more than ten years to a new location where her husband's job took him. Having to leave her friends, relatives, and a home she treasured triggered her feelings of loneliness and depression. Finally, Axis V provides a rating scale for levels of functioning ranging from superior to grossly impaired. Liz would probably obtain a rating of "poor."

No classification system of abnormal behavior is completely satisfactory. Many mental-health professionals object to the idea of pigeonholing people by placing them into diagnostic categories, particularly since many forms of behavior (e.g., dependence on tobacco or caffeine intoxication) that were not formally considered pathological are now labeled abnormal in DSM III. The same criticism applies to childhood disorders. Problem behavior, such as reading difficulties, is included under mental disorders in DSM III. The lifelong effect of acquiring such a label early in life can be devastating (Gamzey, 1978). Many psychologists view diagnostic labels as neither a necessary nor useful step in helping individuals with maladaptive behavior.

Labeling may be dangerous, especially if an incorrect label is affixed to a person. This was well demonstrated by a researcher (Rosenhan, 1973) who asked a group of friends, including three psychologists, a psychiatrist, a pediatrician, a painter, and a homemaker, to present themselves as mental patients at the local hospital and request admission. The only symptom they were instructed to report during the intake interview was that they heard voices sounding "empty, hollow, and thudding." All the people were admitted, even though their particular symptom cannot be found in the psychiatric literature as an indication of a psychiatric disorder. With one exception, all the pseudopatients were labeled schizophrenics.

Alternatives to the Traditional Classification System

Some psychologists, particularly those who endorse the social-learning view of abnormal behavior, are dissatisfied with DSM III because of its neglect of interpersonal behavior. As an alternative to the traditional scheme based on the medical model, Staats (1974) proposed a classification system that groups mental disorders into two categories: behavioral deficits or the lack of appropriate behavior, and inappropriate behavior. Behavioral deficits and inappropriate behavior affect three aspects of a person's behavior—motivation (see Chapter 6), language, and cognition (see Chapter 7)—or his or her actual or instrumental behavior. According to this approach, mental retardation may be classified as a deficit of the language-cognitive repertoire, while the prolonged rocking of the autistic child may be viewed as inappropriate behavior of the instrumental system. Instead of generating a diagnostic label, Staats's classification leads to a descriptive assessment of the person, whose abnormal behavior pattern can be viewed from several perspectives: motivational, cognitive, or instrumental.

A second alternative was suggested by psychologists McLemore and Smith Benjamin (1979). Arguing that a classification system must focus on interpersonal behavior, they attempted to translate the DSM into an interpersonal model. Their model is built on a wide array of social-behavior variables that focus either on the self (busy with own things, maintains contact with others) or on the other person (aggresses, intrudes). As the authors of this classification scheme stated:

> The task of the interpersonal diagnostician is to treat each social category, such as dependence, distrust, or competition, as a window through which to view the other domains of functioning; that is, the diagnostician is interested in the perceptual, cognitive, emotional, and biological processes that affect or derive from social behavior (McLemore and Smith Benjamin, 1979, p. 25).

Still other classification schemes emphasize the importance of disturbed families, deviant subcultures, or violence-prone societies. Psychologists who use these classification methods imply that in some cases of individual abnormality the social environment must also be considered in the diagnostic and intervention process.

The Myth of Mental Illness

For more than two decades psychiatrist Thomas Szasz has been one of the most outspoken and vocal critics of formal diagnosis—medical, psychoanalytic, or otherwise. In his classic treatise "The Myth of Mental Illness" (1960) he argues that there is no such thing as mental illness. Instead Szasz contends that it may be more useful to think of most forms of abnormal behavior as "problems of living." He believes that early psychiatrists deliberately attempted to create new criteria of abnormal behavior so that they could be called illnesses. In his words:

> In modern medicine, diseases were discovered; in modern psychiatry, they were invented. Paresis was proved to be a disease; hysteria was declared to be one (Szasz, 1960, p. 12).

According to Szasz, problems of living are simply types of behavior that deviate from social definitions of normality. Deviations from social norms, however, cannot be established by medical examinations. They must be determined by mental-health professionals or by the disturbed persons themselves in the process of treatment. In other words, what is called "mental illness" in medical terms must be defined by social criteria. Szasz summarizes his anti-mental-illness position as follows:

> Our adversaries are not demons, witches, fate, or illness. We have no enemy whom we can fight, exorcise, or dispel "by cure." What we have are problems in living—whether these be biological, economic, political, or sociopathological. . . . My argument was limited to the proposition that mental illness is a myth whose function is to distinguish and thus render more palatable a bitter pill of moral conflict in human relations (p. 118).

ANXIETY DISORDERS

For the remainder of the chapter we shall examine the major categories of abnormal behavior, beginning with the anxiety disorders and then moving on to personality disorders, the schizophrenias, the affective psychoses, and lastly the organic brain syndrome. Although the medical model seems to predominate in the official classifications systems such as DSM III, anxiety has been traditionally conceptualized in terms of Freud's theory.

Giving a speech is a common anxiety-producing experience. (© *Jim Anderson/Woodfin Camp & Associates*)

Anxiety is a universal experience. All of us experience feelings of unhappiness, insecurity, apprehension, or alarm. Anxiety accompanies many kinds of normal behavior: a first date, a visit to the dentist, a surprise quiz, or a public speech. Usually such feelings are transient and do not render us ineffective, since most of us have learned to cope with anxiety to some extent.

The Nature of Anxiety

While the transient anxiety most of us feel can be linked to specific events, the person who is suffering from an anxiety disorder experiences vague apprehension related to no specific event or sudden feelings of panic. Abnormal anxiety can lead to poor social skills, avoidance of problems, health-related complaints, and a generally negative self-concept. In addition, anxiety may show up in physiological symptoms, such as sweating, rapid breathing, increased heart rate, or raised blood pressure. In most cases the person has some awareness of being or feeling maladjusted without necessarily knowing why. Most anxiety disorders consist of the same psychological problems that disturb "normal" people, but they are exaggerated to the point where they interfere with the person's life adjustment.

Until recently, all anxiety disorders were grouped into a single diagnostic category known as the neuroses. Neuroses included a variety of behavior patterns in which anxiety ranged from mild to severely disabling. Freud, in his extensive writings about the neuroses, initially attributed neurotic behavior to inadequacies in psychosexual development but later changed his views to interpret anxiety as a danger signal serving to alert the ego to pending problems. For Freud, all forms of neurotic behavior were manifestations of excessive anxiety.

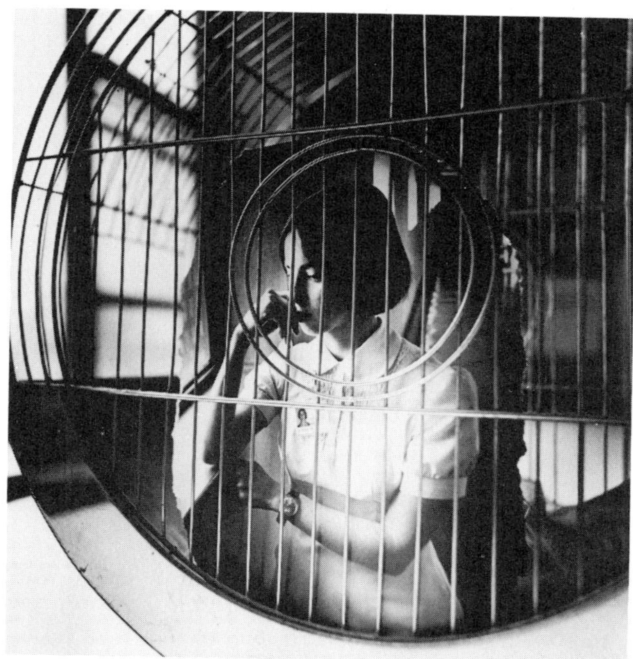

Claustrophobia and acrophobia are common, and treatable, phobic conditions. (© *Arthur Tress/Woodfin Camp & Associates*)

One of the most radical changes in DSM III is the reconceptualization of the neuroses (Nathan & Harris, 1980). Whereas Freud treated the widely divergent patterns he called neuroses as a single category, DSM III, in recognition of the important differences in the various manifestations of anxiety, replaced the term "neuroses" with "anxiety disorders." Included under this heading are three new categories: generalized anxiety disorders, somatoform disorders, and dissociative disorders. While this shift in conceptualization may appear to be trivial, it does imply that anxiety is no longer treated from the traditional Freudian perspective. Nevertheless, the term "neuroses" is so firmly embedded in our thinking about abnormal behavior that it will undoubtedly be used for years to come.

Anxiety disorders are a diverse group of maladaptive behavior patterns in which anxiety, either generalized or limited to specific situations or objects, is the dominant characteristic. The major anxiety disorders are the following: phobic disorders, obsessive-compulsive disorders, and generalized anxiety disorders.

Phobic Disorders

Phobic reactions are triggered by specific situations or objects, such as high places or sharp utensils. A **phobia** is an extreme, morbid, and irrational fear that can severely restrict a person's life. Most phobic individuals are aware that there is no cause for their fear, but they cannot explain why certain circumstances or objects create such intense distress in them.

Most of us have our share of minor fears, such as being afraid of snakes, of walking alone late at night, or of being in closed places. The term "phobic disorder" is used only if the fear is incapacitating and disrupts the person's life in some way. For example, the individual who has a phobic fear of heights may have to pass up a new job that requires frequent air travel.

Phobic disorders are not uncommon. It is estimated in the DSM III that about seven percent of the general population may have been treated for a phobic reaction at some time. Phobias are more common among women than among men (Al-Issa, 1980), partly because phobic behavior is more acceptable in our society for women than for men. A woman who quickly climbs on a chair when she sees a cockroach crawling on the floor is simply laughed at. A man who exhibits the same behavior runs the risk of being called crazy.

There are potentially hundreds of phobias because there is nothing that cannot be an object of morbid dread. Some of the common phobias are:

acrophobia, fear of high places
agoraphobia, fear of open places
claustrophobia, fear of closed places
monophobia, fear of being alone
pyrophobia, fear of fire
zoophobia, fear of animals

One of the more idiosyncratic phobias is called "Arachibutryophobia." It is the fear of peanut butter sticking to the roof of your mouth (Wallechinsky & Wallace, 1975).

Since most phobics do not suffer from any physical disease, the models most commonly applied to the phobias are the learning and psychoanalytic models. According to the learning model, phobias may be viewed as conditioned-anxiety responses. This process was illustrated by the case of little Albert in Chapter 5. If you recall, he was experimentally conditioned to fear a white rat, and this fear generalized to other furry objects. According to learning theorists, the learning processes in this situation provide the basis for later phobic fear of objects similar to the original cause of fear. Psychoanalysts interpret phobias as developing through displacement, a defense mechanism of the ego. When the anxiety aroused by a situation is blocked, it may be displaced to another situation that can be avoided more easily. For example, it may be less troublesome for a man to have a phobia of guns than to become aware of his own urges toward violence. In this case, the phobia protects the person from his own dangerous impulses.

Obsessive-Compulsive Disorders

This behavior pattern refers to persistent, recurrent thoughts (**obsessions**) or actions that the person feels compelled to carry out over and over again (**compulsions**). For instance, one person may be preoccupied with the thought of shouting obscenities, while another may wash his or her hands until the skin is raw. If the person is prevented from entertaining the thought or engaging in the activity, anxiety or even panic may develop. Many obsessive-compulsive individuals come from perfectionist and critical backgrounds, and often thoroughness and punctuality accompany the obsessive-compulsive reaction (Carr, 1974).

Mild forms of compulsive behavior are everyday phenomena. We may keep wondering, after we have left the house, whether we turned the lights off, or we may knock on wood after mentioning our good fortune. Clinical studies suggest that compulsive behavior can vary from minor acts, such as lining up pillows in a precise manner, to elaborate rituals that may take several hours. Consider the following case:

> Mr. R. developed an extensive checking ritual that he performed each evening before going to bed. Not only was his problem time-consuming and very frustrating, but it also created much conflict between him and his wife. Each evening at approximately the same time, Mrs. R. would go to her bedroom and get ready for bed. Mr. R. would then begin his checking in a very systematic manner, examining each room in the house in the same order every night. Mrs. R. had to be in her bedroom before the checking could begin, because Mr. R. was afraid that she might use something after he had checked it or that she might leave her cigarette burning in an ash tray that he had already cleaned. This behavior was extremely annoying to Mrs. R. (Melamed & Siegel, 1975, pp. 826–827).

Generalized-Anxiety Disorders

This is a new diagnostic category that refers to diffuse, chronic anxiety. Freud called this condition **free-floating anxiety.** People who suffer from this type of anxiety disorder continually feel a sense of tension and dread but cannot say what they are afraid of. Eventually this diffuse fear interferes with everyday functioning. The person finds it hard to concentrate, make decisions, and remember commitments; appointments are missed and letters left unmailed. In addition, people with this disorder may develop nervous twitches, headaches, breathing difficulties, clammy hands, and a racing pulse. In other words, they have pervasive "jitters" (Bootzin & Acocella, 1980).

Somatoform Disorders

Somatoform disorders refer to specific, relatively persistent bodily complaints or pain that have no apparent anatomical or physiological basis. There are several types of somatoform disorders. Since the differences among them are usually very subtle, we shall limit our discussion to the major though fairly rare form, the **conversion disorder.** An earlier term for this disorder, conversion hysteria, reflected the Freudian belief that psychological problems can take on the form of physical, or somatic, illness.

Conversion symptoms take a variety of bodily forms, including muscle paralysis, loss of speech, and tremors. Blindness or deafness may occur, either alone or accompanying other symptoms. People with conversion disorders are not faking their symptoms; the symptoms are real. However, they can be distinguished from symptoms of true organic injuries. First, a person with a conversion reaction typically is completely unperturbed by the symptoms and does not demonstrate the anxiety or panic one might expect in a person who suddenly becomes blind or deaf. In addition, conversion disorders fail to clearly follow the symptoms of true physical illnesses. For example, a woman with paralysis from the wrist down, called glove paralysis, did not have a severed nerve in her arm or hand to account for the symptom. Even in muscular paralyses the normal reflexes are retained in the paralyzed area.

The symptoms of conversion disorders can be considered a defense against anxiety. A person with a conversion symptom enacts the role of a person with organic disease and thereby communicates his or her subjective distress. Besides acting out psychological pain, the person may also use his or her "illness" as an excuse to shun responsibilities and attract attention.

Dissociative Disorders

In this category we find conditions that are characterized by sudden, temporary alternations of consciousness or identity. Among the various **dissociative disorders,** the **multiple personality** is the rarest and the most dramatic. In this condition the person alternates between two or more distinctive and well-developed personalities, each of which has its own style, habits, and memories. A famous contemporary case of multiple personality was reported by Thigpen and Cleckley in the popular book *The Three Faces of Eve* (1957); the more recent best-seller *Sybil* (Schreiber, 1974) is about a girl with 16 personalities. The woman described in *The Three Faces of Eve* illustrates the dynamics of the multiple personality:

> Eve White was the original dominant person who had no knowledge of the existence of her second personality, Eve Black, although she had been alternating between the two of them for several years. Whenever Eve Black surfaced all that Eve White could report was that she had "black-outs." Eve Black, on the other hand, was aware of the existence of Eve White, knew everything she did and talked about her with flippancy and contempt. Eve White was bland, quiet, and serious. Eve Black was carefree, mischievous, and uninhibited. She would come out at the most inappropriate times leaving Eve White with hangovers, bills, and a reputation in local bars that she could not explain. Jane, more mature than the other two personalities, apparently developed as a result of the therapeutic process.

Eventually a fourth personality, Evelyn, emerged who seemed to be an integration of the other three personalities.

PERSONALITY DISORDERS

The personality disorders are serious psychological disturbances that nevertheless allow the person to make marginal adjustment because the individual's contact with reality is not greatly impaired. According to DSM III, personality disorders are enduring maladaptive behavior patterns that are acquired over a lifetime. Although the classification system lists a number of different subtypes in this category, it is often difficult to distinguish the personality disorders from other patterns of maladaptive behavior. Most of the research in this diagnostic category has focused on the antisocial personality.

The Antisocial Personality

Antisocial behavior consists of a repetitive pattern of impulsive, often purposeless acts that bring the person into conflict with society. One of the most extensive descriptions of antisocial behavior was provided by Hervey Cleckley (1976) in his book *The Mask of Sanity*. We shall draw from his description in summarizing the major characteristics of the antisocial person.

Guiltlessness. Antisocial behavior is neither neurotic nor psychotic. Although the antisocial person seems to have a clear conception of reality and of society's moral standards, his or her behavior is characterized by an apparent absence of feelings of guilt or responsibility. Antisocial persons chronically break the rules of the family, school, or other social agencies and frequently break the law.

Failure to Learn from Experience. Antisocial persons commit many self-defeating and often criminal acts without regard for the consequences. After being caught cheating, stealing, robbing, or even killing and given the appropriate punishment, the person is likely to repeat the same acts, seemingly unable to profit from prior mistakes. Thus punishment is ineffective in suppressing the occurrence of future antisocial acts. Antisocial persons, in spite of an above-average level of intelligence, continue to show poor judgment and cannot avoid being caught again.

Ability to Make a Good Impression. Antisocial persons impress others as likable, friendly, gutsy, and poised. In conversation they can be convincing and sincere. Frequently they have a superficial charm that makes it easy for them to persuade others to do what they want. They have been described as life's chronic imposters, gifted with an ability to impress other people with their goodness as they exploit them. They may be successful for years as crooked politicians, con men, or prostitutes. Some of them are criminals who are highly respected by their own peer group (Poland, 1974).

Lack of Capacity to Love. Antisocial persons are unable to love or feel a genuine sense of affection or loyalty for another person. Yet they can pretend to love and voice feelings of affection and caring if that will help them to achieve what they are after. Antisocial individuals usually treat their wives, children, parents, and friends as objects to be manipulated for their own pleasure and gains.

Thrill Seeking. Many of the impulsive acts of the antisocial person are performed on the spur of the moment or "for the fun of it." Antisocial individuals continually seek excitement: thefts, robberies, new sexual partners, new domiciles, in short, anything that breaks up their humdrum routine. Committed to this erratic, impulsive style, they lead a hectic life, flitting from one mate to another, from job to job, and from place to place. When their attempts at finding new thrills are frustrated, they are likely to respond with aggression or violence.

Causes of Antisocial Behavior. Research into the causes of antisocial behavior has focused on

APPLICATION

The Profile of an Antisocial Personality: Charles Manson

In 1969 the police discovered the bodies of five individuals, including movie star Sharon Tate, brutally murdered and mutilated in an expensive California home. After a search of several months the police identified 35-year-old Charles Manson as the killer.

Born to a teenage mother who drank heavily and often left him alone at night, Manson spent a good part of his childhood in penal institutions (Bugliosi, 1975). When he was 13, he committed his first violent crime and was sent to a training school for boys for three years. During this period he attempted to run away 18 times. A few years later he was caught taking a stolen vehicle across a state line. After a short time at another training school, Manson was transferred to a high-security institution because he was found holding a razor blade against another boy's throat while sodomizing him.

The years between 1954 and 1967 were spent in and out of federal penitentiaries. During one of his brief stays out of prison, Manson married. His wife later divorced him during one of his subsequent incarcerations. He was released in 1967 at the age of 33 and given permission to move to San Francisco. There he drifted to the Haight-Ashbury section, which was then the haven of "flower children" and hippies. Within a year Manson surrounded himself with a group of followers who called themselves the "Manson family." Drawn to Manson by his remarkable ability to recognize and exploit the vulnerability of others, members of the "family" would do anything Manson asked, including murder. In 1971 Manson and several members of the "family" were sentenced to life imprisonment for the crimes they had committed.

Manson's history shows many of the characteristics of antisocial personalities: lack of respect for social conventions, criminal behavior, lack of genuine emotional ties, manipulation and exploitation of others, and indiscriminate sexual behavior.

Charles Manson has become the prototype of the antisocial personality. (© *United Press International Photos*)

both physiological and learning factors. Some investigators have attributed the antisocial behavior pattern to abnormalities in the brain. Clinical studies indicated that approximately 50 percent of antisocial persons showed abnormal brain-wave patterns. In evaluating these findings, however, we need to consider two additional factors. First, most of the data were collected from individuals who had come to the attention of the law and had been imprisoned. Their experiences in prison may have contributed to their unusual brain-wave pattern. Second, we need to remember that 10 to 15 percent of individuals who are not antisocial also show abnormal EEG patterns (Syndulko, 1978).

Antisocial behavior is often acquired in childhood or adolescence, as illustrated by the case of Charles Manson (see Application). Although most children suffering parental loss or emotional rejection do not become antisocial, many antisocial persons have been raised in disturbed families and have experienced the loss of a parent owing to separation, divorce, or death. The most common pattern is that of boys who are rejected by or lose their father (Rosenthal, 1970). As in so many cases of psychopathology, psychologists suspect an interaction between physiological and psychological causes. Children who are born with subtle neurological problems and who grow up in unstable families in which they are exposed to parental loss or emotional rejection may be particularly prone to acquire antisocial behavior. By the time such a child has reached adolescence, he or she has learned that types of behavior that defy social conventions can bring recognition and prestige.

Other Personality Disorders

In addition to the antisocial personality, several other personality disorders are recognized in the DSM III. We shall briefly summarize the more common ones.

The Narcissistic Personality. This behavior pattern is marked by an exaggerated sense of self-importance, egotism, and selfishness. Narcissistic people are convinced of their own superiority and preoccupied with fantasies of their own brilliance, power, and attractiveness. They exploit others, taking them for granted and expecting to be served without giving in return. While narcissistic people often think they are being loving toward others, they are really concerned only with their own needs.

The Compulsive Personality. A compulsive personality is characterized by the need to be orderly and perfect in whatever is being done. Compulsive individuals are overconscientious and find it difficult to cope with the ambiguities in their lives. They are overconcerned with acting appropriately and with being meticulous at all times. Consequently they find it difficult to relax. They are formal in their dealings with others and incapable of taking genuine pleasure in anything. Although they may have spent an entire year mapping out a family vacation with lists, schedules, rules, and things to do and to take, they return having derived no enjoyment from the trip.

The compulsive personality should not be confused with the obsessive-compulsive disorder. In the compulsive personality, compulsiveness is pervasive and manifested in many everyday activities, whereas in the obsessive-compulsive disorders, compulsiveness is manifested in a single bizarre behavior, such as washing hands or the nightly ritual of Mr. R.

The Histrionic Personality. The histrionic personality is characterized by self-dramatization, self-centeredness, and overreaction. These people tend to be vain and strive to be the focus of attention. Through seductiveness and exaggeration of their own feelings, they try to impress others. Histrionic personalities will faint at the sight of blood, will dominate an entire dinner party with the tale of their recent faith healing, will be so overcome with emotion during a sad movie that they have to be taken home immediately (thus spoiling their companion's evening), or will threaten suicide if a lover's interest cools. To themselves, they seem very sensitive; to others, after the first impression has worn off, they usually seem shallow and insincere (Bootzin & Acocella, 1980). Because their vanity and egocentricity get in the way, these individuals have difficulty in establishing meaningful relationships.

The Dependent Personality. This is a personality pattern marked by the continual need to rely on others to assume responsibility or make decisions. The dependent person lacks self-confidence and resourcefulness and feels helpless. These individuals build their lives around others because they would rather subordinate their own needs than run the risk of not being taken care of or of being rejected. For example, a dependent personality may tolerate a physically abusive spouse to avoid any possibility of being deserted and left to rely on herself or himself. Dependent personalities often become anxious and depressed when left alone for even brief periods.

The Avoidant Personality. This personality pattern describes people who are evasive and fail to face life's challenges. They have a deep mistrust of others and a markedly defeated self-image. Instead of coping with problems, the avoidant personality uses defensive strategies to avoid confrontation or pain. Jane, the high school teacher described at the beginning of this chapter, is likely to be an avoidant personality. Her social withdrawal and low self-esteem are reflected in her severe social isolation. Her desire for affection, which she cannot gain from her students, is redirected at her doll collection. Individuals with avoidant personality disorders are torn between a strong desire for affection and acceptance and an equally strong fear of rejection, a conflict that generates considerable tension.

THE PSYCHOTIC DISORDERS

The psychotic disorders differ sharply from anxiety and personality disorders because of the severely disabling symptoms and loss of contact with reality. The psychotic disorders are commonly divided into functional and organic psychoses. **Functional psychoses** are those in which no clear-cut organic basis exists that might explain the disturbed behavior. This category includes the schizophrenic and affective disorders. In **organic psychoses** a biological or physical cause has been identified. This section will focus on the functional psychoses; the organic psychoses will be discussed in a later section on the organic brain syndromes.

General Psychotic Symptoms

All psychotics have a number of symptoms in common. Typically a person's contact with reality is impaired; psychotics live in their own world of strange, disorganized ideas that make little or no sense to a normal person.

One of the major indications of the break with reality is **disorientation.** The psychotic individual who is disoriented does not know who or where he or she is, or what the date is. Psychologists say that such a person is disoriented to person, place, and time. The following dialogue illustrates disoriented psychotic reasoning:

Doctor: Can you state your name?
Patient: I can and I cannot.
Doctor: What is your name?
Patient: The same as yours, only different.
Doctor: Do you know who I am?
Patient: Of course, you are you and I am I.
Doctor: That is very good, but it is important for our records to obtain correct information.
Patient: Then write in your records that I am the King of Kings and you are my servant.
Doctor: You are not answering my questions.
Patient: I am, but you are not listening.
Doctor: I'll try again. What's today's date?
Patient: Oh, that's easy. It is the 33rd of June, 1933.
Doctor: What time of the day is it?
Patient: Tulip day, late evening.
Doctor: And why are you here?
Patient: To talk to you.
Doctor: But I can't get any information out of you.
Patient: That's because you are doing all the talking. Besides you are blowing my brain. (Coleman, Butcher & Carson, 1980).

Disturbed thinking is a second important symptom of psychoses. Thought disturbances can manifest themselves in a number of different ways. One of the most dramatic manifestations is **delusions,** which are false, persistent beliefs that are uncritically accepted as true and defended in spite of contradictory evidence. The two major types of delusions are delusions of grandeur and delusions of persecution. A person suffering from **delusions of grandeur** (see Application: Psychotic Delusions) believes that he or she is an extremely powerful, gifted, or important individual, such as Christ, Napoleon, or Buddha. In **delusions of persecution** the individual believes that he or she is the victim of a plot in which enemies threaten to kill, hunt, poison, or otherwise abuse him or her. The person may say, "Someone is piping poison through the ventilating system," "My phone is being tapped," "I am being followed," or "My teachers are out to flunk me." Sometimes delusions of grandeur and persecution are integrated so that the individual believes that someone is

APPLICATION

Psychotic Delusions: The New Head of the FBI

A local police department reported the case of a schizophrenic woman, who in a letter to President Carter, requested to be appointed the new director of the FBI. She called herself "General Magnifico" and claimed to be the granddaughter of Queen Victoria and Prince Albert of England, with blood relatives in all the royal families of Europe. Computers at the Pentagon had supposedly rated the "General" as having the highest intelligence score ever obtained by a human being—an IQ of 230.

Other outstanding accomplishments that the "General" claimed included making 47 parachute jumps behind enemy lines during World War II, saving aircraft carriers from being destroyed at Pearl Harbor, and receiving a commisssion from the president as a six-star general.

General Magnifico ended her letter to the president by saying that with her as the director of the FBI, effective control, which had been sadly lacking since the death of J. Edgar Hoover, would be reinstated. The letter was signed "General Magnifico, International Director of the FBI" (McPhatter, 1980).

trying to kill him or her because he or she possesses some special knowledge.

In general, the thought processes of the psychotic individual are disorganized and fragmented. Most psychotics show disruptions in the continuity of their thoughts. As a result the patterns of words they use do not follow the normal rules of logic. Psychotic language may be so disjointed as to be nearly impossible to follow. Among the language disorders of psychotics is the extensive use of **neologisms,** new words that the person invents by combining words or parts of words. One patient, for instance, referred to his doctor as "mediruler," a condensation of the words medicine and ruler, which indicated how this particular patient perceived his relationship with the psychiatrist. Another individual continually referred to his family as MoPoNoLo. This person was raised in a chaotic family where neither his mother nor his father (Mo and Po) loved him (NoLo). A third patient, who was preoccupied with conversations about sex, usually began her discussion with "Glogodivisex," which meant to her "Glory to God in the Divine for permitting me to talk about sex" (Nathan & Harris, 1980).

Psychotic language also contains **word salads,** which are totally incoherent sentences. Psychologist Paul Meehl (1962) pointed out that psychotic language loses much of its communication value, a phenomenon he refers to as "cognitive slippage." Let us look at an example:

Smith: Do you work at the air base? Hm?
Jones: You know what I think of work. I am thirty-three in June, do you mind?
Smith: June?
Jones: Thirty-three years old in June. This stuff goes out the window after I leave the hospital. So I can't get my vocal cords back. So I lay off cigarettes. I'm a spatial condition, from outer space myself, no shit (Haley, 1963, p. 86).

A third category of psychotic symptoms involves perceptual disturbances. As perceptual functions alter, the psychotic person hears and sees things in a distorted way. One frequently observed symptom is the **hallucination** or false perception. Hallucinations can occur in all sensory modalities, but auditory and visual hallucinations are the most common. The person with auditory hallucinations may hear voices that accuse him or her of being a spy, a murderer, or a homosexual.

Psychotics show a wide range of emotional disturbances. Feelings may be flat, meaning that the person remains emotionally unresponsive no matter how exciting the situation is. Or emotional responses may be inappropriate to the situation. For example, a patient who is told of the death of a close relative may break out into uncontrollable laughter. Emotional disturbances such as these make it very difficult for psychotics to function in interpersonal or social settings.

Psychotic behavior is a complicated tangle of cognitive, perceptual, emotional, and interpersonal disturbances. For convenience we have categorized the functional psychoses into two major groups: the schizophrenias and the affective psychoses. Each category encompasses a number of subtypes that may appear as clinically distinct conditions. In reality, however, there is a great deal of overlap in symptoms, which often makes any diagnosis according to subtype difficult.

The Schizophrenias

Probably no other psychological disorder has received more attention than **schizophrenia.** The dramatic break with reality and the bizarre and unusual behavior that characterize schizophrenics have fascinated scientists and lay people alike for centuries. Of all the psychotic disorders, the schizophrenias make up the largest and most important group. The National Institute of Mental Health reports that 25 percent of the patients admitted to mental hospitals each year are diagnosed as schizophrenic.

Disturbed thinking and disorganized language processes, such as those just described, are at the core of schizophrenia. Schizophrenic thinking is often described as autistic, which means that the person's thinking focuses on the self or fantasy to avoid communication and objective reality. Schizophrenic thinking has also been called prelogical in reference to the seemingly primitive, fragmented, incomplete thought processes, which often resemble the cognitive patterns of a young child.

David Berkowitz, who for no apparent motive stalked and killed six people and wounded seven in New York City in 1977, claimed to have experienced auditory hallucinations. A sample of his writing shows the incoherence and violence of his mental state. (© *Wide World Photos; United Press International Photos*)

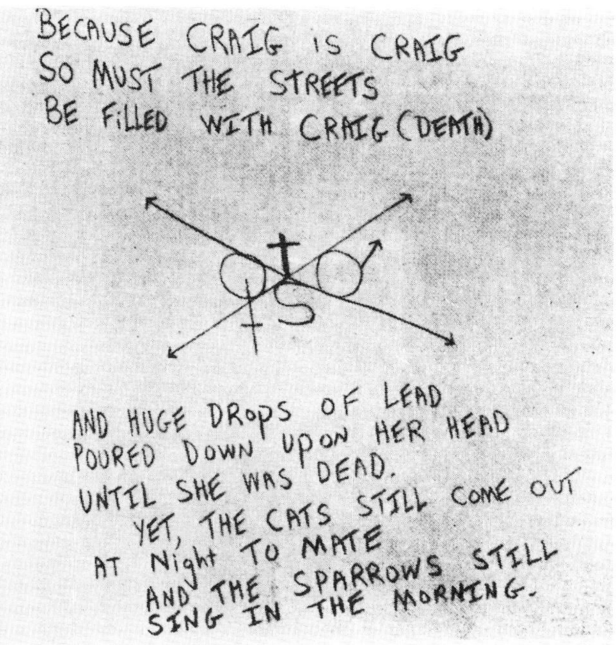

In many cases a specific event precipitates the onset of schizophrenia, which is followed by a gradual decline in personality and intellectual functioning. As the disorder progresses, the schizophrenic becomes increasingly withdrawn, loses interest in regular activities, and becomes preoccupied with private thoughts. A 42-year-old man known to one of the authors, for instance, was admitted to a local mental hospital in an acutely anxious and depressed state. As an extremely conscientious and hard-working family man, he had recently been under a lot of pressure, putting in many hours of overtime at work. At home he had several quarrels with his next-door neighbor. To further complicate the situation, his sexual relations with his wife were ungratifying and frustrating. He began to wonder what his neighbors had against him and whether his wife was having an affair. Eventually he was convinced that his wife and neighbors were involved in a plot against him. His work performance began to deteriorate and eventually he lost his job. Prior to his admission to the hospital, he spent much of the day observing his neighbors from behind closed blinds.

The schizophrenic syndromes have been classified in a number of ways. Traditionally four major categories have been recognized: the paranoid, hebephrenic, catatonic, and simple type. The current DSM III lists three traditional sub-

APPLICATION

The Case of the Genain Sisters

This case history deals with identical quadruplets, all of whom became schizophrenics. When the sisters, Nora, Myra, Iris, and Hester, came to the attention of mental-health professionals, they were in their early twenties. At that time, all four of them displayed in varying degrees the same type of shy, withdrawn schizophrenic behavior. Three of the girls had graduated from high school and held jobs as clerks or typists; the fourth one had dropped out of school and was institutionalized. Eventually, however, the other three also withdrew from social contact and returned home or went to a mental hospital.

Tracing the family history, investigators found that the paternal grandmother of the quadruplets was schizophrenic. Thus it was thought that the sisters had a genetic predisposition to schizophrenia. This predisposition interacted with a pathological family pattern. The family was described as a rigid, closed system in which the girls had felt isolated since early childhood. The atmosphere in the family was characterized by constriction, overcontrol, and hostility (Rosenthal, 1963, p. 551). Parental communications were inconsistent, unclear, and double-binding. Rosenthal believed that the parents failed in even the most elementary tasks of parenthood.

The parents were particularly inconsistent with regard to sexual behavior. Mrs. Genain frantically worried about the evils of masturbation and convinced her husband to try an incredible number of measures, including clitoral circumcision of two of the girls who enjoyed mutual masturbation. Although the parents continually emphasized the dangerous evils of sex, Mr. Genain frequently fondled the girls' breasts. His wife rationalized that he was testing them to see how they would react with boys, with whom, however, they were never allowed to go out. The father also insisted on being present when his daughters dressed, undressed, or changed their sanitary pads during menstruation. Ironically each of the four girls experienced sexual assaults from outsiders, which their father passed off as inconsequential.

Over a period of six years all four girls went through a psychotic breakdown, becoming increasingly disturbed, agitated, and hallucinatory. In all four cases, physical symptoms such as vomiting or insomnia preceded the final breakdown. It may be significant, as Rosenthal pointed out, that in the case of three of the girls deterioration occurred shortly after a man made rather insistent "improper advances."

types of schizophrenia: disorganized, catatonic, and paranoid. In addition, there is an undifferentiated type reserved for patients who cannot be classified into the first three categories and a residual type that describes the individual who is in partial remission (i.e., currently symptom-free) but who has experienced psychotic episodes at one time. Some psychiatric texts list several dozen subcategories.

One of the reasons schizophrenia is categorized in so many different ways is the fact that schizophrenia is a multifaceted, often changing disorder that can take many different forms even in the same person (Haas, 1979). Here we shall look at the three major subtypes upon which traditional as well as current classification systems agree: paranoid, disorganized (hebephrenic), and catatonic.

Paranoid Schizophrenia. The paranoid subtype is not only the most commonly diagnosed form of schizophrenia but also probably the most clearly differentiated subtype. **Paranoid schizophrenia,** as a rule, has a later age of onset (after 35) than the other subcategories. Persons in this category are suspicious of other people and mistrust the world in general. Delusions of persecution are the most dramatic symptoms. Paranoid schizophrenics are convinced that the signals they receive are evidence of serious threats against their life. These delusions come to wholly preoccupy them.

The following case illustrates the delusional system of a paranoid schizophrenic:

> This patient entered a psychiatric hospital after having failed to obtain a body "for his experiments in restoring life." He had been in the army for 16½ months without being hospitalized, despite the fact that he had been psychotic during the entire period. The patient had a number of delusions, including one that people had been trying to kill him for about eight years. According to him, he had been changing into a woman for the last five years and would soon be able to have children. Of interest is that this patient existed in society for quite a while before his paranoid ideas came to be known, resulting in his hospitalization (Salzinger, 1973, p. 4).

Paranoid schizophrenics do not show the intellectual deterioration characteristic of most other forms of schizophrenia. They remain in better contact with the environment and can adjust to hospital routines. They appear interested in the activities and are able to maintain a facade of sanity since many of their motor, affective, and communicative abilities are largely unimpaired.

Disorganized (Hebephrenic) Schizophrenia. Disorganized schizophrenics display the most fragmented behavior of all schizophrenics and probably come closest to the common stereotype of insanity. **Hebephrenia** is characterized by an early age of onset, often in adolescence, and rapid intellectual deterioration. Thinking is severely disorganized and so are emotions and motor behavior. Hebephrenic schizophrenics are noted for immature actions, grimaces, and inappropriate giggles. In many ways, the hebephrenic acts very much like a child as far as temperament, poor self-control, and behavior are concerned.

The clinical picture of disorganized schizophrenia is well illustrated in the case of a divorcée, 32 years of age, who had come to the hospital with bizarre delusions, severe personality decompensation, (i.e., the inability to maintain adequate functioning), a record of alcoholism, and possible incestuous relations with a brother. The following conversation shows typical hebephrenic responses to questioning:

> Doctor: How do you feel today?
> Patient: Fine.
> Doctor: When did you come here?
> Patient: 1416, you remember, doctor (silly giggle).
> Doctor: Do you know why you are here?
> Patient: Well, in 1951 I changed into two men. President Truman was judge at my trial. I was convicted and hung (silly giggle). My brother and I were given back our normal bodies five years ago. I am a police woman. I keep a dictaphone on my body.
> Doctor: Can you tell me the name of this place?
> Patient: I have not been a drinker for 16 years. I am taking a mental rest after a "carter" assignment or "quile." You know, a

"penwrap." I had contacts with Warner Brother Studios and Eugene broke phonograph records but Mike protested. I have been with the police department for 35 years. I am made of flesh and blood - see, doctor (pulling up her dress).

Doctor: Are you married?

Patient: No. I am not attracted to men (silly giggle). I have a companionship arrangement with my brother. I am a "loner" . . . a bachelor (Coleman, Butcher, & Carson, 1980).

Catatonic Schizophrenia. The catatonic schizophrenic is noticeable for his or her motor symptoms. In addition to displaying some of the typical schizophrenic symptoms, catatonics may fluctuate between catatonic excitement and catatonic stupor. During the excited episode, catatonics are agitated, noisy, destructive, and talk excitedly and incoherently. They act as if they are possessed and directed by some super-energizing force. In some cases their extreme hyperactivity can push catatonics toward a condition known as "exhaustion death."

In the stuporous phase the person may remain in a fixed position for extended periods of time. A distinguishing feature of the stuporous phase is the **waxy flexibility** of the catatonic. This is a phenomenon that allows the person to maintain any posture as though molded into a wax statue. The disorder is illustrated in the following case:

> In the admission office the patient showed many mannerisms, lay down on the floor, pulled at his foot, made undirected, violent movements, struck attendants, grimaced, assumed rigid postures, refused to speak, and appeared to be having auditory hallucinations. Later in the day, he was found in the stuporous state. His face was without expression, he was mute and rigid, and paid no attention to those around him or their questions. His eyes were closed and the lids could be separated only with effort. For five days he remained mute, negativistic, and inaccessible, at times staring vacantly into space, at times with his eyes tightly closed (Kolb, 1977, p. 407).

Origins of Schizophrenia

The search for the causes of schizophrenia has been an exhaustive and elusive one. Biological, psychological, and sociocultural factors have all been explored as a possible cause of schizophrenia. We shall look at the causes of schizophrenia in accordance with the three models and look at evidence that supports the notion that schizophrenia can be traced to some biological mechanism (genetic or biochemical), that it can be psychologically caused, or that it is the result of faulty learning.

Genetic Factors. Because a disproportionate number of schizophrenics come from families with a history of schizophrenia, many investigators have been tempted to conclude that genetic factors must play a casual role. One way of studying genetic factors is to compare the incidence of schizophrenia in identical and fraternal twins. Summarizing the literature on twin studies conducted over the past 50 years, Rosenthal (1970) found that members of a pair of identical twins are much more likely to be schizophrenic than members of a pair of fraternal twins. Since identical twins have the same genetic make-up, these data were considered very strong evidence for a genetic theory of schizophrenia. Additional evidence for such an interpretation comes from studies of children who grow up in a schizophrenic family. This line of research, pioneered by Kallman (1953, 1958), indicated that the child of one schizophrenic parent has a 16.4 percent chance of becoming schizophrenic, and the child of two schizophrenic parents a 68 percent chance, as compared with an incidence of less than 1 percent in the general population. Despite numerous criticisms of Kallman's research, later investigators (e.g., Slater & Cowie, 1971) obtained essentially similar results.

Despite the considerable evidence on the side of genetic factors, however, the conclusion that schizophrenia is entirely genetically determined is not warranted. At the present time we do not know how schizophrenia is transmitted genetically. One theory that holds promise is the **diathesis-stress** theory (Meehl, 1962). According to this conceptualization, a genetic predisposition for schizophrenia (the diathesis) interacts with environmental stress to produce the clinical syndrome. The nature and severity of the symptoms depend on the individual's specific predisposition and the type of stress (childbirth trauma, disease, or environmental stress). Schizophrenia, according to this theory, develops in individuals who are genetically predisposed to schizophrenia and who are exposed to particularly stressful experiences for which they have not developed effective coping behavior.

Biochemical Factors. Several theories have been proposed that focus on chemical aberrations in schizophrenics. Most biochemical researchers assume that schizophrenics are victims of an inborn error of metabolism that alters the chemistry of the central nervous system. Of the many different biochemical hypotheses suggested, the **dopamine** hypothesis currently predominates. Stated simply, this theory asserts that schizophrenics suffer from an excessively high concentration of the transmitter substance dopamine in their brains. More specifically, it asserts that schizophrenia is associated with excess activity of those parts of the brain that use dopamine to transmit neural impulses (Snyder, 1976). Major support for the dopamine hypothesis comes from studies on "antipsychotic" drugs (phenothiazine, for example), which have been found effective in controlling schizophrenic symptoms. Snyder (1980) suggested that these drugs work by blocking the brain's receptor sites for dopamine, thereby reducing the activity of those parts of the brain that use dopamine to transmit neural impulses.

Biochemical investigations are complicated because most of the research has been carried out with hospitalized patients who have had poor diets and inadequate exercise and were often heavy smokers. In addition, these patients have been exposed to various biological treatments, such as shock or drug therapy, that profoundly alter biochemical processes. Thus we must be extremely careful in drawing conclusions about observed differences in the biochemistry of institutionalized and noninstitutionalized people. If conclusive evidence for a biochemical explanation for schizophrenia were found, that explanation would likely be a very complex one involving different chemical imbalances not only in different types of schizophrenia but also for different phases of any single case of schizophrenia (Davis, 1975).

Psychosocial Factors. As we have seen, family relationships, especially those between a mother and son, have been regarded as crucial in the development of schizophrenia. One hypothesis focuses on communications between parents and children and the concept of the **double bind** (Bateson, Jackson, Haley, & Weakland, 1956), a situation in which a person is exposed to conflicting communications and punished regardless of the response he or she makes. Let us look at a typical incident:

> A young man who had fairly well recovered from an acute schizophrenic episode was visited in the hospital by his mother. He was glad to see her and impulsively put his arms around her shoulders whereupon she stiffened. He withdrew his arms and asked, "Don't you love me anymore?" He then blushed and she said, "Dear, you must not be so easily embarrassed and afraid of your feelings." The patient was able to stay with her only a few minutes more and following her departure, he assaulted an aide (Bateson et al., 1956, pp. 258–259).

The patient's dilemma is obvious: he cannot show his love for his mother because it makes her feel uncomfortable; but if he does not, he will be criticized by her and feels that he might lose her.

Double-bind situations occur not only in families but also in hospital settings. Mental institutions contain many contradictory elements. The hospital, for instance, fosters dependency and immaturity but expects the patient to become independent and mature in order to obtain a discharge. More recent double-bind studies have focused on the communication patterns of all family members. Overall this research indicates that schizophrenics often come from families that exhibit deviant and confused communication patterns. As with all theories of schizophrenia, the double-bind hypothesis has its problems; it fails to explain, for instance, why one child growing up in a family with disturbed communication patterns develops normally, while another child becomes schizophrenic.

Sociological Factors. The relationship between the incidence of schizophrenia and social class has been demonstrated in numerous studies. In the now classic population survey of New Haven, Connecticut, Hollinshead and Redlich (1958) found a significantly higher incidence of schizophrenia among the lower socioeconomic classes. Although the correlations between social class and schizophrenia are consistent, they are difficult to interpret.

A number of possible explanations have been proposed. Some investigators point to class differences in child-rearing practices that may dispose lower-class children to more intense stress because of harsh, punitive parental treatment. Others believe that the devastating effects of poverty force members of the lower classes to withdraw from the harsh realities of life. Still others maintain that schizophrenics have a tendency to "drift down" into slum areas because of their bizarre behavior and social ineptness. Yet recent evidence (Kohn, 1973) indicates that even though some schizophrenics do suffer a downward slide, most come from lower-class families and never do achieve the higher-class status open to mentally healthy individuals raised in similar circumstances. A last explanation holds that schizophrenics from the middle and upper classes, who can afford private treatment, are less likely to be diagnosed as such than are lower-class individuals dependent upon public care. Thus while it is clear that the incidence of schizophrenia is greater in the lower social strata, it is not clear why this is the case.

The Affective Psychoses

The second major category of the psychotic disorders are the affective psychoses, which are characterized by extreme mood alternations. The two major forms of affective psychoses are manic-depressive psychosis and depression. In addition to the mood disturbances, patients with affective disorders show marked delusions and hallucinations, poor judgment, and various somatic symptoms.

Manic-Depressive Psychosis. The term **"manic-depressive psychosis"** is used to describe a person whose moods swing from normal to extreme elation, from normal to devastating depression or involve both extremes, in which case the condition is classified as **bipolar affective disorder.**

The manic phase is characterized by excitement, joy, and euphoria. The person becomes increasingly overexcited, grandiose, and boastful. The initial feeling of well-being develops into a chaotic and sometimes even frightening experience in which the person becomes hyperactive, moving with great speed from one task to another. Many patients experience the manic state as highly powerful and productive. All systems work at rapid speed, thinking and speech are speeded up, energy seems endless, and moral restraints give way. Although the euphoria is mixed with irritability and restlessness, manics generally see the world as a flamboyant place. The following conversation with a 46-year-old manic woman is typical of this reaction pattern:

Doctor: Hello, how are you today?

Patient Fine, fine, and how are you, Doc? You're looking pretty good. I never felt better in my life. Could I go for a schnapps now? Say, you're new around here. I never saw you before—not too bad. How's about you and me stepping out tonight if I can get that sour old battleship of a nurse to give me back my dress. It's low cut and it'll wow them. Even in this old rag, all the doctors give me the eye. You know I'm a model. Yep, I was No. 1—used to dazzle them in New York, London, and Paris. Hollywood has been angling with me for a contract.

Doctor: Is that what you did before you came here?

Patient: I was a society queen . . . entertainer of kings and presidents. I've five grown sons and I wore out three husbands getting them, about ready for a couple of more now. There's no woman like me, smart, brainy, beautiful, and sexy. You can see I don't believe in playing myself down. If you are good and you know you're good, you have to speak out and I know what I've got.

Doctor: Why are you in this hospital?

Patient: That's just the trouble. My husbands never could understand me. I was too far above them. I need someone like me with the savoir faire, you know, somebody that can get around, intelligent, lots on the ball. Say, where can I get a schnapps around here—always like one before dinner. I've got special recipes like you never ate before . . . sauces, wines, desserts. Boy, it's making me hungry. Say, have you got anything for me to do around here? I've been showing these slowpokes how to make up beds but I want something more in line with my talents.

Doctor: What would you like to do?

Patient: Well, I've been thinking of organizing a show, singing, dancing, jokes. I still can do it all myself but I want to know what you think about it. I'll bet there's some schnapps in the kitchen. I'll look around later. You know what we need here . . . a dance at night. I could play the piano, and teach them the latest steps. Wherever I go, I'm the life of the party (Coleman et al., 1980, p. 377).

The depressive phase of the manic-depressive psychosis is in total contrast to the manic stage. Instead of being elated, optimistic, and highly energetic, the person feels deeply discouraged, apathetic, and depressed. Psychotic symptoms such as disorientation, hallucination, and delusions are often seen. Some individuals go into a depressive stupor where they are oblivious to everything, including food and other physiological needs. In the stuporous phase the person is completely unresponsive and inactive, usually bedridden and artificially fed.

A person suffering from bipolar affective disorder alternates between the manic and the depressed state. The principal characteristic of this disorder is the recurrence of the attacks. Sometimes the person feels "on top of the world" and at other times "down in the dumps" without knowing why. The manic and depressive episodes may last from several weeks to well over a year. Many individuals experience intermittent periods of adaptive functioning before showing the next episode of mania or depression. The bipolar disorder is illustrated in the following case:

Mrs. M. was first admitted to a state hospital at the age of 38, although since childhood she had been characterized by mood swings, some of them extreme to the point of being psychotic. At 17 she suffered from a depression that rendered her unable to work for several months, although she was not hospitalized. At 33, shortly before the birth of her first child, she was greatly depressed. For a period of four days she appeared to be in a coma. About a month later she "became excited" and was entered as a patient in an institution for neurotic and mildly psychotic patients. As she began to improve, she was sent to a shore hotel for one night. On the following day she signed a year's lease on an apartment, bought furniture, and became heavily involved in debt. Shortly thereafter Mrs. M. became depressed and returned to the hospital in which she had previously been a patient. After several months she recovered and, except for relatively mild fluctuations of mood, remained well for approximately two years.

She then became overactive and exuberant and visited her friends, to whom she outlined her plans for reestablishing different forms of lucrative businesses. She purchased many clothes, bought furniture, pawned her rings, and wrote checks without funds. She was returned to a hospital. Gradually her manic symptoms subsided, and after four months she was discharged. For a period thereafter she was mildly depressed. In a

Nearly everyone experiences states of moderate depression. Severe depression, however, may be classified as a psychotic disorder. *(© Marjorie Pickens)*

little less than a year Mrs. M. again became overactive, played her radio until late in the night, smoked excessively, and took out insurance on a car that she had not yet bought. Contrary to her usual habits, she swore frequently and loudly, created a disturbance in a club to which she did not belong, and instituted divorce proceedings. On the day prior to her second admission to the hospital, she purchased 57 hats (Kolb, 1973, pp. 376–377).

Depression. All of us have experienced feelings of **depression** at various times of our lives. For some individuals, however, this mood persists and becomes a serious psychological problem that interferes with everyday functioning. Let us look at a case of severe depression.

E. D., aged 60, was admitted to the hospital because he was depressed, ate insufficiently, and believed that his stomach was "rotting away." The patient [in the premorbid state] was described as a friendly, sociable individual, not quarrelsome, jealous, or critical, and with a sense of humor. He was considered even-tempered, slow to anger, tender-hearted, and emotional.

At 51 the patient suffered from a period of depression and was obliged to resign his position. This period continued for about nine months, after which he seemed to recover fully. He resumed his work but after two years suffered a second period of depression. Again he recovered after several months and returned to a similar position and held it until two months before his admission. At this time he began to worry that he was not doing his work well, talked much of his lack of fitness for his duties, and finally resigned. He spent Thanksgiving Day at his son's in a neighboring city, but while there he was sure that the water pipes in his own house would freeze during his absence and his family would be "turned out into the street." A few days later he was found standing by a pond, evidently contemplating suicide. He soon began to remain in bed and sometimes wrapped his head in his bed clothing to shut out the external world. He declared that he was "rotting away inside" and that if he ate, the food would kill him. He urged the family not to touch the glasses or towels he used lest they become contaminated.

On arrival at the hospital, he appeared older than his years. He was pale, poorly nourished, and dehydrated, with his lips dry, cracked, and covered with sores. His facial expression and general bearing suggested a feeling of utter hopelessness. He was self-absorbed and manifested no interest in his environment. . . . In explaining his presence in the hospital, he said he realized he had been sent by his family because they believed he would benefit by the treatment, but added, "I don't know how they sent me here when they had not the means. My wife cannot pay for me, and by this time she must have been put out of the house" (Kolb, 1973, pp. 375–376).

For many depressives, a lifetime of accomplishments and efficiency becomes meaningless. Feelings of unworthiness, guilt, and suffering predominate, as does the conviction that failure and a bleak future are in store.

Depression can take many forms. DSM III no longer distinguishes between neurotic and psychotic depression. Instead, all affective disorders are grouped into one category. The basic idea in the DSM III was to divide affective disorders into (1) those involving depression, (2) those involving manic patterns, and (3) those involving both, i.e., the bipolar form. These three patterns are further classified according to whether they present a single episode in the person's life or are recurrent.

Two of the most stimulating recent perspectives on depression are Aaron Beck's (1967) cognitive model and Martin Seligman's (1975) concept of **learned helplessness.** Beck ascribes causal significance to illogical thinking in the depressive person. According to his theory, depression results from a negative cognitive set that impairs a person's judgment of reality. These maladaptive cognitive patterns cause a person to evaluate himself or herself as inadequate, unworthy, and helpless. Moreover, depressives tend to see the world as ungratifying, empty, and unpleasant and to view their own future as unpromising and bleak. Beck believes that depression, rather than being a mood disturbance, is a disorder of cognitive distortion.

Seligman argued that important effects occur in people and animals when they encounter environmental circumstances in which they are helpless. According to Seligman, learned helplessness may be a general phenomenon among organisms.

> Laboratory evidence shows that when an organism has experienced trauma it cannot control, its motivation in the face of later trauma wanes. Moreover, even if it does respond and the response succeeds in producing relief, it has trouble learning, perceiving, and believing that the response worked. Finally, its emotional balance is disturbed: depression and anxiety . . . predominate (Seligman, 1975, 22–23).

The now classic experiment was conducted with dogs who were first subjected to a series of inescapable shocks. They were then placed in a shuttlebox, where a warning signal came on before the shock was administered and an escape road was available. These animals did not learn the escape response. In contrast, animals that had not been inescapably shocked learned the task easily. The findings were interpreted as indicating that the experience of having no control over the environment results in learned helplessness. The dogs in Seligman's experiment had developed the expectation that trying to escape the shock was futile, and they therefore gave up and became helpless.

Learned helplessness has been confirmed with humans. Moreover, there are dramatic parallels between the behavior of people who display learned helplessness and the symptoms of depression (see Table 12–6).

In addition to the theories proposed by Beck and Seligman, a number of biological factors have been implicated as causes of depression. It has been found, for instance, that the balance of sodium and potassium inside and outside the neuron (see Chapter 2) is disturbed in depressive individuals, thereby interfering with the transmission of nerve impulses. Hereditary predisposition is suggested by studies indicating that the incidence of affective disorders is considerably higher among relatives of individuals with affective disorders (Kallman, 1958). More recent studies (e.g., Abrams & Taylor, 1974) found that the concordance rate, that is, the extent to which a behavior pattern is shared by two individuals, is higher among family members compared with nonrelated individuals. The available evidence suggests that genetic factors may play a role in the affective disorders.

Suicidal Behavior. One of the most tragic correlates of depression is suicide, which plays a central role in all forms of depression. Even though precise statistics on suicide are difficult to obtain, it has been estimated that each year in the United States between 25,000 and 60,000 people kill them-

Table 12–7. Similarities Between Learned Helplessness and Depression

	Learned Helplessness	*Depression*
Symptoms	Passivity, difficulty learning that responses produce relief, lack of aggression, weight loss, appetite loss, social and sexual deficits, ulcer, and stress.	Passivity, negative cognitive set, introjected hostility, weight loss, appetite loss, social and sexual deficits, ulcer, and stress.
Cause	Learning that responding and reinforcement are independent.	Belief that responding is useless.
Cure	Direct therapy: forced exposure to responses that produce reinforcement.	Recovery of belief that responding produces reinforcement.

Source: Adapted from Seligman (1975).

selves (Epstein, 1974). In addition, another 200,000 individuals attempt suicide but fail. Although it is difficult to predict suicide in a particular individual, psychologists have isolated some of the characteristics of people who take their own lives.

In general, women are more likely to attempt suicide, but men are more likely to succeed in killing themselves. This may reflect a sex difference in the extent of depression or a sex difference in the selected method of dying. Anywhere from two to five times as many women as men are diagnosed as depressed. It may be, as Chesler (1972) argued, that men and women *feel* unhappy, anxious, or depressed in much the same ways but *behave* differently. According to Chesler, women are more likely to assume the culturally available "sick" role when they are under stress. Men and women also differ in the ways they attempt to end their lives. Men are more likely to use drastic or lethal means such as gas, hanging themselves, or jumping from high places, while women prefer pills.

Most depressed individuals do not commit suicide in the midst of their depression, when energy levels are low. Rather, the danger period comes after treatment, or during partial remission, when the person is motivated and energetic enough to take his or her life. It has been observed, for instance, that hospitalized depressive patients have the highest suicide rates when they are allowed to leave the hospital on weekend passes or during the first week after discharge.

One recent attempt to predict suicide focuses on personality elements associated with behavior prior to the suicide and is known as a psychological autopsy. By collecting data that reconstruct a person's life through interviews with spouses, children, friends, physicians, and others who knew the suicide victim well, psychologists have learned as much as possible about the personality and state of mind of the suicide victim. They have learned, for instance, that a middle-aged or elderly man who is divorced, lives alone, and has a history of previous attempts at suicide is a serious candidate for successful suicide.

THE ORGANIC-BRAIN SYNDROMES

In contrast to the schizophrenias and the affective disorders, which are thought to be primarily psychogenic in origin, the organic brain syndromes are biological in origin. Organic brain syndromes are attributable to specific organic causes that interfere with the functioning of the central nervous system. They are usually divided into acute and chronic brain disorders. **Acute brain disorders** are based on chemical changes in the brain that produce temporarily disorganized behavior. The symptoms appear very suddenly and may be

CRITICAL ISSUE

Suicide: Rational or Paranoid?

Suicide raises many legal, moral, and ethical issues. If a person wishes to take his or her life, what obligation or what right do others have to interfere? Thomas Szasz (1976) approaches this question from a controversial perspective when he states:

> In regarding the desire to live as a legitimate human aspiration, but not the desire to die, the suicidologist stands Patrick Henry's famous dictum . . . on its head. In fact, he says, "Give *him* commitment, give *him* electroshock, give *him* lobotomy, give *him* life-long slavery but do not let *him choose* death." By so illegitimizing another person's (not his own) wish to die, the suicide preventor redefines the aspiration of the other as not an aspiration at all (p. 177).

Recently, organized groups have begun lobbying for decriminalization of suicide and the legalization of "mercy killing" (Russell, 1975). These groups are particularly concerned with the issue of artificially prolonging the lives of terminally ill persons whose days are filled with excruciating pain or who are reduced to a vegetative existence. In an attempt to give such people control over their death, these groups have devised a document known as "The Living Will" that allows the terminally ill person to die and not to be kept alive by life-supporting instruments.

A case for rational suicide was made by the American painter Jo Roman, who was told that she had terminal cancer. She planned her death for 15 months, despite attempts to dissuade her by her husband, a professor of psychiatry, and her daughter, a geriatric social worker. Jo insisted that she could not subject herself or those around her to the emotional strains and ravages of terminal cancer. During the 15 months, she wrote a book on suicide and prepared a series of videotapes on the subject. After writing explanatory letters to all her friends, composing her obituary, and bidding farewell to her family, Jo took sleeping pills and a glass of champagne and died quietly.

The case of Jo Roman is different from most right-to-die cases, the majority of whom are near death and in great pain. Jo was neither. In fact, her cancer had not spread to any vital organ. She had stopped chemotherapy because she found the treatment debilitating. To her, ending her life on her own terms was just as important as living it the way she wanted. Her decision was rational in the sense that she wanted to spare herself the pain of watching her body waste away and to protect her family from this painful experience.

At the opposite extreme, a case of irrational, almost paranoid, mass suicide occurred in late 1978 when Reverend Jim Jones enticed, persuaded, and forced over 900 men, women, and children to drink fatal poison in Jonestown, Guyana. The tragedy began when Jones ordered his medical team to bring out a strawberry-flavored drink laced with tranquilizers and cyanide. The babies were given the potion first, and then all others willingly or forcibly drank from the battered tub. Mass confusion occurred while families died with their arms around each other after being directed by a group of armed guards to lie in rows face down. Reverend Jones died the same day from a gunshot wound through his head (Matthews & Harper, 1978).

Prolonged depression can lead to suicidal tendencies. (© *Nancy Hayes/Monkmeyer Press Photo Service*)

caused by infections, toxic substances, or head injuries. **Chronic brain disorders** are caused by progressive degeneration of brain tissue, usually resulting from degenerative diseases and brain tumors. Impaired orientation, loss of memory (especially for recent events), and intellectual deficits are frequent symptoms of the organic brain disorders. Additional impairments occur in the specific area of the brain that is affected. In general, the greater the amount of tissue damage, the greater the impairment of intellectual, sensory, and motor functions.

Degenerative diseases are associated with progressively more serious impairments of both physical and psychological functioning as a result of aging. The diseases that generally develop between the ages of 40 and 65 are known as **presenile dementias;** those that occur after 65 are called the **senile dementias.** In both, progressive deterioration of portions of the central nervous system is responsible for the impairments.

Victims of senile psychosis totally lose the power of communication. (© *Diane Koos Gentry/Black Star*)

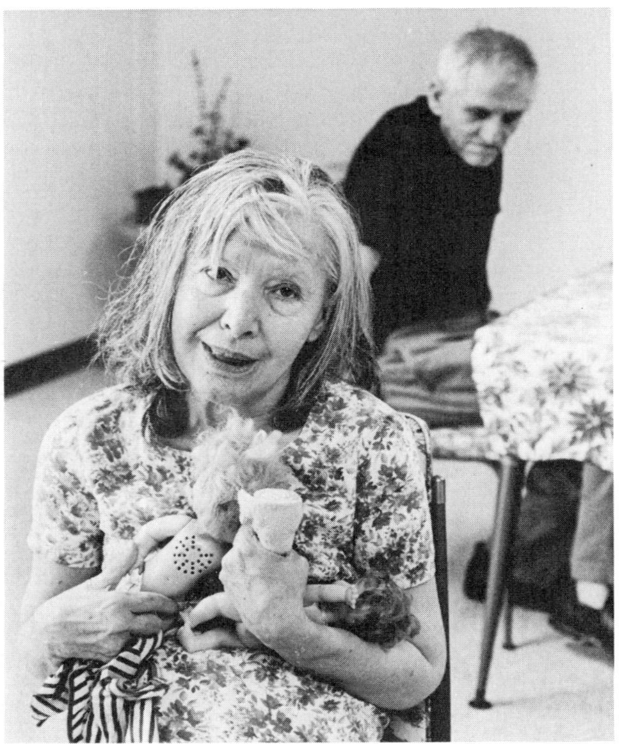

The Presenile Dementias

Four major conditions make up the presenile dementias. One is **Alzheimer's disease,** a disorder characterized by a generalized shrinkage of the brain. As the disease progresses, the person is eventually reduced to a more or less vegetative existence. There is no known cure for this disease, which runs its course in 5 to 10 years. **Pick's disease** is very similar to Alzheimer's disease. Often the two disorders can be distinguished only on the basis of autopsies, which usually reveal a more pronounced degeneration in the frontal and temporal lobes in patients with Pick's disease. Otherwise the clinical picture is similar. As mental deterioration progresses, the person becomes increasingly confused and disorganized. Psychological deficits also include lack of affect and a disturbance of moral and social values. The disease is fatal, with death occurring within two to seven years after the onset of the symptoms.

A rare, genetically transmitted disorder is **Huntington's chorea,** characterized by jerky body movements (chorea) and involuntary muscle spasms. As the disease runs its course, the motor disturbances become more and more severe, and intellectual functions such as memory and concentration become impaired. Presently there is no known cure for Huntington's chorea. By the time death occurs, usually 15 to 20 years after the onset of symptoms, the afflicted person has become totally vegetative.

Parkinson's disease is the most common of the presenile dementias. In contrast to the conditions discussed above, Parkinson's disease is not as a rule associated with a general deterioration of personality and intellect but is evidenced by muscle rigidity and tremors, which become progressively more severe. Although the causes of Parkinson's disease are unknown, physicians in recent years have been successful in treating it with the drug L-dopa, which in many cases brings the tremors and muscular rigidity under control.

The Senile Dementias

The senile dementias, also referred to as senile psychoses, generally appear after age 65. There is a pervasive loss of brain cells in these disorders, which causes the brain to shrink or atrophy. Kolb (1977) estimated that on the average the brain size and weight of a senile 75-year-old man is only 55 percent that of a healthy younger adult. As a result of this general reduction in brain size, the person's thinking becomes illogical and confused, ideas are fragmented, and speech becomes incoherent. Many patients with senile dementia also lose emotional control; in addition, they may become extraordinarily demanding, selfish, and inconsiderate.

The different types of senile dementias are difficult to differentiate because, as the disease progresses, there are many common symptoms that result from the severe organic deterioration of the brain. Often differential diagnosis is not possible until post-mortem examination.

Brain Tumors

Neoplasms, or brain tumors, are abnormal growths of brain tissue that may exert strong pressure on the brain and consequently lead to severe disruption of normal functioning. Brain tumors may be benign or malignant; in the latter case the tumor destroys the surrounding brain tissue. Among the prominent symptoms are clouding of consciousness, disorientation, hallucinations, and a general impairment of intellectual and personality functioning. Sometimes tumors are not discovered until they have progressed beyond controllable proportions because the brain can accommodate slowly expanding neoplasms without showing signs of pathology. Tumors can be removed surgically or controlled with radiation treatment, which destroys the affected brain tissue. Sometimes both methods are used together—surgery to remove the malignant growth and radiation to prevent further spread.

Summary

In this chapter we discussed the clinical picture and causal factors of the major forms of abnormal behavior. The three major models of abnormal behavior are the medical, psychoanalytic, and learning models. Each one makes a number of assumptions about human nature and behavior. No single viewpoint can account for the complexities of abnormal behavior.

Abnormal behavior is classified according to a scheme developed by the American Psychiatric Association that assesses the individual's condition in terms of five axes. Anxiety disorders include the phobic, obsessive-compulsive, generalized, somatoform, and dissociative disorders. Among the personality disorders, the antisocial personality, characterized by callous, unethical, and sometimes criminal behavior, is the most important one. Other personality disorders are the narcissistic personality, characterized by an exaggerated sense of self-importance and selfishness; the compulsive personality, who is overconscientious; the histrionic personality, marked by self-dramatization and overreactivity; the dependent personality, who lacks self-confidence and resourcefulness; and the avoidant personality, who retreats from problems.

Among the psychotic disorders the two major categories are the schizophrenias and the affective disorders. Each of the schizophrenias—the paranoid, hebephrenic, and catatonic—has its distinctive clinical picture. Numerous biological, psychological, and sociocultural theories have been advanced to explain the origins of schizophrenia. No single theory can claim fully to account for the disturbed behavior of schizophrenics. Affective disorders can be of three varieties: the manic, the depressive, or the bipolar type.

Finally, the two main types of organic brain disorders, the presenile dementias and the senile dementias, are caused by varying degrees of deterioration of the brain. Benign and malignant neoplasms impair normal activity in the brain.

Key Terms For Review

acrophobia
acute brain disorders
agoraphobia
Alzheimer's disease
bipolar affective disorder
catatonia
chronic brain disorders
claustrophobia
compulsion
conversion disorder
delusion
delusion of grandeur
delusion of persecution
depression
diathesis-stress theory
disorientation
dissociative disorder
dopamine
double bind
Durham decision
free-floating anxiety
functional psychosis
general paresis
hallucination
hebephrenia
Huntington's chorea
learned helplessness
McNaughten rule
manic-depressive psychosis
monophobia
multiple personality
neologism
neoplasm
obsession
organic psychosis
paranoid schizophrenia
Parkinson's disease
phobia
Pick's disease
presenile dementia
pyrophobia
schizophrenia
senile dementia
somatoform disorder
syndrome
Trepomena pallidum
waxy flexibility
word salad
zoophobia

Suggested Readings

Cofer, D. and Wittenborn, J. Personality characteristics of formerly depressed women. *Journal of Abnormal Psychology*, 1980, 89, 309–314.
The authors report their research, which indicates that formerly depressed women were distinguished from control women by their unhappy outlook and low self-esteem and by having a critical mother and a dependency-fostering father.

Goleman, D. Who's mentally ill? *Psychology Today*, 1978, 12, 34–41.

Goleman points out that one of the consequences of DSM III is to increase "psychiatric territory." Of particular interest in this article are the reports on the impact of lobbying groups in changing some of the categories of DSM III.

Scarf, M. Images that heal: fighting cancer with mental pictures. *Psychology Today*, 1980, 14, 32–46.

The author presents a theory of cancer proposed by Carl Simonton, who suggested that cancer is the result of an emotional reaction such as despair. In his treatment of cancer patients, Simonton emphasizes psychological techniques, among them visualization, to help dealing with emotional conflicts. Scarf also presents a critical analysis of Simonton's theory.

Selye, H. The stress of life. New York: McGraw-Hill, 1978.

The author discusses his conceptualization of stress, how the body responds to stress and how personality breakdown occurs as the result of continued exposure to stress. Selye's own research is presented and the implications of his theory for healthy personality development are discussed.

World Health Organization. Schizophrenia: an international follow-up study. New York: Wiley, 1980.

For this international study 1,200 schizophrenic patients from different countries have been studied to compare the symptoms, course, development, and prognosis of this mysterious disorder.

13

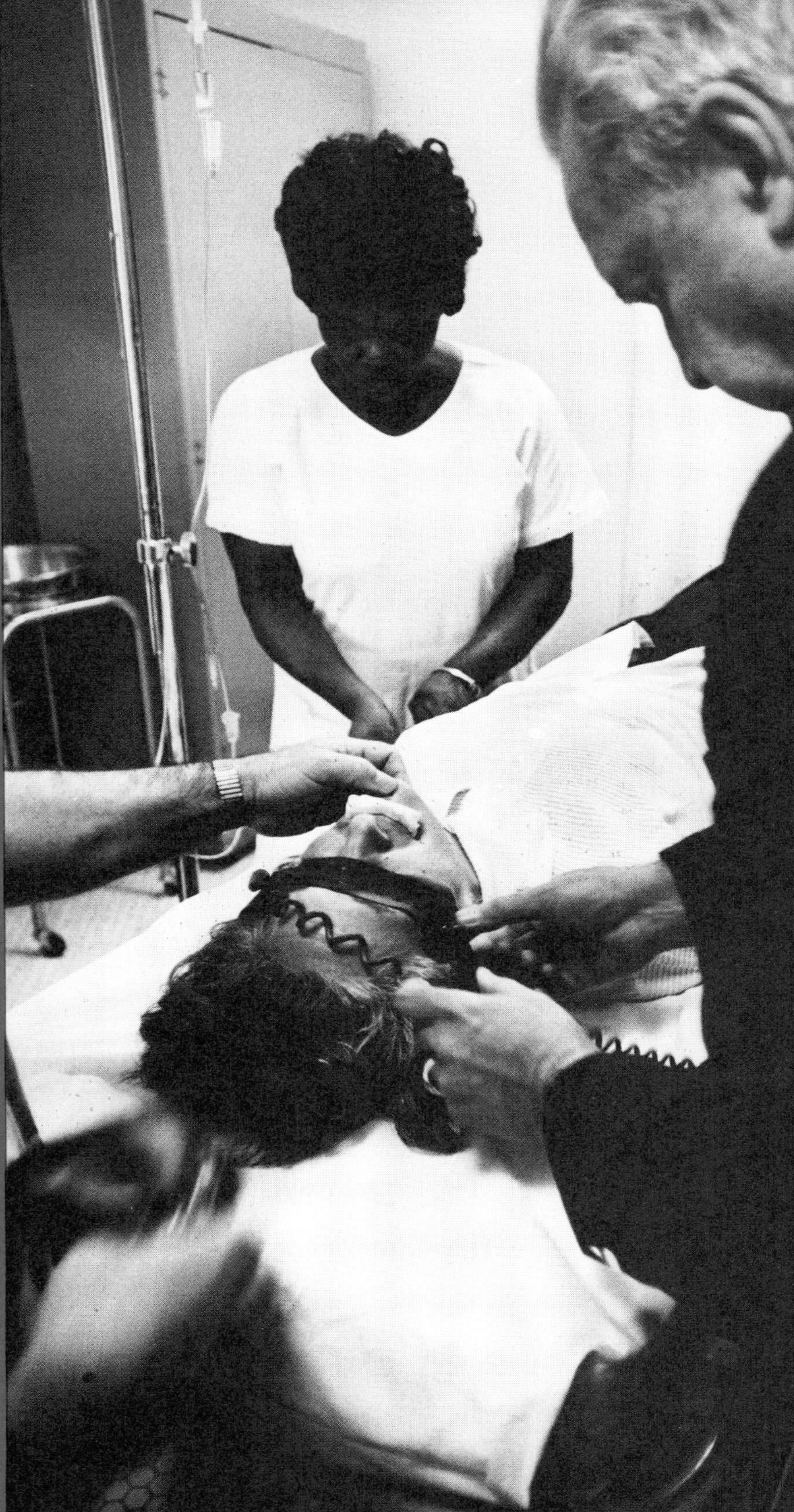

Treatment of Abnormal Behavior

Two years ago I was a confused and lonely woman, who had withdrawn into a private fantasy world for most of my life. For years, I had felt that I needed psychiatric help, but I did not seek help until after fully experiencing the meaning of despair. When I finally made the commitment to myself that I would begin the struggle towards a self-fulfilled life, I entered into a therapeutic relationship with a clinical psychologist.

In my longing for companionship and understanding I sought a deep and meaningful friendship with this man, but my efforts to become close to him were continually frustrated by his professional and distant attitude. At the beginning of therapy I could not understand why he remained so distant, and each time we met I felt hurt and inferior to him. Even though each meeting proved to be a painful experience, and at times I wanted to quit, I kept going to him. I was determined to change and I believed that he would help me. Soon he became so important to me that I began to anticipate each meeting as though it was the only hour during the week with any real meaning.

During our meetings, I often felt as though I were disrobed. His direct gaze intimidated me and I wanted to hide from him. It seemed as though he could see directly through me. To meet his eyes was terribly difficult for me, so I kept my eyes downcast while speaking. As time passed, I gained more courage and began to look directly at him. I spoke freely about myself and he listened. Often he would ask me a question which would plunge my mind into deep thought. His questions taught me to accept responsibility for my actions. At times his questions angered and embarrassed me. Usually at the end of the hour I would leave his office completely engrossed in new avenues of thought. I used his hints, contained in his questions, and I worked hard at trying to understand myself. And I did improve. At first everything had seemed unclear, as if walking into a heavy night mist. But slowly things became clearer to me.

Even my dreams, which had been chaotic and incomprehensible, became more understandable and not nearly so frightening. As I learned about myself, a very slow transformation began. I began to feel that my spirit was undefeatable, and I began to feel beautiful inside.

Slowly the relationship deepened. He always remained the same—distant and professional, but my feelings continually changed. I experienced the gamut of emotions ranging from anger to love. At times I insulted him; at times I told him of my intensely warm feelings for him. Always he remained the same. With time I began to realize that his sameness was very comforting to me. I knew that I could tell him anything and he would understand. Even when I was angry and tried to hurt him, I believed that he would understand and not be angered. I began to love this man of understanding.

What had been physical attraction and infatuation had now changed into a trusting love for another person. In looking back over my two years of therapy, I can say that I am so glad that I have experienced such intense feelings for this person. I had never known a relationship based on trust before, and even though it was painful at times, the trust and respect that I now feel for him is worth the hurt feelings that I first experienced in therapy. And strangely enough, although his behavior has not changed, I no longer feel that he is cold. Rather, I feel that he is a very warm person. I guess I have changed (34-year-old woman).

Changing one's behavior is probably the most difficult task a person can face. We are indeed creatures of habit, and even if we recognize that we are behaving in nonproductive or self-defeating ways, it is often difficult to do anything about it on our own. Many people who recognize that they need help to change consult a mental-health professional, as did the young woman quoted above. When a person does engage professional assistance, he or she is likely to find the process of change to be a highly emotional experience. It can be frustrating, frightening, depressing, exciting, and rewarding.

The statement that began this chapter provides one account of the emotional impact and benefits that may be associated with psychotherapy—a treatment that helps people understand themselves and modify their behavior through their interactions with a therapist. But this is just one of several approaches that mental-health professionals use to treat psychological disorders. Behavior therapy makes use of principles of learning to help people unlearn their maladaptive ways of behaving and to learn new, adaptive behavior. Medical therapies include the use of medication, electroconvulsive therapy, and psychosurgery.

And the personal-growth therapies, such as encounter groups and Gestalt therapy, emphasize authenticity and personal responsibility. In this chapter we shall explore the theory, techniques, and effectiveness of these approaches. Before we do, let us look at the various types of mental-health professionals that provide treatment for abnormal behavior.

THE MENTAL-HEALTH PROFESSIONALS

Treatment of abnormal behavior is not limited to a single professional group. A variety of mental-health professionals are trained to treat psychological problems. Clinical psychologists hold a Ph.D. degree and have had at least four years of graduate training that emphasizes methods of psychological assessment and treatment. They work in a variety of settings, ranging from private practice to university psychological centers to psychiatric hospitals. Psychiatrists hold an M.D. degree and have completed psychiatric residency training following medical school. Because they are medical doctors, they are the only mental-health professionals who can prescribe medication. Psychoanalysts are mostly psychiatrists who in addition to their regular training have spent several years specializing in the techniques of psychoanalysis. Until recently, only psychiatrists were admitted to Institutes of Psychoanalysis for training, but today a few institutes admit clinical psychologists. Both psychiatrists and psychoanalysts work in the same types of settings as do clinical psychologists.

Social workers generally hold a M.S.W. degree, although some have a Ph.D. in social work. Social workers are often employed by mental-health agencies to make contacts with clients' families, friends, or employers. Many social workers are also trained in methods of psychotherapy.

Counseling psychologists may hold either a Ph.D. or an Ed.D. degree. They are most likely to work in schools or other agencies that help people deal with situational problems—such as making career choices or dealing with relationships. Counseling psychologists are less likely to treat individuals with pervasive psychological problems.

In addition to these specialists, many other professionals, such as the clergy, physicians, and teachers, receive some training in the use of psychological treatment methods. Their training tends to be somewhat limited, but they are able to make appropriate referrals when necessary.

While academic degrees and professional certification do provide an index of the training and experiences of the various mental-helath professionals, they do not provide an adequate basis for selecting a psychotherapist. There are both highly skilled and incompetent therapists in every professional category. The best procedure to follow in choosing a therapist is to seek assistance from trusted family members, friends, physicians, or professors. Once in therapy, one should feel free to evaluate the process of therapy. If a person does not feel comfortable with the therapist or the approach being taken or can see no progress after several months of therapy, then it may be time to look for another therapist. One should realize that successful therapy may produce unpleasant feelings or feelings of dislike for the therapist—as happened with the woman whose account opened this chapter. It can be difficult to distinguish between these feelings and the feelings one might have toward an ineffective therapist, so no one should change therapists the first time he or she feels discouraged. But if the negative reactions persist and no explanation for them is offered by the therapist, the client is probably justified in seeking another therapist.

PSYCHOTHERAPY

Without question, the most significant historical figure in the field of psychotherapy is Sigmund Freud (1856–1939). Freud, who received a medical degree from the University of Vienna in 1881, was largely responsible for developing psychological methods of treatment. Prior to his work, the prevailing view was that behavioral disorders were caused by an underlying medical condition. But Freud speculated that one's childhood experiences were largely responsible for the problems one had as an adult. It was necessary to probe the unconscious to uncover the early conflicts producing the mental disorder. The form of psychotherapy Freud evolved is called psychoanalysis. It is a very intensive form of therapy in which the client and the therapist meet from three to five times a week over a period of two to five years. Freud's methods have had a substantial impact on the practice of psychotherapy. Although there is controversy today about the validity of his ideas, psychotherapists owe Freud a debt of gratitude for pointing out the importance of psychological factors in abnormal patterns of behavior.

Since Freud's time countless forms of therapy have been developed. It would be impossible to begin to describe all the therapies in one book, much less in one chapter. The therapies discussed here were selected because they are widely practiced and because they represent major theoretical viewpoints. We shall look at dynamic psychotherapy, client-centered therapy, and rational-emotive therapy in this section.

Dynamic Psychotherapy

Dynamic psychotherapy is an abbreviated form of psychoanalysis that still retains its essential components. Dynamic psychotherapy, also referred to as insight-oriented or intrapsychic psychotherapy, may last anywhere from six months to a year or more, with the client and therapist meeting once or twice a week. The example at the opening of the chapter was one of dynamic psychotherapy.

The goal of dynamic psychotherapy is to bring previously repressed memories into the individual's conscious awareness. As we saw in Chapter 12, Freud believed that unconscious thoughts and feelings influence behavior. For example, according to Freud, boys around the age of four have feelings of sexual desire toward their mothers. These feelings are repressed into the unconscious mind because the boys fear retaliation from their powerful rivals—namely, their fathers. Nonetheless these unconscious memories continue to exert an influence over their behavior. As adults, they may be attracted to women who are similar to their mothers in some way. They may look for a wife who will take care of them—a woman upon whom they can be totally dependent. After clients become aware of these unconscious processes, they are then free to select more adaptive ways of behaving.

Early in the course of therapy, the therapist will attempt to foster the client's **transference** reaction. Transference refers to feelings that one has toward a person to whom they do not realistically apply. These feelings generally have their origin in important past relationships. For instance, the client may come to feel about and react toward the therapist similarly to the way the client felt about and reacted toward his or her father. If this relationship appears to be the source of the client's problems, then the therapist encourages the transference. In this way the therapist will be able to help the client understand his or her emotional reactions.

The woman quoted at the beginning of the chapter obviously had an intense transference reaction. In the early stages of therapy she expected her therapist to give her more attention or to respond more intensely to her. When he did not do this, she became angry at him. It is likely that these reactions reflected problems she had with intimate relationships with men.

The therapist facilitates the transference reaction by remaining as neutral as possible. This means that therapists are very reluctant to answer questions about their personal lives. If a client were to ask a therapist about his or her marital status, the therapist might ask the client if he or she has any preferences or fantasies about the matter. A factual answer would provide a basis in reality for the relationship between the client and therapist. The therapist wants clients to project their own feelings and fantasies onto the therapist. This projection, or transference reaction, is crucial to the course of therapy. Freud recommended that therapists be like a mirror: they should provide clients with the opportunity to see themselves. We could see the therapist described in our opening quotation providing his client with this kind of "mirror."

Once the transference reaction has developed and the therapist has a thorough understanding of the client's personality and problems, the therapist will begin to make **interpretations.** An interpretation is any statement made by a therapist that helps clients become aware of some aspect of their functioning of which they were previously unaware. The format of an interpretation can vary a great deal. It may consist of a simple question, such as "Have you noticed any similarities between your relationship with your wife and your relationship with your mother?" A more elaborate interpretation might consist of a relatively lengthy statement in which the therapist ties together several observations:

> It seems to me that your angry feelings toward Janet (a colleague of the client's) fit a pattern. You reacted the same way when your mother punished you, and you have similar feelings when you have an argument with your wife.

The goal in either case would be to help the clients achieve greater insight into their behavior and feelings.

Experienced dynamic therapists are very cautious in making an interpretation. They do so only if they feel that they have abundant evidence to support it, and then they prepare the client to hear the interpretation through a very gradual process. The most frequent error made by novice therapists is to make too many interpretations on too little evidence (Weiner, 1975). A poorly timed interpretation can be harmful to the process of therapy.

For example, suppose a client begins a therapy session by asking the therapist, "Where did you get that dress? It went out of style ten years ago." If the therapist decides to make an interpretation, she might say, "You seem to be angry at me today." If the dress comment is the only evidence the therapist has for the interpretation, the client will be able to laugh it off or belittle the therapist for "seeing significance in every little comment." If the interpretation is well timed, the therapist might be able to point out that the client was 15 minutes late for the session, that he did not greet the therapist with his customary smile and "Good morning," and that he has not said anything for the past five minutes. In other words, the therapist is able to present enough evidence to force the client to examine his behavior and attempt to understand its causes.

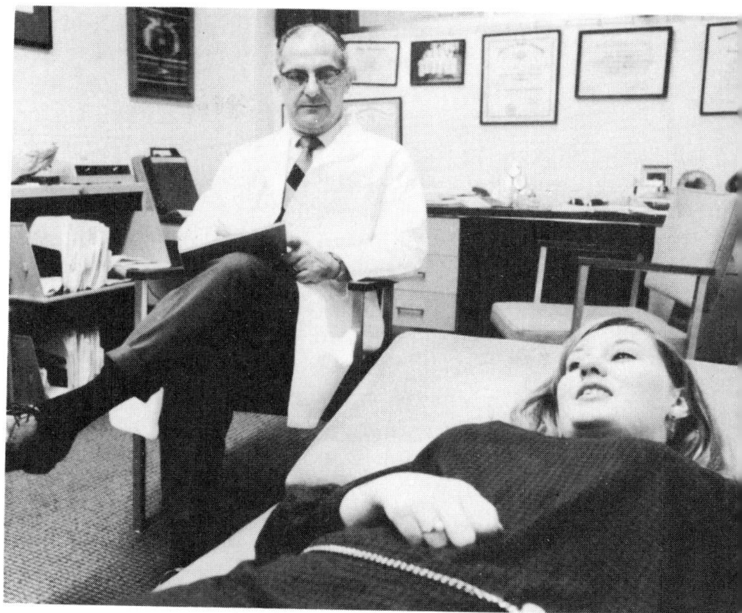

Psychotherapy uses a relaxed atmosphere to allow the client to summon up repressed memories. (© *Van Bucher / Photo Researchers, Inc.*)

The final stage of dynamic psychotherapy is characterized by **working through.** This term describes the therapist's attempts to help clients thoroughly assimilate what they have learned about themselves and learn how to apply this new knowledge to situations that may arise in the future. It is hoped that clients will reach the point where they can serve as their own therapist. They will be able to analyze situations and decide for themselves whether any adjustments in their behavior are necessary.

Dynamic psychotherapy is not necessarily intended to effect changes in clients' behavior. Prominent psychoanalyst Frieda Fromm-Reichman has warned therapists to make no promises of cure. The therapist's task is to increase clients' self-understanding and to bring to consciousness memories of the origins of conflict. Fromm-Reichman suggests that if these goals are being met, improvement in the clients' behavior will occur almost as an aside. But the client alone is responsible for change. Many dynamic therapists do recognize, however, that the primary reason clients come to therapy is to make changes in their lives.

Dynamic psychotherapy is not suitable for everyone. The interactions between therapist and client require that the client have good verbal ability and be reasonably intelligent. This type of therapy also requires clients to discuss many painful and embarrassing aspects of their lives. So clients must be highly motivated to pursue it.

Client-Centered Therapy

The second major form of psychotherapy, **client-centered therapy,*** is based on the belief that all individuals possess an innate drive for positive psychological growth, which is called the drive for self-actualization. A variety of factors can interfere with this growth and cause individuals to become defensive and to lose touch with their true feelings and values. Such individuals experience a state of incongruence between their self-concepts and their experiences. This incongruence results in varieties of inflexible behavior and rigid perceptions of others. (See Chapter 10 for a discussion of Rogers's theory of personality.)

* In 1974 Rogers changed the name of his approach to "person-centered" therapy. This change is intended to reflect the human values his approach incorporates. We have retained the term "client-centered" because in our experience a majority of psychologists continue to use it when referring to this approach to therapy.

To illustrate this idea behind the therapy, consider a 5-year-old boy who is suddenly faced with a baby sister. Because the newcomer means that he will receive less attention from his parents, he will probably on occasion have strong negative feelings toward his sister. He may even hit her and tell her he hates her. If the parents were to say, "You don't hate your sister, you love her," they would be setting the stage for psychological incongruence. The boy will feel that he must love his sister or risk losing the love of his parents, but at the same time he feels real hatred. Rogers suggests that in such a situation the parents should say, "We know you don't like your sister at times, but we will not permit you to hit her." Such an approach teaches the child that there are limits to his behavior and at the same time implies that it is permissible to have angry feelings.

The task of the client-centered therapist is to provide an atmosphere in which clients can resume their drive for personal growth or self-actualization. Rogers places great emphasis on the characteristics of the therapist that are necessary for producing effective results: unconditional positive regard, empathic understanding, and genuineness (Meador & Rogers, 1979).

Unconditional positive regard requires that the therapist value the worth of the client as a human being. There may be occasions when therapists will be repelled by the things clients have done, but it is important to distinguish between the behavior of individuals and the individuals themselves. Rogers believes that many people have low self-esteem because as children they felt rejected by their parents. Therapists must communicate to their clients that while they may disapprove of their behavior, they are not rejecting them as people. If they fail to make this distinction, the clients' feelings of rejection may be perpetuated.

The second characteristic, **empathic understanding,** means that the therapist should try to appreciate and understand the client's emotional experiences. The effective client-centered therapist should be asking, "What would I be feeling if I were saying what the client is saying?" While dynamic psychotherapists place emphasis on clients' achieving intellectual understanding, client-centered therapists believe that emotional understanding is much more important. The clients have problems because they have lost touch with their feelings. It is through the empathic understanding of the therapist that clients are able to integrate their experiences and their feelings.

Finally, the therapist must be **genuine** while performing the therapy. The therapist's verbal and nonverbal communications to the client must be consistent with the therapist's own feelings, reactions, and values. A close and honest relationship between therapist and client is crucial if the client is to grow psychologically. If the therapist is not genuine and puts up facades or plays a role with the client, the client will soon discover it. The client is likely to feel that this relationship is the same as all previous relationships and that there is no point in being honest. This can destroy the process of therapy.

Early in his career, Rogers believed that client-centered therapy is appropriate for all types of clients. In fact, he discouraged any form of psychological assessment of clients because it could create biases and certain expectations on the part of the therapist. Later in his career, after conducting an extensive research project with schizophrenic patients, Rogers concluded that there are some types of individuals for whom client-centered therapy is not appropriate. He now believes that for such therapy to be effective, the client must have some capacity to form a relationship. This eliminates many seriously disturbed clients, who are difficult to treat by any method (Truax & Mitchell, 1978).

Many clients feel frustrated by client-centered therapy during the early stages. Everyone goes into therapy with expectations about what is going to happen. They may expect the therapist to tell them how to solve their problems. Or they may expect to be asked about their childhood and to hear explanations of how their problems developed. Client-centered therapists, however, offer neither solutions nor interpretations. It may take many sessions before clients can appreciate what they are getting from client-centered therapy. The following excerpt provides a flavor of client-centered therapy:

Client: I have really been depressed lately.
Therapist: Tell me about it.
Client: Well . . . ever since my husband left me, I can't seem to get back on the track. I just do not seem to be getting over it.
Therapist: Uh-huh.
Client: . . . I guess I feel so rejected. We were only married two years when he left me for another woman.
Therapist: You are feeling inadequate.
Client: Yes, I am. I must be a real flop of a woman if I can't hold a man's interest for a lousy two years. I just don't know how he could do that to me.
Therapist: You're feeling angry at your husband.
Client: . . . I suppose so. Even if he didn't love me he didn't have to hurt me the way he did.
Therapist: It sounds like you can't decide who to blame for the failure of your marriage—your husband or yourself.
Client: . . . Maybe you're right. Some days I wake up almost in a rage at the way he treated me. Usually, though, I feel depressed. I wonder if I'll ever find someone who will love me.
Therapist: What is it about yourself that makes you feel so unlovable?
Client: I don't know. . .
Therapist: These things can be very painful to talk about. . . . Or even think about.
Client: I know . . . One thing that I can't stop thinking about is my husband calling me a cold bitch. . . That shocked me. I would have never guessed he felt that way.
Therapist: So, you didn't feel cold toward him?
Client: No. I loved him. I always thought we were very compatible.

Rational-Emotive Therapy

Rational-emotive therapy (RET) relies on the therapist to be very active in helping the client to achieve a rational way of viewing life. The rational-emotive therapist tries to teach clients a philosophy of life that promotes more adaptive behavior. RET was developed by psychologist Albert Ellis in the 1950s. Ellis was originally trained in psychoanalytic therapy, but after practicing it for a while he became discouraged with the results. He began experimenting with new techniques and found that as he became more active in the therapy sessions, his clients showed more improvement. Over a period of time, and with gradual adjustment, Ellis arrived at his own theory of psychotherapy.

Ellis's approach can be understood best in terms of what he calls the A-B-C paradigm (Ellis, 1979). The A refers to a situational event, or something that happens to a person. B refers to the cognitions, or what the person thinks about A. And C represents the negative psychological consequences of the situation. To illustrate, A is a situation in which a man was criticized by his boss. B would be the thoughts the man has about his boss's remarks. Perhaps he would say to himself that he is a failure—that he will never achieve success. C then would be the man's feelings of worthlessness and depression.

According to Ellis, most clients come to therapy with the belief that A causes C. That is, the man in the above example attributes his depression to his boss's remarks. Ellis suggests that it is B, not A, that causes C. Thus the man felt depressed because he told himself that he was a failure, not because his boss criticized him.

Ellis believes that the basis of most psychological problems is that people tell themselves irrational and illogical things about the events that happen to them. The man above, for instance, used faulty logic; he generalized from a single criticism to his worth as a total person. Suppose his boss told him that he did a poor job on a particular project. It would be irrational for the man to conclude that he is worthless simply because he performed poorly on one task. Ellis would go even further. He would tell his client that it would be irrational to feel worthless even if the boss had told him that he was the most thoroughly incompetent employee he had ever had. Ellis would suggest to the client that he should replace the thought "I am worthless" with a more logical thought, such as "Even if I am an incompetent employee, I'm still a worthwhile person."

The task of the RET therapist is largely one of education. The therapist must teach clients a new, more rational philosophy of life. This approach requires that the therapist be extremely talkative during the therapy sessions. Unlike the dynamic and client-centered approaches, in which clients are expected to do most of the talking, the RET therapist is likely to talk more than the client. A high level of active involvement is thought to be necessary because the client brings to therapy a set of deeply ingrained beliefs. If clients are to give up these beliefs and adopt a new philosophy of life, the therapist must be very persistent. The approach of the RET therapist is illustrated in the following dialogue.

Therapist: I understand that your problem centers around feeling depressed and lonely.

Client: Yes, my husband divorced me about six months ago, and since then I've been very depressed.

Therapist: Because your husband divorced you?

Client: Yes, it made me feel like a failure. We had been married only two years, and he left me because he was in love with someone else.

Therapist: You seem to be telling yourself that because your husband left you, you're a failure as a woman, that you weren't even interesting enough to keep a husband.

Client: Well, that's true.

Therapist: What's true is that your husband left you for another woman, and that's too bad. It's unfortunate.

Client: Well, that means there must be something wrong with me.

Therapist: Who said so? I'll tell you who said so. You said so. You said to yourself that because your husband left, you must be a failure as a woman. Does that seem logical to you?

Client: You mean I shouldn't feel like a failure just because my husband left?

Therapist: Exactly. It's too bad your marriage didn't work out, but it doesn't mean you're a failure.

Client: But I feel like such a failure.

Therapist: Well, let's suppose for the sake of argument that you were a failure. You were both socially and sexually uninteresting to your husband. What's so terrible about that?

Client: That would be terrible.

Therapist: No, it wouldn't be terrible, it would be too bad. You're telling yourself it would be terrible. At any rate you seem to be saying to yourself that if your husband thought you were sexually inadequate and a boring conversationalist, then those things have to be true.

Client: You mean I shouldn't think I'm a failure just because my husband thinks so.

Therapist: Right. That's the core of your problem. If I do poorly, and my husband thinks I'm inadequate, then I must agree with him and beat myself over the head and get depressed.

Ellis has suggested that clients should have an IQ of at least 120 (compared with the average IQ of 100) if they are to benefit fully from this approach. This is because RET requires clients to make subtle distinctions, such as that between the worth of a specific act and the worth of an individual as a whole. Still, clients with lower levels of intelligence can expect some degree of benefit from this approach. Ellis points out, for example, that mentally retarded individuals can learn that they are worthwhile human beings even though their performance in some areas may be inferior.

Evaluation of Psychotherapy

Nearly a century after Freud began his work there is still no conclusive evidence that psychotherapy produces lasting changes in clients. In the 1950s and 1960s British psychologist Hans Eysenck (1952, 1965) published an extensive review of the available research. He concluded that clients who had received no therapy were no less likely, and perhaps even more likely, to have recovered than clients who had received therapy. Understandably, this conclusion elicited strong reactions from mental-health professionals.

In the 1970s psychologists Allen Bergin and Michael Lambert (1978) addressed the same issue in another comprehensive review of the literature. Their conclusion, while not bringing joy to the hearts of practicing psychologists and psychiatrists, was somewhat more encouraging. They concluded that the results of psychotherapy, on the average, were positive. The average, it must be remembered, includes both very positive and very negative effects. Bergin and Lambert point out that it is more crucial to identify the effective therapists and the effective techniques than it is to determine what the average effect might be. Once the effective therapists and techniques have been identified, the practitioners who achieve less desirable results can attempt to emulate their more successful colleagues. Bergin and Lambert make the important point that the more recent, and methodologically superior, studies find more positive effects than the older studies.

Of the various forms of psychotherapy, which is the most effective? In recent years there has been a fair amount of research comparing the various therapies. Once again it is impossible to arrive at any general conclusions. Part of the problem is that the various therapists do not agree on the criteria that should be used in evaluating the results of therapy. For instance, psychodynamic therapists are concerned about increased insight in their clients, while client-centered therapists look for increases in self-esteem. A second problem in this type of comparative research is that many studies use relatively inexperienced therapists because they are more readily available. It is unfair to make any judgments about either the relative or absolute effectiveness of a therapy if those using it are only advanced graduate students or psychiatric residents. A fair comparison would involve therapists who have completed their training and have had several years of experience.

With these issues in mind, one can begin to appreciate the difficulty involved in assessing the effectiveness of psychotherapy. In his review of the literature, Bergin (1971) estimated that between 65 and 83 percent of clients receiving psychotherapy can expect improvement. He is quick to point out that these are very rough estimates. They are, however, the best we have. One should also keep in mind that these figures are for clients with a variety of disturbances. In psychotherapy, as in medicine, the more severe distrubances are more difficult to treat. It is likely that if improvement rates were listed for specific disorders, we would find that many clients have an extremely good chance for improvement.

BEHAVIOR THERAPY

About the time that Freud's theory had gained wide acceptance, psychologist John Watson (Watson & Rayner, 1920) demonstrated that some psychological disorders could be acquired through learning and speculated that principles of learning could be used in the treatment of such disorders. But this approach did not become popular until the South African psychiatrist Joseph Wolpe, who is often referred to as the father of behavior therapy, published a book describing behavior-therapy techniques in 1958. The growth of behavior therapy since that time has been phenomenal. Now, some 25 years later, behavior therapy has achieved a prominent place in clinical psychology.

Behavior therapy refers to a collection of therapeutic techniques based on the assumption that abnormal behavior is learned in much the same way that normal behavior is learned. The behavior therapist believes that the principles of learning (discussed in Chapter 5) can be used to help clients unlearn inappropriate behavior and replace it with more adaptive and appropriate behavior. Unlike the psychotherapist, the behavior therapist views abnormal behavior itself as the problem and not merely as a symptom of some covert disturbance. For example, the dynamic psychotherapist might argue that a fear of high places reflects an unconscious fear of committing suicide. The behavior therapist would suspect that such a phobia was learned in a relatively straightforward manner. Perhaps as a child, the client observed his or her parents act fearful when in high places.

A second way in which behavior therapy differs from other approaches is that it utilizes different techniques for different types of problems. As we have seen, dynamic psychotherapists rely on interpretation as a basic tool for all types of problems, and client-centered therapists try to help all clients become fully aware of their specific problem. Behavior therapists fit the technique to the nature of the client's problem. Desensitization, which is described below, may be prescribed for a client with a public-speaking phobia. A client with poor social skills may be asked to rehearse more effective responses after the therapist has demonstrated them.

Systematic Desensitization

One of the best-known behavior-therapy techniques is **systematic desensitization (SD).** It was developed by Wolpe and is widely used for the treatment of anxiety-related problems, such as phobias. Fear of animals, fear of flying, and feelings of discomfort in social situations are just a few of the problems that have been successfully treated with SD.

The technique consists of three components. The first is called progressive, or deep-muscle, relaxation. This is a set of exercises in which the client is instructed to tense and then relax the major muscle groups in the body. Between the various exercises, the therapist helps the client achieve relaxing mental imagery as well. Depending on the client's initial level of anxiety, anywhere from one to five or six sessions are required to help the client achieve a deep state of relaxation.

Once the client has mastered the relaxation procedure, the therapist begins the second component of the technique—the construction of an "anxiety hierarchy." This is a list of situations that elicit feelings of anxiety in the client. They are arranged in a "least" to "most" order, so that the first situation will be one that makes the client feel only slightly uncomfortable. The last situation is likely to elicit intense feelings of discomfort. The following hierarchy was developed for a college student with a fear of public speaking:

1. Signing up for speech class next semester.
2. Walking into speech class the first day of the semester.
3. Listening to the instructor lecture about speeches.
4. Listening to the instructor talk about possible topics for speeches.
5. Hearing the instructor assign five speeches for the semester.
6. Working on my speech the week before I'm scheduled to give it.
7. Practicing my speech the night before I'm scheduled to give it.
8. Walking into class the day of my speech.
9. Waiting while the person before me gives his speech.
10. Walking up to the front of the class to give my speech.

Systematic desensitization can help people with a fear of animals. (© *The New York Times*)

The third part of the treatment consists of having the client imagine each situation in the hierarchy for 5 to 30 seconds. The client, while in a state of deep relaxation, begins with the first scene and imagines it in repeated trials until he or she can think about it without experiencing anxiety. Then the client progresses through the hierarchy until all the scenes can be imagined with no emotional arousal. Once this is accomplished, the client will feel considerably more comfortable in related real-life situations.

Although systematic desensitization has proved highly effective for a variety of problems (Rimm & Masters, 1979), there is little agreement as to why it is effective. Wolpe (1976) argues that the effective mechanism is counterconditioning. In other words, the client's anxiety is extinguished because it is incompatible with feelings of relaxation. Other theorists argue that the client's expectations play a major role in the success of the technique (cf. Rimm & Masters, 1979). That is, if clients believe they are receiving meaningful therapy, they are likely to improve. Despite the disagreement over its theoretical mechanism, the technique is widely accepted as an effective therapeutic tool.

Aversion Therapy

One of the most controversial of the behavior-therapy techniques is **aversion therapy**. Aversion therapy involves the administration of a painful or unpleasant stimulus in association with the performance of undesirable behavior by a client. For example, a smoker may receive an electric shock for lighting a cigarette. Aversion therapy may be thought of as punishment for inappropriate behavior.

A majority of clients who receive aversion therapy have requested treatment for problem behavior that they cannot control. Such problems

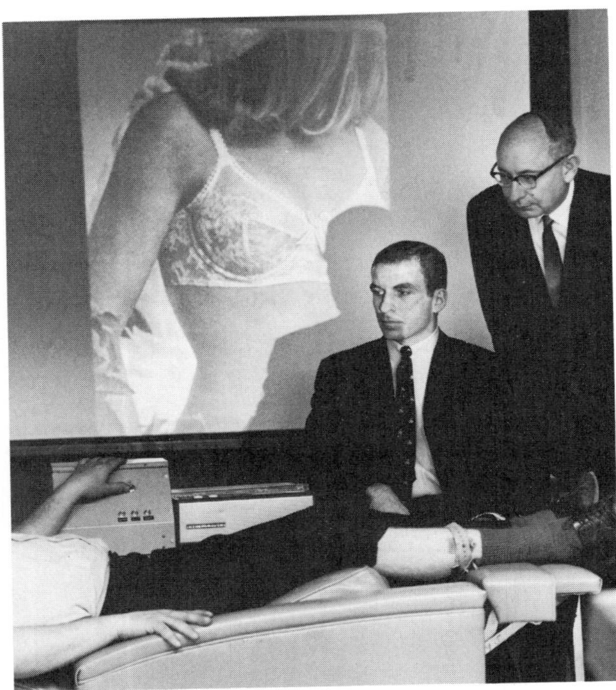

Aversion therapy is highly controversial. This homosexual client receives a shock when he sees a picture of an attractive male but no shock for an attractive female. (© *Bernie Cleff*)

include smoking, alcoholism, overeating, and sexual variations such as pedophilia, exhibitionism, homosexuality, and transvestism. The general procedure requires the client to either perform the undesirable behavior or to look at slides or pictures of situations associated with it in the therapist's consulting room. While the client is doing this, the therapist administers the aversive stimulation. The most common forms of aversive stimulation are electric shock and drugs that produce nausea.

Behavior therapist C. B. Blakemore has presented a case history of a male transvestite that illustrates one type of aversion therapy (Blakemore, Thorpe, Barker, Conway, & Lavin, 1963). The client had dressed in women's clothes for over 20 years and had received six years of psychotherapy that was ineffective. Blakemore treated the man by having him dress in his favorite women's clothing while standing on an electric grid. While the client was dressing he would receive an electric shock. The client received 200 shocks over 400 trials. By not administering the shock on every trial, the therapist hoped to increase generalization to real-life situations. Six months after the therapy was completed, the client reported that he had no urges to wear women's clothes and that he was feeling less anxious than he had felt in years.

Aversion therapy has raised serious ethical considerations. Movies such as *A Clockwork Orange* (1971), in which a man committed suicide after receiving aversion therapy, have instilled fears about unscrupulous behavior therapists forcing individuals to participate in painful behavior therapies. These fears are not completely unfounded. Cotter (1967) has described a program purportedly using behavioral techniques with patients in a Vietnamese mental hospital. Among other things, the patients were coerced into working in an area that was being shelled by the Viet Cong. The "behavioral techniques" consisted of electroconvulsive shocks administered to those who would not work.

The ethical-behavior therapist views such blatant abuse with horror. Nonetheless, the occasional misuse of behavioral techniques is sufficient to create a feeling of mistrust in the general public.

The welfare of the client should always be the first concern of the behavior therapist. This would require that clients participate in such procedures voluntarily and only after the procedures have been fully explained to them. Prominent behavior therapist Leonard Krasner (1971) has pointed out that it is not possible to shape responsible behavior in a client while at the same time treating the client inhumanely.

Evaluation of Behavior Therapy

Behavior therapists have tended to avoid the question of the overall effectiveness of their techniques. Instead they suggest that it is more appropriate to ask what techniques should be used with what problems for which clients by which therapists (Franks & Wilson, 1976). Much of the behavior-therapy literature is concerned with prescribing a specific technique for the treatment of a specific disorder.

Early reports of highly successful applications of behavioral techniques (cf. Bandura, 1969) generated a great deal of enthusiasm. But many of these early studies used volunteer college students as clients rather than "real life" clients. It is much easier to help college students who agree to participate in research dealing with snake phobia than it is to help clients who seek treatment on their own for phobias that seriously hinder their everyday lives. As behavior therapists have moved from university laboratories to clinical settings, they have experienced their share of failures.

The effectiveness of behavior therapy varies with the type of problem treated. It appears to be highly successful in the treatment of phobias, sexual dysfunctions, and social anxieties. It has been very disappointing when it comes to the common problems of smoking and overeating. But behavior therapy is a relatively recent development. Behavior therapists have been dealing with the complex problems found in clinical settings for little more than a decade. The results so far are encouraging enough to suggest that behavior therapists will come closer to solving these problems.

THE MEDICAL THERAPIES

The use of medical or physical methods to produce changes in human behavior can be traced back to prerecorded history. Anthropologists have found remains of skulls that appear to have undergone crude surgery. This surgery consisted of chipping through the skull with tools made of stone. It is believed that individuals who behaved in bizarre or unacceptable ways were subjected to this operation. Supposedly, evil spirits caused the deviant behavior, and the surgery provided a means for these spirits to escape.

Many thousand years later, treatment methods in the United States were no more scientific or humane. In the late eighteenth and early nineteenth century, Dr. Benjamin Rush devised several therapy techniques that were likely to result in physical injury and possibly death. Rush, who is referred to as the father of American psychiatry, believed that behavioral disorders were caused by pathological medical conditions. One such condition was either too much or too little blood being carried to the brain. Rush's treatment for too much blood going to the brain was bloodletting. He reported success in one case by removing 29 pints of blood in 47 sessions. People whose problems were thought to be caused by too little blood were strapped to a large turntable called a gyrator. As the device spun around, it forced blood to the brain, supposedly correcting the undersupply.

Rush is also credited with the invention of the "tranquilizer chair." Violent patients were strapped to an armchair equipped with large wooden blocks that applied pressure to the head. This technique was finally abandoned because it resulted in too many broken bones. Judging from Rush's treatment techniques, one might suspect him of being a sadist. He was, however, genuinely concerned with the welfare of his patients. He chose to try to help people who were being either ignored or subjected to deliberate cruelties.

The early crude surgery and the various devices invented by Benjamin Rush were based on the belief that something physical is responsible for behavioral disorders. This belief still exists, although contemporary theories regarding the nature of the physical cause are considerably more sophisticated (see Chapter 12). Many of these theories focus on anomalies in chemical and electrical activity in the brain. Three forms of treatment based on this belief are the use of drugs, electroconvulsive shock therapy, and psychosurgery.

Drugs

Since they were first introduced in the 1950s, the psychotropic (mind-affecting) drugs have become the most widely used form of medical treatment of mental disorders. Among these medications are the antipsychotic drugs, lithium carbonate, the antidepressant drugs, and the antianxiety drugs.

The **antipsychotic drugs** are frequently used in the treatment of severe disorders such as schizophrenia. The most commonly prescribed antipsychotic drugs are known chemically as phenothiazines. Common brand names include Thorazine, Stelazine, Prolixin, and Mellaril. The psychotropic properties of these drugs were reportedly discovered by accident. They were initially used to control nausea in pregnant women. When they were given to pregnant women in a French mental hospital, it was noted that there were dramatic improvements in their behavior. Since then, the use of phenothiazines for psychotic patients has spread widely.

As you saw in Chapter 12, one theory regarding schizophrenia, the most common of the psychoses, suggests that it is caused by an excess of certain substances that transmit impulses between nerve cells. It is believed that the antipsychotic drugs work by reducing the excess of these neurotransmitter substances. Their effect on patients is to decrease mental and physical excitement, aggressive behavior, delusions, and hallucinations. They do not, however, generally influence thought disorders and inappropriate social behaviors associated with psychosis (Dunner & Somervill, 1977). Schizophrenic patients who take an antipsychotic drug will be considerably less agitated, but they may still be suspicious, think in unusual ways, and have poor interpersonal skills.

A number of studies have documented the effectiveness of these drugs (Casey, Bennett, & Lindley, 1960; Spohn, Lacoursiere, Thompson, & Coyne, 1977). Some researchers call them "magic bullets" and claim that their use has revolutionized the treatment of psychotic patients (Gellhorn & Kiely, 1973). In short, there is little doubt that their use has been of great benefit to millions of patients.

The phenothiazines, however, are not without their problems. They often cause side effects. One involves a disturbance of the part of the nervous system that controls motor behavior. Another side effect, seen mostly in long-time users of the drug, involves spastic movements of the lip, tongue,

The gyrator (left) and "tranquilizer chair" were two of Benjamin Rush's instruments of psychological therapy. (© *The Bettmann Archive, Inc.*)

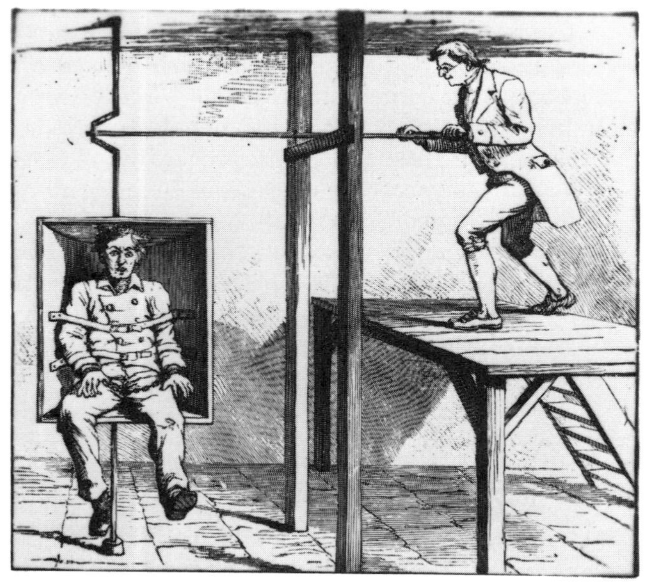

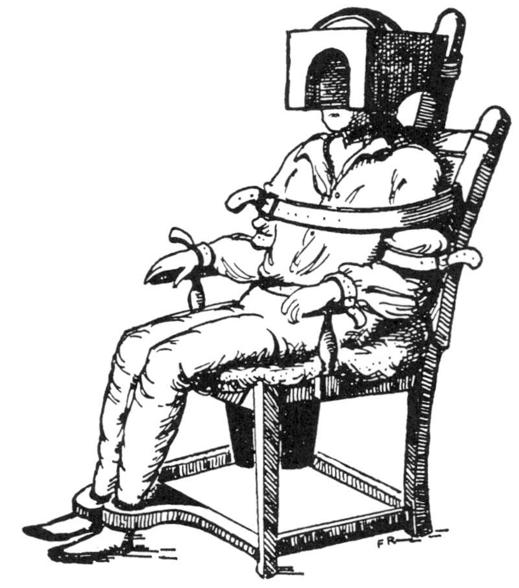

and jaw. There is no known treatment for this condition, and withdrawal from the phenothiazine may only worsen the problem.

Lithium carbonate, although only recently approved for use by the Food and Drug Administration, has become the major treatment for manic-depressive psychosis. This drug controls unrealistic feelings of euphoria, hyperactivity, and impulsivity. Several well-designed research studies have supported its effectiveness as a treatment, and to some extent as a preventive medicine (Prien, Klett, & Caffey, 1973; Quitkin, Rifkin, Kane, Ramos-Lorenzo, & Klein, 1978). Estimates suggest that about 80 percent of patients with acute mania will respond to this medication. As long as care is taken to prescribe the proper dosage, there are relatively few side effects. At higher levels of dosage, however, lithium carbonate can result in loss of balance, confusion, coma, and even death.

The **antidepressant drugs,** sometimes referred to as mood elevators, have been demonstrated to be effective in treating a majority of cases of severe depression (Klerman & Cole, 1965; Hollister, 1972). Common brand names include Elavil, Tofranil, and Marplan. Because their effects are cumulative, two to four weeks of regular medication are necessary before an improvement becomes apparent. Some of the drugs require particularly close medical supervision because their use in combination with certain foods and other medications can lead to strokes.

The **antianxiety drugs** are the most widely used but probably the least effective of the psychotropic drugs. Millions of Americans take drugs such as Valium, Librium, and Miltown. They temporarily reduce unpleasant feelings of anxiety, but there is little evidence they lead to changes in behavior. Many mental-health professionals object to the antianxiety drugs because they reduce any motivation individuals may have to deal with the source of their anxiety. Once clients feel less anxious, they may not see any need to work on their problems in therapy.

In the past few years there have been several reports of abuses of antianxiety drugs in the popular media. Investigative television shows, such as "60 Minutes," have interviewed people who report that they have become addicted to Valium and have suffered as a result. This media attention seems to have produced results that scientific investigators were not able to do with their empirical evidence. News accounts report that prescriptions for drugs such as Valium are down considerably, and the drug companies now caution physicians to consider carefully if a patient will really benefit from taking the drug.

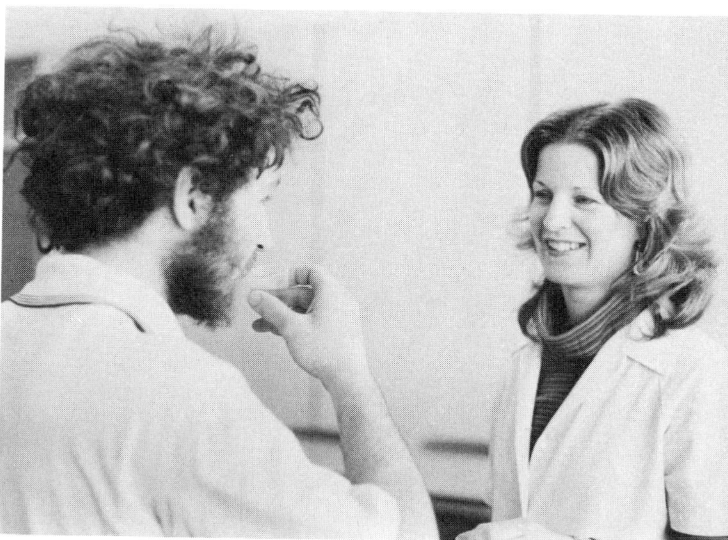

Psychotropic drugs are the leading form of treatment for serious mental disturbance. (© *Kenneth Karp*)

Electroconvulsive Therapy

Electroconvulsive therapy (ECT) was first developed by two Italian physicians in 1938. The procedure involves placing two electrodes on the patient's temples, through which a small electric current is passed. Prior to receiving ECT, patients are administered a barbiturate to induce unconsciousness and a muscle relaxant to reduce the severity of the convulsions. When the electric current is passed between the electrodes, which lasts for about one-half second, the patient experiences

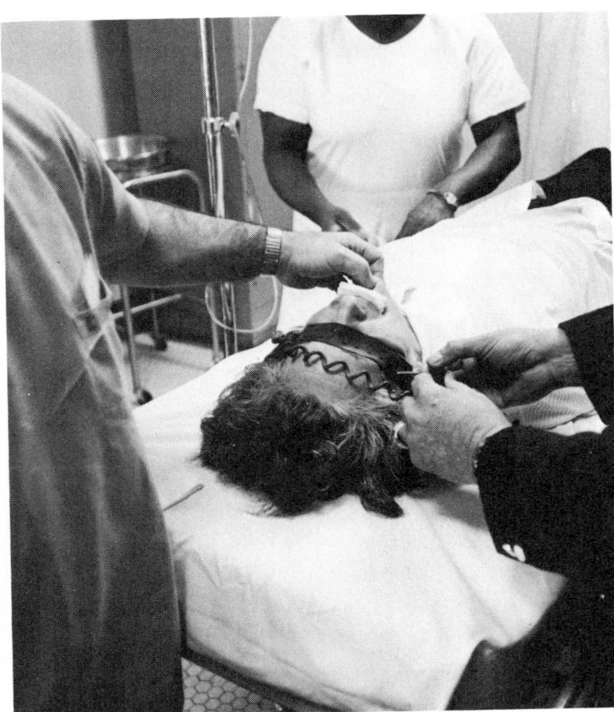

Refinements in the techniques of electroconvulsive therapy have made it a highly effective, though still controversial, method of medical therapy. (© *Magnum Photos, Inc.*)

a convulsion that lasts for about 10 seconds. Virtually all the voluntary muscles contract during this phase. Then, for a period of 30 to 40 seconds, there is a rapid series of alternating contractions and relaxations of the voluntary muscles. The patient awakes a few minutes later and is likely to be confused and disoriented for an hour or so.

ECT is a controversial technique. For many people it elicits images of screaming patients, broken bones, and human zombies. These images are not entirely unjustified since these were common occurrences during the early years of ECT's use. With the advent of modern procedures and medications, however, such scenarios rarely if ever occur. Still, the stigma does remain. You may recall that Senator Thomas Eagleton was dropped as George McGovern's running mate in the presidential elections in 1972 after it was revealed he had received ECT.

Although many psychologists and psychiatrists remain suspicious of ECT, the evidence indicates that it is a rapid and effective treatment for severe depression (Avery & Winokin, 1978; Klerman, DiMascio, & Weissman, 1974). It is used in the treatment of schizophrenia by some psychiatrists, but the evidence fails to justify such application. The mechanism by which ECT operates is not fully understood. In fact, more than 50 theories explaining its effects have been offered. The most reasonable explanation seems to be that ECT induces changes in the biochemistry of brain synapses (Fink, 1979).

While ECT appears to be a highly effective technique in many cases, it is important for therapists and hospital administrators to regulate its application closely. A few years ago ECT was often used as a punishment for the excited or violent behavior of hospitalized patients. Many of these patients received hundreds of treatments, which can lead to significant brain damage (Coleman, Butcher, & Carson, 1980). Used properly and in moderation, ECT appears to be an effective and safe procedure.

Psychosurgery

Psychosurgery is a controversial treatment in which a small area of the patient's brain is destroyed. It was popularized by a Portuguese neurologist named Antonio Egas Moniz in 1935. After hearing of research on the behavioral effects of frontal-lobe brain damage in monkeys, Moniz performed 20 operations in ten weeks on patients who were agitated and violent. His procedure involved drilling two holes through the top frontal portion of the skull. A thin wire was inserted through the holes and rotated so that a small circle was cut through the brain tissue. The procedure was introduced in the United States the following year, and some 40,000 of these operations, called prefrontal lobotomies, were performed through the 1950s. The practitioners of the surgery were generally enthusiastic about the procedure and claimed favorable results. They believed it significantly reduced violence and aggression. Other observers, however, claimed the technique left 40,000 human vegetables in its wake. Ironically, Moniz was eventually shot and paralyzed by a patient whom he had lobotomized for treatment of agitation.

Prefrontal lobotomies are no longer performed because of their profound side effects. In some instances patients were unable to inhibit any impulses; in others, they were unable to experience any emotion. A few patients even died from the operation. It has been replaced by newer, more sophisticated techniques of psychosurgery, which involve inserting a surgical instrument through the eye socket and destroying a very small area of the brain. These new techniques are just as controversial as the older procedures (Valenstein, 1980). Part of the controversy stems from the fact that the professional literature contains conflicting reports on the results of such surgery. For instance, Vernon Mark (1974), a neurosurgeon, has written about the case of Thomas R. According to Mark, psychosurgery was effective in his case. Thomas R. was reported to have had a history of violent rage, attacks, hallucination, and seizures. Prior to surgery he had received three years of psychotherapy, two years of medication, and had been committed to a locked hospital ward at least once. Mark reported that at the time of a four-year follow-up after surgery, there were no rages, attacks, or seizures.

Psychiatrist Peter Breggin (1973) painted quite a different picture of this same case. Breggin, an outspoken critic of psychosurgery, read Thomas R.'s records and interviewed him and his family. Breggin contended that this patient still had problems that were directly attributable to his surgery. Breggin also maintained that, contrary to Mark's account, before his surgery Thomas R. had worked as an engineer, had never been hospitalized, and had never had a diagnosis more severe than "personality pattern disturbance." According to Breggin, after surgery the patient was almost continually hospitalized, was diagnosed as having brain damage and schizophrenia, was frequently violent, and lived in terror that the surgeons would operate on him again.

Such conflicting reports have resulted in strong opposition to psychosurgery in the United States. Because of the potentially severe side effects and the irreversibility of psychosurgery, even advocates of the procedure agree that it should be used only as a last resort. The American Civil Liberties Union has objected to psychosurgery because many of those who receive it are institutionalized patients who cannot give their voluntary and informed consent. Also, some new medication or treatment might be discovered to help these patients. A large number of the 40,000 lobotomized patients would probably have been helped by the phenothiazines that were introduced in the 1950s.

Evaluation of Medical Therapies

There is no question that advances in the physical therapies over the past several decades have revolutionized mental-helath care. The development of the antipsychotic drugs is the most important of these advances. Older mental-health professionals have many horror stories to tell about the back wards of mental hospitals before the introduction of these drugs. The straitjacket, now seen mostly in old movies, was at one time an essential piece of hospital equipment. Today, many people who might have been doomed to spend their lives on one of these back wards 30 years ago are able to return to their families and communities.

The use of drugs, however, is a mixed blessing. Psychotic patients whose bizarre behavior is modified with medication will not necessarily learn skills for dealing with the pressures of everyday life. A schizophrenic patient may no longer have delusions or aggressive episodes after taking medication, but the patient will still require therapy to get along with other people and learn how to apply for a job. All too often, medication is used as a substitute for dealing with basic problems. Physicians must share the blame. It is much easier to write a prescription when a patient complains of anxiety than it is to spend time talking to him

APPLICATION

Confidentiality between Therapist and Client

Most forms of psychotherapy emphasize the importance of the relationship between the therapist and the client. A necessary condition for successful psychotherapy is that the client be able to trust the therapist. An aspect of this trust is confidence that anything said by the client during the course of therapy will be considered private and held confidential. Clients would be unlikely to discuss their personal fears, fantasies, urges, and feelings if they thought the therapist might reveal this information to others. One prominent therapist has stated that "there can be no psychological treatment without complete confidentiality" (Kandler, 1977).

Over the years the legal system has often recognized the importance of therapist-client confidentiality. Recent court decisions, however, have threatened this confidentiality. In *Tarasoff* v. *Regents of University of California* (1974), a client informed his therapist that he was going to murder a young woman, Tatiana Tarasoff. The client did not identify the woman by name, but she was identifiable by the therapist. After the therapy session the therapist conferred with his colleagues, and they decided to have the client committed to a mental hospital for observation. They called the campus police, who took the client into custody. The client impressed the campus police as being rational. He promised to stay away from the woman and was released. Two months later he murdered Tatiana Tarasoff.

The parents of the woman filed suit against the university, the therapist, and his supervisors. The trial judge dismissed the complaint, but an appeal to the Supreme Court of California resulted in a decision in the parents' favor.

This case has elicited strong reactions from the mental-health community. It has been suggested that the case makes therapists agents of the state (Bersoff, 1976). Although on the surface it may appear that therapists are principally concerned with serving their individual clients, their legal responsibility to reveal any information that may avert danger to others means that their first responsibility is to society in general.

Many psychotherapists believe they do have a responsibility to society. A statement endorsed by the Board of Directors of the American Psychological Association (1977) reads:

> Confidential information may be disclosed without authorization from the client only when and to the extent that the psychologist reasonably determines that such disclosure is necessary to protect against a clear and substantial risk of imminent serious injury or disease or death being inflicted by the client on him/herself or on another.

Accordingly, the ethical therapist is justified when he or she violates confidences with clients under some conditions—such as those that occurred in the Tarasoff case.

Not all psychologists agree, however. Max Siegel (1979) of Adelphi University believes that psychologists should not break confidentiality with clients under any circumstances. He has argued that if the therapist in the Tarasoff case had not violated his client's confidence, the client might have remained in therapy and the murder might have been prevented. Siegel stated, "The only potential protection for Ms. Tarasoff was for the psychologist to keep Poddar [the client] in treatment, and this was eliminated when he contacted the police."

The question is, Where does the therapist's responsibility to the client end and his or her responsibility to society begin? Wherever the therapist arbitrarily draws the line, it will sometimes be impossible to make completely satisfactory decisions. But clients should be aware that under current laws, some things they tell their therapist may not be held confidential, unless they have a therapist who is willing to be jailed for contempt of court or be sued for liability.

or her to help find a long-term solution. Drugs should be viewed not as a substitute for therapy but as a way of making it possible for patients to respond to other, more constructive forms of therapy.

ECT has been refined to the point where it is considered to be a relatively painless, rapid, and effective form of treatment for depression. Although there have been many cases in the past in which excessive treatments led to loss of memory and feelings of confusion, modern, and moderate, usage does appear to be a relatively safe procedure.

The one dark spot in the field of physical therapies is psychosurgery. At present there is little, if any, evidence that it is more effective than other available techniques. In fact, there seems to be considerable evidence that it is harmful. Because it is such a drastic and irreversible procedure, little justification can be found for its continued use.

PERSONAL-GROWTH THERAPIES

During the past few decades there has been an almost explosive growth in what can be called the **personal-growth** movement. This movement consists of a number of therapies and techniques for the individual who wants to achieve more satisfaction from life. Such individuals may not have any clearly identifiable problems, but they may have the feeling that something is missing from their lives. Objectively, everything about their lives may seem fine, but they are not really satisfied. Many people who do have clear psychological problems are also attracted to this form of therapy because of its popular appeal. It is in style to spend a weekend in an encounter group. Large numbers of these people are participating in one of the personal-growth therapies.

The personal-growth movement has its origins in the work of social psychologist Kurt Lewin. In 1946 Lewin was commissioned by the State of Connecticut to train leaders who could deal effectively with racial tension. Lewin organized workshops, which were held during the day, and during the evenings the workshop leaders met to discuss the day's events. At the evening sessions the leaders received feedback about their behavior. This open exchange proved to be exciting. For many of the participants, it was probably the first time they were able to learn how they were perceived by others. Before long several of the workshop participants asked if they could attend the evening sessions. The open and honest exchange of feedback that ensued was seen as an invaluable aid in developing effective interpersonal communication skills. These evening sessions led to the development of human-relations training groups, known as T-groups.

During the late 1950s and early 1960s humanistic psychologists suggested that such groups could be useful in promoting general personal growth as well as leadership skills. The intensive interpersonal interactions were viewed as a vehicle for self-discovery. When Carl Rogers lent his prestige to the group experience, the movement gained immeasurably in respectability. These groups are now popularly known as **encounter groups.**

Encounter Groups

The format of encounter groups can vary widely. Some will meet weekly for a few hours over a period of several months. Marathon encounter groups may require participants to spend 48 hours in the same room together. Esalen, the best known of the personal-growth centers, has experimented with having participants spend a summer together. Regardless of the specific format, the general principles governing the groups are much the same.

The basic principle is that the group experience provides participants the opportunity for open, intense, and honest interpersonal relationships. Proponents of the intensive group experience argue that many people feel dissatisfied with their lives because they have fallen into the habit of playing roles with others. For example, a husband may feel that he must be the strong; unemotional leader of the family. Or an employer may feel that he or she must be the tough, autocratic supervisor. Assuming such roles makes it difficult for people truly to know each other. And perhaps more important, after playing a role for a period of time, one cannot help but lose touch with one's own feelings and values. The openness and honesty of the encounter group is thought to break down facades and to help people get in touch with themselves.

The technique used by encounter-group leaders can vary as much as the format. Some leaders prefer an unstructured approach. This type of leader will generally make a few introductory remarks and then may tell the group that it is up to them to take it from there. The leader will simply wait for the group to begin interacting and will serve as a guide once the group members open up to one another.

At the other end of the continuum some leaders play a very active role in the development of the group process. They may use a variety of exercises to help members identify and express their feelings. One simple exercise, called Blind-Touch

CRITICAL ISSUE

The Encounter Movement as a Social Force: Good or Bad?

Psychologists often debate about the effectiveness of the encounter, or personal-growth, therapies. But a broader, and perhaps more important, debate involving not only mental-health professionals but sociologists, philosophers, politicians, religious leaders, and social critics is going on. It concerns the social implications of the encounter movement. Does it reflect a shift from superficial, materialistic values toward a more spiritual, more socially aware life style? Or does it reflect a lack of concern about the practical problems we face? Does the encounter movement reflect the "new narcissism"? Is it a symptom of the "me generation"?

As you might suspect, the answer depends on whom you talk to. Encounter groups have been called both "the greatest invention of the twentieth century" and a "psychic whorehouse." Many believe that the personal-growth therapies can help people achieve increased satisfaction from life without diminishing their social consciences. Others argue that these techniques are based on the premise "If it feels good, do it." They argue that the encounter movement offers an escape from reality.

The issue is more complex than these extreme positions would suggest. A sensitive, competent therapist who conducts an encounter group to help clients learn more about themselves and to improve their interpersonal skills cannot be likened to an authoritarian, self-appointed guru who attempts to coerce followers into accepting the proper values.

Recently two writers reported the results of their extensive interviews with many people who participated in the personal-growth movement during the 1960s and 1970s (Conway & Siegelman, 1978). They made the important distinction between techniques that *facilitate* personal growth and those that *impose* certain values. As an example, the authors contrasted Carl Rogers with Werner Erhard. Rogers, a respected psychologist, attempts to help people fulfill their potential. He does not impose his values upon his clients and believes that the process by which one changes is as important as the end result. Erhard, a former salesman and the founder of a mass encounter therapy called est, tells his clients they are fools if they do not understand and accept his message. It is significant that research has found that encounter leaders who are authoritarian, charismatic, and antagonistic are more likely to have casualties in their groups than helpful, nondirective leaders (Lieberman, Yalom, & Miles, 1973).

If the encounter movement represents an attempt to find meaning and satisfaction from a life style that accepts one's responsibilities to other people, then it must be good—even if its techniques are questionable. But if the encounter movement represents an attempt to find happiness at the expense of personal and social responsibility, then it must be bad—especially if its methods are successful.

Contact, requires group members to move about the room with their eyes closed. As they bump into each other, they are to explore each other's faces, hair, and bodies. The exercise generally encourages feelings of warmth and closeness among participants.

Role playing is also considered a useful exercise. A person who has described a difficult situation but is unable to understand his or her feelings about it may be asked to recreate the experience in the group. Comments by the group members and leader will often illuminate the feelings involved.

Carl Rogers (1970), the most prominent advocate of the intensive group experience, has described the typical sequence of events in encounter groups. At the beginning there is likely to be a great deal of awkward silence, and any conversation tends to be superficial. As the members begin to feel more comfortable, they discuss their feelings about situations that have occurred in the past. The first expression of immediate feelings is likely to be negative. Members might become angry at or critical of one another. Slowly, the group members begin to discuss personally relevant material and to respond in a supportive and therapeutic manner to one another. They abandon their facades. By the end the tone of the group is generally positive. Participants express feelings of liking for and closeness to one another. The members are thought to be ready to interact with other people in a more spontaneous and open, and hence more satisfying, way.

Encounter groups aim to break down barriers to interpersonal communication. (© *Sepp Seitz/Woodfin Camp & Associates*)

Gestalt Therapy

Classifying **Gestalt therapy** as a personal-growth therapy is a somewhat arbitrary decision. The Gestalt approach is really a philosophy of life. Its techniques can be used either with people who have psychological problems or with people who desire personal growth. Since it is closely identified with the personal-growth movement, we will include a discussion of the Gestalt theory in this section.

The basic premise of the Gestalt approach is that people have problems or are dissatisfied with their lives because they have lost touch with their true feelings (Kempler, 1973). This is thought to occur because as young children people learn to do things to win the approval of their parents, teachers, and peers. A child comes to engage in certain activities because they please others, not because he or she really wants to. This is said to result in a split or a polarization between two aspects of the self. One part, called the "top-dog" by Gestalt therapists, tells the person to work hard or to do what is expected by others. The other aspect, called the "under-dog," wants to play—to have fun. The goal of Gestalt therapy is to help clients recognize the conflicts between the two aspects of the self. Once clients are made fully aware of their feelings and can accept the conflicting aspects of their personalities, the painful interactions between the top-dog and the under-dog will diminish.

One way in which Gestalt therapists help clients to recognize the conflicting aspects of the self is by paying attention to body language. This is illustrated in a case history presented by John B. Enright (1970). He discussed a man who was extremely inhibited and had difficulty expressing feelings of any kind. He had suppressed feelings of anger so well that he typically did not even recognize his hostility. In a group therapy session he began to tap his finger on a table while a woman was monopolizing the session. When questioned by the therapist, the man denied having any particular feelings about the woman's talking. The therapist then asked the man to tap his finger harder and harder and louder and louder until he could more fully feel what he was doing. Before long the man's anger mounted. He began pounding the table and shouted that the woman was "just like my wife." The experience enabled the man to understand his excessive control over his feelings of anger and to express such feelings more immediately and hence less violently. Becoming aware of his feelings before they reached an intense state allowed him to make them known in more socially acceptable ways.

The following excerpt from a Gestalt group conducted by psychologist James Simkin provides a flavor of this form of therapy.

Therapist: I'd like to start first with having you say who you are and if you have any programs or expectations.

Jim: Right now I'm a little tense. . . . This morning I was pretty upset because I didn't agree with a lot of the things you were talking about, and I feel pretty hostile toward you.

Therapist: I'm paying attention to your foot now. I'm wondering if you could give your foot a voice.

Jim: My foot a voice? You mean how is my foot feeling? What's it going to say?

Therapist: Just keep doing that, and see if you have something to say, as your foot.

Jim: I don't understand.

Therapist: As you were telling me about feeling hostile this morning, you began to kick and I'm imagining that you still have some kick coming.

Jim: Uh, yeah. I guess maybe I do have some kick left, but I really don't get the feeling that that's appropriate.

Mary: My heart was really racing. It still is. I feel very hot—no life—hot, sweating off anxiety . . .

Therapist: Would you be willing to say what you are experiencing at this moment?

Mary: Well, my whole body is throbbing. I feel my whole . . . well, it's just pulsing. I'm just pulsing.

Therapist: That excites me. I like your pulsing.

Mary: That pleases me.

Lavonne: Right now I'm feeling very tense.

Therapist: Who are you talking to, Lavonne?

Lavonne: I was just thinking about this morning. I was feeling very hostile. I still think I am feeling hostile.

Therapist: I am aware that you are avoiding looking at me.

Lavonne: Yes, because I feel that you are very arrogant.

Therapist: That's true.

Lavonne: And as if I might get into a struggle with you.

Therapist: You might.

Evaluation of Personal-Growth Therapies

There is no doubt that personal-growth therapies can have a significant impact on participants. Advocates of these techniques have no difficulty producing many testimonials from former members who claim that the therapy experience changed their lives. Carl Rogers has called the intensive group experience the most important social invention of the century.

Other mental-health professionals are not nearly so enthusiastic. Psychologist Sigmund Koch (1971) has likened encounter groups to a "psychic whorehouse." He argues that the freedom, flexibility, and closeness that are experienced during the group sessions are superficial.

This position tends to be supported by the available research evidence. For example, one study found that two months after an encounter-group experience, the participants felt that any changes that had occurred had disappeared. The friends and families of the participants failed to notice any changes either at the end of the group experience or two months later (Marks & Vestre, 1974).

There might not be so many objections to the personal-growth therapies if their advocates did not make such extravagant claims. They promise a variety of benefits that research simply fails to substantiate. Even more irritating to the scientifically minded mental-health professional is the tendency of many personal-growth therapists to dismiss research findings. Psychiatrist Andrew Malcolm (1973) has concluded that the encounter-group movement is more like a religion than a professional activity. To a large extent the leaders of the personal-growth therapies seem to be saying that people must have faith in their techniques rather than to be building a foundation based on theory and research.

On the other hand, the fact that millions of people have participated in such experiences would seem to suggest that they have something to offer. Many writers have suggested that our intellectualized and goal-directed society leaves little room for emotional experience. Perhaps personal-growth therapies are a means of satisfying some of our emotional needs. Rather than view these therapies as vehicles for personal growth and behavior change, it may be more appropriate to think of them as vacation-like experiences. People could attend such groups with the goal of feeling emotionally refreshed and invigorated rather than with unjustified hopes of making lasting changes in their lives.

A very real problem with encounter groups is that of casualties. The evidence suggests that a substantial portion of encounter-group participants leave the group worse off than when they entered it. Although encounter-group advocates claim that the risk is negligible, some estimates of casualty rates are as high as 47 percent. A reasonable estimate, however, is that about 8 percent of encounter-group participants will suffer negative psychological effects from the experience (Hartley, Roback, & Abramowitz, 1976).

Many of the casualties occur because participants cannot withstand the confrontations to which they are subjected. Being attacked by other members of the group hurts them rather than helps them. Also, the inhibitions and restraints that encounter-group leaders attempt to eliminate may serve a useful purpose in social relationships. Openness and honesty may make for an exciting and fruitful group experience, but they may get group members into trouble when they return to their everyday lives. Not everyone appreciates an uninhibited expression of feelings and emotions.

SOME THOUGHTS ABOUT PSYCHOTHERAPY AND BEHAVIORAL TREATMENT METHODS

The field of psychotherapy and behavioral change is both discouraging and encouraging at the same time. It is discouraging because after nearly a century there is still controversy regarding the effectiveness of psychotherapy. As we have seen, Eysenck argued in the 1950s that there was no evidence that psychotherapy is effective, and many researchers today still agree with him. It is also discouraging that there is so little agreement among mental-health professionals regarding theories and techniques of behavioral change. Indeed, instead of existing theories and techniques being developed and refined over the years, there has been a proliferation of new schools of thought. While some may view that as positive and healthy, it also makes one wonder if we are any closer to answers than we were 50 years ago.

All is not gloom, however. The introduction of phenothiazines has improved the quality of life for millions of people. There has been remarkable progress in the treatment of a variety of specific problems. For example, most theorists agree that behavior therapy has proved effective and efficient in the treatment of phobias. As recently as the mid-1960s the prevailing view among psychologists was that sexual dysfunctions, such as erectile failure and orgasmic dysfunction, were extremely difficult to treat. Masters & Johnson (1970) led the way in demonstrating that these types of problems could be treated in a very brief period of time with extremely high success rates.

Another encouraging note is that theorists are showing greater willingness to borrow and adapt techniques from other schools of thought. In the 1960s the various schools of thought could be likened to armed camps. Currently it is common to see psychodynamic therapists incorporate some behavioral techniques or behavior therapists borrow from the Gestaltists. Arnold Lazarus, perhaps the leading advocate of a broader approach to therapy, has stated that his presentations were typically greeted with hostility in the early 1970s. By the late 1970s he reported that unfriendly remarks were rare. While there are disadvantages to being too eclectic, it is encouraging to see signs of more openness to new or opposing ideas. It is unlikely that any school of thought has a corner on the truth.

There is good reason to be optimistic about the future of psychotherapy and behavioral change. As psychologists keep reminding themselves, theirs is a comparatively young science. As advances continue to be made in the understanding of psychological and physiological processes, there is every reason to believe that new techniques—both psychological and medical—to alleviate human unhappiness and misery will continue to be developed.

Summary

The four major approaches to the treatment of abnormal behavior are psychotherapy, behavior therapy, medical methods, and personal-growth therapies.

Three important forms of psychotherapy are dynamic psychotherapy, client-centered psychotherapy, and rational-emotive therapy. Dynamic psychotherapy is based on the theory of Freud and is essentially an abbreviated form of psychoanalysis. Its goal is to help clients gain insight into unconscious conflicts that are thought to be influencing their behavior. Client-centered therapy, developed by Carl Rogers, attempts to help clients get in touch with their true feelings and values. To do this, the client-centered therapist creates a warm, accepting atmosphere in which the client is expected to resume psychological growth. Albert Ellis, the pioneer of rational-emotive therapy, believes that psychological problems are caused by the irrational things people tell themselves. His form of therapy promotes a more logical, scientific approach to life.

Behavior therapists assume that abnormal behavior is learned in much the same way that normal behavior is learned. They have developed a variety of techniques to treat many forms of psychological disturbances. Systematic desensitization is used to treat anxiety-related problems, such as phobias, and aversion therapy has been applied to problems such as overeating, smoking, alcoholism, and sexual variations.

The medical therapies are based on the assumption that abnormal behavior is caused by an underlying physical or medical defect. Of these therapies, the most widely used is drugs. Four important types of medication are antipsychotic drugs, lithium carbonate, antidepressant drugs, and antianxiety drugs. The antipsychotic drugs have been shown to be highly effective in the management of schizophrenia, and lithium carbonate is used effectively in the treatment and prevention of manic-depressive psychosis. The antidepressants are successfully used in many cases of severe depression. The antianxiety drugs, while the most widely used, are the least effective. They may reduce unpleasant feelings of anxiety, but they seem to have little effect on behavior. A second type of medical therapy is electroconvulsive therapy. It involves administration of electric current to a sedated patient's temples, which results in convulsions. It appears to be effective in the treatment of depression. Finally, psychosurgery is a controversial procedure that is sometimes used with agitated and violent patients.

The personal-growth therapies include encounter groups and Gestalt therapy. Although their techniques differ, their philosophies are similar. They both emphasize the importance of experience as opposed to intellectual understanding and attempt to help clients get in touch with their true feelings and values.

Research has shown that psychotherapy and the medical therapies (with the exception of psychosurgery) are effective in treating abnormal behavior. The personal-growth therapies do not seem nearly so promising. There is little evidence to suggest that they produce lasting behavioral change.

Key Terms For Review

antianxiety drugs
antidepressant drugs
antipsychotic drugs
aversion therapy
behavior therapy
client-centered therapy
dynamic psychotherapy
electroconvulsive therapy (ECT)
empathic understanding
encounter group
genuine
Gestalt therapy
interpretation
lithium carbonate
personal-growth therapies
psychosurgery
rational-emotive therapy (RET)
systematic desensitization (SD)
transference
unconditional positive regard
working through

Suggested Readings

Barnes, M., & Berke, J. *Two accounts of a journey through madness.* New York: Harcourt Brace Jovanovich, 1972.
A patient and her therapist discuss schizophrenia.

Barton, A. *Three worlds of therapy: Freud, Jung and Rogers.* Palo Alto, Calif.: National Press Books, 1974.
Three forms of psychotherapy are compared and contrasted.

Belkin, G. S. *Contemporary psychotherapies.* Chicago: Rand McNally, 1980.
Principles and procedures of various methods of psychotherapies.

Corsini, R. J. *Current psychotherapies* (2nd ed.). Itasca, Ill.: Peacock, 1979.
The history, concepts, and applications of the major schools of psychotherapy.

Kazdin, A. E. *Behavior modification in applied settings* (Rev. ed.) Homewood, Ill.: Dorsey, 1980.
Kazdin discusses the principles, misconceptions, ethical issues, and techniques associated with operant conditioning as it is applied in clinical settings.

Klerman, G. L. Psychotropic drugs as therapeutic agents. In L. R. Allman & D. T. Jaffe (Eds.), *Readings in abnormal psychology.* New York: Harper & Row, 1976.
This article describes the major psychotropic drugs and the moral and social implications of their widespread use.

14

Attitudes and Attitude Change

Ellen, a college senior majoring in business, was taking introductory psychology as an elective. Her instructor announced that the following week they would begin to talk about attitudes: how they are formed, how they can be changed, and how they influence behavior. This hit a responsive chord in Ellen because lately she had been thinking about some of her own attitudes. The presidential primaries were under way, and she seemed to be experiencing a shift in her political attitudes. She had begun to wonder how she had developed her attitudes in the first place and why they should be changing now.

Ellen had never had more than a passing interest in politics. Her parents had never discussed political issues, although she was aware they were both registered Democrats. She, too, had voted for the Democratic candidates in the mock elections held by her schools—from elementary school on up. She had never examined her reasons for doing so, but when asked she would talk vaguely about the Democratic party and social justice.

This year Ellen was eligible to vote for the first time, and she was more interested than usual in the many candidates. Before the first primary she "knew" she would be supporting the liberal Democratic candidate. But as the campaign progressed, her views began to change. She found herself feeling irritated by some of "her" candidate's comments. She began to wonder if his policies were workable. After the first three or four primaries, she decided that she would not vote for him. In fact, Ellen found herself favoring a Republican candidate.

Ellen was bright and introspective enough to realize that her political attitudes were not completely objective and rational. Because she was only mildly interested in politics, she did not seek out information about each candidate and arrive at a dispassionate decision based on the issues. Ellen realized that she had considered herself to be a Democrat because her parents were Democrats. Now she was curious to know what social forces might be influencing her attitudes toward the current presidential race. Perhaps next week's lecture would provide her with some clues.

As we saw in Chapter 1, social psychology is the study of the effects of groups on the individual. The study of attitudes and attitude change has always been of central interest to social psychologists. In fact, two of the earliest researchers in the field defined social psychology as "the science of attitudes" (Thomas & Znaniecki, 1918). Of course, today social psychology is a much broader discipline than merely the study of attitudes. Social psychology includes the topics of interpersonal attraction, conformity, group processes, and social perception, to name just a few. These topics and others will be presented in the following two chapters. But psychologists continue to be fascinated and, as we shall see, frustrated by the study of attitudes.

One reason for this fascination is that the topic of attitudes is relevant to so many aspects of everyday life. Companies hire advertising firms to influence attitudes so that people will buy their products. Politicians are concerned with voters like our fictitious Ellen whose attitudes toward candidates are far from being completely rational and objective. Many important social issues, such as racism and sexism, can be thought of as a matter of attitudes. Government officials, oil companies, and conservationists all try to influence our attitudes about the energy crisis—often in contradictory ways. Psychologists are not likely to run short of issues to research for some time. And it is hoped that the findings of social psychologists will help us to solve such complex and difficult issues as racism and prejudice so that we may all live together in a more harmonious world.

THE NATURE OF ATTITUDES

An **attitude** can be defined as a combination of cognitive, affective, and behavioral dispositions directed toward a person, idea, or object. Thus there are three components to an attitude. The **cognitive component** refers to the beliefs or factual knowledge about the person, idea, or object. For instance, Ellen may have believed that the conservative Republican candidate's plans for dealing with inflation were sounder than the liberal Democrat's. Ellen's budding dislike for the liberal Democrat's campaign style reflects the **affective component** of her attitude. The affective component refers to one's emotional response to, or feelings toward, a person, idea, or object. These feelings can be either positive or negative. The **behavioral component** of an attitude is one's disposition to do something about one's feelings, beliefs, and knowledge. If Ellen were to work for her candidate's campaign or to vote for him, that would reflect the behavioral component of her attitude. If Ellen believed her candidate's policies were sound, liked him, and voted for him, then we could safely say that her overall attitude toward him was positive.

Consistency among the Components of Attitudes

A good part of the time most of us are probably consistent with regard to the three components of our attitudes. For example, we believe candidate X's policies are reasonable, we like her, and we vote for her. Or, we believe that candidate Y's policies are way out of line, we cannot abide him personally, and we would sooner defect than vote for him. We believe that in general our behavior is consistent with our beliefs and feelings. Most of us, however, can also recognize instances of attitudes in which there is an inconsistency. We may have certain beliefs or feelings about a person or an idea, and yet our behavior does not follow from those beliefs and feelings. For example, we may believe that smoking is harmful to health, we may feel worried about our hacking cough and chest pains, and yet we continue to smoke cigarettes. Or, a male student majoring in engineering may believe that women are not capable of learning that kind of material, yet treat the women in his class with politeness and respect, and even ask one of them for help.

Social psychologists have been aware for some time that the behavioral component of attitudes does not always correspond to the cognitive and affective components. In a classic study Richard LaPiere (1934) discussed his experience of traveling across the country with a young Chinese couple. In covering over 10,000 miles, they stayed in 66 hotels and ate in 184 restaurants. The couple also stayed alone in a few hotels and ate several meals by themselves. In all their travels, the couple were refused accommodations only once. LaPiere and the Chinese couple were for the most part treated courteously and at times graciously. LaPiere was somewhat surprised by this favorable reception, since at the time discrimination was neither illegal nor unusual. Six months after the trip he sent a questionnaire to all the hotels and restaurants they had visited asking if they would serve Chinese persons. Of the 128 replies received, 118 said that they would not.

In another study conducted some 30 years ago (Saenger, 1953), a researcher followed customers who had been served by a black salesperson out into the street. When questioned, many of these customers stated that they would not allow a black person to serve them. Of these, nearly one fourth stated that they had *never seen* a black salesperson in a department store. It would appear that many people are incapable of recognizing the inconsistencies between how they think and feel and how they act. Their beliefs and feelings may be so intense that they deny any evidence that they are behaving in a contradictory fashion.

More recent research conducted in the 1960s and 1970s confirms the very low correlations between beliefs and feelings on the one hand and a specific type of behavior on the other. It has been found, however, that if a *range* of behavior is examined, the relation between cognitions and affect on the one hand and behavior on the other is highly significant (Fishbein, 1967; Fishbein & Ajzen, 1974). Suppose a psychologist is interested in the relation between beliefs and behavior with regard to religion. Say that he or she first gives a group of people a survey measuring the strength of their religious beliefs. Then, their frequency of church attendance is observed. If a majority of the people studied express strong religious beliefs but rarely or never go to church, the psychologist may conclude that there is no relation between beliefs and behavior. But if the psychologist had observed various types of religious behavior, such as praying before meals, reading religious material, contributing to religious organizations, and going to church, the relation between religious beliefs and behavior would probably have been much higher.

Greater consistency between beliefs and behavior has also been found when the attitude being measured is more narrowly defined. For example, in one study, researchers expected that attitudes about air pollution would correspond to the behavior of buying lead-free gasoline; yet this proved not to be so (Heberlein & Black, 1976). In the same study, however, a strong correspondence *was* found between attitudes toward the use of lead-free gasoline and the purchase of such fuel. A person may have strong feelings about air pollution in general without having specific beliefs about the use of lead-free gasoline. Similarly, a person may be highly religious but not think it necessary to go to church. In other words, many researchers have concluded that studies have shown little relation between beliefs and behavior because they used very broad measures of beliefs and very specific measures of behavior. If either very broad or very specific measures of both components are used, then the relation between beliefs and behavior is likely to be significant.

A recent study by social psychologists Mark P. Zanna, James M. Olson, and Russell H. Fazio (1980) suggests that the strength of the link between attitudes and behavior varies from person to person. They examined the relation between attitudes toward religion and religious behavior for individuals who varied on the personality dimension of **self-monitoring.** Self-monitoring refers to the degree to which one looks to situational cues in deciding how to act in a given situation. People who are low self-monitors are thought to make decisions about behavior in accord with their thoughts and feelings, whereas high self-monitors are thought to guide their behavioral choices on the basis of the situations in which they find themselves. Zanna, Olson, and Fazio found that only those individuals who were low self-monitors *and* whose past religious behavior was consistent showed a strong correspondence between their religious attitudes and their religious behavior. All other individuals exhibited very modest relations between attitudes and behavior. In other words, individuals who have a stable pattern of religious behavior are likely to base their decisions about church attendance on their beliefs and feelings. Hence they show consistency between attitudes and behavior. Others, namely the high self-monitors, are more likely to attend church because they are with a friend who does so, and not because they have religious convictions. Thus they can be expected to exhibit less consistency between attitudes and behavior.

As happens so often in psychology, research that set out to answer a relatively simple question has not provided simple, straightforward answers. Rather, it has demonstrated that the question is much more complex that it was originally thought to be. The answer to the question of whether there is consistency between people's attitudes and their behavior appears to be that it depends on the nature of the attitudes being measured, the specific behavior in question, and the particular person involved.

Up to this point, our discussion of attitudes has implicitly assumed that beliefs and feelings influence behavior. Since the early 1970s psychologist Daryl Bem (1972) has been conducting research that supports an alternative theory. Bem has argued that it is our behavior that influences our cognitions and emotions. That is, people come to know of their attitudes through inferences drawn from observing their own behavior. Thus we might say we like tennis because we find ourselves playing the game at every available opportunity. Our reply to the question "Do you like tennis?" is essentially the same as a reply that might be given by a friend: "I guess he does, he is always playing tennis or watching it on television." As we shall see later in the chapter, Bem's theory has important implications for attitude change.

Development of Attitudes

Our attitudes are not always rational and objective, nor are they necessarily based on direct experiences. We are likely to have attitudes toward objects or people to which we have never been exposed. For example, like Ellen, we may have strong feelings about political candidates whom we have never met and about whom we have read very little. Or we may have the attitude that we would never take a vacation in a particular country (e.g., Mongolia), even though we know virtually nothing about it. How, then, do we arrive at our attitudes?

A major part of the socialization process involves the acquisition of attitudes from our parents, peers, and teachers. The factors discussed in Chapter 10 regarding the development of personality traits are essentially the same as those that influence the development of our attitudes. Parents serve as models for their children and reinforce them for exhibiting what are considered to be appropriate attitudes. For instance, parents who strongly disapprove of physical aggression and violence are likely to settle disagreements between themselves through discussion. They may punish their children by putting them in their rooms rather than by spanking them. They may also talk to their children about the virtues of settling arguments peacefully rather than by fighting. And when the parents see their children behave in accord with these attitudes, they will praise them. Studies have found that children share their parents' attitudes on a number of issues, including political beliefs (Jennings & Niemi, 1968), prejudices toward ethnic groups (Epstein & Komorita, 1966), and standards of sexual propriety (Abramson, Michalak, & Alling, 1977).

As children grow older, their peers begin to play an increasingly important role in attitude development. More than one parent has become distraught by the "crazy" attitudes their children bring home from college. Such attitudes are strongly influenced by the person's **reference group,** that is, the group with which he or she identifies. The group functions similarly to the way parents functioned earlier. It provides models of proper attitudes and reinforces the expression of these attitudes.

In a classic study that illustrated the importance of a reference group, T. M. Newcomb (1943) examined the political attitudes of students at Bennington, a women's college in Vermont. At that time Bennington was one of the most expensive colleges in the country, and the majority of students came from affluent, conservative families. The school, however, was known for its intellectual freedom and liberal atmosphere. Newcomb, who was interested in the potential conflict between the parents' and the college's outlook, found that the students became progressively more liberal during their four years at Bennington. For example, in the 1936 presidential elections, over 60 percent of the students' parents favored the Republican candidate, Alf Landon. While only 29 percent of the freshman class favored the liberal Democrat, Franklin Roosevelt, 54 percent of the juniors and seniors supported him. Furthermore, 30 percent of the upperclass students favored socialist or communist candidates.

Parents can have a profound effect on the attitudes of their children. (© *Bob Combs/Rapho Photo Researchers, Inc.*)

Reference groups appeared to be a crucial determinant of views. Those students who maintained strong ties to their families and isolated themselves from college life were likely to retain their conservative political attitudes. Conversely, the students who had become more liberal were usually the most active in campus social activities. In fact, in any college or university one's political attitudes are likely to be influenced by reference groups. For instance, our fictitious Ellen may have become more conservative politically because she was a business major, especially if her professors complained about lowered productivity caused (in their view) by government interference. Or her peers who anticipated making large salaries may have expressed concern about how much in taxes they would have to contribute to welfare. A student majoring in a field such as sociology may become more liberal after hearing professors and fellow students express concern about issues such as prejudice and the social inequalities in our society.

Newcomb found that attitudes developed by college students often endure long after college. (© *Rhoda Galyn / Photo Researchers, Inc.*)

Newcomb was also interested in the long-term effects of the students' college experience. Twenty-five years later he contacted the students and found that they had retained their liberalism (Newcomb, 1967). For instance, 60 percent of the Bennington graduates voted for Democrat John F. Kennedy in the 1960 Presidential election, compared with only 30 percent of non-Bennington women from similar social and economic backgrounds. Also, the students who had remained conservative during their four years of college were likely to vote for Richard M. Nixon, the Republican candidate. Newcomb suggested that once the women had graduated, they sought new reference groups—husbands, jobs, and friends—that would continue to reinforce the political attitudes they had developed in college. It would appear from this study that parents who comfort each other with the thought that their child's radical ideas obtained in college are only a passing phase are likely to be disappointed.

ATTITUDE CHANGE

Every week we are exposed to hundreds of attempts to influence our attitudes. The commercials we see on television or hear on the radio attempt to change our attitudes about certain products. Government leaders and politicians try to change our attitudes about programs and policies. College instructors attempt to change their students' attitudes about aspects of the subject they are teaching. Friends try to change our attitudes about all manner of things, from politics to religion to music. What factors are apt to make these attempts successful? Or, if these attempts are not successful, why are we able to resist such appeals? During the late 1940s and 1950s social psychologists began to examine persuasive techniques of communication. This interest was stirred in part by the use of propaganda during World War II. Reports of brainwashing—the systematic changing of attitudes or beliefs through the use of torture, drugs, or psychological-stress techniques—during the Korean conflict further aroused interest. Research focused on variables such as the source and the nature of the communication, which we shall look at now.

The Source of Persuasive Communications

Advertising firms appear to believe that having well-known individuals endorse a product will help to change attitudes about that product. People are thought to like the idea that their coffee is brewed by the same device that Joe DiMaggio uses, that they use the same camera that James Garner does, or that they have the same tires on their car that Terry Bradshaw has. These celebrities are thought to have high credibility, and high-credibility sources are thought to be capable of producing attitude change.

Social psychologists have confirmed the importance of **source credibility** in producing attitude change. When the source is considered to be knowledgeable and trustworthy, his or her communications are likely to be persuasive. An early example of this effect was provided by Hovland and Weiss (1951). They presented two groups with identical communications. One of the groups was led to believe that the source was credible, while the other group was led to believe the source was untrustworthy. For instance, one communication concerned the practicality of an atomic-powered submarine, a controversial issue at the time. One group was told that the source was Robert Oppenheimer, the physicist who had coordinated the development of the atomic bomb, while the other group was told the source was the Russian state newspaper *Pravda*. In the first instance, 36 percent of the subjects changed their opinion to agree with Oppenheimer, while none of the subjects in the latter instance changed their opinion to agree with *Pravda*.

In addition to expertise and trustworthiness, factors such as physical attractiveness (see Chapter 15 for a discussion on the effects of this variable) and similarity to the receiver can influence the persuasiveness of the communication. Physically attractive individuals tend to be more persuasive than unattractive people (Mills & Aronson, 1965), and sources that are perceived as having experiences similar to the recipient are more credible than sources without such experiences (Berscheid, 1966). Hence Henry Winkler, known as "the Fonz," is likely to be more effective in warning teenagers about the dangers of drug abuse than the president of the American Medical Association.

Virtually all of us have had the experience of expressing attitudes based on something we have read. When questioned about the information, we may have said, "I can't remember where, but I did read it somewhere." This phenomenon of remembering the message but forgetting the source is common and has been called the **sleeper effect.** It was identified in the study just mentioned, in which the feasibility of atomic submarines was supposedly discussed by physicist Robert Oppenheimer and by *Pravda*. The researchers measured the audience's attitudes four weeks after they had been exposed to the message. They found that the group that had been exposed to Oppenheimer had decreased in the extent of their agreement with him, while the group exposed to *Pravda* had increased their level of agreement with the communication. It appears that the sleeper effect reduces the importance of source credibility over time.

In more recent years, the importance of the sleeper effect has been seriously questioned. Many experiments have failed to find that a low-credibility source becomes more influential over time (Gillig & Greenwald, 1974). It is consistently found, however, that the impact of a high-credibility source dissipates over time. Additionally, the sleeper effect can be overcome by reminding the audience of the source of the communication. Currently, social psychologists believe that a person tends to dissociate the source from the message as time passes, but the sleeper effect is not considered to be as common or as potent as previously thought.

There are occasions when the communications from an otherwise credible source will not be persuasive. For instance, if we see a celebrity that we respect and trust endorse a product, we may believe that he or she really uses and likes that product and we may be tempted to try it. But if we see the same celebrity in a number of different commercials, we may strongly suspect that personal gain rather than belief in the product is the motive behind the endorsement. The perceived intentions—or **ulterior motives**—of the source can contribute to his or her persuasive abilities.

This effect of ulterior motives was clearly demonstrated in an experiment that determined that a convicted heroin dealer (generally *not* high in perceived trustworthiness) could be as persuasive as a respected public official (Walster, Aronson, & Abrahams, 1966). In the experiment half of the audience was given a newspaper clipping that argued that convicted criminals were receiving treatment that was too lenient. The article recommended that the police and the courts should be given more power to curb the rising crime rate. The other half of the audience was given an article that took the opposite stand. It argued that the police and courts had too much power and that the rights of defendants needed greater protection. Furthermore, half of each group was led to believe that the source of the article was Joe "The Shoulder" Napolitano, who had been convicted for dealing in heroin. The other half of the audience was told that the source was G. William Stephens, a tough prosecuting attorney. As predicted, the greatest attitude change occurred when Joe "The Shoulder" argued for tougher courts and police, and when the prosecuting attorney argued for protecting the rights of defendants. Sources are most likely to be persuasive when their arguments run counter to their own interests and when no ulterior motives are obvious.

The Communication

Imagine that you are on a debating team. In preparing your speech you would probably ask yourself several questions, such as: Should I present my point of view only and thus minimize confusion, or should I present both points of view in order to seem fair-minded? If given the choice, should I speak first in order to have a fresh impact, or should I speak last so that my views will be perceived as the final word? And, should I base my appeal on logic or on emotion? Social psychologists have attempted to find answers to these questions.

One-sided versus Two-sided Communications. The answer to the first question, whether the debater should make a one-sided or two-sided argument, appears to be that it depends on the audience. One of the first research projects to address this question was conducted during World War II. Shortly before the German surrender, the United States Army became concerned because the prevailing attitude seemed to be that the Japanese surrender would follow shortly. This overconfidence was viewed as a threat to the motivation of the soldiers, and the army wanted to persuade them that the war could last for another two years. Social psychologist Carl Hovland and his colleagues (Hovland, Lumsdaine, & Sheffield, 1949) took this opportunity to design research to examine persuasive communications.

One group of 214 men listened to a radio broadcast that gave a one-sided argument as to why the war with Japan could last longer than anticipated. It cited the problems associated with the distance between the two countries, Japan's access to resources, and the large Japanese army. The two-sided argument, heard by another group of 214 men, included this information but added information about the superiority of the United States Navy and the greater concentrated strength that could be gained in the shift from a two-front to a one-front war. The overall result was that there was no difference between the one-sided and two-sided arguments in producing attitude change.

When the researchers considered characteristics of the audience, however, several important findings emerged. For those whose initial attitudes were consistent with the communication, the one-sided argument was most effective. For these men, the two-sided argument may have raised doubts about their position. For those who were initially opposed to the communication, the two-sided argument was more effective. It may be that these men viewed the one-sided argument as being biased and thus were less vulnerable to it.

The educational level of the men also played an important role. It was found that for men with high levels of education, the two-sided argument produced more attitude change regardless of their initial attitude. For those with less education, the two-sided argument was slightly more effective if they were initially opposed to the communication, but the one-sided argument was overwhelmingly more effective for those who initially favored the communication (see Table 14–1). One possible explanation is that as educational level increases, the ability to evaluate communications critically also increases. A critical audience, therefore, will probably view a one-sided argument as being unfair and insulting to their intelligence. Thus as a debater you would be wise to learn about the audience before structuring your speech.

Primacy versus Recency. If you had your choice in a debate, would you speak first or second? Speaking first may have a **primacy effect**—your message would have an advantage because it would interfere with the assimilation of your opponent's message. On the other hand, speaking second may have a **recency effect**—your message would have an advantage because it would be fresh in the minds of the listeners. Aristotle addressed this question some 25 centuries ago and is reported to have said, "For just as our minds refuse a favorable reception to a person against whom they are prejudiced, so they refuse it to a speech on the other side." In other words, Aristotle believed it was to the debater's advantage to speak first. Others, however, believe that speaking last is an advantage. In courtroom trials, for instance, the defense attorney is thought to have the advantage by being allowed to speak last in order to refute the prosecution's arguments and to then present the defendant's case so that it will be fresh in the minds of the jurors. The question of whether there is a primacy effect or a recency effect has been debated and researched by social psychologists. The answers appears to be, "It depends."

Numerous studies were conducted in the 1950s on this issue, but in many cases the results were inconsistent. Some reported a primacy effect, while others reported a recency effect. One crucial difference between these studies appeared to be the time intervals between the presentation of the two communications and the time interval between the communications and the measurement of attitude change.

In an attempt to resolve the issue, Miller and Campbell (1959) conducted a study in which arguments actually heard at a jury trial were presented in a variety of formats. They found that when the second message immediately followed the first but there was a one-week delay before attitude change was measured, there was a clear primacy effect. A definite recency effect occurred when the second message followed the first message after a week's delay and measurement occurred immediately after the second communication. So, for example, if you were asked a week after hearing a political debate who presented the best argument, your tendency would be to favor the first speaker. If you heard a political speech and a week later heard a rebuttal, your tendency would be to favor the second speaker immediately after hearing the rebuttal. When the two communications and the measurement were presented successively, and when there was a week's delay between the two communications and between the second communication and the measurement, no clear advantage for either primacy or recency was evident. So if these results can be applied to trials where the jury retired to deliberate immediately after hearing the closing arguments, neither the prosecution nor the defense has an advantage. These results could be useful,

Table 14–1. Factors Associated with Attitude Change

In a project designed to change soldiers' attitudes about the potential length of World War II, it was found that attitude change was a function of educational level, initial attitudes, and whether the argument was one-sided or two-sided. The table shows percentages of those who increased their estimate of the length of the war.

	High School Graduate		*Nongraduate*	
	Initially opposed	*Initially favored*	*Initially opposed*	*Initially favored*
One-sided argument	30%	39%	44%	64%
Two-sided argument	44%	54%	51%	-3%

Source: Hovland et al. (1949).

however, to politicians in deciding when to make announcements or hold press conferences.

Appealing to the Emotions: Fear Arousal. A common strategy for attitude change is to use scare tactics. Children are told about the pain of having cavities filled to get them to brush their teeth. Smokers are warned about the life-threatening consequences of their habit to get them to give it up. A classic study conducted by Irving Janis and Seymour Feshbach (1953) seemed to question the idea that inducing fear in the audience is an effective technique of attitude change. They exposed three groups of high school students to messages that emphasized the importance of good dental hygiene. The first group was shown graphic pictures of rotting teeth and diseased gums. The second group saw pictures that were considerably less shocking. The third group heard the lecture but saw no pictures. When questioned a week later, the students in the third group reported more changes in their dental-hygiene practices than students in the other two groups. The researchers concluded that fear arousal can have a boomerang effect—people may become anxious and defensive when exposed to a message designed to elicit fear and thus not pay attention to the content of the message.

The ability to communicate depends largely on a person's understanding of the characteristics of the audience. (© *Black Star*)

Subsequent research found that fear arousal *can* be effective in providing attitude and behavioral change (Dabbs & Leventhal, 1966). The two sides were reconciled to some extent in an experiment conducted by Howard Leventhal (1970). In communications designed to change attitudes about smoking, he found that a fear-arousing message was most effective in generating an intent to stop smoking. The actual number of cigarettes smoked, however, was not reduced unless the fear arousal was accompanied by specific suggestions on how to stop smoking. The suggestions, without the fear element, were ineffective in producing change. So it would seem that fear arousal can be an effective technique of attitude change as long as specific suggestions are made for complying with the communication.

The Audience

As we saw earlier, the effectiveness of a persuasive communication can depend in part on the characteristics of the audience. Along with level of education, researchers have identified a number of characteristics that are related to the degree of attitude change that occurs. These include age, sex, prior attitudes, and self-esteem. The difficulty with this research is that the interrelationships between audience characteristics and source and message variables are so complex that it is virtually impossible to arrive at any generalizations. In a review of this topic William McGuire (1969) of Yale University stated, "The results regarding the relationship between any given individual-difference variable (audience characteristic) and susceptibility to social influence tend to be extremely complex and seemingly contradictory"

CRITICAL ISSUE

Brainwashing: An Extreme Case of Attitude Change

"Brainwashing" is an imprecise term. We tend to use it to describe anyone who tries to instill in others beliefs that we cannot understand. For instance, we may believe that children in other countries are "brainwashed" into accepting the tenets of communism. Children in our country are, of course, "educated" in the virtues of democracy. Parents of children who have joined religious cults claim that their children have been brainwashed. Many parents have even hired consultants to kidnap the children to have them "deprogrammed." Several of the children have in turn filed criminal charges against their parents and the deprogrammers.

The issue of brainwashing came into prominence as the prisoners of war taken in the Korean conflict of the 1950s were returned to this country. Many of these American soldiers had signed confessions of their war crimes and made propaganda broadcasts for their captors. A psychiatrist interviewed many of these men to learn what circumstances could lead to such widespread incidence of what was considered treasonous behavior (Schein, 1956).

Two primary tactics seemed to emerge. First, the Chinese prevented the prisoners from forming close personal ties with one another. Their ability to communicate with other prisoners was limited, and the conversations they were able to have were monitored. The men became distrustful of one another and completely dependent on their captors for information.

The second tactic was the use of rewards and punishments. The men were deprived of adequate food and housing and were told that their lot would improve once they began to cooperate. Beatings and threats of torture and death were also used. These techniques, applied relentlessly, were sufficient to cause many prisoners to do as their captors asked.

Brainwashing was also a concern in 1981, when the American hostages were released from Iran. During their captivity, their docile manner in interviews and their statements that they were being well-treated suggested that brainwashing might have occured. It became apparent, however, that a majority, if not all, of them had not suffered from brainwashing. In fact, many of them had engaged in acts of defiance throughout their captivity. Yet their situation shared many elements with the Korean prisoners of war. They were dependent on their captors for information about the outside world. They had to listen to propaganda about their "crimes." And they were subjected to beatings and threats of death.

Two factors may account for the absence of evidence of brainwashing. First, they were allowed to communicate with one another. Thus they were not as likely to feel isolated as the Korean POWs were. And second, the Iranians were not completely diligent in keeping information about the outside world from them. For instance, several hostages learned of the failed rescue mission when they were allowed to have crossword puzzles. Apparently their captors never thought to look at the news items on the reverse side of the puzzles.

(p. 243). The way in which the characteristic is measured, the prior attitudes of the audience, and the nature of the communication all interact with each other and make it difficult to predict how a particular audience will react to a given message from a specific source.

One issue that social psychologists neglected for many years was the ability of people to resist attempts to change their attitudes. Considering the hundreds of messages to which we are exposed on television, on the radio, and in the newspapers every week, it is amazing that we shift our attitudes so seldom. Throughout the late 1940s and 1950s, researchers were interested in those instances in which attitude changes did occur, but it was not until the 1960s that they began to shift their emphasis and examine resistance to persuasion.

To explain resistance to persuasion, William McGuire (1964) developed the idea of the **inoculation effect.** Using a medical analogy, McGuire and his colleagues reasoned that certain attitudes may be especially open to change because they are accepted so completely that individuals have no defenses against persuasive attempts. McGuire hypothesized that if individuals were exposed to a mild attempt to change these types of attitudes, they would be able to resist full-blown attempts later on. This process would be analogous to inoculation against a virus. The injection of a small dose of the virus stimulates the body to produce antibodies so that it is protected against the disease.

In a test of this inoculation-effect hypothesis, four common beliefs were identified (McGuire & Papageorgis, 1961).

They were:

1. Everyone should get a chest x-ray each year to detect any possible tuberculous symptoms at an early stage of the disease.
2. Penicillin has been, almost without exception, of great benefit to mankind.
3. Most forms of mental illness are not contagious.
4. Every person should brush his or her teeth after each meal.

Three groups of subjects were used in the study. A support group was given information consistent with the four statements. A second group was provided information that mildly attacked these attitudes—that is, they received an "inoculation." A control group received no information about the beliefs. Subsequently, all three groups were exposed to a vigorous attack on their attitudes. Consistent with the hypothesis, the support and control groups showed a significant degree of attitude change, while the inoculation group showed the least amount of change.

These results would seem to hold implications for parents who wish to instill certain attitudes in their children. Providing only one point of view and protecting the child from being exposed to any conflicting information may eventually backfire. For example, some parents may be so concerned that their children adhere to a particular religious doctrine that they never allow their children to be exposed to other points of view. Thus their children never learn how to defend their religious beliefs and may give them up when they are attacked. Parents who want their children to maintain their attitudes may be well advised to provide "inoculations" periodically.

THEORIES OF ATTITUDE CHANGE

Like other psychologists, social psychologists generally believe that theories are extremely useful, and a variety of theories have been developed to aid in the understanding of attitude change and to suggest new approaches to the changing of attitudes. The various theories are not always compatible and in fact are sometimes contradictory, yet each is supported by research. This again reflects the complexity of the topic. Each particular theory seems to work best in certain specific circumstances. Until a more comprehensive theory of attitude change is developed, it may be appropriate to view the theories as complementary to each other rather than as mutually exclusive.

Reinforcement Theory

One of the first theories of attitude change suggested that attitudes are responses and, like other responses, can be acquired by means of the principles of learning (Hovland, Janis, & Kelly, 1953). Thus parents may reward their children for expressing good attitudes and punish them for expressing bad attitudes. Social acceptance and approval is an important form of reinforcement, so adolescents and adults may acquire certain attitudes because they are approved of by peers and colleagues. The Bennington study discussed earlier, in which students' political attitudes became

CRITICAL ISSUE

Attitudes and Politics

Psychologists are not the only ones to struggle with the topic of attitudes. Political scientists have also conducted much research that has addressed the relation between attitudes and various aspects of politics. And like psychologists, they have been puzzled by the relation between the cognitive and behavioral aspects of attitudes.

In a recent article, political scientist Stephen Craig (1980) discussed the possible implications of political discontent. He pointed out that the future of our government depends on the "bonds that tie citizens to their political leaders." In other words, if our government is to continue to function, it must have the support of the people.

This point caused concern among many political scientists during the mid-1960s when a growing distrust of government was accompanied by an increasing number of challenges to its legitimacy. Campus demonstrations and urban riots were common. Political scientists were busy during this period hypothesizing about the connection between the dissatisfaction with government and the consequent unconventional behavior. But the appeal of these hypotheses faded as the 1970s progressed since distrust of the government remained the same, and may have even increased, but the incidence of demonstrations and riots declined dramatically. By 1980, according to Craig, 15 years of rising discontent "appears to have had no systematic consequences at all."

Craig offered several possible explanations for this seeming inconsistency between attitudes and behavior. Although he uses the terms and jargon of political science, many of his conclusions are similar to the findings of psychologists. For instance, he points out that the mixed results of research in this area may be a function of using terms and concepts in too general a way. Several studies that have examined the relation between political attitudes and behavior have focused on unconventional behavior—such as riots and demonstrations. But discontent may also motivate some people to become more active within the existing political structure.

By implication, Craig also addressed the vagueness of the term "political discontent." An attitude survey that finds that the majority are "discontented" may mean very little by itself. One person may believe that nothing can be done to improve the situation. Another may believe that democracy and capitalism are morally bankrupt and that the entire system needs to be changed. And a third person may believe that the system works but that a change in policy is needed. While all three people may be described as being politically discontented, their behavior is likely to be quite different.

Finally, Craig suggests that while attitude surveys indicate rising levels of political discontent, a strong "diffuse support" for our system still exists. This would seem to imply that attitude surveys are misleading because they do not measure specific attitudes. Thus when a majority of people express a lack of confidence in the President, they may be thinking of his specific policies and not of the office. And when people express distrust of the Congress, they may be reacting to specific scandals and not the institution. As psychologists have learned as well, if one wants to find a correspondence between attitudes and behavior, very specific measures of both must be used.

increasingly liberal, illustrates the role of social acceptance and approval. Those students who were most involved in campus activities were the ones whose attitudes were the most liberal. As we shall see shortly, however, other theories can explain the same phenomenon in different terms.

Numerous studies have provided support for a reinforcement theory of attitude change. A typical experiment might require subjects to argue for a point of view that differs from their own—students who are against nuclear power, for example, may be asked to give a speech or write a paper describing the advantages of nuclear power. The reinforcement for doing the assignment could be money, a high grade, or social approval. Several experiments have found that more attitude change does indeed occur when these reinforcers are administered than when they are not (Bostrom, Vlandis, & Rosenbaum, 1961; Scott, 1957, 1959; Wallace, 1966).

In spite of the apparently convincing evidence supporting the reinforcement theory, it has declined in importance over the past decade or two. One difficulty with this line of research is that it is often impossible to distinguish between genuine attitude change and compliance (Insko, 1967). Subjects may go along with the experimenter only to obtain the reward, while their real attitudes remain unchanged. A second reason for this theory's decline is that other theories have generated research that has produced results inconsistent with reinforcement principles. As we shall see, cognitive-dissonance theory suggests that often the least amount of reinforcement can produce the most attitude change.

Cognitive-Consistency Theories

Cognitive-consistency theories suggest that we strive for consistency among our cognitions. Cognitions are our thoughts, the things we know, the things we believe, and the ways in which we think about our own behavior (see Chapter 7). According to these theories one method of producing attitude change is to introduce an inconsistent element into the cognitions. Two well-known cognitive-consistency theories that address this technique are balance theory and cognitive-dissonance theory.

Balance Theory. **Balance theory** suggests that we strive to seek consistency, or balance, among our cognitions. Fritz Heider (1946, 1958), who developed this theory, suggested that a state of balance exists when everything fits together "harmoniously" without stress.

To understand Heider's approach, look at Figure 14–1. The symbol p refers to a person, o refers to another person, and x refers to an object, which can be an attitude, a third person, or an idea. The + and − signs refer to positive and negative feelings. As an example, let our fictitious Ellen be p and her psychology instructor o. In the first figure under balanced relationships, suppose x represents the idea that everyone in our society should have the opportunity to achieve his or her full potential. Both Ellen and her instructor view this idea positively, and Ellen feels positive toward her

Figure 14–1. Heider's balance theory.

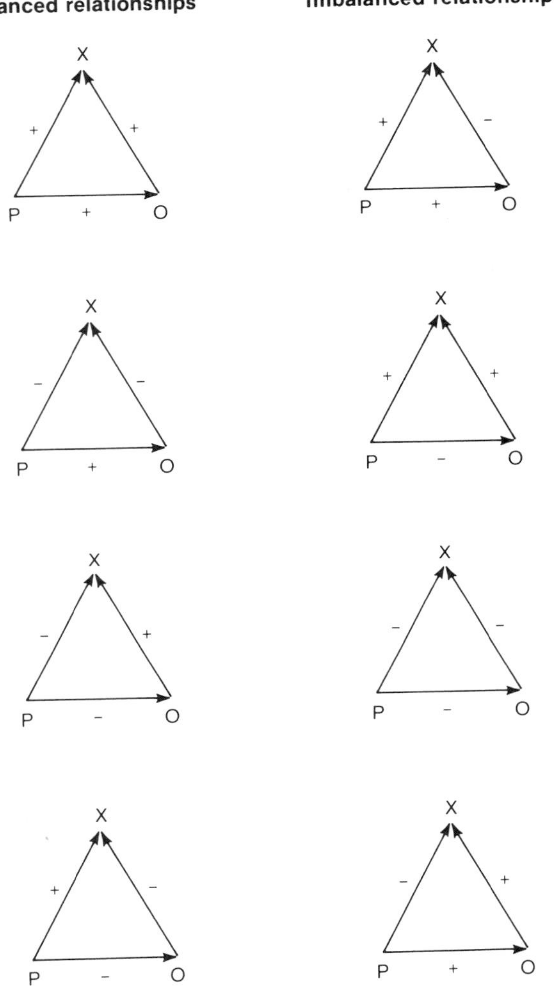

instructor, so a state of balance exists. There would be no pressure for attitude change to occur. In the first figure under imbalanced relationships, suppose *x* is the idea that the best way to insure equal opportunity is through pure capitalism. Ellen's business background inclines her to view this idea positively, but her instructor views it negatively. Because Ellen feels positive about her instructor, a state of imbalance exists. She likes and respects someone who disagrees with her on an important issue. The imbalance would generate stress, which would motivate Ellen to change her attitude toward capitalism or toward her instructor to achieve a harmonious state. The remaining figures illustrate other ways in which relationships can be balanced or imbalanced. You may find it instructive to describe situations to match these figures.

While there is some empirical support for Heider's balance theory, most social psychologists believe it has limited usefulness. First, it can be applied only to three-entity relationships. Second, there is no way to express the relative strength of the sentiments. For instance, in the example above, it would seem that the nature of the imbalanced state would vary depending on the strength of Ellen's feelings about both capitalism and her psychology instructor. And third, the theory does not take into account the fact that the positive and negative feelings are likely to flow in both directions—that is, balance theory does not allow us to predict what effect there would be if Ellen's instructor did not like *her.* Although balance theory does have intuitive appeal, its shortcomings have made psychologists receptive to a more sophisticated cognitive-consistency theory.

Cognitive-Dissonance Theory. A cognitive-consistency theory that could be applied to a wider variety of situations was introduced by Leon Festinger (1957). This theory, called **cognitive dissonance,** was met with much enthusiasm, and hundreds of experiments were conducted in the 15 years following its introduction to test its elements. Although it held great appeal to many social psychologists, others were very critical of it and of much of the research that purportedly supported it. Cognitive dissonance was the focus of a lively controversy throughout the 1960s and early 1970s. Let us explore the theory and why it was controversial.

The basic elements of Festinger's theory are cognitive elements. These include beliefs, opinions, and the things we "know" about various types of behavior, people, objects, or circumstances. Dissonance occurs when two of the elements are inconsistent with each other. So, for example, if a person smokes but reads an article about the health hazards of smoking, cognitive dissonance would be produced. This dissonance, or inconsistency, would generate pressure or tension that serves to motivate the individual to reduce the dissonant state. The person might attempt to stop smoking or, conversely, to collect information that justifies smoking, perhaps concluding that the new low-tar cigarettes are not really that dangerous.

The health warning on cigarette packs could produce a state of cognitive dissonance in a smoker. (*Catherine Noren/Photo Researchers, Inc.*)

The amount of dissonance will be a function of the importance of the cognitive elements and the number of the relevant elements that are dissonant. So if you worked hard on a class project that counted for five percent of your grade and received a D, only a moderate amount of dissonance would be generated because the D was not that important to your final grade. If the same project counted for 50 percent of your grade, the dissonance would be much stronger. Smoking is again a good example. A decade or so ago, when the evidence of the health hazards was just beginning to accumulate, smokers did not have to deal with much dissonance. But as research adds more and more elements—e.g., smoking contributes to lung cancer, heart disease, and emphysema—smokers presumably feel more dissonance because there are more dissonant elements.

Cognitive-dissonance theory can be applied to a variety of situations. One of these is referred to as **postdecisional dissonance,** which is dissonance that occurs when we have been forced to choose among several alternatives and are not sure we have chosen wisely. Suppose upon graduation you have your choice between accepting a job with the federal government or one with a small company. You like the security and regular pay increases the civil-service job provides, but you are concerned about the lack of opportunity to express your creativity or to have a significant impact. The small company promises you the chance to grow with the firm, and if it is successful the rewards will be great. But if the company fails, you will be out of a job. After you make your choice, you will probably experience some dissonance, or what is commonly known as "mixed feelings," because you were forced to forego some attractive opportunities regardless of your decision. You could reduce the dissonance by increasing the attractiveness of the job you selected or by decreasing the attractiveness of the one you rejected. So, if you went with the small company, you might tell yourself that the company has great promise or that job security is not nearly so important as feeling challenged by one's work.

An example of postdecisional dissonance was provided in an experiment where subjects were asked to rank the attractiveness of several household objects, such as a desk lamp (Cottrell, Rajecki, & Smith, 1974). Later, half of the subjects were allowed to choose between their fourth- and fifth-ranked choices, and the other half were simply given their fourth-ranked choice. Upon reranking the various gifts those individuals who were given a choice rated their gift as being more desirable than they had originally. The rankings of those who were not given a choice were unchanged.

Cognitive dissonance can also be applied in situations of **forced compliance,** where an individual is pressured into an action to which he or she is not privately committed. If a student expresses a particular political opinion because it will be approved of by friends, or if a student expresses specific attitudes in class with the hope of attaining a high grade, dissonance should be generated. The degree of the dissonance will be influenced by the extent of the pressure or the size of the reward. For example, if the student knows that by parroting the instructor's attitudes, the course grade will shift from a D to an A, very little dissonance will be aroused since there is strong justification for agreeing with the instructor. If, however, the agreement resulted in a shift only from an A- to an A, there would be little justification for it and hence more dissonance. In the latter case, cognitive-dissonance theory would predict that the student would be likely to experience attitude change. In other words, if one cannot justify behavior by pointing to external pressures, then dissonance will be aroused—and the greater the dissonance, the greater the attitude change.

In a classic experiment that tested this hypothesis, college men were required to spend an hour at a boring task (Festinger & Carlsmith, 1959). After each one had completed the task, the experimenter said that the subject's help was needed to engage the next subject. The subject was asked to tell the next subject how much fun the experiment was and how much he had enjoyed it. Some of the subjects were offered $1.00 for their help, while others were offered $20.00. After the subjects performed their task, they were interviewed and asked to rate how much they had actually enjoyed the experiment.

The different levels of reward were intended to produce varying degrees of dissonance. The subjects who received $20.00 for their cooperation might say to themselves, "I really think the experiment was boring, but for $20.00 I'll tell anyone I loved it." The subjects who received only $1.00 were expected to have more dissonance because they would not have nearly as much justification for expressing an attitude that was inconsistent with what they felt, and thus they would be more inclined to change their attitude. The results supported the hypothesis. Those men who received $1.00 indicated that they enjoyed the experiment more than those who received $20.00. The control group, who were not asked to endorse the experiment, reflected the actual degree to which the experiment was enjoyable.

These results, and others similar to them, are one reason why cognitive-dissonance theory generated so much interest. It predicted results that were inconsistent with learning theory and with what one might expect intuitively. Learning theory would suggest that the larger the reward, the greater the attitude change. Subjects who were paid $20.00 would be expected to state that they enjoyed the experiment the most. This is just the opposite of what occurred.

While advocates of cognitive-dissonance theory were enthusiastic about the results of the Festinger and Carlsmith experiment and others like it, the critics remained unconvinced. Several experiments were conducted in which students were paid to write essays that expressed attitudes counter to their own. Contrary to the results above, these studies tended to support a learning-theory explanation: the greater the reward, the greater the attitude change in the direction of the essay (Elms & Janis, 1965). In addition, there have been several failures to replicate the results of Festinger and Carlsmith, and this calls into question the validity of the theory (cf. Collins, Ashmore, Hornbeck, & Whitney, 1970).

Other psychologists have been critical of cognitive dissonance for theoretical reasons. Daryl Bem (1965, 1967, 1972) has argued that the results that support cognitive-dissonance theory can be explained without invoking the concept of dissonance at all. As you will recall from earlier in the chapter, Bem argues that we infer our attitudes from our behavior or from the circumstances in which we find ourselves. That is, we look to our behavior and find reasons or make attributions for doing the things that we do. Thus if we were to sign up to participate in every available psychology experiment, we would conclude that we must like such activity. Similarly, Bem argues that subjects who were forced to talk about how much they had enjoyed what was really a very boring task would look at their behavior and circumstances to infer their attitudes. Subjects who were paid $20.00 would attribute their statements to the money and would conclude that their saying they enjoyed the experiment had nothing to do with their real feelings. Subjects who were paid only $1.00 might conclude, when looking at their circumstances, "I wouldn't lie for a mere dollar, so I must have enjoyed the experiment." They would attribute their cooperation to their internal state or attitudes. Bem believes that his explanation is scientifically superior because it is simpler—it reaches the same conclusions without using the concept of dissonance. We will discuss attribution theory in more detail in Chapter 15.

Although Bem (1967) has presented data that he believes support his point of view, some theorists have suggested that cognitive-dissonance theory and Bem's attribution theory are really two different ways of saying the same thing and cannot be experimentally distinguished (Greenwald, 1975). Other researchers, however, have suggested that each theory has its usefulness but in different situations. Cognitive dissonance may be most appropriate to situations where the discrepancy between initial attitudes is great, such as telling an outright lie, while self-perception theory may be most accurate when the discrepancy is smaller (Fazio, Zanna, & Cooper, 1977). To use the boring-task experiment as an example, if an individual really hated the experiment, it seems unlikely that the self-perception could be so distorted that he or she would conclude that the experiment must have been enjoyable. Dissonance may serve as the motivator for attitude change in this case. If an individual is pressured into expressing an attitude that is only slightly different from his or her own, then the self-perception theory may account for any resulting attitude change.

The present status of cognitive-dissonance theory is unclear. Currently, little research is being conducted either to support or to refute it. It is one of those issues in psychology that has faded away without having been resolved. And because several of the studies that appeared to support the concept of dissonance employed questionable research practices, such as discarding subjects from experiments whose behavior was not consistent with the theory (Insko, 1967), some social psychologists have concluded that the existing evidence does not support the theory. For example, John Lamberth (1980) has said, "Festinger's ideas were brilliant and they still may receive experimental confirmation. At this time, however, they have not received that confirmation and so dissonance is disappearing from the theoretical scene" (p. 214). Other theorists, however, believe that the evidence is sufficient to conclude that the concept of dissonance can be useful in at least some situations (Fazio et al., 1977; Goldstein, 1980). Cognitive-dissonance theory continues to appeal to many theorists, but they recognize that it is difficult to test empirically. Perhaps future social psychologists will discover innovative research strategies capable of confirming dissonance theory.

The Psychology of Attitude Research

A review of the literature dealing with attitudes and attitude change is interesting because it illustrates a cycle that is familiar to many research areas in psychology. Consider the following: In 1970 fully 20 percent of all the articles that appeared in the *Journal of Personality and Social Psychology*, the most influential social-psychology journal, were concerned with the topic of attitudes. Just seven years later, in 1977, only two percent of the articles appearing in this journal dealt with the topic of attitudes (Lamberth, 1980). If you think that social psychologists have solved all the puzzles and have moved on to new topics, you would be making a reasonable assumption, but you would be wrong.

There are probably more unanswered questions about attitudes and attitude change today than there were 30 years ago. Research has provided many answers, but it has raised many more questions. The limitations of the various theories discussed in this chapter have left researchers with no obvious place to proceed. The frequency of attitude research has declined because social psychologists have lost interest in the topic owing to its complexity.

Part of the difficulty with the topic of attitudes is that there are still unresolved questions concerning its nature. At the beginning of the chapter, we defined an attitude as having three components: cognitive, affective, and behavioral. While this is a commonly accepted definition, various theorists disagree as to the relative importance of interrelations among the three components. As we saw earlier, there is some question about the degree to which the behavioral component follows from the cognitive and affective components. But there is also some controversy about the relation between cognitions and affect, or emotional reaction. A majority of contemporary theorists have assumed that affective responses follow cognitive processing. That is, if we are exposed to a new object or idea, we first evaluate it cognitively and then respond to it emotionally. Recently, social psychologist R. B. Zajonc (1980) has argued that our affective responses occur first. We either like or dislike something and then find reasons for our emotional reaction. Needless to say, this controversy has important implications for the investigation of attitude change.

As in so many areas of research in psychology,

interest in the topic has diminished before the crucial issues have been resolved. Attitudes and attitude change continue to be of vital importance, and clearly there is a need for more answers. It could well be that a spurt of research activity will begin at any time. What seems to be needed is a new theory that will have the impact that cognitive dissonance did to stimulate such research activity.

PREJUDICE

Lest anyone question the importance of attitudes in our everyday lives, consider the issue of prejudice. Because of the negative attitudes directed toward members of minority groups, they have been denied civil rights, educational and employment opportunities, and decent housing, and have had to suffer innumerable indignities. The members of the majority group do not remain unaffected by holding such attitudes. White adults yell obscenities at young black children merely because they are bused to a school that was formerly segregated. Few people would deny that such behavior dehumanizes both the source and the target of such attitudes.

Many of us may like to think that prejudice is largely a thing of the past. We may admit that there are still a number of bigots around, but we believe that most members of our society reject the pejorative stereotypes of minority groups that were common several decades ago. Unfortunately, this does not seem to be the case. In a recent report of attitudes held by high-school students, it was concluded that adolescent bigotry is still rampant (Norman, 1979). After sampling the attitudes of students from three East Coast high schools, it was found that one out of four students believed that Jews were troublemakers, were sloppy, and gave up easily. In schools where Jews constituted a sizable proportion of the student body, over half of the non-Jewish whites agreed with statements such as "Jews think they're better than other students" and "Jews force their beliefs on other students."

Prejudice against blacks appears even more common. A majority of non-Jewish whites believed that blacks were troublemakers, immoral, untrustworthy, sloppy, and conceited. Clearly, the problem of prejudice is still with us. Let us look at what psychologists have learned about prejudice and consider a few examples of attempts to reduce prejudice.

The Nature of Prejudice

Prejudice can be defined as an inflexible attitude toward an individual based solely on that individual's membership in a group. Although we tend to use the term "prejudice" in association with dislike or hatred, it can also refer to positive attitudes. For instance, a man may be prejudiced in favor of women with blonde hair. A crucial element or prejudice, whether it is positive or negative, is stereotypes. The person who believes that all members of a certain minority group are untrustworthy or that "blondes have more fun" bases his or her prejudices on such stereotypes.

A second crucial element of prejudice concerns one's unwillingness to give up stereotypes even

Widespread prejudice in a society often leads to policies of discrimination. (© *Bruce Roberts/Photo Researchers, Inc.*)

APPLICATION

The Jigsaw Route to Learning

Social psychologist Elliot Aronson and his colleagues (Aronson, Blaney, Sikes, Stephan, & Snapp, 1979) have used the principle of common goals to reduce racial tension among children in elementary school. Aronson pointed out that in traditional classrooms only a handful of children are likely to enjoy the school experience. These children are the experts—the ones who can answer the teacher's questions. Many of the other children are likely to remain silent. When they are forced to speak, they may be ridiculed by their classmates and even on occasion by their teachers. In other words, the classroom is a highly competitive atmosphere in which the less capable learn to think of themselves as "losers." Antagonism between the "winners" and the "losers" is likely to develop.

Aronson's approach was to make learning a cooperative enterprise. He divided the children into groups of six and gave each child in the group a portion of the material to be learned. The children would be responsible for sharing their information with their group so that everyone could pass a test. Their task would be analogous to fitting together the pieces of a jigsaw puzzle.

To illustrate how a group might function, Aronson discussed the case of Carlos, a Mexican-American boy who was not very articulate in English. Carlos had learned that he was one of the losers because he had been ridiculed by his classmates when he had attempted to answer the teacher's questions. He began to avoid eye contact with the teacher and stopped trying to answer questions. The teacher tacitly consented to Carlos's strategy and did not call on him or help him.

Carlos did not like it when the cooperative system was introduced because it meant he had to talk to his classmates. In fact, when his turn came to share his information, the other children began to tease him with statements such as "Aw, you don't know it, you're dumb." At this point an observer would intervene with a statement such as "Ok, you can tease him if you want to and that might be fun for you, but it's not going to help you learn about Joseph Pulitzer's middle years. The exam will take place in about an hour."

The other children quickly learned that the only way they would pass the exam was to find out what Carlos knew. They encouraged him to talk and asked questions to draw him out. Carlos began to relax and to communicate more effectively. The other children began to realize that Carlos was not so dumb after all and began to like him. Carlos, in turn, began to view his classmates as friends rather than as tormentors.

The project, for the most part, was a success. Children in the project liked their peers more than children who remained in traditional classrooms. They tended to view their peers as resources and had more positive attitudes toward school. They had more positive self-concepts and felt more important in school than did those in traditional classes. Interestingly, there was not a general reduction in prejudice. The white children liked Carlos more and would like a particular black child more after their participation in the project, but that did not mean they liked all Chicanos or all blacks. But perhaps that is what projects such as this one are all about: getting people to judge others as individuals rather than as members of a group.

when faced with new, conflicting information. The following dialogue provided by Gordon Allport (1954) in his classic book *The Nature of Prejudice* illustrates this point vividly:

Mr. X: The trouble with the Jews is that they only take care of their own group.

Mr. Y: But the record of the Community Chest campaign shows that they gave more generously, in proportion to their numbers, to the general charities of the community than do non-Jews.

Mr. X: That shows they are always trying to buy favor and intrude into Christian affairs. They think nothing of money; that is why there are so many Jewish bankers.

Mr. Y: But a recent study shows that the percentage of Jews in the banking business is negligible, far smaller than the percentage of non-Jews.

Mr. X: That's just it; they don't go in for respectable business, they are only in the movie business or run night clubs (pp. 13–14).

A prejudiced individual is not likely to give up his or her stereotypes simply because they do not agree with the facts.

Attributions of the behavior of the target group made by prejudiced individuals are likely to be different from those made by nonprejudiced persons. Attributions are the reasons or causes that we ascribe to our own behavior and to the behavior of others (see Chapter 15 for a discussion of attribution theory). In order to gain confidence in our understanding of the world, we seem to have a need to make attributions. Thus we may say we failed a test because it was difficult and unfair but that our competitor failed the test because of stupidity and laziness. The former would be an example of making an **environmental attribution**, or external attribution—that is, assigning the causes of a behavior to something outside the individual. The case of the competitor would represent an **internal attribution** or personal attribution—assigning the causes of behavior to something within the person.

As you might guess, prejudiced individuals are likely to make personal attributions about the behavior of minority-group members. For instance, if a prejudiced person were to see a group of young black men hanging around on a street corner in the middle of the day, he or she might think, "They're so lazy and irresponsible. They should be working." A more sympathetic observer might think, "It's too bad our society makes it so difficult for young men like that to find jobs."

A recent study demonstrated that prejudiced whites make personal attributions for the failures of blacks even when the behavior is not part of any cultural stereotype (Greenberg & Rosenfield, 1980). White college men who were prejudiced against blacks were asked to watch videotapes of several white and black actors who displayed varying degrees of extrasensory-perception (ESP) ability. Afterward, the subjects were asked to indicate the reasons for the success or failure of the actors. The college men believed that black actors were successful because they were lucky (external attribution). When the black actors failed on the task, it was supposedly owing to lack of ability (internal attribution). It would seem that prejudiced individuals are not inclined to believe anything favorable about a group about which they hold negative attitudes.

The Acquisition of Prejudice

A number of theories have been developed to explain the existence of prejudice. These theories tend to address different aspects of prejudice and should not be viewed as mutually exclusive. They are all interrelated and must be considered together to understand prejudice. The four major categories of theories are historical, sociocultural, personality, and learning theories.

Historical theories suggest that prejudice has its origins in years of conflict between groups. Many historians stress the importance of economic factors in generating the conflict. This argument can be summarized as follows: "Race prejudice is a social attitude propagated among the public by an exploiting class for the purpose of stigmatizing some group as inferior so that the exploitation of either the group itself or its resources may both be justified" (Cox, 1948, p. 393).

There is some truth to this explanation. There were certainly economic reasons for the institution of slavery and the portrayal of blacks as less than human. The historical or economic explanation, however, fails to explain many cases of prejudice. For instance, people have been prejudiced against the Quakers and Mormons without having any apparent economic motives. Also, majority-group members have been exploited (e.g., factory workers, tenant farmers), yet a tradition of prejudice against them has not developed.

Allport (1954) calls a second category of theories the **sociocultural theories.** One of these theories, the community-pattern theory, emphasizes the basic ethnocentrism, the belief that one's group is superior to all other groups. Prejudices are not limited to groups who vary in skin color; they can exist between Jews and Gentiles, French-

and English-speaking Canadians, various tribes in East Africa (Brewer, 1968), and those with different patterns of speech, such as different social classes in Japan (Klineberg, 1971). Many theorists point to these and dozens of other examples as evidence that groups are likely to relegate some other group to the out-group. By having an out-group, the in-group can minimize its smaller, within-group differences, thereby strengthening in-group solidarity and cohesiveness. Such solidarity and cohesiveness may be useful to achieve national goals or to repel an enemy.

Again this theory has both obvious appeal and obvious limitations. For example, it may explain why Japanese-Americans were treated so unfairly by the United States government during World War II. It may also explain the recent taking of American hostages in Iran. But it does not appear to explain those cases in which the in-group's goals and its prejudices are made mutually exclusive. For instance, why would several cities close their school systems (and give up the goal of educating their children) rather than admit blacks? Or why would South Africa continue its official policy of racial segregation (apartheid) in the face of intense international pressure? Obviously prejudice is more than a vehicle for achieving group cohesiveness.

Personality theories look to variables within the individual to explain prejudice. One variant of this approach suggests that individuals who feel threatened, economically or otherwise, are likely to be prejudiced. They may use minority-group members as scapegoats for their own frustrations and fears. In recent years many articles and television specials have illustrated the prejudices of workers with several years' experience who are laid off, while a minority-group member is kept on the payroll because of equal-opportunity guidelines set down by the federal government. The prejudice of such workers may be viewed as an expression of their frustration, and the minority-group member is a convenient target. This theory, however, does not explain why even rich people, who have no reason to feel threatened, are capable of being prejudiced.

A second variant of this category of theories, and the one that has received the most attention, concerns the concept of the **authoritarian personality** (Adorno, Frenkel-Brunswick, Levinson, & Sanford, 1950). The psychologists who conceptualized this trait were interested in the rise and fall of fascism in Nazi Germany and in the type of person who would blindly follow orders even up to the point of murdering countless people just because they were non-Aryans and considered inferior. The authoritarian personality is one who is rigid, who both fears and wants power, who is fearful of sex, and who views events and issues as falling into clear-cut categories of right and wrong. Such an individual is drawn to the in-group, and all those who do not hold power are automatically in the out-group. Out-group members, including Jews, blacks, Hispanics, and Indians, are regarded as appropriate targets for fear, contempt, and hostility.

While there is much evidence to support the association between the authoritarian personality and prejudice, critics have argued that this explanation neglects the historical and social forces that may serve to shape the authoritarian personality. People do not develop this personality style in a vacuum. There have to be historical and social factors that contribute to its development. Also, people who score low on the measure of authoritarianism are still capable of being prejudiced.

Learning theories view prejudice as a learned attitude. Children acquire attitudes about members of other groups from their parents, peers, and other figures in much the same way that they acquire attitudes about school, sports, and politics. Members of a child's reference group often serve as models and may subsequently reinforce the child's expressions of prejudice.

The media can also transmit attitudes about various groups. For instance, many theorists have pointed out that movies and radio shows of several decades ago served to perpetuate racial stereotypes. Indians were portrayed as untrustworthy and savage, while blacks were portrayed as lazy and stupid.

One of the particularly unfortunate results of

such stereotypes is the effect they can have on minority children. In a study conducted over 30 years ago, black children were given their choice of playing with a white doll or a black doll (Clark & Clark, 1947). Only 32 percent of the children chose the black doll. Fully 59 percent of the black children indicated that the black doll looked "bad."

The more balanced presentation of blacks and other ethnic groups in the media in recent years also seems to have had an effect. Blacks are now portrayed in a variety of roles, and children's shows, such as "Sesame Street," strive to avoid racial stereotypes. In more recent doll-preference studies, it has been found that a majority of black children prefer the black dolls (Harris & Brown, 1971). It may well be that the changes in media portrayals of minority-group members are not directly responsible for the increase in the self-esteem of black children. It could be that the media merely reflect broader changes that have taken place in our society. But it is reassuring to know that minority-group children are not having their self-esteem reduced when they watch television.

Learning theory may account for how prejudice is transmitted from generation to generation, but it does not explain why such attitudes developed in the first place. Also, learning theory has difficulty in explaining why prejudice persists in some individuals whose prejudices result in more punishment than reinforcement.

Once again, we wish to emphasize that no one theory is sufficient to explain all instances of prejudice. Each theory tends to focus on a somewhat limited set of circumstances and may be valid for those circumstances. Psychologists at this time are not able to offer a unified theory of prejudice that can be applied to a variety of situations.

Overcoming Prejudice

Most psychologists recognize that regardless of how much we learn about attitudes or personality, we will probably not be able to eliminate prejudice (Billig, 1976; Goldstein, 1980). Historical, social, and cultural factors play a considerable role in the development and maintenance of prejudice, and it appears unlikely that working with individuals or small groups to change their attitudes will have much of an impact.

In 1971 Harris and Brown found that most black girls preferred to play with black dolls. This study, compared with one made in 1947, is one indication of an increase in the self-esteem of black children. (© *Freda Leinwand / Monkmeyer Press Photo Service*)

Psychologists have not, however, given up hope that they can have an impact on reducing prejudice. Many experiments have been conducted to identify methods of reducing prejudice and improving understanding, and several of these have met with success.

One important principle is that increased contact between the opposing groups can reduce conflict. Nearly 30 years ago a psychology professor had graduate students spend two weeks living and socializing with blacks in Harlem (Smith, 1943). These students developed attitudes toward blacks that were more favorable than those of students who did not have the experience.

Increased contact between "opposing" groups may sometimes help overcome prejudice. (© *Peter Southwick / Stock, Boston, Inc.*)

Increased contact, however, will not always lead to decreased prejudice. As we saw in the study of prejudice among high-school students, increased contact may lead to increased prejudice. Contact between antagonistic groups is likely to be most effective if the group members are equal in status and if the groups have an opportunity for intimate contact. For example, a study of an integrated housing project found that blacks and whites were less prejudiced than residents of segregated projects (Deutsch & Collins, 1951). The residents of the integrated project visited one another, helped when someone was sick, and participated in informal social clubs. In contrast, black and white coal miners in West Virginia, who worked together all day long, were found to go their separate ways when the workday was over (Minard, 1952). The greater intimacy of contact in the housing project was thought to play a major role in reducing prejudice, whereas the miners found their social contacts within their own groups and had little opportunity to achieve intimacy.

A second principle is that when antagonistic groups work toward common goals, conflict is likely to be reduced. This was illustrated in a classic study conducted by Muzafer Sherif (1977). He tried to reduce tensions between two groups of boys, the Rattlers and the Eagles, at a summer camp. At first, the principle of increased contact was used. The boys participated in various social events together and ate together in the dining hall. This approach proved to be unsuccessful. According to Sherif, "In the dining hall line they shoved each other aside, and the group that lost the contest shouted 'Ladies first!' at the winner. They threw paper, food, and vile names at each other at the tables. An Eagle bumped by a Rattler was admonished by his fellow Eagles to brush 'the dirt' off his clothes" (pp. 282, 284).

Sherif was finally successful in reducing tensions when he created "crises," and the two groups were forced to cooperate to resolve them. For instance, the water supply was disrupted, and the Rattlers and the Eagles had to work together to resolve the problem. These common goals did not produce an immediate or complete reversal of attitudes; some bickering and name calling continued after the emergencies were over. But the boys stopped shoving each other in the meal lines, began to sit together, and developed friendships across group lines.

Several theorists have discussed the importance of institutional support if prejudice is to be reduced. Nearly 30 years ago Gordon Allport (1954) presented a convincing argument that our society can effectively enact legislation to reduce prejudice. In fact, laws enforcing equal opportunities in education, employment, and housing can reduce prejudice. One reason such laws are effective is that they promote contact between groups, which may serve to shatter stereotypes. For instance, a white family whose members tend to be prejudiced against blacks may move into a house in an upper-middle-class suburb and find a black family living next door. Because it is difficult to avoid one's neighbors in the suburbs, the two families are likely to engage in small talk on occasion. It is highly likely that the white family will discover that their similarities with the black family are more pronounced than their differences. They may both be concerned about the economy, their children's education, and the record of the local football team. Such an experience is not likely to cause anyone to give up all his or her prejudices, but it will chip away at stereotypes. And it would not have happened if laws protecting freedom of housing had not been enacted. Our society has been serious about combating prejudice only for a generation or so. Perhaps it will be only a few more generations before members of all ethnic groups can live together harmoniously and the barriers of prejudice will be a thing of the past. It may be unrealistic to expect that all vestiges of prejudice will be removed—after all, some people will always believe that blondes have more fun. But it is a realistic goal to strive for a society in which one's opportunities and dignity are not dependent on racial background.

Summary

An attitude can be defined as a combination of cognitive, affective, and behavioral components regarding a person, idea, or object. Cognitions refer to beliefs or factual knowledge, affect refers to emotional reactions, and behavior refers to a person's tendency to act on his or her attitudes. Although this definition of attitude suggests a consistency among the three components, such consistency does not always exist. To a large extent, the degree of consistency that is found will depend on the ways in which the components are measured.

The development of attitudes is influenced by many of the same factors that are responsible for the development of personality. Parents, peers, and teachers all play a major role in shaping one's attitudes. Reference groups are particularly important in shaping attitudes.

Psychologists have conducted much research concerning the effect of the source of a communication on attitude change. When the source has high credibility, is viewed as trustworthy, and is arguing for a position that conflicts with the source's own interests, attitude change is likely to occur. If the source is perceived as having ulterior motives, then the probability of attitude change is reduced or eliminated.

Another body of research has examined the nature of the communication as it relates to degree of attitude change. One-sided versus two-sided arguments, the order of presentation, and the appeal to one's emotions are among the variables that have been examined. The effects of these variables are complex and vary depending on the characteristics of the audience.

Several studies have found that an audience can be made resistant to attitude change if they are exposed to a mild attack upon their existing attitudes. This operates similarly to the way in which an inoculation protects the body against an illness. That is, a mild attack upon one's attitudes will prepare the individual to fend off a vigorous attack at a later time.

Several theories have been developed to help us understand attitude change. Reinforcement theory suggests that one will adopt new attitudes if such changes are rewarded. Cognitive-consistency theories, such as balance theory and cognitive-dissonance theory, suggest that people's attitudes change to produce harmony among various attitudes or between attitudes and behavior. Attribution theory suggests that we look to our environment and our behavior to learn what our attitudes are. No single theory is accepted by all researchers, and it may be that each theory's usefulness is limited to certain situations.

Prejudice is an issue that illustrates the importance and relevance of research on attitudes and attitude change. There are several theories regarding the development of prejudice. Psychologists have attempted to identify techniques to reduce prejudice. While no general solutions have been discovered, several important principles have been offered. First, intimate contact between equal-status members of the conflicting groups can reduce prejudice. Such contact may be effective because unflattering stereotypes are difficult to maintain under such conditions. Second, when members of different groups are required to work together toward a common goal, tensions may be reduced. This principle has been used to reduce prejudice in schoolchildren. Third, institutional support, such as equal-opportunity laws, can help break down stereotyped notions about others.

Key Terms For Review

affective component of attitudes
attitude
authoritarian personality
balance theory
behavioral component of attitudes
cognitive component of attitudes
cognitive-dissonance theory
environmental attribution
forced compliance
historical theories
inoculation effect
internal attribution
learning theories
personality theories
postdecisional dissonance
primacy effect
recency effect
reference group
self-monitoring
sleeper effect
sociocultural theories
source credibility
ulterior motive

Suggested Readings

Allport, G. W. *The nature of prejudice.* Reading, Mass.: Addison-Wesley, 1954.
This book, available in paperback, is dated but considered to be a classic. It provides a comprehensive overview of the topic.

Bachman, J. G., and Johnston, L. D. The freshmen, 1979. *Psychology Today,* September 1979, p. 78 ff.
This article summarizes the results of an attitude survey of nearly 17,000 graduating high-school seniors. Topics surveyed included "the important things in life," career goals, and attitudes toward potential employers and the nation's institutions.

Colman, A. Flattery won't get you everywhere. *Psychology Today,* May 1980, pp. 80–82.
This article describes some of the limitations of flattery. Consistent with find-

ings an attitude research, the status of the source and characteristics of the target influence the effects of flattery.

Norman, M. Adolescent bigotry. In V. J. Derlega & L. H. Janda (Eds.), *Personal adjustment: Selected readings.* Glenview, Ill.: Scott, Foresman, 1979.
This article summarizes a survey of 5,000 high-school students regarding racial prejudice. It found that racial hostility continues to be common.

Silverman, I. On the resolution and tolerance of cognitive inconsistency in a natural-occurring event: Attitudes and beliefs following the Edward M. Kennedy incident. In E. Krupat (Ed.), *Psychology is social.* Glenview, Ill.: Scott, Foresman, 1975.
This article examines the usefulness of cognitive-consistency theory to account for attitude change to a real-life event. It illustrates the complexities involved when one moves from laboratory to field research.

Zimbardo, P. G., Ebbesen, E. B., & Maslach, C. *Influencing attitudes and changing behavior* (2nd ed.). Reading, Mass.: Addison-Wesley, 1977.
A thorough and interesting survey of the existing attitude literature. Available in paperback, the book provides a good background for the serious student.

15

Social Perception, Social Attraction, and Love

Debby was looking forward to the party that her roommate, Sandy, was giving that night. Sandy's older brother was going to be there, and Debby was looking forward to meeting him. Sandy had talked a lot about him. She described him as intelligent, industrious, warm, and practical. She had shown Debby a photograph of him, and his good looks had increased her interest in meeting him. Debby had the feeling that the party might mark the beginning of an interesting relationship.

That night Sandy and Debby were talking together when Sandy's brother, Glen, walked into the room. Debby thought to herself that he looked as good in person as he did in the photograph. Glen stopped to chat with a group of people for a few minutes and then went to the kitchen to fix himself a drink. As he was walking over to Sandy and Debby, he tripped slightly on an end table and spilled his drink on the floor. Debby thought to herself that he might be handsome and a nice person, but he certainly was clumsy.

Debby and Glen were introduced and they sat down to talk. Debby was pleased to learn that they had a lot in common. Glen had graduated the previous year with a degree in sociology, which was Debby's major, too. They both were involved in politics, they liked the same types of novels, and they both loved to play tennis. In fact they made a date to play tennis the following day.

A few weeks later Sandy asked Debby how things were going with Glen. Debby could not have concealed her enthusiasm even if she wanted to. She told Sandy that she had seen Glen almost every day since the night of the party. Glen had told her that he fell in love with her that first night. While Debby had been very much attracted to him from the beginning, she was just beginning to think that she might be in love with him. She listed several of Glen's characteristics and pointed out that her image of an ideal husband shared many of those characteristics. Debby believed that there was a distinct possibility that she and Glen might have a future together. But only time would tell!

Incidents such as this one between Debby and Glen have occurred millions of times. Two people meet, decide they like each other, get to know each other, and develop an intimate relationship. Because these occurrences are so common, we tend to take them for granted. In our more reflective moments, we may wonder what factors cause us to like some people and dislike others upon first meeting them. Why do we begin to like some people more as we get to know them? And why do we fall in love with some people rather than others?

Those questions have fascinated people for centuries. The Greek philosophers speculated about the factors associated with liking and loving. Throughout history writers from Ovid to Shakespeare to Hemingway have explored the bonds that draw people together. And in recent times social psychologists have devoted much energy to unraveling these puzzles. Intensive research concerning social perception and social attraction has been going on for over 30 years. During the last decade or so, social psychologists began for the first time to take a serious interest in romantic love. And people's perceptions of the causes of their own and other people's behavior is one of the most popular topics in social psychology today. So, much of the material in this chapter represents the current interests of many social psychologists.

FIRST IMPRESSIONS

The beginning of research on first impressions is generally accredited to Solomon Asch in the 1940s. Asch was interested in how people form first impressions, an area of research called **impression formation.** In Asch's classic study (1946), he described a hypothetical person to two groups of college students. The first group was told the person was intelligent, skillful, industrious, warm, determined, practical, and cautious. The second group of students was given an identical list of traits except that "warm" was replaced by "cold."

After the students heard the descriptions, they were given a list of other characteristics and asked to check those they thought applied to the person. There were several notable differences in the choices made by the two groups. For instance, of those students who heard the description that included "warm," 91 percent checked "generous," 94 percent checked "good-natured," and 90 percent checked "happy." The corresponding figures for the second group of students were 8 percent, 17 percent, and 34 percent. Asch concluded that the personality trait of warm-cold was responsible for influencing the quality of the overall impression. He tried varying other traits, such as polite-blunt, but did not find nearly so much change in the overall impression.

A few years after Asch's experiment, Harold Kelley (1950) performed a similar study using an actual person. He introduced a guest lecturer to two classes as an industrious, critical, practical, and determined person, who was also described as either "very warm" or "rather cold." The class that heard the lecturer described as being very warm received him more favorably and interpreted his behavior in light of his described warmness. These results appeared to confirm Asch's earlier findings.

Asch reached two general conclusions based on his research. First, people tend to arrive at consistent and integrated first impressions of others. When they are given only a limited amount of information, they tend to fill in the gaps to arrive at a fairly complete and comprehensive image of the individual. So, when they hear a person described as warm, they assume the individual is also generous, good-natured, happy, and sociable. In the anecdote that opened the chapter, Sandy's description of Glen as warm may have caused Debby to assume he had many other desirable traits.

Asch's second conclusion was that traits can be separated into those that are central and those that are peripheral. Central traits, such as warm-cold, have a substantial influence on the overall impression. Peripheral traits, such as polite-blunt, have either no effect or a minor effect on the overall impression.

This second conclusion has been criticized by many theorists. For instance, it has been pointed out that traits such as warm and cold are more highly correlated with the adjectives in the checklist than with others. So the pronounced effects of the warm-cold variation might have been a result of the type of instrument used to measure the overall impressions—that is, the list itself might have brought about the pronounced effect. If different traits were used in the adjective checklist, dimensions such as polite-blunt might appear to have a greater effect on overall impressions than warm-cold. For instance, used in association with traits such as assertive and independent, polite-blunt may have as much effect on overall impressions as warm-cold.

Regardless of the correctness of the idea of central and peripheral traits, Asch's experiment indicates that how a particular trait is interpreted depends on the context in which it occurs. For example, the combination of "cold" and "determined" elicits a different reaction from "warm" and "determined." Cold and determined may suggest a ruthless individual who is not above exploiting others to achieve his or her goals. On the other hand, warm and determined may suggest an individual who pursues goals in an admirable way.

Individual Differences in First Impressions

You have probably had the experience of finding that your first impression of a person differs markedly from that of one of your friends. There is evidence that people vary in the way they tend to evaluate others on first meeting them. One such difference is that some people are predisposed to like everyone they meet. They may focus on the desirable characteristics of others and search for evidence that people possess certain favorable traits. Others have a tendency to dislike people on first meeting them and may try to discover the existence of undesirable characteristics.

The list of adjectives below is similar to one that was developed to measure this tendency to evaluate others in a positive or negative fashion (Kaplan, 1976). Before reading further, check the 12 characteristics that most concern you in evaluating others. (For the moment, ignore the letters that follow the traits.)

sincere (H)	solemn (M)
honest (H)	proud (M)
understanding (H)	prudent (M)
trustworthy (H)	shrewd (M)
intelligent (H)	materialistic (M)
open-minded (H)	eccentric (M)
friendly (H)	boring (L)
gentle (H)	touchy (L)
courteous (H)	boastful (L)
tactful (H)	conceited (L)
well-read (H)	phony (L)
witty (H)	childish (L)
authoritative (M)	nosey (L)
self-possessed (M)	snobbish (L)
skeptical (M)	hostile (L)
forceful (M)	finicky (L)
conservative (M)	stingy (L)
nonchalant (M)	complaining (L)

Now go back and count the number of H's, M's, and L's on the traits you checked. They stand for high, medium, or low in likability (Anderson, 1968). If you have a majority of H's, you probably tend to view people favorably on first meeting them. If most of the adjectives you checked are L's, you are likely to have unfavorable first impressions of others.

It has also been found that certain personality variables may influence our initial evaluations of others. In a series of studies, Janda examined the relation between the degree to which male subjects felt guilty about sexual matters and their first impressions of women (Janda, 1975; Janda, Witt, & Manahan, 1976; Janda, 1981). One finding was that when women played either a warm, friendly role or a cold, unfriendly role, men who were high in sex guilt rated them as equally likable. Low-guilt men, on the other hand, viewed the warm, friendly women as being considerably more likable than the cold, unfriendly women. In other experiments, the men were led to believe that the women either had very permissive sexual attitudes and led a sexually active life, or had very conservative attitudes and did not intend to have sex until they were married. This time the low-guilt men liked both types of women equally well, while the men high in sex guilt liked the sexually conservative women much better than the permissive women. It was concluded that the two groups of men used different dimensions when evaluating women. Men low in sex guilt are more attuned to the sociability of women, while men high in sex guilt are more attuned to the women's sexual attitudes (O'Grady, Janda, & Gillen, 1979). That is, low-guilt men are interested primarily in the warmness or coldness of women and less concerned with whether their sexual attitudes are similar to their own. Men high in sex guilt are primarily concerned with whether women's sexual attitudes are similar to their own.

Physical attractiveness is apt to be the first thing people notice in new acquaintances. (© *Thomas Hopker/Woodfin Camp & Associates*)

Physical Attractiveness

When we first meet someone, we are likely to notice their physical appearance before anything else. While we have been warned that "you can't judge a book by its cover," considerable research has demonstrated that we do just that. We have a strong tendency to be favorably impressed by attractive people and to be less favorably impressed with those who are not so attractive.

In one experiment, college students were asked to rate photographs of men and women who were either high, average, or low in physical attractiveness (Dion, Berscheid, & Walster, 1972). It was found that the attractive people were viewed as having more desirable characteristics, such as being happier, more sensitive, stronger, more poised, more modest, more sociable, and as having a better character than less attractive people. These results occurred regardless of the sex of the person doing the judging and the sex of the person being judged. It would appear that when we first meet someone we consider physically attractive, we are likely to believe that he or she possesses many other desirable characteristics.

The "what is beautiful is good" stereotype applies to children as well. In one study, adult subjects were shown photographs of young children and told of an "incident" in which the child misbehaved in school (Dion, 1972). Children who were physically attractive were thought to be basically well-mannered, unselfish, and sociable, and their misdeed was believed to be a result of their having an "off" day. Unattractive children,

APPLICATION

Don't the Girls Get Prettier at Closing Time?

James Pennebaker and his colleagues at the University of Virginia (1979) have uncovered a rich source of hypotheses available to the social psychologist—country-and-western music. They point out that country-and-western songs have illustrated many principles that later received confirmation from psychological research. For instance, Lefty Frizzel's "If you've got the money, honey, I've got the time" fits in nicely with reinforcement theory. Johnny Cash's "A Boy Named Sue" illustrates cognitive-dissonance theory. And Tammy Wynette's "I was almost persuaded [until seeing] . . . the reflection of my wedding band" is a good example of self-perception theory. Pennebaker suggests that the social psychologist looking for research ideas can get them for a quarter each (three hypotheses for 50¢) from the jukebox at the neighborhood country-and-western bar.

Pennebaker and his colleagues elected to test Mickey Gilley's hypothesis "Don't the Girls Get Prettier at Closing Time?" They argued that this appeared to be a reasonable hypothesis since previous research has shown that as the time to make a decision begins to run out, the differences in attractiveness between the alternatives become blurred. Also, as Gilley points out, "Ain't it funny, ain't it strange, the way a man's opinions change, when he starts to face that lonely night."

To test the hypothesis, 52 men and 51 women in one of three drinking establishments close to campus were approached by a same-sex experimenter and asked if they would answer a couple of questions. The subjects were asked to rate the general level of attractiveness for all the opposite-sex individuals and for all the same-sex individuals. This was done at three different times: 9:00 P.M., 10:30 P.M., and 12:00 midnight. The bars closed at 12:30 A.M.

The results did indeed support Gilley's hypothesis. The only significant result concerned the ratings of the opposite sex between 10:30 and 12:00. The opposite sex was indeed perceived as being more attractive at closing time. In fact, the researchers extended Gilley's hypothesis. While Gilley speculated only about the perceived attractiveness of women, these researchers found that women perceive men as becoming more attractive at closing time as well.

A word of caution in interpreting these results is in order, however. Pennebaker did exclude any subjects from the study who were obviously intoxicated, but it is possible that the ratings taken at 9:00 and 10:30 were more objective since the subjects may have been more sober. Or, in the words of Merle Haggard, at 12:30 the subjects may not have been "feeling any pain at closing time."

who supposedly had engaged in the same misbehavior, were judged to be bratty, antisocial, and maladjusted, and were thought to be likely to cause problems in the future. It seems particularly sad that such stereotypes apply to children, because a self-fulfilling prophecy may result. If teachers and other adults expect unattractive children to be antisocial, they may treat the children in ways that encourage such behavior.

The effects of one's having different expectations for attractive and unattractive individuals was demonstrated in a recent experiment (Snyder, Tanke, & Berscheid, 1977). College men and women were brought into the laboratory and asked to have a telephone conversation to get to know each other. Unknown to the women, the men were shown photographs that were supposedly of the woman with whom they were to talk. Half of the men where shown a picture of an attractive woman, and the other half saw a picture of an unattractive woman. Later, independent judges rated recordings of the conversations for the sociability of both the man and the woman. When the man believed he was talking to an attractive woman, both he and the woman were perceived as being more sociable and likable than when the man believed he was talking with an unattractive woman. Ratings by the women in the experiment showed that those who talked to a man who thought they were attractive believed they had created a more favorable impression than those who talked to a man who believed they were unattractive.

The results of this study suggest that first impressions based on appearances may affect subsequent interactions. Men may relate differently to attractive women than they do to unattractive women, and this difference may elicit different responses in the women. This study would suggest that the social interactions of attractive and unattractive individuals may differ.

G. R. Adams (1977) has outlined a "developmental social psychology of beauty" that suggests how one's appearance can eventually lead to particular personality and behavioral characteristics. First, as we have already seen, people have different expectations about attractive and unattractive individuals. Second, attractive people will be treated more favorably by others. Third, this more favorable treatment will lead to more favorable social images, self-expectations, and interpersonal styles. And, finally, attractive individuals will be more skillful and self-confident in their social interactions.

Adams's hypothesis has received empirical support. Attractive men and women have been found to have greater social skills than unattractive individuals (Goldman & Lewis, 1977; Greenwald, 1977). Furthermore, attractive men have more contact with women and are more satisfied with such contacts than are unattractive men. Also, attractive women have more dates, go to more parties, and have more satisfying opposite-sex relationships than unattractive women (Reis, Nezlek, & Wheeler, 1980).

For those of us who are not "10s," all is not despair. First, in an average group of people there is a great deal of variability in evaluating physical attractiveness. For instance, one study that had two people evaluate a third person for attractiveness found that there was much disagreement. So, while everyone is likely to agree about the relative attractiveness of Farrah Fawcett and Phyllis Diller, individual preferences become much more important for persons who are not at the extremes. Second, while many people think that "what is beautiful is good," people also seem to believe that "what is good is beautiful." When subjects are asked to rate photographs for attractiveness, their ratings are influenced by descriptions of the individual's personality characteristics (Gross & Crofton, 1977). Thus Debby's evaluation of Glen's appearance was probably more favorable after hearing Sandy describe his other positive traits.

ATTRIBUTION THEORY

Most of us are, to some extent, intuitive scientists. We observe the behavior of others, speculate about the motives and causes of their behavior, and make predictions about their future behavior. The process by which we arrive at these social impressions is called **attribution.**

Attribution theory is one of the most vigorously researched topics in social psychology today. Attributions are important because the causes we attribute to the behavior of others can influence our own behavior. To illustrate, suppose a man who tends to be somewhat reserved arrives at a party and sees an attractive woman sitting alone. In speculating about why she is sitting by herself, two possibilities may occur to him. She may not know anyone else at the party and, being somewhat reserved herself, may be reluctant to initiate conversation with others. Or, she may simply be waiting for her date to arrive. If the man settles on the first attribution, he may very well walk over to her and introduce himself. If he decides the second attribution is more likely, he may begin to look around for someone else.

One advantage of attribution theory is that it takes into account the situational factors involved in social perception. Much of the earlier work on first impressions focused on characteristics of the observed or of the observer and ignored environmental factors. Attribution theory suggests that the situation a person is in can have an important effect on how that person is perceived.

As you will recall from Chapter 14, there are two types of attributions: personal, or internal, attributions and environmental, or external, attributions. To use the example of Debby and Glen from the opening of this chapter, Debby viewed Glen as clumsy when he tripped over an end table and spilled his drink. This was a personal attribution. Had Debby blamed the furniture arrangement for Glen's mishap, it would have been an environmental attribution.

Several studies have found that people tend to make personal attributions for the undesirable behavior of others, and to make environmental attributions for similar behavior of their own. Conversely, people tend to make environmental attributions for the success of others, and personal attributions for their own success. Thus if we get into an argument with someone, we assume that they are aggressive and hostile, and that we are forced by the situation to defend our position. Conversely, we may assume that other students have a high grade-point average because they selected undemanding courses and lenient instructors, whereas our own high average resulted from hard work and intellectual prowess.

People tend to make personal attributions about their success. (© *Jim Anderson/Woodfin Camp & Associates*)

The attributions one makes can vary depending on certain personality characteristics. Individuals with high levels of self-esteem tend to follow the pattern described above. If they are successful on a particular task, they make personal attributions (e.g., their skill), and if they fail, they make environmental attributions (e.g., bad luck). Individuals low in self-esteem tend to do just the opposite. They make personal attributions (lack of skill) for their failures and environmental attributions (good luck) for their successes (Arkin, Appelman, & Burger, 1980). It appears that those with low self-esteem cannot believe anything good about themselves, while those with high self-esteem cannot believe anything bad about themselves.

Attribution theory appeals to social psychologists because it poses many complex theoretical issues that need to be solved and because it can be applied to help us understand so many varieties of human behavior. While the theoretical issues are beyond the scope of an introductory psychology text, it may be helpful to examine two situations to which attribution theory has been applied.

Attribution and Responsibility for Rape

Suppose you were a member of a jury at a trial involving rape. The victim, who testified first, stated that after attending a movie with the defendant, she had invited him into her apartment for a drink. While she liked the man, she did not intend to have a sexual relationship with him. She made her wishes explicit, but he forced her to have intercourse with him.

The defendant's version of the events was quite different. He stated that during the evening they had talked about sex. She gave him the feeling that she was very receptive to the idea of having sex with him. When they arrived at her apartment, she played soft music on the stereo and dimmed the lights. The defendant admitted that the victim said she did not want to have sex, but he believed that all the messages she was sending indicated the opposite. The defendant also admitted that he lost control and threatened her to get her to comply, but he claimed that the situation—which she had arranged—was primarily responsible for his behavior.

How would you make attributions of responsibility for the act of rape? Is, as the victim claims, the defendant responsible because he was not able to control his personal impulses? Or is the woman obliged to share responsibility, because the situation strongly influenced the defendant's behavior?

Several experiments have been conducted in recent years to identify the factors that influence perceptions of responsibility for rape. One reason for interest in this area is that it represents an important social issue. A few years ago a majority of people blamed the victims, at least to some extent, for being raped. And as recently as 1977 a Wisconsin judge received national attention when he gave a light sentence to a 15-year-old boy who had raped a high-school girl. The judge stated that the boy reacted "normally" to the scanty clothing worn by teenage girls (*Time,* 1977).

In the past several years many writers, such as Susan Brownmiller (1975), have tried to reverse this stereotype. One view that has been advanced is that as long as the woman makes her wishes explicitly known, the man is completely responsible for the act of rape. But as we shall see, the attributions of responsibility that people make depend on a variety of factors.

Certain characteristics of the victim have been found to influence attributions of responsibility. For instance, in one study a rape case was described to three groups of college students. The only detail that varied was the description of the victim as a married woman, a divorcée, or a virgin. Contrary to what you might expect, the married woman and the virgin were judged to be more responsible than the divorced victim (Jones & Aronson, 1973). In a second study, it was found that while attractive women were perceived as more likely to be victims of rape, unattractive women were judged to be more responsible for the rape (Seligman, Brickman, & Koulack, 1977).

Attribution theory would explain these results as follows: because unattractive, married, and virginal women are perceived to be less likely to be victims of rape, they must have done something to encourage or provoke the rape. For example, in the case of an attractive woman, one could attribute the motive for rape to her attractiveness. Similarly, people seem to expect divorced women to be raped. But in the case of the plain-looking woman, judges attribute the rape to her behavior.

Two recent experiments have examined the role of the victim's sexual responsiveness and style of interacting with men in influencing attributions of responsibility (Janda & Fauber, 1981). In the first experiment, it was found that a victim who was coy and seductive with a man, regardless of whether he was the rapist, was judged to be more responsible for her rape than a nonseductive woman. This was true for both men and women judges, although men tended to attribute even more responsibility to the victim than did the women judges. In the second experiment, a woman who was described as having strong feelings of sexual attraction toward the rapist, yet made her wishes *not* to have intercourse explicitly known, was perceived to share more responsibility than a victim who had no feelings of sexual attraction toward the rapist. Again, this was true for both male and female judges, with males attributing somewhat more responsibility to the victim than the females.

Your decision as a juror might reflect these research findings. Thus if the woman was divorced, attractive, and reported having no sexual feelings toward the defendant, you might attribute responsibility to the defendant and vote for a harsh sentence. If the victim was a virgin and plain-looking and reported feeling sexually attracted to the defendant, you might decide that her behavior or situation or both played an important role in the rape and vote for acquittal or a lenient sentence. It is important to keep in mind that attribution theory does not say anything about the *actual* causes of behavior. It is concerned only with an individual's *perceptions* of the causes. So, the above research says nothing about rape victims' responsibility. It does, however, allow us to learn how people view the victim's contribution to acts of rape.

Attribution and Underachievement

A second area in which attribution theory has been applied concerns underachieving schoolchildren—that is, children who do not work up to their ability. Underachievement is a particularly important problem because it can have a snowball effect. If a first-grade child is capable of mastering first-grade material but does not, he or she will begin the second grade with a clear handicap. The handicap will become more pronounced with each grade, and by the time the child reaches high school, he or she will be hopelessly behind. Solving the problem of underachievement would mean rescuing countless children from living lives well below their potential.

Over the past several years Carol Dweck and her colleagues have conducted research demonstrating that the self-perceptions of underachieving children may be responsible for their low levels of achievement. Dweck has focused on the attributions that such children make for their successes and failures (Dweck & Goetz, 1978).

In one study, children were given a number of problems that were actually insoluble (Dweck & Reppuci, 1973). After a number of trials, the experimenter began to present problems that could be solved. Some children were able to solve the new problems, but many others were unable to solve them even though they had solved similar problems earlier. The difference between the two groups of children seemed to be in their attributions for their previous failures. Children who succeeded in solving problems attributed their previous failures to lack of effort; that is, they believed they did not try hard enough. Children who were not successful tended to blame their failures on their lack of ability (e.g., "I'm not smart enough") or on external factors (e.g., "the problem was too hard").

In a further test of this hypothesis, Dweck (1975) identified a group of children who could not cope with failure and placed them in one of two treatment conditions. In the first, the children were given only success experiences. This treatment is based on the hypothesis that underachievers show poor performance because they lack confidence in their own ability. Accordingly, if they are provided with successful experiences, their self-confidence should increase, which will help them deal with future failures.

In the second treatment condition, children were given **attribution retraining.** These children were administered insoluble problems, and the experimenter would explicitly attribute the failure to lack of effort. The children were told such things as "I don't think you tried hard enough that time" or "You will have to try harder on the next one."

By the end of 25 daily training sessions, children in the attribution-retraining group showed a significant increase in their performance. In fact, most of them performed better on tasks that followed a failure experience. Dweck reported that she overheard several children mutter to themselves things such as "I missed that one, that means I have to try harder," when they encountered failure.

Children in the success-only group did not fare nearly so well. The performance of these children did show improvement as long as they were not exposed to failure. However, many of the children had a more adverse reaction to failure after the training than before. It is important to note that the children's attributions for failure were the most important factor. The children's initial level of proficiency at the tasks used in the research did not affect how they would respond to failure experience. Viewing one's failure as a cue to try harder appears to be crucial in maintaining a high level of performance.

Do People Really Make Attributions?

Although many psychologists are actively researching attribution theory and it seems to be applicable to a variety of phenomena, some researchers have raised serious questions about its importance. Ellen Langer (1978), for example, has questioned the assumption, inherent in attribution theory, that people consciously and constantly process information to make interpretations and decide on courses of action. She feels that attribution theorists such as Franz Heider and Harold Kelley presume "too much mental activity on the part of individuals engaging in many of their everyday activities" (p. 50). Langer suggests that many of the complex types of human behavior result from overlearning or habits and not necessarily from cognitive evaluations of a particular situation.

To illustrate, consider the man who saw a woman sitting alone when he arrived at a party. Langer might argue that his behavior would follow a "script" or routine that he had developed on the basis of past actions, rather than be based on his cognitive evaluations or attributions. That is, if he typically approaches women he is attracted to, he will do so now. If he typically is reluctant to approach women, he will not do so. In other words, past learning rather than current attributions guides our behavior.

Langer believes that many of the findings of attribution research are a product of the research techniques that are used. For example, in the studies described earlier regarding the attribution of responsibility for rape, subjects are typically asked to read or watch a scenario depicting an act of rape. They are then asked to complete a questionnaire containing items such as, "To what degree do you feel the woman was responsible for the rape?" and "To what degree do you feel the man was responsible for the rape?" In other words, the subjects are forced to make attributions. Langer suggests that in real-life situations people may not make such attributions spontaneously.

Langer presents several experiments that support her thesis. In one experiment, undergraduate students at Yale were asked to make attributions regarding their skill at predicting the outcome of a flip of a coin (Langer & Roth, 1975). She found that when students had several "wins" early in the sequence, they viewed themselves as skillful at the task and were confident of future success. Furthermore, fully 40 percent of the subjects believed they could improve their performance with practice. Since, as Langer assumes, Yale undergraduates are intelligent enough to know that the outcome of a coin toss is a purely chance occurrence, attributions regarding skill and practice are nonsensical. Their attributions are a result of "some general rule that says, 'When *asked* about the responsibility for outcomes, attribute positive but not negative outcomes to self.' " (p. 44). Although the subjects believed they were thinking about the task, their attributions suggest they were following a script based on overlearning.

A recent series of experiments addressed this issue by having subjects watch a videotape showing interpersonal interactions, and then asking them to make written reports of what they had seen and their reactions to the scene (Harvey, Yarkin, Lightner, & Town, 1980). This gave subjects the opportunity to make attributions spontaneously. In these experiments it was found that the tendency to make attributions was related to several factors. Subjects made more attributions when the interactions had a serious outcome (e.g., when the actors expressed hostility toward each other), when the subjects anticipated interacting with one of the actors, and when the subjects were asked to imagine that an actor was a close friend. While this study offers evidence that people make attributions spontaneously, it does not answer Langer's questions regarding whether making such attributions actually influences our behavior.

Although this issue awaits resolution from future research, it seems reasonable to assume that the effect of scripts and attributions on behavior depends on the situation. If we encounter a situation that we have faced many times before, it seems likely that our scripts will influence our behavior. So, our decision to approach or not to approach an attractive member of the opposite sex may depend on past learning. In a novel situation, for which we have no script, we will probably think about the situation, make attributions, and act on those attributions. Thus if we are serving on a jury that is hearing evidence regarding rape, we will probably make attributions of responsibility and vote accordingly.

INTERPERSONAL ATTRACTION

The question of why we are attracted to certain individuals has long been of interest. Which is true, that "birds of a feather flock together" or that "opposites attract"? Shall we believe that "absence makes the heart grow fonder" or "out of sight, out of mind"? The question of interpersonal attraction was the subject of one of the earliest scientific studies of behavior, Sir Francis Galton's examination of the marriage patterns of illustrious men in 1870. His results, which suggested that men marry women of equivalent status, supported the "birds of a feather" hypothesis.

CRITICAL ISSUE

Attributions and the Opposite Sex

Attribution theorists believe that everyone is a scientist when it comes to human behavior. We are all interested in why others behave as they do. This is especially true in our interactons with the opposite sex. Most of us have probably asked ourselves questions such as "Do his frequent glances mean that he is interested in meeting me?" or "Does the fact that she wore tight jeans and a low-cut blouse for our date mean that she is interested in having sex with me?" Obviously the attributions we make in situations such as these are likely to influence our behavior. And to avoid embarrassing moments we would like to be able to know if our attributions are valid.

In a recent survey of adolescent attitudes, a group of UCLA researchers found that boys are more likely than girls to misread sexual signals (Zellman, Johnson, Giarrusso, & Goodchilds, 1980). Attributions regarding style of dress were quite different for the boys and the girls. Boys were likely to believe that girls who wore a low-cut top, shorts, tight jeans, or no bra were interested in sex, while girls viewed such apparel as simply being in style. Both boys and girls, however, thought that a see-through blouse on a girl was a sexual come-on. Interestingly, neither boys nor girls attributed sexual motives to boys who wore open shirts, tight jeans, and the like.

Boys were more likely than girls to see sexual implications in the setting of a date regardless of how innocuous the setting was. These situations ranged from those in which the couple "meet for the first time in a public place and go somewhere together" to "go to the guy's house alone when there's nobody home." When on a date, girls who talked about sex, said "I love you," told the boy how good-looking he was, or looked into the boy's eyes were viewed as sexually enticing by the boys. Boys who engaged in such behavior were not as likely to be seen as "coming on sexually" by the girls.

It was interesting to note that factors such as ethnic background, age, and previous dating and sexual experiences had no relation to making attributions of sexual come-ons. Regardless of these factors, the boys were always more likely to see sexual enticement than were the girls. Compared with girls, boys seem to have a more sexualized view of social relationships between the sexes and to be more likely to make incorrect attributions in these relationships.

Many studies regarding interpersonal attraction were conducted throughout the first half of the century, and the topic became the focus of intensive research efforts in the late 1950s. At that time Donn Byrne began a fruitful laboratory research program at the University of Texas exploring the relationship between similarity of attitudes and interpersonal attraction. Over the past 20 years many psychologists have conducted experiments on the topic that have greatly increased our understanding. Let us review what has been learned.

Familiarity

Contrary to folk wisdom, familiarity does not breed contempt. A variety of studies have demonstrated that we tend to like those with whom we come into close contact. This **proximity factor,** as it is called, was convincingly demonstrated in a now classic study by Leon Festinger and his colleagues (Festinger, 1951). They examined the formation of friendships in a housing project for married college students. The project consisted of several small houses arranged in U-shaped courts. All the houses faced the court except the end houses, which faced the street.

The friendships and acquaintances that people choose depend somewhat on the proximity factor. (© *Dennis Black/Black Star*)

Festinger concluded that the major factors influencing the formation of friendships were the distance between houses and the direction in which they faced. Couples were more likely to be friends with a couple next door than with a couple two doors away. Also, people who lived in the end houses had fewer than half as many friends as those whose houses faced the court. It may be disconcerting to realize that our social lives are so dependent on the location of our houses.

A more recent experiment demonstrated that even the anticipation of familiarity or proximity can lead to increased interpersonal attraction (Berscheid, Graziano, Monson, & Dermer, 1976). In this experiment college men and women were told that romantic relationships were being studied. As part of the experiment, the students were asked to date exclusively a person selected for them for either one week or six weeks. After the commitment was made, the students saw a videotape of their prospective date, who was participating in a group discussion.

The results indicated that when the students believed they would be dating the person for six weeks, they liked him or her more than when the commitment was for one week. Apparently, believing that one will be spending a fair amount of time with another person does lead to increased attraction.

Similarity

Perhaps no other principle of interpersonal attraction is as well established as the notion that we tend to like those whom we perceive as having attitudes and values similar to our own. Much of the research supporting this principle has been conducted by Donn Byrne and his colleagues. In his research, subjects are typically given information about a stranger or a hypothetical person and then asked to complete a scale that measures interpersonal attraction. By varying the similarity between the attitudes and values of the subject and those of the stimulus person, the role of attitude similarity can be determined. The consistent and relatively general finding is that the greater the proportion of similar attitudes between the stimulus person and the subject, the greater the subjects' liking for the stimulus person will be (Byrne, 1974). In other words, the more similar another person's attitudes are to our own, the more likely we are to like that person.

A corollary to the principle of similarity and attraction is that we tend to assume that attitude similarity exists when we are attracted to a person on some other basis (Byrne & Wong, 1962). For example, while husbands and wives tend to have similar attitudes, they assume that their attitudes are more similar than they actually are (Byrne & Blaylock, 1963). Probably all of us have had the experience of being attracted to someone on the basis of his or her appearance and assuming that we could be great friends, only to discover later that we have nothing in common with that person.

Several explanations have been offered why similarity leads to attraction. Byrne (1974) suggests that we have a need to validate the "correctness" of our attitudes. We all like to be right, and other people are an important source of validation of our own attitudes and opinions. Thus we are attracted to those who provide evidence that our own attitudes are correct. Byrne points out that we tend to avoid people with dissimilar attitudes because they raise the possibility that we are "stupid, uninformed, immoral, or insane."

A second possible explanation for liking those with similar attitudes is that we can anticipate sharing mutually rewarding activities with them (Berscheid & Walster, 1978). If we discover that another person shares our political views, our love of sports, our fascination with old movies, or any other general interest, we may be attracted to that person because we expect to enjoy those activities with him or her.

People who share attitudes or interests are more likely to like each other. (© *Judy Gurovitz/Photo Researchers, Inc.*)

A third possibility is that we tend to assume that people with similar attitudes will like us. Many experiments have demonstrated that a **reciprocity-of-liking rule** operates: we tend to like those who like us (Jones, 1964). In support of this explanation, Walster and Walster (1963) found that when they asked college students to select a group in which the members would probably like them, the students chose to participate in a group discussion with other students rather than with psychologists or factory workers.

These three explanations should not be viewed as mutually exclusive. It is likely that all three factors contribute to the "similarity leads to attraction" phenomenon.

The influence of similarity is not limited to attitudes. Similarity also appears to be important with respect to a number of physical and psychological characteristics. For instance, it has been found that husbands and wives tend to be similar in their level of physical attractiveness (Berscheid & Walster, 1974), stature (Pearson & Lee, 1903), intelligence (Reed & Reed, 1965), education (Garrison, Anderson, & Reed, 1965), the presence of physical disabilities, such as deafness (Harris, 1912), and a host of social characteristics, such as family background and economic status (Burgess & Wallin, 1943). Overall, the "birds of a feather" hypothesis has received strong support.

There is an important exception to the similarity effect. To illustrate, Byrne (1974) has asked how you might feel if your lover left you for someone very similar to yourself. Or, how would you feel if someone similar was insane or a failure? In such cases the evidence suggests that we prefer dissimilar individuals (Novak & Lerner, 1968). It is easier to rationalize our being jilted for someone completely different from ourselves than for someone who is nearly identical. Also, we might feel threatened if we learned that someone similar to ourselves was a chronic failure or had a history of severe emotional disturbance.

Physical Attractiveness

As we saw earlier, physical attractiveness plays an important role in impression formation. We tend to assume that attractive individuals possess a variety of other desirable characteristics. As you have probably guessed already, physical attractiveness also plays an important role in interpersonal attraction.

One of the first and most ambitious studies illustrating the importance of physical attractiveness involved 750 college freshmen (Walster, Aronson, Abrahams, & Rottman, 1966). The students were told that a computer would select their date for a dance and were asked to fill out questionnaires measuring a variety of social and psychological characteristics. In addition, observers rated their level of physical attractiveness. In actuality, the researchers had assigned dates randomly.

The experiment was conducted to test the similarity hypothesis. It was predicted that students would be most attracted to dates having similar psychological, social, and physical characteristics. Contrary to what was expected, the students, regardless of their own level of attractiveness, preferred the most attractive dates.

Several studies have shown that, given an ideal world, people prefer physically attractive partners (Janda, O'Grady, & Barnhart, 1981; Walster, 1970). In the real world, however, things seem to work somewhat differently. In the real world, one must face the possibility of rejection. And if a not-so-attractive person approaches a potential date who is very attractive, rejection is a very real possibility. It has been found that if people are asked to select a date and are told the date has the option of declining, they will choose someone similar to themselves in physical attractiveness (Berscheid, Dion, Walster, & Walster, 1971). Naturalistic observations have found that dating couples (Murstein, 1972) and same-sex friends (Cash & Derlega, 1978) are similar in their level of physical attractiveness.

A recent article by Douglas Kendrick and Sara Gutierres (1980) suggests there are occasions when beauty can be a social problem. In one of their experiments they asked college men who were watching the television show "Charlie's Angels" to rate a photograph of a woman who was of average attractiveness. These men rated her as being significantly less attractive than did a group of men watching a different program. These results, taken together with other similar findings, suggest that media presentations of extremely attractive women may alter standards of beauty in the real world. This "Farrah factor," as it has been called, may serve to make men more critical of the attractiveness and dating desirability of women with whom they come into contact. Kendrick and Gutierres suggest that this might be a particular problem for unattractive men who are continually exposed to highly attractive women. For instance, a bartender at a Playboy Club may have such a distorted standard of beauty that he will be dissatisfied with the women who go out with him—at least according to the matching hypothesis.

ROMANTIC LOVE

Romantic love is certainly one of the most thought-about forms of social attraction. The number of songs, movies, and novels that focus on love, the flood of letters to advice-to-the-lovelorn columnists, and the everyday conversations of people reflect our interest in and concern about this interpersonal phenomenon. Although romantic love has been a focus of speculation for centuries, it has only been during the past decade or so that psychologists have begun to investigate it. A working definition of romantic love has been offered by Walster and Walster (1978):

> A state of intense absorption in another. Sometimes "lovers" are those who long for their partners and for complete fulfillment. Sometimes "lovers" are those who are ecstatic at finally having attained their partner's love, and momentarily, complete fulfillment. A state of intense physiological arousal.

Let us review what has been discovered about this mysterious state. Bear in mind that the material discussed here and the definition presented above reflect the research conducted by social psychologists. Other psychologists, such as Abraham Maslow and Erich Fromm, have had much to say about the nature of romantic love, but our discussion will be limited to the results of empirical research conducted within the past decade or so.

Liking versus Loving

One issue that psychologists have addressed is whether liking and loving fall on the same continuum or whether they are different. That is, is love a case of intense liking? Or are they different emotions, so that regardless of how much we like a person we may never love him or her?

The tentative answer to these questions seems to be that liking and loving are different forms of social attraction. Berscheid and Walster (1978) argue that there are at least three differences between liking and loving. First, fantasy seems to be an important component of romantic love. Many people enjoy fantasizing about an ideal lover, but few spend any time fantasizing about an ideal friend. Dorothy Tennov (1979), who has questioned and interviewed over 1,000 people about their love experiences, reports that obsessive thoughts and fantasies are the foremost characteristic of romantic love. She provided the following example, which is typical for someone who is experiencing intense feelings of romantic love:

> Stu and I would usually spend the weekend together at his place, and he'd call on Wednesday or Thursday to finalize the plans. My week was spent thinking about what had happened during the previous weekend and trying to plan what would happen during the next one. I don't mean that all I did was lie around thinking about it, but it was a constant part of my thinking no matter what else was going on.

Romantic lovers are deeply absorbed in each other.
(© *Chester Higgins, Jr./Rapho Photo Researchers, Inc.*)

Loving, more than liking, is apt to include ambivalent emotions. (© *Frank Siteman/Stock, Boston, Inc.*)

> A lot of it was planning conversations. If I saw a movie or a book, I'd think about telling Stu about it, actually work out impressive sentences which I'd try to memorize. As I drove to work, I'd imagine that he was in the seat next to me and I'd comment on the scenery, on how I felt about various things. Sometimes I'd sing—and I'd pretend that Stu was listening and admiring and falling more in love with me every minute (pp. 37–38).

It seems doubtful that anyone would have similar fantasies about someone they liked.

A second difference between loving and liking is that love is more likely to be associated with conflicting emotions. Berscheid and Walster reported that when college students had the opportunity to ask psychologists one question about love, the one most frequently asked was, "Can you love and hate someone at the same time?" Tennov found many dramatic examples of this among those she interviewed. One man, for instance, was intensely in love with a woman for several years who never reciprocated his feelings. He would become very angry at himself for being a slave to his feelings and occasionally would have fantasies of physically assaulting her.

A third difference between liking and loving involves the effects of time. Our liking for someone tends to increase as we spend more time with him or her (Homans, 1961), while romantic love appears to be a rather short-lived emotion. An impressive number of experts argue that liking is a better basis for marriage than romantic love because the latter fades with time (McCary, 1978; Reik, 1944; Van Den Haag, 1973). Tennov, on the basis of her interviews, concluded that while romantic love may last as little as a week or as long as a lifetime, the most common duration is between 18 months and three years. Interestingly, in those cases that lasted longer, the object of romantic love never fully reciprocated. In fact, reciprocation often marked the point at which love began to fade.

Zick Rubin (1974) has provided empirical evidence that loving and liking are distinct types of social attraction. He constructed separate personality tests to measure liking and loving and gave them to 182 dating couples. The results suggested that for both men and women there was only a moderate tendency for loving and liking to go together. Loving one's partner did not necessarily ensure a liking for him or her.

These findings, while they may not seem very profound, do have important implications. For instance, they suggest that the research findings discussed in the previous section regarding interpersonal attraction may not apply to romantic love. Similarity of attitudes may indeed lead to increased liking, but as of now, we cannot conclude that it will lead to romantic love. And because romantic love does not lend itself to laboratory research, it may be some time before psychologists have complete answers.

A Theory of Love

As you will recall from Chapter 6, Stanley Schachter proposed a two-component theory of emotion. He suggested that the experience of emotion depends on (1) internal physiological arousal and (2) external cues that suggest a label for that arousal. Recently Walster and Walster (1978) have argued that Schachter's theory of emotion can be used to understand romantic love. They reasoned that people will be especially susceptible to love when they experience a state of physiological arousal and find themselves in a situation that suggests that "love" is an appropriate label for what they are experiencing. Imagine a young couple that ride on a roller coaster together and afterwards look deeply into each other's eyes. They may interpret their internal arousal caused by the ride as love for their partner.

This hypothesis is particularly appealing because bodily arousal can be caused by either positive or negative experiences. Thus fear, frustration, and rejection as well as positive experiences, such as sexual arousal, excitement, and joy, may influence the intensity of love. This theory would explain the paradox of love—that it can lead to agony as well as ecstasy. And it allows us to understand Tennov's observation that the duration of romantic love was usually the longest when the loved one was frustrating or rejecting his or her lover.

Experimental evidence in support of this hypothesis was provided when college men were invited to participate in a learning experiment (Dutton & Aron, 1974). The men were pleasantly surprised to find that their partner for the experiment, actually a confederate of the experimenters, was a highly attractive woman. Their pleasure, however, quickly turned to dismay when they learned that they would be required to receive a series of electric shocks as part of the experiment. Half of the men were told that the shocks would be quite intense and painful (fear condition), while the other half were told that the shocks would be a barely perceptible tingle (control condition). As predicted, the men in the fear condition were more romantically attracted to the confederate than were the men in the control group. Presumably, the attractiveness of the woman led the men to interpret their internal arousal caused by the fear of being shocked as feelings of incipient love.

Men, Women, and the Romantic Ideal

A majority of people in our society subscribe to what is called the **romantic ideal.** That is, they believe they will fall in love with someone, marry that person, and live happily ever after in a state of romantic bliss. Of course, most people realize that often things do not work that way, but they nonetheless think that is the way things *should* work.

It is also generally believed that women are more romantic than men. Women are thought to be the ones who are seeking someone to fall in love with. Once married, they are the ones who try to maintain the romance in their relationship. The media appears to provide ample evidence to support this stereotype. Pulp magazines such as *True Confessions,* romantic novels, and the afternoon soap operas are all aimed at women. Television commercials tell women that if they use the right product they can rekindle feelings of romance in their husbands. Men, on the other hand, are generally thought to be more interested in sexual than romantic gratification. Surprisingly, however, the research evidence suggests just the opposite; men are more romantic than women. A study of the attitudes toward marriage of 1,000 college students hinted at this difference (Kephart, 1967). In response to the question, "If a man [woman] had all the other qualities you desired, would you marry this person if you were not in love with him [her]?" only 24 percent of the women ruled out this possibility, while fully 65 percent of the men said no. Rubin (1973) has found that men are more likely to agree to statements such as "A person should marry whomever he loves regardless of social position" and are less likely to agree with statements such as "Economic security should be carefully considered before selecting a marriage partner." Apparently men, more than women, believe that love is a necessary and sufficient condition for marriage.

In his studies of dating couples, Rubin (Hill, Rubin, & Peplau, 1976; Rubin, 1973, 1974) has provided additional evidence that men are the more romantic sex. He found that men tended to fall in love more readily than women, while women fell out of love more readily than men. Interestingly, men, more than women, were likely to enter a relationship based on the desire to fall in love. Furthermore, when a dating relationship was ended, women were more likely to have initiated the breakup. Men were more distressed by the end of the affair and more likely to suffer from feelings of guilt, depression, loneliness, and unhappiness. Rubin reported that a common reaction of men was a failure to accept the fact that the relationship had ended. They often held on to the hope that the woman would realize that she loved him after all.

Love and Marriage

You may be wondering, What binds a couple together for a lifetime if romantic love is doomed to fade away in a few years. Berscheid and Walster (1978) have coined the term **companionate love** to describe the affection that exists between a man and woman in a long-term relationship. According to these psychologists, companionate love is on the same continuum as liking. It differs from liking only in its intensity of feelings and in the extent to which the lives of the individuals are intertwined.

Romantic love often matures into companionate love. (© *Joel Gordon*)

What Berscheid and Walster may be suggesting is that a couple may be motivated to get married by feelings of romantic love, but if they are to stay married, they must have feelings of companionate love or intense liking for each other. Bernard Murstein (1976) has proposed a model of mate selection, called the stimulus-value-role theory, that is compatible with this idea and with much of the available research on interpersonal attraction. Murstein suggests that in the first stage, the stimulus stage, we will be attracted to a person if he or she is physically attractive to us and creates a good impression. At this point, we may have the feeling that we could fall in love with the person, and we will be motivated to learn more about him or her.

The second and third stages involve more practical considerations. The value stage is characterized by the man and woman learning if they share similar values and attitudes. In the role stage, they discover if they are compatible in the various roles—such as parent, housekeeper, wage earner, and so on—that they will be required to fill as part of a long-term relationship. Murstein's point is that a couple will never progress to the final two stages if the initial attraction does not occur.

It would seem, then, that people do not marry on the basis of romantic love. Rather romantic love serves as an impetus to explore a relationship to determine if marriage is a realistic possibility. If people did marry impulsively on the basis of romantic love, then we probably would not have the rather sizable body of research that finds husbands and wives to be similar with regard to a number of characteristics. So while people may pay lip service to the romantic ideal, they are not blind to the practical considerations involved in marriage. Morton Hunt (1959) summarized this paradox when he wrote;

> Americans are firmly of two minds about it all, simultaneously hardhearted and idealistic, uncouth and tender, libidinous and puritanical. They believe implicitly in every tenet of romantic love and yet they know perfectly well that things don't really work that way (p. 363).

Social psychologists have just begun to explore the form of social attraction that brings men and women together. And with very few exceptions, they have yet to begin to study the nature of the attraction that binds a couple together over long periods of time. This may prove to be one of the most interesting areas of research for psychologists in the 1980s.

Summary

This chapter covered theory and research associated with the areas of social perception and social attraction. The topic of first impressions has been studied since the 1940s. Asch believed certain central traits, such as warmth, strongly influenced the overall first impression. Other researchers disagreed, stating that the results of Asch's research were a product of the methods used.

There appear to be individual differences in forming first impressions. Some individuals focus on negative characteristics, while others look for the positive ones. Also, personality variables, such as sex guilt, influence the way people evaluate others.

Physical attractiveness plays an important role in first impressions. People appear to operate under the "what is beautiful is good" stereotype. They believe that attractive individuals possess many other desirable characteristics. Because attractive individuals elicit certain expectations and reactions from others, they may develop personality traits and behavior that differ from those of unattractive individuals.

Attribution theory is one of the most popular areas of research among social psychologists today. Attributions are the beliefs we hold about the causes of our own and others' behavior. One consistent finding is that we tend to attribute our success to our personal virtues and our failures to circumstances or environmental factors. We tend to do just the opposite with others, making environmental attributions for successes and personal attributions for failures. Two areas of research that attribution theorists have examined are responsibility for rape and the problem of underachieving in school. With regard to rape, married women, virgins, unattractive women, and coy and seductive women are perceived as sharing more responsibility for rape than are divorced or nonseductive women. With regard to underachievement, it has been found that a crucial factor is the attributions for failure that children make. Underachievers can be helped to improve their performance by being taught to attribute their failures to a lack of effort rather than to a lack of ability.

Social psychologists have learned much about interpersonal attraction. We are likely to have as friends those who live near us and those with whom we come into close contact. Perhaps the best-documented principle of interpersonal attraction is that we tend to like those whom we perceive as being similar to ourselves. This holds true for similarities in attitudes, socioeconomic status, and physical characteristics. While people prefer physically attractive individuals, they are apt to form relationships with others who are similar to themselves in this respect.

Romantic love is one form of social attraction that has only recently received attention from research psychologists. Romantic love appears to differ qualitatively from liking in that the former fades with time, is a frequent source of fantasies, and is often associated with conflicting emotions. It has been suggested that Schachter's two-factor theory of emotion can be used to understand romantic love. Contrary to popular belief, research suggests that men may be more romantic than women. The affection that binds men and women together in a long-term relationship has been called companionate love. Romantic love may serve as an impetus to men and women to explore each other's values and attitudes fully to determine if marriage is a realistic possibility.

Key Terms For Review

attribution
attribution retraining
companionate love
impression formation
proximity factor
reciprocity-of-liking rule
romantic ideal

Suggested Readings

Berscheid, E., & Walster, E. Physical attractiveness. In L. Berkowitz (Ed.), *Advances in Experimental Social Psychology*. (Vol. 7). New York: Academic Press, 1974.
Although this article is somewhat dated in terms of the research in the area, it does provide a comprehensive review of the findings that demonstrate that most of us operate under the "what is beautiful is good" stereotype.

Berscheid, E., & Walster, E. *Interpersonal attraction* (2nd ed.). Reading, Mass.: Addison-Wesley, 1978.
This paperback book is both informative and delightful to read. It covers material ranging from interpersonal attraction to romantic love to companionate love.

Goldberg, P., Gottesdiener, M., & Abramson, P. Another putdown of women? Perceived attractiveness as a function of support for the feminist movement. In E. Aronson (Ed.), *Readings about the social animal* (2nd ed.). San Francisco: W. H. Freeman, 1977.
This article illustrates that both men and women are guilty of holding stereotypes of women who support the feminist movement. When asked to select photographs of women who favored women's liberation, both sexes selected unattractive women.

Rubin, Z. *Liking and loving: An invitation to social psychology.* New York: Holt, Rinehart & Winston, 1973.

A fascinating book that provides a historical perspective of the concept of romantic love as well as describing contemporary research. Available in paperback.

Shaver, K. *An introduction to attribution processes.* Cambridge, Mass.: Winthrop, 1973.

A good source for the beginning psychology student who wants to learn about the theory and research regarding attribution processes.

Sigall, H., & Ostrove, N. Beautiful but dangerous: Effects of offender attractiveness and nature of the crime of juridic judgment. *Journal of Personality and Social Psychology,* 1975, *31,* 410–414.

This article illustrates that being physically attractive is not always an advantage. Highly attractive women will receive more severe sentences for some types of crime than less attractive women.

16

Groups

The killings began without warning. Harry Stanley told the C.I.D. (the Army's investigative unit) that one member of Calley's platoon took a civilian into custody and then "pushed the man to where we were standing and stabbed the man in the back with his bayonet. . . . The man fell to the ground and was gasping for breath." The GI then "killed him with another bayonet thrust or by shooting him with a rifle. . . . There was so many people killed that day it is hard for me to exactly recall how some of the people died." Moments after, Stanley saw some old women and some little children—fifteen or twenty of them—in a group around a temple where incense was burning. They were kneeling, crying, and praying, and various soldiers walked by shooting them in the head with their rifles.

There were few physical protests from the people; about eighty of them were taken quietly from their homes and herded together in the plaza area. A few hollered out, "No VC. No VC." But that was hardly unexpected. Calley left Meadlo, Boyce, and a few others with the responsibility of guarding the group. "You know what I want to do with them," he told Meadlo. Ten minutes later . . . he returned and asked, "Haven't you got rid of them yet? I want them dead." . . . Meadlo followed orders: "He stood about ten to fifteen feet away from them and then he and Calley started shooting them. So we went ahead and killed them. Some continued to chant, 'No VC.' Others simply said, 'No, no, no.' " (Hersch, 1970, pp. 49–50).

This passage is not taken from a gruesome novel but is an eye-witness account of the My Lai massacre of 1970, in which more than 100 Vietnamese women, children, and old men were killed by American soldiers under the command of the platoon's leader, Lieutenant William Calley. This event underscores a number of critical aspects of group behavior, including the following of orders, personality characteristics of the group leader, conformity, and group decision making, which we shall seek to understand in this chapter.

Our society is made up of many groups, ranging from the nuclear family to the entire nation. Take a moment and see how many different groups you belong to: your family, a college class, perhaps a club, fraternity, or sorority, a football or tennis team, a social organization, a political party, a church congregation. Throughout life we function in groups: we are born into a family, we go to school in groups, we may get married and have children to form a new group. Membership in groups greatly influences our behavior and our lives because through groups we become participants in larger organizations, cultural institutions, and society as a whole. The study of groups, together with the study of attitudes (see Chapter 14), make up the core of social psychology. Researchers of group behavior, although interested in the personality characteristics of individual group members, are primarily concerned with the relationships among the various people composing the group.

CHARACTERISTICS OF GROUPS

Although many definitions have been offered for the term "group," a simple working definition is "two or more persons who are interacting in such a manner that each person influences and is influenced by each other person" (Shaw, 1976, p. 11). Interaction and intercommunication are characteristics that distinguish groups from mere collections of people, such as those who gather at a bus stop.

Another characteristic of a group is its common set of values and beliefs. When people join or form a group—whether it be to lose weight, overcome a drinking problem, or start a community volunteer service—members are apt to share a philosophy or goals. For example, participants in a weight-control program may determine beforehand how many pounds of weight loss represent satisfactory progress. The members of the group then pursue this goal both individually and collectively. These three features—interaction, shared values and beliefs, and common goals—are key elements in most definitions of groups. A family, a fraternity or sorority, and a congressional committee are examples of groups that possess these three characteristics.

Some groups, such as this Parents Without Partners meeting, are formed because the members share the same concerns. (© *Mimi Forsyth/Monkmeyer Press Photo Service*)

Functions of Groups

Groups serve important emotional and social needs that we cannot satisfy alone. One common reason to join a group is to satisfy a basic need to belong. In exchange for the satisfaction of this need, we accept the fact that some of our behavior will be influenced by the group. Communes, for example, satisfy the emotional needs of their members, who in turn accept the commune's particular political or ideological viewpoint.

Groups also provide us with psychological rewards, such as the enhancement of self-esteem or the attainment of a high-status position, such as group leader.

A third reason for joining a group is that we either like the activities the group is engaged in or like the people who make up the group. Thus a person who joins a bridge club or a fraternity may do so either because he or she has friends who belong to the group, or because he or she enjoys the activities of the group.

People may also join groups to seek and share information. Since we cannot be experts in everything, we turn to others and rely on their expertise to obtain information we need. At the same time, we may be willing to share our knowledge with others who seek us out as a source of information. Sharing information to solve problems or complete a task is an activity that takes place in many groups. Brainstorming, for example, is a means by which members of groups exchange information to come up with new or creative solutions to difficult problems. A school board may use brainstorming to explore ways of handling a teacher shortage, or a government agency may use it to decide on a policy change.

Finally, people join groups because they can accomplish tasks that they could not perform individually. For example, people have grouped together to help the survivors of a natural disaster or to clean up a rundown neighborhood. Collective efforts can produce results that an individual could never achieve alone.

Formation of Groups

Rosenfeld (1976) describes the process of group formation as a four-phase sequence: orientation, conflict, balance, and parting. During the **orientation phase** many group members feel uncomfortable because they are uncertain what they are supposed to know or to do. Each member has joined the group with a certain set of expectations regarding the functions and activities of the group and the kinds of things he or she wishes to gain from the group experience. These expectations have to be confirmed or modified. Through interaction, members learn what is expected of them and what types of behavior are and are not allowed in the group. During the orientation phase, initial anxieties and uncertainties are reduced, and the goals of the group, as well as its social and emotional climate, begin to crystallize. At the end of this initial period of orientation, group members begin to experience a sense of belonging.

During the **conflict phase,** members experience a clash between their own sense of individuality and the rules and standards imposed by the group. If the group is to accomplish its goals, individuals have to subordinate their own needs, desires, or solutions to those agreed upon by the group. Not infrequently members overreact during this period and become hostile and aggressive toward one another, and especially toward the leader.

Successful resolution of the conflict phase leads the group into the **balance phase,** which is characterized by harmony between personal and group identity. The group achieves this state of balance by reaching some form of agreement or compromise between the tasks or goals that must be accomplished and the emotional needs of the members. Ideally, at the end of this phase group members have clearly established their roles, are working enthusiastically toward the group product, and have developed harmonious interpersonal relationships. Some groups fluctuate between the conflict and the balance phase during their entire life span.

Certain groups, such as therapy or consciousness-raising groups, are time-limited. They are formed on the assumption that once the objective is reached, the group will dissolve. During the **parting phase** group members evaluate the extent to which their initial objectives have been met. In groups that have been successful, members leave with the conviction that they did the best job that could be done and that the group served its function well.

Roles in Groups

As the group develops and begins to establish itself, individual differences begin to appear as early as the orientation phase (Shaw, 1976). Some people speak more often than others, some are better organizers or more active than others, and some may be ignored. As a result of these different contributions made by the various group members, each individual begins to assume a different position, or **role,** within the group. Hare (1976) defined role as the "set of expectations which group members share concerning the behavior of a person who occupies a given position in the group" (p. 131). For example, the person who is filling the role of boss on a construction job is expected to see to it that the work gets done.

In many groups the roles are arranged in a hierarchical order. In a work group, for instance, the supervisor may occupy the highest position, the foreman the next highest, and the assembly worker the lowest. Associated with each role are certain functions that the occupant of the role is expected to perform. For example, if at a group meeting the group leader asks who will take notes and all eyes turn to the member who previously volunteered to perform that function, we have a case of clearly visible role expectations. When clear-cut expectations do not exist, roles may be established on the basis of the nature of the group's task. In studies of the roles that develop during the course of jury deliberations, for example, it was found that jurors who participated more and offered most answers were perceived as being more influential (Strodtbeck & Mann, 1956; Strodtbeck, James, & Hawkins, 1957).

Group Norms

Norms are standards or rules of conduct for group members that provide a basis for determining appropriate behavior in otherwise ambiguous situations. In Shaw's (1976) definition, norms are "rules established by the members of the group to maintain behavioral consistency." If a group failed to develop a set of norms, each member would encounter a great deal of frustration trying to figure out what to do and how to do it. Thus norms are used as yardsticks against which the behavior of each individual can be evaluated.

In addition, group norms provide a basis for predicting the behavior of others and thereby enable the individual to anticipate the actions of others. Through norms the performance of a group is regulated as an organized unit, and group life becomes orderly and predictable.

Group norms vary widely from one group to another. Some groups develop general norms that define a range of acceptable behavior; others establish norms that apply to all members regardless of position or status; still others have norms for only certain members, such as the leader.

Types of Norms. Norms can be categorized as formal or informal and as explicit or implicit. Formal norms are those "on the book." They are codified, as in bylaws of an organization or in written statements that are enforced by specified sanctions (i.e., actions to insure compliance). Most formal norms are intended to be taken literally. For example, the formal norms of a fraternity may prescribe the following behavior as appropriate: maintaining good grades, dating women from certain sororities, and being loyal to the fraternity. Deviations from these rules, such as being placed on probation, are likely to evoke punishment.

Informal norms exist in many groups and are sometimes recognized only if they are violated. They represent the way organizations really work on a day-to-day basis. It may be informally understood among a group of workers, for instance, that when the boss asks for a monthly report by Monday, he or she does not expect it to be submitted until Wednesday. The newcomer who turns in the report on Monday may be told by the supervisor to hold on to it until Wednesday. Most of us obey informal social norms such as "Don't come to parties or other social gatherings exactly on time."

A second distinction separates norms into explicit and implicit ones. Explicit norms, although not necessarily put into writing, are nevertheless clearly spelled out so that group members are aware of their specifications. Families, for instance, often set up explicit norms about who is to clean up after dinner or who is to take out the garbage. Attending a church meeting under the influence of alcohol or not attending class meetings regularly are examples of violations of explicit norms.

Implicit norms are usually unstated; like informal norms, they often become clear only when a group member transgresses them. The group member who arrives late at a group meeting and is greeted by hostile glances realizes that he or she has just violated an implicit group norm. Or try taking your mother's seat at the dinner table; someone in your family is bound to say, "That's where Mom is supposed to sit." Sometimes implicit norms supersede explicit norms. For example, a manager in an organization may explicitly tell his or her subordinates to bring their problems to management. But the first worker who follows this advice is labeled a trouble-maker. In the future, the worker will follow the implicit norm, "Don't bring your problems to management or you will be in trouble."

The degree to which group members conform to the norms is critical, since a group cannot function effectively without such conformity. The process by which a group exerts pressure on its members to conform is known as **social control.** Social control occurs whenever one or more individuals attempt to alter the attitudes, behavior, or feelings of others. If group norms are compatible with individual rules of conduct, the group is able to function smoothly since little pressure is necessary to enforce them. However, when individual norms deviate substantially from group norms, one of the major functions of norms, namely to make the behavior of group members predictable, is jeopardized, and conflict and disorganized activity are likely to result. For example, if large numbers of people were suddenly to refuse to comply with governmental orders, chaos would result. Therefore in many groups conformity to norms is rewarded and deviance is punished.

Development of Norms. Some norms develop as simple repetitions of certain behavioral patterns. Think about the norms governing the seating arrangements in any of your classes. After the first few class meetings you and your classmates probably tended to claim the same seat day after day. If you arrive late for class one day to find

Sororities and fraternities often set norms for their members. (© *Hugh Rogers/Monkmeyer Press Photo Service)*

someone else in "your" seat, you probably feel slightly irritated.

However, there is more to the development of norms than simple repetition. Norms develop through interaction and reinforcement. Let us illustrate the development of norms with a well-known laboratory experiment by Muzafer Sherif conducted many years ago (1936). Participants in the study were brought in groups of three into a dark lab room and told that a point of light would appear, move a short distance, and then disappear. The task of the subjects was to estimate the number of inches the light had moved. In actuality, the light was stationary; when shown repeatedly and briefly in a dark room, a light will appear to move. The tendency to perceive motion where none exists is called the **autokinetic effect.**

During the first trials, subjects started out with different judgments, saying that the light traveled 1, 2, 3, 4, 5, or 6 inches. Gradually, however, ex-

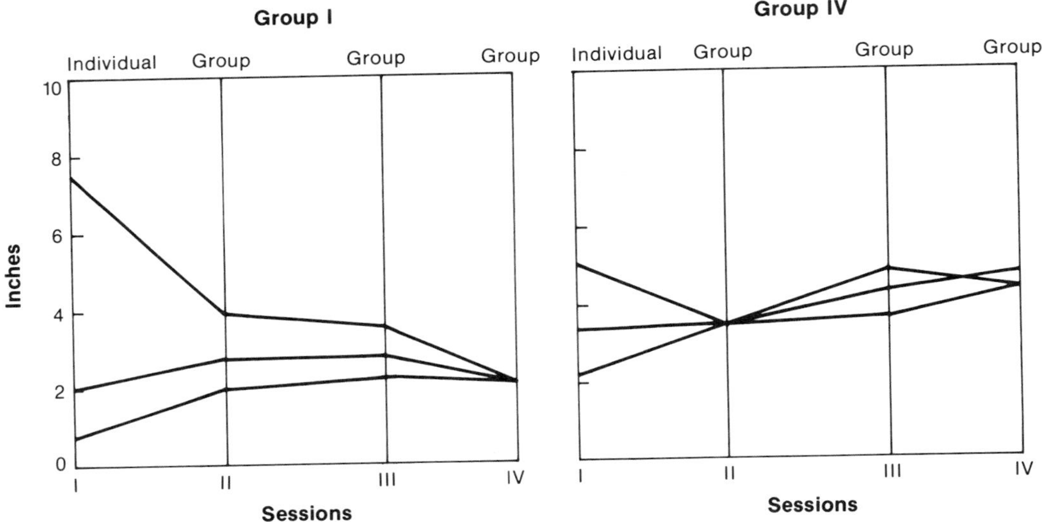

Figure 16–1.

treme values were given up, and the judgments reported by the three individuals in each group converged, coming within an inch of each other. Figure 16–1 shows the convergence of judgments in two groups studied subsequently by Sherif and Sherif (1969).

This convergence of estimates was interpreted as the emergence of a social norm. Sherif suggested that since the light was stationary, the group members had no real basis for judging the amount of movement and apparently looked to one another for comparison.

Other experiments have demonstrated that when subjects who had previously developed their norms on an individual basis were faced with a group situation, their subjective norms gradually converged toward the collective norm. Similarly, if two or more people began the experiment together, the norms they established were carried over into individual judgment situations.

What does this series of experiments tell us? According to Sherif, we have a general tendency to organize our experiences around a **reference norm,** which is a collective product representing the contributions of each group member. With the help of the autokinetic effect Sherif was able to show that a small group of persons, when confronted with an ambiguous social stimulus, progressively reduced differences in their judgments to arrive at a common normative interpretation.

Why do norms emerge at all? Leon Festinger (1950) suggested two reasons. First, the accomplishment of group goals depends on the extent to which the functions and activities of the group members are coordinated. Without regulation and coordination of member behavior, groups would fail to realize their goals. A second reason for the emergence of norms is our need to validate our beliefs and values. Experiments using the autokinetic effect showed that when people cannot depend on physical reality for support, they look to others for social support. The **social-comparison theory** states that in the absence of a physical or objective standard of correctness, we will seek other people as a means of evaluating ourselves (Festinger, 1954). Whether it is our attitude toward Eskimos or a new hairstyle or the latest rock group, we are motivated to evaluate our own beliefs and abilities by comparing them with social reality (Suls & Miller, 1977).

Group Cohesiveness

Group cohesiveness is usually defined as the degree to which individuals are attracted to the group. The most frequently used definition states that group cohesiveness is a "characteristic of the group in which forces acting on members to remain in the group are greater than the total forces acting on them to leave it" (Davis, 1969, p. 78). In other words, groups in which members like one another and want to remain in one another's presence are cohesive; groups in which members are not attracted to one another and groups that are breaking up are said to be low in cohesiveness (Baron & Byrne, 1981). Moreover, as Shaw (1976) pointed out, group members who are attracted to the group work harder to achieve its goals; therefore cohesiveness leads to higher productivity. A close-knit sorority, for instance, is more likely than a less cohesive sorority to make elaborate preparations for the homecoming weekend.

If you examine the groups to which you belong, you will probably find that they differ in their degree of cohesiveness. Perhaps you belong to a sports team whose members are very active and close to one another and whose morale is high. Moreover, the group has set goals, i.e., victories over other teams during the season, that are important to you. All these elements contribute to the cohesiveness of your group and maintain your attraction to it. And perhaps you belong to another group, such as a foreign-language club, in which the members continuously argue and bicker, rarely reaching a consensus. Most of the members in this group do not regularly attend its meetings. Moreover, you often find the activities of this group boring. If you have your choice, you will probably drop out of the second group.

The development of a cohesive group requires constant sensitivity to the satisfaction of group members (Kowitz & Knutson, 1980). Instead of relying on personal needs and desires, group members need to consider one another's needs and wants. Rather than saying, "I want to move on to the next item on the agenda," a group leader concerned with building cohesiveness would say, "I would like us to move on to the next issue, but what do the rest of you think?" In this way the leader speaks honestly for himself or herself while still considering the desires of the group.

In a cohesive group, members are open to influence from one another and listen to one another. Highly cohesive groups also tend to be more active and to experience fewer absences at meetings; in addition, group members are usually concerned about the success of the group.

Measuring Group Cohesiveness. Since group cohesiveness may be reflected by many differences in the behavior of group members, the measures of cohesiveness vary considerably from study to study. Perhaps the most common way of assessing cohesiveness is the **sociometric choice,** in which group members are asked to name the person or persons with whom they would most prefer to interact in a variety of situations. In making their choices, members select associates on various dimensions, such as liking or competence.

A sports team can be a highly cohesive group. (© *Jim Anderson/Woodfin Camp & Associates*)

Applied to the classroom, for instance, the method consists of finding out from each student which members of the class he or she would like to sit next to. Using the reported choices, the experimenter is able to draw up a chart, or **sociogram,** which indicates the positive and negative attitudes of the students toward one another. The number of choices within the group presumably reflects the degree of cohesiveness of the group. The major purpose of the sociometric method is to discover interpersonal attractions and repulsions among various members of the group or the positive and negative feelings members have for one another (Fischer, 1980).

Other measures of cohesiveness include the relative frequency with which the group members use "we" or "I" in their communications and the regularity of their group meetings. Again, it is important to use "I" when speaking for oneself. The use of "we" is often manipulative, as in "We all want this, don't we?"

Cohesiveness and Productivity. As indicated earlier, the greater the degree of cohesiveness in a group, the more productive the group will be. This was demonstrated in a series of investigations performed in the Hawthorne plant of the Western Electric Company, where managers implemented changes in the social dimension of the work group in the hope of increasing output. For example, they allowed some workers to form their own work teams. Members of these teams felt honored to be singled out by management to participate in the research and became motivated by a common goal, namely to improve the working conditions in the plant. As a result, the groups became more cohesive and improved their productivity. (See Chapter 19 for a full description of the Hawthorne studies.)

More recent research has shown that cohesiveness increases productivity only up to a certain point. Fisher (1980), for instance, found that extremely cohesive groups had moderate to low productivity. One explanation may be that members of highly cohesive groups enjoy one another's company so much that they fail to focus on the task to be accomplished. As a result, productivity suffers.

Conformity and Conflict

As we have seen, both conflict and conformity are important group processes. Sometimes demands to conform—to attend class regularly, to do homework, to pay taxes, to observe traffic regulations, to contribute to charity or political campaigns—are in conflict with our own wishes. To agree with the group is to disagree with ourselves, but to agree with ourselves is to disagree with the group. Some degree of nonconformity, referred to by social psychologists as **deviance,** is present in all of us. It becomes apparent when we cross a street against a red light or litter the roadside with cigarette butts and soft-drink cans. In groups, the major consequence of nonconformity is to increase the pressure exerted on the individual to abide by the group's rules.

Conflict between groups is equally important. For example, when labor and management negotiate contracts, workers typically want higher wages, while management wants to hold the line. Or Russia may strive for strategic arms advantage, while the United States wants to ensure its military superiority. Whenever two groups are in conflict, they must find ways of resolving it.

Conformity can be defined as yielding to group pressure. Some psychologists distinguish between two types of conformity: **simple compliance** and **private acceptance.** When a person acts in accordance with a group's norms without believing what he or she is doing, we call it compliance. The person complies with group pressures to conform but retains private attitudes that are inconsistent with the group's norms. In private acceptance, the person not only acts according to group norms but also privately endorses the group's position. Were the men in Calley's platoon merely following orders or did they believe the war justified their actions?

Conformity is often viewed as a type of negative behavior that robs people of their individuality and restricts their creativity. However, conformity is not necessarily bad. In a stable group—whether a family, a work team, or a nation of people—there must be a certain amount of conformity. Otherwise, people would simply follow their own impulses without regard for others, thereby infringing on others' rights and making cooperative enterprises impossible. Nevertheless, group interaction can result in conformity that both the individuals who conform and society might view with some alarm.

Effects of Group Pressure: The Asch Studies

In an experiment by Solomon Asch (1951), presented as a study of visual perception, groups of seven male college students each were asked to judge which of three comparison lines was the same length as a standard line. The standard line was presented on one card and the three comparison lines on another. As you can see from Figure 16–2, the correct comparison line is quite obvious.

The subjects sat around a table and were instructed to report their judgments individually. All but one subject, however, were confederates of the experimenter and had been told in advance to give a certain response. The naive subject (the subject who was not a confederate) was asked to respond last. As the cards were presented, the confederates would sometimes give incorrect responses and sometimes give correct responses. Thus the naive subject sometimes found his own perceptual judgment in conflict with the responses of his peer group and had to decide whether to report the correct answer or go along with the group.

Suppose you were the naive subject. How would you respond if you found yourself in the following situation?

1. You were told by the experimenter that there is only one correct response;
2. You find yourself confronted with two incompatible sets of information, one presented by a majority, your peer group, and the other based on the reality of your senses;
3. You are not allowed to talk with the members of your group; the only communications permitted are the judgments of the comparison line;
4. You feel isolated and confused.

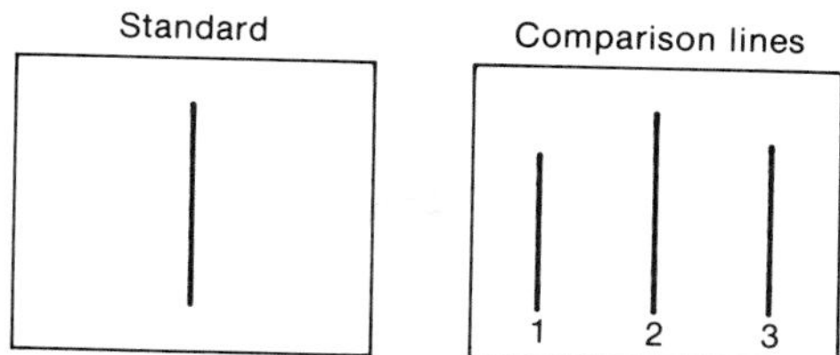

Figure 16–2.

In the original Asch studies, naive subjects conformed, that is, they agreed with incorrect responses, about 32 percent of the time. However, a wide range of individual differences in conformity was observed. While four-fifths of the subjects yielded to the erroneous majority on at least one trial, a significant minority never conformed.

These findings have been replicated in literally hundreds of studies, all of which concluded that conformity in our culture is strong enough that reasonably intelligent people are willing to call white black. Many people found these results disconcerting and even alarming, given the fact that no deliberate attempts were made to influence the subject's judgment. Some suggested that subjects conformed because they were uncertain of the correct choice and were therefore swayed by the majority. In many instances, however, this was not the case. Many subjects were quite certain that their judgment was correct and would have chosen correctly were it not for the presence of the group.

Asch himself (1952) attempted to explain his results as follows: as individuals, we share our environment with others and perceive many events as others do. For example, if it rains on us, it rains as well on those around us. Under such circumstances the pull toward the group and toward perceiving as others do is strong, even if our senses tell us differently.

Group pressure in this Asch experiment is causing the subject to alter a strong opinion. (© *William Vandivert*)

Two limitations of the Asch procedure are often cited. First, Asch's operational definition of conformity was narrow; he referred to public compliance only and did not assess private acceptance of the group's judgment. Although some subjects probably changed their private opinion, apparently many of them conformed to gain the acceptance of the group. However, postexperimental interviews led Asch to conclude that most of those who conformed questioned their own judgment. Second, the experimental situation is unlike circumstances encountered in the real world. Instead of comparing lines against a standard, you might be pressured by your friends to change your opinion about a movie. Or, in a class of students, some may wish to take the final exam early, whereas others may want more time to study. Each side probably attempts to influence the other to conform to its view.

Group Factors in Conformity

What explanations can social psychologists give to account for the hold that the majority had on the naive subject? Three factors that affect conformity are (1) the size of the group, (2) the presence or absence of a unanimous majority, and (3) face-to-face confrontation.

To find out how group size affected conformity, Asch varied the size of the group confronting the naive subject, using 1, 2, 3, 8, and 16 confederates. Asch (1951) observed that the amount of conformity increased with group size until the group consisted of 3 confederates. Then, the effect produced by the size of the group leveled off so that there was no more conformity to a majority of 16 than to a majority of 3 (see Table 16–1).

Asch (1956) also examined the effects of unanimity (complete agreement) on conformity by using two sets of groups: one in which the confederates were unanimous and another in which they disagreed. Breaking the majority's unanimity had a striking effect. Even if only one person defected from a group of 16 confederates and gave the correct response, the amount of conformity was sharply reduced (Morris & Miller, 1975). Giving the subject support of one other person was sufficient to destroy much of the power of the majority.

Is the size of the majority or its unanimity more important? Since conformity does not increase with a unanimous majority of more than three, the size of the majority is important only up to a point. Nonunanimous opinion, then, seems to be more influential in shaping conformist responses. This conclusion is supported by the observation that certain groups, such as authoritarian governments, orthodox religions, or even very strict parents, do not tolerate minor dissent because they are aware of the powerful impact it can have on the group.

Table 16–1. Amount of Conformist Response According to the Size of Unanimous Majorities

Size of the Majority	1	2	3	8	16
Mean number of conformist responses	0.33	1.53	4.0	3.84	3.75

Source: From Asch (1951).

The Milgram Experiments

In the 1960s Stanley Milgram, a social psychologist at Yale University, set out to explain the systematic destruction of the Jews by the Third Reich. Milgram's hypothesis was that Germans have a basic character flaw that makes them obey authority without question, no matter how outrageous the acts they are commanded to commit (Meyer, 1980). Milgram (1963) argued that the building of gas chambers and the production of a daily quota of corpses could not have been carried out on such a massive scale unless a large number of people had readily obeyed.

The result of this theorizing was a series of experiments in which almost 1,000 adults participated. In the first of many studies, volunteer subjects were told that they were participating in a learning experiment designed to study the effects of punishment on memory. The task was to master a series of paired words, such as blue-girl, fat-neck, nice-day. After reading the list once, the subject, designated "teacher," called out the first word in each pair and then a list of four other words from which the learner (a confederate) had to choose the second word of the pair. The punishments were "shocks" delivered by the teacher, who had seen the learner wired to a "shock generator machine" in the adjoining room. The generator had 30 switches labeled from "slight shock" through "danger: severe shock" with the last two switches simply labeled "XXX." The voltage ranged from 15 to 450 volts, from mildly tingling to almost lethal shock.

If the learner gave the correct answer, the teacher was to say "correct" and move on to the next question. If the learner answered incorrectly, the teacher was to say "incorrect," announce the level of punishment, and give the learner the punishing shock. The teacher was continually reminded by the experimenter that the punishments were to increase by 15 volts for each error.

As the learning trials progressed and the shock levels increased, the learner began to pound on the wall of the room where he was supposedly "bound to the electric chair," to cry out in pain, and to plead with the teacher to stop "because of a heart condition." Finally between 390 and 450 volts the learner was no longer heard from. At that point, the teacher turned to the experimenter for help. The experimenter calmly instructed the teacher to treat the absence of a response as a wrong answer and move on to the next higher shock level. Actually the screams and protests of the learner were prerecorded on tape and automatically released in sequence each time the teacher pressed the shock lever.

Of the 40 original subjects, 26, or 65 percent, followed the instructions of the experimenter all the way up to the highest shock level. Some of the obedient subjects, who continued to administer higher and higher levels of shock, did so under considerable stress. Milgram (1963) described one subject as follows:

> I observed a mature and initially poised business man enter the lab smiling and confident. Within twenty minutes he was reduced to a twitching, stuttering wreck, who was rapidly approaching a point of nervous collapse. At one point, he pushed his fist into his forehead and muttered: "Oh God, let's stop it." And yet he continued to follow every word of the experimenter and obeyed to the end (p. 377).

Others were observed to sweat, stutter, tremble, groan, bite their lips, and dig their fingernails into their flesh, and full-blown uncontrollable seizures were recorded for three subjects. The results are summarized in Figure 16–3.

Although these results were obtained in the laboratory, there are many real-life parallels. Many Germans under Nazism and Lieutenant Calley in his defense claimed that they only followed orders from higher authorities.

Since obedience is an important facet of our social life, we must ask why the "teachers" in the Milgram experiments obeyed. After all, the entire experimental procedure from the beginning to the end made no logical sense even to a layman. You might agree that studying the effects of punishment on learning is worthwhile. But to arrive at the lab to find a person strapped to a chair and to be told that you must give him or her extremely

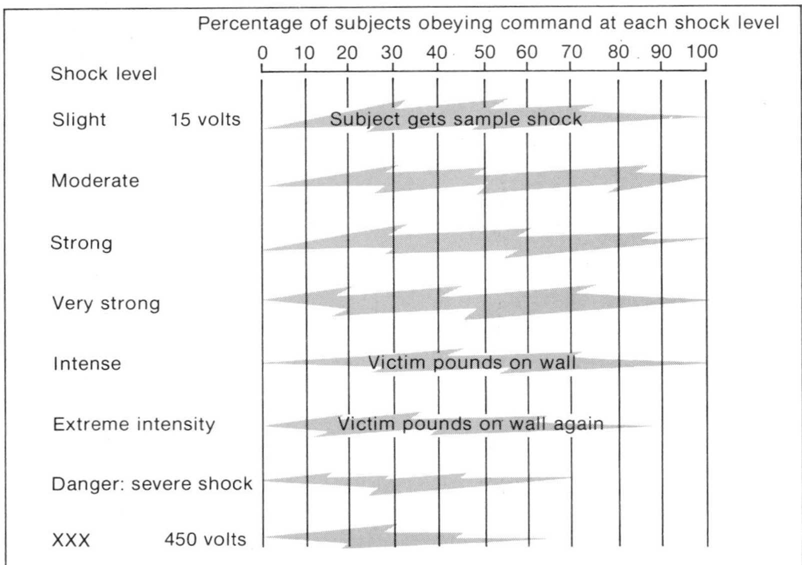

Figure 16–3.

painful and even dangerous shocks would seem to contribute little to the study of such effects, particularly since there is no way that the learner could learn the task in such a short time. The victim screams, pleads to be released, and finally falls silent; but the experimenter insists that the experiment continue. The further the experiment is carried, the more senseless it appears.

One explanation of the subjects' willingness to obey suggested that the prestigious setting of Yale University, where the experiment was conducted, fostered obedience. However, Milgram soon found that it was not necessary for a prestigious institution to sponsor and house the experiment in order to get the same effects. When the study was moved to a rundown office building in a nearby town, the level of obedience did drop, but a considerable number of subjects—48 percent as compared with the 65 percent at Yale—obeyed the experimenter to the end. Milgram concluded that instead of the physical setting, it was the physical presence of the commanding experimenter that was critical in producing the conformity that was observed.

Initially Milgram had planned to carry out his experiment with Americans and then use Germans to verify his hypothesis. However, the results of the first studies showed that Americans might have the same "character flaw" he was looking to find in Germans. Eight years later, variations of Milgram's experimental test of obedience were repeated in Munich (Mantell, 1971). The obedience rate in Germany was not significantly different from Milgram's original sample. As Mantell pointed out, the actual pressures that were brought to bear on a subject in the experiment were relatively mild when compared with the usual military, war, business, or family situation:

> The experimenter had no threats at his disposal which would in any way have impaired or imperiled the individual's physical well-being or the security of his family, job, community prestige, or peer relationships. It is clear that the ethical principles and legal restrictions surrounding laboratory research prohibit the use of threat of physical violence, social ostracism, or any other form of real intimidation. . . . In the absence of threat and the

CRITICAL ISSUE

Deception in Social Psychological Experiments

The Asch and especially the Milgram studies raise an important ethical question: Is the experimenter justified in deceiving research participants? According to the principles set forth by the American Psychological Association (1972), deception refers to misinforming subjects because honest participation may adversely affect a person's willingness to participate in the study. If Milgram had told his volunteers at the outset that they would have to deliver electric shocks to people, most of them would probably have refused to be part of such an experiment.

Deception may be necessary several times in the course of an experiment. Not only may the experimenter have to misrepresent the study to recruit subjects, he or she may have to use further deception, such as employing confederates, to conceal the point of the experiment. Even at the end, the investigator may decide that it is better to leave the subject misinformed about the true nature of the experiment, particularly if similar experiments are planned in the future and disclosure of the study's purpose may bias later subjects and hinder or prevent these further studies.

The APA set forth strict guidelines for studies that involve deception. For example, the experimenter must be able to demonstrate that the research problem is of great importance and that the research objectives cannot be realized without deception. Participants must be allowed to withdraw from the experiment at any time and to withdraw data they have contributed, after the deception is revealed. If the research exposed subjects to mental stress (as the Milgram studies did), the experimenter is obligated to have the subjects treated for any stressful after-effects.

In addition, the guidelines regulating deception studies require the researcher to delineate the procedure used, to clarify the nature of the study, and to explain the rationale for the deception in a post-experimental interview with research participants. This procedure is called **debriefing.** In the Milgram studies (1963, 1973), the two most important topics during debriefing were:

1. Was the debriefing effective in reducing the stress experienced by participants?
2. Was the debriefing effective in helping participants deal with the knowledge that they were capable of harming and possibly killing an innocent person simply on command of the experimenter?

Milgram (1964) stated that his discussion with the participants and the demonstration of the unharmed victim were effective in convincing subjects that, in fact, they had not harmed anyone. In most cases this was sufficient to reduce the stress they experienced. Milgram went even further and later appointed a psychiatrist to interview the subjects most likely to have suffered mental stress. The psychiatrist (Errera, 1972) reported that although several subjects had experienced severe stress during the experiment, he did not find evidence of any traumatic reaction.

Despite the elaborate debriefing procedure, the Milgram studies caused concern on several grounds. First, subjects' rights were violated in that they did not give permission for the experimenter to place them in a distressful conflict situation, and there could have been long-term effects. The Milgram studies could have had a negative effect on the self-concept of subjects since most of them saw themselves as someone who would not inflict pain on others. Also, some subjects may have lost trust in future experiments.

When faced with the necessity to deceive research participants, the investigator has to be able to present sufficient reason for maintaining the deception so that the subject, when informed about it, does not lose confidence in the integrity of the investigator.

The guidelines of the APA have helped reduce the problems associated with deception in experiments, but, as the authors concluded, no guidelines can be offered that would be accepted by all as a solution.

> possibility of personal gain, we are hard-pressed to find adequate explanations for the behavior observed in this experiment (p. 110).

In both the Asch and Milgram studies people acted in a way they would rather not have acted. The two experiments differed, however, in the degree to which participants were pressured to conform. In the Asch studies there were no direct commands, but the group consensus exerted great pressure on the individual. In the Milgram studies pressures to obey the experimenter were open and direct. In both situations the subject looked to others for information. In the Asch studies the naive subject turned to his peers, who were the source of the subject's conflict. In the Milgram studies the experiment itself caused conflict, and the teacher turned to the experimenter for guidance—only to find that the source of information put him deeper into conflict. And while it is hazardous to conclude that the extent of conformity observed in the Asch and Milgram laboratories parallels conformity in real life, these experiments are of considerable social relevance because they shed light on people's potential for engaging in destructive behavior.

The Prisoner's-Dilemma Game

In order to study how individuals try to resolve conflict in groups, researchers have developed conflict games in which incentives both to cooperate and to compete are present at the same time (Rubin & Brown, 1975).

One of the most widely used games is **prisoner's dilemma,** which is based on a problem faced by two "suspects." The rules of the game are derived from the following situation:

> Two suspects who the police believe participated in a murder are taken into custody and separated into different cells. The district attorney (DA) is certain that they are guilty but he does not have enough evidence to convict them. He therefore visits each of them separately; he points out to each prisoner that he has two alternatives, [to confess to] the crime he is held prisoner for or not to confess. If both suspects confess, the DA states that he will book them on some trumped-up minor charge . . . and they will both receive punishment. . . . But if one confesses and the other does not, then the confessor will receive lenient treatment whereas the other will get "the book" thrown at him (Luce & Raiffa, 1957, p. 75).

Let us examine the possible outcomes of the game, which can be represented as a decision matrix, a two-way table in which the outcome for each prisoner is recorded in terms of the prison sentence to be expected. As can be seen from Figure 16–4, the best possible outcome for the pair of suspects would be for both of them not to confess, that is, to make the cooperative response. That way, they will both receive a relatively light sentence. The prisoner's dilemma, however, is that if he trusts the other prisoner completely, he will do best by being untrustworthy himself and confessing. However, neither prisoner can benefit by a selfish choice enough to make up for the harm done to him from a selfish choice made by the other. If both defect—that is, if both confess—both do poorly (Axelrod, 1980). As Figure 16–4 indicates, both of them would get ten years in prison.

The prisoner's dilemma is a paradigm of many social situations in which there are rewards for cooperation and penalties for mutual noncooperation (Snyder, 1971). An obvious example in international politics is that of arms competition. It may be to the advantage of two nations to disarm and not to invest resources in a nuclear missile system. Yet the choice of nations, reflecting repeated findings obtained with individuals in the laboratory, is to select the noncooperative, competitive choice. In fact, as the stakes get higher, the level of cooperation decreases (Gumpert, Deutsch, & Epstein, 1969).

Conflict Resolution

When conflict in a group is not resolved, the group experiences frustration and hostility. Group cohesiveness disintegrates and group goals be-

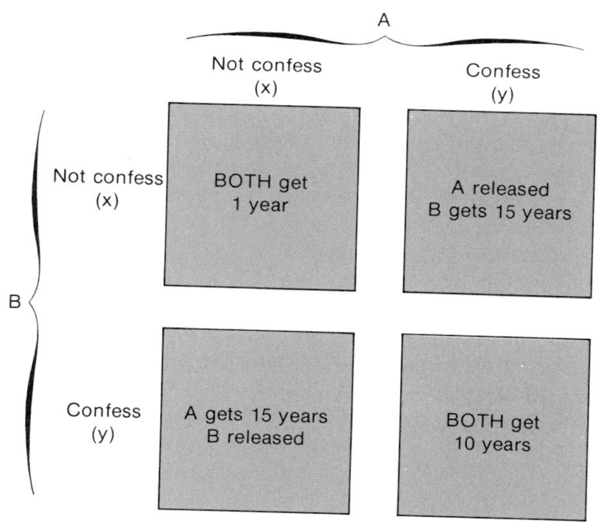

Figure 16–4.

come unobtainable because members of the group have polarized over a specific issue and reached an impasse (Kowitz & Knutson, 1980). At this point conflict may become dysfunctional because it interferes with the productivity of the group and may threaten its survival.

Since conflict can cause a breakdown in the functioning of the group, researchers have looked for ways to resolve conflict. Perhaps one of the most successful examples of conflict resolution was demonstrated in a study based on the concept of **superordinate goals,** that is, important goals that can be attained only through cooperation (Sherif & Sherif, 1953). In this study the experimenters selected members of two summer camps for boys and arranged for group interactions in such a way that one group, the Bull Dogs, interfered with or frustrated the other group, the Red Devils, in an athletic competition. Both groups were then invited to attend a party that had been arranged seemingly for the specific purpose of reducing frustration and group conflict. However, the experimenters had deliberately created a situation to make matters worse. When the Red Devils arrived at the mess hall, they found ice cream and cakes on the table. One half of the refreshments were battered or broken, while the other half was in pristine condition. The Red Devils were told to help themselves to their share and leave the Bull Dogs theirs. Needless to say, the Red Devils served themselves from the half that was in good condition, leaving the Bull Dogs with the messy portion. The Bull Dogs reacted to this treatment as you might predict—calling the Red Devils "pigs" and "bums."

At this point, the experimenters introduced a superordinate goal that could be accomplished only if both groups laid their conflict to rest. For example, the boys were required to recruit the best players from both groups for a campwide softball game to compete against a neighboring camp. The common goal brought the two groups together, generated cohesiveness, and led the two groups to form a new coalition that set out to defeat the boys from the neighboring camp.

The Sherif studies demonstrated that, when managed properly, conflict can serve to increase a group's cohesiveness and generate a feeling of excitement among group members. The introduction of superordinate goals apparently encouraged the two groups of campers to come up with conflict-reducing strategies (such as increased contact with each other, more open communications) that proved effective in solving the problem.

Conflict can also lead to greater productivity because it often forces a stalemate situation on the group that requires some kind of action. In many cities, for instance, groups of citizens have come together to solve local energy crises. Although these groups may disagree about how to handle the problem, with some proposing solar-energy shelters and others arguing for ways to reduce consumption, the flurry of activities generated by many of these groups favorably affects group productivity.

Finally, group conflict helps the group define itself more clearly and specify what the group stands for. Consciousness-raising groups, for instance, often determine their goals after deliberately generating a lot of upheaval among group members just to sharpen members' awareness on issues such as job discrimination or sexual harassment. Similarly, conflict helps members to establish themselves as distinct entities and makes the group more attractive for each member (Rosenfeld, 1976).

Sociologist Georg Simmel (1955) suggested two positive social roles of conflict. First, conflict gives rise to social change. Open conflict between blacks and whites in the Unites States, for instance, has led to many reforms that have benefited blacks. Second, following the motto "One unites in order to fight," conflict between groups may result in a new solidarity and unity within groups. Again, the experience of the two groups of boys in summer camp illustrates this concept. Similarly, the black movement has brought black Americans closer together. Thus conflict can serve as the medium through which problems can be aired and solutions arrived at (Deutsch, 1973).

GROUP DECISION MAKING

Many important decisions are worked out in groups. Political decisions, for instance, are often made by advisory groups, and business decisions are made by boards of directors of large corporations. Most of us, when presented with a problem, seek help from friends and relatives to arrive at a decision.

In the process of pursuing their objectives, groups are faced with the need to make decisions. Group decisions involve an exchange and processing of information, the presentation of arguments, and the attempt to arrive at a consensus. Generally group decisions are the result of a lot of group involvement (Wrightsman & Deaux, 1981). Most group decisions are reached through group discussions, which represent the major means of sharing information. The following example, described first by Kurt Lewin (1943), illustrates the value of group discussions in group decisions:

> During World War II when the price of food and particularly meat had gone up, the government was anxious to persuade the population to consume less expensive meats, particularly variety meats (e.g., brains, kidneys, etc.). Through press and radio appeals housewives were bombarded [with suggestions] to change their steak consumption in favor of variety meats. This turned out to be a very inefficient approach. Lewin argued that instead of appealing to individuals, the government needed to modify group attitudes concerning variety meats. In order to do this, Lewin recommended a group decision-making process as a means of propaganda. He recruited female Red Cross volunteers who understood the relationship between the dietary problem (expense of high quality meat) and the effort of the government to modify meat preferences in order to mobilize all resources. The women were divided into groups of 13 to 17 persons. They were then assigned to two different conditions: half of the group listened to a lady lecturing about the nutritional values of variety meats and discussed menus using these cheaper meats. The lecturer also had ample suggestions of how to eliminate undesirable aspects of variety meats such as odor, appearance, and texture. The other half of the group engaged in a discussion led by an experienced group worker. The discussion brought up the reasons why housewives and their families rejected the consumption of variety meats. After the discussion the group voted on the question of whether they should try to prepare one of the dishes using variety meats during the following week. At the end of the week, home interviews revealed that the lecture had an impact of ten percent on the participants (4 out of 41 housewives had served one of the suggested dishes) while the decision group affected 52 percent. The group discussion with its free interchange of ideas was found to be effective in overruling personal tastes in favor of a group goal (assist the government in its efforts to modify food preferences).

This example demonstrates the importance of three key elements in the collective decision-making process. First, it shows that involving participants in a discussion is more effective than giving them a lecture. Second, it suggests that decisions need to be backed up by a commitment, which was indicated by the fact that over 50 percent of the housewives in the discussion group actually served their families the less expensive meat. This followed directly from the degree of consensus attained by the group. This agreement made the participants feel that "we are all in this together."

Groupthink

Psychologists have long been interested in the differences between individual and group decisions. Because it is assumed that groups are less likely than individuals to "go off the deep end," many decisions are entrusted to groups (Baron & Byrne, 1981). However, recent research findings question this assumption. One phenomenon that appears to distinguish group from individual decision making is groupthink.

Groupthink was a concept developed by Irving Janis (1972) to describe decision making in highly cohesive groups. Janis, in analyzing a number of case studies in which government policy makers made serious errors, defined groupthink as "a mode of thinking that people engage in when they are deeply involved in a cohesive in-group, when the members' strivings for unanimity override their motivation to realistically appraise alternative courses of action" (p. 9). Before we examine the dynamics that lead to its occurrence, let us share with Janis one of his early observations of groupthink:

> In a study of heavy smokers at a clinic set up to help people to stop smoking, Janis noticed the irrational tendency for members to exert pressure on each other to increase their smoking as the time for the final meeting approached. A group member, for instance, took the position that heavy smoking is an almost incurable addiction. The majority of others agreed that no one could be expected to cut down drastically. One heavy smoker, a middle-aged executive, took issue with this consensus, arguing that by using will power he had stopped smoking since joining the group and that everyone should do the same. His declaration was followed by a heated discussion. Most of the others ganged up against the man who deviated from the group consensus. Then, at the beginning of the next meeting, the "deviant" announced that he had made an important decision. "When I joined," he said, "I agreed to follow the two main rules required by the clinic—to make a conscientious effort to stop smoking and to attend every meeting. But I have learned from experience in this group that you can only follow one of the rules, you can't follow both. And so, I have decided that I will continue to attend every meeting but I've gone back to smoking two packs a day and will not make an effort to stop smoking again until after the last meeting." Whereupon the other members beamed at him and applauded enthusiastically, welcoming him back to the fold. No one commented on the fact that the whole point of the meeting was to help each individual to cut down on smoking as rapidly as possible. When this was brought up in a group meeting by Janis, who served as a psychological consultant to the group, the members managed to ignore his comments and reiterated their consensus that heavy smoking was an addiction from which no one could be cured except by cutting down very gradually over a long period of time (Janis, 1972, pp. 8–9).

This observation highlights the dynamics of group decision making as well as the consequences of groupthink. Again, we find the elements of discussion among the smokers, commitment on the part of one group member to follow through with the decision to quit smoking, and finally the overwhelming consensus that heavy smoking is an incurable addiction. The pressures exerted by the group led to groupthink which in turn resulted in the demise of the group.

Factors Facilitating Groupthink. In his studies of major political decisions, such as the escalation of the Vietnam War, the Cuban invasion at the Bay of Pigs, and the decisions made by President Nixon during the Watergate affair, Janis (1972) found that group cohesiveness was the major factor in groupthink. The more cohesive a group of executive decision makers, the greater the likelihood that they will become victims of groupthink. Cohesiveness insulates decision makers from the influence of outside experts and makes them rationalize their present and past decisions. Highly cohesive groups also tend to have an illusion of invulnerability and put great pressure on dissenting members to get them to conform to their views.

APPLICATION

The Escalation of the Vietnam War

In his analysis of foreign-policy decisions that turned into political fiascoes, Janis (1972) searched for symptoms of groupthink. The Vietnam War, culminating in the ultimate decision to bomb North Vietnam, is one example that may at least in part be explained by the groupthink hypothesis.

Between 1964 and 1967 President Lyndon Johnson surrounded himself with a stable group of policy advisors who sometimes called themselves the "Tuesday Lunch Group." The group consisted of policy makers who had all the attributes of well-qualified leaders and more—as sincere Democrats they prided themselves on their humanitarian outlook and ideals. Paradoxically, however, they decided to use aerial bombardment, search and destroy missions, and the use of "whatever violent means are necessary to destroy the enemies' sanctuaries."

Historians, political analysts, and social psychologists recognized the poor quality of the decisions made by the inner circle of policy makers who regularly met with President Johnson to deliberate on what to do about the Vietnam War. The Department of Defense in 1971 published the most thorough analysis (known as the Pentagon Papers) of the Johnson administration's Vietnam War decisions. The authors emphasize time and again the poor quality of the decisions made by the group, particularly the failure to explore the full range of alternatives. The absence of critical debate about Vietnam policies led to the crucial decision made on February 13, 1965, to launch the air war against North Vietnam. As one observer noted, they (Johnson and his group of advisors) tended to conduct the affairs of the state almost as if they were a gentleman's club, and great decisions were often made in the warm camaraderie of a small board of directors deciding what the club's dues are going to be for the next year (Janis, 1972, p. 106).

Janis observed that after Johnson's landslide victory in the presidential election of 1964, self-confidence and a sense of omnipotence pervaded the thinking of Johnson's inner circle. These observations, directly in line with the groupthink hypothesis, suggest that during the deliberations about the escalation of the war, the members of the Johnson group shared the belief that everything would come out all right despite the gloomy predictions of the Central Intelligence Agency. Instead of paying attention to the pessimistic forecasts from experts, who predicted a long, costly involvement, President Johnson optimistically estimated that the "bombing would bring the enemy to the conference table or cause the insurgency to wither from lack of support." If accurate, the assumptions underlying the groupthink hypothesis would explain the erroneous decisions made by Johnson and his inner circle.

According to Janis, the occurrence of the groupthink phenomenon in the escalation of the Vietnam War is supported by the following observations:

1. The group tended to seek consensus instead of critically debating the issues under consideration.
2. Through group interaction and the established climate of cohesiveness, the group generated norms that all members wanted to live up to.
3. At the time when policy decisions had to be made, the group was operating under considerable external stress, namely time pressure. This time pressure generated an increased need for affiliation, a desire to find out what others were thinking about the issues at hand and how they might be dealt with. During the time of the deliberations, group members met more frequently and communicated more than before. Being drawn closely together further increased the group's cohesiveness, which in turn led to an increase in consensus-seeking at the expense of critical thinking. Since all the members of the inner circle were committed to the prior decisions of the group, none of them wanted to challenge the group's policy because it would result in discord and break up the group's unity.

For example, in the group surrounding President Johnson when the Vietnam War was being escalated, members rationalized that aerial destroy missions would bring the enemy to the conference table. Their feeling of immunity to failure not only led them to make bad decisions but also made them prone to defend those decisions with ardor. Deviants in the group were labeled "Mr. Stop-the-Bombing" or "our favorite dove."

Cohesiveness and insulation from external influence are responsible for the development of strong friendship ties and an esprit de corps that characterize groups that have become victims of groupthink. The desire to concur on important issues and to adhere to the group norms is strong enough to override any disagreement or deviance. In groups of this type, individual members are unlikely to take positions that threaten the unity of the group.

Preventing Groupthink. Groupthink interferes with the beneficial effects of cohesiveness because it leads to poor, ill-conceived decisions. Janis proposed that in order to prevent groupthink, leaders of decision-making groups should encourage each group member to function as a critical evaluator and to voice doubts and objections. In addition, the leader must be willing to demonstrate that he or she is open to influence from "deviant" group members. This way the leader reinforces criticism. In cohesive groups, independent subgroups should be set up to work on the same issues and arrive at solutions of the problem under different leaders. These in-groups should actively seek advice from qualified outsiders during their deliberations. Outsiders are likely to challenge the views of the core members of the group, thereby counteracting the complacency of the majority consensus. The president of a company, for instance, who encourages his or her department heads to express their opinions freely and who, in addition, hires a consultant and lets that person interact with the various departments is taking measures to prevent groupthink. These counteracting measures, however, pose one obvious risk: they may lower the group's cohesiveness and its morale.

It should be noted that groupthink is not the same as conformity to group pressures. As we have seen, members of highly cohesive groups are unlikely to deviate from the group's consensus. Conformity requires that deviant members are pressured to concur with the opinion of the group. In groupthink, however, members are not so much deviants as they are willing pawns of the group (Janis, 1972).

Despite the intuitive appeal of Janis's groupthink hypothesis, relatively few tests have been conducted to determine whether groupthink is really operating in the group decision-making process. Research that does exist only partially supports Janis's hypothesis. In a laboratory test of groupthink, for instance, group cohesiveness and leadership style were experimentally manipulated (Flowers, 1977). It was found that a closed leadership style led to few suggestions and a limited use of available facts. However, contrary to Janis's hypothesis, evidence of groupthink was reported in both high-cohesive and low-cohesive groups, suggesting that the phenomenon is more pervasive than Janis thought.

The Risky Shift

Contrary to the widely held notion that groups are more conservative and cautious than individuals, research conducted by Stoner (1961) and later confirmed by many experiments (e.g., Cartwright, 1971; Lamm & Myers, 1977) found that groups, after discussing an issue, show a greater willingness than individuals to make risky decisions. This phenomenon is called the **risky shift.** Most of the research is based on responses to a choice-dilemma questionnaire developed by Kogan and Wallach (1969) (see Table 16–2). This instrument consists of hypothetical choices that must be made, each of which is followed by statements regarding the probability of success of a particular choice.

Table 16–2. Choice-Dilemma Items

1. Ms. F is currently a college senior who is very eager to pursue graduate study in chemistry leading to the Doctor of Philosophy degree. She has been accepted by both University X and University Y. University X has a world-wide reputation for excellence in chemistry. While a degree from University X would signify outstanding training in this field, the standards are so very rigorous that only a fraction of the degree candidates actually receive the degree. University Y, on the other hand, has much less of a reputation in chemistry, but almost everyone admitted is awarded the Doctor of Philosophy degree, though the degree has much less prestige than the degree from University X.

Imagine that you are advising Ms. F. Listed below are several probabilities or odds that Ms. F would be awarded a degree at University X, with the greater prestige.

Please check the *lowest* probability that you would consider acceptable to make it worthwhile for Ms. F to enroll in University X rather than University Y.

——Place a check here if you think Ms. F should *not* enroll in University X, no matter what the probabilities.
——The chances are 9 in 10 that Ms. F would receive a degree from University X.
——The chances are 7 in 10 that Ms. F would receive a degree from University X.
——The chances are 5 in 10 that Ms. F would receive a degree from University X.
——The chances are 3 in 10 that Ms. F would receive a degree from University x.
——The chances are 1 in 10 that Ms. F would receive a degree from University X.

2. Mr. A, an electrical engineer, who is married and has one child, has been working for a large electronics corporation since graduating from college five years ago. He is assured of a lifetime job with a modest, though adequate, salary, and liberal pension benefits upon retirement. On the other hand, it is very unlikely that his salary will increase much before he retires. While attending a convention, Mr. A is offered a job with a small, newly founded company that has a highly uncertain future. The new job would pay more to start and would offer the possibility of a share in the ownership if the company survived the competition of the larger firms.

Imagine that you are advising Mr. A. Listed below are several probabilities or odds of the new company's proving financially sound.

Please check the *lowest* probability that you would consider acceptable to make it worthwhile for Mr. A to take the new job.

——The chances are 1 in 10 that the company will prove financially sound.
——The chances are 3 in 10 that the company will prove financially sound.
——The chances are 5 in 10 that the company will prove financially sound.
——The chances are 7 in 10 that the comapny will prove financially sound.
——The chances are 9 in 10 that the company will prove financially sound.
——Place a check here if you think Mr. A should *not* take the new job no matter what the probabilities.

Source: Baron and Byrne (1981, pp. 576–77), adapted from Kogan and Wallach (1964).

Participants in the experiments, usually seated around a table, were asked first to complete the questionnaire as individuals and then to discuss the items as a group and reach a unanimous decision. The group decision typically involved a higher risk than the average of the decisions made by individuals. The discovery of the risky shift, unexpected as it was, left social psychologists with the task of explaining why individuals in groups tend to shift from a conservative to a risky position. Why would a subject initially believe that Mr. A should not take the new job that was offered him and then change his or her opinion in a group?

For the risky shift to occur, at least two conditions must be present. The first condition is group discussion. Many studies have demonstrated that a collective exchange of information leading to a group consensus is a prerequisite for the risky shift. The second condition is a divergence of initial opinions. Several studies (e.g., Hoyt & Stoner, 1968) have shown that the greater the initial divergence in individual positions, the greater the shift toward riskier decisions.

It has been found, however, that the risky shift does not always occur under these conditions. In studies using choice-dilemma questionnaires, the risky shift was mainly found on items that oriented subjects toward taking chances. By changing the content of the instructions, researchers have been able to produce cautious shifts. Willems and Clark (1969), for instance, produced a cautious shift by eliminating a single word from the traditional instructions. In this study, half of the subjects received instructions used in previous research ("check the lowest probability . . . "), and the other half received neutral instructions ("check the probability . . . "). The risky shift occurred only with the former, risk-oriented instruction.

More recently (Clement & Sullivan, 1970; Knox & Stafford, 1976), cautious shifts have been produced in a variety of naturalistic settings. McCauley and his coworkers (1973), for instance, reported a significant shift to caution for group bettors at a Philadelphia race track.

Such findings make earlier explanations of the risky shift untenable. They proposed that familiarity with the issue under discussion, group leaders who are willing to take risks, or the individual's freedom from taking responsibility for the group's decision are responsible for the risky shift. More recently, the risky shift has been interpreted as a more general phenomenon—a **shift toward polarization** (Lamm & Myers, 1978). According to this interpretation, group discussion produces a shift in individual opinion, but not necessarily in the direction of greater risk. Although group discussion may lead individuals to become more extreme, their change may take either a risky or conservative form. It has been found, for instance, that if the initial opinions of the group tend toward conservatism, then the shift resulting from group discussion will be toward a more conservative position (Myers and Bishop, 1970). The concept of polarization—the tendency of groups to become either more conservative or more risk-oriented depending on the initial opinion of the majority or on the need to reach a consensus—has more or less replaced the concept of risky shift.

In the past, too much reliance has probably been placed upon choice-dilemma problems that describe hypothetical situations. In real-life situations, such as playing blackjack with monetary risks, the relative levels of risk found acceptable by individuals acting independently and in groups seem to be situationally specific. In the real world, shifts toward risk or caution are likely to depend on the circumstances.

LEADERSHIP

Of all the roles available in a group, the leadership role is the most important and most valued. When thinking about leadership and leaders, various questions come to mind. Why and how do people come to power? Why do people zealously follow some leaders and not others? What constitutes good leadership? What differentiates leaders from followers?

The central attribute of leadership is influence. The person who is able to initiate group activities and supervise the accomplishment of group goals, who provides guidelines and sustains the efforts of the members, and who makes decisions and gives orders is usually perceived as the leader of the group. To become a leader, a person must want to lead, must have certain skills, and must be reinforced by the group (Kowitz & Knutson, 1980). In most groups, leaders emerge gradually through a process of elimination. Usually the longer a leader is in power, the more likely his or her leadership is to be accepted by the group members.

Certain situations are particularly conducive to the emergence of leaders: in ambiguous or stressful circumstances or in crisis situations groups are particularly prone to seek a leader. For example, Thomas Jefferson in the United States, Oliver Cromwell in England, Joseph Stalin in Russia, and Fidel Castro in Cuba were leaders who emerged during revolutionary crises and continued in power after the revolution.

The Trait Approach versus the Situational Approach

Reading the early literature on leadership, one gets the impression that leaders are born. Although some early writers suggested that leaders acquire the necessary characteristics of their role while actually leading, they assumed that leaders possess certain inherent leadership traits. Bird (1940), for instance, identified intelligence, initiative, a sense of humor, and extroversion as traits of leadership. Observations of world leaders such as Jomo Kenyatta, Indira Gandhi, Charles de Gaulle, and Golda Meir, to name just a few, seemed to substantiate the belief that some persons are born to lead. Such leaders seem to share certain qualities, such as will power, boundless energy, and a genuine concern for the welfare of their people. This approach became known as the **trait approach,** or the great man theory of leadership. It implied that we can render groups more effective by selecting leaders who possess leadership traits.

Although the trait approach does not enable us to predict who will become leaders and who will not, we can make some generalizations with respect to traits. Some characteristics, such as intelligence or general skills, have been found in many leaders. Group leaders, to a greater extent than other group members, have also demonstrated traits such as sociability, popularity, motivation, self-confidence, and sensitivity to the needs of others. It should be pointed out, however, that for each study reporting a positive correlation between a specific trait and leadership, there is another one indicating the absence of any such relationship. For example, many studies relate superior height, weight, or energy to leadership. As we know, however, leaders such as Napoleon, Hitler, or Mohandas Gandhi were neither taller nor heavier than their followers.

Research has shown that leaders must not be too different from the rest of the group. In most cases, group members prefer their leader to be one of them. With respect to intelligence, for instance, Gibb (1969) noted that if too much discrepancy exists between the leader's level of intelligence and the average intelligence level of the group, the leader's success in initiating and maintaining his or her role may be hampered. As Gibb stated, "The evidence suggests that every increment in intelligence means wiser government but that the crowd prefers to be ill-governed by people it can understand" (p. 218).

One rather elusive trait that many people associate with leadership is **charisma.** Charisma is difficult to define. For most of us, it refers to a person's mysterious ability to control others and to accomplish goals even in the face of great obstacles. Charismatic leaders possess magnetic qualities that cause followers to play into their hands. Most of us would describe John F. Kennedy and Fidel Castro as charismatic, but not Richard Nixon and Gerald Ford. In fact, managers in the Nixon presidential campaigns spent a great deal of time trying to make him more charismatic, only to find that charisma is difficult to attain.

Fidel Castro and John Kennedy are thought by many to be charismatic leaders. (© *Burt Glinn / Magnum Photos; Cornell Capa / Magnum Photos*)

Since it seems impossible to measure charisma objectively, we have no data supporting or refuting charisma as an essential leadership trait.

Overall, research testing the assumptions of the trait approach has been disappointing. We have learned from these studies that we know very little about the personality of leaders. Psychologists have concluded that the trait concept of leadership is of little value in selecting leaders. The more prevalent belief today is that leadership is primarily determined by the situation. According to this view, which can be called the **situational approach,** the leader is one who best grasps the psychosocial climate of contemporary events. It has been suggested that Fidel Castro is a leader in whom the trait and the situational approaches are integrated (Marlowe, 1975).

The situational theory of leadership argues that the person most likely to emerge as leader in any given setting is the individual whose special skill and competence are suited to the goals the group is set up to accomplish. In other words, it is the particular task and the particular situation rather than a few crucial traits that determine who becomes a leader. The situational approach to leadership implies that a person who acts effectively as a leader in one situation may well have to settle for a less demanding role in another situation.

Nevertheless, the trait approach to leadership endures. Just ask a friend who is not taking an introductory course in psychology to describe a leader. The response will probably focus on some presumed trait, since most of us have been taught to think of our leaders as supermen or superwomen endowed with highly desirable personality characteristics.

Leadership Style

Leadership style refers to varieties of behavior that characterize the leader's activities. This behavior may or may not reflect personality attributes of the leader (Fiedler, 1967).

Psychologists describe two broad categories of leadership style: **task-oriented leadership** and **socially oriented leadership.** The task-oriented leader is concerned with efficiency and with guiding the group toward its goal. The socially oriented leader concentrates on social and emotional group processes, such as helping to boost the morale of the group and to release tension when the group is confronted with problems. Effective leaders typically use both styles comfortably.

Another way of defining leadership style is by arranging leaders' behavior along a continuum ranging from autocracy on one end to laissez-faire leadership at the other. Leadership studies conducted in the 1930s under the supervision of Kurt Lewin (Lewin et al., 1939) brought forth three leadership styles: autocratic, democratic, and laissez-faire. The **autocratic leader** is one who makes all the decisions for the group and exerts close control over the group's activities. Under autocratic leadership, group members become increasingly dependent on their leader, who makes himself or herself indispensable to the group. Autocratic leaders overemphasize the task dimensions of their group and keep group participation at an absolute minimum.

Along the middle of the continuum we find the **democratic leader,** who solicits the input of the group and encourages members to share in the decision-making process. While democratic leaders usually have as much power as autocratic leaders, they use their power in a different way. Democratic leaders permit participation of all group members and encourage interaction and involvement of the group in the accomplishment of the group's goals. Instead of functioning in their own best interests, democratic leaders are concerned with the welfare of the group and tend to emphasize the social-emotional dimension of the group.

The other extreme of the continuum is occupied by the **laissez-faire leader.** This style of leadership implies that the leader leads through not leading at all. The laissez-faire leader allows the group to make all decisions. In a way, the laissez-faire leader acts as a member of the group. Because of the difficulty in assessing this type of leadership, we are essentially left with the autocratic and democratic styles. Table 16–3 summarizes the various positions leaders can take along the leadership continuum.

Leaders can, of course, choose behavioral styles between the ends of the continuum, or they can choose different positions at different times. Most leaders select a style somewhere between the autocratic and democratic extremes, based on an assessment of the situation, their own skills, and the characteristics of the group (Fiedler, 1971).

Effective Leadership

Research on leadership styles has raised the question about the relative effectiveness of the different styles. Comparisons between autocratic and democratic leaders have revealed some differences between groups functioning under each of the two styles. For example, groups with a democratic leader reported more satisfaction with the interpersonal atmosphere in the group, while groups with authoritarian leaders were more efficient and productive. However, productivity and group satisfaction were interrelated. Group members who experienced greater satisfaction with a democratic leader also tended to work harder to achieve the group's goals or to increase its productivity. By the same token, productive groups under autocratic leadership experienced pride in their accomplishments and hence an increase in satisfaction. Again, this indicates that depending on the particular situation, both democratic and autocratic leaders can generate productivity in their groups and at the same time create a basis for interpersonal and emotional satisfaction.

Moreover, leadership style seems to be affected by particular circumstances, including features of the group itself (such as its role structure), the nature of the task and the group's interest in it, and the physical and general cultural setting in which the group operates. If Hitler, for instance, had espoused his ideas in the United States rather than

Table 16–3. The Leadership Continuum

Leader-Centered Autocratic						Group-Centered Democratic
1	2	3	4	5	6	7
Leader decides; announces decisions.	Leader decides, sells decisions.	Leader presents ideas; invites questions.	Leader presents tentative ideas that are subject to change.	Leader presents alternatives; group decides.	Leader defines boundaries; group decides.	Group defines boundaries and decides.

Source: Adapted from Napier and Greshenfeld (1973).

in Germany, he might have been committed to a penal institution or a mental hospital. In Germany, however, the time and the situation were right for Germans to become followers of a leader like Hitler, who exemplified an extreme autocratic, leader-centered approach.

In an attempt to identify the components of effective leadership, Fred Fiedler (1967) proposed a model known as the **contingency model of leadership effectiveness.** This theory predicts that the leader's contribution to group effectiveness is dependent on characteristics of both the leader and the situation. According to Fiedler, there is no one type of successful leader. Some circumstances may call for the authoritarian style. Imagine yourself bleeding and in pain on the operating table in an emergency room, and you hear the surgeon say to his or her team, "Now, we have a problem here; let us get together and discuss what we should do with this patient." Other circumstances may call for a permissive, democratic leader. A leader of a therapy group, for instance, may be very permissive and encourage individual members to express themselves honestly, and he may be concerned with rewarding interpersonal experiences.

According to Fiedler's model, the identification of leadership style is based on the extent of the leader's esteem for the least preferred coworker (LPC). A paper-and-pencil test requires the leader to think about all the people with whom he or she has worked and to select the person he or she liked least. This person is the least preferred coworker. Fiedler thought of the LPC score as an indication of a leader's emotional reaction to people with whom he or she could not work well.

In an extensive series of studies, Fiedler (1958, 1971) found that leaders with high LPC scores, that is, those who perceived their least preferred coworker in a relatively favorable manner, tend to be permissive, relaxed, less directive, and more concerned with the group's needs for successful interpersonal relationships than with the accomplishment of the group's goals. For this type of leader, satisfaction comes from friendly group relations. In contrast, the leader with a low LPC score perceives the least preferred coworker in a highly negative, rejecting manner and is primarily motivated by successful task completion. This type of leader tends toward an autocratic leadership position. The more officially sanctioned power this leader has, the easier it is for him or her to lead.

Fiedler compared democratic and autocratic leaders on the basis of leader-member relations, the structure of tasks, and the leader's power. He concluded that a human-relation-oriented leader is most effective when leader-member relations are good, the task structure is ambiguous, and the leader's power is weak. Task-oriented leaders are most effective when there are good leader-member relations, and when there is a clear task structure and strong power.

The general conclusion we can draw from Fiedler's massive research is that there is no such thing as one effective leader for all situations. The task, the power of the leader, and leader-follower relationships, as well as the specific political situation, all play an important role in determining the degree of effectiveness that any given leader will be able to have.

Summary

Membership in groups is an important aspect of our social life. Most of us are attracted to groups because they satisfy needs, such as the need to belong or the desire to take part in certain activities. As groups are formed and establish themselves, they go through various phases. They also assign roles and develop group norms of some kind, formal or informal, explicit or implicit. These norms provide the rules or standards regulating the behavior of group members. An important way in which groups differ is their degree of cohesiveness.

Adherence to group norms is labeled conformity. Investigations conducted by Solomon Asch and Stanley Milgram examined the dynamics of conformist behavior. The Asch studies showed that group judgments can have a profound influence on individual judgments, often to the point that many of us are willing to betray the reality of our senses to go along with the opinion of the majority. Both group size and unanimity affect conformity; when unanimity is broken by one dissenter, conformity is sharply reduced. The Milgram experiments showed that many people are willing to inflict pain on others simply because they are required by an experimenter to do so. These studies raised many serious questions concerning obedience in real life. Conformity situations often put an individual in conflict because the person has to choose between two opposing value systems. Conflicts can also occur between groups. Experimental resolutions of group conflict have used threats or superordinate goals.

Since many important social and political decisions are made in groups, psychologists have studied the processes that influence group decisions. Two specific phenomena are groupthink and the risky shift. In groupthink a decision-making body develops a problem-solving approach that is closed to critical input of both deviant group members and outsiders. Groupthink is particularly common in cohesive groups and has been responsible for major foreign-policy fiascoes. Contrary to what one might expect, groups have been found to make riskier decisions than individuals are willing to make. The polarization hypothesis, which suggests that groups move in the direction of the majority's initial orientation, accounts for both cautious and risky shifts in group decisions.

Whenever groups develop, the problem of leadership emerges. In the past, numerous studies were conducted to identify the traits characterizing leaders. Today psychologists believe that leadership cannot be defined only by some combination of traits. Fiedler's contingency model of leadership combines leadership style and situational variables in an attempt to predict leadership effectiveness. This model is important because it specifies what kinds of behavior are likely to be the most effective in a given situation of leadership.

Key Terms For Review

autocratic leader
autokinetic effect
balance phase
charisma
conflict phase
conformity
contingency model of leadership effectiveness
debriefing
democratic leader
deviance
group cohesiveness
groupthink
laissez-faire leader
norms
orientation phase
parting phase
prisoner's dilemma
private acceptance
reference norm
risky shift
role
shift toward polarization
simple compliance
situational approach
social-comparison theory
social control
socially oriented leadership
sociogram
sociometric choice
superordinate goals
task-oriented leadership
trait approach

Suggested Readings

Billig, M. *Social psychology and intergroup relations.* New York: Academic Press, 1976.
This book focuses attention on topics and issues that are not conventionally discussed by social psychologists. Topics include game theory, group ideology, the context of intergroup relations, and social identity.

Carlsmith, M., Ellsworth, P., & Aronson, E. *Methods of research in social psychology.* Reading, Mass.: Addison-Wesley, 1976.
This book discusses research methods and issues in social psychology, including nonexperimental research, deception, ethics, and postexperimental interviews.

Fiedler, F., & Chemers, M. *Leadership and effective management.* Chicago: Scott, Foresman, 1974.
The authors present a comprehensive review of the leadership research and provide an excellent background for those who would like to learn more on this topic.

Milgram, S. *Obedience to authority.* New York: Harper & Row, 1973.
This book presents a detailed description of the author's extensive research on obedience. The results of Milgram's findings are reviewed in the context of the social implications of this important body of research.

Strickland, L. (Ed.). *Soviet and Western perspectives in social psychology.* New York: Pergamon Press, 1979.
This book, the outcome of an international conference of social psychologists, highlights the differences in East-West orientations in social psychology. Topics include American and Soviet theories and methodologies, the development of social psychology in the USSR, and comparative social psychology.

17

Human Sexual Behavior

Lisa came from a typical family that included, along with her mother and father, an older sister and a younger brother. When asked to recall her childhood memories and experiences related to sex, Lisa reports that nothing in particular stands out in her mind. She has vague memories that when she was 5 or 6 years old she wanted to marry her father when she grew up. She does not remember very much specific information about sex given to her by her parents except for when her mother explained menstrual cycles when Lisa was approaching puberty. She also recalls that in her early teenage years she had the strong belief that premarital sex was wrong, although she cannot remember either of her parents saying anything explicit about it.

Near the end of her freshman year in college Lisa had her first experience of sexual intercourse. She had some conflicts about it, but she believed that she would marry the boy when they graduated so it seemed okay. Her ambivalent feelings were also evident in that she did not use any birth control for the first two months of her sexual relationship. To do so, Lisa believed, would cheapen the relationship. She did seek contraception when she realized that she was not ready to be a parent and that she was not sure that she wanted to marry her boyfriend.

Lisa had two other premarital affairs before she married at age 23. Although she enjoyed these relationships and had an orgasm on occasion, she was puzzled by the urgency for sex her partners seemed to feel. After six months of marriage she began to appreciate such feelings. She had a satisfying sexual relationship with her husband, had orgasm regularly, and eagerly anticipated upcoming sexual encounters.

Her sexual life progressed smoothly for several years. Then, when her husband was going through a stressful job transition, problems began to develop. During this period, her husband had little interest in sex, but to please Lisa he would engage in intercourse. On these occasions he would have an orgasm very rapidly, leaving Lisa feeling frustrated and unsatisfied. After a few months, Lisa began to approach each sexual encounter with the fear that she again would be left unsatisfied, and she was finding it increasingly difficult to become sexually aroused. When her husband's job situation improved and he resumed his typical pattern of sexual response, Lisa still was unable to experience orgasm. Several more months passed with no improvement, so Lisa and her husband consulted a clinical psychologist who specialized in sexual problems. The consultation proved helpful, and the problem was well on its way to being resolved within a brief period of time.

There is nothing unusual about Lisa's sexual history. It is so typical, in fact, that the average person may not even be prompted to ask questions about it. But human sexual behavior is extremely complex, and the psychologist would be aware of several issues raised by Lisa's history. For example, how did Lisa develop her attitudes toward sex? How typical is her pattern of sexual behavior? What role, if any, do hormones play in Lisa's interest in sex? Why was Lisa unable to enjoy sex after her husband's problems were resolved? In the past decades psychologists and other specialists have been conducting research to answer these and other questions.

In this chapter we shall examine patterns of sexual behavior and various types of sexual dysfunctions and variations. But first let us see how biological, psychological, and social factors contribute to human sexual behavior.

BIOLOGICAL FACTORS

Clearly, there is a biological basis for sexual behavior. Both animals and humans are motivated to seek sexual release, and coitus (sexual intercourse) is necessary for the survival of the species. Still, numerous myths regarding the biological basis of sexual behavior have been popular at one time or another. For example, in the latter part of the nineteenth century, when sex manuals began to appear, husbands were cautioned to keep their "animalistic" desires under control so as not to harm their wives' delicate natures. This view of women as biologically asexual creatures persisted well into the twentieth century. As recently as the 1950s a book entitled *Kinsey's Myth of Female Sexuality* (Bugler & Kroger, 1950), which was written to refute current ideas that millions of women were having and enjoying sex, was quite influential in some scientific and professional circles.

Researchers today recognize that both men and women need and enjoy sex, and these researchers are studying more sophisticated issues. Two such issues are the physiology of sexual arousal and the biological basis of sexual drive and interest.

Physiology of Sexual Arousal

In the middle 1950s William Masters and Virginia Johnson (1966) began to investigate the physiological changes that accompany sexual arousal in men and women. They observed and recorded the responses of over 1,200 men and women during some 10,000 sexual-response cycles, including intercourse and masturbation. Their research helped to make the study of human sexuality respectable. It dispelled myths and provided objective information about the physiology of sexual arousal.

One important finding was that the physiological responses of men and women are very similar and that this holds true regardless of whether the stimulation is masturbation or coitus. Two major responses for both sexes are the swelling of the genitals through collecting of blood there and an increase in muscle tension.

Although the pattern of sexual arousal varies from person to person, Masters and Johnson suggested that the sexual response cycle can be divided into four stages. These are excitement, plateau, orgasm, and resolution. The **excitement phase,** which can last from several minutes to several hours, is characterized by elevation and enlargement of the genital areas. In women vaginal lubrication and enlargement of the clitoris occurs, and in men the penis becomes enlarged and erect. During the **plateau phase,** increases in heart rate, blood pressure, muscular tension, and glandular secretions all accompany increases in subjective sexual arousal, that is, the person's mental readiness for sex. Women, more so than men, may experience a coloring of the body, called sex flush, during this stage. **Orgasm,** the third phase, refers to the very intense, pleasurable release from sexual tension. Rhythmic contractions in the genital areas occur every eight-tenths of a second for both men and women. In men this is accompanied with ejaculation—a sudden release of semen. During the **resolution phase,** the body gradually returns to its normal preexcitement state.

Masters and Johnson's (1966) research destroyed the myth that women have less interest in and less capacity for sexual response. The resolution phase differs for men and women. Men enter a **refractory period** during which they are incapable of having erection or orgasm. This period, which varies from one man to another, can last from a few minutes to several hours and tends to increase with age. Women, on the other hand, do not enter into a refractory period; they are able to have multiple orgasms. In fact, several women reported that they would have 20 orgasms or more when masturbating and would stop only when physically exhausted. Women clearly have greater sexual capacity than men do. Masters and Johnson (1970) suggested that the view of women as asexual may have evolved because men feel threatened by the superior sexual capacity of women.

Masters and Johnson have been pioneers in sex therapy. (© *Magnum Photos*)

A second myth that was shattered concerned the issue of vaginal versus clitoral orgasm in women. Sigmund Freud believed that these two forms of orgasm existed and that women who had clitoral orgasms were emotionally immature. This view, which persisted until Masters and Johnson's work, undoubtedly caused many women grief. Why were they not able to achieve the more mature, and supposedly more satisfying, vaginal orgasm? Masters and Johnson demonstrated that all female orgasms are the same physiologically, regardless of whether they are achieved by intercourse or by masturbation. Of course, there may be subjective differences between orgasms that are achieved in different ways, but the clitoris is almost always involved in both types of orgasm.

Physiological Basis of the Sexual Drive

As you will recall from Chapter 9, the sex hormones (estrogen in women and testosterone in men) play an important role in the development of gender identity. These hormones are also important to sexual drive and interest (Beach, 1977). Research with animals has shown that estrogen is crucial for females to accept and cooperate sexually with males. The degree of control that estrogen exerts varies from species to species. Animals such as rats, mice, and hamsters will rarely, if ever, cooperate in copulation if estrogen is absent. In more complex animals, such as monkeys and chimpanzees, sexual readiness is clearly related to estrogen levels in the system, but copulation does occur even when there are low levels of this hormone.

There is some doubt that these findings from animal research can be generalized to women (Money, 1977). Studies investigating women's sex drive across the menstrual cycle, when estrogen levels vary, typically produce unclear or contradictory results (Greenblatt & McNamara, 1976). At present, there is no conclusive evidence that sex in women is related to estrogen levels. (This holds true for adult women who have not experienced medical problems involving hormones either prenatally or prior to puberty. For a discussion of such effects, see Chapter 9.)

In males, both animal and human, testosterone levels are related to the ability to develop penile erections and to ejaculate. Clinical cases involving men who are deprived of testosterone usually find that there is a reduction in sexual drive and interest. And those men who have deficient levels of this hormone often report an increase in their sex drive after receiving supplemental injections (Money & Ehrhardt, 1972).

Recent research has found that testosterone may also be responsible for sex drive in women. Certain medical conditions require administration of this hormone to women, and they often report an increase in their sex drive. This finding has led John Money (1977) to refer to testosterone as the "libido" hormone. For women, as well as men, some critical level of testosterone appears to be necessary for sexual drive and interest. Once that level has been reached, additional dosages will not produce additional increases in sex drive.

Important as hormones are to providing a basis for sexual drive, social-learning experiences are more important, particularly with humans. Some men whose hormone levels are reduced by castration, accidentally or surgically, maintain their sexual interest and ability for several years. Furthermore, hormones have no effect on the direction of sex drive. For example, attempts to orient homosexual males toward heterosexuality by administering testosterone to them have not been successful. Such men may experience an increase in sex drive, but they remain homosexual.

To sum up, biological factors can be viewed as providing a basis for human sexual response. Men and women experience fairly specific physiological changes during the sexual-response cycle, and their biological heritage provides an impetus for seeking sexual release. The biological impetus, however, is subject to modification by environmental forces. Two individuals who are similar biologically may behave quite differently sexually. One person may remain chaste for his or her entire life with little difficulty, while the other may desire frequent intercourse with a variety of partners. The next two sections will explore the factors that act on our biological heritage.

PSYCHOLOGICAL FACTORS

Individuals express their sexuality and gratify their sexual drives in an almost infinite variety of ways. Lisa, portrayed at the beginning of the chapter, probably represents a fairly typical pattern of sexual behavior. But she might be viewed as prudish by some people who believe that a wider variety of activities is important to sexual satisfaction. Others might be shocked by Lisa's premarital affairs. They might feel that occasional intercourse within the context of a traditional marriage is the only appropriate way of satisfying sexual urges.

Differences in sexual behavior and attitudes generally have their origins in childhood. As part of the process of personality development, children acquire sexual attitudes and values that will influence their adult sexual behavior. Personality theorists do not always agree on why this is so (see Chapter 10), but there is little doubt that, to some extent, psychological factors contributing to sexual behavior are based on childhood experiences.

Development of Sexual Attitudes

Sol Gordon (1976), a widely respected sex educator, has written that all parents engage in sex education whether they are aware of it or not. This education can begin as early as age one or two, when children begin to show an interest in their own genitals and those of their playmates, run through the house with no clothes on, and so on. Children of parents who are accepting of such displays of sexual interest will learn attitudes that are quite different from those of children whose parents punish any sign of sexual interest. Parents also provide sex education by the way they express (or do not express) affection toward each other, by their reactions to televised shows related to sex, and by their willingness to answer questions about sex. These are but a few examples of indirect methods of sex education, which probably have as much psychological impact as do more explicit methods.

People who have acquired the attitude that sex is vulgar and dirty are considered to have **sex-negative attitudes** (LoPiccolo, 1978). In extreme cases, as we shall see later in the chapter, sex-negative attitudes, or sexual guilt, can contribute to sexual problems, but they can also influence behavior in less dramatic but important ways (Janda & Klenke-Hamel, 1980).

Clinical psychologist Donald Mosher (1965, 1966) has developed a scale to measure sex guilt and a hypothesis to account for behavioral differences between high-guilt and low-guilt individuals. He has suggested that high-guilt people behave in accord with internalized standards of right and wrong, while low-guilt people look for external cues to see how others will react. When faced with a decision to behave in a sexual manner, the high-guilt person will decide whether such behavior is acceptable according to his or her own standards. The low-guilt person will evaluate the situation to determine whether a sexual response will be met with approval or disapproval. If approval is expected, the sexual response will be made; if disapproval is expected, it will not be made.

To illustrate, consider a woman who has an opportunity to have an extramarital affair. If she has a high level of sex guilt, she will reflect on her standards of morality. She may decide (as most high-guilt people do) that extramarital sex is wrong, and hence she will not enter into the affair. If the woman is low in sex guilt, she will consider external factors. What is the probability that the affair will be detected? How will her relationship with her family be affected? Her answers to such questions will influence her decision.

In an experiment designed to test Mosher's hypothesis, college women were administered a word-association test containing numerous sexual **double-entendre words** (e.g., "screw," "broad"). The test was administered under two different conditions. In one, an experimenter was present in the room; in the other, the experimenter was absent and the subjects made their responses into a tape recorder. The latter condition was designed to reduce subjects' possible fears of disapproval for making sexual responses (e.g., "make love," "woman"). As Mosher hypothesized, women who received high scores on his measure of sex guilt tended to make about the same number of sexual responses in both conditions. They appeared to be responding in accord with their internalized standards of proper behavior. The women who scored low on the guilt scale, however, made significantly more sexual responses when the experimenter was absent from the room. Their behavior was more sensitive to situational cues (Janda & O'Grady, 1976).

This difference in sensitivity to external cues extends to ways in which high- and low-guilt men perceive women (Janda, 1975; Janda, Witt, & Manahan, 1976). In one experiment men were asked to interact with a woman who was trained to play one of two roles. For half of the men she played a warm, friendly, approachable role. For the other half, she acted cold, distant, and unapproachable. Ratings of the woman by the male subjects indicated that the low-guilt men reacted much more favorably to her when she played the warm and friendly role than when she played the cold and distant role. The men high in sex guilt, however, rated the woman in the two roles equally favorably. Perhaps men high in sex guilt are unable to detect cues given by women that signal an interest in pursuing a relationship. Sex guilt seems to influence the ability simply to establish relationships with members of the opposite sex, as well as influence more direct sexual behavior.

Interpersonal attraction involves many biological, psychological, and social factors. (© *Eric Kroll/Taurus Photos*)

Patterns of Sexual Arousal

Psychological factors also affect patterns of sexual arousal. Men and women can become aroused by a wide variety of stimuli. Some men find full-figured women highly arousing, while others prefer slender, willowy women. Some women are sexually aroused by intelligence and scholarliness in a man, while others are interested in athletic, muscular men. Some individuals are aroused by articles of clothing, such as high-heeled boots or black leather garments. In more unusual patterns, people respond sexually to the infliction of pain or to individuals with amputated limbs.

An interesting example of individual preferences can be seen in actress Shelley Winters's revelation of how she and Marilyn Monroe compared notes about the men they would like to seduce. Winters was interested in men who were known for their physical sex appeal, such as Burt Lancaster, Clark Gable, and Errol Flynn. Monroe was more interested in men such as Albert Einstein who had achieved eminence in their field.

Various psychological theories have been developed to explain these differences. Psychoanalytic theorists would suggest that sexual preferences have their origins in one of the early psychosexual stages (see Chapter 10). A man or woman may be attracted to individuals who possess characteristics similar to those of the mother or father. These theorists would suggest that Lisa's desire to marry her father when she was very young was part of a typical developmental process and would influence her choice of a husband.

A social-learning theory of how patterns of sexual arousal are acquired would use the concept of classical conditioning. According to one hypothesis (McGuire, Carlisle, & Young, 1965), individuals, particularly males, can acquire unusual patterns of sexual arousal by masturbating to relevant fantasies. Consider the reported case of a young man who was attracted to prepubescent girls (Staats, 1974). As a young boy he engaged in sex play with girls his own age. These activities came to a halt when his parents moved. After puberty, when he began to masturbate, his fantasies centered on a nine-year-old girl of his previous experience. By pairing the pleasure of orgasm with the image of a young girl, he established a pattern of becoming sexually aroused in response to prepubescent girls. When he was 19 years old, he attempted to have intercourse with an aging prostitute, but the circumstances and the woman were so unappealing that he became repelled by the idea of having sex with a mature woman. His masturbation fantasies of the nine-year-old girl continued, and he became increasingly obsessed with the idea of having sex with young girls. The combination of his childhood sexual experiences, which produced material for fantasies, and his unfortunate attempt at a more mature heterosexual relationship was sufficient to produce the variant pattern of sexual arousal in this man.

The investigations of how sexual attitudes are developed and how patterns of sexual arousal are established are just two examples of the type of research that has been done in an attempt to understand the role of psychological factors in human sexual behavior. This area of research is important because it helps us see how our biological heritage can be shaped. It also has important practical implications. For instance, it makes Lisa's sexual problem with her husband more understandable and readily treatable. As recently as 15 years ago, Lisa probably would have been told that the chances of solving her problem were very poor (Hastings, 1967).

SOCIAL FACTORS

As we have seen in many instances, the society in which we live exerts a powerful influence on our behavior. Our sexual behavior and attitudes are no exception. We tend to behave sexually as others in our group do. Of course, within any group there is individual variability, but meaningful generalizations can be made about the sexual behavior of specific societies and specific subgroups within a society.

Differences within Cultures

Until the middle part of this century we knew more about the sexual behavior of people in primitive societies than we did about the behavior of people in our own country. The Victorian influence was strong up to this time, and most behavioral scientists were reluctant to collect objective information for fear of losing their jobs. Then, in 1938, Dr. Alfred Kinsey was asked to coordinate a new course in marriage at Indiana University. Kinsey found that he could not answer many questions from his students about patterns of sexual behavior, and his visits to the library convinced him that no one else could either.

As a result, he developed an extensive questionnaire of sexual behavior and recruited a team of interviewers. His work culminated in the publication of two volumes, *Sexual Behavior in the Human Male* (1948) and *Sexual Behavior in the Human Female* (1953). They summarized the results of interviews with over 10,000 men and women. His books not only provided the first reliable index of sexual behavior in the United States, but they also revealed relationships between a variety of social factors and sexual behavior.

Kinsey found that a person's religious affiliation, ethnic group membership, and social class all serve to shape his or her sexual behavior. The most meaningful factor, according to Kinsey, is social class. Using educational level as an index of social class, Kinsey found substantial differences in sexual behavior between those with at least some college and those with eight years of education or less (Kinsey, Pomeroy, & Martin, 1948; Kinsey, Pomeroy, Martin, & Gebhard, 1953).

Lower-class males were found to be more likely to engage in premarital sex and in extramarital sex in the early years of marriage than upper-class males. Upper-class males were more likely to masturbate, engage in oral sex, and have intercourse in a lighted room.

Relationships between social class and sexual behavior were not nearly so strong for women. The upper-class women were somewhat more likely to have engaged in masturbation, homosexual activities, and extramarital affairs. They were also more likely to experience orgasm during premarital and marital intercourse. For both lower-class and upper-class women, petting and premarital intercourse were strongly related to age at marriage. The older a woman was when she married, the more likely she was to have engaged in such activities, regardless of her social class.

A striking factor that emerged from the Kinsey studies was the tendency of the lower classes to subscribe to a double standard of sexuality. Lower-class males sought premarital experiences not only for pleasure but also as proof of their sexual prowess. Lower-class women generally acceded to sexual demands in an effort to win their partner's love, even though they were fearful of losing their reputation and might have derived little pleasure from such experiences.

This pattern underwent little change after marriage. The lower-class male still appeared to be primarily interested in his own gratification. Foreplay was likely to be very brief and unvaried, and intercourse occurred in one or two basic positions and was likely to be completed quickly. It is not surprising that lower-class women reported less interest and enjoyment in sexual activities than did middle- and upper-class women (Rainwater, 1965).

The sexual relationship between a man and a woman in the upper classes tended to be an extension of a love relationship. Sex was more likely to be viewed as a cooperative activity that is pleasurable to both the man and the woman. Upper-class couples tended to use more varied techniques and positions for foreplay and intercourse and were likely to spend more time engaging in these activities.

There is some evidence that social-class differences in sexual behavior may be diminishing. In a survey sponsored by the Playboy Foundation in the early 1970s, it was found that differences between social classes were generally small and in some cases nonexistent. For example, in 1948 Kinsey found that only 15 percent of high school males engaged in cunnilingus (oral stimulation of the female genitals), while 45 percent of college males did. In 1972 the corresponding figures were 56 percent and 66 percent (Hunt, 1974). A second finding was that the difference between upper- and lower-class men in duration of foreplay had completely disappeared. In 1972 both groups reported an average of 15 minutes of such activity. While it is difficult to know precisely what these data mean, they do seem to reflect a relaxation of the double standard and a greater acceptance of sexuality—particularly of women's sexuality—in the lower social classes.

Differences among Cultures

Because most of us have lived in only one society, we tend to believe that our standards of sexual behavior are normal and that anything that deviates from these standards must be abnormal. Cross-cultural research of sexual behavior illustrates that quite different standards of "normal" sexual behavior can evolve in different societies.

One end of a continuum of sexual permissiveness is represented by the Mangaian—a Polynesian society. These people place a high value on sexual activity. Children have their first sexual encounter during early adolescence, often in the same one-room hut in which the parents are asleep. (If they are, in fact, awake, fathers are careful to feign sleep so as not to frighten away the daughters' night visitors.) Both boys and girls are concerned with learning to be skillful lovers, and it is reported that all Mangaian women have orgasm regularly. The Mangaian view sex as a completely natural and valuable aspect of life (Marshall, 1971).

The other end of the continuum is represented by Inis Beag—an Irish folk community marked by its sexual repression. These people believe that only men have sexual urges. Women find intercourse painful or unpleasant, but it is a mortal sin for a wife to refuse her husband's advances. Marital intercourse involves virtually no foreplay, takes place with the participants wearing underclothes, and is quickly completed. Most of the men are not even aware that women are capable of having an orgasm. Nor are the people of Beag aware of numerous sexual activities that we consider common, such as tongue kissing, oral sex, and manual manipulation of genitals. To these people, intercourse is something that men must engage in periodically, but there is little joy to be derived from it (Messenger, 1971).

Cross-cultural research also points up the degree to which variant forms of sexual behavior are practiced. To use one example, our society generally views homosexuality as a form of sexual deviation, although tolerance toward it may be gradually increasing. We also tend to categorize people as being either homosexual or heterosexual, and we (including many mental-health professionals) believe that it is very difficult for a homosexual to become heterosexual. In other societies, such as the Mangaian, homosexuality is virtually unheard of. In still others, such as the Marind Anim, young boys are *expected* to go through a period in their lives during which they are exclusively homosexual. When they reach adulthood, they marry and are thereafter exclusively heterosexual. Clearly, ideas of what is "normal" in homosexual behavior are culturally determined.

Cross-cultural research has also shown that there are virtually no sexual taboos that are universal. Incest may be one exception, but even incest is defined so differently across cultures that to speak of it as a universal taboo is misleading. Some cultures permit marriage between first cousins, while others prohibit sexual contact with any blood relative. The value of cross-cultural research is that it demonstrates the powerful role that social standards play in shaping people's sexual behavior.

PATTERNS OF SEXUAL BEHAVIOR

As mentioned earlier, Kinsey first provided us with a reliable body of data about the patterns of sexual behavior in our society. In this section we shall review Kinsey's findings and note those areas in which significant changes appear to have occurred during the past 30 years. But first a few words about the problems of doing research in sexual behavior are in order.

Methods of Research

It is notoriously difficult to collect reliable information on sexual behavior. Perhaps the most obvious problem is that the researcher must rely on respondents to answer questions truthfully. But some people may conceal certain of their sexual experiences out of embarrassment, while others may exaggerate their experiences in an attempt to impress the interviewer. Kinsey did include several crosschecks in his questionnaire to detect misrepresentations, so it was probably not a major problem in his surveys.

A second problem, and one that does affect Kinsey's surveys, is that of representativeness. If one is to generalize from a sample to a population, then the relevant characteristics of the sample must be representative of the population in general. Characteristics such as social class, age, religion, and ethnic-group membership are all related to sexual behavior. So the sample should be subdivided along these lines in the same proportion as the population.

Kinsey's methods of generating a sample resulted in having some groups, such as Protestants, young people, and college-educated people, overrepresented, while other groups were under-represented. He attempted to correct for this statistically, but critics have nonetheless been able to charge that Kinsey's samples are not truly representative of the nation's population.

Despite these shortcomings, there is little doubt that Kinsey's data are the best available. Since his investigations other major surveys of sexual behavior have been conducted, but few have approached the level of sophistication achieved by Kinsey.

Masturbation

At the time of Kinsey's findings, the prevailing view of masturbation (at least the view expressed publicly) was that it was virtually a perversion. His results indicated, however, that the percentage of those who had ever masturbated was about 92 percent for males and 62 percent for females. Obviously, many people must have believed that they were the only ones engaged in this activity.

Recent data suggest that there has been little change in the percentage of individuals who have ever masturbated. There is some indication, however, that both boys and girls are beginning to masturbate at an earlier age. For example, Kinsey reported that 45 percent of males and 13 percent of females had masturbated by the age of 13 while a survey in 1972 found that 63 percent of males and 33 percent of females had done so (Hunt, 1974).

The incidence of heterosexual petting appears to have undergone little change since Kinsey's surveys. (© *Marjorie Pickens*)

Heterosexual Petting

The incidence of heterosexual petting (physical contact that leads to sexual arousal excluding intercourse) appears to have undergone little change since Kinsey's surveys. He reported that 88 percent of young women and 89 percent of young men had had petting experiences. Hunt's 1972 survey indicated only slightly higher percentages, 90 percent for young women and 95 percent for young men.

Hunt's data do suggest, however, that heterosexual petting is becoming a less important form of sexual activity for unmarried men and women. For example, Kinsey found that married women reported having eight petting partners prior to marriage; the corresponding figure in Hunt's survey was only three. Kinsey did not collect information about the number of petting partners for males, but Hunt found that younger respondents had fewer premarital petting partners (12) than did the older males (15).

Hunt's explanation for his finding is that unmarried people are engaging in intercourse earlier than they did a generation ago. In the 1920s, when sexual attitudes were beginning to become more permissive, heterosexual petting developed as a compromise between premarital chastity and the new permissiveness. Men and particularly women viewed petting as a way to gratify their sexual

CRITICAL ISSUE

What "Turns On" Men and Women?

In the course of adding to scientific knowledge of human sexuality over the past century, "experts" have actually contributed to sexual myths. For instance, Sigmund Freud lent credence to the notion that female sexuality is quite different from male sexuality. And Havelock Ellis, who wrote many books about sex around the turn of the century and was considered a sexual radical, supported the notion that masturbation can result in a variety of psychological and medical ills. The views of these men only show that scientists are not free from cultural influences; Freud, Ellis, and others were undoubtedly influenced by the Victorian ethic that was prevalent at the time they did their work.

Of more current interest are myths supported by Alfred Kinsey concerning differences between men and women in patterns of sexual arousal. Although Kinsey made many invaluable contributions to scientific knowledge, his biases led him to make interpretations of his data that were not entirely accurate. For instance, he noted that women tended to report that they were sexually aroused by tactile stimulation, while men reported that they found visual stimuli highly arousing. Kinsey's training in biology and zoology led him to believe that this reflected a basic biological difference between men and women. A related myth that is widely accepted is that women find depictions of sex within a context of a love-romance relationship exciting, while men are aroused by portrayals of casual sex.

These "facts" were generated by asking people about their reactions. Women's reports indicated that they did not find sexually explicit photographs or films as arousing as did men. But rather than reflecting women's biological difference from men, this may represent their lesser experience with such stimuli or their desire to respond to the survey in a socially acceptable way. Recent research shows that men and women are very similar in what they find sexually arousing.

As one example, college men and women were asked to watch a film in which a couple make love. Although all subjects viewed the same film, one-third of the men and women were told that the couple was married (marital sex), one-third were told that the couple had just met that night (casual sex), and one-third were told the woman was a prostitute and the man was her customer (commercial sex). Contrary to what Kinsey might have predicted, there were no differences between sexual arousal of men and women. And both men and women found the film to be most arousing when they were told it was casual sex (Fisher & Byrne, 1978). Beginning with the work of Masters and Johnson, current research has found that the similarities in sexual responses of men and women are more evident than are the differences.

desires until they married. A generation later, young people viewed petting as an acceptable compromise for a shorter period of time before moving on to intercourse.

Sexual Intercourse

There appear to have been significant changes in the incidence of premarital intercourse over the past generation. Kinsey reported that 71 percent of males and 33 percent of females had engaged in premarital intercourse by the age of 25. Hunt reported that the corresponding figures for 24-year-olds were 90 percent and 75 percent. There is also evidence that in the 1970s both men and women were having intercourse at an earlier age.

The most dramatic changes have occurred in the rates for women. This seems to indicate a relaxation of the double standard. In fact, Hunt reported that nearly 60 percent of young women believed that it is acceptable to have premarital intercourse when strong affection exists. A survey conducted in 1959 reported that only 15 percent of young women approved of such behavior (Reiss, 1967).

More people today than in previous generations think of sex as an activity to be enjoyed. (© *Joel Gordon*)

These changes do not necessarily signal a sexual revolution. The number of premarital partners of both men and women has remained virtually unchanged over the past generation. More than half of all women have only one sexual partner, presumably the husband-to-be, prior to marriage. Men have an average of six premarital partners. So while the current generation of young people may be more willing to have premarital intercourse, they are not engaging in many casual affairs. Sociologist Ira Reiss (1967) has coined the term "permissiveness with affection" to describe current standards of sexual morality. Men and women view premarital intercourse as acceptable if it occurs in an intimate relationship.

The frequency of marital intercourse has slightly increased over the past generation. Kinsey reported that in his youngest group, aged 16 to 25, the median frequency of intercourse was 2.45 times a week. His oldest respondents, aged 56 to 60, had a median frequency of once every two weeks. The corresponding figures for 1972 were 3.25 times a week and once a week.

Perhaps of more significance, Hunt reported data suggesting that married couples are using more varied techniques of foreplay (such as oral sex) and a wider range of coital positions, and they are taking longer for both foreplay and intercourse. Women in the 1970s reported having orgasm more regularly than women a generation earlier. In contrast to Kinsey's findings, Hunt reported that many young women desired to have intercourse more often than they did, rather than less often. These changes would seem to suggest that married persons, particularly women, view sexual activity with less conflict and derive more satisfaction from it than did married persons in times past.

As in many of the other changes in sexual attitudes and behavior, changes in extramarital intercourse have been greater for women than for men. While there was virtually no difference between the Kinsey and Hunt surveys in the percentage of men who had extramarital affairs, Kinsey reported that only 9 percent of married women had had such a relationship by the age of 25, while Hunt found that 24 percent of married women between the ages of 18 and 24 had had an extramarital affair. Once again, the changes that have occurred over the past generation seem to reflect a relaxation of the double standard.

A review of all these changes in sexual behavior gives little evidence that the much touted sexual revolution has taken place. Important changes have occurred, but they do not seem to reflect a break from traditional values. The majority of people continue to take sexual relationships seriously. They do, however, seem to have a less puritanical view of sexual activities. And they seem to be developing a view that sex is an activity to be enjoyed rather than one that is merely a means of reducing tension.

The most important changes have occurred in women. The behavior of men does not appear to have changed substantially since Kinsey's surveys, but women's sexual behavior is becoming similar to that of men. If the current trends continue, the double standard may soon be a thing of the past.

SEXUAL DYSFUNCTIONS

Sometimes individuals experience problems that disrupt their pattern of sexual behavior. For one reason or another, the individual is unable to engage in or enjoy sexual activities. These **sexual dysfunctions,** as they are called, are quite common and are not to be confused with sexual variations, or variant forms of sex that some people consider to be "abnormal" (such as exhibitionism and sado-masochism).

Masters and Johnson (1970) have estimated that in half of all marriages persons experience some form of sexual dysfunction, just as Lisa did in the example given at the opening of this chapter. Because many people associate sexual prowess and responsiveness with the concepts of masculinity and feminity, the consequences of sexual dysfunction can be quite far-reaching. Severe depression and anxiety and the break-up of long-standing marriages are not uncommon in such cases.

As recently as the mid-1960s, cases of sexual dysfunction were thought to be extremely difficult to treat. They were viewed as symptoms of underlying personality disturbance requiring years of therapy to correct. Now, however, most psychologists view such disorders as learned (see Chapter 12), and a majority of cases respond well to brief, structured forms of treatment. Over the past decade or two, clinical psychology has made great strides in developing techniques to treat sexual dysfunctions.

Varieties of Sexual Dysfunctions

The four most common forms of sexual dysfunctions are erectile failure and premature ejaculation in men and orgasmic dysfunction and vaginismus in women.

Erectile Failure. Some men are unable to achieve or maintain an erection for a sufficient period of time to complete sexual intercourse. The term **erectile failure** has been offered for this discussion as a substitute for the older, more common term, "impotence" (LoPiccolo, 1978). "Impotence" has become an emotional word over the years; in any case, the term "erectile failure" is more precise.

Virtually every man has occasions when he is unable to achieve an erection. Preoccupation with money matters, fatigue, or lack of interest in his partner can all contribute to an inability to have an erection. These occasional failures do not constitute a dysfunction. It is only when the man consistently has erectile failure that it becomes classified as dysfunction. Masters and Johnson (1970) have drawn an arbitrary dividing line at 25 percent. If a man is unable to achieve or maintain erection on 25 percent of his attempts to have intercourse, then professional consultation may be necessary.

Masters and Johnson have made the distinction between primary and secondary cases of erectile failure. In primary cases, the man has never been able to have intercourse, although he may have erections at other times, such as when masturbating. In secondary cases, the man has had at least some successful experiences. Secondary erectile failure may be specific to a particular partner. Some men, for example, are unable to have intercourse with their wives but have no problem in extramarital relationships. The converse situation can also occur.

The moment at which the erection is lost varies from case to case. Some men lose their erection the moment their partner indicates her willingness to have intercourse. Others may lose it at the sight of a naked partner. Attempts at penetration may result in loss of the erection. And in some cases, penetration may be achieved but the erection will be lost almost immediately thereafter. Needless to say, it is extremely frustrating to the man (to say nothing of the attitude of the woman) to want to have intercourse but to be unable to do so.

Premature Ejaculation. It is difficult to arrive at a satisfactory definition of **premature ejaculation.** In general, it refers to a man's having orgasm sooner than he or his partner would like. But experts cannot agree how long the period between penetration and ejaculation should be. Suggested time intervals have ranged from 30 seconds to 10 minutes. Definitions based on time have obvious problems. Many couples may find rapid intercourse highly exciting and mutually satisfying. It would be absurd to classify the man in such cases as a premature ejaculator simply because he failed to meet some expert's criterion.

In an attempt to move away from a stop-watch approach, Masters and Johnson have defined premature ejaculation as an ejaculation that occurs before the man's partner has an orgasm on 50 percent of their encounters. This definition has obvious shortcomings as well. Many women fail to reach orgasm for reasons other than their partner's pattern of ejaculation. In such cases, according to Masters and Johnson's definition, even the man who is able to have intercourse for extended periods of time would be labeled a premature ejaculator.

However it is defined, premature ejaculation is clearly a serious problem for many men. Some may ejaculate at the sight of their partner's unclothed body. Other men ejaculate when their partner fondles their genitals. Still others may ejaculate upon penetration or seconds later. This pattern greatly diminishes their pleasure and virtually ensures that the woman will not reach orgasm through intercourse.

Orgasmic Dysfunction. The woman who is unable to have an orgasm during intercourse is said to have an **orgasmic dysfunction.** This term has come to replace "frigidity" for the same reasons that "erectile failure" is used in place of "impotence." The severity of orgasmic dysfunction varies greatly from case to case. Some women may derive no pleasure from intercourse and may in fact experience feelings of disgust. Others may become highly aroused during foreplay and intercourse but seem to get "stuck" during the plateau phase of the sexual response cycle.

As with erectile failure, a distinction can be made between primary and secondary orgasmic dysfunction (Masters & Johnson, 1970). Primary cases involve women who have never experienced orgasm in intercourse or through any other means of stimulation. Secondary cases involve women who have had some successful sexual experiences. Such women may have had orgasms through masturbation or petting but are unable to do so during intercourse. As in Lisa's case, some women may have had orgasms during intercourse in the past but are no longer able to do so. As with men, the dysfunction may occur only with a particular partner. A woman may have orgasms during intercourse with her husband but be unable to have them in extramarital relationships.

For both men and women the ability to have sexual intercourse is not necessarily related to feelings of love and affection. While most people would agree that sex with a loved partner is more gratifying, many people can function effectively with partners they have little feeling for or may even dislike. These same individuals may experience problems when attempting to have intercourse with partners they love.

Vaginismus. **Vaginismus** involves an involuntary contraction of the muscles surrounding the vaginal entrance. The contractions can be so severe as to make sexual intercourse impossible. The contractions can occur in response to imagined, anticipated, or attempted sexual intercourse. Many married women who seek treatment for this disorder have never had intercourse.

Women suffering from this disorder can vary greatly in terms of their level of sexual responsiveness. Some women may find any form of sexual contact unpleasant and never experience erotic sensations. Others may become highly aroused during foreplay and even have orgasm in response to clitoral stimulation. They may want to have intercourse but are prevented by the involuntary muscle contractions.

Probable Causes of Sexual Dysfunctions

Until the 1960s sexual dysfunctions were generally explained on the basis of psychoanalytic theory. Each specific dysfunction was thought to represent some particular set of conflicts about sex. For example, premature ejaculation was thought to represent intense unconscious feelings of hatred toward women. Premature ejaculation supposedly allowed the man to express his sadistic impulses toward a woman while at the same time depriving her of the opportunity to derive pleasure from the act. Similar interpretations were offered for the other forms of sexual dysfunction.

Relatively few experts in the field of human sexuality still subscribe to these psychoanalytic interpretations. It has become generally accepted that specific experiences can lead to sexual dysfunction in people who are otherwise psychologically well adjusted. Thus the sexual dysfunction is itself the problem and not merely symptomatic of some deeper and more mysterious problem. A variety of specific experiences can result in a sexual dysfunction, but most of them operate by creating negative attitudes toward sex or instilling performance anxiety. These in turn interfere with successful sexual functioning.

Negative Attitudes toward Sex. As we saw earlier in the chapter, some parents may create feelings of guilt about sex in their children. If this sense of guilt is intense enough, it can interfere with effective sexual functioning. Masters and Johnson (1970) described several cases in which negative attitudes toward sex, or sexual guilt, were thought to be the causal factor in sexual dysfunction.

As one example, a couple sought treatment because their marriage had not been consummated after nine years. The wife came from a family that emphasized strict obedience to religious tenets. Her father, who dominated the family, firmly believed that sex and sin were synonymous. He censored all newspapers, magazines, and radio programs to ensure that the children were never exposed to any suggestion of sexuality. He closely supervised his daughter's social life when she was a teenager and permitted her to date only in groups attending well-chaperoned church activities.

The patient remembered her mother as an unemotional woman whose only purpose in life seemed to be to cook, clean, care for the children, and wait on the father. When the patient had her first menstrual period, she was terrified and ran home to her mother, who informed her that it was a "curse" that she would have to endure every month. The only other mention of sex was on the patient's wedding day, when the mother told her she would have to allow her husband certain "privileges." What these privileges were was left unclear, but the mother did state they would be painful. Her reward for serving her husband would be to have children.

The woman's husband came from an almost identical background. On the wedding night, when intercourse was attempted, the woman was trying to maintain her modesty, while her husband searched for the proper place to insert his penis. It never occurred to her to cooperate in this venture. As her mother promised, the woman did experience pain when intromission was attempted. During the early months of marriage the couple tried to make love almost nightly, but the woman's vaginismus made it impossible. For several years prior to treatment, attempts at consummation occurred three or four times a year.

This is, of course, an extreme example, but many women are incapable of having orgasms or of deriving pleasure from intercourse because they were brought up to believe that "nice girls" are not interested in sex. Men, too, are sometimes troubled by feelings of sex guilt, but not to the same extent. Even puritanical parents are likely to recognize that their sons are going to be interested in sexual matters. They may place strict limits on their son's sexual behavior, but boys are generally allowed to develop an acceptance of their sexuality. Girls often grow up believing that even sexual feelings are improper. When they marry and face the prospect of regular sexual relations, such women are incapable of suddenly reversing their negative attitudes toward sex.

Performance Anxiety. The second major causal factor in cases of sexual dysfunction is performance anxiety—concerns about one's sexual competence and expertise. The sexual functioning of both men and women can be impaired by performance anxiety, although it tends to be more prevalent among men. In our society men are expected to be the initiators and experts with regard to sex. And as women are increasingly demanding sexual satisfaction, many men have developed fears about their ability to perform in a satisfactory way.

Performance anxiety can develop from a variety of experiences. Masters and Johnson (1970) reported several cases in which the man was humiliated by an older, more experienced woman during his first attempt at intercourse. These women, often prostitutes, may have laughed or made derogatory comments about the size of his genitals or his fumbling approach. Such experiences generated sufficient performance anxiety so that the next attempt at a sexual encounter was doomed to failure, even if it was with a sympathetic and supportive partner.

The most common occurrence, according to Masters and Johnson, was an experience of failure associated with alcohol. They described a composite case history of a middle-aged man who was relatively successful in his occupation. This man had gradually increased his level of social drinking over the years. On an evening following unusually heavy drinking, he attempted to have intercourse with his wife. His intoxicated state rendered him impotent, but he suspected that his "problem" might have been caused by his advancing years. After worrying about his failure for a few days, he decided to test himself again with his wife. Because he approached the encounter with the fear that he might fail, he was impotent once again. After only a few such failures an enduring pattern of sexual dysfunction can be established, even after years of successful and gratifying sexual functioning. If men or women are anxious about how they are performing sexually, it is virtually impossible for them to function effectively.

Treatment of Sexual Dysfunctions

Since Masters and Johnson (1970) published the details of their highly effective treatment method, a variety of programs have been developed that incorporate and supplement their techniques. Four ingredients appear to be essential in these treatments: (1) reversing negative attitudes and correcting misconceptions about sex; (2) reducing performance anxiety; (3) improving communication between sexual partners; and (4) giving advice on specific techniques.

Reversing Negative Attitudes and Correcting Misconceptions. Masters and Johnson achieved this goal by holding roundtable discussions. After the husband and wife have each been extensively interviewed by a same-sexed therapist, all four individuals meet together to discuss issues that have been raised. These issues may include what the woman can expect from sex, the frequency of intercourse, or sexual functioning beyond middle age. The crucial goal is to get both partners committed to work toward a mutually satisfying sexual relationship.

Many therapists continue to use a similar approach in dealing with negative attitudes and misconceptions. In recent years, however, it has been found that the same goals can be met as effectively, and more efficiently, in group therapy. These groups may consist of several couples (Kaplan, Kohl, Pomeroy, Offit, & Hogan, 1978), or they may consist of only men or only women (Schneidman & McGuire, 1978). Generally the therapist will introduce certain material, and through group discussions the participants usually develop less puritanical views of sex and acquire useful factual information.

Reducing Performance Anxiety. One effective method of reducing performance anxiety, developed by behavior therapists in the 1950s, is *in vivo* desensitization. *In vivo* desensitization requires people to face their fears in real-life situations under controlled conditions so that their anxiety can be reduced. The basic procedure is to ask the couple to engage in extended periods of mutual caressing and nongenital foreplay. Intercourse is forbidden during these sessions. This allows the couple to experience erotic sensations without the pressure of having to perform sexually. Many impotent men have an erection in the presence of their partner for the first time in years during these sessions.

Several therapists have found the use of erotic films and videotapes to be useful in reducing anxiety and inhibitions (Schneidman & McGuire, 1978). By watching sexual activities under relaxed and nondemanding circumstances, couples often find performance anxiety lessening. Systematic desensitization (see Chapter 13) has also been shown to be effective in many studies (Husted, 1978; Kockott, Dittmar, & Nusselt, 1978). In these studies clients are asked to imagine themselves engaging in various sexual activities while in a deep state of relaxation. Once they can imagine such scenes without feeling anxious, they can experience such activities in a more relaxed manner. The goal of these techniques is to help the individual to stop evaluating his or her performance so that erotic sensations are free to develop.

Improving Communication. Many cases of sexual dysfunction could be prevented if only the couple could tell each other about their needs and their likes and dislikes. For example, many men enter a sexual relationship with little knowledge of what it takes to please their partners. Such men may engage in only cursory foreplay and then have their orgasm quickly. Faced with this situation, many women have chosen not to tell their partners that they need more foreplay to prepare them for intercourse. After many disappointing experiences, frustration can build to the point where orgasm for the woman is impossible even if sufficient stimulation were to occur. In Lisa's case, improved communication with her husband played an important role in solving her problem. Once she began to talk about her feelings, they were able to deal with the situation in a less defensive and more productive way.

Masters and Johnson encouraged partners to communicate during the roundtable discussions. The partners were also instructed to provide each other with feedback during the sessions of extended foreplay. Often, simply the assurance from a therapist that it is permissible to talk about one's sexual feelings and preferences is sufficient to improve communication. In some cases, however, additional techniques are required.

For individuals who are particularly reluctant to communicate their sexual needs, the behavioral technique of assertion training may be employed (Lazarus, 1976). To illustrate, imagine the case of a young woman who cannot bring herself to ask her husband to modify his sexual technique even though she recognizes that it is important for her to do so. The therapist would first suggest ways in which she might phrase the request. Next, the woman would be encouraged to practice verbalizing these requests in the presence of the therapist. The therapist might then point out ways she could make such requests more effective. With additional practice the woman is likely to feel less anxious and will probably be able to talk to her husband about her sexual needs.

Offering Advice about Techniques. Along with the three techniques described above, therapists will also offer advice about specific sexual techniques as required. For example, men may be informed about the importance of clitoral stimulation in women's sexual arousal. Or the couple may be taught the "squeeze technique" if the problem centers on premature ejaculation. In this technique the woman is instructed to squeeze her partner's penis when he has the urge to ejaculate. The woman-above position for intercourse is recommended in cases where the woman has difficulty reaching orgasm. This position will allow her to control the pace and movements of intercourse.

As we have said, remarkable progress has been made in the treatment of sexual dysfunction. While the chances of success vary from case to case, it is not uncommon for treatment programs to report success rates of from 80 to 90 percent. Of equal importance, the development of innovative and efficient techniques over the past 5 to 10 years (cf. LoPiccolo & LoPiccolo, 1978) has made effective therapy affordable for thousands of people.

SEXUAL VARIATIONS

While a majority of people in our society seek sexual gratification through sexual intercourse with similarly aged members of the opposite sex, there are sizable numbers of individuals whose sexual interests focus on inanimate objects, children, or members of their own sex. Others associate sexual pleasure with emotions that most people consider unrelated to sex, such as pain, humiliation, fear, and anger. These patterns of sexual behavior, which the majority of our society consider to be unusual, are called sexual variations.

As we saw in Chapter 12, it is difficult to make distinctions between what is normal and what is abnormal, or deviant, behavior. The same difficulty occurs with regard to sexual behavior. A variety of definitions of abnormal sexual behavior have been offered, but none of these is uncritically accepted by all experts. Let us look at one authoritative definition of sexual deviations provided by the American Psychiatric Association (1968):

> This category is for individuals whose sexual interests are directed toward objects other than people of the opposite sex, toward sexual acts not usually associated with coitus or toward coitus performed under bizarre circumstances as in necrophilia, pedophilia, sexual sadism, and fetishism. Even though many people find their practices distasteful they remain unable to substitute normal sexual behavior for them. This diagnosis is not appropriate for individuals who perform deviant sexual acts because normal sexual objects are not available to them.

In 1974 the American Psychiatric Association voted to remove homosexuality per se as a form of sexual deviation. In its place was substituted "sexual orientation disturbance," which includes only those homosexuals who have conflicts about their sexual orientation or who wish to change it. Also, in the most recent edition of the *Diagnostic and Statistical Manual* (American Psychiatric Association, 1980), the term "sexual deviation" is not used. Specific forms of sexual variations are included under the general heading of psychosexual disorders.

While this definition has intuitive appeal, there are problems with it. As just one example, consider the case of fetishism—a sexual variation in which an individual attaches much erotic significance to an inanimate object or some specific body part. Suppose a man was greatly aroused sexually by black net stockings and had little interest in having intercourse unless his partner wore them. Further suppose that this man married a woman who enjoyed wearing erotic clothing and that she readily agreed to wear black net stockings during their sexual encounters. Is it logical to conclude that this man has a sexual deviation, even though he has a sex life that is satisfying to both him and his partner and does no one any harm?

Many cases, of course, are not so ambiguous. The fetishist who derives gratification by stealing women's clothing and masturbating while viewing or holding the article of clothing and who has no interest in heterosexual intercourse would be viewed as abnormal by almost everyone. But there is always the problem of drawing the arbitrary line between normality and abnormality. For this reason, many writers have chosen to use the term "sexual variations" rather than "sexual deviations." This term recognizes that certain types of sexual behavior may be unusual but does not necessarily label them as abnormal. Let us examine some of the major categories of sexual variations.

Homosexuality

Homosexuality can be defined as having an erotic attraction to, and engaging in sexual behavior with, a member of the same sex. The term "lesbian" is sometimes used to describe homosexual women. The term "homosexual" is misleading, however, because it suggests an "either-or" phenomenon. It suggests that one is either homosexual or heterosexual. In fact, both Kinsey's and Hunt's data indicate that the individual who is exclusively homosexual for his or her entire life is relatively rare. It is more accurate to view homosexuality as falling along a continuum. The majority of individuals who are labeled homosexual

Attitudes toward homosexuality have undergone considerable change over the last 50 years. (© *Michael Hanulak/Black Star; Michael Abramson/Black Star*)

actually have a mixture of homosexual and heterosexual interests and behavior.

It is difficult to estimate the degree to which homosexuality occurs, since many people who have homosexual experiences are reluctant to discuss them. Kinsey created a furor in the late 1940s and early 1950s when he stated that 37 percent of men and 13 percent of women had at least one homosexual experience by the age of 45. Many people interpreted these figures as meaning that one-third of all men were either homosexual or had homosexual tendencies. Actually, many of the homosexual experiences that Kinsey uncovered were isolated ones, occurred in early adolescence, and had no lasting significance. Hunt (1974), while recognizing the difficulties inherent in surveys, concluded from his data that from one to three percent of men are "more or less" exclusive homosexuals, and another three to seven percent have at least occasional homosexual experiences. Among his female respondents, three percent of single women and one percent of married women reported having at least one homosexual experience within one year prior to the survey. Hunt makes the important point that there is no evidence that homosexuality has increased over the past several decades.

Views of homosexuality have undergone considerable change over the past 50 years. A generation or two ago, most people viewed homosexuality as sinful and perverted. Homosexuals had to be careful to conceal their sexual orientation lest they lose their jobs, alienate their families, and face other unpleasant social consequences. During the past decade homosexuals have been "coming out of the closet" and demanding their rights. Their efforts, as measured by recent court cases, have not always been successful, but there is little doubt that our society now has more tolerance for homosexuality. Many psychotherapists are now willing to treat homosexuals who do not wish to change their sexual orientation but only wish to feel comfortable with it (see Critical Issue, below). And some popular writers have proposed that sexual liberation includes the ability to enjoy homosexual as well as heterosexual relationships (Kerr, 1977).

It is impossible to make any generalizations about homosexuals. As a group, they are every bit as diverse as heterosexuals (Bell & Weinberg, 1978). Some are promiscuous; others prefer stable, intimate relationships. Some are psychologically disturbed, while many others seem well adjusted and have made outstanding personal achievements. Some are only interested in orgasm through genital stimulation, while others enjoy varied and prolonged foreplay. A few gay men and women may fit the "queen" or "dyke" stereotypes, but most are indistinguishable from heterosexuals in their appearance and mannerisms. In short, just about everything that can be said of heterosexuals (with the obvious exception of penile-vaginal intercourse) can also be applied to homosexuals. People are men and women first, and homosexuality is just one of many ways in which they may vary.

There are a variety of theories concerning the development of a homosexual orientation. Psychoanalytic theorists generally believe that one's sexual orientation is determined in early childhood. They argue that failure to resolve the Oedipal conflict, at around age four or five, can result

CRITICAL ISSUE

Should Homosexuals Be Treated?

Although homosexuality is no longer considered the sin and perversion it was a generation ago, most people, including mental-health professionals, continue to view it as something less than normal. Many clinical psychologists and psychiatrists accept homosexuals for treatment only if the goal is to reverse their sexual orientation, and many studies have found that such treatment can be successful.

These professional activities are a curious contrast to the views of many sex researchers. Some 30 years ago certain sex researchers asserted that experiences shape sexual orientation (Ford & Beach, 1951). More recent researchers have carried this theme even further. They believe that there is nothing inherently abnormal about homosexuality; it should be viewed as falling on one end of a continuum of normal sexual behavior (Marmor, 1976).

In response to this apparent paradox between what mental-health professionals profess to believe about the nature of homosexuality and how they treat their clients, behavior therapist Gerald Davison (1976, 1978) has asserted that psychotherapists should refuse to attempt to change a homosexual's orientation even if he or she requests such help. Davison's point is that if we really believe that homosexuality is within the range of normal sexual functioning, then we should not treat it as if it were abnormal. After all, therapists have not developed techniques for the heterosexual who wishes to be homosexual or bisexual. If Davison were to see a homosexual in therapy, he would attempt to help that person accept his or her sexuality and to deal with any associated guilt or anxiety.

As you might suspect, Davison's arguments were not met with equanimity. Some therapists (e.g., Bieber, 1976) maintained that homosexuality is in fact a psychological disturbance and should be treated as such. A more moderate position suggests that therapists explore the feelings and motives of their homosexual clients and allow the clients to decide between the goals of feeling more comfortable with their homosexuality and changing their sexual orientation (Hoffman, 1977). This controversy is likely to continue for some time. It is of interest, however, because it reflects the relationship between professional practice on the one hand and theory and cultural values on the other.

in a homosexual orientation. The little boy who fails to identify with his father may acquire homosexual preferences.

Social-learning theorists believe that a variety of experiences, not only in childhood but during adolescence and adulthood as well, may contribute to a homosexual orientation. To illustrate, imagine a teenage girl who is intimidated by boys. If this girl engages in sex play with one of her girlfriends, she is likely to find it pleasurable. Because she feels uncomfortable with boys, she may pursue sexual relationships with women as she grows older.

Martin Hoffman (1977), in a review of the theories of homosexuality, concluded that we simply do not know its causes. It could be that different homosexuals develop their sexual orientation in response to different experiences. Some may have had problems identifying with the opposite-sex parent during early childhood. Others may turn to homosexual relationships because of unpleasant heterosexual experiences during their adolescence. At present, we cannot say with any certainty why some people prefer heterosexual experiences and others prefer homosexual relationships.

Bisexuality

Participation in both heterosexual and homosexual behavior is called **bisexuality.** Although Freud wrote about bisexuality around the turn of the century, it has only been in recent years that behavioral scientists have become interested in this phenomenon. The neglect of bisexuality seems to be a result of the popular belief that people are either heterosexual or homosexual. People who engage in both types of behavior are thought to be denying their true nature. Interestingly, this view is held by heterosexuals, homosexuals, and some experts on human sexuality (Bieber, 1976; Blumstein & Schwartz, 1976, 1977).

The term "bisexuality" is somewhat misleading because it suggests that individuals are equally aroused by or interested in both kinds of relationships. This may be the case for some individuals, but many others have a clear preference for one type of relationship over the other. Or they may view the two types of relationships as being completely different. For the bisexual, comparing homosexuality and heterosexuality may be like comparing apples and oranges. For example, some women prefer to have sexual relationships with other women, but they may sleep with a man if they feel an emotional rapport with him. The difference in the way a bisexual may perceive homosexual and heterosexual experiences is vividly illustrated in the following quotation:

> I'm straight, but I need outlets when I'm away from home and times like that. And it's easier to get with men than women. So I go into the park or a rest station on the highway and get a man to blow me. I would never stay the night with one of them, or get to know them. It's just a release. It's not like sex with my wife. It's just a way to get what you need without making it a big deal. And it feels less like cheating (Blumstein & Schwartz, 1977, p. 39).

This quotation also illustrates an interesting finding that has come out of research of the bisexual experience. Notice that the man said he was "straight" even though he had frequent homosexual experiences. In interviews with 156 men and women who had bisexual experiences, sociologists Philip Blumstein and Pepper Schwartz (1970, 1977) found many instances of an inconsistency between respondents' self-label and their sexual behavior. Some, like the man quoted above, labeled themselves heterosexual even though they had frequent homosexual experiences. Other labeled themselves homosexual despite their interest in having occasional heterosexual affairs. Still others labeled themselves bisexual even though their sexual behavior was almost exclusively limited to either heterosexuality or homosexuality. For instance, one woman thought of herself as bisexual even though she was happily married and had had two brief homosexual affairs ten years earlier.

Blumstein and Schwartz also found that a person's self-label was not always predictive of future behavior. For instance, several people had once thought of themselves as exclusively homosexual. They then married and remained exclusively heterosexual for 10 to 15 years. Upon obtaining a divorce, they became exclusively homosexual again. These cases suggest that a person's sexual orientation may be less resistant to change and much more flexible than was once thought.

Sadism and Masochism

Sadism involves deriving sexual pleasure from inflicting pain on another person, while **masochism** involves deriving pleasure from receiving pain in a sexual context. Sadists and masochists may engage in elaborate rituals with many accessories, such as ropes, whips, chains, leather collars, or hot wax. Or the sadomasochistic relationship may be more psychological, with one partner assuming the "master" role and the other the "slave" role.

In extreme forms sadomasochism is relatively rare, although Kinsey found that one-fourth of all men and women responded erotically to being bitten during sexual activity. Also, surveys have found that between three and ten percent of respondents find sadomasochistic stories sexually arousing (Hunt, 1974). Of course, one's sexual fantasies do not always correspond to what one would actually do in real life.

Exhibitionism

Exhibitionism, deriving sexual pleasure from exposing one's genitals, is a common, and almost exclusively male, sexual variation. Women who wear clothing that reveals much of their body are thought to be sexy but not deviates.

There are different types of exhibitionists, but the most common is the man who compulsively exposes himself time and again (Gebhard, Gagnon, Pomeroy, & Christenson, 1965). These men seem unable to control their behavior, even though they may have a regular sexual life, have been arrested, and risk a prison sentence for any future arrests. Most exhibitionists are relatively harmless, and their primary goal is to shock or frighten their victims. Only about one in ten has either attempted or seriously considered rape.

Voyeurism

Voyeurism refers to the derivation of sexual pleasure from watching nudes or sexual activities, during which the voyeur will often masturbate. Once again this is a predominantly male variation; approximately one woman is arrested for every ten men.

Voyeurism is another good example of the difficulties inherent in drawing a line between the normal and abnormal. Most men and women enjoy looking at attractive members of the opposite sex. Films portraying explicit sexual relations do not have difficulty finding an audience. The person who is likely to be brought to the attention of legal authorities and mental-health professionals is the one who takes risks (e.g., peeping into private homes) to satisfy his voyeuristic urges and who finds it difficult to establish a heterosexual relationship.

Pedophilia

People who suffer from **pedophilia,** the desire for sexual contact with children, are nearly always men. As is the case with most sexual behavior, there is no typical child molester. Some men are interested in prepubescent girls exclusively; others are interested only in boys; still others do not care about the gender of the child. Sexual activity is generally limited to caressing and fondling the genitals, although some pedophiliacs do attempt intercourse. Most cases do not involve force or violence; in only three percent of the cases is the child physically harmed (McCaghy, 1971). Pedophilia is viewed as one of the most despicable of the sexual variations since the adult takes advantage of the child's powerlessness and naiveté.

A variety of other sexual variations are so rare that there has been virtually no relevant research conducted. For example, coprophilia and urophilia involve an association between sexual arousal and excrement or urine. Apotemnophilia is a condition in which individuals are sexually aroused by partners with an amputated limb or have sexual fantasies of themselves with an amputated arm or leg. These and other variations illustrate the infinite variety of ways in which one's biological drives can be shaped by experience.

Causes of Sexual Variations

Opinions vary as to how people acquire sexual variations. Psychoanalytic theorists tend to emphasize internal conflict, whereas social-learning theorists stress the principles of modeling and reinforcement. To use fetishism as an example, imagine a man who is aroused by women's black underwear. A social-learning theorist may argue that the fetish developed under chance associations. Perhaps as an adolescent the man used photographs of women wearing black underwear as a masturbation aid. Or he may have "borrowed" such garments from his mother or sister for the same purpose. If this individual lacks the social skills necessary to form heterosexual relationships, the black underwear may gradually become the focal point of his sexual activities.

Psychoanalytic theorists would be interested in the man's unconscious reasons for selecting black underwear as a sexual object. Perhaps the man divides women into two categories—"good" women and "bad" women. Black is arousing because it represents the "bad" or sexual woman. Psychoanalytic theorists believe that sexual conflicts and fears of inadequacy play a role in most variations. So the man may use women's underwear to become aroused because the women themselves are too threatening.

One interesting question is why many sexual variations are predominantly male disorders. Voyeurism, exhibitionism, and pedophilia are rarely seen in women. One explanation is that women can express these unusual urges in socially acceptable ways so that they do not come to the attention of law-enforcement officials or mental-health professionals. A woman who has the desire to expose herself can work as an erotic dancer. A woman who wears pants and a shirt goes unnoticed, while a man who wears a dress in public may be arrested.

While this explanation may have some value, it falls short of explaining this sex difference entirely. Women dancers who wear scanty clothing do not generally have the same compulsive need to expose their bodies as do male exhibitionists. And it is no more acceptable for a woman to molest young children than it is for a man.

A more reasonable hypothesis has been offered by Rook and Hammen (1977). They argue that the physiological differences between men and women can lead to different patterns of sexual arousal. Adolescent boys, even if they are sexually inexperienced, can readily recognize when they are sexually aroused—by their erection. Inexperienced girls, however, cannot identify their bodily signs of arousal as readily. Thus, because adolescent boys have frequent evidence of their arousal and girls do not, boys are more likely than girls to associate arousal with a wide variety of stimuli. While plausible, this hypothesis awaits empirical support.

Treatment of Sexual Variations

Behavioral methods of treatment have been most successful in treating individuals with sexual variations. They typically involve a combination of aversion therapy to reduce the attractiveness of the variant stimuli and techniques to increase the individual's ability to initiate and engage in heterosexual activities (Fischer & Gochros, 1977).

As an example, Kushner (1977) reported the case of a 33-year-old man who had had a fetish for women's panties since the age of 12. He would masturbate while wearing the panties, which he took from clotheslines. In treatment, the man received electric shocks to the fingertips while looking at pictures of women's panties, while holding a pair of panties, or while imagining himself wearing the panties. After 14 weeks of therapy the man reported that he was no longer troubled by the fetish and was, in fact, having difficulty imagining situations involving panties while masturbating. The next phase of treatment was aimed at the man's problem of erectile failure. Desensitization and specific suggestions about nonthreatening pleasuring activities (as recommended by Masters and Johnson) were successful in resolving this problem. Eighteen months after treatment, the man reported that he was married, had a family, and had a satisfactory sexual relationship with his wife.

Summary

Human sexual behavior is influenced by biological, psychological, and cultural factors. Physiological research has established that the sex hormones—estrogen in females and testosterone in males—play a role in sexual drive and interest. Estrogen is crucial for female animals, and testosterone appears to be the "libido" hormone for both male and female humans. Physiological research has also found that men and women have similar bodily reactions during the sexual-response cycle.

Learning plays a major role in determining how one's biological heritage will be expressed. Learning shapes sexual attitudes and can result in the development of sexual guilt and anxiety. Psychological factors can also shape one's pattern of sexual arousal. For example, males may develop unusual arousal patterns as a result of boyhood fantasizing during masturbation.

Finally, the culture or subculture in which one lives will influence sexual behavior. Kinsey found that there were substantial differences in sexual behavior between the lower socioeconomic groups on the one hand and the middle and upper socioeconomic groups on the other, although more recent research indicates these differences may be disappearing. Cross-cultural research shows widely divergent patterns of sexual behavior, from the inhibited and joyless sexuality of Inis Beag to the uninhibited and highly pleasurable sexuality of the Mangaian.

Alfred Kinsey's survey provided the first reliable information about American patterns of sexual behavior. Many of his findings were shocking and controversial since they indicated that large numbers of people were behaving in ways that were inconsistent with publicly stated standards of morality. More recent surveys have found that the sexual behavior of men has changed relatively little, but women's behavior has changed dramatically. The relaxation of the double standard appears to be the most meaningful change in sexual behavior in the past 25 years.

One major development in the field of clinical psychology has been the introduction of techniques to treat sexual dysfunctions. Erectile failure and premature ejaculation in men and orgasmic dysfunction and vaginismus in women often can be treated successfully in a brief period of time using techniques developed by behavior therapists and sex researchers Masters and Johnson. Sexual dysfunctions usually result from negative attitudes toward sex or performance anxiety. Treatment procedures generally involve (1) reversing negative attitudes and correcting misconceptions, (2) reducing performance anxiety, (3) improving communication between couples, and (4) providing information about specific sexual techniques.

Most psychologists today recognize the difficulty in making arbitrary distinctions between the sexually normal and abnormal. Hence the term "sexual variations" has come to replace the term "sexual deviations" to describe atypical behavior. Homosexuality, once considered a sin and perversion, is now viewed with more tolerance. As a group, homosexuals are as diverse as heterosexuals. Other sexual variations such as sadism, masochism, exhibitionism, voyeurism, and pedophilia illustrate the diversity of ways in which an individual's biological heritage can be expressed. Psychoanalytic theorists generally believe that sexual variations represent unconscious conflicts, while social-learning theorists believe that they are acquired through learning experiences. Behavioral methods appear to be effective in treating sexual variations. They employ techniques to reduce the attractiveness of the variant stimuli and to increase ability to initiate and engage in heterosexual behavior.

Key Terms For Review

bisexuality
erectile failure
excitement phase
exhibitionism
homosexuality
masochism
orgasm
orgasmic dysfunction
pedophilia
plateau phase
premature ejaculation
refractory period
resolution phase
sadism
sex-negative attitudes
sexual dysfunction
vaginismus
voyeurism

Suggested Readings

Belliveau, F., & Richter, L. *Understanding human sexual inadequacy*. New York: Bantam Books, 1970.
This book explains Masters and Johnson's work with sexual dysfunction in a style that the lay person can understand.

Brecher, R., & Brecher, E. *An analysis of human sexual response*. New York: Signet Books, 1966.
This paperback book describes Masters and Johnson's research regarding normal human sexuel functioning.

Freedman, M. *Homosexuality and psychological functioning*. Belmont, Calif.: Brooks/Cole, 1971.
Written for the beginning psychology student and the general public, this short book provides an overview of homosexuality.

Hunt, M. *Sexual behavior in the 1970s*. Chicago: Playboy Press, 1974.
Hunt reports the results of a sexual-behavior survey sponsored by the Playboy Foundation. Comparisons with Kinsey's surveys are made and interpreted.

Klenke-Hamel, K. E., & Janda, L. H. *Exploring human sexuality*. New York: D. Van Nostrand, 1981.
This book surveys the basic topics and research in the area of human sexuality.

Money, J. *Love and love sickness*. Baltimore: The Johns Hopkins University Press, 1980.
Money presents his research regarding biological disorders of sex and its implications for a variety of sociosexual issues.

18

Violence and Aggression

John could tell it was going to be one of those days. He and his wife had had an argument the night before about the monthly bills, and John knew from his wife's stony silence while she prepared breakfast that she was still angry. This made John feel irritable as well, and when his wife placed his eggs in front of him, he commented that he didn't know how much longer he could face eggs for breakfast. His wife replied icily, "You're welcome to fix breakfast yourself if you're not satisfied with what I make." The dismal mood was only reinforced when their four-year-old son came into the kitchen complaining that he was too tired to dress himself. John, whose patience was wearing thin, gave his son a swat and told him to get back to his room and get dressed.

Breakfast passed without further incident, and without further conversation, and John dropped his son off at nursery school on his way to work. When he arrived at work, his secretary informed him that his boss, Mr. Kirby, was waiting to see him. This did nothing to improve John's mood, since he was sure last month's drop in sales would be the topic of conversation.

John was not wrong, and Mr. Kirby, in his typical style, raked John over the coals for a full 30 minutes without ever raising his voice. John was told, although very subtly, that his competence as a sales manager was questionable and his future with the company uncertain. On his way out of Mr. Kirby's office, John, preoccupied with his own thoughts, bumped into his secretary and broke her glasses. After apologizing profusely and promising to pay for a new pair, John went into the restroom to try to pull himself together. After kicking the wall a few times, he began to feel better. He promised himself that he would make the best of the day and would get to work on improving sales in his territory. He couldn't help thinking, however, that he just wanted to make it through the day without further damage.

Everyone has days like John's when nothing seems to go right, when **aggression** seems to play a major role. Since aggression seems to be a common theme in everyday interactions, an impressive number of personality theorists have suggested that aggression is an important motive for behavior. Theorists do not, however, agree on what causes aggressive behavior. Some argue that it is an innate drive and an inevitable form of human behavior. Others argue that aggression is a type of learned behavior, pointing to societies where aggression is rare. Although literally hundreds of books and thousands of articles have been written about aggression, we are far from understanding it. Nevertheless, behavioral scientists have learned much about aggression. In this chapter we shall consider some of their major findings.

THE PROBLEM OF DEFINITION

Think about the anecdote that opened this chapter. How many instances of aggression can you identify in it? Was the silence between John and his wife an act of aggression? Was John's comment about the eggs or his wife's retort aggressive behavior? What about John's spanking his son, his colliding with his secretary, or his kicking the restroom walls? And was John's boss being aggressive when he questioned John's competence as a sales manager?

The answers to these questions depend on which definition of aggression you accept. And few, if any, varieties of human behavior are as difficult to define. Albert Bandura (1973), a noted aggression researcher, has called the study of aggression a "semantic jungle." Anyone who thinks about aggression for a moment or two can undoubtedly think of many examples of behavior that are quite different but still fall under the label of aggression. For example, dropping a nuclear bomb on Hiroshima and making a sarcastic remark to a friend may both be thought of as acts of aggression. Although many attempts have been made, it is virtually impossible to arrive at a scientifically sound definition that would apply to both acts.

One definition that was widely accepted for many years was provided by Arnold Buss (1961). He defined aggression as any "response that delivers noxious stimuli to another organism" (p. 1). This definition covers virtually all the incidents involving John during his disastrous morning. Because the term "noxious stimuli" can include both physical and psychological stimuli, and because the acts were noxious to the recipient, Buss would agree that the wife's stony silence, the boss's verbal attack, and John's swatting his son were all instances of aggressive behavior. Buss's definition, however, would suggest that John's bumping into his secretary was an act of aggression too, even though it was accidental and John felt bad about it. Also, some behavior would not be classified as acts of aggression using Buss's definition, even though most people would view them as such. John's kicking of the wall would not be an act of aggression since another organism was not involved. If a "hit man" shot at, but missed, his intended victim, it would not be an aggressive act since the victim did not experience noxious stimulation.

The obvious problem with Buss's definition is that the intent of the aggressor is not considered. Buss chose not to include the concept of intent because it is an unobservable condition and hence difficult to subject to rigorous analysis. But as we have seen throughout this text, human cognitions have regained scientific respectability, and most theorists today believe that the notion of intent is crucial to the concept of aggression.

Robert Baron is one of these theorists. He defines aggression as "any form of behavior directed toward the goal of harming or injuring another living being who is motivated to avoid such treatment" (1977, p. 7). Baron recognizes that many examples of behavior cannot be readily classified by using his definition. For example, when John spanked his child, was his intent to hurt the child or to teach him to dress himself in the morning? Using Buss's definition, John's behavior was clearly an act of aggression, but Baron's definition leaves us unsure. Baron points out that our legal system must wrestle with similar questions every day. For instance, the newspaper reporter who writes unflattering things about public figures cannot be held responsible for libel unless there was malicious intent. So juries are asked to decide whether the reporter was acting aggressively or simply presenting what he or she perceived as the facts (even though the perception may have been incorrect).

Along with attempting to arrive at a general definition of aggression, several theorists have proposed ways of conceptualizing various types of aggressive acts. Buss (1961), for example, suggested that aggression can vary along three dimensions: physical-verbal, active-passive, and direct-indirect. These dimensions can result in eight combinations, which are illustrated in Table 18–1; they appear to cover almost any conceivable act of aggression.

One important distinction that has been made by several theorists is that of hostile versus instrumental aggression (Baron, 1977; Buss, 1971; Feshbach, 1964). **Hostile aggression** is behavior in which the primary goal is to harm or injure the recipient. John's sarcastic comment to his wife would be an example. He did not expect to gain anything from his wife; he wanted only to make her feel bad.

Instrumental aggression is behavior that is intended to obtain certain objectives and is not intended specifically to harm the recipient. Mr. Kirby's attack on John was motivated by a desire to increase profits rather than to injure John's feelings.

While some theorists find this distinction useful, others have criticized it as being false. Bandura (1973) argues that both hostile and instrumental aggression are aimed at achieving specific goals, even though the nature of the goals may differ. Hence it would be appropriate to use the term "instrumental aggression" in both cases. In response to this point, Dolf Zillman (1979) has used the terms "annoyance-motivated aggression" and "incentive-motivated aggression."

Table 18–1. Buss's Categories of Aggression

Type	*Example*
Physical-active-direct	Hitting another person.
Physical-active-indirect	Hiring a "hit man" to kill another person.
Physical-passive-direct	Demonstrators engaging in a sit-in to prevent business executives from reaching their offices.
Physical-passive-indirect	Strikers refusing to return to work.
Verbal-active-direct	Insulting another person.
Verbal-active-indirect	Spreading vicious gossip about another person.
Verbal-passive-direct	Giving another person the "silent treatment."
Verbal-passive-indirect	Failing to speak up in another person's defense when he or she is unfairly criticized.

Source: Buss (1961).

These terms distinguish between the two types of aggression while avoiding the problem of defining goals.

By now you should have a sense of the difficulties inherent in defining aggression and conceptualizing the wide variety of forms that aggressive acts can take. Perhaps the most reasonable position is the one taken by Russell Geen (1976) of the University of Missouri. He believes that it may be impossible to formulate a single definition of aggression. Geen approaches the study of aggression by adopting an operational definition of aggression suited to the type of aggression he is dealing with. In a child-abuse situation, for example, he may look at the intensity of verbal attacks and frequency of physical abuse. He then attempts to learn as much as possible about the variables associated with that type of aggression. This appears to be a logical approach, because it is very likely that research findings regarding a specific form of aggression cannot be generalized to all acts of aggression. For instance, the factors associated with violent and unpredictable physical attacks upon children may be quite different from the factors associated with subtle verbal attacks upon one's colleagues. In other words, when we use the term "aggression," we are talking about a class of behavior whose differences may be as important as its similarities. With this in mind, let us review the factors that contribute to aggressive behavior.

BIOLOGICAL FACTORS

Recall the opening case history in Chapter 2 of Charles Whitman, who shot and killed 13 people on the campus of the University of Texas. His autopsy revealed a brain tumor that was thought to have contributed to his outburst of violence. This case illustrates what is perhaps the oldest tradition among behavioral scientists—to look for innate or biological explanations for aggressive behavior. There are several varieties of biological theories, but essentially they all state that it is human nature to be aggressive. This tradition in psychology began with William James, who posited 32 different instinctual patterns, of which aggression was one (James, 1890).

The early part of the twentieth century was marked by an attempt to explain many types of human behavior by instincts. In fact, one theorist claimed to have identified 5,684 behavior patterns that were instinctive (Bernard, 1924, 1926). But as instincts were being used to explain virtually all forms of human behavior, theorists recognized that instincts had little explanatory value. It does not help to understand a behavioral pattern when we say that it is caused by instincts—especially when we say the same about 5,000 forms of behavior. The proliferation of instincts had the effect of reducing their importance as an explanation for aggression. Nonetheless, many people persist in their attempt to explain aggression in biological terms. The most influential of these are psychoanalysts, ethologists, psychologists, and other researchers who point to the influence of the sex chromosomes and the sex hormones.

Psychoanalysis

As you will recall from Chapter 10, Sigmund Freud, the father of psychoanalysis, believed that two instincts motivate human behavior: the death instinct, or thanatos, and the life instinct, or libido. In contrast to other theorists who believed aggression is an instinct directed toward others, Freud believed that the destructive, or death, instinct was directed toward the self—that is, toward returning the self to its original inanimate form. In order to avoid self-destruction, the individual is forced to direct aggression toward others through defense mechanisms.

Perhaps the most important element of Freud's theory of aggression is that of catharsis. **Catharsis** refers to the weakening or elimination of the aggressive impulses by substituting some form of less destructive or nondestructive behavior. For example, a husband who yells at his wife may experience a catharsis of his aggressive impulses so that he is less likely to assault her physically.

Some psychoanalytic theorists have suggested that surgeons or dentists have chosen their profession as a vehicle for expressing their aggressive impulses in a socially appropriate way. And a few theorists suggest that violence on television is desirable because of its cathartic effect.

Some practicing psychotherapists use Freud's theory as a basis for treatment. For instance, the following advertisement appeared in a professional newsletter in 1980:

> ENCOUNTERBATS: cloth-covered foam bats with hand-guards, for professional, institutional, or home use. For anger or for fun. $38.50 per pair.

Psychotherapist George Bach, who has written the best-selling books *The Intimate Enemy* (Bach & Wyden, 1968) and *Creative Aggression* (Bach & Goldberg, 1974), believes that the use of such bats in marriage counseling will drain off aggressive impulses. Bach recommends that couples feel free to express their hostility verbally as well. At one point, he recommended to women, "Don't be afraid to be a real shrew, a real bitch! Get rid of your pent-up hostilities! Tell them where you're really at! Let it be total, vicious, exaggerated hyperbole!"

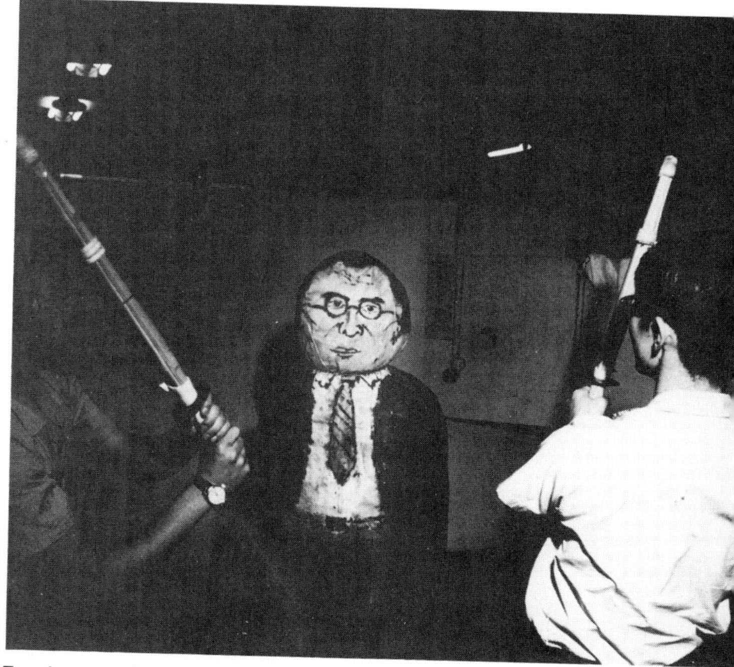

Employees of Matsushita Electric Company in Japan achieve catharsis by going to the self-control room and taking a few swings at an effigy of the boss. *(© Paolo Koch / Rapho Photo Researchers, Inc.)*

The catharsis hypothesis has been subjected to experimental tests. A typical experiment might involve a confederate who commits aggression against subjects either by making insulting remarks or by administering electric shocks. Subjects are then allowed to reply in kind, and their hostility level is compared to that of subjects given the same treatment but not allowed to respond to the confederate. A few studies have found that allowing subjects to respond to the confederate's insults does have a cathartic effect (Doob & Wood, 1972; Rosenbaum & deCharms, 1960). Several other studies, however, suggest just the opposite. For example, in one study the confederates administered excessive electric shocks to the subjects (Geen, Stonner, & Shope, 1975). Some of the subjects were allowed to administer shocks to the confederate in return on two different occasions, while others had no such opportunity. The subjects who administered the most intense shocks expressed the greatest hostility toward the confederates on rating scales. It seems that one act of aggression, rather than reducing hostility, may serve to increase it.

Bach's techniques do not appear to be supported by the available evidence. It has been found that couples who freely express aggression verbally are more likely than those who do not to use physical violence (Straus, 1974). In a review of the experimental research, psychologist Michael Quanty (1976) has concluded that aggressive responses can have a cathartic effect, but only for individuals who have a history of being reinforced for responding in such a way. For example, many married couples have the expectation that they will "kiss and make up" after having a fight. So their feelings of hostility may be lessened after expressing aggression. But it is the overall pattern they have established that reduces hostility rather than the cathartic effect of expressing aggression per se. For many other individuals who have come to behave in an aggressive fashion, committing an aggressive act may serve to promote further aggression.

Freud himself was not very specific about the effect that catharsis would have on the strength of the aggressive impulses. The notion that catharsis could keep thanatos at manageable levels is based on other theorists' interpretations of Freud's theory and not on what Freud had to say about the issue (Jakobi, Selg, & Belschner, 1971). Freud himself believed that aggression and violence were inevitable. His theory presented a very pessimistic view of the destiny of the human race.

Ethology and Aggression as Instinct

Freud's theory of aggression gradually lost favor because it was not explicit and lacked supporting evidence. Aggression as instinctive behavior regained respectability, however, during the 1950s and 1960s with the work of ethologists, such as the Nobel Laureate Konrad Lorenz (1966, 1974). **Ethology** is the scientific study of animal behavior. Ethologists direct much of their research toward identifying certain behavioral patterns that appear to result from the organism's evolutionary heritage. Lorenz believes that aggression is part of both animals' and humans' evolutionary heritage. Hence he agrees with Freud's view that aggression is instinctive. But he was more specific than Freud about how aggression operates, and he was more concerned with gathering supporting evidence.

Baring of the teeth by a baboon acts as an aggression-releasing stimulus for other baboons. (© *Irven Devore)*

Lorenz hypothesized that aggression stems from a fighting instinct that is found in humans and many animals. The energy for this instinct is continually and spontaneously generated by the organism. So, aggressive energy is thought to accumulate gradually over time.

One of Lorenz's most important contributions was identifying special aggression-releasing stimuli for a variety of animals. **Aggression-releasing stimuli** are varieties of behavior or postures assumed by an animal that elicit aggression from other animals. A baboon baring its canine teeth, shown on this page, is an example of a releasing stimulus. According to Lorenz's theory, this behavior will elicit aggression from other baboons as long as they have sufficient aggressive energy accumulated.

An important aspect of the theory is that if the organism does not have the opportunity to act aggressively periodically, the energy will build until aggression can be elicited by less potent releasing stimuli or, ultimately, in the absence of any releasing stimuli. In contrast to Freud, who was not very specific about the effect of catharsis, Lorenz clearly believed that periodic episodes of minor aggressive acts can prevent the occurrence of more destructive aggression.

Along with aggression-releasing stimuli, Lorenz hypothesized the existence of **inhibitory stimuli**—varieties of behavior or postures assumed by an animal that inhibit aggression in other animals. For example, the male baboon presents his hindquarters for mounting by another male in an act of appeasement that reduces the probability of further aggression. An important inhibitory stimulus for many animals, including humans, is cries of distress. For example, an inexperienced turkey hen will attack any animal of reasonable size if it approaches her brood. She will even attack her own chicks, but the "distress cries" serve as an inhibitory mechanism. Deafened hens, however, will peck at their chicks and actually kill them (Lorenz, 1966).

Lorenz believes that the fighting instinct has survival value for both humans and animals. Fighting to protect territory ensures the even distribution of a species over a particular area. It ensures that the strongest and best members of a species will have the best areas, thus increasing their chances of survival. The fighting instinct also allows the fittest members to mate and thus results in strong and aggressive offspring. Somewhat paradoxically, Lorenz suggests that the fighting instinct may reduce intra-species fighting by leading to the establishment of "pecking orders," with the strongest and most aggressive at the top. These pecking orders serve to stabilize interaction among the animals.

Humans have problems with their aggressive instincts, according to Lorenz, because their ability to inflict harm on others has outstripped their innate inhibitory mechanisms. Lorenz speculates that during the early stages of human evolution, natural inhibitors, such as cries of distress, were effective in preventing extreme destructiveness. With the invention of various long-range weapons, such as guns and guided missiles, the balance between the fighting instinct and the innate inhibitors was lost.

Lorenz is much more optimistic than Freud was regarding the control of destructive aggression in humans. Because he believes that catharsis can reduce the energy associated with the fighting instinct, he believes that people can keep their aggressive impulses under control by engaging in or viewing nondestructive aggressive activities. For instance, Lorenz would suggest that playing in or even watching a football game would serve this purpose.

Certain aspects of Lorenz's theory are well accepted. Many ethologists have presented strong evidence for the existence of releasing mechanisms in lower vertebrates (Eibl-Eibesfeldt, 1970; Marler & Hamilton, 1968; Tinbergen, 1951). That the existence of such mechanisms demonstrates that aggression is instinctive, however, is a matter of conjecture. Many biologists and psychologists believe that learning factors have not been convincingly ruled out (Lehrman, 1970; Schneirla, 1959; Zillman, 1979).

Lorenz's generalizations from animals to people have been supported by some psychologists but questioned by many others. Some theorists have argued that there are both releasing and inhibitory mechanisms for humans. In his best-selling book *The Naked Ape,* Desmond Morris (1968) argued that men who stick out their chests or wear clothes that make them appear taller are exhibiting a display of threat. Morris also offered practical applications of the theory. For example, he suggested that if we are stopped for a traffic violation, we should show ourselves to be submissive to the police officer in words, posture, and gesture. We should also move away from our cars to prevent feelings of territorial rivalry from developing.

As Zillman (1979) points out, such advice is pure speculation. There is no empirical evidence supporting the idea that humans have innate releasing or inhibitory mechanisms or that aggression itself is innate. For example, no one has presented convincing evidence that sticking out one's chest is a releasing mechanism. Also, a principle that is well accepted among behavioral scientists is that as we move up the scale from the lower to the higher animals, learning plays an increasingly important role in the development of all kinds of behavior.

Physiological Influences

Kenneth Clark (1971), past president of the American Psychological Association, has stated that aggression is a disease. Furthermore, he believes that we know enough about the physiological basis of aggression to develop drugs and surgical techniques to control it in order "to assure psychological health and moral integrity [that is] imperative for the survival of human society" (p. 35).

Clark's view certainly is not without appeal. A world where human brutality and destructiveness are controlled by antiaggression pills seems preferable to what we have now. But is it possible? Let us review what is known about the physiological basis of aggression.

Brain Centers. As you will recall from Chapter 2, certain areas of the brain do seem to be associated with aggressive behavior in both animals and humans. Fifty years ago physiologist W. R. Hess (1932) found that electrical stimulation of certain areas of the brain in cats elicited aggressive behavior. Shortly after that, other researchers found that the removal of certain portions of the brains of monkeys resulted in a great reduction in viciousness (Kluever & Bucy, 1937). It was this research that led to the practice of psychosurgery with violent people. Unfortunately for both the monkeys and the people, the side effects were severe. Patients who received these early operations were often referred to as human vegetables (see Chapter 13 for a more detailed discussion of psychosurgery).

More recently, inhibitory areas of the brain have been identified. José Delgado (1967) has provided dramatic evidence of this by stopping a charging bull in his tracks through remote-control stimulation of the bull's brain. He has also changed the pecking order in a monkey colony by installing a lever that controlled the inhibitory area of the dominant male monkey's brain (Delgado, 1963). The subordinate monkey would halt his tormentor's attacks by pressing the lever. The subordinate monkey no longer had to avoid his boss or display submissive gestures when around him.

While there appears to be little doubt that certain areas of the brain located in the limbic system (see Chapter 2) are associated with the stimulation and inhibition of aggressive behavior, the evidence does not allow us to conclude that these areas of the brain are the source of aggressive behavior. It could be that stimulation of a particular area results in pain, or fear, or perhaps unfamiliar and unpleasant sensations, and that these reactions provoke the aggressive behavior (Scherer, Abeles, & Fischer, 1975). In the case of Delgado's charging bull, perhaps motor behavior that is incompatible with attacking was elicited (Valenstein, 1973). The most reasonable conclusion appears to be that certain brain areas play a role in aggressive behavior but are not a unique source of aggressiveness. Other factors, such as learning, are likely to contribute to aggressiveness as well.

Sex Hormones and Chromosomes. People have known for centuries that castration of animals, such as bulls and roosters, renders them less aggressive. In fact castration, which results in reduced levels of the male sex hormone testosterone, has been used with some success in some countries to treat prison inmates jailed for violent sex crimes (Moyer, 1971). Controlled research with monkeys also presents convincing evidence that testosterone plays a role in aggressive behavior (Joslyn, 1973; Rose, Haladay, & Burnstein, 1971). In an extensive review of the literature on sex differences, Maccoby and Jacklin (1974) concluded that "males are more aggressive than females in all human societies for which evidence is available" (p. 242). They suggested that hormonal factors as well as social-learning factors account for this difference.

Although many theorists believe that the evidence linking testosterone and aggression is quite strong, there are dissenters. For instance, John Money (1980), one of the foremost experts on biological aspects of human sexuality, concludes that "all told, among human beings, there is no substantial experimental evidence that sex hormones, either before birth or at puberty, are directly responsible for sexual differences in aggression, assertion, or dominance" (p. 159). Money points to cases of boys and girls who were exposed to abnormally high levels of testosterone in the uterus. During childhood these individuals are more active than their peers, but they are no more hostile, threatening, or aggressive. Money

CRITICAL ISSUE

Sex and Aggression: Is There a Link?

The idea that aggressive tendencies can be expressed in sexual activities has been with us for some time. Freud was very interested in this connection and provided many examples of how one expresses anger through sexual behavior. Hostility was thought to account for many forms of sexual problems.

During the past decade, many studies have examined the effects of sexual arousal on aggressive behavior. As is so often the case, the nature of the relationship depends on the situation. Typical findings are that when men are exposed to mildly arousing erotic stimuli, they will act less aggressively than men who have not been exposed to such material. Sexual arousal seems to be incompatible with feelings of anger and hostility. On the other hand, men who are insulted or angered (e.g., told that an essay they had written was of poor quality) prior to viewing erotica will show elevated levels of aggressiveness. Also, highly arousing forms of erotica seem to lead to increases in aggression for both angered and nonangered men.

One goal of such research is to answer questions, posed by the National Institute of Mental Health, about the conditions that lead to sexual attacks against women. A recent study by Edward Donnerstein (1980) provides a good example of research that attempts to deal with this issue. Donnerstein asked 120 men to view one of three films: a neutral, erotic, or aggressive-erotic film. Half of the subjects were angered prior to viewing the film by either a male or a female confederate. After viewing the film, subjects were given an opportunity to deliver electric shocks to the confederate. Of course, no electric shocks were actually delivered.

The results found that men who viewed the aggressive-erotic film (which depicted an act of rape) showed higher levels of aggression toward the female confederate than men who viewed the erotic film. This was particularly true for those men who were angered before viewing the film. Interestingly, viewing the erotic film led to increased aggression against the male confederate but not against the woman.

One must always be cautious in generalizing from laboratory research to real-life behavior, but these findings do have important implications. They are consistent with those of the Presidential Commission on Obscenity and Pornography (1971), which concluded there is no evidence of a relationship between pornography in general and subsequent sex crimes. Donnerstein's results, however, raise the possibility that specific types of erotic material—namely aggressive erotica—may contribute to such crimes. One can imagine a man who tends to be socially inept and consequently is rejected by women. If this man, who probably feels anger toward women, is exposed to pornography that depicts aggression against women, he may be more likely to commit such acts. The outrage over the "snuff" films—pornographic films in which a character was actually murdered—may well be justified.

believes that the aggressiveness of the lower vertebrates is rather strictly under the control of hormones. But as we move up to the higher vertebrates, learning factors can eliminate the effect of the sex hormones.

Money also discusses the belief that the male sex chromosome plays a role in aggressiveness. This belief was buttressed by reports that an unusually high proportion of men jailed for violent crimes had the abnormal XYY configuration (Jacobs, Brunton, & Melville, 1965). Several theorists have discounted the importance of the Y or the extra Y chromosome in violent crimes (Bandura, 1973; Shah, 1970). It has been pointed out that many men with XYY configuration do not get into difficulty because of their aggressiveness and that prisoners with the XYY configuration are not more violent than normal prisoners. An indirect connection between XYY and aggressiveness is also possible. The XYY configuration can result in lowered intelligence and an above-average physical stature. These differences may lead to differences in socialization, which in turn may be responsible for higher levels of aggressiveness.

All the evidence regarding biological bases of aggression suggests that Clark's proposal that aggression be controlled medically is certainly not an impossibility, but neither is it an immediate possibility. Aside from the ethical issues involved (who would decide who has to take the aggression-controlling pill?), a majority of psychologists believe that it is unlikely that pills or electrodes can eliminate destructive human aggression. As we shall see shortly, certain social factors are influential in the formation of aggressive behavior.

An important point to keep in mind is that the research regarding the brain and hormones says nothing about the source of aggression, even in the lower vertebrates. Areas of the brain and hormones may mediate the expression of aggression, but it would be misleading to think of such factors as controlling or causing aggressive behavior. The question of what *causes* aggression may be unanswerable or best left to philosophers. Psychologists may have to limit themselves to unraveling the relative contributions of biological and environmental factors and the various ways in which they can interact with one another.

THE VIOLENT INDIVIDUAL

One truism in psychology is that the best predictor of future behavior is past behavior, and this certainly applies to aggression. We can conclude that people who have behaved aggressively in the past are likely to behave aggressively in the future. We cannot, however, predict with any de-

None of these attempted or actual assassins of Presidents or Presidential candidates was on the Secret Service list of potential killers. Left to right: Sirhan Sirhan, Arthur Bremer, Lynette (Squeaky) Fromme, Sara Jane Moore. *(© Wide World Photos; Wide World Photos; United Press International Photos; United Press International Photos)*

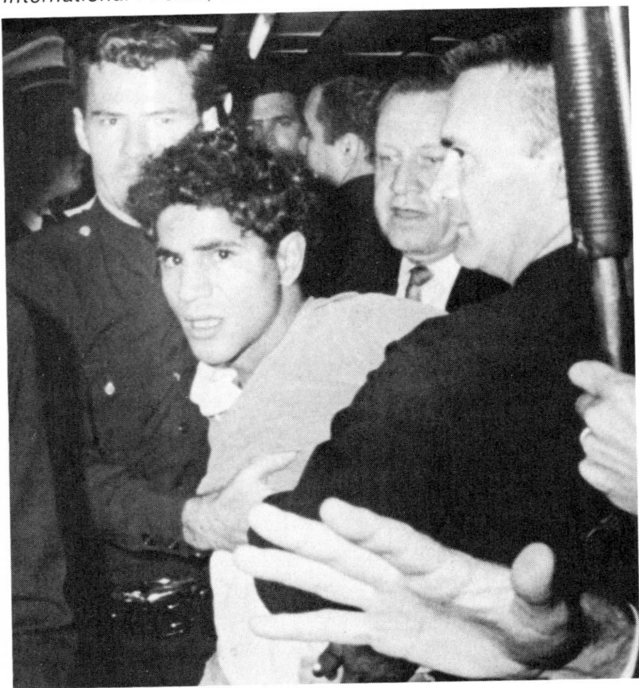

gree of accuracy who will be violent and who will not on the basis of personality characteristics. Recall the discussion of personality traits in Chapter 10. Many psychologists have attempted to measure a variety of personality traits to be able to predict future behavior, but these attempts have not met with much success. This holds true for the trait of aggressiveness with its potential for violence. In spite of intensive efforts by researchers (cf. Edmunds & Kendrick, 1980), no one has been able to construct a test that measures aggressiveness with any substantial degree of validity.

A Supreme Court decision in 1966 (*Baxtrom* v. *Harold*) provided a dramatic example of the difficulty of identifying potentially violent people. In that year there were 967 patients in New York hospitals for the criminally insane who had not committed crimes. These individuals, all of whom were judged to be potentially violent by psychiatrists, were considered too dangerous to be in regular mental hospitals. The Supreme Court ruled that these patients should be transferred to regular mental hospitals. Hospital officials and employees greeted the arrival of the patients with trepidation. They were convinced that the patients would assault others and would have to be sent back to the hospitals for the criminally insane. Four years later, only 26 of the 967 patients had been sent back because of threatening behavior (Steadman & Cocozza, 1975). The psychiatrists were correct in their predictions in fewer than three percent of the cases.

A more recent example of the difficulty of identifying individuals with the potential for violence concerns the attempted assassination of President Ronald Reagan by John Hinckley. Although the Secret Service keeps a list of some 25,000 people

who are believed to pose a threat to the president, and a second list of 300 to 400 considered to be especially dangerous, Hinckley's name was not included. In fact, none of the individuals who have made assassination attempts on Presidents or Presidential candidates since 1963—Sirhan Sirhan, Arthur Bremer, Lynette (Squeaky) Fromme, Sara Jane Moore, and John Hinckley—had been included on the list (*Time*, 1981).

It is puzzling that it is so difficult to identify individuals with a potential for aggression and violence, because in many ways aggression does seem to be a trait. Leonard Eron (1980) has pointed out that people who are aggressive are likely to act that way in many situations. Children who are aggressive at home are usually aggressive at school. People who are verbally aggressive are usually physically aggressive. Furthermore, one can predict the aggressiveness of 18- and 19-year-olds by measuring their aggressiveness at age eight. The fact remains, however, that no one has been able to construct a test that measures the aggressive personality.

The difficulty of predicting who will be violent on the basis of personality characteristics has led psychologists to focus their efforts on identifying social conditions and learning factors that are likely to elicit aggression in people in general. Let us consider some examples of their work.

SOCIAL FACTORS

One reason for the appeal of instinct and physiological theories of aggression is that they seem to make instances of incredible brutality understandable. How could the Nazis murder millions of people? How could some American soldiers in Vietnam kill innocent women and children? How can some parents torture helpless infants until they are disfigured or dead? Or how can we hear about such incidents on the evening news without being stricken with horror?

It is tempting to believe that these things could not happen unless there was something about our nature that caused us to be aggressive. Yet, as we have suggested, a substantial number of psychologists believe that we are not born to be aggressive, but rather learn to be that way. These theorists, generally referred to as social-learning theorists, recognize that physiological factors may mediate the expression of aggression, but they believe that our environment and learning experiences play the crucial role. Take the case of John that opened this chapter. His aggressiveness with his wife and children are understandable in terms of his environment. It would seem difficult to argue that he was sarcastic to his wife or spanked his child as a result of innate aggressiveness. Let us review the evidence supporting their position.

Frustration and Aggression

It is commonly said that frustration leads to aggression. This notion was first suggested by John Dollard and his colleagues in 1939 (Dollard, Doob, Miller, Mowrer, & Sears, 1939). They presented a simple and straightforward alternative to the instinct theory and the biological theory of aggression. They suggested that (1) frustration always leads to some form of aggression and (2) aggression is always the result of frustration. Their hypothesis had an immediate impact and continues to be seen frequently in the popular literature. Aggression researchers, however, were quick to reject it.

Probably everyone can think of instances in which frustration does *not* lead to aggression. Consider students who are frustrated by receiving a poor grade on an exam after studying hard for it. Some students probably will become aggressive, making hostile remarks about the professor or displacing their aggression onto a roommate. But others will respond to the frustration by vowing to study even harder. Still others may withdraw and shrug it off. Aggression need not always result from frustration, either. The hired killer or the soldier may kill to get money or to follow orders.

This is not to say that frustration cannot lead to aggression. A leading researcher in the field, Leonard Berkowitz (1969), has modified Dollard's

APPLICATION

Violence against Children: Toward Prevention

"Sometimes she would make me mad, and I would hit her before I knew it, I would hit her with the belt, I'd use the switch or sometimes I'd hit her in the mouth or face and push her down." This quotation is taken from a mother's statement given the night her two-year-old daughter died from a beating.

Incidents such as this are depressingly common. Over 200,000 cases of child abuse are reported every year. Many more go unreported. Surveys suggest that the actual incidence of child abuse in the United States may exceed two million cases a year (Straus, 1979). The tragedy of defenseless infants and children being punched, kicked, bitten, burned, stabbed, and even killed by those on whom they are completely dependent is almost beyond comprehension.

During the past decade the problem of child abuse has received increasing attention, and many programs have begun that provide help for parents who have a tendency to abuse their children. Self-help groups, hotlines, and public-awareness campaigns have undoubtedly made an invaluable contribution. Unfortunately, these agencies and services typically are not involved until a child has been abused at least once.

A recent article by Barton Schmitt (1980), a pediatrician, offers the possibility that many potential cases of child abuse can be prevented. Schmitt summarized research that has been conducted at Colorado General Hospital in Denver. He pointed out that while many of the traditional indices of high-risk families, such as unemployment and conflict between the husband and wife, can be useful in predicting child abuse, direct observation of the mother-child interactions while on the maternity ward can be extremely valuable. Schmitt advises that physicians and nurses be sensitive to three questions: "How does the mother look?" "What does she say?" "What does she do?"

Mothers who look sad, depressed, angry or agitated may have the potential for neglecting or abusing their child. If they express anger or disappointment about the baby or say things such as that the baby is ugly, mean, or bad, the staff should take notice. Finally, mothers who avoid looking at or holding their babies or who handle them roughly or with minimal warmth should be considered high risks, particularly if they display anger when the infant cries or spank the infant.

These signs were used to identify 50 high-risk cases. Half of the cases received the usual services, while the other half were enrolled in a coordinated medical-care program. As part of this program, the hospital staff made frequent telephone calls to the families to inquire how things were going and to offer suggestions in case there were problems. A public-health nurse made weekly visits and offered guidance for child care and appropriate discipline techniques. During particularly difficult periods, such as when the child was ill or was having toilet-training problems, the staff kept in touch with the parents daily.

At the end of two years, the program proved to be a success. There were no cases of child abuse in the group that received the coordinated medical-care program. In the control group, 20 percent of the children received serious injuries as a result of child abuse. As Schmitt suggests, we do not have to wait until the child has been abused before taking action. By making simple behavioral observations and utilizing existing medical services for high-risk cases, we can reduce the incidence of child abuse dramatically.

original position and has suggested that under some conditions there is an increased probability of aggressive behavior following frustration. Several experiments appear to support this notion (Berkowitz & Geen, 1967; Harris, 1974). Many other experiments, however, failed to find that frustration produced aggression (Buss, 1963, 1966; Taylor & Pisano, 1971), and still others found that frustration may even serve to *reduce* aggression on occasion (Gentry, 1970; Rule & Hewitt, 1971).

For example, a student who is frustrated by studying hard for an exam and then failing it may become depressed and withdraw from the course to avoid the instructor. Is this another instance in which psychologists have managed to make a seemingly simple issue extremely complex?

The difficulty in arriving at any conclusions based on the available research is that so many variables are involved. The degree of frustration, the nature of the frustration, and the way in which subjects could express their aggression are just a few of the important considerations. Robert Baron (1977) offers a tentative resolution of this issue. He suggests that the link between frustration and aggression depends on two factors: (1) the magnitude of frustration and (2) the degree to which the frustration is perceived to be arbitrary or unexpected. Zillman, in an extensive review (1979), came to much the same conclusion. He suggested that when frustration is perceived as arbitrary or unexpected, the victim will interpret it as a personal attack. And it is when frustration is coupled with a personal attack that the frustration is likely to lead to aggressive behavior.

Frustration is one cause of aggression. *(© Stephanie Fitzgerald/Peter Arnold, Inc.)*

Consider the following example: You have been working hard to assemble a piece of equipment to meet a deadline that your boss has set for you. You have all the pieces laid out and arranged for the final assembly when your boss walks through the room, bumps into the table, and knocks over all the pieces. Although he apologizes profusely, you know that several hours' work has been wasted. Compare your reaction to that scenario with one in which your boss comes into the room, berates you for your slowness, and intentionally knocks all the pieces to the floor.

Here is a second example: Your boss has given you a choice of three bonuses for completing an important job: a week's paid vacation, a $500 bonus, or a weekend cruise to the Bahamas. You have your heart set on the cruise but would be very happy to receive the $500. Suppose your boss says that she is sorry but the cruise is booked solid and she has to give you your second choice of the $500 bonus. Now suppose that your boss says that she has decided (without consulting you) that you will receive the week's vacation with pay. How would your reactions differ?

If you are like the majority of subjects in psychological experiments, you would be more likely to express aggression in the latter outcome in both examples. In these cases it is likely that you would perceive your boss's frustrating actions as insulting in the first example and arbitrary in the second. Experiments using similar situations have confirmed these speculations (Mallick & McCandless, 1966; Worchel, 1974).

Roger Brown and Richard Herrnstein (1975) have coined the phrase "illegitimate disappointment of legitimate expectations" to describe this phenomenon. They argue that we develop expectations about how we will be treated by others. When we do not receive the treatment we expect—that is, when we are frustrated—we will become aggressive if we perceive the disappointment to be illegitimate or arbitrary. Table 18–2 provides several examples of legitimate and illegitimate disappointments of legitimate expectations.

Learning and Aggression

Albert Bandura has conducted a number of influential studies dealing with aggression. Many of them have used young children as subjects and illustrate the importance of observational learning, or modeling (see Chapter 5), on the acquisition and expression of aggressive behavior. His research has shown that children can learn to be aggressive by observing models behaving in aggressive ways.

In one study, Bandura had young children observe a model act aggressively toward a Bobo doll—a large inflated plastic toy with a weighted bottom. The model engaged in unusual, aggressive behavior, sitting on the doll, punching it in the nose, hitting it on the head with a toy hammer, and kicking it around the room. After observing the model, the children were allowed to play in a room containing a Bobo doll and a variety of other toys, many of which had been used by the model in the assaults against the Bobo doll. The children generally acted toward the doll in a highly aggressive fashion, often assaulting it exactly as the model had done (Bandura, Ross, & Ross, 1963a, 1963b).

Further research demonstrated that observing an aggressive model does not mean that the child will always act aggressively. Bandura makes the important distinction between acquisition and performance of behavior. If the children observed a model who was rewarded for acting aggressively toward the doll, then they would be likely to follow suit. Conversely, if they saw the model being punished for such behavior, they would not act aggressively. All children, however, could imitate the model's behavior when asked to do so. In other words, all the children learned the aggressive behavior, but they copied it only when they saw the model rewarded (Bandura, 1965).

Justifications for Aggression

Bandura's theory emphasizes the importance of cognitive factors—people's thoughts and beliefs—in regulating aggressiveness. One interesting as-

Table 18–2. Legitimate and Illegitimate Disappointments of Legitimate Expectations

Illegitimate Disappointments	*Legitimate Disappointments*
1. After you have waited to see your doctor for over two hours, she walks into the examining room with a cheery "How are you today?"	1. After you have waited to see your doctor for over two hours, she arrives, apologetic, and tells you about an emergency operation she had to perform.
2. After many attempts you finally manage to flag down a taxi only to be told that the driver does not want to go to the airport.	2. After many attempts you finally manage to flag down a taxi only to be told the driver cannot go to the airport because he has to return home to tend a sick child.
3. Just as you are about to walk out the door to pick up your date for the New Year's Eve party, she calls to cancel with no explanation.	3. Just as you are about to walk out the door to pick up your date for the New Year's Eve party, she calls from the hospital to tell you she was in an accident.
4. After you have been holding a towel around a leaking pipe for three hours, the plumber arrives with beer on his breath and pool chalk on his fingers.	4. After you have been holding a towel around a leaking pipe for three hours, the plumber arrives and tells you how his truck caught on fire.
5. Your application for a promotion from secretary to administrative assistant is turned down and given to Miss Smith, who is known for her tight sweaters and "creative" spelling.	5. Your application for a promotion from secretary to administrative assistant is turned down and given to Miss Jones, who is known for her intelligence and willingness to work long hours.

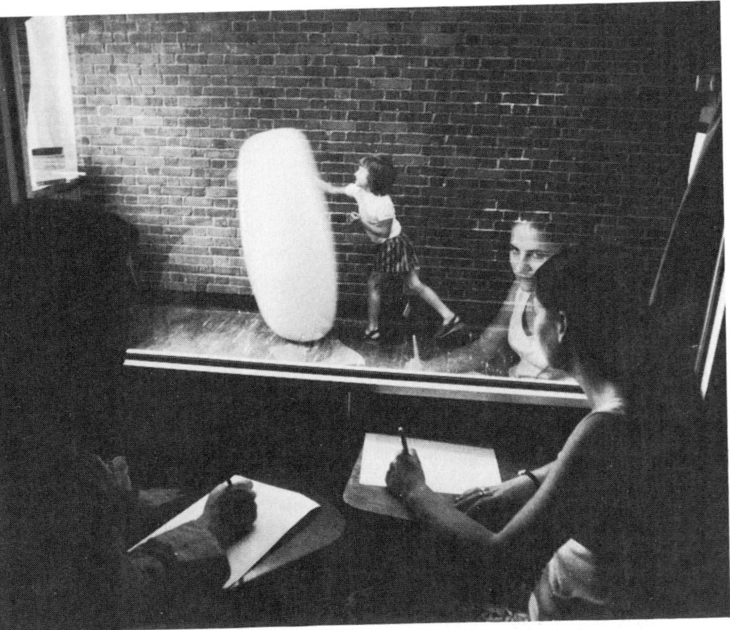

These young children mimic the behavior of a model they have watched pummeling a Bobo doll. *(Cary Wolinsky / Stock, Boston, Inc.)*

pect of this theory is how cognitions can justify cruel and destructive acts of aggression. Bandura (1973) has written, "By engaging in a variety of self-deceptive cognitive maneuvers, humane, moral people can behave cruelly without self-condemnation" (p. 238). Examples of processes by which this can occur, as suggested by Bandura, are as follows:

1. *Slighting aggression by advantageous comparison.* This occurs when a person compares his or her actions with more hideous deeds in order to minimize the meaning of the aggression. A child may say, "Well, maybe I pushed her, but anyone else would have beaten her up." A terrorist may say, "Yes, we shot them, but we did not torture them first."
2. *Justification of aggression in terms of higher principles.* Examples might include the executions of dissidents in politically unstable countries or the bombing of civilians to preserve democracy. The idea here is that the ends justify the means.
3. *Displacement of responsibility.* The war atrocities of Vietnam, the mass murders of the Nazis, and the behavior of ordinary people in Stanley Milgram's research (see Chapter 16) are explained by the principle "I was only following orders."
4. *Diffusion of responsibility.* The violence of mobs provides an example of this principle. A person can avoid feeling responsible if he or she is only one of a large group of people.
5. *Dehumanization of victims.* Much aggression is justified by the view that the victims are less than human. Blacks and the Vietnamese are painfully aware of this principle.
6. *Attribution of blame to victims.* Many studies have found that people tend to justify their aggression by believing they were forced into it by the victim; that is, "He only got what was coming to him."
7. *Misrepresentation of consequences.* People may justify their aggression by emphasizing the benefits and minimizing the negative aspects. For example, a teacher may justify her hostile and sarcastic remarks to a student by pointing out that they made him work harder. She may not mention the fact that the student no longer participates in class discussions.
8. *Graduated desensitization.* This is a gradual process by which nonaggressive persons may become increasingly aggressive. Initially, they may engage in only mildly aggressive behavior. As their discomfort with this behavior disappears, they may engage in progressively more aggressive actions.

Although Bandura has posited these self-deceptive maneuvers that allow people to engage in aggressive behavior without feeling guilty or uncomfortable, he and other social-learning theorists do not regard aggression as inevitable. Unlike the Freudians and the ethologists, who view aggression as part of human nature, social-learning theorists believe that it is possible to learn to be nonaggressive. They point to anthropological evidence that demonstrates that aggression is not inevitable. We shall review an example of this evidence later in the chapter.

The Paradox of Aggression

You might argue that Bandura's research, which was conducted in a laboratory setting, does not have any relevance to real-life situations. Critics have pointed out that because the Bobo doll is an inanimate object, the children's behavior is not really aggression at all—it is a form of play (Klapper, 1968). Also, you might argue that in real-life situations children are more likely to be punished than rewarded for aggressive behavior.

While it is true that hitting a Bobo doll is not the same as hitting a playmate, the two may go together. It has been found that children who are highly aggressive with a Bobo doll and other toys are judged by their peers and teachers to be high in general aggressiveness (Johnston, DeLucca, Murtaugh, & Diener, 1977). So Bandura's use of the Bobo doll does seem to have implications for real-life situations.

With regard to the second point, aggressiveness in young children is often reinforced by the effect of the aggression on the victim even though it is punished by an adult. To illustrate, the aggressive behavior of a group of nursery-school children was observed for a period of 26 weeks (Patterson, Littman, & Bricker, 1967). The researchers were particularly interested in the relative occurrences of rewards and punishments for aggression. Rewards might include the victim's crying and running away or giving up a toy or piece of candy. Punishments might include being verbally reprimanded by the teacher or put in a corner. It was found that aggression was rewarded much more often than it was punished. Children who were aggressive when they began nursery school remained that way, and children who tended to be passive initially showed a striking increase in their level of aggressiveness.

As Bandura has pointed out, in many ways children are presented with a paradox when it comes to socialization experiences related to aggression. Many parents are likely to talk to their children about the virtues of getting along with others and punish them for expressions of aggressiveness (although more than one father has reacted with pride when his son has beaten up the neighborhood bully). But these children watch their own parents interact and learn quickly that the one who is the most aggressive is likely to get his or her way. In fact, the children may be the victims of aggression when their parents are supposedly teaching them not to be aggressive. How many children have been spanked for hitting their little brothers or sisters? Our society may talk about the virtues of pacifism, but often the lesson children learn is that to get what they want, they have to be aggressive.

Children's play can often include imitating violent acts. *(© Marjorie Pickens)*

TELEVISION AND VIOLENCE

During the past decade there has been a growing concern about the potential effects of televised

Some theorists feel that violence on television inculcates a violence ethic in children. *(© Patricia Hollander Gross/ Stock, Boston, Inc.)*

portrayals of violence and aggression. This concern was stimulated in part by Bandura's findings that children were more likely to behave aggressively after they watched aggressive models on a television monitor in a laboratory setting. The concern has been fueled by several dramatic incidents that have occurred in the past few years. The televised movie *Fuzz* depicted adolescents dousing derelicts with gasoline and setting them on fire. Several such incidents actually occurred during the following week. Another TV movie showed a young girl being sexually assaulted with a soft-drink bottle. Within a few days a virtually identical crime was committed. In another instance a teenage boy pleaded innocent by reason of insanity after brutally murdering an elderly woman. His defense was based on the idea that watching television shows containing violence ("Kojak" was his favorite) led him to believe that violence and its consequences were unreal.

Is there a connection between violence portrayed on television and the commission of acts of violence and aggression? Many people certainly believe so. It has been pointed out that the average child can expect to see over 10,000 people killed on television between the ages of 5 and 15 (Liebert, Neale, & Davidson, 1973). Various organizations of concerned parents monitor television shows and, by pressuring sponsors and the networks, attempt to remove particularly violent shows. And any parent who has watched cartoons with children on Saturday morning cannot help feeling discomforted by the ingenious ways in which the characters harm one another.

Psychologists have come to much more tentative answers. It is virtually impossible to conduct the kind of research that would provide a definitive answer. At the very least it would require that a large group of children be randomly assigned to one of two groups, one that received a steady diet of televised violence and one that was not exposed to such programs. Their environments would have to be identical in all other respects. This means the influence of parents would have to be eliminated. Obviously such a research project will probably never be conducted. So tentative answers are the best that we can hope for.

The results of a number of laboratory studies leave little doubt that viewing violence on television can lead to aggressive behavior in the observer (Geen, 1976). This has been found to be true with both children and adults. It is important to keep in mind that viewing violence will not insure that the observer will behave in similar ways. The consequences of the model's behavior and the degree to which the model's aggression is portrayed as justified will also have an influence.

It also appears that observing violence on television increases one's tolerance for such behavior in real-life situations. In one study a group of third- and fourth-grade children watched either a violent detective show or an excerpt from an exciting baseball game (Drabman & Thomas, 1979). The children were then led to believe that they were responsible for watching some preschool children over a television monitor. The adult experimenter explained that he had to leave for a few minutes, and he asked his subjects to come and get him if the preschoolers began to cause trouble. The older children were actually watching a videotape that showed two young children taunting, pushing, fighting, and crying. The fight became progressively worse until it appeared the camera was destroyed. As predicted, children who had viewed the detective show were significantly slower to summon adult aid than were the children who had seen the baseball game. The researchers speculated that prolonged exposure to televised violence might breed indifference to real-life violence.

Studies such as these, important as they are, do not answer many important questions. For instance, most of these studies used relatively brief excerpts from violent films. What is the effect when the violent scenes are part of a longer show with a plot? Since some studies have found that the effects of observing violence dissipate rather quickly, will watching a violent television show at night have an effect on a child's behavior in school the next day? Or one might ask what the cumulative effects of viewing violence over 10 to 15 years might be, since laboratory studies obtain results after a mere 10- to 15-minute exposure.

These questions can only be answered by research carried out in naturalistic settings, and, as we have mentioned, such research is extremely difficult to do. The findings of studies that have attempted to answer these questions tend to be open to more than one interpretation. For instance, one study found that third-grade children who preferred violent television shows were rated ten years later as being more aggressive than their peers who preferred nonviolent shows (Eron, Huesmann, Lefkowitz, & Walder, 1972). While this study, which is one of the most ambitious of its type, shows a relationship between viewing habits and aggressiveness, it says nothing about causation. It could be that third-grade boys who preferred the violent shows valued aggressiveness and made attempts to become more aggressive as they grew older.

In his review of this issue, Russell Geen (1976) has concluded that naturalistic studies tend to support the more conclusive laboratory research. Viewing violence on television does seem to be related to aggressiveness, although the causal link has not yet been firmly established. Other arguments against excessive violence on television can be made, however. It has been suggested that such shows teach children that aggression and violence is an appropriate and normal response to frustration or conflict (Thomas & Drabman, 1978). Furthermore, people who watch such shows overestimate the potential for violence in their own lives. Because they believe they are likely to be victims of violent actions, they tend to be generally fearful (Gerbner & Gross, 1976). So even if children do not learn to be violent by watching such shows, they may come to believe that they live in a dangerous society.

A common line of defense taken by the television and movie industry is that they are only giving people what they want. And although there is evidence that shows could be made less violent without losing their appeal (Diener & DeFour, 1978), there is undoubtedly some truth to their statement. If we were a society that truly abhorred violence, it is doubtful that many of the current television shows and movies could find an audience. This is not to suggest that parents should not continue in their efforts to modify media fare. Perhaps the struggle reflects a gradual change in our society's values regarding violence and aggression.

ARE AGGRESSION AND VIOLENCE INEVITABLE?

Anthropologist Ashley Montagu (1976) pointed out that there have been 14,600 wars during the 5,600 years of recorded human history—about 2.6

per year. During this period some 185 generations of humans have lived, but only about ten have experienced uninterrupted peace. Although it is often difficult to define wars and although wars vary greatly in intensity and destructiveness, this record leads many people to agree with Freud's assertion that aggression and violence are inevitable. It also lends considerable weight to the ethologists' point of view that aggression is instinctual in human beings.

Yet there is good reason to believe that it is possible to prevent or control aggression and violence. As we have seen, social-learning theorists believe that aggression is a learned form of social behavior. And if people can learn to be aggressive or violent, they can also learn to be gentle and cooperative. Regulation of the environment will eradicate aggression. Although history indicates that the presumed aggressive tendencies in the social environment are deeply engrained, they would seem to be easier to change than human instinct.

Anthropologists have described societies in which aggression and violence are rare or virtually nonexistent. For example, E. Richard Sorenson (1978) described the South Fore people of New Guinea as follows:

> Infants rarely cried . . . older children typically enjoyed deferring to the interests and desires of the younger; sibling rivalry was virtually undetectable. A responsive 'sixth sense' seemed to attune the hamlet mates to each other's interests and needs. They were not likely to directly ask, inveigle, bargain, or speak out for what they needed or wanted. More often subtle, even fleeting expressions of interest, desire, and discomfort were quickly read and helpfully acted on by one's associates. A spontaneous urge to share food, affection, work, trust, and pleasure characterized the daily life. Aggression and conflict within communities was unusual and the subject of considerable comment when it occurred (pp. 14–15).

Sorenson has speculated about the child-rearing practices that contribute to the gentleness and cooperative spirit among the Fore people. Young infants remain in almost continual body contact with their mother or other caretakers. They are not put down when the mother has to prepare a meal or carry a heavy load. This means that the baby's needs, such as for food, stimulation, and comfort, are gratified immediately without any obstacles. Sorenson suggests that this provides developing children with a sense of security and confidence that their needs will be met. Thus they do not view others as competitors. They do not have the feeling that they must be aggressive to get what they want.

Sorenson's naturalistic observations do not constitute scientific proof regarding the relation between child-rearing practices and adult personality characteristics. His hypothesis seems plausible, however, and certainly merits the research attention of psychologists.

A second observation of Sorenson's is consistent with psychological research. He points out that the South Fore children do not have any models for aggression, nor are they rewarded for aggressive behavior. When infants or young children engage in "accidental" or "experimental" aggression, they are regarded with affectionate amusement. Their acts of aggression are considered to be immature behavior. If the behavior persists until it becomes painful, the subject will move away from the young child and try to divert him or her by affectionate playfulness. No displays of anger or displeasure were observed nor were the children punished or chastised.

With regard to the practice of not reinforcing aggressive behavior, Sorenson wrote:

> The young children's experimental and accidental aggressive behavior did not persist: their nascent or accidental aggressive motions failed to find a place in the daily life style. Anger, squabbling, and fighting did not become natural to their lives. Momentary expressions of anger, as might occur during "accidents" in rough play, were quickly dissipated. Conflict over "things" was typically sidetracked by behavioral habits of cooperative deference or settlement (p. 24).

These observations are consistent with social-learning theory. If we do not learn aggression by observing others, and if our aggressive actions fail to be reinforced, there is no reason for us to be aggressive. This means, of course, that Freud and the ethologists were wrong: aggression is not instinctual or inevitable (Baron, 1977). As Montagu (1978) has stated, "Whatever genetic potentialities we may have for aggressive behavior, early conditioning in cooperative behavior and the discouragement of anything resembling aggressive behavior seems to make an individual, and a society, essentially unaggressive and cooperative. That being so, the lesson, I think, is clear" (p. 9).

Summary

Aggression can be defined as behavior that is directed toward the goal of harming or injuring another living being who is motivated to avoid such treatment. This definition, however, leaves room for ambiguity, since goals and motives are not always apparent. Aggression may be most accurately conceptualized as a class of behavior rather than as a single type of behavior. A nuclear attack and a sarcastic remark both may be called acts of aggression, but they are different in important ways. Several theorists have distinguished between hostile aggression, which is intended to harm or injure the target, and instrumental aggression, which is intended to obtain other rewards and not specifically to harm the target. Zillman has offered the more precise terms of annoyance-motivated and incentive-motivated aggression.

One major class of theories of aggression can be referred to as biological theories. One variant is psychoanalysis, which suggests that aggression is an innate drive directed toward the destruction of the self. Ethologists believe that aggression is instinctive and, because of its survival value, has become part of our evolutionary heritage. There is probably more empirical support for the ethologists' position, but it is far from conclusive. Most psychologists do not believe that aggression is instinctive for humans.

Both of these theories involve the concept of catharsis—the idea that major acts of aggression can be prevented by draining off aggressive energies in numerous minor acts of aggression. A large body of research suggests that catharsis is not a viable concept. The effects of catharsis depend on the specific learning history of the individual. Minor acts of aggression may actually lead to increased aggression in some cases.

Other biological theories point to the importance of certain brain centers and the male sex hormones and chromosomes in influencing aggression. There is strong evidence that these factors are important in animals, but in humans their role is less clear. Most psychologists believe that they may set the stage for aggressive behavior but that their influence can be overcome by learning factors.

The hypothesis that frustration leads to aggression has had great appeal. Once again, empirical evidence is lacking. Aggression is just one of many ways in which people may react to frustration. Their response depends on their specific learning history. It has been found, however, that frustration is likely to lead to aggression when the frustration is perceived to be arbitrary or a personal attack. This phenomenon has been called "illegitimate disappointments of legitimate expectations."

Social-learning theorists have provided a large body of research that attests to the importance of learning in acquiring and performing aggressive behavior. People learn aggressive behavior by observing others engage in it. They learn that aggression is an appropriate response to stress or frustration. They engage in aggressive behavior because of the rewards that are obtained for doing so. One's cognitions play an important role in aggressive behavior, and Bandura has outlined ways in which decent, moral people can justify their acts of violence and brutality.

Research attesting to the effects of modeling has led many parents, educators, and psychologists to be concerned about media portrayals of violence and aggression. Laboratory research justifies these concerns. Viewing aggressive films and television shows seems to lead to increases in aggression and a greater tolerance for aggression. The results of naturalistic studies are equivocal, but on the whole they are consistent with the laboratory research. In addition, violence in the media results in overestimation of the actual incidence of violence in society and in excessive fearfulness about being a victim of violence.

Anthropological evidence suggests that societies can develop norms of nonviolence. The Fore people are noted for their cooperativeness, mutual caring, and absence of aggressive behavior. It has been suggested that their pacifistic nature results from their failure to model aggression for children or to provide any rewards for acts of aggression.

Key Terms For Review

aggression
aggression-releasing stimuli
catharsis
ethology
hostile aggression
inhibitory stimuli
instrumental aggression

Suggested Readings

Baron, R. A. *Human aggression.* New York: Plenum Press, 1977.
This book, written in a style that is both interesting and understandable, provides an excellent introduction to the topic of aggression.

Frodi, A., Macaulay, J., & Thome, P. R. Are women always less aggressive than men? A review of the experimental literature. *Psychological Bulletin,* 1977, *84,* 634–660.
This article reviews the evidence regarding the commonly held belief that men are generally more aggressive than women. The authors conclude that in some situations and with some forms of aggression, women may be just as aggressive as men.

Geen, R. G., & O'Neal, E. D. *Perspectives on aggression.* New York: Academic Press, 1976.
This book contains nine articles that explore in depth various issues related to

violence and aggression. Topics include moral judgment of aggressive behavior, interracial aggression, and violence in the mass media.

Marsh, P. *Aggro: The illusion of violence.* Toronto: J. M. Dent & Sons, 1978.
A provocative book in which Marsh uses his observations of British gangs to make the point that aggression is inevitable and instinctual and has the potential to be socially useful. It provides an alternative view to that expressed in the chapter.

Montagu, A. *Learning non-aggression.* New York: Oxford University Press, 1978.
This book contains a collection of articles describing various societies in which aggression is minimal or nonexistent. They offer the possibility that aggression is not inevitable.

Zillman, D. *Hostility and aggression.* Hillsdale, N.J.: Lawrence Erlbaum, 1979.
Written for the serious student, this text provides an in-depth review of the theory and research in the area.

19

Applications of Psychology

The French physician Dr. Alain Bombard sailed from Europe to North America in an inflatable craft. He set out on his voyage to prove his theory that a person could survive by relying solely on the resources of the ocean for food and water. After studying the food value of fish and sea plants and drinking small amounts of salt water each day at home for many months, Bombard embarked on his tiny craft without any food or water supplies. He managed to catch plenty of fish with his homemade hooks and found all the vitamins and carbohydrates needed for survival by eating plankton and small plants. He also showed that dehydration is not necessary, since he was able to quench his thirst by drinking small amounts of seawater, catching rainwater, and squeezing water from the fish he caught.

When Bombard realized that he had conquered his food and water problem and his small craft was doing an excellent job, he began fighting the effects of isolation. He wrote:

> *The solitude . . . started to affect me. . . . I began to understand the difference between solitude and isolation. Moments of isolation in ordinary life can soon be ended; it is just a question of going out of the door into the street or dialing a number on the telephone to hear the voice of a friend. Isolation is merely a matter of isolating oneself, but total solitude is an aggressive thing and slowly wears down its victim. It seemed sometimes as if the immense and absolute solitude of the ocean's expanse were concentrated on the top of me, as if my beating heart were the center of gravity of a mass which was at the same time nothingness. The day I dropped the tow off Las Palmas I thought that solitude was something I was able to master, once I had become accustomed to its presence. I had been too presumptuous. It was not something I carried with me, it could not be measured by the confines of*

> *myself or the boat. It was a vast presence which engulfed me. Its spell could not be broken, any more than the horizon was finite. And if from time to time I talked aloud in order to hear my own voice, I felt even more alone, a hostage to silence (Bombard, 1953, p. 140).*

Meeting the challenge to live from the ocean was thus not the only ordeal; much more difficult was the struggle to combat the isolation and loneliness created by the environment. At times Bombard heard voices, imagined objects, and developed a form of paranoia (Bombard, 1953).

In the previous chapters we have introduced a variety of concepts derived from several areas of psychology, including perception, learning, motivation, personality, and group processes. These concepts are not simply theoretical constructs, but are used every day in the real world. While we have attempted throughout the book to give examples of how these concepts apply to real-life situations, this chapter is devoted to illustrating in depth how principles drawn from a broad spectrum of general psychology work in the real world.

Applied psychologists are found in many professions, both in the private and public sector. They work in business to help manufacturers test the effectiveness of their advertising or conduct opinion surveys that are used in the design of new products. They work in educational institutions where they assess educational readiness or educational achievement at all levels. They are found in the medical profession and help physicians recognize the importance of emotional, motivational, and attitudinal factors in various types of physical disorders. And they appear in courtrooms as expert witnesses. Today applied psychologists are increasingly working with members of other professions as consultants or as trainers of other personnel. To give the student an idea of the kinds of work with which applied psychologists are concerned, we have selected three areas where applications to daily living are particularly clear: environmental, industrial, and community psychology.

ENVIRONMENTAL PSYCHOLOGY

More than twenty years ago **environmental psychology** emerged as a new area of specialization. It reflects the growing public concern about the deteriorating environment, from air and water pollution to the depletion of natural resources. In the broadest sense, environmental psychology is concerned with our relationships and interactions with the physical world, both natural and man-made.

Dr. Bombard's experience at sea falls into the domain of environmental psychology. Bombard's voyage was a dramatic demonstration that the environment can have profound effects on our behavior. Most of us are not exposed to the natural environment for such extended periods of time as Dr. Bombard was. Instead we have to cope with the effects of the built environment—our homes, highways, and commercial buildings. Sometimes we are unaware of our physical surroundings but other times we keenly recognize their effects. Being caught in a traffic jam with cars honking horns, living near an airport under jetliners taking off and landing, or working in a nonairconditioned office during the summer can affect our dispositions, our hearing, and our ability to work.

Environmental psychology is concerned with identifying the effects of the environment on behavior. Environmental psychologists assume that the physical character of a setting—whether an office, classroom, playground, or city street—elicits specific kinds of behavior. Humans are affected by three aspects of their environment: personal space, crowding, and architectural design.

Personal Space

All of us tend to keep regular interpersonal distances when interacting with others. We stand closer or farther away from other people depending on who they are and the nature of the interaction. **Personal space** may be thought of as a "bubble" of space that we have around us and consider our own property. If another person violates our space, we may be uncomfortable or even angry (Horowitz, Duff, & Stratton, 1964).

A casual observation of people conversing can show some of the dynamics of personal space and interpersonal distance. If two acquaintances are talking and one of them leans too close to the other, the other is likely to compensate by backing up, thereby increasing the distance between them. By the same token, should the distance between them become too great, one will quickly narrow the gap by moving closer.

Edward Hall (1959, 1966) coined the term **proxemics** to denote the study of people's use of space. Hall called our attention to the messages we submit by the way we perceive and structure space. In his well-known book *The Hidden Dimension,* Hall defined four interpersonal distances, or spatial zones, that people observe in their interactions with others. Each is divided into a near and a far phase.

The first zone, called **intimate distance,** ranges from zero to 18 inches. The near phase is the zone in which lovemaking or direct physical aggression takes place. The far phase is used for interactions in which touching is permissible and in which conversation is carried on in very low voices. The second zone, **personal distance,** is 18 to 48 inches, a distance that comfortably separates two individuals. It is the distance of social interactions between friends that do not involve physical contact. The near phase of personal distance, for instance, may be the distance people maintain at a crowded cocktail party.

The third zone, **social distance,** extending from 4 to 12 feet, is used in more formal interactions where personal involvement is substantially reduced. It is the distance people use to insulate themselves from others. Businesspersons maintain this distance in their interactions. Hall observed, for instance, that desks in offices of company presidents are large enough to keep subordinates or visitors at the far phase of social distance. This distance may also be used for interviewing applicants or conducting formal negotiations.

Living near an airport can adversely affect the environment. *(© Michael Philip Manheim/Photo Researchers, Inc.)*

Top left: Whispering takes place at intimate distance. Top right: Ordinary conversation usually occurs at personal distance. Bottom: Interaction between strangers often occurs at public distance. *(© Erika Stone; Richard Falvar/Magnum Photos, Inc.; S. Oristaglio/Photo Researchers, Inc.)*

The final zone is **public distance,** the near phase of which extends from 12 to 25 feet away from the person. Communication at this phase is always quite formal and is essentially one-way. Hall believed that interpersonal distances beyond 25 feet preclude any possibility of interaction. A distance of 25 feet or more is almost automatically set around important public figures when they deliver formal presentations. An example of public distancing is described in Theodore White's

The Making of the President 1960:

> Kennedy loped into the cottage with his light, dancing step, as young and lithe as springtime, and called a greeting to those who stood in his way. Then he seemed to slip from them as he descended the steps of the split-level cottage to a corner where his brother Bobby and brother-in-law Sargent Shriver were chatting, waiting for him. The others in the room surged forward on impulse to join him. Then they halted. A distance of perhaps thirty feet separated them from him, but it was impassable. They stood apart, these older men of long-established power, and watched him. He turned after a few minutes, saw them watching him, and whispered to his brother-in-law. Shriver now crossed the separating space to invite them over. First Averell Harriman; then Dick Daley; then Mike DiSalle; then, one by one, he let them all congratulate him. Yet no one could pass the little open distance between him and them uninvited, because there was this thin separation about him, and the knowledge they were there not as his patrons but as his clients. They could come by invitation only, for this might be a President of the United States (p. 171).

One of the most important determinants of the use of personal space is the relationship that exists between the individuals. In general, the more intimate the relationship, the closer people stand. Friends stand closer than strangers, and men and women who are sexually attracted to each other stand closer than friends (Allgeier & Byrne, 1973). Having an infinite amount of personal space, as experienced by Dr. Bombard during his transatlantic voyage, can be very stressful.

Personality factors also affect our use of space. People with certain personality disturbances tend to use larger interpersonal distances (Lett, Clark, & Altman, 1969). A number of studies have shown that autistic children, schizophrenics, and emotionally disturbed individuals require more personal space than normal individuals do. Normal persons with high achievement motivation keep larger personal spaces than less achievement-oriented persons (Altman & Vinsel, 1977). Another personality correlate of spatial behavior is self-esteem. Individuals with a positive self-concept approach others more closely than do those with a negative self-concept (Stratton, Tekippe, & Flick, 1973).

Studies on sex differences suggest that men require more personal space than women. If you observe a pair of women, you almost always find them standing closer than men. However, sex differences in interpersonal distance must be considered in terms of whether persons of the same or opposite sex are interacting (Altman, 1975). A number of studies have reported that male-female pairs are usually closer to each other than same-sex pairs. The sexes also differ in their reactions to violations of personal space. Males generally appear to be more upset than females when their personal space is invaded, although both sexes are bothered (Heimstra & McFarling, 1978).

Cross-cultural differences also exist in the use of personal space. Germans are known for their large zones of personal space and are supposedly less flexible in their spatial behavior than Americans. Hall (1966) made a similar observation when he noted that Germans go to great lengths to protect their personal space with heavy walls, solid fences, and closed doors. Mediterranean Europeans and Arabs, on the other hand, display a great tolerance for closeness and prefer to maintain "intimate," or "personal," distances, to use Hall's terms.

Differences in spatial behavior among subgroups in the United States are less consistent, although similarities among members of a given group tend to produce closer interpersonal distances. For example, people of similar age stand closer to one another than people of different ages (Willis, 1966). Similarly, individuals of the same race tend to interact at closer distances than individuals of different races (Frankel & Barrett, 1971). According to Scherer (1974), one of the best predictors of within-group distance seems to be social class; it has been consistently observed that lower-class individuals maintain closer interaction distances than those from the middle class.

Conflicting preferences in personal distances can have important consequences, especially when people interact on a regular basis. For example, among ghetto populations, which often represent a mixture of races and ethnic backgrounds, cultural differences in spatial norms may force some people to interact at distances so close as to cause stress (Schmidt, Goldman, & Feimer, 1979).

Crowding

Environmental psychologists distinguish between two related concepts: density and crowding. Density is a physical concept, while crowding refers to a psychological experience. Stokols (1972) defines **density** as the area available to the number of individuals present. **Crowding,** on the other hand, refers to the subjective feeling of having too little space. To feel crowded, a person must perceive disparity between the amount of space he or she requires and the amount of space available. Stokols argues that high density, while a necessary condition for the experience of crowding, does not always produce that experience. Both Stokols (1976) and Altman (1975) believe that density is perceived as crowding only when a person feels that his or her activities are being interfered with. We may not feel crowded at a party or a concert; yet we may feel very crowded if, during the concert intermission, we find long lines of people waiting to get into the restroom. Thus crowding is determined by both one's individual needs and the situation.

Crowded subways can lead to stressful behavior *(© Stock, Boston, Inc.)*

Epstein (1981) points out that as the number of people populating a given environment increases, the task of managing that environment may distract the person from achieving his or her goals. In addition, unavoidable social interactions may be distracting. Thus increasing the number of occupants in the space available may also increase the number of potentially conflicting goals that may create group conflict. This conceptualization of crowding again recognizes the fact that high density alone does not lead to stress reactions. Instead, when a person labels a setting as crowded, he or she is actually attributing the problems experienced to the presence of others.

Animal Research on Crowding. Zoologists and experimental psychologists interested in animal behavior were the first to note the physical changes in animals living in high population densities. Two classic studies were conducted by John Christian (Christian, Flygger, & Davis, 1961) and John Calhoun (1962). Christian's study took advantage of a naturally occurring high-density situation among deer on James Island in Chesapeake Bay. In 1916 a small group of Sitka deer had been released on the island. Since there was an adequate food supply and no predators, the deer population increased steadily to about 300 in 1955. During that year, Christian killed five deer to examine the internal organs, all of which were found to be in good shape. Then something strange happened. During the first three months of 1958 over half of the population (161 animals) died, and in 1959 additional deaths occurred until finally the deer population stabilized at around 80.

Since there was ample food on the island for the 300 animals, starvation had to be ruled out as a cause of death. Furthermore, no epidemic was reported during the mass deaths of 1958 and 1959. Examinations of tissues of animals who died during this period revealed some striking abnormalities, however. Compared with the deer examined earlier, the adrenal glands of these animals showed considerable increases in weight. Since the adrenal glands are particularly active under conditions of stress, Christian proposed a relationship between population density and adrenal gland size and reasoned that the high density during 1958–1959 led to increased stress, which in turn led to metabolic disturbances that were the cause of the mass mortality.

Calhoun (1962) studied the behavioral effects of density under more controlled conditions. Working with Norway rats, Calhoun constructed a series of pens with connecting ramps (see Figure 19–1), each of which was equipped with food, drinking bottles, and nest-building material to accommodate 40 to 50 rats. After 32 rats were placed in the pen, the population was allowed to increase to about 80 animals.

As the density in the pen increased, striking behavioral distortions were observed; usually beginning when the population density reached roughly twice the size that a pen could comfortably accommodate. Among female rats, nest-building was disrupted. Instead of carrying their infants from one place to another, they simply picked the pups up and dropped them at various places in the pen. Many female animals were unable to carry their pregnancy to full term. Infant mortality skyrocketed; 96 percent of infants in the densely populated pens died before weaning.

Sexual behavior became highly unusual. Females were almost continuously pursued by packs of males, regardless of whether they were in heat or not. Some male rats apparently could not discriminate between appropriate and inappropriate sex partners, harassing juveniles as well as females not in heat. Other males were not only hyperactive and hypersexual but also engaged in homosexual activities. Some were even cannibalistic; in their chase after females in heat, they would discover dying or dead infants and devour them.

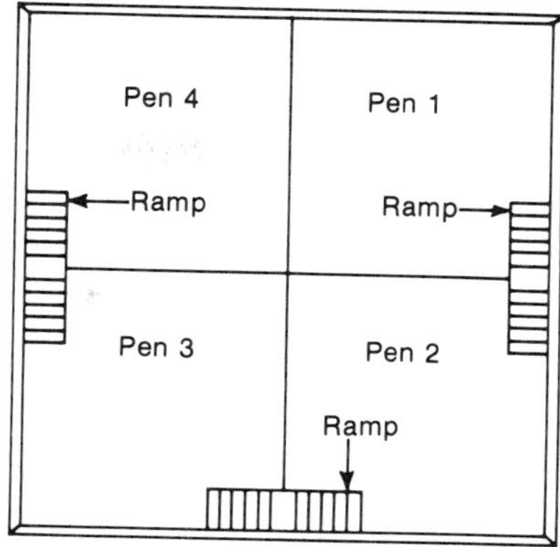

Figure 19–1. Design of Calhoun's rat pens.

The results of the Christian and Calhoun studies clearly indicated that high-density animal populations adequately supplied with resources show signs of physiological disturbances and display frequent and deviant sexual and maternal behavior. These findings have aroused considerable speculation about the possible effects of density and crowding on humans.

Effects of Crowding on Humans. Many urban high-density areas, especially ghettos, suffer from a number of social problems, including poverty, high crime rates, juvenile delinquency, family disorganization, disease, and high mortality. As a result of the findings regarding animals, environmental psychologists became interested in studying the relationship between crowding and human behavior. Could it be that living in overcrowded areas was responsible for the numerous social pathologies found in high-density neighborhoods?

The usual way to assess the effects of population density on humans is to obtain a measure of crowding and record the number and types of social problems. Schmitt (1966), for instance, conducted a study in Honolulu using population per acre, average number of persons per room, and average household size as density measure. He reported a strong positive correlation between high density and a number of indicators of social pathology, such as death rate, adult crime rate, admissions to mental hospitals, and number of illegitimate births. It is difficult to draw firm conclusions from this study because only a physical measure of density was included, and we cannot be sure that the residents also felt crowded. Many other variables, such as cultural background, temperature, and noise, determine subjective feelings of crowding.

Other studies failed to find any degree of association between crowding in urban settings and social pathologies. In one series of studies, for instance, the number of people per square mile was correlated with the number of crimes committed in the same metropolitan area. Taking only these two factors, density and crime, into account, a small but significant correlation was observed. However, when other factors that tend to be highly correlated with crime, such as income, poverty, education, and ethnicity, were controlled for, the relationship between density and crime rate disappeared entirely (Freedman, 1975).

One of the most interesting studies demonstrating the contradictory findings relating crowding with social pathologies was conducted in Hong Kong (Mitchell, 1971). In this city the average resident reportedly shares a 400-square-foot dwelling with ten or more persons. This averages out to 40 or less square feet per person, which is less than one-half of the 85 square feet per person considered a minimum in households (Committee on the Hygiene of Housing, American Public Health Association, 1950). Moreover, in many cases the dwellings are shared by unrelated individuals. Yet despite these spatial deficits, Mitchell found a relatively low rate of social pathology and no emotional disorders related to density. Thus it remains highly uncertain whether there is a causal relationship between crowding and social or psychological problems. In contrast to animals, people are apparently able to find ways to reduce the stress associated with crowded living (Fischer, Baldassare, & Ofshe, 1975). For example, a person may temporarily escape the effects of an overcrowded house by visiting a friend's home or a neighborhood bar.

Architectural Design

Personal space and crowding are two aspects of the living environment with which we come in daily contact. A third is the architectural design of rooms, buildings, and cities. As Raskin (1974) pointed out, "Most of mankind spends the major part of its time indoors, in environments of its own creation, emerging only once in a while to plant a radish, chop down a tree, or complain about the weather. We are born indoors, live, love, bring up our families, worship, work, grow old, sicken and die indoors. . . . Man-created environment consisting of hospitals, schools, residences, office buildings, and churches is what we call architecture" (p. 3). To illustrate, we have selected two examples of the built environment: the college campus with its dormitories and classrooms, and large-scale public housing.

College Dormitories and Classrooms. Until recently the design and layout of college buildings were largely determined by the administrators, who were primarily concerned with building costs and intended functions. Today many university administrators seek the advice of environmental psychologists to help solve design problems and improve the physical environment of the campus, particularly for buildings such as dormitories and classrooms.

Baum, Valins, and their colleagues investigated the effects of dormitory architecture on students' social behavior. In their studies they compared two types of dormitories: corridor-type dorms and suite-type dorms. The older model of a college dormitory is the corridor type, with single rooms lined up along a common long corridor. Many of the more recently built dormitories use the suite-type arrangement, with four or six students sharing a suite.

Although the amount of space allocated to each student in the two types of dormitories was approximately the same, the designs had different effects on residents. The long-corridor residents were more likely to experience feelings of crowding (Baum & Valins, 1977) and unwanted social interaction than were suite residents. Corridor residents also felt more helpless and acted more competitive than did students living in accommodations of a different architectural variety (Baum, Aiello, & Calesnick, 1978). Corridor residents were less apt to participate in local residential groups, such as bridge clubs or softball teams, and were less able to reach a consensus when working with others on a group task (Baum, Harpin, & Valins, 1975). Students living in suites were found to be more friendly and outgoing. Many of them saw the group as a "family." Suite residents were also more disposed to participate in local residential groups, primarily within their suite units.

While the suite dorm has the advantage of reducing crowding in shared areas, it may not be the answer to all the living needs of students. At many colleges students are assigned arbitrarily to their quarters without regard to roommate preferences. Such random assignment may create hostility, resentment, and eventually disrupted interpersonal relations if students are placed in a suite where they find out that they cannot get along with one another. Many students find it easier to adjust to one other person than to four to six others (Corbett, 1973). Optimally, a college would cater to both the student's need for privacy and his or her need for satisfying social interactions, since both studying and socializing take place in the dormitory environment.

The classroom presents its own design problems. Many classrooms are ugly, sterile, or dull, with their standard arrangement of chairs lined up in straight rows facing the blackboard. Smaller seminar classes are usually held in rooms with portable chairs placed around a large rectangular or circular table. When asked to rate their classrooms, students are often overwhelmingly negative in their comments. The rooms are described as boxed in, stuffy, cramped, and impersonal.

Psychologist Robert Sommer and design instructor Helge Olsen (1980) recently introduced the concept of the "soft classroom." With the help of half a dozen enthusiastic students, they redecorated a dreary "hard" classroom, constructing tiered wooden benches with colorful foam-rubber cushions and adding decorative items, such as a multicolored carpet, mobiles, and plants. The "soft classroom" not only elicited strong positive feelings from students and instructors, but also resulted in classroom participation two to three times as high as that in the best seminar classes. Although the remodeling was considered highly successful, the research team encountered one unexpected problem, namely maintenance. Custodians, usually trained to take care of classrooms with tile floors and fixed steel or plastic furniture, were not trained to clean carpets. Other maintenance tasks, such as fastening the straps holding the cushions to the benches, were considered "women's work" that the custodians did not see as part of their job. Sommer and Olsen concluded that this problem could have been avoided if the team had involved janitors in the selection of items that required out-of-the-ordinary maintenance.

While it may be tempting to conclude from this research that the "soft classroom" was responsible for the increased student participation, a word of caution is necessary. In the Sommer and Olsen study, no control group was included in the experimental design. Thus we cannot rule out alternative explanations. It is conceivable, for instance, that the attention the students received from an experimenter and a designer, or the mere fact that they participated in research, influenced their classroom behavior. More controlled studies are needed that relate classroom designs to educational outcomes.

Dormitories and classrooms are particularly important environments for college students. Other subgroups of our population have entirely different environmental needs. Let us now consider the housing needs of lower-class families.

Public Housing for the Urban Poor. Slums and ghettos are characterized by overcrowding, a lack of privacy, the absence of civic amenities, and political and social unrest (Karan, Bladen, & Singh, 1980). During the 1950s and 1960s a large number of high-rise buildings were constructed to replace

The Pruitt-Igo housing project failed to meet the needs of the people for which it was built. *(© United Press International Photos)*

some of the dilapidated one-or two-story buildings occupied by slum dwellers. Experience with some of these high-rise buildings has raised the question whether such housing is a good environment for people. The case of the Pruitt-Igo project in St. Louis, Missouri, provides some interesting answers about high-rise housing.

The Pruitt-Igo Housing Project consisted of 43 buildings of 11 stories each containing some 3,000 apartments. The new complex offered more space per person than the dwellings residents had previously occupied as well as playgrounds for the children. The architects failed, however, to make provisions for space both outside and inside the buildings where people could congregate.

Because of the overcrowded conditions inside most slum dwellings, residents are dependent on outside areas for social exchange. Yet the designers of Pruitt-Igo made no allowances for such semipublic spaces. Consequently, the families living in Pruitt-Igo retreated into their apartments. Although 78 percent of the residents were satisfied with their apartments, only 49 percent were satisfied with living in the project. In contrast, inhabitants of run-down dwellings beset with problems of heat and cold, poor plumbing, and dangerous electrical wiring are usually dissatisfied with their housing but satisfied with their neighborhoods (Yancy, 1971).

When Pruitt-Igo residents were asked why they were dissatisfied, they complained about the lack of space both inside and outside the buildings. Mothers complained that there were no inside areas where children could play under their supervision. A mother who lived on the 10th floor could not supervise her child on the street or playground. The only public spaces inside the high-rise buildings were stairwells, which many mothers feared because they represented dangerous and uncontrollable space. For teenagers the stairwells were private enough for sexual intercourse; they could also hide muggers and other undesirables.

The Pruitt-Igo project taught city planners an important lesson: housing designed for the urban poor must take into account the ways that slum dwellers have adapted to the problems of poverty, deprivation, and the dangers of ghetto living. As it appears unlikely that the world's population growth will decrease appreciatively, it becomes more and more important to acknowledge the inevitability of high-density living in the future and to plan environments in ways that will reduce the adverse consequences of such living. As for Pruitt-Igo, the multimillion-dollar project was eventually demolished by the city because crime, vandalism, and deterioration made the buildings so unsafe that no one was willing to live in them.

Many other areas are awaiting the investigations of environmental psychologists, such as the spatial layouts of cities, transportation systems, litter problems, rush-hour commuting, and gasoline shortages. In some of these areas, environmental psychologists are already actively involved. For example, they have explored the effectiveness of different kinds of litter receptacles and of signs warning against littering. Similarly, environmental psychologists are beginning to be engaged in research on energy conservation. Studies are now being conducted on the development of psychological strategies for reducing energy consumption in homes and businesses. Undoubtedly environmental psychologists will make significant contributions in the future that will improve the quality of environments and consequently of our lives.

INDUSTRIAL PSYCHOLOGY

Harry Schneider was vice-president of production of a medium-sized tool-manufacturing firm. He was known to be from the school of "hard knocks" and ran a tight ship in his department. Although the company did not have a serious turnover problem, it was obvious to Harry that the productivity of the hourly workers had to be increased if the company were to prosper.

After discussing his concern with other management personnel, Harry found himself at a loss. The company was paying top wages for the region and offered excellent working conditions and a generous package of fringe benefits. Yet the assembly workers barely put in their eight-hour day. Harry decided to call in an industrial psychologist as a consultant.

Like environmental psychology, **industrial psychology** is a relatively new area of specialization. In this country it started around the beginning of this century, when Walter Dill Scott gave an address discussing the potential application of psychological principles to the field of advertising (Ferguson, 1963). It developed over the past 60 years and has branched out in many subdivisions, such as personnel psychology, consumer psychology, social-industrial psychology, and engineering psychology. All these branches are concerned with the application of psychological principles to problems of work.

The majority of industrial psychologists can be found in five settings: government, industry, academia, consulting firms, and research organizations (Landy & Trumbo, 1976). Regardless of the type of setting, the responsibilities of most industrial psychologists are diversified and continually changing with the changing needs and demands of work settings. For example, with the introduction of the word processor, the work space of many offices had to be redesigned to accommodate the new piece of equipment.

The Hawthorne Studies

One of the most important early events in industrial psychology was a series of studies that began in 1924 and extended over 15 years. Management at the Hawthorne plant of the Western Electric Company in Chicago had a concern similar to Harry Schneider, that is, worker productivity. More specifically, management wanted to find out how various working conditions, such as illumination, influence productivity.

Common sense says that it is difficult to work in darkness or under the glare of a bright light; consequently the best level of illumination for the job must be somewhere in between. To determine this optimal level, illumination studies were conducted on female workers who were asked to perform their jobs under various lighting conditions. However, much to the bewilderment of both managers and researchers, productivity improved no matter what changes in lighting the experimenters made in any direction. Even when poor lighting conditions were reinstated, worker performance continued to improve instead of dropping back to the earlier level. In fact, when the experimenters only pretended to change the lights by replacing bulbs with others of the same intensity, the workers expressed pleasure with the "increased" illumination and increased their work output. Also examined were the effects of rest periods, pay rates, and the provision of company lunches on rates of performance. Regardless of the working conditions studied, the results were equally striking: productivity continued to rise whether relevant working conditions were improved or worsened.

Eventually, it became obvious that something beside better illumination, pay rates, or company lunches was causing the increase in productivity. This variable turned out to be a very complex human factor. In their efforts to secure the cooperation of the worker in this series of investigations, the experimenters made the conditions as pleasant as possible for the employees. For example, instead of being closely supervised, the employees worked in small groups of coworkers of their choice. They were also assigned to a comfortable and cheerful work space and received a great deal of attention from the experimenters and important plant personnel. The mere fact of being observed, receiving attention from management, and being able to interact with those who conducted the experiment were uncontrolled variables that served as an important stimulus for increased productivity.

Despite the methodological limitations of the Hawthorne studies (no attempt was made, for instance, to employ control data from output records of women who were not put under special experimental conditions), these studies made important contributions to our understanding of human behavior in organizations. They also highlight the need for controlling attitudinal variables in the design of psychological experiments (Anastasi, 1979). The **Hawthorne effect,** referring to the influence that participation in an experiment may have on the subject's behavior, has been evoked in many experiments. Earlier in the chapter, for example, we described the results of a "soft classroom," which could also be interpreted as being a function of the Hawthorne effect. Similarly, the industrial psychologist consulting with the tool-manufacturing company may point out to Harry that a program instituted to increase productivity may be successful solely because of the Hawthorne effect.

The Hawthorne studies are often viewed as the beginning of the human-relations movement in organization, which focuses on the human element in the workplace. An important human element of any job is the degree of satisfaction a person derives from his or her work.

Job Satisfaction

Job satisfaction is probably one of the most thoroughly researched concepts in industrial psychology. A recent estimate by Locke (1976) suggested that over 3,000 articles or dissertations have been written to date, and the number is rising yearly. One of the main reasons for studying the topic is the widely held view that job satisfaction leads to high work productivity. Although this view has been questioned, the degree of satisfaction and fulfillment people derive from their work is not only an important consideration in itself but has, as we shall see, important consequences for the organization.

Determinants of Job Satisfaction. Job satisfaction has been defined as a pleasurable or positive emotional state resulting from the appraisal of one's job or job experience (Locke, 1976). As such, job satisfaction is a function of the characteristics of both the individual and the job.

Among the characteristics of the worker that contribute to job satisfaction are age, race, education, and training. For instance, most of the evidence regarding the relationship between age and job satisfaction—holding such factors as occupational level constant—indicates that there is a positive age-job satisfaction relation. Job satisfaction seems to increase with age up to the preretirement years (approximately the early 60s); thereafter most workers report a sharp decline in job satisfaction (Quinn, Staines, & McCullough, 1974).

One of the most important determinants of job satisfaction is, not surprisingly, the nature of the work itself. There are many reasons why people like their jobs per se. One person may be satisfied with the work because he or she brings the right skills, education, or training to the job. Another person may enjoy the opportunities the job affords, such as travel or social contacts. For some people, a challenging job is in itself sufficient reason for satisfaction. Stimulating work is particularly important for individuals with high educational or skill levels who become easily bored with

Work environment is one of the most important factors in job satisfaction. *(© Paul Conklin/Monkmeyer Press Photo Service; Ken Karp)*

routine tasks or jobs that require little effort or skill. For workers in low-status positions that offer little challenge, other factors such as high pay must be involved if the job is to lead to satisfaction.

Pay is, of course, important to almost everyone. Employees who believe they are inequitably or inadequately paid tend to be dissatisfied with their jobs. However, some studies indicate that pay is not a paramount concern. Opsahl and Dunnette (1966), for instance, reported that when they asked 42,000 individuals to rank ten job factors in order of importance, pay came in sixth.

One difficulty in assessing the importance of money for job satisfaction is that money may not only have different meanings for different workers, but it may also mean much more than the goods and services it buys (Lawler, 1971). For many people money earned from the job serves as a symbol of status and achievement or as an indicator of their value to the organization.

Opportunities for advancement are another source of job satisfaction. Like money, promotions have a symbolic value as well as a financial one: they can mean status and prestige, not only in the organization but also in the larger community. In many cases promotion within the organization is the external recognition of successful job performance (Gruneberg, 1979).

Many other determinants of job satisfaction could be mentioned: job security (the guarantee of steady employment); benefits such as medical or life insurance, vacation time, and retirement provisions; job involvement; the type of supervision; and the opportunities for social interactions. All these variables are probably examined by the industrial psychologist engaged by Harry, the production manager, when he or she tries to pinpoint the productivity problem with the hourly workers.

Consequences of Job Satisfaction and Dissatisfaction. Satisfied workers are important from the standpoint of organizational effectiveness. A satisfied work force is associated with few grievances and good labor-management relations; a dissatisfied one with turnover, absenteeism, withdrawal, counterproductive behavior, and poor mental or physical health.

Absenteeism is probably the easiest and least painful way for workers to show their dissatisfaction. Lyons (1972) found that not only does job dissatisfaction increase the likelihood that the worker will withdraw from the work situation by absenting himself or herself but also that absenteeism was a predictor of future termination of employment. Even more conclusive is the evidence concerning the relationship between job satisfaction and turnover. Employees who leave their jobs typically report substantially lower levels of job satisfaction than those who stay.

Ideally the characteristics of the job match the needs of the worker. Since different workers have different needs—some may value having a variety of tasks, others may care most about using their skills—a job that offers a high degree of satisfaction to some workers may make others dissatisfied (Anastasi, 1979).

Engineering Psychology

Although **engineering psychology** and industrial psychology are related, they differ in their approach to the worker and his or her job (Chapanis, 1976). Whereas the industrial psychologist is oriented to fitting the worker to the job through selection procedures or training, the engineering psychologist, or human-factors specialist, is concerned with fitting the job to the worker. This is accomplished through the design of equipment and the work environment.

An example of fitting the job to the worker comes from the early days of engineering psychology. During World War II complex machines, such as high-speed aircraft, rockets, and radar-equipped instruments, severely taxed the capabilities of operators (Alluisi & Morgan, 1976). It soon became apparent that selection and training procedures alone could not produce highly efficient operators. The equipment itself needed to be redesigned. In cooperation with engineering psychologists, industrial designers and professionals from other occupations redesigned the equipment so that the task of the operator was less confusing and easier to manage.

The essential job of human-factors specialists is to see that industrial systems are designed to allow operators to run them with minimum error and maximum efficiency (Dunnette & Kirchner, 1965). To this end, they study the effects of ventilation, noise, and illumination. They improve the design of the workplace to make it safer. They design such diverse products as household appliances, aircraft display panels, computer consoles, and space suits. They may investigate the effects of working in shifts on performance or the manning of a commercial jetliner with a cockpit crew of two versus three. Some of the most challenging problems for the human-factors specialist are the design of complicated human-machine systems and the integration of the person into such systems (Chapanis, 1976).

The Human-Machine System

People and machines make up systems that interact with each other. The characteristics of human-machine systems, which combine the functions of the human operator with the functions of the equipment, are usually described in terms of engineering terminology, as shown in Figure 19–2. To illustrate, consider a driver and an automobile. Each human-machine system needs certain inputs, which are referred to as the information-receiving, or sensing, function. In some human-machine systems, the information received is displayed, as in the gas gauge in cars. The driver checks the gauge to see whether there is enough

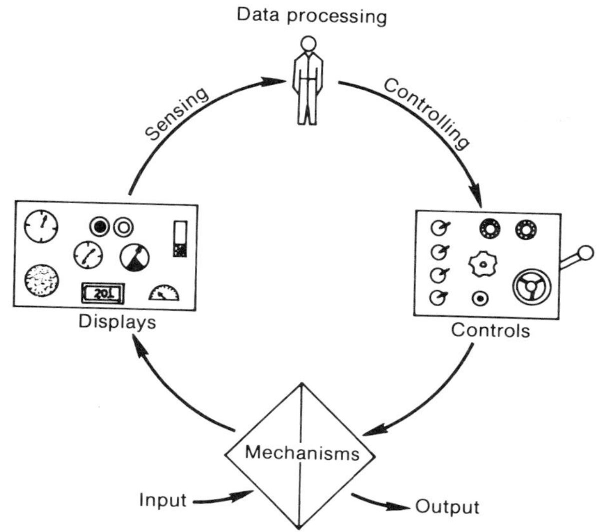

Figure 19–2. General structure of a human-machine system.

gas to operate the vehicle. On the basis of the information received, the driver decides whether or not to put the car on the road. Engineering psychologists refer to this function as information, or data-processing, function, which usually involves making a decision. The third function in a human-machine system is some kind of output, which is often produced by operating a control such as the accelerator.

The task of the human-factors specialist is to build into the design of human-machine systems those features that will maximize human efficiency as well as the efficiency of the system (Landy & Trumbo, 1976). One of the major objectives of such systems is to adapt the equipment to the sensory and motor capacities of the operators. For example, when the instrumentation panels for spacecraft were designed, engineering psychologists took careful measures of various bodily dimensions, such as maximum arm reach, strength of grip, and knee height, to assure that the placement of panels and controls was within optimal reach for the operator.

Most human-machine systems have distinct developmental stages (see Figure 19–3). Let us examine these stages by assuming that a hospital has engaged a human-factors specialist to help develop a sophisticated laboratory for various clinical tests. This is the purpose of the system. Once the purpose of the system has been identified, the engineering psychologist will assign the different functions of the system to either the people or the machines. For example, he or she may decide at this point that people will be in charge of getting slides, test tubes, or chemicals to the lab, while machines will perform the analyses, such as urinalyses or blood tests.

As pointed out by Chapanis (1965), humans excel at some jobs and machines excel at others.

Figure 19–3. Stages in the development of a human-machine system.

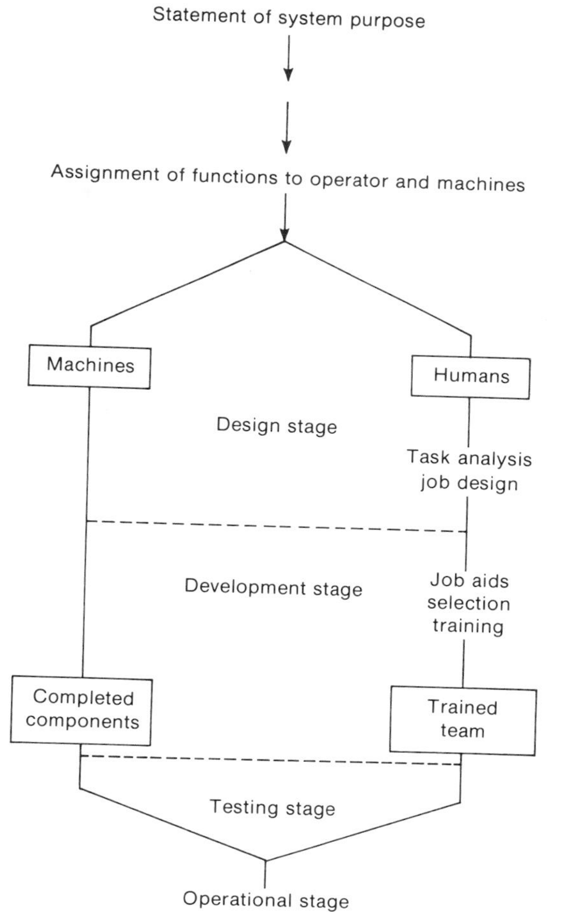

The human operator, for instance, is able to handle unexpected events, whereas it is difficult to program machines to anticipate all possible events. Machines, on the other hand, show few performance decrements even over relatively long periods of time, whereas people tend to show decrements after fairly short time periods because of boredom, fatigue, or distractions. In allocating functions to people or machines, the human-factors specialist attempts to maximize the effectiveness of the system.

During the next phase, engineering psychologists working with engineering designers concentrate their efforts on the design of the necessary equipment. Many hardware problems are attacked at this stage—the actual design or redesign of the equipment, the design of controls and display, and the design of the physical work space and its surrounding environment. During this phase specific jobs connected with the equipment are also designed, such as the tasks involved in the laboratory analysis of blood or urine specimens.

After the basic human-machine system has been designed, personnel are selected and trained while the equipment development continues. The developmental process culminates in the completion of all components of the system. In our example of the hospital laboratory this would mean completing an actual machine model and preparing a team of operators. The operators would be trained to place the specimens in the test equipment and to interpret the results from the various indicators on the machine.

Finally, the system needs to be tested and evaluated before it is put into actual operation. Changes in design after the system goes into operation can be extremely costly. It is important that the system is evaluated against its original planning specifications. This evaluation usually includes a cost analysis of the system based on the cost of hardware, operating expenses, costs resulting from accidents, errors, breakages, costs of personnel selection and training, and the system's potential social costs, such as pollution (Chapanis, 1976).

The Work Environment. Part of human-machine systems is the physical environment in which the equipment is operated and maintained. Physical surroundings include the work space and the arrangement of the equipment. People work in many different kinds of spaces—from the plumber working under a stopped-up sink, to the astronaut in his capsule, to the factory worker at his position on the assembly line, to the minister in his pulpit (McCormick, 1976). In the design of many of these work spaces, it is important to determine body dimensions. Sitting height, for example, is a basic factor in seat-to-roof dimensions of automobiles.

In addition to the physical features of the workplace, three environmental factors affect the performance of the worker: noise, illumination, and atmospheric conditions.

Human-factors specialists define noise as an "auditory stimulus or stimuli bearing no informational relationship to the presence or completion of the task" (Burrows, 1960). A common complaint of students and workers alike is that they cannot do their jobs because it is too noisy around them. Yet while some studies show that noise produces a decrement in performance, others show no effect, and still others show an increment in performance. Performance on simple repetitive tasks does not appear to be affected by noise, whereas performance on tasks calling for speed and skill or a high level of perceptual accuracy is likely to be adversely affected by noise (McCormick, 1976). The finding that noise enhances performance can be attributed to the increase in attention caused by an increase in noise intensity (Warner, 1961), that is, the extra noise made the worker more alert with respect to the environment.

Prolonged exposure to high levels of noise can impair hearing. Sound is measured in terms of sound pressure level, or decibels (db). Figure 19–4 depicts the decibel readings of typical noise environments. Continuous exposure to noise levels of 80 db and above can result in hearing loss. Companies operating such noisy environments are required by the Occupational Safety and Health Administration (OSHA) to provide their workers with protective devices, such as earplugs or earmuffs, to use baffles and sound absorbers where possible, and to install rubber mountings on machines.

As we saw in the discussion of the Hawthorne studies, the establishment of optimal illumination levels for different types of work has been of interest to industrial psychologists for many years. Since many circumstances require special illumination, it is difficult to establish general illumination-level recommendations. Human-factors specialists, however, have developed a procedure for deriving illumination requirements for various tasks (Blackwell, 1972).

In addition to noise and illumination a number of atmospheric conditions affect the efficiency of workers. They include air temperature, humidity, air movement, and radiant temperature (i.e., the temperature of walls, ceilings, and other surface areas).

Extremes of heat and cold have both been found to affect worker productivity adversely. A serious problem in industrial settings such as mines and mills is heat stress. It is not only likely to be detrimental to performance, but it also may result in dehydration, which can lead to weight loss from water depletion. Extreme cold affects the performance of manual tasks, because cold fingers are less dextrous. In work places where extreme temperatures are unavoidable, their adverse effects can be reduced by permitting workers to acclimatize themselves gradually or by selecting personnel who can tolerate extreme conditions.

Human Factors and the Handicapped. Human-factors engineering has benefited many disabled people who depend on mechanical aids to get around in the environments of the nonhandicapped. They may suffer from motor impairments, blindness, or deafness. Human-factors specialists work together with special educators, audiologists, speech therapists, engineers, and designers in the development of assistive devices that are not only as useful as possible but are also technologically feasible, affordable, satisfactory to the user's body image, and safe.

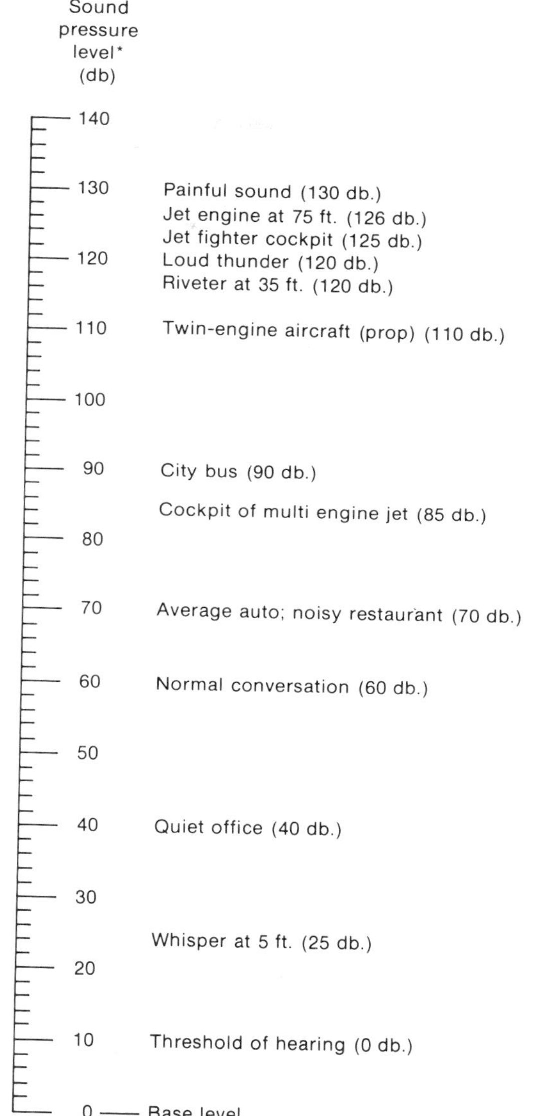

Figure 19–4. Decibel levels for selected sounds.

The report of the National Research Council's Committee on National Needs for the Rehabilitation of the Physically Handicapped (1976) recognized the importance of a multidisciplinary approach to the problem of helping the handicapped:

Work involving repetition of simple tasks is less affected by noise than other types of work. *(© Erich Hartmann/Magnum Photos, Inc.; Peter Southwick/Stock, Boston, Inc.)*

> The intellectual resources and perspective of engineering, the physical sciences, and the behavioral sciences need to be integrated more effectively into biomedical research and development relating to the physically handicapped. Many of the devices and procedures that have potential for the alleviation of handicapping conditions require the application of sophisticated engineering principles and techniques as well as awareness of the psychological and social factors that enter into their acceptance (p. 4).

Recent years have seen some advances that have significantly reduced the barriers to fully productive lives for many handicapped people. For instance, in 1973 Congress created the Architectural and Transportation Compliance Board to enforce compliance with federal statutes requiring that buildings be accessible to handicapped people. This mandate led to the installment of ramps, graduated paths, and automatic doors, and to the removal of architectural barriers, such as curbs and escalators, in many cities and on many campuses. If the handicapped person is to gain satisfaction from working and independent living, special aids and living environments need to be designed. Let us illustrate the application of human-factors concepts for one particular handicapped population, namely those with motor impairments.

The National Council estimated that there are 10 million Americans with motor deficits. These deficits result from a variety of conditions, such as cerebral palsy, muscular dystrophy, Parkinson's disease, multiple sclerosis, or deformed and paralyzed limbs. Lack of mobility often drastically diminishes the ability of these people to get or hold a paying job. Although the advent of computer networks has made it possible to bring jobs to some people with immobilizing handicaps, the majority of them have to rely on assistive devices or mechanical aids to get to work or perform a job.

Three mechanical aids that are available for persons with motor disabilities are prostheses, orthoses, and wheelchairs. A **prosthesis** is a substitution for a nonexisting limb or part of a limb. While the prosthesis is supposed to replace the lost limb, it does not reestablish the freedom of motion of the original limb. **Orthoses** support and sometimes motivate a paralyzed limb (Sheridan & Mann, 1978). The wheelchair, which remains the major mode of locomotion for paralyzed persons as well as for those who have lost both legs, has greatly enhanced the rehabilitation of these individuals (Glaser et al., 1980), enabling them both to hold a regular job and to maintain independent life.

Assistive devices, many of which were developed after World War II to rehabilitate men who had lost limbs in battle, pose a continuing challenge for the human-factors specialist. First, as Sheridan and Mann pointed out, each case of motor impairment is different. The differences can be in sensory loss, reduced muscle capability, or in what is anatomically missing. This means that many assistive devices, such as a stump socket or a cable-operated prosthesis for the above-elbow amputee, must be custom fitted. Other parts such as external cosmetic elements, must come in a variety of sizes to ensure a good fit for the handicapped person.

In addition to designing a device that functionally replaces a part of the human body, the human-factors specialist needs to consider psychological needs. Many physically handicapped men and women are very sensitive about their appearance and often resent having to be hooked up to mechanical gadgets. Although hardly any research has been done to examine how handicapped persons incorporate mechanical devices into their body image, it would seem that the ease and naturalness with which the mechanical part allows the person to move around contribute considerably to the person's satisfaction. In fact, the integration of design features into the body is regarded by many human-factors psychologists as essential for many motor assistive devices (Sheridan & Mann, 1978), because only through effective integration can an effective human-machine system be attained.

Many motor-impaired individuals prefer to live independently in home-like residences rather than to be given over to custodial care in large institutions. Independent living enables them to perceive themselves and be perceived by others as responsible and self-reliant. Describing an experiment in independent living with wheelchair-bound paraplegics, Rice et al. (1978) called attention to modifications in interior design that are necessary for paraplegics to function adequately. Such modifications may be slight but they are important in daily living. For example, shower stalls would have enough turn-around space for the disabled person and for the attendant who must often be present. Bathroom and kitchen sinks must be positioned so as to provide for knee space beneath. Any exposed drains or pipes below sinks must be specially insulated because they can become hot enough to burn the knees or legs of paraplegics. This insulation is particularly important because paraplegics cannot feel the burn and only discover it when it is too late.

Handicapped people often make successful adjustments to the work environment. *(© Freda Laimwand/Monkmeyer Press Photo Service)*

The physically handicapped person who has little or no use of his or her hands poses special problems to the human-factors specialist. Manipulating objects such as doorknobs, combs, toothbrushes, or eating utensils is often impossible without special hand- or arm-operated instruments. To help these individuals, human-factors specialists are designing tools that can be manipulated electronically.

Work and Mental Health

Work of some sort, though not necessarily paid employment, is important for the mental health of most of us. It provides us with a sense of purpose and a means of satisfying ambitions and pursuing interests (Gardner & Taylor, 1975). However, work is not done in isolation. It brings into play social relationships, the job itself, and the immediate environment.

Stress at Work. For most people, at some time during their working careers, this complex set of working relationships causes stress. Stress can manifest itself physically, behaviorally, or psychologically. Physical reactions to stressful work conditions include fatigue, headaches, sweating, and various types of psychophysiological disorders, such as ulcers and high blood pressure. An extensive review of the medical-psychological literature found many studies that reported a relationship between coronary disease and job complaints, such as boredom, feeling ill at ease, and interpersonal conflict (Jenkins, 1971). It was also noted that individuals who are highly competitive, impatient, perfectionistic, and unable to relax are more prone to heart attack.

Symptoms of work-related stress also take behavioral forms, such as quarrelsomeness, poor quality of work, reduced productivity, accident proneness, absenteeism, and job changes. Workers who have been at the same job for many years, who are conscientious and methodical, and who see their job as the major source of satisfaction are especially vulnerable to mental breakdown under stress (Schilling, 1975).

Until recently, relatively little attention has been paid by the occupational-health professions to psychosocial sources of stress (Cox, 1979). One psychological factor that has been linked to mental health, however, is job satisfaction. Dissatisfaction with one's work is stressful for many people. Dissatisfaction implies conflict, since it means that the person is doing work he or she would prefer to avoid (Locke, 1976). Moreover, dissatisfaction at work breeds frustration and anger, feelings that are not conducive to psychological well-being.

The Mental Health of the Industrial Worker. Many people today are engaged in mass-production work. On most assembly lines the work is repetitive, requiring the same low level of skill and offering little opportunity for advancement. Benyon (1975), after interviewing assembly-line workers at the Ford Motor Company, found that the majority of employees viewed their jobs as dull, monotonous, tedious, and lacking in any intrinsic value. They said they endured it for the money and felt they were paid to put up with the boredom. Walker and Guest (1952) reported the following worker's comment:

> The assembly line is no place to work, I can tell you. There is nothing more discouraging than having a barrel beside you with 10,000 bolts in it and using them all up. Then you get a barrel with another 10,000 bolts and you know that every one of those 10,000 bolts has to be picked up and put exactly in the same place as the last 10,000 bolts (p. 54).

Many people who work on assembly lines never see the finished product. As a result, they often feel alienated from their jobs and believe that their work is meaningless.

Comparing the mental health of car-assembly workers in Detroit with white-collar workers, Kornhauser (1965) found that the automobile workers were much more poorly adjusted in terms of anxiety, tension, self-esteem, hostility, and personal morale. The differences in mental health

CRITICAL ISSUE

Sexual Harassment in the Work Place

For many years sexual harassment has been a common, recurring problem of working women. Recent surveys, interviews, and conversations with women have shown that many working women have been victims of sexual harassment sometime during their career.

The problem of sexual harassment is not a recent phenomenon. More than 100 years ago, Louisa May Alcott, author of *Little Women,* wrote that while she was working as a paid companion to an elderly woman, the woman's brother wanted Alcott to provide "personal" services to him (Goodman, 1978). But it is only recently that sexual harassment has surfaced publicly and has become a critical area of concern for organizations.

As an increasing awareness of the nature and pervasiveness of sexual harassment developed, federal guidelines were put forth to prevent and eliminate the use of sexual favors in return for being promoted or just keeping one's job. For example, the Equal Employment Opportunity Commission (EEOC) of the United States recognized sexual harassment as a form of sex discrimination and issued the following guidelines on sexual harassment (Section 1604.11):

> Unwelcome sexual advances, requests for sexual favors, and other verbal or physical conduct of a sexual nature constitute sexual harassment when (1) submission to such conduct is made either explicitly or implicitly a term or condition of an individual's employment; (2) subjection to or rejection of such conduct by an individual is used as the basis for employment decisions affecting such individuals, or (3) such conduct has the purpose or effect of unreasonably interfering with an individual's work performance or creating a hostile or offensive working environment.

The guidelines clearly assert that unwelcome sexual advances are unlawful and they specify the conditions under which such advances are civil-rights violations.

When sexual harassment exists, women are required, generally as a result of their inferior economic status, to make intimately personal decisions concerning job-related behavior. The crude phrase "put out or get out" describes what such decisions involve (Biles, 1981).

Some forms of sexual harassment are blatant; others are subtle. They range from verbal harassment or abuse, to subtle pressures for sexual activities, to attempted rape. Because most women are reluctant to subject themselves to public embarrassment and the likely retaliation of employers, the problem of sexual harassment is probably more serious than the number of formal complaints would suggest.

It should be noted that sexual harassment is not limited to males sexually harassing females, although this form of harassment is probably the most common one. It has been suggested that as women move into managerial positions in which they wield power, the number of women committing sexual harassment may increase (Greenlaw & Kohl, 1981). Similarly, the EEOC guidelines also apply to homosexual harassment.

In order to deal with the problem, many federal, state, and local agencies and many businesses in the private sector are attempting to provide organizational climates to discourage sexual harassment. Many of these organizations have already implemented programs that are designed to identify and minimize the problems of sexual harassment and discrimination.

Sexual harassment is found not only in the work place but also on college campuses. Here, too, sexual harassment takes a variety of forms—from telling degrading jokes, to pestering a student for a date, to pressuring a student into having a sexual relationship. Cases involving a professor attempting to trade a grade for sexual favors have been heard before a federal appeals court. Women students, like working women, are finally speaking out on a problem that, like rape, went unreported for years. On most college campuses today, channels have been established to handle student complaints of sexual harassment.

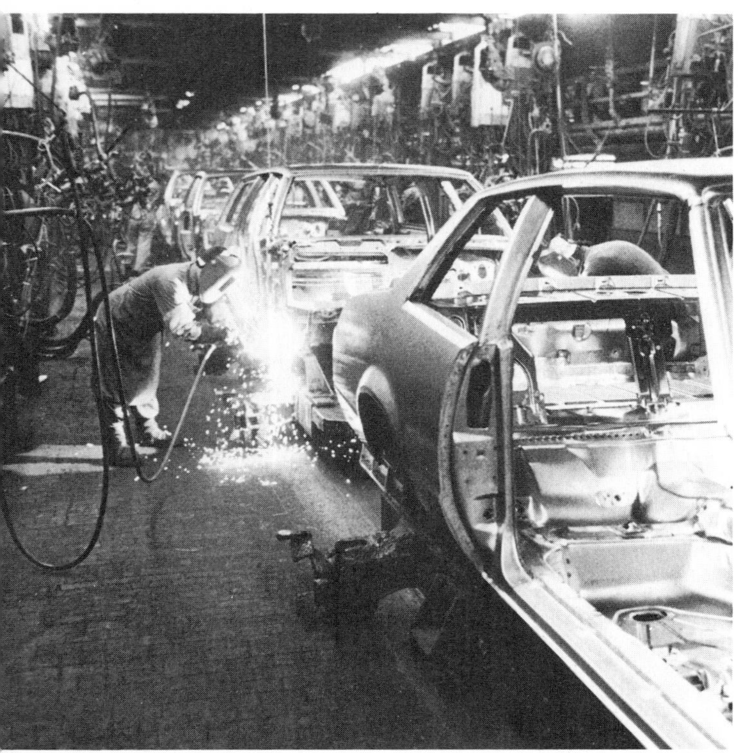

Many assembly-line workers find their environment tedious. *(© Peter Conklin/Monkmeyer Press Photo Service)*

between the automobile-assembly workers and the white-collar workers could not be accounted for by differences in educational level or other job prerequisites. Instead, it seemed that the assembly-line workers, although comparatively well paid, tended to regard their jobs and themselves with contempt. They felt trapped in dead-end positions and dreamed of being their own bosses in a small business or trade. The effects of monotonous, seemingly meaningless work were not only detrimental to the mental health of the employees, but they tended to spill over to other areas of life, such as relations with family and friends.

Executive Mental Health. Production-line workers and employees in low-status occupations are not the only ones who suffer from poor mental health as a result of their jobs. Executives who are hard-driving, competitive, and strongly committed to their jobs can also be afflicted by physical and psychological problems. Frequently they are "workaholics": result-oriented, aggressive individuals who feel intensely the pressures to meet deadlines and maintain high productivity levels (Friedman & Rosenman, 1974). When these individuals are examined psychologically, the high-pressure exterior is often found to mask a dependent personality. Such people are far more prone than the average person to ulcers and heart disease.

It is regrettable that we have so little data regarding the relation between work and mental health. It has been found, however, that workers with more highly skilled jobs tend to be better adjusted than those with assembly-line or unskilled jobs. The factors found to contribute most heavily to adjustment were feelings that a job provided a chance to use acquired abilities and was interesting (Prien et al., 1979).

Industrial Psychologists as Mental-Health Specialists. Some large companies and a few labor unions are beginning to utilize the services of industrial psychologists trained as mental-health specialists and have experimented with the installation of mental-health services in their organizations. Psychologists in these firms provide consultation services to management and diagnostic or psychotherapeutic services to employees with job-centered problems. Turnover, absenteeism, and alcoholism among members of the work force are major problems in many organizations that require the attention of psychologists.

Industrial psychologists are just beginning to appraise the personality factors that bear directly on a person's fitness or nonfitness for work. Achieving a good person-job fit requires an extensive analysis of the skills and personal qualities needed to perform the job successfully. If psychologists are successful in achieving the person-job fit, they will increase the number of fortunate men and women who presently have jobs they enjoy and that provide opportunities for self-expression and a sense of achievement.

COMMUNITY PSYCHOLOGY

Let us look at some typical activities community psychologists engage in. Diane was a community mental-health worker in a large state institution for the mentally retarded. However, most of her time was spent in rural areas supervising residents who had been discharged from the institution after community placements were found for them. Because her clients were functioning at a low level and were expected to learn very little in terms of independent living skills, Diane's major responsibility was to ensure that their physical needs were met.

Diane experienced many frustrations and much stress on her job, which were partly owing to work overload and partly to lack of support and organizational conflict within the institution. She was not only responsible for the supervision of over 90 clients spread over a two-county area, but she had to take care of an additional 50 inpatients still awaiting discharge from the institution. Most of her time was spent in crisis management such as finding a placement for a new client within 48 hours.

In addition to having a heavy caseload, Diane felt that she received little support from the institution, which because of its medical orientation, considered community mental-health workers as "transportation aides." The only positive aspects of her job were the rewarding relationships Diane was able to establish with other community mental-health workers employed by local agencies (adapted from Cherniss, 1980).

Community psychology and the community mental-health movement are often called the "third revolution" in the field of mental health. The French physician Philippe Pinel led the first revolution during the eighteenth century, when he unchained the residents of a mental hospital in Paris and advocated more humane treatment for the mentally ill. The second revolution was initiated by Freud, who emphasized the importance of intrapsychic processes in personality (see Chapter 10) and the role of psychological factors in certain disorders.

Community psychology stresses the role of social, institutional, and political determinants of behavior. According to this branch of psychology, changing individual behavior often requires changes in social institutions (Bernstein & Nietzel, 1980). For example, although individuals may agree that people with mental problems should live in the community whenever possible, it takes social agencies and other institutions to see to it that "deinstitutionalization" takes place. Since it is assumed that social, institutional, and political factors are to a considerable degree responsible for individual adjustment problems, community psychologists attempt to alleviate mental-health problems by working to change the communities into which the person must fit.

Like industrial psychologists, community psychologists can be found in many capacities and settings. They may serve as consultants to a city council, as members of urban-planning teams, or as directors of social-service agencies or citizens' advocate groups. They may train volunteers to operate hotlines at crisis centers, develop aftercare programs to ease the transition of former mental patients into less restrictive community facilities such as halfway houses or sheltered workshops, or design mental-health services for rural or urban-ghetto populations. In this section we shall trace the growth of the community mental-health movement and look at some examples of how the concept of community mental health is put into practice.

Community Mental Health

In 1963 President John F. Kennedy first called upon Congress to provide for a "new, bold" approach to the treatment of mental disorders and the promotion of mental health in this country. This call resulted in the Community Mental Health Center Act, also known as the Kennedy Bill, which provided massive federal funding for the construction of nationwide community mental-health centers. These centers were to promote programs for early detection of psychological problems in the community and develop a delivery system of services that would keep patients in the community, thereby avoiding the "warehousing" (traditional custodial care) of large numbers of chronic patients in mental institutions (Bloom, 1973).

The development of community mental-health programs may be summarized as follows:

> The community mental-health movement in the U.S. reached its fruition during the decade of the 1960s. For the country as a whole that decade was characterized by large scale general trends of social

CRITICAL ISSUE

Burnout in Community Mental Health

The problem of burnout among men and women employed in community mental-health services is a complex social psychological phenomenon that was unheard of a few years ago, although it probably existed long before the term was coined. Maslach (1976) defined burnout as the "loss of concern for people with whom one is working" in response to job-related stress. As Table 19–1 illustrates, there are many different symptoms of burnout.

As Cherniss (1980b) pointed out, one of the best ways of defining burnout is through examples. Consider the following two cases:

> *Example 1.* Mary Smith was a social worker employed in a community mental-health center. It was her first job since receiving her Master's in social work. Like most new social workers, she began with great expectations. She was idealistic, committed, and hopeful. After eight months on the job, she became discouraged and demoralized about the lack of motivation and change in so many of her clients. She wanted to do family therapy, but she could never get a whole family to come together for treatment. She was expected to spend part of her time doing consultation and education in the community. But she was not even sure what that work entailed and certainly did not feel competent when she tried to do it. Going to work became more and more unpleasant. She began getting colds and flus frequently. She was less sympathetic and responsive with clients, except in one or two cases that were more interesting and successful than others. She had expected that being a therapist and counselor in a mental-health agency would be as fascinating as it had seemed in the books she read in college. But she became bored during many sessions with clients. She eventually quit and went back to graduate school to work on a Ph.D. in psychology.

> *Example 2.* In its early days, a particular group home for youths was an exciting, innovative program. The staff was one big, happy family. No one cared about the extra hours worked. There was tremendous dedication to the youths who were thought to have great potential to change and grow. However, over time, the staff became frustrated. They were irritated by what they considered insensitive and inept administrators who were never around but made all the important decisions and were paid twice as much as the rest for working half as hard. The frequent delays in receiving paychecks and the red tape they had to go through whenever the staff wanted to do something for a resident seemed to be further indication for the lack of administrative support. There was also increasing jealousy and rivalry among the staff. Cliques and conflicts emerged: afternoon versus morning staff; professionals versus paraprofessionals; black versus white. Absenteeism and turnover increased. The staff rarely worked past their regular shift and became angry if they had to stay a few minutes longer because someone on the next shift was late. They began asking at staff meetings how

reform. In such a period of reform, the emphasis is on a revitalized humanistic concern for the disadvantaged, the oppressed and powerless . . . it is not surprising that community mental health took place at the same time as the war on poverty, advances in civil rights, the phenomenon of the "flower people," the student rebellions, and the various liberation fronts, for, as social and historical movements, they all stand in kinship relation to one another (Hersch, 1972, p. 749).

As this statement indicates, community psychology is not only concerned with the impact of social problems on the individual but is actively

much physical force was permitted in dealing with disruptive behavior. They also began asking why tranquilizers were not used more to help control the youths' behavior. Many members drank heavily when they came home. Many of them were having marital problems (Cherniss, 1980, pp. 14–15).

A number of factors residing both in the individual and the work setting have been found to contribute to burnout. Many community mental-health workers have to carry an extremely heavy caseload. Being responsible for other people's psychological well-being is stress-producing in itself. In addition, in many cases the mental-health worker is unable to help clients. One social worker described her experience with a welfare client as follows:

> You get very frustrated with a case like this. A woman had five or six children living in her house. The husband moved out and was living in a garage. He was working and not giving the wife a cent to buy food, to heat the house, or anything for the kids. But according to the Department of Social Services [welfare], he was living on the premises, he was working, and therefore they did not qualify for welfare. And there was nothing they could do (Cherniss, 1980a).

Administrators and supervisors of mental-health programs are gradually realizing that burnout is a personnel problem that deserves serious attention and are making attempts to reduce it. Such attempts include decreasing the demands made on mental-health workers, scheduling burnout checkups for employees, and allowing workers to escape temporarily from the demands of the job.

Table 19–1. Signs of Job Stress and Worker Burnout in Human Service Programs

1. High resistance to going to work every day.
2. A sense of failure.
3. Anger and resentment.
4. Guilt and blame.
5. Discouragement and indifference.
6. Negativism.
7. Isolation and withdrawal.
8. Feeling tired and exhausted all day.
9. Frequent clock-watching.
10. Great fatigue after work.
11. Loss of positive feelings toward clients.
12. Postponing client contacts; resisting client phone calls and office visits.
13. Stereotyping clients.
14. Inability to concentrate on or listen to what client is saying.
15. Feeling immobilized.
16. Cynicism regarding clients; a blaming attitude.
17. Increasingly "going by the book."
18. Sleep disorders.
19. Avoiding discussion of work with colleagues.
20. Self-preoccupation.
21. More approving of behavior-control measures, such as tranquilizers.
22. Frequent colds and flus.
23. Frequent headaches and gastrointestinal disturbances.
24. Rigidity in thinking and resistance to change.
25. Suspicion and paranoia.
26. Excessive use of drugs.
27. Marital and family conflict.
28. High absenteeism.

Source: Adapted from Berkeley Planning Associates (1977), Freudenberger (1974), Maslach (1976), and Schwartz and Will (1961), in Cherniss (1980, p. 17)

involved in the solution of community problems that are not necessarily restricted to mental health and mental disorders.

The Kennedy Bill specified that a broad range of mental-health services be made available to everyone in the community. Each mental-health center was to serve 75,000 to 200,000 individuals and be located within or very near the community it served. The bill provided funding for the construction of the community mental-health centers and for staff salaries for a period of four years. After that time it was expected that federal funding would be replaced by local funding. For many centers, especially those located in poor communities, this turned out to be a problem.

In order to qualify for federal funds a community mental-health center had to provide the following five services: (1) inpatient care, (2) outpatient care, (3) partial hospitalization (e.g., for a person working during the day and returning to the hospital at night), (4) around-the-clock emergency service, and (5) consultation and education. Each center could specify the exact nature of the services offered in the five categories and develop programs based on local needs and resources. No person was to be denied services because of the inability to pay.

Although community mental-health programs may offer traditional forms of treatment, the ultimate goal is to modify the social system so as to prevent the occurrence of mental disorders. Community psychologists argue that in the long run preventive efforts will be more efficient and effective than individual treatment administered after the onset of psychological problems or dysfunctions (Phares, 1979).

Gerald Caplan (1964), one of the most influential early community psychologists, identified three types of prevention: primary, secondary, and tertiary. **Primary prevention** refers to the attempt to reduce and eventually eliminate mental disorders in the population by taking measures to counteract harmful factors before they lead to psychological disturbances (Gibbs, Lachenmeyer, & Sigal, 1980). Examples of such preventive measures are removing stressful environmental conditions, such as noise and pollution; conducting research on populations at risk, such as the studies of children growing up in schizophrenic families (see Chapter 12); and using amniocentesis to assess reproductive abnormalities.

Secondary prevention is aimed at the reduction of the rate of mental disorders through early detection. Identifying afflicted individuals in the community as early as possible allows community psychologists to treat them before the disturbance becomes too severe. In practice, this often means reducing the duration or the severity of existing disorders. In contrast to primary-prevention programs, which are mainly aimed at groups or communities, secondary programs are designed for subgroups or individuals who are identified as being at risk for particular problems.

Finally, **tertiary prevention** focuses on the person who has suffered from a mental disorder, has been treated for it, and is trying to readjust to community life. Tertiary prevention aims at reducing or minimizing the negative after-effects of hospitalization. Examples of tertiary prevention are occupational rehabilitation programs that provide training for former mental patients in skills that will qualify them for jobs.

Attention has also been called to the need for preventive programs for college students, who, as a group, may be subject to many stressful situations and who constitute a high-risk group (Bloom, 1971). For many students, the college experience represents the first extended separation from parents, the home community, and its social support system. First-year students, moreover, are exposed for the first time to difficult and competitive academic demands and are apt to experience anxiety and conflict over matters such as occupational choice, sexual behavior and values, and social competencies. It is therefore not surprising to learn that the incidence of emotional disorders is higher among college students than among the population at large (Reid, 1970).

Designing programs that could potentially reach a large segment of this vulnerable population is not easy. The preferred preventive strategy would be to reduce the stress of college life by offering guidance on how to deal with unavoidable stress (Heller & Monahan, 1977). However, it seems unlikely that, for instance, psychologists or counselors could convince college students to plan a moratorium on their sexual behavior because of sexual conflicts that are bound to occur. Many universities, recognizing the difficulties of students that arise from the situational stress of college life, have established mental-health clinics on campus to help students in times of distress. On most campuses, counseling for stress-related problems, academic or personal, is free of charge.

Crisis Intervention

A man threatens to commit suicide. A woman is severely beaten by her husband. A father of a large family loses his job. All these events may be defined as crises—situations in which the person in distress requires immediate help. Crisis intervention is an important aspect of community mental health since it provides around-the-clock emergency services, as outlined by the Community Mental Health Act.

Although many of us can handle crises without experiencing a personality breakdown, some individuals need professional help to manage crises such as failing grades, the breakup of a relationship, children running away from home, and other transitory problems. In crisis intervention, the central goal is to alleviate the person's problem as rapidly as possible through immediate counseling.

Crisis intervention can be distinguished from other forms of psychotherapy (see Chapter 13) in two ways. First, crisis intervention is not concerned with the person's past or his or her usual ability to cope. Instead, after a rapid assessment of the nature of the crisis, the emphasis is on the person's reaction to it. Second, crisis intervention is usually limited to a few contacts. Frequently one or two sessions are enough to clarify the crisis situation and help the person toward a successful resolution. In some cases there may be four to ten sessions.

Suicide prevention is an important type of crisis intervention. *(© Van Bucher/Photo Researchers, Inc.)*

Successful crisis intervention requires crisis centers and crisis workers. Obviously a person in an acute crisis is unlikely to travel many miles to reach an office or talk to secretaries who want to set up a file before assistance can be rendered. Particularly significant has been the establishment of free clinics to provide crisis-management assistance. Most of these clinics are staffed by individuals who have been trained in crisis assistance and who work under the supervision of clinical psychologists.

Suicide prevention is one of the most visible forms of crisis intervention. In the United States there are approximately 200 suicide-prevention services in operation, most of which consist of 24-hour hotlines manned by volunteer paraprofessionals. The prototype of this kind of service is the Los Angeles Suicide Prevention Center, established by Schneidman and Farberow in 1958. The major task of the suicide-prevention worker is to assess the likelihood that the caller will seriously attempt to take his or her life. Farberow (1974) described several important steps that the worker tries to follow when answering calls. First, the prevention worker has to establish a relationship with the caller to determine the nature of the problem. In many cases this means listening nonjudgmentally, assuring the caller of interest and concern. Since many individuals in suicidal crises are confused and unable to differentiate between major and minor problems, clarification of the main problem is important. The crisis worker tries to help the caller to realize that his or her assessment of the situation is impaired by acute distress.

After establishing the relationship and focusing on the problem, the worker must evaluate the potential for suicide. This is done by comparing the information obtained from the caller against a checklist of critical items including sex, age, marital status, and prior suicide attempts. As you will recall from Chapter 12, males who are middle-aged, divorced, living alone, and have previously threatened to commit suicide are the most serious potential candidates for suicide. Once the self-destructive potential of the caller has been assessed, the suicide-prevention worker attempts to determine the emotional resources of the individual and formulates a therapeutic plan based on this information. Often crisis workers are able to persuade the caller to come to the center to discuss the problem in person. This is a positive sign indicating that the caller is willing to listen and to accept help.

Although suicide-prevention centers have been successful in reducing the number of suicides, prevention remains difficult. First, less than a third of suicidal individuals seek psychological assistance. Second, the majority of people who do come to the centers do not follow up initial visits by seeking further help. In a follow-up of 53 persons who commited suicide after contact with the Cleveland Suicide Prevention Center, it was reported that none had contacted the center or another agency prior to death (Sawyer, Sudak, & Hall, 1972).

Community Psychology in the Ghetto

Before the advent of community mental health, minority groups, particularly lower-class urban black people, received few, if any, psychological services. Traditional psychotherapy is very costly and tends to be most successful with highly verbal individuals, making it difficult to render such treatment to poor blacks.

Community psychologists recognized that social, economic, and environmental factors make a major contribution to the development of psychological disorders among the urban poor. People who live in rundown neighborhoods under conditions of social deprivation not only lack personal and social skills but also find few sources of psychological reinforcement or interpersonal gratification in their environment. Such conditions make the struggle for mental health much more difficult.

Since slum residents, because of the stress of poverty, are at the greatest risk of developing mental disorders, they became a high-priority target population for the community mental-health movement. This resulted in two types of mental-health centers for ghetto residents: those that concentrated on rendering services to the most seriously disturbed among the poor, and those that developed social-action programs aimed at producing changes in the social fabric of their lives (Reiff, 1974).

The South Bronx in New York City in 1968 was a blighted slum area on every index of social pathology, such as deteriorated housing, crime, violence, drug addiction, infant mortality, and physical decay. Its population was 70 percent Puerto Rican, most of whom did not speak English. The median school years completed was 8.6, and the rate of delinquency per 1,000 youths was 320.5.

As part of the community mental-health movement, the South Bronx received a mandate to develop community mental-health services as outlined by the Kennedy Bill. In addition to the five essential services—inpatient, outpatient, emergency room, partial hospitalization, and community consultation and education—a municipal antipoverty program, called the Neighborhood Service Center Demonstration Program, was developed. This program consisted of neighborhood centers located in storefronts, each of which provided mental-health services for the residents of five slum blocks (approximately 25,000 people). The function of these centers was to serve as "social first-aid stations" where residents could bring their problems or get assistance, such as with application forms for housing projects or public assistance.

The varied activities of the neighborhood centers included the following: direct services—providing assistance in finding employment and housing, giving advice and counsel, finding resources, and offering psychological support; community services—organizing community meetings and socials, tenants' groups, and task and welfare committees; community education—organizing and conducting campaigns (voter registration, dissemination of information about job opportunities, planned parenthood, and surplus foods, and publication of a newsletter); social planning—convening meetings with representatives of welfare, police, school, and family agencies (Kaplan & Roman, 1973, p. 90).

The Neighborhood Service Center Demonstration Program operated for three years, serving over 12,000 new clients and over 20,000 revisits. It became a model for similar mental-health services in other ghetto areas.

One of the major reasons, then, why the community mental-health movement failed to score major successes in urban ghetto areas has been due to the conflict of values. Most community psychologists come from white, middle-class backgrounds and value systems and attempt to practice traditional psychotherapy on people for whom this approach is unsuitable. This value disparity between providers and recipients of mental-health services has led many professionals to believe that the urban poor are resistive and untreatable (Goldberg, 1973). If community psychology is to make any inroads with slum dwellers, more community mental-health centers need to be placed in ghetto areas and more community psychologists need to be trained who share the value system of that segment of the population.

A Critical Evaluation of Community Mental Health

Recent years have seen a growing concern with the quality and effectiveness of community mental-health programs, and many evaluations have been done. Typically these evaluations focus on such questions as how much it costs to run the center, how many people are aware of the services provided, and what the impact of these services is on mental health and related problems of area residents.

It appears that one of the gravest criticisms of community mental health is that its promises have been oversold and its accomplishments exaggerated. One of the reasons is simply a matter of numbers: of the 2,000 comprehensive community mental-health centers projected by the 1963 act, only about 650 have been completed (Fiester, 1978).

On a qualitative level, a controversial critique of community mental health issued by Ralph Nader's group argued that the centers are based on a good and recommendable set of ideas that are poorly implemented. Nader's group also pointed out that many centers are controlled by psychiatrists and psychologists who still receive little training in the skills required for community mental-health activities.

Other critics (e.g., Bernstein & Nietzel, 1980) believe that community psychologists are still stuck in the rut of arguing with clinicians about the ills of the medical model rather than getting on with the development of effective community intervention programs. As a result, community mental health simply places "old wine" (treatment under the medical model) into "new bottles" (comprehensive community mental-health centers). In spite of the quest for a variety of nontraditional services, inpatient and outpatient services make up the bulk of most centers' activities. A recent survey by Bloom (1977) indicated that only about seven percent of the staff's time is spent in actual community services.

The chief aim of community psychology was to develop preventive techniques and programs, particularly with regard to primary prevention. In spite of all good intentions and investments, however, few examples of effective primary prevention stand out. Cowen (1977) views the failure in the area of primary prevention as follows:

> Psychologists have done very little in the area of primary prevention. Measured by what we as psychologists have achieved, the concept is all aura and no substance. Although we agree overwhelmingly that 'it' is great, many of us cannot identify 'it' in concrete form. The time has come to call our own bluff. We either continue, ostrich-like, to play word games that help us momentarily to feel righteous and avant-garde, or we must roll up our sleeves and start new, qualitatively different brands of [prevention] programming and research (p. 489).

Cowen's critique reflects a thorough disillusionment with the current state of community psychology. He shares with others (e.g., Nietzel, Winett, MacDonald, & Davidson, 1977) the assumption that community psychologists must or should be distinguished by the attitudes about how social problems should be conceptualized. The development of effective intervention programs for treating and preventing such problems has to follow from such conceptualization if community mental health is to succeed.

Summary

Applied psychology attempts to put psychological principles to work in the real world—to give, as George Miller (1969) put it, "psychology away to the people who need it—and that includes everybody." Three important branches of applied psychology are environmental, industrial, and community psychology.

Environmental psychologists have studied the effects of the use of personal space, crowding, and architectural design on human behavior. They have found that interpersonal distancing depends on the type of interaction, the degree of intimacy between two persons, the characteristics of the situation, and cultural orientations. Research has shown that crowding can lead to serious physiological and behavioral disorders among animals. The effects of crowding on humans, however, are less clear. Environmental psychologists have become involved in the design of classrooms, dormitories, and public housing that reflect the needs of those who use or live in them.

Because work may fulfill or frustrate important human needs, industrial psychologists have attempted to identify what makes people satisfied or dissatisfied with their jobs. The Hawthorne studies conducted in the 1920s and 1930s were among the first attempts to investigate the relationship between working conditions and productivity. Job satisfaction is determined by the characteristics of both the job and the person. Most of us work because we derive extrinsic rewards (pay, recognition) as well as intrinsic rewards (self-esteem, a sense of purpose) from our work.

Human-factors, or engineering, psychologists are industrial psychologists who attempt to make the human-machine system function as efficiently as possible. They are involved in the assignment of tasks to machines or humans and the design of equipment and physical surroundings and are concerned with the effects of illumination, noise, and atmospheric conditions. Human-factors specialists have been instrumental in improving the quality of life of the handicapped by designing assistive devices, such as prostheses, orthoses, and wheelchairs.

Stress related to one's job can take both physiological forms (ulcers, high blood pressure) and behavioral forms (fatigue, absenteeism). Industrial workers and business executives alike suffer from disorders arising from occupational stress. Organizations are beginning to use the services of industrial psychologists to counteract the effects of stress on their employees.

Community psychology emphasizes the need to change social institutions that contribute to mental disorders. Thus the community psychologist is concerned not only with the problems of the individual but also with the social surroundings in which they occur. An important function of community mental-health programs is crisis intervention, and a prime-target population of community psychologists is the urban poor. Critics have suggested that if community programs are to succeed, psychologists will have to change their outlook, values, and techniques.

Key Terms For Review

community psychology
crowding
density
engineering psychology
environmental psychology
Hawthorne effect
industrial psychology
intimate distance
orthosis
personal distance
personal space
primary prevention
prosthesis
proxemics
public distance
secondary prevention
social distance
tertiary prevention

Suggested Readings

Anastasi, A. *Fields of applied psychology*. New York: McGraw-Hill, 1979.
After outlining the field of applied psychology, the author presents a detailed description of specialty areas such as organizational engineering, environmental, consumer, clinical, and counseling psychology. Special emphasis is given to the various methodologies in the applied field.

Cooper, C., & Payne, R. (Eds.). *Stress at work*. New York: Wiley, 1978.
The purpose of this book is to bring together what is known presently about occupational stress and health. The authors identify sources of stress in both blue-collar and managerial jobs, and make recommendations for dealing with job-related stress.

Heimstra, N., & McFarling, L. *Environmental psychology*. Monterey, Calif.: Brooks/Cole, 1978.
The authors discuss major aspects of environmental psychology, including the impact of rooms and housing on behavior, commercial environments, city living, natural parks, and wilderness areas and outdoor recreation.

20

Appendix: Statistics and Research Methods

Beth was a sophomore psychology major who was enrolled in the Experimental Methods in Psychology course. One of the course requirements was to design and conduct a psychological experiment. Beth had been fascinated by the lectures she had heard in Introductory Psychology about physical attractiveness, and she decided to do her research on that topic.

Beth was interested in the studies that found that one's self-esteem was related to one's choice of dating partners. She had noticed that among her own women friends, those who seemed to have very high self-esteem dated more attractive men than those who had low self-esteem, regardless of their own level of attractiveness. To test the hypothesis that women with high self-esteem prefer more attractive dates than women with low self-esteem, Beth first administered a self-esteem inventory to 24 women. Scores on this scale could range from 0 to 50. She next divided the women into two groups based on their self-esteem scores and their physical attractiveness so that the groups differed in self-esteem but were of equivalent attractiveness. The attractiveness of the women was determined by having a friend unobtrusively categorize each woman as attractive, average, or unattractive as she signed up to participate in the experiment.

Beth then brought the women into the laboratory individually and told them that she was interested in studying the process by which men and women get to know each other. Each woman was to select a photograph of a college man that she would like to get to know. Beth explained that the photographs were of men who had volunteered to participate in the study and that a date would be arranged between the woman and the man she selected. Actually, the photos were taken from a college yearbook and were selected to reflect a wide range of physical attractiveness. A group of students had previously rated each photograph on a 10-point attractiveness scale. After the woman selected a photograph, she was told the actual purpose of the experiment and all her questions were answered.

When Beth completed her experiment, she arranged the data she had collected in tabular form, as shown in Table 20–1. Now all she had to do was figure out whether her results supported her hypothesis.

Statistics could provide her with the answer. This chapter presents an overview of statistical and research methods. Of course, one chapter is not sufficient for you to learn how to do statistics or design experiments. But it can familiarize you with some of the concepts and help you appreciate the difficulties of psychological research. Beth's data will be used in our numerical examples.

STATISTICS AND DATA ANALYSIS

It is virtually impossible to live in our society without being exposed to statistics. We hear that "seven out of ten doctors recommend Brand X," "the president has an approval rating of 42 percent," "the polls indicate that the Democratic candidate will win the election." A knowledge of statistics helps us evaluate such statements.

There are two general purposes of statistics. The first is to summarize a body of data. For instance, it is more convenient and more readily understandable to say that the Major League batting champion had a batting average of .342 than to say he had 212 hits in 620 times at bat. When statistics are used in this way, they are called descriptive statistics.

The second general purpose of statistics is to allow us to make inferences about our data. Pollsters, for example, wish to make predictions about forthcoming elections. And Beth would like to make statements about the dating choices of all college women and not just of those women who participated in her experiment. Statistical techniques that allow us to make such statements are referred to as inferential statistics. They enable us to arrive at generalizations. Let us look at examples of both kinds of statistics.

Descriptive Statistics

Descriptive statistics are used to organize and present data in a convenient and understandable way. Descriptive statistics can take a variety of forms, but three types are of particular importance to the psychologist: measures of central tendency, measures of variability, and measures of association.

Measures of Central Tendency. The word "average" is used by most people when they are speaking of a measure of central tendency. We talk about average salaries, average test scores, average rainfall, and so on. Because the word "average" can be used in so many ways, psychologists prefer to use the more precise concepts of the mean, the median, and the mode. These three measures of central tendency define the center of a set of data in slightly different ways.

The **mean** is the arithmetic average. It is usually what people are referring to when they use the term "average." The mean is obtained by adding together the scores in a set of data and then dividing by the total number of scores. The mathematical formula is:

$$\overline{X} = \frac{X_1 + X_2 + \ldots + X_n}{N} = \frac{\Sigma X}{N}$$

where $\overline{X}$ = the symbol used for the mean
N = the number of scores
Σ = the Greek capital letter *Sigma*, the mathematical sign indicating that the scores are to be added together
X_1, X_2 = scores from the first and second observations or pieces of data.

As an example, suppose Beth was curious about the average level of attractiveness of the men selected by the women in her experiment. She would plug the data she obtained into the above formula as follows:

$$\overline{X} = \frac{6 + 5 + \ldots + 8}{24} = \frac{172}{24}$$

$$\overline{X} = 7.17$$

The second measure of central tendency, the **median**, is the score above and below which half of all scores fall. In other words, the median is the midpoint of a distribution, or set of scores. To find the median of her data on the men's attractiveness, Beth would arrange the scores from lowest to highest and find the midpoint of that distribution. In this case, the median would be 7.

The mode is the simplest and the least frequently used measure of central tendency. The **mode** is the score that occurs with the greatest frequency. In Beth's experiment, there are two modes, since photographs with ratings of 7 and 8 were both selected by five women (see Table 20–1).

Earlier we mentioned that the word "average" can be used in several ways. To illustrate, imagine a small but prosperous company that pays the following salaries:

President	$60,000
Foreman	50,000
Worker A	10,000
Worker B	8,000
Worker C	8,000

The following statements could be made about this situation:

The average salary is $27,200.
The average employee earns $10,000.
The average salary is $8,000.

All three statements could be made without any of the speakers being intentionally dishonest. The first statement uses the term "average" as the arithmetic mean. This would be the favored statistic if one wished to show how generous the company was. The second statement uses the median as the measure of central tendency, and the company does not appear overly generous. The

Baseball fans are well-acquainted with the usefulness of statistics, such as batting average. *(© Wide World Photos)*

Table 20–1. Results of Self-esteem and Dating Choice Experiment

Low Self-esteem Group			*High Self-esteem Group*		
Subject Number	**Self-esteem Score**	**Attractiveness Score of Dating Choice**	**Subject Number**	**Self-esteem Score**	**Attractiveness Score of Dating Choice**
1	12	6	13	29	7
2	12	5	14	30	8
3	14	5	15	30	7
4	18	6	16	32	7
5	18	8	17	33	9
6	20	7	18	35	6
7	21	6	19	35	9
8	22	4	20	35	8
9	22	8	21	37	10
10	24	7	22	37	9
11	24	6	23	39	9
12	25	7	24	41	8
Mean	19.33	6.25		34.42	8.08
Standard Deviation	4.40	1.16		3.59	1.11

Mean Self-esteem score for all women	=	26.88
Standard deviation	=	8.54
Mean Attractiveness score of dating choice for all women	=	7.17
Standard deviation	=	1.46

last statement uses the word "average" to mean normal or typical—that is, the mode. The modal salary is indeed $8,000, which makes the company look stingy.

The point of the example is that different statistics will be obtained by using different measures of central tendency. And it is quite possible for union officials and management or for political opponents to cite statistics that are accurate but appear to be contradictory. Hence the cynical belief, held by many people, that one can use statistics to prove anything. While that is not true, it certainly is possible to use statistics that support one's position and ignore statistics that do not. Consequently, the careful consumer or voter or newspaper reader wants to know all of the relevant statistics. And psychologists, in reporting their research results, have a responsibility to present sufficient statistics so that the reader can evaluate whether the researcher's conclusions are justified. Statistics do not lie but, on occasion, people may use them misleadingly.

Measures of Variability. Suppose you took a test and were told that the mean score was 70 and your score was 85. You may be pleased to know that you scored above average, but you probably would want to know how much above average your score was. The **standard deviation,** the most frequently used measure of variability, could provide you with this information. This statistic allows one to make statements about the degree to which a particular score deviates from the mean. Table 20–2 provides an example of the calculation of the standard deviation. This table uses a variety of data that are taken from ten school children in the third grade.

Before we illustrate the calculation of the standard deviation for Beth's data, we must introduce the concept of the **normal distribution.** We assume that most human characteristics are distributed in the manner shown in Figure 20–1. That is, a majority of people are near the mean, or average, and as the distance from the mean increases, the number of people decreases. This distribution is also called a "bell-shaped curve" because of its appearance. All bell-shaped curves, like this one, are symmetrical. As an example, imagine that Figure 20–1 represents the distribution of scores obtained by 1,000 people who took

Table 20–2. Height of Ten Third-grade Children and Calculation of the Standard Deviation

Child	*Height*	*Mean* ($\bar{X}$)	*Deviation from Mean* ($X - \bar{X}$)	*Squared Deviation from Mean* $(X - \bar{X})^2$
Jim	56″	50″	6	36
John	54	50	4	16
Bob	54	50	4	16
Sally	53	50	3	9
Chris	52	50	2	4
Michael	50	50	0	0
Tammy	48	50	−2	4
Ellen	46	50	−4	16
Barbara	44	50	−6	36
Janet	43	50	−7	49
Total	500″			186
	Mean = 50.0″			

To calculate the standard deviation, use the formula:

$$s = \sqrt{\frac{\Sigma(X - \bar{X})^2}{N}}$$

$$s = \sqrt{\frac{(56-50)^2 + (54-50)^2 + \ldots + (43-50)^2}{10}}$$

$$s = \sqrt{\frac{36 + 16 + \ldots + 49}{10}}$$

$$s = 4.3 \text{ inches}$$

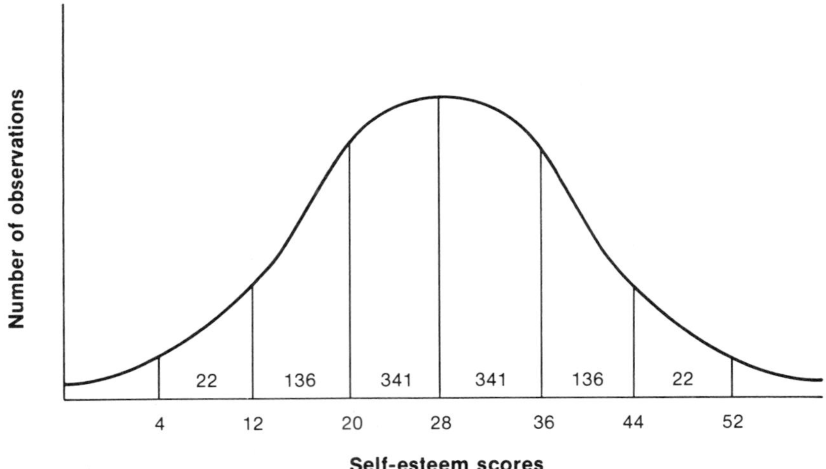

Figure 20–1.

the self-esteem inventory used by Beth in her experiment. The mean score obtained by the 1,000 people was 28, and the standard deviation was 8. The number in each segment of the distribution is the number of people who obtained self-esteem scores in that interval. Hence, of 1,000 people, 341 obtained scores between 28 and 36, 136 obtained scores between 36 and 44, and so on.

The scores on the self-esteem inventory can be expressed in standard deviation units, called *z* **scores,** using the following formula:

$$z = \frac{X - \overline{X}}{s}$$

where z = standard deviation unit
X = raw score
$\overline{X}$ = mean score
s = standard deviation

A self-esteem score of 44 would become:

$$z = \frac{44-28}{8} = 2$$

Therefore, we know that a person who received a self-esteem score of 44 scored 2 standard deviations from the mean. From Figure 20–1, you can see that out of 1,000 people, this individual with a score 2 standard deviations above the mean scored higher than 977 of them. Only 23 out of 1,000 people would receive scores that were higher than 44.

Statistical tables have been compiled that can tell us the percentage of cases that fall above and below a given z score. So if we wanted to know how many people could be expected to receive scores below 30 on the self-esteem inventory, we would first find the z score:

$$z = \frac{30-28}{8} = .25$$

Looking up the value of .25 in the appropriate table, we obtain a percentage of 59.87. Thus we know that of 1,000 people, about 599 can be expected to have scores of below 30 on the inventory.

Z scores are useful because they can be used to compare one score with another. For example, suppose you received a test score of 90 in a sociology course and a score of 75 on a physics exam. These numbers would provide you with no information about your performance relative to the rest of the class. If, however, your sociology instructor had told you that the mean was 95 and the standard deviation 5, you would know that your z

score was −1 ($z = \frac{X - \overline{X}}{s} = \frac{90-95}{5} = -1$). In other words your score was one standard deviation unit below the mean. Suppose for your physics class, the mean was 65 and the standard deviation 5. This time your z score would be +2. Relative to your classmates, then, your score on the physics exam was actually better than your score on the sociology test.

This discussion is intended to give you the flavor of the standard deviation. Its purpose is to describe the variability that exists in a distribution of scores. Once the mean and standard deviation are known, one can know how a particular score compares with others.

Now, let us illustrate the calculation of the standard deviation for Beth's data. As shown in Table 20–2, it involves adding together the squared deviations from the mean and dividing by the total number of observations. Suppose Beth is curious about the variability of self-esteem scores of her 24 subjects. She would use the formula:

$$s = \sqrt{\frac{\Sigma(X-\overline{X})^2}{N}}$$

Substituting her data, she would have:

$$s = \sqrt{\frac{(12-26.88)^2 + (12-26.88)^2 + \ldots + (41-26.88)^2}{24}}$$

$$s = \sqrt{\frac{(-14.88)^2 + (-14.88)^2 + \ldots + (14.12)^2}{24}}$$

$$s = 8.54$$

To find the range of the self-esteem scores of her subjects, Beth uses the z score formula:

$$z = \frac{X - \overline{X}}{s} = \frac{12-26.88}{8.54} = -1.74$$

where X = the lowest score.

$$z = \frac{X - \overline{X}}{s} = \frac{41-26.88}{8.54} = +1.65$$

where X = the highest score.

She now knows that her subjects' scores range from 1.74 standard deviations below the mean to 1.65 standard deviations above the mean.

As an additional example of the meaning of the standard deviation, consider the data presented in Table 20–2. There, we found that the standard deviation of the height of ten third-grade children was 4.3 inches. Suppose we sampled children from the entire school from kindergarten through the sixth grade. The mean height may still be 50 inches, but because we will have some small kindergarten children and some tall sixth-graders in our sample, the standard deviation will be larger than for the third-grade children. Figure 20–2 illustrates the distribution of scores for third-graders only, and for children of all grades. Notice that the difference between the two standard deviations of 4.3 inches and 8 inches reflects the difference between the shapes of the bell-shaped curves. The larger the standard deviation, the more variability there is among the scores.

Correlation: Measure of Association. Beth is curious about the relationship between her subjects' self-esteem scores and their choices of a date. To get a rough idea of whether a relationship exists, she plots a scatter diagram (Figure 20–3). This is done by placing the range of possible scores for self-esteem on the horizontal axis, which is called the x axis. The range of possible scores for physical attractiveness of the men is plotted on the vertical axis—called the y axis. The points in the scatter diagram are plotted so that each point represents two scores: one on self-esteem and one on physical attractiveness of the date selected. For example, to plot the point for subject number 1 from Table 20–1, Beth would go across the x axis until she reached the score of 12, and then move straight up until she reached the point that corresponds to 6 on the y axis. As you can see, it does appear that there is a slight tendency for attractiveness of dating choice to increase as self-esteem scores increase. But it is impossible to make any precise statements describing the relationship by visual inspection of the data.

The **correlation coefficient,** symbolized as r, is the statistic that allows us to describe in a precise

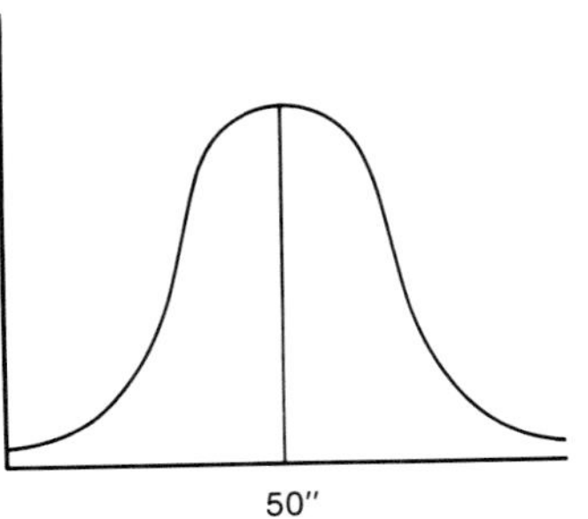

Third Grade Children
Mean = 50 inches
Standard Deviation = 4.3 inches

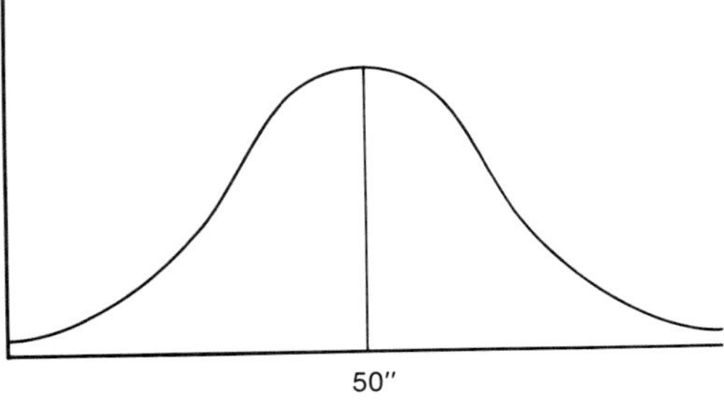

All Children Grades K through 6
Mean = 50 inches
Standard Deviation = 8 inches

Figure 20–2.

manner the degree of association between two sets of scores. Correlations can range from −1.00 to +1.00. An r of +1.00 would indicate a perfect positive relationship, and an r of −1.00 would indicate a perfect negative relationship. An r of .00 would indicate that there was no relationship between the two sets of scores. A positive correlation means that as scores on one variable increase, scores on the second variable increase as well. For example, as Beth's scatter diagram suggests, as one's self-esteem increases, so does the attractiveness of one's dating choices. A negative correlation would indicate that as scores on one variable increase, scores on the second variable decrease. For example, an increase in the frequency of toothbrushing may be associated with a decrease in the incidence of cavities. Some examples of scatter diagrams and their corresponding correlation coefficients are provided in Figure 20–4 on the opposite page.

Several types of correlation coefficients have been developed for a variety of types of data. Beth has selected the **Pearson product moment correlation coefficient** to measure the degree of association between self-esteem scores and attractiveness of dating choice. This correlation coefficient is appropriate for her data and is most frequently used. The formula is as follows:

$$r = \frac{\frac{\Sigma XY}{N} - \overline{XY}}{(s_x)(s_y)}$$

where X = self-esteem scores
$\overline{X}$ = mean for self-esteem
s_x = standard deviation for self-esteem
y = attractiveness scores
$\overline{Y}$ = mean for attractiveness
s_y = standard deviation for attractiveness
N = number of subjects

The first step would be to calculate the means and standard deviations for both sets of scores. Once these are obtained (see Table 20–1), they are substituted in the formula as follows:

$$r = \frac{\frac{(12 \cdot 6) + (12 \cdot 5) + \ldots + (41 \cdot 8)}{24} - (26.88)\,(7.17)}{(8.54)\,(1.46)}$$

$$r = \frac{\frac{4832}{24} - 192.73}{12.47}$$

$$r = .69$$

The correlation coefficient of .69 indicates that there is a moderately positive relationship between self-esteem scores and attractiveness of dating choice.

A word of caution is in order regarding the interpretation of correlations. There is a tendency for people to assume that if two variables are highly correlated, then one causes the other. But such a conclusion is unwarranted. The number of tattoos and the number of motorcycle accidents may be correlated, but it is not logical to conclude that tattoos cause motorcycle accidents or that motorcycle accidents cause tattoos.

Incidentally, this has been a line of defense of the tobacco industry. They argue, and rightly so, that a correlation between smoking and the incidence of various diseases does not prove that smoking causes these diseases. Of course, other

Figure 20–3.

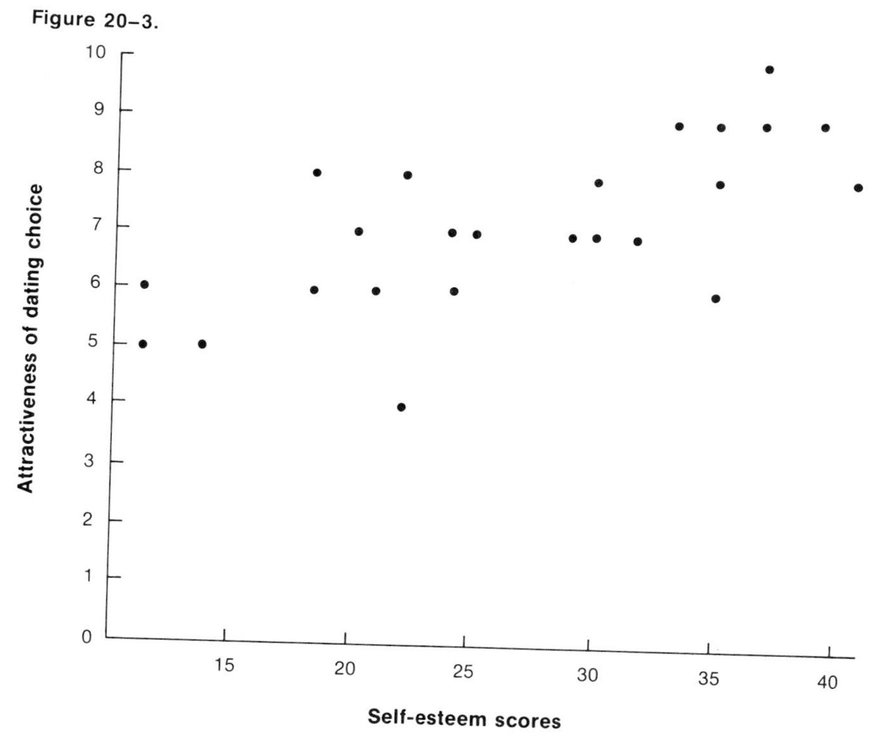

Figure 20–4.

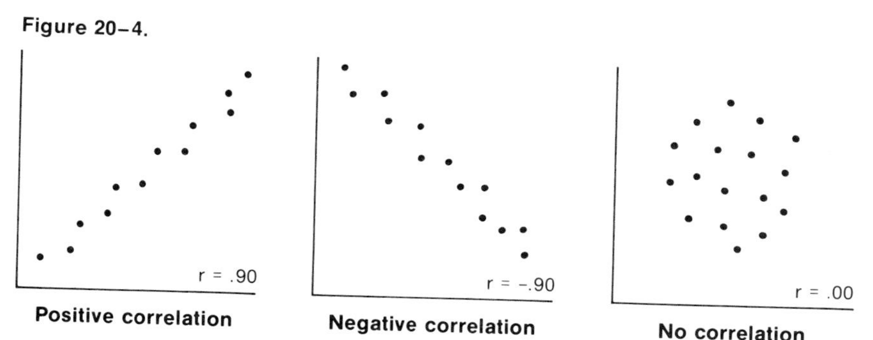

lines of evidence strongly suggest that smoking does indeed cause medical problems, but strictly speaking the tobacco industry is correct: correlation does not prove causation. We shall discuss the limitations of correlational research in more detail later in the chapter.

Inferential Statistics

Psychologists are not satisfied simply to describe their data. Even if Beth can say that the mean attractiveness of the dating choices of her low-self-esteem women is 6.25 and the mean for the high-self-esteem women is 8.08, her task is unfinished. The crucial question would be: Does this difference between the means reflect a significant difference? If Beth were to conduct the experiment with 24 other women, would she obtain similar results? If you were to flip a coin ten times, and heads appeared on six of those tosses, you would not conclude that there is a greater probability of heads appearing than tails. You would know that if you were to flip the coin ten more times, the incidence of heads and tails would probably be different.

Inferential statistics are techniques that help us to decide whether differences, such as the one Beth obtained, are meaningful. If Beth were to repeat her experiment with 24 different subjects, the mean scores of the two groups of women might differ simply through chance. The question then becomes: Is the observed difference a result of uncontrolled variables or chance factors, or is it a meaningful difference that we could expect to observe again if the experiment were repeated? Inferential statistics provide the answers to these types of questions.

***Student's* t.** It would take several weeks in a statistics course to cover all of the concepts involved in inferential statistics, but let us provide a brief example of what Beth might do with her data. When Beth designed her experiment, she was proposing two mutually exclusive hypotheses. The first, always referred to as the null hypothesis, would be:

> Null Hypothesis: There is no difference between the mean attractiveness of dating choices of women with high and low self-esteem.

The second hypothesis, called the alternate, or experimental, hypothesis, would be:

> Alternate Hypothesis: There is a difference between the mean attractiveness of dating choices of women with high and low self-esteem.

Inferential statistics would allow us either to reject or to fail to reject the null hypothesis. If we can reject the null hypothesis, then we can accept the alternate hypothesis.

The inferential statistic that Beth has selected to use is called the student's *t*, or the ***t*-test.** The formula is*

$$t = \frac{\overline{X}_1 - \overline{X}_2}{\sqrt{\dfrac{s_1^2 + s_2^2}{N-1}}}$$

where $\overline{X}_1$ = mean of attractiveness scores for high self-esteem women

$\overline{X}_2$ = mean of attractiveness scores for low self-esteem women

s_1^2 = the square of the standard deviation (called the variance) for attractiveness scores for high self-esteem women

s_2^2 = the square of the standard deviation for attractiveness scores for low self-esteem women

N = the number of subjects per condition

By substituting the means and standard deviations of the ratings of the men selected by the high and low self-esteem women, you would have:

* Actually, a slightly different formula would be used. This formula would provide a biased estimate of the difference between the means and would be used only if the samples were of infinite size. In the interests of simplicity, we shall let you learn about biased and unbiased estimates when you take a statistics course. Also, a slightly different formula would be used if there were an unequal number of subjects in the two conditions.

$$t = \frac{8.08 - 6.25}{\sqrt{\dfrac{1.11^2 + 1.16^2}{11}}} = \frac{1.83}{.48} = 3.81$$

The last step would be to look up the t value of 3.81 in the appropriate statistical table. This table, which is found in the back of every statistics book, gives the probability of obtaining such a result on the basis of chance alone. For a t value of 3.81, we discover that by chance alone Beth could expect the results she obtained in fewer than 1 time out of 100. In other words, Beth can be 99 percent certain that the difference she obtained was meaningful. Psychologists tend to use a probability level of 95 percent as a standard. Since Beth's results exceed that standard, she would be justified in rejecting the null hypothesis and concluding that women high in self-esteem are likely to select more attractive prospective dates than women who are low in self-esteem.

As you are well aware by now, most psychological experiments are considerably more complex than one that compares two groups of subjects. And, as you might guess, the statistical techniques used for these experiments are more complex than the t-test. But the basic goal is the same: being able to infer that an obtained result reflects a reliable and meaningful difference. If, as in Beth's case, the statistical tests do indicate this, the psychologist can conclude that his or her results are statistically significant.

RESEARCH METHODS

Statistics are only a tool, and the statistical results of an experiment can only be as good as the research methods that produced those results. A researcher may obtain results that are highly significant from a statistical point of view, but they may be meaningless or trivial if the experiment was not well designed or properly conducted.

Suppose a researcher hypothesized that schizophrenia results in slowed reaction times. This researcher went to the local psychiatric hospital and tested 30 schizophrenic patients. As a comparison, he tested 30 college sophomores in an introductory psychology class. A t-test indicated a highly significant difference between the two groups. Can he conclude that schizophrenia does result in slowed reaction times?

No, of course not. A number of differences between hospitalized schizophrenics and college students could be responsible for the difference in reaction times. For example, the patients are almost certain to be taking medications that could affect reaction times, they live in a less stimulating environment than college students, they are likely to be older than the students, and they may not be as motivated to perform well on the task. Clearly, this would be a case in which statistically significant results were rendered meaningless by poor research design. Let us review the major

Correlation does not prove causation in the case of cigarette smoking and lung cancer. *(© Leif Skoogfors / Woodfin Camp & Associates)*

types of research and the issues and potential problems associated with each.

Laboratory Research

A majority of the experiments described in this text are examples of **laboratory research.** In this type of research, psychologists bring subjects—either animals or people—into their laboratories, and observe their behavior under controlled conditions. The general goal of laboratory research is to observe the effects of an independent variable on a dependent variable. The **independent variable** is controlled and manipulated by the researcher so that its effects on the subjects' behavior can be observed. The behavior to be observed is the **dependent variable.** In Beth's experiment, self-esteem was the independent variable and the women's dating choices the dependent variable.

Laboratory research is the most common source of data for psychological statistics. *(© Mimi Forsyth/Monkmeyer Press Photo Service)*

The advantage of laboratory research is that researchers can exert a great deal of control over the conditions. This allows them to have confidence that it was in fact the independent variable that influenced the dependent variable. Suppose, for example, that a psychologist was interested in the effects of hunger (or, more precisely, food deprivation) on evaluations of the taste qualities of various kinds of foods. The researcher decides to compare three groups of people—the very hungry, the moderately hungry, and the sated. One strategy would be to visit the campus cafeteria and test people prior to lunch, immediately after lunch, and in the middle of the afternoon. While it seems reasonable to conclude that prior to lunch people will be very hungry, it could be that some individuals had coffee and a Danish late in the morning. Even if the psychologist were to ask prospective subjects when they last ate, they may forget about the Danish that was consumed two hours earlier.

A better laboratory research strategy might involve asking people to come to the researcher's lab immediately upon getting up in the morning. All participants would eat breakfast upon arriving, and the calorie content of the meal would be carefully controlled. Then, one group (the sated group) would be tested upon completion of the meal, another group (moderately hungry) would be tested three hours later, and a third group (very hungry) would be tested at the end of six hours. In this way the psychologist would be confident that it was in fact food deprivation that caused any observed differences in the ratings of food made by the participants.

Control Groups. Suppose you wanted to test the effectiveness of a new tranquilizer in reducing anxiety. You identify a group of highly anxious people, give them a week's supply of the pills, and find that they are significantly less anxious at the end of the week. The tranquilizer must be effective—right?

As you probably suspect, the answer is "not necessarily." It could be that your participants were anxious in response to a specific situation. The passage of time and not the pill might have lowered their anxiety levels. In order to have more confidence in the tranquilizer, you would want to include a control group. A **control group** would be similar in all ways to the group receiving the medication except that they would not be exposed to the independent variable—namely, the tranquilizer. If, at the end of a week, the group receiving the medication was significantly less anxious than the control group, you could be more confident that the medication was responsible.

In this example, your task would still be incomplete. Physicians are well acquainted with the **placebo effect.** If people receive a treatment that they believe to be effective, they are likely to show improvement on that basis alone. To determine whether the tranquilizer was effective because of its medicinal properties or because of the placebo effect, you would have to include a second control group. This control group would be told that they were receiving a tranquilizer, but they would actually receive an inert substance—a placebo. Then, if the group that actually received the tranquilizer was less anxious than both control groups, the researcher could be confident that the tranquilizer was an effective antianxiety agent.

Experimenter Bias. Even though scientific research calls for objectivity, psychologists are subject to the same biases and distorted perceptions as anyone else. They want their experiments to yield the predicted results. Few psychologists would intentionally distort their data, but very few are capable of being 100 percent objective about their own research. Relatively subtle types of behavior exhibited by the experimenter, such as gestures, tone of voice, and eye movements—behavior that the experimenter is not even aware of—may influence the participants.

In the tranquilizer example just described, experimenter bias could be an important problem. If the anxiety level of participants was determined by having researchers interview them or observe their behavior, the researchers may tend to make more favorable judgments for those subjects who were known to have received the tranquilizers. Again, this does not necessarily reflect an intentional bias. Researchers simply are not immune to the possibility that their personal desires will influence their perceptions.

Psychologists are well aware of the problem of experimenter bias and build in protections against it in their research designs. In the food-deprivation study, the researcher might ask colleagues or assistants to conduct the taste tests. They would not be informed of the hypothesis of the experiment or of the experimental condition of the various participants.

The same procedure could be used in the tranquilizer experiment. Those who judged the subjects' anxiety level would not be informed which group the participants were in until all the data were collected. Controlling for experimenter bias is one more step toward insuring that statistically significant results are indeed meaningful.

Field Research

While laboratory research allows experimenters to control the situation, there is always the question of whether the results can be generalized to naturalistic situations. Will subjects who respond to a stimulus in a particular way in the laboratory respond in the same way in their everyday lives? **Field research** gives up the control provided by the laboratory in order to gain the meaningfulness of naturalistic settings.

Consider an experiment conducted by psychologist Jerry Wiggins (Wiggins, Wiggins, & Conger, 1968). He was interested in the relationship between personality characteristics in men and their preferences for various body types in women. He constructed a series of silhouettes in which size of breasts, buttocks, and thighs were varied. Thus it was possible to present the men with silhouettes of women with all possible combinations of characteristics—small breasts, small buttocks, and large thighs; large breasts, small buttocks, and small thighs; and so on. Wiggins did find several relationships between personality characteristics and body-type preferences. For instance, men who tended to be moralistic preferred small-breasted silhouettes.

As interesting as Wiggins's results are, we have no idea whether the men's preferences for silhouettes in a laboratory setting have any correspondence to their preferences in naturalistic settings. Are moralistic men more likely to ask a small-breasted woman to dance at a party than they are to ask a large-breasted woman? Or does breast size become irrelevant in such a setting?

In order to learn whether the laboratory results can be generalized to real-life behavior, we would have to conduct a field experiment. A researcher might employ a female confederate who, with the judicious use of padding, can vary her body characteristics. She may sit alone in a library or cafeteria and identify the personality characteristics of the men who approach her. Or the researcher might frequent a few parties and evaluate the personalities of the men and the body type of their dates. Obviously, researchers give up a great deal of control over the situation when they conduct field research, but they gain a great deal of realism.

It is important to remember that the use of control groups and the issue of experimenter bias apply to field research as well as to laboratory research. If field research is properly designed, the results can be as meaningful as, and often more meaningful than, the results of laboratory research.

Correlational Research

Correlational research refers to strategies that attempt to discover whether two variables are associated with each other. Beth's experiment and Wiggins's experiment are both examples of correlational research. Beth wanted to discover whether there was a relationship between self-esteem and attractiveness of dating choices, and Wiggins was interested in the correlation between personality characteristics and preferences for feminine body types. It is important to note that the researcher's choice of a statistic to test the results of an experiment does not necessarily bear a relation to the nature of the research strategy. Beth used a *t*-test in her experiment, but her research design is correlational in nature. Conversely, it is possible, although rarely done, to use a correlation coefficient to describe the results of an experiment that is not correlational.

In our discussion of the correlation coefficient we noted that correlation does not prove causation. This means that Beth's conclusion must be limited to stating that there is a relationship between the self-esteem of women and their dating choices. She cannot conclude that self-esteem causes dating choice. It could be that both self-esteem and attractiveness of dating choices are caused by some third variable—such as earlier parent-child interactions or previous heterosexual experiences.

You might be wondering why researchers even bother with correlational research if their conclusions are so severely limited. The answer is that on many occasions there are no alternatives. Ethical standards prevent researchers from conducting the type of research that would provide conclusive answers for a variety of issues. For example, suppose one wanted to test the hypothesis that parents who belittle the efforts of their children to achieve independence will reduce their self-esteem. The only realistic research strategy is the correlational method. One would observe the nature of the parent-child interactions and determine whether a relation with the child's self-esteem exists.

It is impossible to obtain conclusive proof of cause-and-effect relationships using correlational methods. But it is possible to build a very strong case for cause and effect using nothing but correlational methods. Thus very few people doubt that smoking or exposure to asbestos can cause cancer in humans even though the evidence is correlational. If we suspect that A causes B, if numerous experiments conducted by many researchers under a variety of conditions find that A and

B are correlated, and if we can eliminate the causative role of any third variable, it is reasonable to suggest that A does cause B.

Experimental Research

When possible, **experimental research** is the first choice of research psychologists. The basic strategy is to manipulate the independent variable A to see whether it affects the dependent variable B. If every time A is presented, B follows, we can conclude that A causes B. In contrast to correlational research, which allows us to determine whether A and B vary together, experimental research allows us to make statements about cause-and-effect relationships.

To illustrate, let us consider Beth's experiment again. As we have said, it was a correlational study since she identified a relationship between self-esteem in women and the attractiveness of their dating choices. She could have conducted an experimental study by manipulating the self-esteem of her subjects and observing the effects on dating choices. Researchers have manipulated self-esteem by having subjects "overhear" someone talking about them, by giving them either favorable or unfavorable feedback from a personality test, or by forcing a comparison between themselves and another individual. By using these methods, it is possible to produce temporary increases or decreases in self-esteem.

Such manipulation points to the important issue of ethical concerns in experimental research. Is the researcher justified in lowering the self-esteem of subjects to advance scientific knowledge? We shall discuss this issue in more detail later in the chapter, but it should be noted here that ethical considerations apply to correlational research as well as experimental research. They are more likely to be of concern in experimental studies, however, since the researcher is manipulating the environment of the subjects.

Although we tend to think of laboratory research as being experimental and field research as being correlational, this need not be the case. While it may be more difficult to manipulate the independent variable in field research, it certainly is not impossible.

As one example, social psychologists have studied the "foot in the door" phenomenon in naturalistic settings. The foot-in-the-door principle posits that if people comply with a request for a small favor, they are more likely subsequently to comply with a request for a large favor. To conduct an experimental study, a researcher would select a pool of participants and randomly assign half of them to an experimental group and half to the control group. The researcher would knock on the doors of the experimental subjects and ask for a small favor, such as asking them to sign a petition to combat airport noise. Next the researcher would approach the participants in both groups and ask for a large favor. The participants might be asked to spend three hours stuffing envelopes for the campaign against airport noise. If significantly more people in the experimental group than in the control group agreed to stuff envelopes, the researcher would have evidence for a cause-and-effect relationship.

Developing a Research Program

Many questions that interest psychologists can never be answered conclusively. Ethical and practical considerations prevent psychologists from conducting the kind of research that would provide definitive answers. A good example concerns the topic of violence and aggression, which was covered in Chapter 18. As we indicated in that chapter, it is impossible to prove conclusively that a steady diet of televised violence and aggression during childhood causes aggression and violence in the viewers. One would have to recruit a group of newborn babies, randomly assign them to an experimental or a control group, and rear them under identical conditions with the exception of their exposure to violent or nonviolent television shows. This, of course, will never be done.

The only realistic alternative is to use a variety of research methods to test various aspects of the hypothesis. As you will recall, a variety of field and laboratory experiments, both correlational and experimental, have been conducted with regard to the television-violence issue. Some studies have required about an hour's time from each subject, while others have followed subjects over ten years. This research has resulted in a fairly coherent picture. At the very least, it has prompted one prominent researcher to assert, "Significant overall reduction of violence and mayhem on the television screen would, I believe, lower the level of violence in American society." (Eron, 1980, p. 250). The available evidence does leave room for disagreement, and not all researchers are convinced that reducing violence on television and in the movies would have a significant impact on our society. Nevertheless, a comprehensive research program that utilizes a variety of methods in a variety of settings can provide us with a sound basis for making informed decisions, even though we cannot obtain conclusive answers.

ETHICS IN RESEARCH

Recently the public has become increasingly concerned about the use of animal and human participants in scientific research—and rightly so. In many instances researchers have abused their subjects in ways that border on the incredible. Bacterial gases have been released in cities. People have been administered psychotropic drugs, such as LSD, without being informed. In one study, men with syphilis were not informed of their condition or offered treatment so that researchers could study the long-term effects of the disease. In another, soldiers were ordered to allow themselves to be exposed to radiation. All these investigations have taken place in the name of science.

We like to believe that only a few unethical researchers allow such things to take place. But there is an unfortunate tendency to stretch or bend ethical standards when it comes to gathering support for scientific hypotheses. Suppose Beth believed people should never feel bad as a result of their participation in research. Consequently, she designed her study to be correlational so that she would not have to lower the self-esteem of any of her subjects. But, upon submitting her results to a professional journal for publication, she was told by the editor that her findings were inconclusive because of their correlational nature. Will Beth be able to accept with equanimity the fact that a year's worth of work will not be brought to fruition? Or will she decide that the next time around she will not worry so much about her subjects' feelings? Clearly, it would help Beth if she had a well-defined set of ethical principles to serve as a guide.

In response to numerous abuses of human participants in the past and from a desire that people should not be harmed as a result of their participation in research, several agencies have published guidelines for ethical conduct. One goal of such guidelines is to help researchers like Beth. When one has worked long and hard on a problem, it is difficult to be objective when evaluating the ethics of a questionable research procedure.

A second important reason for establishing ethical principles is that many experiments call for procedures that result in an ethical dilemma. Ethical guidelines may not provide clear-cut answers, but at least they lead to review boards. A review board, usually made up of one's colleagues, will discuss the proposed research and ensure that the researcher is not letting scientific interests overshadow the welfare and safety of subjects.

A typical dilemma might concern a conflict between two clinical psychologists, one who is research oriented and one who is service oriented. Suppose Dr. Smith, who is employed at a university counseling center, wants to discover whether the techniques used by the center for treating depression are effective. Being research minded, Dr. Smith proposes a study in which every other student who seeks treatment for depression will actually receive treatment. The remaining students will be placed in a no-treatment control group. By comparing the two groups at the end of six months, Dr. Smith will be able to offer scientific proof regarding the effectiveness of the center's treatment methods.

The research-review committee, which includes a service-minded clinical psychologist, is horrified by Dr. Smith's proposal. The members do not see how any depressed students can be denied treatment. First, their tuition helps to support the center. Second, there is a real possibility that some depressed students who are denied treatment may become worse and attempt suicide. Dr. Smith argues that the center cannot continue to offer treatment that has not been proved to be effective.

The ethical dilemma here is that both Dr. Smith and the committee are right. It is unethical to use techniques that are not supported by scientific evidence, and it is unethical to deny treatment to depressed students in the name of science. The existence of a set of ethical principles and a review board to enforce them, however, will promote discussion that may result in a more satisfactory decision than either research-minded or service-minded psychologists would arrive at on their own. The committee and Dr. Smith may conclude that the risks of withholding a potentially effective treatment are greater than the risk of providing an ineffective treatment. They may agree that Dr. Smith should conduct his research but that a no-treatment control group should not be part of it.

In other situations, the decision may be the opposite. For example, if the treatment is a new medication that has serious side effects, a review committee may decide that a no-treatment control group is essential. Since the risks of using such a medication are severe, it should not be used unless there is conclusive evidence that it is effective.

The American Psychological Association, the Department of Health and Human Services, and many state legislatures are among the organizations that have defined ethical treatment of research participants. The various guidelines differ in some respects, but they all include two general principles.

First, human research participants can be included in experiments only if they give their informed consent. This principle has three main implications. The first is that individuals cannot be coerced into participating in an experiment. At one time, students enrolled in introductory psychology courses were commonly required to participate in a given number of experiments, thereby providing professors and graduate students with a readily available pool of subjects. The coercion was justified by stating that participation in research was a valuable learning experience. Opinion has since shifted, and during the middle 1970s the "learning experience" rationale began to be viewed as a rationalization for making researchers' lives easier. Current ethical practice dictates that students can receive extra credit for participating in research but that they must be provided with an alternative means of meeting the course requirements. Not even college freshmen should or can be forced to participate in research if they choose not to.

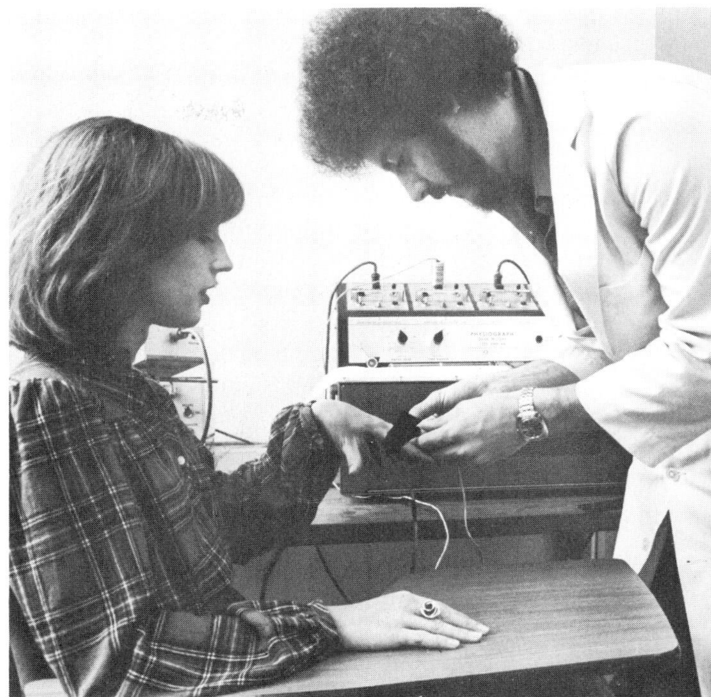

Ethical considerations require the experimental psychologist to obtain informed consent from his or her subjects. *(© Sybil Shelton/Monkmeyer Press Photo Service)*

A second implication is that prospective subjects must be told of any risks involved or of any procedures that might influence their decision to participate. They must be informed if electric shock, drugs with side effects, and situations producing stress are to be used in the experiment. But there are many situations that are not clear cut. For instance, if Beth were to decide to manipulate the self-esteem of her subjects, would she have to inform them of this? Would ethics require her to tell each woman, "I will be trying to make you feel bad about yourself in this experiment?" If Beth were to make such a statement, she would probably undermine the whole experiment. Fully informing participants about the nature of an experiment may make it virtually impossible to conduct the experiment.

As you know from reading this text, in many experiments psychologists initially deceive their subjects. The justification is that such experiments do not expose participants to stresses any more severe than those they face in their day-to-day lives. Moreover, the effects are temporary, and the researcher assumes the responsibility of discussing the experiment with the participant after it is completed. The researcher does take every precaution to insure that the participants do not leave with any lingering unpleasant feelings. Researchers who employ deception argue that it is more unethical not to do the research. These arguments are not convincing to everyone. Some institutions and researchers categorically state that the use of deception is unethical.

A third implication of the informed-consent principle is that people should not be involved in experiments without their knowledge. This happens frequently in field research. For example, several experiments have been conducted in which the behavior of motorists stopped for red lights has been observed. In one, a researcher stood on the curb and stared at the driver and then observed how quickly the motorist drove away once the light turned green. Of course, none of the motorists observed had agreed to participate in the experiment. And it is possible that such an experiment would upset a driver. For instance, a woman might be so flustered by a strange man staring at her that she would drive off in a fright and hit a pedestrian. Again, many investigators justify such research on the grounds that it increases scientific knowledge and in the long run benefits society. But such research certainly raises difficult ethical problems.

The second general ethical principle is that researchers must protect the welfare and dignity of all research participants. Many of the implications of this principle overlap with those of the first principle. For instance, the ethical researcher is especially sensitive to any experimental procedures that could cause participants distress. This principle would go one step further and prohibit any procedures that are clearly dangerous, even if participants give their informed consent. Thus if an experiment calls for the use of electric shock, it would not be sufficient to forewarn participants of the potential dangers. The researcher would have to insure that the participants would not be harmed. If a participant has a heart attack after receiving a series of electric shocks, the researcher does not escape responsibility by having a signed consent form.

One important implication of this principle concerns confidentiality and protection of privacy. Virtually all researchers promise participants that anything they say or do during the experiment will be held confidential. It is necessary to make such guarantees to increase the likelihood that participants feel free to be open and honest. Many experiments deal with personal topics, such as religion, politics, sexuality, and fears. Few people would be willing to share such personal information if they believed there was the possibility of it becoming public knowledge.

In a large majority of cases there is no difficulty in protecting confidentiality and anonymity of research participants. Often only the experimenter knows the participant's name, and any written observations or test results are coded so that the participant cannot be identified later. But difficult situations arise. Suppose a researcher who is conducting an experiment about aggression explains the experiment to a participant. The participant then volunteers that he has been having obsessive thoughts about killing someone. The experimenter, who is aware of ethical responsibilities, attempts to refer the participant to the university counseling center. The participant angrily refuses and states that he would never have mentioned his fantasies except for the promise of confidentiality. What does the experimenter do?

In this case most researchers probably would decide that it is more unethical not to do something about the situation than it is to break the promise of confidentiality. But where does one draw the line? What about a participant who volunteers that he or she is using hard drugs—or soft drugs? Or a participant who reports thoughts of committing suicide—or one who reports moderate depression? Once again, there are no easy answers.

The existence of clearly defined ethical principles and review boards to enforce them does not guarantee that no abuses will occur. As we have seen, there are many situations that require that an ethical principle be violated. But such principles make researchers aware of and sensitive to their responsibilities to research participants. At the very least, ethical principles promote discussions with one's colleagues that, it is hoped, result in fewer instances of unethical behavior. It does seem safe to say that fewer abuses will take place with such guidelines than without them.

Summary

Statistics are tools for evaluating the results of psychological research. Descriptive statistics are convenient ways of summarizing data. The mean, median, and mode are measures of central tendency. The mean is the arithmetic average, the median is the midpoint of a distribution of scores, and the mode is the most frequently occurring score. The standard deviation is a measure of variability. It allows us to make statements about how much above or below the mean a particular score is. The correlation coefficient is a measure of association. It provides an index of the strength of the relationship between two sets of scores.

Inferential statistics allow us to make conclusions about the meaning of our data. Student's *t*, or the *t*-test, allows us to ascertain whether the difference between two means is significant or whether it could have occurred on the basis of chance alone.

For statistics to have meaning, research methods must be well designed. The psychologist has several basic strategies from which to choose. Laboratory research allows tight control over relevant variables but may be somewhat artificial. Field research, which takes place in naturalistic settings, provides more realism, but the researcher gives up some control. Psychologists must use correlational research in studying many problems. It involves observations to determine whether two variables are associated with each other. It does not allow for conclusions about cause-and-effect relationships. Experimental research, which manipulates variable A to observe its effects on B, allows for cause-and-effect conclusions. But ethical considerations and practical limitations prevent the use of the experimental method for many problems. Often researchers must use a combination of strategies to generate answers to a problem.

Researchers who use humans as subjects must be sensitive to ethical issues. Several codes of ethics have been proposed, and all include two basic principles. First, people who participate in research must do so on the basis of informed consent. Second, researchers must strive to protect the welfare and dignity of human research participants. These principles generate many situations in which researchers must choose the least unethical of two courses of action. The existence of ethical principles has generated review boards to administer and enforce them. While codes of ethics and review boards do not do away with abuses, they do serve to make researchers sensitive to the ethical issues inherent in their experiments.

Key Terms For Review

control group
correlation coefficient
correlational research
dependent variable
descriptive statistics
experimental research
field research
independent variable
inferential statistics
laboratory research
mean
median
mode
normal distribution
Pearson product moment correlation coefficient
placebo effect
standard deviation
***t*-test**
***z* scores**

Suggested Readings

American Psychological Association. *Ethical Principles in the Conduct of Research with Human Participants.* Washington, D.C.: American Psychological Association, 1973.
This publication provides a complete statement of the ethical principles along with actual cases to illustrate the principles. It is "must" reading for anyone who plans to engage in research.

Bruning, James L., and Kintz, B. L. *Computational Handbook of Statistics,* Glenview, Ill.: Scott, Foresman, 1977.
This paperback book is extremely useful for the beginning psychology student. It provides detailed, step-by-step examples of how to calculate a variety of statistics.

Conrad, Eva, and Maul, Terry. *Introduction to Experimental Psychology.* New York: John Wiley, 1981.
This book provides a comprehensive introduction to research methods for the serious student.

Couch, James V. *The Fundamentals of Statistics for the Behavioral Sciences.* New York: St. Martin's Press, 1982.

An excellent introductory statistics text that discusses the procedures and the use of the basic statistical techniques.

Reich, John W. *Experimenting in Society: Issues and Examples in Applied Social Psychology*. Glenview, Ill.: Scott, Foresman, 1982.

This paperback book provides an interesting introduction to the practical problems and ethical issues of conducting research with people.

Tanur, Judith M. *Statistics: A Guide to the Unknown*. San Francisco: Holden-Day, 1972.

Written for those without special knowledge of statistics, this paperback book provides numerous examples of the difficulties of applying and interpreting statistics. Examples of issues discussed range from the health hazards of smoking to predicting the weather. Students from a variety of disciplines will find material of interest in this book.

Glossary

absolute threshold the minimum amount of energy necessary to be perceived

acceptance the final stage in the process of adjusting to death, during which the person is neither angry nor depressed

accommodation according to Piaget's theory of intellectual growth, the process of changing one's cognitive repertoire when new information demands such change

accommodation the visual process whereby the lens changes shape to focus light

achievement motivation our desire to accomplish something of value or importance through effort and to meet standards of excellence in what we do

acrophobia an irrational fear of high places

activity theory a theory of aging proposing that the more active old people remain, the more successfully they age

adjustment definition a formal definition of personality that views the individual as struggling to find his or her identity and to adjust to the environment

adrenal glands endocrine glands located on the surface of the kidneys

affect a term used to describe the observable component of an emotion, such as giggling or crying

affective component of attitudes the emotional response to a person, idea, or object

aggression-releasing stimuli behavior or postures assumed by an animal that elicit aggression from other animals

agoraphobia an irrational fear of open places

alcohol a substance that depresses many of the activities of the brain

alcoholic hallucinosis auditory hallucinations associated with alcoholic intoxication

alpha waves brain waves with a frequency of 8–12 cycles per second, which are produced when a person is in a relaxed waking state

Alzheimer's disease an organic brain disorder characterized by shrinkage of the brain

amniocentesis the insertion of a needle into the amniotic cavity for the purpose of drawing a sample of the amniotic fluid

amphetamine a drug that produces a stimulating effect by releasing epinephrine in the brain

amphetamine psychosis a psychotic-like state induced by excessive intake of amphetamines

amygdala a structure in the limbic system concerned with the control of emotionality

androgen the sex hormone produced by the testes and adrenal gland

androgyny behavior including masculine and feminine characteristics; freedom from sex-role stereotypes

anger the second phase in the process of adjusting to death during which anger is the predominant reaction

anima according to Carl Jung, the feminine aspect of a man's personality

animus according to Carl Jung, the masculine aspect of a woman's personality

anterograde amnesia failure to remember events occurring after an operation

antianxiety, antidepressant, antipsychotic drugs a group of mind-affecting drugs used in the treatment of severe psychological disorders

anxiety a vague, subjective feeling of apprehension; irrational fear

approach-approach conflict a situation in which a person must choose between two equally desirable alternatives

approach-avoidance conflict a situation in which

a person has motives to approach and avoid a single goal

archetypes in Jung's analytic theory of personality, universal thought patterns associated with the collective unconscious

arrangement definition a formal personality definition that puts personality traits into some kind of order to arrive at a total description of the person

assimilation according to Piaget's theory of intellectual growth, the process of incorporating new stimuli into one's cognitive repertoire

assumptions the behavior, dimensions, or events with which a theory is concerned, as well as the types of behavior that the theory attempts to predict

attentional processes processes based on the notion that people cannot learn much by observation unless they attend to and perceive accurately the significant features of the behavior to be modeled

attitude a combination of cognitive, affective, and behavioral dispositions directed toward a person, idea, or object

attribution the process whereby people ascribe causes to their own behavior and that of other people

attribution retraining procedures that encourage a person to view his or her successes and failures as resulting from personal efforts

auditory canal the part of the outer ear that concentrates sound waves

aura a period of unusual feelings or perceptions that occurs before a person lapses into an overwhelming sleep

authoritarian personality an individual who is rigid, fears power, but wants it, is fearful of sex, and is likely to be prejudiced

autocratic leader one who makes all the decisions for the group and exerts close control over the group's activities

autokinetic effect the tendency to perceive motion where none exists

autonomic nervous system a division of the peripheral nervous system concerned with the regulation of involuntary responses

aversion therapy a behavior-therapy technique used to eliminate undesirable behavior

avoidance-avoidance conflict a situation in which a person must choose between two equally undesirable alternatives

avoidance conditioning the presentation of an aversive event, which is signaled by a discriminative stimulus

axon the part of the neuron that electrically transmits the nerve impulse

babbling prespeech sounds rich in both vowels and consonants

Babinski reflex the reflex that occurs in response to tickling the sole of an infant's foot

balance phase the third phase of group formation during which there is harmony between personal and group identity

balance theory a theory of attitude change that suggests that people strive to seek consistency or balance among their cognitions

barbiturates drugs that depress the central nervous system and act as sedatives

bargaining the third stage in the process of adjusting to death, during which the person tries to make some "bargain" to postpone his or her death

basal age in the Stanford-Binet, the highest age level at which a child can answer all items correctly

behavioral component of attitudes the disposition to act in accordance with one's feelings and beliefs about a person, idea, or object

behavioral potential in Rotter's theory of personality, the probability of the occurrence of a given response under certain environmental conditions

behaviorism the school of psychology that suggests that observable behavior is the only meaningful topic of study in a scientific discipline

behavior therapy a form of therapy that utilizes principles of learning to change behavior

biofeedback a training procedure in which a person receives information about changes in some bodily response and tries to modify the response

biological aging readily apparent and fairly predictable effects of aging in which the body of the older person shrinks in size and has a reduced ability to recover from stress

biological death when the heart stops beating, when breathing stops, or when the electrical activity of the brain ceases

bipolar affective disorder a term used to describe a person whose moods swing between extremes of elation and depression

bisexuality a sexual variation in which one engages in both homosexual and heterosexual behavior

bonding attachment of the infant to the primary caretaker

brain a portion of the central nervous system that consists of three sections: forebrain, midbrain, and hindbrain

brainstorming a problem-solving technique in which people share their ideas about possible solutions to a problem

caffeine a widely used stimulant found in coffee, tea, and cola drinks

Cannon-Bard theory a theory of emotion that suggests that the subjective experience of emotion and physiological changes occur simultaneously

castration anxiety in the psychoanalytic phallic stage, a boy's fear that his sexual attraction to his mother will bring him into conflict with his father, and that his father will punish him for his "incestuous" desires by removing his penis

catatonia a subcategory of schizophrenic behavior characterized by bizarre motor behavior

catharsis a process of weakening or eliminating aggressive impulses by substituting some form of less destructive or nondestructive behavior

ceiling age in the Stanford-Binet Intelligence Scale, the lowest age level at which a child answers all times incorrectly

central nervous system a portion of the nervous system consisting of the brain and spinal cord

cerebellum a part of the hindbrain concerned with the organization of bodily movements

cerebrospinal fluid fluid in the cerebral ventricles and the central canal of the spinal cord

cerebrum a large and important part of the forebrain consisting of the neocortex and the corpus callosum

chaining the process of linking entire series of operant responses

chain technique a method to improve memory that emphasizes continuity of cue words and links them together in such a way that each word gives you a recall cue for the next cue word in the chain

character a dimension of personality that is evaluated by others as either ethical and moral or the reverse

charisma a magnetic quality in leaders that attracts followers

chromosomes microscopic particles carrying genes for general body and sex characteristics. Chromosomes occur in pairs in the nucleus of every human cell

chronic brain disorders caused by progressive degeneration of brain tissue, usually resulting from degenerative diseases and brain tumors

chunking grouping separate bits of information into larger units to facilitate remembering

classical conditioning a procedure in which a conditioned stimulus—through repeated pairings with an unconditioned stimulus—comes to elicit a conditioned response

claustrophobia an irrational fear of closed places

client-centered therapy based on Rogers's theory, a form of therapy that attempts to promote psychological growth

clinical psychologist a Ph.D. who has specialized in clinical psychology during graduate training

clinical psychology the branch of psychology that specializes in the assessment and treatment of psychological disorders

cloning asexual reproduction in which all descendants from a single cell are genetic carbon copies of one another

cocaine a powerful stimulant derived from the leaves of the coca plant

cochlea a fluid-filled tube in the inner ear that transforms mechanical energy into neural activity

cognition how a person gathers knowledge about

the world around him and how he stores, retrieves, and uses that knowledge

cognitive component of attitudes beliefs or factual knowledge about a person, idea, or object

cognitive-dissonance theory a theory of attitude change that suggests that inconsistencies in a person's thoughts about something generate tension and the subsequent desire to reduce that tension

collective unconscious in Jung's analytic theory of personality, universal experiences shared by humans throughout time

community psychology stresses the role of social, institutional, and political determinants of behavior

companionate love intense liking; the affection that exists between a man and a woman whose lives are deeply intertwined

compensation a defense mechanism in which a person overcomes weakness in one area of personality by excelling in another

complex in Jung's analytic theory of personality, thoughts and memories with a common theme that are associated with the personal unconscious

compulsion an irresistible impulse to repeat an irrational act over and over again

concrete operations according to Piaget's theory of cognitive development, the third stage of intellectual growth during which higher-order thought processes develop

conditioned response a reflex action given in response to the conditioned stimulus alone

conditioned stimulus a stimulus that acts upon the senses in order to evoke a desired response

conditioning when a response is consistently followed by a reinforcing event

conduction deafness a hearing impairment caused by conditions that prevent the inner ear from being activated

cones photoreceptive cells in the retina that are primarily responsible for vision in bright light and for color vision

conflict phase the second phase of group formation during which members experience a clash between their own sense of individuality and the rules and standards imposed by the group

conformity yielding to group pressures

conservation the principle that solids and liquids can be transformed in shape without changing their mass or volume

consolidation the transformation of information from temporary to permanent memory storage

contingency model of leadership effectiveness a theory of leadership proposed by Fiedler that suggests that characteristics of leaders and the situation interact to determine effective leadership

continuous reinforcement rewarding an organism for every desired response

control group a group participating in an experiment that is not exposed to the independent variable, thus providing a means for comparison

conventional morality according to Kohlberg, the level of moral development during which children and adults obey rules for their own sake

conversion disorder a condition in which psychological problems manifest themselves as physical illness

cooing the vocal productions of infants during the second half of the first year that consist of long vowels

cornea the part of the outer covering of the eye that gathers and concentrates light

corpus callosum a fiber tract connecting the two cerebral hemispheres

correlation coefficient the statistic that provides an indication of the degree of association between two sets of scores

correlational research strategies that attempt to discover whether two variables are associated with each other

cost contingencies (or fines) the withdrawal of reinforcers that have already been earned

crowding the subjective feeling of having too little space

cumulative record a record of any and all behavior that occurs in a Skinner box

cutaneous senses the skin senses of pressure, warmth, coldness, and pain

debriefing a requirement under the guidelines regulating deception studies requiring the researcher to delineate the procedure used, to clarify the nature of the study, and to explain the rationale for the deception in a post-experimental interview with research participants

decay theory a theory of forgetting that suggests that memories fade over time

defense mechanism unconscious processes used to protect one's self against anxiety

delirium tremens a disoriented state associated with alcohol intoxication that usually begins after a period of nondrinking and is preceded by restlessness and insomnia

delta waves the high-altitude, slow waves of 1–2 cycles per second that occur during the third NREM stage of sleep

delusion a psychotic symptom referring to false, persistent beliefs uncritically accepted as true

delusion of grandeur a false belief of psychotic individuals that they are extremely important or powerful

delusion of persecution a false belief of psychotic individuals that others are plotting to harm them

democratic leader one who solicits the input of the group and encourages members to share in the decision-making process

dendrites branching fibers arising from the body of the nerve cell

denial a defense mechanism in which a person refuses to acknowledge unacceptable impulses

denial and isolation the first stage in the process of adjusting to death in which the person refuses to believe his impending death

density the area available to the number of people present

deoxyribonucleic acid (DNA) genetic material contained in the nucleus of living cells

dependent variable the variable that is left free to vary in a research project; researchers manipulate independent variables in order to examine their effects on dependent variables

depression an affective disorder characterized by hopelessness, lethargy, and physical complaints

depression the fourth stage in adjusting to impending death during which the person has a sense of sadness that life will soon be over

descriptive statistics statistics that are used to organize and present data in a convenient and understandable way

developmental psychology the branch of psychology that focuses on the relation between age and behavior

deviance any behavior that does not conform to a group's accepted norms

diatheses-stress theory a theory of schizophrenia that suggests that genetic predisposition and environmental stress interact to produce schizophrenic symptoms

differential-emotion theory a theory that suggests that certain fundamental emotions are innate and that each has its own specific neurological pattern

digit-letter system a system to help memorize sequences by breaking up numbers and converting them into words

disengagement theory a theory of aging proposing that aging is characterized by withdrawal of the old person from his or her activities

disorientation a state of mental confusion with respect to time, place, and self-identity

dissociative disorder a condition in which a person experiences temporary alterations of consciousness

distinctiveness definition a formal definition of personality that equates personality with unique and individual aspects of behavior

Doctor of Psychology an academic degree in clinical psychology that emphasizes practical applications rather than research skills

dopamine a transmitter substance in the central nervous system that has been linked with schizophrenia

double approach-avoidance conflict a situation in which a person must choose between two alternatives, both of which have positive and negative elements

double bind a situation in which a person is exposed to conflicting messages

Down's syndrome a chromosomal disorder leading to mental retardation; also called mongolism

drive a term used to describe motivational states, such as hunger and thirst, that have a physiological basis

duplicity theory the hypothesis that there are two visual systems, one associated with rods and the other with cones

Durham decision a law stating that an accused is not responsible for his or her criminal behavior if the unlawful act was the product of a mental disorder

dynamic psychotherapy based on Freud's theory, a form of psychotherapy that attempts to help clients understand their unconscious conflicts

eardrum the part of the outer ear that transmits sound waves to the middle ear

eclectic a theorist who uses ideas from a variety of approaches or schools of thought

ectogenesis embryonic development outside the body of the mother

ego the mediating force that balances the demands of the id and the external realities

egocentricity a characteristic of the preoperational child, who is unable to see the world from someone else's perspective

ego psychology neo-Freudian theories of personality that emphasize the conscious, rational processes of the ego

Electra complex in psychoanalytic theory, the female version of the Oedipal complex

electrical stimulation a technique to measure an animal's behavior as a function of electrical charges in the brain by passing small amounts of electrical current through intact brain tissue

electroconvulsive therapy (ECT) a therapy technique in which an electric current is applied to a patient's temples

electrode a thin wire used to apply electrical current to brain tissue

electroencephalogram (EEG) recording of electrical potential generated by the brain

emotion the term used by psychologists to refer to feelings such as joy and sadness; a complex concept involving physiological changes, activity in the brain, and subjective evaluations

empathic understanding a quality of therapists that enables them to understand and appreciate clients' feelings

empirical definitions the operations by means of which a theory can be tested

encoding the formation of a memory trace

encounter group a personal-growth therapy that emphasizes open, honest, and intense interpersonal relationships

endocrine gland a ductless gland that releases hormones into the bloodstream

engineering psychology fitting the job to the worker through the design of equipment and the work environment

engram the electrochemical circuit that memory presumably leaves in the brain

engrossment a father's emotional involvement with his baby and resulting sense of self-esteem

enkephalin a transmitter substance that mimics the effects of opiates

environmental attribution the belief that outside factors are the causes of a person's behavior

environmental psychology the science concerned with our relationships and interactions with the physical world, both natural and man-made

epinephrine a hormone secreted by the adrenal medulla that causes an increase in sympathetic arousal

erectile failure a man's inability to have or maintain an erection sufficient to have sexual intercourse

erogenous zones in psychoanalytic theory, the pleasure-producing areas of the body, such as the mouth and genitals

eros according to psychoanalytic theory, the life instincts

esteem needs in Maslow's hierarchy, the need to see oneself as adequate, competent, and useful

estrogen the sex hormone produced chiefly by the ovaries

ethology the scientific study of animal behavior

excitement phase the first stage of sexual arousal characterized by vaginal lubrication and enlargement of the clitoris in women and by elevation and enlargement of genital area in men

exhibitionism a sexual variation in which one derives pleasure from exposing one's genitals

expectancy according to Rotter "the probability held by the individual that a particular reinforcement will occur as a function of a specific situation or situations"

experimental psychology the branch of psychology concerned with the determinants of behavior such as learning, memory, or cognition. It also refers to an approach to research that can be applied to any topic in psychology

experimental research research that supports statements about cause-and-effect relationships

expressive aphasia a speech disorder in which the person has difficulty expressing thoughts in speech or writing

extinction the repeated presentation of the conditioned stimulus without the unconditioned stimulus, resulting in the gradual decrease, and finally extinction, of the conditioned response

extraversion in Jung's analytic theory of personality, the attitude toward people and action

field research research done in natural settings

fixation in psychoanalytic theory, development arrested at an earlier stage of psychosexual development

fixed-interval schedule a schedule in which reinforcement depends on the passage of a set period of time

fixed-ratio schedule a schedule in which the experimenter determines a fixed number of responses that must occur before reinforcement is delivered

flashback the spontaneous recurrence of some aspect of a psychedelic drug experience

formal operation according to Piaget's theory of cognitive development, the fourth stage of intellectual growth during which abstract thought develops

fovea the depressed spot at the back of the eye where the greatest concentration of cones is found

free association a psychoanalytic technique in which a person is encouraged to say whatever comes to mind

free-floating anxiety diffuse, chronic anxiety where the person continually feels a sense of tension and dread but cannot say what he or she is afraid of

frontal lobe a part of the cerebral hemispheres involved in learning, memory, and performance

fully functioning self the culmination of personality development in which an individual is open to experience, is free of defenses, and has unconditional positive regard for self and others

functional fixation an obstacle to successful problem solving that occurs when people fixate on an inappropriate solution

functionalism the school of psychology that suggests that the workings of the mind help us to adapt to everyday occurrences

functional psychosis a psychotic behavior pattern that lacks an organic cause

generalization gradient the gradual drop in response strength associated with the decreasing similarity to the original conditioned stimulus

generalized and conditioned reinforcers learned reinforcers, such as affection, approval, and attention, that are rewarding for many different types of behavior

generalized-anxiety disorder a condition in which a person suffers from chronic, diffuse anxiety

general paresis an advanced stage of syphilitic infection in which brain tissues are progressively destroyed

genetics the study of heredity

genuine a characteristic of therapists that enables them to be open and honest about their personal feelings, reactions, and values with clients

Gestalt psychology the school of psychology that suggests that our conscious experience of the world is more than the sum of its individual elements

Gestalt therapy a personal-growth therapy based on the premise that problems result when one loses touch with one's true feelings

gonad glands glands secreting sex hormones; ovaries in the female, testes in the male

grasping reflex a reflex that causes a baby to close its fingers firmly over any object placed on the palm

group cohesiveness the degree to which individuals are attracted to a group

groupthink a process operating in cohesive groups that leads to erroneous decisions

hallucination false perceptions, often auditory or visual, frequently experienced by psychotics

hallucinogens (psychedelic drugs) drugs, such as marijuana and LSD, that produce hallucinations

Hawthorne effect the influence that participation in an experiment may have on the subjects' behavior

hebephrenia a subcategory of schizophrenic behavior characterized by rapid intellectual deterioration

hermaphroditism a clinical condition in which the individual is born with ambiguous sex characteristics

hierarchical definition a formal definition of personality that interprets personality traits as stages of development that appear in fixed order

higher-order conditioning the neutral stimulus is presented with, and then replaced by, a new stimulus, while the response remains the same

historical theories with regard to prejudice, the idea that prejudice has its origins in years of conflict between groups

histrionic personality a behavior pattern characterized by self-dramatization and self-centeredness

holophrastic speech single-word utterances that express the meaning of an entire sentence

homosexuality a sexual variation in which one is erotically attracted to, and engages in sexual behavior with, members of the same sex

hormones chemical substances secreted by the endocrine glands to control physiological processes

hostile aggression aggressive behavior in which the primary goal is to harm or injure another person

humanistic psychology a school of psychology that suggests that humans can grow psychologically beyond their past experiences. This school emphasizes variables such as goals, values, and aspirations

Huntington's chorea organic brain disorder characterized by jerky body movements and intellectual and memory impairments

hydrocephalus a clinical condition resulting from excess cerebrospinal fluid in the brain; associated with mental retardation

hypermetropia farsightedness. Hypermetropia occurs when the lens cannot accommodate to close objects

hypnosis a trance-like state in which the subject is highly susceptible to suggestion

hypothalamus a structure in the brain controlling arousal, emotionality, the regulation of food and water intake, and temperature

hypothyroidism a malfunctioning of the thyroid that results in dwarfism

id in psychoanalytic theory, the part of personality concerned with basic physiological needs

implantation the attachment of the fertilized egg to the lining of the uterus

impression formation the process by which we construct ideas about what another person is like

imprinting a process by which a newborn animal forms a relatively permanent bond with the parent during a critical period in the young animal's life

incentive an environmental cue that elicits goal-directed behavior

incus a bone in the middle ear that transmits sound waves

independent variable a variable that the experimenter in a research project manipulates in order to determine its effects upon a dependent variable

individual differences a focus of study for psychologists who are interested primarily in the differences, such as in intelligence, that exist among people

industrial psychology the application, through selection procedures or training, of psychological principles to problems of work

inferential statistics statistics that allow one to generalize beyond one's sample to a larger population

inferiority-superiority concept perceived feelings of inferiority, whether from biological, psychological, or social weakness, produce the need to become superior

inhibitory stimuli in instinctual theories of aggression, behavior or postures assumed by an animal that inhibit aggression in other animals

inoculation effect with regard to attitude change, the idea that a mild attack on a person's beliefs will make him or her resistant to later, more intense attacks

insomnia a sleep disturbance characterized by difficulty in falling or remaining asleep

instrumental aggression aggressive behavior in which the primary goal is to obtain specific objectives rather than to harm the recipient

interactionist perspective a theory of language development that suggests that both biological and environmental factors contribute to language acquisition

interference theory the theory that forgetting occurs when other similar material we have learned interferes with the recall of the material we want to remember

intermittent schedule of reinforcement reinforcement is given on some occasions and not on others

internal attribution the belief that the causes of a person's behavior lie within the individual

interposition a cue to depth perception that involves the blocking of one figure by another

interpretation a statement made by a therapist that helps clients become aware of an aspect of their functioning they were previously unaware of

intimate distance the first spatial zone, from zero to 18 inches, in which lovemaking or direct physical aggression takes place

introversion in Jung's analytic theory of personality, the attitude toward inner directedness and self

iris the colored membrane in the eye that, to some extent, controls the amount of light entering the eye

James-Lange theory a theory of emotion that suggests that emotions result from physiological changes

junk-box theory a theory of forgetting that suggests that memory loss is due to retrieval failure

just noticeable differences (jnd) the smallest difference that can be perceived between two stimuli

kinesthesis the sensory system that informs us about the position and movement of our body parts

Klinefelter's syndrome a chromosomal disorder in males resulting in underdeveloped sex organs and sterility

laboratory research research in which psychologists bring subjects into their laboratories and observe their behavior under controlled conditions

laissez-faire leader one who leads through not leading at all by allowing the group to make all decisions

language-acquisition device according to Chomsky, a prewired system in the brain that predisposes the nervous system to receive and process language

latent learning learning that takes place in the absence of reinforcement

law of effect Thorndike's law that states that the future frequency of a response is related to its past consequences

learned helplessness a phenomenon in which animals or humans act as though they believe they can do nothing to change their situation

learning relatively permanent changes in behavior as a result of training or experience

learning theories theories that view prejudice as a learned attitude

learning-theory perspective assumption that children learn to imitate the speech responses of their parents through reinforcement

learning without awareness the learning of one set of behavior on a verbal level and another opposing set on a nonverbal level

lens the part of the eye located behind the pupil that controls the degree to which light is bent

lesion a technique for studying brain-behavior relationships

libido according to psychoanalytic theory, sexual energy, which motivates much of human behavior

limbic system a collection of structures in the forebrain concerned with the control of emotions

linear perspective the phenomenon in which parallel lines appear to converge as they recede into the distance

lithium carbonate a drug that controls unrealistic feelings of euphoria, hyperactivity, and impulsivity; used in the treatment of manic-depressive psychosis

long-term memory (LTM) the memory process that stores information permanently

lysergic acid diethylamide (LSD) a psychedelic drug that may produce psychotic-like symptoms

McNaughten rule a British court decision stating that an insanity defense can be made if it can be proved that the accused did not know what he or she was doing at the time of the crime

magnitude estimation a method used to scale physical energy as it relates to sensory experience

malleus a bone in the middle ear that transmits sound waves

manic-depressive psychosis an affective disorder characterized by alternating moods of euphoria and profound sadness or by one of these moods

marijuana a psychedelic drug that produces a state of euphoria and enhances sensory input

masochism a sexual variation in which sexual pleasure is derived from receiving pain in a sexual context

mean a measure of central tendency; the arithmetic average

median a measure of central tendency; the score above and below which half of all scores fall

meditation sustained, contemplative thinking

medulla a part of the hindbrain located above the spinal cord and involved in autonomic processes such as respiration, heart action, and gastrointestinal functions

menarche first menstruation

menopause the cessation of menstruation, which marks the end of a woman's reproductive ability

mental age in intelligence testing, a score obtained by a child that is equivalent to the average performance of children of that particular mental age

metaneeds in Maslow's theory of personality, the growth needs

metapathology in Maslow's theory of personality, psychological deficiencies stemming from unfulfilled growth needs

method of loci a memory device based on assigning each item to a physical location

mnemonics the use of mental devices to improve memory

mode a measure of central tendency; the score that occurs with the greatest frequency

modeling behavior mimicking the behavior of others

monophobia an irrational fear of being alone

moral anxiety in psychoanalytic theory, the fear of one's conscience

morality of constraint according to Piaget, the stage of moral development during which moral judgments are built on punishment; also called heteronomous morality

morality of cooperation according to Piaget, the stage of moral development during which moral judgments are based on underlying intentions and reciprocity; also called autonomous morality

Moro reflex the startle response of the newborn

morpheme the smallest meaningful unit of a language

motivation complicated motivational principles, such as instincts, drives, needs, or other internal states, that must be present if certain types of behavior are to be maintained

motive a condition that causes an individual to engage in goal-oriented activities

motor-reproduction process an observational-learning process concerning the conversion of symbolic representations into appropriate actions

multiple personality a condition in which a person alternates between two or more distinctive personalities

myelin sheath a fatty protein substance surrounding some axons

myopia nearsightedness that occurs when the lens cannot accommodate to distant objects

narcissistic personality a behavior pattern characterized by egotism and selfishness

narcolepsy a sleep disorder in which sudden and irresistible urges to sleep occur erratically

nativistic perspective a theory of language development that suggests that language acquisition is an innate ability

need for acceptance in Maslow's hierarchy, the need to be liked, loved, and to belong

need for achievement an acquired motive that makes one strive for success

neocortex part of the forebrain; composed of frontal, parietal, occipital, and temporal lobes

neologism meaningless words coined by a psychotic

neoplasm a brain tumor

nerve deafness a hearing impairment resulting from damage to the cochlea or the auditory nerve

neuron the basic cell of the nervous system

neurotic anxiety in psychoanalytic theory, the fear that the id impulses will gain control over the ego

neurotic triad in the MMPI, three scales, Hs, D, and Hy

neutral stimulus a stimulus that will not produce the unconditioned response when presented alone initially

nicotine a widely used psychoactive agent most commonly found in tobacco

nocturnal emission the ejaculation of semen during sleep

norepinephrine a transmitter hormone secreted by the adrenal medulla

normal distribution in statistics, where a majority of people are near the average or mean; also called "bell-shaped curve"

norms in psychological testing, scores that are derived from the scores obtained by a representative group of people. Normative scores give raw test scores meaning

norms standards or rules of conduct for group members that provide a basis for determining appropriate behavior in otherwise ambiguous situations

object permanence the knowledge that objects continue to exist even if they can no longer be seen

observational learning learning how to behave based on examples of the behavior of other people

obsession persistent, recurrent thoughts that a person cannot bar from consciousness

occipital lobe a part of the cerebral hemisphere in control of visual information

Oedipal complex in psychoanalytic theory, the unconscious sexual desires in children for the parent of the opposite sex

olfactory epithelium a membrane that contains the receptor cells for the sense of smell

omnibus definition a formal personality definition that includes everything about an individual

operant behavior the class of responses not elicited by specific stimuli

operant conditioning learning by the complex interplay of voluntary responses and their consequences

opponent-process theory a theory of color vision that suggests that activity in a photoreceptive cell is either increased or decreased depending on the wavelength of light that strikes it

optic chiasma the point at which optic fibers from the right and left eyes cross over before they reach the brain

organic psychoses disorders in which a biological or physical cause has been identified

organism in Rogers's theory of personality, the totality of all experiences

orgasm the third stage of sexual arousal, characterized by intense pleasurable release from sexual tension

orgasmic dysfunction an inability of a woman to have an orgasm during sexual intercourse

orientation phase the first of the four-phase process of group formation during which many group members feel uncomfortable because they are uncertain about what they are supposed to know or do

orthoses devices that support and sometimes motivate a paralyzed limb

overgeneralization extending the meaning of words beyond their actual definition

paradoxical cold a phenomenon that occurs when the skin's temperature receptors are activated

paranoid schizophrenia a subcategory of schizophrenic behavior characterized by suspiciousness and delusions of persecution

parasympathetic nervous system a division of the autonomic nervous system concerned with energy conservation

parietal lobe a part of the cerebral hemispheres that coordinates sensory input

Parkinson's disease a presenile organic brain disorder characterized by muscle rigidity and muscle tremors

parting phase the fourth and final phase of group formation during which the group members evaluate the extent to which their initial objectives have been met

peak experience a feeling of awe and pleasure elicited by everyday events and experienced by self-actualized individuals

Pearson product moment correlation coefficient symbolized as *r*, the most commonly used correlation coefficient

pedophilia a sexual variation in which one is sexually aroused by children and seeks sexual contact with them

pegword system a memory trick in which each word to be remembered is attached to a pegword in a rhyme

penis envy in the psychoanalytic phallic stage, a girl's feeling that she has lost something valuable, i.e., the penis, which causes her to turn to her father, who has the "prized" organ, to compensate for her "deficiency"

perception the processes by which we organize and interpret information received by our senses

perceptual constancies processes of perceptual organization that allow us to see the world as a stable and consistent place

period of the embryo the second stage of prenatal development lasting approximately six weeks, during which the major organ systems develop

period of the fetus the third stage of prenatal development lasting from approximately two months after conception to birth

period of the ovum the first stage of prenatal development during which the fertilized egg travels from the fallopian tube to the uterus

peripheral nervous system the second major division of the nervous system, serving both sensory and motor functions, which connects the central nervous system with the rest of the body

persona in Jung's analytic theory of personality, the mask a person wears when playing various roles

personal distance the second spatial zone, from 18 to 48 inches, a distance that comfortably separates two people

personal-growth therapies therapies that are intended to help people derive increased satisfaction from their lives

personality theories theories that look to variables within the individual to explain prejudice

personal space the "bubble" of space that we have around us and consider our own property

personal unconscious in Jung's analytic theory of personality, forgotten experiences, thoughts, and memories

phenomenal field a person's inner world of experiences

phobia an intense maladaptive fear of an object or situation

phoneme an elementary sound of a language roughly corresponding to the letters of the alphabet

phonology the sound system of a language

physiological needs in Maslow's hierarchy, motives, such as hunger or thirst, with a biological basis

physiological psychology the branch of psychology concerned with the biological bases of behavior

Pick's disease an organic brain disorder characterized by degeneration of frontal and temporal lobes

pinna the fleshy, protruding part of the outer ear

pituitary gland the master gland that regulates the activities of the other endocrine glands

placebo effect in medicine and psychotherapy, inert treatments that are effective as a result of the beliefs or expectations of those receiving the treatments

plateau phase the second stage of sexual arousal characterized by increases in heart rate, blood pressure, muscular tension, and glandular secretions

pleasure principle striving for the immediate gratification of primitive drives and operating on the assumption that whatever satisfies an impulse is good and whatever blocks or frustrates such satisfaction is bad

pons part of the hindbrain that forms a bridge from the medulla to the cerebellum

postconventional morality according to Kohlberg, the level of moral development in which morality is based on self-selected principles

postdecisional dissonance dissonance that occurs when a person has been forced to choose among several alternatives and is not sure the right one was selected

preconscious according to psychoanalytic theory, the level of awareness that contains easily accessible repressed thoughts and feelings

preconventional morality according to Kohlberg, the level of moral development that emphasizes external control

premature ejaculation a condition in which a man has an orgasm sooner than he or his partner would like

preoperational stage according to Piaget's theory of cognitive development, the second stage of intellectual growth during which symbolic thought develops

presenile dementia an organic brain disorder associated with aging

primacy effect with regard to attitude change, the tendency for the communication presented first to be more persuasive than later communications

primary prevention the attempt to reduce and eventually eliminate mental disorders in the population by taking measures to counteract harmful factors before they lead to psychological disturbances

primary reinforcer a stimulus that a deprived organism will approach, such as food for a hungry animal

prisoner's dilemma in conflict resolution, a game that combines incentives for both competition and cooperation

private acceptance when a person acts according to group norms and privately endorses the group's position

proactive interference interference produced by knowledge acquired before the information to be recalled

progesterone a hormone secreted by the ovaries that prepares the uterus for implantation of the fertilized egg and for the nourishment of the embryo during the early stages of prenatal development

progestin a drug once prescribed for pregnant women to alleviate discomforts of pregnancy

projection a defense mechanism in which a person ascribes unacceptable feelings or thoughts to others

prosthesis a substitution for a nonexisting limb or part of a limb

proxemics the study of people's use of space

proximity factor the principle that suggests that we tend to like those individuals who are geographically close to us

psychiatrist an M.D. who has completed specialized training in the treatment of psychological disorders

psychoactive drug a drug that influences the processing of sensory information and the function of the brain

psychoanalysis a theory of personality and method

of psychological treatment based on the idea that unconscious, repressed memories of childhood experiences are the basis of the motives, desires, and fantasies that influence adult behavior

psychological aging measured by the capacity of the older person to adapt to the demands of the environment and of other people

psychological dependence the desire to continue taking a drug when a person discovers that he or she derives pleasure, a greater sense of well-being, or a new state of awareness from it

psychological situation the concept that behavior does not take place independent of a context but is influenced by specific situations

psychophysical stage the stage, characterized by an awareness of self and an awareness of the social environment, in which most people spend their lives

psychophysics the study of the relationship between physical stimuli and subjective experience

psychosocial death the way we feel about our own impending death and about the death of those close to us

psychosurgery a controversial technique in which a small area of a patient's brain is destroyed in an attempt to eliminate types of behavior such as aggression and agitation

public distance the fourth and final spatial zone, from 12 to 25 feet, in which communication is formal and essentially one-way

pupil the dark circle that admits light in the center of the eye

pyrophobia an irrational fear of fire

rapid eye movements (REM) eye movements that are characteristic of human sleep during periods of dreaming

rational-emotive therapy (RET) a form of therapy that requires the active participation of the therapist in helping clients achieve a rational approach to life

rationalization a defense mechanism in which a person attempts to justify a behavior with inaccurate excuses

reaction formation a defense mechanism in which a person turns his or her feelings into their opposites

reality anxiety in psychoanalytic theory, the fear of real dangers in the external world

reality principle in psychoanalytic theory, the functioning principle of the ego

recall the first of the three principal ways to measure memory, in which the individual is able to reproduce material from memory

recency effect with regard to attitude change, the tendency for communication presented last to be more persuasive than earlier communications

receptive aphasia a speech disorder in which the person has difficulty understanding written or spoken communication

reciprocity-of-liking rule the principle that suggests that we tend to like those who like us

recognition the second of the three principal ways to measure memory, in which the individual perceives something as familiar because he or she remembers encountering it before

reference group a group that a person identifies with and that influences his or her attitudes

reference norm a collective product representing the contributions of each group member

reflex an innate, spontaneous response to certain environmental events

refractory period a period following a man's orgasm during which he is incapable of having an erection or orgasm

regression a defense mechanism in which a person retreats to an earlier stage of development

rehearsal a memory aid in which the material to be remembered is repeated over and over

reinforcement reward that evokes certain behavior

reinforcement value the value an individual attaches to different types of rewards, determined, in part, by past experiences

relearning the third of the three principal ways to measure memory, in which the individual learns material faster the second time than the first time, showing that he or she has some memory of the material

reliability in psychological testing, the consistency of test scores when an individual is given one test or equivalent forms of the test on two different occasions

repression a defense mechanism in which a person blocks unacceptable impulses or thoughts from entering consciousness

resolution phase the fourth stage of sexual arousal, during which the body returns to its normal preexcitement state

respondent behavior a reflex that is evoked by a stimulus

retentional processes processes that retain activities of the model in memory either through verbal coding or imagery

reticular activating system (RAS) a set of fibers that extends from the brainstem to the thalamus; important for maintaining wakefulness

retina the back of the eye upon which light is focused

retrieval the memory process that consists of an active search for information in short- or long-term memory

retroactive interference interference produced by knowledge acquired after the information to be recalled

retrograde amnesia failure to remember events occurring before an operation

reversibility the ability to reverse mental actions

risky shift a shift towards risky decisions observed in groups following group discussions

rods photoreceptive cells in the retina that are primarily responsible for vision in dim light

role as defined by Hare, the "set of expectations which group members share concerning the behavior of a person who occupies a given position in the group"

role-playing techniques in psychological assessment, a technique in which clients are asked to simulate their problem behavior in the therapist's consulting room

romantic ideal the belief that we will fall in love, get married, and live happily ever after

rooting reflex when a baby's cheek is touched, its head will turn toward the finger and the mouth will make sucking movements

sadism a sexual variation in which sexual pleasure is derived from inflicting pain on another person

safety needs in Maslow's hierarchy, the need to avoid physical and psychological abuse

sample in psychological testing, the sample of the examinee's behavior provided by the items on the test

schedule of reinforcement the prescribed period of time between rewards for desired behavior

schizophrenia a group of behavior disorders characterized by disturbed thought processes, blunted affect, and social withdrawal

school phobia an unrealistic fear of going to school

sclera the outer covering of the eye, which serves a protective function

secondary prevention aimed at the reduction of mental disorders through early detection

secondary reinforcer a stimulus that reinforces because it was initially associated with a primary reinforcer

self a person's self-concept and sense of identity

self-actualization the highest level in Maslow's hierarchy, pertaining to the need for personal development

self-monitoring a personality dimension that refers to the degree to which one looks to his or her beliefs and feelings in arriving at decisions about how to act in a given situation

semantics the study of the meaning of words and sentences

senile dementia an organic brain disorder associated with old age; also called senile psychosis

sensation the activity in the central nervous system and the sensory receptors that receive, process, and analyze physical energy

sense of equilibrium (vestibular sense) the sense that helps us maintain balance

sensory deprivation an experimental situation in which the subject receives severely restricted sensory input

sensory information store memory concerned with the reception of information through the senses

sensory-motor stage according to Piaget's theory of cognitive development, the first stage of intellectual growth, during which the rudiments of intelligence emerge

serial ordering arranging objects according to some dimension, such as height and weight

serotonin a transmitter substance in the brain

sex-negative attitudes the belief that sex is vulgar and dirty; also referred to as sex guilt

sex-role transcendence a wider range of acceptable behavior for men and women

sexual dysfunction an inability to engage in or derive pleasure from sexual activities

shadow in Jung's analytic theory of personality, the archetype that reflects the primitive side of personality

shift toward polarization the hypothesis that group discussion leads individuals to become either more risky or more cautious in their decisions

short-term memory the memory process that temporarily stores a limited amount of information

sigma the mathematical sign indicating that a group of scores are to be added together

signal-detection theory the study of the factors that influence a person to signal perception of a stimulus

simple compliance when a person acts in accordance with a group's norms without believing what he or she is doing

situational approach the view that the leader is one who best grasps the psychosocial climate of contemporary events

sleeper effect the tendency of people to remember a communication but forget the source, and hence to be more influenced by a low-credibility source as time passes

sleep spindles brain waves with a frequency of 14–16 cycles per second that are characteristic of stage 2 sleep

social aging measured by the social roles and habits maintained by the older person

social-comparison theory the theory that in the absence of a physical or objective standard of correctness, we will seek other people as a means of evaluating ourselves

social control the process by which a group exerts pressure on its members to conform

social distance the third spatial zone, from 4 to 12 feet, that is used in formal interactions, where personal involvement is substantially reduced

socially oriented leadership the leader concentrates on social and emotional group processes

social phase begins shortly after birth and is characterized by an awareness of others, mainly the parents

social psychology the branch of psychology that focuses on the behavior of individuals within the context of groups

sociocultural theories with regard to prejudice, the idea that prejudice is caused by social and cultural beliefs, such as the belief that one's group is superior to all others

sociogram a chart that indicates the positive and negative attitudes individuals have toward one another

sociometric choice a method of assessing cohesiveness in which group members are asked to name the person or persons with whom they would most prefer to interact in a variety of situations

somatic nervous system a division of the peripheral nervous system concerned with the regulation of the body's external environment

somatoform disorder a condition in which a person suffers bodily pains but has no physical problems

somnambulism sleepwalking

source credibility with regard to attitudes, the degree to which the source of a communication is perceived to be knowledgeable and trustworthy

spatial ability visual perception of figures arranged in space; believed to be sex-linked

spinal cord the part of the central nervous system contained within the spine

spiritual phase awareness goes beyond physical and material awareness of the self and others, encompassing both the social and the psychophysical phase

spontaneous recovery the spontaneous reappearance of the conditioned response when presented with the conditioned stimulus sometime after extinction first occurred

standard deviation the statistic that describes the amount of variability in a set of scores. It allows one to determine the degree to which a score deviates from the mean

standardization in psychological testing, the development of procedures to insure that all examinees take the test under identical conditions and of test norms, which make possible interpretation of relative test performance

stapes a bone in the middle ear that transmits sound waves

state-dependent learning a concept suggesting that something learned in state of awareness A can be forgotten in state B and be recalled again in state A

stereotaxic instrument an instrument designed to hold the head of a laboratory animal in a rigid position during brain surgery

stereotype according to Wrightsman, "a relatively rigid, oversimplified conception of a group of people in which all individuals in the group are labeled with the so-called group characteristic"

steroids hormones released by the adrenal cortex

stimulus discrimination in classical conditioning, when an organism responds differently to previous generalized stimuli

stimulus generalization in classical conditioning, when an organism that has been conditioned to respond to one stimulus responds to similar stimuli that have not been paired with the original unconditioned stimulus

storage the holding or retention of encoded information while it is not being used

stranger anxiety the fear of strangers in infants of about 7 months old

structural analysis the process of identifying and clarifying the ego state involved in a given situation

structuralism the school of psychology that attempts to break down complex conscious experiences into fundamental components

style of life a plan that directs the way goals will be pursued and individual inferiorities overcome

sublimation a defense mechanism in which a person channels unacceptable thoughts or feelings into productive endeavors

successive approximation a method of operant conditioning that trains an animal to come closer and closer to the desired response

sucking reflex an oral reflex necessary for survival

superego in psychoanalytic theory, the part of personality that reflects conscience and societal codes of morality

superordinate goals group goals that can only be attained through cooperation

superstitious behavior according to Skinner, some response totally irrelevant to the reinforcing event that is strengthened by being accidentally paired with the reinforcement

swimming reflex when infants are placed under water, they can swim for a short time, exhaling slowly, until there is no more air in their lungs

switchboard theory the theory that forgetting occurs when neurons turn off engrams, the interconnected electrochemical circuits thought to exist in the brain

sympathetic nervous system a division of the autonomic nervous system concerned with emergency reactions

synapses the gap between neurons that is filled with transmitter substances

syndrome a cluster of symptoms

syntax rules for putting words into grammatically intact sentences

systematic desensitization a behavior-therapy technique used to treat anxiety-related problems, such as phobias

task-oriented leadership the leader is concerned with efficiency and with guiding the group toward its goal

taste buds sense receptors, located primarily on the tongue, that are responsible for taste

telegraphic speech speech that consists largely of meaningful or content words

temperament a biologically based personality dimension that can be described in such terms as irritable, nervous, or sensitive

temporal contiguity in classical conditioning, the

closeness in time in pairing the neutral and unconditioned stimuli

temporal lobe a part of the cerebral hemisphere that contains major auditory reception areas

tertiary prevention aims at reducing or minimizing the negative after-effects of hospitalization

test bias a characteristic of a test in which it either overpredicts or underpredicts the performance of a particular group of people

testosterone the male sex hormone that induces and maintains male secondary sex characteristics

thalamus in the brain, a cluster of nuclei that relays impulses to and from the cortex and the rest of the central nervous system

thanatos according to psychoanalytic theory, the death instincts

thyroid a gland lying on the side of the thorax that secretes the hormone thyroxin and controls the rate of body metabolism

time-out a temporary withdrawal of all positive reinforcers used to decrease undesirable behavior

token economy contingent reinforcement whereby tokens are rewarded when the behavior is satisfactory and withheld when it is unsatisfactory

tolerance a physiological process whereby the body requires increasingly larger amounts of a drug to experience an effect

trait a personality characteristic that directs behavior; usually inferred from overt actions

trait approach to leadership a theory suggesting that leaders possess certain personality traits that predispose them for leadership positions

transactional analysis (TA) a personality theory introduced by Eric Berne in which the conceptualization of human relationships is straightforward, stressing basic human needs directly related to everyday observable behavior

transduction the process by which the sense receptors transform physical energy into neural energy

transference feelings of the client toward the therapist that do not realistically apply because they originate in important relationships in the client's past

translocation an error in chromosomal replication whereby one chromosome becomes attached to another

Trepomena pallidum the infectious agent for syphilis

trichromatic theory a theory of color vision that suggests that there are three types of cones, each associated with a primary color

t-test an inferential statistic that allows one to determine if the difference between the means of two groups of scores is meaningful and reliable

Turner's syndrome a chromosomal disorder in women resulting in short stature and sterility

two-factor theory of avoidance the theory that both classical and operant conditioning are involved in avoidance learning

ulterior motive in regard to attitude change, a self-interested motive on the part of a source of communication

unconditional positive regard a quality of a therapist that enables him or her to value a client as a human being

unconditioned response a response that occurs without prior training

unconditioned stimulus a stimulus that occurs without prior training

unconscious motivation according to psychoanalysis, thoughts, feelings, and urges that are repressed but continue to exert an influence over behavior

underextension defining words too narrowly

vaginismus an involuntary contraction of the vaginal muscles that prevents a woman from having sexual intercourse

validity in psychological testing, the degree to which a test measures what it is intended to measure

variable-interval schedule a schedule in which the time between reinforcement is varied and unpredictable

variable-ratio schedule reinforcement in which the ratio of responses to rewards can be determined in the long run through averaging, but is unpredictable in the short run

ventricles the protective system of canals in the brain and spinal cord containing cerebrospinal fluid

visual cliff an experimental apparatus used in the study of depth perception

voyeurism a sexual variation in which one derives sexual pleasure from watching nudes or sexual activities

waxy flexibility a symptom of catatonic schizophrenia that refers to the maintenance of bizarre postures for long periods of time

Weber's law a law stating that to hear a 50 decibel sound, it would require 5 more decibels, or 1/10 of that sound, before one noticed a difference in loudness

Whorf hypothesis the notion that linguistic differences cause cognitive, perceptual, or behavior differences

withdrawal symptoms symptoms that occur when a person who is physically dependent on drugs is deprived of them

word salad incoherent sentences characterizing the speech of psychotics

working through a stage near the end of therapy where the therapist attempts to help the client assimilate what he or she has learned from therapy

Zeitgeist the sociocultural climate of a given society at a given time

zoophobia an irrational fear of animals

z scores a type of standard score that is expressed in standard deviation units

References

Chapter 1

Goleman, D. 1,528 little geniuses and how they grew. *Psychology Today*, February 1980, 28 ff.

Graziano, A. M., & Mooney, K. C. Family self-control instruction for children's nighttime fear reduction. *Journal of Consulting and Clinical Psychology*, 1980, *48*, 206–213.

Hebb, D. O. What psychology is about. APA invited address presented at the annual meeting of American Psychological Association, Montreal, Canada, August 29, 1973.

Hebb, D. O. What psychology is about. *American Psychologist*, 1974, *29*, 71–79.

James, W. *The principles of psychology* (2 vols.). New York: Holt, 1890.

Johnson, R. C., Cole, R. E., Bowers, J. K., Foiles, S. V., Nikaido, A. M., Patrick, J. W., & Woliver, R. E. Hemispheric efficiency in middle and later adulthood. *Cortex*, 1979, *15*, 109–110.

Overmier, J. B., & Seligman, M. E. P. Effects in inescapable shock upon subsequent escape and performance learning. *Journal of Comparative and Physiological Psychology*, 1967, *63*, 23–33.

Rodin, J., & Langer, E. J. Long-term effects of a control relevant intervention with the institutionalized aged. *Journal of Personality and Social Psychology*, 1977, *35*, 897–902.

Seligman, M. E. P. *Helplessness: On depression, development, and death.* San Francisco: Freeman, 1975.

Seligman, M. E. P., & Maier, S. F. Failure to escape traumatic shock. *Journal of Experimental Psychology*, 1967, *74*, 1–9.

Watson, J. B. Psychology as the behaviorist views it. *Psychological Review*, 1913, *20*, 158–177.

Woods, P. J. (Ed.). *Career opportunities for psychologists: expanding and emerging areas.* Washington, D.C.: American Psychological Association, 1976.

Woods, P. J. (Ed.). *The psychology major. Training and employment strategies.* Washington, D.C.: American Psychological Association, 1979.

Chapter 2

Bardwick, J. *Her body, the battleground: In the female experience.* Del Mar, Calif.: CRM Publications, 1973.

Briggs, R., & King, T. Transplantation of living nuclei from blastula cells into enucleated frogs' eggs. *Proceedings of the National Academy of Sciences*, 1952, *38*, 455–463.

Bruce, L. *Fundamentals of physiological psychology.* New York: Holt, 1977.

Buck, C. Knowing the right from the left. *Human Behavior*, 1976, *5* (6), 29–35.

Dobzhansky, T. *Heredity and the nature of man.* New York: New American Library, 1964.

Ganong, W. *Review of medical physiology* (7th ed.). Los Altos, Calif.: Lange Medical Publications, 1975.

Gazzaniga, M. *The bisected brain.* New York: Appleton-Century-Crofts, 1970.

Grossman, S. *Essentials of physiological psychology.* New York: Wiley, 1973.

Gwynne, P., Clifton, T., Hager, M., Begley, S., & Gastel, B. All about that baby. *Newsweek*, August 7, 1978, 68–72.

Hamerton, J., Canning, N., Ray, M., & Smith, S. A cytogenetic survey of 14,069 newborn infants. *Clinical Genetics*, 1975, *8*, 223–243.

Jacobs, P., Brenton, M., Melville, M., Brittain, R., & McClemont, W. Aggressive behavior, mental subnormality and the XYY male. *Nature* (London), 1965, *208*, 1351–1353.

Karp, L. *Genetic engineering: Threat or promise?* Chicago: Nelson-Hall, 1977.

Levinthal, C. *The physiological approach in psychology.* Englewood Cliffs, N.J.: Prentice-Hall, 1979.

The madman in the tower. *Time,* August 12, 1966.

Marinari, K., Lesher, A., & Doyle, M. Menstrual cycle status and adrenocortical reactivity to psychological stress. *Psychoneuroendocrinology,* 1976, *1,* 213–218.

Mart, J. Embryology: Out of the womb—into the test tube. *Science,* 1973, *182,* 811–814.

Mertens, T. *Human genetics.* New York: Wiley, 1975.

Milner, B. Hemispheric specialization: Scope and limits. In F. Schmitz & F. Worden (Eds.), *The neurosciences: Third study program.* Cambridge, Mass.: M.I.T., 1974.

Milner, P. *Physiological psychology.* New York: Holt, 1970.

Money, J., & Ehrhardt, A. *Man and woman, boy and girl.* Baltimore: Johns Hopkins, 1972.

Nash, J. *Developmental psychology: A psychobiological approach.* Englewood Cliffs, N.J.: Prentice-Hall, 1970.

Nyhan, W. *The heredity factor.* New York: Grosset & Dunlap, 1971.

Owen, D. The 47, XYY male: A review. *Psychological Bulletin,* 1972, *78,* 209–233.

Paige, K. Effects of oral contraceptives on affective fluctuations associated with the menstrual cycle. *Psychosomatic Medicine,* 1971, *33,* 515–537.

Penfield, W. *The mysteries of the mind.* Princeton, N.J.: Princeton, 1975.

Rose, R., Holiday, J., & Bernstein, T. Plasma testosterone, dominance rank, and aggressive behavior in male rhesus monkeys. *Nature,* 1971, *231,* 366–368.

Rose, S. *Brain consciousness.* New York: Knopf, 1973.

Sage, W. The split brain lab. *Human Behavior,* 1976, *5* (6), 24–28.

Schmeck, H. New gene machines speeding up the pace of biological revolution. *New York Times,* March 24, 1981, 4.

Schwartz, M. *Physiological psychology* (2nd ed.). Englewood Cliffs, N.J.: Prentice-Hall, 1978.

Slater, E., & Shields, J. Genetical aspects of anxiety. In M. Lader (Ed.), *Studies of anxiety.* Ashford, England: Headley Brothers, 1969.

Snyder, S. Mind over matter. *Psychology Today,* 1980, *14* (1), 66–76.

Sperry, R., & Gazzaniga, M. Language following surgical disconnection of the hemispheres. In F. Darley (Ed.), *Brain mechanisms underlying speech and language.* New York: Grune & Stratton, 1967.

Steptoe, P., & Edwards, R. Birth after the re-implantation of a human embryo. *Lancet,* 1978, *8085,* 366.

Thomas, L. On cloning a human being. *New England Journal of Medicine,* 1972, *291,* 1296–1297.

Timiras, P. Estrogens as organizers of CNS function. In Influence of hormones on the nervous system. *Proceedings of the International Society of Psychoendocrinology.* Basel, Switz.: Karger, 1971.

Toran-Allerand, C. Sex steroids and the development of the newborn mouse hypothalamus and preoptic area in vitro: Implications for sexual differentiation. *Brain Research,* 1976, *106,* 407–412.

Unger, R. *Female and male.* New York: Harper & Row, 1979.

Valenstein, E. *Brain control.* New York: Wiley, 1973.

Watson, J. *The double helix.* New York: New American Library, 1968.

Watson, J. *Molecular biology of the gene.* New York: Benjamin, 1970.

Watson, J. Moving toward the clonal man: Is this what we want? *Atlantic,* May 1971, 50–53.

Weintraub, J. *The human nervous system.* New York: Appleton-Century-Crofts, 1980.

Weintraub, P. The brain: His and hers. *Discover,* April 1981, 15–20.

Windle, W. *The spinal cord and its reaction to traumatic injury.* New York: Marcel Dekker, 1980.

Chapter 3

Aarons, C. Sleep-assisted instruction. *Psychological Bulletin,* 1976, *83* (1), 1–40.

Alcoholism: New victims, new treatment. *Time,* April 22, 1974, 75–81.

Amarose, A., Schuster, C., & Muller, T. An animal model for the evaluation of drug-induced chromosome change. *Oncology,* 1973, *27,* 550–562.

Barber, T. *Hypnosis: A scientific approach.* New York: Van Nostrand, 1969.

Barber, T. *Advances in altered states of consciousness and human potentialities* (Vol. 1). New York: Psychological Dimensions, 1976.

Becker, H. Becoming a marijuana user. *American Journal of Sociology,* 1953, *59,* 236–242.

Bennett, T. *Brain and behavior.* Monterey, Calif.: Brooks/Cole, 1977.

Berecz, J. Treatment of smoking with cognitive conditioning therapy: A self-administered aversive technique. *Behavior Therapy,* 1976, *7,* 641–648.

Bernstein, D., & McAlister, A. The modification of

smoking behavior: Progress and problems. *Addictive Behaviors*, 1976, *1*, 89–102.

Brown, B. *New mind, new body.* New York: Harper, 1974.

Campbell, A. *Seven states of consciousness.* New York: Perennial Library, Harper & Row, 1974.

Carlin, A., Bakker, C., Malpern, L., & Post, R. Social facilitation of marijuana intoxication: Impact of social set and pharmacological activity. *Journal of Abnormal Psychology*, 1972, *80*, 132–140.

Chandhuri, H. *Philosophy of meditation.* New York: Philosophical Library, 1965.

Cohen, M., & Marmillo, M. Chromosomal damage in human leukocytes induced by lysergic acid diethylamide. *Science*, 1967, *155*, 1417–1419.

Crothers, T. Alcoholic trance. *Popular Science Monthly*, 1884, *26*, 189–191.

Davidson, J., & Davidson R. (Eds.). *The psychobiology of consciousness.* New York: Plenum, 1980.

Dement, W. C. *Some must watch while some must sleep.* San Francisco: Freeman, 1974.

Dement, W. C., & Kleitman, N. The relation of eye movements during sleep to dream activity: An objective for the study of dreaming. *Journal of Experimental Psychology*, 1951, *53*, 339–346.

Dishotsky, N., Coughman, W., Mogar, R., & Lipscomb, W. LSD and genetic damage. *Science*, 1971, *172*, 431–440.

Dorrance, D., Janiger, O., & Teplitz, R. Effect of peyote on human chromosomes. *Journal of the American Medical Association*, 1975, *234*, 299–302.

Ellinwood, E. Amphetamine psychosis: A multidimensional process. *Seminars in Psychiatry*, 1969, *6*, 208–226.

Eriksson, M., Catz, C., & Yaffee, S. Drugs in pregnancy. In H. Osofsky (Ed.), *Clinical obstetrics and gynecology: High risk pregnancy with emphases upon maternal and fetal well-being* (Vol. 16). New York: Harper & Row, 1973.

Fischman, M., Schuster, R., & Resnekov, L. Cardiovascular and subjective effects of intravenous cocaine administration in humans. *Archives of General Psychiatry*, 1976, *33*, 983–989.

Fisher, C., Kahn, E., Edwards, A., & Davis, D. A psychophysiological study of nightmares and night terrors: Physiological aspects of the stage-4 night terror. *Journal of Nervous and Mental Disease*, 1973, *57*, 75–98.

Foulkes, D. Do you think all night long? In R. Woods & H. Greenehouse (Eds.), *The new world of dreams.* New York: Macmillan, 1974.

Freud, S. The interpretation of dreams. In *The Standard Edition* (Vols. 4 & 5). London: Hogarth, 1953. (First German edition, 1900).

Garfield, P. *Creative dreaming.* New York: Ballantine, 1974.

Girando, D. D., & Girando, D. A. *Drugs: A factual account.* Reading, Mass.: Addison-Wesley, 1973.

Goleman, D. *The varieties of the meditative experience.* New York: Dutton, 1977.

Goodman, L., & Gilman, A. *The pharmaceutical basis of therapeutics* (5th ed.). New York: Macmillan, 1975.

Hall, C. S. *The meaning of dreams.* New York: McGraw-Hill, 1966.

Hartman, E. *The biology of dreaming.* Springfield, Ill.: Charles C. Thomas, 1967.

Heron, W. The pathology of boredom. *Scientific American*, 1957, *196*, 52–56.

Hilgard, E. Pain as a puzzle for psychology and physiology. *American Psychologist*, 1969, *24*, 103–113.

Hilgard, J. *Personality and hypnosis: A study of imaginative involvement.* Chicago: University of Chicago Press, 1970.

Hintzman, D. *The psychology of learning and memory.* San Francisco: Freeman, 1978.

Hunt, W., & Matarazzo, J. Three years later: Recent developments in the experimental modification of smoking behavior. *Journal of Abnormal Psychology*, 1973, *81* (2), 107–114.

James, W. *The principles of psychology.* New York: Dover, 1950. (originally published 1890)

Jones, E. *The life and work of Sigmund Freud.* New York: Basic Books, 1953.

Joyce, J. *Ulysses.* New York: Random House, 1934.

Josephson, B., & Ramachandran, V. *Consciousness and the physical world.* New York: Pergamon, 1980.

Kanfer, F. Self-monitoring: Methodological limitations and clinical applications. *Journal of Consulting and Clinical Psychology*, 1970, *35*, 148–152.

Lichtenstein, E., & Penner, M. Long-term effects of rapid smoking treatment. *Addictive Behaviors*, 1977, *2*, 117–124.

Loftus, E. Alcohol, marijuana and memory. *Psychology Today*, 1980, *14* (1), 42–56.

Ludwig, A. Altered states of consciousness. In C. Tart (Ed.), *Altered states of consciousness*, New York: Wiley, 1969.

McFall, R., & Hammen, C. Motivation, structure, and self-monitoring: Role of non-specific factors in smoking reduction. *Journal of Consulting and Clinical Psychology*, 1971, *37*, 80–86.

McKean, M. *The stop smoking book*. San Luis Obispo, Calif.: Impact, 1976.

Miller, N. *Biofeedback and self-control*. Chicago: Aldine, 1973.

Millon, T., & Millon, R. *Abnormal behavior and personality: A biosocial learning approach*. Philadelphia: Saunders, 1974.

Muses, C., & Young, A. (Eds.) *Consciousness and reality: The human pivot point*. New York: Dutton, 1974.

Ornstein, R. *The psychology of consciousness*. San Francisco: Freeman, 1972.

Ornstein, R. (Ed.) *The nature of human consciousness*. San Francisco: Freeman, 1973.

Ornstein, R. *The psychology of consciousness* (2nd ed.). New York: Harcourt Brace Jovanovich, 1977.

Overton, D. State-dependent learning produced by alcohol and its relevance to alcoholism. In B. Kissin & H. Begleiter (Eds.), *Physiology and behavior: The biology of alcoholism* (Vol. 2). New York: Plenum, 1972.

Pahnke, W. N., & Richards, W. A. Implications of LSD and experimental mysticism. In C. Tart (Ed.), *Altered states of consciousness*. Garden City, N.Y.: Doubleday, 1972.

Payne, B. *Getting there without drugs*. New York: Viking, 1973.

Pomerlau, O., & Pomerlau, C. *Break the smoking habit: A behavioral program for giving up cigarettes*. Champaign, Ill.: Research, 1977.

Ray, O. *Drugs, society, and human behavior*. St. Louis: Mosby, 1978.

Rice, J. *Ups and downs*. New York: Macmillan, 1972.

Rubin, F. *Learning and sleep*. Bristol, England: John Wright & Sons, 1971.

Sarbin, T., & Nucci, L. Self-reconstitution processes: A proposal for reorganizing the conduct of confirmed smokers. *Journal of Abnormal Psychology*, 1973, *81* (2), 182–195.

Schuman, M. The psychophysiological model of meditation and altered states of consciousness: A critical review. In J. Davidson & R. Davidson (Eds.), *The psychobiology of consciousness*. New York: Plenum, 1980.

Schwartz, M. *Physiological psychology*. Englewood Cliffs, N.J.: Prentice-Hall, 1978.

Select Committee Report to the FDA. *Tentative evaluation of the health aspects of caffeine as a food ingredient*. Bethesda, Md.: Life Sciences Research Office, Federation of American Societies for Experimental Biology, 1976.

Shick, J. F., & Smith, D. E. Analysis of the LSD flashback. *Journal of Psychedelic Drugs*, 1970, *3*, (1), 31–34.

Smith, D. E. Acute and chronic toxicity of marijuana. *Journal of Psychedelic Drugs*, 1968, 2 (1), 9–13.

Smith, G. M., & Beecher, H. K. Amphetamine sulfate and athletic performance. *Journal of the American Medical Association*, 1959, *170*, 542–557.

Synder, S. H. *Madness and the brain*. New York: McGraw-Hill, 1974.

Spiegelberg, F. *Spiritual practices of India*. New York: Citadel, 1962.

Tart, C. T. *On being stoned: A psychological study of marijuana intoxication*. Palo Alto, Calif.: Science and Behavior Books, 1971.

Tart, C. T. (Ed.) *Altered states of consciousness*. Garden City, N.Y.: Doubleday, 1972.

Teyler, T. *Altered states of awareness: Readings from Scientific American*. San Francisco: Freeman, 1972.

U.S. Department of Health, Education, and Welfare. *Smoking and health: A report of the Surgeon General*. Washington, D.C.: U.S. Public Health Service, Office on Smoking and Health, January 1979.

U.S. Public Health Service. *Smoking and health: Report of the Advisory Committee to the Surgeon General of the Public Health Service*. Washington, D.C.: Department of Health, Education, and Welfare, 1964.

Van de Castle, R. *The psychology of dreaming*. New York: General Learning Press, 1971.

Wallace, R., & Benson, H. The physiology of meditation. *Scientific American*, 1972, *226* (2), 84–90.

Webb, W. B. *Sleep: The gentle tyrant*. Englewood Cliffs, N.J.: Prentice-Hall, 1975.

Weil, A. The marriage of the sun and the moon. In N. Finberg, *Altered states of consciousness*. New York: Macmillan, 1977.

Williams, R., Karacan, T., & Hursch, C. *EEG of human sleep*. New York: Wiley, 1974.

Wolberg, L. R. *Hypnosis: Is it for you?* New York: Harcourt Brace Jovanovich, 1972.

World Health Organization. Seventh report by the Expert Committee on Addiction-producing drugs. Technical Report Series No. 116, 1957.

Wyatt, R., Fram, D., Buchbinder, R., & Snyder, F. Treatment of intractable narcolepsy with a monoamine oxidase inhibitor. *New England Journal of Medicine*, 1971, *285*, 987–991.

Zinberg, N. *Altered states of consciousness*. New York: Macmillan, 1977.

Chapter 4

Amoore, J. E., Johnson, J. W., Jr., & Rubin, M. The stereo chemical theory of odor. *Scientific American,* 1964, *210,* 42–49.

Bekesy, G. von. Duplexity theory of taste. *Science,* 1964, *145,* 834–835.

Blakemore, C., & Cooper, G. F. Development of the brain depends on visual environment. *Science,* 1970, *228,* 477–478.

Campos, J. J., Langer, A., & Krowitz, A. Cardian responses on the visual-cliff in prelocomotor human infants. *Science,* 1970, *170,* 196–197.

Cherry, E. C. Some experiments on the recognition of speech, with one and with two ears. *Journal of the Acoustical Society of America,* 1953, *25,* 975–979.

Coles, M. G., Gale, A., & Kline, P. Personality and habituation of the orienting reaction: Tonic and response measures of electrodermal energy. *Psychophysiology,* 1971, *8,* 54–63.

Coren, S., Porac, C., & Ward, L. M. *Sensation and perception* New York: Academic, 1979.

Eysenck, H. J. *The biological basis of personality.* Springfield, Ill.: Thomas, 1967.

Eysenck, H. J. *Eysenck on extraversion.* New York: Wiley, 1973.

Galanter, E. Contemporary psychophysics. In R. Brown, E. Galanter, E. Hess, & G. Mandler (Eds.), *New directions in psychology.* New York: Holt, 1962.

Glass, D. C., Cohen, S., & Singer, J. E. Urban din fogs the brain. *Psychology Today,* May 1973, 94–99.

Goldiamond, I. Statement on subliminal advertising. In R. Ulrich, T. Stachnik, & J. Mabry (Eds.), *Control of human behavior* (Vol. 1). Glenview, Ill.: Scott, Foresman, 1966.

Hall, E. T. Learning the Arabs' silent language. *Psychology Today,* August 1979, 44 ff.

Halsam, D. Individual differences in pain threshold and level of arousal. *British Journal of Psychology,* 1967, *58,* 139–142.

Hering, E. *Outlines of a theory of the light sense.* (L. M. Hurvich & D. Jameson, trans.) Cambridge, Mass.: Harvard, 1964. (originally published 1878)

Hess, E. H. Attitude and pupil size. *Scientific American,* 1965, *212,* 46–54.

Hubel, D. H. The visual cortex of the brain. *Scientific American,* 1963, *209,* 54–62.

Hubel, D. H., & Wiesel, T. N. Receptive fields, binocular interaction and functional architecture in the cat's visual cortex. *Journal of Physiology,* 1962, *160,* 106–154.

Kimura, K., & Beidler, L. M. Microelectrode study of taste receptors of rat and hamster. *Journal of Cellular and Comparative Physiology,* 1961, *58,* 131–140.

Kirtley, D. D. *The psychology of blindness.* Chicago: Nelson-Hall, 1975.

Kroaner, V. Man and outer space: An international symposium in Yerevan. *Space World,* January 1972, 48 ff.

McClelland, D. C., & Liberman, A. M. The effects of need for achievement on recognition of need-related words. *Journal of Personality,* 1949, *18,* 236–251.

Postman, L., Bruner, B., & McGinnies, E. Personal values as selective factors in perception. *Journal of Abnormal and Social Psychology,* 1948, *43,* 142–154.

Rock, I., & Victor, J. Vision and touch: An experimentally created conflict between the two senses. *Science,* 1964, *143,* 574–596.

Secret voices. *Time,* September 10, 1979, 71.

Siddle, D. A., Morish, R. B., White, K. D., & Mangen, G. L. Relation of visual sensitivity to extraversion. *Journal of Experimental Research in Personality,* 1969, *3,* 264–267.

Stelmack, R. M., Achorn, E., & Michand, A. Extraversion and individual differences in auditory evoked response. *Psychophysiology,* 1977, *14,* 368–374.

Stevens, S. S. The direct estimation of sensory magnitudes—loudness. *American Journal of Psychology,* 1956, *69,* 1–25.

Stevens, S. S. *Psychophysics and social scaling.* Morristown, N.J.: General Learning, 1972.

Tees, R. C. Effect of visual deprivation on development of depth perception in the rat. *Journal of Comparative and Physiological Psychology,* 1974, *86,* 300–308.

Treisman, A. M. Strategies and models of selective attention. *Psychological Review,* 1969, *76,* 282–299.

Turnbull, C. Some observations regarding the experiences and behavior of the Bambuti pygmies. *American Journal of Psychology,* 1961, *74,* 304–308.

Von Senden, M. *Raum-und Gestaltauffassung bei operierten vor und nach der Operation.* Leipzig: Barth, 1932. cited in P. G. Zimbardo, *Psychology and Life,* Glenview, Ill.: Scott, Foresman, 1979.

Von Senden, M. *Space and sight: The perception of space and shape in congenitally blind patients before and after operation.* London: Methven, 1960.

Walk, R. D. Can the duckling respond adequately to

depth? Paper presented at the 33rd meeting of the Eastern Psychological Association, Atlantic City, April 1962.

Walk, R. D. Class demonstration of visual depth perception with the albino rabbit. *Perceptual and Motor Skills*, 1964, *18*, 219–224.

Walk, R. D., & Gibson, E. J. A comparative and analytic study of visual depth perception. *Psychological Monographs*, 1961, *75*, 1–44.

Wright, R. H., & Burgess, R. E. Molecular coding of olfactory specificity. *Canadian Journal of Zoology*, 1975, *53*, 1247–1253.

Zotterman, Y. Thermal Sensations. *Handbook of Physiology, Section 1: Neurophysiology*, 1959, *1*, 431–458.

Chapter 5

Ayllon, T., & Azrin, N. H. The measurement and reinforcement of behavior of psychotics. *Journal of the Experimental Analysis of Behavior*, 1965, *8*, 357–383.

Azrin, N., & Holz, W. Punishment. In W. K. Honig (Ed.), *Operant behavior: Areas of research and application.* New York: Appleton-Century-Crofts, 1966.

Bandura, A. *Social learning theory*. Englewood Cliffs, N.J.: Prentice-Hall, 1977.

Bandura, A., & Jeffery, R. Role of symbolic coding and rehearsal processes in observational learning. *Journal of Personality and Social Psychology*, 1973, *26*, 122–130.

Baum, M. Extinction of an avoidance response in rats via response prevention (flooding): A test of residual fear. *Psychological Reports*, 1971, *28* (1), 203–208.

Bennett, P., & Maley, R. Modification of interactive behaviors in chronic mental patients. *Journal of Applied Behavior Analysis*, 1973, *6*, 609–620.

Bolles, R. C. Species-specific defense reactions and avoidance learning. *Psychological Review*, 1970, *77*, 32–48.

Bolles, R. C. The role of stimulus learning in defensive behavior. In S. Hulse, H. Fowler, & W. Honig (Eds.), *Cognitive processes in animal behavior*. Hillsdale, N.J.: Erlbaum, 1978.

Carpenter, F. *The Skinner primer*. New York: Free Press, 1974.

Chomsky, N. *Language and mind*. New York: Harcourt Brace Jovanovich, 1972.

DiCara, L. V. Learning in the autonomic nervous system. *Scientific American*, 1970, *222*, 30–39.

Fancher, R. *Pioneers of psychology*. New York: Norton, 1979.

Ferster, C. B., & Skinner, B. F. *Schedules of reinforcement*. New York: Appleton-Century-Crofts, 1957.

Foreyt, J. P., & Kennedy, W. A. Treatment of overweight by aversion therapy. *Behavior Research and Therapy*, 1971, *9*, 28–34.

Hulse, S., Egeth, H., & Deese, J. *The psychology of learning*. New York: McGraw-Hill, 1980.

Kazdin, A. Response cost: The removal of conditioned reinforcers for therapeutic change. *Behavior Therapy*, 1972, *3*, 533–546.

Kazdin, A. *The token economy*. New York: Plenum, 1977a.

Kazdin, A. *Behavior modification in applied settings*. Homewood, Ill.: Dorsey, 1977b.

Kazdin, A., & Bootzin, R. The token economy: An evaluative review. *Journal of Applied Behavior Analysis*, 1972, *5*, 343–372.

Kirchner, A., Pear, J., & Martin, B. Shock as punishment in a picture-naming task with retarded children. *Journal of Applied Behavior Analysis*, 1971, *4*, 227–233.

Libb, J., & Clements, C. Token reinforcement in an exercise program for hospitalized geriatric patients. *Perceptual and Motor Skill*, 1969, *28*, 957–958.

Lovell, B. *Adult learning*. London: Croom, Helm, 1980.

Miller, N. Learning of visceral and glandular responses. *Science*, 1969, *163*, 434–445.

Mowrer, O. H. On the dual nature of learning: A reinterpretation of conditioning and problem solving. *Harvard Educational Review*, 1947, *17*, 102–148.

Nye, R. *What is B. F. Skinner really saying?* Englewood Cliffs, N.J.: Prentice-Hall, 1979.

Patterson, G. An application of conditioning techniques to the control of a hyperactive child. In L. Ullman & L. Krasner (Eds.), *Case studies in behavior modification*. New York: Holt, 1965.

Pavlov, J. P. *Conditioned reflexes.* (G. V. Anrep, trans.) London: Oxford, 1927.

Rescorla, A. Pavlovian second-order conditioning: Some implications for instrumental behavior. In H. Davis & H. Hurwitz (Eds.), *Operant-Pavlovian interactions.* Hillsdale, N.J.: LEA, 1977.

Rescorla, R. Some implications of a cognitive perspective on Pavlovian conditioning. In S. Hulse, H. Fowler, & W. Honig (Eds.), *Cognitive processes in animal behavior.* Hillsdale, N.J.: Erlbaum, 1978.

Rescorla, R. Aspects of the reinforcers learned in second-order Pavlovian conditioning. *Journal of Experimental Psychology: Animal Behavior Processes*, 1979, *5*, 79–95.

Reynolds, G. *A primer of operant conditioning*. Glenview, Ill.: Scott, Foresman, 1968.

Sachs, D. Behavioral techniques in a residential nursing home facility. *Journal of Behavior Therapy and Experimental Psychiatry*, 1975, *6*, 123–127.

Seligman, M. On the generality of the laws of learning. *Psychological Review*, 1970, *77*, 406–418.

Skinner, B. F. Two types of conditioned reflex: A reply to Konovski and Miller. *Journal of General Psychology*, 1937, *16*, 272–279.

Skinner, B. F. Superstition in the pigeon. *Journal of Experimental Psychology*, 1948, *38*, 168–172.

Skinner, B. F. *Science and human behavior*. New York: Macmillan, 1953.

Skinner, B. F. *Walden Two*. Toronto: Collier-Macmillan Canada, 1970.

Skinner, B. F. *Cumulative record* (3rd. ed.). New York: Appleton-Century-Crofts, 1972.

Skinner, B. F. *The shaping of a behaviorist*. New York: Knopf, 1979.

Solomon, R., Kamin, L., & Wynne, L. Traumatic avoidance learning. *Journal of Abnormal Social Psychology*, 1953, *48*, 291–302.

Solomon, R., & Wynne, L. Traumatic avoidance learning: The principles of anxiety and partial irreversability. *Psychological Review*, 1954, *61*, 353–385.

Swenson, L. *Theories of learning: Traditional perspectives/contemporary developments*. Belmont, Calif.: Wadsworth, 1980.

Thorndike, E. Animal intelligence: An experimental study of the associative process in animals. *Psychological Monographs*, 1898, *2*, No. 8.

Tolman, E., & Honzik, C. Introduction and removal of reward and mate performance in rats. *University of California Publications in Psychology*, 1930, *4*, 257–275.

Upper, D. A "ticket" system for reducing ward rule violations on a token economy program. *Journal of Behavior Therapy and Experimental Psychiatry*, 1973, *4*, 137–140.

Watson, J., & Rayner, R. Conditioned emotional reactions. *Journal of Experimental Psychology*, 1920, *3*, 1–14.

Wingfield, A. *Human learning and memory*. New York: Harper & Row, 1979.

Chapter 6

Anand, B. K., & Brobeck, J. R. Hypothalamic control of food intake in rats and cats. *Yale Journal of Biological Medicine*, 1951, *24*, 123–140.

Arnold, M. B. *Emotion and personality* (Vol. 1). New York: Columbia, 1960.

Atkinson, J. W., & Feather, N. T. *A theory of achievement motivation*. Huntington, N.Y.: Krieger, 1966.

Atkinson, J. W., & Litwin, C. H. Achievement motive and test anxiety conceived as motive to approach success and motive to avoid failure. *Journal of Abnormal and Social Psychology*, 1960, *60*, 52–63.

Bateson, G., Jackson, D. D., Haley, J., & Weakland, J. Doublebind hypothesis of schizophrenia. *Behavioral Science*, 1956, *1*, 251–264.

Beach, F. A., & Ranson, T. W. Effects of environmental variation on ejaculatory frequency in male rats. *Journal of Comparative and Physiological Psychology*, 1967, *64*, 384–387.

Cannon, W. B. The James-Lange theory of emotion: A critical examination and an alternative theory. *American Journal of Psychology*, 1927, *39*, 106–124.

Cannon, W. B. Hunger and thirst. In C. Murchison (Ed.), *The foundations of experimental psychology*. Worcester, Mass.: Clark University Press, 1929.

Crockett, H. J. The achievement motive and differential occupational mobility in the U.S. *American Sociological Review*, 1962, *27*, 191–204.

Deci, E. L. Intrinsic motivation, extrinsic reinforcement, and inequity. *Journal of Personality and Social Psychology*, 1972, *22*, 113–120.

Delgado, J. M. R. *Physical control of the mind: Toward a psycho-civilized society*. New York: Harper & Row, 1971.

Duffy, E. *Activation and behavior*. New York: Wiley, 1962.

Frey, W. H. Not-so-idle tears. *Psychology Today*, January 1980, 91–92.

Haggard, E. A., & Isaacs, F. S. Micromomentary facial expressions as indicators of ego mechanisms in psychotherapy. In L. A. Gottschalk & A. H. Averback (Eds.), *Methods of research in psychotherapy*. New York: Appleton-Century-Crofts, 1966.

Hess, W., & Akert, K. Experimental data on the role of hypothalamus in the mechanism of emotional behavior. *Archives of Neurological Psychiatry*, 1955, *73*, 127–129.

Horner, M. The motive to avoid success and changing aspirations of college women. In J. M. Bardwick (Ed.), *Readings on the psychology of women.* New York: Harper & Row, 1972.

Izard, C. E. *Patterns of emotions.* New York: Academic, 1972.

Izard, C. E. *Human emotions.* New York: Plenum, 1977.

James, W. What is emotion? *Mind,* 1884, *4,* 188–204.

Lange, K. *The emotions.* (Istar A. Haupt, trans., K. Dunlap, Ed.) Baltimore: Williams and Wilkins, 1922. (originally published in Denmark, 1885)

Lazarus, R. S. Emotions and adaptation: Conceptual and empirical relations. In W. Arnold (Ed.), *Nebraska symposium on motivation,* Lincoln: University of Nebraska Press, 1968.

Lewin, K. A dynamic theory of personality. (K. E. Zever & D. K. Adams, trans.) New York: McGraw-Hill, 1972.

Lindsley, D. B. Psychophysiology and motivation. In M. R. Jones (Ed.), *Nebraska Symposium on Motivation.* Lincoln: University of Nebraska Press, 1957.

Lowell, E. L. The effect of need for achievement on learning and speed of performance. *Journal of Psychology,* 1–52, *33,* 31–40.

Maher, B. A. *Principles of psychopathology.* New York: McGraw-Hill, 1966.

Marshall, G., & Zimbardo, P. G. The affective consequences of inadequately explained physiological arousal. *Journal of Personality and Social Psychology,* 1979, *37,* 970–988.

Maslach, C. Negative emotional biasing of unexplained arousal. *Journal of Personality and Social Psychology,* 1979, *37,* 953–969.

Maslow, A. H. Self-actualizing and beyond. In A. H. Maslow (Ed.), *The farther reaches of human nature.* New York: Viking, 1972.

McClelland, D. C. *The achieving society.* Princeton, N.J.: Van Nostrand, 1961.

McClelland, D. C., Atkinson, J. W., Clark, R. A., & Lowell, E. L. *The achievement motive.* New York: Appleton-Century-Crofts, 1953.

Miller, N. E. Liberalization of basic S-R concepts: Extensions to conflict behavior, motivation and social learning. In S. Koch (Ed.), *Psychology: A study of a science* (Vol. 2). New York: McGraw-Hill, 1959.

Mower, O. H. *The crisis in psychiatry and religion.* Princeton, N.J.: Van Nostrand, 1961.

Mussen, P. H., Conger, J. J., & Kagen, J. *Child development and personality.* New York: Harper & Row, 1974.

Nisbett, R. Hunger, obesity and the ventromedical hypothalamus. *Psychological Review,* 1972, *79,* 433–453.

Olds, J. Commentary on positive reinforcement produced by electrical stimulation of septal areas and other regions of rat brain. In E. S. Valenstein (Ed.), *Brain stimulation and motivation: Research and commentary.* Glenview, Ill. Scott, Foresman, 1973.

Sarason, I. Test anxiety, general anxiety, and intellectual performance. *Journal of Consulting Psychology,* 1957, *21,* 485.

Schachter, S. The assumption of identity and peripheralist and centralist controversies in motivation and emotion. In M. B. Arnold (Ed.), *Feelings and emotions.* New York: Academic, 1970.

Schachter, S. Nicotine regulation in heavy and light smokers. *Journal of Experimental Psychology: General,* 1977, *106,* 5–12.

Schachter, S., & Rodin, J. *Obese humans and rats.* Washington, D.C.: Erlbaum/Halsted, 1974.

Schachter, S., & Singer, J. E. Cognitive, social and physiological determinants of emotional states. *Psychological Review,* 1962, *69,* 379–399.

Schemmel, R., Michelsen, O., & Gill, J. L. Dietary obesity in rats: Influence of diet, weight, fat accretion in seven strains of rats. *Journal of Nutrition,* 1970, *100,* 1041–1048.

Schwartz, G. E., Fair, P. L., Greenberg, P. S., Freedman, M., & Keliman, J. L. Facial electromyography in the assessment of emotion. *Psychosomatic Medicine,* 1974, *11,* 237.

Solarz, A. K. Effects of hydration on the running and drinking performance of thirsty rats. *Journal of Comparative and Physiological Psychology,* 1958, *51,* 146–151.

Stein, A. H., & Bailey, M. M. The socialization of achievement orientation in females. *Psychological Bulletin,* 1973, *80,* 345–366.

Suinn, R. M. Anxiety and intellectual performance: A partial failure to replicate. *Journal of Consulting Psychology,* 1965, *29,* 81.

Teevan, R. C., & McGhee, P. E. Childhood development of fear and failure motivation. *Journal of Personality and Social Psychology,* 1972, *21,* 345–348.

Teitelbaum, P. *Physiological psychology: Fundamental principles.* Englewood Cliffs, N.J.: Prentice-Hall, 1967.

Tomkins, S. S. *Affect imagery, consciousness* (Vol. 1 & 2) New York: Springer, 1962.

Tschukitscheff, I. P. Uber den Mechanismus der Hungerbewegungen des Magens. I Einflues des "satten" und "Hunger"—Blutes auf die periodische Tatigkeit des Magens. *Archiv Fur die Gesamte Psychologie,* 1930, *223,* 251–264.

Valins, S. Cognitive effects of false heart-rate feedback. *Journal of Personality and Social Psychology,* 1966, *4,* 400–408.

Wurterbottom, M. R. The relation of need for achievement to learning experience in independence and mastery. In J. W. Atkinson (Ed.), *Motives in fantasy, action, and society.* Princeton, N.J.: Van Nostrand, 1958.

Young, P. T. *Motivation and emotion: A survey of the determinants of human and animal activity.* New York: Wiley, 1961.

Chapter 7

Atkinson, R., & Shiffrin, R. The control of short-term memory. *Scientific American,* 1971, *225,* 82–91.

Beatty, J. *Introduction to physiological psychology.* Monterey, Calif.: Brooks/Cole, 1975.

Bijou, S. *Child development: The basic stage of early childhood.* Englewood Cliffs, N.J.: Prentice-Hall, 1976.

Bloom, L., Rocissano, M., & Hood. L. Adult-child discourse: Developmental interaction between information processing and linguistic knowledge. *Cognitive Psychology,* 1976, *8,* 521–528.

Bower, G. Analysis of a mnemonic device. *American Scientist,* 1970, *58,* 496–510.

Brown, R. *A first language: The early stages.* Cambridge, Mass.: Harvard, 1973.

Brown, R., & Hanlon, C. Derivational complexity and order of acquisition in child speech. In J. R. Hayes (Ed.), *Cognition and the development of language.* New York: Wiley, 1970.

Bruner, J. S. From communication to language: A psychological perspective. *Cognition,* 1975, *3,* 255–287.

Bruner, J. S., & Kenney, H. On multiple ordering. In J. Bruner, R. Oliver, & P. Greenfield (Eds.), *Studies in cognitive growth.* New York: Wiley, 1966.

Bruner, J., Oliver, R., & Greenfield, P. *Studies in cognitive growth.* New York: Wiley, 1966.

Chomsky, N. *Language and mind.* New York: Harcourt Brace Jovanovich, 1968.

Christen, F., & Bjork, R. On updating the loci in the Method of Loci. Paper presented at the Psychonomic Society, St. Louis, Mo., November 1976.

Dale, P. *Language development: Structure and function.* Hinsdale, Ill.: Dryden Press, 1972.

Dellas, M., & Gaier, E. Identification of creativity: The individual. *Psychological Bulletin,* 1970, *73,* 55–73.

Dillard, J. L. *Black English.* New York: Random House, 1972.

Frances, S. Sex differences in nonverbal behavior. *Sex Roles,* 1979, *5* (4), 519–535.

Friedman, H., DiMatteo, M., & Mertz, T. Nonverbal communication on television news: The facial expressions of broadcasters during coverage of a presidential election campaign. *Personality and Social Psychology Bulletin,* 1980, *6* (3), 477–485.

Fuerst, B. *Stop forgetting.* New York: Doubleday, 1972.

Gagné, R. *The conditions of learning.* New York: Holt, 1977.

Gardner, B., & Gardner, A. Comparing the early utterances of child and chimpanzee. In A. Pick (Ed.), *Minnesota Symposia on Child Psychology* (Vol. 8). Minneapolis: The University of Minnesota Press, 1974.

Gardner, H. *The shattered mind.* New York: Knopf, 1975.

Gardner, R., & Gardner, B. Teaching sign language to a chimpanzee. *Science,* 1969, *165,* 664–672.

Geschwind, N. Language and the brain. *Scientific American,* 1972, *220,* 76–83.

Greenfield, P. M., & Smith, J. *The structure of communication in early language development.* New York: Academic, 1976.

Greeno, J. G. The structure of memory and the process of solving problems. In R. L. Solso (Ed.), *Contemporary issues in cognitive psychology: The Loyola Symposium.* Washington, D.C.: Winston, 1973.

Greeno, J. G. Hobbits and orcs: Acquisition of a sequential concept. *Cognitive Psychology,* 1974, *6,* 270–292.

Groninger, L. D. Imagery and subjective categorization effects on long-term retention and retrieval. *Bulletin of the Psychonomic Society,* 1974, *3,* 261–263.

Halliday, M. A. *Learning how to mean: Exploration in the development of language.* London: Arnold, 1975.

Henley, N. Power, sex, and nonverbal communication. In B. Thorne and N. Henley (Eds.), *Language and sex: Difference and dominance.* Rowley, Mass.: Newbury House, 1975.

Henley, N., & Freeman, J. Sexual politics in interpersonal behavior. In J. Freeman (Ed.), *Women: A feminist perspective.* Palo Alto, Calif.: Mayfield, 1975.

Hewes, G. Language origin theories. In D. Rumbaugh (Ed.), *Language learning by a chimpanzee: The Lana Project.* New York: Academic, 1977.

Higbec, K. L. *Your memory.* Englewood Cliffs, N.J.: Prentice-Hall, 1977.

Jackson, K. F. *The art of solving problems.* New York: St. Martin's, 1975.

Jakobson, R. *Child language, aphasia and phonological universals.* The Hague: Mouton, 1968.

Kaplan, E., & Kaplan, G. The prelinguistic child. In J. Elliot (Ed.), *Human development and cognitive processes.* New York: Holt, 1971.

Klausmeier, H. *Cognitive learning and development: Information processing and Piagetian perspectives.* Cambridge, Mass.: Ballinger, 1979.

Knapp, M. *Nonverbal communication in human interaction.* New York: Holt, 1972.

Labov, W. The logic of nonstandard English. In F. Williams (Ed.), *Language and poverty.* Chicago: Markham, 1970.

Lashley, K. In search of the engram. Society for Experimental Biology, 1950, *Symposium No. 4,* 454–482.

Lefrancois, G. *Of children.* Belmont, Calif.: Wadsworth, 1980.

Lenneberg, E. *Biological foundations of language.* New York: Wiley, 1967.

Maccoby, E. E., & Jacklin, C. N. *The psychology of sex differences.* Palo Alto, Calif.: Stanford University Press, 1924.

Mehrabian, A. *Nonverbal communication.* Chicago: Aldine-Atherton, 1972.

Miller, E. *Clinical neuropsychology.* Baltimore: Penguin, 1972.

Miller, G. A. The magic number seven, plus or minus two: Some limits on our capacity to process information. *Psychological Review,* 1956, *63,* 81–97.

Miller, G. A., Galanter, E., & Pribram K. *Plans and the structure of behavior.* New York: Holt, 1960.

Montague, W. Elaborate strategies in verbal learning and memory. In G. Bower (Ed.), *The psychology of learning and motivation* (Vol. 6). New York: Academic, 1972.

Moskowitz, B. A. The acquisition of language. *Scientific American,* 1978, *239* (5), 92–108.

Moss, H. A. Sex, age, and state as determinants of mother-infant interaction. *Merrill-Palmer Quarterly,* 1967, *13,* 19–36.

Nelson, K. Structure and strategy in learning to talk. *Monographs of the Society for Research in Child Development,* 1973, *38,* (1–2, Whole No. 149).

Oller, D., & Warren, J. On the phonological capacity. *Lingua,* 1976, *39,* 183–199.

Parnes, S., & Harding, H. *A sourcebook for creative thinking.* New York: Scribner, 1962.

Philips, J. *The origin of intellect: Piaget's theory.* San Francisco: Freeman, 1969.

Piaget, J. *The construction of reality in the child.* New York: Basic Books, 1954.

Piaget, J. *The child's conception of the world.* London: Routledge, 1960.

Premack, A. J., & Premack, D. Teaching language to an ape. *Scientific American,* 1972, *227,* 92–99.

Premack, D. Language in chimpanzees? *Science,* 1971, *172,* 808–822.

Pribram, K. *Languages of the brain.* Englewood Cliffs, N.J.: Prentice-Hall, 1971.

Puff, R. *Memory organization and structure.* New York: Academic, 1979.

Rotman, B. *Jean Piaget: Psychologist of the real.* Ithaca, N.Y.: Cornell University Press, 1977.

Rumbaugh, D. M., Gill, T. V., von Glasersfeld, E., Warner, H., & Pisani, P. Conversations with a chimpanzee in a computer-controlled environment. *Biological Psychiatry,* 1975, *10,* 627–641.

Scheerer, M. Problem solving. *Scientific American,* 1963, *108,* 118–128.

Shallice, T., & Warrington, E. Independent functioning of verbal memory stores: A neurophysiological study. *Quarterly Journal of Experimental Psychology,* 1970, *22,* 261–273.

Skinner, B. F. *Verbal behavior.* New York: Appleton-Century-Crofts, 1957.

Slobin, D. T. Children and language: They learn the same way all around the globe. *Psychology Today,* July 1972, 71–82.

Tagatz, G. *Child development and individually guided education.* Reading, Mass.: Addison-Wesley, 1976.

Thomas, J. An analysis of behavior in the hobbits-orcs problem. *Cognitive Psychology,* 1974, *6,* 257–269.

Torrance, E. P. Education and creativity. In C. W. Taylor (Ed.), *Creativity: Progress and potential.* New York: McGraw-Hill, 1964.

Vinacke, W. E. *The psychology of thinking.* New York: McGraw-Hill, 1974.

Vygotsky, L. *Thought and language.* Cambridge, Mass.: M.I.T., 1962.

Whorf, B. *Language, thought and reality.* New York: Wiley, 1956.

Willis, F., & Hamin, H. The use of interpersonal touch in securing compliance. *Journal of Nonverbal Behavior,* 1980, *5* (1), 49–55.

Wilson, E. Animal communication. *Scientific American,* 1972, *227* (3), 52–60.

Chapter 8

Ambron, S., & Brodzinsky, D. *Life span human development.* New York: Holt, 1979.

Anderson, A. "Old" is not a four-letter word. In C. Borg (Ed.), *Readings in human development, 79/80.* Sluice Dock, Guilford, Conn.: Dushkin Publishing Group, 1979.

Bayless, R. *Voices from beyond.* Secaucus, N.J.: University Books, 1976.

Bloom, M. *Life span development.* New York: Macmillan, 1980.

Blum, B. (Ed.) *Psychological aspects of pregnancy, birthing, and bonding.* New York: Human Sciences Press, 1980.

Bower, T. *Human development.* San Francisco: Freeman, 1979.

Bowlby, J. Separation anxiety. *International Journal of Psychoanalysis,* 1960, *41,* 89–113.

Butler, R. *Why survive? Being old in America.* New York: Harper & Row, 1975.

Center of Disease Control. *Abortion surveillance: Annual summary.* Atlanta: 1977.

Chiriboga, D., & Thurnher, M. Concept of self. In M. Lowenthal, M. Thurnher, & D. Chiriboga (Eds.), *Four stages of life.* San Francisco: Jossey-Bass, 1975.

Clayton, R. *The family, marriage, and social change.* Lexington, Mass.: Heath, 1975.

Craig, G. *Human development.* Englewood Cliffs, N.J.: Prentice-Hall, 1976.

Cumming, E., & Henry, W. *Growing old.* New York: Basic Books, 1961.

Darnley, F. Adjustment to retirement: Integrity or despair? *The Family Coordinator,* 1975, *24* (2), 217–226.

Dennis, W. *Children of the creche.* New York: Appleton-Century-Crofts, 1973.

Douglas, J., & Ross, J. Age of puberty related to educational ability, attainment and school leaving age. *Journal of Child Psychology and Psychiatry,* 1964, *5,* 185–196.

Elkind, D. *A sympathetic understanding of the child six to sixteen.* Boston: Allyn & Bacon, 1971.

Erikson, E. *Childhood and society.* New York: Norton, 1963.

Fantz, R. The origin of form-perception. *Scientific American,* 1961, *204,* 66–72.

Faust, M. Developmental maturity as a determinant in prestige of adolescent girls. *Child Development,* 1960, *31,* 173–184.

Feifel, H. *New meanings of death.* New York: McGraw-Hill, 1977.

Fiore, C., & Landsburg, A. *Death encounters.* New York: Bantam, 1979.

Flaste, R. Career ambitions: Keeping the options open. *New York Times,* February 27, 1976, 15.

Gibson, E., & Walk, R. The "visual cliff." *Scientific American,* 1960, *202,* 64–71.

Goren, C., Sarty, M., & Wer, P. Visual following and pattern discrimination of face-like stimuli by newborn infants. *Pediatrician,* 1975, *56,* 544–549.

Greenberg, M., & Morris, N. Engrossment: The newborn's impact upon the father. *American Journal of Orthopsychiatry,* 1974, *44* (4), 520–531.

Harlow, H., & Harlow, M. The effect of rearing conditions on behavior. *Bulletin of the Menninger Clinic,* 1962, *26,* 213–224.

Helms, D., & Turner, J. *Exploring child behavior.* Philadelphia: Saunders, 1976.

Hoffman, M. L. Moral development. In P. Mussen (Ed.), *Carmichael's manual of child psychology.* New York: Wiley, 1970.

Holcomb, W. Spiritual cases among the aging. In M. Spencer & C. Dow (Eds.), *Understanding aging: A multidisciplinary approach.* New York: Appleton-Century-Crofts, 1975.

Hutt, J. Auditory discrimination at birth. In S. Hutt & C. Hutt (Eds.), *Early human development.* Oxford: Oxford University Press, 1973.

Janda, L., & Klenke-Hamel, K. *Human sexuality.* New York: Van Nostrand, 1980.

Jones, M. The later careers of boys who are early or late maturing. *Child Development,* 1957, *28,* 113–128.

Jones, M. Psychological correlates of somatic development. *Child Development,* 1965, *36,* 899–911.

Kagan, J., Kearsley, R., & Zelazo, S. *Infancy: Its place in human development.* Cambridge, Mass.: Harvard University Press, 1978.

Kearsley, R. The newborn's response to auditory stimulation: A demonstration of orienting and defensive behavior. *Child Development,* 1973, *44,* 582–591.

Keleman, S. *Living your dying.* New York: Random House, 1975.

Klaus, M., & Kennell, J. *Maternal-infant bonding.* St. Louis: Mosby, 1976.

Kohlberg, L. The development of moral character and moral ideology. In M. Hoffman & L. Hoffman (Eds.),

Review of child development research (Vol. 1). New York: Russell Sage, 1964.

Kohlberg, L. The child as a moral philosopher. *Psychology Today*, 1968, *2* (4), 25–30.

Kubler-Ross, E. *On death and dying*. New York: Macmillan, 1969.

Leboyer, F. *Birth, without violence*. New York: Knopf, 1975.

LeFrancois, G. *Of children: An introduction to child development*. Belmont, Calif.: Wadsworth, 1980.

Lorenz, K. Z. *King Solomon's ring*. New York: Crowell, 1952.

Marks, A. Understanding adolescent pregnancy. In B. Blum (Ed.), *Psychological aspect of pregnancy, birthing, and bonding*. New York: Human Sciences Press, 1980.

McKenzie, S. *Aging and old age*. Glenview, Ill.: Scott, Foresman, 1980.

Meek, G. *After we die, what then?* Franklin, N.C.: Metascience, 1980.

Monthly Vital Statistics Report: Advance Report. Final notability statistics 1976 (DHEW Pub. No. [PHS] 78–1120. Vol. 26, No. 12, Suppl). Washington, D.C.: U.S. Government Printing Office, 1978.

Moody, R. *Life after death*. New York: Bantam/Mockingbird, 1975.

Moody, R. *Reflections on life after death*. Harrisburg, Pa.: Bantam/Mockingbird, 1977.

Neugarten, B. Adaptation and the life cycle. *Journal of Geriatric Psychiatry*, 1970, *4*, 71–87.

Neugarten, B. Personality and aging. In J. Birren & K. Schaie (Eds.), *Handbook of the psychology of aging*. New York: Van Nostrand Reinhold, 1977.

Nilsson, L. *A child is born*. New York: Delacorte, 1977.

Peck, R. Psychological development in the second half of life. In B. Neugarten (Ed.), *Middle age and aging*. Chicago: University of Chicago Press, 1968.

Piaget, J. *Language and thought of the child*. New York: Harcourt Brace Jovanovich, 1926.

Piaget, J. *The moral development of the child*. New York: Harcourt Brace Jovanovich, 1932.

Pines, M. Invisible playmates. *Psychology Today*, 1978, *12* (4), 38–42, 106.

Rest, J. The hierarchical nature of moral development: The study of patterns of comprehension and preference with moral stages. *Journal of Personality*, 1974, *41* (1), 92–93.

Rogers, D. *The adult years*. Englewood Cliffs, N.J.: Prentice-Hall, 1979.

Rogers, K. The mid-career crisis. *Saturday Review*, January 20, 1973, 37–38.

Schreiber, H. Die Krise in der Mitte des Lebens. Muenchen, West Germany: Bertelsmann Verlag Gmbh, 1977.

Shah, F., Zelnik, M., & Kanter, J. Unprotected intercourse among unwed teenagers. *Family Planning Perspectives*, 1975, *7* (1), 39–44.

Sheehy, G. Catch-30 and other predictable crises of growing up adult. *New York* magazine, February 18, 1974, 30–46.

Sheehy, G. *Passages: The predictable crises of adult life*. New York: Dutton, 1976.

Shertzer, B., & Stone, S. *Fundamentals of guidance* (3rd Ed.). Boston: Houghton Mifflin, 1976.

Siegel, R. The psychology of life after death. *American Psychologist*, 1980, *35* (10), 911–931.

Siegel, R. Accounting for "after life" experiences. *Psychology Today*, 1981, *15* (1), 64–75.

Smith, B. *Aging in America*. Boston: Beacon Press, 1973.

Sorenson, R. C. *Adolescent sexuality in contemporary America*. New York: World, 1973.

Stern, D., & Wasserman, G. Maternal language behavior to infants. Symposium presented at the Society for Research in Child Development, San Francisco, 1979.

Tanner, J. Growing up. *Scientific American*, 1973, *229* (3), 34–43.

Turner, J., & Helms, D. *Life span development*. Philadelphia: Saunders, 1979.

Veevers, J. Voluntary childlessness and social policy: An alternative view. *The Family Coordinator*, 1974, *23*, 397–406.

Wheeler, D. *Journal to the other side*. New York: Ace, 1976.

Zelnik, M., & Kanter, J. Survey of female adolescent sexual behavior. Conducted for Commission of Population, Washington, D.C., 1972.

Chapter 9

Alper, T. Achievement motivation in college women: A now-you-see-it-now-you-don't phenomenon. *American Psychologist*, 1974, *29*, 194–203.

Basow, S. *Sex-role stereotypes: Traditions and alternatives*. Monterey, Calif.: Brooks/Cole, 1980.

Bear, S., Berger, M., & Wright, L. Even cowboys sing the blues: Difficulties experienced by men trying to adopt nontraditional sex roles and how clinicians can be helpful. *Sex Roles*, 1979, *5* (2), 191–198.

Bem, S. The measurement of psychological androgyny. *Journal of Consulting and Clinical Psychology*, 1974, *42* (2), 155–162.

Bem, S. Sex role adaptability: One consequence of psychological androgyny. *Journal of Personality and Social Psychology*, 1975, *31* (4), 634–643.

Bem, S. On the utility of alternate procedures for assessing psychological androgyny. *Journal of Consulting and Clinical Psychology*, 1977, *45*, 196–205.

Bianchi, E., & Reuther, R. *From machismo to mutuality: Essays on sexism and woman-man liberation.* Ramsey, N.J.: Paulist Press, 1976.

Biller, H. The father and personality development: Paternal deprivation and sex-role development. In M. Lamb (Ed.), *The role of the father in child development.* New York: Wiley, 1976.

Block, J. *Another look at sex differentiation in the socialization behaviors of mothers and fathers.* New York: Psychological Dimension, 1978.

Broverman, T., Broverman, D., Clarkson, F., Rosenkrantz, P., & Vogel, S. Sex role stereotypes: A current appraisal. *Journal of Social Issues*, 1972, *28*, 59–78.

Deaux, K. *The behavior of men and women.* Monterey, Calif.: Brooks/Cole, 1976.

Diamond, M. Sexual identity and sex roles. *The Humanist*, March–April, 1978, 16–19.

Dominick, J., & Rauch, G. Image of women in TV network commercials. *Journal of Broadcasting*, 1972, 16.

Dweck, C., & Reppucci, D. Learned helplessness and reinforcement responsibility in children. *Journal of Personality and Social Psychology*, 1972, *25*, 109–116.

Dwyer, C. Children's sex role standards and sex role identification and their relationship to achievement. Unpublished doctoral dissertation, University of California at Berkeley, 1973.

Ehrhardt, A., & Money, J. Progestin-induced hermaphroditism: IQ and psycho-sexual identity in a study of ten girls. *Journal of Sex Research*, 1967, *3*, 83–100.

Erikson, E. Inner space and outer space: Reflections on womanhood. *Daedalus*, 1964, *93*, 582–606.

Fagot, B. Sex differences in toddler's behavior and parental reaction. *Developmental Psychology*, 1974, *10*, 56–57.

Fagot, B. Consequences of moderate cross-gender behavior in preschool children. *Child Development*, 1977, *48*, 902–907.

Federbush, M. The sex problems of school math books. In J. Stacey, S. Bereaud, & J. Daniels (Eds.), *And Jill came tumbling after: Sexism in American education.* New York: Dell, 1974.

Finz, S., & Waters, J. An analysis of sex role stereotyping in daytime television serials. Paper presented at the Meeting of the American Psychological Association, Washington, D.C., September 1976.

Forisha, B. *Sex roles and personal awareness.* Glenview, Ill.: Scott, Foresman, 1978.

Franzwa, H. Female roles in women's magazine fiction, 1940–1970. In R. Unger & F. Denmark (Eds.), *Woman: Dependent or independent variable?* New York: Psychological Dimensions, 1975.

Freud, S. *New introductory lectures on psychoanalysis.* New York: Norton, 1965. (First German edition, 1933).

Gagnon, J., & Simon, W. *Sexual conduct: The social origins of human sexuality.* Chicago: Aldine, 1973.

Gardner, J. Sesame Street and sex role stereotypes. *Women*, 1970, *1*, 3.

Geshuri, Y. Discriminative observational learning: Effects of observed reward and dependency. *Child Development*, 1975, *46*, 550–554.

Gunther, B. Who are we? *Playboy*, 1972, *19*, 139.

Hartley, R. Sex-role pressures and the socialization of the male child. *Psychological Reports*, 1959, *5*, 457–468.

Hartnett, O., Boden, G., & Fuller, M. *Sex role stereotyping.* New York: Tavistock, 1979.

Hartup, W. Peer interaction and social organization. In P. H. Mussen (Ed.), *Manual of Child Psychology*, 3rd Ed. New York: Wiley, 1970.

Heilbrun, A. Sex role, instrumental-expressive behavior and psychopathology in females. *Journal of Abnormal Psychology*, 1968, *73*, 131–136.

Heilbrun, A. Measurement of masculine and feminine sex role identities as independent dimensions. *Journal of Consulting and Clinical Psychology*, 1976, *44*, 183–190.

Hetherington, E. M. Effects of father absence on personality development in adolescent daughters. *Developmental Psychology*, 1972, *7*, 303–326.

Hetherington, E. M., & Parke, R. *Child psychology: A contemporary viewpoint.* New York: McGraw-Hill, 1979.

Horner, M. Toward an understanding of achievement-related conflicts in women. *Journal of Social Issues*, 1972, *28*, 157–176.

Hubbard, R., & Love, M. *Genes and gender II: Pitfalls in research on sex and gender.* New York: Gordian Press, 1979.

Hyde, J., & Rosenberg, B. *Half the human experience.* Lexington, Mass.: Heath, 1980.

Jung, C. Anima and animus. In *Two essays on analytical psychology: Collected works of C. Jung* (Vol. 7). New York: Bollinger Foundation, 1953.

Jung, C. *The portable Jung.* J. Campbell (Ed.). New York: Viking, 1971.

Kaplan, A. Clarifying the concept of androgyny: Implications for therapy. *Psychology of Women Quarterly,* 1979, *3,* 223–230.

Keniston, K., & Keniston, E. An American anachronism: The image of women and work. *The American Scholar,* 1964, *33* (5), 355–375.

Kessler, S., & McKenna, W. *Gender: An ethnomethodological approach.* New York: Wiley, 1978.

Kohlberg, L. A cognitive developmental analysis of children's sex-role concepts and attitudes. In E. Maccoby (Ed.), *The development of sex differences.* Palo Alto, Calif.: Stanford University, 1966.

Kohlberg, L., & Ullian, D. Stages in the developmental of psychosexual concepts and attitudes. In R. Friedman, R. Richart, & R. Van de Wiele (Eds.), *Sex differences in behavior.* New York: Wiley, 1974.

Komarovsky, M. Cultural contradictions and sex roles: The masculine case. *American Journal of Sociology,* 1973, *78* (4), 873–884.

Kramer, C. Women's speech: Separate but unequal? *Quarterly Journal of Speech,* February 1974, 14–24.

LeFrancois, G. *Of children: An introduction to child development.* Belmont, Calif.: Wadsworth, 1980.

Levin, R., & Levin, A. Sexual pleasures: The surprising preferences of 100,000 women. *Redbook,* September 1975, 51–58.

Maccoby, E., & Jacklin, C. *The psychology of sex differences.* Palo Alto, Calif.: Stanford University Press, 1974.

McClelland, D., Atkinson, J., Clark, R., & Lowell, E. *The achievement motive.* New York: Appleton-Century-Crofts, 1953.

Mead, M. Cultural determinants of sexual behavior. In W. C. Young (Ed.), *Sex and internal secretions* (Vol. II). Baltimore: Williams & Wilkins, 1961.

Mischel, W. Sex-typing and socialization. In P. Mussen (Ed.), *Carmichael's manual of child psychology* (Vol. 2). New York: Wiley, 1970.

Money, J. Human hermaphroditism. In F. A. Beach (Ed.), *Human sexuality in four perspectives.* Baltimore: Johns Hopkins University Press, 1977.

Money, J., & Ehrhardt, A. *Man and woman, boy and girl.* Baltimore: Johns Hopkins University Press, 1972.

Mussen, P., & Distler, L. Child-rearing antecedents of masculine identity and kindergarten boys. *Child Development,* 1960, *31,* 89–100.

Nickols, J. *Men's liberation: A new definition of masculinity.* New York: Penguin Books, 1975.

Nielson Television 78. Chicago: A. C. Nielson, 1978.

Parke, R. Family interactions in the new-born period: Some findings, some observations, and some unresolved issues. In K. Riegel & J. Meacham (Eds.), *The developing individual in a changing world* (Vol. 2). The Hague: Mouton, 1976.

Parke, R., & Sawin, D. The family in early infancy: Social interactional and attitudinal analysis. Paper presented at the Society for Research in Child Development, New Orleans, March 1977.

Pingree, S., Hawkins, R., Butler, M., & Paisley, W. A scale for sexism. *Journal of Communication,* 1976, *26,* 193–200.

Pleck, J. The male sex role: Definitions, problems and sources of change. *Journal of Social Issues,* 1976, *32* (3), 155.

Rebecca, M., Hefner, R., & Oleshansky, B. A model of sex-role transcendence. *Journal of Social Issues,* 1976, *32,* 197–206.

Rheingold, H., & Cook, K. The content of boys' and girls' rooms as an index of parents' behavior. *Child Development,* 1975, *46,* 459–463.

Rossi, A. Equality between the sexes: An immodest proposal. *Daedalus,* 1964, *93,* 607–652.

Roszak, B., & Roszak, T. *Masculine/feminine.* New York: Harper & Row, 1969.

Rubin, J., Provenzano, F., & Luria, Z. In the eye of the beholder: Parents' view on sex of newborns. *American Journal of Orthopsychiatry,* 1974, *44,* 512–519.

Sauls, J., & Larson, R. Exploring national assessment data using singular value decomposition. Education Commission of the States, Denver, April 1975.

Schaffer, K. *Sex roles and human behavior.* Cambridge, Mass.: Winthrop, 1981.

Serbin, L., & O'Leary, K. How nursery schools teach girls to shut up. *Psychology Today,* 1975, *8,* 96–104.

Stafford, R. Hereditary and environmental components of quantitative reasoning. *Review of Educational Research,* 1972, *42,* 183–201.

Stasz-Stoll, C. *Female and male: Socialization, social roles, and social structure.* Dubuque, Iowa: Brown, 1974.

Sutton-Smith, B., & Sovasta, M. Sex differences in play and power. Paper presented at Eastern Psychological Association, Boston, April 1972.

Tavris, C., & Offir, C. *The longest war: Sex differences*

in perspective. New York: Harcourt Brace Jovanovich, 1977.

Tresemer, D. Fear of success: Popular but unproven. *Psychology Today,* 1974, 82–85.

U.S. Department of Labor, Women's Bureau. *Occupations of employed women, April 1977.* Washington, D.C., 1977.

Weitzman, L. *Sex role socialization.* Palo Alto, Calif.: Mayfield Publishing Co., 1979.

Wesley, F., & Wesley, C. *Sex role psychology.* New York: Human Sciences Press, 1977.

Wrightsman, L. *Social psychology* (2nd Ed.). Monterey, Calif.: Brooks/Cole, 1977.

Chapter 10

Adler, A. *Social interest: A challenge to mankind.* New York: Putnam, 1964 (Originally published, 1938).

Adler, A. Superiority and social interest: A collection of later writings. H. Ansbacher & R. Ansbacher (Eds.). New York: Viking, 1973.

Allport, G. *Personality: A psychological interpretation.* New York: Holt, 1937.

Bandura, A. Behavioral modifications through modeling procedures. In L. Krasner and C. Ullman (Eds.), *Research in behavior modification.* New York: Holt, 1965.

Bandura, A. Behavior theory and the models of man. *American Psychologist,* 1974, *29,* 859–869.

Bandura, A., & Walters, R. *Social learning and personality development.* New York: Holt, 1963.

Berne, E. *The structure and dynamics of organizations and groups.* Philadelphia: Lippincott, 1963.

Berne, E. *Games people play.* New York: Grove, 1964.

Binswanger, L. *Being in the world: Selected papers of L. Binswanger.* New York: Basic, 1963.

Carlson, R. Where is the person in personality research? *Psychological Bulletin,* 1971, *75,* 203–219.

Chiang, H., & Maslow, A. *The healthy personality.* New York: Van Nostrand, 1977.

Corsini, R. (Ed.) *Current theories of personality.* Itasca, Ill.: F. E. Peacock, 1977.

DiCaprio, N. *Personality theories: Guides to living.* Philadelphia: Saunders, 1974.

Evans, R. *Carl Rogers, the man and his ideas: A dialogue.* New York: Dutton, 1975.

Ewen, R. *An introduction to theories of personality.* New York: Academic, 1980.

Eysenck, H., & Wilson, G. *Know your own personality.* New York: Penguin, 1978.

Fischer, S., & Greenberg, R. *Scientific credibility of Freud's theory and therapy.* New York: Basic, 1977.

Forer, E. *The birth order factor.* New York: Pocket Books, 1977.

Franke, V. *Man's search for meaning.* New York: Pocket Books, 1963.

Franke, V. *The will to meaning: foundations and applications of logotherapy.* Cleveland: World, 1969.

Freud, A. *The ego and the mechanisms of defense* (Rev. Ed.). New York: International Universities Press, 1966. (First German edition, 1936)

Freud, S. *New introductory lectures. In Vol. XXII of the Standard Edition.* London: Hogarth, 1961.

Freud, S. *On the history of the psychoanalytic movement* Vol. 14. New York: Norton, 1967. (Originally published in London by Hogarth Press, 1914)

Freud, S. *An outline of psychoanalysis.* Translated and edited J. Strachey. New York: Norton, 1969. (First German edition, 1933)

Glasser, W. *Reality therapy.* New York: Harper & Row, 1965.

Glasser, W. *The identity society.* New York: Harper & Row, 1975.

Gore, R., & Robber, J. A personality correlate of social action. *Journal of Personality,* 1963, *31,* 58–64.

Greenwald, H. *Direct decision therapy.* New York: Knapp, 1975.

Hall, C., & Lindzey, G. *Theories of personality* (3rd Ed.). New York: Wiley, 1978.

Harris, T. *I'm OK, You're OK.* New York: Harper & Row, 1969.

Hartmann, H. *Essays on ego psychology: Selected problems in psychoanalytic theory.* New York: International Universities Press, 1964.

Hogan, R. *Personality theory: The personological approach.* Englewood Cliffs, N.J.: Prentice-Hall, 1976.

James, M., & Jongeward, D. *Born to win: Transactional analysis with Gestalt experiments.* Reading, Mass.: Addison-Wesley, 1977.

Kempler, W. Gestalt therapy. In R. Corsini (Ed.), *Current psychotherapies.* Itasca, Ill.: F. E. Peacock, 1973.

Kline, P. *Fact and fantasy in Freudian theory.* London: Methuen, 1972.

Kopp, S. *This side of tragedy.* Palo Alto, Calif.: Science and Behavior, 1977.

Lazarus, R., & Monat, A. *Personality* (3rd Ed.). Englewood Cliffs, N.J.: Prentice-Hall, 1979.

Levinson, D. *The seasons of a man's life.* New York: Knopf, 1978.

Maddi, S. The search for meaning. In M. Page (Ed.), *Nebraska Symposium on Motivation.* Lincoln: University of Nebraska Press, 1970.

Maddi, S. *Personality theories* (3rd Ed.). Homewood, Ill.: Dorsey, 1976.

Marx, M., & Hillix, W. *Systems and theories in psychology.* New York: McGraw-Hill, 1979.

Maslow, A. Toward a humanistic biology. *American Psychologist,* 1969, *24,* 8, 734–735.

Maslow, A. Self-actualizing people. In G. Levitas (Ed.), *The world of psychology.* New York: Braziller, 1963.

Mischel, W. *Personality and assessment.* New York: Wiley, 1968.

Mischel, W. On the empirical dilemmas of psychodynamic approaches: Issues and alternatives. *Journal of Abnormal Psychology,* 1973, *82,* 335–344.

Monte, C. *Beneath the mask: An introduction to theories of personality.* New York: Praeger, 1977.

Moulton, R. A survey and reevaluation of penis envy. *Contemporary Psychoanalysis,* 1970, *7,* 84–104.

Naditch, M., Gargon, P., & Michael, P. Denial, anxiety, locus of control and the discrepancy between aspirations and achievement as components of depression. *Journal of Abnormal Psychology,* 1975, *84,* 1–9.

Perls, F. *Gestalt therapy verbatim.* Lafayette, Calif.: Real People Press, 1969.

Pervin, L. *Current controversies: Issues in personality.* New York: Wiley, 1978.

Prociuk, T., & Lussier, R. Internal-external locus of control: An analysis and bibliography of two years of research (1973–1974). *Psychological Reports,* 1975, *37,* 1323–1337.

Rogers, C. *Client-centered therapy: Its current practice, implications, and theory.* Boston: Houghton Mifflin, 1951.

Rogers, C. A theory of therapy, personality and interpersonal relationships as developed in the client-centered framework. In S. Koch (Ed.), *Psychology: A study of a science* (Vol. 3). New York: McGraw-Hill, 1959.

Rogers, C. *On becoming a person: A therapist's view of psychotherapy.* Boston: Houghton Mifflin, 1961.

Rotter, J. *Social learning and clinical psychology.* Englewood Cliffs, N.J.: Prentice-Hall, 1954.

Rotter, J. Generalized expectancies for internal vs. external control of reinforcement. *Psychological Monographs,* 1966, *80* (Whole No. 609).

Rotter, J. Some implications of social learning theory for the practice of psychotherapy. In D. Levis (Ed.), *Learning approaches to therapeutic behavior change.* Chicago: Aldine, 1970.

Sartre, J. *Being and nothingness.* Translated by H. Barnes. New York: Philosophical Library, 1956.

Schachter, S. *The psychology of affiliation.* Palo Alto, Calif.: Stanford University Press, 1959.

Schultz, D. *Theories of personality.* Monterey, Calif. Brooks/Cole, 1981.

Shlien, J. Phenomenology and personality. In J. Wepman & R. Heine (Eds.), *Concepts of personality.* Chicago: Aldine, 1963.

Simon, H. *The sciences of the artificial.* Cambridge, Mass.: M.I.T., 1969.

Skinner, B. Behaviorism at fifty. *Science,* 1953, *140,* 951–958.

Skinner, B. *About behaviorism.* New York: Knopf, 1974.

Steiner, J. *Treblinka.* Translated by H. Weaver. New York: Simon & Schuster, 1967.

Chapter 11

Anastasi, A. *Psychological Testing* (4th ed.), New York: Macmillan, 1976.

Boring, E. G. *A history of experimental psychology* (Rev. ed.) New York: Appleton-Century-Crofts, 1950.

Campbell, D. P. *Handbook for the Strong Vocational Interest Blank.* Palo Alto, Calif.: Stanford University Press, 1971.

Campbell, D. P. *Manual for the SVIB-SCII* (2nd ed.), Palto Alto, Calif.: Stanford University Press, 1977.

Campbell, J. T., Crooks, L. A., Mahoney, M. H., & Rock, D. A. *An investigation of source of bias in the prediction of job performance: A six-year study.* Princeton, N.J.: Educational Testing Service, 1973.

Cole, N. S. Bias in selection. ACT Research Report No. 51. Iowa City, Iowa: American College Testing Program, 1972.

Gardner, J. W. *Excellence.* New York: Harper, 1961.

Hathaway, S. R., & McKinley, J. C. *The Minnesota Multiphasic Personality Inventory manual, revised.* New York: Psychological Corporation, 1967.

Jensen, A. R. How much can we boost IQ and scholastic

achievement? *Harvard Educational Review*, 1969, *39*, 1–123.

Kennedy, W. A., Nelson, W., Lindner, R., Moon, H., & Turner, J. The ceiling of the new Stanford-Binet. *Journal of Clinical Psychology*, 1960, *17*, 284–286.

Linn, R. L. Test bias and the prediction of grades in law school. *Journal of Legal Education*, 1975, 27, 293–323.

Maloney, M. P., & Ward, M. P. *Psychological assessment: A conceptual approach*. New York: Oxford, 1976.

Marks, P. A., Seeman, W., & Haller, D. L. *The actuarial use of the MMPI with adolescents and adults*. Baltimore: Williams & Wilkins, 1974.

Nader releases ETS report, hits tests as poor predictors of performance. *APA Monitor*. February 1980, 1 ff.

Scarr-Salapatek, S. Race, social class, and IQ. *Science*, 1971, *174*, 1285–1295.

Spearman, C. *The abilities of man*. New York: Macmillan, 1927.

Temp, G. Test bias: Validity of the SAT for blacks and whites in thirteen integrated institutions. *Journal of Educational Measurement*, 1971, *8*, 245–251.

Thurstone, L. L. Primary mental abilities. *Psychometric Monographs*, 1938, No. 1.

Turnbull, W. APA and the war on testing. *APA Monitor*, March 1980, 2.

Twentyman, C. T., & McFall, R. M. Behavioral training of social skills in shy males. *Journal of Consulting and Clinical Psychology*, 1975, *43*, 384–395.

Vinitsky, M. A forty-year follow-up on the vocational interests of psychologists and their relationship to career development. *American Psychologist*, 1973, *28*, 1000–1009.

Chapter 12

Abrams, R., & Taylor, M. Unipolar mania: A preliminary report. *Archives of General Psychiatry*, 1974, *30* (4), 441–443.

Al-Issa, J. *The psychopathology of women*. Englewood Cliffs, N.J.: Prentice-Hall, 1980.

American Psychiatric Association. Committee on Nomenclature and Statistics. *Diagnostic and statistical manual of mental disorders* (2nd Ed.). Washington, D.C.: American Psychiatric Association, 1968.

American Psychiatric Association. Task Force on Nomenclature and Statistics. DSM-III draft. *Diagnostic and statistical manual of mental disorders* (3rd Ed.). Washington, D.C.: American Psychiatric Association, January 15, 1980.

Bandura, A. Behavior theory and the models of man. *American Psychologist*, 1974, *29* (12), 859–869.

Bateson, G., Jackson, D., Haley, J., & Weakland, J. Towards a theory of schizophrenia. *Behavioral Science*, 1956, *1*, 251–264.

Beck, A. *Depression: Causes and treatment*. Philadelphia: University of Pennsylvania Press, 1967.

Bootzin, R., & Acocella, J. *Abnormal Psychology*. New York: Random House, 1980.

Bugliosi, V., with Gentry, C. *Helter skelter*. New York: Bantam, 1975.

Carr, A. Compulsion neurosis: A review of the literature. *Psychological Bulletin*, 1974, *81*, 311–318.

Chesler, P. *Women and madness*. New York: Avon, 1972.

Cleckley, H. *The mask of sanity* (5th Ed.). St. Louis: Mosby, 1976.

Cofer, D., & Wittenborn, J. Personality characteristics of formerly depressed women. *Journal of Abnormal Psychology*, 1980, *89*, 309–314.

Coleman, J., Butcher, J., & Carson, R. *Abnormal psychology and modern life*. Glenview, Ill.: Scott, Foresman, 1980.

Davis, J. Critique of single amine theories: Evidence of a cholinergic influence in the major mental illnesses. In D. Freedman (Ed.), *Biology of the major psychoses*. New York: Raven, 1975.

Davison, G., & Neale, J. *Abnormal psychology* (2nd Ed.). New York: Wiley, 1978.

Durham, V. J. *United States*, 214 F 2d 862, 876 (D. C. Cir. 1954).

Epstein, H. A sin or a right? *New York Times Magazine*, Sept. 8, 1974, 91–94.

Eysenck, H., & Rachman, S. *The causes and cures of neurosis*. London: Routledge & Kegan Paul, 1965.

Gamzey, N. DSM-III: Never mind the psychologist; is it good for children? *The Clinical Psychologist*, 1978, *31*, 1–6.

Goldstein, M., Baker, B., & Jamison, K. *Abnormal psychology*. Boston: Little, Brown, 1980.

Goleman, D. Who is mentally ill? *Psychology Today*, 1978, *12*, 34–41.

Haas, K. *Understanding adjustment and behavior*. Englewood Cliffs, N.J.: Prentice-Hall, 1975.

Haas, K. *Abnormal psychology*. New York: Van Nostrand, 1979.

Haley, J. *Strategies of schizophrenics.* New York: Grune & Stratton, 1963.

Hollingshead, A., & Redlich, F. *Social class and mental illness.* New York: Wiley, 1958.

Kallman, F. *Heredity in health and mental disorders.* New York: Norton, 1953.

Kallman, F. The use of genetics in psychiatry. *Journal of Mental Science,* 1958, *104,* 542–549.

Kohn, M. Social class and schizophrenia: A critical review and reformulation. *Schizophrenia Bulletin,* 1973, *7,* 60–79.

Kolb, L. *Modern clinical psychiatry* (9th Ed.). Philadelphia: Saunders, 1977.

Leo, J. Psychoanalysis reaches a crossroad. *New York Times,* August 4, 1968, 1, 56.

Maher, B. *Principles of psychopathology.* New York: McGraw-Hill, 1966.

Mathews, T., & Harper, C. The cult of death. *Newsweek,* December 4, 1978, 38–40.

McLemore, C., & Smith, B. J. What happened to interpersonal diagnosis: A psychosocial alternative to DSM-III. *American Psychologist,* 1979, *34* (1), 17–34.

McPhatter, B. Psychotic delusions: The new head of the FBI. *Personal Communication,* 1980.

Meehl, P. Schizotaxia, schizotypy, and schizophrenia. *American Psychologist,* 1962, *17,* 827–838.

Melamed, B., & Siegel, L. Self-directed in vivo treatment of an obsessive compulsive checking ritual. *Journal of Behavior Therapy and Experimental Psychiatry,* 1975, *6,* 31–35.

Nathan, P., & Harris, S. *Psychopathology and society.* New York: McGraw-Hill, 1980.

Poland, R. *Human experience: Psychology of growth.* St. Louis: Mosby, 1974.

Price, R. *Abnormal behavior: Perspectives in conflict.* New York: Holt, 1978.

Rosenhan, D. On being sane in insane places. *Science,* 1973, *179,* 250–258.

Rosenthal, D. *Genetic theory and abnormal behavior.* New York: McGraw-Hill, 1970.

Russell, O. *Freedom to die: Moral and legal aspects of euthanasia.* New York: Human Sciences Press, 1975.

Salzinger, K. *Schizophrenia: Behavioral aspects.* New York: Wiley, 1973.

Sarbin, T. The scientific status of the mental illness metaphor. In C. Plog & R. Edgerton (Eds.), *Changing perspectives in mental illness.* New York: Holt, 1969.

Scarf, M. Images that heal: Fighting cancer with mental pictures. *Psychology Today,* 1980, *14,* 32–46.

Schreiber, F. *Sybil.* New York: Warner, 1974.

Schwitzgebel, R. L., & Schwitzgebel, R. K. *Law and psychological practice.* New York: Wiley, 1980.

Seligman, M. *Helplessness: On depression, development, and death.* San Francisco: Freeman, 1975.

Selye, H. *The stress of life.* New York: McGraw-Hill, 1978.

Slater, E., & Cowie, V. *The genetics of mental disorders.* London: Oxford, 1971.

Snyder, S. The dopamine hypothesis of schizophrenia: Focus on the dopamine receptor. *American Journal of Psychiatry,* 1976, *133* (2), 197–202.

Snyder, S. *Biological aspects of mental disorders.* New York: Oxford, 1980.

Staats, A. *Social behaviorism.* Homewood, Ill.: Dorsey, 1974.

Syndulko, K. Electrocortical investigations of sociopathy. In R. Hare & D. Schalling (Eds.), *Psychopathic behavior: Approaches to research.* Chichester, England: Wiley, 1978.

Szasz, T. The myth of mental illness. *American Psychologist,* 1960, *15,* 113–118.

Szasz, T. The ethics of suicide. In B. Wolman & H. Krauss (Eds.), *Between survival and suicide.* New York: Gardner, 1976.

Thigpen, C., & Cleckley, H. *The three faces of Eve.* New York: McGraw-Hill, 1957.

Wallechinsky, R., & Wallace, J. *The people's almanac.* Garden City, N.Y.: Doubleday, 1975.

World Health Organization. *Schizophrenia: An international follow-up study.* New York: Wiley, 1980.

Chapter 13

American Psychological Association, Task Force on Privacy and Confidentiality. *Final Report.* Washington, D.C.: Author, 1977.

Avery, D., & Winokin, G. Suicide, attempted suicide, and relapse rates in depression. *Archives of General Psychiatry, 35,* 749–753.

Bandura, A. *Principles of behavior modification.* New York: Holt, 1969.

Bergin, A. E. The evaluation of therapeutic outcomes. In A. E. Bergin & S. L. Garfield (Eds.), *Handbook of psychotherapy and behavior change.* New York: Wiley, 1971.

Bergin, A. E., & Lambert, M. J. The evaluation of therapeutic outcomes. In S. L. Garfield & A. E. Bergin

(Eds.), *Handbook of psychotherapy and behavior change* (2nd ed.). New York: Wiley, 1978.

Bersoff, D. N. Therapists as protectors and policemen: New roles as a result of Tarasoff? *Professional Psychology*, 1976, *7*, 267–273.

Blakemore, C. B., Thorpe, J. B., Barker, J. C., Conway, C. G., & Lavin, N. T. The application of faradic aversion conditioning in the case of transvestism. *Behaviour Research & Therapy*, 1963, *1*, 29–44.

Breggin, P. R. Psychosurgery (letter to the editor). *Journal of the American Medical Association*, 1973, *226*, 1121.

Casey, J. F., Bennett, I. V., Lindley, C. J., Hollister, L. E., Gordon, M. H., & Springer, N. N. Drug therapy in schizophrenia. *AMA Archives of General Psychiatry*, 1960, *2*, 210–220.

Coleman, J. C., Butcher, J. N., & Carson, R. C. *Abnormal psychology and modern life* (6th ed.). Glenview, Ill.: Scott, Foresman, 1980.

Conway, F., & Siegelman, J. *Snapping: America's epidemic of sudden personality change.* New York: Lippincott, 1978.

Cotter, L. H. Operant conditioning in a Vietnamese mental hospital. *American Journal of Psychiatry*, 1967, *124*, 23–28.

Dunner, D. L., & Somervill, J. W. Medical treatments. In D. C. Rimm & J. W. Somervill (Eds.), *Abnormal Psychology*, New York: Academic, 1977.

Ellis, A. Rational-emotive therapy. In R. Corsini (Ed.), *Current psychotherapies.* (2nd Ed.). Itasca, Ill.: Peacock, 1979.

Enright, J. B. An introduction to Gestalt techniques. In J. F. Fagan & I. L. Shepard (Eds.), *Life techniques in Gestalt therapy*. New York: Perennial Library, 1970.

Eysenck, H. J. The effects of psychotherapy: An evaluation. *Journal of Consulting Psychology*, 1952, *16*, 319–324.

Eysenck, H. J. The effects of psychotherapy. *International Journal of Psychiatry*, 1965, *1*, 97–178.

Fink, M. *Convulsive therapy: Theory and practice.* New York: Raven, 1979.

Franks, C. M., & Wilson, G. T. *Annual review of behavior therapy: Theory and practice* (Vol. 4). New York: Brunner/Mazel, 1976.

Gellhorn, E., & Kiely, W. F. Autonomic nervous system in psychiatric disorder. In J. Mendels (Ed.), *Biological psychiatry*. New York: Wiley, 1973.

Hartley, D., Roback, H. B., & Abramowitz, S. I. Deterioration effects in encounter groups. *American Psychologist*, 1976, *31*, 247–255.

Hollister, L. E. Drug therapy: Mental disorders—antipsychotic and antimanic drugs. *New England Journal of Medicine*, 1972, *286*, 984–987.

Kandler, H. O. Issues of confidentiality in psychiatry. *Newsletter, Society for Adolescent Psychiatry*, New York, May 1977.

Kempler, W. Gestalt therapy. In R. Corsini (Ed.), *Current psychotherapies.* Itasca, Ill.: Peacock, 1973.

Klerman, G. L., & Cole, J. Clinical pharmacology of imipramine and related antidepressant compounds. *Pharmacological Review*, 1965, *17*, 101–141.

Klerman, G. L., DiMascio, A., Weissman, M., et al. Treatment of depression by drugs and psychotherapy. *American Journal of Psychiatry*, 1974, *131*, 186–191.

Koch, S. The image of man implicit in encounter groups. *Journal of Humanistic Psychology*, 1971, *11*, 112.

Krasner, L. Behavior therapy. In P. H. Mussen & M. R. Rosenweig (Eds.), *Annual review of psychology*. California Annual Reviews, Inc.: 1971.

Lieberman, M. A., Yalom, I. D., & Miles, M. B. *Encounter groups: First facts.* New York: Basic, 1973.

Malcolm, A. *The tyranny of the group*. New York: Clark, Irwin, 1973.

Mark, V. H. The continuing polemic of psychosurgery (letter to the editor). *Journal of the American Medical Association*. 1974, *227*, 943.

Marks, M. W., & Vestre, N. D. Self-prescription and interpersonal behavior changes in marathon and time-extended encounter groups. *Journal of Consulting and Clinical Psychology*, 1974, *42*, 729–733.

Masters, W. H., & Johnson, V. E. *Human sexual inadequacy*. Boston: Little, Brown, 1970.

Meador, B. D., & Rogers, C. R. Person-centered therapy. In R. Corsini (Ed.), *Current psychotherapies* (2nd Ed.). Itasca, Ill.: Peacock, 1979.

Prien, R. F., Klett, C. J., & Caffey, E. M. Lithium prophylaxis in recurrent affective illness. *American Journal of Psychiatry*, 1974, *131*, 198–203.

Quitkin, F., Rifkin, A., Kane, J., Ramos-Lorenzo, J. R., & Klein, D. F. Prophylactic effect of lithium and imipramine in unipolar and bipolar II patients: A preliminary report. *American Journal of Psychiatry*, 1978, *135*, 570–572.

Rimm, D. C., & Masters, J. C. *Behavior therapy: Techniques and empirical findings* (2nd Ed.). New York: Academic, 1979.

Rogers, C. R. *Carl Rogers on encounter groups.* New York: Harper & Row, 1970.

Siegel, M. Privacy, ethics, and confidentiality. *Professional Psychology*, 1979, *10*, 249–258.

Spohn, H. E., Lacoursiere, R. B., Thompson, K., & Coyne, L. Phenotherazine effects on psychological and psychophysiological dysfunction in chronic schizophrenics. *Archives of General Psychiatry*, 1977, *34*, 633–644.

Tarasoff v. *Regents of University of California*, 13C 3d 177, 529 P. 2d 533, 118 Cal. Rptr. 129 (1974).

Truax, C. B., & Mitchell, K. M. Research on certain therapist interpersonal skills in relation to process and outcome. In S. L. Garfield & A. E. Bergin (Eds.), *Handbook of psychotherapy and behavior change* (2nd Ed.). New York: Wiley, 1978.

Valenstein, E. S. *The psychosurgery debate: Scientific, legal, and ethical principles.* San Francisco: Freeman, 1980.

Watson, J. B., & Rayne, R. Conditioned emotional reactions. *Journal of Experimental Psychology*, 1920, *3*, 1–14.

Weiner, I. B. *Principles of intensive psychotherapy*. New York: Wiley, 1975.

Wolpe, J. *Psychotherapy by reciprocal inhibition*. Palo Alto, Calif.: Stanford University Press, 1958.

Wolpe, J. Conditioning is the basis of all psychotherapeutic change. In A. Burton (Ed.), *What makes behavior change possible?* New York: Brunner/Mazel, 1976.

Chapter 14

Abramson, P., Michalak, P., & Alling, C. Perception of parental sex guilt and sexual behavior and arousal of college students. *Perceptual and Motor Skills*, 1977, *45*, 337–338.

Adorno, T. W., Frenkel-Brunswik, E., Levinson, D., & Sanford, R. W. *The authoritarian personality*. New York: Harper, 1950.

Allport, G. W. *The nature of prejudice*. Reading, Mass.: Addison-Wesley, 1954.

Aronson, E., Blaney, N., Sikes, J., Stephan, C., & Snapp, M. Busing and racial tension: the jigsaw route to learning and liking. In V. J. Derlega & L. H. Janda (Eds.), *Personal adjustment: Selected readings*. Glenview, Ill.: Scott, Foresman, 1979.

Bem, D. J. An experimental analysis of self-persuasion. *Journal of Experimental Social Psychology*, 1965, *1*, 199–218.

Bem, D. J. Self-perception: An alternative interpretation of cognitive dissonance phenomena. *Psychological Review*, 1967, *74*, 183–200.

Bem, D. J. Self-perception theory. In L. Berkowitz (Ed.), *Advances in experimental social psychology* (Vol. 6). New York: Academic, 1972.

Berscheid, E. Opinion change and communicator-communicatee similarity and dissimilarity. *Journal of Personality and Social Psychology*, 1966, *4*, 670–680.

Billig, M. *Social psychology and intergroup relations*. New York: Academic, 1976.

Bostrom, R., Vlandis, J., & Rosenbaum, M. Grades as reinforcing contingencies and attitude change. *Journal of Educational Psychology*, 1–61, *52*, 112–115.

Brewer, M. B. Determinants of social distance among east African tribal groups. *Journal of Personality and Social Psychology*, 1968, *10*, 279–289.

Clark, K. B., & Clark, M. P. Racial identification and preference in Negro children. In T. M. Newcomb & E. L. Hartley (Eds.), *Readings in social psychology*. New York: Holt, 1947.

Collins, B. E., Ashmore, R. D., Hornbeck, F. W., & Whitney, R. Studies in forced compliance: XIII and XV in search of a dissonance-producing forced compliance paradigm. *Journal of Representative Research in Social Psychology*, 1970, *1*, 11–23.

Cottrell, N. B., Rajecki, D. W., & Smith, D. U. The energizing effects of post decision dissonance upon performance of an irrelevant task. *Journal of Social Psychology*, 1974, *93*, 81–92.

Cox, O. C. *Caste, class, and race*. New York: Doubleday, 1948.

Craig, S. C. The mobilization of political discontent. *Political Behavior*, 1980, *2*, 189–209.

Dables, J. M., & Leventhal, H. Effects of varying the recommendations in a fear arousing communication. *Journal of Personality and Social Psychology*, 1966, *4*, 525–531.

Deutsch, M., & Collins, M. E. *Interracial housing: A psychological evaluation of a social experiment*. Minneapolis: University of Minnesota Press, 1951.

Elms, A. C., & Janis, I. Counternorm attitudes induced by consonant versus dissonant conditions of role playing. *Journal of Experimental Research in Personality*, 1965, *1*, 50–60.

Epstein, R., & Komorita, S. Childhood prejudice as a function of parental ethnocentrism, punitiveness, and outgroup characteristics. *Journal of Personality and Social Psychology*, 1966, *3*, 259–264.

Fazio, R. H., Zanna, M. P., & Cooper, J. Dissonance

and self-perception: An integrative view of each theory's proper domain of application. *Journal of Experimental Social Psychology*, 1977, *13*, 464–479.

Festinger, L. *A theory of cognitive dissonance.* Palo Alto, Calif.: Stanford University Press, 1957.

Festinger, L., & Carlsmith, J. M. Cognitive consequences of forced compliance. *Journal of Abnormal and Social Psychology*, 1959, *58*, 203–210.

Fishbein, M. Attitude and the prediction of behavior. In M. Fishbein (Ed.), *Readings in attitude theory and measurement.* New York: Wiley, 1967.

Fishbein, M., & Ajzen, J. Attitudes toward objects as predictors of single and multiple behavior criteria. *Psychological Review*, 1974, *81*, 59–74.

Gillig, P. M., & Greenwald, A. G. Is it time to lay the sleeper effect to rest? *Journal of Personality and Social Psychology*, 1974, *29*, 132–139.

Goldstein, J. H. *Social psychology.* New York: Academic, 1980.

Greenberg, J., & Rosenfield, D. Whites' ethnocentrism and their attributions for the behavior of blacks: A motivational bias. *Journal of Personality*, 1980, *48*, 643–657.

Greenwald, A. G. On the inconclusiveness of "crucial" cognitive tests of dissonance vs. self-perception theories. *Journal of Experimental Social Psychology*, 1975, *11*, 490–499.

Harris, S., and Brown, J. R. Self-esteem and racial preference in black children. *Proceedings of the 79th Annual Convention of the American Psychological Association*, 1971, *6*, 259–260.

Heberlein, T. A., & Black, J. S. Attitude specificity and the prediction of behavior in a field setting. *Journal of Personality and Social Psychology*, 1976, *33*, 474–479.

Heider, F. Attitudes and cognitive organization. *Journal of Psychology*, 1946, *21*, 107–112.

Heider, F. *The psychology of interpersonal relations.* New York: Wiley, 1958.

Hovland, C. I., Janis, I. L., & Kelly, H. H. *Communication and persuasion.* New Haven, Conn.: Yale University Press, 1953.

Hovland, C. I., Lumsdaine, A. A., & Sheffield, F. D. *Experiments on mass communication.* Princeton, N.J.: Princeton University Press, 1949.

Hovland, C., & Weiss, W. The influence of source credibility on communication effectiveness. *Public Opinion Quarterly*, 1951, *15*, 635–650.

Insko, C. *Theories of attitude change.* New York: Appleton-Century-Crofts, 1967.

Janis, I. L., & Feshbach, S. Effects of fear-arousing communications. *Journal of Abnormal and Social Psychology*, 1953, *48*, 78–92.

Jennings, M., & Niemi, R. The transmission of political values from parent to child. *American Political Science Review*, 1968, *62*, 169–184.

Klineberg, O. Black and white in international perspective. *American Psychologist*, 1971, *26*, 119–128.

Lamberth, J. *Social psychology.* New York: Macmillan, 1980.

LaPiere, R. T. Attitudes vs. actions. *Social Forces*, 1934, *13*, 230–237.

Leventhal, H. Findings and theory in the study of fear communications. In L. Berkowitz (Ed.), *Advances in experimental social psychology* (Vol. 5). New York: Academic, 1970.

McGuire, W. J. Inducing resistance to persuasion: Some contemporary approaches. In L. Berkowitz (Ed.), *Advances in experimental social psychology* (Vol. 1). New York: Academic, 1964.

McGuire, W. J. The nature of attitudes and attitude change. In G. Lindzey & E. Aronson (Eds.), *Handbook of social psychology* (2nd ed.), Reading, Mass.: Addison-Wesley, 1969.

McGuire, W. J., & Papageorgis, D. The relative efficacy of various types of prior belief-defense in producing immunity against persuasion. *Journal of Abnormal and Social Psychology*, 1961, *62*, 327–337.

Miller, N., & Campbell, D. Recency and primacy in persuasion as a function of the timing of speeches and measurements. *Journal of Abnormal and Social Psychology*, 1959, *59*, 1–9.

Mills, J., & Aronson, E. Opinion change as a function of the communicator's attractiveness and desire to influence. *Journal of Personality and Social Psychology*, 1965, *1*, 173–177.

Minard, R. D. Race relations in the Pocahontas Coal Field. *Journal of Social Issues*, 1952, *8*, 29–44.

Newcomb, T. M. *Personality and social change.* New York: Dryden, 1943.

Newcomb, T. M., Koenig, T. K., Flacks, R., & Warwick, D. *Persistence and change: Bennington College and its students after 25 years.* New York: Wiley, 1967.

Norman, M. Adolescent bigotry. In V. J. Derlega & L. H. Janda (Eds.), *Personal Adjustment: Selected readings.* Glenview, Ill.: Scott, Foresman, 1979.

Saenger, G. *The social psychology of prejudice: Achieving intercultural understanding and cooperation in a democracy.* New York: Harper, 1953.

Schein, E. H. The Chinese indoctrination program for prisoners of war. *Psychiatry,* 1956, *19,* 149–172.

Scott, W. Attitude change through reward of verbal behavior. *Journal of Abnormal and Social Psychology,* 1957, *55,* 72–75.

Scott, W. Attitude change by response reinforcement: Replication and extension. *Sociometry,* 1959, *22,* 328–335.

Sherif, M. Experiments in group conflict. In E. Aronson (Ed.), *Readings about the social animal* (2nd Ed.), San Francisco: Freeman, 1977.

Smith, F. T. *An experiment in modifying attitudes toward the Negro.* New York: Teachers College, Columbia University, 1943.

Thomas, W. I., & Znaniecki, F. *The Polish peasant in Europe and America.* (Vol. 2). Boston: Badger, 1918.

Wallace, J. Role reward and dissonance reduction. *Journal of Personality and Social Psychology,* 1966, *3,* 305–312.

Walster, E., Aronson, E., & Abrahams, D. On increasing the persuasiveness of a low prestige communicator. *Journal of Experimental Social Psychology,* 1966, *2,* 325–342.

Zajonc, R. B. Feeling and thinking: Preferences need no inferences. *American Psychologist,* 1980, *35,* 151–175.

Zauna, M. P., Olson, J. M., & Fazio, R. H. Attitude-behavior consistency: An individual difference perspective. *Journal of Personality and Social Psychology,* 1980, *38,* 432–440.

Chapter 15

Adams, G. R. Physical attractiveness research: Toward a developmental social psychology of beauty. *Human Development,* 1977, *20,* 217–239.

Anderson, N. H. Likableness ratings of 555 personality-trait words. *Journal of Personality and Social Psychology,* 1968, *9,* 272–279.

Arkin, R. M., Appelman, A. J., & Burger, J. M. Social anxiety, self-presentation, and the self-serving bias in casual attribution. *Journal of Personality and Social Psychology,* 1980, *38,* 23–35.

Asch, S. E. Forming impressions of personality. *Journal of Abnormal and Social Psychology,* 1946, *41,* 258–290.

Berscheid, E., Dion, K., Walster, E., & Walster, G. W. Physical attractiveness and dating choice: A test of the matching hypothesis. *Journal of Experimental Social Psychology,* 1971, *7,* 173–189.

Berscheid, E., Graziano, E., Monson, T., & Dermer, M. Outcome dependency: Attention, attribution and attraction. *Journal of Personality and Social Psychology,* 1976, *34,* 978–989.

Berscheid, E., & Walster, E. Physical attractiveness. In L. Berkowitz (Ed.), *Advances in experimental social psychology,* (Vol. 7). New York: Academic, 1974.

Berscheid, E., & Walster, E. *Interpersonal attraction.* (2nd Ed.). Reading, Mass: Addison-Wesley, 1978.

Brownmiller, S. *Against our will: Men, women and rape.* New York: Simon & Schuster, 1975.

Burgess, E. W., & Wallin, P. *Engagement and marriage.* Philadelphia: Lippincott, 1953.

Byrne, D. *An introduction to personality* (2nd Ed.). Englewood Cliffs, N.J.: Prentice-Hall, 1974.

Byrne, D., & Blaylock, B. Similarity and assumed similarity of attitudes between husbands and wives. *Journal of Abnormal and Social Psychology,* 1963, *67,* 636–640.

Byrne, D., & Wong, T. J. Racial prejudices, interpersonal attraction and assumed dissimilarity of attitudes. *Journal of Abnormal and Social Psychology,* 1962, *65,* 246–252.

Cash, T. F., & Derlega, V. J. The matching hypothesis: Physical attractiveness among same-sexed friends. *Personality and Social Psychology Bulletin,* 1978, *4,* 240–243.

Dion, K. K. Physical attractiveness and evaluation of children's transgressions. *Journal of Personality and Social Psychology,* 1972, *24,* 207–213.

Dion, K. K., Berscheid, E., & Walster, E. What is beautiful is good. *Journal of Personality and Social Psychology,* 1972, *24,* 285–290.

Dutton, D., & Aron, A. Some evidence of heightened sexual attraction under conditions of high anxiety. *Journal of Personality and Social Psychology,* 1974, *30,* 510–517.

Dweck, C. S. The role of expectations and attributions in the alleviation of learned helplessness. *Journal of Personality and Social Psychology,* 1975, *31,* 674–685.

Dweck, C. S., & Goetz, F. E. Attributions and learned helplessness. In J. H. Harvey, W. Ickes, & R. F. Kidd (Eds.), *New directions in attribution research* (Vol. 2). New York: Wiley, 1978.

Dweck, C. S., & Rappucci, N. D. Learned helplessness

and reinforcement responsibility in children. *Journal of Personality and Social Psychology,* 1973, *25,* 109–116.

Festinger, L. Architecture and group membership. *Journal of Social Issues,* 1951, *1,* 152–163.

Garrison, R. J., Anderson, V. E., & Reed, S. C. Assortive marriage. *Eugenics Quarterly,* 1968, *15,* 451–463.

Goldman, W., & Lewis, P. Beautiful is good: Evidence that the physically attractive are more socially skillful. *Journal of Experimental Social Psychology,* 1977, *13,* 125–130.

Greenwald, D. P. The behavioral assessment of differences in social skills and social anxiety in female college students. *Behavior Therapy,* 1977, *8,* 925–937.

Gross, A. E., & Crofton, C. What is good is beautiful. *Sociometry,* 1977, *40,* 85–90.

Harris, J. A. Assortive mating in man. *Popular Science Monthly,* 1912, *80,* 476–492.

Harvey, J. H., Yarkin, K. L., Lightner, J. M., & Town, J. P. Unsolicited interpretation and recall of interpersonal events. *Journal of Personality and Social Psychology,* 1980, *38,* 551–568.

Hill, C. T., Rubin, Z., & Peplan, L. A. Breakups before marriage. The end of 103 affairs. *Journal of Social Issues,* 1976, *32,* 147–168.

Homans, G. C. *Social behavior: Its elementary forms.* New York: Harcourt Brace Jovanovich, 1961.

Hunt, M. *The natural history of love.* New York: Knopf, 1959.

Janda, L. H. Effects of guilt, approachability of examiner and stimulus relevance upon sexual responses to thematic apperception stimuli. *Journal of Consulting and Clinical Psychology,* 1975, *43,* 369–374.

Janda, L. H. Effects of sex guilt on interpersonal pleasuring. *Journal of Personality and Social Psychology,* 1981, *40,* 201–209.

Janda, L. H., & Fauber, R. Attribution of responsibility for rape as a function of the victim's behavior. Unpublished manuscript. Old Dominion University, 1981.

Janda, L. H., O'Grady, K. E., & Barnhart, S. A. Effects of sexual attitudes and physical attractiveness of person perception of men and women. *Sex Roles,* 1981, *7,* 189–199.

Janda, L. H., Witt, C. G., & Manahan, C. Effects of guilt and approachability of examiner upon associative sexual responses. *Journal of Consulting and Clinical Psychology,* 1976, *44,* 986–990.

Jones, C., & Aronson, E. Attribution of fault to a rape victim as a function of the respectability of the victim. *Journal of Personality and Social Psychology,* 1973, *26,* 415–419.

Jones, E. E. *Ingratiation: A social psychological analysis.* New York: Appleton-Century-Crofts, 1964.

Jones, E. E., & Nisbett, R. E. *The actor and the observer: Divergent perceptions of the causes of behavior.* Morristown, N.J.: General Learning Press, 1971.

Kaplan, M. F. Measurement and generality of response dispositions in person perception. *Journal of Personality,* 1976, *44,* 179–194.

Kelley, H. H. The warm-cold variable in first impressions of persons. *Journal of Personality,* 1950, *18,* 431–439.

Kendrick, D. T., & Gutierres, S. E. Contrast effects and judgments of physical attractiveness: When beauty becomes a social problem. *Journal of Personality and Social Psychology,* 1980, *38,* 131–140.

Kephart, W. M. Some correlates of romantic love. *Journal of Marriage and the Family,* 1967, *29,* 470–474.

Langer, E. Rethinking the role of thought in social interaction. In J. H. Harvey, W. Ickes, & R. F. Kidd (Eds.), *New directions in attribution research* (Vol. 2). New York: Wiley, 1978.

Langer, E., & Roth, J. Heads I win, tails, it's chance: The illusion of control as a function of the sequence of outcomes in a purely chance task. *Journal of Personality and Social Psychology,* 1975, *32,* 951–955.

McCary, J. L. *McCary's human sexuality* (3rd Ed.). New York: Van Nostrand, 1978.

Murstein, B. Physical attractiveness and marital choice. *Journal of Personality and Social Psychology,* 1972, *22,* 8–12.

Murstein, B. Who will marry whom? *Theories and research in marital choice.* New York: Springer, 1976.

Novak, D. W., & Lerner, M. J. Rejection as a function of perceived similarity. *Journal of Personality and Social Psychology,* 1968, *9,* 147–152.

O'Grady, K. E., Janda, L. H., & Gillen, H. B. A multidimensional scaling analysis of sex guilt. *Multivariate Behavioral Research,* 1979, *14,* 415–434.

Pearson, K., & Lee, A. On the laws of inheritance in man. I. Inheritance of physical characteristics. *Biometrika,* 1903, *2,* 372–377.

Pennebaker, J. W., Dyer, M. A., Caulkins, R. S., Litowitz, D. L., Ackreman, P. L., Anderson, D. B., & McGraw, K. M. Don't the girls get prettier at closing time: A country and western application to psychology. *Personality and Social Psychology Bulletin,* 1979, *5,* 122–125.

Rape and culture. *Time.* September 12, 1977, 41.

Reed, E. W., & Reed, S. C. *Mental retardation: A family study.* Philadelphia: Saunders, 1965.

Reik, T. *A psychologist looks at love.* New York: Farrar and Rinehart, 1944.

Reis, H. T., Nezlek, J., & Wheeler, L. Physical attractiveness in social interaction. *Journal of Personality and Social Psychology,* 1980, *38,* 604–617.

Rubin, Z. *Liking and loving: An invitation to social psychology.* New York: Holt, 1973.

Rubin, Z. From liking to loving: Patterns of attraction in dating relationships. In T. L. Huston (Ed.), *Foundations of interpersonal attraction.* New York: Academic, 1974.

Seligman, C., Brickman, J., & Koulack, D. Rape and physical attractiveness: Assigning responsibility to victims. *Journal of Personality,* 1977, *45,* 554–563.

Snyder, M., Tanke, E. D., & Berscheid, E. Social perception and interpersonal behavior: On the selffulfilling nature of social stereotypes. *Journal of Personality and Social Psychology,* 1977, *35,* 356–366.

Tennow, D. *Love and limerence.* New York: Stein & Day, 1979.

Van Den Haag, E. Love or marriage? In M. E. Lasswell & T. E. Lasswell (Eds.), *Love, marriage, family: A developmental approach.* Glenview, Ill.: Scott, Foresman, 1973.

Walster, E. Effects of self-esteem on liking for dates of various social desirabilities. *Journal of Experimental Social Psychology,* 1970, *6,* 248–253.

Walster, E., Aronson, V., Abrahams, D., & Rottman, L. The importance of physical attractiveness in dating behavior. *Journal of Personality and Social Psychology,* 1966, *4,* 508–516.

Walster, E., & Walster, G. W. Effect of expecting to be liked on choice of associates. *Journal of Abnormal and Social Psychology,* 1963, *67,* 402–404.

Walster, E., & Walster, G. W. *Love.* Reading, Mass.: Addison-Wesley, 1978.

Zellman, G. L., Johnson, P. B., Giarrusso, R., & Goodchilds, J. D. Sexuality: Misreading the signals. *Psychology Today,* October 1980, 28.

Chapter 16

American Psychological Association. Ethical principles in the conduct of research with human participants. Washington, D.C., 1973.

Asch, S. Effects of group pressure upon modification and distortion of judgment. In H. Guetzkow (Ed.), *Groups, leadership, and men.* Pittsburgh: Carnegie Press, 1951.

Asch, S. Social psychology. New York: Prentice-Hall, 1952.

Asch, S. Studies of independence and conformity. A minority of one against a unanimous majority. *Psychological Monographs,* 1956, *70,* 9, Whole No. 416.

Axelrod, R. Effective choice in Prisoner's Dilemma. *Journal of Conflict Resolution,* 1980, *24,* 1, 3–25.

Baron, R., & Byrne, D. *Social psychology: Understanding human interaction.* Boston: Allyn & Bacon, Inc., 1981.

Billig, M. *Social psychology and inter-group relations.* New York: Academic, 1976.

Bird, C. *Social psychology.* New York: Appleton-Century-Crofts, 1940.

Carlsmith, M., Ellsworth, P., & Aronson, E. *Methods of research in social psychology.* Reading, Mass.: Addison-Wesley, 1976.

Cartwright, D. Risk taking by individuals and groups. An assessment of research employing choice dilemmas. *Journal of Personality and Social Psychology,* 1971, *20,* 361–378.

Clement, D., & Sullivan, D. No risky shift effect with real groups and real risks. *Psychonomic Science,* 1970, *18,* 243–245.

Davis, J. *Group performance.* Reading, Mass.: Addison-Wesley, 1969.

Deutsch, M. *The resolution of conflict.* New Haven, Conn.: Yale University Press, 1973.

Errera, P. Statement based on interviews with "forty worst cases" in the Milgram obedience experiment. In J. Katz (Ed.), *Experimentation with human beings.* New York: Russell Sage, 1972.

Festinger, C. Informal social communication. *Psychological Review,* 1950, *57,* 271–282.

Festinger, L. A theory of social comparison processes. *Human Relations,* 1954, *7,* 117–140.

Fiedler, F. *Leader attributes and group effectiveness.* Urbana: University of Illinois Press, 1958.

Fiedler, F. *A theory of leadership effectiveness.* New York: McGraw-Hill, 1967.

Fiedler, F. *Leadership.* New York: General Learning Press, 1971.

Fiedler, F., & Chemers, M. *Leadership and effective management.* Chicago: Scott, Foresman, 1974.

Fisher, A. *Small group decision making: Communication and the group process.* New York: McGraw-Hill, 1980.

Flowers, M. A laboratory test of some implications of Janis's groupthink hypothesis. *Journal of Personality and Social Psychology,* 1977, *35,* 888–896.

Gibb, C. Leadership. In G. Lindzey and E. Aronson (Eds.), *The handbook of social psychology*, Vol. IV. Reading, Mass.: Addison-Wesley, 1969.

Gumpert, P., Deutsch, M., & Epstein, E. Effect of incentive magnitude on cooperation in the prisoner's dilemma game. *Journal of Personality and Social Psychology*, 1969, *11*, 66–69.

Hare, P. *Handbook of small group research*. New York: Free Press, 1976.

Hersh, S. *Cover-up: The army's secret investigation of the massacre at My Lai*. New York: Random House, 1972.

Hoyt, G., & Stoner, J. Leadership and group decisions involving risk. *Journal of Experimental Social Psychology*, 1964, *4*, 275–284.

Janis, T. *Victims of groupthink: A psychological study of foreign policy decisions and fiascoes*. Boston: Houghton Mifflin, 1972.

Knox, R., & Safford, R. Group caution at the race track. *Journal of Experimental Social Psychology*, 1976, *12*, 317–324.

Kogan, N., & Wallach, M. Risk taking: A study in cognition and personality. New York: Holt, 1964.

Kowitz, A., & Knutson, T. *Decision making in small groups*. Boston: Allyn & Bacon, 1980.

Lamm, H., & Myers, D. Group-induced polarization of attitudes and behavior. In L. Berkowitz (Ed.), *Advances in experimental social psychology*. New York: Academic, 1978.

Lewin, K. Behind food habits and methods of change. *Bulletin of the Research Council*, 1943, No. 108.

Lewin, K., Lippitt, R., & White, R. Patterns of aggressive behavior in experimentally created social climates. *Journal of Social Psychology*, 1939, *10*, 271–299.

Luce, R., & Raiffa, H. *Games and decisions*. New York: Wiley, 1957.

McCauley, C., Stitt, C., Woods, K., & Lipton, D. Group shift to caution at the race track. *Journal of Experimental Social Psychology*, 1973, *9*, 80–86.

Mantell, D. The potential for violence in Germany. *Journal of Social Issues*, 1971, *27* (4), 101–112.

Marlowe, L. *Social psychology*. Boston: Holbrook, 1975.

Meyer, P. If Hitler asked you to electrocute a stranger, would you? In *Psychology 80/81, Annual Editions*. Sluice Dock, Guilford, Conn.: Duskin, 1980.

Milgram, S. Behavioral study of obedience. *Journal of Abnormal and Social Psychology*, 1963, *67*, 371–378.

Milgram, S. Issues in the study of obedience: A reply to Baumrind. *American Psychologist*, 1964, *19*, 848–852.

Milgram, S. *Obedience to authority*. New York: Harper & Row, 1973.

Morris, W., & Miller, R. The effects of consensus-breaking and consensus-preempting on reduction of conformity. *Journal of Experimental Social Psychology*, 1975, *11*, 215–223.

Myers, D., & Bishop, G. Discussion effects on racial attitudes. *Science*, 1970, *169*, 778–779.

Napier, R., & Gershenfeld, M. *Groups: Theory and experience*. Boston: Houghton Mifflin, 1973.

Rosenfeld, L. *Now that we are all here: Relations in small groups*. Columbus, Ohio: Merrill, 1976.

Rubin, J., & Brown, B. *The social psychology of bargaining and negotiation*. New York: Academic, 1975.

Shaw, M. *Group dynamics: The psychology of small group behavior*. New York: McGraw-Hill, 1976.

Sherif, M. *The psychology of social norms*. New York: Harper & Row, 1936.

Sherif, M., & Sherif, C. *Groups in harmony and tension*. New York: Harper & Row, 1953.

Simmel, G. *Conflict*. New York: Free Press, 1955.

Snyder, G. Prisoner's dilemma and chicken models in international politics. *International Studies*, 1971, *15*, 66–103.

Stoner, J. *A comparison of individual and group decisions involving risk*. Unpublished master's thesis. Massachusetts Institute of Technology, School of Industrial Management, 1961.

Strickland, L. (Ed.) *Soviet and Western perspectives in social psychology*. New York: Pergamon, 1979.

Strodtbeck, F., James, R., & Hawkins, C. Social status in jury deliberations. *American Sociological Review*, 1957, *22*, 713–718.

Strodtbeck, F., & Mann, R. Sex role differentiation in jury deliberations. *Sociometry*, 1956, *19*, 3–11.

Suls, J., & Miller, R. (Eds.) *Social comparison processes: Theoretical and empirical perspectives*. Washington, D.C.: Halsbeck-Wiley, 1977.

Willems, E., & Clark, R. Shift toward risk and heterogeneity of groups. *Journal of Experimental Social Psychology*, 1971, *7*, 304–312.

Wrightsman, L., & Deaux, K. *Social psychology in the 1980s*. Monterey, Calif.: Brooks/Cole, 1981.

Chapter 17

American Psychiatric Association. *Diagnostic and statistical manual of mental disorders*. (2nd Ed.), Washington, D.C.: APA, 1968.

American Psychiatric Association. *Diagnostic and statis-*

tical manual of mental disorders (3rd Ed.), Washington, D.C.: APA, 1980.

Beach, F. A. Hormonal control of sex-related behavior. In F. A. Beach (Ed.), *Human sexuality in four perspectives.* Baltimore: Johns Hopkins University Press, 1977.

Bell, A. P., & Weinberg, M. S. *Homosexualities.* New York: Simon & Schuster, 1978.

Bergler, E., & Kroger, W. *Kinsey's myth of female sexuality: The medical facts.* New York: Grune & Stratton, 1954.

Bieber, I. A discussion of "Homosexuality: The Ethical Challenge." *Journal of Consulting and Clinical Psychology,* 1976, *44,* 163–166.

Blumstein, P. W., & Schwartz, P. Lesbianism and bisexuality. In S. Gordon & R. W. Libby (Eds.), *Sexuality today and tomorrow.* North Scituate, Mass.: Duxbury, 1976.

Blumstein, P. W., & Schwartz, P. Bisexuality: Some social psychological issues. *Journal of Social Issues,* 1977, *33,* 30–45.

Davison, G. C. Homosexuality: The ethical challenge. *Journal of Consulting and Clinical Psychology,* 1976, *44,* 157–162.

Davison, G. C. Not can but ought: The treatment of homosexuality. *Journal of Consulting and Clinical Psychology,* 1978, *46,* 170–172.

Fischer, J., & Gochros, H. L. *Handbook of behavior therapy with sexual problems: Vol. I.* New York: Pergamon, 1977.

Fisher, W. A., & Byrne, D. Sex differences in response to erotica? Love versus lust. *Journal of Personality and Social Psychology,* 1978, *36,* 117–125.

Ford, C., & Beach, F. *Patterns of sexual behavior.* New York: Harper & Row, 1951.

Gebhard, P. H., Gagnon, J. H., Pomeroy, W. B., & Christenson, C. V. *Sex offenders: An analysis of types.* New York: Harper & Row, 1965.

Gordon, S. Freedom for sex education and sexual expression. In S. Gordon & R. W. Libby (Eds.), *Sexuality today and tomorrow.* North Scituate, Mass.: Duxbury, 1976.

Greenblatt, R. B. & McNamara, P. Endocrinology of human sexuality. In B. J. Sadock, H. I. Kaplan, & A. M. Freedman (Eds.), *The sexual experience.* Baltimore: Williams & Wilkins, 1976.

Hastings, D. W. Sexual potency disorders of the male. In A. M. Freedman & H. I. Kaplan, (Eds.), *Comprehensive textbook of psychiatry.* Baltimore: Williams & Wilkins, 1967.

Hoffman, M. Homosexuality. In F. A. Beach (Ed.), *Human sexuality in four perspectives.* Baltimore: Johns Hopkins University Press, 1977.

Hurt, M. *Sexual behavior in the 1970's.* New York: Dell, 1974.

Husted, J. R. Desensitization procedures in dealing with female sexual dysfunction. In J. LoPiccolo & L. LoPiccolo (Eds.), *Handbook of sex therapy.* New York: Plenum, 1978.

Janda, L. H. Effects of guilt, approachability of examiner and stimulus relevance upon sexual responses to thematic apperception stimuli. *Journal of Consulting and Clinical Psychology,* 1975, *43,* 369–374.

Janda, L. H. & Klenke-Hamel, K. E. *Human Sexuality.* New York: Van Nostrand, 1980.

Janda, L. H., & O'Grady, K. E. Effects of guilt and response modality upon associative sexual responses. *Journal of Research in Personality,* 1976, *10,* 457–462.

Janda, L. H., Witt, C., & Manahan, C. The effects of guilt and approachability of examiner upon associative sexual responses. *Journal of Consulting and Clinical Psychology,* 1976, *44,* 986–990.

Kaplan, H. S., Kohl, R. N., Pomeroy, W. B., Offit, A. K., & Hogan, B. Group treatment of premature ejaculation. In J. LoPiccolo & L. LoPiccolo (Eds.), *Handbook of sex therapy.* New York: Plenum, 1978.

Kinsey, A. C., Pomeroy, W. B., & Martin, C. E. *Sexual behavior in the human male.* Philadelphia: Saunders, 1948.

Kinsey, A. C., Pomeroy, W. B., Martin, C. E., & Gebhard, P. H. *Sexual behavior in the human female,* Philadelphia: Saunders, 1953.

Kockett, G., Dittmar, F., & Nusselt, L. Systematic desensitization of erectile impotence: A controlled study. In J. LoPiccolo & L. LoPiccolo (Eds.), *Handbook of sex therapy.* New York: Plenum, 1978.

Kushner, M. The reduction of a long-standing fetish by means of aversive conditioning. In J. Fischer & H. L. Gochros (Eds.), *Handbook of behavior therapy with sexual problems: Vol 11.* New York: Pergamon, 1977.

Lazarus, A. A. *Multimodal behavior therapy.* New York: Springer, 1976.

LoPiccolo, J. Direct treatment of sexual dysfunction. In J. LoPiccolo & L. LoPiccolo (Eds.), *Handbook of sex therapy,* New York: Plenum, 1978.

LoPiccolo, J., & LoPiccolo, L. *Handbook of sex therapy.* New York: Plenum, 1978.

Marshall, D. S. Sexual behavior on Mangaia. In D. S. Marshall & R. C. Suggs (Eds.), *Human sexual behavior.* Bloomington, Ind.: Institute for Sex Research, 1971.

Masters, W. H. & Johnson, V. E. *Human sexual response.* Boston: Little, Brown, 1966.

Masters, W. H., & Johnson, V. E. *Human sexual inadequacy.* Boston: Little, Brown, 1970.

McCaghy, C. H. Child molesting. *Sexual Behavior,* 1971, *1,* 16–24.

McGuire, R. J., Carlisle, J. M., & Young, B. G. Sexual deviations as conditioned behaviour: A hypothesis. *Behaviour Research and Therapy,* 1965, *2,* 185–190.

Messenger, J. C. Sex and repression in an Irish folk community. In D. S. Marshall, & R. C. Suggs (Eds.), *Human sexual behavior.* Bloomington, Ind.: Institute for Sex Research, 1971.

Money, J. Human hermaphroditism. In F. A. Beach (Ed.), *Human sexuality in four perspectives.* Baltimore: Johns Hopkins University Press, 1977.

Money, J., & Ehrhardt, A. A. *Man and woman, boy and girl.* Baltimore: Johns Hopkins University Press, 1972.

Mosher, D. L. Interaction of fear and guilt in inhibiting unacceptable behavior. *Journal of Consulting Psychology,* 1965, *29,* 161–167.

Mosher, D. L. The development and multitrait-multimethod matrix analysis of three measures of three aspects of guilt. *Journal of Consulting Psychology,* 1966, *30,* 25–29.

Rainwater, L. *Family design.* Chicago: Aldine, 1965.

Reiss, I. L. *The social context of premarital permissiveness.* New York: Holt, 1967.

Rook, K. S., & Hammen, C. L. A cognitive perspective on sexual arousal. *Journal of Social Issues,* 1977, *33,* 7–29.

Schneidman, B., & McGuire, L. Group therapy for nonorgasmic women: Two age levels. In J. LoPiccolo & L. LoPiccolo (Eds.), *Handbook of sex therapy.* New York: Plenum, 1978.

Staats, A. W. Social behaviorism. Homewood, Ill.: Dorsey, 1975.

Chapter 18

Bach, G. R., & Goldberg, H. *Creative aggression.* New York: Doubleday, 1974.

Bach, G. R., & Wyden, P. *The intimate enemy.* New York: Avon, 1968.

Bandura, A. Vicarious processes. A case of no-trial learning. In L. Berkowitz (Ed.), *Advances in experimental social psychology* (Vol. 2). New York: Academic, 1965.

Bandura, A. *Aggression: A social learning analysis.* Englewood Cliffs, N.J.: Prentice-Hall, 1973.

Bandura, A., Ross, D., & Ross, S. A. Imitation of film mediated aggressive models. *Journal of Abnormal and Social Psychology,* 1963a, *66,* 3–11.

Bandura, A., Ross, D., & Ross, S. A. Vicarious reinforcement and imitative learning. *Journal of Abnormal and Social Psychology,* 1963b, *67,* 601–607.

Baron, R. A. *Human aggression.* New York: Plenum, 1977.

Berkowitz, L. The frustration-aggression hypothesis revisited. In L. Berkowitz (Ed.), Roots of aggression: *A re-examination of the frustration-aggression hypothesis.* New York: Atherton, 1969.

Berkowitz, L., & Geen, R. G. Stimulus qualities of the target of aggression: A further study. *Journal of Personality and Social Psychology,* 1967, *5,* 364–368.

Bernard, L. L. *Instinct: A study of social psychology.* New York: Holt, 1924.

Bernard, L. L. *An introduction to social psychology.* New York: Holt, 1926.

Brown, R., & Herrnstein, R. J. *Psychology.* Boston: Little, Brown, 1975.

Buss, A. H. *The psychology of aggression.* New York: Wiley, 1961.

Buss, A. H. Physical aggression in relation to different frustrations. *Journal of Abnormal and Social Psychology,* 1963, *67,* 1–7.

Buss, A. H. Instrumentality of aggression, feedback, and frustration as determinants of physical aggression. *Journal of Personality and Social Psychology,* 1966, *3,* 153–162.

Buss, A. H. Aggression pays. In J. L. Singer (Ed.), *The control of aggression and violence.* New York: Academic, 1971.

Clarke, K. B. The pathos of power: A psychological perspective. Paper presented at the American Psychological Association, Washington, D.C., 1971.

Delgado, J. M. R. Cerebral heterostimulation in a monkey colony. *Science,* 1963, *141,* 161–163.

Delgado, J. M. R. Aggression and defense under cerebral radio control. In C. D. Clements & D. B. Lindsley (Eds.), *Brain Function, (Vol. 5). Aggression and defense.* Berkeley: University of California Press, 1967.

Diener, E., & DeFour, D. Does television violence enhance program popularity? *Journal of Personality and Social Psychology,* 1978, *36,* 333–341.

Dollard, J., Doob, L., Miller, N. E., Mowrer, O. H., &

Sears, R. R. *Frustration and aggression.* New Haven: Yale University Press, 1939.

Donnerstein, E. Aggressive erotica and violence against women. *Journal of Personality and Social Psychology,* 1980, *39,* 269–277.

Doob, A. N., & Wood, L. E. Catharsis and aggression: Effects of annoyance and retaliation on aggressive behavior. *Journal of Personality and Social Psychology,* 1972, *22,* 156–162.

Drabman, R. S., & Thomas, M. H. Does TV violence breed indifference? In V. J. Derlega & L. H. Janda (Eds.), *Personal Adjustment: Selected readings.* Glenview, Ill.: Scott, Foresman, 1979.

Edmunds, G., & Kendrick, D. C. *The measurement of human aggressiveness.* New York: Halsted Press, 1980.

Eibl-Eibesfeldt, I. Ethology: *The biology of behavior.* New York: Holt, 1971.

Eron, L. D. Prescription for reducing aggression. *American Psychologist,* 1980, *35,* 244–252.

Eron, L. D., Husemann, L. R., Lefkowitz, M. M., & Walder, L. O. Does television violence cause aggression? *American Psychologist,* 1972, *27,* 253–263.

Feshbach, S. The function of aggression and the regulation of aggressive drive. *Psychological Review,* 1964, *71,* 257–272.

Geen, R. G., Stonner, D., & Shope, G. L. The facilitation of aggression by aggression: A study in response inhibition and disinhibition. *Journal of Personality and Social Psychology,* 1975, *31,* 721–726.

Geen, R. G. The study of aggression. In R. G. Geen and E. C. O'Neal (Eds.), *Perspectives on aggression.* New York: Academic, 1976a.

Geen, R. G. Observing violence in the mass media: Implication of basic research. In R. G. Geen and E. C. O'Neal (Eds.), *Perspectives on aggression.* New York: Academic, 1976b.

Gentry, W. D. Effects of frustration, attack, and prior aggressive training on overt aggression and vascular processes. *Journal of Personality and Social Psychology,* 1970, *16,* 718–725.

Gerbner, G., & Gross, L. The scary world of TV's heavy viewer. *Psychology Today,* April 1976, 41 ff.

Harris, M. B. Mediators between frustration and aggression in a field experiment. *Journal of Experimental Social Psychology,* 1974, *10,* 561–571.

Hess, W. R. Beitrage zur physiologie des hirnstammes: I Teil Die Methodik der lokalisierten reizung und ausschaltung subkorfikaler hirnabschnitte. Leipzig: Georg Thieme, 1932.

Jacobs, P. A., Burnton, M., & Melville, M. M. Aggressive behavior, mental subnormality, and the XY male. *Nature,* 1965, *208,* 1351–1352.

Jakobi, U., Selg, H., & Belschner, W. Tuebmodelle der Aggression. In H. Selg (Ed.), Zur Aggression verdammt?: *Psychologische Ansatze einer Fruedensforschung.* Stuttgart: Kohlhammer, 1971.

James, W. *The principles of psychology.* New York: Holt, 1890.

Johnston, A., DeLuca, D., Murtaugh, K., & Diener, E. Validation of a laboratory play measure of child aggression. *Child Development,* 1977, *48,* 324–327.

Joslyn, W. D. Androgen-induced social dominance in infant female rhesus monkeys. *Journal of Child Psychology and Psychiatry,* 1973, *14,* 137–145.

Klapper, J. T. The impact of viewing "aggression": Studies and problems of extrapolation. In O. N. Larsen (Ed.), *Violence and the mass media.* New York: Harper & Row, 1968.

Kluever, H., & Bucy, P. C. "Psychic blindness" and other symptoms following bilateral temporal lobectomy in rhesus monkeys. *American Journal of Physiology,* 1937, *119,* 352–353.

Lehrman, D. S. Semantic and conceptual issues in the nature-nurture problem. In L. R. Aronson, E. Tobach, D. S. Lehrman, & J. S. Rosenblatt, (Eds.), *Development and evolution of behavior: Essays in memory of T. C. Schneirla.* San Francisco: Freeman, 1970.

Liebert, R. M., Neale, J. M., & Davidson, E. S. *The early window: Effects of television on children and youth.* New York: Pergamon, 1973.

Lorenz, K. *On aggression.* New York: Harcourt Brace Jovanovich, 1966.

Lorenz, K. *Civilized man's eight deadly sins.* New York: Harcourt Brace Jovanovich, 1974.

Maccoby, E. E., & Jacklin, C. N. *The psychology of sex differences.* Palo Alto, Calif.: Stanford University Press, 1974.

Mallick, S. K., & McCandless, B. R. A study of catharsis of aggression. *Journal of Personality and Social Psychology,* 1966, *4,* 591–596.

Marler, P., & Hamilton, W. J. *Mechanisms of animal behavior.* New York: Wiley, 1968.

Money, J. *Love and love sickness.* Baltimore: Johns Hopkins University Press, 1980.

Montagu, A. *The nature of human aggression.* New York: Oxford, 1976.

Montagu, A. *Learning non-aggression.* New York: Oxford, 1978.

Morris, D. *The naked ape.* New York: McGraw-Hill, 1968.

Moyer, K. E. The physiology of aggression and the implications for aggression control. In J. L. Singer (Ed.), *The control of aggression and violence.* New York: Academic, 1971.

Patterson, G., Littman, R., & Bricker, W. Assertive behavior in children: A step toward a theory of aggression. *Monographs of the Society for Research in Child Development,* 1967, *32,* 113.

Quanty, M. B. Aggression catharsis: Experimental investigations and implications. In R. G. Geen & E. C. O'Neal (Eds.), *Perspectives on aggression.* New York: Academic, 1976.

Rose, R. M., Haladay, J. W., & Burnstein, R. S. Plasma testosterone, dominance rank, and aggressive behavior in rhesus monkeys. *Nature,* 1971, *231,* 366–368.

Rosenbaum, M. E., & de Charms, R. Direct and vicarious reduction of hostility. *Journal of Abnormal and Social Psychology,* 1960, *60,* 105–111.

Rule, B. G., & Hewitt, L. S. Effects of thwarting on cardiac response and physical aggression. *Journal of Personality and Social Psychology,* 1971, *19,* 181–187.

Scherer, K. R., Abeles, R. P., & Fischer, C. S. *Human aggression and conflict.* Englewood Cliffs, N.J.: Prentice-Hall, 1975.

Schmitt, B. D. The prevention of child abuse and neglect: A review of the literature with recommendations for application. *Child Abuse and Neglect,* 1980, *4,* 171–177.

Schneirla, T. C. An evolutionary and developmental theory of biphasic processes underlying approach and withdrawal. In M. R. Jones (Ed.), *Nebraska Symposium on Motivation, 1959.* Lincoln: University of Nebraska Press, 1959.

Shah, S. A. *Report on the XYY chromosomal abnormality.* Washington, D.C.: U.S. Government Printing Office, 1970.

Sorenson, E. R. Cooperation and freedom among the Fore of New Guinea. In A. Montagu (Ed.), *Learning non-aggression.* New York: Oxford, 1978.

Steadman, H. J., & Cocozza, J. J. We can't predict who is dangerous. *Psychology Today,* January 1975, 33 ff.

Straus, M. A. Leveling, civility, and violence in the family. *Journal of Marriage and the Family,* 1974, *36,* 13.

Straus, M. A. Family patterns and child abuse in a nationally representative American sample. *Child Abuse and Neglect,* 1979, *3,* 213–225.

Taylor, S. P., & Pisano, R. Physical aggression as a function of frustration and physical attack. *Journal of Social Psychology,* 1971, *84,* 261–267.

Thomas, M. H., & Drabman, R. S. Effects of television violence on expectations of others' aggression. *Personality and Social Psychology Bulletin,* 1978, *4,* 73–76.

Time. April 13, 1981, p. 43.

Tinbergen, N. *The study of instinct.* Oxford: Clarendon, 1951.

Valenstein, E. S. *Brain control.* New York: Wiley, 1973.

Worchel, S. The effect of three types of arbitrary thwarting on the instigation to aggression. *Journal of Personality,* 1974, *42,* 301–318.

Zillman, D. *Hostility and aggression.* Hillsdale, N.J.: Erlbaum, 1979.

Chapter 19

Allgeier, A., & Bryne, D. Attraction toward the opposite sex as a determinant of physical proximity. *Journal of Social Psychology,* 1973, *90,* 213–219.

Alluisi, E., & Morgan, B. Engineering psychology and human performance. *Annual Review of Psychology,* 1976, *27,* 305–330.

Altman, T. *The environment and social behavior: Privacy, personal space, territory and crowding.* Monterey, Calif.: Brooks/Cole, 1975.

Altman, T., & Vinsel, A. Personal space: An analysis of E. T. Hall's proxemics framework. In T. Altman and J. Wohlwill (Eds.), *Human behavior and environment* (Vol. 2). New York: Plenum, 1977.

Anastasi, A. *Fields of applied psychology.* New York: McGraw-Hill, 1979.

Baum, A., Aiello, J., & Calesnick, L. Crowding and personal control: Social density and the development of learned helplessness. *Journal of Personality and Social Psychology,* 1978, *36,* 1000–1011.

Baum, A., Harpin, E., & Valins, S. The role of group phenomena in the experience of crowding. *Environment and Behavior,* 1975, *7,* 2, 185–198.

Baum, A., & Valins, S. *Architecture and social behavior.* Hillsdale, N.J.: Erlbaum, 1977.

Benyon, H. *Working for Ford.* Harmondsworth, Middlesex, England: Penguin, 1973.

Berkeley Planning Associates. *Evaluation of child abuse*

and neglect demonstration projects 1974–1977. Volume IX: Project management and worker burnout. Unpublished report. Springfield, Va.: National Technical Information Service, 1977.

Bernstein, D., & Nietzel, M. *Introduction to clinical psychology.* New York: McGraw-Hill, 1980.

Biles, E. A program guide for preventing sexual harassment in the workplace. *Personnel Administrator,* 1981, *26,* 49–56.

Blackwell, H. A human factors approach to lightening recommendations and standards. In *Proceedings of the Sixteenth Annual Meeting of the Human Factors Society.* Santa Monica, Calif., 1972.

Bloom, B. A university freshman preventive intervention program: Report of a pilot project. *Journal of Consulting and Clinical Psychology,* 1971, *37,* 235–242.

Bloom, B. *Community mental health: A historical and critical analysis.* Morristown, N.J.: General Learning Press, 1973.

Bloom, C. *Community mental health: A general introduction.* Monterey, Calif.: Brooks/Cole, 1977.

Bombard, A. The voyage of the Hertique. New York: Simon and Schuster, 1953.

Burrows, A. Acoustic noise, an informational definition. *Human Factors,* 1960, *2,* 3, 163–168.

Calhoun, J. Population density and social pathology. *Scientific American,* 1962, *206,* 139–148.

Caplan, G. *Principles of preventive psychiatry.* New York: Basic, 1964.

Chapanis, A. On the allocation of function between men and machines. *Occupational Psychology,* 1965, *39,* 1–11.

Chapanis, A. Engineering psychology. In M. Dunnette (Ed.), *Handbook of industrial and organizational psychology.* Chicago: Rand McNally, 1976.

Cherniss, C. *Professional burnout in human service organizations.* New York: Praeger, 1980.

Christian, J., Flyger, V., & Davis, D. Phenomena associated with population density. *Proceedings of the National Academy of Science,* 1961, *47,* 428–449.

Committee on the Hygiene of Housing, American Public Health Association. *Planning the home for occupancy: Standards for healthful housing series.* Chicago, Public Administration Service, 1950.

Cooper, C., & Payne, R. (Eds.). *Stress at work.* New York: Wiley, 1978.

Corbett, J. Are suites the answer? *Environment and Behavior,* 1973, *5* (4), 413–420.

Cowen, E. Psychologists in primary prevention: Blowing the cover story. An editorial. *American Journal of Community Psychology,* 1977, *5,* 481–490.

Cox, T. *Stress.* Baltimore: University Park, 1979.

Dunnette, M., & Kirchner, W. *Psychology applied to industry.* Englewood Cliffs, N.J.: Prentice-Hall, 1965.

Epstein, Y. Crowding stress and human behavior. *Journal of Social Issues,* 1981, *37,* 1, 126–144.

Farberow, N. *Suicide.* Morristown, N.J.: General Learning Press, 1974.

Ferguson, L. *The heritage of industrial psychology.* Hartford, Conn.: Finlay, 1963.

Fiester, A. JCAH standards for accreditation for community mental health service programs: Implications for the practice of psychology. *American Psychologist,* 1978, *13,* 1114–1121.

Fischer, C., Baldassare, M., & Ofshe, R. Crowding studies and urban life: A critical review. *Journal of the American Institute of Planners,* 1975, *41,* 406–418.

Fox, W. Human performance in the cold. *Human Factors,* 1970, *9,* 3, 203–220.

Frankel, A., & Barrett, J. Variations in personal space as a function of authoritarianism, self-esteem, and racial characteristics of a stimulus situation. *Journal of Consulting and Clinical Psychology,* 1971, *37,* 95–98.

Freedman, J. *Crowding and behavior.* New York: Viking, 1975.

Freudenberger, H. Staff burnout. *Journal of Social Issues,* 1974, *30,* 159–165.

Friedman, M., & Rosenman, R. *Type A behavior and your heart.* New York: Knopf, 1974.

Gagne, R. *Psychological principles in system development.* New York: Holt, 1962.

Gardner, W., & Taylor, P. *Health at work.* New York: Wiley, 1975.

Gibbs, M., Lachenmeyer, J., & Sigal, J. *Community psychology.* New York; Gardner, 1980.

Glaser, R., Barr, S., Laubach, L., Sawka, M., & Suryaprasad, A. Relative stress of wheelchair activity. *Human Factors,* 1980, *22* (2), 177–180.

Goldberg, C. *The human circle: An existential approach to the new group therapies.* Chicago: Nelson-Hall, 1973.

Goodman, J. Sexual demands on the job. *Civil Liberties Review,* March/April 1978, 55–58.

Greenlaw, P., & Kohl, J. Sexual harassment: Homosexuality, bisexuality, and blackmail. *Personnel Administrator,* 1981, *29,* 59–62.

Gruneberg, M. *Understanding job satisfaction.* London: MacMillan, 1979.

Hall, E. *The silent language.* Garden City, N.Y.: Doubleday, 1959.
Hall, E. *The hidden dimension.* Garden City, N.Y.: Doubleday, 1966.
Heimstra, N., & McFarling, L. *Environmental psychology.* Monterey, Calif.: Brooks/Cole, 1978.
Heller, K., & Monahan. *Psychology and community change.* Homewood, Ill.: Dorsey, 1977.
Hersch, C. Social history, mental health, and community control. *American Psychologist,* 1972, *27,* 749–754.
Horowitz, M., Duff, D., & Stratton, C. Body-buffer zone: Exploration of personal space. *Archives of General Psychiatry,* 1964, *11,* 651–656.
Jenkins, D. Psychologic and social precursors of coronary disease (II). *New England Journal of Medicine,* 1971, *284,* 307–317.
Kaplan, S., & Roman, M. *The organization and delivery of mental health services in the ghetto.* New York: Praeger, 1973.
Kazan, P., Bladen, W., & Singh, G. Slum dwellers' and squatters' images of the city. *Environment and Behavior,* 1980, *12* (1), 81–100.
Kornhauser, A. *Mental health of the industrial worker: A Detroit study.* New York: Wiley, 1965.
Landy, F., & Trumbo. *Psychology of work behavior.* Homewood, Ill.: Dorsey, 1976.
Lawler, E. *Pay and organizational effectiveness: A psychological view.* New York: McGraw-Hill, 1971.
Lett, E., Clark, W., & Altman, T. *A propositional inventory of research on interpersonal distance (Research Report No. 1).* Bethesda, Md.: Naval Medical Research Institute, 1969.
Locke, E. The nature and causes of job satisfaction. In M. Dunnette (Ed.), *Handbook of industrial and organizational psychology.* Chicago: Rand McNally, 1976.
Lyons, T. Turnover and absenteeism: A review of relationship and shared correlates. *Personnel Psychology,* 1972, *25,* 271–281.
Maslach, C. Burned-out. *Human Behavior,* 1976, *5,* 16–22.
McCormick, E. *Human factors engineering and design.* New York: McGraw-Hill, 1976.
McGee, T.. *Crisis intervention in the community.* Baltimore: University Park, 1974.
Mitchell, R. Some implications of high density housing. *American Sociological Review,* 1971, *36,* 18–29.
National Research Council. *Science and technology in the service of the physically handicapped. Vol. 1.* Washington, D.C.: National Academy of Sciences, Committee on National Needs for the Rehabilitation of the Physically Handicapped, 1976.
Nietzel, M., Winett, R., MacDonald, M., & Davidson, W. *Behavioral approaches to community psychology.* New York: Pergamon, 1977.
Opsahl, R., & Dunnette, M. The role of financial compensation in industrial motivation. *Psychological Bulletin,* 1966, *66,* 94–118.
Phares, J. *Clinical psychology.* Homewood, Ill.: Dorsey, 1979.
Prier, E., Jones, M., Miller, L., Gulkin, R., & Sutherland, G. *Mental health in organizations.* Chicago: Nelson-Hall, 1979.
Quinn, R., Staines, G., & McCollough, M. *Job satisfaction: Is there a trend?* Washington, D.C.: U.S. Department of Labor, 1974.
Raskin, E. *Architecture and people.* Englewood Cliffs, N.J.: Prentice-Hall, 1974.
Reid, K. Community mental health on the college campus. *Hospital and Community Psychiatry,* 1970, *21,* 387–389.
Reiff, R. Social responsibility of community mental health centers. In D. Evans, & W. Claiborn, *Mental health issues and the urban poor.* New York: Pergamon, 1974.
Rice, D., Hinton, H., & Conover, D. A small group independent living experiment for the physically handicapped. *Human Factors,* 1978, *20* (3), 365–370.
Robinson, S. Littering behavior in public places. *Environment and Behavior,* 1976, *8* (3), 363–384.
Sawyer, J., Sudak, H., & Hale, S. A follow-up study of 53 suicides known to a suicide prevention center. *Life-Threatening Behavior,* 1972, *2* (4), 227–238.
Scherer, S. Proxemic behavior of primary school children as a function of their socioeconomic class and subculture. *Journal of Personality and Social Psychology,* 1974, *29,* 800–805.
Schilling, R. (Ed.). *Occupational health practice.* Boston: Butterworths, 1975.
Schmidt, D., Goldman, R., & Feimer, N. Perceptions of crowding. *Environment and Behavior,* 1979, *11* (1), 105–130.
Schmitt, R. Density, health and social disorganization. *Journal of the American Institute of Planners,* 1966, *32,* 38–40.
Schwartz, M., & Will, G. Intervention and change on a mental hospital ward. In W. Bennis, K. Benne, &

R. Chin (Eds.), *The planning of change.* New York: Holt, 1961.

Sheridan, T., & Mann, R. Design of control devices for people with severe motor impairment. *Human Factors,* 1978, *20,* 3, 321–338.

Sommer, R., & Olsen, H. The soft classroom. *Environment and Behavior,* 1980, *12* (1), 3–16.

Stokols, D. On the distinction between density and crowding: Some implications for future research. *Psychological Review,* 1972, *79,* 275–277.

Stokols, D. The experience of crowding in primary and secondary environments. *Environment and Behavior,* 1976, *8* (1), 49–86.

Stratton, L., Tekippe, D., & Flick, G. Personal space and self-concept. *Sociometry,* 1973, *36,* 424–429.

Walker, C., & Guest, R. *The man on the assembly line.* Cambridge, Mass.: Harvard University Press, 1952.

Warner, H. Effects of intermittent noise on human target detection. *Human Factors,* 1969, *11* (3), 245–250.

White, T. *The making of the president 1960.* New York: Atheneum, 1961.

Willis, F. Initial speaking distance as a function of speaker's relationship. *Psychonomic Science,* 1966, *5,* 221–222.

Worchel, S., & Cooper, J. *Understanding social psychology.* Homewood, Ill.: Dorsey, 1976.

Yancey, W. Architecture, interaction, and social control: The case of a large-scale public housing project. *Environment and Behavior,* 1971, *3* (1), 3–18.

Chapter 20

Eron, L. D. Prescription for reduction of aggression. *American Psychologist,* 1980, *35,* 244–252.

Wiggins, J. S., Wiggins, N., & Conger, J. C. Correlates of heterosexual somatic preferences. *Journal of Personality and Social Psychology,* 1968, *10,* 82–90.

Name Index

Subject Index